JAPAN

JONATHAN DEHART

Contents

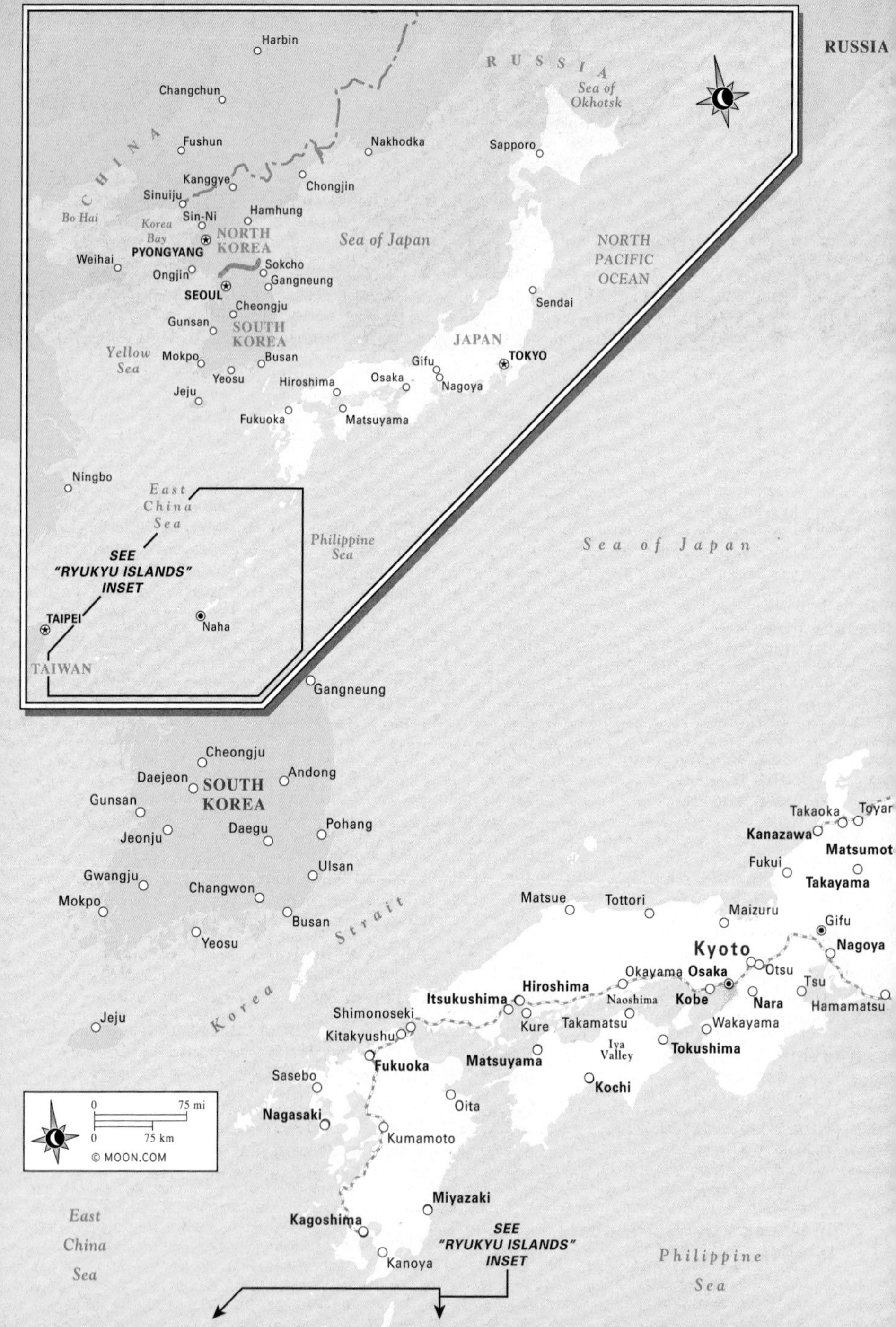
RUSSIA
Harbin
Changchun
CHINA
Fushun
Kanggye
Sinuiju
Sin-Ni
Bo Hai
Korea Bay
NORTH KOREA
PYONGYANG
Hamhung
Chongjin
Nakhodka
RUSSIA
Sea of Okhotsk
Sapporo
Sea of Japan
NORTH PACIFIC OCEAN
Weihai
Ongjin
Sokcho
Gangneung
SEOUL
Cheongju
Gunsan
SOUTH KOREA
Sendai
JAPAN
Yellow Sea
Mokpo
Busan
Yeosu
Jeju
Gifu
TOKYO
Nagoya
Osaka
Hiroshima
Fukuoka
Matsuyama
Ningbo
East China Sea
Philippine Sea
SEE "RYUKYU ISLANDS" INSET
TAIPEI
Naha
TAIWAN
Sea of Japan
Gangneung
Cheongju
Daejeon
SOUTH KOREA
Andong
Gunsan
Jeonju
Daegu
Pohang
Ulsan
Gwangju
Changwon
Mokpo
Busan
Yeosu
Korea Strait
Jeju
Takaoka
Toyar
Kanazawa
Matsumot
Fukui
Takayama
Matsue
Tottori
Maizuru
Gifu
Kyoto
Nagoya
Okayama
Osaka
Otsu
Hiroshima
Itsukushima
Naoshima
Kobe
Nara
Tsu
Hamamatsu
Shimonoseki
Kure
Takamatsu
Wakayama
Kitakyushu
Iya Valley
Tokushima
Fukuoka
Matsuyama
Sasebo
Kochi
Oita
Nagasaki
Kumamoto
0 75 mi
0 75 km
© MOON.COM
Miyazaki
East China Sea
Kagoshima
SEE "RYUKYU ISLANDS" INSET
Kanoya
Philippine Sea

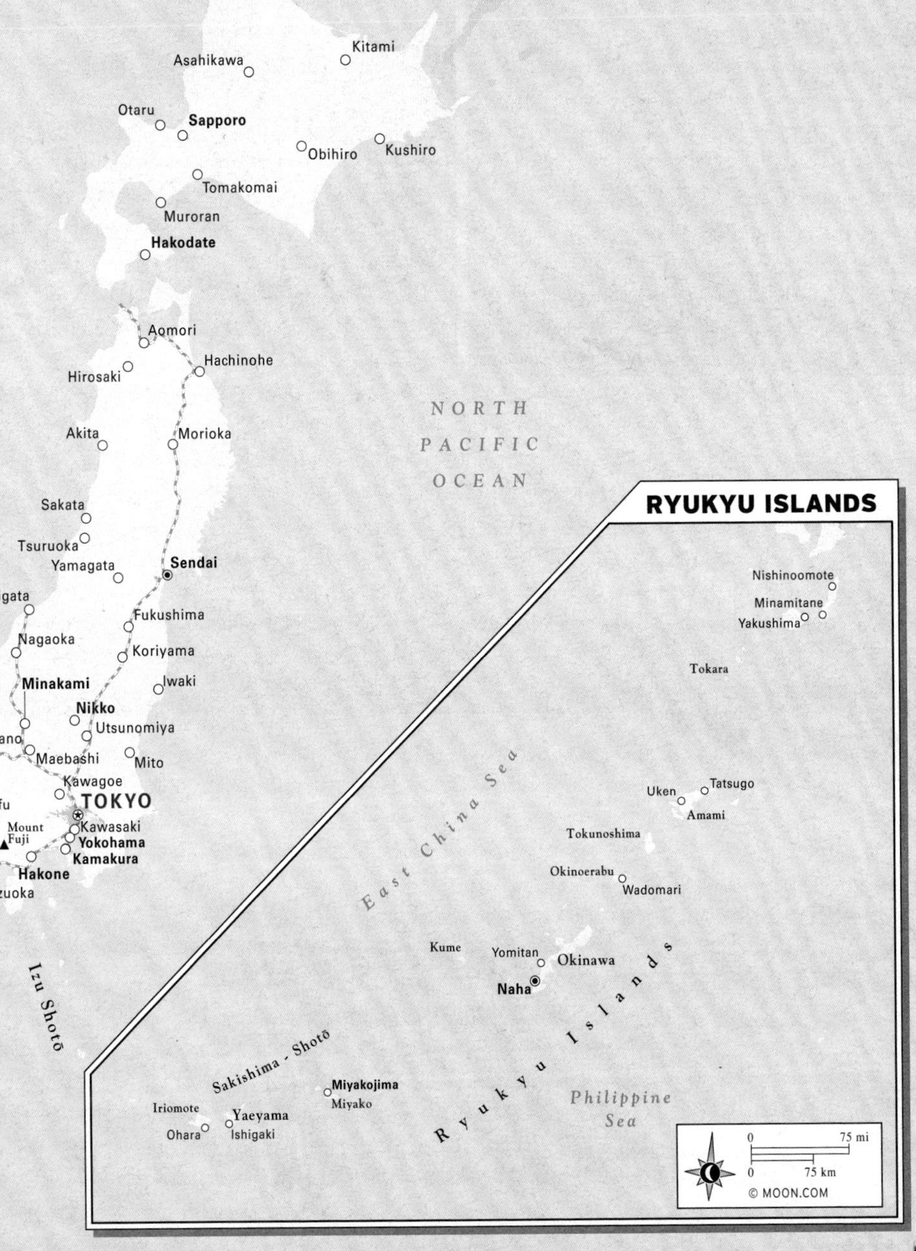
JAPAN
La Perouse Strait
Sea of Okhotsk
Kitami
Asahikawa
Otaru
Sapporo
Obihiro
Kushiro
Tomakomai
Muroran
Hakodate
Aomori
Hachinohe
Hirosaki
NORTH PACIFIC OCEAN
Akita
Morioka
Sakata
Tsuruoka
Yamagata
Sendai
Niigata
Fukushima
Nagaoka
Koriyama
Iwaki
Minakami
Nikko
Utsunomiya
Maebashi
Mito
Kawagoe
TOKYO
Kofu
Mount Fuji
Kawasaki
Yokohama
Kamakura
Hakone
Izu Shotō
RYUKYU ISLANDS
Nishinoomote
Minamitane
Yakushima
Tokara
East China Sea
Uken
Tatsugo
Amami
Tokunoshima
Okinoerabu
Wadomari
Kume
Yomitan
Okinawa
Naha
Ryukyu Islands
Sakishima - Shotō
Miyakojima
Miyako
Iriomote
Yaeyama
Ohara
Ishigaki
Philippine Sea
0
75 mi
0
75 km
© MOON.COM

DISCOVER

Japan

Dusk falls on Shibuya, where trendy Tokyoites amass at the world's busiest crossing. The walk signal turns green and a scramble ensues, resembling a human pinball machine. Meanwhile, in the ancient capital of Kyoto, a geisha's wooden clogs make a distinct clicking sound as she whisks along the cobblestones of Pontochō alley.

Tradition and modernity have a unique way of mingling in Japan. Kyoto, and on a slightly smaller scale Kanazawa, on the western coast of Central Honshu, are treasure troves of traditional culture, from temples to tea ceremonies, though the rush of tourists reminds you that the present is never far away. Hypermodern Tokyo and Osaka are urban dreamworlds of pop culture, cutting-edge technology, quirky fashion, and contemporary art, but traditional theater performances of kabuki and *Noh*, and serene parks, temples, and gardens allow you to find pockets of Zen even in the heart of the urban metropolis.

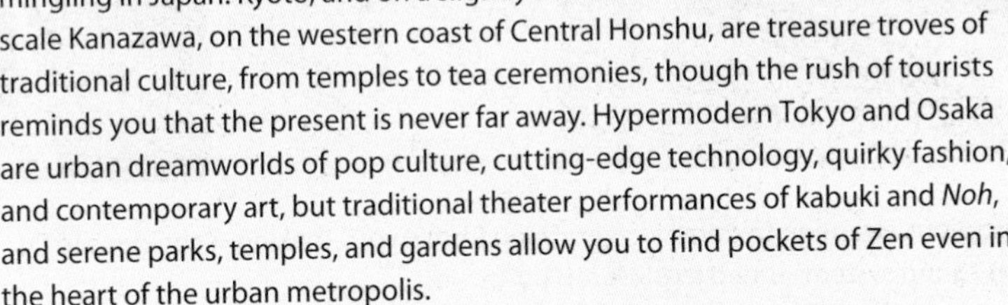

The food is another study in contrasts. Whether it's a sidewalk ramen stall in Fukuoka, a countryside *izakaya* (Japanese pub) in a hamlet in the Japan Alps, or a sushi spread in Hokkaido, Japanese cuisine deserves all the praise that it gets. A deep sense of craftsmanship, as well as connoisseurship, informs Japan's

Clockwise from top left: Kurama-dera temple in Kyoto; *yukata*; Kenroku-en; seafood at Kuromon Ichiba; *maneki-neko*; Tazawa-ko in winter.

fastidious attention to detail in everything from sword-making techniques to DJ bar sound systems tuned to pin-drop perfection.

Japan's natural wonders exert as much pull as its culture. For a country of its size, the range of terrain is striking—from the sweeping vistas of Hokkaido and the Japan Alps of Central Honshu, to the mist-shrouded peaks of Shikoku and the volcanoes of Kyūshū in the south. This landscape means access to hiking and hot springs year-round, and skiing in winter. The string of islands southwest of Kyūshū, the largest being Okinawa, add a dash of subtropical spice, including world-class beaches and scuba diving. And when cherry blossoms blanket the entire country in soft pink petals every spring, friends throw *hanami* (flower viewing) parties under the colorful branches.

Above all else, the hospitality of the people—from dark-suited office workers striving to power Japan Inc., to robotics whizzes, renegade chefs, purple-haired punk rockers, and teens seeking transcendence by dressing like their favorite anime characters—is what makes a trip to Japan special. The Japanese have a history of dusting themselves off and rebuilding after setbacks, from the ashes of World War II to the aftermath of the March 2011 Tohoku earthquake and tsunami. Most recently fueled by Tokyo's 2020 Olympics, there is a buzz of optimism in the air, and people are eager to share their good cheer and their country's subtle spell.

Clockwise from top left: Kyoto couple in traditional *yukata;* nigiri sushi; Kuniga-kaigan coast; Osaka's Dōtombori.

大阪王将
大阪名物元祖焼餃子
NIKOH BLDG
王将

14 TOP EXPERIENCES

1 Taking a deep dive into **Tokyo nightlife,** from watching epic robot battles and singing karaoke to bar-crawling through warrens of drinking dens and sipping award-winning cocktails (page 132).

2 **Staying in a *ryokan*** (traditional inn), one of the best ways experience Japan's singular art of hospitality, or *omotenashi* (page 345).

3 Walking in the footsteps of monks on a pilgrimage to **Dewa Sanzan** (page 468), **Kumano Kodō** (page 404), or the **88-Temple Pilgrimage Route** (page 552).

4 Sipping **Japanese whisky**—the best in the world—at a cocktail bar in Tokyo (page 140) or at the Suntory Yamazaki Distillery in Osaka Prefecture (page 379).

5 Strolling through the sculpted beauty and serenity of **Kenroku-en** (page 242) and **Ritsurin-kōen** (page 549), just two of Japan's famous gardens.

6 Getting up close and personal with geothermal **Kyūshū,** from the massive volcano **Aso-San** (page 646) to the hot springs at resorts like **Kurokawa Onsen** (page 654).

7 Sitting shoulder-to-shoulder with locals in **Tokyo's** boisterous **culinary alleyways** (*yokochō*), drinking beer, eating grilled or stewed nibbles, and making new friends (page 118).

8 **Island hopping in the Inland Sea,** from artistic Naoshima to other quaint, welcoming nearby islands, and connecting with a quieter, slower side of Japan (page 557).

9 Indulging in ***kaiseki ryōri*** (traditional haute cuisine), a feast of seasonal dishes that represents the upper end of Japan's culinary spectrum (page 332).

10 Hiking, skiing, and snowboarding through Japan's wild side in Hokkaido's remote national parks, such as **Daisetsuzan** (page 524) or **Shiretoko** (page 536).

11 Relaxing on the remote beaches of the **Kerama Islands,** snorkeling or scuba diving in the cyan waters of Japan's tropical far-south (page 704).

12 People-watching and popping into the boutiques and department stores of Tokyo's **Harajuku** (page 108) and **Akihabara** (page 78) to get a taste of Japan's unique youth culture.

13 Donning a *yukata* (lightweight kimono) at a traditional festival, such as **Awa Odori** in Shikoku (page 566) or **Nebuta Matsuri** in Tohoku (page 480).

14 Finding **Kyoto's quiet side,** veering away from the crowds to discover the calmer temples and shrines of Japan's refined ancient capital (page 295).

Planning Your Time

Where to Go

Tokyo

The high-octane capital should be top priority for any first visit to the country. Tokyo is **quintessential modern Japan,** a pop-cultural and economic juggernaut, and base of the national government. The dynamic city is a feast for the senses, with world-class **food, nightlife,** and **shopping.** It's also the most networked **transport hub** in Japan, with two international airports and extensive rail links to the rest of the country.

Around Tokyo

The region surrounding Tokyo offers a number of enticing **side trips** that are perfect if you have limited time. South of Tokyo is Japan's second largest city, cosmopolitan **Yokohama,** with a buzzing nightlife scene, and the ancient seaside feudal capital of **Kamakura,** with its rich Buddhist heritage. West of there, **Hakone** and **Izu** are good picks for an ***onsen* (hot spring)** experience, with Japan's most famous peak, **Mount Fuji,** looming nearby. Northeast of Tokyo is the alpine town of **Nikkō,** an ancient center of mountain worship with flamboyant temples, shrines, and mausoleums.

Central Honshu

With the lion's share of the country's highest peaks, the **Japan Alps** offer excellent **hiking** in warmer months and abundant powder for **skiing** and **snowboarding** in winter. Tucked into valleys, rural hamlets oozing rustic charm and historic centers like **Matsumoto** and **Takayama**

Mount Fuji

welcome visitors to their charming townscapes. To the west, beside the Sea of Japan, the city of **Kanazawa** offers a low-key alternative to Kyoto, with its samurai and geisha quarters and dreamy old garden of **Kenroku-en.**

Kyoto

Alongside the modern capital of Tokyo, the ancient capital of Kyoto should be top priority for any first journey to Japan. This is the best place to explore **traditional culture,** to see **geisha,** to try a **tea ceremony,** to **shrine- and temple-hop,** to eat ***kaiseki ryori*** (haute Japanese cuisine), to stay in a high-end ***ryokan,*** and to gaze at various styles of **gardens,** from landscape to raked gravel. Step away from the top sights to discover a slower, more local side of the city, beyond the tourist throngs.

Kansai

A great complement to Kyoto, the Kansai region is home to **Osaka,** a fun place to eat, drink, and carouse with legendarily friendly locals. Nearby, the small town of **Nara,** home to the famed **Great Buddha of Todai-ji,** is a great place to see traditional Japan, minus Kyoto's crowds. The attractive port city of **Kobe** is known for its high-end beef and jazz, while **Himeji** has Japan's best castle. Farther afield, you'll discover spiritual hot spots like **Kōya-san** and the **Kumano Kodō pilgrimage route.**

Western Honshu

The urbanized, sun-drenched southern coast along the gorgeous **Inland Sea** is home to the vibrant, modern incarnation of **Hiroshima,** as well as the famed "floating" *torii* shrine gate of **Miyajima's Itsukushima-jinja.** This is

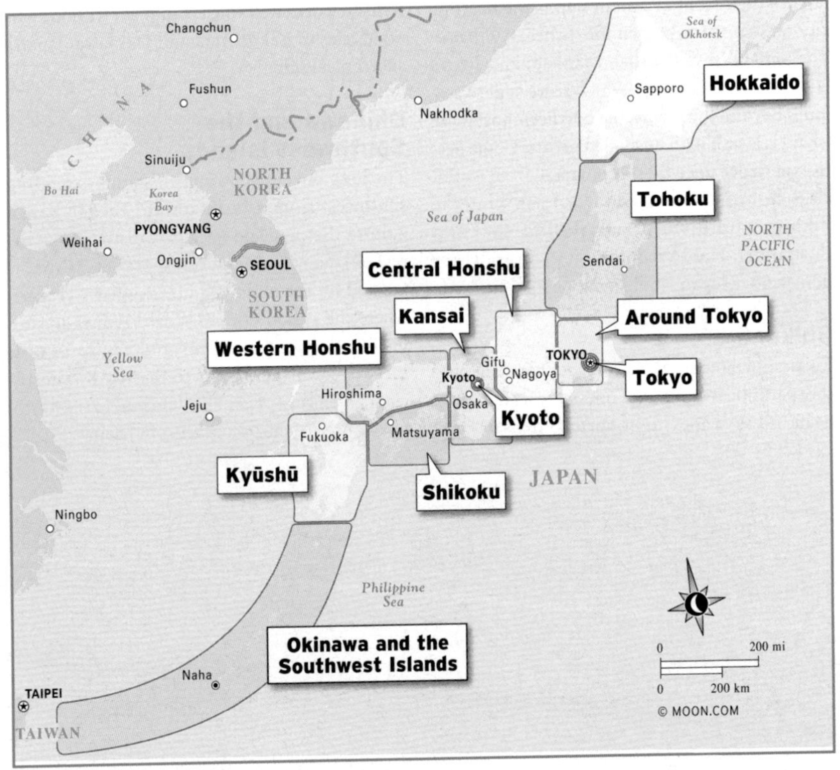

juxtaposed against a mellow northern shore on the Sea of Japan side where the heart of "old Japan" still beats strong. Picturesque historic towns like **Matsue** and the **Izumo Taisha** grand shrine offer the chance to see a slower, simpler, more local side of Japan free of tourist hype.

Tohoku

Located on the northern end of Honshu, Tohoku is a mountainous region steeped in legend. Here you'll find spiritual **pilgrimage routes,** mountaintop **temples,** stunning natural vistas, hidden **hot springs,** and some of the best **summer festivals** in Japan. It's also the home of the pine-covered islands of **Matsushima.** This is a wonderful region to explore if your goal is to go where the vast majority of tourists don't.

Hokkaido

Japan's final frontier's main hub is the bustling city of **Sapporo,** known for its hearty cuisine. The remainder of the island's inhabitants live in laid-back fishing towns, which serve superb seafood. Beyond the towns, the northernmost main island is awash with unspoiled nature. Come here to experience the wild side of Japan, from world-class **skiing** and **snowboarding** in winter to **hiking, wildflowers,** and **wildlife-spotting** in summer. Not to mention, it's culturally the homeland of Japan's indigenous people, the **Ainu.**

Shikoku

Rustic and remote, with a gorgeous coastline, and the sparkling **Inland Sea,** one of the world's most beautiful seascapes, to its north, Shikoku is best known for its arduous **88-temple pilgrimage circuit** that runs clockwise around the island and can be done in part or in full. The rugged interior is best explored in the **Iya Valley** region, where vine bridges and hillside hamlets of thatched-roof houses beckon. And in August, **Awa Odori,** Japan's most exciting traditional summer festival, takes place in Tokushima.

Kyūshū

Volcanic, subtropical, and spiritual, Kyūshū has deep ties to Shinto myth. It's also where Japan first encountered the West when Portuguese sailors made landfall in 1543. Today you can eat **street food** in **Fukuoka;** stroll through dynamically reborn **Nagasaki;** sip **shochu** in **Kagoshima;** peer into the caldera of an active **volcano** or relax in an ***onsen,*** of which there are more than on any other island in Japan. A trip to Kyūshū works well when combined with the emerald isles of Yakushima and Okinawa, Japan's subtropical side.

Okinawa and the Southwest Islands

The long bow of subtropical islands extending southwest from Kyūshū toward Taiwan have a culture, diet, and laid-back pace distinct from the rest of Japan. The main transport hub, **Naha,** is located on the main island, **Okinawa-Hontō,** where the region's ties to **World War II** are still visible. **Remote beaches** and **scuba diving** meccas cover the islands to the south. The ancient green **forests** of **Yakushima,** to the north, boast some of the best **hiking** in Japan.

Know Before You Go

When to Go

Most of Japan has four distinct seasons, interspersed by a few rainy periods, though the country's diverse geography means the climate varies. **Spring** (roughly late-March through mid-June) and **autumn** (October through early December) are the most pleasant times of year to visit the country on the whole. That said, it's a year-round destination, with each season offering its own draw.

SPRING

Spring begins to creep northward from Kyūshū around **early to mid-March** and hits most of Honshu soon after. Spring tends to be **cool** (8-24°C/46-75°F in Tokyo)—gradually warming through **April** and **May**—with patches of rain. **Cherry blossoms** start to bloom from around early to mid-March in Kyūshū, late March in Tokyo, and around early May in Hokkaido, where spring temperatures range -1-17°C (30-63°F). Overall, it's a great time to visit.

Except for Hokkaido, most of Japan is wet throughout **June,** when the hit-and-miss ***tsuyu* (rainy season)** takes hold. Overcast skies with patches of rain and the occasional all-day shower are the norm during this period, though there are plenty of sunny days in between, too.

SUMMER

From **July** through **September** things can be downright **stifling,** with furnace-like temperatures (23-31°C/73-88°F in Tokyo) and high humidity throughout much of the country, save for Hokkaido, which is slightly cooler (14-26°C/57-79°F). While less amenable than spring, the months of July and August can be a fun time to visit the country due to a plethora of vibrant **festivals** held throughout this sweltering period. Among the best are **Fukuoka's Hakata**

Nyūtō Onsen in Tohoku

Nebuta Matsuri float

Gion Matsuri (first half of July), **Kyoto's Gion Matsuri** (most of July, culminating on July 17), **Osaka's Tenjin Matsuri** (July 25), **Aomori's Nebuta Matsuri** (Aug. 2-7), **Akita's Kanto Matsuri** (Aug. 3-6) and **Tokushima's Awa Odori** (Aug. 12-15). If you're visiting the country during any of these bashes, **book accommodations well in advance** (three months or more, to be safe).

AUTUMN

In **September** and **early October**, massive **typhoons** whip through Okinawa, then move northward through Kyūshū, Shikoku and Honshu, but normally stop short of Hokkaido. These turbulent storms have been known to wreak havoc on parts of Japan, with torrential rain and even devastating floods on occasion. These extreme cases aside, it's perfectly safe to travel during this time of year. Just be sure to keep an eye on the weather forecast if you'll be in the country then.

Autumn proper starts from around **early October** and lasts through **November** in Tohoku and Hokkaido (fall temperatures range 1-6°C/34-62°F in Sapporo), extending into the first half of **December** for much of Honshu, Shikoku, and Kyūshū (10-22°C/50-72°F in Tokyo). This is one of the most pleasant times to visit Japan. As temperatures drop, **blazing foliage** ripples through the country, with November being the highpoint. Rates for accommodations do spike around this time in scenic places, so **book ahead** if you plan to head into nature around this time.

WINTER

Winter sets in from **mid-December** through **mid-March,** with temperatures varying significantly across the country (2-12°C/36-54°F in Tokyo, -8-2°C/18-36°F in Sapporo). Okinawa never really has winter proper—temperatures range 14-19°C (57-66°F) even in January.

The Sea of Japan side of Honshu is frigid, windy, and snowy, while the Pacific side is cold, dry, and crisp, with clear skies and little snow. Meanwhile, Hokkaido and the western half of Tohoku have some of **the heaviest average snowfalls** on Earth. Legendary powder also accumulates in the Japan Alps. This means great skiing and snowboarding. There are also excellent **winter festivals,** with the huge **Sapporo Snow Festival,** the intimate **Otaru Snow Light Path Festival,** and the dramatic, fiery **Nozawa Onsen Dosojin Matsuri** atop the list.

HANAMI AND OTHER BUSY TIMES

High season in Japan includes ***hanami*** (cherry blossom viewing) season (roughly late March through early April), the **Golden Week** holidays (April 29-May 5), **Ōbon** (roughly August 10-17), and the height of the **kōyō** (autumn foliage) craze in November. To avoid crowds, it's best not to visit the country during these periods, as trains, highways, and hotels will overflow with domestic travelers from around the time the cherry blossoms start to bloom, around early to mid-March in Kyūshū, late March in Tokyo, and early May in Hokkaido.

SLOWER MONTHS

Less hectic months include **June,** the **dead of summer** (July, August besides Ōbon, and September), **October,** and **December.** Aside from ski resorts, which do brisk business, the period of **January** through **March** is **low season** for the rest of the country. Deals can be had during any of these off months, especially if you plan several months ahead.

Things generally remain in operation throughout the year, the one exception being the **New Year holidays** (December 29-January 3), when everything but convenience stores, some chain restaurants, and most accommodations (at elevated rates) remain open. While experiencing Japan's New Year traditions is one point in favor of visiting over the New Year holidays, it's probably best to come at another time.

Passports and Visas

To enter Japan, you'll need a **passport** valid for the duration of your trip from the date of your arrival in the country. Although you may not be

Philosopher's Path in Kyoto

skiing at Mount Zaō

asked to show it, you're legally obligated to have an onward ticket for either a flight or ferry out of Japan, for a return trip or a future leg of the journey elsewhere. So have something in hand just in case.

If you're coming from the US, Canada, the UK, most European countries, Australia, or New Zealand, you'll be granted a **90-day single-entry visa** on arrival. South African citizens will need to apply for a **90-day tourist visa** at their closest embassy or consulate. For passport holders from the UK, Ireland, and a number of other European countries (Germany, Austria, Switzerland, Lichtenstein), it's possible to extend your visa for another 90 days. This requires a trip to the closest immigration bureau and paying a ¥4,000 fee. For a list of the 68 nations that are not required to apply for a visa before arriving in Japan, visit www.mofa.go.jp/j_info/visit/visa/short/novisa.html.

What to Take

One of the beautiful things about Japan is its well-stocked **convenience stores.** These one-stop shops, selling anything from toiletries and undershirts to bento-box meals and portable phone chargers, umbrellas, cosmetics, and more, are ubiquitous throughout urbanized Japan, making it easy to pick up anything you've forgotten to pack.

Nonetheless, there are a few items you'd be wise to bring. For one: **shoes** that are easy to take on and off (**slip-ons** work best). You'll find yourself likely taking off your shoes much more than you're used to—in someone's home, in a temple, etc. Also pack any **medications** and accompanying **prescriptions** you may need. Be sure to check Japan's strict laws on medication before traveling with medicine. The **US Embassy** provides helpful information on their website about this matter: https://jp.usembassy.gov/u-s-citizen-services/doctors/importing-medication.

The electrical outlets in Japan are the same shape as those in the United States, so travelers with devices from the UK or Europe may need a plug adapter. The voltage is 100V; many modern electronics are dual voltage, so a converter may not be necessary, but check your devices to be sure.

It also pays to be aware of Japan's love of

gift-giving. This is especially important if you plan to meet anyone who may invite you to their home. It need not be expensive. Some kind of a sweet snack or beverage that can be shared, a recording of interesting music, or some kind of decorative item would all do. A little gift goes a long way in Japan.

Planning Ahead

There are a few things that need to be in order before you leave for Japan. First things first, if you plan to get a **Japan Rail Pass** (www.japanrailpass.net), a great value if you plan on making full use of the country's extensive train network, **you must purchase it before traveling to Japan.** You cannot buy a JR Pass once you are in Japan.

If you're planning to travel to some of the more remote parts of Japan and want to rent a car, make sure you've already gotten your **international driver's license** (IDP, aka international driving permit). To learn more about the process of obtaining an IDP, visit https://internationaldrivingpermit.org, which provides country-by-country information on the process of applying. It doesn't hurt to **book your rental car before your trip** to avoid hassle later.

It also pays to make **reservations** for some meals, attractions, or events, such as a sumo tournament or sporadically held *Noh* theater performance, a few months in advance. Some **popular attractions,** such as Tokyo's Ghibli Museum and Kyoto's "moss temple" Saihō-ji, only allow a set number of visitors per day; you'll need to book your place at these attractions up to a few months in advance as well. If you're determined to snag a seat at a world-class sushi counter, *kaiseki ryōri* restaurant, or any other truly **world-famous restaurants,** some of the wait times are shocking. Aim to book seats months in advance.

Finally, if you happen to be visiting anywhere during a **festival** or one of the **high seasons,** try to book everything—accommodation, rental car, even *shinkansen* (bullet train) tickets—as far in advance as you can (think three, or even six months ahead).

Transportation

GETTING THERE

The vast majority of travelers will arrive in Japan via one of **four main airports:** Tokyo's Narita Airport or Haneda Airport, Osaka's Kansai International Airport, or Nagoya's Chubu Centrair International Airport. It's also possible to enter the country by sea, with **hydrofoils** and **ferries** shuttling daily between **Busan, South Korea,** and **Fukuoka.** Ferries also make the trip between **Shanghai** and both **Osaka** and **Kobe.**

GETTING AROUND

Once you're on the ground, transportation options are profuse, from trains and planes to buses, ferries, and rental cars.

BY TRAIN

Japan's most efficient mode of transport is its **extensive railway** network. You'll be able to get where you're going aboard a train—whether of the **local, rapid,** or ***shinkansen*** (bullet train) variety—in the vast majority of cases. Traveling short distances within a city or town is also often best done by train, whether above-ground or subway.

If you plan to rely heavily on the rail network, consider buying a **Japan Rail Pass** (www.japanrailpass.net) before you get to Japan. This pass—which offers unlimited trains on the Japan Rail (JR) network nationwide in increments of one, two, and three weeks—is a steal if you maximize it.

BY BUS

Buses are another option for traveling both long distances and just within town. Although less comfortable than trains, buses are sometimes the only means of reaching some **far-flung destinations.** They are also generally **cheaper** than trains, making them a good option if you're on a serious budget and don't mind the journey taking a bit more time.

BY TAXI

Taxis are abundant. That said, fares are **expensive.** They are best used either for only

short distances within a town or city when there's no cheaper means of getting around, you're in a rush, or you have money to burn.

BY CAR

A rental car will be invaluable if you're venturing well **off the beaten path.** This is especially the case when traveling in **rural Hokkaido, Tohoku, Shikoku's deep interior,** or some parts of **Kyūshū** and **Okinawa.** Trains still run through some parts of these regions, but their frequency and reach can sometimes be frustratingly limited. (Driving is on the **left,** like in the UK.) If you plan to drive, you must get an **international driving permit (IDP)** before arriving. Visit https://internationaldrivingpermit.org for country-by-country information on the process of applying.

BY AIR

If you're short on time, consider using the country's far-reaching **domestic flight network.** This can prove particularly useful for trips to or from the northern or southern edges of the country, such as **Hokkaido, Kyūshū,** or **Okinawa.**

BY BOAT

In terms of experience, taking a **ferry** will add a new dimension to any trip within Japan. If you happen to be traveling between Shikoku and Kyūshū, Kyūshū and Okinawa, or Honshu and Hokkaido, there are some ferry operators that make overnight journeys. High-speed, jet-propelled **hydrofoils** (aka jetfoils) also make shorter journeys (e.g., from Kagoshima to Yakushima, or from Niigata to Sado-ga-shima).

The main things to consider before hopping on a ferry is whether your trip timeline is generous enough to accommodate the **slower pace** and whether you're prepared to potentially deal with a bit of **seasickness.** One advantage of ferries is the feasibility of carrying a bicycle, motorbike, or rental car on board for an added fee.

shinkansen (bullet train) in Kyūshū

Sensō-ji temple

The Best of Japan

This two-week itinerary is a good choice for visitors making their first journey to Japan and can be done largely by train (local, express, and bullet train), with a few legs of the trip done by rental car or ferry. It covers the two major "must-visit" cities of Tokyo and Kyoto, and the two important regions in which these cities are located—Kantō, or Greater Tokyo, and Kansai to the south—while also passing through beautifully mountainous Central Honshu, or Chūbu. You'll see urban jungles, traditional temples, gorgeous scenery, fascinating historic sites, and you'll eat very well along the way.

If this itinerary seems a bit ambitious, you could leave off Kanazawa and the Japan Alps and give yourself a buffer day or two in Tokyo and Kyoto.

This itinerary starts with your first full day in Japan, and so the day you arrive at either Narita or Haneda, just plan on getting to your accommodation and sleeping off some jetlag.

Tokyo

For your time in Tokyo, the western districts of Shinjuku or Shibuya or the upscale area around Tokyo Station would each be a good place to base yourself.

DAY 1

Get acquainted with Tokyo's modern side by exploring Shinjuku, Shibuya, and Harajuku. Start at **Meiji Jingū,** Tokyo's most impressive shrine, then wander through the side streets of the sprawling district of **Harajuku,** ground zero for youth fashion in Japan. Proceed down **Omotesando** and its high-end shops to **Aoyama,** where you'll find the **Nezu Museum's** collection of premodern Asian art and a wonderful garden. Make your way to **Shibuya,** the beating heart of Japanese youth culture and home to the world's busiest intersection, and finish your night with dinner and drinks at a lively *izakaya* in trendy **Ebisu.** After you've eaten, go for **cocktails** or to one of the city's many excellent **DJ bars** nearby.

DAY 2

Start the day by exploring the slower, old-school neighborhoods on the east side of town. Begin with a trip to the colorful Buddist temple **Sensō-ji** in **Asaskusa,** then head west to **Ueno,** famed for its massive park and the **Tokyo National Museum,** which houses the world's largest collection of Japanese art. Proceed to nearby **Akihabara,** the best spot to glimpse some of Japan's quirky subcultures, chief of them being *otaku*, a catch-all word for all things geek. Take the subway to **Tokyo City View** in the entertainment district of **Roppongi** for striking views of the concrete jungle below. End the day in **Shinjuku,** eating dinner in the smoky alleyway of hole-in-the-wall restaurants that is **Omoide Yokochō,** followed by a bar crawl through **Golden Gai's** drinking dens.

Kanazawa and the Japan Alps

DAY 3

In the morning, take the bullet train from Tokyo to Kanazawa, a 3-hour ride, arriving in time for lunch. Spend the day immersing yourself in the rich heritage of this alluring city, which rose to prominence during the Edo period (1603-1868). There's the beautiful garden **Kenroku-en,** considered Japan's best; the stately castle **Kanazawa-jō;** the well-preserved **Nagamachi samurai quarter;** and the atmospheric geisha district of **Higashi Chaya-gai.** Get a good night's sleep for a busy next day.

DAY 4

Get an early start and take the bullet train to Toyama (25 minutes), then transfer to a limited express train to the mountain town of Takayama (1.5 hours). You'll spend the next day exploring Takayama, but first, head out for a day hike in **Kamikōchi,** a beautiful corner of the Japan Alps. Rent a car and drive east for about 1 hour on Route 158 to the Akandana parking lot near Hirayu Onsen. Access Kamikōchi proper by bus or taxi (20-30 minutes) from there. The trail that runs along the **Azusa River,** from the beautifully situated **Kappa-bashi bridge** to the campground and lodge of **Tokusawa** (4 hours round-trip), is a good choice. Have lunch at the

Kamikōchi

Kyoto

farmhouse in Ainokura

restaurant beside **Myōjin-ike pond,** which you'll pass on the hike. After returning to your car, drive 30 minutes north to **Shin-Hotaka Ropeway.** Board the two double-decker cable cars and ascend 800 meters (2,624 feet) to the top of **Nishi-Hotaka-dake** (2,909 meters/9,543 feet) to enjoy stunning panoramas of the Northern Alps. (Note: Activies like the hike and ropeway aren't feasible during winter, roughly November-March.) Descend and drive to your *ryokan* of choice in the **Shin-Hotaka Onsen area,** just a few minutes drive south of the ropeway. Enjoy an evening of relaxation at one of the area's hot-spring *ryokan*, where you'll eat dinner and soak to your heart's content.

DAY 5

After having breakfast at your inn, drive roughly 1 hour southwest, back to **Takayama,** following routes 475, 471, and 158. Spend the first half of the day meandering through Takayama's old atmospheric merchant's quarter, **Sanmachi Suji.** After lunch—a meal centered on the town's famed **Hida beef** is a good pick—venture in your rental car into the countryside west of town to the **Shirakawa-gō** region, famed for its traditional thatched-roof farmhouses, which are open to the pubic and offer a picturesque glimpse of rural life in premodern Japan. Begin in **Ogimachi,** 1 hour northwest of Takayama and the most famous and accessible of these folk villages. Continue deeper into the surrounding countryside, driving 30 minutes north to **Suganuma,** then another 15 minutes beyond that to **Ainokura.** Stay overnight at one of the many evocative **farmhouses** in the area, but be sure to book well in advance: They fill up fast.

Kyoto

For your time in Kyoto, Gion or downtown make convenient bases.

DAY 6

Head back to Kanazawa and drop off your rental car. Then, hop on a bullet train bound for Kyoto, a 2.5 hour ride that should get you to town in time for lunch. After you've arrived, check into your room and spend the remainder of your daylight hours exploring a few of the city's major sights.

Consider the hillside temple of **Kiyomizu-dera,** the majestic Pure Land Buddhist temple of **Chion-in,** and maybe **Nijo-jō** castle. In the evening, splurge on a once-in-a-lifetime dinner at a ***kaiseki ryōri*** restaurant, followed by cocktails or **whisky** at one of Kyoto's discerning purveyors of the spirit.

DAY 7

Discover Kyoto's less crowded side on your second day in the city. Head to **Arashiyama's** famous **bamboo grove,** and be sure to visit the less crowded **Okochi-Sanso Villa,** once home to a Japanese movie star and famed for its sublime gardens and traditional architecture. The atmospheric temples of **Jōjakkō-ji, Nison-in, Giō-ji,** and **Adashino Nenbutsu-ji** are all within 20 minutes' walk north of the villa, with a fraction of the crowds that visit the grove. Backtrack to the **Katsura-gawa** and have lunch at one of the eateries lining the river. After lunch, make your way to **Ryōan-ji** to check out the temple's rock garden and some of the other famous sights in the area, such as the gold-leaf-covered **Kinkaku-ji.** Plan on having dinner in the **Gion district.** Consider seeing a **geisha performance** after dinner, followed by a stroll down the dreamy, lantern-lit alleyway of **Pontochō.**

Kōya-san

DAY 8

In the morning, make your way north to visit some of the spiritual gems of the **Higashiyama** neighborhood, from important Zen temple **Nanzen-ji** to **Ginkaku-ji,** the silver companion to golden Kinkaku-ji, and the contemplation-inducing **Philosopher's Path.** After having lunch in the area, depart Kyoto, making your way to the mountain hermitage of **Kōya-san,** roughly 3.5 hours south of Kyoto by limited express train, via Osaka. Once you've arrived at the remote mountain hermitage, check into your ***shukubō*** (temple lodging), where you'll be based for a night. In the remaining daylight, explore Kōya-san's temples and the atmospheric cemetery of **Okuno-in.** For dinner, eat like a monk with a feast of ***shōjin-ryōri*** (Buddhist vegetarian fare) at your temple-cum-lodging.

Kōya-san

Arashiyama Bamboo Grove in Kyoto

Hiroshima-style *okonomiyaki*

Himeji and the Inland Sea

DAY 9

After an early breakfast at your *shukubō,* leave Kōya-san and begin your journey west, toward the "art island" of Naoshima. This picturesque island in Japan's gorgeous Inland Sea has developed a reputation for its eclectic modern art museums, sculptures dotting the landscape, and charming villages. But first, take the local train to Shin-Osaka, then hop on the bullet train to **Himeji,** 3.5 hours into your journey, to pay a visit to Japan's greatest fortress, **Himeji-jō** (aka "White Heron" castle). Have lunch before continuing west to Okayama by *shinkansen* (20 minutes), transfer to the JR Uno-port line, and ride until the port of Uno (45 minutes). There, board a 20-minute **ferry** to Naoshima.

DAY 10

Wake up early and have breakfast at one of Naoshima's charming **cafés.** Get a **bicycle** so you can explore the island's buzzing art scene on two wheels. Start at the **Art House Project,** empty houses transformed into works of art in the old village of Honmura, then head to museum-cum-hotel **Benesse House** and the **Chichū Art Museum,** built directly into the earth. This stretch of coast offers dramatic views of the sun as it dips below the Inland Sea.

DAY 11

Take a 20-minute ferry from Naoshima to the less-crowded neighboring island of Teshima. Explore the island's **experimental art sights,** cleverly integrated into the landscape. After having **lunch** at one of Teshima's many charming cafés, make your way back to the mainland via ferry to Uno port and travel by a series of trains west to Hiroshima, about 1.5 hours total travel time. For dinner, try the city's signature spin on ***okonomiyaki,*** a delicious savory pancake.

Hiroshima and Miyajima

DAY 12

Visit Hiroshima's **Peace Park** in the morning for a sobering lesson on one of the darkest moments in Japan's history. Next, take the JR San'yō line from Hiroshima Station to Miyajimaguchi Station (25 minutes), before walking to the nearby

Onsen: The Art of Skinny Dipping

Whether in the pool of a countryside inn, an *onsen* resort, a co-ed, open-air pool (aka *rotenburo*), don't be anxious—bathing etiquette remains the same.

- **Slip out of your shoes** at the door. There will usually be lockers or shelves for shoes, and a locker just outside the changing rooms for any valuables. It goes without saying, but having your phone or snapping photos anywhere beyond this point is an absolute no-no.

- Enter the appropriate **changing room** (men: 男; women: 女) and leave your clothing in a locker or basket. No clothing of any kind is acceptable in the bathing area.

- You absolutely must bathe before getting into the pool. Scrub yourself down in the **separate area for washing,** oftentimes with small plastic or wooden stools. Rinse yourself and the space as a courtesy to the next person.

- Most *onsen* will either provide or rent you a small **towel** and a larger towel for drying after you leave the bath, but some simple *onsen* don't provide towels or soap, in which case you'll need to bring your own. It's fine to use a small towel for modesty purposes on your way to enter the bath, although many simply mill about freely without concern.

- **Ease into the water** up to your shoulders—don't splash—and never put your head underwater. If you have long hair, either wrap it into the towel or tie it with a hairband. Likewise, keep the small towel out of the water, leaving it beside the bath or folding it up on your head while you soak.

- It's perfectly fine to have casual conversation, but **don't be rowdy.** Alcohol is frowned upon—though nice in moderation if you've got a private bath in your own room.

- When you exit the bath, **wipe off excess water** before you return to the changing room to dry off and get dressed. You've successfully navigated an *onsen*!

A quick word on **tattoos:** Many *onsen* facilities have a strict policy against them due to their unfortunate association in with *yakuza* (mafia). The best policy is to cover any smaller tattoos you may have with waterproof band-aids or medical tape. Keep them concealed when dealing with staff at the entrance and reception desk. To be sure of an *onsen*'s tattoo policy, simply call ahead—or have your hotel's reception desk or concierge do so for you.

Here's a list of Japan's top *onsen*:

- **Shin-Hotaka Onsen:** Tucked away deep in the mountains east of the town of Takayama, this *onsen* area is famed for its co-ed bath, Shin-Hotaka-no-yu, set beside a river and surrounded by mountains swathed in forest (page 274).

- **Kinosaki Onsen:** This quintessential *onsen* village beside the Sea of Japan is about 2.5 hours north of Kyoto by train. Don a *yukata* (lightweight kimono) and *geta* (wooden clogs), and bath-hop your way around the picturesque town (page 397).

- **Nyūtō Onsen:** Escape from the modern world at this remote jewel in the depths of Tohoku. Famed for its milky-white pool and old-school mixed bathing. This is my personal favorite (page 474).

- **Dōgo Onsen:** This fabled *onsen* in Shikoku's Matsuyama inspired filmmaker Hayao Miyazaki, who is said to have drawn inspiration from the Dōgo Onsen Honkan for the ethereal bathhouse in his animated masterpiece *Spirited Away* (page 578).

- **Kurokawa Onsen:** Located north of the vast caldera of Aso-san, this idyllic *onsen* village sits in a remote valley in the heart of Kyūshū; its well-preserved atmosphere makes it among one of Japan's prettiest *onsen* towns (page 654).

ferry terminal for the 10-minute trip to nearby **Miyajima** and **Itsukushima-jinja,** famed for its "floating" *torii* shrine gate. By mid-afternoon, return to Hiroshima and hop on a bullet train to **Osaka,** less than 1.5 hours' ride east, where you'll stay for the night. Spend the evening soaking up Osaka's brash nighttime vibe in its **Dōtombori** neighborhood on the south side of town.

Osaka and Shuzen-ji Onsen

DAY 13

After waking up at a suitably late hour—allowing yourself to recover if things got rowdy the night before—spend the late morning exploring Osaka's north side (perhaps riding to the top of **Umeda Sky Building** for 360-degree vistas of Japan's third largest metropolis) and have lunch before hopping on the bullet train to start the long journey back toward Tokyo. On the way, stop at the hot-spring mecca of **Shuzen-ji Onsen,** located a few hours by southwest of Tokyo. To reach Shuzen-ji from Osaka, take the *shinkansen* from Shin-Osaka Station to Atami (2 hours 20 minutes), then transfer to the limited express Odoriko (40 minutes). Stay for the night at a ***ryokan*** (traditional inn), soaking in ***onsen* baths**, donning a *yukata* (lightweight kimono), and enjoying Japan's legendary spirit of hospitality (*omotenashi*).

Tokyo

DAY 14

After a leisurely breakfast at your *ryokan* and a final *onsen* soak, make your way back to Tokyo by train by lunchtime and check into your accommodation for the night. Revisit any parts of the city that particularly spoke to you, or take care of any remaining **souvenir shopping** before your return flight home the next day.

Japan's Wild North: Hokkaido

Hokkaido is Japan's last frontier, a vast wilderness, save for its energetic capital of Sapporo and earthy fishing towns dotting its shore. This is the best place to go if your aim is to discover Japan's untamed side. Given that this itinerary involves plenty of time spent walking through nature, it's best suited to the warmer months (roughly May through October), with summer (July-August) being prime time.

Hakodate

DAY 1

Arrive in Hakodate on a connecting flight from Tokyo. Begin your day at the **morning market** for a seafood breakfast before hopping on the tram to the east side of town and the star-shaped **Fort Goryōkaku,** the first Western-style fortress built in Japan. Get back on the tram to the west side of town for lunch in the historic **Motomachi** neighborhood and to explore its 19th-centry architecture. Before sunset, hop on the **Mount Hakodate Ropeway** and get in position to see the city's lights flicker, ending the day by heading to dinner on **Daimon Yokōcho,** an alley lined with eateries a quick walk southeast of Hakodate Station.

Tōya-ko and Noboribetsu Onsen

DAY 2

Start your day early, traveling by train northeast for 2 hours to pristine lake **Tōya-ko.** Stop at the **Volcano Science Museum** to experience a simulated eruption, then take the nearby ropeway to the top of **Usu-zan** for wide-open vistas of Tōya-ko and nearby **Shōwa-shinzan,** Japan's youngest volcano. Follow the **Kompirayama Walking Trail,** which begins near Tōya-ko Visitor Center on the southwest side of the lake, where you'll see glimpses of industrial carnage—apartment blocks, bridges, roads, and more—destroyed when Usu-zan erupted in 2000. After taking in this sobering sight, travel to **Noboribetsu Onsen** to stay overnight at one of the *ryokan* in this famed hot-spring town.

Sapporo

DAY 3

In the morning, take a 75-minute train ride north to Sapporo, Hokkaido's bustling capital. Begin your exploration of the city at **Hokkaido Jingū,** the island's most important shrine. Have **ramen** or **soup curry** for lunch downtown, then explore the highlights of the city center—the long, central park of **Ōdōri-kōen,** the red-brick, 19th-centry **Former Hokkaido Government Office,** and the **Hokkaido University Botanical Garden**—on foot. For another nighttime city view, head to **Mount Moiwa,** southwest of downtown, and ascend by ropeway and cable car. For dinner, try **Genghis Khan** (Mongolian BBQ) and wash it down with **locally brewed beer.** If you've got energy, head to the city's huge entertainment district, **Susukino,** Japan's rowdiest nightlife zone north of Tokyo.

Otaru

DAY 4

Take the train west to the old port town of Otaru and its charming **canal district,** fronted by atmospheric 19th-century warehouses and the **Otaru City Museum.** Continue to **Nichigin-dōri,** once Hokkaido's most important financial district, when Otaru made a mint as a 19th-century herring center. The town is still renowned for its fresh catch, so plan on eating lunch at one of its excellent **sushi** shops. As dusk approaches, get dinner at Otaru's canal-side **brewery** before heading back to Sapporo.

Daisetsuzan National Park

DAY 5

Hop on the train from Sapporo 1.5 hours to **Asahikawa,** the gateway to Daisetsuzan National Park, the largest national park in Japan, with some of its most rugged scenery. Rent a car and drive 1 hour east to **Asahidake Onsen,** where you'll stay for the night. Take one of the more manageable **hikes** in the Asahidake Onsen area, accessed via the **Daisetsuzan**

Mount Hakodate Ropeway

soup curry

Asahidake Ropeway, before winding down in the evening with a hot-spring bath in the village.

DAY 6

Drive about 2 hours northeast to **Sōunkyō Onsen.** Consider hiking to the top of **Mount Kurodake,** with a little help from the **Kurodake Ropeway,** accessed near the Sōunkyō Visitor Center, before staying overnight at the charming hot spring resort.

Shiretoko National Park

DAY 7

Get an early start and drive roughly 4 hours east to the southern edge of Shiretoko National Park, which occupies a remote peninsula in northeast Hokkaido. Spend the day exploring the park's wealth of **hiking trails, wildlife-watching** opportunities, and open-air ***onsen* pools.** Spend the night in the town of **Rausu** on the east coast, a good base for exploring the park.

Kushiro Wetlands

DAY 8

In the morning, drive about 3 hours southwest to the Kushiro Wetlands, where you can see Hokkaido's famed **red-crested cranes** in their native habitat. End your trip by driving 45 minutes west of the marshlands to **Kushiro Airport,** from where you can either fly to Sapporo or Tokyo.

Sapporo Snow Festival sculpture

killer whales near Shiretoko National Park

Top Temples and Shrines

monk at Okuno-in

Priests and monks have been meditating, chanting, studying, and performing rituals at temples and shrines across Japan for millennia. These spiritual sanctuaries range from humble and rustic to flamboyant and colorful, even plated with gold. In the case of **Shinto,** the form of nature worship native to the archipelago, halls of worship are known as shrines (with names that include *-jinja, -jingū, -gū, -hongū, Taisha*, etc.), while in the case of the imported faith of **Buddhism,** they're known as temples (with names that include *-tera, -dera, -ji, -in*, etc.). Here are some outstanding representations of the country's religious architecture.

- **Meiji Jingū:** Tokyo's top shrine is set within an expansive swathe of green in the heart of the city that makes for a pleasant stroll and reprieve from the din outside (page 67).
- **Fushimi Inari-Taisha:** With a famous walking path lined by thousands of vermillion *torii* gates, this complex in southeast Kyoto is the head shrine dedicated to Inari, the god of rice (page 301).
- **Kinkaku-ji:** Originally the house of a retired shogun, the upper two floors of this Zen Buddhist temple in Kyoto are coated in gold leaf, inspiring the name "the Golden Pavilion" (page 316).
- **Tōdai-ji:** This temple in Nara is the largest wooden structure on earth, and it's only two-thirds the size of the original. It houses a 15-meter- (45-foot-) tall bronze Daibutsu (Great Buddha) (page 385).
- **Okuno-in:** Set amid soaring cedar trees, the cemetery, temple, and mausoleum is full of fierce guardian deities, moss-encrusted stone monuments, and stone lanterns (page 403).
- **Ise-Jingū:** Shinto's holiest shrine, Ise's spell is woven through its sheer simplicity. The shrine has been dismantled and rebuilt every 20 years for the past 1,300 years (page 406).
- **Itsukushima-jinja:** This shrine on the island of Miyajima near Hiroshima is famed for its *torii* gate that seemingly floats on the Inland Sea during high tide (page 426).
- **Yamadera:** This remote temple complex sprawls over a mountainside in deep Tohoku, reached by a steep path lined by stone lanterns and Buddhist statuary (page 460).

From Beaches to Volcanoes: Kyūshū and Okinawa

Kyūshū is a fantastic representation of classic Japan—volcanos, *onsen*, great food, and attractive cities—and an appealing alternative to the usual Tokyo and Kyoto itinerary. Meanwhile, Okinawa and the string of islands extending beyond is decidedly un-Japanese: laid-back vibes, white-sand beaches, and a distinct culture and heritage. On this trip, you'll take trains, rental cars, ferries, and planes. It's a great choice if you'd like to discover a balmy, subtropical side of Japan that you may not have realized exists.

Fukuoka

DAY 1

After you've flown from Tokyo to Kyūshū's largest metropolis of Fukuoka, begin your journey through Japan's southernmost main island by exploring this thoroughly modern city with a cosmopolitan vibe. Start your day near **Hakata Station,** exploring the city's primary spiritual sights: **Tōchō-ji,** known for its huge wooden Buddha statue, and **Kushida-jinja,** a shrine revered by many as the city's spiritual heart. Visit the **Fukuoka Asian Art Museum,** the **Fukuoka Castle Ruins,** and **Fukuoka City Museum** to dig a bit deeper into the important history of the city and its vibrant present. Head to the rows of ***yatai* (street food)** stalls along the riverfront on **Nakasu Island** and **Tenjin.**

Nagasaki

DAY 2

Hop on the train for a 2-hour ride to Nagasaki. A quick ride on the city's efficient tram network takes you to the sobering **Peace Park,** which commemorates the nuclear bombing of the city during World War II. After leaving the park, head south by tram to the atmospheric district of **Teramachi ("Temple Town")** and visit **Sōfuku-ji,** a temple that demonstrates the clear Chinese influence long felt in the city. The nearby **Chinatown** (Shinchi) will allow you to literally taste China's imprint on the city. Next, head up the **Dutch Slope,** a neighborhood that shows another foreign group's influence. It's lined with 19th-century Western architecture, and is home to **Ōura Cathedral** and **Glover Garden.** Traipse downhill to **Dejima,** an artificial island created to accommodate Dutch traders during the 17th century. For dinner, try ***shippoku,*** Nagasaki's spin on haute *kaiseki ryōri*. End the day with a trip to the top of **Inasayama-kōen,** across the bay from downtown, to see the city's lights flicker on.

Kurokawa Onsen

DAY 3

In the morning, rent a car near Nagasaki Station and drive 3 hours eastward, making your way to the pristine hot spring village of **Kurokawa Onsen**, set deep in a lush valley in a remote corner of Kumamoto Prefecture, north of the vast caldera of Aso-san. Check into your ***ryokan*** of choice, don a ***yukata*** (lightweight kimono) and spend the day vegging out in your room, soaking in your *ryokan's* tubs, and bath-hopping around the charming town. Eat a lavish dinner at your inn and sleep well.

Aso-san and Kagoshima

DAY 4

After breakfast at the inn and a final morning soak, drive to Aso-san to admire the views across the vast windswept **caldera.** Continue driving south for 3.5 hours to the laid-back city of Kagoshima, where you'll stay for the night. Head over to the pretty gardens of **Sengan-en** and be sure to also visit the nearby **Shoko Shuseikan** factory, where Japan's industrial revolution kicked off. For dinner, try one of

Kagoshima's specialties, such as ***kurobuta*** (black pork) or ***shabu-shabu*** (hot pot), followed by a proper introduction to the prefecture's beloved beverage of choice, ***shōchū***.

Yakushima

DAY 5

Start the day with a brief trip to **Sakurajima** (Japan's very own Vesuvius), crossing the bay by ferry. This active volcano is a daily presence for Kagoshima residents, before whom it belches smoke and ominously looms. Return to downtown Kagoshima for lunch, then head to the ferry terminal again—this time to board the **jet foil** to Yakushima. After arriving in Yakushima, rent a car at Miyanoura Port and drive to your accommodation for the night. Get settled in and rest well—you'll need the energy for the next day.

DAY 6

Wake up early—you will explore the emerald island of Yakushima for the whole day. Drive around the island and explore the beautiful **Ōkonotaki waterfall** or **Yakusugi Land,** a park that makes the island's famed giant Yakusugi trees more accessible, and **Hirauchi Kaichu Onsen,** a hot-spring pool on the south side of the island that can only be accessed at low tide. For something more substantial, consider the 3-4 hour hike through the lush **Shiratani Unsuikyō ravine,** which inspired anime maestro Hayao Miyazaki's masterful film *Princess Mononoke.* Return to your hotel for a good night's sleep.

Naha

DAY 7

Return by jet foil to Kagoshima in the morning. Head to **Kagoshima Airport** and fly to Naha, the capital of Okinawa Prefecture. Plan on eating somewhere with a traditional musical performance of Okinawa's wistful three-stringed instrument, the ***sanshin.*** Be sure to try Okinawa's potent booze, the spirit known as ***awamori.***

statue in Nagasaki Peace Park; sculpture by Seibo Kitamura

Furuzamami Beach

Kerama Islands

DAY 8

Start the day early with a trip by jet foil to **Zamami-jima,** one of the islands in the Kerama island chain, less than an hour west of Naha. While away a few hours on **Furuzamami Beach** before taking a boat 15 minutes southwest to **Aka-jima. Swim, snorkel,** or simply saunter around this mellow sliver of land, which teems with the petite **Kerama deer.** As the afternoon wears on, hop on a jet foil from Aka-jima directly back to Naha. When the time comes, head to **Naha Airport** and fly to Tokyo for your flight home.

Tokyo 東京

Tokyo is more than a city. Japan's sprawling

capital bursts at the seams with a population of 37 million to form the largest metro area on the planet. The dizzying metropolis organically congeals around a cluster of hubs the size of cities themselves, giving Tokyo a labyrinthine quality. With the neon nightscapes of Shinjuku and Shibuya evoking *Blade Runner* in the west, the ancient temples and wooden houses of Ueno and Asakusa in the east, and palpable energy coursing throughout, Tokyo packs a strong sensory punch.

The city's dynamism is inextricably linked to its history of continuous reinvention. Long before its ascent on the world stage, Tokyo was a small fishing hamlet known as Edo, located on the banks of the Sumida River. Its clout began to grow when Tokugawa Ieyasu, founder

Highlights

Look for ★ to find recommended sights, activities, dining, and lodging.

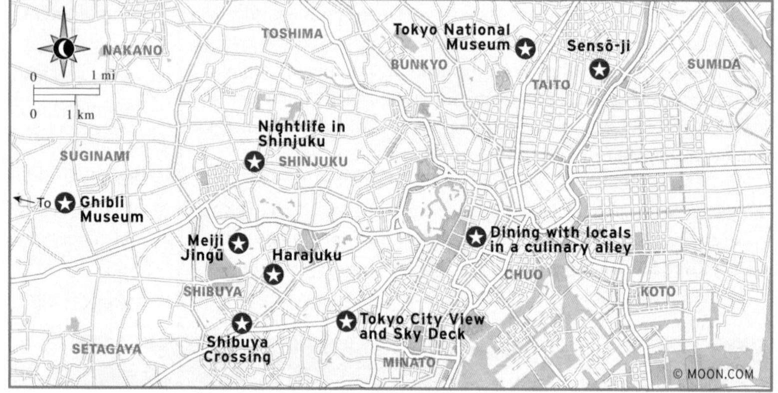

★ **Ghibli Museum:** This fantastical museum dedicated to Japan's most beloved anime studio, Studio Ghibli, sits within Inokashira-kōen, one of Tokyo's most appealing parks (page 64).

★ **Harajuku:** Ground zero for Japan's colorful youth fashion scene, this neighborhood is full of hip boutiques clustered around the busy thoroughfare of Omotesandō and tucked down a dense tangle of pedestrian-friendly backstreets (page 64).

★ **Meiji Jingū:** Surrounded by forest, this majestic Shinto shrine provides an oasis of calm just beyond the fashionable throngs of Harajuku (page 67).

★ **Shibuya Crossing:** Simply crossing the world's busiest pedestrian intersection will leave you gobsmacked by Tokyo's formidable pulse (page 69).

★ **Tokyo City View and Sky Deck:** Tokyo City View offers one of the most thrilling ways to get the lay of the land. Ascend to the Sky Deck on the building's roof for windowless views in all directions (page 75).

★ **Sensō-ji:** Tokyo's most famous temple houses a golden image of the Buddhist Goddess of Mercy (page 78).

★ **Tokyo National Museum:** If you only have time for one museum in your Tokyo itinerary, make it this one—it holds the world's largest collection of Japanese art (page 82).

★ **Dining with locals in a culinary alley:** Take a seat beside locals at a hole-in-the-wall eatery in one of Tokyo's numerous *yokochō* (culinary alleys) for a meal and an experience you won't forget (page 118).

★ **Nightlife in Shinjuku:** Tokyo's most eclectic nightlife zone offers experiences from robot battles to pub crawls through the tumbledown bars of Golden Gai (page 134).

of the Tokugawa shogunate, chose to base his government in Edo Castle in 1603. By the mid-18th century, Edo's population swelled to 1 million, making it the world's largest city at the time.

The city was renamed Tokyo (Eastern Capital) in 1868, when the official capital migrated from Kyoto and the Tokugawa shogunate's rule came to an end. It was this pivotal year when political power returned to the emperor via the Meiji Restoration, and Japan opened up to the world beyond after enforcing a policy of self-isolation for more than 250 years. Tokyoites eagerly lapped up the new influences from abroad, from fashion to philosophy, and the contours of the present city began to take shape. This then unraveled following the Great Kanto Earthquake of 1923 and subsequent firebombing during World War II. But once again Tokyo proved its mettle, serving as the main engine of Japan's "economic miracle" during the 1950s and '60s. But the growth didn't last; the country's "bubble economy" finally popped in the late 1980s, and a malaise descended that lingers to this day.

Economic indicators may paint a sluggish picture, but Tokyo's street life tells another story. The capital's culinary offerings are truly world-class, from mom-and-pop ramen shops to lavish sushi spreads. Tokyo is also the best place in Japan to watch traditional Kabuki and *Noh* theater performances, as well as sumo. The city oozes style, with high-end fashion offerings as well as Harajuku's quirky collection of youth-oriented labels. It's also home to one of the world's most singular pop culture industries, most visible in the gadget paradise of Akihabara's "Electric Town." Moreover, Tokyo simply works. Compared with other major cities, it's positively spic and span. Well-stocked vending machines and convenience stores are reassuringly never more than a few blocks away. And trains full of dapper commuters rarely miss a beat.

But no trip to Tokyo is complete without experiencing Tokyo like a local: Wander away from any busy station area and you'll soon discover a dense network of communities with fiercely maintained traditions, where denizens shop at the neighborhood store and rowdy homegrown festivals mark the passing of time. These many villages are, in many ways, the backbone of Tokyo, and reveal the city at its most hospitable. Embrace the warm welcome, then enjoy getting lost.

ORIENTATION

Although Tokyo is commonly thought of as a city, it is in fact one of Japan's 47 prefectures. It's divided into 23 special wards, which function as cities themselves, and Tokyo includes 39 municipalities to the west and the far-flung Izu and Ogasawara island chains. More than 9 million people live in the 23 special wards, and 13 million reside within the prefecture. The greater metropolitan area is home to a whopping 37.8 million, making it the most populous metro area on the planet.

Wrapping your mind around this massive slice of humanity is daunting, but it's helpful to think of Tokyo not in terms of officially drawn lines but rather as a vast collection of neighborhoods that have grown around a matrix of railway stations. It's worth remembering Tokyo's roots as a cluster of fishing settlements, which expanded over the centuries to form Tokyo's major hubs.

Navigating all of this is admittedly a big task. Thankfully, the excellent train and subway system can get you within a short walk of just about anywhere in the city. Key among the railway lines are the roughly ovular **Yamanote Line,** which wraps around the city, and the **Chūō Line,** which pierces through the center of the city, running east to west. Most travelers stick to major hubs dotting the Yamanote Line or inside this loop, with occasional forays west to some of the city's more free-spirited haunts.

Previous: Shibuya Crossing; Meiji Jingū's inner garden; Sensō-ji.

Greater Tokyo

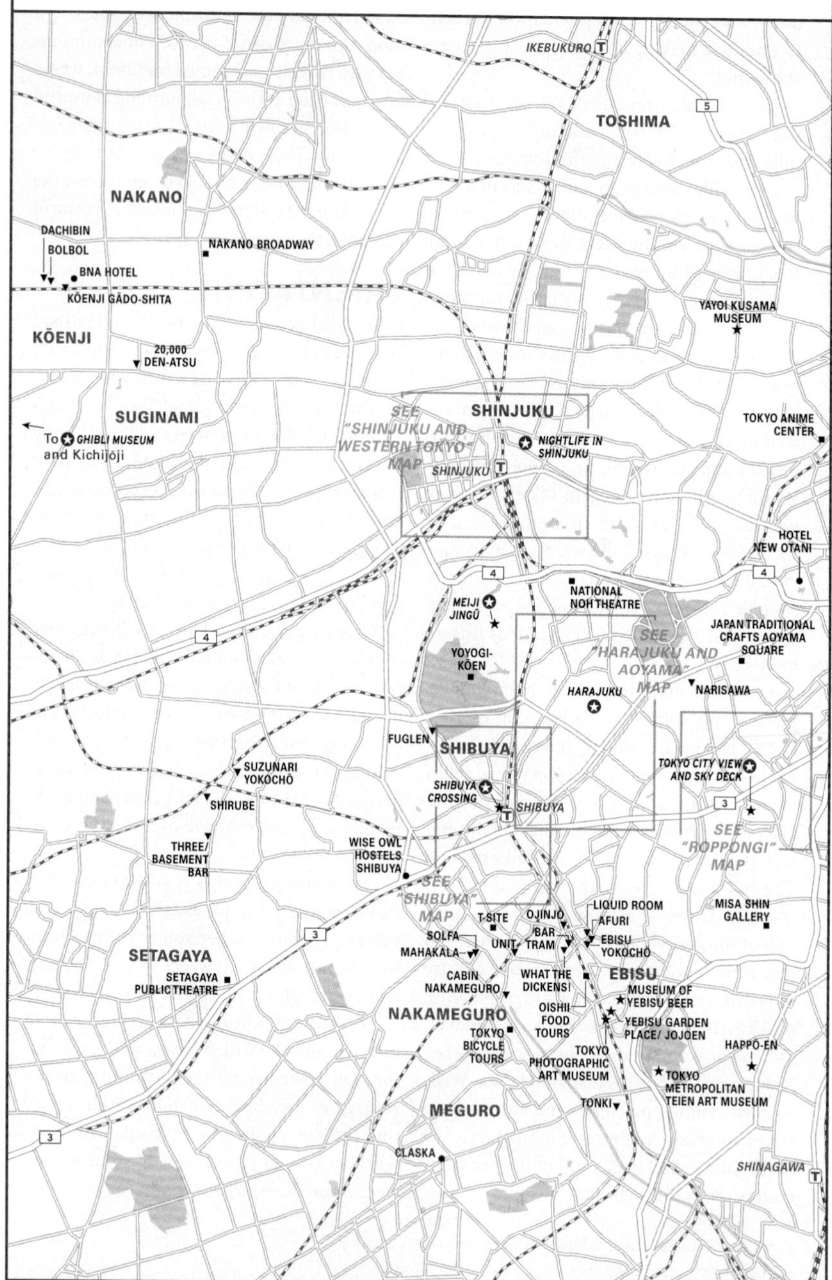

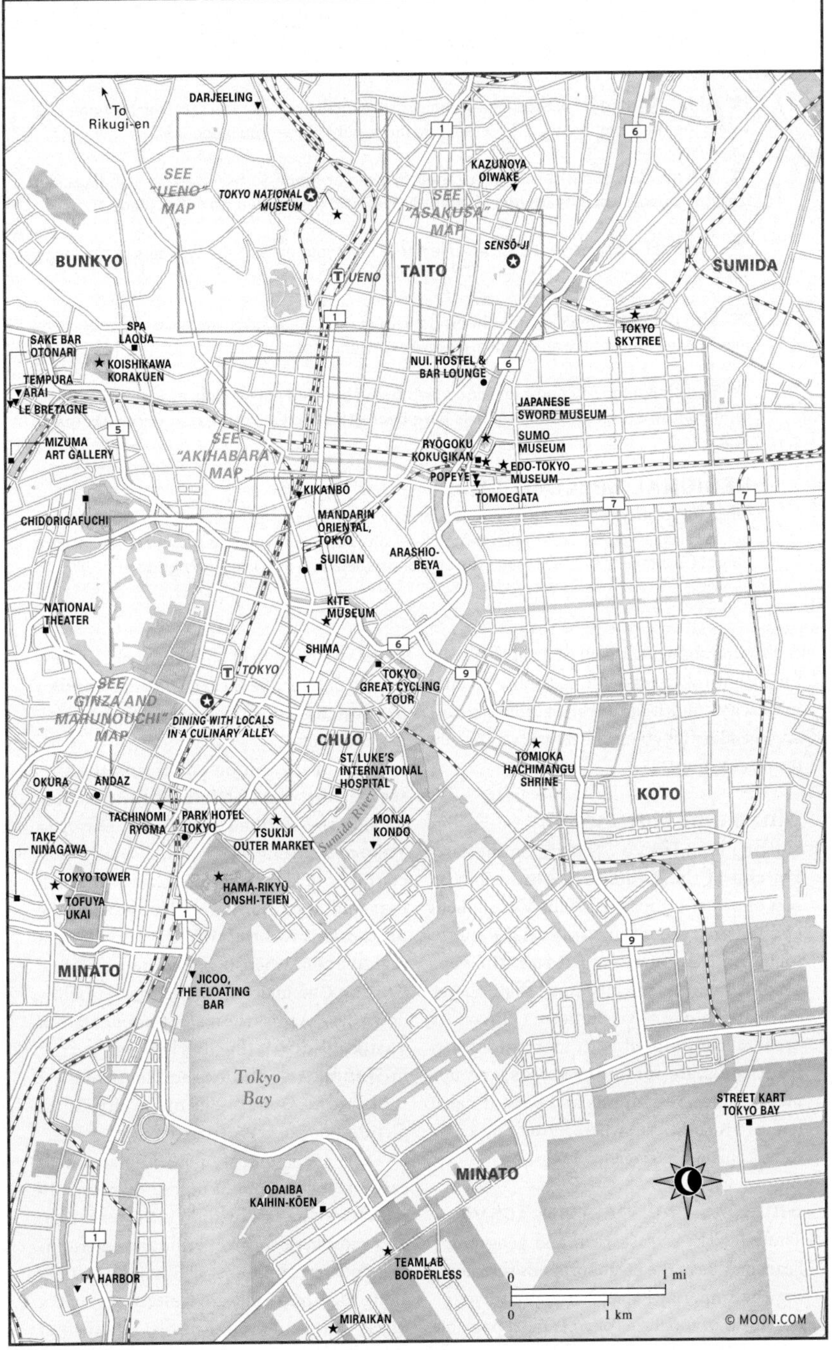

DARJEELING
To Rikugi-en
SEE "UENO" MAP
TOKYO NATIONAL MUSEUM
KAZUNOYA OIWAKE
SEE "ASAKUSA" MAP
SENSŌ-JI
BUNKYO
UENO
TAITO
SUMIDA
TOKYO SKYTREE
SPA LAQUA
SAKE BAR OTONARI
KOISHIKAWA KORAKUEN
TEMPURA ARAI
LE BRETAGNE
NUI. HOSTEL & BAR LOUNGE
JAPANESE SWORD MUSEUM
MIZUMA ART GALLERY
SEE "AKIHABARA" MAP
RYŌGOKU KOKUGIKAN
SUMO MUSEUM
EDO-TOKYO MUSEUM
POPEYE
TOMOEGATA
KIKANBŌ
CHIDORIGAFUCHI
MANDARIN ORIENTAL, TOKYO
SUIGIAN
ARASHIO-BEYA
NATIONAL THEATER
KITE MUSEUM
SHIMA
TOKYO
TOKYO GREAT CYCLING TOUR
SEE "GINZA AND MARUNOUCHI" MAP
DINING WITH LOCALS IN A CULINARY ALLEY
CHUO
TOMIOKA HACHIMANGU SHRINE
ST. LUKE'S INTERNATIONAL HOSPITAL
OKURA
ANDAZ
KOTO
TACHINOMI RYOMA
PARK HOTEL TOKYO
TSUKIJI OUTER MARKET
Sumida River
MONJA KONDO
TAKE NINAGAWA
TOKYO TOWER
TOFUYA UKAI
HAMA-RIKYŪ ONSHI-TEIEN
MINATO
JICOO, THE FLOATING BAR
Tokyo Bay
STREET KART TOKYO BAY
MINATO
ODAIBA KAIHIN-KŌEN
TEAMLAB BORDERLESS
TY HARBOR
MIRAIKAN
0
1 mi
0
1 km
© MOON.COM

Best Restaurants

★ **Ginza Kyubey:** For the quintessential sushi experience, reserve a seat at the counter and watch the chefs prepare their delectable creations right before you (page 113).

★ **Nihon Saisei Sakaba:** It's all about the pig at Nihon Saisei Sakaba, a standing-only *izakaya* (Japanese pub) that serves essentially every pig part, grilled, on a stick (page 117).

★ **Sakurai Japanese Tea Experience:** Open your eyes to the wonders of tea (page 122).

★ **Shirube:** The open kitchen churns out classics and innovative fare to a boisterous clientele, making dinner here an essential *izakaya* experience (page 122).

★ **Tonki:** For the city's best *tonkatsu* (deep-friend breaded pork cutlet), head to this revered restaurant where generations of chefs have been artfully creating the dish since 1939 (page 126).

REGIONAL SPECIALTIES

While Tokyo offers everything under the sun, the city is where sushi originated as ***nigiri*** (sashimi, or raw fish, placed on a bed of rice). Another specialty born in the capital is ***monjayaki,*** a savory pancake containing hunks of meat, seafood, and vegetables, all cooked on a griddle.

Finding someone fluent in English can be tough, but Tokyo residents and police on duty in the city's multitude of *koban* (police boxes) are legendary for going out of their way to help overseas visitors.

Ginza and Marunouchi

Starting near **Tokyo Station,** on the eastern end of the **Yamanote Line,** Tokyo's seat of power is most visible in Marunouchi and the area around the **Imperial Palace,** including **Nihonbashi Bridge,** the geographic heart of the city since the Edo period. South of Tokyo Station is Ginza, its broad avenues lined with luxury **fashion boutiques, department stores,** and upmarket cafés, restaurants and bars. It's also home to **Kabuki-za,** where most of the city's Kabuki plays are staged.

Shinjuku and Western Tokyo

Though Tokyo's historical and geographic heart may lie in the neighborhoods surrounding the Imperial Palace, in many ways the heartbeat of modern Tokyo is most palpable in the western hub of Shinjuku, once a sleepy suburb of Edo. The sheer energy of **Shinjuku Station,** the world's busiest railway terminal, is tremendous.

West of the station you'll find the skyscraper district of **Nishi-Shinjuku.** Just outside the station's east exit is **Omoide Yokochō (Memory Lane),** a smoky, raucous pair of lanes tightly packed with small bars and restaurants. A short walk to the northeast is **Kabukichō,** the city's largest nightlife zone where in one corner you'll find **Golden Gai,** an iconic collection of tumbledown bars. Across the major thoroughfare of **Yasukuni-dōri** is the city's lively gay quarter in **Shinjuku Ni-chōme,** and south of there is **Shinjuku Gyoen,** one of the city's most picturesque pockets of green.

There are a number of other notable areas easily reached from Shinjuku. Just over 10 minutes to the east by train is **Kagurazaka,** an atmospheric former geisha and entertainment quarter. And west of Shinjuku Station, along the Chūō Line, are **Nakano,** an *otaku* (geek culture) haven; **Kōenji,** a hotbed of

Best Accommodations

★ **Aman:** Massive yet understated rooms reminiscent of a *ryokan* (traditional inn), each with a *yuzu*-infused stone bathtub and outstanding views of the city at night, offer a high-end respite from the city (page 144).

★ **Park Hyatt Tokyo:** This legendary hotel in a prime location amid the skyscrapers of western Shinjuku boasts amazing service, spectacular views of Mount Fuji, and as seen in the film *Lost in Translation*, one of the most dazzling cocktail bars in the world (page 144).

★ **Hotel New Otani:** A city within the city with a deep sense of history, this hotel has a gorgeous garden, complete with a dramatic waterfall (page 145).

★ **Gate Hotel Kaminarimon:** In the heart of Asakusa, this hotel is ideally situated for sightseeing in the historic part of town and has a great restaurant, terrace, and bar (page 148).

★ **Hanare:** A wonderful *ryokan* in the heart of the charming Yanaka neighborhood includes staff eager to help you explore the city and full of helpful suggestions (page 148).

counterculture; and **Kichijōji,** home to luxuriant **Inokashira-kōen** and the whimsical **Ghibli Museum.**

Harajuku and Aoyama

Just south of Shinjuku, Harajuku is hallowed ground for youth trends and streetwear, and sacred gound of a different kind given the location of what is perhaps the city's grandest shrine, **Meiji Jingū,** just behind Harajuku Station. Neighboring Aoyama is a fashion mecca as well, catering to a much more sophisticated and well-heeled class. Architecture buffs will appreciate the hodgepodge of iconic buildings dotting the wide leafy avenue of of **Omotesandō**—the Champs-Elysées of Tokyo—which runs through the heart of both neighborhoods.

Besides fashion, both areas are home to a number of museums, featuring everything from woodblock prints to Buddhist statuary.

Shibuya

Like Shinjuku, Shibuya is one of the best nodes on the Yamanote Line to experience Tokyo at full tilt. Stepping into the fray at **Shibuya Crossing** is one of the most intensely urban experiences to be had on earth. The bulk of the action is found in the congested streets of **Center Gai** and in the alleys leading away from the station up the hill known as **Dogenzaka.** Counterculture nexus **Shimokitazawa** is directly accessible from Shibuya.

Ebisu and Around

At the southwestern corner of the Yamanote Line is upmarket Ebisu, which forms a low-key, sophisticated triangle with neighboring districts **Daikanyama** and **Nakameguro,** chock-full of hip fashion boutiques and excellent options for drinking and dining.

Besides bars and restaurants, there are also a handful of worthwhile **museums** in the area, including Tokyo's largest photography exhibition space.

Roppongi

Inside the southern side of the Yamanote Line, a number of cosmopolitan hubs sustain a large share of Tokyo's expat community. Roppongi is at the center of this zone, offering a mix of posh eateries, world-class **art museums,** and one of the city's highest concentrations of **nightlife,** some of it seedy. Nearby, **Azabu** is packed with fine dining establishments and exclusive shops.

Addresses in Tokyo

Addresses in Japan can be baffling to the uninitiated. General elements include the **prefecture, municipality,** and **three numbers** separated by dashes. The piece that's notably missing is a street name. Though some major thoroughfares do have names, such as Tokyo's Meiji and Yasukuni-dōri, most streets are unnamed.

Instead, addresses are organized by **district, block,** and **building,** indicated by the three numbers following the prefecture and municipality. Compounding the confusion, districts and blocks tend to be numbered in a relatively logical geographic progression, while the buildings that make up the blocks aren't numbered according to their physical placement in the block but rather according to when they were built, with the oldest building on a given block being numbered 1, and so on.

As an example, take the Nezu Museum's address: 6-5-1 Minami-Aoyama, Minato-ku, Tokyo. Minato-ku is the ward that Minami-Aoyama is a part of, and Tokyo is the prefecture. The "6" refers to district number 6 of the area known as Minami-Aoyama, the "5" refers to the block number within that district, and the "1" is the building number.

If you're a bit confused, you're not alone. Even taxi drivers end up scratching their heads and doing a few extra laps around an area before finding some destinations—mercifully often stopping the taxi meter at the point where they lose their way so as not to hike up the fare. It helps immensely to have a **printed map** of where you're going, a clear set of directions based on **landmarks,** or best yet, a data-only SIM card so you can simply punch an address into **Google Maps,** which will get you where you're trying to go.

Akihabara

Northwest of Rippongi, Ginza, and Marunouchi is the geeked-out zone of Akihabara, devoted almost entirely to supplying the **gadgets** for all manner of quirky hobbies, along with **idol group performances,** cosplay, anime, manga, and more.

Asakusa

In the northeastern corner of the Yamanote Line, Asakusa is Tokyo at its old-school best. Like most other parts of the city, much of the area was razed during World War II, but the narrow zigzagging streets, temples, aged wooden houses, and shops evoke an earlier time. Across the Sumida River, the neighborhood of **Ryōgoku** is the nation's foremost center for the ancient sport of sumo.

Ueno

Just northwest of Asakusa is Ueno, a historical and cultural hot spot. The expansive grounds of **Ueno-kōen**—Tokyo's largest park—are home to a number of major museums, from natural history to modern art, with the excellent **Tokyo National Museum** topping the list.

Tokyo Bay Area

To the east, Tokyo Bay is surrounded by a diverse assortment of neighborhoods that would not exist without Herculean land reclamation efforts. Across the bay from Tsukiji is **Odaiba,** a manmade island with a number of interesting **museums** and a seaside park that offers some of the best nighttime views of the city.

PLANNING YOUR TIME

A good introduction to Tokyo can be had in as little as two or three days; this gives you enough time to see the highlights of the main part of the city, and leaves you time to sample the vast culinary, nightlife, and shopping options. With the luxury of an additional day or two, you can go a bit off the beaten path and explore the more local side of the city. Plan to stay in either **Shibuya** or **Shinjuku** in the west side of town if you want access to the more clamorous modern side of the city. In the east, **Ueno** and **Asakusa** are good bases if you'd like to see an older, slower part of the city. Meanwhile, **Marunouchi** and **Ginza** have a glut of luxury hotels. The bulk of the city's sights and activities are concentrated in these parts of the city, as well as in some trendy residential pockets south and west of town.

Note that in Tokyo opening times for venues vary greatly, and many shops, museums, and even restaurants are closed on certain days each week. Further, some popular sights like **Tokyo Skytree** fill up fast, so it pays to arrive at or just before opening time to beat the rush, or show up from late-afternoon on, after crowds have dispersed—with the added bonus of a twilight view if you stick around. Other attractions like the **Ghibli Museum,** as well as many popular restaurants, require bookings weeks or even a month or more in advance. Consult the official website of any given attraction beforehand. Pre-planning is key.

Weather in the Tokyo area varies significantly by season. **Spring** and **autumn** are the most pleasant times of year, with mild temperatures and the arrival of gorgeous cherry blossoms shaking off the vestiges of winter by late March-early April, and beautiful foliage on display when leaves change color in autumn. **Summer** is humid and can be sweltering, punctuated by intermittent typhoons June-August, but it's also a fun time to visit, to attend traditional festivals and large music events. Winter is cold, but snow is rare; crisp temperatures around 5°C (41°F) and mostly blue skies are the norm, and, as it's off-season, prices for flights and rooms tend to drop.

Itinerary Ideas

TOKYO ON DAY 1

1 Start at Harajuku Station. Curl around the backside of the station and proceed down the gravel path that leads to Tokyo's grandest shrine, **Meiji Jingū.** Explore the shrine's grounds and inner sanctum.

2 After backtracking to the towering *torii* gate that marks the entrance to the shrine, walk down **Omotesandō,** taking in architecture along the famous shopping street and exploring quirky fashion boutiques tucked in backstreets.

3 Continue to the end of Omotesandō, entering the posh Aoyama neighborhood, where you'll come to **Nezu Museum.** Explore both the collection of East Asian art and religious artifacts in the museum itself, then meander through the beautiful garden behind it.

4 For lunch, backtrack to **Maisen,** one of the city's better purveyors of *tonkatsu* (breaded pork cutlet), set in a chicly renovated bathhouse on a Harajuku side street.

5 After lunch, walk 12 minutes southeast to **Sakurai Japanese Tea Experience.** Get to know the ancient tradition of Japanese tea at this decidedly modern, very stylish tearoom.

6 With your appreciation for the humble tea leaf enhanced, walk southwest (about 20 minutes) to Shibuya Station. Once you've arrived, behold the maelstrom of **Shibuya Crossing.**

7 Spend a bit of time meandering through the belly of the beast in the pedestrian-only **Center Gai** area. Simply strolling amid the throngs and buildings chockablock with restaurants, cafés, and shops will give you a visceral sense of Tokyo's pulse.

8 While you're in Center Gai, stop by **Purikura no Mecca** to take some self-portraits

Itinerary Ideas

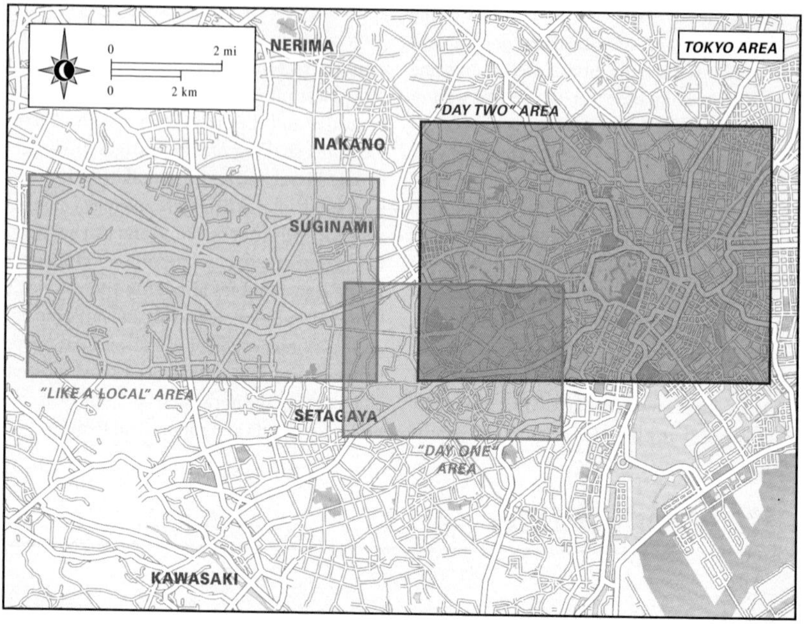

TOKYO AREA

0 2 mi
0 2 km

NERIMA
"DAY TWO" AREA
NAKANO
SUGINAMI
"LIKE A LOCAL" AREA
SETAGAYA
"DAY ONE" AREA
KAWASAKI

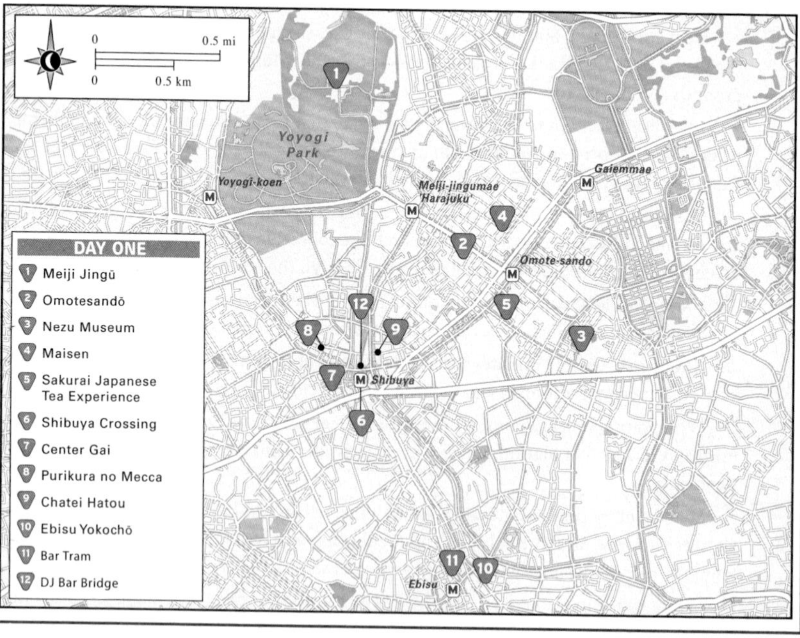

0 0.5 mi
0 0.5 km

Yoyogi Park
Yoyogi-koen
Meiji-jingumae 'Harajuku'
Gaiemmae
Omote-sando
Shibuya
Ebisu

DAY ONE

1. Meiji Jingū
2. Omotesandō
3. Nezu Museum
4. Maisen
5. Sakurai Japanese Tea Experience
6. Shibuya Crossing
7. Center Gai
8. Purikura no Mecca
9. Chatei Hatou
10. Ebisu Yokochō
11. Bar Tram
12. DJ Bar Bridge

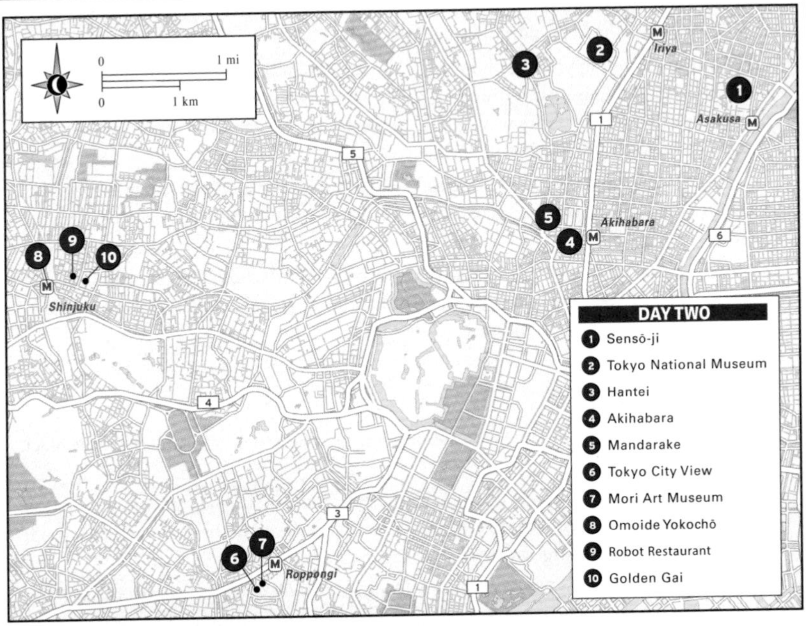

0
1 mi
0
1 km
Iriya
Asakusa
1
5
Akihabara
6
8
9
10
Shinjuku
4
3
6
7
Roppongi
1
DAY TWO
1 Sensō-ji
2 Tokyo National Museum
3 Hantei
4 Akihabara
5 Mandarake
6 Tokyo City View
7 Mori Art Museum
8 Omoide Yokochō
9 Robot Restaurant
10 Golden Gai

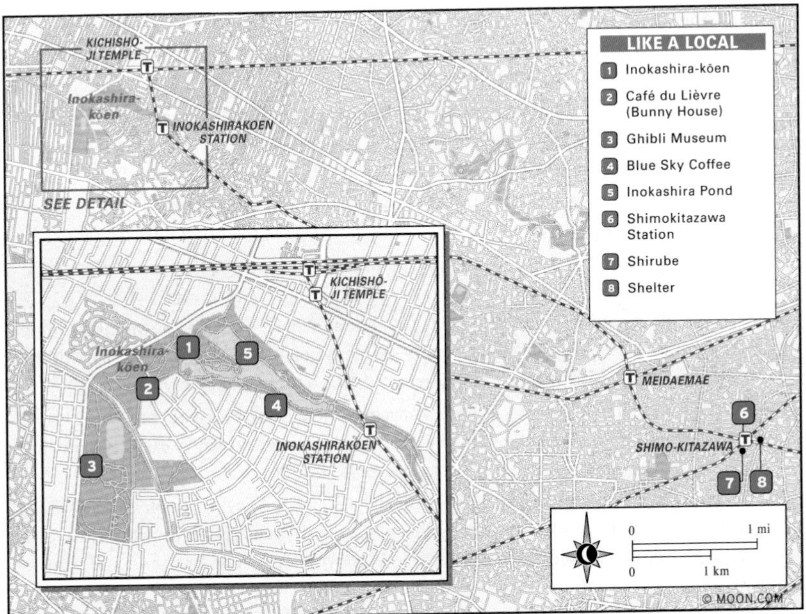

KICHISHŌ-JI TEMPLE
Inokashira-kōen
INOKASHIRAKOEN STATION
SEE DETAIL
LIKE A LOCAL
1 Inokashira-kōen
2 Café du Lièvre (Bunny House)
3 Ghibli Museum
4 Blue Sky Coffee
5 Inokashira Pond
6 Shimokitazawa Station
7 Shirube
8 Shelter
KICHISHŌ-JI TEMPLE
Inokashira-kōen
INOKASHIRAKOEN STATION
MEIDAEMAE
SHIMO-KITAZAWA
0
1 mi
0
1 km

in one of these singular photo booths that are all the rage among Japan's youth. Note that you might not be admitted if you're a guy traveling solo or in a male-only group.

9 Take a coffee break—and a step back in time—at **Chatei Hatou,** an excellent old-school *kissaten* (tea-drinking place) about a 10-minute walk east of Center Gai, on the opposite side of the Meiji-dōri thoroughfare.

10 As dinner time approaches, hop on the Yamanote Line at Shibuya Station to the stylish neighborhood of Ebisu. Have dinner in rowdy and boisterous **Ebisu Yokochō,** a covered alleyway of no-frills eateries serving grilled meats and vegetables on sticks and in stews, and plenty of booze to wash it all down.

11 If you've got the energy, go for drinks after dinner. For a relatively tame night, **Bar Tram,** a dimly lit bar with a speakeasy vibe known for its absinthe-base cocktails, is a good pick.

12 If you plan on a bigger night, take the train back to Shibuya, which takes on a rowdier air after dark. **DJ Bar Bridge,** located a stone's throw from Shibuya Station, is a great starting point for a night out in the area.

TOKYO ON DAY 2

1 Start your day at the famed, boisterous temple of **Sensō-ji** in Asakusa, on the older eastern side of town.

2 Hop on the Ginza subway line at Asakusa Station and make your way to Ueno Station and **Tokyo National Museum,** a 10-minute walk northwest of the station. Inside, you'll encounter the world's largest collection of Japanese art.

3 Cross Ueno Park to **Hantei** (about a 15-minutes walk west) for a lunch of *kushiage*, battered and deep-fried meat and vegetables on sticks, in a charming Meiji period home.

4 From here, hop on the train at Nezu Station, right outside Hantei. Ride to Nishi-Nippori Station on the Chiyoda subway line, then transfer to the Yamanote line to Akihabara Station, the heart of **Akihabara.**

5 Spend the next few hours getting lost in Akihabara's warren of quirky pop culture. A good starting point is **Mandarake,** a one-stop shop for geeks that sells everything from anime and manga to vintage figurines and cosplay attire.

6 Taking the Hibiya line from Akihabara, make your way to Roppongi. Head to **Tokyo City View** in the Roppongi Hills complex for stellar views of the city as dusk begins to fall.

7 Just underneath Tokyo City View is the **Mori Art Museum,** one more worthwhile stop for the day.

8 From Roppongi Station, hop on the Ōedo line and make your way to Shinjuku as dinnertime approaches. Eat and drink at one of the many hole-in-the-wall options in **Omoide Yokochō,** one of Tokyo's most atmospheric *yokochō* (culinary alleyways).

9 For a mindblowing spectacle, walk 7 minutes east to **Robot Restaurant** in the neon-drenched red-light district of Kabukichō after dinner. There's no way to easily sum up this epically kitsch, yet technologically stunning, robot showdown.

10 If you're still going strong, follow this up with a bar crawl through **Golden Gai.** Visitors have thronged to this former black market in recent years to drink their way through a warren of 200 tumbledown bars—each with its own décor, ethos, and regular characters.

TOKYO LIKE A LOCAL

1 Begin your day in the mid- or even late morning in the appealing suburb of Kichijōji, about 15 minutes west of Shinjuku on the Chūō line. Once you arrive, walk south of the station to the lovely, leafy grounds of **Inokashira-kōen.**

2 Have lunch at the whimsical **Café du Lièvre (Bunny House),** which serves a nice selection of Japanese-style curry dishes.

3 After lunch, continue walking south through the less-crowded side of the park to the **Ghibli Museum.** Enjoy taking a tour through this playful, artful ode to Studio Ghibli.

4 When you leave the museum, backtrack to Inokashira-kōen. Get a coffee to-go from **Blue Sky Coffee.**

5 If you're so inclined, rent one of the swan boats and ply the waters of **Inokashira Pond.** But beware: According to legend, the goddess Benzaiten, who resides in the shrine at the southwest corner of the pond, will invoke a jealous curse on any couple who boat through the placid waters.

6 Make your way back to Kichijōji Station, stopping to peruse any shops that may catch your eye on the way. Take the Keio-Inokashira line to **Shimokitazawa Station** (15 minutes, express train) and meander through streets lined by eateries and boutiques with an edgier, countercultural leaning.

7 For dinner, eat at the lively, innovative *izakaya* **Shirube.** Reserve a day ahead to be safe.

8 After dinner, check out the live music scene in Shimokitazawa at **Shelter.**

Sights

GINZA AND MARUNOUCHI
銀座, 丸の内

After a large fire that swept through Tokyo in 1872, the government hired a foreign architect to oversee the construction of some 1,000 brick buildings in the area—only about 20 such structures stood elsewhere in the city at the time. Today, Ginza is synonymous with glitz. It's also conveniently located within easy reach of the buzzing business district of Marunouchi, where you'll find the **Imperial Palace** and the revamped **Tokyo Station** building, which evokes the early 20th century with its appealing facade of red brick and stone. **Nihonbashi,** the geographic heart of the city since the Edo period, is also a brief stroll away. Of historic importance, the **Nihonbashi Bridge,** about a 5-minute walk north of Nihonbashi Station, has served as the starting point (marking kilometer zero) for the national network of highways. Originally wooden when built in the early Edo period (1603-1868), today you'll encounter a Meiji period (1868-1912) stone reconstruction, with an expressway running overhead.

Just outside the north side of Yurakuchō Station, the **Tokyo International Forum** is a soaring architectural masterpiece. An ode to natural light envisioned by Uruguayan architect Rafael Viñoly, the ship-like east wing has a spellbinding ceiling of glass and steel. About 15 minutes' walk northwest of the Imperial Palace grounds, or 7 minutes west of Kudanshita Station, sits the **Yasukuni Jinja,** a shrine that honors Japan's war dead, historically charged due to associations with Japan's World War II sins. Finally, about 10 minutes' walk east of Tokyo Station, the **Artizon Museum** (www.artizon.museum),

Ginza and Marunouchi

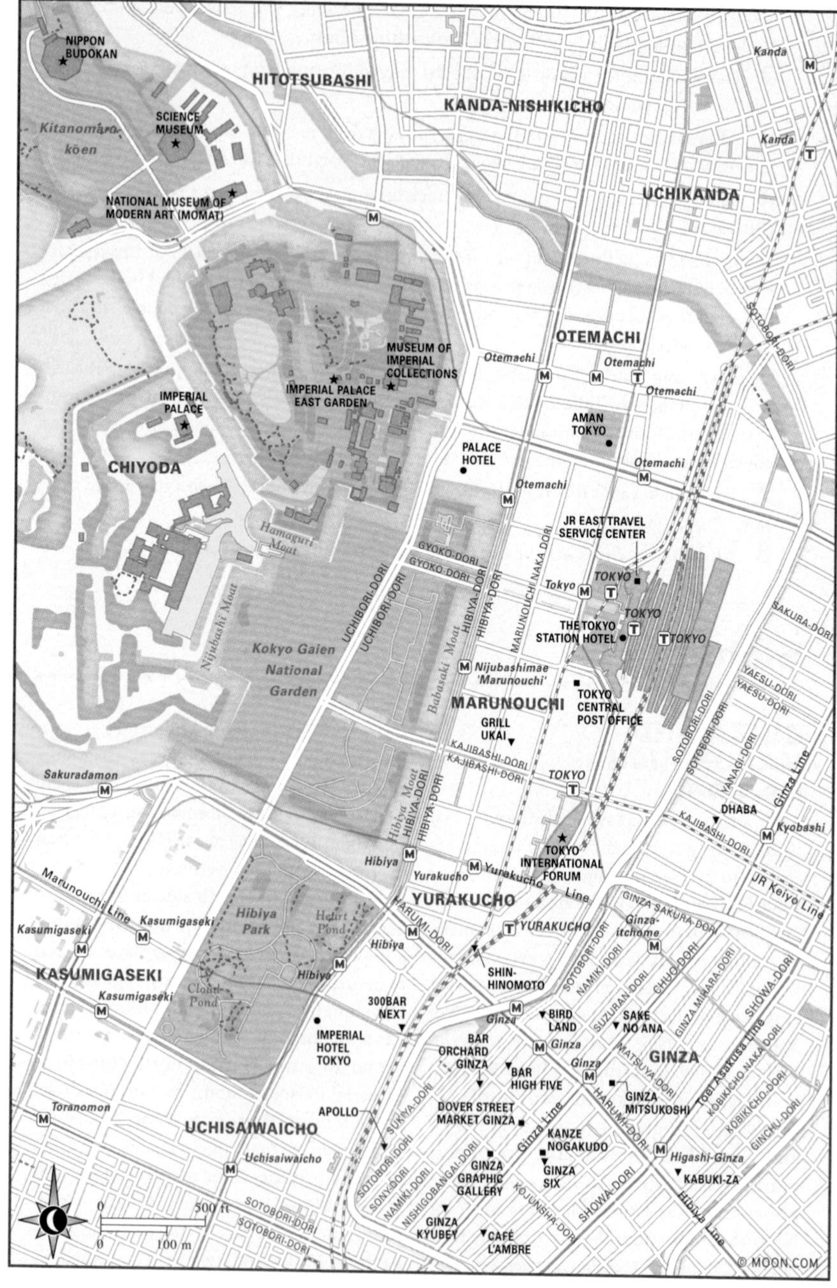

formerly the Bridgestone Museum of Art, is set to reopen in January 2020 after an extensive renovation. The museum's collection features a host of European masters—Picasso, Kandinsky, Matisse—with a strong showing of French impressionists, from Monet to Renoir.

Imperial Palace
皇居

1-1 Chiyoda, Chiyoda-ku; tel. 03/3213-1111; http://sankan.kunaicho.go.jp/english/guide/koukyo.html; tours 10am, 1:30pm Tues-Sat; free; take Chiyoda line to Ōtemachi Station, exit C13b

Located in the geographic heart of Tokyo, the Imperial Palace is integral to the city, yet also feels separate from it. Its construction was kicked off by Tokugawa Ieyasu, the first shogun, in 1590. In its heyday, it was the world's largest castle. Today, only the inner circle of the original complex survives. After being damaged by fire in 1945, the current palace was rebuilt in 1968.

Japan's imperial family resides on the western grounds, which are only open to the public on the emperor's birthday (February 23) and the day after New Year's Day (January 2) when thousands of Japanese waving miniature flags flood in to catch a glimpse of the emperor and a few family members waving to the masses from a palace balcony.

While most of the imperial domain remains hermetically sealed to the public, the Imperial Household Agency does give two daily tours, each lasting a little more than an hour, and delving a bit deeper into the palace grounds. Note that tours aren't offered during official functions, on public holidays, or during afternoons from late July through August, or December 28-January 4. Spots can be reserved online or by phone as early as a month before you plan to arrive. You can also try your luck and arrive the day of with a photo ID in hand to inquire whether spots are still available; ask at the tour office next to Kikyo-mon (Kikyo Gate).

Imperial Palace East Garden
皇居東御苑

1-1 Chiyoda, Chiyoda-ku; tel. 03/3213-1111; www.kunaicho.go.jp/e-event/higashigyoen02.html; 9am-4pm daily, Nov.-Feb., 9am-5pm Mar.-mid-Apr., 9am-6pm mid-Apr.-Aug., 9am-5pm Sept., 9am-4:30pm Oct., closed Mon. and Fri., closed Tues. if national holiday falls on Mon.; free; take Chiyoda line to Ōtemachi Station, exit C13b

After either taking a private tour of the palace grounds or capturing a few snapshots in front of Niju and Megane bridges, proceed to the flawless grounds of the Imperial Palace East Garden. The garden is best entered via Ote-mon (Ote Gate), just west of Ōtemachi Station and roughly a 15-minute walk west of Tokyo Station's Marunouchi North Exit. Take time to visit the **Museum of Imperial Collections** (9am-3:45pm daily Nov.-Feb., 9am-4:45pm Mar.-mid-Apr., 9am-5:45pm mid-Apr.-Aug., 9am-4:45pm Sept., 9am-4:15pm Oct., closed Mon., Fri., closed Tues. if national holiday falls on Mon; free) just beyond Ote-mon, showing off a small selection of the imperial family's more than 9,000 pieces of Japanese art.

The garden itself is a fine example of a Japanese garden. In its Ninomaru section, meander along the winding paths, over lightly arched bridges, and past stone lanterns, cherry trees, azaleas, and a teahouse. Basking in the pleasant scene, note the stone base of what was once the main tower of Edo Castle, still standing on the lawn. Climb the steps and see the surroundings from atop the last remnants of what was once the world's largest keep. Or climb the nearby Shiomizaka (tide-viewing slope) for a broader view onto the bustling commercial district of Ōtemachi.

Two-hour walking tours are offered free of charge by the JNTO Tourist Information Center at 1pm on Wednesday, Saturday, and Sunday. Arrive at the center before 1pm to join.

National Museum of Modern Art (MOMAT)
国立近代美術館

3-1 Kitanomaru-kōen, Chiyoda-ku; tel. 03/5777-8600; www.momat.go.jp/am/; 10am-5pm Tues.-Thurs. and Sun., 10am-8pm Fri.-Sat.; adults ¥500, free for children, free on 1st Sun. of month; take Tōzai line to Takebashi Station, exit 1b

This massive collection of Japanese art stretches from the turn of the 20th century onward, focusing heavily on the works of modernist Japanese painters, as well as some international artists, with photography, video pieces, sculptures and more also on show. The key theme illustrated by the artworks being shown is the evolution of modern Japan from the Meiji period (1868-1912) onward. Part of the appeal of visiting the museum its its location beside the walls of the Imperial Palace and its moat, lined with cherry trees that color the area pink in spring, and foliage blazes during autumn. Alongside the permanent collection, shown acros three floors, the ground floor hosts changing special exhibitions, between which the museum shuts its doors, so check the website to see if an exhibition is ongoing before making the trip.

Crafts Gallery
国立近代美術館工芸館

1 Kitanomaru-kōen, Chiyoda-ku; tel. 03/3211-7781; www.momat.go.jp/cg; 10am-5pm Tues.-Sun.; adults ¥210, free for children, free on 1st Sun. of month; take Tōzai line to Takebashi Station, exit 1b

Located about 7 minutes' walk west of MOMAT is this annex, housed in a handsome Western-style brick building constructed during the Meiji period (1868-1912) that once served as the base of the palace guards. Today, the complex contains a diverse collection of arts and crafts dating from the late-19th century on, from around Japan and abroad, with a focus on *mingei* (folk crafts) and Japan's most significant artisans, some of whom are deemed living national treasures. Mediums include ceramics and textiles to lacquerware, woodwork, bamboo, metalwork, glassware and more, displayed in rotating exhibitions.

Kite Museum
凧の博物館

5F Taimeiken, 1-12-10 Nihonbashi, Chūō-ku; tel. 03/3275-2704; www.taimeiken.co.jp/museum.html; 11am-5pm Mon.-Sat.; ¥200; take Asakusa, Ginza, Tozai lines to Nihonbashi Station, exits A4, C5

There is a dilettantish quality to this collection of kites—some 300 in total—covering

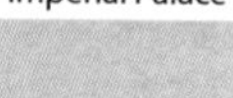

Imperial Palace

nearly every square inch of the walls and ceilings of this unique museum. Paper kites, stretched across bamboo frames, pop with colorful scenes of samurai and other legendary figures, both from Japan and elsewhere in Asia. The collection was amassed by Shingo Modegi, who once owned the restaurant on the building's first floor. Aside from a brief English pamphlet available at the museum's front desk, there isn't much in the way of description or context. If the prospect of walking through a few rooms chock-full of colorful Asian kites sounds appealing, this museum could be worth a quick stop.

SHINJUKU AND WESTERN TOKYO
新宿

Tokyo Metropolitan Government Building
東京都庁

2-8-1 Nishi-Shinjuku, Shinjuku-ku; www.metro.tokyo.jp/ENGLISH/OFFICES/observat.htm; 9:30am-11pm daily, last entry 10:30pm; free; take JR lines to Shinjuku Station west exit, or Ōedo line to Tochōmae Station, exit A4

The Tokyo Metropolitan Government Building is the brainchild of Pritzker Prize-winning architect Tange Kenzo. The headquarters of the city's army of civil servants, this colossal structure has dominated western Shinjuku's skyline since it opened in 1991. Kenzo drew inspiration from Notre Dame in Paris, as evidenced in the archetypal twin-tower form, but this is where the similarities to Paris's medieval masterpiece end. (Note that across town Tokyo Tower stands as an unsightly 20th-century ode to another Paris icon, the Eiffel Tower.)

What the glass-and-granite Tokyo Metropolitan Government Building lacks in old-world charm, it makes up for in stunning views. Reach either of the two towers' observation decks via an elevator on the ground floor of Building 1, which also houses a tourist office that offers free tours of the complex (weekdays only except for national holidays and the first and third Tuesday every month; first-come, first-served). At 202 meters (662 feet) high, both observatories offer similar views, but it's worth noting that the southern tower tends to be less crowded. The northern tower's main advantage is that it stays open later (the South deck closes at 5:30pm on its open days; the North deck is closed on the second and fourth Monday of every month, while the south deck is closed on the first and third Tuesday of every month). Excellent views are possible by day or night. On clear days, you can catch a glimpse of Mount Fuji some 100 km (62 mi) to the west. Alternatively, arrive at dusk and watch the gray urban expanse transform into a twinkling sea of lights below.

Samurai Museum
侍サムライミュージアム

2-25-6 Kabukichō, Shinjuku-ku; tel. 03/6457-6411; www.samuraimuseum.jp/en/index.html; 10:30am-9pm; ¥1,500 adults, ¥750 children 3 and up, children under 3 free; take JR, Odakyu, Keio lines to Shinjuku Station, east exit, or take Marunouchi, Shinjuku lines to Shinjuku-Sanchōme Station, exit B3

Smack in the middle of Tokyo's largest red-light district isn't where you'd expect an institution dedicated to the illustrious, disciplined way of the samurai to thrive, but the success of the Samurai Museum has proved otherwise. Set amid Kabukichō's maze of hostess clubs, love hotels, and alleys prowled by persistent touts, a full kit of armor greets visitors at the entrance to this hit museum.

Well-presented samurai garb is on display, largely devoid of protective glass, making the experience of seeing the feudal artifacts all the more visceral. English-speaking guides and signage are thankfully on hand. Alongside a range of armor and iron helmets adorned with flamboyant crests in the shapes of dragons, horns, and animals, there are also several rooms displaying weaponry wielded by Japan's former warrior class, from swords and bows and arrows to the matchlock muskets that came into use after being introduced from abroad.

You can even suit up yourself for free. And

Shinjuku and Western Tokyo

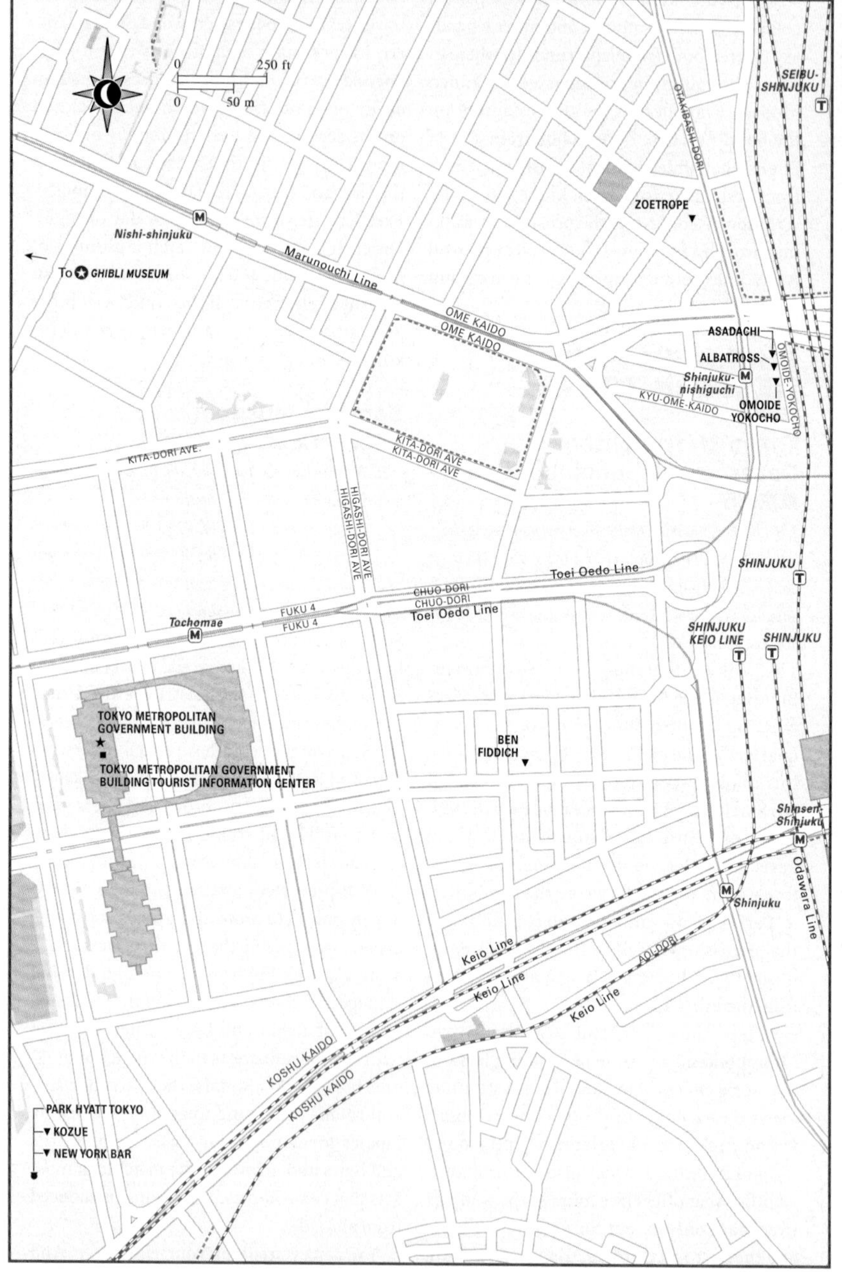

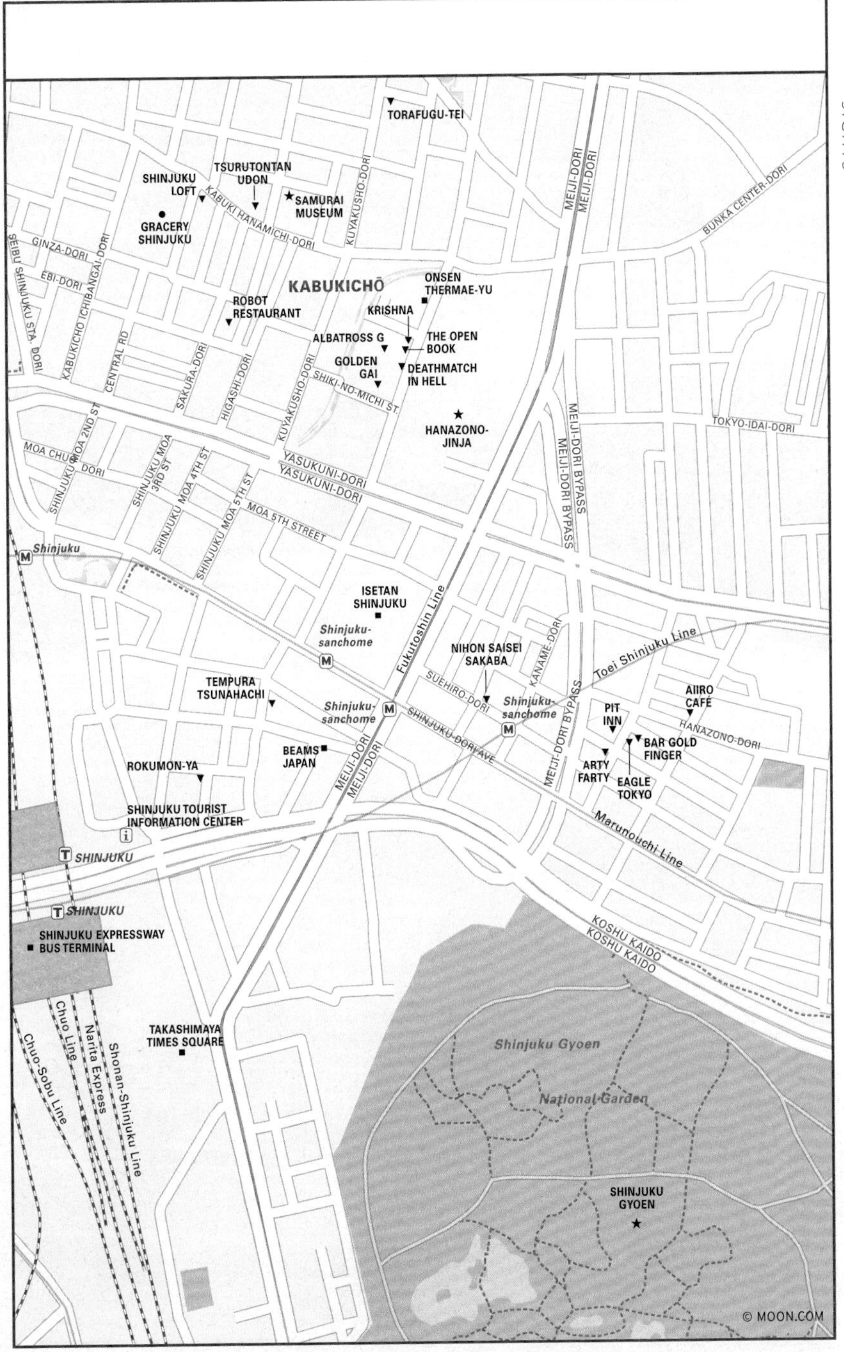
TORAFUGU-TEI
SHINJUKU LOFT
TSURUTONTAN UDON
SAMURAI MUSEUM
GRACERY SHINJUKU
KABUKI HANAMICHI-DORI
KUYAKUSHO-DORI
MEIJI-DORI
BUNKA CENTER-DORI
GINZA-DORI
EBI-DORI
SEIBU SHINJUKU STA. DORI
KABUKICHO ICHIBANGAI-DORI
KABUKICHŌ
ONSEN THERMAE-YU
ROBOT RESTAURANT
KRISHNA
ALBATROSS G
THE OPEN BOOK
GOLDEN GAI
DEATHMATCH IN HELL
CENTRAL RD
SAKURA-DORI
HIGASHI-DORI
SHIKI-NO-MICHI ST.
HANAZONO-JINJA
MEIJI-DORI BYPASS
TOKYO-IDAI-DORI
MOA CHUO DORI
SHINJUKU MOA 2ND ST
SHINJUKU MOA 3RD ST
SHINJUKU MOA 4TH ST
SHINJUKU MOA 5TH ST
YASUKUNI-DORI
MOA 5TH STREET
Shinjuku
ISETAN SHINJUKU
Fukutoshin Line
Shinjuku-sanchome
NIHON SAISEI SAKABA
KANAME-DORI
Toei Shinjuku Line
TEMPURA TSUNAHACHI
SUEHIRO-DORI
AIIRO CAFÉ
PIT INN
HANAZONO-DORI
SHINJUKU-DORI AVE
BAR GOLD FINGER
BEAMS JAPAN
ARTY FARTY
EAGLE TOKYO
ROKUMON-YA
SHINJUKU TOURIST INFORMATION CENTER
Marunouchi Line
SHINJUKU
KOSHU KAIDO
SHINJUKU EXPRESSWAY BUS TERMINAL
Chuo Line
Narita Express
Shonan-Shinjuku Line
Chuo-Sobu Line
TAKASHIMAYA TIMES SQUARE
Shinjuku Gyoen
National Garden
SHINJUKU GYOEN
© MOON.COM

1

2

if you prefer to see someone with a bit more dexterity play the part, an armored actor with legit sword skills gives a demonstration four times a day (2pm, 3pm, 4pm, 5pm).

Hanazono-jinja
花園神社

5-17-3 Shinjuku, Shinjuku-ku; tel. 03/3209-5265; www.kanko-shinjuku.jp.e.xm.hp.transer.com/spot/-/article_369.html; 8am-8pm daily; free; take JR, Odakyu, Keio lines to Shinjuku Station, east exit, or take Marunouchi, Shinjuku lines to Shinjuku-Sanchōme Station, exit B3

Hanazono-jinja is located in a very unlikely spot for a shrine: abutting Tokyo's largest red-light district. Entering the shrine grounds from Yasukuni-dōri, you walk between two copper lion statues standing guard at the entrance before passing down a cobblestone path flanked by wooden lanterns painted vermillion. A multistory building stands on either side, nearly always covering the path in shadow. Inside, you'll discover a main prayer hall and a handful of sub-shrines dotting the grounds, including a fertility shrine with phalluses of wood and stone and Geino Asama shrine, which is frequented by entertainers and celebrities of all stripes who have come to pray to the god of media and entertainment.

Dedicated to the fox god Inari, overseer of money and success, the shrine is a magnet for proprietors of businesses, aboveboard and not, and entertainers who work in neighboring Kabukichō. It's said that yakuza, the Japanese mafia, who have a stronghold in the area, often run food stalls and other businesses at the shrine's lively festivals, including the Reitaisai Matsuri, which falls on the closest weekend to May 28 every year. And on every January 8, those who purchased talismans for success in business during the previous year line up to toss their old charms into a fire. It's worth stopping by the shrine for a break from the wicked ways of nearby Golden Gai and Kabukichō.

1: Shinjuku Gyoen **2:** the view from the Tokyo Metropolitan Government Building

Shinjuku Gyoen
新宿御苑

11 Naito-machi, Shinjuku-ku; tel. 03/3350-0151; www.env.go.jp/garden/shinjukugyoen/english; 9am-4:30pm Tues.-Sun. Oct. 1-Mar. 14, 9am-6pm Tues.-Sun. Mar. 15-June 30 and Aug. 21-Sept. 30, 9am-7pm Jul. 1-Aug. 20, closed Mon. if Tues. is a holiday; ¥500 adults, ¥250 university and high school students, free for children aged 15 and younger; take Marunouchi line to Shinjuku Gyoen-mae Station, exit 1

This 150-acre green space is Tokyo's biggest garden and one of its best situated, in the heart of Shinjuku. What makes Shinjuku Gyoen unique is its diversity of landscaping styles. A formal French garden occupies the northern part, which is defined by neat lines of carefully planted trees and flowers. The south is a classically Japanese garden complete with stone lanterns, ponds with islands reachable by arched bridges, and a welcoming teahouse. A typically English-style open lawn sprawls across the center. The grounds are also home to a greenhouse growing subtropical plants, including orchids, an imperial villa dating to 1869, and Taiwan-kaku Pavilion, built to celebrate Emperor Hirohito's wedding in 1927.

The garden is at its most beautiful in spring when hundreds of cherry trees blossom, filling the garden with an ocean of pink petals. The onset of autumn also injects added color to the already beautiful scene, when the leaves of the garden's more than 20,000 trees transform into a mosaic of color. Note that alcohol and sports are prohibited in the garden, but picnics are ideal.

Yayoi Kusama Museum
草間彌生美術館

107 Bentenchō, Shinjuku-ku; tel. 03/5273-1778; https://yayoikusamamuseum.jp; 11am-5pm Thurs.-Sun.; adults ¥1,000, children age 6-18 ¥600; take Ōedo line to Ushigome-Yanagichō Station, east exit, or Tozai line to Waseda Station, exit 1

For full immersion in a surreal, polka-dotted landscape housing mirrored infinity rooms, loudly colored geometric and patterned paintings, and multitudinous phallic sculptures, head to the Yayoi Kusama Museum. The five-story white building full of windows and warm light stands out markedly from the drab apartment blocks surrounding it. The museum hosts two exhibitions per year, drawing on the artist's prodigious body of work. Active since the 1950s, and once a figure in New York City's avant garde in the 1970s, Kusama has honed a singular style that has made her one of Japan's most famous contemporary artists. Here work is inspired by the hallucinatory visions of forms superimposed on the world around her, which she's experienced since childhood.

Two floors are dedicated to Kusama's paintings, one floor houses installations for visitors to lose themselves in, and the top floor has a reading room where fans of the artist, known for her trademark bob-cut red wig, can read up on her life and work. The museum admits ticket holders according to six 90-minute time slots daily (11am-12:30pm, noon-1:30pm, 1pm-2:30pm, 2pm-3:30pm, 3pm-4:30pm, 4pm-5:30pm). Tickets are often sold out months in advance. If you plan to visit, book your spot early through the official website.

★ Ghibli Museum
三鷹のジブリ美術館

1-1-83 Shimorenjaku, Mitaka-shi; tel. 0570/05-5777; www.ghibli-museum.jp; 10am-6pm Wed.-Mon.; ¥1,000 adults, ¥100-700 children; take Chūō Line running west from Shinjuku's JR Station to reach both Mitaka Station and Kichijōji Station, which sit beside each other, Chūō, Sōbu lines to Mitaka, south exit, or Kichijōji, park exit

If you're only going to visit one sight outside downtown, make it the Ghibli Museum. Arriving at the whimsical facade of the complex on the edge of the heavily wooded Inokashira-kōen, you'll fittingly feel as if you've just wandered into the imagination of legendary anime director Hayao Miyazaki. It's a must-see for Ghibli fans and doesn't disappoint even those with only a passing interest in Miyazaki or Studio Ghibli films. The museum, located just west of downtown in the suburb of Mitaka, is a seamless ode to Miyazaki's vision, which has produced classic films such as *Spirited Away* and *Princess Mononoke*.

The first floor showcases animation techniques, original Ghibli drawings, and a richly illustrated history of the art form; there's also a theater playing short Ghibli flicks that are only viewable at the museum. Special thematic exhibitions, such as the place of food in Ghibli films, are featured on a rotating basis on the second floor. The rooftop boasts a garden inhabited by Ghibli characters, including a towering robot soldier from *Castle in the Sky*, and there's even a giant cat bus brought to life from Miyazaki's hallmark *My Neighbor Totoro*, and both adults and kids can hop aboard.

Adding to the fantastical impact of the museum itself is the surrounding, which could easily be home to many of the imaginary characters portrayed in Studio Ghibli films, with the mysterious yet adorable rabbit-like forest spirit Totoro atop the list.

Note that the museum is extremely popular and limits the number of its daily visitors. Tickets are only valid for the date and time you book and can be purchased up to four months in advance. Reserve as early as you can within that timeframe. Ghibli Museum can be reached either via bus from Mitaka Station (¥320 round trip, ¥210 one-way; 10 minutes one way), or via a 20-minute walk from Kichijōji Station. I recommend the latter option, which greatly enhances the experience.

★ HARAJUKU AND AOYAMA
原宿, 青山

Harajuku and Aoyama have deep roots in the world of fashion, and the city's grandest shrine, **Meiji-dōri.** Buildings of note

1: bus stop sign for the Ghibli Museum at Mitaka Station 2: the Ghibli Museum 3: Meiji Jingū

1

2

3

Harajuku and Aoyama

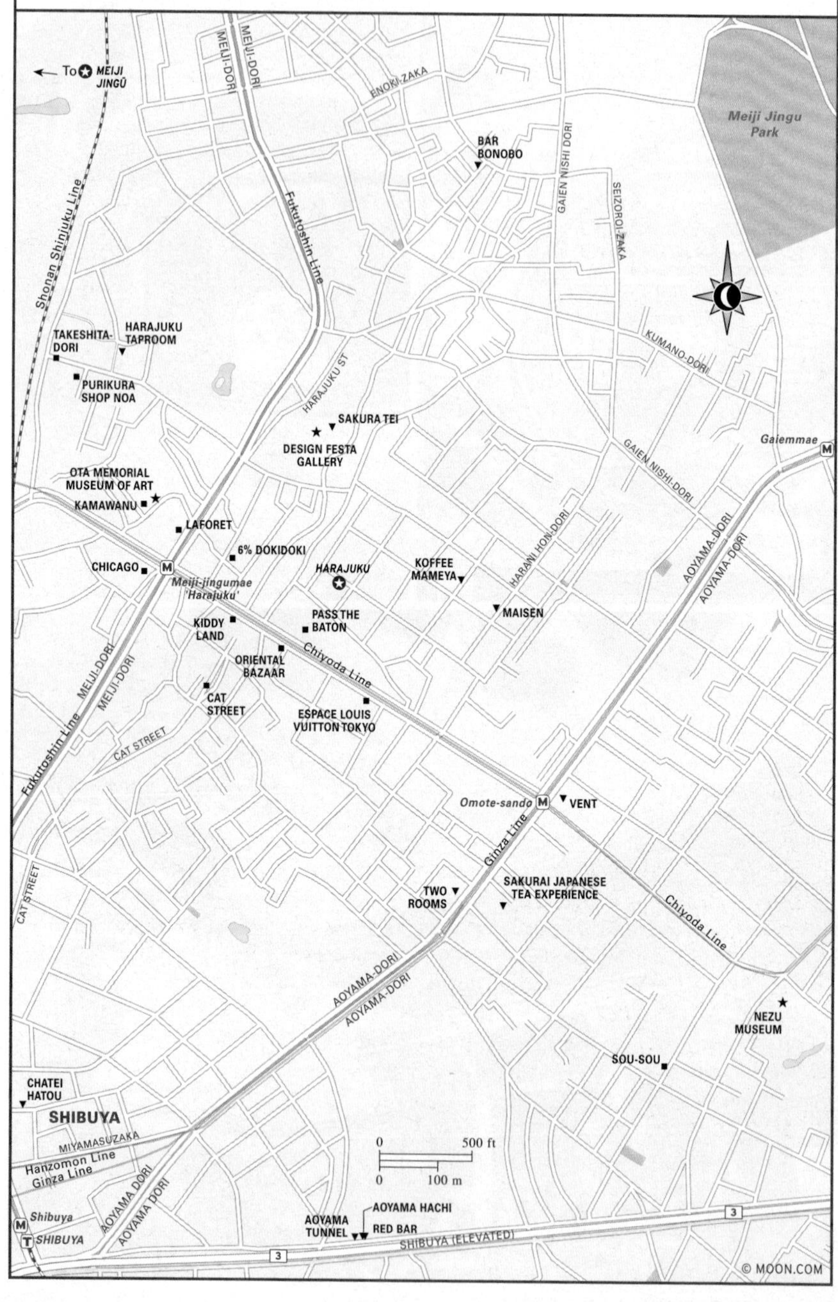

Japan's Big Three of Fashion

As you walk down Omotesandō, which is lined with architecturally stunning designer shops, you'll pass the flagships of the designers that make up Japan's big three names in fashion when you reach the Aoyama area on the southeastern end of the avenue.

ISSEY MIYAKE

Crossing the large four-way intersection with Aoyama-dōri, you'll come to the Issey Miyake shop (3-18-14 Minami Aoyama, Minato-ku; tel. 03/5411-5007; www.isseymiyake.com; 11am-8pm daily) on the first corner on the left. Exploding on the scene in the late 1980s, he became famous for his experimental approach, involving fresh uses of fabric, geometric forms, and materials ranging from rough and natural to brightly colored plastic.

REI KAWAKUBO

Cross the street at the crosswalk and enter the flagship of legendary fashion label **Comme des Garcons** (5-2-1 Minami Aoyama, Minato-ku; tel. 03/3406-3951; www.comme-des-garcons.com; 11am-8pm daily). This label was launched in the early 1980s by renowned designer Rei Kawakubo, another of Japan's big three, alongside Miyake. Here you'll find her renegade-chic style on full display. Fashion aside, the striking building, with its dramatic lines and spare interior, is worth a visit in its own right.

YOHJI YAMAMOTO

Finally, continue up the right side of the street to see the flagship of the third name in Japan's high-fashion trinity, Yohji Yamamoto (5-3-6 Minami Aoyama, Minato-ku; tel. 03/3409-6006; www.yohjiyamamoto.co.jp; 11am-8pm daily), who is renowned for his tailoring, which incorporates Japanese techniques onto distinctive black flowing garments.

along the area's main drag, **Omotesandō,** include the **Dior** store, located a few minutes' walk south of Meiji-dōri, designed by Pritzker Prize-winning duo Sejima Kazuyo and Nishizawa Ryūe; **Louis Vuitton**, just up the hill from Dior and resembling a giant pile of trunks connected by a maze of corridors; and **Tod's**, just a few buildings up from Louis Vuitton, which architect Itō Tokyo designed to play on the theme of Zelkova trees with its intersecting concrete beams.

Another great place for urban strolling is the jam-packed pedestrian shopping street of **Takeshita-dōri,** Harajuku at its most youthful and saccharine, directly in front of Harajuku Station's Takeshita exit. Some of the hippest boutiques are located along **Cat Street,** located near the intersection of Meiji-dōri and Omotesandō, about a 7-minute walk southeast of Harajuku Station's Omotesandō exit, and in the tangle of backstreets to the north of Omotesandō and east of Meiji-dōri.

★ Meiji Jingū
明治神宮

1-1 Yoyogi Kamizonochō, Shibuya-ku; www.meijijingu.or.jp; sunrise-sunset daily; free; take Yamanote line to Harajuku Station, Omotesandō exit, or Chiyoda, Fukutoshin lines to Meiji-Jingūmae Station, exit 2

One of Tokyo's most iconic Shinto shrines, Meiji Jingū is set in a sprawling swath of green just a stone's throw from one of Tokyo's hyperkinetic youth meccas. Exiting Harajuku Station, cross a bridge over the train tracks and walk until you reach the large *torii* gate with the imperial crest in its lintel. Offer a light bow for good measure before crossing the threshold, delineating the sacred space from the din outside, and be sure to remain on either side of the gravel pathway, as the middle is reserved for the gods. Notice the city sounds fade as you venture down the shaded trail, deeper into a forest of towering camphor trees.

Continue following the path until you

come to the second *torii* gate, which stands 12 meters (39 feet) high—the largest of its type in Japan—made of 1,500-year-old cypress trees felled on Mount Alisan in Taiwan. Just after you pass through the second gate, you'll see the entrance to **Meiji Jingū Gyoen**, a traditional garden with a pond inhabited by colorful carp. The garden was designed by the Emperor Meiji, in whose name the shrine was built, for his wife Empress Shoken. The garden is a riot of white and purple in mid-June, when more than 100 types of iris bloom.

Exit the garden and continue walking along the main path toward the shrine until you reach a third *torii* gate, which leads to the courtyard's entrance. After ritually purifying yourself at the fountain in front of the shrine's inner gate, enter the courtyard where clusters of trees considered spiritually significant are festooned with thick straw ropes to drive away evil spirits. Nearby, notice the countless wooden tablets hanging from wooden frames, inscribed with the wishes of the faithful, as well as strips of fortune-telling paper tied to metal wires en masse, releasing the buyers from unwelcome fortunes. It's not uncommon to see a *miko*, or shrine maiden, glide past, adorned in red trousers and a white kimono top. Or even a Shinto wedding if your timing is lucky.

The **Honden** (central hall) is the courtyard's centerpiece, with its cypress-wood exterior and gently curved copper-clad roof offset by bronze lanterns hanging from its eaves.

To see Meiji Jingū at its most lively, visit during festivals. Foremost among these is the New Year, when some 3 million people mob Meiji Jingū for *hatsumode*, their first Shinto shrine trip of the new year, to pray for a successful year ahead. Meanwhile, musical performances and dances are staged in the shrine's courtyard April 29-May 3 and November 1-3. And on November 15, children ages three, five, and seven flock to the shrine wearing pint-sized kimono for Shichi-go-san, a holiday that marks a rite of passage for girls ages three and seven, and boys ages three and five.

Although the shrine is being restored ahead of its 100-year anniversary in 2020, most of the structure and grounds can still be explored.

Ota Memorial Museum of Art
浮世絵 太田記念美術館

1-10-10 Jingūmae, Shibuya-ku; tel. 03/3403/0880; www.ukiyoe-ota-muse.jp/eng; 10:30am-5:30pm Tues.-Sun.; admission varies by exhibition; take Yamanote line to Harajuku Station, Omotesandō exit, or Chiyoda, Fukutoshin lines to Meiji-Jingūmae Station, exit 5

Just behind the Laforet complex, a purveyor of youth fashion, the Ota Memorial Museum of Art is an inviting space to immerse yourself into the rich world of ukiyo-e (woodblock prints). This popular Japanese art form, which exploded in the 17th through the 19th centuries, was deeply rooted in the "floating world" of Kabuki, beautiful courtesans, and sumo wrestlers, all of whom were often depicted in the works. Wanderers traversing dramatic landscapes, the natural world, historical scenes, folk tales, and erotica were also prominent subject matter. Seeing the intricate lines of the prints, realism in many of the faces, and exquisite attention to detail, it's hard not to draw parallels to Japan's modern-day obsession with caricature in the forms of manga and anime.

Kamawanu, an excellent shop in the basement, sells aesthetically pleasing *tenugui*, thin cotton hand towels with beautifully dyed designs.

Nezu Museum
根津美術館

6-5-1 Minami-Aoyama, Minato-ku; tel. 03/3400-2536; www.nezu-muse.or.jp/en; 10am-5pm Tues.-Sun.; ¥1,300 adults, ¥1,000 students, free for children; take Chiyoda, Ginza, Hanzomon lines to Omotesandō Station, exit A5

This sublime museum has excellent exhibitions, a relaxing café with beautiful garden views of wisteria and irises, and a dazzling mix of traditional and modern architecture. Combined, these elements create an understated ambience exuding elegance; you sense you've stumbled onto something special.

The Nezu Museum first opened in 1941, standing on the same land where once stood the private residence of late Tobu Railway founder Nezu Kaichiro, whose private collection of Japanese and Asian art served as the foundation for the museum's collection. After the original museum was destroyed during World War II, the current structure, designed by Kengo Kuma, reopened in 2009.

The collection includes more than 7,000 artworks from across Japan and East Asia, including exquisite bronze statutes from China's Shang and Zhou dynasties, Japanese paintings, and Korean ceramics. The café overlooking the lush garden in back offers good options for a light lunch or afternoon tea. And the 17,000-square-meter Japanese garden beckons visitors to stroll and discover two traditional teahouses, and myriad stone lanterns and Buddha statues.

SHIBUYA
渋谷

As recent as the early years of the Meiji period (1868-1912), Shibuya was open countryside with a reputation for producing excellent tea. Today at **Shibuya Crossing,** pedestrians briskly walk in all directions, bombarded by advertisements and music clips playing on television screens mounted on glass and steel shopping complexes.

Shibuya is in the midst of an ambitious spate of development: A major commercial complex known as **Shibuya Stream** opened in 2019, and a skyscraper called **Shibuya Sky,** with a massive rooftop terrace with views of Shibuya Crossing and Tokyo as a whole, was set to open in November 2019.

Four stops away on the Keio-Inokashira Line is the counterculture nexus of **Shimokitazawa,** home to artisanal coffee shops, storied hole-in-the-wall venues for indie rock gigs, and vintage clothing shops.

★ Shibuya Crossing
渋谷スクランブル交差点

2-2 Dogenzaka, Shibuya-ku; www.sibch.tv; take JR lines to Shibuya Station, Hachikō exit

Seen from above, Shibuya Crossing, aka "the scramble," resembles a giant free-for-all, with hordes of cell phone-wielding pedestrians amassing and then rushing in every direction each time the walk signal turns green. When you visit, you're propelled into the current and become part of the flow. For maximum impact, try coming on a Friday night or anytime Saturday, when the trend-conscious masses come out to shop, eat, and play.

This is Tokyo at its rawest, the perfect visceral place to soak in the sheer energy of the world's largest metropolis. It's also the gateway to a district at the heart of Japanese youth culture, thriving in the teeming streets of Shibuya's **Center Gai;** it's also where you'll find an entry point to **Dogenzaka,** a district bursting at the seams with options for dining and nightlife of every shade, as well as one of Tokyo's most well-known agglomerations of love hotels.

In the frantic square next to the crossing is perhaps Tokyo's most beloved meeting point: the bronze statue of legendarily loyal dog **Hachikō.** The canine came to meet his master, a professor, at the station as he returned home from work every day, and continued to make his daily trek to Shibuya Station nearly a decade after his master died in 1925.

EBISU AND AROUND
恵比寿

Ebisu is a sophisticated neighborhood that provides welcome relief from the chaos of nearby Shibuya. But don't expect too much peace and quiet. While the area's streets are relatively calm, they still hum with foot traffic, as a slightly more mature mix of locals and expats congregate in the evening to eat and drink at the area's impressive array of restaurants and drinking dens.

Ebisu has long been associated with food and, more specifically, drink, as its very origin is linked to the founding of a brewery

Shibuya

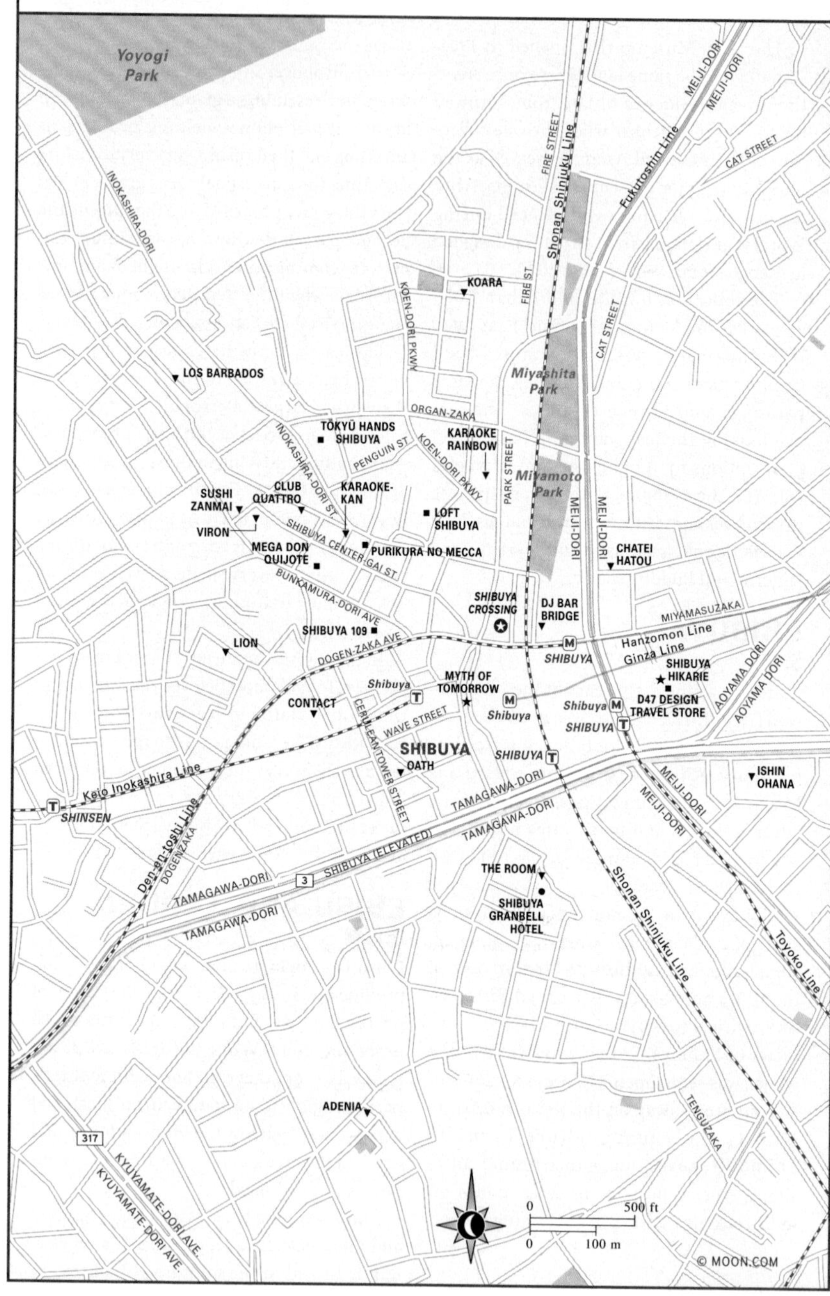
Yoyogi Park
INOKASHIRA-DORI
FIRE STREET
Shonan Shinjuku Line
MEIJI-DORI
Fukutoshin Line
CAT STREET
KOARA
KOEN-DORI PKWY
FIRE ST
LOS BARBADOS
Miyashita Park
ORGAN-ZAKA
TŌKYŪ HANDS SHIBUYA
KARAOKE RAINBOW
PENGUIN ST
INOKASHIRA-DORI ST
PARK STREET
Miyamoto Park
SUSHI ZANMAI
CLUB QUATTRO
KARAOKE-KAN
LOFT SHIBUYA
VIRON
SHIBUYA CENTER-GAI ST
MEGA DON QUIJOTE
PURIKURA NO MECCA
CHATEI HATOU
BUNKAMURA-DORI AVE
SHIBUYA CROSSING
DJ BAR BRIDGE
MIYAMASUZAKA
SHIBUYA 109
Hanzomon Line
LION
DOGEN-ZAKA AVE
SHIBUYA
Ginza Line
SHIBUYA HIKARIE
Shibuya
MYTH OF TOMORROW
CONTACT
D47 DESIGN TRAVEL STORE
AOYAMA DORI
CERULEAN TOWER STREET
WAVE STREET
SHIBUYA
OATH
ISHIN OHANA
Keio Inokashira Line
TAMAGAWA-DORI
SHINSEN
Den-en-toshi Line
DOGENZAKA
SHIBUYA (ELEVATED)
3
THE ROOM
SHIBUYA GRANBELL HOTEL
Toyoko Line
ADENIA
TENGUZAKA
317
KYUYAMATE-DORI AVE.
0
500 ft
100 m
© MOON.COM

Views of Shibuya

To fully grasp the scale of Shibuya Crossing's foot traffic, head to the hallway linking the JR station to the Keio-Inokashira line on the second floor of the **Shibuya Mark City** commercial complex. Windows lining the passageway offer views of the frenzy below. You'll also be able to see the ***Myth of Tomorrow,*** a vivid mural by Taro Okamoto, dramatically depicting Japan's traumatic relationship with nuclear weapons, and more recently power.

Another good vantage point is **Shibuya Hikarie** (2-21-1 Shibuya, Shibuya-ku; tel. 03/5468-5892; www.hikarie.jp; 10am-9pm daily; free), a complex of boutiques, eateries, and artistic offerings accessible from Shibuya Station's east exit; from the 11th floor, you'll have a view of the spectacle of the fabled Shibuya Scramble, set within a wider view of Shibuya as a whole.

There's also a plexiglass-enclosed viewing platform in **Mag's Park** (1-23-10 Jinnan, Shibuya-ku; https://magnetbyshibuya109.jp/en/mags-park; 11am-11pm daily, last entry 10:30pm; ¥1,000), a rooftop space that opened in 2018 atop the **Shibuya 109-2** department store. Its location on one corner of the scramble gives unimpeded views of the intersection.

for Yebisu Beer in the late 1920s. "Yebisu" is the archaic name of the god of prosperity, Ebisu, embodied in a jolly looking statue next to the train station. **Yebisu Garden Place** (4-20 Ebisu, Shibuya-ku; tel. 03/5423-7111; www.gotokyo.org/en/kanko/shibuya/spot/40163.html; daily; free), site of the **Museum of Yebisu Beer** (B1F Sapporo Beer Headquarters, Yebisu Garden Place, 4-20-1 Ebisu, Shibuya-ku; tel. 03/5423-7255; www.sapporobeer.jp/english/brewery/y_museum; 11am-7pm Tues.-Sun., tasting salon last order 6:30pm, closed Tues. if Mon. is holiday) is a city witin a city, with a pleasing blend of greenery, shops, and cultural offerings oriented around a spacious central square.

The nearby neighborhoods of **Daikanyama** and **Nakameguro** have a similar vibe, with a heavy emphasis on high-end fashion boutiques and hipster cafés. The mellow streets of both areas are worth wandering for the sake of putting yourself in serendipity's way.

Tokyo Photographic Art Museum
東京都写真美術館

Yebisu Garden Place, 1-13-3 Mita, Meguro-ku; tel. 03/3280-0099; https://topmuseum.jp; 10am-6pm Tues.-Wed. and Sat.-Sun., 10am-8pm Thurs.-Fri.; entry fee varies by exhibition; take Yamanote line to Ebisu station, east exit, or Hibiya line to Ebisu Station, exit 1

Tokyo's premier photography museum, colloquially shortened to **TOP Museum,** is housed in a four-story building toward the back of Ebisu Garden Place. The space boasts a library, studio, research laboratory, film screening hall, and multimedia gallery. Its permanent collection includes works by greats such as Ansel Adams, W. Eugene Smith, and Gustave Le Gray, as well as Japan's own photographic legends, such as Nobuyoshi Araki and Daido Moriyama, among many others.

A café on the museum's first floor, run by the trendy Maison Ichi bakery in nearby Daikanyama, provides a space to relax with a beverage or light meal after enjoying the visual feast.

Tokyo Metropolitan Teien Art Museum
東京都庭園美術館

5-21-9 Shirokanedai, Minato-ku; tel. 03/3443-0201; www.teien-art-museum.ne.jp; 10am-6pm daily, last entry 5:30pm, closed the 2nd and 4th Wed. each month, closed Thurs. if Wed. falls on holiday; entry fee varies by exhibition, garden only ¥200 adults, ¥160 college students, ¥100 high school and junior high school students; take Yamanote line to Meguro Station east exit, or Mita, Namboku lines to Shirokanedai Station, exit 1

The Tokyo Metropolitan Teien Art Museum's main draw is the building itself. Completed in 1933, the mansion is a stunning example of art deco architecture, with both a rose garden

teamLab Planets TOKYO
TOYOSU
大盛堂書店
TAISEIDO
三千里
1
2
3

and a Japanese landscape garden. The mansion was formerly the residence of Emperor Hirohito's uncle, Prince Asaka Yasuhiko, and Princess Nobuko, Emperor Meiji's eighth daughter. Prince Asaka returned from a stint in 1920s Paris, inspired to build a modern home, and enlisted French architect Henri Rapin and glass designer René Lalique, along with a team of Japanese architects, to produce the dazzling result. In 2014, the structures were restored and a new annex was added by artist Sugimoto Hiroshi. A visit to the museum today means exploring the enchanting mansion, with its crystal chandeliers and lush grounds, just as much as seeing whatever exhibition—likely in the decorative arts genre—is taking place at the time.

Happo-en
八芳園

1-1-1 Shirokanedai, Minato-ku; tel. 03/3443-3111; www.happo-en.com/banquet; 10am-10pm daily; free; take Namboku, Mita lines to Shirokanedai Station, exit 2

Happo-en, which means "garden of eight views," is aptly named: It looks beautiful from any angle. Serene paths wind through the beautifully landscaped garden, which has a pond at its heart and is dotted by bonsai trees, some of which are centuries old. A stone lantern said to have been carved by the warrior Taira-no Munekiyo some 800 years ago also stands on the grounds, which were originally the residence of an advisor to the shogun during the early 17th century. The current design was largely realized in the early 20th century by a business magnate who acquired the land and built a Japanese villa, which can still be seen near the garden's entrance. With a large banquet hall on-site, it's no surprise the garden is one of the most popular places in Tokyo for couples to tie the knot. Note that small sections of the garden may be closed off if a wedding is underway.

Muan (tel. 03/3443-3775; www.happo-en.com/banquet/plan_en/detail.php?p=837; 11am-4pm daily), a teahouse, is also tucked away in the garden, offering sets of *matcha* (powdered green tea with a highly caffeinated kick) and Japanese-style sweets, as well as small tea ceremonies if you book ahead. Overlooking Happo-en is also the excellent **Thrush Café** (tel. 03/3443-3105; www.happo-en.com/restaurant/thrushcafe; 10am-10pm Mon.-Fri., 9am-10pm Sat.-Sun., food last order 8pm, drink last order 9:30pm), which offers a more substantial menu for a meal in the serene setting.

ROPPONGI
六本木

During the Sino-Japanese War (1894-1895) and the Russo-Japanese War (1905), Rippongi area was used as a military training ground. Following World War II, Occupation forces moved into newly empty barracks, leading to the development of the sort of nightlife associated with overseas GIs—hence the neighborhood's slightly seedy reputation.

The area has since been developed into an upscale district, with luxury shops, world-class art museums, and towering mega-complexes **Roppongi Hills** (9-7-1 Akasaka, Minato-ku; tel. 03/3475-3100; www.roppongihills.com; 11am-9pm daily; free) and **Tokyo Midtown** (9-7-1 Akasaka, Minato-ku; tel. 03/3475-3100; www.tokyo-midtown.com; 11am-9pm daily; free) giving it a cosmopolitan sheen. As the sun falls, however, the area running south from **Roppongi Crossing** on **Gaien-Higashi-dōri** fills with shady touts who serve as a reminder that the underbelly still remains. If you can politely but firmly ignore the unsavory characters milling about at night, you'll discover that the area boasts some fantastic dining options and watering holes.

Roppongi has also become Tokyo's main hub for contemporary art, with its "Art Triangle" of the **Mori Art Museum,** the **Suntory Museum of Art,** and the **National Art Center, Tokyo. 21_21 Design Sight** (9-7-6 Akasaka, Minato-ku; tel. 03/3475-2121; www.2121designsight.jp; 10am-7pm daily

---

1: Shibuya Crossing **2:** Tokyo Skytree **3:** Tokyo Metropolitan Teien Art Museum

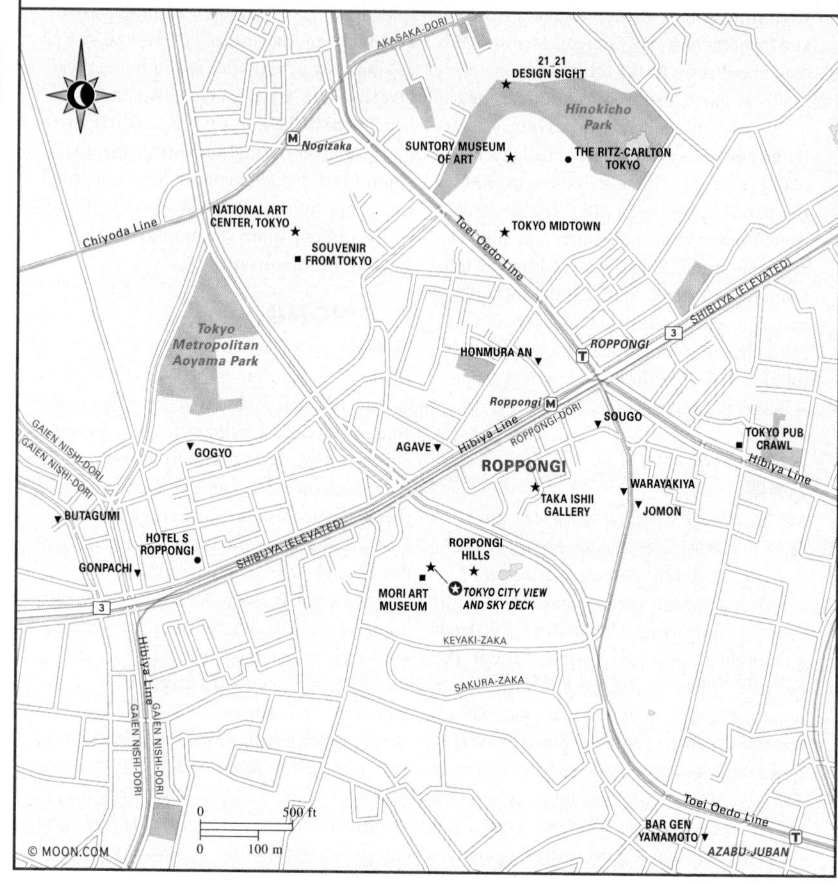

(last entry 6:30pm), closed Thurs. and New Year holidays; ¥1,200 adults, ¥800 university students, ¥500 high school students, free junior high and under) an art space right behind Tokyo Midtown, is also worth a visit.

Close by, the posh neighborhoods of **Akasaka** and **Azabu** boast great restaurants and swanky cocktail bars, minus the unsavory bits.

Mori Art Museum
森美術館

53F Roppongi Hills Mori Tower; 6-10-1 Roppongi, Minato-ku; tel. 03/6406-6000; www.mori.art.museum/jp; 10am-10pm (last entry 9:30pm) Wed.-Mon., 10am-5pm (last entry 4:30pm) Tues., ¥1,800 adults, ¥1,200 students, ¥600 children; take Hibiya line to Roppongi Station, exit 1C or Ōedo line to Roppongi Station, exit 3

If only you visit one contemporary art museum during your time in Tokyo, make it the Mori Art Museum. This stellar museum consistently hosts sophisticated exhibitions on a range of relevant themes and media from Japan and abroad in a fantastic space designed by American architect Richard Gluckman. Past exhibitions have showcased Japanese visionaries such as Aida Makoto and Takashi Murakami, Chinese hell-raiser Ai Wei Wei, and modern Southeast Asian and Middle Eastern art. Note that the museum is closed between exhibitions, so please check the schedule on the website before going.

★ Tokyo City View and Sky Deck
東京シティビュー

52F Roppongi Hills Mori Tower; 6-10-1 Roppongi, Minato-ku; tel. 03/6406-6652; https://tcv.roppongihills.com/jp; 10am-11pm (last entry 10:30pm) Mon.-Fri. and holidays, 10am-1am (last entry midnight) Fri.-Sat. and day before holidays; admission included with ticket to Mori Art Museum; take Hibiya line to Roppongi Station, exit 1C, or Ōedo line to Roppongi Station, exit 3

One story beneath the Mori Art Museum is the 52nd-floor Tokyo City View, which offers an almost 360-degree view of the city. Admission is included with the ticket for Mori Art Museum and vice versa. And for an even more unimpeded view, another ¥500 on top of the admission you've already paid for the Mori Art Museum or Tokyo City View allows you to ride an escalator to the rooftop **Sky Deck** for a view without windows.

Suntory Museum of Art
サントリー美術館

3F Tokyo Midtown Galleria, 9-7-4 Akasaka, Minato-ku; tel. 03/3479-8600; www.suntory.com/sma; 10am-6pm Wed.-Thurs. and Sun.-Mon., 10am-8pm Fri.-Sat.; fees vary by exhibition; take Ōedo line or Hibiya line (via underground walkway) to Roppongi Station, exit 8, or Chiyoda line to Nogizaka Station, exit 3

Standing at the western edge of Tokyo Midtown is the Suntory Museum of Art, a "lifestyle art" showcase featuring beautifully crafted everyday objects such as lacquerware, glass, ceramics, and textiles. The museum, designed by architect Kengo Kuma, holds the largest assortment of arts and crafts in Japan. It also has a room where tea ceremonies are held every other Thursday at 1pm, 2pm, and 3pm for up to 50 people total for the day (¥1,000 each; up to two tickets per person). Tickets are sold on the day from the museum's third-floor reception desk. Check the website to confirm which days the ceremonies will be held (www.suntory.com/sma/rental/teaceremonyroom.html). There's also a café specializing in morsels from the city of Kanazawa, renowned for its traditional crafts. The gift shop carries exquisitely designed tableware and glassware, some done in the geometric Edo Kiriko style.

National Art Center, Tokyo
国立新美術館

7-22-2 Roppongi, Minato-ku; tel. 03/5777-8600; www.nact.jp/english; 10am-6pm Wed.-Thurs. and Sun.-Mon., 10am-8pm Fri.-Sat., closed Wed. if Tues. is holiday for exhibitions organized by National Art Center, Tokyo, 10am-6pm Wed.-Mon. for exhibitions organized by artist associations; fees vary by exhibition; take Ōedo line to Roppongi Station, exits 7, 8

With the biggest exhibition space of any art museum in the country, the National Art Center, Tokyo houses 12 galleries in a striking building designed by the late architect Kurokawa Kisho. Standing in front of the massive structure, the curved green windows of its front wall appear to undulate as it allows natural light to flood the soaring atrium. The museum doesn't have a collection of its own. Instead, it hosts meticulously curated shows ranging from the surrealist mindscapes of Salvador Dalí to the polka-dot infused world of Yayoi Kusama, alongside a host of other exhibitions overseen by various art collectives and associations throughout Japan. The museum also boasts two restaurants, a café, and a stellar gift shop, **Souvenir From Tokyo.**

Tokyo Tower
東京タワー

4-2-8 Shiba-kōen, Minato-ku; tel. 03/3433-5111; www.tokyotower.co.jp/en.html; 9am-11pm daily; ¥1,200 adults, ¥700 junior high and elementary school students; take Ōedo line to Akabanebashi Station, Akabanebashiguchi exit

Finished in 1958, Tokyo Tower was originally intended to commemorate the city's phoenix-like rise after World War II. Its

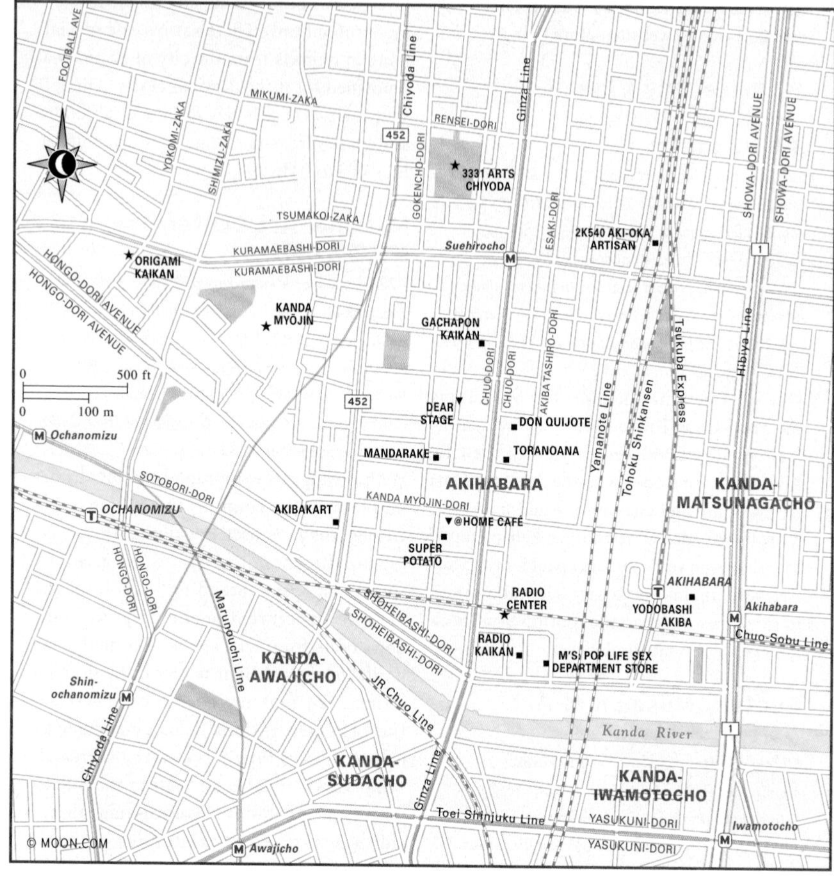

resemblance to the Eiffel Tower is overt, as is the fact that it stands 13 meters taller than its Parisian inspiration. The structure still serves as a radio and television broadcast tower, but the words "tourist trap" are admittedly hard to avoid when thinking of it today. Its extra attractions—a wax museum, an aquarium, and an exhibit dedicated to the anime program *One Piece*—only reinforce this impression. People still flock to it nonetheless, and the white and orange behemoth remains one of the most recognizable points in the city's skyline. The observation decks of the Tokyo Metropolitan Government Building, Tokyo Skytree, or Tokyo City View provide more sweeping views. But if you feel the pull of vintage charm, Tokyo Tower still offers thrilling views of the Minato area skyline at night.

AKIHABARA AND AROUND
秋葉原

Akihabara has long been associated with commerce, from bicycles and radios during World War II to a flourishing black market that specialized in supplying radios to information-starved civilians in the postwar years. Whether you indulge in one of the obsessions catered to by the neighborhood's myriad niche shops or not, a visit will surely leave you feeling you've experienced a bona fide slice of a subculture that is singularly Japanese. If you crave a break from all the gadgets, the nearby classical garden of **Koishikawa Kōrakuen** is well worth a detour too.

Kanda Myōjin
神田明神

2-16-2 Sotokanda, Chiyoda-ku; tel. 03/3254-0753; www.kandamyoujin.or.jp; free; take Chūō, Sōbu, Marunouchi lines to Ochanomizu Station, exit 1, or Yamanote, Hibiya lines to Akihabara Station, Electric Town exit

It's somewhat counter-intuitive that one of Tokyo's oldest shrines, Kanda Myōjin, has become so deeply associated with Akihabara, Tokyo's most technology-crazed neighborhood. Founded in AD 730, the current shrine is in fact a concrete re-creation of the original one. It is dedicated to three gods: Ebisu (god of commerce and fishermen), Daikokuten (guardian of farmers, harvests, and wealth), and Masakado (full name: Taira no Masakado, a guardian deity). Visitors to the shrine typically come to pray for luck in marriage and business.

Passing through the shrine's magnificently carved vermillion gate today, you'll soon discover indicators of its proximity to "Electric Town," such as *omamori* (amulets purchased for blessing or protection at temples and shrines) to protect electronic gadgets and a glut of *ema* (wooden prayer plaques) adorned with precise hand-drawn portraits of supplicants' favorite anime and manga characters alongside their prayers. This isn't the only fun aspect of the shrine. In mid-May during oddly numbered years, the Kanda Matsuri, seen as one of Tokyo's top-three festivals, begins at the shrine and then spills out into the area's streets.

Origami Kaikan
おりがみ会館

1-7-14 Yushima, Bunkyō-ku; tel. 03/3811-4025; www.origamikaikan.co.jp; 9:30am-5:30pm Mon.-Sat.; fees vary; take Chūō, Sōbu, Marunouchi lines to Ochanomizu Station, exit 1

Established in 1859, Origami Kaikan is regarded as the place where the art of origami paper-folding was born. The building houses an exhibition space, a workshop where you can see origami paper being created, and a shop devoted to origami papers, books, and more. There are also Japanese-language classes on origami priced according to the class's level of difficulty on any given day.

Koishikawa Kōrakuen
小石川後楽園

1-6-6 Koraku, Bunkyō-ku; tel. 03/3811-3015; www.tokyo-park.or.jp/teien/en/koishikawa/index.html; 9am-5pm daily; ¥300; take Chūō, Sōbu, Ōedo, Tōzai, Namboku, Yurakuchō lines to Iidabashi Station, east exit (JR station) and exit C3 (subway)

West of Akihabara on the Chūō Line is the station of Iidabashi, the closest stop to one of Tokyo's most beautiful Japanese-style gardens: Koishikawa Kōrakuen. The origin of this Edo-period garden dates back to 1629 when it was four times as large and the property of Yorifusa Tokugawa, head of the influential Mito Tokugawa clan. The original garden was larger than the current incarnation, but its essence remains. Landscapes from Chinese legend and Japan's natural wonders are re-created in miniature throughout the garden, which erupts in colorful plum blossoms in February and irises in June. The changing color of leaves in autumn is also a draw. The grounds are graced by a lotus pond, small waterways, and bridges, including the famous Full-Moon Bridge (Engetsu-kyo).

ASAKUSA AND AROUND
浅草

At the heart of the city's old downtown, Asakusa first emerged as a neighborhood

TOP EXPERIENCE

Geek Paradise: Akihabara and *Otaku* Culture

The district of Akihabara is ground zero for all things geek, or *otaku*, in Japan. Long before geekdom invaded these streets, however, the area was home to a post-World War II black market where tech-savvy university students known as "radio boys" sold transistor radio parts—often pilfered from the occupation forces—to information-starved citizens.

Throughout the 1960s, Akihabara expanded its reach beyond the humble radio and became the premier destination for popular new items like televisions, refrigerators, and washing machines. Since the mid-1980s, Akihabara has exploded into full geek mode. This is the place to find performances by idol groups—pop music groups composed of teenage girls who have been picked, preened and marketed for mass appeal—cafés where patrons are served coffee by cosplay butlers and maids, and high-rise buildings full of shops selling anime, manga, plastic figurines, video games, and more.

- For a glimpse of Akihabara of old, head to the rundown, two-floor **Radio Center** (1-14-2 Sotokanda, Chiyoda-ku; tel. 03/3251-0614; www.radiocenter.jp; 10am-7pm daily; free; take Yamanote, Chūō lines to Akihabara Station, Electric Town exit) under the Sōbu line train tracks. Here you'll find tumbledown shops peddling parts for all manner of electronic devices.
- Aside from wandering the neighborhood's many fascinating shops, to get a taste of the Akihabara of today head to **@Home Café** (1-11-4 Sotokanda, Chiyoda-ku; tel. 03/5207-9779; www.cafe-athome.com/en; 11am-10pm daily), the easiest place to wrap your head around the country's maid café phenomenon.
- Akihabara's branch of **Don Quijote** (4-3-3-Sotokanda, Chiyoda-ku), a maze-like chain store selling everything under the sun at cheap prices, also hosts daily performances (go to http://ticket.akb48-group.com/home/top.php for tickets) by idol group AKB48 in an event space on its top floor.
- For a glimpse into the wondrous world of *gachapon*, or toys dispensed in capsules from vending machines, head to the **Gachapon Kaikan** (3-15-5 Sotokanda, Chiyoda-ku; tel. 03/5209-6020; www.akibagacha.com; 11am-7pm daily), where avid collectors zealously part ways with ¥100 coins in their quest for figurines and models of everything from animals to mushrooms.

during the early part of the Edo period. The area's location northeast of the shogun's castle was believed to place it in an unlucky direction, according to principles of Chinese geomancy. Thus, Shogun Tokugawa Ieyasu called for the construction of the great temple of **Sensō-ji** in 1590 to keep evil spirits at bay. Across the Sumida River, the neighborhood of **Ryōgoku** centers around sumo, with restaurants serving the style of hot pot that accounts for the bulk of the wrestlers' diet, training stables, a museum, and the **Ryōgoku Kokugikan** stadium.

★ Sensō-ji
浅草寺

2-3-1 Asakusa, Taitō-ku; tel. 03-3842-0181; www.senso-ji.jp; temple grounds always open, main hall 6am-5pm daily Apr.-Sept., 6:30am-5pm Oct.-Mar.; free; take Ginza, Asakusa lines to Asakusa Station, exit 1

Tokyo's oldest temple, Sensō-ji, or Asakusa Kannon, also serves as a testament to the capital's turbulent past. Originally completed in AD 645, the temple is said to have been inspired by two fishermen brothers who miraculously found a golden statue of Kannon, the Buddhist goddess of compassion, wrapped in nets they had cast into the nearby Sumida

Akihabara game

- To see idols in the making, check out live music performance space **Dear Stage** (DEMPA Bldg., 3-10-9 Sotokanda, Chiyoda-ku; tel. 03/5207-9181; http://dearstage.com; 6pm-10:50pm Mon.-Fri., 5pm-10:50pm Sat.-Sun. and holidays; ¥1,000 entry for main stage area). Performances take place in the evenings, when there are also two upper floor bars staffed by bubbly young women in maid outfits (¥500 per hour).
- For an English map to help you navigate the delightfully baffling labyrinth of Akihabara, head to Akiba Info at the **Tokyo Anime Center** (4F Akihabara UDX, 4-14-1 Sotokanda, Chiyoda-ku; tel. 03/5298-1188; https://animecenter.jp; 11am-7pm daily). If you're keen to peek behind Tokyo's geek curtain but feel timid, check out the well-rated **Akihabara Anime & Manga Culture Guided Tour** (www.getyourguide.com; 2.5 hours; ¥4,400).

River. It is said that the golden object still resides in the temple, but that it remains hidden from sight.

The temple was mostly razed during World War II bombing raids, but it has been fully reconstructed. Its current iteration is made of concrete rather than wood, but the atmosphere remains intact. Enter the grounds via the imposing **Kaminari-mon** (Thunder Gate), recognizable by its giant red lantern and flanked by statues of Fujin and Raijin, the rather wrathful-looking deities of wind and thunder. Crossing the threshold, amble along **Nakamise-dōri,** a row of shops and food stalls hawking charms, traditional crafts and rice crackers and red bean cakes.

At the far end of Nakamise-dōri, where the shops end, stands a second large gate called **Hozo-mon,** and just beyond it is the temple's main hall, **Kannon Hall.** Worshippers gather around a large cauldron to bathe in the smoke, believed to impart good health. If you're inclined, buy a bundle of incense sticks to light and place in the cauldron yourself. Looming to the left of Kannon Hall is a five-story pagoda. And to the east of Kannon Hall is **Asakusa-jinja,** a shrine built in 1649 to commemorate the two fishermen who

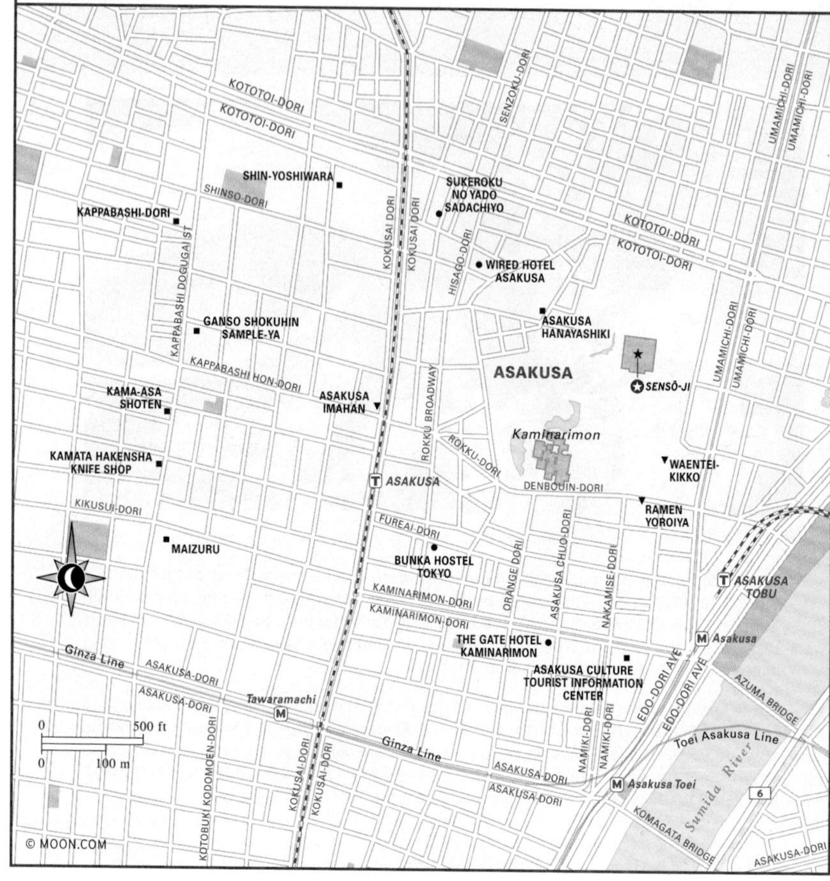

snagged the golden statue of Kannon almost 1,400 years ago.

With more than 30 million annual visitors, it's no surprise that the temple is jam-packed any day of the week. Avoid visiting on weekends, and instead, try to go in the late afternoon or after dusk when crowds are thinner.

Tokyo Skytree
東京スカイツリー

1-1-2 Oshiage, Sumida-ku; tel. 03/5302-3470; www.tokyo-skytree.jp/en; 8am-10pm daily; Tembo Deck ¥2,100 Mon.-Fri., ¥2,300 Sat.-Sun. and holidays, Tembo Galleria ¥1,000 Mon.-Fri., ¥1,100 Sat.-Sun. and holidays; take Hanzōmon line to Oshiage Station, Tokyo Skytree exit

Given Tokyo's massive dimensions, the city has a decidedly low-rise skyline. As the world's tallest freestanding tower, Tokyo Skytree dramatically bucks this trend. Rising 634 meters above a swath of buildings near the east bank of the Sumida River, Sky Tree opened in 2012 to serve as the capital's new and improved television broadcasting tower. The only man-made structure taller is the 830-meter (2,723-foot) Burj Khalifa in Dubai (which is considered a skyscraper rather than tower). The structure itself, a central pillar enmeshed in a giant steel frame, incorporates principles of traditional Japanese and temple architecture in its delicate balance of both convex and concave curves.

But the tower's real draw is the 310 restaurants and shops situated around its base in a complex called Tokyo Skytree Town, and two dizzyingly high observation decks. Reaching these fantastically high perches isn't cheap. A ticket to the Tembō Deck—standing 350 meters (1,148 feet) with 360-degree views, a glass-floor paneled section, and a snack bar—sets an adult back ¥2,060. Another ¥1,030 sends you via high-speed elevator to the Tembō Galleria, which is 100 meters (328 feet) higher and includes a 110-meter-long (360-foot) glass floor. Though the difference in height between the two decks is noticeable, it doesn't necessarily feel like it is worth the extra yen. Daytime views from either platform are stunning and reach all the way to Mount Fuji when the sky is clear. Arriving just before dusk ensures an awesome view, as the vast blanket of Tokyo's twinkling lights is seemingly endless. Purchase tickets on the fourth floor, where current wait times are indicated in English. Try showing up in the morning or at night to avoid the crowds. Weekend queues can also be discouragingly long.

Japanese Sword Museum
刀剣博物館

1-12-9, Yokoami, Sumidaku; tel. 03/6284-1000; www.touken.or.jp/english; 9:30am-5pm Tue.-Sun.; adults ¥1,000, students ¥500, ages 15 and under free; take Sōbu, Ōedo lines to Ryōgoku Station, west exit (JR station) or exit A1 (subway station)

If you enjoy geeking out on history or samurai cinema, the Japanese Sword Museum is well worth visiting. Its collection of blades came into being thanks to the Ministry of Education's creation of a society and museum dedicated to keeping Japan's rich tradition of sword-making alive after *katana* seized by US occupation forces were returned to Japan in 1948. Dozens of steel specimens, displaying exceptionally high levels of craftsmanship and decorative flourishes, as well as a large collection of handles and sheaths, are on display with clear English signage. Armor and other artifacts from the Heian and Edo periods are also on show. While the impressive collection offers a glimpse of an important slice of Japanese history and craftsmanship, those with a more casual level of interest might prefer a trip to Shinjuku's Samurai Museum.

Sensō-ji

From the third floor, step out on the landing to look over the neighboring **Former Yasuda Garden,** which dates to the late 17th century and is free to enter.

Edo-Tokyo Museum
江戸東京博物館

1-4-1 Yokoami, Sumida-ku; tel. 03/3626-9974; www.edo-tokyo-museum.or.jp/en; 9:30am-5:30pm Tues.-Sun., until 7:30pm Sat., closed Tues. if Mon. is a holiday; adults ¥600, college students ¥480, high school and junior high school students ¥300, elementary school students and younger free; take Ōedo line to Ryōgoku Station, exits A3, A4, or Sōbu line, west exit

For an engaging overview of Tokyo's history from feudal days to modern metropolis, the Edo-Tokyo Museum is your best bet. Despite having an exterior resembling a massive spaceship, the museum's displays illustrate the dramatic ups and downs of the city's past, from the 1923 Great Kanto Earthquake and subsequent citywide fires to incineration by American B-29 bombers during World War II. All of this, followed by the dramatic transformation that swept the city, and country via the post-World War II "economic miracle," and then the subsequent popping of the bubble economy, have molded the city into what it is today. These traumas and transformations are powerfully illustrated through a wide range of displays, including miniature models of entire city districts, a reconstruction of a typical post-World War II apartment, and a hodgepodge of items from daily life, such as vehicles and household objects. Some exhibits are interactive.

English signs are ubiquitous, and English-speaking volunteer guides are available for part of the day (10am-3pm daily), reservable on the spot at the 6th-floor Permanent Exhibition Volunteer Guide Reception Center or by phone two weeks in advance. It's also possible to take a self-guided tour with an English-language audio guide, available for a ¥1,000 deposit. Traditional cultural demonstrations are provided on some Saturdays as well. Choose your course and leave the museum with a deeper appreciation for the historical journey of the multilayered city around you.

UENO
上野

It is said that the edge of Tokyo Bay once ended where the extensive grounds of **Ueno-kōen** and **Ueno Station** stand on reclaimed land today. Elsewhere in Ueno you'll discover **Ameya-Yokochō,** a former postwar black market that is now a warren of open-air shops, smoky restaurants grilling chicken and offal, and stalls hawking cheap clothing and other goods. West of Ueno you'll discover the laid-back streets of **Yanaka,** a charming neighborhood full of mom-and-pop restaurants, shops selling locally made crafts, art galleries, old-school cafés, and a number of serene temples and shrines. Take the Yamanote Line a few stations to the west and alight at Komagome Station to explore **Rikugi-en,** one of the city's most scenic stroll gardens, dating to the Edo period.

★ Tokyo National Museum
東京国立博物館

13-9 Ueno-kōen, Taitō-ku; tel. 03/5777-8600; www.tnm.jp/?lang=en; 9:30am-5pm Tues.-Thurs. and Sun., 9:30am-9pm Fri.-Sat., closed on Tues. if Mon. is holiday; adults ¥620, college students ¥410, ages 18 and under free; take Yamanote line to Ueno Station, Ueno-kōen exit

At the Tokyo National Museum you'll see the most extensive collection of Japanese art on the planet, including Buddhist sculptures, swords, *Noh* masks, delicate ceramics, colorful kimonos, and sacred scrolls. All told, there are more than 110,000 pieces in the collection, with around 4,000 items on display at any one time.

After passing through an opulent entrance, explore the backbone of the collection, housed in the Honkan (Japanese Gallery). This 25-room space, which hosts rotating exhibitions of Japanese arts and antiquities, is in the middle of three main buildings, with the five-floor Toyokan on the right exhibiting arts

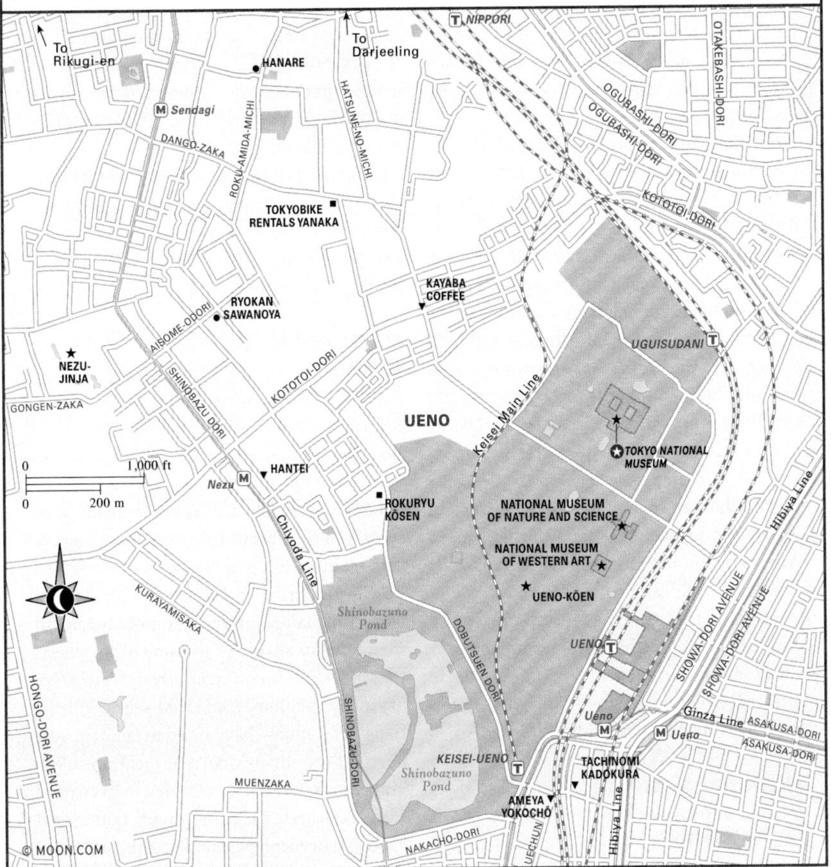

from China, Korea, Southeast Asia, Central Asia, India, and Egypt; and the oft-closed Hyokeikan, constructed in 1909 to honor the Taisho Emperor's wedding, on the left.

Behind the Honkan is the Heiseikan, which displays artifacts from prehistoric Japan in the Japanese Archaeological Gallery, occasionally hosts special exhibitions of Japanese art, and houses a gift shop and a few eateries. Behind the Hyoeikan is the newest addition to the museum, the Gallery of Hōryū-ji Treasures. This spectacular collection shows off some of the objects from Hōryū-ji, a 7th-century temple in built in Nara Prefecture. If you're pressed for time, focus on exploring the Honkan and the Gallery of Hōryū-ji Treasures, with the Toyokan being a potential bonus.

Beyond the galleries, a garden and several teahouses can be found behind the Honkan, but these facilities are only open to the public in spring (mid-Mar.-mid-Apr.), when its cherry trees explode with pink petals, and in autumn (late Oct.-early Dec.), when the leaves become a riot of earth tones. Note that excellent English signage and audio tours are available for the museum's main collections, but are not always available for special shows.

National Museum of Nature and Science
国立科学博物館

7-20 Ueno-kōen, Taito-ku; tel. 03/5777-8600; www.kahaku.go.jp/english; 9am-5pm Tues.-Thurs. and Sun., 9am-8pm Fri.-Sat.; ¥630; take Yamanote line to Ueno Station, Ueno-kōen exit

From dinosaur bones to a large chunk of a meteorite that fell into China in the 16th century to the stuffed body of *the* Hachikō, inspiration for the dog-shaped statue in Shibuya Crossing, the National Museum of Nature and Science is the best place to get a glimpse of the natural forces underlying the Japanese archipelago.

Spread across two buildings, the Japan Gallery and the Global Gallery, this museum has collections on subjects such as outer space, evolution, and Japan's flora and fauna. There's also good coverage of the crucially important role that rice has played in the development of human society in Japan, the ancient Jomon and Yayoi civilizations, the indigenous Ainu people, and those of the Ryūkyū islands southwest of Kyūshū.

Multilingual touch screen displays are conveniently available throughout the museum, along with optional English audio tours (¥300). This is a good rainy-day option for those traveling with kids.

National Museum of Western Art
国立西洋美術館

7-7 Ueno-kōen, Taitō-ku; tel. 03/5777-8600; www.nmwa.go.jp/en; 9:30am-5:30pm Tues.-Thurs. and Sun., 9:30am-8pm Fri.-Sat.; ¥500; take Yamanote line to Ueno Station, Ueno-kōen exit; take Yamanote line to Ueno Station, Ueno-kōen exit

This is Japan's only national museum solely focused on Western art, and the building is as big an attraction as the collection itself. Finished in 1959, the complex is the brainchild of French architect Le Corbusier, whose ideas exerted an immense influence on modern Japanese architecture. The structure's uniqueness was officially recognized in 2016 when it was added to the UNESCO World Heritage List for cultural heritage.

The art collection was amassed by Matsukata Kojiro, a shipping magnate who accrued a huge collection of Western art over the course of his life, from medieval icons to Jackson Pollock. French impressionists make a particularly strong showing, especially Monet, with whom Matsukata was a personal friend.

English-language signage is present throughout the museum, and an English-language pamphlet and map about the building's unique properties can be picked up at the front desk.

Nezu-jinja
根津神社

1-28-9, Nezu, Bunkyō-ku; tel. 03/3822-0753; www.nedujinja.or.jp; 6am-5pm daily; free; take Chiyoda line to Nezu Station, exit 1

With its long tunnel of red torii gates, koi ponds, some 3,000 azaleas that explode with color in spring, beautiful grounds, and an ornate main building reminiscent of the famed Tōshō-gū shrine in Nikkō outside Tokyo, Nezu-jinja is one of Tokyo's more beautiful shrines. This shrine is also one of the country's oldest; the main structure dates to 1706, having miraculously survived World War II. In fact, it is said to have stood in Sendagi, just north of the shrine's current location; 1,900 years ago, before being relocated to its current spot to celebrate the fifth shogun Tsunayoshi choosing his nephew Ienobu as his successor. The shrine can get crowded during spring, but the best thing about Nezu-jinja is its relative lack of popularity, compared to big-name religious sites in the city like Meiji Jingū, and Sensō-ji. For these reasons, it's worth going just a bit out of the way to see it, especially if you won't be venturing outside Tokyo.

Rikugi-en
六義園

6-16-3 Hon-komagome, Bunkyō-ku; tel. 03/3941-2222; www.tokyo-park.or.jp/teien/en/rikugien; 9am-5pm; ¥300, free for children and local

---

1: Tokyo National Museum **2:** Nezu-jinja

1

2

junior high students; take Yamanote, Namboku lines to Komagome Station, exit 2

Another historic site worth a detour if you're in the Ueno area is Rikugi-en. Stretching across 89,000 square meters (957,988 square feet), this Edo-period garden was designed by Yoshiyasu Yanagisawa, a high-ranking administrator who received the plot from the fifth shogun Tsunayoshi Tokugawa. The sprawling garden is crisscrossed by winding paths and features miniaturized re-creations of 88 gorgeous landscapes immortalized in Japanese poetry, which Yanagisawa cherished. The garden is gorgeous any time of year, but it really comes alive during spring when cherry blossoms turn the grounds pink, and in autumn when the leaves transform into a riot of reds, yellows, and browns.

TOKYO BAY AREA
東京湾

Until recently the area's most famous site was by far the hallowed **Tsukiji Fish Market,** which closed in September 2018. The new market, which opened in Toyosu in October 2018, remains the world's largest bazaar of fish mongers, but it's unfortunately a somewhat sterile affair compared to its predecessor in Tsukiji. Though it's safe to give the new market in Toyosu a pass, it is still possible to visit Tsukiji's **Outer Market** of seafood shops and mom-and-pop sushi counters.

Just south of Tsukiji is the famed **Hama-rikyū Onshi-teien,** a villa set in a pristine garden. Architecture buffs should take note of the **Nakagin Capsule Tower** (8-6-10 Ginza, Chuo-ku), about 7 minutes' walk north of Hama-rikyū Onshi-teien. The singular structure looks like a series of large concrete building blocks with round windows.

Across the bay lies the hyper urbanized development of **Odaiba.** Linked to the rest of Tokyo either by the scenic **Rainbow Bridge** or the fully automated **Yurikamome New Transit Monorail,** Odaiba is a hodgepodge of family-friendly museums, shopping centers, and **Ōedo Onsen Monogatari,** a popular *onsen* (hot spring) theme park. One of Odaiba's biggest draws is its position as a jumping-off point for a cruise on the bay, whether by day or night, offering great views of the city. If you make the trip to Odaiba, pass by the 19.7-meter-tall (65-foot) **Unicorm Gundam Statue** (1-1-10 Aomi, Taitō-ku; tel. 03/6380-7800; 10am-9pm daily; free), towering over the **DiverCity Tokyo Plaza** (http://mitsui-shopping-park.com/divercity-tokyo). The life-size statue from the anime series *Mobile Suit Gundam* about giant robots "performs" at select times each day when its head moves and eyes light up, and mist wafts through the area as music plays.

Tsukiji Outer Market
築地場外市場

www.tsukiji.or.jp/index.html; take Hibiya line to Tsukiji Station, exits 1, 2, or take Ōedo line to Tsukijishijō Station, exit A1

To the chagrin of many foodies and urban anthropologists, the colorful, chaotic inner side of the legendary Tsukiji Fish Market, once the site of legendarily intense morning tuna auctions, closed in fall 2018. The market relocated to a massive, sterile new building, **Toyosu Market,** in the area known as Toyosu southeast of Tsukiji. Thankfully, Tsukiji's outer market, which once spilled into the streets just northeast of the former inner market, has remained in operation. It's perhaps the one place in the world where sushi for breakfast comes recommended.

Starting from mid-morning to early afternoon, stalls sell edibles ranging from freshly bought oysters to sweet yet savory rolled omelets alongside sit-down restaurants and shops hawking pottery and kitchenware of excellent quality. The bulk of these stalls are housed in the newly rebuilt **Tsukiji Uogashi** complex (6-27-1 Tsukiji, Chūō-ku; tel. 03/3544-1906; https://uogashi.tsukiji-dainaka.com; 9am-2pm daily).

To glean a bit more insight into the fish business and be guided directly to the best spots for nibbles in Tsukiji, check out the highly rated tour of Tsukiji Outer Market run by **Japan Wonder Travel** (https://japanwondertravel.com/products/tokyo-foodrink-tour-tsukiji-fish-market; 3 hours from 8:30am daily; ¥9,500). Sterile though it may be, it is still possible to get a glimpse of the goingson of Toyosu Market. To have a guide tell you what's what, consider the tour of both the new facility in Toyosu and Tsukiji Outer Market run by Japan Wonder Travel (https://japanwondertravel.com/products/tokyo-foodrink-tour-toyosu-tsukiji-fish-market; 3.5 hours from 8:30am daily; ¥11,500) or the one covering the same terrain by **Ninja Food Tours** (www.ninjafoodtours.com/tokyo-food-tours/tsukiji-fish-market; 3 hours from 9am daily; ¥8,800).

Hama-rikyū Onshi-teien
浜離宮恩賜庭園

1-1 Hama Rikyū-teien, Chūō-ku; tel. 03/3541-0200; www.tokyo-park.or.jp/teien/en/hama-rikyu/index.html; 9am-5pm (last entry 4:30pm) daily; ¥300; take Ōedo, Yurikamome lines to Shiodome Station, exit 10, or take Ginza, Asakusa lines to Shimbashi Station, Shiodome exit

Once upon a time, the Tokugawa shogunate hunted on the land that Hama-rikyū Onshi-teien occupies today. On an island and surrounded by a walled moat, the garden is reachable via the Minamimon Bridge or by boat from Asakusa. Like all things with deep roots in Tokyo's past, the garden has seen its share of radical transformations, having been flattened during World War II. Today Shiodome's skyscrapers loom just beyond it, but the garden is sealed off from the city, embodying a deep sense of calm.

Strolling through the grounds, a stone's throw from Tsukiji Market, the space strikes a perfect balance between water and landscape, with numerous native species of vegetation, from hydrangeas to wizened black pines. One pine is said to be 300 years old. Ducks swim in a large central pond that contains two islands, linked by attractive wooden bridges. On one of the islands stands **Nakajima no Ochaya,** (9am-4:30pm daily; tea ¥510) an inviting teahouse with one of the best views in the city.

To reach the garden from Asakusa by boat (35 minutes; ¥1,040, which includes garden entrance fee; 1-2 boats per hour), take the Sumida River Line operated by **Tokyo Cruise** (http://www.suijobus.co.jp/en). Head to **Asakusa Pier** (1-1 Hanakawado, Taito-ku), which sits beside the Sumidagawa a stone's throw from Asakusa Station (Ginza, Tobu, Asakusa lines). The **Hama-rikyū Pier** is actually located within the garden itself. Note that boats traveling in the opposite direction, from Odaiba Seaside Park to Asakusa, do not stop at the garden. However, it is possible to travel from Hama-rikyū to Hinode Pier (5 minutes; ¥210), from where it's possible to then travel to the pier at **Odaiba Seaside Park** (20 minutes ¥520). For more information, from timetables and routes to pier locations, visit the Tokyo Cruise website.

Miraikan
日本科学未来館

2-3-6 Aomi, Koto-ku; tel. 03/3570-9151; www.miraikan.jst.go.jp/en; 10am-5pm Wed.-Mon.; adults ¥630, 18 years and under ¥210; take Yurikamome line to Telecom Center Station

Miraikan, or the National Museum of Emerging Science and Innovation, is a great museum with interactive exhibitions focused on robots and and life sciences. There's a globe hanging over the lobby that depicts climate change in action via 851,000 LEDs dotting its 6.5-meter (21-foot) circumference, as well as great displays on outer space and genetics. The museum feels somewhat geared toward kids, but it's fun and interesting for adults, too, and provides good English-language information on its exhibits. You'll get the chance to experience just that in an exhibit on some of the world's most sophisticated androids. As you interact with the androids on display, you may find yourself contemplating consciousness and what it really means to be human.

teamLab Borderless
チームラボボーダレス

1-3-8 Aomi, Kōtō-ku; tel. 03/6406-3949; https://borderless.teamlab.art; 10am-7pm Mon.-Fri., 10am-9pm Sat.-Sun. and holidays, closed 2nd and 4th Tues. every month; adults ¥3,200, children ¥1,000; take Yurikamome line to Aomi Station

Where is digital art and technology heading, and to what extent will we be able to interface with it? Since it opened in 2018, this groundbreaking digital art museum has sought to explore that question in a fun, interactive space that has proven a major hit with the Instagram set worldwide. Essentially, everyting in the mueum is interactive—touching the artworks *is* encouraged for once!—and art is created, with your participation, in real time. The museum is the brainchild of a collective of digital artists and "ultra-technologists" comprised of CG animators, mathematicians, architects, musicians, and engineers. More than 50 works of art are spread over a massive 10,000-square-meter (107,639 square feet) space, ranging from morphing flowers, waterfalls of light, swimming whales, and samurai on the march, to a room with bean bag chairs and a meditative display of waves crashing endlessly before you.

If you're active on social media, chances are you've seen images of the **Forest of Resonating Lamps,** in which the mirrored walls, floor, and ceiling, from which hang myriad motion-sensing, color-changing lamps, conjure an otherworldly realm beyond space and time. In the **Athletics Forest** you can jump, climb, and bounce in a variety of innovative exhibits that produce art in response to your actions. You can also draw and color your own animal or fish on paper, which is then digitized and set loose on the walls of the **Future Park,** or drink a cup of tea (¥500) that will overflow with blooming digital flowers in the **En Tea House.**

This is a fantastic place to go for a playful escape and is a particularly wonderful choice if you have kids—though adults will have fun too. A few notes: Wear pants (the floors are mirrored in some rooms) and comfortable shoes (the Athletic Forest only admits those wearing flat shoes). Also try to dress in a lighter shade; holograms don't interact well with black surfaces. Aim to go from the late afternoon on, when it tends to be a bit less crowded. Finally, the number of tickets sold on a given day is limited, so buy yours online (https://ticket.teamlab.art/#) at least a few weeks in advance.

Entertainment and Events

The performing arts have a rich history in Tokyo, stretching back to the hedonistic *ukiyo* (floating world) that took shape during the Edo period, in which samurai and sumo wrestlers engaged with geishas in teahouses as merchants filled their pockets. It's worth noting that the word, loaded with connotatios of extravagance, transgression, and, indeed, ennui, also produced a great deal of art, from poetry and music to painting—the name of the woodblock prints known as *ukiyo-e* literally means "pictures of the floating world."

It was during this period when Kabuki, a traditional form of theater with flamboyant costumes, rivieting music, and extravagant stage sets, was in its heyday. Today, the capital is still the best place in the country to see Kabuki, which continues to thrive, as well as traditional arts like the more rarefied *Noh* form of dance theater, known for its music and poetry. Today, edgy forms of dance and theater such as *butō* also flourish at the fringes of the performance arts scene.

For more information on other Japanese performing arts, go to the **Performing Arts Network Japan** website (www.performingarts.jp/index.html). Another useful resource is the official site of the **Japan Arts Council** (www.ntj.jac.go.jp/english.html), where it's also possible to get tickets for performances at Japan's national theaters. To get a sense of the city's edgier contemporary performing arts scene, check out **Tokyo Stages** (https://tokyostages.wordpress.com), compiled by Tokyo-based arts writer and translator William Andrews.

THEATER

KABUKI-ZA

4-12-15 Ginza, Chūō-ku; tel. 03/3545-6800; www.kabukiweb.net/theatres/kabukiza; ¥4,000-20,000 full performance, ¥800-2,000 one act; take Hibiya, Asakusa lines to Higashi-Ginza Station, exit 3

The place to see Kabuki in Tokyo is the esteemed Kabuki-za. Its exterior evokes a flavor of drama that is decidedly Japanese: the sweeping curves of its roof, pillars dotting its exterior walls, and an arched entryway reminiscent of a shrine over which paper lanterns hang. Even if you don't have time to watch a Kabuki performance, pay a visit to the marvelous Ginza landmark.

Showtimes tend to run either from 11am to around 3:30pm or 4:30pm to 9pm. If sitting through a full performance sounds daunting, it's also possible to watch just one act, for which 90 seats and 60 standing positions at the back of the theater are reserved on the day of each performance.

Booking tickets to see either a full three or four-hour performance, or just a single act, is simple thanks to the official English-language website, which offers a clear breakdown of the various scheduled plays and showtimes. If you prefer to reserve tickets over the phone, just dial 03/6745-0888. There is usually an English-speaking member of staff available 10am-6pm daily. If you plan to attend a full performance, it's best to book a few months in advance if you hope to snag a good seat, either online or by phone. If you plan to attend a single act, be sure to arrive a few hours in advance of the time you'd like to watch, and inquire at the ticket counter about a seat or standing spot.

When you reserve your place, be sure to rent a headset if you'd like a running interpretation of the performance in English (¥500 with ¥1,000 refundable deposit for one act, ¥1,000 and personal ID for full performance). And if you plan to see a full performance and think you'll get hungry, bring something to snack on, or perhaps even a bento box meal. On the fifth floor of the complex behind the theater, you'll find a gallery showcasing Kabuki-related memorabilia and outfits, and an excellent **café,** which is a good place to relax while waiting for a performance to begin or during intermission.

NATIONAL THEATRE

4-1 Hayabusa-chō, Chiyoda-ku; tel. 03/3265-7411; www.ntj.jac.go.jp; ¥1,800-12,800, headsets with English-language interpretation ¥700 with refundable ¥1,000 deposit; take Hanzōmon line to Hanzōmon Station, exit 1

Tokyo's top traditional performance space stages not only kabuki, but also *bunraku*, a form of theater using oversized puppets that originated in Osaka, as well as *gagaku* (imperial court music) concerts.

KANZE NŌGAKUDŌ

Ginza Six B3F, 6-10-1 Ginza, Chūō-ku; tel. 03/6274-6579; www.kanze.net; take Ginza, Hibiya, Marunouchi lines to Ginza Station, exit A3

The Kanze Nogakudo, a *Noh* theater found in the third-level basement floor of Ginza Six. It's the new incarnation of the Kanze association, which held performances at a renowned theater in Shibuya from its inception in 1901 until 2017, when the company relocated. In its current home, you can catch performances featuring just the final acts of three *Noh* plays. This is a good way to receive an enjoyable, not overwhelming introduction to this highbrow form of dance theater. Unfortunately, a *Noh* performance is not as easy to catch as Kabuki. Performances at Kanze Nogakudo are often sold out months in advance, and there is no English-language website for booking tickets. If you'd like to try to see a show, call at least two months in advance to talk with an English speaker; there are a few on staff. Tickets usually start from around ¥4,000 and performances, which last two to three hours, tend to be held only on weekend afternoons from 1pm. Note that it's also possible to catch the last act of a play from the unrerseved seating section by purchasing a special ticket on the day of a performance for ¥3,000.

NATIONAL NOH THEATRE

4-18-1 Sendagaya, Shibuya-ku; tel. 03/3423-1331; www.ntj.jac.go.jp; ¥2,800-5,000; take Sōbu line to Sendagaya Station or the Ōedo line to Kokuritsu-kyogijō Station

The National Noh Theatre is another place in Tokyo to see *Noh* performances acted out on a beautiful stage crafted from cypress wood. Shows are sporadic, but when they take place, this is a great venue to see one as it offers English-language translation on a screen provided at each seat. Check the English-language website for details on show times and prices, which vary by performance.

SETAGAYA PUBLIC THEATRE

Carrot Tower, 4-1-1 Taishido, Setagaya-ku; tel. 03/5432-1526, ticket reservations tel. 03/5432-1515; www.setagaya-pt.jp; ¥5,000-7,500; take Tokyū Den-en-toshi line from Shibuya Station to Sangenjaya Station

This theater stages contemporary spins on *Noh* and is the home base of the Sankai Juku *butō* troupe, making it one of the better places in the city to see contemporary drama and *butō*. The auditorium is shaped like an open-air theater, harkening back to ancient Greece. **Theatre Tram** is a smaller space also located within the complex that hosts edgier, experimental performances.

SUIGIAN

B1F 2-5-10 Nihonbashi-Muromachi, Chūō-ku; tel. 03/3527-9378; https://suigian.jp/en; 11am-11:30pm Mon.-Sat., 11am-9pm Sun.; cover ¥5,000-12,000; take Ginza, Hanzomon lines to Mitsukoshi-mae Station, exit A6

This dinner theater stages a range of introductory performances (40 minutes each) of various arts, from *Noh* and *kyōgen* to formal court dances. A square stage with a bonsai tree painted in the backdrop is surrounded by a space where the audience wines and dines on comfortable sofas and chairs. This is a classy place for an introduction to Japan's traditional arts in an intimate setting. Seats during the three daily performances (from 11:15am, 1:45pm, and 7pm) are broken down into various categories and cost between ¥5,000 and 12,000. For an additional charge, you get a sushi meal (¥4,158) or a sushi meal with a Japanese sweet and tea (¥5,940) during these three showtimes. Reservations are required for the meal and the seats during those hours. From 8:30pm Mon.-Sat., it becomes a first-come, first-serve bar and lounge with an a la carte menu, but sushi meals are no longer served. A ¥3,000 per person table charge is applied during lounge hours, which includes one drink.

TOKYO TAKARAZUKA THEATER

1-1-3 Yurakuchō, Chiyoda-ku; tel. 0570/00-5100; https://kageki.hankyu.co.jp/english/index.html; ¥3,500-12,500, take Yamanote line to Yurakuchō Station; or take Chiyoda, Hibiya, Mita lines to Hibiya Station

The Tokyo outpost of the Takarazuka Revue, based in the town of its namesake near Kōbe, features all female roles, markedly contrasting the all-male trend in traditional arts. The performers fit into one of five troupes of around 80 members each: *hana* (flower), *tsuki* (moon), *yuki* (snow), *hoshi* (star), *sora* (cosmos), and a sixth group of superstars known as *senka* who rotate in and out of the other five troupes. Think: grand, flamboyant, musical, dance, extravaganza. Check the website for the performance schedule.

ART GALLERIES

If you're into art, Tokyo provides ample choices for gallery hopping. The following galleries stand out for their cutting-edge work by artists both Japanese and international. For extensive gallery listings, exhibition information, and more, **Tokyo Art Beat**

1: Kabuki-za 2: festival participants carry an *omokishi* (portable shrine) 3: festival crowd 4: dancers in Kōenji's Awa Odori

1

2

(www.tokyoartbeat.com) is an excellent resource. And if you're really keen to dive deep into Tokyo's art world, it's worth looking at the **Grutt Pass** (www.rekibun.or.jp/grutto/english.html), a coupon booklet for more than 70 museums around the city.

DESIGN FESTA GALLERY

East: 3-20-2, West: 3-20-18, Jingū-mae, Shibuya-ku; tel. 03/3479-1442; www.designfestagallery.com; 11am-8pm daily; free; take Yamanote line to Harajuku Station, Omotesandō exit, or take Chiyoda, Fukutoshin lines to Meiji-Jingūmae Station, exit 5

Design Festa Gallery is the brainchild of three local artists who had a vision for a dilapidated apartment block in Harajuku's backstreets. Spread across three floors, some of the rooms are overseen by the creators themselves, who rent space from the gallery. The gallery space offers a glimpse into Tokyo's art scene at the young, grass-roots level, and is connected to **Design Festa,** the country's largest art and design fair held twice a year. If you're thirsty or hungry after perusing the eclectic offerings, there's also a funky café and an *okonomiyaki* (savory pancake) restaurant on-site.

TAKE NINAGAWA

2-12-4 Higashi-Azabu, Minato-ku; tel. 03/5571-5844; www.takeninagawa.com; 11am-7pm Tues.-Sat.; fee varies by exhibition; take Namboku, Ōedo lines to Azabun-Jūban Station, exit 6

This gallery often features pioneering young Japanese artists.

TAKA ISHII GALLERY TOKYO

3F Complex 665, 6-5-24 Roppongi, Minato-ku; tel. 03/6434-7010; www.takaishiigallery.com; 11am-7pm Tues.-Sat.; fee varies by exhibition; take Hibiya line to Roppongi Station, exit 3

Taka Ishii Gallery showcases work by big-name Japanese and international photographers. Past exhibits have included Nobuyoshi Araki, Daido Moriyama, and Thomas Demand.

MIZUMA ART GALLERY

2F Kagura Bldg., 3-13 Ichigayatamachi, Shinjuku-ku; tel. 03/3268-2500; http://mizuma-art.co.jp; 11am-7pm Tues.-Sat.; fee varies by exhibition; take Yurakucho, Namboku lines to Ichigaya Station, exit 5, or Tozai, Yurakuchō, Namboku lines to Iidabashi Station, exit B3

This edgy gallery is now in its third incarnation in Ichigaya. It has featured some big names over the years, including Aida Makoto, O JUN, Jun Kurashige, and many more.

ESPACE LOUIS VUITTON TOKYO

7F Louis Vuitton Omotesandō, 5-7-5 Jingū-mae, Shibuya-ku; tel. 03/5766-1094; www.espacelouisvuittontokyo.com; noon-8pm during exhibitions; free; take Ginza, Hanzomon, Chiyoda lines to Omotesandō Station, A1, or Chiyoda, Fukutoshin lines to Meiji-Jingūmae Station, exit 4

On the 7th floor of the Omotesandō Louis Vuitton store, is an airy, well-lit space that has hosted shows by artists from Japan, as well as from Finland, India, the United States, and Brazil.

GINZA GRAPHIC GALLERY

1F DNP Ginza Bldg., 7-7-2 Ginza, Chūō-ku; tel. 03/3571-5206; www.dnp.co.jp/gallery/ggg_e; 11am-7pm Mon.-Sat.; free; take Ginza, Hibiya, Marunouchi lines to Ginza Station, exit A2

Run by a Japanese printing giant, the Ginza Graphic Gallery focuses on the best in design and graphic arts.

MISA SHIN GALLERY

1F 3-9-11 Minami-Azabu, Minato-ku; tel. 03/6450-2334; www.misashin.com; noon-7pm Tues.-Sat.; fee varies by exhibition; take Mita, Namboku lines to Shirokane-Takanawa Station, exit 4

This gallery has hosted shows by some heavy-hitting luminaries, including architect Arata Isozaki and Ai Weiwei.

3331 ARTS CHIYODA

6-11-14 Sotokanda, Chiyoda-ku; tel. 03/6803-2441; www.3331.jp; 10am-9pm daily; fee varies by exhibition; take Ginza line to Suehirocho Station, exit 4, or take Yamanote, Sōbu lines to Akihabara Station, Electric City exit

This experimental art space is housed in a former junior high school. The facility includes

Purikura

Purikura, a shortened form of "print club," is a massive industry in Japan that attracts giggling teens en masse to take cutesy photos with friends. They are essentially photo booths, but the photos can be souped up with various digital enhancements. Often located in game centers (arcades), *purikura* booths are popular nationwide, although major cities like Tokyo and Osaka command a particularly large number of them. They have also made their way to teen hangouts outside Japan.

HOW IT WORKS

Many of booths have a preset theme; for example, a dessert-themed booth may add little digital slices of cake to your photos. Insert money in the slot outside and step inside. After you've input the settings of your choice—doe eyes and rosy cheeks, perhaps—strike a silly pose and let the camera do its work. After the images have been taken, you'll have the option to do further editing with a stylus in an editing booth outside. Once you've modified your photos to your liking, simply press the "end" button that appears on the screen to print them out. Voila: a cheap, quirky souvenir.

PURIKURA PLACES

To try out a *purikura* booth, a few good bets include **Purikura no Mecca** (3F, 29-1 Udagawachō, Shibuya-ku; open 24/7; take Yamanote line to Shibuya Station, Hachikō exit) and **Purikura Land Noa** (1-17-5 Jingūmae, Shibuya-ku; tel. 03/6206-8090; 8am-11:30pm daily; take Yamanote line to Harajuku Station, Takeshita exit) on Takeshita-dōri. Here you'll find collections of *purikura* booths to snap away to your heart's content.

Note that some *purikura* spots loosely enforce a rule that prohibits men, whether solo or in a group, from entering without at least one woman accompanying them. You'll be less likely to face an issue in an arcade than in a place solely dedicated to the booths.

private galleries, a large exhibition space, and recording studios, and the schoolyard is now a public park. As with many of Tokyo's galleries, it also has an attractive café and a gift shop stocked with locally created pieces. If you want to feel the pulse of Tokyo's creative world, be sure to pay a visit to this inspired hub.

FESTIVALS AND EVENTS

The following is a list of events, from celebrations of contemporary art to centuries-old rites, that take place in Tokyo throughout the year. It's by no means comprehensive, but these are some of the city's biggest conventions and best bashes.

Spring

ART FAIR TOKYO

Citywide; https://artfairtokyo.com; early Mar., 1-day pass ¥4,000 for one, ¥6,000 for two

Art Fair Tokyo provides a great chance to dive into Tokyo's art scene, with some 150 galleries participating every March, normally for about a week during the first half of the month. It is a four-day event that requires purchasing a ticket to attend. Participating galleries and museums offer discounted admission for those holding an Art Fair pass.

TOKYO RAINBOW PRIDE

Yoyogi-kōen and around; http://tokyorainbowpride.com; first week of May; free

Thousands suit up in fancy attire for a parade with floats to celebrate LGBTQ pride at Tokyo Rainbow Pride. The parade goes from Yoyogi-kōen toward Shibuya Station. A festival is also held in Yoyogi-kōen.

DESIGN FESTA

Tokyo Big Sight; http://designfesta.com; May, Aug., and Nov.; ¥800 one day, ¥1,000 for one-day tickets bought day of entry, ¥1,500 two days, ¥1,800 for two-day tickets bought day of entry; take the Rinkai line to Kokusai-Tenjijo Station or the Yurikamome line to Kokusai-Tenjijo-Seimon Station

Taking place three times a year, in May, August and November, Design Festa is a massive event showcasing the work of the city's newest crop of artists and designers. As the name indicates, it's linked to the Design Festa Gallery in Harajuku. It takes place over a weekend at **Tokyo Big Sight,** (3-11-1 Ariake, Kōtō-ku; tel. 03/5530-1111; www.bigsight.jp/english), a massive exhibition space in Odaiba made of four upside-down pyramids on massive pillars resembling something out of *Star Wars*. There's plenty of food and amenities, but the point is the performances, workshops, and artwork on display.

KANDA MATSURI

Kanda Myōjin and around; closest weekend to May 15, in odd numbered years; free

Kanda Matsuri is one of Tokyo's three biggest festivals. Thousands flood the streets all the way from Kanda to Nihombashi and Marunouchi, with hundreds of floats and *omikoshi* (portable shrines) carried by sweaty participants to the great shrine of **Kanda Myōjin.** It's a spectacle to behold. The festival begins Friday afternoon before the weekend closest to May 15 and goes until around early evening. Saturday's festivities begin from around noon and last till late afternoon. Sunday starts around 6am and goes all the way through evening.

SANJA MATSURI

Asakusa-jinja and around; www.asakusajinja.jp/en/sanjamatsuri; third weekend of May; free

The largest festival in Tokyo, drawing a crowd of almost 2 million, this three-day bash takes place as the temperatures heat up in the third weekend of May each year, beginning from Friday afternoon. It celebrates the three founders of Tokyo's most famous Buddhist temple, **Sensō-ji** in Asakusa, which sits next to the Shinto shrine of **Asakusa-jinja** (2-3-1 Asakusa, Taitō-ku), where the three founders are enshrined. The most visually stunning aspect is about 100 elaborate *mikoshi* (portable shrines), which symbolically house deities, being paraded through the nearby streets by men and women decked out in Edo-period attire in the hopes of bringing prosperity to the area. The neighborhood around Sensō-ji is overlflowing with *yatai* (foot stalls), games, and plenty of locals beating drums, playing bamboo flutes, and milling around in *yukata* (lightweight kimono). The festivities culminate on Sunday when three massive *mikoshi* owned by Asakusa-jinja make their rounds.

ROPPONGI ART NIGHT

Roppongi; www.roppongiartnight.com; last weekend of May; free

During the last weekend of May each year, Roppongi, where three major contemporary art museums are clustered, hosts a two-day overnight event showcasing art, design, film, music, and live performances. Walk through the district, from Roppongi Hills to Tokyo Midtown to the National Art Center, and explore. Stalls selling food and drinks dot the area too, giving it a lively, even rowdy atmosphere as the night wears on.

Summer

SUMIDAGAWA FIREWORKS

Asakusa; www.sumidagawa-hanabi.com; 7pm, last Sat. of Jul.; free

The Sumidagawa Fireworks is Tokyo's largest fireworks show, on the banks of the Sumida River. Crowds of up to 1 million around Askusa, the center of the action, are intense, and the displays awesome. To get a good spot, plan on arriving several hours before of the show. Even then, be prepared to jostle for a decent position.

COMIKET

Tokyo Big Sight; www.comiket.co.jp; early Aug., late Dec.; free

This one's for the *otaku* out there. Comic Market, or Comiket, is Tokyo's largest manga sale, held twice a year in August and December. Each edition takes place over the course of four days at **Tokyo Big Sight**

Japan's Biggest Music Festival

Japan's biggest music festival doesn't take place in Tokyo, but rather at a ski resort in Niigata Prefecture, about two hours away. Over a three-day weekend in late July, **Fuji Rock Festival** (www.fujirockfestival.com) draws around 100,000 people for an always-impressive lineup of shows. Big-name international bookings (think: Bob Dylan, The Cure, The Chemical Brothers, etc.) routinely perform at this massive festival with seven stages spread across a huge area at then-off-season Naeba Ski Resort (202 Mikuni, Yuzawa, tel. 025/789-4117, www.princehotels.co.jp/ski/naeba).

To reach Naeba from Tokyo Station, take the JR Joetsu *shinkansen* to Echigo-Yuzawa Onsen Station, roughly one hour and 15 minutes on the train (¥6,870). Local buses regularly run from the station to Naeba, a 40-minute trip (¥650). In a pinch, a taxi ride from the station to Naeba will set you back about ¥7,000.

(3-11-1 Ariake, Kōtō-ku; tel. 03/5530-1111; www.bigsight.jp/english), which also hosts Design Festa. Hordes of cosplayers and manga fans, to the tune of 200,000, gather for the event, so be prepared for serious crowds.

ASAKUSA SAMBA CARNIVAL

Asakusa; www.asakusa-samba.org; last Sat. of Aug.; free

You'd think you were in Brazil at the Asakusa Samba Carnival, a huge celebration with music, floats, and flamboyantly costumed dancers with the requisite tail feathers. The event serves as a reminder of the deep historic ties between Brazil and Japan: Brazil is home to the biggest Japanese diaspora of any country in the world. In celebration, around 20 teams parade down Asakusa's major thoroughfare of Umamichi-dōri, moving past the Kaminarimon gate of Sensō-ji temple in the direction of Tawaramachi. The lively festival draws some 500,000 spectators.

KŌENJI AWA ODORI

Kōenji; www.koenji-awaodori.com; last weekend of Aug.; free

Kōenji Awa Odori is a pulsating, fun, and rowdy *matsuri* (festival). This is by far Tokyo's best *awa-odori* dance festival, which take place in August during O-bon season, when Buddhist tradition holds that the ancestors return to the world of the living. The festival's roots are actually in Tokushima, Shikoku, where the heaving progenitor has been going strong for more than 400 years. Although not quite as large as the one in Tokushima, more than 1 million people flock to the suburb of Kōenji to watch as troupes of drummers, flutists, shamisen players, and dancers weave through the neighborhood's streets. This is one of my personal favorites. The street parade begins around 5pm and ends around 8pm or 9pm, although people stick around and eat at the neighborhood's restaurants under the train tracks and drink into the night. All you have to do is ride the Chūō line west of Shinjuku to Kōenji (about 7 minutes) and you will be immediately propelled into the action as you exit the station.

Fall

TOKYO JAZZ FESTIVAL

Multiple venues; www.tokyo-jazz.com; Sept.; from ¥3,800 depending on seat class and event, free performances also held

Tokyo Jazz Festival brings together a world-class lineup of jazz stars from Japan and abroad for Japan's biggest jazz event. It's definitely recommended for serious devotees of the art. It takes place over a weekend, usually around the end of August or early Septemeber, mostly in Shibuya and Harajuku, with some outdoor performances in **Yoyogi-kōen** and some indoor performances at **NHK Hall** (2-2-1 Jinnan, Shibuya-ku), among other venues in Shibuya and around (see website). Tickets go on sale starting around late June and sell out relatively fast, so keep an eye on the website if you're keen to attend. Note that there are some free performances in Yoyogi-kōen.

TOKYO GAME SHOW

Makuhari Messe's International Conference Hall; http://expo.nikkeibp.co.jp; mid-Sept.; adults ¥1,500 (one-day pass purchased in advance), ¥2,000 (one-day pass bought same day), children under 12 free

Tokyo Game Show is one of the world's top gaming conferences. Thousands of video game enthusiasts flock to this gathering to discover what's to come in the world of gaming. Events take place over a weekend (two days) in the event hall (2-1 Nakase, Mihama-ku, Chiba-shi; www.m-messe.co.jp/en), located about 40 minutes by train east of Tokyo Station in Chiba Prefecture.

Sports and Recreation

Tokyo's sights, food, nightlife, and shopping will probably be more than enough to keep you busy during your time in the city, but if you feel the need for some recreation, there are plenty of things to do. A number of great parks can be found throughout the city. Aside from Tokyo Disneyland and DisneySea, which are both located outside Tokyo proper, there's a classic amusement park, **Asakusa Hanayashiki,** in the heart of the old part of town. You can cycle through the city, or catch a sumo tournament. Other possibilities include navigating Tokyo's streets in a go-kart while dressed in a cosplay outfit or taking cutesy pictures in a *purikura* (photo sticker) booth.

PARKS

Tokyo is often portrayed as a jungle of neon and concrete. And while that reputation isn't totally unfounded, there are actually some wonderful green spaces scattered around the city.

CHIDORIGAFUCHI
千鳥ヶ淵

From 2-chōme Kudanminami to 2-chōme Sanbanchō; tel. 03/5211-4243; www.gotokyo.org/en/spot/45/index.html; free; take Hanzōmon, Shinjuku, Tōzai lines to Kudanshita Station, exit 2

An area worth checking out just beyond the palace grounds is Chidorigafuchi, which runs along the western side of Hanzo Moat, one of 12 at the palace. Chidorigafuchi is divided into three sections: the **Chidorigafuchi Greenway,** which runs south to the **Chidorigafuchi National Cemetery,** the burial site of 352,297 unidentified casualties of World War II, including civilians who died from air raids and the atomic bombs dropped on Hiroshima and Nagasaki. Farther south of the cemetery, there's also a park area, **Chidorigafuchi-kōen.**

The Chidorigafuchi Greenway, lined by cherry trees, is one of the Tokyo's most quintessential *hanami* (cherry blossom viewing) spots. In the middle of the green expanse, you'll find a boathouse where it's possible to rent paddle-boats between April and November and ply the moat (30 minutes; ¥500). During *hanami* season, when the trees lining the moat explode into a riot of pink, expect considerable wait times for boat rentals and limited space to snap pictures amid the legion of photographers.

INOKASHIRA-KŌEN
井の頭恩賜公園

1-18-31 Gotenyama, Musashino-shi; www.kensetsu.metro.tokyo.jp/jimusho/seibuk/inokashira/en_index.html; 24 hours daily; free; take Sōbu, Chūō, Inokashira lines to Kichijōji Station, Kōen exit

If you want to get a bit outside downtown, Inokashira-kōen is highly recommended. This lovely park is located in the bustling suburb of Kichijōji, which always hovers near the top of any list of Tokyo's most desirable places to call home. The park has a central walking loop that circles a large pond, where you can rent paddle boats shaped like large swans. On weekends, performers attract crowds and

1: shrine at Ueno-kōen 2: swan boats on the pond at Inokashira-kōen 3: lotus in Shinobazu Pond 4: Chidorigafuchi cherry blossoms

花園稲荷神社
花園稲荷神社
奉納
花園稲荷神社
1
2
3
4

locals sell their wares, from jewelry to photographs and paintings. On an island at the western edge of the park's large pond, you'll find **Inokashira Benzaiten,** a shrine dedicated to Benzaiten, patron of the arts, who is the only goddess among Japan's eight gods of luck and an incarnation of the Hindu goddess Sarasvati. At the back of the park, you'll find the immensely popular **Ghibli Museum.** There are also some excellent cafés and restaurants in and around Inokashira, so take your time and enjoy this special place.

YOYOGI-KŌEN
代々木公園

2-1 Yoyogi Kamizonocho, Shibuya-ku; www.yoyogipark.info; 24 hours daily; free; take Yamanote line to Harajuku Station, Omotesandō exit; Chiyoda line to Yoyogi-Kōen Station, exit 3

Perhaps Tokyo's most popular public park is Yoyogi-kōen. There are often large weekend festivals held here during spring and summer, and the place is absolutely jam-packed with revelers during *hanami* (cherry-blossom viewing), when the sprawling green space erupts in color as the park's myriad cherry trees blossom. The park is also known as a place for street performers of all kinds, including the famed rockabilly dancers who congregate every Sunday to bust a move to 1950s rock tunes at the park's main entrance near Harajuku Station.

UENO-KŌEN
上野公園

5-20 Ueno-kōen, Taitō-ku; tel. 03/3828-5644; www.tokyo-park.or.jp/park/format/index038.html; 5am-11pm daily; free; take Yamanote line to Ueno Station, Ueno-kōen, Shinobazu exits

This sizable public park is dotted with shrines and temples. It contains Shinobazu Pond, stocked with abundant lotus flowers and waterfowl, and Japan's oldest zoo. Ueno-kōen is also blessed with a large proliferation of cherry trees that burst colorfully to life each spring to make the park one of the city's most popular spots for *hanami.*

The park's real draw is its abundance of museums, with Tokyo National Museum at the head of the pack. The National Museum of Nature and Science and National Museum of Western Art are also worth a visit.

ODAIBA KAIHIN-KŌEN
お台場海浜公園

1 Daiba, Minato-ku; tel. 03/5500-2455; www.tptc.co.jp/en/c_park/01_02; 24 hours daily; take Yurikamome line to Odaiba Kaihin-kōen Station

Across the Rainbow Bridge from the rest of the city, you'll find Odaiba Kaihin-kōen. This seaside park reminds you that Tokyo is in fact a maritime city—something that's easy to forget. Take in some of the best views of Tokyo from across the bay from this 800-meter-long (2,624-foot) man-made beach, complete with walking paths, a promenade, and even a Statue of Liberty knockoff. This popular date spot is especially romantic at dusk, as the Rainbow Bridge and city light up and petite cruise boats fill the bay. Windsurfing and kayaking are permitted, and the necessary equipment can be rented at the boathouse next to the beach, but swimming is forbidden.

SIGHTSEEING TOURS

The most rewarding discoveries in Tokyo often come through serendipity and wandering on your own, but sometimes a tour can help unlock facets of the city.

Walking Tours

For basic walking tours, **Tokyo Metropolitan Government Tours** (www.gotokyo.org/en/tourists/guideservice/guideservice/index.html; average 3 hours; free or only covering costs incurred by guides) and **Tokyo Systemized Goodwill Guide (SGG) Club** (http://tokyo-sgg.jp/guide.html; average 1.5-2 hours; free) provide good options.

FOOD TOURS

With more eateries than any city on the planet, it's no surprise that Tokyo is full of food tours. A few operators giving tours of the city's culinary scene are **Food Tours Tokyo** (http://foodtourstokyo.com; average 3 hours; ¥18,000 for group of up to 4, ¥4,500 pp for group over 4, food costs of about ¥5,000-6,000 not included, costs incurred by guide must be covered), **Japan Wonder Travel** (https://japanwondertravel.com; average 3 hours; ¥9,000-14,500, includes some food and drinks), **Ninja Food Tours** (www.ninjafoodtours.com; 2-3.5 hours; ¥7,500-10,800, includes some food and drinks) and **Oishii Food Tours** (www.oishiitours.com; 3.5 hours; ¥12,000-15,000, includes some food and drinks), each offering a number of tours according to neighborhood and theme.

NIGHTLIFE TOURS

Then there's drinking. If you're interested in joining a tour down the rabbit hole that is nightlife in Tokyo, here are a few to consider.

Night Out Tokyo Tour by **Backstreet Guides** (https://thebackstreetguides.com; 6 hours Wed., Fri., Sun.; ¥13,000, includes some food and drinks) starts with a few sights, followed by yakitori and drinks in Shibuya then Shinjuku, and ends with an introduction to the rowdy district of Roppongi with a few photo ops.

Tokyo Pub Crawl (http://tokyopubcrawl.com; from 7pm until late Fri., Sat., sometimes Tues.; men ¥3,000, women ¥2,500 if paid in advace, includes 3-4 welcome shots, some drinks between bars and 40-50 percent discounts on drinks at bars visited, does not include cover charges) is just what the name suggests: Friendly staff plugged into the nightlife scene lead a large gathering of people on a group pub crawl. It's a great way to meet people, including locals and fellow travelers, and has loads of repeat customers.

Kanpai Tokyo: Shinjuku Drinks and Neon Lights by **Tokyo Urban Adventures** (www.urbanadventures.com; 2.5-3 hours; ¥11,065, includes snacks, two drinks) leads customers through a tour of Shinjuku's endless array of bars and restaurants, with a focus on the red-light district of Kabukichō and the drinking dens of Golden Gai.

But my personal recommendation is to go deeper than all of these tours with **"Shibuya Stray Cat"** Tatsuya (www.airbnb.com/experiences/64941; 5 hours; ¥10,500, includes drinks), a seasoned journalist, bona fide character, and Tokyo old hand who has been drinking and befriending his way through Shibuya's backstreets for decades. Alongside being a gregarious, boisterous host and guide, Tatsuya's perspective on the colorful neighborhood stretching back to the 1970s is truly fascinating. As a bonus, his tours veer well off the beaten track.

CULTURAL TOURS

For culturally focused street-level introductions to neighborhoods around Tokyo, **Gaijin Tours** (www.gaijintours.com; 2-4 hours; ¥4,000-20,000) offers a number of interesting options, from exploring the pop-cultural maze of Akihabara to the old-school neighborhood of Yanaka, west of Ueno.

If you're a keen street photographer, check out **Eyexplore** (www.eyexplore.com; 2.5 hours; ¥9,900-28,000, other tours as high as ¥120,000). This outfit offers photography walking tours with a variety of themes, including the city at night, architecture, and temples.

For a glimpse of Tokyo's spooky side, **Haunted Tokyo Tours** (www.hauntedtokyotours.com; 2-3 hours a few times weekly, check schedule on website for details; ¥4,500) leads curious urban explorers on walks deep into some of Tokyo's less frequented corners, with tours bearing names like Blood of Samurai, Freak Show, and Ghosts & Goblins of Old Tokyo. More than just an introduction to the supernatural legends that have arisen throughout Tokyo's turbulent history, they provide excellent historical background and will take you into pockets of the city you would not likely see otherwise.

Bus Tours

City bus tours are available from a few providers. **Hato Bus Tours** (www.hatobus.com; tel. 03/3435-6081; 4 hours; adults ¥5,000-12,000,

The Lowdown on Sumo

There aren't too many sports more deeply associated with Japan in the popular imagination than sumo. The sport is deeply rooted in ancient Shinto rites meant to entertain the gods in hopes of a good harvest. And in many ways, it remains more ritual than action even today.

The match itself, when it finally comes, sometimes lasts only seconds, but in rare cases can stretch to around a minute. The first man who leaves the ring or touches its earthen surface with any part of his body but the soles of his feet loses the match. Unlike professional boxing, where opponents face off according to their weight classes, it's every man for himself in the sumo ring. Hence the effort to pack on the pounds by alternating calorie-rich meals with long naps.

Here are the best ways to catch a glimpse into the fascinating world of sumo during your time in Tokyo.

CATCH A MATCH

The best place to see a sumo match is at **Ryōgoku Kokugikan** (1-3-28 Yokoami, Sumida-ku; tel. 03/3623-5111; take Sōbu line to Ryōgoku Station, west exit). Fifteen-day tournaments are held three times a year in Tokyo (Jan., May, and Sept.), The day kicks off around 8am, but it gets interesting around 3pm when the top wrestlers begin to enter the ring. The tournaments usually end around 6pm. Buy your tickets a month in advance (http://sumo.or.jp/en; http://buysumotickets.com; or http://sumo.pia.jp/en; ¥3,800-14,800). There's also a box office near the station's main entrance that sells a few hundred tickets for nosebleed seats (¥2,100) on the day of each match, but you'll need to arrive no later than 5:30am or 6am to have a shot at landing one.

Tournaments are also held once a year in Osaka (Mar.), Nagoya (Jul.), and Fukuoka (Nov.). Advance tickets (book a month beforehand; ¥2,500-12,300) can be purchased at online: http://sumo.or.jp/en, http://buysumotickets.com, and http://sumo.pia.jp/en.

Upon entering the arena, look up. The roof suspended above the ring is the roof of a Shinto shrine. The bulk of the activity taking place under this sacred cover consists of the referees intoning chants and the wrestlers cleansing their mouths with water, throwing salt to symbolically purify the ring (where women are not allowed to enter—a controversy surrounding sumo), and repeatedly performing the choreographed show of strength known as *shiko,* in which they squat, clap their hands, raise each leg, and stamp each foot. You can rent a headset that provides English-language commentary (¥100 with ¥2,000 deposit) to help you make sense of it all.

EAT *CHANKO NABE*

The calorie-dense hot pot loaded with vegetables, seafood, and meat is scarfed down by wrestlers daily. Try **Tomoegata** (2-17-6 Ryōgoku, Sumida-ku; tel. 03/3632-5600; www.tomoegata.com; 11:30am-2pm/5pm-10:30pm Mon.-Fri., 11:30am-2pm/4:30pm-10:30pm Sat.-Sun., holidays), located

children ¥3,160-8,000 for Tokyo tours) in Hamamatsucho is the best-known provider, offering English-language half-day and full-day tours of Tokyo, as well as points of interest around the capital from Kamakura and Nikkō to Mount Fuji and Hakone. **Gray Line** (www.jgl.co.jp/inbound; tel. 03/3595-5948; ¥4,900-9,800 adults, ¥2,600-6,600 children 6-11) offers both half-day and full-day tours of Tokyo's major sights. Tours depart from Dai-Ichi Hotel in Shinbashi, although pickup from some major hotels can be arranged. **Skybus** (www.skybus.jp; tel. 03/3215-0008; four times daily; ¥1,600 adults, ¥700 children) gives tours lasting roughly an hour through various areas of the city in red double-decker buses with open tops. If you just want a quick introduction, this is the way to go.

Bike Tours

If you're interested in combining a tour with a bike ride, try **Tokyo Bicycle Tours** (www.

sumo wrestling ring

in the heart of sumo territory in Ryōgoku. Alternatively, you can get a small bowl of the stuff (¥300) in the basement of the Ryōgoku Kokugikan on a tournament day.

VISIT THE SUMO MUSEUM

This museum (1F Ryōgoku Kokugikan, 1-3-28 Yokoami, Sumida-ku; tel. 03/3622-0366; www.sumo.or.jp/en; 10am-4:30pm Mon.-Fri., sporadically closed Mon. and national holidays; free) houses memorabilia and woodblock prints related to the sport. It also holds special exhibitions six times a year. Note that the museum closes between special exhibitions and is only open to tournament ticketholders during the grand tournaments held at the Ryōgoku Kokugikan three times a year (Jan., May, and Sept.) in Tokyo. Before making the trip, check the museum's schedule online (http://sumo.or.jp/EnSumoMuseum/schedule) to be safe.

VISIT TOMIOKA HACHIMANGU SHRINE

At this shrine (1-20-3 Tomioka, Koto-ku; tel. 03/3642-1315; www.tomiokahachimangu.or.jp; 24 hours daily; free; take Ōedo, Tōzai lines to Monzen-nakachō Station, exit 1) sumo bouts were held for about 100 years during the Edo period. Monuments bearing the names of wrestlers who became *yokozuna* (grand champions) and *ozeki* (second-highest rank) dot the grounds. Look to your right as you enter and find the humblingly massive handprints in stone of some sumo superstars. It's also an impressive shrine in its own right.

tokyobicycletours.com; 3-6.5 hours; ¥5,000-9,000), which offers tours of central Tokyo and the Tokyo Bay area by reservation only, for a minimum of two riders. Another solid option is the **Tokyo Great Cycling Tour** (1-3-2 Shinkawa, Chūō-ku; tel. 03/4590-2995; www.tokyocycling.jp; 1.5-6 hours; adults ¥5,000-13,000, ages 12 and under ¥2,500-6,500), which offers a bit wider range of cycling routes.

ONSEN

ONSEN THERMAE-YU

1-1-2 Kabukichō, Shinjuku-ku; tel. 03/5285-1726; www.thermae-yu.jp; 11am-9am; ¥2,405 Mon.-Fri., ¥1,870 surcharge from midnight-9am Mon.-Fri., ¥2,750 surcharge from midnight-9am Sat.-Sun. and holidays, ¥880 surcharge on Sat.-Sun. and holidays; take Marunouchi, Fukutoshin, Shinjuku lines to Shinjuku-Sanchōme Station, exit E1, or Chūō, Sōbu lines to Shinjuku Station, east exit

Besides the spic-and-span sex-separated

indoor and outdoor pools at this impressive new *onsen* complex, there are also saunas, a beauty salon, and various exfoliation scrub-downs, as well as a bar, café, and eatery on site. The water is pumped in daily from Izu Peninsula, southwest of Tokyo. A good choice in the heart of Kabukichō. Tattoos aren't permitted.

SPA LAQUA

5-9F Tokyo Dome City, 1-1-1 Kasuga, Bunkyō-ku; tel. 03/5800-9999; www.laqua.jp; 11am-9am, last entry 8am; adults ¥2,900, children 6-17 years old ¥2,090, ¥1,980 surcharge from 1am-6am, ¥350 surcharge Sat.-Sun. and holidays; take Marunouchi line to Kōrakuen Station, exit 2

Real *onsen* water is piped into the stylish indoor and outdoor pools at this hot-spring complex in the center of town from 1,700 meters (5,577 feet) beneath the earth, said to bestow health benefits such as improved circulation. This huge complex is spread across five floors, which also house facilities for treatments ranging from Thai massages to Korean body exfoliation scrubbing sessions. No tattoos allowed.

ROKURYU KŌSEN

3-4-20 Ikenohata, Taitō-ku; tel. 03/3821-3826; 3:30pm-11pm Tues.-Sun.; ¥460; take Chiyoda line to Nezu Station, exit 2

This old-school bathhouse tucked down a quiet sidestreet just west of Ueno-kōen is a great place to go if your aim is to experience a local neighborhood public bath known as a *sentō*. The ambience here is real, from the arched entryway that resembles a shrine to the old tiles and the mural of the famed bridge of Kintai-kyō in remote Yamaguchi Prefecture. The piping hot water is loaded with healthy minerals, too.

ŌEDO ONSEN MONOGATARI

2-6-3 Aomi, Kōtō-ku; tel. 03/5500-1126; https://daiba.ooedoonsen.jp; 11am-9am daily, last entry 7am; adults ¥2,720, children age 4-12 ¥1,058, Mon.-Fri., ¥2,936 Sat.-Sun. and holidays, ¥2,160 surcharge 2am-5am; take Yurikamome line to Telecom Center Station; or Rinkai line to Tokyo Teleport Station, then board shuttle

Change your street clothes for a *yukata* (lightweight kimono) and get acquainted with the *onsen* experience at this kitschy, surprisingly family-friendly hot-spring theme park across Tokyo Bay in Odaiba. This massive complex has gender-separated indoor and outdoor baths fed with water from beneath Tokyo Bay, and a mixed outdoor foot bath wherein small fish chomp away dead skin on your feet. There are also food stalls, old-school festival games, and restaurants in a kitschy recreation of Tokyo as it once looked in the old days. No tattoos allowed.

BAY CRUISES

Stand at banks of the Sumida-gawa in Asakusa during the evening and you will most likely see a number of low-slung boats festooned with paper lanterns gliding in both directions on the river. These are traditional houseboats known as *yakatabune*. It's possible to ride one of these crafts up and down the Sumida-gawa, and around the contours of Tokyo Bay, eating and drinking as you go. While the food is hit-or-miss, the views of the city from the water are romantic. Thoroughly modern compact cruise boats also sail the waters around Tokyo.

Choosing a *yakatabune* or cruise provider can be daunting, given the sheer number of them and the language barrier (some do have English-language reservation services). To get a sense for what a *yakatabune* tour is, and what your options are for reserving a spot on one, visit the website of the **Tokyo Yakatabune Association** (www.yakatabune-kumiai.jp/en/index.php).

FUNASEI

1-16-8 Kita-Shinagawa, Shinagawa-ku; tel. 03/5770-5131; www.funasei.com; 2.5 hours; adults from ¥10,800, children ¥4,000-8,000

This *yakatabune* (traditional houseboat) cruise provider operates six traditional boats and one private charter yacht, seating 20 to 120, depending on the craft. The boats depart from Shinagawa and sail northward, up the Sumida-gawa to Tokyo Skytree in Asakusa, before returning via Odaiba. The meals served on board are Japanese—tempura, sashimi, and more—and booze is unlimited. Note that the laiason by phone is an English-speaking travel agency. Inquire directly with them about cruise schedules and availability.

VINGT ET UN

1-12-2 Kaigan, Minato-ku; tel. 03/3436-2121; www.vantean.co.jp; departs noon, 4:20pm, 7:20pm; 2 hours; ¥5,500-9,600 adults, ¥4,400-7,600 children for noon and 4:20pm cruises; ¥9,800-15,300 adults, ¥7,800-12,200 children for 7:20pm cruise; take Yurikamome line to Takeshiba Station, or Yamamote, Keihin-Tōhoku lines to Hamamatsuchō Station, or Ōedo, Asakusa lines to Daimon Station

Departing from Takeshiba Pier at the mouth of the Sumida-gawa, this operator doesn't use *yakatabune*, but instead plies the waters of Tokyo Bay with a mini-cruise ship that can transport up to 700 sails. The boats move southward, passing under the Rainbow Bridge, before going to Odaiba and then continuing south to Haneda Airport, then return. You'll have the choice of three set meals of tasty French fare.

Shopping

GINZA AND MARUNOUCHI
銀座, 丸の内

Ginza is home to an array of shops dedicated to high-end fashion and luxury goods, both produced in Japan and overseas. Think world-class brands in sophisticated boutiques and swanky, sprawling emporiums offering an entire city's worth of consumer opulence under one roof.

Fashion

DOVER STREET MARKET GINZA

6-9-5 Ginza, Chūō-ku; tel. 03/6228-5080; http://ginza.doverstreetmarket.com; 11am-8pm daily; take Ginza line to Ginza Station, exit A2

If this seven-floor complex feels like a shopping mall as seen through the eyes of a design renegade with avant-garde sensibilities, that's because it is. Legendary designer Rei Kawakubo, whose label Comme des Garçons exploded onto the world's runways in the 1980s, has revived Ginza's fashion cred with Dover Street Market Ginza, a bleeding-edge, high-concept shopping mall brimming with top-end brands from Japan and overseas.

GINZA SIX

6-10 Ginza, Chūō-ku; http://ginza6.tokyo; 10:30am-8:30pm daily; take Ginza, Hibiya, Marunouchi lines to Ginza Station, exit A3

Ginza's largest shrine to commerce is enormous, with 241 brands under one very exclusive roof. You'll also find an exquisitely designed Tsutaya Books on the sixth floor and even a *Noh* theater in the basement. Splash out some serious cash and you can even hire a personal stylist to advise you on your shopping spree.

SHINJUKU AND WESTERN TOKYO
新宿

While Shinjuku has a hodgepodge of everything, from vinyl records to punk-rock fashion shops, department stores are the defining feature. A number of mammoth electronics stores also dot the area.

Souvenirs

BEAMS JAPAN

3-32-6 Shinjuku, Shinjuku-ku; tel. 03/5368-7300; www.beams.co.jp/global/shop/j; 11am-8pm; take Yamanote line to Shinjuku Station, east exit

The Beams Japan flagship carries some of Japan's best designs, from fashion to art and

Food Underground: Discover Japan's *Depachika*

A typical Japanese department store (*depato*) is 5-10 floors high, with women's fashion on the first couple of floors, fashion and sports gear for men on the floors above that, and lifestyle items, stationery, and furniture on the next few floors. A restaurant floor is at the top, usually offering an impressive range of cuisines, including Italian, Korean, Chinese and Japanese. Some department stores turn their rooftops into beer gardens in warmer months.

The floor that proves to be the biggest revelation for many is the basement level, where you'll typically find an extensive gourmet food hall known as a *depachika*. Excellent seasonal produce, sushi, tempura, bento box lunches, tofu, fresh ginger, yakitori, *tonkatsu*, croquettes, premade salads, sandwiches, cheese, Western and Japanese desserts… the list goes on.

For the full *depato* experience, with an emphasis on the best subterranean food halls, check out the following department stores:

- **Ginza Mitsukoshi** (4-6-16 Ginza; Chūō-ku; tel. 03/3562-1111; www.mitsukoshi.co.jp; 10am-8pm Mon.-Sat., 10am-7:30pm Sun. and last day of holiday periods; take Ginza, Hibiya, Marunouchi lines to Ginza Station, exits A7, A8, A11) has a vast array of decadent culinary options in its sprawling basement food hall. After stocking up on nibbles, head to the rooftop garden to eat them.
- **Isetan Shinjuku** (3-14-1 Shinjuku, Shinjuku-ku; tel. 03/3352-1111; https://isetan.mistore.jp/store/index.html; 10am-8pm; take Marunouchi, Shinjuku, Fukutoshin lines to Shinjuku-Sanchōme Station, exits B3, B4, B5; or Chūō, Sōbu lines to Shinjuku Station, east exit; or Ōedo line to Shinjuku Station, exit 1) is the flagship of this hip chain. It's renowned for its artistic, attention-grabbing window displays, but the show-stopper here is its opulent *depachika*. Caviar, giant legs of Iberico ham, Japanese sweets, and a stunning array of booze, from champagne to whisky and *nihonshū* (commonly reffered to, incorrectly, as *sake*).
- **Takashimaya Times Square** (5-24-2 Sendagaya, Shibuya-ku; tel. 03/5361-1111; www.takashimaya-global.com; 10am-8pm Sun.-Thurs., 10am-8:30pm Fri.-Sat.; take Chūō, Sōbu lines to Shinjuku Station, South Exit) has a swanky sensibility, as evidenced from the glut of luxury brands sold throughout its floors selling fashion. Head down to the basement to see how this is applied to food. Take note of the haute bento box meals prepared by the chefs at *kaiseki ryōri* purveyor Kikunoi. There's a rooftop garden here too.

housewares. It also houses a gallery that exhibits works by photographers and artists. If you get hungry while browsing the shop's six floors, head to the basement, where you'll find a restaurant serving Japanese takes on Western staples and curry, as well as a café.

Electronics

YODOBASHI CAMERA SHINJUKU WEST

1-11-1 Nishishinjuku, Shinjuku-ku; tel. 03/3346-1010; 9:30am-10pm; take Yamanote line to Shinjuku station, west exit

In a city overflowing with electronics emporiums, where to begin? Yodobashi Camera Shinjuku West, the flagship store of this appliance retail giant, is a safe bet. A stone's throw from Shinjuku Station's west exit, this store will delight gadget lovers with its vast range of products. Note that a deluge of shoppers flood into the aisles on weekends. The outpost in Akihabara, **Yodobashi Akiba** (1-1 Kanda Hanaoka-chō, Chiyoda-ku; 9:30am-10pm; take Yamanote line to Akihabara, Shōwa-tōriguchi exit) is equally epic.

HARAJUKU AND AOYAMA
原宿, 青山

These neighborhoods are home to the highest concentration of trendsetting shops in the city. Funky Harajuku caters to the young.

But if you head down Omotesandō toward Aoyama, you'll be dazzled by some of the most bleeding-edge high fashion anywhere, artfully displayed in stunning boutiques.

Fashion

LAFORET

1-11-6 Jingūmae, Shibuya-ku; tel. 03/3475-0411; www.laforet.ne.jp; 11am-8pm; take Yamanote line to Harajuku Station, Omotesandō exit

For a quick introduction to youth fashion trends, come to LaForet in Harajuku. Inside you'll find a smorgasbord of boutiques hawking brightly colored clothes for hip young things, as well as various exhibitions and events. Check out the goth-lolita offerings and local labels Monomania and H>Fractal, all found in the basement, and the legendary, bleeding-edge **GR8** on floor 2.5, incongruously fronted by a traditional garden with stone lanterns and bonsais.

CHICAGO

2F Mansion 31, 6-31-15, Shibuya-ku; tel. 03/6427-5505; 11am-8pm daily; take Yamanote line to Harajuku Station, Omotesandō exit

A fixture in Harajuku's always evolving fashion landscape, Chicago has the largest selection of vintage threads of any branch in the chain. The strong suit here is vintage kimonos and lighter cotton versions called *yukata*, which are sold at prices that won't break the bank.

6%DOKIDOKI

2F TX101 Bldg., 4-28-16 Jingūmae, Shibuya-ku; tel. 03/3479-6116; www.dokidoki6.com; noon-8pm daily; take Yamanote line to Harajuku Station, Omotesandō exit

Vivid clothing and accessories, adorned in unicorns, hearts, and ice-cream cones assault your vision at 6%Dokidoki, which translates to "6% Excitement." It's no shock to learn the shop's founder Sebastian Masuda often works with Kyary Pamyu Pamyu, a J-Pop starlet who is *kawaii* (cute) incarnate. Come here for the full Harajuku experience. Seeing is believing.

SOU-SOU

1F A-La Croce Bldg., 5-4-24Minami-Aoyama, Minato-ku; tel. 03/3407-7877; http://sousounetshop.jp; 11am-8pm daily; take Ginza, Hanzōmon lines to Omotesandō Station, exit B1

Sou-Sou is a Kyoto brand that injects modern flare into classic Japanese fashions. At its outpost in trendy Aoyama, you'll find a range of excellent souvenir options from cool T-shirts and split-toe trainers to *yukatas* designed with a modern twist.

Secondhand

PASS THE BATON

B2F Omotesandō Hills West, 4-12-10 Jingūmae, Shibuya-ku; tel. 03/6447-0707; www.pass-the-baton.com; 11am-9pm Mon.-Sat., 11am-8pm Sun., holidays; take Ginza, Hanzōmon lines to Omotesandō Station, exit A2, or Chiyoda, Fukutoshin lines to Meiji-Jingūmae Station, exit 5

Pass the Baton is a unique consignment shop tucked away in the basement of **Omotesandō Hills,** though it's accessed via a separate door at street level. Clothing, bags, antiques, furniture, and art fill the store. The shop aims to pass well-loved items from one person to the next; it provides a link between owners by attaching a personal anecdote to each item.

Toys

KIDDY LAND

6-1-9 Jingūmae, Shibuya-ku; tel. 03/3409-3431; www.kiddyland.co.jp/harajuku; 11am-9pm Mon.-Fri., 10:30am-9pm Sat.-Sun., holidays; take Yamanote line to Harajuku Station, Omotesandō exit, or Chiyoda, Fukutoshin lines to Meiji-Jingūmae Station, exit 4

Kiddy Land is a monument to toys. The enormous shop is chockablock with characters from Studio Ghibli and Disney films, Doraemon dolls, Godzilla models, Star Wars figures, and Sanrio mascots. If you're buying gifts for kids, this shop ticks all boxes.

Souvenirs

ORIENTAL BAZAAR

5-9-13 Jingūmae, Shibuya-ku; tel. 03/3400-3933; www.orientalbazaar.co.jp/en; 10am-7pm Fri.-Wed.; take Yamanote line to Harajuku Station, Omotesandō

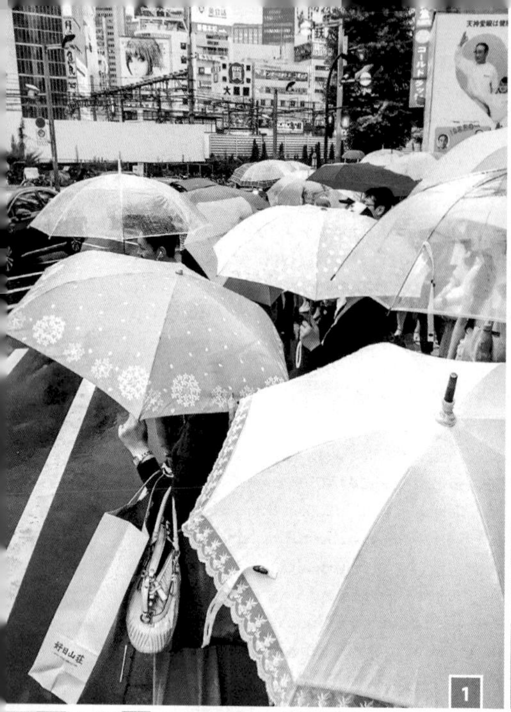

1

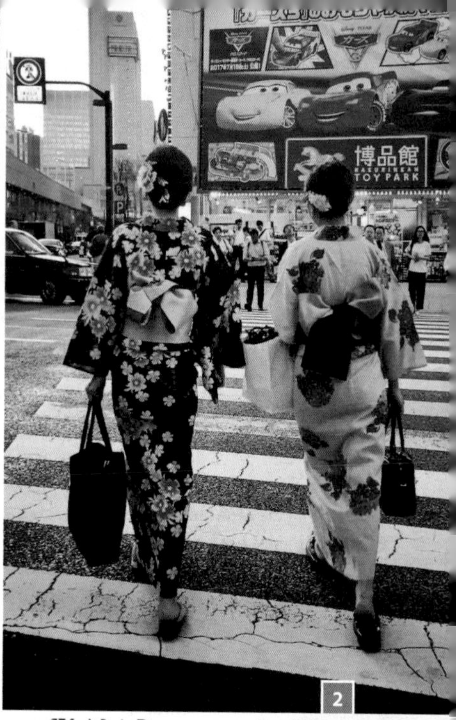
博品館
TOY PARK

2

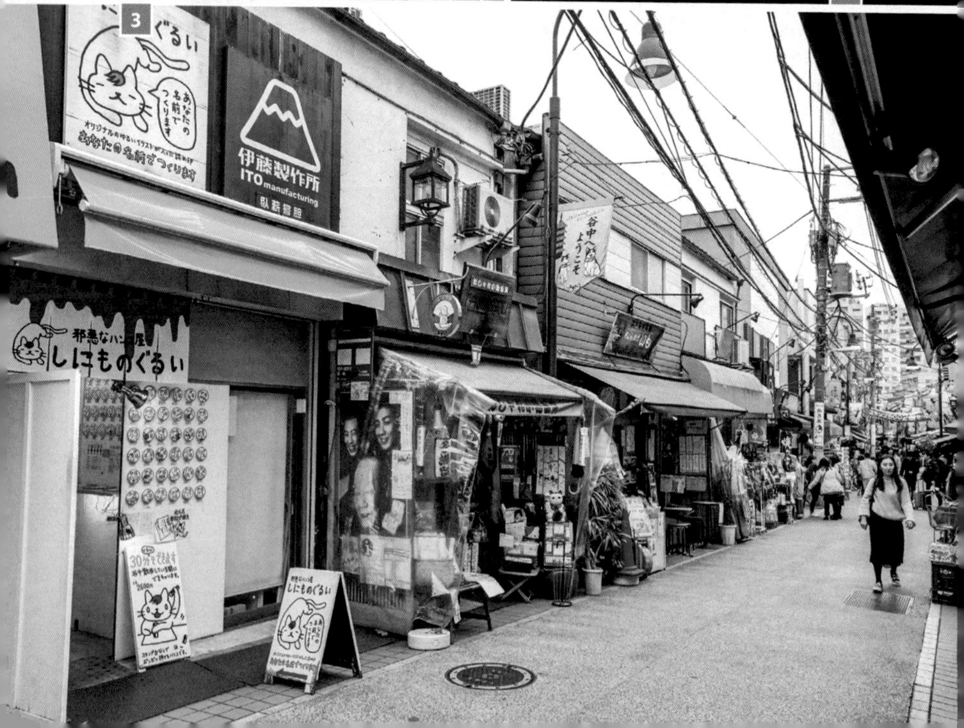
あなたの名前でつくります
伊藤製作所
ITO manufacturing
邪悪なハンコ屋
しにものぐるい
谷中へようこそ

3

exit, or Chiyoda, Fukutoshin lines to Meiji-Jingūmae Station, exit 4

Harajuku's Oriental Bazaar is a one-stop souvenir shop with English speaking staff and reasonable prices. If you have limited time and want to take home a few items, they have it all: origami earrings, sake cup sets, tableware, antiques, *yukata*, *ukiyo-e* prints.

JAPAN TRADITIONAL CRAFTS AOYAMA SQUARE

1F Akasaka Oji Bldg., 8-1-22 Akasaka, Minato-ku; tel. 03/5785-1301; http://kougeihin.jp; 11am-7pm daily; take Ginza, Hanzōmon lines to Aoyama Itchōme Station, exit 4 north

Another excellent one-stop shop is Japan Traditional Crafts Aoyama Square, a showcase for traditional crafts from all over Japan that receives funding from the government. Crafts on sale incorporate a wide range of materials, from lacquer and textiles to bamboo, metal, ceramics, and glass. Artisans practice their craft in the store, which features their work on a rotating basis. Items sold here are of a uniformly high quality. Check the artist schedule online.

SHIBUYA
渋谷

A number of large, eclectic shops carrying quirky lifestyle goods, as well as a number of youth fashion retailers, can be found in Shibuya. Teenybopper fashion emporium **Shibuya 109,** housed in an iconic multi-floor tower just west of Shibuya Crossing (2-29-1 Dōgenzaka, Shibuya-ku; 10am-9pm daily), is the neighborhood's most recognizable fashion landmark. Affordable designer items can be found, too, if you know where to look.

Souvenirs

TŌKYŪ HANDS SHIBUYA

12-18 Udagawa-chō, Shibuya-ku; 03/5489-5111; https://shibuya.tokyu-hands.co.jp; 10am-9pm daily; take Yamanote line to Shibuya, Hachikō exit

It's all about household items at Tōkyū Hands Shibuya, from the useful to the downright bizarre. The eight-floor Shibuya branch of this quirky purveyor of miscellaneous goods is Tokyo's largest, with everything from sundry materials for DIY projects to kitchenware shaped like cartoon characters, light fixtures, and more than 400 types of toothbrushes. If you can dream it, Tōkyū Hands likely has it.

LOFT SHIBUYA

18-2 Udagawa-chō, Shibuya-ku; tel. 03/3462-3807; www.loft.co.jp; 10am-9pm; take Yamanote line to Shibuya, Hachikō exit

Like Tōkyū Hands Shibuya, Loft Shibuya is dedicated to providing great products for seemingly every aspect of life. Seasonal items with a Japanese sensibility, such as folding fans for summer, occupy the ground floor, while the other six floors carry everything from stationery and watches to kitchenware, furniture, and art. The items and ambience here feel slightly more upmarket than Tōkyū Hands.

MEGA DON QUIJOTE SHIBUYA

28-6 Udagawa-chō, Shibuya-ku; tel. 03/5428-4086; www.donki.com/en; 24 hours daily; take Yamanote line to Shibuya Station, Hachikō exit

This 24/7 discount shop is massive. Cheaper in its offerings than Tōkyū Hands and Loft, Mega Don Quijote Shibuya, or "Donki," carries everything from discount groceries in the basement to clothing, household items, and gadgets. Its shelves overflow with cheap gift possibilities like *matcha*-flavored Kit Kats, Japanese snacks and knives, and funky socks. It's worth checking out this shop if you're planning to bring home gifts in bulk.

D47 DESIGN TRAVEL STORE

8F Shibuya Hikarie, 2-21-1, Shibuya, Shibuya-ku; tel. 03/6427-2301; www.hikarie8.com/d47designtravelstore; 11am-8pm daily; take Yamanote line to Shibuya Station, east exit

As the name suggests, the D47 Design Travel Store features the unique flavors, arts, and specialties of the 47 prefectures that comprise

1: rainy day in Shinjuku **2:** shopping in Ginza **3:** Yanaka shopping street

TOP EXPERIENCE

Youth Fashion

Harajuku has been a center of fashion and youth culture since at least the 1990s, and its heyday was well documented in photographer Shoichi Aoki's legendary magazine, *FRUiTS* when creativity flourished in the neighborhood's then-pedestrian-only smaller streets. Although recent years have seen *FRUiTS* cease publication (resulting in declarations of the demise of Harajuku as a global fashion hub) and car traffic flowing through those streets that were once youth hangouts, the neighborhood's fashion landscape is far from dead, but rather, in a state of flux.

A host of new fashion leaders are establishing themselves in the scene, such as Peco and Aiba Runa, whose brand **RRR By Sugar Spot Factory** and social media imprint have made her one of Harajuku's new stars. Similarly, new magazines, such as *Fanatic* and *Melt Magazine*, are popping up. For an easy-to-access look down the rabbit hole that is Japan's fashion subcultural universe, as well as other quirky bits of obscure travel, peruse the blog of writer and TV host **La Carmina** (www.lacarmina.com/blog).

Although not as prevalent as they once were, many lively fashion subcultures continue to be visible in Harajuku's streets:

- **Cosplay:** "Costume play" is about dressing as an anime, manga, or video game character, and is the most widely recognizable of Harajuku's subcultures.
- ***Kawaii:*** The "cute" aesthetic is infused into a vast number of styles, which sometimes mix and match cute with childish, even grotesque elements for visual shock-factor. The *kawaii* aesthetic extends far beyond the realm of fashion. Perhaps no other country has placed such emphasis on the culture of cuteness as Japan. The most universally recognizable manifestation of this aesthetic is the iconic character Hello Kitty.
- **Lolita:** Another major trend with roots in Harajuku, this genre sees mostly young women donning knee-high stockings and knee-length skirts with petticoats, sometimes adding a corset

the Japanese archipelago. Japan may not be a huge country geographically speaking, but a trip to this store will likely impress you with the true extent of its diversity.

EBISU AND AROUND
恵比寿

There's a hip pocket of town located upon a hill between Ebisu and Shibuya called **Daikan-yama.** The streets, lined with trendy boutiques and cafés, beg to be strolled. This is one of many places where stylish locals shop.

T-SITE

17-5 Sarugaku-chō; tel. 03/3770-2525; https://store.tsite.jp/daikanyama; 7am-2am daily; take Tōkyū Tōyoko line to Daikanyama Station

This has to be among the world's coolest bookstores. The design of the complex, which appears to be enmeshed in a knit exterior of countless letter Ts, has won awards for architecture firm Klein Dytham. There's a solid selection of books and magazines on travel, art, architecture, food, and culture, including some in English, and **Anjin,** a chic café and lounge-bar, is on the second floor. A great place to chill for a few hours.

OKURA

20-11 Sarugaku-chō, Shibuya-ku; tel. 03/3461-8511; www.hrm.co.jp/okura; 11:30am-8pm Mon.-Fri., 11am-8:30pm Sat.-Sun. and holidays; take Tōkyū Tōyoko line to Daikanyama Station

Situated on a fashionable street behind T-Site, Okura is a great place to get acquainted with Japan's centuries-old indigo dyeing tradition. The threads here are all made using old-school indigo dyeing techniques. A mix of old and modern-style attire are sold, from *tabi* or headdress, Victorian-style. There are numerous spins on this style, from **Gothic Lolita** to **Punk Lolita** and beyond.

- ***Gyaru:*** Based on the English word "gal," the key elements include hair dyed blond or brown, heavy makeup, provocative clothing, and a bit of a devil-may-care attitude to go with it.
- **Visual *kei:*** The "visual style" trend has roots in a Japanese rock movement akin to glam rock. Young male followers suit up in loud outfits and sport flashy hairstyles and makeup.
- **Fairy *kei:*** "Fairy style" is one of numerous fashion tribes that formed on Ura-Hara, as Harajuku's backstreets are known. It doesn't get much more saccharine than this: pastel hair bows, decorative stars, babies, angels and polka dots, leg warmers, tights, baggy shirts, oversized glasses and more. Stop by **Spank!** (4F Nakano Broadway, 5-52-15 Nakano, Nakano-ku; tel. 08/03404-3809; http://spankworld.jp/index.html; 12:30pm-7:30pm Thurs.-Tues.), the store that hatched this trend.
- **Dolly *kei:*** This style is inspired by European fairy tales and religious symbols, filtered through a Harajuku lens.
- **Genderless *kei:*** A relatively new development, this style draws on flourishes of *kawaii* to blur the boundaries of gender. Boys have been the predominant force in this movement, which idealizes a slim figure, bright eyes, makeup, expertly coifed hair, painted eyebrows, showy clothing, and plenty of *kawaii* accoutrements from hats to handbags.
- **Decora:** In this style, accessories, legwarmers, and knee-socks are layered over each other to the point of overpowering the rest of an already quirky outfit, funky dental mask and tutu included.

(split-toed socks) to jackets, jeans, T-shirts, and scarves. The tastefully rustic building that houses the shop is a pleasure to explore too. As there's no English sign, look out for the squat, traditional-style shopfront, which normally has some indigo-dyed specimen on display out front.

AKIHABARA
秋葉原

Akihabara is the preeminent place to experience the wonderful and wacky world of *otaku* culture. Here you'll find all manner of electronic products and parts, multistory complexes filled with anime and manga, video game emporiums, maid and butler cafés, a shocking number of vending machines, and plenty of cosplayers milling about.

Souvenirs

2K540 AKI-OKA ARTISAN

5-9 Ueno, Taito-ku; www.jrtk.jp/2k540; 11am-7pm Thurs.-Tues.; take Yamanote line to Akihabara Station, Akihabara Electric Town exit, Yamanote line to Okachimachi Station, south exit 1, or Ginza line to Suehirocho Station, exit 2

2K540 Aki-Oka Artisan is a unique space under rail tracks that houses a smattering of shops selling both traditional goods and quirkier, more modern items. The eclectic emporium's name derives from its distance from Tokyo Station—2 km and 540 meters (about 1.5 mi)—and its location between Akihabara and Okachimachi. The key thread tying its shops together is the fact that they all sell wares made in Japan, from kaleidoscopes and hats to figurines, sneakers, furniture, and toys. The space also holds occasional hands-on workshops related to traditional crafts.

Nakano Broadway: An Akihabara Alternative

If you're seeking a less touristy slice of the *otaku* pie that offers just as much, if not more, than Akihabara, consider heading **to Nakano Broadway** (5-52-15 Nakano, Nakano-ku, Tokyo; store hours vary, but most are roughly open noon-8pm), a huge collection of shops hawking *otaku* goods just north of Nakano Station on the Chūō Line, less than 10 minutes from Shinjuku Station. The area has become increasingly popular in recent years, but hasn't yet succumbed to the deluge of duty-free shops catering to the tourists now flooding into Akihabara daily. The most appealing aspect of Nakano Broadway is that all the shops you would want to see are located under one sprawling roof, rather than scattered around a hectic neighborhood. Further, the alleyways snaking off the main shopping arcade are infused with a whiff of nostalgia and are enjoyable to explore in their own right, should you want to wander a bit after taking in the *otaku* emporium.

- If you feel the call to visit Nakano, make a beeline for the flagship **Mandarake** store, spread across several floors; Mandarake Henya (4F) specializes in vintage collectibles.
- At Nakano Broadway you'll also find four establishments owned by artist **Takashi Murakami,** famous for his collaborations with Louis Vuitton, among other things: Bar Zingaro (2F), which sells great coffee; contemporary art gallery and shop Hidari Zingaro (3F); contemporary ceramics showcase Oz Zingaro (4F); and *otaku*-influenced art space pivix Zingaro (2F).
- After you've navigated your way through this *otaku* warren, sing karaoke with maids at **Anison Karaoke Bar Z** (301 No. 2 Sankyō Bldg., 5-57-9 Nakano, Nakano-ku; tel. 03/6454-0790; 6pm-11:30pm daily), or visit the quirky **Daikaiju Salon** (1F Lions Mansion Nakano, 1-14-16 Arai, Nakano-ku; tel. 03/5942-7382; http://daikaijyu-salon.com; 3pm-11pm Mon.-Fri., 1pm-11pm Sun.), a bar and café overflowing with figurines, art, and more revolving around Japan's pantheon of monsters, located about five minutes' walk north of Nakano Broadway. Note that patrons must order at least one food or drink item per hour.

Pop Culture

RADIO KAIKAN

1-15-16 Sotokanda, Chiyoda-ku; www.akihabara-radiokaikan.co.jp; 10am-8pm daily; take Yamanote, Sōbu, Hibiya lines to Akihabara Station, Electric Town exit

A 10-story tower to geekdom with deep historical roots, stretching back to the years immediately following the war when radios were a premium item, Radio Kaikan carries a hodgepodge of figurines, dolls, manga, trading cards, and much more. Even if you don't plan to buy anything, it's worth stopping to peruse the merchandise to get a sense of the jaw-dropping extent of the depth and breadth of hobbies catered to in Akihabara.

MANDARAKE

3-11-12 Sotokanda, Chiyoda-ku; tel. 03/3252-7007; http://mandarake.co.jp; noon-8pm daily; take Yamanote, Sōbu, Hibiya lines to Akihabara Station, Electric Town exit

Mandarake is an eight-floor shop at Akihabara's epicenter that has it all: manga, anime, cosplay items, rare art, dolls, *doujinshi* (a wildly popular genre of self-published manga that's often highly risqué), video games, consoles, vintage figurines and models, card games, and loads of toys. If you don't find what you need at Radio Kaikan, try Mandarake instead.

TORANOANA

4-3-1, Sotokanda, Chiyoda-ku; www.toranoana.jp; 10am-10pm daily; take Yamanote, Sōbu, Hibiya lines to Akihabara Station, Electric Town exit

The seven-floor flagship of Toranoana (Tiger's Cave) is a towering complex dedicated almost exclusively to the art of caricature, moving or still, whether drawn by professionals or obsessive fans. This is the place to go to see anime and manga in all of its wild—sometimes downright shocking—diversity. This spot is a haven for devotees of self-published manga known as *doujinshi,* which often features highly risqué themes and artwork. Fair warning: Themes and imagery become increasingly adult in nature as you ascend to the higher levels of the shop.

SUPER POTATO

3F-5F Kitabayashi Bldg., 1-11-2 Sotokanda, Chiyoda-ku; tel. 03/5289-9933; www.superpotato.com; 11am-8pm Mon.-Fri., 10am-8pm Sat.-Sun., holidays; take Yamanote, Sōbu, Hibiya lines to Akihabara Station, Electric Town exit

There may be no better spot for retro video games on earth than the awesomely named Super Potato. This secondhand bazaar of 8- and 16-bit games, from the Super Mario Brothers to Sonic the Hedgehog and Link (The Legend of Zelda), packs a surprisingly powerful nostalgic punch for those who came of age at the dawn of the video game era in the 1980s. Even if you don't buy anything, stopping by this shop is like stepping into a museum dedicated to the heroes and heroines of your lost youth. Be sure to have a few coins handy to play a few rounds of old-school arcade games on the 5th floor.

M'S: POP LIFE SEX DEPARTMENT STORE

1-15-13 Sotokanda, Chiyoda-ku; tel. 03/3252-6166; www.ms-online.co.jp; 10am-11pm daily; take Yamanote, Sōbu, Hibiya lines to Akihabara Station, Electric Town exit

It's an open secret that everyone who has spent any amount of time exploring Akihabara's maze of curiosities has snuck into M's: Pop Life Sex Department Store. If nothing else, I'd be remiss not to mention this one for its, ahem, value as a cultural case study. While the name speaks for itself, the sheer scale of the shop and its happy-go-lucky atmosphere are worth marveling at. Its seven floors are overflowing with sex toys, lingerie, costumes, whips, chains, life-sized dolls, DVDs—basically every imaginable product catering to the flesh. And it all feels normalized, with shoppers perusing merchandise as if they're in a sporting goods store.

ASAKUSA
浅草

True to its locale in the heart of old-school Tokyo, Asakusa is a great place to find traditional crafts and souvenirs that you would associate with Japan. It's also a good place to indulge in a bit of kitsch.

Souvenirs

SHIN-YOSHIWARA

102, 3-27-10 Nishiasakusa, Taito-ku; www.shin-yoshiwara.com; noon-6pm daily; take Ginza line Tawaramachi Station, exit 3

This cheeky souvenir shop is a one-off. Inspired by the carnal essence of Yoshiwara, Edo's legendary red-light district that once stood in the same area, designer Yayoi Okano decided to open Shin-Yoshiwara, a shop that sells traditional items with a sassy twist. Here you'll find Japanese hair ornaments shaped like voluptuous nude women, ceramic dishes etched with two female breasts containing the characters of the shop's name inside them, *ukiyo-e* style prints depicting tatted-up *yakuza* at public baths, and more. Okano's sexy merchandise initially received a mixed response from locals, but feelings have slowly warmed and the shop's reputation has grown.

Kitchenware

KAPPABASHI-DŌRI

take Ginza line to Tawaramachi Station, exit 3

A short walk from Senso-ji brings you to Kappabashi-dōri, a busy road lined with store after store dedicated to the culinary arts. Starting at the corner of Asakusa Dori and running along Shinbori Dori, you'll find shops selling tableware, knives, crockery, plastic food models, signage for restaurants, utensils, and more. Some stores worth a look include knife emporiums **Kama-Asa Shoten** (2-24-1 Matsugaya, Taito-ku; tel. 03/3841-9355; www.kama-asa.co.jp; 10am-5:30pm daily) and **Kamata Hakensha**

Top Souvenirs

yukata and folding fan: two popular souvenirs

If you can dream it, you can likely buy it in Tokyo. What follows should give you a starting point for thinking about what to take home from your trip.

FUNKY FASHION

Try **Beams Japan** (page 103) in Shinjuku or any boutique in Harajuku's youth fashion mecca **LaForet** (page 105).

KIMONOS AND *YUKATA*

Head to **Chicago** (page 105) in Harajuku for vintage options, Jotaro Saito in **Ginza Six** (page 103) for high-end, and **Sou-Sou** (page 105) in Aoyama for traditional items with a contemporary twist.

CRAFT AND DESIGN

For traditional crafts like lacquerware, folding fans, and ceramics, check out **Oriental Bazaar** (page 105) or **Japan Traditional Crafts Aoyama Square** (page 107). For great contemporary design, try **D47 Design Travel Store** (page 107) or **2K540 Aki-Oka Artisan** (page 109).

HOUSEWARES

Tokyo is home to a number of multi-floor "lifestyle goods" emporiums like **Loft Shibuya** (page 107) and **Tōkyū Hands Shibuya** (page 107) where everything under the sun is on sale. The famed shopping street **Kappabashi-dōri** (page 111) has a huge selection of knives, kitchenware, and crowd-pleasing fake plastic food samples.

POP CULTURE PICKS

For items like manga and anime merchandise, head to **Mandarake** (page 110) or **Toranoana** (page 110). For retro video games, check out **Super Potato** (page 111).

GADGETS

Go to **Yodobashi Camera Shinjuku West** (page 104).

Knife Shop (2-12-6 Matsugaya, Taito-ku; tel. 03/3841-4205; www.kap-kam.com; 10am-6pm Mon.-Sat., 10:30am-5:30pm Sun.), and shops selling hyperreal plastic food models and other kitchen-related souvenirs of all kinds, such as **Ganso Shokuhin Sample-ya** (3-7-6 Nishiasakusa, Taito-ku; tel. 0120-171-839; www.ganso-sample.com; 10am-5:30pm daily) and **Maizuru** (1-5-17 Nishiasakusa, Taito-ku; tel. 03/3843-1686; www.maiduru.co.jp; 9am-6pm daily). When you spot the huge head of a chef protruding from atop the Niimi building, you'll know you've come to the right place.

Food

It's not a stretch to say that Tokyo may have the best food on the planet. The level of mastery among chefs, premium ingredients, and sheer number of cooking styles found in Japanese cuisine put the city in a league of its own. Japan's capital boasts more Michelin stars than any other city on earth, to the chagrin of Paris and New York. And where the Big Apple is said to have about 30,000 restaurants, some estimates put that number at 300,000 for Tokyo.

Embarking on a voyage into this vast culinary seventh heaven can be a life-changing experience. Japanese cooking aims to bring out the natural flavors inherent in a given preparation; so rather than dowsing dishes in a heavy layer of sauce, food is more likely to be lightly dipped in *shoyu* (soy sauce) or seasoned with a pinch of sea salt. An aesthetic sense is also a fundamental tenet—hence, the importance of seasonality and presentation. It's routine to see food so beautifully presented in elegant vessels made of lacquer, stone, wood, clay, ceramic, or glass that the meal is nearly elevated to art.

Restaurant options run the gamut, from **sushi** and **sashimi** to Japanese-style hot pot dishes **sukiyaki** and **shabu-shabu.** ***Kaiseki*** is a multicourse affair that evolved from the tea ceremony, comprising appetizers through a series of dishes that have been grilled, raw, fried, simmered and steamed, and ending with a light seasonally appropriate dessert. ***Okonomiyaki*** is a savory pancake cooked on a grill in front of you.

Then there are meals cooked over an open flame, such as ***yakiniku*** and ***robatayaki.*** Noodles, from **ramen** and ***udon*** to summer favorites ***somen*** and **soba,** are ubiquitous and served in a staggering variety of broths.

Highly evolved **foreign cuisines** are also readily on offer, from French and Italian to Indian, with chefs routinely going overseas to study their cuisine of choice before coming back to open their own shop and putting twists on the menu.

GINZA AND MARUNOUCHI
銀座, 丸の内

Sushi

★ GINZA KYUBEY

7-6 Ginza 8-chōme, Chūō-ku, Tokyo; tel. 03/3571-6523; www.kyubey.jp/en; 11:30am-2pm and 5pm-10pm; lunch ¥5,500-23,000, dinner ¥10,000-30,000; take Ginza line to Shimbashi Station, exit 3

Ginza Kyubey is the ideal spot for the full sushi experience. Take a seat at the counter and watch as master chefs work their magic in front of you. Although this place is not cheap, the prices feel commensurate with the ambience and fare. One of the great things about Kyubey is that the atmosphere isn't stuffy, which can sometimes be the case at high-end sushi shops, where a small number of customers sit at one counter as the master does his work, and people converse in hushed tones. By contrast, Kyubey seats more 17 and has a relatively lively atmosphere, striking the right balance of high quality and friendly ambience. Reservations, made via your hotel concierge,

Izakaya and *Kissaten*

There are a few eating establishments central to social life in Japan that you may be encountering for the first time if it's your first visit to the country: *izakaya* and *kissaten*. Here's how to make the most of a visit at either one.

Note that many *izakaya* and *kissaten* allow smoking. Steer clear if you're hypersensitive to being in a smoky environment. Otherwise, just accept it as the price of admission into this unique side of Japan's culinary and social life.

IZAKAYA

These gathering places are essentially akin to a pub, but different in subtle ways; there's really no exact equivalent in the West. Alcohol is central to the experience, from the volume quaffed to the fact that the food served tends to pair well with booze. Think lots of small plates bearing skewers of grilled meat (chicken, pork, etc.), french fries, small servings of stew, sashimi, salads, and more. The alcohol on offer usually includes draft beer, sake (aka *nihonshū*), and shōchū.

There are many spins on the general *izakaya* concept, from an open space with many separate tables to those with private rooms where people sit on tatami floors, or with their legs tucked under a table in a space below the level of the floor. Another common format is the *tachinomi* (literally: stand-drink) where people hover around a long or wrap-around bar, or congregate at small separate tables, eating and drinking on their feet. There's often a seating charge (normally around ¥300-500), for which you'll generally receive a small dish known as otōshi. It tends to be a small boiled item or a concoction that includes a bit of fish or meat. Truthfully, sometimes you won't be thrilled by what you receive, but there's no way around it. Finally, many *izakaya* impose a time limit (normally around two hours), and the option of *tabehōdai* (all you can eat) and/or a *nomihōdai* (all you can drink) for a flat fee (around ¥4,000 is common). Essentially, you'll be able to fill up as much as possible while you're on the clock, but when your time is up, your party will have to make way for the next group.

KISSATEN

Another unique enterprise found throughout Japan without an exact overseas counterpart is the *kissaten*. These are essentially nostalgic cafés dating to the Shōwa period (1926-1980), with the dated decor—dark, aged wood or tile dating to the 1950s—and old-school preparation methods to prove it. At a *kissaten*, you can expect to receive a proper cup of coffee that's been meticulously and slowly prepared by a master of the bean, often with the use of tools that are all but extinct. Try to visit one of these time capsules while you're in Japan. Given the rarefied nature of such a space, expect to pay a bit more than you normally would for a caffeine hit. A safe benchmark is something in the range of ¥700, or even more. Savor it—don't swill it down and run.

are recommended. If this restaurant is fully booked, try the branch at Hotel New Otani.

Yakitori

BIRD LAND

Tsukamoto Sozan Bldg. B1F, 4-2-15 Ginza, Chūō-ku; tel. 03/5250-1081; http://ginza-birdland.sakura.ne.jp; 5pm-9:30pm Tues.-Sat., closed national holidays; courses ¥6,300-8,400; take Ginza, Marunouchi, Hibiya lines to Ginza Station, exit C6

Bird Land is a chic yakitori restaurant that uses the best free-range chickens. No part of the chicken is wasted, from the liver that gets turned into pâte to the organs, roasted up and put on sticks before being glazed in sauce or simply salted. The menu also features a nice selection of imported beer and wine to wash it all down. The shop is compact and popular, so either try to make a reservation or show up late, after the dinner rush passes.

Izakaya

SHIN-HINOMOTO

2-4-4 Yūrakuchō, Chiyoda-ku; tel. 03/3214-8021; http://shin-hinomoto.com; 5pm-midnight Mon.-Sat., closed Sun.; courses ¥4,500; take Yamanote,

Yūrakuchō lines to Yūrakuchō Station, Hibiya exit

Alongside being owned by a Brit, Shin-Hinomoto, aka Andy's Fish, has another twist: It's under the train tracks, so don't be surprised if you feel a rumble each time the cars on the Yamanote Line roll overhead. This is a great place to go for the full *izakaya* experience, complete with cramped quarters, lively customers exclaiming "*kanpai*" ("cheers") with each round of drinks, and cheap but tasty grub. The menu is heavily weighted toward seafood and is helpfully available in English. As you enter the restaurant, there's a cubby hole lined with vending machines selling booze sitting to the right side of the entrance. The sidewalk here is a favorite place for salarymen to congregate for a canned alcoholic beverage of choice after leaving the office. Reserve a day or two ahead to be safe—by telephone only—especially if you're visiting on the weekend.

SAKE NO ANA

3-5-8 Ginza, Chūō-ku, Tokyo; tel. 03/3567-1133; www.sakenoana.com; 11:30am-11pm Mon.-Sat., 11:30am-10pm Sun. and holidays; lunch sets ¥1,050-2,200, dinner courses ¥5,400-6,480; take Ginza, Marunouchi, Hibiya lines to Ginza Station on, A13 exit

Sake no Ana puts a premium on serving food that goes best with sake. This restaurant is a fantastic place to go for a crash course on the Japanese rice-based brew, thanks to an in-house sake sommelier, Sakamoto-san, who is happy to give you a taste-based tour by pairing different varieties with dishes like a *natto* (fermented soy bean) omelet or deep-fried fugu (puffer fish)

TACHINOMI RYOMA

ALC Bldg. 1F, 2-13-3 Shimbashi; tel. 03/3591-1757; 4:30pm-12:30am Mon.-Sat., closed holidays; ¥4,000; take Yamanote, Ginza, Asakusa lines to Shimbashi Station, Karasumori exit

This welcoming *tachinomi* (standing-drinking) in the heart of the salaryman stronghold of Shimbashi, bordering Ginza's southern edge, has an extensive shōchū menu with more than 100 varieties. It's a great place to sample a number of varieties with a booze-friendly menu of choices like *karage* (fried chicken) and sashimi. The bartenders here really know their stuff and are happy to make suggestions.

Steakhouse

SHIMA

3-5-12 Nihonbashi, Chūō-ku; tel. 03/3271-7889; www.jimu-uke.co.jp/shima_site; noon-1pm (last order) and 6pm-9pm (last order), closed Sun. and two irregular days each month; lunch ¥8,000, dinner ¥23,000; take Ginza line to Kyobashi Station, exit 6

If you want to go big on one steak meal in Tokyo, Shima is an excellent choice. The immaculately marbled beef, sourced from a Kyoto farm, is phenomenal. Thanks to the warm presence of Chef Oshima Manabu, a Kyoto native, the atmosphere at this discrete basement eatery is friendly, too. Patrons seated at the counter can be heard chatting away with the chefs. It's not cheap, but for some Tokyo eateries charge three to four times as much for a similar meal. Reservations required for dinner. Call ahead a week or more in advance to be safe.

GRILL UKAI

Marunouchi Park Bldg. Marunouchi Brick Square 2F, 2-6-1 Marunouchi, Chiyoda-ku; tel. 03/5221-5252; www.ukai.co.jp/english/grill; 11am-1:30pm (last order) and 6pm-9pm (last order) Mon.-Fri., 11am-2pm (last order) and 6pm-9pm (last order) Sat., 11am-2pm and 6pm-8pm Sun. and holidays; lunch ¥3,780-6,800, dinner ¥7,560-12,960; take Yamanote line to Tokyo Station, Marunouchi South exit

Grill Ukai is a gourmet steakhouse that serves mouthwatering multicourse meals. The kitchen uses top-notch meats and seafood, from premium cuts of wagyu and lobster to Iberico pork. Separated from the bustling streets outside, the dining space is blessed with loads of windows and overlooks a leafy courtyard.

International

DHABA

Sagami Bldg. 1F, 2-7-9 Yaesu, Chūō-ku; tel. 03/3272-7160; www.dhabaindia.com/dhaba/index.html;

11:15am-3pm and 5pm-10:30pm Mon.-Fri., 11:30am-3pm (last order 2:30pm) and 5pm-10pm (last order 9pm) Sat.-Sun. and holidays; lunch ¥1,200, dinner ¥2,200; take Ginza line to Kyobashi Station, exit 5

Dhaba is a splendid South Indian restaurant that has it all: chefs recruited straight from Tamil Nadu and Kerala, a soothing ambience thanks to dark blue walls and a turquoise floor, and knock-out food. The menu's range is impressive too, from lemon prawn curry served with delectably thin puri to a mean masala dosa. And perhaps most importantly, the chefs don't tone the spice down to suit local tastes. If northern Indian fare is more to your liking, check out nearby sister shop **Khyber** (Ginza 1-chōme Bldg. 1F, 1-14-6 Ginza, Chūō-ku; from ¥1,000).

Café

CAFÉ L'AMBRE

8-10-15 Ginza, Chūō-ku; tel. 03/3571-1551; www.cafedelambre.com; noon-10pm (last order 9:30pm) Mon.-Fri., noon-7pm (last order 6:30pm) Sat.-Sun. and holidays; ¥1,000; take Yamanote line to Shimbashi Station, exit 1

This legendary coffeehouse in the heart of Ginza has been caffeinating the masses since 1948, though its interior looks more recent. Although some old-school Tokyo coffeehouses can be a bit full of themselves, this is a relaxed place for a caffeine hit and conversation. The English-language menu offers more than 30 varieties, including some exotic concoctions. How about coffee with Cognac?

SHINJUKU AND WESTERN TOKYO
新宿

Street Food

OMOIDE YOKOCHŌ

1-2-11 Nishi-Shinjuku, Shinjuku-ku; http://shinjuku-omoide.com; take Yamanote line to Shinjuku Station, west exit

This atmospheric alley, lit by red lanterns and filled with smoke, is packed with small, gritty bars and restaurants serving down-and-dirty fare consisting of animal parts and vegetables cooked over an open flame, washed down with prodigious amounts of booze. It once lacked public restrooms—hence its colloquial name "Piss Alley." Thankfully, restrooms with dubious levels of privacy are now crammed into one part of the alley, but everything else remains more or less unchanged. The colorful lanes run alongside the train tracks on the west side of Shinjuku Station, though the area is best reached via a tunnel that cuts under the train tracks near the East Exit. Talk of redevelopment is frequent, but for now the structures still stand in all their dilapidated glory.

As for picking a restaurant, **Asadachi** (1-2-14 Nishi-Shinjuku, Shinjuku-ku; noon-11pm Tues.-Sun.) is a lively spot. Beware of the more mysterious entries on the rather unconventional menu; those include exotic fare such as raw pig testicles and grilled salamander. But don't worry—plenty of other options exist, including grilled fatty salmon belly, mushrooms and grated daikon (radish), and boiled tripe. Asadachi, recognizable for its turtle shells hanging over the counter (yes, they serve them too) is only one of dozens of options in the alleyway. The best way to dine in Omoide Yokochō is to stroll the lane and take a seat at any counter that draws you. And for drinks, try **Albatross** (1-2-11 Nishi-Shinjuku, Shinjuku-ku; 5pm-2am Sun.-Thurs., 5pm-5am Fri.-Sat.), a classic watering hole decked out in chandeliers and red velvet that occupies three cramped floors. The top floor is a partially covered rooftop balcony with *Blade Runner*-like views of Shinjuku at night. Note that a ¥300 per person table charge applies.

Okonomiyaki

ROKUMON-YA

Hironaga Bldg. B1F, 3-35-13 Shinjuku, Shinjuku-ku; tel. 03/3356-6824; www.rokumonya.com/hon; 11:30am-2:30pm and 5:30pm-midnight (last order 10:45pm) Mon.-Fri., noon-2:30m and 5pm-midnight Sat., noon-2:30pm and 4pm-11pm Sun.; plates ¥980-1,680, courses ¥3,680-4,580; take Yamanote line to Shinjuku Station, south exit

If you feel like going on a culinary adventure, descend the staircase at this seemingly off-the-radar joint, request a seat at the counter, and watch the chefs prepare your food in front of you. Rokumon-ya has a loyal following, for good reason. It offers various styles of *okonomiyaki,* including the Hiroshima variety, which includes noodles on top. There's no English menu, but the friendly staff will help you order, and you really can't go wrong. Reservations are recommended.

Tempura

TEMPURA TSUNAHACHI

3-31-8 Shinjuku, Shinjuku-ku; tel. 03/3352-1012; www.tunahachi.co.jp/en; 11am-10:30pm (last order 10pm) daily; lunch ¥1,512, dinner ¥2,484-5,400; take Yamanote line to Shinjuku Station, south exit

Tempura Tsunahachi is the perfect place to eat excellent tempura that doesn't break the bank. Housed in an old wooden building, the shop has been serving customers from kabuki actors to pro baseball stars since 1923. If you go for lunch, sets start from ¥1,500, which is downright cheap for the level of quality compared to other similar spots. Don't be shocked if there's a queue out front when it opens for lunch. This a great, cost-effective option if you're willing to wait.

Udon

TSURUTONTAN UDON

Amimoto Bldg. B1F, 2-26-3 Kabukichō, Shinjuku-ku; tel. 03/5287-2626; www.tsurutontan.co.jp/shop/shinjuku-udon; 11am-8pm daily; ¥880-1,980; take Yamanote line to Shinjuku Station, east exit

Tsurutontan Udon boasts an expansive menu packed with photos of the numerous creative spins the shop puts on this wheat flour-based noodle dish. It's a good choice for a meal before or after a night out. There are both hot and cold dishes, prepared using both Japanese and overtly Western flavors like carbonara.

Izakaya

★ NIHON SAISEI SAKABA

Marunaka Bldg. 1F, 3-7-3 Shinjuku, Shinjuku-ku; tel. 03/3354-4829; http://ishii-world.jp/nihonsaisei/shinjuku3; 3pm-midnight (last order 11:30pm); ¥3,000; take Marunouchi, Fukutoshin, Toei Shinjuku lines to Shinjuku 3chome Station, exit C3

It's all about the pig at Nihon Saisei Sakaba, a standing-only *izakaya* that serves essentially every pig part, grilled, on a stick. This Shinjuku institution has a friendly, gritty ambience, with smoke wafting into the street where customers stand around makeshift tables made of empty beer crates and drink from frosty mugs. Have a look at the English menu: colon, spleen, womb, even birth canal. Don't worry; there are standard grilled bits, too. For a fun night out with the chance to mingle with fellow customers, this spot is hard to beat.

Kaiseki

KOZUE

Park Hyatt Tokyo 40F, 3-7-1-2 Nishinjuku, Shinjuku-ku; tel. 03/5323-3460; http://restaurants.tokyo.park.hyatt.co.jp/en/koz.html; 11:30am-2:30pm and 5:30pm-9:30pm; lunch ¥2,300-10,000, dinner ¥13,000-22,000; take Ōedo line to Tochomae Station, exit A4

Kozue serves haute Japanese cuisine in a setting blessed by fabulous views on the 40th floor of the Park Hyatt Toyko. The high-end *kaiseki* restaurant serves seasonal fare—for instance, fugu in winter, freshly foraged mushrooms in autumn—in artisan-made earthenware, porcelain, and lacquer dishes. Views of the city at night are outstanding year-round, and on clear afternoons you'll be able to see Mount Fuji. It's a spectacular dining experience. Book either online or over the phone a few days in advance to be on the safe side. Book a week or more ahead and make a special request for a window seat for stellar views.

KŌENJI
高円寺

Located less than 10 minutes west of Shinjuku on the Chūō and Sobu lines, Kōenji is known for its counterculture leanings. It's also a fantastic place for a night out eating and drinking among locals.

TOP EXPERIENCE

★ Navigating Tokyo's Culinary Alleys

One of the great experiences of any trip to Tokyo is a visit to the city's atmospheric alleyways known as *yokochō,* preferably, with a twofold agenda: eating grilled meats and swilling back draft beer alongside locals. Smoky, crowded, friendly, sometimes even rowdy, the alleys offer a wonderful way to get up close and personal with Tokyo's earthier and historic side, as well as to make connections with the locals. As an added bonus, you get amazing food at a bargain price. Don't be afraid of the offal. It can be surprisingly good.

A growing trend of new shops opening in some of the city's trendier *yokochō* has added a buzz around them in recent years. So you've come at a fortunate time. Lucky you, these amazing alleyways are scattered all around the city. Besides **Omoide Yokochō** (page 116), **Harmonica Yokochō** (page 120), **Kōenji Gādo-shita** (page 118), and **Ebisu Yokochō** (page 125), here are some other culinary alleyways worth visiting:

- **Yūrakuchō Gādo-shita** (2-3 Yūrakuchō, Chiyoda-ku): "Beneath the girder" is the literal meaning of *Gādo-shita,* which makes perfect sense when you enter this ramshackle restaurant zone. Extending north and south of Yūrakuchō Station—moving toward Tokyo station to the north and Shimbashi Station to the south—this extensive network of watering holes, yakitori (skewers of grilled chicken), and *izakaya* specializing in fish and more is a lively after-work hub for office workers keen to blow off steam on weekday evenings. To see the densest cluster of restaurants, walk southward from Yūrakuchō Station's central west exit, cross the major east-west artery of Harumi-dōri, and you'll begin to smell grilled meat and see tipsy salarymen emerging from under the tracks of the JR Yamanote line on your left.

- **Nombei Yokochō** (1-25-10 Shibuya, Shibuya-ku): "Drunkard's Alley," which sits about 1-minute walk from Shibuya Crossing, is another classic *yokochō.* Like Omoide Yokochō, it's firmly on the tourist radar but retains its old-school atmosphere. To reach it from Shibuya Station's Hachiko exit, cross Shibuya Station to the corner where you'll see Magnet by Shibuya 109. Here, turn right and walk under the train tracks. You'll see the alleyway on your left, lined with hanging lanterns. A few spots to be aware of are **Tight** (1-25-10, Shibuya-ku; tel. 03/3499-7668; www.2004-tight.com; 6pm-2am Mon.-Sat.), an appropriately named bar squeezed into a remarkably tiny space, and **Bar Piano** (tel. 03/5467-0258; opening times vary, but generally 8pm-late daily), which was visited by the late globe-trotting chef, writer, and food personality Anthony Bourdain.

Izakaya

DACHIBIN

3-2-13 Kōenji-Kita, Suginami-ku; tel. 03/3337-1352; www.dachibin.com; 5pm-5am daily; ¥3,000 take Chūō, Sobu lines to Kōenji Station, north exit

Dachibin serves great Okinawan fare made with ingredients sourced from the southern islands, including a healthy list of *awamori,* their fiery variety of *shōchū.* The atmosphere is rowdy and inviting, the staff friendly, and once a month there's a live jam session featuring the *sanshin,* a three-stringed instrument native to Okinawa. This place has been doing a brisk business for more than three decades.

Street Food

KŌENJI GĀDO-SHITA

3-chōme Kōenji-Minami, Suginami-ku; ¥3,000; take Chūō, Sobu lines to Kōenji Station, north exit

Perhaps the most legitimate street food option of Tokyo's vast array of alleyways known as *yokochō,* Gādo-shita is a hodgepodge of smoky, boisterous bars and restaurants with seating both inside and out, running along the train tracks west of Kōenji Station. It gets rowdy on weekends and is a great place for a night out with locals in one of Tokyo's most bohemian neighborhoods.

Omoide Yokochō, Shinjuku's famed culinary alley

- **Suzunari Yokochō** (1-45-15 Kitazawa, Setagaya-ku): Housed in an old theater complex, this cluster of about 15 bars and eateries in Shimokitazawa is a good spot to go if you happen to be in this countercultural enclave later in the evening, perhaps before or after a gig at one of the nearby live houses. A good spot for a drink with locals and alternative types here is **Ghetto** (1-45-16 Kitazawa, Setagaya-ku; 8:30pm-5am daily).
- **Ameya Yokochō** (4 to 6 Ueno, Taito-ku): This jumble of streets beside and under the elevated train tracks a few minutes' walk south of Ueno Station is known as "Ameyoko" by locals. This name stems from the fact that an abundance of candy (*ame*) was sold in these alleyways during the postwar years. *Ame* also denotes "America," from where black-market goods were also hawked in the area's shops following the war. The market has an indoor mall, where you'll find all manner of cheap clothing and sneakers, and a semi-outdoor side. The latter begs to be explored. Here, some 500 stalls and hole-in-the-wall eateries line the open-air marketplace that is one of Tokyo's most sprawling and bustling.

International

BOLBOL

3-2-15 Kōenjikita Suginami; tel. 03/3223-3277; http://bolbol.jp/english.html; 11:30am-3pm and 5pm-11pm Thurs.-Mon.; lunch ¥650-1,000, dinner ¥1,000-4,600; take Chūō, Sobu lines to Kōenji Station, north exit

BolBol offers excellent Persian food and is run by a friendly owner from Iran and his Japanese wife. The atmosphere evokes Iran, from the Persian rugs on the floor to the ornate tableware and instruments hanging on the wall. Try the dinner course, which includes buttered rice, lamb, and chicken on skewers, grilled tomatoes, and pickled vegetables. Combine it with draft beer or wine. If you're so inclined, relax with a hookah after dinner. Belly dance shows that encourage participation from willing audience members are held on Friday and Saturday nights. The showtimes for these performances vary, but are usually from 8pm or later.

KICHIJŌJI
吉祥寺

Located 15 minutes west of Shinjuku on the Chūō and Sobu lines, Kichijōji routinely ranks as one of Tokyo's most desirable places to live.

One reason for its popularity is its array of excellent restaurants, many of them centered in the boisterous warren of alleys north of the station known as **Harmonica Yokochō.**

Yakitori

TETCHAN

1-1-2 Honchō, Musashino-shi; tel. 0422/20-5950; 4pm-11pm Mon.-Fri., 3pm-11pm Sat.-Sun.; ¥3,000

If you plan to eat among the numerous eateries spread throughout the maze of Harmonica Yokochō, try Tetchan, a funky yakitori joint designed by famed architect Kengo Kuma with risqué wall art downstairs. This lively spot has a handful of tables, a long wrap-around bar that looks onto the kitchen, and a few standing tables. The menu includes a tasty range of grilled chicken on skewers, a bit of pork, lamb, and beef, and vegetable side dishes.

Soup Curry

ROJIURA CURRY SAMURAI

2-27-2 Kichijōji-Honchō, Musashino-shi; tel. 0422/27-6043; http://samurai-curry.com; 11:30am-3:30pm and 5:30pm-10:30pm daily; ¥1,500; take Chūō, Keio-Inokashira lines to Kichijōji Station, north exit

Here, you'll find excellent ingredients, from Hokkaido-sourced vegetables to thick cuts of fatty pork, with no additives and a surprisingly spicy kick: This soup curry restaurant with roots in Sapporo is the real deal. The list of customizable options is extensive, from cheese topping to extra helpings of vegetables like burdock root and okra. The *sakusaku* (crispy) broccoli is amazingly flavorsome. Beware: even at the lower end of the spice spectrum—there are 10 levels—you'll likely be putting out the fire with regular sips of water.

International

CAFÉ DU LIÈVRE (BUNNY HOUSE)

1-19-43 Gotenyama, Musashino-shi; tel. 0422/43-0015; 10am-7pm (last order 6pm) Mon.-Fri., 8:30am-8pm (last order 7pm) Sat.-Sun. and holidays; ¥1,000-2,000; take Chūō, Sōbu, Keio-Inokashira lines to Kichijōji Station, park exit

Set in the forested backside of **Inokashira-kōen,** this charming café with accents of French decor is a great stop for a bite either on the way to or after visiting the nearby **Ghibli Museum.** Using high-quality buckwheat flour sourced from Hokkaido, the restaurant and café whips up tasty galettes with toppings like eggs, pesto, tomatoes, mushrooms, and other veggies. There are also sweet crepes and a handful of tasty curry-and-rice dishes.

Cafés

BLUE SKY COFFEE

4-1-1 Inokashira, Mitaka-shi; http://blueskycoffee.jp; 10am-6pm Thurs.-Tues., closed on some rainy days; ¥250; take Chūō, Sōbu, Keio-Inokashira lines to Kichijōji Station, park exit, or Keio-Inokashira line to Inokashira-kōen Station

Housed in charmingly worn wooden building, this café sits right in the heart of Inokashira-kōen. They brew great coffee using top-notch equipment and sell a smattering of sweets, too. A great spot for a coffee to-go in the park.

HARAJUKU AND AOYAMA

原宿, 青山

Okonomiyaki

SAKURA TEI

3-10-1 Jingūmae, Shibuya-ku; tel. 03/3479-0039; www.sakuratei.co.jp/en; 11am-midnight; lunch ¥1,050-1,500; take Yamanote line to Harajuku Station, Takeshita exit

Connected to **Design Festa Gallery** is a bright, lively restaurant called Sakura Tei. While some *okonomiyaki* joints cook the dish for you, here you do it yourself on a teppanyaki plate at your table. Don't fret; there's a photo guide at each table instructing you how to properly get the job done. The English-language menu includes both *okonomiyaki* and *monjayaki* (batter topped with meat, vegetables, and seafood, then cooked to a loose texture resembling a scrambled egg), from classics like pork, kimchi, and seafood medleys, to the experimental, like a carbonara version.

Fugu: Eating the World's Deadliest Fish

Few foods strike fear into the hearts of diners quite the same way as fugu, puffer fish, and for good reason. Its potent tetrodotoxin is said to be 1,000 times more lethal than cyanide—and there's no antidote. It's an understatement to suggest that extreme care during preparation is wise.

fugu sashimi

Eating fugu was banned outright in Japan between 1570 and 1870. Even today, the imperial family is forbidden from partaking. This hasn't stopped the rest of the population from consuming some 10,000 tons of the fish annually. Commonplace though this may be, there is still a real sense of risk in eating this dish. It's no surprise that chefs must pass a rigorous licensed exam before being allowed to separate the edible parts from the toxin-infused areas, including the fugu's liver, which is both the most toxic and considered most delicious by some. Although the Japanese government banned serving the poisonous organ in 1984, daredevils who love the fish consume the liver for the tingling it produces on the lips, which is in fact the first sign of poisoning.

WHERE TO TRY FUGU

While fugu is often associated with the culinary worlds of Japan's Kansai region and the southern island of Kyūshū, the delicacy is widely available at well-known and pricey high-end restaurants in Tokyo. If you've got an appetite for danger and want to try your luck, check out **Torafugu-tei's Shinjuku branch** (Metro Bldg. B1F, 2-11-7 Kabukichō, Shinjuku-ku; tel. 03/3209-2919; www.torafugu.co.jp/en/shinjuku_honten/; take JR Yamanote line to Shinjuku Station, east exit) or **Shibuya branch** (1F King Bldg., 5-6 Maruyama-chō, Shibuya-ku; tel. 03/3462-7929; www.torafugu.co.jp/en/shibuya/; lunch 11:30am-2pm daily, last order 1:30pm; 5pm-midnight Mon.-Sat., last order 11pm; 4pm-11:30pm Sun. and holidays, last order 10:30pm; take JR Yamanote line to Shibuya Station, Hachikō exit or Keio-Inokashira line to Shinsen Station, south exit).

Tonkatsu

MAISEN

4-8-5 Jingūmae, Shibuya-ku; tel. 0120/428-485; https://mai-sen.com; 11am-10:45pm (last order 10pm) daily; ¥1,580-5,000; take Ginza, Hanzomon, Chiyoda lines to Omotesandō Station, exit A2

Set in what used to be a bathhouse, with soaring ceilings and a small garden in back, Maisen is a popular and excellent *tonkatsu* restaurant located amid the back lanes of Harajuku. You can choose from a range of pork dishes, from *hire katsu* (pork filet) to *rosu katsu* (pork loin). Set meals come with a small dish of pickled radish, rice and soup.

International

NARISAWA

2-6-15 Minami Aoyama, Minato-ku; tel. 03/5785-0799; www.narisawa-yoshihiro.com/en/openning.html; noon-3 pm (last order 1pm) and 6pm-8pm (last order 7pm), Tues.-Sat. with other sporadic closings; lunch ¥27,000, dinner ¥32,400; take Ginza, Hanzomon, Ōedo lines to Aoyama-itchome Station, exit 5

At Narisawa, creativity and attunement to nature are the hallmarks of the culinary creations of pioneering chef Yoshihiro Narisawa. Working away in his immaculate Aoyama kitchen, Narisawa brings a singular sensibility to a host of European cooking techniques—primarily French. He forages his own herbs and adds seasonal touches to every meal. His visually striking creations range from *wagyu* beef to edible soil, and a range of innovative desserts. The restaurant has an extensive selection of wines and cheeses too. Reservations for a given month are accepted from the beginning of the month prior through the restaurant's website. In other words, if you want to reserve a table in September, you can reserve from August 1. Be prepared to act promptly when the reservation period officially opens.

Cafés

★ SAKURAI JAPANESE TEA EXPERIENCE

Spiral Bldg. 5F, 5-6-23 Minami-Aoyama, Minato-ku; tel. 03/6451-1539; www.sakurai-tea.jp; 11am-11pm; tea ¥1,400, tasting course ¥4,800; take Ginza, Hanzomon lines to Omotesandō Staion, exit B1

Owner Shinya Sakurai takes his tea seriously. After spending 12 years becoming a master in the realm of tea, he finally felt ready to open his exceptional Aoyama café, Sakurai Japanese Tea Experience. This attractive café, which doubles as a chic, innovative tea-ceremony space, is stocked with jars containing tea leaves sourced from around Japan, which Sakurai personally travels to procure. There's an area to sit and quaff your brew of choice, with samples of single varieties priced at ¥380 each. For the full experience, including the opportunity to sit back and watch the master at work, try a tasting course of five different tea varieties; it costs ¥4,800 but is worth it. As you wait for your brew to reach peak drinkability, Sakurai will share details surrounding the delicate coaxing that each type of leaf requires for optimal preparation. The range of options is eye-opening, with some tea served with surprising accents, like lime, or infused with spirits. Some tea leaves can be eaten after being prepared. Paired with a traditional Japanese sweet, the combination is exquisite.

KOFFEE MAMEYA

4-15-3 Jingūmae, Shibuya-ku; tel. 03/5413-9422; www.koffee-mameya.com; 10am-6pm daily; from ¥450; take Ginza, Hanzomon lines to Omotesandō Station, exit A2

Koffee Mameya is the new incarnation of once legendary Omotesandō Koffee, which closed in 2015. Fortunately, the same impeccable standards of quality have been maintained. There's no seating at this popular bean specialist, but it's a great place to grab a coffee or espresso to go while exploring Harajuku's backstreets. If you want to purchase beans to brew at home, 15-20 types are available, sourced from five roasteries.

SHIBUYA AND AROUND 渋谷

Sushi

SUSHI ZANMAI

34-5 Udagawachō, Shibuya-ku; tel. 03/5784-2820; www.kiyomura.co.jp/shops/detail/43; open 24 hours; plates ¥213-594, set meals ¥1,274-3,348; take Yamanote line to Shibuya Station, Hachikō exit

In terms of bang for buck, Sushi Zanmai is a gem. With branches all over Tokyo, this 24-hour sushi shop just beyond Shibuya's pedestrian-only Center Gai area, near the Hachiko exist (and Shibuya Crossing), scores huge points for convenience. It also has a relaxed vibe, making it a great place to savor your meal in comfort. The tuna is phenomenal.

Izakaya

★ SHIRUBE

Pinecrest Kitazawa 1F, 2-18-2 Kitazawa, Setagaya-ku; tel. 03/3413-3785; 5:30pm-midnight (food last order 11pm, drink last order 11:30pm) daily; ¥4,000; take Keio-Inokashira, Odakyu lines to Shimokitazawa Station, south exit

On a side street in Shimokitazawa, just south of Shibuya on the Keio-Inokashira line, Shirube is the place to come for the quintessential *izakaya* experience. Pull aside the

1: Harmonica Yokochō 2: yakitori 3: Sakurai Tea Experience 4: *izakaya* in Kōenji

1
ハモニカ
キッチン
中華メニュー
1品全て500円,ダブル1,000円
2
3
4
お氣軽に

white curtains in front of the door that read "Izaka-ya-ism," slip off your shoes inside, and take a seat. At the center of the buzzing restaurant is its large open kitchen, where you can see the energetic team of chefs at work. The friendly staff will be happy to help you navigate the diverse menu, also available in English, which features classics such as sashimi, *nikujaga* (stewed beef with potatoes and onions), dumplings, braised pork, and more. These staples are complemented by a number of innovative fusion dishes like cheese tofu and avocado-tuna dip with toast. The simplest (and most recommended) option is the ¥4,000 *nomihōdai* (all you can drink) plan, which comes with a set meal and lasts 90 minutes. The place gets packed, so reservations are recommended.

International

VIRON

Tsukada Bldg. 1-2F, 33-8 Udagawachō, Shibuya-ku; tel. 03/5458-1770; bakery 9am-10pm, breakfast 9am-11am, lunch noon-2pm, café 3pm-5pm, dinner 7pm-10:30pm; pastries from ¥200, lunch ¥2,000, dinner ¥8,000; take Yamanote line to Shibuya Station, Hachikō exit

Walking through the red entrance of Viron, you may feel as if you've been transported to France. Inside you'll find more red, from the chairs to the curtains. The freshly baked bread is made using flour from France. On the second floor, you'll find a brasserie serving food on par with any great Parisian bistro. Dishes from all regions of France come in generous portions. The desserts are excellent, as are the breakfasts.

LOS BARBADOS

104, 41-26 Udagawachō, Shibuya-ku; tel. 03/3496-7157; www7b.biglobe.ne.jp/~los-barbados; noon-3pm and 6-11pm Mon.-Sat.; plates ¥700-1,100; take Yamanote line to Shibuya Station, Hachikō exit

This eight-seat restaurant and bar is an off-the-radar gem in the backstreets of Shibuya, serving surprisingly good African and Middle Eastern fare, including some solid vegetarian options. The cozy space is run by a friendly Japanese couple, Daisuke and Mayumi Uekawa, who developed a passion for the region after spending extended time in central Africa. It's also a bar with a good selection of beer, wine, and rum.

ADENIA

1-7 Hachiyama-chō, Shibuya-ku; tel. 03/5489-5151; www.adenia.jp; 11:30am-2:30pm and 6pm-9:30pm; lunch ¥1,200-3,800, dinner ¥2,400-12,000; take Yamanote line to Shibuya Station, west exit

Adenia is a small brasserie near Shibuya Station that serves excellent meals with main dishes of meat and seafood. Chef Masafumi Irie was formerly the Park Hyatt Tokyo's sous chef, so you're in good hands. Lunch plates, which include salad and fries, are a bargain. The space is tiny, so booking ahead is wise.

Cafés

CHATEI HATOU

1-15-19 Shibuya, Shibuya-ku; tel. 03/3400-9088; 11am-11pm daily; ¥1,000; take Yamanote line to Shibuya Station, east exit

With an entrance reminiscent of a lodge in the Alps, Chatei Hatou is a venerable café extolled by serious coffee drinkers the world over, including Blue Bottle Coffee CEO James Freeman. Upon entering, the master selects the cup you'll use from among an eclectic array standing on a shelf behind the counter. A cup from the impressive menu may cost upwards of ¥1,500, but if you want a real *kissaten* experience, it's worth it.

LION

2-19-13 Dogenzaka, Shibuya-ku; tel. 03/3461-6858; 11am-10:30pm daily; ¥1,000; take Yamanote line to Shibuya Station, west exit

Less a place for socializing—talking is discouraged, in fact—and more of an experience, Lion is unique. Patrons sip coffee in pew-like seats facing a towering set of speakers at the back of the café. Classical music wafts through the space, split between a ground floor and a balcony, like a church. Arrive, drink a coffee, and soak in the unlikely ambience at this singular monument to coffee and classical tunes atop Shibuya's "love hotel hill."

FUGLEN

1-16-11 Tomigaya, Shibuya-ku; tel. 03/3481-0884; www.fuglen.com; 8am-10pm Mon.-Tues., 8am-1am Wed.-Thurs., 8am-2am Fri., 9am-2am Sat., 9am-midnight Sun.; café from ¥250, bar from ¥1,250; take Chiyoda line to Yoyogi-kōen Station, exit 2

A sister cafe to Oslo's fashionable coffee spot of the same name, Fuglen is the central nexus in Tomigaya, an enclave for in-the-know locals on the backside of Shibuya. Although it's firmly on the hipster map, this bar and café has the substance to complement its style. Seating includes a counter, a few tables, and a sofa. They serve excellent coffee and a range of tasty baked goods. From 7pm, they sell well-made cocktails that make for good aperitifs.

EBISU AND AROUND
恵比寿

Street Food

EBISU YOKOCHŌ

1-7-4 Ebisu, Shibuya-ku; www.ebisu-yokocho.com; 5pm-late daily; ¥3,000; take JR Yamanote line to Ebisu Station, east exit

Tokyo may lack the cred of a city like Bangkok, but you can find pockets of good, gritty street food. In Ebisu Yokochō, a bustling arcade with a retro feel, small *izakaya* line a narrow concrete foot path, selling everything from grilled fish and yakitori to *yakisoba,* even raw horse and whale. Somewhat out of sync with the DIY decor—rickety stools, tables made of beer crates—there are even a few wine bars. It gets rowdy on Friday nights when people meet to wash away the cares of the workweek over frosty pints of beer. While you must order drinks from the store where you're seated, it's possible to order food from other establishments from within the *yokochō.*

Ramen

AFURI

1117 Bldg. 1F, 1-1-7 Ebisu; Shibuya-ku; tel. 03/5795-0750; http://afuri.com; 11am- 5am daily; ¥1,000; take Yamanote line to Ebisu Station, west exit

Just outside the backdoor of the always boisterous Ebisu Yokochō, you'll find the flagship of hit ramen shop Afuri. Soup stock here is infused with a mix of chicken, seaweed, and seafood, in varying degrees of fattiness. The most popular variety is *shio* (salt-based) ramen. I recommend selecting the citrus yuzu-infused *shio* broth with thick hunks of *chashu* (pork belly). The thin noodles and surprisingly light broth leave you feeling satisfied without the food coma triggered by some varieties of ramen.

Yakiniku

JOJOEN

Ebisu Garden Place Tower 38F and 39F, 4-20-3 Ebisu, Shibuya-ku; tel. 03/3473-8989; www.jojoen.co.jp/shop/jojoen/ebisu; 11:30am-10:30pm daily; lunch ¥2,600-5,800, dinner ¥9,000-15,000; take Yamanote line to Ebisu Station, east exit

The Ebisu branch of Jojoen, perched on the 38th floor of the Ebisu Garden Place Office Tower, combines the chain's stellar *yakiniku* with spectacular views. It's a great choice for lunch before heading out to explore the area, or for dinner before a night out. Meat lovers will surely leave satisfied. Reserve ahead to get a window seat.

Izakaya

OJINJO

2-2-10 Ebusi, Shibuya-ku; tel. 03/5784-1775; www.facebook.com/OJINJO; 5pm-12:30am Mon.-Thurs., 5pm-12:30am Fri., 4pm-12:30am Sat.-Sun. and holidays; ¥4,000

This lively *izakaya* hidden down a side street in Ebisu is renowned for the quality and variety of its lemon-infused *chūhai* (aka lemon sour), or *shōchū* mixed with soda and freshly squeezed lemon juice. With a menu containing six spins on the classic *izakaya* beverage (with crushed ice, mint, etc.), it's a great place to get acquainted with this commonly quaffed cocktail, which is often flavored with other types of fruit juice, such as grapefruit, plum, and more. The *shōchū*-friendly food menu is likewise diverse, from Okinawa stir-fries and grilled fish to oysters.

MAHAKALA

Maison Aoba 102, 1-17-5 Aobadai, Meguro-ku; tel. 03/3463-5147; www.mahakala-nakameguro.com; 6pm-midnight Tues.-Fri.; 3pm-midnight Sat.-Sun. and holidays; skewers ¥100-300, plates ¥350-900, seating charge ¥300 per person; take Tōkyū Tōyoko line to Nakameguro Station, main exit

Mahakala, an atmospheric restaurant along the leafy banks of the Meguro River, serves dishes originating from Kansai, including Osaka's famed *kushikatsu* (deep-fried cutlets of meat, seafood, and vegetables on skewers). Another item on the menu worth noting is *ikatamayaki,* a dish from Kobe consisting of a savory pancake made of eggs and grilled with squid in a bonito-based broth. The restaurant also serves scrumptious desserts. Reserve a a day or two ahead to be safe.

★ TONKI

1-1-2 Shimomeguro, Meguro-ku; tel. 03/3491-9928; 4pm-10:45pm Wed.-Mon., closed third Mon. every month; ¥1,900; take Yamanote line to Meguro Station, west exit

Serving *tonkatsu* since 1939, Tonki is an institution, a short walk from Meguro Station. The entrance may look commonplace, but slide open the wooden door, lift the curtain, and you'll enter a surprisingly expansive first floor, with an open kitchen full of diligent chefs at work and surrounded by a counter on three sides. Queues are commonplace, especially for a seat on the first floor, where customers can watch the masterful chefs perform. For quicker seating, choose the second floor. Set meals, including rice, trimmings, and miso soup, are ¥1,900 for both fatty and lean cuts of pork.

ROPPONGI
六本木

Izakaya

GONPACHI

1-13-11 Nishi-Azabu, Minato-ku; tel. 03/5771-0170; www.gonpachi.jp; 11:30am-3:30am (food last order 2:45am, drink last order 3am); lunch ¥1,000-3,500, dinner ¥4,500-8,900; take Ōedo, Hibiya lines to Roppongi Station, exit 2

This towering *izakaya* is said to be the restaurant that inspired a particularly gory scene in the film *Kill Bill.* Gonpachi has garnered a reputation as a lively spot with a wide-ranging menu of countryside standards like yakitori and grilled fish. Adding to the atmosphere are a soundtrack of the three-stringed shamisen and servers in traditional coats. There is a more upscale sushi restaurant with an open terrace on the third floor as well.

WARAYAKIYA

Roppongi Gordy Bldg. 1F, 6-8-8 Roppongi, Minato-ku; tel. 03/6778-5495; www.diamond-dining.com/shops/warayakiya; 5pm-5am Tues.-Sat., 5pm-11pm Sun.-Mon. and holidays; ¥3,980; take Ōedo, Hibiya lines to Roppongi Station, exit 3

Warayakiya is a great *izakaya* focused on a grilling method that uses straw instead of charcoal. This style originates from Kōchi Prefecture on the Pacific side of Shikoku. With the leaping fire reaching temperatures up to 900°C (1,652°F), it's worth getting a counter seat so you can watch the chefs expertly sear fish, meat, and vegetables to perfection. The seared bonito is a hit, and the place is lively and often packed, so booking ahead is recommended.

JOMON

1F Fujimori Bldg., 5-9-17 Roppongi, Minato-ku; tel. 03/3405-2585; http://teyandei.com/?page_id=18; 5:30pm-11:45pm Mon.-Fri., 5:30pm-5am Sat.-Sun. and holidays; course ¥3,980, set of 8 skewers ¥1,780; take Ōedo or Hibiya Line to Roppongi Station, exit 3

Right across the street from Warayakiya is another excellent choice for dinner: Jomon. This *izakaya*'s specialty is grilled skewers of meat, fish, and vegetables, preferably washed down with a healthy dose of beer. Or if you're in the mood for something stronger, perhaps *nihonshū* or *shōchū.* When the place fills up, it buzzes with a friendly vibe. Sit at the bar or facing the street in one of the nooks fronted by floor-to-ceiling windows that are usually left open during warmer months. Individual skewers cost from ¥250, with plates starting from about ¥600. Expect to spend about ¥5,000 per person total.

Japanese Convenience Stores

From a citydweller's perspective, Japanese convenience stores (*konbini*) are one of the wonders of the modern world. Ubiquitous (more than 50,000 individual stores dot the archipelago), operating at all hours, and remarkably diverse in their offerings, these smooth-operating institutions can be an unexpected revelation for many foreign travelers.

The biggest *konbini* chains, in order of market share, are **7-Eleven, Family Mart,** and **Lawson. Natural Lawson,** a Lawson spinoff that has been gaining steam in recent years, stocks products made with healthier ingredients. There's also a smattering of smaller players such as **MiniStop, New Days, Circle K Sunkus,** and **Daily Yamazaki.** Food and drinks are the main thing on sale, from snacks and canned coffee to *bento* (boxed meals): sandwiches, salads, *onigiri* (rice balls), candy, dairy products, ice cream and frozen food, beverages of every kind (soft drinks that change with the season, energy drinks, vitamin drinks, alcohol, etc.), warm foods like fried chicken and *oden* (a variety of foods boiled in soy-flavored broth), snacks, instant noodles, bread, and more. Recently, many *konbini* have started selling surprisingly good (and cheap at around ¥100-200) coffee (café latte, Americano, etc.).

Convenience stores in Japan also tend to stock a surprising array of products used in daily life: batteries, household goods, toiletries, cosmetics, body care products, neckties, undershirts, pantyhose, and umbrellas. Some bigger convenience stores even have areas where patrons can sit down and eat the food they've bought in the store, while a small number of them in upscale areas have even been known to set up alfresco seating areas in warmer months. Alongside edibles and drinks, there are always well-stocked magazine racks, filled with serialized manga and women's magazines sitting next to pornography (sealed shut with tape).

Soba

HONMURA AN

7-14-18 Roppongi, Minato-ku; tel. 03/5772-6657; www.honmuraantokyo.com/eng/index.html; noon-2:30pm and 5:30pm-10pm Mon.-Fri., noon-2:30pm and 5:30pm-9:30pm Sat.-Sun. and holidays; lunch ¥1,600, dinner ¥7,400; take Ōedo, Hibiya lines to Roppongi Station, exit 4b

Honmura An elevates the humble buckwheat noodle to an art form. Owner Koichi Kobari returned to Tokyo from New York in 2007 to take over his late father's soba shop, leaving a legion of disappointed fans in his wake. The shop defies the image of soba as being something eaten on the fly or from a bento box, and encourages diners to savor the noodles, which are served both hot and cold. The menu fluctuates by season and is fully bilingual. Prices are shockingly cheap for the quality of the food. A ¥350 seating charge applies at dinner. Reserve over the phone up to a month in advance, then be sure to reconfirm your reservation the day before you are scheduled to dine.

Tonkatsu

BUTAGUMI

2-24-9 Nishiazabu, Minato-ku; tel. 03/5466-6775; www.butagumi.com/nishiazabu/about.php; 11:30am-3pm and 6pm-10:30pm (last order 9:30pm) Tues.-Sun.; lunch ¥1,500-2,800, dinner ¥1,900-10,000; take Chiyoda line to Nogizaka Station, exit 5

With a menu offering pig from Japan to Spain, Butagumi is an excellent place to get your high-grade *tonkatsu* fix. The shop is slightly off the beaten path in a small side street off of Nishi-Azabu, but it's worth hunting down. The chefs know how to get the balance with the breading just right: not too oily, even light. Refillable shredded cabbage, rice, and miso soup round out the resoundingly satisfying meal.

Kaiseki

TOFUYA UKAI

4-4-13 Shiba Kōen, Minato-ku; tel. 03/3436-1028; www.ukai.co.jp/english/shiba; 11:45am-3pm and 5pm-7:30pm (last order) Mon.-Fri., 11am-7:30pm (last order) Sat.-Sun. and holidays; closed two Mon. every month; lunch ¥5,940-7,960, dinner ¥10,800-16,200; take Ōedo Line to Akabanebashi Station, Akabanebashiguchi exit

Tofuya Ukai, just a stone's throw from Tokyo Tower, is the best place to taste the wonders of tofu. Impressively, this *kaiseki* restaurant even makes its own tofu at a shop in the foothills of the Okutama mountain range west of Tokyo. Set amid readily visible gardens with ponds teeming with colorful carp, the restaurant is set within a relocated sake brewery that was originally built in Yamagata Prefecture more than 200 years ago. Staff in kimonos serve up to 500 guests in the wooden complex's 55 tatami-mat private rooms. Book ahead for a seat and to settle on your dining course, which must be determined beforehand.

Vegetarian

SOUGO

Roppongi Green Bldg. 3F, 6-1-8 Roppongi, Minato-ku; tel. 03/5414-1133; www.sougo.tokyo; 11:30am-3pm lunch, 2pm-5pm café time, 6pm-11pm dinner, 11pm-5am bar; lunch ¥1,500-5,000, cafe time ¥600-1,200, dinner ¥8,000-10,000; take Ōedo or Hibiya Line to Roppongi Station, exit 3

A stellar vegetarian option in a city with limited choices for those who don't eat meat, Sougo has garnered a reputation for its accessible *shōjin-ryōri,* or vegetarian food eaten by Buddhist monks. It's offered at a price and level of accessibility sadly lacking at most restaurants serving the spiritually inspired cuisine. Bucking tradition, there is an open kitchen fronted by a bar. The menu is seasonal and experimental, and incorporates some nonvegan items such as dashi stock and even cheese. Vegan meals can be ordered a day beforehand.

Ramen

GOGYO

1-4-36 Nishi-Azabu, Minato-ku; tel. 03/5775-5566; www.ramendining-gogyo.com/nishiazabu; 11:30am-3pm and 5pm-3am Mon.-Fri.; 11.30am-4pm and 5pm-3am Sat., 11:30am-4pm and 5pm-midnight Sun. and holidays; ¥1,000; take Hibiya or Ōedo Line to Roppongi Station, exit 2

The atmosphere at Gogyo is surprisingly polished for a ramen joint, with comfy chairs and stylish wooden tables. And in the open kitchen, there's the occasional sudden dance of flames as the chefs prepare the unique variety of "burnt" ramen. You have a choice of heavy soy sauce and miso broths, topped with a layer of partially burned fat for a rich kick. Side dishes are also tasty, including some exceptionally good salads. Sometimes there's a queue, but it moves reasonably fast.

KAGURAZAKA (IIDABASHI STATION)
神楽坂 (飯田橋駅)

The neighborhood of Kagurazaka, near Iidabashi station in the center of the city, has great ambience and a variety of dining options. It's also recognized as a geisha quarter, though not on the level of what's found in, say, Kyoto.

Tempura

TEMPURA ARAI

Kagurazaka AGE Bldg. B1F, 4-8 Kagurazaka, Shinjuku-ku; tel. 03/3269-1441; http://tempura-arai.jp/en.html?lang=1; noon-2:30 and 5pm-1am; a la carte ¥500-2,000, dinner course ¥10,000; take Chūō line to Iidabashi Station, west exit

In the basement of a building on a quiet backstreet of Kagurazaka is the stellar Tempura Arai. The atmosphere is chic and modern, but the menu consists of the classics—plenty of seafood and vegetables—done superbly. Also on offer is a nice selection of California wines and seasonal sakes. The space is small enough that you can hear your food sizzling from your seat. An English menu is available.

International

LE BRETAGNE

4-2 Kagurazaka, Shinjuku-ku; tel. 03/3235-3001; www.le-bretagne.com/e; 11:30am-10:30pm (last order) Tues.-Fri., 11am-10:30pm (last order) Sat., 11am-10pm (last order) Sun.; ¥1,000-3,000; take Chūō line to Iidabashi Station, west exit

This excellent creperie is great for a casual meal

before or after meandering through the atmospheric lanes of Tokyo's French quarter. Owned by a native of Brittany, the sweet and savory galettes, made with buckwheat, hit the spot.

AKIHABARA
秋葉原

Ramen

KIKANBŌ

2-10-9 Kajichō, Chiyoda-ku; tel. 03/6206-0239; http://kikanbo.co.jp; ¥1,000; 11am-9:30pm Mon.-Sat., 11am-4pm Sun.; take Chūō, Sōbu lines to Kanda Station, east exit, or walk 8 minutes south of Akihabara Station, Electric Town exit

"Ogre's iron club" is the literal meaning of this restaurants name. After experiencing the kick from a bowl of ramen at this well-loved noodle spot, you'll understand why. You'll have to choose your spice level (1 to 5) for *kara* (chili) and *shibi* (*sansho* pepper, akin to the mouth-numbing pepper served in much Sichuan-style Chinese cuisine). The broth is made from a mix of miso, meat and fish, and the noodles are topped with hunks of pork and other fixings (bean sprouts, baby corn, optional boiled egg for ¥100). The fiery theme is reinforced by an all-black interior, demon masks hanging from the walls and *taiko* (traditional drum) soundtrack. Recommended for those with a penchant for spice, but proceed with caution.

ASAKUSA
浅草

Shabu-Shabu/Sukiyaki

ASAKUSA IMAHAN

3-1-12 Nishi-Asakusa, Taito-ku; tel. 03/3841-1114; www.asakusaimahan.co.jp/english; 11:30am-9:30pm (last order 8:30pm) daily; lunch ¥1,500-10,000, dinner ¥8,000-25,000; take Tsukuba Express to Asakusa Station, exit A2, or Ginza Line to Tawaramachi Station, exit 3

Take a seat at the Asakusa branch this butcher-cum-sukiyaki restaurant. Watch as the server places succulent cuts of perfectly marbled wagyu into a soy-based soup in the pot on your table, heated by a flame, with mushrooms, tofu, green onions, and other vegetables. When the dish is cooked just enough, pull out a slice of beef and dip it in the small dish of raw free-range (and perfectly safe) egg. It's pricey but delicious.

Kaiseki

WAENTEI-KIKKO

2-2-13 Asakusa, Taito-ku; tel. 03/5828-8833; www.waentei-kikko.com/index_e.html; 11:30am-1:30pm and 5pm-9pm Thurs.-Tues.; lunch ¥2,500-3,500, dinner ¥6,800-13,800; take Ginza or Asakusa Line to Asakusa Station, exit 1

Set in an old house near Senso-ji, Waentei-kikko has tatami-mat floors, sliding doors framed with translucent paper, dark wooden rafters, and most importantly, four daily performances (12:15pm, 1:30pm, 6:30pm, and 8pm) by Fukui Kodai, one of the restaurant's managers and a master at the three-stringed Tsugaru-shamisen. The restaurant serves seasonal, set meals for both lunch and dinner, the former more casual in a bento box and the latter in the form of a *kaiseki* course. This is a wonderful way to experience traditional Japanese music in an intimate setting. Reservations recommended.

RAMEN YOROIYA

1-36-7 Asakusa, Taitō-ku; tel. 03/3845-4618; https://yoroiya.jp; 11am-8:30pm daily; ¥1,000; take Ginza or Asakusa Line to Asakusa Station, exit 1

The ramen at this Asakusa institution is delicious, and service is fast, friendly, and (mostly) off the tourist track. Ramen Yoroiya specializes in ramen served in a *shoyu* (soy sauce-based) broth. This style of ramen, usually topped with a double-yolk boiled egg, originated right in the neighborhood. While it's less crowded than many eateries around Sensō-ji, which can be rammed during lunch hours, a queue sometimes forms during peak hours. It moves relatively quickly, but to avoid this, arrive early or in mid-afternoon after the rush passes. English menu available.

UENO AND AROUND
上野

Kushiage

HANTEI

2-12-15 Nezu, Bunkyo-ku; tel. 03/3828-1440; http://hantei.co.jp; 11:30am-3pm and 5pm-11pm daily; closed Mon. or Tues. if Mon. is a holiday; lunch ¥3,200-4,300, dinner from ¥5,000-7,000; take Chiyoda Line to Nezu Station, exit 2

Pull back the curtain and step inside Hantei, set in an old three-story wooden building that hints at what the rest of this charming neighborhood once looked like. *Kushiage,* or deep-fried vegetables, meat, and fish on sticks is the specialty at this old-school restaurant. Lunch courses consist of either 8 or 12 skewers. For dinner, servers bring out six sticks at first, with the option to call for six additional sticks (¥1,500) or three (¥800) at a time. Diners also have the option of adding either white rice, pickles, and red-bean miso soup, or rice topped with kelp and seaweed and pickles (¥600).

Izakaya

TACHINOMI KADOKURA

Forum Aji Bldg. 1F, 6-13-1 Ueno, Taito-ku; tel. 03/3832-5335; http://taishoen.co.jp/kadokura; 10am-11:30pm Mon.-Sat., 10am-10pm Sun.; a la carte ¥150-600; take Yamanote Line to Ueno JR station, Iriya exit, or Hibiya or Ginza Line to Ueno subway station, exit 5a

Stand alongside locals at Tachinomi Kadokura, a no-frills bar that serves cheap, delicious pub fare: sashimi, a fried and breaded ham cutlet, an omelette with vegetables grilled on a hotplate at your table. It all goes down well with beer. An English menu is available.

International

DARJEELING

3-10-3 Nishi-Nippori; Arakawa-ku; tel. 03/5685-0267; https://akr4118853167.owst.jp; 11am-11pm daily; ¥1,050-2,400; take Keihin-Tōhoku, Yamanote, Keisei lines to Nippori Station, north exit

Darjeeling is chockablock with statues of Hindu deities, geometrically patterned tapestries, elaborate bronze candleholders, intricately carved furniture, paintings of peacocks, and even a sitar hanging on the wall. The gracious owner attentively presents the delicious north Indian food on beautiful tablewear. A great place for lunch or dinner after strolling around the atmospheric Yanaka neighborhood.

Café

KAYABA COFFEE

6-1-29 Yanaka, Taitō-ku; tel. 03/3823-3545; http://taireki.com/en/kayaba.html; 8am-11pm Mon.-Sat., 8am-6pm Sun.; a la carte ¥250-600, lunch sets ¥1,000; take Keihin-Tōhoku, Yamanote, Keisei lines to Nippori Station, north exit, or Chiyoda line to Nezu Station

Housed in a traditional wooden home built in 1916, Kayaba Coffee was founded by Kayaba Inosuke and his wife Kimi in 1938. This charming institution is a stellar example of a *kissaten*, as Tokyo's retro coffee houses are known. About 5 minutes' walk west of Ueno-kōen, this café is a local landmark with its ambience intact, from the yellow sign out front and retro furniture to the dark wood paneling and brick counter. The menu consists of classic *kissaten* fare like egg sandwiches and, of course, great coffee. Notes that queues do form sometimes, particularly during weekend lunch hours.

TOKYO BAY AREA
東京湾

Sushi

SUSHIKUNI

4-14-15 Tsukiji, Chūō-ku; tel. 03/3545-8234; https://ameblo.jp/sushikuni; 10am-3pm and 5pm-9pm Thurs.-Tues.; lunch ¥2,000-3,000, dinner ¥5,000-6,000; take Ōedo line to Tsukijishijō Station, exit A1

A stand-out in Tsukiji Outer Market, Sushikuni is known for its *kaisen-don*, or raw fish served overtop rice. The specialties here are *ikura* (salmon roe) and *uni* (sea urchin roe). Queues do form, but they move relatively fast.

Robot Restaurant

Shinjuku's Robot Restaurant

Robot Restaurant (Shinjuku Robot Bldg. B2F, 1-7-1 Kabukichō, Shinjuku-ku; tel. 03/3200-5500; www.shinjuku-robot.com; 4pm-11pm daily; ¥8,000; take Shinjuku, Ōedo Marunouchi lines to Shinjuku-Sanchome Station, exit B3 or E1; or take JR lines to Shinjuku Station, east exit) must be experienced to be fully comprehended. But to give an idea, four 90-minute shows happen nightly in a basement in Kabukichō, featuring women in bikinis riding mechanical flame-spewing dragons and towering robots, engaged in a war with a legion of other robots, all set amid a heavily mirrored landscape, drenched in eye-searing neon and with a nonstop din of music and battle sounds (earplugs definitely recommended). As the show approaches the crescendo, audience members are given glowsticks, which they wave in concert with the bikini-clad warriors.

This singular spectacle cost a whopping ¥10 billion to create, which is perhaps reflected in the hefty price of admission. You can book your tickets online in advance, or at the venue. Note that if you opt for the latter, there are often discount vouchers available at tourist information centers and some accommodations that can shave as much as ¥2,000 off the cost of admission. "Restaurant" is a misnomer; the food here is on par with a convenience store bento. Ditto for the drink menu, which extends to canned alcoholic drinks and bottles of tea. Note that this has very much become a "tourist-only" affair, but if you enjoy a zany spectacle for its own sake, go for the show and leave with your mind blown.

International

TY HARBOR

2-1-3 Higashi-Shinagawa, Shinagawa-ku; tel. 03/5479-4555; www.tysons.jp/tyharbor/en; 11:30am-2pm and 5:30pm-10pm Mon.-Fri., 11:30am-3pm and 5:30pm-10pm Sat.-Sun. and holidays; lunch ¥1,300-3,200, dinner ¥1,300-5,800; take Tokyo Monorail or Rinkai Line to Tennozu Isle Station, central exit

For a maritime city, Tokyo admittedly has few options for wining and dining with a view of the bay. TY Harbor remedies that. It includes a chic bar serving dark and light California-style beers, and a restaurant serving Western cuisine, from steaks and salads to burgers made with fine cuts of wagyu beef.

Monjayaki

MONJA KONDO

3-12-10 Tsukishima, Chūō-ku; tel. 03/3533-4555; www.monja.gr.jp/kondohonten.html; 5pm-10pm Mon.-Fri., noon-10pm Sat.-Sun.; lunch ¥1,500, dinner ¥2,500; take Ōedo line to Tsukishima Station, exit 8

Doing brisk business since 1950, Monja Kondo is said to be Tokyo's first restaurant to serve *monjayaki*, the Tokyo-born cousin of *okonomiyaki*, the savory pancake-like dish with stronger ties to Osaka and Hiroshima. Monja Kondo's menu boasts a whopping 90 toppings to choose from, and friendly staff are on standby to help you cook your meal at your table's teppanyaki grill.

Bars and Nightlife

TOP EXPERIENCE

GINZA AND MARUNOUCHI
銀座, 丸の内

Bars

BAR HIGH FIVE

Efflore Ginza 5 Bldg. B1F, 5-4-15 Ginza, Chūō-ku; tel. 03/3571-5815; www.barhighfive.com; 5pm-1am Mon.-Sat. (last entry 11:30pm); table/cover charge ¥1,000; take Ginza, Marunouchi, Hibiya lines to Ginza Station, exit B5

Located in a basement, amid the Ginza area's glitz, is Bar High Five, with mixologist extraordinaire Hidetsugu Ueno at the helm and a long counter facing an impressive wall of bottles. In addition to world-renowned cocktails, the bar offers a serious selection of scotch and whisky. The owner speaks fluent English, too. This probably won't be the best choice if you're looking to socialize—the atmosphere is a bit buttoned-down and there's a clearly written list of rules (posted in English on the bar's website) that must be upheld by customers. But if you're a keen connoisseur of nuanced drinks, this is among the very best bars in all Asia.

BAR ORCHARD GINZA

6-5-16 Ginza, Chūō-ku; tel. 03/3575-0333; www.facebook.com/barorchardginza; 6pm-midnight Mon.-Fri., 6pm-11pm Sat.; table/cover charge ¥1,000; take Ginza, Marunouchi, Hibiya lines to Ginza Station, exit B9

Bar Orchard Ginza is an excellent bar near Ginza Station that has made a name for itself by putting unique spins on old-school principles of mixology. Cocktails here make heavy use of seasonal fruits and range from orthodox to innovative, depending on your request. The friendly couple who run the bar employ techniques like using liquid nitrogen in frozen cocktails to give creations a little extra zing.

300BAR NEXT

Murasaki Bldg. B1F, 1-2-14 Yūrakuchō, Chiyoda-ku; tel. 03/3593-8300; www.300bar-next.com; noon-2am Mon.-Thurs., and noon-4am Fri.-Sat., noon-11pm Sun. and holidays; take Ginza, Hibiya, Marunouchi lines to Ginza Station, exit C2, or Yamanote, Yūrakuchō lines to Yūrakuchō Station, Hibiya exit

For a budget option in Ginza—yes, you read that right—300Bar Next can't be beat, with all drinks and food costing only ¥300 per item. If you happen to be in Ginza and don't feel like splashing out, this is your best option. The bartenders are friendly and know their drinks (and make a mean mojito), and the crowd is lively and welcoming. It's a fun place to warm up for a big night out.

SHINJUKU AND WESTERN TOKYO
新宿

Bars

BEN FIDDICH

Yamatoya Bldg. 9F, 1-13-7 Nishi-Shinjuku, Shinjuku-ku; tel. 03/6279-4223; www.facebook.com/BarBenfiddich; 6pm-3am Mon.-Sat., closed holidays; take JR lines to Shinjuku, west exit

At Ben Fiddich there are roots and spices in jars, perfectly sculpted ice cubes, pestles and mortars, and organic mixing ingredients sourced from bar master Hiroyasu Kayama's family farm in neighboring Saitama Prefecture. What you won't find is a menu; just sit back with an open mind and let the bar master work his magic.

NEW YORK BAR

Park Hyatt, 3-7-1-2 Nishi-Shinjuku, Shinjuku-ku; tel. 03/5323-3458; http://tokyo.park.hyatt.com; 5pm-midnight Sun.-Wed., 5pm-1am Thurs.-Sat.; ¥2,500 cover charge after 8pm Mon.-Sat., or after 7pm Sun.; take Ōedo line to Tochōmae Station, exit A4

Made famous by Sofia Coppola's film *Lost in Translation,* this bar is a true gem and offers some of the most dazzling views of the city at night. Perched on the 52nd-floor of the Park Hyatt Tokyo, in Shinjuku's skyscraper district, New York Bar is the pinnacle of elegance, with its dark wood and floor-to-ceiling windows from which Mount Fuji can be glimpsed on clear days. Here you'll find top-notch cocktails; an array of booze, including the most varieties of wine from the United States in Japan; and excellent steak and pizza.

SAKE BAR OTONARI

B1F Otori Bldg., 5-35 Kagurazaka, Shinjuku-ku; tel. 080/7954-5357; 5pm-midnight; take Chūō line to Iidabashi Station, west exit

Sake Bar Otonari is a great little *tachinomi* (standing bar) in Kagurazka, near Iidabashi Station on the Sobu Line 10 minutes' train ride from Shinjuku. It has a stellar selection of sake from around Japan and excellent food, with the bar focusing on ham. The remainder of the menu comes from an excellent *izakaya* next door. The atmosphere is lively, and the staff and customers are foreigner-friendly. This is a highly recommended jumping-off point into the world of sake.

HARAJUKU AND AOYAMA
原宿, 青山

Bars

HARAJUKU TAPROOM

2F, 1-20-13 Jingūmae, Shibuya-ku; tel. 03/6438-0450; http://bairdbeer.com/ja/tap/harajuku.html; 5pm-midnight Mon.-Fri., noon-midnight Sat.-Sun.; take Yamanote line to Harajuku Station, Takeshita exit

A stone's throw from the youth fashion catwalk of Takeshita-Dōri isn't the most likely spot for a craft beer bar to thrive, but Harajuku Taproom, by Baird Brewing, manages to do just that. Its restaurant has an *izakaya*-inspired menu and serves 15 of Baird Brewing's fantastic microbrews. On weekends and national holidays, it opens at noon for lunch.

TWO ROOMS

3-11-7 Kita-Aoyama, Minato-ku; tel. 033/498-0222; www.tworooms.jp; 11:30am-2am Mon.-Sat., 11:am-10pm Sun.; take Ginza line to Omotesandō Station, exit B2; or take Fukutoshin line to Kitasandō Station

Two Rooms is a sleekly decorated bar with excellent fish grilled teppanyaki-style, succulent steaks, a motherlode of wine, and a plush outdoor terrace with spectacular views of the city. It's popular as both a sophisticated nightlife spot and a restaurant. On weekends, Two Rooms serves an amazing brunch.

BAR BONOBO

2-23-4 Jingūmae, Shibuya-ku; tel. 03/6804-5542; http://bonobo.jp; 6pm-3am Mon.-Tues., 9pm-3am Wed.-Thurs., 10pm-6am Fri.-Sat.; cover charge ¥1,000 (includes one drink); take Yamanote line to Harajuku Station, Takeshita exit

Bar Bonobo, tucked away on a Harajuku backstreet, is a converted two-story house with a great sound system and friendly vibe. There's a bar on the first floor, a DJ booth upstairs where various music events are held, and a rooftop terrace. A bit off the beaten path, it's worth the detour if you're looking for a laid-back place with a slightly underground feel.

Clubs

VENT

Festa Omotesandō Bldg. B1F, 3-18-19 Minami-Aoyama, Minato-ku; tel. 03/6804-6652; http://vent-tokyo.net; 11pm-late on nights with events; fee varies; take Ginza, Chiyoda, Hanzomon lines to Omotesandō Station, exit 4

Great DJ lineups and a dance floor with a spectacular acoustics sound system are the main selling points at Vent. This newcomer to Tokyo's electronic music scene is located at the corner of Omotesandō and Aoyama Dori. Its chic interior is minimal and contains a lounge that provides a great place to socialize and drink without being drowned in decibels. These elements tend to attract an aurally savvy crowd who are in-the-know yet friendly. Both local DJs and big names from overseas are routinely scheduled to spin.

☆ Shinjuku Nightlife Districts

Tokyo offers a great variety of nightlife, but Shinjuku stands above the crowd in terms of depth and variety. Served by the world's busiest train station, the area is home to Kabukichō, the city's biggest red-light district; Golden Gai, a warren of more than 200 small bars; and the city's gay quarter centered in Shinjuku Ni-Chōme. Nearby Shinjuku San-chōme also boasts a number of eateries and watering holes with a more local crowd and a bit more elbow room than what you'll find in Kabukichō or Golden Gai.

KABUKICHŌ
歌舞伎町

Tokyo's largest red-light zone, neon-drenched Kabukichō ("Kabuki Town") occupies a 360,000-square-meter (89-acre) area just north of Yasukuni-dōri. Once known as Tsunohazu, it was a residential zone that was razed during World War II bombing raids. Postwar plans to resurrect the area as a family-friendly entertainment center with a kabuki theater never materialized. Instead, host and hostess bars, strip clubs, soaplands (brothels masquerading as bathhouses), and love hotels proliferated, and the *yakuza* (Japanese mafia) and Chinese investors moved in. By the 1990s, Kabukichō had become a *fuzoku* (pink trade) zone, which it remains to this day. Despite its seedy reputation, there are security cameras dotting the area and it's a safe place for a stroll if you keep your wits about you and ignore the persistent touts. "Cleanup" efforts are ongoing, as exemplified in the recent opening of the large Toho cinema and shopping complex right in the heart of the action. Definitely go to the unmissable, uncharacterizable **Robot Restaurant** (Shinjuku Robot Bldg. B2F, 1-7-1 Kabukichō, Shinjuku-ku), but otherwise, just walking around the neighborhood, taking in its atmosphere, and then moving on to Golden Gai is the best way to experience the area.

GOLDEN GAI
ゴールデン街

This warren of more than 270 ramshackle bars in the heart of Kabukichō is one of the city's best places for a pub crawl. Although it's a fading tradition, roving musicians called *nagishi* occasionally do still wander the alleys strumming the accompanying guitar riffs for customers who request songs they wish to sing (¥1,000 per tune is the standard rate). The one thing to bear in mind during a night out in the seven dilapidated lanes that comprise Golden Gai (1 Kabukichō, Shinjuku-ku; 7pm-late daily) is that space is at a premium. This means that most of the bars slap you with a "table charge," generally ranging from ¥500 to ¥1,000 per person, and some of the more secretive spots greet newcomers with a slight chill.

With this in mind, the alleyways are pure ambience, evoking a time when postwar Tokyo was just coming back into its own, and the vast majority of the bars are friendly and welcome visitors with open arms. Here are a few good bars to start with:

- **Albatross G** (1-1-7 Kabukichō, Shinjuku-ku; tel. 03/3203-3699; www.alba-s.com; 5pm-2am Sun.-Thurs., 5pm-5am Fri.-Sat.), staffed by very friendly bartenders.
- **Deathmatch in Hell** (Goldengai 3rd street, 1-1-8 Kabukichō, Shinjuku-ku; tel. 090/2524-5575; 8pm-3am Mon.-Sat., closed holidays), with metal and horror movie themes and a fun crowd.
- **Krishna** (Paresu Bldg. 2F, 1-1-5 Kabukichō, Shinjuku-ku; tel. 03/5287-2561; http://krishuna.com; 7pm-5am daily), a slightly bigger second-floor bar run by two female backpackers and friends with impeccable taste in music.

Shinjuku at night

- **The Open Book** (1-1-6 Kabukichō, Shinjuku-ku; tel. 080/4112-0273; www.facebook.com/theopenbook2016; 7pm-1:30am Mon.-Sat.), a lemon *chūhai* (shōchū, soda and lemon juice) specialist, hidden behind a large, unmarked wooden door with a wall overflowing with books.

To get to Golden Gai, take Shinjuku, Ōedo Marunouchi lines to Shinjuku-Sanchome Station, exit B3 or E1; or take JR lines to Shinjuku Station, east exit.

SHINJUKU-NICHŌME
新宿二丁目

Just a few minutes' walk from Golden Gai is Ni-Chome, Tokyo's friendly, compact, gay district. Foreign-friendly and easily accessible options include:

- The male-only **GB** (Shinjuku Plaza Bldg. B1F, 2-12-13 Shinjuku, Shinjuku-ku; tel. 03/3352-8972; 8pm-2am Mon.-Fri., 8pm-3am Sat., 7pm-midnight Sun.), which is attached to a hotel.
- Female-only **Bar Gold Finger** (2-12-11 Shinjuku, Shinjuku-ku; tel. 03/6383-4669; www.goldfingerparty.com; 6pm-late).
- Open-air spot **AiiRO Café** (2-18-1 Shinjuku, Shinjuku-ku, http://aliving.net/aiirocafe; 6pm-2am Mon.-Thurs., 6pm-5am Fri.-Sat., 6pm-midnight Sun.), which hosts drag queen and dance performances on weekends.
- The chic standing bar **Eagle Tokyo** (2-12-3 Shinjuku, Shinjuku-ku; tel. 03/6874-0176; www.eagletokyo.com; 6pm-1am Sun.-Thurs., 6pm-5am Fri-.Sat.), which welcomes all.
- Perhaps the most popular of the lot, **Arty Farty** (2F, 2-11-7 Shinjuku, Shinjuku-ku; www.arty-farty.net; 6pm-1am), which requires women to come with a gay friend for admission on weekends when the dance floor gets jumping.

To get to Shinjuku-nichōme take Marunouchi line to Shinjuku-sanchōme, exits C5, C8.

Live Music in Tokyo

Live music is played at a mind-boggling range of venues all throughout Tokyo. There are thriving local scenes across all genres, and world-class acts routinely perform in the city. Here's where to start to check out the city's myriad "live houses," as they are usually referred to in Japan:

- **Pit Inn** (B1, 2-12-4 Shinjuku, Shinjuku-ku; tel. 03/3354-2024; www.pit-inn.com/index.html; 2:30pm, 7:30pm; hours and fee vary by event; take Marunouchi line to Shinjuku-sanchōme Station, exit C5): An eminent jazz spot imbued with history and blessed by a consistently stellar lineup of both Japanese and overseas artists. There are daily matinee and evening shows.
- **Shinjuku Loft** (Tatehana Bldg. B2F, 1-12-9 Kabukichō, Shinjuku-ku; tel. 03/5272-0382; http://www.loft-prj.co.jp; 3pm-10pm; hours and fee vary by event; take Yamanote line to Shinjuku Station, east exit): A stalwart of Tokyo's live music scene. One room hosts the main show and a smaller one near the bar hosts more intimate performances.
- **20,000 Den-Atsu** (B1 L-Grazia Higashi-Kōenji, 1-7-23-Kōenji-Minami, Suginami-ku; www.den-atsu.com; one-drink minimum ¥500; hours and fee vary by event; take Marunouchi line to Higashi-Kōenji, exit 3): This legendary punk-rock venue from Kōenji was reborn after its former location burned down in 2009. For punk in Tokyo, this is your best bet.
- **Club Quattro** (Udagawa-chō, 32-13; tel. 03/3477-8750; www.club-quattro.com/shibuya/, hours and fee vary by event; take Yamanote Line to Shibuya Station, Hachikō exit): Don't let its location at the heart of Tokyo's teenybopper nexus fool you. Both the intimate space itself and the Japanese and international artists it hosts are high-caliber, covering genres from rock to world music.
- **Shelter** (Senda Bldg. B1F, 2-6-10 Kitazawa, Setagaya-ku; tel: 03/3466-7430; www.loft-prj.co.jp/SHELTER/index.html; hours and fee vary by event): Shelter is a compact venue at the center of Shimokitazawa's vibrant rock scene. Domestic and occasional overseas acts jam here nightly. Go early to be sure you get in.

SHIBUYA
渋谷

Bars

ISHINOHANA

B1F, 3-6-2 Shibuya, Shibuya-ku; tel. 03/5485-8405; http://ishinohana.com; 6pm-2am Mon.-Sat., cover charge ¥500; take Yamanote line to Shibuya Station, east exit

It's all about seasonality at Ishinohana, evidenced by the owner's obsession with fresh produce at this cocktail den near Shibuya Station. This bar is also thankfully devoid of the pomp on display at some of Ginza's swankier cocktail lounges. There's a menu with myriad takes on the martini and another featuring only infinite variations on the mojito. Exotic fruits and vegetables are injected into classics, alongside a host of cocktails originating from this shop, including the award-winning Claudia, a martini infused with caramel syrup and pineapple juice.

Clubs

CONTACT

2-10-12 Dogenzaka, Shibuya-ku; tel. 03/6427-8107; www.contacttokyo.com; times and fee vary by event; take Yamanote line to Shibuya Station, Hachikō exit

Contact is a great choice for discriminating clubbers. There's a clear separation between the dance space and the bar area. A no-drinks policy is in effect on the dance floor, where flashes of lasers and strobes penetrate air cooled by mist machines, all enveloped by a superb sound system. This venue is the latest entry by organizer Global Hearts, who made a mark in Tokyo's electronic music scene with now-closed Yellow and Air. Keep an eye on the website; major international DJs routinely perform.

- **Three** (5-18-1 Daizawa, Setagaya-ku; tel. 03/5486-8804; www.toos.co.jp/3; hours and fee vary by event) and **Basement Bar** (5-18-1 Daizawa, Setagaya-ku; tel. 03/5481-6366; http://toos.co.jp/basementbar; 6pm-midnight) sit side-by-side in the same building. Basement Bar provides a space for indie rockers to jam on the cheap, and Three does the same, with a lounge for a little class. Rough around the edges, they are vital outposts in Tokyo's indie scene.

- **What the Dickens** (4F, 1-13-3 Ebisu-Nishi, Shibuya-ku; tel. 03/3780-2099; www.whatthedickens.jp; 5pm-midnight, closed Mon.; no cover): This foreigner-friendly faux British pub (shepherd's pie and fish and chips included) is a favored haunt of Tokyo's expat community and a healthy number of Japanese regulars too. Local acts jam every evening.

- **Unit** (Za House Bldg., 1-34-17 Ebisu-Nishi, Shibuya-ku; tel. 03/5459-8630; www.unit-tokyo.com; hours and fee vary by event; take Tōkyū Tōyoko line to Daikanyama Station, main exit): Here you can see anyone from local indie rockers to DJs. The three-floor space allows you to take a break or switch up the tempo as needed. Check the schedule before making the trip.

- **Liquid Room** (3-16-6 Higashi, Shibuya-ku; tel. 03/5464-0800; www.liquidroom.net; hours and fee vary by event; take Yamanote line to Ebisu Station, west exit.): Liquid Room's focus is largely live music, although the owners do sometimes organize club nights. Artists from around Japan and from overseas routinely perform, and tickets vanish quickly.

- **Kazunoya Oiwake** (5-37-7 Asakusa, Taitō-ku; tel. 03/3874-0722; www.kazunoya-oiwake.com; 5:30pm-midnight Tues.-Sun., performances 7pm and 9pm; cover charge ¥2,000, plus 1 food item and 1 drink; take Tsukuba Express train to Asakusa Station, exit 1): This is a great place to eat and drink while listening to a master pluck the quintessentially Japanese three-stringed Tsugaru-shamisen, an instrument from northern Japan that resembles a banjo.

THE ROOM

Daihachi Tohto Bldg. B1F, 15-19 Sakuragaoka-chō, Shibuya-ku; tel. 03/3461-7167; www.theroom.jp; time and fee vary by event; take Yamanote line to Shibuya Station, south exit

The Room, owned by members of crossover jazz-electronic outfit Kyoto Jazz Massive, is a basement club that strikes the right balance of feeling slightly underground while still managing a warm welcome. You'll find a nicely lit bar for socializing and a dimly lit dance floor for busting a groove next door. Events are a mix of DJ sets and energetic live performances of jazz, house, or a fusion of various elements—sometimes by Kyoto Jazz Massive themselves. The entrance can be a little hard to locate. Look for the red sign beckoning you to venture downstairs.

Karaoke

KARAOKE-KAN

30-8 Udagawa-chō, Shibuya-ku; tel. 03/3462-0785; 11am-6am daily; ¥173 per 30 minutes daily (until 7pm), ¥533 per 30 minutes Mon.-Thurs. (after 7pm), ¥653 per 30 min. Fri.-Sun. (after 7pm); take Yamanote Line to Shibuya Station, Hachikō exit

Although karaoke chain Karaoke-kan (http://karaokekan.jp/index.html) has branches around major station areas all over Tokyo, its branch in Shibuya's **Center Gai** is the most famous of them all, due to Bill Murray's famous crooning session in *Lost in Translation,* which was filmed at this branch. The scene that featured Murray's warbling was filmed in hallowed rooms 601 and 602, and if you're keen to snag either of these rooms, you'll need to reserve ahead by a day or two by phone or in person. Note that you can sing freely for as long as you want from

11am-7pm on any day for ¥1,760, or at nighttime (11pm-5am) for ¥1,986 (Sun.-Thurs.) and ¥2,653 (Fri.-Sat.).

KARAOKE RAINBOW

Shibuya Modi 8F, 1-21-3 Shibuya, Shibuya-ku; tel. 03/6455-3240; www.karaoke-rainbow.com/pc/shop/shibuya.html; 11am-5am daily; ¥140 per 30 minutes (until 7pm), ¥380 per 30 minutes (after 7pm), first hour free Mon.-Fri. (until 7pm) and Mon.-Thurs. (after 7pm); take Yamanote Line to Shibuya Station, Hachikō exit

Karaoke Rainbow is a chic karaoke spot in Shibuya with a large English-language catalog of songs. It nicely dodges the garish neon and worn rooms seen in many chains, instead taking its style cues from, say, Brooklyn: art on the walls, plants, street lamps, and benches in the corridors. Note that while you do get a free hour of crooning before 7pm on Mon.-Fri. and even after 7pm on Mon.-Thurs., you'll still need to buy a drink during the first hour.

DJ Bars

DJ BAR BRIDGE

Parkside Kyodo Bldg. 10F, 1-25-6 Shibuya, Shibuya-ku; tel. 03/6427-6568; 8pm-5am daily; cover charge ¥1,000 (includes one drink); take Yamanote line to Shibuya Station, Hachikō exit

On the 10th floor of a building next to Shibuya Station, DJ Bar Bridge boasts views of the pedestrian scramble below, a friendly crowd, affordable drinks, and a great roster of resident DJs. Most important, its sound system is fantastic. Given its convenient location, this is a great place to begin a night in the area.

OATH

Tosei Bldg. B1F, 1-6-5 Dogenzaka, Shibuya-ku; tel. 03/3461-1225; www.djbar-oath.com; cover charge ¥1,000 (includes one drink); 8pm-5am Mon.-Thurs., 8pm-8am Fri.-Sat., sometimes open Sun.; take Yamanote line to Shibuya Station, Hachikō exit

Descend the stairs and enter this compact club, a vital node in Tokyo's underground scene that hosts performances by a long list of regular local DJs. Opulent chandeliers hang from the ceiling and ornately kitsch mirrors are mounted on the walls. After paying the cover charge, drinks are priced at a reasonable ¥500. But the real draw is the great sound system.

AOYAMA TUNNEL

Aoyama Bldg. B1F, 4-5-9 Shibuya, Shibuya-ku; http://aoyama-tunnel.com; 8pm-8am Tues.-Sat.; cover charge ¥1,000 (includes one drink); take Ginza, Chiyoda, Hanzōmon lines to Omotesandō Station, exit B1, or Yamanote line to Shibuya, Hachikō exit

Aoyama Tunnel is the ideal environment for an all-nighter. Cheap drinks, a good DJ list, and stellar sound keep the revelers coming. It's about a 10-minute trek from Shibuya station up a busy main road rammed with traffic, but once you arrive you'll enjoy yourself. For a change of pace, head upstairs to the worn (and storied) multifloor club of **Aoyama Hachi** (Aoyama Bldg. 1F-4F, 4-5-9 Shibuya, Shibuya-ku; tel. 03/5766-4887; www.aoyama-hachi.net; hours and fee vary by event) or next door on the first floor, the afterhours hot spot **Red Bar** (tel. 03/5888-5847; 8am-8pm daily; cover charge ¥1,000, includes one drink), which is bathed in red light as the name suggests, and scope out the vibe.

KOARA

Koritsu Bldg. B1F, 1-13-15 Jinnan, Shibuya-ku; tel. 03/6423-0644; www.koara-tokyo.com; 9pm-5am Mon.-Thurs., 9pm-6am Fri.-Sat., 5pm-11pm Sun.; cover charge ¥1,000 pp (includes one drink); take Yamanote line to Shibuya Station, Hachikō exit

Audiophiles take note: Koara is a cubbyhole-sized club on a quiet side street of Shibuya with one of the best sound systems in town. Although only a few dozen people pack the place out, it has a reputation for occasionally hosting a big-name DJ passing through. More than likely, though, the tunes will be provided by an upstart local spinner. There's no cover charge on many nights, and drinks are affordably priced.

Safety After Dark

A serious issue with drink spiking and subsequent credit card fraud persists in Tokyo, perpetuated by certain shady bars and street touts in the nightlife hub of **Roppongi,** particularly on the stretch of **Gaien-Higashi-dōri** that leads from Tokyo Midtown south through Roppongi Crossing and toward Tokyo Tower, and in the red-light zone of **Kabukichō** in Shinjuku. Unfortunately, travelers are often unwitting victims. Along with countless reports of such incidents of drink spiking followed by use of the unconscious victims' credit cards, some tourists have reported being beaten up. The problem is so prevalent that the embassy of the United States, among others, routinely issues warnings about the practice on its website.

As a general rule of thumb, if a tout, often from overseas, approaches you on the sidewalk and attempts to lure you into a bar or club for "one free drink," to mingle with members of the opposite sex, or really anything else, politely but firmly decline and move on. Be warned that some of them can be quite aggressive with their pitch. If they persist, ignore them and keep walking. Under no circumstances should you follow one of them to a private venue, often behind a suspiciously discreet door many floors above street level. As an extra precaution, if you plan to go out for a big night on the town and think you may end up in Kabukichō or Roppongi, consider taking a cash amount you're confident will cover your needs, but leave your credit and debit cards behind.

EBISU AND AROUND
恵比寿

Bars

BAR TRAM

Swing Bldg. 2F, 1-7-13 Ebisu-Nishi, Shibuya-ku; tel. 03/5489-5514; http://small-axe.net/bar-tram; 7pm-3am Mon.-Thurs., 7pm-4am Fri.-Sat., 7pm-2am Sun.; cover charge ¥500; take Yamanote line to Ebisu Station, west exit, or take Hibiya line to Ebisu Station, exit

Bar Tram and sister bar **Bar Trench** (102 DIS Bldg., 1-5-8 Ebisu-Nishi, Shibuya-ku; tel. 03/3780-5291; http://small-axe.net/bar-trench; 7pm-2am Mon.-Sat., 6pm-1am Sun. and holidays; cover charge ¥500) specialize in herbal liqueur and absinthe-infused cocktails. Dimly lit atmospheric hideouts with a whiff of 19th-century Paris about them, both bars are a short walk from Ebisu Station, and just around the corner from each other. The bartenders are dressed for the job—white shirt, necktie, vest—of navigating more than 70 varieties of the green fairy at Bar Tram alone. Bar Trench boasts the largest collection of bitters in Japan and has an equally quirky list of cocktail names. Monkey Gland, anyone?

Clubs

SOLFA

1-20-5 Aobadai, Meguro-ku; tel. 03/6231-9051; www.nakameguro-solfa.com; 5pm-5am daily; fee varies by event; take Tōkyū Tōyoko line to Nakameguro Station, main exit

Located in the hip neighborhood of Nakameguro, one train stop or a 15-minute walk from Ebisu Station, Solfa is a wonderfully intimate nightclub. The dance floor accommodates up to 100 people, and the lounge can squeeze in a bit more. DJs on deck usually play artfully chosen techno and house. If you feel like going to a more discerning club that isn't an overwhelmingly crowded, sweaty affair, this one's for you.

ROPPONGI
六本木

Bars

AGAVE

DM Bldg. B1F, 7-18-11 Roppongi, Minato-ku; tel. 03/3497-0229; http://agave.jp; 6:30pm-2am Mon.-Thurs., 6:30pm-4am Fri.-Sat.; take Hibiya, Ōedo lines to Roppongi Station, exit 2

Frida Kahlo paintings, Zapata posters, and Mexican tunes waft through a room with orange stone walls. There's a humidor full of cigars, and behind the bar, an array of some 450

TOP EXPERIENCE

Japan's Award-Winning Whiskies

In an archetypal Japanese development, akin to the way Toyota and Honda first sought to copy Western carmakers and ultimately ended up besting them in some cases, Japan has fully supplanted Scotland as the world's whisky king in recent years.

Japan's first domestically distilled malt whisky was bottled in 1924 by at **Suntory Yamakazi Distillery** in Osaka Prefecture (page 379). Suntory founder Shinjiro Torii dreamed of introducing his home country to Scotch. He succeeded in striking the right balance for Japanese taste buds and Suntory took off.

Don't be discouraged by stratospheric prices like ¥722,098 for a bottle of the Chichibu Whisky Matsuri 2017 and ¥315,917 per bottle of Hakushu 25 Year Old. A number of excellent bars allow you to sample some of Japan's best whiskies from Suntory as well as those from Nikka Whisky Distilling and the small Chichibu distillery that has taken the world by storm. A few great places to see what all the fuss is about are:

- **Zoetrope** (3F, 7-10-14 Nishi-Shinjuku, Shinjuku-ku; 7pm-4am Mon.-Sat.; ¥1,000 cover charge), a film buff's bar with more than 300 bottles of domestic whisky.
- **Cabin Nakameguro** (Riverside Terrace 101, 1-10-23 Naka-Meguro, Meguro-ku; tel. 03/6303-2220; www.cabintokyo.com; 7pm-late Mon.-Thurs., 7pm-2am Fri.-Sat., last order 1am, closed on holidays), which has a great whisky menu and is located in a trendy part of town.
- **Apollo** (B1F, 8-2-15 Ginza, Chūō-ku; tel. 03/6280-6282; 6pm-2am Mon.-Fri., 6pm-midnight Sat.), a classy spot in Ginza with a deep whisky selection and a jazz soundtrack, all overseen by friendly, erudite bartenders.

varieties of tequila and mescal. You'd swear you were in Mexico, but Agave is in fact a basement with the ambience of an upscale cantina. It's located near Roppongi's main drag and is seriously committed to the drink derived from the blue-leafed plant after which it's named. Beware that a single pour from the cheaper end of the menu starts at around ¥1,000, while rarer offerings go for upwards of ¥9,000.

BAR GEN YAMAMOTO

1-6-4 Azabu-Juban, Minato-ku; tel. 03/6434-0652; http://genyamamoto.jp; 3pm-11pm Tues.-Sat., closed Aug. 18-28; cover charge ¥1,000; take Namboku, Ōedo lines to Azabu-jūban Station, exit 5B

About five minutes' walk southeast of the massive Roppongi Hills complex in the affluent neighborhood of Azabu-Juban, you'll find legendary cocktail wizard Gen Yamamoto at work. Bar Gen Yamamoto is a model of simplicity: eight seats at the bar, no soundtrack, minimalist interior. It's just Yamamoto mixing renowned cocktails using seasonal fruits and vegetables from around Japan: lemons and tomatoes from Shikoku, pears from Hokkaido, grapes from Okayama. Rather than measuring everything like a chemist in a lab, he masterfully eyeballs most ingredients in his concoctions. For the full range of flavors, from sweet to savory, try one of the tasting sets of four, six, or seven drinks (¥4,600, ¥6,800, or ¥7,900). It's not cheap, but the quality and craft are phenomenal.

ASAKUSA
浅草

Bars

POPEYE

2-18-7 Ryōgoku, Sumida-ku; tel. 03/3633-2120; www.lares.dti.ne.jp/~ppy; 5pm-11:30pm Mon.-Fri., 3pm-11:30pm Sat.; take Sōbu line to Ryōgoku Station, west exit

Popeye has 70 beers on tap, with the bulk brewed by Japanese craft outfits. In fact, the microbrew mecca has more Japanese microbrews on tap than any other bar worldwide. Try to get a place at the counter, where the approachable staff will be happy to guide you in your journey through the islands' best offerings. Be warned that many of the beers aren't cheap, and the British pub fare leaves something to be desired. But if you're a craft brew aficionado and unearthing hidden gems is your aim, this is the best spot in the capital to explore Japan's microbrew scene.

TOKYO BAY AREA
東京湾

Night Cruise

JICOO, THE FLOATING BAR

2-7-104 Kaigan, Minato-ku; tel. 0120/049-490; www.jicoofloatingbar.com; 8pm-11pm Thurs.-Sat.; ¥2,600 entry; take Yurikamome line to Hinode Station; Yamamote, Keihin-Tohoku lines or Tokyo Monorail to Hamamatsucho Station, or Asakusa, Ōedo lines to Daimon Station

This futuristic looking boat, complete with bar, DJ deck, and multicolored lights, offers nighttime cruises through Tokyo Bay from Hinode Pier to Odaiba, taking in dazzling views of Rainbow Bridge along the way. Jicoo, The Floating Bar leaves Hinode Pier at 8pm, 9pm, and 10pm on Thursday, Friday, and Saturday nights. The music and vibe on Thursday and Friday nights are mellower, while Saturday nights get a bit rowdier. It's a fun alternative to partying on land and a good way to see Tokyo's lights from the water.

Accommodations

When choosing accommodation in Tokyo, the most important factor is convenience. The most popular areas are the zone surrounding Tokyo Station, centered on **Ginza** and **Marunouchi,** and in the western part of the city, **Shinjuku** and **Shibuya.** The draws of these core areas are proximity to the city's best food, shopping, and nightlife. Further, Tokyo, Shibuya, and Shinjuku stations are on the Yamanote line, which runs in a loop around the city, while Ginza has several subway links (Ginza, Hibiya, Marunouchi lines).

Roppongi is also a solid base in the heart of downtown with good subway links (Oedo, Hibiya lines). That said, it's very much "on" 24 hours a day and can feel somewhat seedy at nighttime, particularly along the main drag of Gaien-Higashi-dōri. As such, it's best suited to night owls and those traveling without kids. The same caveat applies to Shinjuku's Kabukichō district—it's a very colorful area, but it doesn't' score the highest marks for family friendliness at nighttime.

Another area worth considering is the older side of town in the city's northeast, centered on **Ueno** and **Asakusa.** These two neighborhoods have more affordable options and plenty of local character but are also less central.

If you end up staying outside of these core areas, aim to at the very least find a room near a station on the Yamanote loop line, the east-west Chūō/Sōbu line, or a subway station not too far from the city's core, encompassing the area inside the Yamanote line. For example, the bohemian neighborhood of **Kōenji,** located on the Chūō and Sōbu lines is a good pick for those seeking an offbeat, local vibe.

GINZA AND MARUNOUCHI
銀座, 丸の内

¥20,000-30,000

HOTEL RYUMEIKAN TOKYO

1-3-22 Yaesu, Chūō-ku; tel. 03/3272-0971; www.ryumeikan-tokyo.jp; ¥24,000 d; take Yamanote line to Tokyo Station, Yaesu North exit

Next to Tokyo Station, Hotel Ryumeikan Tokyo is a branch of the Ryokan Ryumeikan Honten, which has been running since 1899. The rooms are petite but smart, and feature

Nights on the Fringe: Tokyo Subcultures

For those who approach a new city with the sensibility of a cultural anthropologist, nightlife in Tokyo is fertile ground. The city's fetish and goth scene often appears as performance art at events and venues for alternative types. Many journalists, photographers, and even academics show up in street clothes, too, but those committed enough to in costume (wigs, masks, latex, platform boots, etc.) will normally gain cheaper entry. A few good places to take the plunge into Tokyo's subterranean nightlife scene include:

- **Decabar Z** (Shinko Bldg. 5F, 1-2-13 Kabukichō, Shinjuku-ku; tel. 03/6273-8415; www.tokyo-decadance.com/decabarz; 6pm-midnight Sun.-Mon., 6pm-5am Tues.-Thurs., 6pm-6am Fri.-Sat.) in Shinjuku is the most easily accessible place where alternative types congregate. You'll know it by the huge mural at the entrance inspired by the anime series *Dragon Ball Z*. To learn more, keep an eye on the official Facebook page (www.facebook.com/tokyodecadance.official; time and fee vary) and its public group page (www.facebook.com/groups/tokyo.decadance). These events are usually announced about a month in advance.
- **Department H** (https://ameblo.jp/department-h; first Sat. of month; starts midnight and goes all night; ¥5,000) is among Tokyo's most famous fetish parties. Held on the first Saturday of every month at **Tokyo Kinema Club** (1-1-14 Negishi, Taitō-ku; tel. 03/3874-7988), a former cabaret theater in Uguisudani, one stop from Ueno on the Yamanote line, legions of alt types flock to the event in all manner of costume. Besides the thrill of dressing up, there's a cosplay discount of ¥2,000. There's no bar on site, so you'll have to bring your own drinks.
- **Midnight Mess** (www.facebook.com/groups/midnightmesstokyo; time, fee, and place vary) is another heavy hitter in the goth underground scene. Keep an eye on its Facebook page for upcoming events. Here, you'll see more eye-popping fetish cosplay attire and intense performances, including *shibari*.

KINBAKU

There are often S&M-flavored stage performances, with the art of *kinbaku* (Japanese rope bondage; literally: to bind tightly) being among the most popular, usually done with an accompanying shamisen player or a punishing electronic soundtrack in a nightclub environment. This art form has become so influential that Madonna has used it in her performances and Anthony Bourdain featured it in an episode of his CNN series *Parts Unknown*. Here are a few places to catch a *kinbaku* show:

- **Studio Six** (1002 BIG Office Plaza, 2-62-8 Higashi-Ikebukuro, Toshima-ku; tel. 090/1208-9889; http://osadasteve.com/studio6_en.html; performances 7pm every Sat.; ¥15,000, ¥20,000 with photo permission), located in Ikebukuro, 10 minutes north of Shinjuku on the Yamanote Line, is a *kinbaku* space run by German-born *kinbaku* master Osada Steve, a big name in the Japanese bondage scene. Osada holds performances at the studio on Saturday nights. Note that you might encounter nudity, and the performances can be erotically charged.
- **Ichinawa Salon** (Takadanobaba Rihimu B1F, 3-7-5 Takada, Toshima-ku; tel. 03/6914-0074; http://shibari.jp/event/ichinawasalon.html; ¥2,000 women, ¥5,000 men; 7pm-11pm 3rd Tues. every month) is a friendly salon where world-famous *shibari* artist Hajime Kinoko schools newbies in the art. It costs ¥1,000 to watch the proceedings and ¥4,000 to join the class. For an introduction to the man and his rope art, check out the documentary about him done by *Vice Japan*, "Bondage Art with Kinoko Hajime," on YouTube.

free Wi-Fi access. Helpful staff are ready to assist you in sending your luggage to the airport so you don't have to carry it with you. This is a good option for those wanting an affordable place to sleep, but not much else.

¥30,000-40,000

PARK HOTEL TOKYO

1-7-1 Higashi-Shimbashi, Minato-ku; tel. 03/6252-1111; www.parkhotel-tokyo.com; ¥36,000 d; take Yamanote, Ginza, Asakusa lines to Shimbashi Station,

Shiodome exit for JR station, exit 1d for subway station, or take Yurikamome, Ōedo lines to Shiodome Station, exits 7, 8

The Park Hotel Tokyo is a Design Hotel with reasonable rates—not an easy find in Tokyo. The first hotel in the capital launched by Berlin-based Design Hotels, this property in Shiodome boasts a floor with more than 30 rooms, each uniquely painted by Japanese artists. The walls of these special rooms feature contemporary takes on everything from Mount Fuji and the book *Tale of Genji* to samurai and kabuki. The hotel even has pillow consultants on staff and collaborates with pillow maker Lofty to provide guests with versions that offer maximum rest.

Over ¥40,000

IMPERIAL HOTEL TOKYO

1-1-1 Uchisaiwaicho, Chiyoda-ku; tel. 03/3504-1111; www.imperialhotel.co.jp; ¥47,200 d; take Chiyoda, Hibiya, Mita lines to Hibiya Station, exits A5, A13, or Yamanote, Yūrakuchō lines to Yūrakuchō Station, Hibiya exit

The Imperial Hotel Tokyo has more history coursing through its halls than just about any other hotel in the city. It has been standing on its current site, overlooking the Palace, Hibiya Park, and Ginza, in some form since 1890. Its second incarnation, which opened (and remained standing) the same day that the 1923 Great Kanto Earthquake struck the capital, was designed by Frank Lloyd Wright. Its current main building opened in 1970 and boasts 13 restaurants and three bars, including the superb Imperial Lounge Aqua and the legendary Old Imperial Bar, originally designed by Frank Lloyd-Wright and still graced by the same furniture and motifs. The hotel's proximity to Hibiya, Ginza, and Yūrakuchō stations ensures easy access to anywhere in the city.

TOKYO STATION HOTEL

1-9-1 Marunouchi, Chiyoda-ku; tel. 03/5220-1111; www.thetokyostationhotel.jp; ¥52,600 d; take Yamanote line to Tokyo station, Marunouchi South exit

The Tokyo Station Hotel is housed in an Important Cultural Property, the iconic red-brick and newly restored Tokyo Station. Here, you'll find a superb in-house French restaurant, a number of quality casual joints, and an excellent cocktail bar. Further, the hotel's concierge is known to outperform the competition when it comes to nailing difficult restaurant reservations. So consider staying here if a high-end culinary tour is on your agenda.

PALACE HOTEL

1-1-1 Marunouchi, Chiyoda-ku; tel. 03/3211-5211; https://en.palacehoteltokyo.com; ¥124,600; take Chiyoda line to Ōtemachi station, exit C13b

The recently revamped historic Palace Hotel is long on views, with its south-facing rooms with balconies—a rare luxury in Tokyo—overlooking the Imperial Palace moat and gardens, with the skyscrapers jutting skyward in the backdrop. The spacious rooms have earth-tone decor that exudes a hushed elegance in harmony with the green space sprawling outside the window. It's also within walking distance of Hibiya Park and the shopping districts of Ginza and Yūrakuchō, and it has phenomenal Japanese and Western food on-site. Cultural events are often held in the lobby to reflect the seasons, such as traditional rice cake-making performances on New Year's Day and cherry blossom events in spring.

MANDARIN ORIENTAL, TOKYO

2-1-1 Nihonbashi Muromachi, Chūō-ku; tel. 03/3270-8800; www.mandarinoriental.com; ¥150,000 d; take Ginza, Hanzomon lines to Mitsukoshimae Station, exit A8

Stellar service and stunning views are just a couple of the strong suits at the Mandarin Oriental, Tokyo. Many materials in the hotel were sourced from local artists, and design flourishes throughout invoke the spirit of Japan, from paper hanging lanterns to understated flower arrangements. On-site are also a renowned spa, a slew of high-end restaurants ranging from Mediterranean to Cantonese, great bars, and an excellent pastry shop. What's more, the surrounding neighborhood of Nihonbashi is being redeveloped to become a new hot spot by 2020. Mount Fuji can be seen from the lobby on clear days, and at night, Mandarin Bar has some of the best views in the city.

★ AMAN

The Ōtemachi Tower, 1-5-6 Ōtemachi, Chiyoda-ku; tel. 03/5224-3333; www.aman.com; ¥100,000-330,000 d; take Marunouchi line to Ōtemachi station, exit A5

Luxury resort giant Aman operates an exclusive hotel on the top six floors of Ōtemachi Tower. The lavish 84-room property is a departure for Aman, being its first in an urban setting. While the brand is a haven for celebrities who want to keep a low-profile, this hotel is in the heart of the bustling Ōtemachi business district, only a short walk from Tokyo Station. Friendly, attentive staff are ready to guide you to deluxe facilities, including fine dining, a two-floor spa, a lounge, and a café. And the rooms are massive.

SHINJUKU AND WESTERN TOKYO
新宿

¥20,000-30,000

BNA HOTEL KŌENJI

2-4-7-Kōenjikita, Suginami-ku; info@bna-hotel.com; www.bna-hotel.com; ¥21,000 d; take Chūō, Sōbu lines to Kōenji station, north exit

The BnA Hotel boutique hotel is the brainchild of the Bed & Art (BnA) Project, an initiative aimed at combining art and hospitality. Located in Kōenji, a countercultural hub west of Shinjuku, the hotel pays a portion of all proceeds to the artists who have poured their energy into the rooms, which are works of eccentric, graphics-driven art. The check-in desk also functions as a café and bar where local creatives congregate, and a gallery complete with DJ setup is found on the basement level. Note that there are only two rooms, so book well in advance if this concept sounds intriguing.

GRACERY SHINJUKU

1-19-1 Kabukichō, Shinjuku-ku; tel. 03/6833-2489; http://shinjuku.gracery.com; ¥25,000 d; take Yamanote line to Shinjuku Station, east exit

The Gracery Shinjuku is for Godzilla fans. A 12-meter (39-foot) statue of the monster bellows and exhales smoke on the hour noon-8pm on the hotel's 8th-floor terrace. Set in the heart of Shinjuku's Kabukichō entertainment district, the 30-floor tower offers guests at the higher levels impressive views of Tokyo—just like the monster would have. The rooms, of which there are almost 1,000, are small but well designed. For serious fans, there's a room with a statue of the creature inside.

Over ¥40,000

★ PARK HYATT TOKYO

3-7-1-2 Nishi-Shinjuku, Shinjuku-Ku; tel. 03/5322-1234; http://tokyo.park.hyatt.com; ¥144,600 d; take Ōedo line to Tochōmae station, exit A4

Park Hyatt Tokyo is a rock-star hotel that owes much of its fame to Sofia Coppola's 2003 film *Lost in Translation,* staring Bill Murray as jaded action star Bob Harris, fresh in Tokyo to film a whisky commercial. It's hard not to visualize scenes from the movie when passing through the lobby, taking a dip in the pool, or perhaps most of all, having drinks in the supremely atmospheric New York Bar. Clean lines and minimalist decor imbue the hotel with understated elegance, and Mount Fuji can be glimpsed on clear days.

SHIBUYA
渋谷

Under ¥10,000

WISE OWL HOSTELS SHIBUYA

4-9-10 Aobodai, Meguro-ku; tel. 03/5738-0180; http://wiseowlhostels.com; ¥5,000 single bunk bed in mixed dorm; ¥10,315 twin bunk bed in private room; take Den-en-toshi line to Ikejiri-Ōhashi Station, north exit

Wise Owl Hostels comes with all the hipster amenities: artisanal coffee, an organic restaurant, and a bar. It's also convenient, with a wide range of sleeping arrangements for backpackers, couples, and families on a budget, all within walking distance of Shibuya, Nakameguro, and Daikanyama. Wooden walls and black-out blinds ensure maximum privacy for dorm beds, and all mattresses are high-quality. Free Wi-Fi is available throughout—not a bad package for the price.

¥20,000-30,000

SHIBUYA GRANBELL HOTEL

15-17 Sakuragaoka-cho, Shibuya-ku; tel. 03/5457-2681; www.granbellhotel.jp; ¥21,700 d; take Yamanote line to Shibuya station, south exit

Located just a stone's throw from Shibuya Station, the Shibuya Granbell Hotel is a good option for those on a midrange budget who want to be near the action. Room design is several cuts above a standard budget hotel, thanks to the involvement of the same company responsible for decking out the fashionable Claska. Think funky pop-art prints adorning curtains, minimalist color schemes, and appliances with a hip edge. Top-floor suites can be booked for longer-term stays. Free Wi-Fi is available in all rooms, which is a good thing given the hotel's popularity among young movers and shakers.

EBISU AND AROUND

恵比寿

¥30,000-40,000

CLASKA

1-3-18 Chūō-cho, Meguro-ku; tel. 03/3719-8121; www.claska.com/en; ¥30,250 d; take Tōkyū Tōyoko line to Gakugei Daigaku station, east exit

Design is the key word at Claska, where Japanese elements infuse each of the 20 rooms. Galleries, art studios, a shop, and event spaces are found on some of the floors, and the rooftop is graced by a terrace. A ground-floor restaurant serves Japanese and European fare, and some of the rooms can be reserved on a weekly basis for longer-term guests. The one downside is that it's a bit far at around 2 km (1.25 mi) from the nearest station, Meguro, so guests may end up using taxis.

ROPPONGI AND AROUND

六本木

¥20,000-30,000

HOTEL S ROPPONGI

1-11-6 Nishi-Azabu, Minato-ku; tel. 03/5771-2469; http://hr-roppongi.jp; ¥27,045 d; take Hibiya line to Roppongi Station, exit 2

Sleek Japanese aesthetics in many of the rooms and a shared ground-floor lounge with computers, periodicals, and art books give Hotel S Roppongi a sophisticated sheen. The well-designed hotel shares space with serviced apartments and restaurants. The Zen suite comes with a round bathtub made of Hinoki cypress. Located a stone's throw from Nishi-Azabu crossing, a diverse range of eateries and nightlife options are close at hand. The only drawback is that it's about a 10-minute walk from the nearest train station, Roppongi.

Over ¥40,000

★ HOTEL NEW OTANI

4-1 Kioi-cho, Chiyoda-ku; tel. 03/3265-1111; www.newotani.co.jp/en/tokyo; ¥45,980 d; take Ginza, Marunouchi lines to Akasaka-Mitsuke Station, exit 7

One of the biggest hotels in Japan, the Hotel New Otani is like a small city with a long, colorful history. It was used as the backdrop for the corporate villain's HQ in the 1965 James Bond film *You Only Live Twice*. There are more than 30 places to wine and dine, a plethora of gift shops, fashion boutiques, a spa, florist, supermarket, even a dentist and a doctor. The high point is the 400-year-old, 10-acre garden brimming with trees, flowers, koi ponds, and a surprisingly large waterfall. One drawback: the swimming pool is open in summer only.

ANDAZ

1-23-4, Toranomon, Minato-ku; tel. 03/6830-1234; https://tokyo.andaz.hyatt.com; ¥115,515 d; take Ginza line to Toranomon Station, exit 4

Atop Tokyo's second tallest building and most recent skyscraper development project, Toranomon Hills, the Andaz is notable for its superb views and rooftop bar that hosts a variety of seasonal events. Chic, contemporary Japanese flourishes, such as lanterns and washi

1
2
3
4
503
5

paper dividers grace the lounge. And thanks to the hotel's boutique sensibility, there's no need to visit a check-in desk; instead, friendly staff wielding small electronic tablets are happy to serve you anywhere you may meet. The area may feel too business-like for some, but it's set to undergo a significant sprucing-up by 2020.

THE RITZ-CARLTON TOKYO

Tokyo Midtown, 9-7-1 Akasaka, Minato-ku; tel. 03/3423-8000; www.ritzcarlton.com; ¥193,00 d; take Ōedo, Hibiya lines to Roppongi Station, exit 8, or Chiyoda line to Nogizaka Station, exit 3

The Ritz-Carlton Tokyo is a five-star gem in the center of bustling Roppongi. The luxury property occupies the upper floors of Tokyo Midtown, the city's tallest building, giving the rooms sweeping views of the city and Mount Fuji. Modern design elements, from chandeliers with an edge to large works of contemporary art, and incorporations of marble and dark wood throughout give the hotel a luxurious ambience. Expansive rooms offer guests more than 50 square meters (538 square feet) of space—large indeed by Tokyo standards. Dining options range from French to *kaiseki,* and afternoon tea is served in the soaring lobby where piano music drifts in the air. The exceptional staff cater to any need that may arise.

ASAKUSA
浅草

Under ¥10,000

BUNKA HOSTEL TOKYO

1-13-5 Asakusa, Taitō-ku; tel. 03/5806-3444, http://bunkahostel.jp; ¥2,555 single bunk bed in mixed dorm; take Tsukuba Express to Asakusa Station, exit 4

Bunka Hostel Tokyo appeals to backpackers who want a bit more comfort. Housed in a renovated office building in the heart of Asakusa, the hostel has options ranging from bunk beds to family rooms. It also offers a shared dining room, free Wi-Fi, and an *izakaya* on the first floor, open to guests and non-guests alike.

1: exterior of the Park Hyatt Tokyo **2:** Kozue at the Park Hyatt **3:** Tokyo at night **4:** capsule hotel

NUI. HOSTEL & BAR LOUNGE

2-14-13 Kuramae, Taitō-ku; tel. 03/6240-9854; https://backpackersjapan.co.jp; ¥3,500 single bunk bed in mixed dorm, ¥9,000 twin bunk bed in private room; take Ōedo line to Kuramae Station, exit A7

Nui. Hostel & Bar Lounge is roughly a 15-minute walk from Asakusa, set in the trendy district of Kuramae. This is another hostel with all the right touches, including a first-floor bar-café that draws guests and non-guests together and creates a nice social buzz. Mixed dorms and doubles share bathrooms and a kitchen, and Wi-Fi is free. Common areas close at midnight.

¥10,000-20,000

WIRED HOTEL ASAKUSA

2-16-2 Asakusa, Taitō-ku; tel. 03/5830-7931; http://wiredhotel.com; ¥16,000 d; take Ginza line to Asakusa Station, exit A

With design and branding by a Portland-based creative outfit, Wired Hotel Asakusa ticks all the artisanal boxes. On the first floor you'll find a café-bar open to all and serving soy-based snacks, naturally. Single rooms, doubles, and even a penthouse suite ensure that all types of travelers' needs are met. Decor feels more New York studio than old-school Tokyo, but this boutique hideaway is indeed in the middle of Asakusa, the heart of the city's old downtown district.

SUKEROKU NO YADO SADACHIYO

2-20-1 Asakusa, Taitō-ku; tel. 03/3842-6431; www.sadachiyo.co.jp/en; ¥18,800 d; take Ginza line to Asakusa, exit 1

Sukeroku no Yado Sadachiyo is a modern *ryokan* that does a great job at invoking the spirit of Edo, with its staff wearing kimonos and classic *ryokan-style* rooms, complete with tatami-mat floors, paper shoji sliding screens, antiques, and alcoves with paintings of geisha and samurai. Guests sleep on futons and have the option to don a *yukata.* While there are both wooden and stone communal baths, rooms also have private bathrooms with a shower and toilet. Traditional Japanese meals are served during breakfast and dinner. It's a short walk from Sensō-ji, to boot.

¥20,000-30,000

★ GATE HOTEL KAMINARIMON

2-16-11, Kaminarimon, Taitō-ku; tel. 03/6263-8233; www.gate-hotel.jp; ¥28,614 d; take Ginza line to Asakusa Station, exit 2

Located just across from Sensō-ji's iconic Kaminarimon Gate, the Gate Hotel Kaminarimon hotel designed by Shigeru Uchida, a renowned designer whose mastery extends from architectural interiors to furniture and urban planning, offers a stylish option in the heart of old Tokyo. The lobby shares the 13th floor with an eatery specializing in French fusion cuisine. One floor up, there's also a terrace and bar. May-October guests can take an elevator to the rooftop for excellent views of Tokyo Skytree and surroundings. For those seeking a good option in the old part of town, this hotel offers great bang for buck.

UENO AND AROUND
上野

¥10,000-20,000

RYOKAN SAWANOYA

2-3-11 Yanaka, Taitō-ku; tel. 03/3822-2251; www.sawanoya.com; ¥11,880 d; take Chiyoda line to Nezu Station, exit 1

Ryokan Sawanoya is another great Yanaka-area inn. At this family-run *ryokan,* the traditional touches are all in place: tatami floors, Japanese-style ceramic and cypress-wood baths (both shared and private in some rooms), paper lanterns, futons in place of beds, and traditional dance performances at select times. The affable owners are happy to help, providing a slew of travel information, local recommendations, and bicycle rentals to guests. What's more, there is English-language information throughout the *ryokan,* educating guests on such topics as bathing etiquette.

¥20,000-30,000

★ HANARE

3-10-25 Hagiso, Yanaka, Taitō-ku; tel. 03/5834-7301; http://hanare.hagiso.jp; ¥22,000 d; take Chiyoda line to Sendagi, exit 2

Hanare is a gem in the heart of Yanaka, one of Tokyo's most charming neighborhoods. This *ryokan* is run by wonderful staff who encourage guests to get out and experience the city. They're always armed with suggestions for the best shrines, public baths, bike rentals, mom-and-pop restaurants, and traditional craft shops. All five rooms have tatami floors, and the bathroom is shared. The inn shares a building with a café, a gift shop, and a gallery.

Information and Services

TOURIST INFORMATION

The easiest way to gather information is from your hotel's front desk, but if you're hitting the pavement and need to stop somewhere for additional help, there are a number of tourist information centers scattered around Tokyo. Thankfully, many are located in areas you'll likely pass through as you explore.

In the Marunouchi area, you'll find the Japan National Tourism Organization's **JNTO Tourist Information Center** (3-3-1 Marunouchi, Shin-Tokyo Building, Chiyoda-ku; tel. 03/3201-3331; www.jnto.go.jp; 9am-5pm daily; take Chiyoda line to Nijubashimae, exit 1). Here you can get information not only on Tokyo but also on Japan as a whole. There are also branches at Narita Airport terminals 1 and 2. Also in Marunouchi is the **JR East Travel Service Center** (1-9-1 Marunouchi, Tokyo Station, Chiyoda-ku; www.jreast.co.jp/e/customer_support/service_center_tokyo.html; take JR Yamanote line to Tokyo, Marunouchi North exit). Here you can get English information and book getaways within Japan.

In Shinjuku, you can pick up information in English on various practicalities at the **Tokyo Metropolitan Government Building Tourist Information Center** (2-8-1 Nishi-Shinjuku, Shinjuku-ku, Tokyo Metropolitan Government Building 1F; tel. 03/5321-3077; 9:30am-6:30pm daily; take Ōedo line to Tochomae, exit A4). The **Shinjuku Tourist Information Center** is outside the South East Exit of JR Shinjuku Station (3-37-2 Shinjuku, Shinjukuku; tel. 03/3344-3160; www.kanko-shinjuku.jp/office/-/index.html; 10am-7pm daily).

And for help with navigating the eastern districts of Ueno and Asakusa, your best bet is the **Asakusa Culture Tourist Information Center** (2-18-9 Kaminarimon, Taitō-ku; tel. 03/3842-5566; 9am-8pm daily; take Ginza line to Asakusa, exit 2).

BANKS AND CURRENCY EXCHANGE

ATMs are ubiquitous throughout Tokyo, from convenience stores to banks. To the chagrin of many travelers, however, they often don't cooperate with foreign-issued cards, even when they bear the logos of Visa, MasterCard, American Express, Plus, or any other major card.

For currency exchange, most banks such as **Mizuho, Mitsubishi UFJ,** and **Sumitomo Mitsui** do the job, but only on weekdays 9am-3pm. If you need to exchange currency, it's best to handle it upon arriving at an international airport. You can also exchange money in Marunouchi at **Exchangers** (1F Shin-Tokyo Bldg.; 3-1 Marunouchi, Chiyoda-ku; tel. 03/6269-9466; www.exchangers.co.jp; 10am-4pm daily).

POSTAL SERVICES

Japan's postal service is efficient and dependable, and Tokyo has local branches in every district, typically open 9am-5pm Monday-Friday and Saturday 9am-noon. Sending packages via airmail to the United States normally takes about one week, while surface deliveries require a month or two.

For the best service, go to any ward's central post office, which will have English-speaking staff. These larger main branches also tend to have longer hours of operation, such as 9am-9pm on weekdays and 9am-7pm on weekends. Your best bet is **Tokyo Central Post Office** (2-7-2 Marunouchi, Chiyoda-ku; tel. 03/3217-5231; Tokyo Station, Marunouchi South Exit), which operates 24 hours.

Also note that **FedEx** (tel. 0120-003/200 toll free; www.fedex.com) has locations dotted around the city's major business districts. Rates aren't cheap, but this is a reliable way to send a package overseas.

INTERNET ACCESS

It's a common complaint that Tokyo has a dearth of Wi-Fi in public spaces like cafés compared with other cities. There's truth to this, but the situation is improving. Signal strength varies, but Wi-Fi is available on subway station platforms, in some convenience stores, and even on the streets of some neighborhoods. Many shops and attractions provide Wi-Fi for customers as well. Starbucks provides Wi-Fi after completing a free registration, but the connection can be patchy. Further, most hotels provide Wi-Fi for guests, sometimes for a fee, or at least have shared computers connected to the Internet in the lobby.

Free Wi-Fi Japan (www.flets.com) allows you to connect at various hot spots around Tokyo after registering and getting log-in credentials online or at a tourist center. **Travel Japan Wi-Fi** (http://japanfreewifi.com) allows access at some 200,000 spots around Japan for iOS and Android devices after registering online. There's also **Japan Connected** (www.ntt-bp.net), an app that lets you connect to a broad range of hot spots around the country without having to log in to each one.

These options are not recommended for good, steady connectivity though. The best way to ensure you remain connected is by renting a pocket Wi-Fi either at the airport on arrival—there are numerous providers with clear English signage—or via **Japan**

Wireless (http://japan-wireless.com), which ships devices to travelers who have already checked into their hotels.

There are also Internet cafés, which will have computer booths that you can typically rent in 30-minute or one-hour increments.

PHARMACIES AND MEDICAL SERVICES

For emergency fire and ambulance services, dial 119. Most operators don't speak English, but will transfer you to someone who does. A multilingual service that can connect you to English-speaking doctors of various kinds is the **Tokyo Metropolitan Health and Medical Information Center** (tel. 03/5285-8181; www.himawari.metro.tokyo.jp; 9am-8pm daily). Call the number and request English assistance. They will put you in touch with an operator who can help.

Aside from seeking assistance from one of these services, English-speaking physicians are limited. For emergency room services with English-speaking care, go to **St. Luke's International Hospital** (9-1 Akashi-cho, Chūō-ku; tel. 03/3541-5151; http://hospital.luke.ac.jp; take Hibiya line to Tsukiji, exit 3).

DIPLOMATIC SERVICES

The **US Embassy and Consulate** (1-10-5 Akasaka, Minato-ku; tel. 03/3224-5000; http://jp.usembassy.gov; take Namboku line to Tameike-Sanno, exit 13) is open weekdays 8:30am-5:30pm.

The **Embassy of Canada to Japan** (7-3-38 Akasaka, Minato-ku; tel. 03/5412-6200; www.canadainternational.gc.ca/japan-japon; take Ginza, Ōedo, Hanzōmon lines to Aoyama-Itchōme Station, exit 4) is open weekdays 9am-5:30pm.

The **British Embassy Tokyo** (No. 1 Ichiban-chō, Chiyoda-ku; tel. 03/5211-1100; www.gov.uk/world/organisations/british-embassy-tokyo; take Hanzōmon line to Hanzōmon Station, exit 4) is open weekdays 9:30am-4:30pm.

The **Australian Embassy Tokyo** (2-1-14 Mita, Minato-ku; tel. 03/5232-4111; https://japan.embassy.gov.au; take Ōedo, Nanboku lines to Azabu-jūban Station, exit 2, or take Mita, Asakusa lines to Mita Station, exit A3) is open weekdays 9am-12:30pm and 1:30pm-5pm.

The **New Zealand Embassy, Tokyo** (20-40 Kamiyama-chō, Shibuya-ku; tel. 03/3467-2271; www.nzembassy.com/japan; take Chiyoda line to Yoyogi-kōen Station, exit 1) is open weekdays 9am-5:30pm.

The **South African Embassy in Japan** (Hanzōmon First Building 4F, 1-4 Kojimachi, Chiyoda-ku; tel. 03/3265-3366; www.sajapan.org; take Hanzōmon line to Hanzōmon Station, exit 3a) is open weekdays 9am-5:30pm.

USEFUL WEBSITES

Tokyo Cheapo (www.tokyocheapo.com) is a great resource packed with tips on how to make your yen go further in Tokyo.

TimeOut Tokyo (www.timeout.jp/en/tokyo) offers extensive listings of the best events, restaurants, bars, and more. Check the calendar for events that will be taking place when you're going to be in Tokyo. They also publish a free quarterly print edition.

Savvy Tokyo (https://savvytokyo.com) is a lifestyle website geared toward women living in Japan, operated by the same media outfit that runs Gaijinpot. Another solid resource.

Tokyo Art Beat (www.tokyoartbeat.com) is the best website for keeping tabs on happenings in Tokyo's art scene. There are extensive gallery and museum listings.

Go Tokyo (www.gotokyo.org/en) offers information on things to do, shopping, transportation, accommodations and just about anything else you'll need for your time in the capital.

Tokyo Dross (http://tokyodross.blogspot.jp) provides extensive gig listings with an underground bent. This is a source you should check out if you're keen to experience the best musical offerings in the city, from electronic to punk.

Tokyo Jazz Site (http://tokyojazzsite.com) is a fantastic website dedicated to exploring the capital's deep jazz scene, from old-school cafés with extraordinary sound systems to underground haunts well off the tourist path.

Transportation

GETTING THERE

Air

Tokyo is served by **Narita Airport** (tel. 0476-34-8000; www.narita-airport.jp) and **Haneda Airport** (03/6428-0888; www.tokyo-airport-bldg.co.jp/en). Narita is about 60 km (37 miles) east of the city, and Haneda is south of the city near the Tokyo Bay. Haneda, Japan's busiest airport, is undeniably more convenient than Narita, but more international flights come and go from the latter.

Note that Narita has three terminals, with terminals one and two handling international flights and terminal three catering to budget airlines. Be careful to confirm the right terminal for your departing flight; going to the wrong terminal is a common mistake and can result in lost time. If you accidentally go to the wrong terminal, don't panic; free shuttle buses run between the three terminals every 15-30 minutes (7am-9:30pm), departing from the ground floor of each one. If anything is unclear, there are information desks with English-speaking staff all across the airport who can point you in the right direction.

Whether arriving via Narita or Haneda, if you plan to get to Tokyo by train, it may be worth sending your baggage to your destination in Tokyo via one of many courier services available at both airports, as navigating the trains with luggage can be challenging. Simply inquire about the nearest **luggage courier service** at an information desk if you don't see one. Signage is clear and in English. If you choose to use such a service, ask the staff at the kiosk about how to send your baggage back to the airport on your return trip.

Narita

FROM NARITA AIRPORT

The trip into Tokyo from Narita by bus takes 1.5-2 hours, depending on traffic. By train, it takes 36-80 minutes, depending on which hub is your destination.

BUS

Taking the bus from Narita is straightforward, with tickets being sold at counters in the arrivals hall. One of the most popular bus services is the **Airport Limousine Bus** (www.limousinebus.co.jp/en; ¥3,200 adults, ¥1,600 children), which runs at scheduled times to a number of major hotels and major train stations in the capital. The average journey takes around 1.5 hours, or a bit more in heavy traffic. Tickets can be purchased in all terminals, and most staff speak English. This service is particularly good for those staying at a hotel that is directly linked to the Airport Limousine's route, or at least very near a station where the bus stops.

Another bus option from Narita is the **Keisei Bus Tokyo Shuttle** (www.keisei-bus.co.jp/inbound/tokyoshuttle/en/; ¥1,000), which is a good budget option. This service runs every 20 minutes 6am-11pm. Tickets are sold at the Keisei Bus Counter in the arrivals lobby, with one bus stop at terminal 1 and two bus stops at terminal 2. The list of destinations isn't as extensive as it is for the Limousine Bus, but the price is lower and it gets the job done by taking passengers to Tokyo Station, Sukiyabashi crossing in the heart of Ginza, and Shinonomeshako in Koto-ku, east of Odaiba. If you happen to be flying late at night or in the early morning, it's worth noting that Keisei buses also run from Tokyo Station to terminals 2 and 3 less frequently from 11pm-6am (¥2,000). Inquire at the ticket counter or check the website for more information.

One more option worth considering is **Access Narita** (tel. 0120-600-366; www.accessnarita.jp; 7:25am-10:45pm; ¥1,000 adults, ¥500 children 6-12, free for children 5 and under), which is available at all three terminals and allows you to buy a ticket as you board the bus. The bus runs three times an hour and takes passengers to either Tokyo Station or Sukiyabashi crossing in Ginza.

When you leave the airport, look for the blue sign for Access Narita and head there. From terminal 1, go to the South Wing exit and then find bus stop no. 31; for terminal 2, go to either the North Exit 3, bus stop no. 2, or Domestic Flights exit, bus stop no. 19; and for terminal 3, head to bus stop no.2 near the bus shelter area.

TRAIN

By far one of the simplest options for reaching Tokyo from the airport by train is the **Narita Express** (www.jreast.co.jp/e/nex; 7:45am-9:45pm; adults ¥3,070-3,250, roughly have for children). The Narita Express (N'EX) runs to a host of stations downtown, including Tokyo, Shinjuku, Shibuya, Ikebukuro, and Shinagawa. All seats are reserved and can be purchased at an airport N'EX counter, with trains leaving approximately every 30 minutes. One-way fares start from ¥3,070 to Tokyo Station (1 hour), but the best deal is the return-trip fare of ¥4,070 for adults and ¥2,030 for children under the age of 12, available to foreign travelers, which must be used within two weeks. Note that JR passes are valid for the leg of the journey covered by JR, as long as the seats for the journey have been reserved at a JR ticket counter.

The **Keisei Skyliner** (www.keisei.co.jp; 7:30am-10pm) is actually quicker than N'EX, but the destinations are more limited, with half-hourly trains making the roughly 40-minute trip to either Ueno or Nippori station. One-way tickets for both destinations are ¥2,520 and must be reserved at the Keisei ticket counter in either Narita terminal 1 or 2. After arriving at either Ueno or Nippori, you'll then have the option of transferring to the JR Yamanote line or, in the case of Ueno, taking the subway Ginza or Hibiya lines. Note that Keisei offers a deal called the Skyliner & Tokyo Subway Ticket that allows travelers to purchase a one-way or return ticket on the Skyliner along with receiving a subway pass for between one and three days. If your destination happens to be in the northeastern part of Tokyo, the Skyliner makes sense, but the N'EX offers easier access to other parts of the city.

For those on a tighter budget, the **Keisei Main line** (6:30am-10:30pm) offers a rapid train every 20 minutes (¥1,030) that takes about 65 minutes to reach Nippori and just over 70 minutes to reach Ueno at the northeastern corner of the JR Yamanote line, both for the same price. This line essentially takes the same path as the Skyliner, but makes extra stops. Another option offered by Keisei is the **Narita Sky Access Express,** (5:40am-11pm; ¥1,290-1,520), which runs every 40 minutes and follows the same route as the Keisei Main line, but veers southwest at Aoto Station and travels to Nihonbashi Station (59 minutes), Shimbashi (62 minutes), and Shinagawa (72 minutes), all of which are connected to the convenient Ginza line, among others.

TAXI

Taking a taxi from Narita is, simply put, not economical. But if money is no object, you can take a cab at a fixed rate of ¥20,000-22,000, with a surcharge of 20 percent 10pm-5am, to most places in downtown Tokyo (60-90 minutes). Taxis from the airport can be paid with credit card. To catch a taxi, head to taxi stand no. 15, just outside Terminal 1, south exit S2. For more information, see www.narita-airport.jp/en/access/taxi.

From Haneda Airport

Although the city is closer to Haneda, many of the flights coming into the airport arrive late at night, which means trains into Tokyo may have already stopped running. By bus, the journey is 30-90 minutes, depending on traffic, and by train, it takes as little as 15 minutes. The good news is that buses run late into the night from Haneda, and taxis are significantly more affordable than from Narita.

BUS

Haneda has similar bus options, though the ride is shorter and fares are cheaper. The simplest option by bus is the **Airport Limousine**

Bus (www.limousinebus.co.jp/en; ¥950-1,250 adults depending on destination, half-price for children). Some of the hubs the bus links to include Shinjuku, Shibuya, Roppongi, and Ginza. Travel times are 20-90 minutes, depending on traffic and the distance of the destination. Late-night options include buses that run from Haneda to **Shinjuku Bus Terminal** (12:20am, 1am) and Shibuya Station (12:15am, 12:50am, 2:20am). Note that prices double midnight-5am.

TRAIN

Making the trip into Tokyo from Haneda Airport by train is an even briefer affair, with the **Tokyo Monorail Haneda Airport Line** (www.tokyo-monorail.co.jp/english; 5am-midnight; ¥500 one-way) running local, rapid, and express service trains between Haneda Airport and JR Hamamatsucho Station on the southeastern side of the JR Yamanote line. Trains run every 5-10 minutes, and the ride to JR Hamamatsucho Station only takes about 15 minutes.

Another rail option from Haneda to Tokyo is the **Keikyū Airport Express** (tel. 03/5789-8686; www.haneda-tokyo-access.com/en; 5:30am-midnight; ¥300-500), which stops at Haneda's domestic and international terminals. This train runs several times hourly to Shinagawa Station in about 15 minutes, and then some of the trains continue on along the Toei Asakusa subway line to stations such as Ginza and Asakusa. Aside from the Asakusa line, Shinagawa is a major hub with a plethora of lines linked to it, including the Yamaote line, Yokosuka line, and the Keihin-Tohoku line, among others.

TAXI

It's more reasonable to take a taxi from Haneda than from Narita Airport (though it's still not cheap), with taxis running to some of Tokyo's major hubs for ¥5,600 (to **Ginza**) at the lower end of the scale, up to ¥8,500 (to **Ikebukuro**) at the higher end. Note that a surcharge of 20 percent applies for all rides 10pm-5am. Taxis from the airport can be paid for with credit card. You can get a taxi at the **first-floor curbside area,** reachable by escalator from the arrival lobby on the second floor (www.haneda-airport.jp/inter/en/access/taxi.html).

Train

Tokyo is by far the most connected city in Japan when it comes to train travel. There are three main train stations in the city that travelers arrive at when traveling by *shinkansen* (bullet train), which is the simplest, most pleasant and most efficient way of reaching the city by train.

Tokyo Station is the final station for bullet trains traveling to the capital from all over the country, whether from **Kyoto** (average 2 hours 15 minutes; ¥14,170), **Shin-Osaka** (average 2.5 hours; ¥14,720), **Hiroshima** (4 hours; ¥19,440), **Hakata** (Fukuoka's main station; 5 hours; ¥23,390), **Nagoya** (1 hour 40 minutes; ¥11,300), **Kanazawa** (3 hours; ¥14,380), **Sendai** (1.5 hours; ¥11,410), or Hakodate's **Shin-Hakodate-Hokuto Station** (6 hours 15 minutes; ¥23,430).

Shinagawa Station, on the south side of downtown, is one stop before Tokyo for bullet trains coming from **Kyoto, Osaka, Hiroshima, Kyūshū,** and all other stops to the west.

Meanwhile, the hub of **Ueno** on the northeast side of town, which also serves as a *shinkansen* terminal, receives trains coming from the northeast (**Tohoku** and **Hokkaido**) before they finally reach Tokyo.

Generally speaking, Tokyo Station is a safe bet for your terminus of choice, as the station is also linked to the **Yamanote line,** which runs in a loop around Tokyo's downtown, and the **Chūō** and **Sōbu** lines, which run east-west through the city, as well as the **Marunouchi** subway line. That said, Ueno, serviced by the **Yamanote, Hibiya,** and **Ginza** lines, may be worth considering as your terminus if you're heading in the city's north or east, and Shinagawa, on the

Yamanote and **Toei Asakusa line,** may be a good pick if you're heading to somewhere in the city's south or west.

While it's possible to make the trip on a wide range of train types operating at the local level—local, express, rapid, limited express, etc.—in most cases, doing so will increase cost and complexity exponentially, with frequent transfers.

Bus

If you're arriving in Tokyo domestically by land, thanks to the **JR Highway Bus** (03/3844-1950; www.jrbuskanto.co.jp) and a few other highway bus companies you can travel between the capital and other major cities around Japan overnight for less than you'd pay for a train ticket. But you get what you pay for, as journeys are significantly prolonged on the road. Further, some buses have toilets, while others don't, although all make stops for restroom breaks.

JR Highway Bus terminals in Tokyo are located near the new south exit of **Shinjuku Station** (6:20am-midnight) and the Yaesu South Exit of **Tokyo Station** (6am-12:30am). As there's no easy English-language ticketing website for JR Highway Bus, your best bet is to inquire about tickets directly at the JR ticket window at one of these terminals.

Perhaps the most popular bus route into Tokyo is from **Kyoto,** from where JR operates night buses that depart daily, usually from midnight. The trip takes around 7.5 hours and costs ¥9,000-9,500. Another popular trip is from **Osaka,** which takes about 8 hours and costs ¥9,500-10,000.

Among the numerous private bus operators, discount player **Willer Express** (https://willerexpress.com/en), stands out, offering some trips between Tokyo and Kyoto or Osaka for as little as ¥3,000. A sampling of other routes includes **Kanazawa** to Tokyo (8.5 hours, from ¥6,900) and **Nagoya** to Tokyo (6 hours, ¥5,500). Conveniently, Willer Express has an English-language website that provides all essential details and allows online booking.

On the website of **Kosoku Bus** (www.kosokubus.com/en), you'll find bus trips for as little as ¥2,800 (Osaka to Tokyo) or ¥2,980 (Kyoto to Tokyo). This website allows you to search for and purchase tickets in English for a variety of routes and providers around the country. Other routes you can book seats for on the website include journeys to Tokyo from **Hiroshima** (13 hours, from ¥8,600), **Nagoya** (5.5 hours, ¥3,000), and **Sendai** (6 hours, from ¥2,800).

Note that private operators often start and end journeys at terminals elsewhere in Tokyo, beyond the highway bus terminals at Shinjuku and Tokyo stations. Just be sure to know how to navigate to or from the departure or arrival point, wherever it is in the city, before setting off. Also note that Tokyo is a good jumping-off point for highway bus journeys to elsewhere in the country. To get a sense of the kinds of trips that can be taken from Shinjuku Station's bus terminal, for example, visit http://shinjuku-busterminal.co.jp/en/search.

Car

Renting a car might make sense for some journeys beyond the capital into or from more remote areas that may be less accessible, or completely inaccessible, by train. That said, rather than driving all the way to Tokyo from somewhere far-flung, a more likely scenario will involve traveling first out of Tokyo to some regional hub, then renting a car there to travel farther afield. Once you've driven your way through the more remote leg of your journey, your best bet will be to then drop off your rental car at the nearest major train hub, then simply go to Tokyo by rail.

GETTING AROUND

Tokyo has, bar none, one of the best public transport systems of any major global city. Buses, trains, subway lines, and taxis shuttle millions around the city daily. There are also growing numbers of cyclists and plenty of people putting their drivers licenses to use, too. But for the vast majority of travelers, the city's vast network of above-ground trains and subway lines are sufficient for all of their transportation needs.

Train

While Tokyo's train system can feel daunting, don't fret. It's actually not that difficult to navigate once you've grasped a few key things. For starters, the two most important above-ground JR lines (covered by the Japan Rail Pass) for most travelers to the city will be the oval-shaped **Yamanote Line** that runs around the core of the city, and the **Chūō Line** that shoots directly through the Yamanote Line, linking Tokyo's eastern and western suburbs. Key stations on the Yamanote Line include **Tokyo, Shinagawa, Shibuya, Shinjuku,** and **Ikebukuro,** while major stations on the Chūō Line, from east to west, include **Tokyo, Shinjuku,** and the western suburb of **Mitaka.** Most trains run roughly from around 5am to midnight, with some running a bit later than that.

There are a number of private lines that you may occasionally need to use to reach some more local stations. Some key ones to be aware of include the **Keio-Inokashira Line,** which runs between Shibuya and Kichijōji with Shimokitazawa in between; the **Tōkyū Tōyoko Line**, linking Shibuya to Daikanyama, Nakameguro, and, much farther along, Yokohama; the **Odakyu Line,** which links Shinjuku to Shimokitazawa; and the **Yurikamome Line,** which links Odaiba to the rest of downtown across Tokyo Bay. Again, the Suica or Pasmo can be used freely on these lines. Of course, you can also simply purchase a ticket too.

TICKETS

While the easiest way to navigate different train and subway lines is by simply getting a **Suica** (www.jreast.co.jp/e) or **Pasmo** (www.pasmo.co.jp/en) card as soon as you begin to use Tokyo's public transport system, it's also possible to buy paper tickets for these trains as you go. To do this, calculate your price based on the fare chart on the wall above ticket machines at all stations. Generally speaking, single fares within Tokyo for the JR lines range from ¥130 to around ¥390, with fares increasing if you ride beyond the bounds of Tokyo proper. If your route involves transferring to the subway or to other private lines, this will also raise the total fare. There will usually be an English-language station breakdown, but the easiest way to calculate fares is by planning ahead, using the website **Hyperdia** (www.hyperdia.com), which allows you to calculate rail fares anywhere in the country, adjusting for date and either the intended time of departure or arrival.

If you plan on traveling heavily within the city for a day, using a mix of JR lines, Toei lines, and Tokyo Metro lines, there is a special ticket called the **Tokyo Combination Ticket** (www.jreast.co.jp/e/pass/tokyo_free.html; ¥1,590 adults, ¥800 children), which allows unlimited travel for one calendar day on all 13 subway lines, all JR East lines (excluding those with reserved seats), the Nippori-Toneri Liner, Tokyo Toei streetcars, and even the Toei Bus system. This ticket can be purchased through the ticket machines at some JR East reserved-seat ticket machines, JR Ticket Offices (Midori no Madoguchi), and the JR EAST Travel Service Centers, located next to the New South Gate Exit of Shinjuku Station, next to Marunouchi North Gate of Tokyo Station and near East Exit of Ikebukuro Station. This ticket can also be purchased at Tokyo Metro and Toei Subway stations, with some exceptions. Note that the ticket will not work outside Tokyo's core metropolitan area. For example, this means that it wouldn't cover travel to Mitaka, where the Ghibli Museum is located, as this is a stand-alone city within Tokyo Metropolis.

Subway

A total of 13 color-coded subway lines, operated by **Tokyo Metro** (www.tokyometro.jp/en) and **Toei** (www.kotsu.metro.tokyo.jp/eng), both government-run, crisscross the city. The fare for one-way journeys is

¥170-240 (¥90-120 for children) for Tokyo Metro lines, and ¥180-320 (¥90-160 for children) for Toei lines.

One thing to keep in mind is that changing between lines operated by Tokyo Metro and Toei requires a special transfer ticket, which can be slightly complicated for the uninitiated. The easiest way to handle all the tricky transfers between different rail lines is by purchasing either a **Suica** (www.jreast.co.jp/e) from a JR ticket machine or a **Pasmo** (www.pasmo.co.jp/en) from a Tokyo Metro ticket machine.

If you'll be using the Tokyo Metro system heavily over a 24-hour period, it's worth looking into the **Tokyo Metro 24-Hour Ticket** (www.tokyometro.jp/en; ¥600 adults, ¥300 children). You can buy this ticket at any Tokyo Metro station and use it for unlimited travel on any Tokyo Metro line. For even greater access, including both the Tokyo Metro and Toei subway lines, there's also a special deal called the **Common One-Day Ticket for Tokyo Metro & Toei Subway Lines** (www.tokyometro.jp/en; ¥900 adults, ¥450 children). This ticket allows unlimited travel on all subway lines for one calendar day, either on the day of purchase for a same-day ticket or for any day within six months of the date of purchase for the advance ticket option.

Bus

Bus stops dot every area of the city, with **Toei** (www.kotsu.metro.tokyo.jp/eng) buses linking every corner. No matter how far you ride, all fare is capped at ¥210 (¥110 for children). Simply hop aboard, drop your money (in coins) into the electronic box next to the driver's seat at the front of the bus and ride until your intended stop. If you've only got bills on hand, a machine that changes ¥1,000 notes is at the front of every bus, but you won't get any money back if you drop more than the required fare in coins into the box. While buses are plentiful and easy to use, the train and subway networks are so convenient that buses tend only to be necessary in special cases outside the city center where train lines may not reach.

Bicycle

Tokyo's streets are mercifully safe thanks to drivers' conscientiousness. While you should be cognizant of pedestrians, sidewalks around town are generally considered acceptable places to navigate a bicycle too. Some guesthouses and *ryokan* rent bikes to guests, and there are also a number of bike rental services around town.

Take a look at **Tokyobike Rentals Yanaka** (4-2-39 Yanaka Taitō-ku; tel. 03/5809-0980; https://tokyobikerentals.com; 10am-7pm Wed.-Mon.), a bicycle designer with a hipster bent located in Yanaka. Advance bookings are required via the website, which is bilingual, with a one-day rental priced at ¥3,000 and ¥1,500 for each extra day.

Taxi

Taxis in Tokyo are pricey, starting at ¥410 for the first 1.059 km (0.6 mi), after which the fare jumps ¥80 for each additional 237 meters (777 feet). Moreover, a surcharge of 20 percent is often applied 10pm-5am. Fares quickly reach ¥3,000 or potentially much more, depending on the destination. With rates like these, taxis rarely make economic sense unless you're splitting the fare with other passengers and not going too far. That said, they are an option for late-night rides after the train and subway lines stop running. Mercifully, the vast majority accept credit cards. There are a few taxi companies with English-speaking services, including **MK Taxi** (03/5547-5547; www.tokyomk.com) and **Nihon Kotsu** (03/5755-2336; www.nihon-kotsu.co.jp). For more information on taking taxis in Tokyo, see the website of the **Tokyo-Taxi Hire Association** (www.taxi-tokyo.or.jp).

Car

Driving a car in Tokyo rarely makes sense due to the oftentimes tricky network of one-way streets and significant difficulty and expense associated with finding parking. The excellent train and subway systems make driving unnecessary.

If you do plan to get around in a car, parking is only had at a premium, starting at ¥100-500 per 30 minutes, to upward of ¥2,800 for 12 hours, or more for 24 hours. The actual parking lots range from self-service lots to underground car parks, often attached to department stores or other large shops, and the very Japanese phenomenon of the parking tower, in which cars are mechanically lifted and lowered by attendants who effectively stack them in shelves.

You can find parking space, gauge the rates, and know whether there is any vacancy at www.parkme.com/tokyo-jp-parking. Beware that it's ill-advised to try and park beside the street if there is no parking meter present, as police sometimes patrol for illegally parked cars. Likewise, don't park in the lot of a restaurant or business where you're not actually a customer, which can result in a fine.

Boat

Tokyo Cruise (www.suijobus.co.jp/en; adults ¥210-1,720, roughly have for children) operates boats down the Sumida-gawa, starting from Asakusa in the north, with piers in locations around the Tokyo Bay area, including inside the park grounds of Hama-rikyū Onshi Teien, in Toyosu, and over in Odaiba Kaihin-kōen (Seaside Park). The boats run from 9:50am until about 6pm. Check the website for fares and timetables.

Around Tokyo

For visitors craving a break from the bustle of Tokyo, Japan's excellent public transport provides easy access to a number of destinations perfectly suited for a day trip or an overnight stay.

Only 30 minutes from Tokyo by train to the south, the cosmopolitan port city of Yokohama offers a fascinating look into Japan's history. After being near the scene of Commodore Perry's second arrival in 1854, Japan became open to trade and the city rose as an international port. The spirit of international exchange is strongly felt in its expansive Chinatown, too. After dark, the city's burgeoning craft beer and live jazz scenes offer the promise of a great night out.

For a dose of traditional culture and relaxation, head just south of Yokohama to the beachside town of Kamakura, Japan's first feudal

Highlights

Look for ★ to find recommended sights, activities, dining, and lodging.

★ **Barhopping in Yokohama:** Yokohama's accessible, low-key nightlife is mostly known for its craft beer and live jazz. Check out the neighborhoods of Kannai, Bashamichi, and Noge (page 174).

★ **Great Buddha at Kōtoku-in:** The temple of Kōtoku-in houses the famed bronze Daibutsu (Great Buddha), which stands 11.4 meters (37 feet) tall (page 181).

★ **Tōshō-gū:** Nikkō's colorful main shrine, built in the 17th century, is one of the most ornately decorated in Japan (page 188).

★ **Outdoor Adventure in Minakami:** This mountainous region north of Tokyo, pierced by the Tone River, provides ample options for outdoor adventure enthusiasts, from whitewater rafting in spring to canyoning in summer (page 195).

★ **Hakone Yuryō Onsen:** In a tranquil forest setting, this *onsen* features both communal and private baths, as well as a restaurant serving food cooked in a traditional Japanese sunken hearth (page 203).

★ **Mount Fuji:** Japan's most sacred peak looms larger in the national psyche than perhaps any other mountain on earth (page 210).

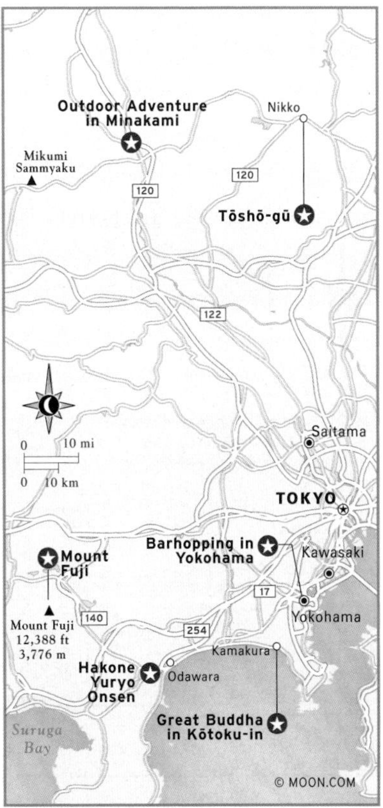

Around Tokyo

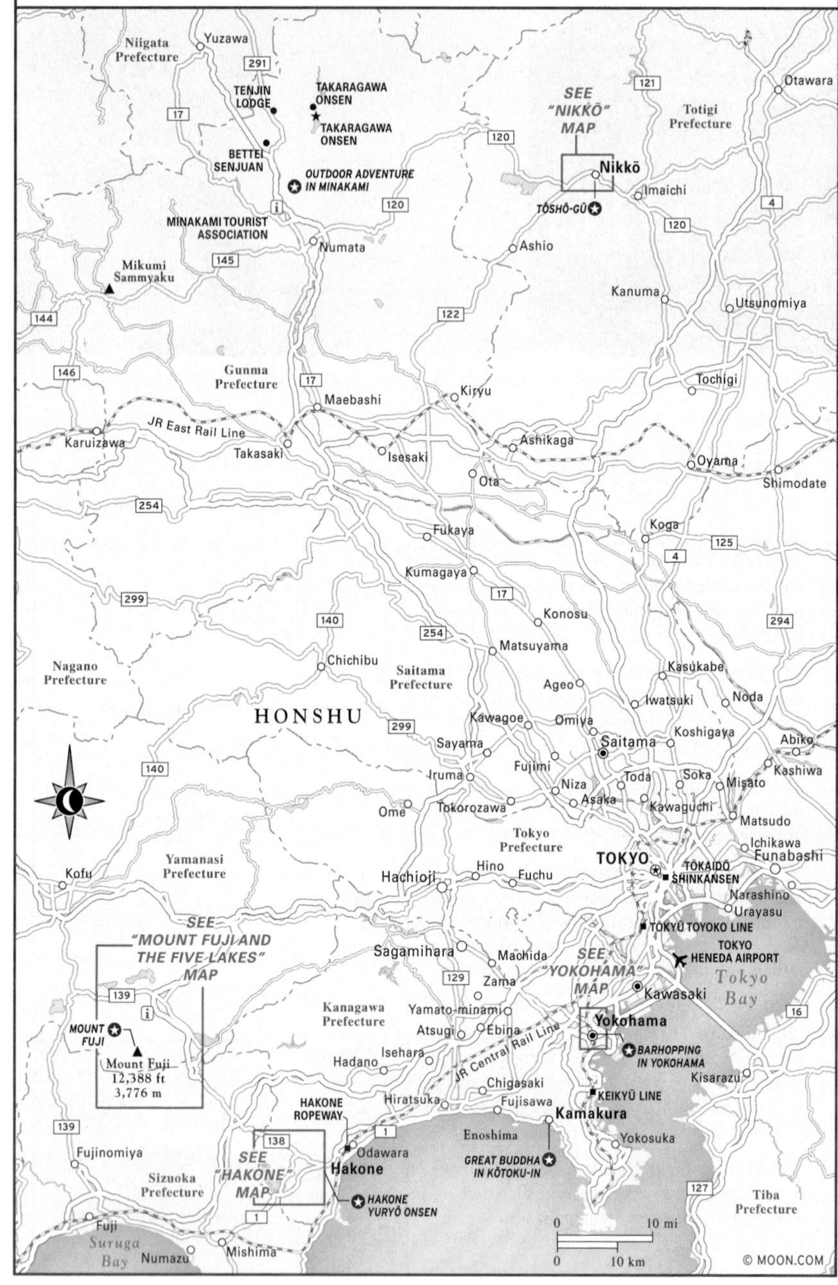

Best Restaurants

★ **Araiya:** This is the place to sample Yokohama's famed beef hot-pot, a fixture of the city's culinary scene since the Meiji period (1868-1912) (page 173).

★ **Tsuruya:** This mom-and-pop shop has served broiled eel on rice since 1929 and was once a favorite of Nobel Prize-winning novelist Kawabata Yasunari, who lived nearby (page 184).

★ **Masuda-ya:** This restaurant serves set course meals revolving around tofu skin, a silky delicacy and a specialty in Nikkō (page 191).

★ **Meiji-no-Yakata:** Housed in an atmospheric 19th-century villa tucked away in a leafy park in Nikkō, this Western-style restaurant is a Meiji-period time capsule (page 192).

★ **Amazake-Chaya:** Set in a 17th-century teahouse with a thatched-roof, this charming pit stop on the Old Hakone Highway serves nibbles and cups of *amazake-chaya*, a surprisingly refreshing infusion made of fermented rice (page 207).

★ **Sanrokuen:** Diners occupy cushions on the wooden floor, grilling skewers of meat, seafood, and mountain vegetables over a sunken hearth at this countryside gem near Lake Kawaguchi (page 218).

REGIONAL SPECIALTIES

In Nikkō, try ***yuba,*** or tofu skin, prepared in myriad ways, from being served with noodles to deep-fried or in *gyoza.*

capital. The earthy town has lovely seaside views and is dotted with temples, including Kotoku-in, which houses the famed bronze Daibutsu (Great Buddha). The town is surrounded by green hills lined with hiking trails.

North of the capital, a slightly more grandiose pocket of history is found in Nikkō, home to a collection of temples and shrines set among lofty cedar trees. The mountain town, which gained prominence during the Edo period (1603-1868), is 2.5 hours from Tokyo by train.

For spectacular views of Mount Fuji, take a train about two hours west of Tokyo to the countryside town of Hakone, nestled in the beautiful Fuji-Hakone-Izu National Park. Here, too, visitors can book a room in *a ryokan,* peruse art museums in lush outdoor settings, and soak in an *onsen.* Other places to get your *onsen* fix within a day trip of Tokyo include Minakami's Takaragawa Onsen (two hours northwest of Tokyo) and the rugged Izu Peninsula's Shuzenji (100 km/62 mi southwest of Tokyo). Izu also offers some prime beachfront, difficult to find in the Tokyo region.

To get up close and personal with Mount Fuji, head to the mountain itself. Official climbing season runs from July through August. To bask in the mountain's presence from the comfort of a hot spring, the Fuji Five Lakes form an arc around its northern base. Among them, Lake Kawaguchi is an accessible, pristine vantage point with a wealth of excellent hotels built for the sole purpose of relaxing within close range of the almost perfectly symmetrical peak.

Previous: large communal bath at Hakone Yuryō Onsen; Tōshō-gū; Great Buddha at Kōtoku-in

Best Accommodations

★ **Nikkorisou Backpackers:** This hostel, three minutes' walk from Shin-kyō, is run by an excellent host, with funky artwork and friendly guests (page 193).

★ **Bettei Senjuan:** This intimate *ryokan* run by a hospitality dream team boasts phenomenal views of Mount Tanigawa and private open-air baths (page 198).

★ **Fukuzumiro:** This dreamy late-19th-century Hakone gem filled with imaginative woodwork is the perfect place to unplug and recharge (page 207).

★ **Gōra Kadan:** Wander the incense-scented halls, dine on haute cuisine, soak in a private bath, and bask in the tranquil sylvan ambience at this premium *ryokan* in the heart of Hakone (page 208).

★ **Shuhokaku Kogetsu:** The *onsen* at this high-end escape beside Lake Kawaguchi, a *sakura* (cherry blossom) hot spot in spring, offers stunning views of Mount Fuji (page 220).

★ **Asaba Shuzenji Ryokan:** This historic *onsen ryokan*, founded in 1675, has sumptuous rooms with private baths, rustic open-air baths, and an outdoor *Noh* stage surrounded by forest and water (page 223).

ORIENTATION

To the North

Nikkō, in Tochigi Prefecture, and Minakami, in Gunma Prefecture, lie to the north of Tokyo, both about 2.5-3 hours from the capital city by train. Nikkō, with its location closer to the Tohoku *shinkansen* line, makes a good stopover for people headed to the northeastern reaches of Japan.

To the South

Yokohama and Kamakura, both in Kanagawa Prefecture, lie to the south of Tokyo and are within commuting distance from the city.

Fuji-Hakone-Izu National Park

Moving farther south/southwest, Fuji-Hakone-Izu National Park (**富士箱根伊豆国立公園**, www.fujihakoneizu.com) covers 1,227 square km (474 square mi) and comprises Hakone, Fuji Five Lakes, the Izu Peninsula, and Mount Fuji itself. The park spreads across parts of three prefectures: Yamanashi, Shizuoka, and Kanagawa.

PLANNING YOUR TIME

If your trip is largely confined to Tokyo, you don't need to go too far to get a well-rounded taste of what Japan has to offer. **Yokohama** is only 30 minutes to the south of Tokyo by train, and **Kamakura** is only another 30 minutes south from there. Both cities are easy day trips, and neither requires an overnight stay. Yokohama tends to be somewhat busy any day of the week, while the pace of Kamakura shifts from relatively sleepy on weekdays to boisterous and oftentimes overcrowded on weekends, with beaches filling up from the second half of June through the first half of September. Plan accordingly, avoiding the weekends if possible.

Venturing slightly farther, on a long day trip, it's possible to visit **Nikkō's** temples and shrines, as well as the *onsen* towns of **Minakami, Hakone,** the **Izu Peninsula,** and the **Mount Fuji** and **Fuji Five Lakes region.** But to really soak up the experience at any of these places, an overnight stay is recommended. The return trip from any of these is enough to exhaust a seasoned traveler. And considering that all of these destinations are geared toward downtime, rushing back to the hubbub of Tokyo defeats the purpose.

Transportation to any of these places can be arranged at the last minute, even day-of. Overnight stays require more planning. All of these destinations are popular with Japanese urbanites in need of escape, especially Hakone. Try to arrange *onsen* stays as far in advance as possible—even six months or more. *Ryokan* reservations spike in Japan around cherry blossom season (early April), when autumn foliage pops (mid-November), and during Golden Week (April 29-May 5) and Ōbon holidays (mid-August). If you avoid popular *onsen* during those times, you'll increase the chances of getting your preferred room.

It's not an issue in Yokohama and Kamakura, but keep in mind that many businesses close down quite early in small towns and *onsen* resorts. It's not uncommon to step out for dinner in the early evening and discover that everything is closed. Be sure to check the opening hours on the official website of any restaurant, shop, or attraction before making a trip.

As for the best seasons to visit any of these destinations, weather in most of the region is essentially the same as it is in Tokyo, but in the higher elevations of Nikkō, Minakami, Hakone, and the area surrounding Mount Fuji, winters are much colder, often bringing snow. These conditions make late November through March is the cheapest time to travel to these colder zones.

Itinerary Ideas

DAY TRIP TO YOKOHAMA

1 Leave Shibuya Station on the Tōkyū Toyoko Line in the mid-morning, aiming to arrive at Motomachi-Chūkagai Station, in the heart of **Chinatown,** by around 11am to slightly beat the afternoon rush. Eat lunch at **Tung Fat,** and then spend a little time exploring Chinatown's nooks and crannies.

2 Walk about 10 minutes northeast to the harbor. Stop by the **NYK Hikawamaru,** a ship moored in the harbor that was built in the 1930s and has all the period stylings intact. Step in and explore this piece of maritime history.

3 Speaking of history, if you'd like to learn more about Yokohama's long engagement with the West and the city's own development, walk about 10 minutes northwest, staying near the harbor, to the **Yokohama Archives of History.**

4 Head to the Minato Mirai area next. First visit the quirky **Cup Noodles Museum,** where you can direct the creation of your own one-off cup of noodles yourself for a nominal fee of ¥300.

5 Personalized Cup Noodles in hand, ascend to the observation deck atop nearby **Landmark Tower** for sweeping views over the city and harbor.

6 As dinnertime starts to approach, choose **Araiya,** a great spot to try Yokohama's spin on beef hot pot, located near Minato Mirai.

7 Go on a **bar crawl** through the districts of **Kannai, Bashamichi,** and **Noge.** You can begin from any of these and move around in the direction you choose. They are all located within about 15 minutes' walk of one another.

Itinerary Ideas

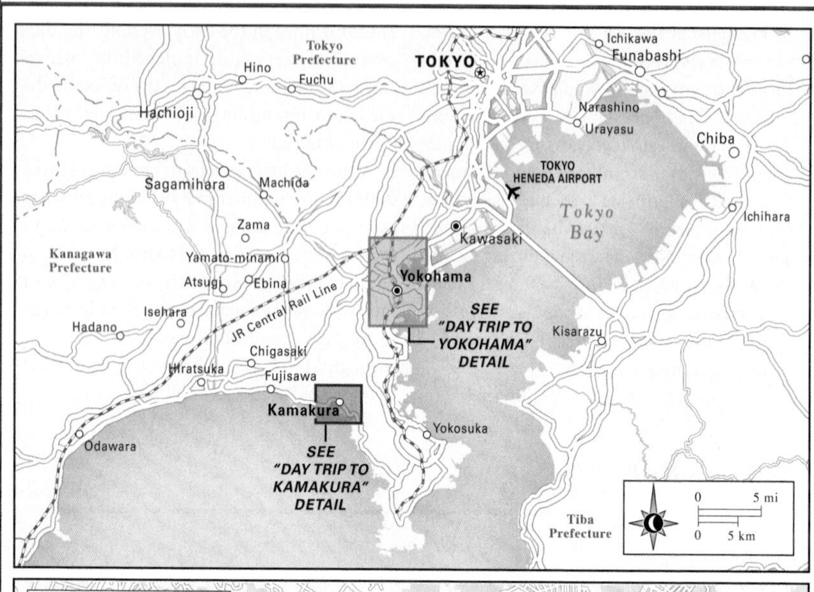

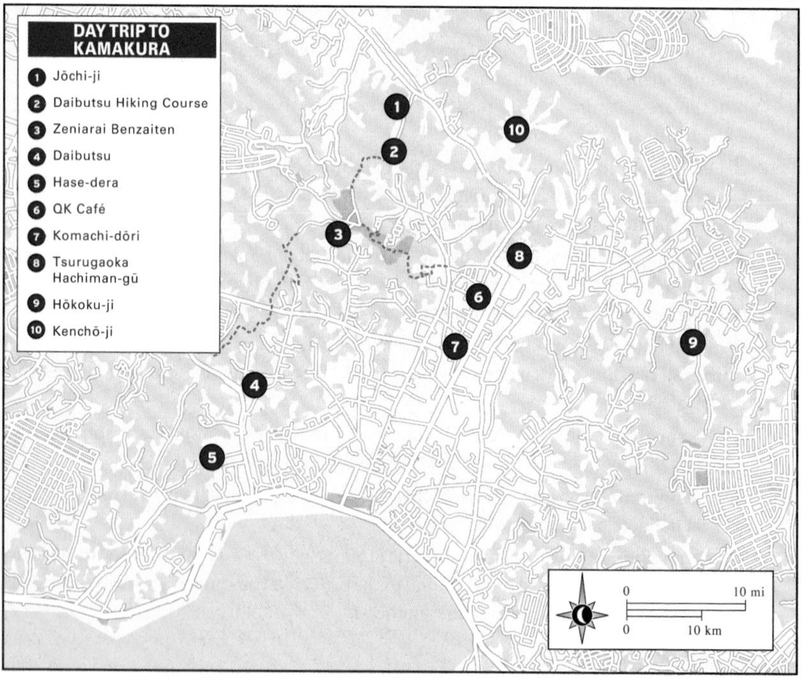

DAY TRIP TO KAMAKURA

1. Jōchi-ji
2. Daibutsu Hiking Course
3. Zeniarai Benzaiten
4. Daibutsu
5. Hase-dera
6. QK Café
7. Komachi-dōri
8. Tsurugaoka Hachiman-gū
9. Hōkoku-ji
10. Kenchō-ji

0 10 mi
0 10 km

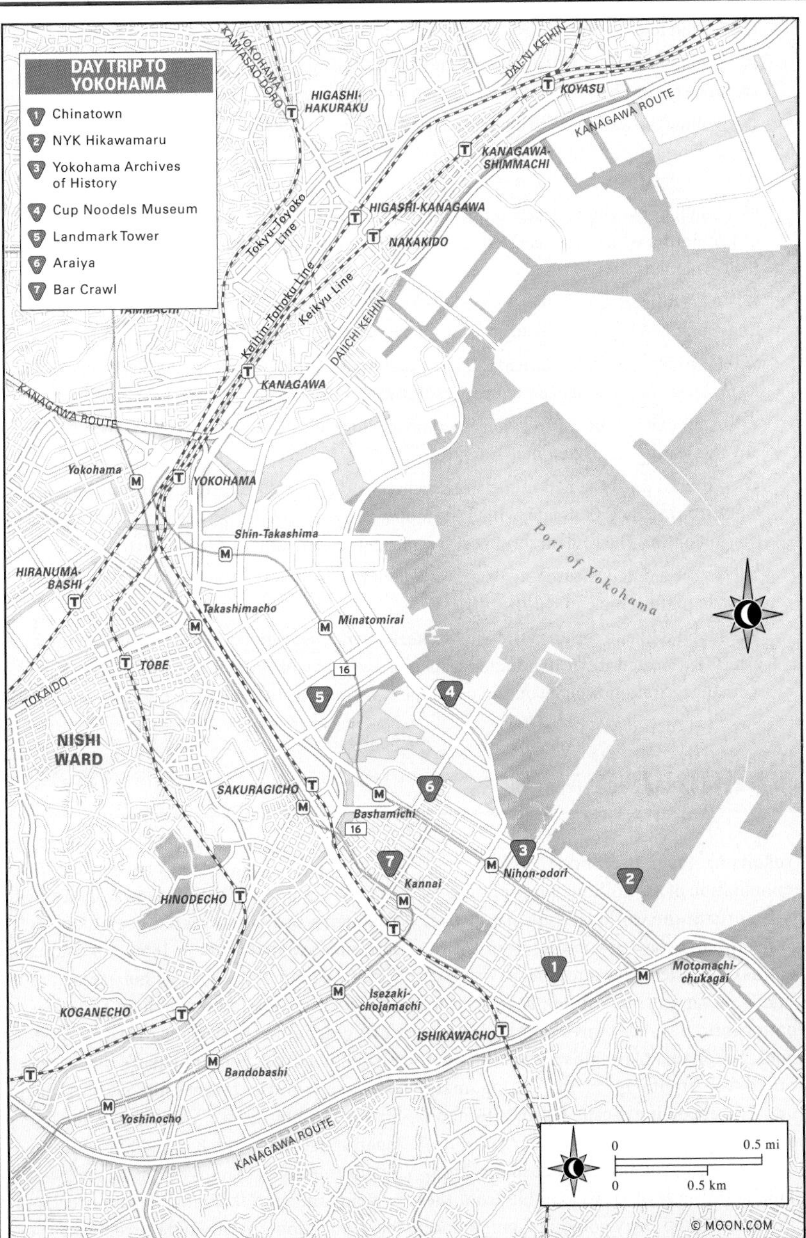
DAY TRIP TO YOKOHAMA
1 Chinatown
2 NYK Hikawamaru
3 Yokohama Archives of History
4 Cup Noodels Museum
5 Landmark Tower
6 Araiya
7 Bar Crawl
Port of Yokohama
NISHI WARD
KOYASU
HIGASHI-HAKURAKU
KANAGAWA-SHIMMACHI
HIGASHI-KANAGAWA
NAKAKIDO
KANAGAWA
YOKOHAMA
Yokohama
Shin-Takashima
HIRANUMA-BASHI
Takashimacho
Minatomirai
TOBE
SAKURAGICHO
Bashamichi
Nihon-odori
Kannai
HINODECHO
Motomachi-chukagai
Isezaki-chojamachi
KOGANECHO
ISHIKAWACHO
Bandobashi
Yoshinocho
KANAGAWA ROUTE
DAI-NI KEIHIN
DAIICHI KEIHIN
YOKOHAMA KAMIASAO DORO
Tokyu-Toyoko Line
Keihin-Tohoku Line
Keikyu Line
TOKAIDO
16
0 0.5 mi
0 0.5 km
© MOON.COM

DAY TRIP TO KAMAKURA

1 Begin your exploration of Kamakura in the north side of town, starting from Kita-Kamakura Station. Aim to arrive by around 10am. First, walk about six minutes' west of the station to the temple of **Jōchi-ji.**

2 After exploring the temple's grounds and slowing down to Kamakura time, find the entrance to the **Daibutsu Hiking Course,** located next to the temple grounds.

3 Follow the well-marked course, passing a number of small temples tucked away in the forested hills around the seaside town. Take special note of **Zeniarai Benzaiten,** a shrine set into a grotto with a sacred spring.

4 You'll know you've reached the end of the hiking course when you reach the temple of Kotoku-in, which houses the famed **Daibutsu** (Great Buddha) statue, after which the trail is named.

5 After admiring the 90-ton spectacle, walk 10 minutes south to **Hase-dera,** a temple known for its 11-faced, 9-meter-tall (30-foot) wooden visage of Kannon, goddess of mercy.

6 From here, walk to Hase Station on the Enoden train line. Ride this local railway to Kamakura Station and head to nearby **QK Café** for lunch.

7 After eating lunch, stroll along the famed shopping street of **Komachi-dōri,** alert for any interesting shops that may catch your eye.

8 Proceed until the end of the street, where you'll reach the entrance to **Tsurugaoka Hachiman-gū.** This shrine, which sits atop a cliff overlooking the ocean, is dedicated to the god of war, Hachiman, serving as a reminder of Kamakura's deeply martial past.

9 To see a magical bamboo grove, walk about 20 minutes deeper into the eastern part of town to the temple of **Hōkoku-ji.**

10 If you'd like to see one last temple, check out **Kenchō-ji,** Japan's first-ever Zen monastery. It's located about 30 minutes' walk northwest of Hōkoku-ji, in the direction of Kita-Kamakura Station, where you can catch the train back to Tokyo for the night.

Yokohama 横浜

Yokohama, Japan's second-largest city with a population of 3.7 million, is one of the biggest ports in the world. It's ultimately part of the urban sprawl emanating from Tokyo, but has a relaxed pace and a sense of space that is lacking in the capital, thanks to its panoramic bayside views and wide avenues. Yokohama maintains a good buzz but rarely feels frantic or overwhelming, making it an appealing escape for an afternoon or evening.

In a word, Yokohama is cosmopolitan. This defining trait is inseparable from the city's past as the entry point for Commodore Perry's black ships, which heralded the end of Japan's 250-year period of self-isolation and the signing of the Kanagawa Treaty in Yokohama in 1854. Declared one of Japan's five international ports in 1858, Yokohama became a booming silk trade hub, as well as a channel for foreign technology and ideas during the powerfully transformative Meiji period. It was the home of Japan's first brewery, bakery, and ice cream shop. Sakuragichō Station, still in service, was the terminus of Japan's first train, which ran to Shinbashi in Tokyo.

Remnants of Yokohama's legacy are visible throughout the city today, from its Port Museum and the moored Nippon Maru to the graceful 19th-century Victorian homes of the affluent hillside neighborhoods of Motmoachi and Yamate, where early foreign residents did their best to make themselves feel at home.

The city's melting-pot heritage is also evident in the meandering lanes of dumpling shops, temples, and teahouses of its Chinatown, Japan's largest and a great place to dine. Other dining hot spots include the areas of Kannai, Bashamichi, and Noge: boozy neighborhoods infused with faded Shōwa-period (1925-1989) charm. A number of craft beer pubs in these areas make for a great night of bar hopping, rounded out by the excellent jazz clubs that opened in the decades following its rebirth from the ashes of World War II.

But Yokohama is far from being stuck in the past. The future-facing bayside development Minato Mirai 21, smack in the middle of downtown, loom large in the city's image today. But wander away from the harbor, and historic alleys remain.

ORIENTATION

Compared to Tokyo, most of Yokohama's highly walkable streets are mercifully uncrowded. The main entry point into the city is **Yokohama Station,** located at the northern side of town, with the modern bayside development of **Minato Mirai** and the adjacent man-made island of **Shinkō** to the southeast.

South of Minato Mirai and Shinkō is the wide boulevard of **Nihon-ōdōri,** once the key roadway of Yokohama. Continuing eastward the bay leads to the waterfront park of **Yamashita-Kōen,** with **Chinatown** (Motomachi-Chūkagai) to the southwest. South of Chinatown is the charming shopping district of **Motomachi,** where much of Yokohama's foreign population lived in the 19th century; many of the city's pioneering foreign residents are buried in the **Yokohama Foreign General Cemetery.** Overlooking it all is **Yamate,** a historic district full of 19th-century buildings atop a bluff just south of Motomachi.

Heading northwest of Yamate, either on foot (20 minutes) or one stop on the train from **Ishikawachō Station** (10 minutes' walk northwest of Yamate) on the Negishi line, you'll arrive at the neighborhoods of **Kannai, Bashamichi,** and **Noge,** all packed with great options for eating and drinking.

SIGHTS

Minato Mirai 21
みなとみらい 21

http://minatomirai21.com

Minato Mirai 21 is an ambitious urban development next to the bay in downtown Yokohama, including a smattering of shops restaurants, museums, hotels, one of Japan's highest observation decks, and even a small amusement park. At the heart of this "harbor of the future," as its name literally means, you'll find the bulk of the structures that make up Yokohama's skyline.

YOKOHAMA PORT MUSEUM AND NIPPON MARU
横浜みなと博物館、帆船日本丸

2-1-1 Minato Mirai, Naka-ku; tel. 045/221-0280; www.nippon-maru.or.jp; 10am-5pm Tues.-Sun., closed on Tues. when Mon. is a holiday; ¥600 adults, ¥300 children; take JR Negishi line, Yokohama Subway line to Sakuragichō Station

While Yokohama does have a cultured side, in truth the city is more mercantile than avant-garde. To get a sense of its role as a center of maritime commerce, visit the Yokohama Port Museum. While the museum may feel slightly dry if you're not a history buff, the accompanying tour of the anchored 1930 ship, the **Nippon Maru,** is worth the price of admission. Originally launched as a training vessel for officers of the merchant marine, the elegant ship was then used for training during World War II, and as a transport ship following the war. Its history comes alive as you amble along the deck and through its halls. At 97 meters (318 feet) long, the ship is quite a sight when its sails are raised.

Yokohama

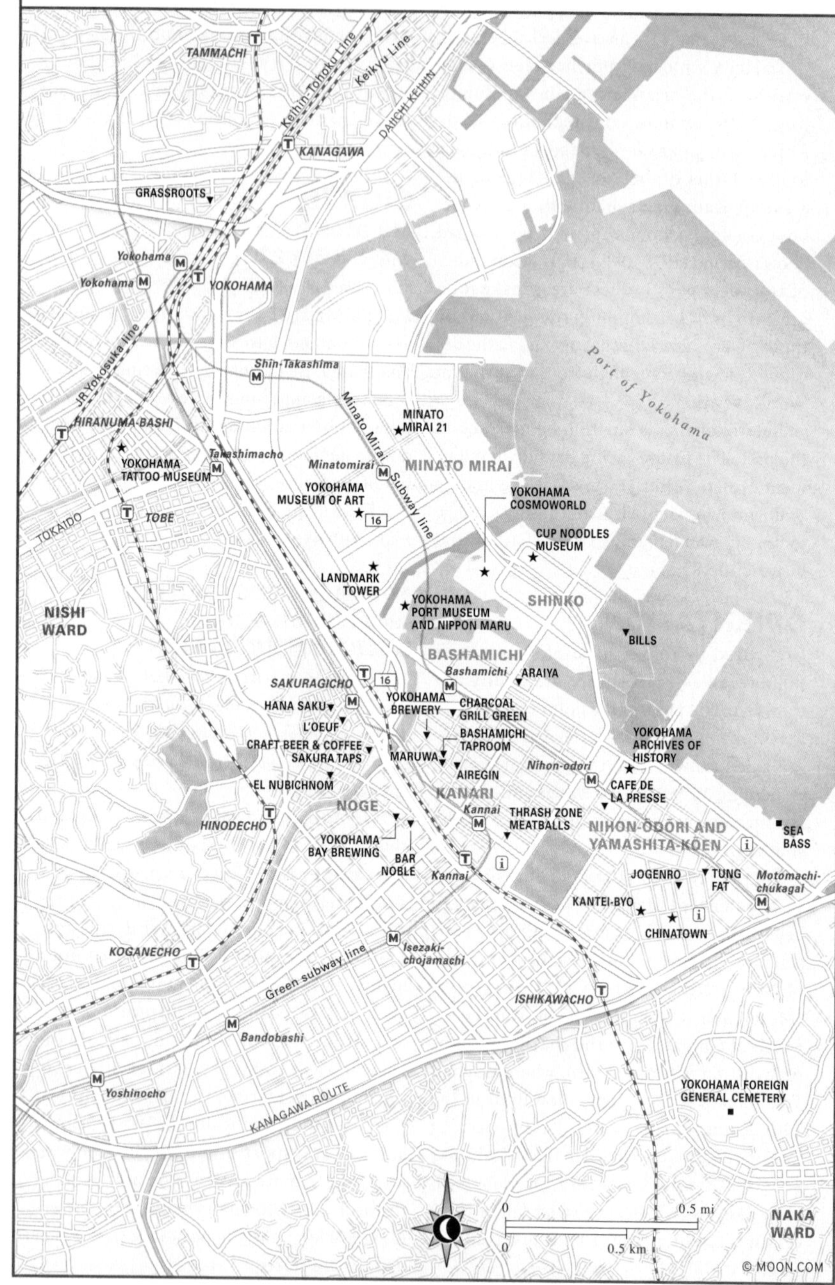
TAMMACHI
Keihin-Tohoku Line
Keikyu Line
DAIICHI KEIHIN
KANAGAWA
GRASSROOTS
Yokohama
Yokohama
YOKOHAMA
JR Yokosuka line
Shin-Takashima
Port of Yokohama
Minato Mirai Subway line
MINATO MIRAI 21
HIRANUMA-BASHI
YOKOHAMA TATTOO MUSEUM
Takashimacho
Minatomirai
MINATO MIRAI
YOKOHAMA MUSEUM OF ART
YOKOHAMA COSMOWORLD
16
TOKAIDO
TOBE
CUP NOODLES MUSEUM
LANDMARK TOWER
NISHI WARD
YOKOHAMA PORT MUSEUM AND NIPPON MARU
SHINKO
BILLS
BASHAMICHI
Bashamichi
ARAIYA
SAKURAGICHO
16
HANA SAKU
YOKOHAMA BREWERY
CHARCOAL GRILL GREEN
L'OEUF
BASHAMICHI TAPROOM
CRAFT BEER & COFFEE SAKURA TAPS
MARUWA
YOKOHAMA ARCHIVES OF HISTORY
AIREGIN
Nihon-odori
EL NUBICHNOM
KANARI
CAFE DE LA PRESSE
NOGE
Kannai
THRASH ZONE MEATBALLS
HINODECHO
NIHON-ŌDŌRI AND YAMASHITA-KŌEN
SEA BASS
YOKOHAMA BAY BREWING
BAR NOBLE
Kannai
JOGENRO
TUNG FAT
Motomachi-chukagai
KANTEI-BYO
CHINATOWN
Isezaki-chojamachi
KOGANECHO
Green subway line
ISHIKAWACHO
Bandobashi
Yoshinocho
KANAGAWA ROUTE
YOKOHAMA FOREIGN GENERAL CEMETERY
0
0.5 mi
0
0.5 km
NAKA WARD
© MOON.COM

LANDMARK TOWER
ランドマークタワー

2-2-1 Minato Mirai, Nishi-ku; tel. 045/222-5015; www.yokohama-landmark.jp

The 296-meter-high (971-foot) Landmark Tower is worth a visit for its **Sky Garden** (69F The Landmark Tower Yokohama; tel. 045/222-5030; www.yokohama-landmark.jp/skygarden/web/english; 10am-9pm Sun.-Fri. (last entry 8:30pm), 10am-10pm Sat. and summer holidays (last entry 9:30pm); ¥1,000 adults, ¥500 elementary and junior high students, ¥800 high school students and over 65, ¥200 children over 4 years old). At 273 meters (895 feet) above the ground, this observation deck is the best place to survey the development, as well as Mount Fuji and Tokyo when the sky is clear. The elevator, which climbs at a speed of 750 meters (2,460 feet) per minute, ensures that the ride to the top is fun, too.

YOKOHAMA MUSEUM OF ART
横浜美術館

3-4-1 Minato Mirai, Nishi-ku; tel. 045/221-0300; http://yokohama.art.museum/eng/index.html; 10am-6pm Fri.-Wed., closed Thurs.; ¥500 adults, ¥300 university and high school students, free for children under 12; take Minato Mirai line to Minato Mirai Station, exit 3

A showcase of contemporary art and photography, the Yokohama Museum of Art is another one of Minato Mirai 21's major draws. The space features western and Japanese artists, with exhibitions ranging from conservative to groundbreaking (check the schedule). As an added bonus, the building was designed by Pritzker Prize winner Tange Kenzo—something worth appreciating as you pass through the rays of natural light beaming into the courtyard entrance from a soaring skylight.

Shinkō

YOKOHAMA COSMOWORLD
横浜コスモワールド

2-8-1 Shinkō, Naka-ku; tel. 045/641-6591; http://cosmoworld.jp; 11am-9pm Mon.-Fri., 11am-10pm Sat.-Sun.; ¥300-800 for most rides; take Minato Mirai line to Minato Mirai Station, exit 3, or JR Negishi line, Yokohama Subway line to Sakuragichō Station

As you'll notice from the high perch of Landmark Tower, development has spilled across a small inlet to Shinkō, an artificial island containing restaurants, shops, and more. The most notable point of interest on this manmade addition to Yokohama's waterfront is Yokohama Cosmoworld, a small but lively amusement park famed for the **Cosmo Clock 21,** a Ferris wheel that stands 112.5 meters (369 feet) above the crowds and has a massive clock plastered to its side. One rotation on the ride, which was the world's tallest Ferris wheel when it opened, takes 15 minutes and offers stunning views of the city below. It's an ideal attraction if you're traveling with kids.

CUP NOODLES MUSEUM
カップヌードルミュージアム

2-3-4 Shinkō, Naka-ku; tel. 045/345-0918; www.cupnoodles-museum.jp; 10am-6pm Wed.-Mon., closed Wed. if Tues. is holiday; take Minato Mirai line to Minato Mirai Station, exit 3, or JR Negishi line, Yokohama Subway line to Sakuragichō Station

Also in the Shinkō district, the Cup Noodles Museum is a surprisingly inspirational ode to the humble instant meal, a staple among college students worldwide. Following a sleek visual presentation, including anime clips on cup-noodle creator Momofuku Ando's journey toward fast-food superstardom, you can oversee the creation of your own signature noodle variety for a nominal fee (¥300), including the packaging and toppings. With advance reservations, you can even learn to knead your own instant noodles. This is a fun option for those traveling with kids.

Nihon-ōdōri and Yamashita-Kōen
日本大通り, 山下公園

Heading south of Minato Mirai and Shinkō brings you to the roughly northeast-southwest avenue of Nihon-ōdōri. This historic thoroughfare was once the heart of Yokohama, reflected in some of the grand architecture

1

2

seen in the buildings, some of which date to the 19th century. Sitting at the northeast edge of this avenue is the **Yokohama Archives of History.** Running alongside the harbor just east of this historic street is the waterfront park of **Yamashita-Kōen,** with the **NYK Hikawamaru,** a 1930s-era ship has all the period fixings intact and can be entered and explored.

YOKOHAMA ARCHIVES OF HISTORY
横浜開港資料館

3 Nihonnodori, Naka-ku, Yokohama; tel. 045/201-2100; www.kaikou.city.yokohama.jp/en/index.html; 9:30am-5pm, Tues.-Sun., closed Tues. if Mon. is holiday; ¥200 adults, ¥100 children; take Minatomirai line to Nihonodori Station, exit 3

This one's for the history buffs. If you want to get a sense of what Japan was like when it was first opening up to the wider world after the arrival of Commodore Perry's black ships, the Yokohama Archives of History museum includes more than 200,000 artifacts from that pivotal historical time, up through the beginning of the Showa period (1926-1989). Maps, newspaper clippings, photographs, prints, models of ships, and more allow you to peer into Yokohama's past.

Adding to the museum's historical significance is the fact that it is situated in the same building where the Treaty of Kanagawa was signed between the shogunate and the US government on March 31, 1854, bringing an end to Japan's 250-year lockdown. One tree in the museum's inner courtyard is supposedly an offspring of the incense tree seen in many sketches of Perry's dramatic arrival at that very spot.

Chinatown
横浜中華街

As with many port cities, Yokohama is home to a bustling Chinatown. Just as the city was one of Japan's first ports to welcome foreign trade, many Chinese were seeking to escape political turmoil at home—a fortuitous alignment of events. Among the Chinese who wound up in Yokohama were those who fled Shanghai after the Opium War and found new life as go-betweens who helped Western merchants navigate the tricky waters of Japan's unfamiliar business customs.

Chinatown, or Yokohama Chūkagai, remains vital in part thanks to China's ascent in recent decades. Its main draw today is its sheer energy and some 200 eateries, which generate a steady flow of foot traffic, especially on weekends. Stores hawk a mix of items, from touristy trinkets and lanterns to tea. A walk through the neighborhood and a meal make for an enjoyable change of pace.

KANTEI-BYO
关帝庙

140 Yamashitachō, Naka-ku; tel. 045/226-2636; www.yokohama-kanteibyo.com; 9am-7pm daily; free; take Minato Mirai line to Motomachi-Chūkagai Station, or JR Negishi line to Ishikawacho Station

One sight worth a stop if you're in the area is Kantei-byo, a temple dedicated to Guan Yu, a Han war general from China's Three Kingdoms period who is now seen as a guardian of wealth—hence the temple's reputation as a spiritual haven among those running businesses in the area. Facing the temple's opulent gate, you'll notice the dragons on its roof and the hanging red lanterns. Walk up the first set of steps, lined with stone dragons, past two guardian dogs, and up another staircase to the main hall. Inside, under a ceiling festooned with myriad shimmering golden ornaments, Guan Yu is powerfully seated at the center, ready to help the faithful in business.

Note the location of the temple, too. If you draw a straight line from Chinatown's main north and south gates, as well as between the main east and west gates, Kantei-byo lies at the intersection of these two lines: Feng Shui is in full effect, maximizing the power of this sacred spot to boost the neighborhood's bottom line.

1: Minato Mirai at night **2:** Yokohama Chinatown

Yokohama Tattoo Museum and Japan's Legacy with Ink

From ocean waves rolling over an arm to a flamboyant tiger on one's back, Japanese tattoos, or *irezumi* (literally: insert ink), are among the most sought-after styles among ink aficionados. A traditional Japanese tattoo job calls for a major commitment of time and money, potentially involving tens of thousands of dollars and continuous weekly visits for as long as five years. The artist and client hold ongoing discussions about the design, and the master has right to refuse service.

When this dance is carried to its conclusion, a full-body suit covers the arms, legs, chest, and back—only ending in places where clothing stops. There are complex social reasons for this. While tattoos are a matter of fashion in the West, and foreign enthusiasts may clamor for a place under the needle of a great master, the art is weighed down by taboo in Japan—an irony, given its deep history with the art.

In the ancient past, Okinawan women tattooed their hands with talismans and shamanic symbols using a blend of ink and the island's very own firewater, *awamori*. Japan's indigenous Ainu people have an ancient tradition of using soot from the fireside to mark their faces and arms with designs intended to ward off evil spirits and ensure safe passage into the afterlife. The modern tattoo tradition took root on the islands more recently, during the Edo period (1603-1868), in the red-light zones of Edo and Osaka. During this period, the motifs we think of as "Japanese" today began to emerge. The explosion of woodblock prints (*ukiyo-e*) in the art world grew hand in hand with tattooing.

Although the art form was strictly banned, members of the underclass, from dock workers to fire fighters and palanquin bearers, proudly rebelled and got inked in droves. The *yakuza* (mafia) got inked as well, fueled by the belief that tatting up—painful, permanent—took courage, loyalty, and, as a bonus, disregard for the law. Furthermore, the cost accrued from a full-body suit came to be viewed as a signifier of financial success.

This historical mix of reasons took hold in the public's imagination, and the art form still has never achieved social acceptability. Even today, tattooing remains a very private affair, done discretely and by appointment only. Most *onsen* and fitness centers still ban those sporting ink.

The **Yokohama Tattoo Museum** (1-11-7 Hiranuma, Nishi-ku; tel. 045/323-1073; www.ne.jp/asahi/tattoo/horiyoshi3; noon-6pm Wed.-Mon.; ¥1,000; take Keikyū line for Kanazawa-Bunko to Tobe station), run by legendary master Horiyoshi III and his wife, is an excellent place to go for a nuanced view of the rich history and impressive level of skill that goes into this art form. The cramped space is positively overflowing with tools of the trade and related memorabilia. Note that the museum is closed on the 1st, 10th, and 20th of every month.

To learn more, check out *Japanese Tattoos: History, Culture, Design*, by Brian Ashcraft (with Hori Benny).

ENTERTAINMENT AND EVENTS

YOKOHAMA JAZZ PROMENADE

tel. 045/211-1510; http://jazzpro.jp/english; first full weekend of early Oct., performances 9am-10pm; one-day ticket ¥5,000 adults, ¥1,000 junior high and high school students, free for primary school students and younger

Japan's biggest jazz festival, Yokohama Jazz Promenade transforms the port city into one giant stage. Jazz bands from Japan and abroad jam in the streets, in the city's numerous jazz clubs, and at large venues like Minatomirai Hall, Yokohama Kannai Hall and Motomachi's main shopping street, among many others. See the website for a schedule and information about getting tickets.

FOOD

Shinkō

BILLS

Yokohama Red Brick Warehouse Bldg. 2, 1-1-2 Shinkō, Naka-ku; tel. 045/650-1266; http://billsjapan.com; 9am-11pm Mon.-Fri., 8am-11pm Sat.-Sun. and holidays; ¥2,000-¥3,000; take Minatomirai line to Minatomirai Station

Just south of Yokohama in Minato Mirai,

the dining options are chain-heavy. But one stands out: Bills. This branch of the Australian breakfast juggernaut Bills Japan seats 120 and does a good job of pleasing the masses until midday with its expertly done pancakes, and scrambled or poached eggs. Lunch and dinner options include pasta, burgers, sandwiches, curries, salads, and more.

Noge

HANA SAKU

2-60 Hanasakichō, Naka-ku; tel. 045/325-9215; http://kulakula.info/hanasaku/index.html; 5pm-11:30pm daily; ¥180-880 per plate; take subway Blue line to Sakuragi-chō, south exit 1

An *izakaya* in Sakuragichō with a minimalist interior of clean lines, wood and metal, Hana Saku is all about sake. The bartender is happy to introduce patrons to the wonders of sake, from sweet to dry, choosing from more than 20 varieties. The food menu is based on Kyoto-style side-dishes of pickled and cooked vegetables, grilled meats and stews, and creative takes on tofu.

Nihon-ōdōri and Yamashita-Kōen

CAFÉ DE LA PRESSE

Yokohama Media & Communications Center 2f, 11 Nihon-ōdōri, Naka-ku; tel. 045/222-3348; http://www.alteliebe.co.jp; 10am-8pm Tues.-Sun.; drinks ¥480-900, food ¥800-1,800; take subway Blue line to Nihon-ōdōri, exit 3

A French-style café on Yokohama's historic tree-lined boulevard Nihon-ōdōri neighborhood, Café de la Presse is located on the second floor of the Yokohama Media & Communications Center. It's good for a pit stop if you're in the area, whether it's for a caffeine hit, cocktail, or an aperitif. The menu includes a good selection of western dishes, from quiches and sandwiches to soups and salads, as well as European desserts.

Bashamichi

★ ARAIYA

4-23 Kaigan-dōri, Naka-ku; tel. 045/226-5003; www.araiya.co.jp; 11am-2:30pm and 5pm-10pm daily; ¥2,000-4,000 lunch, ¥7,500-12,500 dinner; take Minatomirai line to Bashamichi Station, 6 Akarenga Soko exit

Araiya has a menu of rice bowls topped with strips of beef and sukiyaki, and extensive shabu-shabu courses. But its signature dish, *gyū-nabe,* consists of lean cuts of beef, leeks, shiitake mushrooms, and thin strands of jelly made from *konnyaku* (a plant from the taro family). The dish is cooked in a delicately balanced sauce that is both sweet and savory in a cast-iron pot at the table and dipped in raw egg, and the result is delicious.

CHARCOAL GRILL GREEN

6-79 Benten-dōri, Naka-ku; tel. 045/263-8976; www.greenyokohama.com; 11:30am-2pm and 5pm-11:30pm Mon.-Fri., 11:30am-3pm and 5pm-11:30pm Sat.-Sun.; ¥1,400-4,800; take Minatomirai line to Bashamichi Station, exit 3

Charcoal Grill Green is a bistro in the heart of Bashamichi, focused on charcoal-grilled meat (chicken, lamb, steak, duck) and seafood, as well as a good range of salads, soups, and other starters. The drink menu has a good selection of local craft beers and wines from California. This is a good place for either a few bites with drinks or a full meal.

MARUWA

5-61 Sumiyoshichō, Naka-ku; tel. 045/641-0640; 11:30am-2pm and 5:30pm-8pm Mon.-Fri., 11:30am-2pm Sat.; ¥1,000-2,000 for lunch, ¥2,000-3,000 for dinner; take Minatomirai line to Bashamichi Station, exit 5

For perhaps the best *tonkatsu* in the city, head to Maruwa in Bashamichi. The shop's no-frills décor and lack of music allow you to fully direct your attention to the delectable breaded cutlets of pork. At lunchtime, be ready for a queue. Arrive around 11:15 to avoid standing in a long line. Alternatively, come for dinner when it's less crowded (though pricier). All meals include miso soup, pickled vegetables, and refillable rice and shredded cabbage.

Chinatown

TUNG FAT

148 Yamashitachō, Naka-ku; tel. 045/681-7273; www.douhatsu.co.jp; 11am-9:30pm daily, closed first and third Tues. every month; ¥2,700-3,600 for lunch set meals, ¥4,860-16,200 for dinner courses; take Minatomirai line to Motomachi-Chūkagai Station, exit 1

Found on Chinatown's main drag, Chūkagai-ōdōri, Tung Fat (aka Dohatsu) is another tried-and-true Cantonese option. Known for its seafood, the shop routinely attracts a long queue, especially during lunchtime. Look for the display of ducks, chickens, offal, and sausage hanging behind the window.

JOGENRO

191 Yamashitachō, Naka-ku; tel. 045/641-8888; www.jogen.co.jp/jgr_yokohama; 11:30am-10:30pm Mon.-Thurs. and Sun., 11:30am-11pm Fri.-Sat. and the day before any holiday; ¥1,100-3,300 lunch sets, ¥4,500-20,000 for dinner courses; take Minatomirai line to Motomachi-Chūkagai Station, exit 2

Chinatown's maze of eateries is not solely devoted to Cantonese-style cooking. To shake things up Shanghai-style, try Jogenro. This restaurant sprawls across five floors, each with its own theme. Opulent furniture and decor you'd expect to see in a colonial townhouse in early-20th-century Shanghai evoke the Pearl of the Orient. The menu includes a solid range of soup dumplings, as well as stir-fried and grilled meats, vegetables, noodles, and rice.

★ BARS AND NIGHTLIFE

Yokohama's craft beer zone is primarily centered in the neighborhoods of Kannai, Bashamichi, and Noge, all of which sit within walking distance of each other. Kannai is in the most southeast position of the group, with Bashamichi northeast of there, while Noge is northwest of Kannai, across the Ōka River. It's possible to walk across the entire area in 10-15 minutes.

Kannai

THRASH ZONE MEATBALLS

2-15-1 Tokiwacho, Naka-ku; 3pm-10pm Mon.-Fri., 1pm-9pm Sat.-Sun.; take subway Blue line to Kannai Station, exit 3

If Yokohama's nightlife could be summed up in a few words, they would be "craft beer and jazz." Thrash Zone Meatballs is a good spot to begin a bar hop through Yokohama's craft beer zone. The local brews at this concrete-walled, sparsely decorated drinking den are hoppy and strong, and served alongside meatballs—by themselves or in a bun—made with a healthy dose of cheese and spice. As the shop's name suggests, patrons enjoy this mix to a soundtrack of thrash metal.

BAR NOBLE

2-7 Yoshidachō, Naka-ku; tel. 045/243-1673; http://noble-aqua.com; 6pm-1:30am daily; table charge ¥800 per person; take Blue line to Kannai Station, exit 6, JR Negishi line to Kannai Station, Isezakichō exit

If you're feeling like a cocktail, head to Bar Noble. You'll get a whiff of the sort of sophistication emanating from Ginza's swanky cocktail strongholds here, down to the dapper bartenders. Ambient lighting, a Zelkova countertop, and tunes lightly wafting from unseen speakers deepen the spell. With more than 500 types of booze on the shelf, rest assured, the bartenders know how to mix a drink. Try Great Sunrise, the bar's signature cocktail, which won the World Cocktail Championship in November 2011. This deep-yellow concoction is meant to signify the hope of a new day following the March 11 Tōhoku earthquake and tsunami.

YOKOHAMA BAY BREWING KANNAI

2-15 Higashidōri, Naka-ku; tel. 045/341-0450; www.yokohamabaybrewing.jp; 4:30pm-11pm Mon.-Fri., 1pm-11pm Sat.-Sun.; take JR Negishi or Blue line to Kannai Station

Back on the craft beer circuit, one minute up the road from Bar Noble you'll find the excellent Yokohama Bay Brewing. This shop was opened in 2011 by Suzuki Shinya, trained in the Czech Republic and Germany and formerly the head brewer of Yokohama Brewery. Of the seven or so beers on tap, four or five are carefully selected from local outfits around Japan; the others are Suzuki's creations, always anticipated by his diehard fans. Simple bar nibbles are also on the menu.

Bashamichi

BASHAMICHI TAPROOM

5-63-1 Sumiyoshichō, Naka-ku; tel. 045/264-4961; https://bairdbeer.com; 5pm-midnight Mon.-Fri., noon-midnight Sat.-Sun and holidays; take subway Blue line to Kannai Station, exit 3

Seven minutes' walk northeast of Yokohama Bay Brewing Kannai, you'll find another craft-beer gem, the three-floor Bashamichi Taproom, run by Shizuoka-based Baird Brewing Company. Around 20 beers, from light lagers to punchy ales and dark, honeyed stouts are on tap at the ground-floor bar. There's a spacious second-floor seating area and a rooftop terrace that beckons in warmer months. The kitchen also whips up excellent platters of barbecued tender pork, beef brisket, and ribs, smoked overnight in an oven imported from Texas and flavored with sauces made in house.

YOKOHAMA BREWERY

6-68-1 Sumiyoshichō, Naka-ku; tel. 045/641-9901; www.yokohamabeer.com; 11:30am-3pm and 6pm-11pm Mon.-Fri., 11:30am-11pm Sat., 11:30am-9pm Sun.; take Minato Mirai line to Bashamichi Station, exit 3

Two minutes up the road from Bashamichi Taproom, you'll find the city's oldest craft-beer brewery, Yokohama Brewery. Founded in 1995, the brewpub serves a range of pilsners and sweeter Belgian-style beers. Above the brewery is Umaya, a restaurant serving Western and Asian cuisine.

AIREGIN

5-60 Sumiyoshichō; tel. 045/641-9191; www.airegin.yokohama; 7pm-10:30pm daily; ¥2,500 cover charge includes one drink; take Blue line to Kannai Station, exit 8

Airegin (Nigeria spelled backward) is a standout in the city's vibrant jazz scene. Originally opened as a jazz *kissa* (jazz café) in Shinjuku, Tokyo, by a jazz-loving couple in 1969, it relocated to Yokohama where became established as a stalwart in the local scene. This archetypal jazz joint is cozy and smoky, and draws a dedicated crowd of connoisseurs. Look for the large yellow sign on the sidewalk. It's located a few doors down from Bashamichi Taproom.

Noge

CRAFT BEER & COFFEE SAKURA TAPS

1-16-1 Hanasakichō, Naka-ku; tel. 045/334-8873; http://sakurataps.com; 5pm-11pm Mon.-Fri., 3pm-11pm Sat., 3pm-10pm Sun.; take subway Blue line to Sakuragichō Station, exit 1

Craft Beer & Coffee Sakura Taps, or Sakura Taps for short, is another worthy stop on Yokohama's craft beer trail. Just across the Ōka River in the old-school, slightly dilapidated district of Noge, Sakura Taps has eight (mostly Japanese) craft beers on tap, and munchies like grilled meats and vegetable fritters. Note that if you're willing to swill your beer standing up, you receive a discount of ¥50-200 per glass, depending on the size.

EL NUBICHNOM

1-1 Miyagawachō, Naka-ku; tel. 045/231-3626; https://ameblo.jp/el-nubichinom; 5:30pm-10:30pm Mon. and Wed.-Thurs., 5:30pm-11:30pm Fri., 3pm-11:30pm Sat., 3pm-8pm Sun.; take subway Blue line, JR lines to Sakuragichō Station, exit 1

El Nubichnom claims to be the world's smallest craft-beer bar. This standing-only bolthole of a bar, overlooking the Ōka River, is run by a friendly, passionate beer judge named Kaji-san. Five or six Japanese craft brews are on tap at any given time, and often include some rare ones. Sizes include 200ml (¥700) and 400ml (¥1,400); prices drop to ¥600 and ¥1,100, respectively, during happy hour (which begins when the bar opens and bizarrely runs until 30 minutes before closing). This is a fun, cramped spot for a drink or two.

Note that the two-story building that

houses El Nubichnom is also home to an array of bars. To see the options on the second floor, ascend the staircase on either side of the building to the corridor that runs along the back of the building, where you'll find the entrances to all second-floor bars.

L'OEUF

2-23-4 Miyagawachō, Naka-ku; tel. 045/315-5517; https://oeuf-yokohama.jimdo.com; 6pm-midnight Wed.-Sat., 5pm-midnight Sun.; take subway Blue line, JR lines to Sakuragichō Station, exit 1, or Keikyū line to Nogechō Station

Swing open the massive wooden door and step inside the unique space that is L'oeuf. The bar's dark-wood interior has a European flavor, inspired no doubt by the decade its owner, Ikuo Mitsuhashi, spent in Paris as a pantomime artist. Next to the door is a piano, and at the center of the room is a pole for dance performances. The bar, run by the friendly English and French-speaking Mitsuhashi-san, is in the back and there's additional seating upstairs.

DOWNBEAT BAR

1-43 Hanasakichō, 2F Miyamoto Bldg., Naka-ku; tel. 045/241-6167; www.yokohama-downbeat.com; 4pm-11:30pm Mon.-Sat.; cover charge for some events; take subway Blue line, JR lines to Sakuragichō Station, exit 2

A good place to end the journey through Yokohama's jazz landscape is at one of the best jazz joints in the city, Downbeat Bar is a classic old-school jazz *kissa* with dim lighting and worn posters plastered on the walls and ceiling. Tunes chosen from a gold mine of some 3,700 records are played through a stellar sound system. It also hosts gigs sometimes.

Around Yokohama Station

GRASSROOTS

Watanabe Bldg. B1F, 2-13-3 Tsuruyachō; tel. 045/312-0180; http://grassroots.yokohama; 5pm-2am daily; occasional cover charge; take JR lines to Yokohama Station, northwest exit

A good alternative to craft brew and jazz is Grassroots. DJs spin, artists show their work, and musicians jam at this cool basement venue a few minutes' walk from Yokohama Station. A respectable menu of pub food and beers from around the globe is also on offer. Check the event schedule, which varies by night.

INFORMATION AND SERVICES

For information on the city in English, your first port of call in Yokohama is the **Yokohama Station Tourist Information Center** (tel. 045/441-7300; 9am-7pm daily). Located about 7 minutes' walk from Nihon-ōdōri Station, near the western edge of Yamashita-Kōen, **Yokohama Convention & Visitors Bureau** (Sangyō-Bōeki Center 1F, 2 Yamashita-chō; tel. 045/221-2111; www.welcome.city.yokohama.jp/eng/convention; 9am-5pm Mon.-Fri.; take subway Blue line to Nihon-ōdōri, exit 3) is well stocked with English-language maps and flyers and is run by friendly English-speaking staff. And for information on Chinatown, head to the **Chinatown 80** (80 Yamashita-chō; tel. 045/681-6022; 10am-8pm Sun.-Thurs., 10am-9pm Fri.-Sat.; take Minatomirai line to Motomachi-Chūkagai, exit 2).

There are also a few good local resources online. **Yokohama Seasider** (www.yokohamaseasider.com) has event listings, interviews with local movers and shakers, restaurant, café and bar recommendations, and more. Last but not least, the **Yokohama Official Visitor's Guide** (www.yokohamajapan.com) has activity recommendations, listings of all kinds, and transportation information.

TRANSPORTATION

Getting There

The train ride from Tokyo to Yokohama is easy and surprisingly quick. There are a number of options for getting to Yokohama, but for simplicity's sake I recommend starting your journey from either Shibuya, Shinjuku, Tokyo, or Shinagawa station.

If you leave from Shibuya station, take the **Tōkyū Toyoko Line** straight to **Yokohama**

Station, continuing as the **Minato Mirai Line** until **Motomachi-Chukagai** (the best stop to access Chinatown). If your destination is Yokohama Station itself, be sure to catch the express or **limited express train** from Shibuya Station, which can deposit you at Yokohama Station in as little as 30 minutes. The fares for these faster rides are the same as the local train (¥280 one way). If you need to go to a station in downtown Yokohama that is not serviced by express or limited express trains, you can transfer to a local train at Yokohama Station.

Also departing from Shibuya Station is the **JR Shonan Shinjuku Line** (20 minutes; ¥400). The **JR Shonan Shinjuku line** departs from JR Shinjuku Station. The ride to Yokohama Station costs ¥570 one way and takes about 30 minutes.

Two other Tokyo hubs with easy access to Yokohama are **Tokyo** and **Shinagawa station**. The **JR Tōkaidō line**, **JR Yokosuka line** and **JR Keihin-Tohoku line** all run between both stations and Yokohama. A ride on the JR Tōkaidō line from Tokyo Station to Yokohama takes around 25 minutes and costs ¥480 one way; the fare from Shinagawa is ¥300 and the journey takes 20 minutes. The JR Yokosuka Line costs ¥480 and takes about 30 minutes from Tokyo; from Shinagawa, the 20-minute trip costs ¥300. And the ¥480 journey aboard the JR Keihin-Tohoku line from Tokyo to Yokohama takes roughly 40 minutes, while the 30-minute trip from Shinagawa costs ¥300.

Getting Around

SUBWAY

Many of Yokohama's sights, clustered around Minato Mirai 21 and the areas of Motomachi and Chinatown, are within walking distance of each other. The city is served by a subway system with two easily navigable lines, simply called the **Blue and Green lines,** which run north-south (¥210-520).

TRAIN

There is also the local aboveground **JR Negishi line** that runs through the city. But chances are, you won't even need to use these lines. The vast majority of sights you'll likely visit in Yokohama are easily accessed from stops on the Minato Mirai line, which is simply the continuation of the Tokyū Toyoko line that runs directly to Yokohama from Shibuya.

BUS

In addition to train and subway lines, there's an **Akai-Kutsu** bus service (www.yokohamajapan.com/information/getting-around-yokohama/akaikutsu.php), which shuttles visitors to popular sights in the Minato Mirai 21, Chinatown, and Motomachi areas. Buses leave from Sakuragichō station, located on the Blue subway line and JR Negishi line. A quick trip on one of these buses costs ¥220 for adults and ¥110 for children ages 11 and under, which you can pay when you get on the bus, and station announcements are made in English.

WATER TAXI

Finally, one fun way to see the city and get around a bit is by taking a short trip by boat across the bay. The **Sea Bass** (www.yokohama-cruising.jp; 10am-7pm daily) water taxi service stops at piers near Sogō Department Store outside the east exit of Yokohama Station, Minato Mirai 21, the Akarenga retail zone, and Yamashita-Kōen park near Chinatown. Starting from the pier near Yokohama Station east exit, the ride to Minato Mirai 21 takes about 10 minutes (¥400 adults, ¥200 children), about 15 minutes to Akarenga (¥580 adults, ¥290 children), and roughly 15 minutes to Yamashita-kōen (¥700 adults, ¥350 children).

Kamakura

One hour south of Tokyo by train, Kamakura is the closest place to the capital to deeply experience Japanese Buddhism in its various forms. Located in compact area next to the ocean, hemmed in by mountains laced with hiking trails on, the city is home to more than 80 temples and shrines. If you're going to make only one trip beyond Tokyo, make it Kamakura.

Modern-day Kamakura has the feeling of a beach town, which it is. Down-to-earth locals, artisan cafés, and restaurants selling health-conscious food vaguely evoke coastal California. Surfers and sunbathers fill the beaches along the coast heading toward Enoshima, west of town. However, especially on holidays and weekends, the lively shopping street of Komachi-dōri and the town's more popular temples and shrines are thronged with tourists.

The vast majority of Kamakura's religious complexes were built during the Kamakura Period (1185-1333) by monks who absconded from China during the Song Dynasty, when the climate began to turn against Buddhism. During this brief window of time, Japan's first shogun, Minamoto no Yoritomo (1147-1199), chose to base his rather makeshift government in the city after wresting power from Kyoto.

Kamakura's temple construction boom occurred alongside the spread of Buddhism, particularly Zen, in Japanese society. The city's five most important Zen temples, in order of importance, are Kenchō-ji, Engaku-ji, Jufuku-ji, Jōchi-ji, and Jōmyō-ji. While all five temples remain standing, the two most worth visiting are Kenchō-ji and Engaku-ji, both located within walking distance of Kita-Kamakura Station. In truth, this hardly scratches the surface. If you're keen to temple hop all day, ask the kind staff at the tourist information center next to Kamakura Station for more information on the town's many gems.

The town begs to be explored on foot. Next to the grounds of Jōchi-ji you'll find the trailhead to the Daibutsu Hiking Course, a pleasant hike leads southward through the mountains to the iconic Great Buddha statue at the temple of Kotoku-in.

ORIENTATION

Kamakura's time in the political spotlight was turbulent and brief, but its spiritual legacy is readily visible today, with clusters of temples and a handful of key shrines located throughout the city. The main concentrations can be accessed on foot or by bus from **Kita-Kamakura Station** in the north, **Kamakura Station** in the city center, where you'll also find the major shopping thoroughfare of **Komachi-dōri**, and **Hase Station** in the southwest, where you'll find the Great Buddha at Kotoku-in. Beyond the religious sights, the trails weaving through the hills surrounding the city and around the nearby Shōnan coast give a chance to experience a quieter side of Japan, without going far from Tokyo.

SIGHTS

Kita-Kamakura

ENGAKU-JI
円覚寺

409 Yamanouchi; tel. 0467/22-0478; www.engakuji.or.jp/top.html; 8am-4:30pm daily Mar.-Nov., 8am-4pm daily Dec.-Feb.; ¥300 adults, ¥100 children; take JR Yokosuka line to Kita-Kamakura Station

Of Kamakura's five great Zen temples, Engaku-ji is the biggest. Founded in 1282 by Hōjō regent Tokimune, the complex originally had more than 40 sub-temples on its grounds, of which 17 are still standing. The temple's bell, cast in 1301, is Kamakura's biggest and today is only rung to celebrate the new year.

Attesting to the temple's deep antiquity, the Shozoku-in sub-temple showcases some of the best touches of Zen architecture from

China's Sung Dynasty of any temple in Japan and contains a tooth of the Buddha. Note that this building is not open to the public for most of the year, but can be glimpsed through a gate at other times. Yasunari Kawabata, the first Japanese writer to win the Nobel Prize for literature, set much of his novel *Thousand Cranes* on the temple's grounds, dense with history and ambience. Also, legendary film director Yasujiro Ozu is buried in the temple's cemetery.

Before leaving, be sure to relax and sip a tea at the teahouse (8am-4:30pm daily Mar.-Nov., 8am-4pm daily Dec.-Feb.) located on the grounds near the large bell. English menu available.

KENCHŌ-JI
建長寺

8 Yamanouchi; tel. 0467/22-0981; www.kenchoji.com; 8:30am-4:30pm; ¥500 adults, ¥200 children; take JR Yokosuka line to Kita-Kamakura Station

Kenchō-ji is Japan's oldest Zen monastery, founded by the Hōjō regent Tokiyori in 1253 and constructed by Rankei Doryu, a Chinese priest who came to spread the message of Zen in Japan. Only 10 buildings now dot the grounds (there were about 49 sub-temples and seven main halls at its peak) but vestiges of its once great status remain, from a bell cast in 1255 and classified a National Treasure to an atmospheric grove of juniper trees as old as 700 years that are said to have sprung from seeds from China and been planted by Rankei himself. Other interesting elements include an effigy of Jizō Bosatsu, guardian of criminals, a grim reminder of the area's use as an execution ground long ago, and a pond shaped like the character for "spirit."

On Friday and Saturday (www.kenchoji.com/zazen; 4:30pm-5:30pm), the temple holds free crash courses on *zazen* (seated meditation), open to all, in Japanese. Even if you don't understand the instructions, it's perfectly acceptable to show up and join in, following visual cues. Show up about 15 minutes before 4:30pm to join. Brace yourself: You'll be sitting in a certain position for more than 30 minutes.

Central Kamakura

TSURUGAOKA HACHIMAN-GŪ
鶴岡八幡宮

2-1-31 Yukinoshita; tel. 0467/22-0315; www.tsurugaoka-hachimangu.jp; 5am-8:30pm daily Apr.-Sept., 6am-8:30 daily Oct.-Mar.; free

Given Kamakura's samurai legacy, steeped in power struggle and war, it's appropriate that the first shogun, Minamoto Yoritomo, chose to put the god of war, Hachiman, front and center at the city's largest shrine. Tsurugaoka Hachiman-gū sits at the top of a high bluff, with great views of the city and coast.

The design and layout of the shrine were so colored by Minamoto's battle-hardened worldview that even the bridges cutting through the pond on its grounds were meant to symbolize the fissure between the eternally feuding Minamoto and Taira clans. Other associations with the shrine are equally dramatic. In 1219, the shrine's head priest Kugyo hid in a ginkgo tree on the grounds, waiting to take his uncle by surprise and murder him. It's also the setting where shogun Yoritomo commanded the lover of an exiled samurai to dance before him and his wife.

KAMAKURA NATIONAL TREASURE MUSEUM

2-1-1 Yukinoshita; tel. 0467/22-0753; www.city.kamakura.kanagawa.jp/kokuhoukan; 9am-4:30pm Tues.-Sun.; ¥400 adults, ¥200 children; take JR Yokosuka line to Kamakura station, east exit

Have a look at the marvelous collection of Buddhist statuary held at the Kamakura National Treasure Museum behind the pond on the shrine's grounds. The works on display range from wild-eyed temple guardians brandishing swords to beatific, haloed Boddhisatvas and Jizō, as the oft-bibbed stone statues of the protector of children, travelers and unborn are known.

1

2

3

East Kamakura

HŌKOKU-JI

報国寺

2-7-4 Jomyo-ji; tel. 0467/22-0777; www.houkokuji.or.jp; 9am-4pm daily; ¥300; take bus 23, 24, 36 from Kamakura Station to sixth stop for Jōmyō-ji

Hōkoku-ji, a Rinzai temple built in 1334, is a slight detour, but its atmospheric bamboo grove makes the trip worthwhile. While you're there, stop at the space with a roof in the grove to sit and slow down with a cup of green tea and a sweet (¥600). The temple is also home to a raked rock garden, a smattering of Buddhist statuary, and a small teahouse in a pavilion. While sitting, clearing the mind, and doing nothing may not appeal to all, the temple holds basic Zen seated meditation sessions on Sunday mornings (7:30am-10:30am; free) for those who'd like to add a little Zen to their lives.

Hase

HASE-DERA

長谷寺

3-11-2 Hase; tel. 0467/22-6300; www.hasedera.jp/en; 8am-5pm Mar.-Sept., 6am-5:30pm Oct.-Feb.; ¥300; take Enoshima Dentesu line to Hase Station

At Hase-dera, a veritable storeroom of evocative Buddhist relics, an 11-faced Kannon, the goddess of mercy, with a colorful backstory is the temple's centerpiece. Legend states the statue now at Hase-dera in Kamakura was one of two Kannon statues carved from a camphor tree found by a monk named Tokudo Shonin in AD 721 in a village called Hase near Nara. The other one now stands in Hase-dera near Nara. The one in Kamakura is said to have washed ashore on a nearby beach after having been cast into the ocean near Osaka in the faith that it would resurface. Hase-dera in Kamakura was built to commemorate its miraculous discovery.

Along with this multifaced statue of the bodhisattva of compassion, 33 other carvings at the temple depict Kannon's range of avatars. The complex also houses a sutra library, a bell cast in 1264, and an army of stone jizō statues clad in red bibs encircling a hall dedicated to the guardian of children and travelers. Walk past the jizō and enter the cave beyond. Inside you'll find a serene candlelit space and exquisite reliefs of Buddha and other sacred figures carved into the walls. If you only visit one other temple in Kamakura besides Kotoku-in, make it this one.

1: Engaku-ji **2:** Kenchō-ji **3:** tea at Hōkoku-ji temple

★ Great Buddha at Kōtoku-in

高徳院

4-2-28 Hase; tel. 0467/22-0703; www.kotoku-in.jp/en; 8am-5:30pm Apr.-Sept., 8am-5pm Oct.-Mar.; ¥200 adults, ¥150 children; take Enoshima Dentesu line to Hase Station

An 11.3-meter-tall (37-foot), 81-tonne (90-ton) bronze statue of Amida Buddha, the Great Buddha at Kōtoku-in (aka Daibutsu) is a symbol of Kamakura itself. Said to be based on the famed gold-encrusted Buddha occupying Tōdai-ji in Nara, the Buddha's calm pose is accentuated by its palms, facing upward in a mudra known as the *jobon-josho*, believed to maximize potential enlightenment.

This tranquility is impressive, given the fact that the Daibutsu, about a 10-minute walk from Hase-dera, has seen its fair share of calamity, from earthquakes to tidal waves and fires. The original sat in a large hall, destroyed by a monumental typhoon that leveled the city in 1494. Today, it remains seated in blissful meditation—its 1-meter-wide (3.3-foot) eyes half-closed—wearing the same expression of serenity it had when it was cast in 1252. Pay an extra ¥20 to enter the statue itself and see the impressive bronze-work from the inside; there's even a stairway leading to shoulder-height.

SPORTS AND RECREATION

Hiking

If you are interested in hiking around Kamakura but the Daibutsu Hiking Course seems prohibitively crowded, there are other hiking trails in the hills around Kamakura. Pick up information about other options

1
2

and maps, or ask questions to the English-speaking staff, at the **Kamakura City Tourist Association** (1-1-1 Komachi; tel. 0467/22-3350; www.trip-kamakura.com; 9am-5pm daily), which sits just beside Kamakura Station's east exit.

DAIBUTSU HIKING COURSE

Hiking Distance: 3 km (1.9 mi)
Time: 1-1.5 hrs
Information and maps: Visitor Center
Trailhead: Jōchi-ji

If you aren't concerned with ticking the box next to every temple on Kamakura's vast list, the **Daibutsu Hiking Course** is a great way to explore the city's riches on foot. The route links the temple of **Jōchi-ji** (1402 Yamanouchi; tel. 0467/22-3943; https://jochiji.com/en; 9am-4:30pm daily; ¥200 adults, ¥100 children), located about 8 minutes' walk southwest of **Kita-Kamakura Station**, in the north with the **Daibutsu** (Great Buddha) in the south, passing the atmospheric shrine of **Zeniarai Benten** (2-25-16 Sasuke; tel. 0467/25-1081; 8am-4:30pm daily; free) on the way. You'll also take in **Genjiyama Park** (4-7-1 Ogigayatsu, Kamakura; open 24/7; free), the neighboring **Kuzuharagaoka Shrine** (5-9-1 Kajiwara, Kamakura; tel. 0467/45-9002; open 24/7; free), and **Sasuke Inari Shrine** (2-22-10 Sasuke; tel. 0467/22-4711; 24/7; free). From the shrine, the hike continues for about 20 more minutes, at which point you find yourself at the foot of the temple of **Kōtoku-in** and its famed **Great Buddha.**

Cycling

GROVE KAMAKURA

2-1-3 Yuigahama; tel. 0467/23-6667; www.grovekamakura.com; 10am-7pm, closed Wed

While Kamakura is an ideal city to explore on foot, there are options for bicycle rentals for those who would like to cover more terrain. Grove Kamakura, located about 8 minutes' walk from Kamakura Station, rents front-suspension bikes for ¥2,500 and dual suspension bikes for ¥3,000 per day.

JR BUS TECH

1-1 Komachi; tel. 0467/24-2319; www.jrbustech.co.jp/kamakura; 8:30am-5pm, until 5:30pm Apr.-Aug. on holidays, closed Jan. 1-3

JR Bus Tech has two locations: the one near Kamakura Station, and one near Hase Station (2-14 Hase, Kamakura-shi; tel. 0467/24-3944; www.jrbustech.co.jp/kamakura; 9:30am-5pm, until 5:30pm Apr.-Aug. on holidays, closed Jan. 1-3). Both shops offer a range of bicycle types and possible rental timeframes, with a basic one-speed bicycle costing ¥1,800 for any rental of more than four hours.

FOOD

Kita-Kamakura

KAMAKURA HACHINOKI

350 Yamanouchi; tel. 0467/23-3723; www.kitakamakura-en.com; 11:30am-2:30pm Mon.-Fri., 11am-3pm Sat.-Sun. and holidays, 5pm-7pm Thurs.-Tues., dinner only by reservation a day early; ¥3,600-4,500 lunch, ¥6,800-14,250 dinner; take JR lines to Kita-Kamakura Station

Kamakura Hachinoki is a Michelin-starred restaurant serving *shōjin ryōri* (Buddhist vegetarian cuisine traditionally reserved for Zen monks). Set in an old Japanese house, with tatami mats and exquisite old wooden furniture, the meal is a multicourse banquet. Allow a full evening to properly enjoy it. English menu available.

KITA-KAMAKURA EN

501 Yamanouchi; tel. 0467/23-6232; www.Kita-Kamakura-en.com; 11:30am-2pm lunch, 2pm-5pm teatime, 5pm-8pm dinner Tues.-Sun.; ¥5,000 lunch average, ¥10,000 dinner average; take JR lines to Kita-Kamakura Station, west exit

This fantastic family-run *kaiseki* restaurant overlooks a pond and Zen temple grounds. Kita-Kamakura En is a simple space with an earthy color scheme, free of the stuffy atmosphere often associated with *kaiseki*. Set courses change with the seasons, and ingredients are sourced from around the country. On

1: Hase-dera **2:** Great Buddha at Kōtoku-in

the second floor of the ochre building outside Kita-Kamakura Station's main exit. Reserve a month or more in advance. Alternatively, stop by at teatime if it's fully booked.

Central Kamakura

LATTERIA BEBE

11-17 Onarimachi; tel. 0467/81-3440; http://latteria-bebe.com; 11am-9pm Tues.-Sun.; ¥850-2,200; take JR, Enoden lines to Kamakura Station

Latteria Bebe is an excellent pizzeria owned by two brothers who apprenticed as chefs in Italy (one making pizza, the other cheese). Set in an old wooden house about 5 minutes' walk from Kamakura Station, the restaurant has a wood-fire oven and offers on-site cheese workshops where guests make their own mozzarella. The menu includes seasonal ingredients and local seafood. Lunch sets are a good value. Book ahead a few days in advance if possible; otherwise, be prepared to wait. Limited English spoken.

WANDER KITCHEN

10-15 Onarimachi; tel. 0467/61-4751; http://wanderkitchen.net; noon-8pm daily; ¥1,000; take JR, Enoden lines to Kamakura Station

Down a quiet side street near Onari shopping street, Wander Kitchen is a cozy, chic spot for a casual lunch or dinner. Its affordably priced menu casts a wide net, from spicy Southeast Asian and Indian curries to European and Latin American fare. Friendly staff are ready to help you navigate the Japanese menu. Look for the pink flamingo at the entrance to the small side street. Free Wi-Fi.

QK CAFÉ

1-6-28 Yukinoshita; tel. 0467/53-7669; 11am-7pm Wed.-Mon.; ¥1,000; take JR, Enoden lines to Kamakura Station

QK Café, a short walk north of Kamakura Station, is a good option for herbivores. This welcoming café sells bento box lunches loaded with locally sourced vegetables. Work by local artists adorns the walls and quirky souvenirs are scattered about. A daily happy hour (5pm-7pm) offers locals and travelers a chance to mingle. Friendly staff are happy to advise visitors to the city.

★ TSURUYA

3-3-27 Yuigahama; tel. 0467/22-0727; http://tsuruya-en.com/about.html; 11:30am-7pm Wed.-Mon.; ¥2,200-4,400; take Enoden line to Wadazuka Station

It's all about eel at Tsuruya. This Michelin-starred restaurant has been serving a simple menu since 1929 consisting of broiled eel atop rice—either in a stylish wooden box or a bowl—or with rice on the side, delicately flavored with a variety of dipping sauces. The shop has literary associations thanks to the fact it was frequented by novelist Kawabata Yasunari, the first Japanese writer to win the Nobel Prize for literature, who lived in the area toward the end of his life. It's advisable to book a few days in advance.

Hase

MATSUBARA-AN

4-10-3 Yuigahama; tel. 0467/61-3838; http://matsubara-an.com; 11am-9pm daily; ¥2,000-3,000 lunch, ¥3,000-4,000 dinner; take Enoden line to Yuigahama Station

Set in an atmospheric old Japanese house, Matsubara-an is a soba restaurant firmly on the foodie map. Guests have a choice between a chic indoor dining area and outdoor seating in a quiet garden. The restaurant makes its own noodles, which it serves both *kake* (hot) and *zaru* (cold), along with sides like tempura and sashimi. Lunch sets come with starters like roast duck and veggies with *bagna cauda* (Italian hot garlic and anchovy) dip. Reserve a few days in advance for dinner; lunch is first-come, first-served.

KANNON COFFEE KAMAKURA

3-10-29 Hase; tel. 0467/84-7898; 10am-6pm daily; ¥500-1,000; take Enoden line to Hase Station

Three minutes' walk from Hase-dera and five minutes on foot from the Great Buddha, Kannon Coffee Kamakura serves quality coffee and good affordably priced lunches. The shop's dedication to bread is evidenced in the fact that yeast is made on-site. Mildly sacrilegious pastries made in the shape of the Great Buddha are among the more popular items on the menu.

SOMETARO

3-12-11 Hase; tel. 0467/22-8694; www.okonomi-sometaro.com; 11:30am-9pm Thurs.-Mon.; ¥1,000 average; take Enoden line to Hase Station

Just around the corner from Kannon Coffee you'll find Sometaro, a great *okonomiyaki* restaurant. Here you can cook your own fully customizable savory pancake (toppings include cheese, kimchi, egg, and more) or *yakisoba* (stir-fried soba noodles) on a hotplate at your table. If you're new to the process, affable staff are happy to help you get the job done.

GOOD MELLOWS

27-39 Sakanoshita; tel. 0467/24-9655; http://goodmellows-en.com; 10:30am-6:30pm Wed.-Mon.; ¥1,200; take Enoden line to Hase Station

About 12 minutes' walk from Hase-dera, Good Mellows is a great beachside option serving reasonably priced burgers, beers, and the kinds of sides you'd expect to see at a bar stateside (buffalo wings, fries, salads). The burgers can be customized with a range of toppings (pineapple, avocado, bacon, and a slew of cheeses). English menu available. The place closes early, so it's better as an option for lunch.

INFORMATION AND SERVICES

Exit Kamakura Station's east exit and you'll be right in front of the **Kamakura City Tourist Association** (1-1-1 Komachi; tel. 0467/22-3350; www.trip-kamakura.com; 9am-5pm daily). Here you'll find English-language maps, pamphlets, and booklets on the town's history and culture. The center has friendly English-speaking staff who are happy to answer questions. The website **Kamakura Today** (www.city.kamakura.kanagawa.jp/visitkamakura/en/) also provides good information in English about the town's sights, food, shopping, and more.

TRANSPORTATION

Getting There

The **JR Yokosuka line** runs from Tokyo to Kamakura in just under an hour (¥940) and from Shinagawa, stopping at Yokohama en route, in about 45 minutes (¥730). Catching the same train from **Yokohama Station** takes about 25 minutes (¥350).

Another option is the **JR Shonan Shinjuku line,** which directly links Shinjuku and Shibuya to Kamakura in roughly an hour (¥940). Note that, in order to reach Kamakura station on this train, you'll need to transfer at Ofuna, unless you catch a train bound for Zushi.

If you're traveling to Kamakura from one of Japan's other major hubs in Kansai or even farther west, take the **Tōkaidō** ***shinkansen*** from **Shin-Osaka** (3 hours; ¥14,990), passing through Kyoto, Nagoya, and a cluster of other stations before reaching Shin-Yokohama Station. There, you'll transfer to the JR Yokohama Line bound for Sakuragichō, where you'll transfer again to the JR Shōnan-Shinjuku line or the JR Yokosuka line, either of which goes directly to both Kita-Kamakura and Kamakura Station.

Getting Around

The beautiful thing about Kamakura is its sheer walkability. That said, if you want to save a bit of time, you can get around the city and its major sightsclustered around Kita-Kamakura, Kamakura, and Hase stations—by taking the train.

Aside from the JR lines that connect Kita-Kamakura and Kamakura stations, the **Enoden (Enoshima Electric Railway) line** is a classic old-school tram that goes from Kamakura station to Hase, near the Great Buddha, before moving slowly on through the city's coastal neighborhoods. If you want to dig a bit deeper and make a trip to Enoshima, you'll need to take the Enoden to reach the island west of Kamakura proper.

There is also a network of city buses leaving from Kamakura Station and connecting to all the main sights. And if you're in a rush and want to save time when going to a slightly isolated temple or shrine, such as Zeniarai Benten or Houkoku-ji, a brief taxi ride is also an option.

Finally, the **Kamakura Free Kankyo Tegata** is a special ticket deal that allows you to ride freely on any bus running through the city, as well as most stretches of the Enoden line (¥550 adults, ¥280 children). These passes can be purchased at tourist information centers in Kamakura Station, near the east exit of Enoden Kamakura station, Hase Station, and handful of sights around town, including the gift shop at Engaku-ji.

Nikkō 日光

Nikkō (Light of the Sun), a mountainous realm located 125 km (78 mi) north of Tokyo, is dissected by the Daiya River and neighbored to the west by the gleaming alpine Lake Chūzen-ji and holy Mount Nantai. Nikkō was long believed to be the domain of forest spirits; some shrines in this area date back to the 8th century.

This hallowed status inspired Tokugawa Ieyasu (1542-1616), founder of the Tokugawa Shogunate, to have his tomb built there. Ieyasu's grandson, Tokugawa Iemitsu (1604-1651) built the grand mausoleum of Tōshō-gū for his grandfather in 1634, and was later himself enshrined in Nikkō at Taiyūinbyō. UNESCO has declared Nikkō a World Heritage site.

During the Meiji period (1868-1912), when Japan began to open up, central Nikkō, east of most the religious and historical sights, became the summer escape of choice among many foreign diplomats and merchants escaping the heat of Tokyo. Among these residences was Meiji-no-Yakata, once the grounds of a summer villa owned by American trader F.W. Horn, now filled with swanky restaurants.

Nikkō's treasures don't stop at the cultural. The greater area is part of Nikkō National Park, including dazzling Lake Chūzen-ji, some 10 km (6 mi) west of downtown, surrounded by waterfalls and hiking trails through dense old-growth forest, as well as the tranquil hot-springs of Yumoto Onsen, set deep in the mountains. These natural riches are a short bus ride from central Nikkō, worth exploring if you can stay overnight.

Nikkō can unfortunately be inundated by crowds. The town is at its most packed on weekends and holidays, particularly from May to October. Your best is either to visit on a weekday or stay overnight and get an early start on sightseeing.

ORIENTATION

Nikkō is compact, with a population just over 80,000. The town's wealth of temples and shrines are all bunched together roughly 2 km (1.2 mi) northwest of **JR Nikkō** and **Tobu-Nikkō stations.** The gateway to the town's grandiose religious structures is the famed **Shin-kyō,** an arched bridge over the Daiya-gawa river, located about 1.6 km (1 mi) from the town's two main railway stations. You can reach this point either by taking a bus (5 minutes; ¥200) or simply taking the 30-minute walk.

Once you've crossed the famed Shin-kyo, the first major sight you'll come to is the temple of **Rinnō-ji**, followed by **Tōshō-gū.** Another 5-minute walk west of Tosho-gu brings you to **Futarasan-jinja,** Nikkō's most ancient sight, with **Taiyuinbyō Temple,** where Ieyasu's grandson is enshrined, another 15 minutes' walk westward from there.

A worthy detour from Nikkō's core sightseeing district is the ethereal ravine known as the **Kanmangafuchi Abyss,** a pathway lined with stone lanterns and stone guardian Jizo statues along the southern bank of the Daiya-gawa, just about 30 minutes on foot from the town's major cluster of temples and shrines.

Nikkō

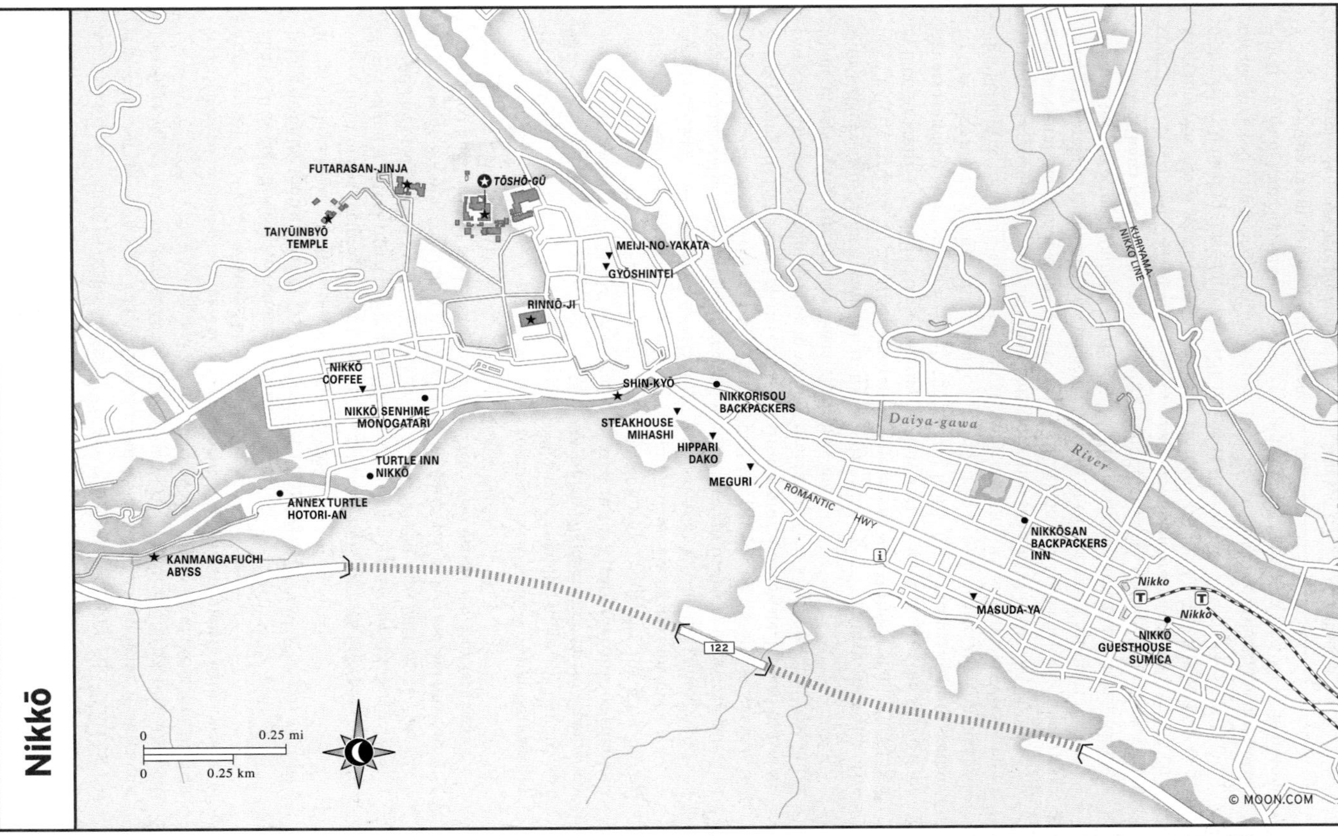
FUTARASAN-JINJA
TŌSHŌ-GŪ
TAIYŪINBYŌ TEMPLE
MEIJI-NO-YAKATA
GYŌSHINTEI
RINNŌ-JI
KURIYAMA-NIKKO LINE
NIKKŌ COFFEE
NIKKŌ SENHIME MONOGATARI
SHIN-KYŌ
NIKKORISOU BACKPACKERS
STEAKHOUSE MIHASHI
HIPPARI DAKO
Daiya-gawa River
TURTLE INN NIKKŌ
MEGURI
ANNEX TURTLE HOTORI-AN
ROMANTIC HWY
NIKKŌSAN BACKPACKERS INN
KANMANGAFUCHI ABYSS
Nikko
MASUDA-YA
Nikkō
NIKKŌ GUESTHOUSE SUMICA
122
0
0.25 mi
0
0.25 km
© MOON.COM

SIGHTS

Shin-kyō (Sacred Bridge)
神橋

Kamihatsuishimachi, Nikkō; tel. 0288/54-0535; www.shinkyo.net/english; 8am-5pm daily Apr.-Sept., 8am-4pm daily Oct.-mid-Nov., 9am-4pm daily mid-Nov.-Mar.; ¥300; from Nikkō Station or Tōbu Nikkō Station, take a Tōbu bus to Shin-kyō bus stop

Your survey of Nikkō's wonders begins at Shin-kyō (Sacred Bridge), a vermillion arched bridge spanning the banks of the Daiya-gawa. It sits at the entrance to the area of Nikkō where most of the temples and shrines are clustered and is actually part of **Futarasan-jinja.** The bridge is said to mark the spot where Shōdō Shōnin, a Buddhist priest who introduced Buddhism to Nikkō, crossed the river atop two snakes in AD 766.

Rinnō-ji
輪王寺

2300 Sannai, Nikkō; tel. 0288/54-0531; www.rinnoji.or.jp; 8am-5pm Apr.-Oct., 8am-4pm Nov.-Mar.; ¥400 adults, ¥200 children, or ¥900 for multi-entry ticket to Taiyūinbyō; take JR Nikkō line to Nikkō Station and Tōbu Nikkōline to Tōbu Nikkō Station, then take a Tōbu bus to Nishisando bus stop

After crossing the Daiya-gawa on the backs of two serpents, Shōdō Shōnin went on to found Rinnō-ji, a sprawling temple of the Tendai sect with 1,200 years of history behind it. In the main hall—a striking black, green and vermillion structure—you'll find three towering figures standing 8 meters (26 feet) tall and representing manifestations of the Buddha, with Senju, the thousand-armed version of Kannon, the goddess of mercy, on the right; Amida Nyorai, the Buddha who guides believers to paradise, in the middle; and Bato-Kannon, the protector of animals, on the left. For an additional fee of ¥300, you can also enter the treasure hall (8am-5pm Apr.-Oct., 8am-4pm Nov.-Mar.), which contains around 6,000 relics linked to the temple, as well as the nearby stroll garden Shōyō-en (8am-5pm Apr.-Oct., 8am-4pm Nov.-Mar.).

North of the main hall is a sub-temple known as Goho-tendo, where the faithful offer up prayers, written on wooden plaques, which are burned and released to the heavens. Three of the Seven Gods of Luck of Chinese folklore are enshrined in Goho-tendo: Daikoku-ten and Bishamon-ten, bestowing wealth and a bountiful harvest, and Benzai-ten, the goddess of the arts. South of the main hall is the abbot's quarters, complete with a beautiful Edo-period garden.

★ Tōshō-gū
東照宮

2301 Sannai, Nikkō; tel. 0288/54-0560; www.toshogu.jp; 8am-4:30pm Apr.-Oct., 8am-3:30pm Nov.-Mar.; ¥1,300 adults, ¥450 children; take JR Nikkō line to Nikkō Station and Tōbu Nikkōline to Tōbu Nikkō Station, then take a Tōbu bus to Nishisando bus stop

Tōsho-gū is a UNESCO World Heritage site and shrine complex, originally built in 1617 for which Nikkō is famous. No expense was spared in the creation of this ostentatious complex, which enshrines Tokugawa Ieyasu, founder of the Tokugawa shogunate.

Make your way up the Omotesandō and walk through the large stone *torii* gate. Just past the pagoda up a stone staircase is the **Omotemon** shrine gate, flanked by two intimidating deva kings meant to protect the holy site.

In this first square beyond the Omotemon, you'll find a stable housing a white sacred horse. Above the stable door is the iconic panel that has come to symbolize Nikkō, which depicts three monkeys—one covering its ears, one its eyes, one its mouth—sending the message of "Hear no evil. See no evil. Speak no evil." The precise origin of this imagery is uncertain, but it's believed that it came to Japan via a Chinese Buddhist monk in the 8th century. At the back of this square is a sutra library, which is closed to the public. The **Nikkō Tōshō-gū Museum of Art** (2301 Sannai, Nikkō; tel. 0288/54-0560; www.toshogu.jp/shisetsu/bijutsu.html; 9am-5pm Apr.-Oct., 9am-4pm

1: Shin-kyō **2:** Tōshō-gū **3:** Rinnō-ji

1
2
3

Nov.-Mar.; ¥800 adults, ¥400 children) is found at the end of a path that branches off to the right from the courtyard beyond the Omotemon.

Proceeding from this first courtyard, make your way to the second flight of stone stairs. On your right, you'll see a bell tower; on the left, a drum tower and **Yakushi-do,** a temple dedicated to the Buddha's ability to heal sickness, known for the *Crying Dragon* painted on its ceiling. Continue to the top of the stairs where you'll find the mesmerizing 11.3-meter-tall (37-foot) **Yomeimon** (Gate of Sunlight), a National Treasure and example par excellence of the Momoyama style of architecture and sculpture derived from Chinese Ming Dynasty aesthetics. So close to perfection was this gate that those who built inverted the last beam to avoid making the gods jealous.

Across the Yomeimon, to the right is the **Kaguraden,** a space for religious dances and Shinto weddings. On the left is a storage room for portable shrines used in traditional festivals. And on the opposite side of this courtyard is the gate that leads to the shrine's inner sanctum. This gate, known as the **Karamon** (Chinese Gate), is another opulent National Treasure that leads to the main inner courtyard. After slipping off your shoes, you can enter the main hall and the prayer hall, as far you may go into Tōshō-gū itself. Deeper into the complex is the inner chamber and innermost chamber, closed to visitors.

Back in the plaza just inside the Yomeimon gate, on the right you'll encounter one more symbol of Nikkō, the **Sakashitamon** (Gate of the Sleeping Cat). Cross through this gate bearing the image of a sleeping feline and climb 207 steps to reach Tokugawa Ieyasu's actual tomb. The monument itself is relatively mundane, but the pristine surroundings are worth seeing.

Futarasan-jinja

日光二荒山神社

2307 Sannai, Nikkō; tel. 0288/54-0535; www.futarasan.jp; 8am-5pm daily Apr.-Oct., 9am-4pm daily Nov.-Mar.; ¥200 adults, ¥100 children; from Nikkō Station or Tōbu Nikkō Station , take a Tōbu bus to Nishisando bus stop

The first thing to note about Futarasan-jinja is its age. Founded by Shōdō Shōnin in AD 782, this shrine is the spiritual guardian of Nikkō. This feels appropriate, considering that the shrine was built to honor the gods of three sacred mountains surrounding the area: Mount Nantai, Mount Nyoho, and Mount Tarō. The Futarasan-jinja complex next to Tōshō-gū is, in fact, one of three locations, with other shrines including Chugushi-jinja, on the banks of nearby Lake Chūzen-ji, and Oku-miya atop Mount Nantai. Without the pomp of its neighbor, it exudes a sense of calm and relative simplicity.

Entering via a bronze *torii* gate, you'll discover an ornate gate decorated and carved in much the same way as the Karamon (Chinese Gate) of Tōshō-gū. The same applies to the Haiden (prayer hall), featuring paintings of dragons and lions, beyond the gate. The current incarnation of the Honden (main hall) of the shrine is the oldest structure in Nikkō, dating to 1619. Feel your eyes drawn to the room's centerpiece: a 2.7-meter-tall (9-foot) altar adorned with natural scenes of animals and flowers, containing a wooden statue of Tokugawa Iemitsu, grandson of Ieyasu.

Taiyūinbyō Temple

大猷院廟

tel. 0288/54-0531; 8am-4:30pm Apr.-Oct., 8am-3:30pm Nov.-Mar.; ¥550 adults, ¥250 children, or ¥900 for multi-entry ticket to Rinno-ji; take JR Nikkō line to Nikkō Station and Tōbu Nikkōline to Tōbu Nikkō Station, then take a Tōbu bus to Nishisando bus stop

This temple is the mausoleum of Iemitsu Tokugawa, third of the Tokugawa shoguns and grandson of Ieyasu. Similar in style and layout to neighboring Tōshō-gū, Iemitsu had Taiyūinbyō built at a slightly smaller scale in deference to his larger-than-life grandfather enshrined next door.

Another difference between the two ornate

complexes is that while Tōshō-gū is a shrine, Taiyūinbyō is a temple; more specifically a sub-temple of Rinnō-ji. It's worth noting that before the Meiji period, there was less effort to draw a clear line between Buddhism and Shintō. Before Japan's push to modernize, the two religions mingled freely, as reflected in many old religious structures throughout the country, including Taiyūinbyō.

Mirroring its grander neighbor, Taiyūinbyō is entered by following a path west of Tōshō-gū until reaching a vermillion gate, through which you encounter a second gate protected by two celestial kings, each holding up one hand and keeping the other down—gestures meant to receive those with pure hearts and repel those without—then, a bell tower on the right and a drum tower on the left. Passing next through the Karamon gate, you come to the prayer hall. Inside, marvel at the pillars and walls adorned with gold lacquer, carvings, and more. Beyond this is the main hall, which can only be observed from outside, and Iemitsu's mausoleum itself.

Taiyūinbyō's visual impact cannot compare with Tōshō-gū, but the overall effect in terms of stillness and the setting within a dense forest of cryptomeria give this smaller complex a special atmosphere all its own.

Kanmangafuchi Abyss
憾満ヶ淵

free; from Nikkō Station or Tōbu Nikkō Station, take Tōbu bus to Tamozawa bus stop

To see a less crowded site, cross the bridge over the Daiya-gawa near Tamozawa Villa. Running along the southern bank of the river you'll find a wooded path lined with some 70 moss-encrusted stone statues of Jizō (guardian of children and travelers) adorned with red bibs and crocheted caps. This path, always open and free of charge, is known as the Kanmangafuchi Abyss. A tradition calls the stone figures lining the path "Bake Jizō" (Ghost Jizō), due to the belief that one always arrives at a different number when counting them while walking up the path and then recounting them on the journey back.

Although the walk from Tōshō-gū to the Kanmangafuchi Abyss takes about 30 minutes, or 20 minutes from Shin-kyō, heading west from Shin-kyō along the northern bank of the Daiya-gawa and crossing a bridge from the north to south side of the river on the way, the slight detour is worth it. Imbued with serenity, it's one of the most atmospheric spots in Nikkō and will feel like a respite from the crowds. If you're not walking from a nearby sight, the path begins after passing through a residential area near the Tōbu bus stop for Tamozawa.

FOOD

Nikkō's restaurant options are mostly clustered in the downtown area between JR and Tobu-Nikkō stations and Shin-kyo. There are also a few good options within the prime sightseeing area where all of the famed temples and shrines are located. The offerings extend from locally sourced wagyu beef to meals featuring strips of locally made *yuba* (tofu skin), a staple in *shōjin-ryōri* eaten by Buddhist monks.

Downtown

★ MASUDA-YA

439-2 Ishiyamachi; tel. 0288/54-2151; www.nikko-yuba.com; 11am-3pm Fri.-Wed.; ¥3,900-5,200; take JR Nikkō line to Nikkō Station and Tōbu Nikkō line to Tōbu Nikkō Station

Masuda-ya is the place in central Nikkō to try *yuba*. These sheets of bean curd are a specialty that was once reserved for royals and priests in Nikkō and Kyōto, which are both known for the dish. Set in a cozy space overlooking a Japanese garden, the restaurant serves a *kaiseki* course with a variety of plates combining yuba with local produce, eggs, trout, pickles, rice, and more. If you're in Nikkō, it's worth trying this unique cuisine. Lunch only.

MEGURI

909 Nakahatsuishimachi; tel. 080/9343-0831; www.facebook.com/yasaicafemeguri/; 11:30am-6pm Sat.-Wed.; ¥1,500 average; from Nikkō Station or Tōbu Nikkō Station, take a Tōbu bus to Shin-kyō bus stop

For a more hip, contemporary and casual option, Meguri serves excellent vegan curries, tempura, soups, cakes, and more. The restaurant, run by a friendly young couple, has tatami floor-seating and a mural of birds, flowers, and trees across the ceiling. The dining area is small, and food is sold on a first-come, first-served basis, so show up early if you plan to eat lunch here. Roughly 5 minutes' walk from Shin-kyō; look for a sign outside that says "Oriental Fine Arts."

HIPPARI DAKO

1011 Kamihatsuishimachi; tel. 0288/53-2933; noon-5pm, 6:30pm-8:30pm daily; ¥500-1,000; from Nikkō Station or Tōbu Nikkō Station, take a Tōbu bus to Shin-kyō bus stop

Hippari Dako is a greasy-spoon joint with a long history of attracting foreign diners. The copious number of business cards, student ID cards, and random notes scrawled onto scraps of paper plastered all over its walls and ceiling attests to this. Part of its appeal is a cost-effective menu—a rarity in Nikkō—of simple items like grilled dumplings, ramen, yakisoba, curry udon (thick wheat-flour noodles), and yakitori.

STEAKHOUSE MIHASHI

1115 Kamihatsuishimachi; tel. 0288/54-3429; www.meiji-yakata.com/en/mihashi/; 11:30am-8pm Fri.-Wed.; ¥1,800-10,000; from Nikkō Station or Tōbu Nikkō Station, take a Tōbu bus to Shin-kyō bus stop

Another eatery in the same family, Steakhouse Mihashi is a casual restaurant that serves locally sourced wagyu beef steaks and fresh vegetables on sizzling platters. The mushroom steak made from locally grown *maitake* brazed in house-made sauce is tasty. Conveniently located up a hill near Shin-kyō.

Heritage Area

★ MEIJI-NO-YAKATA

2339-1 Sannai; tel. 0288/53-3751; www.meiji-yakata.com; 11am-7:30pm daily Apr.-late Nov., 11:30am-7:30pm daily late Nov.-Mar.; ¥1,500-8,000; from Nikkō Station or Tōbu Nikkō Station , take Tōbu bus to Nishisando bus stop

Meiji-no-Yakata is an institution. Set in a stone cottage with soaring ceilings and hardwood floors, it was once the home of 19th-century American merchant F.W. Horn, who brought the gramophone to Japan. A short walk from Rinno-ji, this restaurant serves Western fare, from roast lamb to steaks and stews made with locally sourced beef, and fish caught in nearby Lake Chūzen-ji—the very types of dishes being introduced to Japan when Horn called the place home. This is an enjoyable place to dine on the sort of Western-style cooking that emerged during the Meiji era. English menu available.

GYŌSHINTEI

2339-1 Sannai; tel. 0288/53-3751; www.meiji-yakata.com; 11am-7pm Fri.-Wed. Apr.-late Nov., 11:30am-7:30pm Fri.-Wed. late Nov.-Mar.; ¥3,800-5,500; from Nikkō Station or Tōbu Nikkō Station, take Tōbu bus to Nishisando bus stop

Owned by the same group that runs Meiji-no-Yakata, and located on the same property, Gyōshintei veers away from meat and instead focuses on *shōjin ryōri*, featuring liberal helpings of local produce and *yuba*, or tofu skin. Even the soup stock is free of animal products. Tatami-mat-floored rooms, calligraphy scrolls, ikebana arrangements set into alcoves, and views onto a garden dotted by bonsai trees and moss-covered rocks create a calm atmosphere, appropriate for a meal traditionally made for monks. If you crave a little extra protein, the *kaiseki* courses include a bit of fish.

NIKKŌ COFFEE

3-13 Honchō; tel. 0288/53-2335; http://nikko-coffee.com; 10am-6pm Tues.-Sun., closed first and third Tues. every month or next day if Tues. falls on public holiday; ¥600 coffee, ¥1,500 lunch; from Nikkō

Station or Tōbu Nikkō Station, take a Tōbu bus to Nishisando bus stop

Nikkō Coffee is set in an old rice store that's been spruced up with antique furniture, exposed rafters, and retro lighting. Tucked down a backstreet, this is a good spot for a caffeine hit, snack, or light lunch, with options like sandwiches, galettes, and curries.

ACCOMMODATIONS

Under ¥10,000

NIKKŌSAN BACKPACKERS INN

1-362-8 Inarimachi; tel. 0288/53-5016; www.nikkosanbackpackersinn.com; ¥2,600 dorm, ¥6,500 double; take JR Nikkō line to Nikkō Station and Tōbu Nikkō line to Tōbu Nikkō Station

Nikkōsan BackPackers Inn is a stylish new hostel with a relaxed atmosphere near Nikkō Station, with mixed and female-only dorm rooms, as well as private singles and doubles. All rooms share a bathroom. Friendly, knowledgeable staff are happy to suggest itinerary options and give recommendations for restaurants and other destinations around town. It's a good place to meet fellow travelers, too.

NIKKŌ GUESTHOUSE SUMICA

5-12 Aioichō; tel. 090/1838-7873; www.nikko-guesthouse.com; ¥3,000 dorm, ¥8,000 double, ¥14,000 private apartment; take JR Nikkō line to Nikkō Station and Tōbu Nikkō line to Tōbu Nikkō Station

Set in a nicely revamped house, Nikkō Guesthouse Sumica is a chic hostel run by a friendly couple who are eager to make guests feel at home and give suggestions for your journey. Room choices include dorms and tatami-mat doubles. All rooms share a bathroom. Note that the inn enforces an 11pm curfew.

★ NIKKORISOU BACKPACKERS

1107 Kamihatsuishimachi; tel. 080/9449-1545; http://nikkorisou.com; ¥3,000 dorm, ¥8,000 double; from Nikkō Station or Tōbu Nikkō Station, take a Tōbu bus to Shin-kyō bus stop

Near Shin-kyō and within easy reach of the main shrine complex of Tōshō-gū, Nikkorisou Backpackers is a laid-back guesthouse with a shared bathroom and dorm rooms, both mixed and female-only, as well as tatami-mat and Western-style doubles. All guests can use a shared kitchen. Bicycles can be rented for ¥500 a day.

¥10,000-20,000

ANNEX TURTLE HOTORI-AN

8-28 Takumichō; tel. 0288/53-3663; www.turtle-nikko.com/hotori-an; ¥13,100 double with bathroom

Near the southwestern edge of the Tōshō-gū area, Annex Turtle Hotori-an is notable for its shared *onsen* bath overlooking the river. Both Japanese tatami and Western-style rooms with private baths are available. Western-style breakfast can be served in-room upon request. If rooms are all booked, also check at the original **Turtle Inn Nikkō** (2-16 Takumichō; tel. 0288/53-3168; www.turtle-nikko.com/turtle; ¥11,300 double with bathroom), located nearby.

Over ¥40,000

NIKKŌ SENHIME MONOGATARI

6-48 Yasukawa-chō; tel. 0288/54-1010; www.senhime.co.jp/en; ¥45,000 d with 2 meals

Located about 7 minutes' walk west of Shin-kyō and about 10 minutes' walk south of the temple and shrine district, this well-appointed hotel has both Western and tatami rooms with views of the surrounding mountains and Daiya-gawa river. There are shared, sex-separated open-air *onsen* baths and saunas, and some rooms have private outdoor baths, too. Great Japanese dinner and a breakfast that can be either Japanese or Western-style are included. Contact the hotel directly to compare rates, which are sometimes cheaper than you'll find on booking websites.

INFORMATION AND SERVICES

For English-language maps and help with finding food and accommodation around town, stop by the information desk at **Tōbu-Nikkō Station** (tel. 0288/22-1525;

8:30am-5pm daily). Downtown, the more well-stocked **Nikkō Kyōdo Center** (591 Goko-machi; tel. 0288/54-2496; www.achikochi-kanko.jp; 9am-5pm daily) is located about 15 minutes' walk up the main strip from the JR and Tōbu stations on the left side of the road. You'll have better luck finding English-speaking staff here, particularly from 10am to 2pm.

TRANSPORTATION

Getting There

Starting from Asakusa Station in **Tokyo,** take the **Tobu Nikkō Line,** which offers limited-express (*tokkyu*) trains (1 hour 50 minutes; ¥2,750) roughly twice an hour, and rapid (*kaisoku*) trains (2.5 hours; ¥1,360). It's possible to book a seat on the spot for either type of train, but you may have to change trains at Shimoimaichi Station if you opt for the cheaper rapid option. Also note that sitting in one of the two cars at the back of the rapid train is wise, as the train often splits at a station along the way, leaving only the two cars at the rear to continue on to Nikkō.

Alternatively, if you happen to be traveling with a JR Pass you can take the **JR Utsunomiya line,** which departs from Shinjuku Station, and goes to Utsunomiya Station. From here, you can take the JR Nikkō line the rest of the way. Note that this option is only economical if you're using a JR pass, which will cover the cost of the entire journey. Similarly, you can take the **JR Tohoku** *shinkansen* from either Tokyo or Ueno station, again transferring to the JR Nikkō Line at Utsunomiya, using the JR Pass.

Reaching Nikkō from **Kansai** (Osaka, Kyoto) or **Nagoya** involves first going to Tokyo via the Tōkaidō *shinkansen,* then taking one of the routes from the capital described above. Coming from Shin-Osaka, for example, is roughly a 5-hour journey, costing approximately ¥19,000, depending on which route you take from Tokyo.

Getting Around

The bulk of Nikkō's sights are located about 20 minutes' walk northwest of both **Tobu Nikkō** and **JR Nikkō stations.** Buses (¥200) run from both station areas also run to Shin-kyō, Tosho-gu and all surrounding sights.

It's worth knowing about a few special passes that can save a bit of money on transportation, not only within Nikkō but also for the journey to and from Tokyo. The **Nikkō City Area Pass** (www.tobu.co.jp/foreign/en/pass/twoday.html; ¥2,0400 for adults, ¥610 for children) covers round-trip train fare between Asakusa and Nikkō (excluding limited-express trains) and unlimited local train and bus rides within certain areas of Nikkō for two days. The **Nikkō All Area Pass** (www.tobu.co.jp/foreign/en/pass/all.html; ¥4,600 for adults and ¥1,180 for children Apr. 20-Nov. 27, ¥4,230 for adults and ¥1,060 for children Nov. 28-Apr. 19) offers a four-day option that covers round-trip fare between Tokyo and Nikkō (limited express not included), as well as more extensive bus travel, including to Chūzen-ji *onsen* and Yumoto *onsen*, northwest of the shrine area in the vicinity of Lake Chūzen-ji.

To check fares for other bus trips beyond Nikkō's shrine area, check the Tobu Bus website (www.tobu-bus.com/en/nikko). And be sure to pick up a clear English-language map—an invaluable resource for visualizing transportation logistics in the area—at either Nikkō's JR or Tobu station.

Minakami and Around 水上

The *onsen* town of Minakami at Gunma Prefecture's wild northern fringe is perhaps the most well-rounded slice of nature within close range of Tokyo. Located a little less than two hours from the capital by train and local bus, the area surrounding the town itself is home to 18 *onsen* pumping volcanically heated water into a plethora of appealing baths, including Takaragawa Onsen, one of Japan's best places to soak in lush surroundings.

The area is also a known quantity among adventure sports enthusiasts, thanks to the beautifully rugged terrain, centered on **Mount Tanigawa** (1,977 meters/6,486 feet), one of Japan's 100 Famous Mountains. This means trekking and rock climbing in the warmer months and skiing in winter. Running through the area is the Tone River, which whips up some of Japan's best white water in spring when snow from the surrounding mountains melts. Opportunities for rafting are abundant from April through June, and for canyoning when it heats up in summer.

A quick word on food options, of which there are few in the area. Your best bet is to eat at your *ryokan* or lodge of choice if you plan to stay overnight in the area. Otherwise, ask for a few recommendations at the tourist information center. Among the area's smattering of restaurants, some only operate seasonally, so that's your best bet.

TAKARAGAWA ONSEN 宝川温泉

1899 Fujiwara; tel. 0278/75-2614; www.takaragawa.com; 9am-5pm daily; ¥2,000 adults, ¥1,500 children, bath towel ¥100, face towel ¥200; take bus heading from Minakami Station toward Takaragawa Onsen (every 1.5 hours), every second or third bus stops directly at Takaragawa Onsen (40 minutes; ¥1,150), while others only go as far as Takaragawa Iriguchi bus stop (30 minutes, ¥1,050), from where you must walk 20 minutes or take courtesy car (no reservation required)

Beside a river flowing through a splendid landscape of forested mountains, Takaragawa Onsen is not only one of Japan's largest outdoor baths, it's one of the most magical. Three large mixed baths and one for women only dot the side of the Takara River, upstream from the Tone River—a breathtaking scene. Recently, the *onsen* has instated a new policy that requires all guests to wear a bathing suit in the mixed area. This is very "un-Japanese," though it may make this a more comfortable *onsen* for some bathers.

Luxuriating in the steamy pools is likely all you will feel like doing once you've arrived, but the dense forest surrounding the baths is crisscrossed with inviting trails begging to be explored. If you choose to venture out, you'll likely find yourself gravitating back to the baths beside the burbling stream. Close your eyes and ease yourself in. This is what the *onsen* experience is all about.

★ SPORTS AND RECREATION

A slew of adventure sports tour outfits are active in the Minakami area, thanks to the mountainous terrain and presence of the Tone River. There are excellent English-speaking guides that lead white-water rafting tours on the waterway during spring (Apr.-June), when the rapids pick up, with May being the wildest time. During summer, when the Tone tames a bit and the heat spikes, the attention shifts to canyoning, or traversing canyons by walking, swimming, climbing, and rappelling.

Rafting and Canyoning

Among the area's tour providers, **Canyons** (tel. 0278/72-2811; www.canyons.jp) stands out, offering half-day rafting trips for ¥9,500, full-day journeys for ¥16,000, and canyoning tours from ¥8,500 to ¥9,500, depending

1

2

on location. Other good options for rafting and canyoning include **I Love Outdoors** (tel. 0278/72-1337; http://iloveoutdoors.jp), which does half-day rafting expeditions for ¥8,000 and half-day canoeing trips from ¥6,500. One more outfit worth checking out is **H20 Guide Services** (tel. 0278/72-6117; http://h2o-guides.jp), which also offers guided rafting (¥8,000 half-day, ¥13,000 full-day in May only) and canyoning trips (¥8,000).

Hiking

If you'd like to try to make the ascent up Mount Tanigawa itself, be sure to do some research first. There are also some good guides in the region, but they only speak Japanese (https://mmga.jp). At a glance, it may seem like it would be a straightforward climb, but the peak is tricky and has taken more than 800 lives, dwarfing the number of unfortunate climbers who have died on Everest. If you're keen to try, you can start either from the service road that runs up the mountain to the left of the Tanigawa-dake Ropeway, or save yourself the first 600 meters (1,968 feet)—roughly 2.5 hours—of huffing and puffing by riding the gondola and then continuing up the peak from there.

If you opt for the latter, Mount Tanigawa will be the peak looming to your right when you reach the top of the ropeway. Just follow the trail that starts from the righthand side from that point, which leads to **Tomanomimi** (1,963 meters; 6,440 feet), the first of two peaks, after about 2 hours of hiking. Before you reach the top, you'll come to **Kata no Koya** (tel. 090/3347-0802; https://twitter.com/gunmanooyama), a lodge where you can make a pit stop for drinks and food. From here, you can either simply turn around and return, or you can press on to Mount Tanigawa's second peak, **Okinomimi** (1,977 meters; 6,486 feet), following the same trail. This second peak is only a few minutes' walk beyond the first. Unless you are a highly experienced hiker with suitable gear, simply returning from this point is recommended.

Note that hiking season runs from May through October or November, depending on when snow begins to fall. For two detailed hike reports, check out the one at the always informative **Hiking In Japan** blog (https://japanhike.wordpress.com/2008/04/09/mt-tanigawa). To see a map (Japanese only) that shows what the hike looks like from the top of the ropeway to the highest peak (Okinomimi), visit www.tanigawadake-rw.com/tanigawadake. Stop by the **Minakami Tourist Association** (page 199) for more information on potential hikes in the area.

TANIGAWA-DAKE ROPEWAY
谷川岳ロープウェイ

www.tanigawadake-rw.com; tel. 0278/72-3575; 8am-5pm Mon.-Fri. and 7am-5pm Sat.-Sun. and holidays Apr.-Nov., 8:30am-4:40pm daily Dec.-Mar.; ¥1,230 one-way, ¥2,060 round-trip

The mountains present adventure of a different variety. The Tanigawa-dake Ropeway is a gondola that transports you to the top of Tenjin-daira, a ski resort area roughly 1,500 meters (4,921 feet) up Mount Tanigawa. A number of hiking trails, open from May through November and ranging from easy to grueling, start from this point. Even if you don't plan to trek, it's worth boarding one of the gondolas and enjoying the fantastic vista of the dramatic terrain that surrounds Minakami. A bus to the bottom of the ropeway (Ropeway Ekimae bus stop) departs hourly from Minakami Station (20 minutes; ¥750). You can also reach the lower station of the ropeway by taking the train from Minakami Station to Doai Station (8 minutes; ¥240), although these trains run infrequently. From Doai Station, it's a 15-minute walk uphill to the lower station of the ropeway.

Mountain Biking

For mountain biking enthusiasts, **MTB Japan** (tel. 0278/72-1650; www.mtbjapan.com) provides half-day (¥6,000) and full-day (¥10,000

1: Takaragawa Onsen **2:** hikers on Mount Tanigawa

including lunch) downhill tours through the area's stunning mountain trails, passing waterfalls, running along lakes, and ploughing full speed ahead downhill. It's worth noting that MTB Japan arranges tours with other operators, combining mountain biking with canyoning, canoeing, or kayaking. For bona fide thrill seekers, they can even arrange for paragliding or bungee jumping. Inquire for details. On that note, **Bungy Japan** has English speaking staff and does bungee jumps (tel. 0278/72-8133; www.bungyjapan.com; ¥9,000 for first jump) from the 42-meter-high (137-foot) Suwakyō Bridge above the Tone River.

Skiing

In winter, Minakami is a destination for powder hounds in search of a fix near Tokyo. Water-sports tour provider **Canyons** excels again here, offering chances to traipse through the snowy landscape with snowshoes (¥6,000 half-day, ¥9,500 full-day) from January through March. The family-run **Tenjin Lodge** at Mount Tanigawa's base also provides a variety of skiing tours, from backcountry skiing (¥15,000 full-day, ¥5,000 for gear) to snowshoeing (¥7,000 adults, ¥5,000 children under 12). Tenjin Lodge opens its rooms to tour members and nonparticipants alike.

JAPAN SNOW ADVENTURES

45 Yubiso; tel. 080/9083-2172; http://japansnowadventures.com

Canyons also arranges backcountry skiing tours of varying difficulty levels with Japan Snow Adventures. Note that Canyons also offer accommodation packages at its Alpine Lodge for those joining a tour (¥2,500 Sun.-Fri., ¥4,500 Sat. and public holidays, includes breakfast).

ACCOMMODATIONS

Under ¥10,000

TENJIN LODGE

220-4 Yubisa; tel. 0278/25-3540; www.tenjinlodge.com; ¥6,500 per person for double room; From Tokyo, take Joetsu Shinkansen to Echigo-Yuzawa Station, then take JR Joetsu line to Doai Station, pickup from Minakami Station also available on request

If your aim is to venture into the mountains around Minakami, whether for skiing in winter or trekking during the warmer months, Tenjin Lodge is a great option. This friendly, family-run lodge has Japanese and Western-style rooms and shared male and female bathrooms, and serves up tasty home-cooked breakfasts (¥800) and dinners (¥1,200), from pasta to Southeast Asian and Korean food. Sometimes they also do a good barbecue at the riverside next to the inn (¥2,000). As a bonus, the hosts are passionate about the outdoors and offer a variety of adventure tours in the area, from trekking to skiing.

¥20,000-30,000

TAKARAGAWA ONSEN ŌSENKAKU

1899 Fujiwara; tel. 0278/75-2121; www.takaragawa.com; ¥22,500 with two meals and shared bathroom; take bus from Minakami Station to Takaragawa Iriguchi bus stop (30 minutes, ¥1,150), then walk 20 minutes, or take bus (every second or third bus goes to onsen (40 minutes, ¥1,150)

If you plan to visit the pools at Takaragawa Onsen and feel like extending it for an overnight stay, the easiest place to do so is at Takaragawa Onsen Ōsenkaku. This old-school inn, attached to the famed baths, is so close to the river you can hear water gurgling from some of the rooms. Guests have 24-hour access to the *onsen* baths, which allows you to sneak in a late-night soak after most bathers have gone to sleep. Request in advance for the inn to send a car to pick you up from Minakami Station.

Over ¥40,000

★ BETTEI SENJUAN

614 Tanigawa; tel. 0278/20-4141; www.senjyuan.jp; ¥80,000 with two meals; take a taxi from Minakami

Bettei Senjuan is a discrete boutique *onsen* resort at the foot of Mount Tanigawa. With only 18 exquisite rooms, guests are so well tended to that it's easy to forget others are sharing the inn. The rooms' elegant decor comes in Japanese and Western-style, and each has an expansive private open-air *onsen* tub with stunning views of the surrounding mountains. Dinner is a multicourse *kaiseki* affair served in a private dining room. A library with a fireplace is a tempting alternative to the bath during winter. This is the quintessential luxury *ryokan* experience.

INFORMATION AND SERVICES

MINAKAMI TOURIST ASSOCIATION

1744-1 Tsukiyono, Minakami-machi; tel. 0278/62-0401; http://enjoy-minakami.com/en; 8:30am-4:30pm Jun.-Oct., 9am-4:30pm Nov.-May

Stop by the Minakami Tourist Association to ask questions you may have about outdoor activities in the area, recommendations for food or accommodations, or transportation logistics. The staff are helpful and speak English. The complex is located next to Jōmō Kōgen Station on the Joetsu *shinkansen* line, a 25-minute bus ride from Minakami Station, from where you'll access the bulk of the region's attractions. The association's English-language website also provides a wealth of useful information.

GETTING THERE AND AROUND

Minakami is best reached from **Tokyo.** Starting from **Ueno Station,** either take the **Joetsu** *shinkansen* (50 minutes; ¥4,810) or **JR Takasaki line** (1 hour 40 minutes; ¥1,980) via Omiya or Ageo station to **Takasaki**, where you'll change to the Jōetsu line and ride until you reach **Minakami** (1 hour 10 minutes; ¥990). Alternatively, starting at either Tokyo (¥6,020) or Ueno Station (¥5,810), take the Joetsu *shinkansen* to **Jōmō Kōgen Station**. The trip from either stop takes roughly 1 hour. From Jōmō Kōgen, it's a 25-minute bus ride (¥620) to Minakami.

The area's *onsen* and other attractions can be accessed by bus or taxi.

Hakone 箱根

With its wealth of natural beauty, from verdant mountains to a plethora of *onsen,* Hakone has been a known quantity since as the 16th century. It is said that Hideyoshi Toyotomi (1537-1598), the great samurai warrior and one of Japan's "three unifiers," treated himself to a bit of R&R in Hakone following the Siege of Odawara in 1590. He could think of no better option than relaxing in the soothing waters after conquering nearby Odawara Castle, then the world's largest, and ousting the Hōjō clan to become the new ruler of Japan.

Located in the heart of **Fuji-Hakone-Izu National Park** (www.fujihakoneizu.com), Hakone's natural splendor and diverse artistic offerings—many of them displayed outdoors—are understandably a draw to busy 21st-century Tokyo-ites too. The traditional approach to exploring Hakone is to make a loop, completed via a succession of quirky transportation options, from a quaint local train line and a cable car to a ropeway over a dramatically vaporous valley and a galleon-like sightseeing boat on Lake Ashi (Ashi-no-ko), which occupies a caldera and offers stunning views of Mount Fuji looming in the backdrop.

While it's fun, following this well-worn path can admittedly feel a bit formulaic. It pays to follow your own curiosity in Hakone and blaze your own trail, perhaps highlighting the art museums in the area, including the standout Hakone Open-Air museum and Okada Museum. Or, perhaps the simplest plan of all is vegging out in an *onsen* resort and gorging on haute cuisine while wearing only a robe and slippers for a few days straight.

Hakone

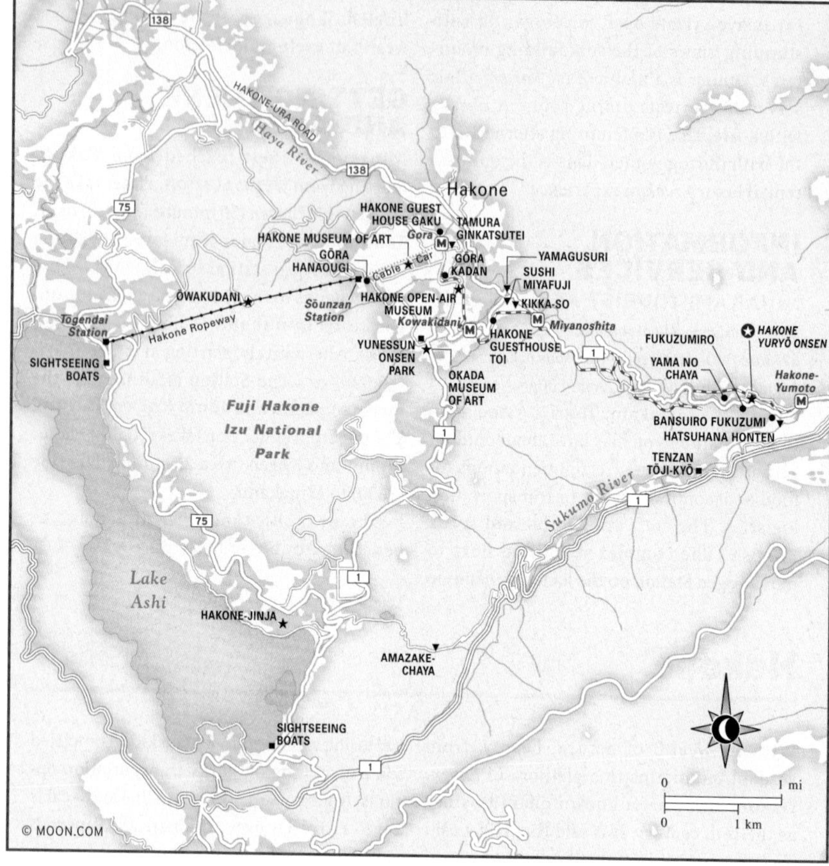

With so many things to do in one place, it's no wonder that Hakone is a destination of choice for day trips and weekend escapes from the capital. The upside of this is that a trip to the area is certain to be a good mix of relaxation and stimulation. The downside is that the place becomes inundated on weekends and any day during holidays and peak season. To minimize the impact of crowds on your experience in Hakone, come on a weekday and hit the popular spots early in the day.

ORIENTATION

Approaching from Odawara, you'll enter Hakone aboard the Hakone-Tōzan line. The first stop of note is **Hakone-Yumoto,** a town on the eastern edge of Hakone. The primary draw here is the wealth of *onsen* options, including **Hakone Yuryō Onsen** and **Tenzan Tōji-kyō.** Back on the Hakone-Tōzan line, if you continue west you'll come to **Miyanoshita,** a good area to

1: Hakone-Jinja **2:** sulphur vents of Ōwakudani **3:** visitors at Hakone Open-Air Museum

1

2

3

stop for a bite to eat or stay overnight, and **Kowakidani,** where you'll find the stunning **Okada Museum of Art** and the fun **Yunessun Onsen Park.** Push farther west on the Hakone-Tōzan railway line to its final two stops, **Chōkoku-no-mori,** where you'll find the crowd-pleasing **Hakone Open-Air Museum,** and **Gōra**, home to the **Hakone Museum of Art** and a good area to sleep if you plan to stay at one of the area's many *ryokan*. From there, a cable car links Gōra to **Sōun-zan,** from where hiking trails begin and the **Hakone Ropeway** descends to **Lake Ashi** at Hakone's southwestern edge, hovering above the dramatically volcanic landscape of **Ōwakudani** below. The towns of **Moto-Hakone** and **Hakone-machi** are situated on the southeastern side of Lake Ashi.

SIGHTS

Around Kowakidani

OKADA MUSEUM OF ART

岡田美術館

493-1 Kowakudani; tel. 0460/87-3931; www.okada-museum.com/en; 9am-5pm daily; ¥2,800 adults and university students, ¥1,800 children; from Hakone-Yumoto station, take bus to Koakien bus stop

Since it opened in 2013, the Okada Museum of Art has been wowing visitors with its collection of East Asian art, both ancient and modern, from Chinese pottery to Japanese scrolls. Situated on a mountain blanketed in forest, the museum is the creation of casino magnate Kazuo Okada, a self-professed art lover who began to set aside pieces with the express intention to one day open a museum. He succeeded brilliantly. The result is this cutting-edge structure spread over five floors, behind which you'll find a lush stroll garden and laid-back café. There's also a footbath at the entrance where museum-goers can refresh themselves before gawking at the many beautiful artistic specimens in the private collection for the next few hours.

Around Gōra

HAKONE OPEN-AIR MUSEUM

箱根 彫刻の森美術館

1121 Ninotarira; tel. 0460/82-1161; www.hakone-oam.or.jp; 9am-5pm daily; ¥1,600 adults, ¥1,200 university and high school students, ¥800 middle school and elementary school students; take electric train to Chōkoku-no-Mori Station

Japan does art in natural settings exceptionally well, and Hakone Open-Air Museum is a superb example. Imagine traipsing through a sculpture garden dotted by works by masters both European and Japanese, from Miró and Rodin to Henry Moore and Morie Ogiwara, set against a backdrop of verdant mountains and valleys. You've just pictured this refreshing museum in your mind's eye.

For Picasso fans, there's a pavilion devoted entirely to his work, with some 300 pieces. Another noteworthy work is the Symphonic Sculpture, a spiral staircase encased by a colorful swirl of glass, leading up to a viewing platform where the lush natural surroundings can be appreciated.

Those traveling with kids will be relieved to find Zig Zag World, a sculpture-inspired playground. And if you want to soak and relax after a day spent walking, there's even an outdoor foot bath.

HAKONE MUSEUM OF ART

箱根美術館

1300 Gōra; tel. 0460/82-2623; www.moaart.or.jp/hakone; 9:30am-4:30pm daily Apr.-Nov., until 4pm Dec.-Mar.; ¥900 adults, ¥400 high school students, junior school students and younger free; take Hakone Tozan cable car to Gōra Station

Exquisite Asian pottery and art, a traditional teahouse, and an enigmatic moss garden that crackles with color in autumn are some of the discoveries that await at the Hakone Museum of Art. Built on the collection of art aficionado Okada Mokichi (1882-1955), some of the earthenware pieces date as far back as the Jomon period (13,000-300 BC).

Around Sōun-zan

ŌWAKUDANI

大湧谷

tel. 0460/84-5201; www.kanagawa-park.or.jp/owakudani; cable car 9am-5pm daily Mar.-Nov., 9am-4:15pm daily Dec.-Feb.; ¥820 with Hakone Free Pass, ¥1,550 round-trip without Hakone Free Pass; from Gōra Station, ride Hakone-Tōzan to Sōun-zan Station, transfer to cable car and ride one stop to Ōwakudani Station

Ride in a cable car over this geologically tortured landscape. Ōwakudani means "Valley of Hell," named for the desolate, steamy valley emitting the strong scent of sulfur that formed 3,000 years ago when Kamiyama erupted, an event that also created the nearby Lake Ashi. If the sulfur fumes get to you, consider that the Japanese government's Ministry of the Environment concluded that the stench ranks among Japan's most prevalent 100 odors. The upshot of all this is that the area is known to turn out tasty *onsen tamago*: eggs boiled until turning black in the sulfurous springs.

Southern Lake Ashi

HAKONE-JINJA

箱根神社

80-1 Motohakone; tel. 0460/83-7123; http://hakonejinja.or.jp; 9am-4pm daily; from Hakone-Yumoto Station, take Hakone Tōzan bus (line H) to Hakone-jinja Iriguchi bus stops

Built in 757, Hakone-jinja is a picturesque shrine on the shore of Lake Ashi; it is at its most dramatic when it's shrouded in mist. To reach the shrine, take the five-minute stroll from the Moto-Hakone boat pier and continue along an ascending path lined by lanterns and marked by an imposing and very photogenic *torii* gate. Definitely stop by this shrine if you're exploring the Lake Ashi area.

ONSEN

Around Hakone-Yumoto

★ HAKONE YURYŌ ONSEN

箱根湯寮

4 Tōnosawa; tel. 0460/85-8411; www.hakoneyuryo.jp/english; 10am-9pm Mon-Fri, 10am-10pm Sat.-Sun. and holidays; ¥1,500 adults, ¥750 children; take shuttle bus, which leaves every 15 minutes from Hakone-Yumoto station, or Hakone-Tōzan line to Tōnosawa Station

For the classic countryside *onsen* experience within easy reach of Tokyo, Hakone Yuryō Onsen ticks all boxes. Surrounded by lushly forested hills, the outdoor baths here are excellent, with serene views of foliage on all sides and baths ranging from large single-sex communal pools to 19 private open-air ones rented by the hour (from ¥4,000). Book a private bath up to a month in advance by phone. Alongside baths, massages are offered in relaxation rooms, and an on-site restaurant serves food cooked over an *iori* (open hearth).

As is the case with most *onsen,* if you're sporting any ink you will need to keep it under wraps at the reception desk. Further, the communal baths will not be an option. Conceal what tattoos you have until reaching your reserved private bath, however, and you'll still be able to enjoy the experience.

TENZAN TŌJI-KYŌ

天山湯治郷

208 Yumoto-chaya; tel. 0460/86-4126; www.tenzan.jp; 9am-10pm daily; ¥1,300 adults, ¥650 children; take shuttle bus "B" from Hakone-Yumoto Station; located 500 meters past Okada Hotel

If you're sporting a significant amount of ink, this sprawling *onsen* complex, which doesn't have a policy against tattoos, is your best bet in Hakone. Tenzan Tōji-kyō has indoor and outdoor baths, uniquely designed and surrounded by lush foliage, set at a range of temperatures, from merely warm to exfoliation-inducing. For maximum relaxation, head to one of the complex's saunas or massage rooms.

Around Kowakidani

YUNESSUN ONSEN PARK

根小涌園ユネッサン

1297 Ninotaira; tel. 0460/82-4126; www.yunessun.com/en; 9am-7pm Mar.-Oct., until 6pm Nov.-Feb.; ¥2,500 adults, ¥1,400 children; from Gōra, Hakone-machi, or Hakone-Yumoto, take a bus to Kowakien

If you've ever dreamt of dunking yourself in

The Hakone Loop

Getting around Hakone is part of the fun of making the trip. Seeing the region's sights involves a combination of jumping between local trains, cable cars, ropeways, buses, and boats. A caveat: While this—or something similar—is the "classic" way to see Hakone, in truth it's a bit cookie-cutter (read: touristy). If there are specific things that appeal to you in the area that don't fit neatly into this route, the best way to see Hakone can actually be limiting the number of things you see and do, while maximizing down time, perhaps soaking in an *onsen*.

CABLE CAR AND ROPEWAY

The Hakone-Tōzan railway, which begins at Odawara, stops in the heart of Hakone at Gōra. From there, most visitors take a 10-minute ride on the Hakone-Tōzan cable car 1.2 km (0.75 mi) to Sōun-zan Station. At Sōun-zan you have the option of floating over Ōwakudani (Great Boiling Valley) aboard the **Hakone Ropeway** (1-15-1 Shiroyama, Odawara; tel. 0460/32-2205; www.hakoneropeway.co.jp/foreign/en; 9am-5pm Feb.-Nov. and 9am-4:15pm Dec.-Jan.; ¥1,600 adults, ¥800 children Sōun-zan to Ōwakudani round-trip, covered by Hakone Freepass). Gondolas on this line depart about once every minute and carry up to about 18 passengers.

Exiting the infernal valley, proceed along the ropeway to Tōgendai on the northeastern shore of the alpine Lake Ashi. The entire journey, from Sōun-zan to Tōgendai, takes about 30 minutes (¥1,450 adults, ¥730 children Sōun-zan to Tōgendai one-way, covered by Hakone Freepass).

BOAT

After floating over the volcanic landscape of Ōwakudani on board the ropeway, exit at Tōgendai and head for the dock if you want to take a cruise over the gorgeous Lake Ashi. Cruise boats connect Tōgendai to Hakone-machi and Moto-Hakone on the other side of Lake Ashi. The trips from both Tōgendai to Hakone-machi and from Tōgendai to Moto-Hakone take 30 minutes one-way (¥1,000 adults; ¥500 children), while the shorter jaunt between Hakone-machi and Moto-Hakone is roughly 10 minutes long (¥360 adults; ¥180 children).

Boats operated by **Hakone Sightseeing Boats** (www.hakone-kankosen.co.jp/foreign/en;

a massive bathtub full of coffee, tea, or something harder like wine, Yunessun Onsen Park gives you that chance. There are also waterslides, mixed open-air baths with sweeping views of nature, and numerous other options for immersing yourself in hot rejuvenating liquid concoctions at this hot spring theme park—bathing suit required.

For a more traditional *onsen* experience, the adjoining **Mori-no-Yu** (11am-7pm Mon.-Fri., 11am-8pm Sat.-Sun. and holidays; ¥1,500 adults, ¥1,000 children) offers single-sex, clothing-optional bathing both in and outdoors, including tubs under gazebos amid traditional gardens, and private baths that can be rented for ¥5,000 per hour.

If you'd like to experience the whole gamut, admission to both parts of the park is ¥3,500 adults, ¥1,800 children. And if you're too relaxed to bother leaving after all that soaking, there are four official hotels connected to the park. Tattoos, no matter how small, are not permitted at Yunessun.

FOOD

Around Hakone-Yumoto

HATSUHANA HONTEN

635 Yumoto; tel. 0460/85-8287; www.hatsuhana.co.jp; 10am-7pm Thurs.-Tues.; ¥1,000-1,400; take Hakone Tōzan railway to Hakone-Yumoto Station

Set in an old wooden building overlooking the Hayakawa River, Hatsuhana Honten has been serving its distinctive style of soba noodles since 1934. When wheat flour was scarce during World War II, the restaurant's owner tried making the noodles with only

mountain ropeway

9:30am-5:30pm daily Mar. 20-Nov. 30, 10am-4:40pm daily Dec. 1-Mar. 19), covered by the Hakone Freepass, and **Izuhakone Sightseeing Boats** (www.izuhakone.co.jp/ashinokoboatcruise/info/en.html; 8:30am-5pm daily year-round), not covered by the Hakone Freepass, run between Hakone-machi and Moto-Hakone on the lake's south side, and between its northern shore ports of Tōgendai and Kojiri.

Given the ¥1,000 fare for a one-trip across Lake Ashi, it makes most economic sense simply to get a Hakone Freepass, not only for this cruise, but for all legs of your journey in Hakone. These boats can become very crowded with tourists, especially during summer and on national holidays, so give them a pass if you're trying to avoid crowds.

buckwheat flour and eggs, then dipping them in mineral-rich sticky yam called *jinenjo.* An unexpected hit, the recipe survives to this day. Try the original seiro soba, known for its distinctive chewy texture, made without water and dipped in sticky yam.

Miyanoshita

KIKKA-SO

359 Miyanoshita; tel. 0460/82-2211; www.fujiyahotel.jp; 11:30am-4pm and 5:30pm-7pm daily; ¥6,000; take Hakone Tōzan railway to Miyanoshita Station

Set in an annex of the historic Fujiya Hotel, which was once a villa used by the Imperial Family, Kikka-So serves excellent multicourse *kaiseki* meals at dinner time. Appreciating the traditional Japanese garden and building itself adds an aesthetic dimension to the experience. Book at least a few days in advance for either lunch or dinner. Reservations required for dinner. For something more casual (and less pricey), try afternoon tea at the Fujiya's equally refined **Orchid Lounge** (9am-10pm daily; ¥1,000-2,300).

SUSHI MIYAFUJI

310 Miyanoshita; tel. 0460/82-2139; www.miyanoshita.com/miyafuji/; 11:30am-2:30pm and 5:30pm-7:30pm Thurs.-Mon.; ¥1,500-2,000; take Hakone Tōzan railway to Miyanoshita Station

Sushi Miyafuji is an old-school family-run sushi joint that brings in fish from the port of Odawara daily. The most popular items on its menu are rice bowls topped with fish, including the *aji-don* (rice bowl topped with brook trout) and the fisherman's bowl (horse

1
2
3
4

mackerel and squid over rice). Located five minutes' walk up a slope from the Fujiya Hotel.

YAMAGUSURI

224 Miyanoshita; tel. 0460/82-1066; http://yamagusuri.com; 10am-8:30pm Mon.-Fri., 7am-8:30pm Sat.-Sun. and holidays; ¥1,380-2,680; take Hakone Tōzan railway to Miyanoshita Station

For a healthy, well-rounded meal, Yamagusuri (Mountain Medicine) is a good bet. Choose from an appealing range of set meals, including grilled fish, mountain vegetables, locally sourced eggs, miso soup, and brown rice topped with grated yam. Don't let the slippery texture of the yam put you off. It's delicious and packed with nutrients. Enjoy the medicinal fare while surveying the lush valley outside the dining room window.

Around Gōra

TAMURA GINKATSUTEI

1300-739 Gōra; tel. 0460/82-1440; www.ginkatsutei.jp; 11am-3pm and 5pm-9pm daily; ¥1,250-2,000; take Hakone Tōzan railway to Gōra Station

Tamura Ginkatsutei is a popular lunch spot, easily spotted by the long line that often forms in front. If you don't mind taking a number and standing in line, you're in for a treat. Besides serving excellent *tonkatsu* (breaded pork cutlet), the shop's signature dish is tofu *katsuni* (deep-fried tofu stuffed with ground pork and boiled in a broth with egg). Note that the restaurant calls numbers in Japanese. Just show the servers at the door your number and they will get you when your turn comes if you don't stray too far when waiting. Thankfully the menu is available in English.

Southern Lake Ashi

★ AMAZAKE-CHAYA

395-1 Futoko-yama; tel. 0460/83-6418; www.amasake-chaya.jp; 7am-5:30pm daily; ¥250-750; from Moto-Hakone bus stop or Hakone-Yumoto bus stop, take Hakone Tōzan bus to Amazake Chaya bus stop

From the Moto-Hakone bus stop on the southern shore of Lake Ashi, walk 30 minutes up the cedar-lined Old Hakone Highway—once a segment of the Tōkaidō Highway that linked Edo and Kyoto—until you reach the charming thatched-roof Amazake-Chaya. This 360-year-old teahouse serves the same sweet brew made from fermented rice (*amazake*), that it did in Edo days. The drink is imbibed cold, hot, and at room temperature, depending on season, and can have low or no alcohol content, depending on the recipe.

ACCOMMODATIONS

Around Hakone-Yumoto

BANSUIRO FUKUZUMI

643 Yumoto; tel. 0460/85-5531; www.2923.co.jp; ¥28,000 with two meals; take Hakone Tōzan railway to Hakone-Yumoto Station

With a history stretching back to 1625 and old-school ambience intact, Bansuiro Fukuzumi weaves a spell on guests. Rebuilt now several times, the current iteration of this majestic old inn is a product of the Meiji period, when Japanese and Western architectural styles were often blended in experimental ways. Hence, wood, stone, and metal coexist seamlessly in the same building. It was no surprise that this inn—one of Hakone's oldest—was declared an important cultural property in 2002. The cuisine offered is similarly excellent, and there are private *onsen* baths to boot.

★ FUKUZUMIRO

74 Tōnosawa; tel. 0460/85-5301; www.fukuzumi-ro.com; doubles from ¥44,000 with two meals; from Hakone-Yumoto Station, take Hakone Tōzan railway to Tōnozawa Station

Fukuzumiro is another old-school gem, in business since 1890. Next to the Hayakawa River, the atmospheric property sprawls across three floors with 17 rooms, each with its own unique flourishes. Creativity is built into the *ryokan*'s exquisite woodwork—look for the "lucky bat" carvings scattered throughout—and the inn is known as a

---

1: outdoor communal bath **2:** room at Hakone Yuryō Onsen **3:** private bath at Hakone Yuryō Onsen **4:** irori, or sunken hearth, at Hakone Yuryō Onsen

retreat for writers and artists, including novelists Natsume Sōseki, Nobel Laureate Yasunari Kawabata, and actor Tsumasaburo Bando. Food courses featuring a range of seafood and vegetables are delivered to guests' rooms.

YAMA NO CHAYA

171 Tōnosawa; tel. 0460/85-5493; https://luxury-ryokan.com; ¥37,400 with two meals; from Hakone-Yumoto Station, take Hakone Tōzan railway to Tōnozawa Station

Yama No Chaya is a boutique *ryokan* situated next to a suspension bridge over the Hayakawa River. Everything is under one roof at this magnificent *ryokan,* with 12 types of rooms to choose from, featuring private wooden balconies for moon viewing and some with private open-air *onsen* baths. All *onsen* water is drawn from a spring on the hotel's property. For those sporting ink, note that tattoos are permitted here. Shuttle bus service runs from Hakone-Yumoto Station. Book as far in advance as possible.

Around Kowakidani

HAKONE GUESTHOUSE TOI

278 Miyanoshita; tel. 0460/83-8309; http://hakone-guesthouse.com; ¥3,500 dorm, ¥9,000 double without bathroom; from Hakone-Yumoto Station, take Hakone Tōzan bus to Kamisokokura bus stop, or take Hakone Tōzan railway to Kowakidani Station

Hakone Guesthouse Toi is a rare thing: a budget accommodation option in Hakone. This minimalist hostel opened in 2016 and has the trendy amenities that are becoming de rigueur in a new breed of hostel that's become increasingly fashionable. Expect wood paneling, an on-site café/bar with pour-over coffee, young, energetic staff and a laid-back vibe. Room options include private singles, doubles, and dorms (including female-only). Bathrooms are shared.

Around Gōra

HAKONE GUEST HOUSE GAKU

1380-385 Gōra; tel. 0460/83-8223; www.hakonegaku.com; ¥3,500 dorm, ¥13,000 double without bathroom; from Hakone-Yumoto Station, take Hakone Tōzan railway to Gōra Station

Hakone Guest House Gaku is a clean, quiet hostel run by friendly staff who are eager to help. Options include tatami rooms for large groups and families, as well as dorm-style rooms. All guests share a bathroom, and have access to a kitchen, as well as a first-floor lounge with a dart board and pool table. There's also a fourth-floor rooftop balcony where the occasional barbecue takes place, offering panoramic views of the surrounding mountains. Some English spoken.

★ GŌRA KADAN

1300 Gōra; tel. 0460/82-3331; www.gorakadan.com; ¥100,000 with two meals; take Hakone Tōzan railway from Hakone-Yumoto Station to Gōra Station

Gōra Kadan is a legendary *ryokan* so luxurious, the premium price tag actually feels justified. Top-notch *kaiseki* cuisine is presented like art in a European-style building, where flower-scented incense infuses the halls. Gorgeous tatami rooms filled with antiques and separated by sliding rice-paper walls, have private gardens, open-air baths. And, of course, the hospitality is refined to the hilt. No detail is missed, no edges left unsmoothed. Amenities include a pool, spa, and salon. This property is world-class in every sense. If you can manage to book a room—do so as far in advance as possible—this is the Hakone hotel worthy of a serious splurge.

Around Sōun-zan

GŌRA HANAOUGI

1300-681 Gōra; tel. 0460/87-7715; https://gorahanaougi.com; ¥80,000 with two meals; take Hakone Tōzan railway from Hakone-Yumoto Station to Gōra Station, then take Hakone Tōzan cable car to Sōun-zan Station

Gōra Hanaougi is exactly what an *onsen* resort should be: relaxing, discrete, and hospitable. Entering the lobby, with its lofty ceiling, handcrafted wooden chandeliers, and a sunken hearth, you'll be greeted by attentive staff, who smile and check you in to one of a variety of room types; rooms may feature expansive terraces, futons on tatami floors, or Western beds. The core appeal is that every room has its own open-air bath and views of the leafy mountainside just beyond. Food options are top-notch and include mountain-foraged vegetables, local wagyu beef, and seasonal seafood. Shuttle service is available from Gōra Station on request.

INFORMATION AND SERVICES

There is a **tourist information center** at Hakone-Yumoto Station (706-35 Yumoto Hakone-machi; tel. 0460/85-8911; www.hakone.or.jp; 9am-5:45pm) where you can ask questions of helpful English-speaking staff, and pick up English-language maps and more. Online, **https://hakone-japan.com** provides plenty of information on things to see and do in Hakone.

TRANSPORTATION

Getting There

To reach Hakone from Tokyo, take the **Odakyū line** from **Shinjuku Station** to **Hakone-Yumoto Station.** The speedy Romance Car reaches Hakone-Yumoto in 90 minutes (¥2,330), while the *kyūkō* (express) train will get you there in 2 hours (¥1,220). Note that you may need to change trains at Odawara if you take the cheaper express train.

If you have a JR Pass, you can also take the **JR Tōkaidō Shinkansen** (Kodama, Hikari trains only) about 30 minutes to **Odawara Station.** You can then transfer to the local **Hakone-Tōzan line**—not covered by the JR Pass—to go to Hakone-Yumoto, where you can access the rest of the Hakone area.

If you plan to travel from Tokyo to the Hakone region and see a number of its sights, the **Hakone Freepass** (www.odakyu.jp/english/passes/hakone/; ¥5,700 adults, ¥1,500 children for two-day pass, ¥6,100 adults, ¥1,750 children for three-day pass) could make sense. This pass allows you to travel round-trip between Shinjuku and Hakone-Yumoto, and then make your way around Hakone using the area's various modes of transportation (local train, cable car, Hakone Ropeway, boat). It also allows you to see many of the area's attractions at discounted rates. You can buy the two-day or three-day pass at any Odakyū train station or buy the two-day passonline (www.japan-rail-pass.com/pass-regional/east/hakone-free-pass?ap=j0095g).

If you're combining travel from Tokyo to both Kamakura and Hakone, the **Hakone Kamakura Pass** (www.odakyu.jp/english/passes/hakone_kamakura/; ¥7,000 adults, ¥2,250 children) allows you to stretch your yen by covering your round-trip between Shinjuku, Kamakura, and Hakone, and giving free access to all Odakyū trains, buses, boats, cable cars, and ropeways around Hakone, as well as the Enoden railway that links Kamakura and Enoshima. The pass also gives you access to many area attractions at discounted rates. Valid for three days, the pass is only available at Shinjuku Station's Odakyū Sightseeing Service Center.

A similar option also exists for those seeking to travel from Tokyo and explore both Hakone and Mount Fuji and the Five Lakes region. The **Fuji Hakone Pass** (https://www.odakyu.jp/english/passes/fujihakone/) allows you to travel freely for three days within the Fuji-Hakone area, and receive discounts at more than 90 attractions throughout the area. You have the option to include round-trip train fare from Shinjuku (¥9.780 adults, ¥3,590 children) or to begin using the pass from Odawara Station, round-trip to Tokyo not included, on the Odakyū and JR lines (¥7,180 adults, ¥2,290 children). You can buy this pass at the Odakyū Sightseeing Service Center in either Shinjuku Station or Odawara Station.

If you're traveling to Hakone from Kansai, beginning from **Shin-Osaka Station** catch the **Tōkaidō Shinkansen "Kodama" train,** which you'll ride until Ōdawara Station (3 hours 20 minutes; ¥12,850). Here, transfer to the Hakone-Tōzan Railway bound for Hakone-Yumoto (15 minutes; ¥320), where you'll be able to access the rest of the region.

Getting Around

The local train line servicing the Hakone area is the **Hakone-Tōzan line,** which connects Odawara to Gōra, a one-hour journey, stopping at Hakone-Yumoto, Tōnosawa, Kokakidani, and near the Hakone Open-Air Museum and Okada Museum of Art, among other stations, along the way.

From the Hakone-Tōzan line's terminus at Gōra, where you'll find the Hakone Art Museum, the classic route includes taking the **Hakone-Tōzan Cable Car** to Sōun-zan. From here, take the **Hakone Ropeway** to Ōwakudani, where plenty of steaming and bubbling volcanic activity is in full view, and then to Tōgendai on the shore of Lake Ashi. Tōgendai is the jumping-off point for a **boat cruise,** which offers excellent views of Mount Fuji when the sky is clear (colder months, early morning, and late afternoon are the best times to catch a glimpse of the peak). Take the boat to Hakone-machi, from which you can either walk to Hakone-jinja or continue by boat to Moto-Hakone, located near the Hakone-jinja. From here, return to Hakone-Yumoto by **bus.** Although it's certainly possible to buy tickets as you go for all of these modes of transportation, the most economical way to get around Hakone is to purchase one of the passes that covers round-trip fare between Tokyo and Hakone, and covers all modes of transportation within Hakone, as discussed above.

★ Mount Fuji 富士山

The Japanese have a word to describe the rush of emotion that ensues in the moments just before the first rays of the sun break over the horizon when viewed from a mountain top: *go-raiko.* The phrase, roughly meaning "honorable coming of the light," seeks to capture a feeling that is hard to pin down, an innate sense that witnessing the sunrise from a mountain peak is an extraordinary, even spiritual experience. Seeing the sky fill with the colors of dawn followed by sunrise from atop Mount Fuji, Japan's highest peak at 3,776 meters (12,388 feet), is the ultimate way to grasp the essence of *go-raiko* and to understand why the mountain holds such sway over the national psyche.

Since time immemorial, Mount Fuji has stood as nature's most sacred spot in Japan. The goddess of Mount Fuji, Princess *Konohamasakuya*—daughter of the mountain god and deity of all volcanoes—is honored at small shrines dotting its slopes. The privilege to climb to the summit was not granted for laypeople until about 150 years ago. Women were not permitted to make the ascent until 1868. Even today, steadfast hikers with mystical leanings approach the mountain only after purifying themselves at Sengen-jinja, a shrine in a dense old-growth forest at the mountain's base. Today, the inner sanctum of Sengen-jinja still stands atop the peak, serving as a reminder of these sacred roots.

Rather than a trickle of holy men, weekend warriors and overseas travelers now crowd the mountain, which is the crowning jewel of **Fuji-Hakone-Izu National Park.** The summit is flush with the same amenities you'd expected to find in any Japanese town, from 24-hour ramen stalls to a weather station and even a post office. But those who witness sunrise from the summit cannot deny the deeper stirrings felt by seekers who made the same journey centuries ago.

HIKING

For most travelers, glimpsing Mount Fuji from afar is enough. But during the official climbing season from the start of July until the end of August, well-established paths to the summit beckon to those keen to get up close and personal with the sacred peak. Once you've reached the top, the amenities available my shock you. You can mail a postcard, buy a charm at a shrine, circumnavigate the

Mount Fuji and the Five Lakes

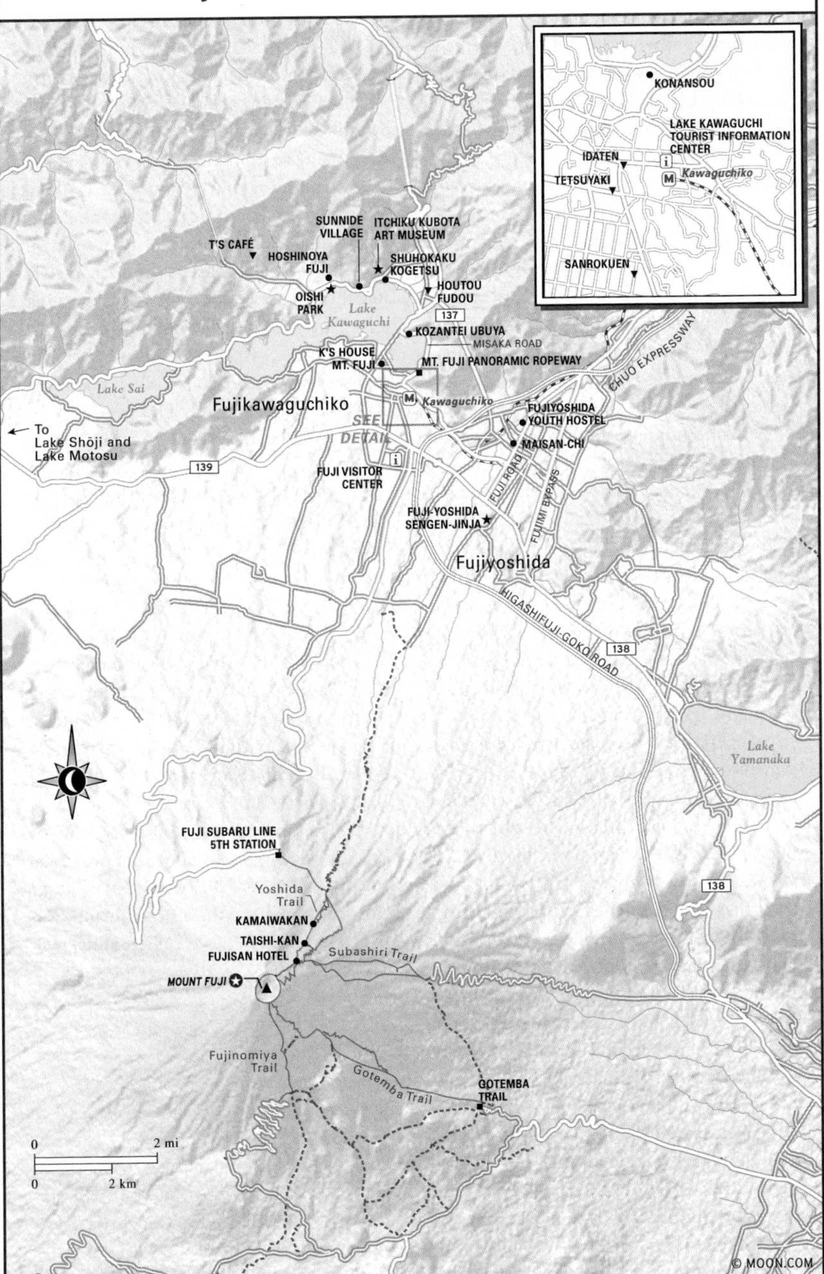

volcanic crater (a 2-hour walk), and slurp ramen at a food stall perched near the caldera's rim. Mount Fuji is one of the most climbed mountains in the world. But don't let the legions of grannies and middle-aged salarymen fool you—the ascent can be arduous. As the old adage goes: "A wise man climbs Fuji once; a fool climbs it twice."

If you'd like to climb Fuji, the popular **Yoshida trail** runs along the mountain's north face in Yamanashi Prefecture, while the **Subashiri** runs up the eastern face, and the less popular **Fujinomiya** and **Gotemba** trails line the south face in Shizuoka Prefecture. Each trail is broken into 10 stations, with the fifth being where most climbers start their ascent. Given Fuji's immense popularity, you might find yourself sharing the slopes with loads of hikers, particularly on weekends during the climbing season, with the Ōbon holidays in mid-August being the busiest time. Foot traffic can be so heavy that queues form at bottlenecks in the trail. Although merging with the crowd is part of the journey, it's helpful to climb on a weekday, preferably in July, and to undertake the majority of the ascent overnight.

Temperature differences between the base and summit are as much as 20°C (68°F) in summer. Although Mount Fuji's last eruption was in 1707, its soil still contains a thick layer of granular volcanic ash, prone to shifting as you walk. Wear sturdy boots suited for hiking, a hat that can be fastened to prevent losing it in the wind, sunscreen, gloves, sunglasses, a headlamp if you're hiking at night, sufficient water (3 liters is wise), vitamin-infused drinks, calorific snacks, and a trash bag. In short, prepare for the unexpected. Thick wool socks and waterproof clothes could save you from a multihour slog while drenched in the rain.

Depending on where you start and which trail you take, the journey from one of the main fifth stations up the top half of Mount Fuji is usually a five to six-hour affair. Most begin the journey at night—around 8pm if they're starting from the first station, or 11pm if they're starting from the fifth station—and walk until morning. Another popular way to make the ascent is to start in the afternoon, stay in a hut overnight at the seventh or eighth stage, then proceed to the summit in the early morning. Walking at either of these times allows hikers to avoid the sun at its peak and to see the sunrise from the top.

Be mindful of your own condition along the way. Around the time you enter the eighth stage, altitude sickness becomes a real concern. If you begin to feel nauseous or uncharacteristically exhausted, don't ignore the warning signs. Turn back if these symptoms arise.

Making the ascent outside of July and August requires legit skills hiking in icy conditions, and the capacity and gear to handle extremes. Hikers keen to summit Fuji during the off-season should register with local authorities at the **Lake Kawaguchi Tourist Information Center** (3641-1 Funatsu; 0555/72-6700; www.fujisan.ne.jp; 8:00am-6:00pm) and keep an eye on the weather forecast, respecting the risk involved. Finally, hire a guide. **Fuji Mountain Guides** (042/445-0798; www.fujimountainguides.com; ¥44,000 per person for 2-day tours), run by bilingual American guides, offer tours year-round. **Discover Japan Tours** (www.discover-japan-tours.com/en; ¥10,000 per person, 2-day tours) offer tours for groups of at least two. Other resources packed with Fuji tips include the online guide **Climbing Mount Fuji** (www17.plala.or.jp/climb_fujiyama) and the official **Mount Fuji Climbing website** (www.fujisan-climb.jp).

YOSHIDA TRAIL

Distance: 15 km (9 mi)

Time: 9-12 hours

Information and maps: Fuji-Yoshida Tourist Office or Fuji Visitor Center; www.japan.travel/en/spot/2328

Trailhead: Subaru Line Fifth Station

By far the most popular route to the top of Fuji involves starting from the fifth station of the well-trodden Yoshida trail. Known as the **Subaru Line Fifth Station** (aka **Kawaguchi-ko Fifth Station** or

Yoshidaguchi Fifth Station), this station sits at an elevation of 2,305 meters (7,562 feet) and is by far the most developed of the mountain's fifth stations, including the most mountain huts (20) of all major routes. Following this route involves an ascent (7.5 km/4.5 mi) to the top of 6-7 hours and a descent (7.5 km/4.5 mi) of about 3-5 hours. The fifth station can be reached by bus from either Kawaguchiko Station or Fujisan Station.

While starting at the fifth station will more than likely be all you need to scratch your Fuji itch, for experience seekers with a slightly masochistic bent, it's entirely possible to climb Fuji the same way that spiritual pilgrims of yore once did. In the town of Fuji-Yoshida, near the lake of Lake Kawaguchi at the mountain's eastern base, pilgrims gravitate to **Fuji-Yoshida Sengen-jinja** (aka Kitaguchi Hongū Fuji Sengen-jinja; 5558 Kami-Yoshida; tel. 0555/22-0221; www.sengenjinja.jp; 24 hours), a shrine dedicated to the mountain's chief deity, Princess Konohanasakuya. The Yoshida trail, which goes from the base to the summit, starts from this shrine. Sticklers for tradition swear by this trail, which entails roughly a 12-hour, 19-km (11.8-mi) ascent from base to summit, followed by a descent that takes 3-5 hours.

SUBASHIRI TRAIL

Hiking distance: 14 km (8.75 mi)
Time: 10-12 hours
Information and maps: www.japan.travel/en/fuji-guide/mt-fuji-subashiri-trail; www.alltrails.com/trail/japan/shizuoka/mount-fuji-trail-subashiri-trail
Trailhead: Subashiri Fifth Station

On the south face of the mountain, the Subashiri trail begins from the **Subashiri Fifth Station** (1,950 meters/6,398 feet) and has relatively well-developed infrastructure with 12 huts along the way. This is the second-best option overall, and is particularly appealing if you happen to be coming from Lake Yamanaka rather than Lake Kawaguchi. It winds through forests and is less crowded. In fact, it merges with the more accessible, developed, and crowded Yoshida Trail from the eighth station onward. The ascent (8 km/5 mi) takes around 7-9 hours, while the descent (6 km/3.75 mi) takes about 3 hours.

To reach Subashiri Fifth Station, take the JR Tokaido line from Tokyo to Kozu (1.25 hours; ¥1,320), then transfer to the JR Gotemba line and ride until Gotemba Station (50 minutes; ¥670). From Gotemba, take the bus to Subashiri Fifth Station (1 hour; ¥1,540 one way, ¥2,060 round trip).

ACCOMMODATIONS

Reserving a space at one of Mount Fuji's mountain huts can be tricky during climbing season. Fuji Mountain Guides (www.fujimountainguides.com/mountain-hut-reservations.html) offers a reservation service for a nominal fee of ¥1,000.

KAMAIWAKAN

Yoshida trail, seventh station; tel. 080/1299-0223; http://kamaiwakan.jpn.org; ¥8,000, depending on day and meal option

Clean and revamped, Kamaiwakan is a good option at 2,790 meters (9,153 feet) with free Wi-Fi and two optional meals. Some English is spoken. Book two months ahead.

TAISHI-KAN

Yoshida trail, eighth station; tel. 0555/22-1947; www.mfi.or.jp/w3/home0/taisikan; ¥9,000, depending on day

Taishi-kan is a tried-and-true mountain hut for Fuji hikers. It sleeps 350 hikers in sleeping bags. Two meals (including vegetarian and halal on request) are included in the price. Check-out time is 5am. Soft drinks and snacks are sold. Some English is spoken. Book two months in advance.

FUJISAN HOTEL

Yoshida trail, eighth station; tel. 0555/22-0237; www.fujisanhotel.com; ¥8,000, depending on day and meal option chosen

Fujisan Hotel is a very popular option, given its location at the 3,400-meter (11,154-foot) junction of the Lake Kawaguchi and Subashiri trails. The lodge will hold onto your bag while you walk the final 60 minutes of the path to

1
2

the summit. Breakfast and dinner are optional. Book two months in advance.

INFORMATION AND SERVICES

For maps and English-language information on the area, visit **Fuji-Yoshida Tourist Office** beside (Fuji-Yoshida) Fujisan Station (tel. 0555/22-7000; 9am-5pm), or **Fuji Visitor Center** (6663-1 Funatsu; tel. 0555/72-0259; 8:30am-7pm late July-Aug. 26, 8:30am-6pm Aug. 27-Sept., 8:30am-5pm rest of year) on the north face of the mountain south of Lake Kawaguchi.

TRANSPORTATION

Getting There

Straddling the border of Yamanashi and Shizuoka prefectures, Mount Fuji is within easy reach of Tokyo by bus or train. The main transit hubs for accessing the Mount Fuji area include the town of **Fuji-Yoshida** and **Lake Kawaguchi,** which are served by buses and trains from Tokyo.

TRAIN

To come via train, starting from **Shinjuku,** take the **Chūō Line** west to **Otsuki.** The limited express (*tokkyū*) train takes 1 hour and 10 minutes (¥2,360), while the regular (*futsū*) train takes about 1 hour and 30 minutes (¥1,3400) and may require a transfer at Takao Station. From Otsuki, transfer to the **Fuji Kyūkō** line. The ride to the town of Fuji-Yoshida (Fujisan Station) takes 50 minutes (¥1,040), while the ride to Lake Kawaguchi is only about 5 minutes longer (¥1,170). Note that this route makes the most economic sense if you're traveling with a JR Pass, as the entire ride will be covered.

BUS

If you'd rather take a bus—in some ways the simpler option—buses operated by **Keiō Dentetsu** (tel. 03/5376-2222; http://highway-buses.jp; ¥2,000 adults, ¥1,000 children) and **Fujikyū Express** (http://bus-en.fujikyu.co.jp/highway; ¥2,000 adults, ¥1,000 children) depart once or twice hourly from the **Shinjuku Highway Bus Terminal** (Shinjuku Station west exit; https://highway-buses.jp/terminal/shinjuku.php) and run to both the town of Fuji-Yoshida (Fujisan Station) and Kawaguchiko Station. The journey to either stop takes about 1 hour and 40 minutes.

If you want to take a bus from downtown Tokyo straight to the fifth station, Keiō Dentetsu runs buses directly to the mountain from Shinjuku Highway Bus Terminal (tel. 03/5376-2222; http://highway-buses.jp; ¥2,900 adults, ¥1,450 children one way). Note that you must reserve a seat in advance.

If you're coming from the west—Shin-Osaka in the west through Kyoto and Nagoya to the east—board the **Tōkaidō *shinkansen* Kodama line** and ride until **Mishima Station**. From Shin-Osaka to Mishima, for example, the journey is just over 2 hours and costs ¥12,300. From the south exit of Mishima Station, catch a **Fujikyūkō bus** (http://bus-en.fujikyu.co.jp/highway) to Kawaguchiko Station. This last leg of the journey takes anywhere from an hour and a half to more than 2 hours, depending on road conditions, and costs ¥2,300 one way.

Getting Around

Once you've arrived in either the hub of Fuji-Yoshida (Fujisan Station) or Kawaguchiko Station, buses connect to the five lakes and other area attractions.

To get farther up the mountain by bus, you can travel about one hour from either Kawaguchiko Station or Fujisan Station to the **Subaru Fifth Station** (¥1,570 one-way, ¥2,300 round-trip). During the official climbing season, buses run to the fifth station 7am-8pm, and return 8am-9pm. Note that buses run much less frequently throughout the rest of the year—roughly from 9am until a bit after 3pm. For more details about timetables and fares, see the Fujikyū Yamanashi website

1: Mount Fuji and Lake Yamanaka **2:** hiking the Yoshida trail on Mount Fuji

(http://bus-en.fujikyu.co.jp/route/). All buses running to the fifth station are in operation from mid-April until early December.

Buses bound for Lake Yamanaka run once or twice an hour from both **Kawaguchiko Station** and Fujisan Station, stopping at **Fujiyoshida Sengen-jinja** along the way. Step off at **Kitaguchi Hongu Fujisengen Jinja-mae bus stop,** which is directly in front of a tree-lined path that leads to the shrine. The ride to this stop from Kawaguchiko Station takes 15 minutes, and about 5 minutes from Fujiyoshida Station.

Fuji Five Lakes 富士五湖

Five lakes surrounding the iconic peak teem with visitors, particularly in summer, reaching fever pitch during climbing season. **Lake Yamanaka**, is a favorite for water sports lovers, while **Lake Sai** is a good place to camp and, in summer, to swim. **Lake Shōji**, the smallest of the five, and **Lake Motosu**, famed for its appearance on the ¥1,000 note, are both west of Lake Sai. Farther from Tokyo than the other three lakes, they offer fewer amenities and don't warrant a detour for those with limited time. Chief among these are **Lake Kawaguchi** on the north face of the mountain, the most developed and easy to access from Tokyo, and therefore the one covered here.

Along with the neighboring town of Fuji-Yoshida, the town surrounding Lake Kawaguchi makes for a good overnight stay before or after climbing Fuji. Of the five lakes at the base of the revered volcano, Kawaguchi is the one worth a stop for those on a short trip, due to its easy access from Tokyo and its well-developed infrastructure. The town is teeming with *onsen* resorts, most offering unobstructed views of Fuji, which looms to the south. The southern shore is admittedly touristy and can become jammed with visitors during summer. But the lake's east side and less-developed northern shore offer spectacular views of the mountain and are home to a few museums worth visiting. Lake Kawaguchi is a great choice if you want to appreciate Fuji at a distance, preferably while lounging around a *ryokan* clad in a *yukata* or soaking in an *onsen* tub.

SIGHTS

Itchiku Kubota Art Museum

2255 Kawaguchi; tel. 0555/76-8811; www.itchiku-museum.com; 9:30am-5:30pm Wed.-Mon. Apr.-Nov., 10am-4:30pm Wed.-Mon. Dec.-Mar., closed Wed. if holiday falls on Tues., open daily Oct.-Nov.; ¥1,600 adults, ¥900 college and high school students, ¥400 junior high and elementary students; from Kawaguchiko Station take Kawaguchiko bus (Kawaguchiko line) to Itchiku Kubota Art Museum bus stop

In addition to admiring the views of Mount Fuji, there's also a museum near the lake that's worth visiting. The Itchiku Kubota Art Museum showcases textiles woven by master artist Kubota Itchiku (1917-2003), who elevated the kimono to stunning heights. The museum itself is housed in a pyramidal building and presents Kubota's stunning vision in the artwork called Symphony of Light, containing 80 kimonos, of which 30 are shown at any one time. Each hefty garment in this work is three to four times heavier than a normal kimono and incorporates dyeing techniques dating to the 14th-17th centuries. There's a café with a glass beads gallery on site (coffee or tea ¥500), as well as a garden with a teahouse on the grounds (10am-2:30pm daily; tea ¥1,000, tea with sweets sets ¥1,300-2,500).

1: Lake Kawaguchi from the top of the Mount Fuji Ropeway **2:** passengers boarding the ropeway car

1
2

SPORTS AND RECREATION

MOUNT FUJI PANORAMIC ROPEWAY

1163-1 Azagawa; tel. 0555/72-0363; www.mtfujiropeway.jp; ¥500 adults and ¥250 children one-way, ¥900 adults and ¥450 children round-trip

At the southeastern edge of Lake Kawaguchi, the Mount Fuji Panoramic Ropeway will transport you 1,104 meters (3,622 feet) up to a viewing deck with superb views of Mount Fuji. You won't get views of Japan's most famous peak better than this.

MOUNT MITSUTŌGE

Hiking Distance: 14.1 km (8.8 mi)

Time: 6.5 hours

Information and maps: Kawaguchiko Tourist Information Center; https://ridgelineimages.com/hiking/mt-mitsutoge

Trailhead: Mount Fuji Panoramic Ropeway viewing deck

If you feel like a long day-hike, try this fantastic path to Mount Mitsutōge (1,786 meters/5,859 feet), which starts from the viewing platform. The journey talks about 6.5 hours round-trip and offers not only stellar views of Fuji, but also a 360-degree panorama of the entire region, stretching from Tokyo to the Southern Alps. It's a fairly grueling day-hike, so be sure to take enough water and snacks to sustain you for the day.

You can either return on the path you took to the summit, or continue to Mitsutōge Station. The total time required for the hike is roughly similar either way. If you opt for the latter, trains run on the Fuji Kyūkō line from Mitsutōge Station directly back to Kawaguchiko Station (25 minutes; ¥550). Pick up a map at the Kawaguchiko Tourist Information Center.

FOOD

★ SANROKUEN

3370-1 Funatsu; tel. 0555/73-1000; 11am-9pm Fri.-Wed., last order 9pm; ¥2,100-4,200; take Fuji Kyūkō line to Kawaguchiko Station

A 15-minute walk from Kawaguchiko Station, Sanrokuen is an atmospheric restaurant set in a thatched-roof house, built 150 years ago. Guests sit on the floor around a sunken hearth and slow-grill five-course sets of meat, fish, vegetables, and tofu on spears over an open charcoal pit. While rainbow trout, duck, pork, beef, and a variety of delicious local vegetables feature heavily on the menu, some items are not your everyday fare. Barbecued jellyfish anyone? This is a good choice for a unique, homey meal with friendly hosts. It's wise to book a week in advance or more to ensure a seat. English is spoken.

TETSUYAKI

3486-1 Funatsu; tel. 070/4075-1683; https://tetsuyaki.business.site; noon-2pm and 5pm-9:30pm Mon.-Tues., 5pm-9:30pm Wed.-Sat.; ¥800-1,000; take Fuji Kyūkō line to Kawaguchiko Station

Two minutes' walk from Kawaguchiko Station, Tetsuyaki offers good, greasy-spoon options on a budget-friendly menu. You'll find chicken and rice dishes, steak and fries, *okonomiyaki*, ginger pork, and booze. It's a good option if you're searching for a bite after dark, as many restaurants close early around town.

IDATEN

3486-4 Funatsu; tel. 0555/73-9218; http://ida-ten.jp; 11am-10pm daily; ¥880-1,180; take Fuji Kyūkō line to Kawaguchiko Station

Generous portions of tempura are the focus of the menu at Idaten. Sit in a counter seat for a view of the kitchen, where you can see the chefs at work. Optional sets include rice, miso soup, and udon. English menu is available. This is a good choice if you're on the south side of the lake, near Kawaguchiko Station.

HOUTOU FUDOU

707 Kawaguchi; tel. 0555/76-7011; www.houtou-fudou.jp/index.html; 11am-7pm daily; ¥1,050; take Fuji Kyūkō line to Kawaguchiko Station, then take Kawaguchiko "retro bus" (Kawaguchiko line) to Kawaguchiko Music Forest bus stop

Houtou Fudou, on the eastern shore of the lake, is a good restaurant to sample *houtou*, a dish that includes flat noodles akin to udon in a bowl of miso-based stew and vegetables. This dish is a specialty of Yamanashi Prefecture and a local favorite. Along with *houtou*, the menu also includes soba noodles, minced tuna with rice, *basashi* (raw horse meat), and *inari* sushi (sweetened tofu pouches stuffed with sushi rice).

T'S CAFÉ

Ridge E 1F, 1477-1 Ōishi; tel. 0555/25-7055; www.fujioishihanaterasu.com; 10am-6pm daily in summer, 10:30am-5pm daily in winter; ¥700-1,200; take Fuji Kyūkō line to Kawaguchiko Station, then take Kawaguchiko "retro bus" (Kawaguchiko line) to Kawaguchiko Natural Living Center bus stop

Tucked away in Fuji Ōishi Hanaterrace—a cluster of shops next to Ōishi Park dedicated to locally produced foods and goods—T's Café offers a reasonably priced menu of drinks, snacks, light meals, and ice cream, all made using locally sourced ingredients. Views of lavender fields and Mount Fuji are an added bonus. This is a good pick if you're on the lake's north shore.

ACCOMMODATIONS

FUJIYOSHIDA YOUTH HOSTEL

3-6-51 Shimoyoshida, Fujiyoshidashi; tel. 0555/22-0533; www.jyh.or.jp/e/i.php?jyhno=2803; ¥3,200 dorm; take JR Chūō line to Otsuki Station, and then take Fuji Kyūkō railway to Shimoyoshida Station

Given that its no-frills rooms are private, the name Fujiyoshida Youth Hostel is a bit of a misnomer. Guests share a clean bathroom and sleep on futons on tatami-mat floors in the six rooms of this tiny inn, which is a Japanese-style home run by a family who lives on the first floor. The owners are extremely hospitable and are happy to help with local recommendations. This is a solid budget option in the town of Fuji-Yoshida, away from the more touristy Lake Kawaguchi. Breakfast is available for an additional ¥600.

K'S HOUSE MT. FUJI

6713-108 Funatsu; tel. 0555/83-5556; https://kshouse.jp; ¥3,300 dorm, ¥8,400 private room without bathroom, ¥8,800 private room with bathroom; take Fuji Kyūkō line to Kawaguchiko Station

Popular among backpackers and hikers who are in town to climb Mount Fuji, K's House Mt. Fuji offers clean, cozy Japanese-style private rooms with tatami-mat floors and dorm-style rooms, including some that are female-only, at reasonable rates. Guests have access to a shared lounge and kitchen, and the hostel is close to a convenience store, supermarket, and a few eateries. It's located only a 3-minute walk from the south side of the lake. This is a solid budget option for those seeking to meet fellow travelers.

SUNNIDE VILLAGE

2549-1 Ōishi; tel. 0555/76-6004; www.sunnide.com; ¥36,000 room with two meals; take Fuji Kyūkō line to Kawaguchiko Station, then take Kawaguchiko "retro bus" (Kawaguchiko line) to Sunnide Resort/Nagasaki Park Entrance bus stop

A more affordable option on the north side of the lake, Sunnide Village is a resort complex of midrange budget hotel rooms and appealing cottages, all with sweeping views of Fuji. Guests also have access to a luxuriant outdoor bath with stellar views.

KONANSOU

4020-2 Funatsu; tel. 0555/72-2166; www.konansou.com; ¥42,000 with two meals; take Fuji Kyūkō line to Kawaguchiko Station

Konansou is a *ryokan* with modern Japanese and Western-style rooms, some with private outdoor bathtubs, at the southeastern corner of Lake Kawaguchi. There are fantastic views of Mount Fuji and the lake throughout the hotel. Alongside gender-separated indoor and outdoor public *onsen* baths, there is a rooftop garden with an *onsen* footbath and private *onsen* baths that can be reserved in 50-minute increments. Guests can opt for a breakfast buffet and dinner plan comprising *kaiseki* fare, either eaten in the restaurant or delivered to the room.

★ SHUHOKAKU KOGETSU

2312 Kawaguchi; tel. 0555/76-8888; www.kogetu.com; ¥45,000 with two meals; pickup from Kawaguchiko Station available for guests

The biggest draw at this plush *onsen ryokan* is the stunning view of Fuji, seen from both the men's and women's open-air pools. Sitting on the northern shore of Lake Kawaguchi, this luxury spot has all the bells and whistles you'd expect—top-notch hospitality, *kaiseki* meals made with the finest seasonal ingredients served directly to the rooms, and large, well-appointed Japanese-style rooms with views of the lake and peak looming beyond. There's also a stunning garden and a private lakeside beach. If you've got the cash, this is a worthy splurge.

KOZANTEI UBUYA

10 Asakawa; tel. 0555/72-1145; http://www.ubuya.co.jp; ¥58,000 with two meals; take Fuji Kyūkō line to Kawaguchiko Station; hotel shuttle bus available from there upon request

Kozantei Ubuya is a high-end *ryokan* on the east side of Lake Kawaguchi with phenomenal lakeside views of Mount Fuji from its indoor and outdoor *onsen* baths. Antifogging windows in the bathrooms of even standard suites offer unhindered vistas of the famed peak. Spacious rooms come in both Japanese and Western styles, and deluxe suites have private outdoor bathtubs. Optional breakfast and dinner are prepared with locally sourced ingredients.

HOSHINOYA FUJI

1408 Ōishi; tel. 050/3786-1144; https://hoshinoya.com; ¥135,000 with two meals; take Fuji Kyūkō line to Kawaguchiko Station, then take taxi directly to Hoshinoya Fuji or Kawaguchiko "retro bus" (Kawaguchiko line) to Lake Kawaguchi Natural Living Center bus stop

While it's certainly not cheap, Hoshinoya Fuji is glamping at its most refined. In a nod to the beautiful natural surroundings, guests receive bags filled with a map, headlamp, and binoculars at check-in. Concrete cubic "cabins" with floor-to-ceiling windows and chic, minimalist decor surrounded by trees, dot a mountain hillside on the north side of Lake Kawaguchi. All rooms offer superb views of Mount Fuji. Dining, a campfire space for roasting marshmallows, a library with wood stove, and other luxuries are found in the Cloud Terrace, located above the guest quarters. Who knew the great outdoors could be so lavish. Book as far in advance as possible, as it tends to be booked out months in advance.

INFORMATION AND SERVICES

Just outside Kawaguchiko Station, on your right-hand side as you exit the station, the **Kawaguchiko Tourist Information Center** (3641-1 Funatsu; tel. 0555/72-6700; 9am-5pm daily) has English speakers on staff, as well as pamphlets about the area's *onsen* and maps for its hiking trails.

TRANSPORTATION

As Kawaguchiko Station is one of the major gateways to Mount Fuji itself, making a trip to Lake Kawaguchi, which is next to Kawaguchiko Station, means taking the same route you would if you were traveling to Mount Fuji, as described above. This applies to both train and bus routes.

Likewise, if you are coming to Lake Kawaguchi from Kansai (Osaka, Kyoto), or a closer hub, such as Nagoya, you would follow the same route as the one described above to reach Mount Fuji from the west.

Izu Peninsula

伊豆半島

Occupying the southern fringe of **Fuji-Hakone-Izu National Park,** the craggy, scenic Izu Peninsula has many of the same draws as Hakone: *onsen,* beaches, and decent waves, within easy reach of Tokyo. The peninsula's easy access from the capital makes it a favorite during summer for Tokyoites, but there are fewer tourists from overseas in Izu than Hakone. The bulk of the overdevelopment—and overcrowding—is concentrated around the resort town of Atami on the northeastern coast, but venture beyond Atami and you'll discover a few gems.

SHIMODA AND AROUND

For history and beaches, head 75 km (47 mi) south of Atami to the coastal town of **Shimoda,** where the American Commodore Perry docked his black ships in 1854 during his trip to open up Japan through gunboat diplomacy. The nearby beaches are among the best in the greater Tokyo region.

Sights

RYŌSEN-JI

3-12-12 Shimoda; tel. 0558/22-0657; www.izu.co.jp/~ryosenji; 24 hours daily; free

This small temple is located about 15 minutes' walk south of Izukyū-Shimoda Station. This is where Perry and members of the collapsing Tokugawa shogunate inked a treaty that led to the opening of Shimoda's port in 1854. The temple's **Museum of the Black Ship** (3-12-12 Shimoda; tel. 0558/22-2805; www.mobskurofune.com; 8:30am-5pm daily; ¥500 adults, ¥250 children), has an intriguing collection of woodblock prints of Perry and his crew. East of Ryōsen-ji, the atmospheric cobblestone **Perry Street** is lined by old homes now housing boutiques, antique shops, cafés, and restaurants, fronting a willow-draped canal crisscrossed by narrow footbridges.

Beaches

From mid-July through August, when lifeguards are on duty during daylight hours,

Shimoda

beaches surrounding Shimoda fill up with university students and families, dotted by snorkeling and bodyboard rental shops, food stands, and public toilets.

SHIRAHAMA

Shirahama Kaigan bus stop, 4.5 km (2.8 mi) northeast of Izukyū-Shimoda Station

This beach is intensely popular for its clear waters, which are safe for swimming and snorkeling.

SOTOURAHAMA

Sotoura Guchi bus stop

If you're looking for a calmer experience, Sotoruahama, located in an inlet about 2.5 km (1.6 mi) south of Shirahama, is significantly less crowded than other beaches in this area.

KISAMI ŌHAMA

Ōhama Kaigan bus stop, 4.8 km (3 mi) southwest of Izukyū-Shimoda Station

This beach is the second-most popular after Shirahama.

Surfing

In addition to the shops below, **Irie Coffee & Sea in Shirahama** also offers equipment rentals and lessons.

SHIRAHAMA MARINER

2752-16 Shirahama; tel. 0558/22-6002; https://mariner.co.jp/school/rental-e.html; 9am-9pm daily; Shirahama Kaigan bus stop

This shop in Shirahama rents surfboards (¥3,000-4,000) and wet suits (¥2,000) and gives bilingual surf lessons (¥6,000-8,000).

REAL

1612-1 Kisami; tel. 0558/27-0771; https://realsurf.jp; Kisami bus stop

A 15-minute walk north of Kisami Ōhama, this shop offers bilingual surf/stand-up paddle lessons (¥9,000) and rents surfboards (¥4,000) and wet suits (¥2,500). Check out their website for a good rundown of the top surf spots.

Food

IRIE COFFEE & SEA

1737 Shirahama; tel. 0558/36-4333; 10am-7pm daily; lunch ¥1,000

At the northern end of Shirahama, this café has a simple menu consisting of good coffee and tasty chicken dishes, from fried (karage) to jerk (Jamaican-style). It doubles as a surf shop (surfboard rentals ¥4,000, surfing lessons ¥8,000).

CAFÉ MELLOW

1891-1 Kisami; tel. 0558/27-2327; https://cafe-mellow.com; 11am-11pm Wed.-Mon., closed every second Wed.; ¥1,000-1,500

In the Kisami area, try **Café Mellow, located** a few minutes' walk inland from Kisami Ōhama. It serves simple, hearty fare like burgers, pizzas, pasta, curry, salads, and a range of rice dishes.

Accommodations

GARDEN VILLA SHIRAHAMA

2644-1 Shirahama; tel. 0558/22-8080; www.gardenvilla.jp/13_english; ¥38,600 d with dinner; Itami bus stop

This friendly family-owned hotel facing the ocean is located a 10-minute walk from Shirahama beach. It has a terrace, swimming pool and poolside bar (open Jul.-Sept.), and two open-air *onsen* baths overlooking the ocean.

ERNEST HOUSE

1893-1 Kisami; tel. 0558/22-5880; www.ernest-house.com; ¥28,080 double

Next door to Café Mellow is this charming, family-run guesthouse with simple, tidy rooms, bicycles for rent, and an excellent breakfast basket (¥1,080 adults, ¥864 children) that can be carried to the beach as a picnic if desired.

Information and Services

For more information, English-language maps, and help with booking accommodations, head to the **Shimoda Tourist Association** (1-1 Sotogaoka; tel.

0558/22-1531; www.shimoda-city.com; 8:30am-5pm daily), located 3 minutes' walk southeast of Izukyū-Shimoda Station. The friendly English-speaking staff there are happy to help. The website is handy, too.

Transportation

You can ride the half-hourly **Odoriko limited express** (tokkyū) train directly from Tokyo Station to **Izukyū-Shimoda Station** (2.5-3 hours; ¥6,760). Alternatively, you can take the *shinkansen* to **Atami** (45 minutes; ¥4,270), then transfer to the Odoriko limited express train from there to Izukyū-Shimoda (1.25 hours; ¥3,790). If your arrival in Atami doesn't coincide with a limited express train, it's also possible to take the local JR Itō line to **Itō Station** (25 minutes; ¥330), then transfer to the Izukyū line to Izukyū-Shimoda Station (1 hour 5 minutes; ¥1,650). JR passes only cover the journey as far as Itō. Once you've reached Izukyū-Shimoda Station, the beaches are all within a 10-minute ride on one of the **local buses** that depart regularly from in front of Izukyū-Shimoda Station (within ¥360).

SHUZEN-JI ONSEN

In a pristine forest in Izu's northern interior, the tranquil escape of Shuzen-ji Onsen straddles the Katsura River, beside an atmospheric bamboo grove. The town was visited by Kōbō Daishi (aka Kūkai), the founder of the Shingon school of Buddhism, and **Shuzen-ji** temple (964 Shuzen-ji; tel. 0558/72-0053; http://shuzenji-temple.com; 8:30am-4pm daily; temple free, treasure hall ¥300), is said to have been founded by Kūkai more than 13 centuries ago. For a serene bathing experience, minus Hakone's theme park vibe, Shuzen-ji doesn't disappoint.

Onsen

Tokko-no-yu (24 hours daily; free), the most historically significant bath in town, is said to have been created by Kūkai. It's now a riverside footbath.

Hako-yu (925 Shuzen-ji; tel. 0558/72-5282; noon-9pm daily; ¥350), located south of the river just east of Tokko-no-yu, is a clean, modern complex with cedar interiors, easily identified by its watchtower.

Food and Accommodations

NANABAN

761-1-3 Shuzen-ji; tel. 0558/72-0007; 11am-4pm Fri.-Wed.; ¥630-1,890

This soba restaurant is known for its *zendera* soba, which comes with a fresh stalk of wasabi root to grate and mix with sesame to add some kick to the cold noodles.

ARAI RYOKAN

970 Shuzen-ji; tel. 0558/72-2007; http://arairyokan.net; ¥53,900 d with two meals

This *ryokan* is an atmospheric time capsule, once favored by artists, kabuki actors, and intellectuals. Established in 1872, the inn's wooden interior and classic tatami rooms—some with riverside views—evoke another time. There are shared, sex-separate *onsen* baths and private baths can be reserved. Food is seasonal and top-notch.

★ ASABA SHUZENJI RYOKAN

3450-1 Shuzen-ji; tel. 0558/72-7000; www.asaba-ryokan.com/en; ¥165,000 d with two meals

Reflected in the price tag, this *ryokan* does everything right: mouthwatering *kaiseki* cuisine, expansive rooms with private bathtubs, views of bamboo groves, private gardens, and even a *Noh* stage. There are shared indoor baths and open-air baths surrounded by forest—both separated by sex. Private baths that can be used freely around the clock by guests.

Transportation

To reach Shuzen-ji Onsen, take the *shinkansen* from Tokyo Station to **Mishima Station** (50 minutes; ¥4,600), then transfer to the Izu-Hakone railway bound for **Shuzen-ji Station** (35 minutes; ¥520).

From Shuzen-ji Station, hop on the bus to **Shuzen-ji Onsen** (10 minutes; ¥220). Before you take the bus to Shuzen-ji Onsen, stop by the **Tourist Information Center** (631-7 Kashi-wakubo; tel. 0558/72-0271; www.shuzenji.info; 9am-5pm daily) in Shuzen-ji Station where an English-language map of the village is available.

Central Honshu

Located at the geographical center of Japan,

Central Honshu, or Chūbu as it's called in Japanese, draws visitors with its access to nature (especially the Japan Alps, a vast chain of mountain ranges that cuts through the center of Honshu), its proliferation of *onsen* (hot spring baths), and its abundance of well-preserved historic towns. The most popular of the region's many storied cities is Kanazawa, home to charming teahouses, a former samurai quarter, and Kenroku-en, one of Japan's finest gardens.

In the mountains that spread across the region's interior, a cluster of small cities offers a glimpse of a more traditional way of life. Takayama boasts a well-preserved merchants' quarter, crisscrossed by streams, along with Hida-no-Sato, a cluster of thatched roof houses

Highlights

Look for ★ to find recommended sights, activities, dining, and lodging.

★ **Higashi Chaya-gai:** The myriad tea houses lining the cobblestone paths of Kanazawa's geisha district offer an evocative glimpse of the past (page 241).

★ **Kenroku-en:** Kanazawa's famed castle garden is widely regarded as one of the country's best designed landscapes (page 242).

★ **Sanmachi Suji:** Takayama's well-preserved riverside merchant's quarter lures you into its many museums, galleries, shops, and eateries (page 253).

★ **Matsumoto-jō:** The country's oldest wooden castle, nicknamed "Crow Castle" for its iconic black walls, Matsumoto-jō is an immaculate representation of a classical Japanese fortress (page 263).

★ **Hiking in Kamikōchi:** This highland valley offers some of the most breathtaking alpine scenery in all of Japan. Rivers course through verdant forests, and *onsen* offer relaxation to weary hikers (page 268).

★ **Walking Japan's Medieval Highway:** Ramble along a rural section of Japan's famed medieval highway, the Nakasendō, between the well-preserved Edo-period (1603-1868) towns of Tsumago and Magome (page 272).

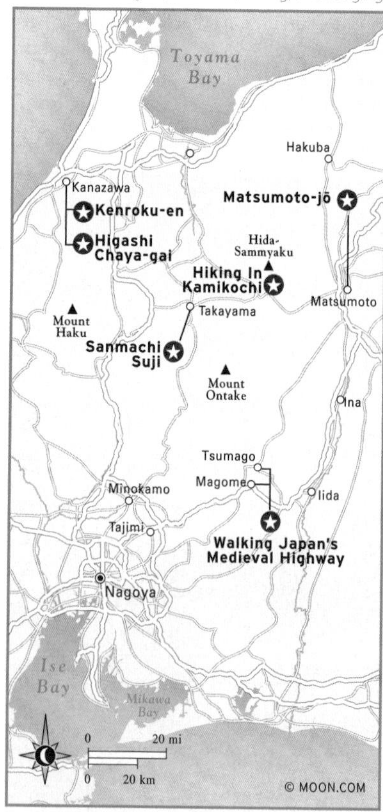

rebuilt to evoke Japan's rural past. Matsumoto is blessed with a lovely alpine backdrop and is home to one of Japan's most famous castles. And Nagano boasts a temple that has long been the destination of pilgrims and offers lodging for travelers, too.

More rural, the Shirakawa-gō region is graced by hamlets of thatched roof houses that may inspire romantics to have flights of fancy. The bucolic scene is especially magical in winter when snow blankets the landscape, and the windows of those charming A-frame houses glow softly in the evening.

Even deeper within the mountains, the legendary riverside *onsen* of Shin-Hotaka-no-Yu beckons hot springs enthusiasts to one of Japan's most wild places to soak in the open air. Bathing is mixed, so it's only suitable for those with an exhibitionist streak (optional modesty towel not withstanding). On the far side of a mountain near the remote pool, the Kamikōchi region offers some of the country's best terrain for hikers. And in winter, when the mountains are enveloped in a thick quilt of snow, powder lovers flock to the region's world-class ski slopes.

Meanwhile, in the south, the mercantile city of Nagoya is a convenient, no-frills transit hub. Its rich, if cloying, culinary options, often slathered in sweet sauce, inject a bit of flavor into an otherwise bland cityscape. Hop aboard a local train bound for the Kiso Valley, however, and enjoy a change of scenery. This alpine pass, dotted by atmospheric towns that once stood along the medieval Kyoto-Tokyo highway known as the Nakasendō, is best experienced on foot, traipsing between the old post towns of Tsumago and Magome against a backdrop of jagged peaks.

ORIENTATION

Central Honshu is Japan's vast heartland, sandwiched between the Greater Tokyo conurbation known as Kanto to the east and the nation's similarly sprawling historic heart in the region of Kansai (Kyoto, Osaka, and around) to the west. Aichi prefecture—home to **Nagoya,** the region's largest city with a population of 2.3 million—sprawls along the southwestern Pacific coast, bordered on the north by landlocked Gifu prefecture. The prefectures of Fukui and Ishikawa, home to the historic towns of **Kanazawa** and **Toyama** make up the Japan Sea side. Meanwhile, Nagano prefecture commands a large swath of Central Honshu's rugged core.

The primary feature of Central Honshu is its abundance of mountains. A series of ranges, collectively called the **Japan Alps,** run through the center of the region, tapering off near both the Pacific and the Japan Sea coasts. This craggy interior can be easily accessed from the greater Tokyo area, Nagoya in the south, or Kanazawa in the north. The towns of **Takayama,** located in Gifu prefecture, and **Matsumoto** and **Nagano,** both in Nagano prefecture, are the main hubs in the Alps region.

PLANNING YOUR TIME

How long you'll want to devote to Central Honshu will depend on whether you plan to explore its mountainous interior or simply head to one of the region's coastal hubs. It's best viewed as a place to spend two or three days exploring some of Japan's natural beauty—hiking in the warmer months or skiing in winter—as you shuttle between greater Tokyo (Kanto) and Kansai. That said, if you don't plan to visit Kansai's historical gems, Kyoto and Nara, Central Honshu's older towns—most notably **Kanazawa**—provide a good dose of traditional Japan. It's possible to see Kanazawa's top sights in an afternoon, but spending one or two nights will give you a chance to take it all in.

Although it's easy to access from Tokyo and Kansai's major hubs, thanks to its large *shinkansen* (bullet train) station, **Nagoya** is best viewed as a transit point and less as a base. The city does have a handful of minor points

Previous: Matsumoto Castle; statue at Kenroku-en; Higashi Chaya-gai.

Best Restaurants

★ **Yabaton Honten:** In business for seven decades, this Nagoya shop does one decadent thing and nails it: a local dish called *miso-katsu,* which is *tonkatsu* (breaded and fried pork cutlet) covered in sweet miso sauce (page 237).

★ **Atsuta Horaiken Honten:** This venerable local spot serves a thinly sliced eel over rice, a Nagoya specialty, in nostalgic surroundings (page 238).

★ **Otome Sushi:** This popular Kanazawa sushi joint brings the region's seafood and tipple made at its diverse constellation of *sake* breweries under one roof (page 250).

★ **Kyōya:** This Takayama favorite serves countryside grub—think vegetables foraged in the nearby mountains and BBQ—in a cozy, farmhouse-like interior (page 258).

★ **Sakurajaya:** At this restaurant, which sits a bit outside downtown Takayama, an innovative chef brings knowhow and ingredients you'd expect to find in a German kitchen, fused with those of Japan (page 258).

★ **Kobayashi Soba:** This stylish eatery in the heart of Matsumoto serves a wide range of soba—cold, in warm soup, with duck—and tempura with the freshest of trimmings, down to wasabi grated at the table (page 265).

REGIONAL SPECIALTIES

The industrial city of **Nagoya** is known for dishes liberally slathered in sauce or steeped in sweetened flavors. A prime example is ***hitsumabushi,*** or thinly sliced saltwater eel flavored with soy-based sauce atop a bed of rice. Another local dish in this vein is ***miso-nikomi*** udon, a style of thick udon noodles served in a viscous miso broth. Then there's ***miso-katsu,*** or breaded and deep-fried cuts of fatty pork slathered in a sweetened miso-based sauce.

of interest if you happen to be in town for a day, as well as plenty of decent accommodation options, but it's not the most vibrant place to stay more than one night.

If you're heading into the mountains, it pays to stop in one of the region's provincial hubs, like **Takayama** or **Matsumoto.** They're worth a day of exploration and an overnight stay, or can serve as bases for exploring the surrounding countryside; take a day hike, completing the **Tateyama-Kurobe Alpine** route, or seeing the thatched-roof houses of **Shirakawa-gō.** The city of **Nagano,** home of **Zenkō-ji** temple, is an entry point to a cluster of rustic, secluded *onsen,* and hiking or winter sports options. Though Shirakawa-gō, **Shin-Hotaka-no-Yu Onsen,** the **Kamikōchi** region, and the numerous *onsen* surrounding Nagano city are accessible by bus, you'll end up losing time if you take public transportation, because departures are sporadic. With a car, however, staying in the Japan Alps overnight in a remote *onsen ryokan* allows you to appreciate their magic.

The mountains running through the middle of the region heavily influence the weather, especially in winter. While the Pacific side has relatively dry and sunny but cold winters, the Japan Sea side gets a heavy dump of snow in winter. There are excellent resorts for **skiing** and **snowboarding** throughout the Alps. Book rooms a few months in advance for popular ski resorts like **Hakuba, Nozawa,** and **Shiga Kōgen.** Similarly, accommodations book up fast for some of the bigger **festivals** in the region, such as the Takayama Matsuri, and during the popular **autumn leaves** viewing season that peaks in November.

Best Accommodations

★ **Flatt's:** Slow down to savor ocean views, ingenious meals, and genuine warmth at this charming bed-and-breakfast run by a gregarious Australian chef and his local wife on the quiet eastern shore of the Nōto Peninsula (page 248).

★ **Asadaya:** With brilliant service, Edo-period chic, and exquisite cuisine, this is the finest *ryokan* in Kanazawa (page 251).

★ **Takimi No Ie:** This discreet *ryokan* along the Nakasendō brings all of Japan's rural pleasures under one roof, from the sunken hearth where guests are served locally sourced meals to a secluded *onsen* bath surrounded by natural splendor (page 273).

★ **Sumiyoshi-ya:** This nostalgic, rustic *ryokan* is a wonderful place to immerse yourself in the quintessential hot-spring village of Nozawa Onsen (page 280).

★ **Backcountry Lodge Hakuba:** Run by a friendly couple, this homey lodge is a relaxed place to base yourself in the Hakuba Valley, and to kick back and read by the fire after a day on the slopes (page 286).

Nagoya

Nagoya, Japan's fourth-largest city with a population of 2.3 million, has the unenviable distinction of being considered by many to be Japan's most boring major city. This bad rap can be traced to the 1980s when the TV star and comedian Tamori, in his trademark black sunglasses, began to knock the city as a middling place lacking zest, sophistication, or distinguishing traits of any kind. The city's image took another hit in 2016 when its own residents rated it in a survey as being among the least desirable destinations of eight cities across Japan, in a variety of categories, prompting the media to have a Nagoya-bashing field day. Ouch.

One thing to keep in mind is that vast swaths of Nagoya were reduced to rubble during World War II, wiping out most traces of historical charm that may once have graced its streets. The city's manufacturing might—it was a major producer of Japan's legendary Zero fighter planes—made it a prime target for Allied bombers. The gray cityscape that arose from the ashes hasn't helped matters. But if you find yourself in the much-maligned metropolis, don't despair. After hearing the unfair press, you'll likely be pleasantly surprised. Its refreshingly diverse range of attractions, down-to-earth residents, surprisingly green downtown, and local dishes that pair well with beer will engage and satiate you.

The city's strong suit is its sturdy mercantile backbone. This is reflected in some of its better-known attractions, such as the Toyota Commemorative Museum of Industry and Technology and SCMAGLEV and Railway Park, a hit with children and train geeks. Stellar museums and parks, important spiritual sites, and a reproduction castle are also scattered around the city. Given its convenient location between Kanto and Kansai, from which it can easily be reached by *shinkansen*, Nagoya is an ideal jumping-off point for journeys into the Japan Alps.

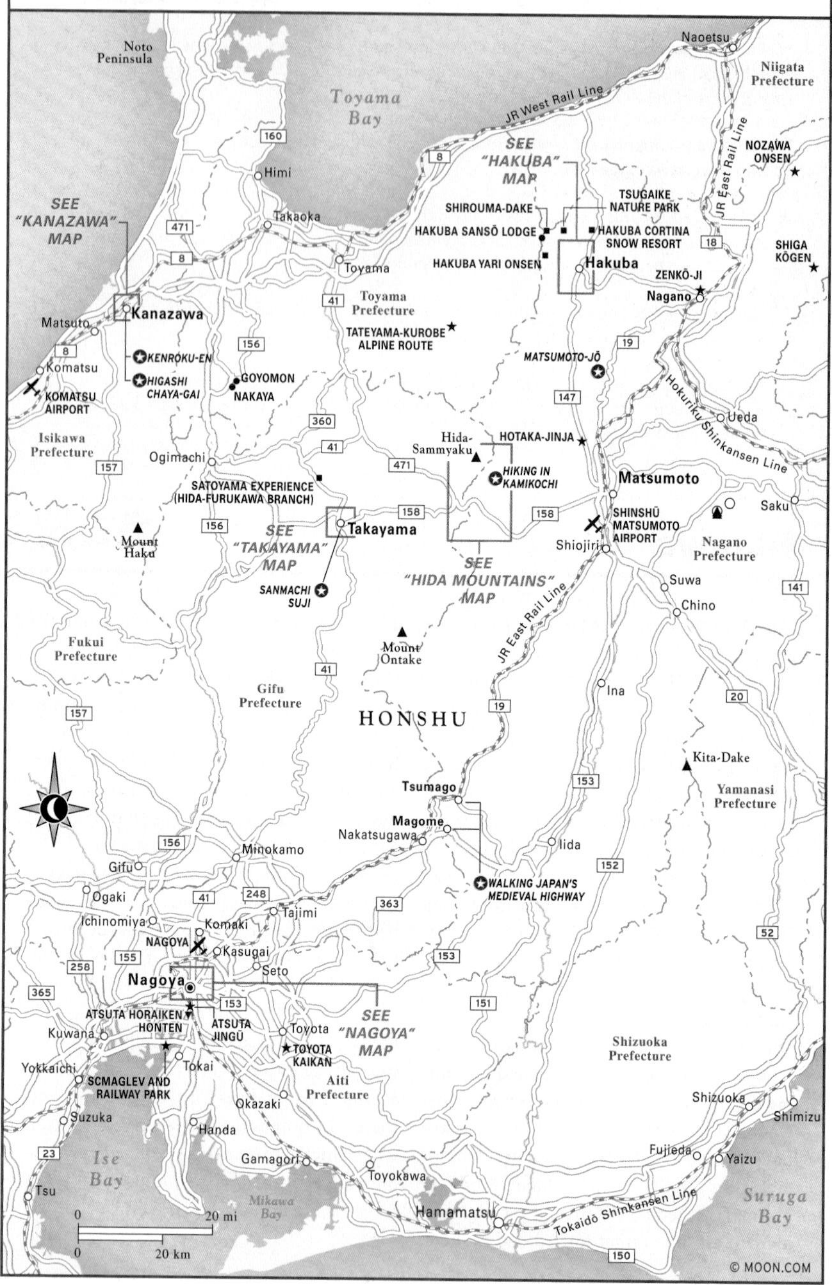

CENTRAL HONSHU
NAGOYA

SIGHTS

NORITAKE NO MORI
ノリタケの森

3-1-36 Noritake-shinmachi, Nishi-ku; tel. 052/561-7290; www.noritake.co.jp/eng/mori; 10am-6pm Tues.-Sun., closed Tues. if Mon. is a holiday; free (some attractions inside garden cost money); take Higashiyama subway line to Kamejima Station

This is a good stop for anyone with a penchant for porcelain. For more than a century, Noritake has been in the ceramics business, and Noritake no Mori (Noritake Garden) occupies the grounds where the company's factory once stood. Aside from serving as an appealing patch of green northeast of Nagoya Station, you'll find a **Craft Center** (tel. 052/561-7114; 10am-5pm Tues.-Sun., closed Tues. if Mon. is holiday; adults ¥500, children free), where you can see porcelain production in action—or make your own—and the **Noritake Gallery** (052/562-9811; 10am-6pm Tues.-Sun., closed Tues. if Mon. is holiday; free), which showcases a wide range of Noritake handiwork, from tablewear and vases to electronic and industrial gadgets. There are also a restaurant and a café on-site, where patrons eat and drink from an array delicate porcelain tablewear.

TOYOTA COMMEMORATIVE MUSEUM OF INDUSTRY AND TECHNOLOGY
トヨタ産業技術記念館

4-1-35 Noritake-shinmachi, Nishi-ku; tel. 052/551-6115; www.tcmit.org; 9:30am-5pm Tues.-Sat., closed Tues. if Mon. is holiday; adults ¥500, high school and junior high school students ¥300, elementary school students ¥200; take Meitetsu Nagoya line to Sako Station

You might be surprised to learn that, before Toyota was mass-producing more cars than any automaker on earth, the automotive giant was actually a manufacturer of weaving technology. Come here to learn more about the company's fascinating history, including its journey from making textile machinery to revolutionizing the economy-car industry and establishing itself as a leader in robotics. This museum, housed in the former base of the company's weaving operations, is a testament to Nagoya's industrious spirit. English-language signage and audio tours ensure full comprehension. For true lovers of the automobile, **Toyota Kaikan** (1 Toyota-chō, Toyota; tel. 0565/29-3355; www.toyota.co.jp/en/about_toyota/facility/toyota_kaikan; 9:30am-5pm Mon.-Sat., tours from 11am; free), located in Toyota city outside Nagoya, shows off the company's ever-impressive array of new tech with 2.5-hour factory tours. Note that the free tours require advance reservation online or by phone.

NAGOYA-JŌ
名古屋城

1-1 Honmaru, Naka-ku; tel. 052/231-1700; www.nagoyajo.city.nagoya.jp; 9am-4:30pm daily; adults ¥500, children free; take Meijo subway line to Shiyakusho Station

With two golden dolphins adorning the roof of its *donjon* (main keep), lovely grounds dotted by teahouses and a stunning newly reopened palace complex, Nagoya-jō cuts a striking profile. Entering the grounds of the fortress, shielded by massive stone walls, requires crossing two moats. Once inside the main keep, five floors house a range of exhibits, from replicas of the massive female dolphin adorning the roofline, to re-creations of the city's streetlife during the Edo period when the castle was constructed. Be sure to go all the way to the top, where vistas of Nagoya stretch in all directions.

The castle's legacy underlines Nagoya's historical importance. No less than Oda Nobunaga (1534-1582), the great warrior famed for unifying half of Japans' provinces; Toyotoi Hideyoshi (1536-1598), who completed the mammoth task begun by his predecessor Oda; and Tokugawa Ieyasu (1543-1616), who founded the mighty Tokugawa shogunate that reigned throughout the Edo period (1603-1868), were all born in the area. It was the last of these three towering figures, Tokugawa, who called for the construction of

Nagoya

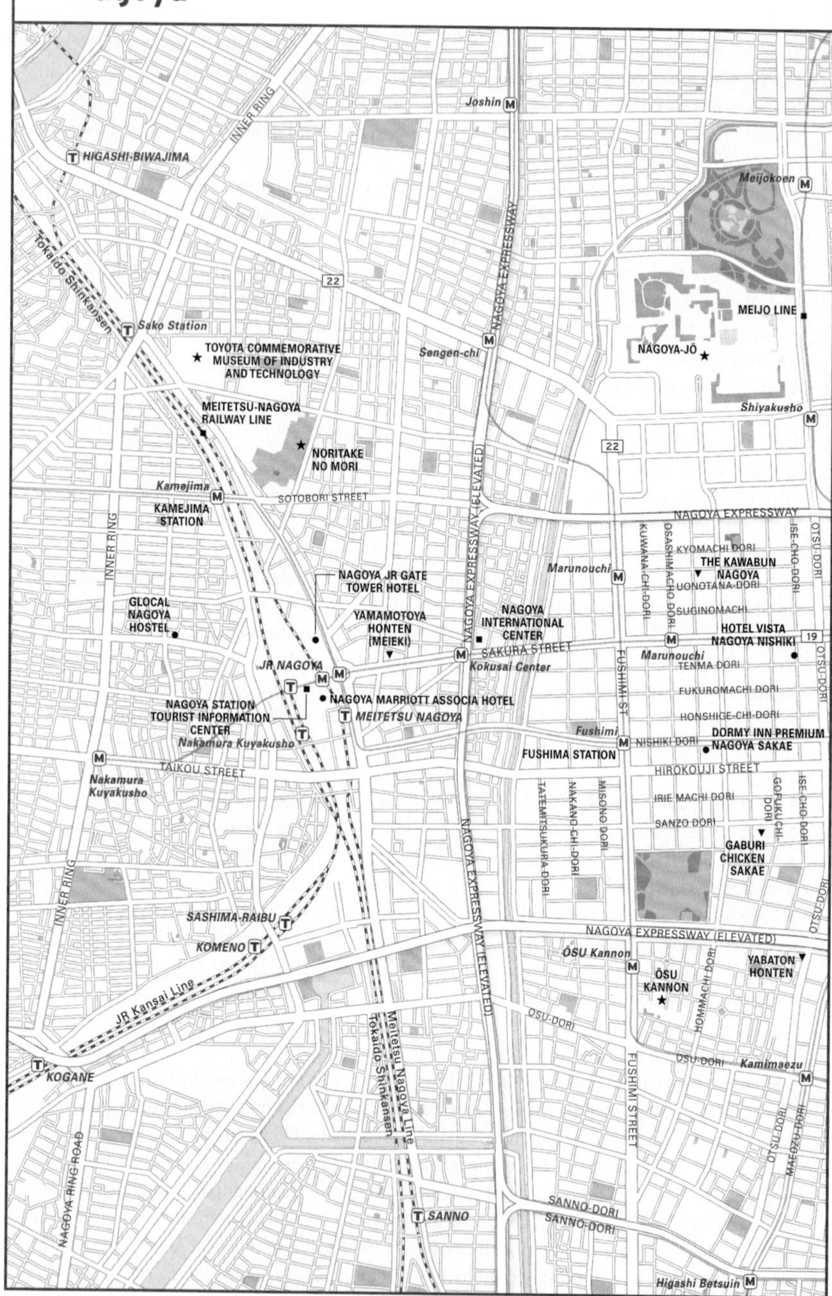

Joshin
HIGASHI-BIWAJIMA
INNER RING
Meijokoen
Tokaido Shinkansen
NAGOYA EXPRESSWAY
22
MEIJO LINE
Sako Station
TOYOTA COMMEMORATIVE MUSEUM OF INDUSTRY AND TECHNOLOGY
Sengen-chi
NAGOYA-JŌ
MEITETSU-NAGOYA RAILWAY LINE
Shiyakusho
NORITAKE NO MORI
Kamejima
SOTOBORI STREET
KAMEJIMA STATION
NAGOYA EXPRESSWAY (ELEVATED)
KYOMACHI DORI
KUWANA-CHI-DORI
OSASHIMACHO DORI
ISE-CHO-DORI
OTSU-DORI
THE KAWABUN NAGOYA
Marunouchi
UONOTANA-DORI
NAGOYA JR GATE TOWER HOTEL
SUGINOMACHI
GLOCAL NAGOYA HOSTEL
YAMAMOTOYA HONTEN (MEIEKI)
NAGOYA INTERNATIONAL CENTER
HOTEL VISTA NAGOYA NISHIKI
19
SAKURA STREET
Kokusai Center
TENMA DORI
JR NAGOYA
FUSHIMI ST
FUKUROMACHI DORI
NAGOYA MARRIOTT ASSOCIA HOTEL
MEITETSU NAGOYA
HONSHIGE-CHI-DORI
NAGOYA STATION TOURIST INFORMATION CENTER
Fushimi
NISHIKI DORI
DORMY INN PREMIUM NAGOYA SAKAE
Nakamura Kuyakusho
FUSHIMA STATION
TAIKOU STREET
HIROKOUJI STREET
TATEMITSUKURA-DORI
NAKANO-CHI-DORI
MISONO DORI
GOFUKU-CHI-DORI
IRIE MACHI DORI
SANZO DORI
GABURI CHICKEN SAKAE
SASHIMA-RAIBU
NAGOYA EXPRESSWAY (ELEVATED)
KOMENO
ŌSU Kannon
YABATON HONTEN
ŌSU KANNON
HOMMACHI-DORI
JR Kansai Line
Meitetsu Nagoya Line
Tokaido Shinkansen
OSU-DORI
Kamimaezu
KOGANE
FUSHIMI STREET
OTSU-DORI
MAEZU-DORI
NAGOYA RING ROAD
SANNO-DORI
SANNO
Higashi Betsuin

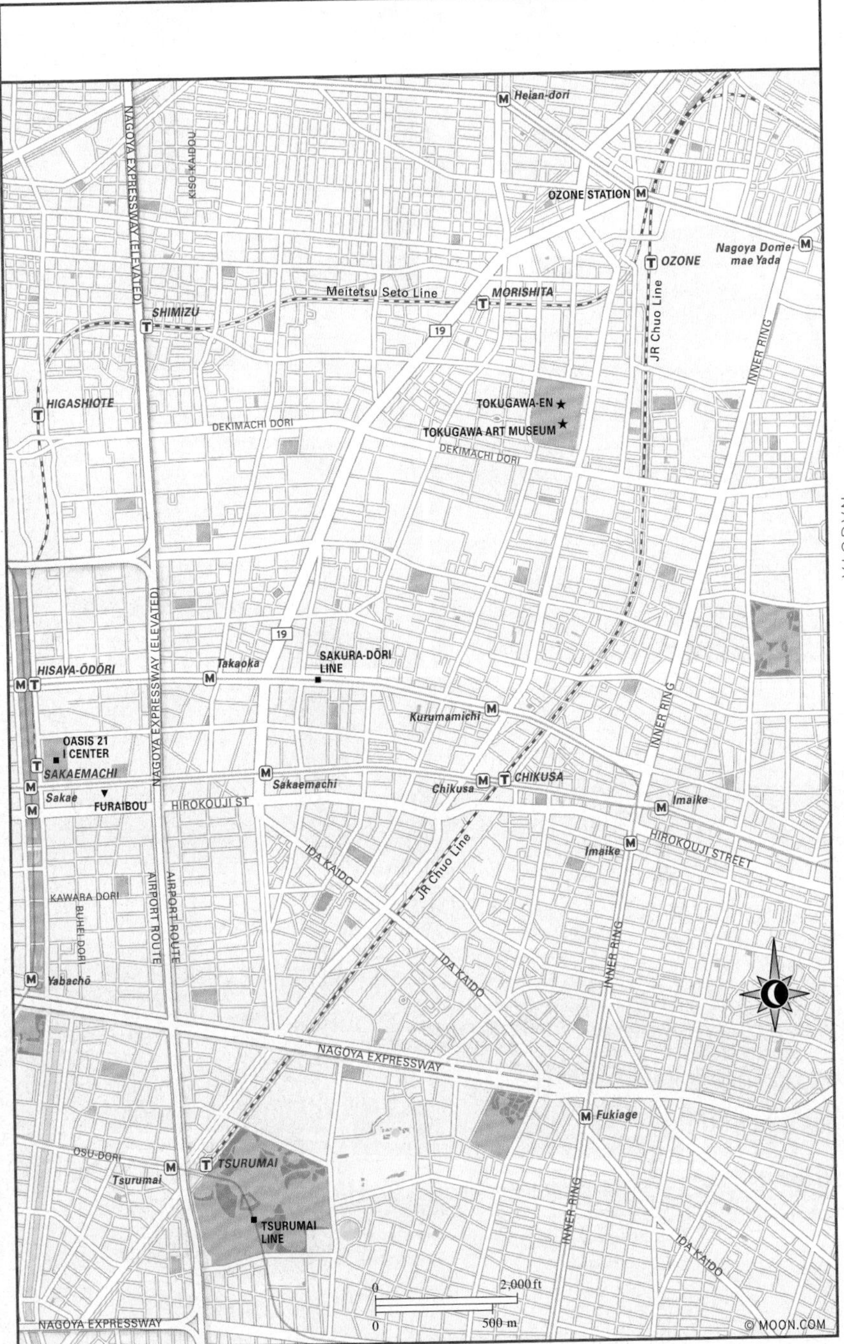
Heian-dori
OZONE STATION
Nagoya Dome-mae Yada
OZONE
MORISHITA
Meitetsu Seto Line
SHIMIZU
19
JR Chuo Line
INNER RING
NAGOYA EXPRESSWAY (ELEVATED)
KISO-KAIDOU
HIGASHIOTE
TOKUGAWA-EN
TOKUGAWA ART MUSEUM
DEKIMACHI DORI
DEKIMACHI DORI
19
SAKURA-DŌRI LINE
Takaoka
HISAYA-ŌDŌRI
Kurumamichi
INNER RING
OASIS 21 I CENTER
SAKAEMACHI
Sakaemachi
Chikusa
CHIKUSA
Sakae
FURAIBOU
HIROKOUJI ST
Imaike
Imaike
HIROKOUJI STREET
IDA KAIDO
JR Chuo Line
KAWARA DORI
BUHEI DORI
AIRPORT ROUTE
AIRPORT ROUTE
IDA KAIDO
INNER RING
Yabachō
NAGOYA EXPRESSWAY
Fukiage
OSU-DORI
Tsurumai
TSURUMAI
TSURUMAI LINE
INNER RING
IDA KAIDO
0
2,000 ft
0
500 m
NAGOYA EXPRESSWAY
© MOON.COM

1
2
3

Nagoya-jō in 1609, to serve as the base of the Owari branch of the Tokugawa family.

The castle has been undergoing an ambitious redevelopment program. The palace (**Honmaru Goten**), also on the grounds, reopened to visitors in June 2018, after a lengthy rebuilding project using time-honored materials and techniques. With its elegant entrance, immaculate tatami rooms, and beautifully painted sliding doors, the building is one of the best examples of classical Shoin architecture in the country.

TOKUGAWA ART MUSEUM
徳川美術館

1017 Tokugawa-chō, Higashi-ku; tel. 052/935-6262; www.tokugawa-art-museum.jp; 10am-5pm Tues.-Sun., closed Tues. if Mon. is holiday; adults ¥1,400, university and high school students ¥700, junior high and elementary school students ¥500; take JR Chūō line to Ozone, or Meguru loop bus to stop 11

To glean some sense of the power wielded by the Owari branch of Tokugawa Ieyasu's lineage, which was based in Nagoya, be sure to visit this excellent museum. Built on the grounds where the Owari family once resided, the museum contains some 10,000 precious artifacts possessed by the Owari line of the Tokugawa family.

Six exhibition halls showcase armor and weapons of war, a re-created teahouse with exquisite utensils, household items that would have once graced the reception chambers and living quarters of a palace, a *Noh* theater with a collection of haunting masks, and perhaps most impressive of all, a scroll of *The Tale of Genji* dating to the 12th century. The scroll is only exhibited briefly each year to preserve the delicate parchment, but videos revealing its intricate details stand ready at other times.

TOKUGAWA-EN
徳川園

1001 Tokugawa-chō, Higashi-ku; tel. 052/935-8988; www.tokugawaen.aichi.jp; 9:30am-5:30pm Tues.-Sun., closed Tues. if Mon. is holiday; adults ¥300; take JR Chūō line to Ozone, or Meguru loop bus to stop 11

If you check out the Tokugawa Art Museum, be sure to stop at this lovely garden next door. It's at its most resplendent in spring, when peonies (mid- to late April) and irises (late May to early June) bloom, and in autumn when foliage turns fiery red, bright yellow, and earthy brown. The Tokugawa family donated the garden—once a place of respite for retired feudal lords—to the city in 1931, but it was subsequently decimated by Allied bombs in 1945. Restored in 2001 and reopened in 2004, today the garden is beautifully landscaped once more, complete with bodies of water crisscrossed by bridges, meandering footpaths, and a waterfall. This is a great stop to slow down and contemplate how the ruling class once lived.

ŌSU KANNON
大須観音

2-21-47 Ōsu, Naka-ku; tel. 052/231-6525; www.osu-kannon.jp; 24 hours a day; free; take Tsurumai subway line to Ōsu Kannon Station

Within this popular temple stands a wooden statue of Kannon, Buddhist goddess of mercy, sculpted by Kobo Daishi (aka Kūkai), founder of the Shingon school of Buddhism and one of Japan's most important spiritual figures. Originally built in Gifu Prefecture, north of Nagoya, this popular hall of worship was moved to its current location by Tokugawa Ieyasu in the early 17th century. Although originally built at the end of the Kamakura Period (1192-1333), its current incarnation was born in 1970. Despite the relative youth of the structure, beneath its main hall is a library that holds some 15,000 ancient texts, including what is considered the oldest copy of the *kojiki,* a handwritten chronicle of Japan's mythical history. Just next to the temple, you'll find the Osu Shopping Street, a covered shopping area crammed with hundreds of cafés, restaurants, and shops hawking all manner of goods, from things geek to cheap threads.

1: Nagoya-jō **2:** Tokugawa-en **3:** Atsuta Jingū

Around Nagoya

ATSUTA JINGŪ
熱田神宮

1-1-1 Jingū, Atsuta-ku; tel. 052/671-4151; www.atsutajingu.or.jp; 24 hours a day; free; take Meitetsu Nagoya line to Jingū-mae Station, or Meijo subway line to Jingū-nishi Station

This shrine, tucked away in a leafy grove in the south of Nagoya, is among the most important sites in Shinto. It has hallowed status because it houses the sacred sword known as Kusanagi, which legend says was bestowed upon the royal family by Amaterasu Omikami, the sun goddess herself, Shinto's chief deity. Along with the mirror (symbolizing wisdom and held in Ise Jingū) and the jewel (embodying the virtue of benevolence and kept at the Imperial Palace in Tokyo), the sword at Atsuta Jingū, denoting valor, is one of the three Imperial Regalia of Japan. The shrine buildings are modeled on the style of Ise Jingū. Similar to Ise's evasive mirror, the sacred sword within the inner sanctum of Atsuta Jingū is never put on public display.

SCMAGLEV AND RAILWAY PARK
リニア・鉄道館　～夢と想い出のミュージアム～

3-2-2 Kinjofuto, Minato-ku; tel. 052/389-6100; http://museum.jr-central.co.jp; 10am-5:30pm Wed.-Mon., closed Wed. if Tues. is holiday; adults ¥1,000, children ¥500, shinkansen simulator ¥500; take Aonami line from Nagoya Station to Kinjofuto Station

Train geeks, rejoice. The entire history of Japan's sophisticated engagement with train technology is explored in this excellent museum, from early steam locomotives and the iconic bullet train (*shinkansen*) to futuristic, lighting-fast maglev trains that approach speeds of almost 600 km (373 mi) per hour. A massive, elaborate miniature train set runs through an exceedingly realistic diorama of Japan's major train hubs. Elsewhere, almost 40 actual train cars can be examined up close, from underneath and inside. Simulators let you experience what it's like to be at the controls, to open and close doors for passengers, or to be at the helm of a *shinkansen*. Note that you'll need to reserve a spot to try any of the simulators, which cost anywhere from ¥100 to ¥500 per turn, 45 minutes in advance.

There's a strong educational component geared toward kids throughout, and an English-language audio guide can be rented for ¥500. This is a highly recommended stop if you have a keen interest in trains.

FOOD

YAMAMOTOYA HONTEN (MEIEKI)

1st Horiuchi Bldg. B1F, 3-25-9 Meieki; tel. 052/565-0278; http://yamamotoyahonten.co.jp; 11am-10pm daily; ¥700-1,600; take JR lines to Nagoya Station

A local specialty, the thick udon here is served in a heavy, flavorful miso broth. Unlike a lot of Japanese fare, it's not subtle, but this is part of its appeal for many foreign palates. Other options to go with the noodles include tempura, oysters, locally raised chicken, and *kurobuta* (black pork), as the intensely flavorsome variety of Berkshire Pork that originated in the English countryside is known in Japan, among others.

FURAIBOU

Gourmet Bldg. Aeri 1F, 4-5-8 Sakae, 1F Airy Bldg., Naka-ku; tel. 052/241-8016; www.furaibou.com; 5pm-midnight Mon.-Thurs., 5pm-1am Fri.-Sat.; ¥3,000-4,000 average; take Higashiyama and Meijo lines to Sakae Station

This restaurant serves another down-and-dirty Nagoya specialty that will feel somewhat like home for many Western travelers: chicken wings (*tebasaki*). Nagoya's take on the classic beer food is deep-fried and basted in a sweet, lightly spicy sauce, with a pinch of sesame and seasoning. The menu also extends to sashimi, noodles, and more. Note that it can get smoky at times.

GABURI CHICKEN SAKAE

3-12-11 Sakae, Naka-ku; tel. 052/262-8739; https://gabuchiki.com/shop/view/39; 5pm-3am Mon.-Sat.,

Pachinko

Chances are you'll encounter a pachinko parlor during your time in urban Japan. Luridly bright, smoky, deafening, and utterly inscrutable to the uninitiated, pachinko is one of Japan's more mystifying pastimes. For sheer shock value, step inside. Myriad silver ball bearings ricochet through a pinball-like glass box filled with a variety of obstacles and carefully arranged brass pins. Bored salarymen and office ladies sit before the machines for hours on end.

HOW TO PLAY

Insert money or a prepaid card into the desired machine to receive a throng of tiny silver balls. Next, pull a lever to release a stream of the balls through the machine's maze. If one of the spheres released manages to ping a specific spot, the player gets a chance to receive more balls to play again. The more balls you've got, the higher your chance of winning. Most machines have a digital screen that plays short animations to escalate tension as a potential jackpot looms. To emerge victorious, players must trigger three matching symbols or numbers on the screen. Varying levels of wins are possible, depending on how many times the player manages to align these numbers, facing increasingly challenging odds as they pull the lever.

PACHINKO'S HISTORY

Since the first commercial pachinko parlor opened in Nagoya in 1948, the garish establishments have popped up like mushrooms around the country. Today, the pachinko industry is astoundingly large, with more revenue than all gambling in Las Vegas, Macau, and Singapore combined. Gambling is illegal in Japan, but pachinko found a loophole: If a player hits a jackpot, a flood of the small silver orbs fills a tray that they can exchange for prizes at an on-site gift shop. These prizes can then be exchanged for money at a separate window outside the parlor. These cash-exchange windows evade the law by nominally separating the prizes from the parlors themselves. Previously run by the *yakuza* (mafia), now they are tightly regulated.

PACHINKO AND *ZAINICHI*

Some 80 percent of all pachinko parlors are owned by ethnic Koreans, who, despite being born in Japan, are still considered foreign residents. The community, known as *zainichi,* is often subject to discrimination, and pachinko is their largest economic foothold in Japan. The randomness of the game is brilliantly used as a metaphor for the vagaries of fate in Korean-American author Min Jin Lee's novel *Pachinko,* which traces four generations of a Korean family from pre-World War II Japanese-occupied Korea to a *zainichi* neighborhood in Osaka, where one generation of the fictional family runs a parlor of its own.

4pm-3am Sat., 4pm-midnight Sun. and holidays; dishes ¥350-990; about 10 minutes' walk from the Sakae subway station

While Furaibou is a good place for a sit-down meal, Gaburi is a fun, boisterous fried-chicken spot with a cheaper, more booze-friendly menu. Drink options are weighted toward various spins on the highball (whisky-soda), mixed with lemon, cola, and more. In the heart of the nightlife zone, this is a fun place for a bite before a big night out.

★ YABATON HONTEN

3-6-18 Ōsu, Naka-ku; tel. 052/252-8810; www.yabaton.com; 11am-9pm daily; ¥1,300-1,900; take Meijo line to Yabachō Station

With a logo featuring a portly pig, the chain's signature dish is clear: *miso-katsu* (juicy pork, breaded and deep-fried, then slathered in sweet, savory miso sauce, and served with shredded cabbage). In business since 1947, this restaurant is most noted for pushing this dish into Japan's culinary consciousness.

THE KAWABUN NAGOYA

2-12-30 Marunouchi, Naka-ku; tel. 052/222-0020; www.thekawabunnagoya.com; lunch 11am-2pm Mon. and Wed.-Fri. except holidays, dinner 5:30pm-10pm Mon. and Wed.-Fri., 6:30pm-10pm Sat.-Sun. and holidays; lunch ¥1,200-5,000, dinner ¥4,500-10,000

Housed in a traditional home boasting views onto a lovely garden with a pond, this classy restaurant serves great Italian food. It's ideal for families, couples, or groups who want a quality meal in elegant surroundings, with chic furniture and subdued lighting. The seasonal Italian menu includes pasta, salmon, and steak. Lunch sets are a good value. Sumptuous multicourse dinners are complemented by an extensive wine list. To be safe, reserve a day or more ahead for dinner.

Around Nagoya

★ ATSUTA HORAIKEN HONTEN

503 Godo-chō, Atsuta-ku; tel. 052/671-8686; www.houraiken.com/honten; 11:30am-2pm and 4:30pm-8:30pm Thurs.-Tues., closed every 2nd and 4th Thurs.; dishes ¥550-950, set meals ¥2,500-5,500; take Meijo subway line to Temmachō Station

Hitsumabushi, or thinly cut eel drizzled in a soy-based sauce and served over rice (¥3,600), has been served to patrons in this vaunted restaurant's tatami-floored rooms since 1873. Add scallion, wasabi, and seaweed for extra zing. There's also an a la carte menu and various other set meals beyond eel (assorted tempura and more). It draws a crowd, particularly in summer, so you may have to wait for a seat. A recommended local favorite.

ACCOMMODATIONS

Under ¥10,000

GLOCAL NAGOYA HOSTEL

1-21-3 Noritake, Nakamura-ku; tel. 052/446-4694; www.facebook.com/hostelnagoya; dorms ¥3,200, private ¥12,500; less than 10 minutes' walk west of JR Nagoya Station

This hip hostel has a café, bar, where fellow travelers and locals congregate, and friendly English-speaking staff who are keen to introduce you to their city. Each dorm room sleeps four people, and one floor is women-only. All rooms share showers and toilets, which are grouped on one floor. There's also a shared kitchen and lounge, and coin laundry. A fantastic choice for budget travelers who want to socialize.

¥10,000-20,000

HOTEL VISTA NAGOYA NISHIKI

3-3-15 Nishiki, Naka-ku; tel. 052/951-8333; https://nagoya-nishiki.hotel-vista.jp/ja; from ¥10,080 d with breakfast; take Meijo or Sakuradōri subway line to Hisaya-ōdōri Station

Situated amid the buzz of Sakae's north side, this modern hotel has compact, well-maintained rooms with spacious bathrooms. Staff at the front desk speak English and are happy to help. Breakfast buffet available. Nagoya TV Tower and the northern edge of Hisaya-ōdōri-kōen are a 5-minute walk away.

DORMY INN PREMIUM NAGOYA SAKAE

2-20-1 Nishiki, Naka-ku; tel. 052/231-5489; www.hotespa.net; ¥12,000 d with breakfast; take Higashiyama and Tsurumai lines to Fushimi Station

This sharp hotel is a great pick if you're planning to spend real time in the entertainment district of Sakae, which is walkable from the hotel. This branch is a cut above the norm when it comes to ambience compared to most Dormy Inn properties, and its rooms are petite but clean. It also has an appealing shared bath on-site to complement the petite yet well-appointed en-suite bathrooms.

NAGOYA JR GATE TOWER HOTEL

1-1-3 Meieki, Nakamura-ku; tel. 052/566-2111; www.associa.com/ngh; ¥18,000 d (room only), breakfast ¥2,700 per person; directly connected to JR Nagoya Station; lobby is on the 15th floor of the JR Gate Tower

Clean, bright, modern rooms with great views come stocked with all the amenities you'll likely want. There's a sumptuous breakfast spread in the hotel's stylish restaurant, serving 120 dishes, both Western and Japanese. There's also a fitness center.

¥30,000-40,000

NAGOYA MARRIOTT ASSOCIA HOTEL

JR Central Towers Office, 1-1-4 Meieki, Nakamura-ku; tel. 052/584-1111; www.marriott.com; ¥30,000 d (room only), ¥35,500 (with breakfast); in the JR Central Towers, right above JR Nagoya Takashimaya Department Store and JR Nagoya Station

Perhaps the city's most luxurious digs, this hotel stands above Nagoya Station, offering stellar vistas over the city. The decor has a European flair, rooms are airy and plush, and nine restaurants are on-site. There's a fitness center with a fabulous pool, and the service is stellar, and the concierge is ready at hand to assist with anything. If you're seeking convenience and amenities, this is arguably the best choice in town. If you're traveling off season or reserve well in advance, reasonable deals can be discovered.

INFORMATION AND SERVICES

The most convenient place to stop for English maps and pamphlets is the **Nagoya Station Tourist Information Center,** located right on the central concourse (1-1-4 Meieki, Nakamura-ku; tel. 052/541-4301; 8:30am-7pm daily). In the heart of the Sakae entertainment district, there's the **Oasis 21 i Center** (Oasis 21 B1F, 1-11-1 Higashisakura, Higashi-ku; tel. 052/963-5252; 10am-8pm daily), on the basement floor of the towering Oasis 21 complex linked to Sakae Station. About 7 minutes' walk east of Nagoya Station, the **Nagoya International Center** (1-47-1 Nagono, Nakamura-ku; tel. 052/581-0100; www.nic-nagoya.or.jp; 9am-7pm Tues.-Sun.) has a library stocked with some 30,000 volumes in various languages and is run by friendly bilingual staff, who are happy to help with local recommendations.

As for online resources, go to the **Nagoya Pocket Guide** website (www.nagoyapocket-guide.com) for food and nightlife listings, as well as transport information. **Nagoya-Info** (www.nagoya-info.jp) provides a good breakdown of things to see, do, and eat, including helpful brochures available for download. Check the local English zine **Nagmag** (https://nagmag.jp) for event listings and recommendations for food, nightlife, and more.

TRANSPORTATION

Getting There

TRAIN

Towering over the western side of downtown, the mammoth complex housing **JR Nagoya Station** contains rambling department stores and food courts. The station is served by the ***shinkansen;*** other **JR lines;** the **Kintetsu line,** which leads southwest into Mie Prefecture and the Kii Peninsula; and the **Meitetsu line,** which runs north to Inuyama. The six lines of the city's subway network also pass through the station, and a large bus terminal sits out front.

The *shinkansen* links Nagoya to Japan's main hubs, including **Tokyo** (1 hour 45 minutes; ¥11,300) **Shin-Osaka** (50 minutes; ¥6,680), **Kyoto** (35 minutes; ¥5,910), **Hiroshima** (2 hours 15 minutes; ¥14,430), and beyond. The JR Chūō line's Shinano limited express runs north to **JR Matsumoto Station** (2 hours, 10 minutes; ¥6140) and **JR Nagano Station** (3 hours 15 minutes; ¥7,460). To reach **JR Takayama Station,** take the Hida limited express on the JR Takayama line (2 hours 30 minutes; ¥6,140).

If you've got a little time before your next connection, note that **Sky Promenade** (4-7-1 Meieki; tel. 052/527-8877; www.midland-square.com; adults ¥750, children ¥500; 11am-9:30pm daily), one of Japan's highest viewing platform without a roof, covers floors 44-46 of the Midland Square complex, rising above the station.

AIR

If you're coming to Nagoya from most points on Honshu, taking a train is likely your best bet. This is especially true if you've got a JR pass. But if you're coming from abroad, it's worth checking into flights. Nagoya's main airport is **Central Japan International Airport** (tel. 056/938-1195; www.centrair.jp), which is much calmer than Tokyo's airports, and very conveniently located. Around 30 international flights from Asia, North America, and Europe, and domestic flights to about 20 locations across Japan come through this airport.

Chūbu Centrair, as it's often called, sits on an artificial island about 40 km (25 mi) south of downtown in the bay of Ise-wan. It's become something of a draw for locals with its collection of restaurants and its *onsen* **Fū-no-yu** (tel. 0569/38-7070; www.centrair.jp/interest/visit/relax/bath.html; adults ¥1,030, elementary school students ¥620, children age 6 and under ¥210; 8am-10pm daily). To reach downtown, take the speedy **Meitetsu Airport Line** to Nagoya Station (28 minutes, ¥1,230).

Getting Around

SUBWAY

Nagoya is well-connected belowground, with six subway lines (¥200-330). One-day passes for unlimited subway travel can be purchased at ticket counters or machines across the city (adults ¥740, children under 12 ¥370). The yellow color-coded **Higashiyama line** and red **Sakura-dōri lines** are particularly useful, as they thread through downtown's core areas such as Sakae and the neighborhood surrounding Ōsu Kannon.

BUS

A far-reaching bus system serves Nagoya, with the **Me-guru** (www.nagoya-info.jp/en/routebus; single rides for adults ¥210, children ¥100; one-day pass adults ¥500, children ¥250) doing a one-way circuit around the city's core sites. These buses run at roughly 30-60-minute intervals 9:30am-5pm Tuesday through Sunday.

Note that passes, sold at ticket counters and windows, allow unlimited travel for a day on both the subway system and bus network (adults ¥850, children under 12 ¥430). On weekends, public holidays, and the 8th of each month, prices drop (adults ¥600, ¥300 children under 12).

Kanazawa

Many towns in Japan are called "Little Kyoto," but Kanazawa is most deserving. Its wealth of historical sights and charm can be traced to its past status as the base of the mighty Maeda samurai clan. During the Edo period, this feudal superpower ruled over the Hokuriku region, encompassing modern-day Fukui, Ishikawa, Toyama, and Niigata prefectures. Largely thanks to the region's abundant rice production, the clan's wealth and might were second only to the shogunate-founding Tokugawa clan itself.

Around this significant seat of feudal power arose a great city of cobblestone streets, geisha districts lined with teahouses, a samurai quarter, a bustling market, a castle, and one of Japan's loveliest landscape gardens, **Kenroku-en.** Like Kyoto, Kanazawa's historic treasures are well-preserved, as it escaped bombing during World War II. Today, the city of 450,000 is the capital of Ishikawa Prefecture. In addition to its feudal-era charm, it also boasts an energetic, though manageable, fish market and an excellent contemporary art museum.

Most of the attractions in Kanazawa are located east of Kanazawa Station. The **Higashi Chaya-gai** geisha district is slightly southeast of the station, with the Omi-chō Market located almost due west from there. A short walk south, you'll find **Kanazawa-jō Kōen** and next to it, the dazzling Kenroku-en landscape garden and the **21st Century Museum of Contemporary Art.** South of the city, the Teramachi temple district is home to the quirky "Ninja Temple" **Myōryū-ji.**

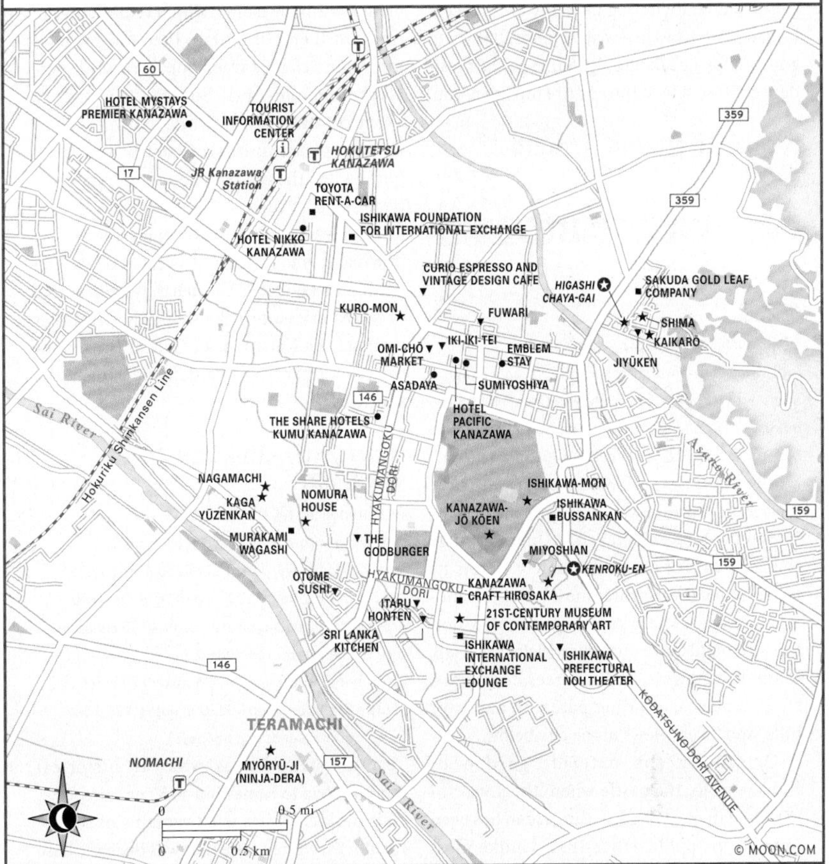

SIGHTS

★ Higashi Chaya-gai

東茶屋街

Located northeast of Omi-chō Market, across the Asano-gawa, you'll find Higashi Chaya-gai, an atmospheric district that's still the haunt of the occasional geisha. Wooden teahouse exteriors are fronted by narrow slats, and old gaslight lamps line the pedestrianized streets. A weeping cherry tree presides over a busy point where geisha once met with clients and today young couples wearing *yukata* stroll with ice cream cones. Amble the streets and follow your curiosity where it leads.

SHIMA

志摩

1-13-21 Higashiyama; tel. 076/252-5675; www.ochaya-shima.com; 9am-6pm daily; adults ¥500, children age 16 and under ¥300

If you feel the urge to see where the geisha working in the district's numerous teahouses once lived, visit the two-story former geisha residence known as Shima. This building, built in 1820 and officially designated an

Important Cultural Property by the Japanese government, is strewn with implements of the geisha trade, including an array of impeccably lacquered and bejeweled combs. It's worth going in for a peak into a genuine geisha's residence if this side of the culture intrigues you.

Kenroku-en and Around
兼六園

TOP EXPERIENCE

★ KENROKU-EN
兼六園

1-1 Marunouchi; tel. 076/234-3800; www.pref.ishikawa.jp/siro-niwa/kenrokuen/e; 7am-6pm daily Mar.-mid-Oct., 8am-5pm daily mid-Oct.-Feb.; ¥310 adults, ¥100 children; take the Kanazawa Loop Bus to bus stop LL9 or RL8 (20 minutes, ¥200 one way), or take the Kenroku-en Shuttle Bus to bus stop S8 (20 minutes, ¥200 one way; ¥100 weekends and holidays)

Welcome to Kenroku-en, a meticulously shaped patch of green that safely claims its place among Japan's three most beautiful landscape gardens. The expansive grounds are dotted with ponds, streams, an artificial waterfall, fountains, flowers, various trees, teahouses, stone lanterns, winding paths up and over hills, and lovely views of the city below.

Originally the exterior garden of Kanazawa-jō, the castle where the powerful Maeda clan once resided, the garden has been open to the public since 1871. Unlike most landscape gardens, which often feel like nature in bite-sized miniature, these extensive grounds take a bit of time to explore properly. Hidden nooks abound throughout the sprawling open terrain. The ponds, waterfalls and streams are fed by a complex system built in 1632 that deftly redirects water from a far-away river. Ancient trees, weather-beaten stones, and moss-encrusted lanterns are ubiquitous throughout the grounds.

Seasonality is another key element of Kenroku-en's beauty. Winter—not usually a time you'd associate with viewing a garden—presents a starkly beautiful scene, as a thick blanket of snow covers the long limbs of trees and stone lanterns that dot the garden. As winter comes to an end, mid-February brings plum blossoms, which remain on the trees until end of March, then the garden's numerous cherry trees pop with pink petals around mid-April. Summer is primarily a time of deep green, while autumn colors bring a pleasing mix of earthy and fiery tones when the garden's abundant maple foliage starts to turn.

No matter the season, it's enjoyable to slow down and enjoy a tea and sweet at one of the garden's teahouses. Alternatively, stop at one of the eateries along the shopping street that starts at the Katsurazaka Gate at the northeastern corner of the garden and runs to the southeast.

KANAZAWA-JŌ KŌEN
金沢城公園

1-1 Marunouchi; tel. 076/234-3800; www.pref.ishikawa.jp/siro-niwa/kanazawajou/e; castle 9am-4:30pm daily, park grounds 5am-6pm daily Mar.-mid-Oct., 6am-4:30pm daily mid-Oct.-Feb.; grounds free, buildings ¥310 adults, ¥100 children; take the Kanazawa Loop Bus to bus stop LL9 or RL8 (20 minutes, ¥200 one way), or take the Kenroku-en Shuttle Bus to bus stop S8 (20 minutes, ¥200 one way; ¥100 weekends and holidays)

To understand Kanazawa's vast historical wealth, a trip to Kanazawa-jō Kōen is in order. This park encircles what remains of the resplendent, white castle that was once the base of the mighty Maeda Clan. From 1583 until the end of the Edo period, this powerful family ruled the fiefdom of Kaga, the second largest and richest of all domains during the long period of Tokugawa rule. Ravaged by fire over the centuries, most recently in 1881, the only original structures left standing are two storehouses and the **Ishikawa-mon** gate, which faces the northern edge of Kenroku-en. The main keep was incinerated in 1602 and never reconstructed.

A drawn-out process of rebuilding the

1: Kenroku-en **2:** Kanazawa-jō Kōen **3:** winter at Kenroku-en **4:** Higashi Chaya-gai

1

2

3

4

various structures of the fortress is underway. So far a pair of reconstructed turrets connected by a narrow storehouse, which can be entered for a small fee, the **Kahoku-mon** gate and the **Hashizume-mon** gate have been completed. If approaching from Omi-chō Market, the **Kuro-mon** gate at the northwest corner of the castle grounds is the closest entrance. If you're coming from Kenroku-en, enter via the Ishikawa-mon gate. A visit just before closing, at dusk, is particularly atmospheric, as the white castle is lit from below, while a slightly unnerving number of crows swarm overhead, cawing and congregating along the roof.

21ST-CENTURY MUSEUM OF CONTEMPORARY ART, KANAZAWA
金沢21世紀美術館

1-2-1 Hirosaka; tel. 076/220-2800; www.kanazawa21.jp; 10am-6pm Tues.-Thurs. and Sun., 10am-8pm Fri.-Sat.; price varies by exhibition; take the city bus from Kanazawa Station to Hirosaka bus stop (10 minutes, ¥200) or the Kanazawa Loop Bus to bus stop RL9 or LL8 (20 minutes, ¥200)

Kanazawa's attractions aren't limited to the feudal era. At the 21st-Century Museum of Contemporary Art, Kanazawa, creativity veers in more untamed directions. Showing modern art from Japan and abroad, the massive circular building that houses the exhibitions is a work of art itself. The slightly baffling lack of a clear entrance or exit is part of the fun. Various doors exist around the round structure—take your pick. There are usually a few paid exhibitions to choose from, as well as a few free permanent installations; the most popular by far is the social media-friendly *Swimming Pool* by Argentine artist Leandro Erlich. Looking down into this "pool" from above is free. Going "underwater" to look up and see the blurry outlines of people standing above the distorted glass display overhead can be done for a fee.

Check out the exhibition schedule to see what catches your interest. The museum is easily accessible on foot from both Kenroku-en and Kanazawa-jō Kō en.

Nagamachi
長町

Ambling through the narrow cobblestone lanes of Nagamachi, bear in mind that this was once the domain of Kanazawa's burgeoning samurai class. In feudal times, the elite warriors convened behind the numerous private gates, plotting, carousing, and meditating.

NOMURA HOUSE SAMURAI RESIDENCE
武家屋敷跡 野村家

1-3-32 Nagamachi; tel. 076/221-3553; www.nomurake.com; 8:30am-5pm daily Apr.-Sept., 8:30am-4:30pm Oct.-Mar.; adults ¥550, high school students ¥400, junior high and elementary school students ¥250; from Kanazawa Station take any city bus from bus stop 7-11 to Korinbo bus stop (10 minutes, ¥200), or from Omi-chō Market walk 15 minutes southwest, or walk 20 minutes west of Kanazawa-jō Kōen

The streets themselves ooze ambience, but to get a glimpse of life behind the scenes, head to the Nomura House, once home to a prominent samurai family. This renovated home boasts a lovely garden with a pond stocked with fat, colorful koi.

KAGA YŪZENKAN
加賀友禅館

2-6-16 Nagamachi; tel. 076/264-2811; www.kagayuzen-club.co.jp; 9:30am-5pm Thurs.-Mon., closed Dec.-Feb.; ¥350; from Kanazawa Station take any city bus from bus stop 7-11 to Korinbo bus stop (10 minutes, ¥200), or from Omi-chō Market walk 15 minutes southwest, or walk 20 minutes west of Kanazawa-jō Kōen

Swing by the Kaga Yūzenkan, a kimono-dyeing workshop. Although the building is thoroughly modern, the silk-dyeing technique has a long history in Kanazawa, and some of the kimonos on display are stunning. With an advance reservation, it's possible to try your hand at the delicate art yourself for ¥4,000.

Teramachi
寺町

Teramachi (literally: Temple Town) is a neighborhood brimming with temples in the south of town, across the Sai-gawa. What little historical ambience is left in the area is a bit underwhelming, except for **Myōryū-ji** (Oddly Built Temple, aka Ninja-dera, or Ninja Temple). While the temple was never actually the haunt of cloaked assassins, some uniquely concealed defense mechanisms incorporated into the structure of the complex inspired its name.

MYŌRYŪ-JI (NINJA-DERA)
妙立寺

1-2-12 Nomachi; tel. 076/241-0888; www.myouryuji.or.jp; 9am-4pm Mon.-Fri., 9am-4:30pm Sat.-Sun. and holidays; ¥1,000 adults, ¥700 children; take the left loop of the Kanazawa Loop Bus to Hirokoji bus stop (LL5), from there, it's about 4 minutes' walk south

Like most structures of historical import in Kanazawa, Ninja-dera was built by the Maeda Clan. Although it looks like a temple, it doubled as a secret outpost where agents could hide and escape to warn Kanazawa-jō of approaching invaders. Some of the temple's ingenious devices include tunnels said to be linked to underground passages that lead all the way to Kanazawa-jō, hidden chambers, booby traps, and confusingly arrayed sets of stairs and passageways meant to throw off would-be intruders.

This clever defensive approach was developed in response to the Tokugawa Shogunate's stringent building codes, meant to prevent regional fiefdoms from gaining the military upper hand. Among the regulations was the stipulation that a temple could be no taller than three stories. Once you pass through the main chamber of Ninja-dera, however, you'll discover that the structure is in fact four stories. If you count hidden subterranean levels, this number jumps to seven. The *seppuku* room is a self-locking chamber specifically designed to give a lord a secret place to commit ritual suicide rather than face capture, before setting the entire temple ablaze with a flame kept burning in the room.

You can join a guided Japanese-language tour of the temple if you reserve via phone up to a month in advance. A helpful English-language pamphlet also does a good job of introducing the singular temple.

ENTERTAINMENT AND EVENTS
Performing Arts
ISHIKAWA PREFECTURAL NOH THEATER

4-18-3 Ishibiki; tel. 076/264-2598; www.pref.ishikawa.lg.jp/nougakudo/nougakudoutop.html; 9am-5pm Tues.-Sun., last entry 4:30pm; price varies by performance

Kanazawa is among the best places in Japan to see the beautifully arcane spectacle of *Noh* drama. This theater, constructed of cypress and topped with a roof resembling a Shinto shrine, hosts hourlong performances with breaks for *kyogen* (comedic intermissions) on Saturday evenings during summer. There are daylong performances once monthly throughout the rest of the year. Inquire with the city's tourist information center for more details. Inquire far in advance of your trip to find out your chances of catching one of the sporadic performances. Even if you're not keen to see a performance, you can pop in to admire the stage as long as there are no rehearsals taking place that day. It's a 5-minute walk from the Dewamachi bus stop.

KAIKARŌ

1-14-8 Higashiyama; tel. 076/253-0591; www.kaikaro.jp; 10am-5pm daily to tour residence; ¥750 adults, high school students and younger ¥500 to tour residence

Full geisha entertainment with a *kaiseki* (multicourse meal) in Higashi Chaya-gai. The price is on a sliding scale, depending on the number of diners, but for a group of 10, the cost is ¥28,000 per person, excluding drinks, for the company of three geisha and a full-course spread. Check the website (www.kaikaro.jp/eng/experience.html#Enyukai) and inquire by phone for details.

1

2

Festivals

KAGATOBI DEZOMESHIKI
加賀鳶出初式

Kanazawa Castle, 1-1 Marunouchi; tel. 076/234-3800; www.pref.ishikawa.jp/siro-niwa/kanazawajou/e; Jan. 6; free

With the nation's traditional architecture being built almost entirely of wood, the role of the firefighter looms large in Japan's history. In the dead of winter every year, scantily clothed firefighters perform acrobatic feats linked to ancient firefighting maneuvers, precariously perched on bamboo ladders in front of Kanazawa Castle.

HYAKUMANGOKU MATSURI
百万石祭

http://100mangoku.net; early June; free

The city's biggest festival, spanning three days in early June each year, commemorates Kanazawa's founding by Lord Maeda Toshiie on June 14, 1583. A procession of locals in 16th-century attire marches through the streets, a special tea ceremony is held in a variety of styles, *Noh* is performed in the ethereal glow of torch light, 1,500 floating lanterns drift down the lazy Asanogawa, and thousands of youngsters advance through the streets bearing red lanterns and beating *taiko* drums. The main event of the festival, the Hyakumangoku parade, takes place on the first Saturday of June, and the other events are held on the day prior and the day after.

SHOPPING

Kanazawa's range of shopping options is geared toward traditional arts and crafts. The highest density of sprawling department stores is found in the Kōrinbō and Katamachi neighborhoods, particularly along the bustling **Hyakumangoku-dōri** thoroughfare that runs north-south to the west of Kanazawa Castle Park. For a discerning selection of artfully made local items—including gold leaf, intricately painted Kutani pottery, and roughly hewn ceramics—head to the **Hirosaka** shopping street, which runs east-west between Kōrinbō and Kenroku-en, along the southern edge of Kanazawa Castle Park. If you're after something hip or offbeat, try some of the boutiques along the **Tatemachi** shopping street, a short walk southwest of the 21st Century Museum of Contemporary Art.

KANAZAWA CRAFT HIROSAKA

1-2-25 Hirosaka; tel. 076/265-3320; www.crafts-hirosaka.jp; 10am-6pm Tues.-Sun., closed Tues. if Mon. is a holiday

This elegant shop sells a plethora of refined regional arts and crafts under one roof. This is a great place to find a striking conversation piece to take home with you. It's located next to the north side of the 21st Century Museum of Contemporary Art.

ISHIKAWA BUSSANKAN

2-20 Kenrokumachi; tel. 076/222-7788; https://kanazawa-kankou.jp; 9:30am-5:50pm Mon.-Fri. and 8:50am-5:50pm Sat.-Sun. and holidays Mar.-May, 8:50am-5:50pm daily Jun.-Oct., 9:50am-5:50pm Wed.-Mon. Dec.-Feb.

This four-story shop sells reasonably priced traditional arts, crafts, and edibles in a laid-back setting. On the basement level, there are displays on *taiko* drums and sweets production. Workshops held on the third floor teach guests about crafts from making drums and confections to applying gold leaf and glass etching.

SAKUDA GOLD LEAF COMPANY

1-3-27 Higashiyama; tel. 076/251-6777; https://goldleaf-sakuda.jp; 8:30am-6pm daily

Come to this fun shop for anything gilded: chopsticks, folding fans, owl figurines, gold-flecked tea sets, etc.. And if you're a golfer, you can even get gold-leaf coated golf balls. It's a short walk north of the main entrance to the Higashi Chaya-gai teahouse district.

MURAKAMI WAGASHI

2-3-32 Nagamachi; tel. 076/264-4223; www.wagashi-murakami.com; 9:15am-5pm daily; around

1: Nagamachi **2:** Hyakumangoku Matsuri

Driving the Noto Peninsula

North of Kanazawa, the Noto Peninsula (能登半島) is an appendage of land protruding some 100 km (62 mi) into the Sea of Japan. The dramatic coastline is dotted by fishing hamlets, craggy cliffs, quiet beaches, and rustic shrines and temples. It makes for a very appealing day trip from Kanazawa for those looking to see a wilder side of Japan deeply in touch with the rhythm of the seasons.

To properly explore this rugged stretch of oceanfront, rent a car in Kanazawa—an English GPS system is a lifesaver—then head north.

Shiroyone Senmaida Rice Terraces

- Begin by driving up the Noto-Satoyama Kaidō (Expressway) along the west coast of Noto, passing along the **Chirihama Nagisa Driveway,** an 8-km (5-mi) stretch of sand about 40 km (65 mi) north of Kanazawa that's a beach-party zone in summer in addition to being a road.

- Continue north along the Noto-Satoyama Expressway until it meets route 249. **Myōjō-ji** (Yo-1 Takidanimachi, Hakui-shi; tel. 0767/27-1226; http://myojoji-noto.jp; 8am-5pm Apr.-Oct., 8am-4:30pm Nov.-Mar.; adults ¥500, junior high and elementary students ¥300), a 1.2-km (0.7-mi) detour off of 249, is an important temple of the Nichiren Buddhist sect, constructed in 1294. The temple's most prominent building is the five-story pagoda, which can be seen from a distance.

- Continue north along the stretch of coastline between Fukūrako and Sekinohana. This spectacular shoreline is known as the **Kongō Coast.** Soak up the vista of the gnarled rock formations along this jagged section of beach. For this stretch of the drive, use routes 36 and 49; it will take an extra 10 minutes, but it hugs the coast and offers a more scenic ride than 249.

- From Sekinohana, merge back onto 249 and continue north 14.3 km (8.9 mi) to **Sōji-ji Soin** (1-18 Monzen, Monzen-machi, Wajima-shi; tel. 0768/42-0005; https://noto-soin.jp; ¥400), an atmospheric Zen temple with a history stretching back to 1321. The temple accepts staying guests who are given the chance to participate in monks' regimented daily activities such as *zazen* (seated meditation; from 4am), morning prayers (from 5am) and feasting on *shōjin-ryōri* (Buddhist vegetarian cuisine). A night with two meals costs ¥6,500 per person. You can also join a guided *zazen* session (¥1,000, including temple admission) or eat a monk's meal without staying overnight (¥2,500-3,500). Inquire in advance about joining any upcoming *zazen* sessions or to book a night.

- Continue along route 249 until reaching the **Shiroyone Senmaida Rice Terraces** (99-5 Shiroyone-machi, Wajima-shi; tel. 0768/23-1146; http://senmaida.wajima-kankou.jp; 24 hours daily; free). Some 2,000 highly photogenic, terraced rice fields lead like vast steps down to the Sea of Japan. Returning from here to Kanazawa, the total drive takes about 5.5 hours. If you go all the way to the very northern tip of the peninsula, the full journey takes just shy of 7 hours.

After coming this far you may want to ease more into Noto-time at ★ **Flatt's** (27-26-3 Yanami, Noto-chō; tel. 0768/62-1900, http://flatt.jp, ¥16,500 per person for a room with two meals), a wonderful bed-and-breakfast located near route 249 on the eastern side of the peninsula, a 62.6-km (38.9-mi) drive from the Shiroyone Senmaida Rice Terraces. The B&B is run by an Australian chef and his Japanese wife. Aside from cozy rooms with oceanside views, the food is stellar: Japanese for breakfast, Italian with a twist for dinner. All meals for non-staying guests must be booked at least one day in advance. Accommodations must be booked by phone.

the corner from the Nomura House in the heart of the Nagamachi samurai district

This historic shop is the best place in town to find colorful, exquisitely packaged *wagashi* (traditional Japanese sweets), made in the shapes of flowers, fish, rabbits, and more. Made with ingredients like *mochi* (rice cake), *azuki* (red-bean paste), and sesame, the confections here are much more subtle than most Western sweets. To bring out the delicate flavors, pair one of these treats with a cup of green tea.

FOOD

Around Omi-chō Market

OMI-CHŌ MARKET

50 Kamiomichō; tel. 076/231-1462; https://ohmicho-ichiba.com; 9am-5pm daily; free; walk 15 minutes southeast of Kanazawa Station, or take the city bus to Musashigatsuji bus stop

This fish market is a hive of commerce, with all manner of seafood being haggled over and consumed on the spot. Particularly lively in the morning, Omi-chō is a great, down-to-earth alternative market to Tokyo's sometimes overwhelming Tsukiji Market or Kyoto's Nishiki Market, which is routinely crammed with tourists. It's a good place to gawk at the freshest catches and perhaps have lunch at one of the many eateries on-site if your appetite is stirred. Its central location makes it a worthwhile stop on your way to other attractions around town.

IKI-IKI-TEI

Omicho Ichiba-kan 1F, 88 Aokusa-machi; tel. 076/222-2621; 7:00am-5:00pm (until all food is sold) Fri.-Wed.; From ¥1,000; on a corner near the market entrance closest to Kanazawa Station

This little joint in Omi-chō Market is routinely elbow-to-elbow with diners eating fish sourced from stalls nearby. They serve great set meals and *donburi* (rice bowls) of both sushi and sashimi. If you're visiting the market in the morning, try to arrive as soon as the shop opens for a sushi breakfast. Otherwise, be prepared to queue or place an order and wander the market until the appointed time the shop staff recommends for you to return.

FUWARI

2-6-57 Owari-chō; tel. 076/207-3417; www.facebook.com/fuwari.ip; 5pm-11pm Tues., Thurs., and Sun., 5pm-1am Fri.-Sat.; ¥4,000 average; 3 minutes' walk northeast of Omi-chō Market

This stylish restaurant, housed in an atmospheric wooden building, is another great spot to sample local seafood, from grilled to raw. Also on the menu (English version available) are beef, tempura, yakitori, and vegetable medleys. The experience is highly visual, with dishes beautifully presented on artfully made tableware. The service is friendly and attentive, and the drinks menu is extensive. Highly recommended. Reserve a day or more in advance.

CURIO ESPRESSO AND VINTAGE DESIGN CAFÉ

1-13 Yasuecho; 076/231-5543; www.facebook.com/CurioEspresso; 8am-5pm Mon. and Wed.-Fri., 9am-5pm Sat., 9am-3pm Sun.; ¥1,000-2,000; 5 minutes' walk north of Omi-chō Market

Discerning coffee drinkers, head to this stylish café for a caffeine hit. The menu includes an extensive range of brews, from espressos to flat-whites, alongside a good range of sandwiches that make for a good light breakfast or lunch. The amiable staff is happy to make local recommendations too.

Higashi Chaya-gai

JIYŪKEN

1-6-6 Higashiyama; tel. 076/252-1996; www.jiyuken.com; lunch 11:30am-3pm Wed.-Mon., dinner 5pm-9pm Mon.-Fri. and 4:30pm-9pm Sat.-Sun. and holidays, closed 3rd Mon. of month; ¥720-1,855

Near the entrance to the Higashi Chaya-gai district, and set amid dessert shops and teahouses, this faintly nostalgic diner serves classics from Japan's *yoshoku* repertoire. This style of cooking was born when Western influence flooded into Japan during the Meiji period (1868-1912). Dishes include "hamburg" (beef patty), *omuraisu* (omelet stuffed with ketchup-infused rice), and all manner of vegetables, meat, and seafood breaded and fried, from *tonkatsu* to *korokke* (croquette). It fills up at lunch time, so you may have to wait for a bit. There's an English menu, and some of the staff speak English.

Kenroku-en and Around

ITARU HONTEN

3-8 Kakinokibatake; tel. 076/221-4194; www.itaru.ne.jp; 5:30pm-11:30pm Mon.-Sat.; plates from ¥300, courses ¥3,000-6,000; 5 minutes' walk west of the 21st Century Museum of Contemporary Art

For a boisterous *izakaya* (pub) experience, this popular local spot fits the bill. Patrons sit along an L-shaped counter facing the open kitchen where the chefs chop, mix, sear, and season a creative selection of dishes. Food is heavily weighted toward seafood, from sushi and sashimi platters to fish served in stews or basted and grilled. There are also nonseafood items on the menu, as well as an extensive *sake* list. Reserve a day or more ahead if you can.

SRI LANKA KITCHEN

3-6 Kakinokibatake; tel. 076/223-6255; https://srilankacurrykanazawa.wordpress.com; 11:30am-2:30pm and 6pm-10pm daily; lunch ¥780-1,480, dinner ¥2,000-3,000, a la carte from ¥300; 5 minutes' walk west of the 21st-Century Museum of Contemporary Art, on same street as Itaru Honten

This Sri Lankan joint is a great place for a break from Japanese cuisine. It serves excellent vegetarian and meat-based curries, and a broad menu extending to vegan fare. For a great lunch, try the set served on a banana leaf (¥1,280). In the evening, try one of the bang-up dinner courses. The menu is in Japanese, but the friendly staff speak English.

MIYOSHIAN

1-11 Kenroku-machi; tel. 076/221-0127; http://miyoshian.net; 9:30am-4:30pm Thurs.-Tues., closed irregularly; tea sets ¥700, bento set lunches ¥1,500-3,000; 4 minutes' walk south of the entrance at the north of the garden.

An atmospheric spot in Kenroku-en for a potent cup of *matcha* (green tea) and a sweet, or for a *bento* box lunch of local dishes. It sits beside a serene backdrop of a waterfall and pond. Tatami-floor seating only.

Nagamachi

★ OTOME SUSHI

4-10 Kigura-machi; tel. 076/231-7447; lunch noon-2pm daily, dinner seatings at 5pm and 7pm Mon.-Tues. and Thurs.-Sat.; lunch from ¥10,000, dinner from ¥18,000 (sushi); shop is tucked down a side street and lacks English signage, so arrival by taxi is recommended

If you're keen to splurge on sushi, you won't go wrong at this high-end specialist near the Nagamachi samurai quarter. With access to exceptional fish and a meticulous master who grew up around the docks, this sushi joint ticks all the boxes. Relax into its wooden interior—counter seats and a private room are available—and get acquainted with the region's oceanic bounty. The deep *sake* selection features labels from within the region. There's no English menu, but the staff speak limited English and do their best to guide you through the meal. The bill will reflect the quality, so budget accordingly. Reserve a few days or more in advance either by phone or via the reservation website Table All (www.tableall.com/restaurant/89).

THE GODBURGER

2-12-10 Korinbo; tel. 076/205-2925; www.facebook.com/Gbhamburgerman; noon-4pm and 6pm-10pm Thurs.-Tues.; ¥1,000-2,000

This trendy modern burger shop, run by friendly staff, sits beside a stream just east of Nagamachi's samurai residences. The menu includes a good range of toppings—chili beans, avocado, bacon, fried egg—as well as a veggie burger option. This is a good place for a delicious, casual meal on the go between Kenroku-en and Nagamachi or Kanazawa Castle, or if you just feel like a burger and fries.

ACCOMMODATIONS

Under ¥10,000

HOTEL PACIFIC KANAZAWA

46 Jikkenmachi; tel. 076/264-3201; www.hotel-pacific.jp; ¥5,000 single, ¥8,000 d; 3 minutes' walk southeast of Omi-chō Market

Set in a prime location, this clean, current hotel has a chic little caféon the first floor, amiable bilingual staff, and 31 trim, well-appointed rooms (both tatami and Western) with tiny en-suite showers. Bicycles can be rented for an additional charge.

EMBLEM STAY

1-2-8 Owari-chō; tel. 076/222-7333; http://emblem-group.com; ¥6,400 d with shared bath, ¥8,800 d with en suite bath; 5 minutes' walk east of Omi-chō Market

Friendly English-speaking staff, reasonable rates, and a stellar location make this modern, minimalist hostel and hotel a good pick for exploring the town on foot. The rooms are trim, without an inch of unused space, but are well laid-out and stocked with the essentials. There are twin rooms, doubles, rooms for up to four or six, and four-person dorms, both mixed and female-only. Some rooms share a bathroom, as well as a kitchen, lounge, and an on-site bar serving drinks and light food (3pm-midnight daily). Rooms with *en suite* baths and kitchens are also available.

HOTEL MYSTAYS PREMIER KANAZAWA

2-13-5 Hirooka; tel. 076/290-5255; www.mystays.com/en/hotel/kanazawa/mystays-premier-kanazawa; ¥8,000 d; on the western side of JR Kanazawa Station, 5 minutes' walk

This smart, modern hotel has sprawling rooms by Japanese budget-hotel standards, each with a desk, seating area, and a bit of floor space left over. Amenities include a fitness room, a nicely balanced breakfast buffet, and a café beside the entrance. The English-speaking staff are warm and happy to help. Pound for pound, this is one of the city's best values.

¥10,000-20,000

SUMIYOSHIYA

54 Jukken-machi; tel. 076/221-0157; https://sumiyoshiya-ryokan.com; ¥12,400 d without meals, ¥14,400 d with breakfast, ¥22,000 d with two meals

Pristine tatami rooms, warm English-speaking staff, and reasonable rates make this midrange *ryokan* just north of Kanazawa Castle Park and east of Omi-chō Market a great place to stay without breaking the bank. The hotel serves both Japanese and Western breakfasts, and exquisite Japanese dinner spreads. Some rooms have private baths and toilets, while others have private toilets but share a bath. There are also free bicycle rentals.

THE SHARE HOTELS KUMU KANAZAWA

2-40 Kamitsutsumi-chō; tel. 076/282-9600; www.thesharehotels.com/kumu; doubles from ¥15,400; 10 minutes' walk east of the Nagamachi samurai quarter on Route 157

This fresh, modern hotel has a café on the first floor and a chic, artsy interior. Rooms include both dorms and spacious private rooms, many with tatami platform lounge areas with floor cushions for seats. The optional breakfast buffet includes good Western-style basics (eggs, sausage, baked goods). There's a rooftop balcony with good views of the surrounding area and bicycles for rent for staying guests. This hotel has a slightly grown-up vibe, so you may want to stay somewhere else if you're traveling with kids.

Over ¥40,000

★ ASADAYA

23 Jitsuken-machi; tel. 076/231-2228; www.asadaya.co.jp; single ¥65,000 pp, doubles ¥46,000 pp; 3 minutes' walk southeast of Omi-chō Market

In business for more than 140 years, this is Kanazawa's top *ryokan*. It offers only four guest rooms, and you can rest assured that Japan's legendary spirit of *omotenashi* (service as an art form) is alive and well here. With antique screens depicting mystical landscapes, flower arrangements tucked into alcoves, and tatami floors throughout, the ambience is akin to the set of a samurai movie. Three of the rooms have en-suite baths. The other one gets first dibs on the shared family bathing facilities. The immaculate *kaiseki* meals are presented on gorgeous tableware and made with locally sourced, seasonal ingredients. If you've got the cash to splurge, this is the best place in town to do so. Book as far in advance as possible to get one of the few rooms.

INFORMATION AND SERVICES

Your first port of call for information on the city is the fantastic **Tourist Information Center** (tel. 076/232-6200; www.kanazawa-tourism.com; 8:30am-8pm daily) in Kanazawa Station. Here you'll be greeted by English-speaking staff (until 7pm daily) and can even get set up with a free bilingual guide by the **Goodwill Guide Network** (tel. 076/232-3933; www.kggn.jp). There are ample English pamphlets and maps of the city.

About six minutes on foot southeast of Kanazawa Station, on the third floor of the Rifare Building (1-5-3 Honmachi; tel. 076/262-5931; www.ifie.or.jp; 8:30am-8pm Mon.-Fri., 8:30am-5pm Sat.-Sun.) you'll find the **Ishikawa Foundation for International Exchange.** This is a meeting point for locals who want to practice English with travelers who are keen for local insights. There's also plenty of English printed matter on the city and region. Close to Kenroku-en, the foundation also heads up the **Ishikawa International Exchange Lounge** (1-8-10 Hirosaka; tel. 076/221-9901; 10am-5pm Mon.-Fri., 10am-4pm Sat.), which hosts a variety of language classes and talks on different aspects of Japanese culture.

For an up-to-date rundown on things to see and do, and places to eat and drink, be sure to pick up a copy of the English tourist zine ***Eye on Kanazawa*** (http://eyeon.jp). The free paper, accompanied by a good website, is carried at the Tourist Information Center in Kanazawa Station and other pick-up points around town.

TRANSPORTATION

Getting There

TRAIN

In 2015, the grand, expansive new **Kanazawa Station** opened on the western side of town to serve the then newly launched Hokuriku *shinkansen* line. This train line has shortened the trip from **Tokyo** by a full hour (2.5 hours; ¥14,320), making Kanazawa easier to reach than ever before.

Coming from **Nagoya,** Shirasagi limited express trains zip to Kanazawa (3 hours; ¥7,530), while Thunderbird limited express trains run between Kanazawa and **Shin-Osaka Station** (2 hours 40 minutes; ¥7,850), passing **Kyoto** en route (2 hours 15 minutes; ¥7,100).

AIR

Komatsu Airport (tel. 076/121-9803; www.komatsuairport.jp), located about 30 km (18.6 mi) southwest of Kanazawa, services flights from around Japan and a few other Asian hubs, including **Seoul** and **Shanghai.** Hourly buses run between the airport and **Kanazawa Station** (www.hokutetsu.co.jp; 50 minutes; ¥1,130), stopping in the Katamachi area in the heart of Kanazawa on the way.

BUS

JR Highway Bus (www.kousokubus.net/JpnBus/en) operates routes between Kanazawa and **Tokyo, Osaka** and **Kyoto,** among other cities. It's possible to travel to and from Nagoya by highway bus through **Hokutetsu Kankō** (tel. 076/237-5115; www.hokutetsu.co.jp). The same operator, along with **Nōhi Bus** (www.nouhibus.co.jp) also services **Takayama,** via Gokayama and Shirakawa-gō. See the relevant websites for detailed routes, timetables and fares.

Getting Around

There's a city-run bicycle rental system known as **Machi-nori** (www.machi-nori.jp), but the system is unfortunately a bit of a headache and the bicycles are best suited to those with, shall we say, diminutive frames. However, Kanazawa is so compact, it's really a **walking** city. Most of the sights are concentrated around the central districts of Katamachi and Kōrinbō—both within about 15 minutes' walk of Kanazawa Station—or a bit farther north in the Higashi Chaya-gai tea district.

BUS

Buses leave from the **terminal** next to the station's east exit. Any bus leaving from bus stop nos. 7, 8, or 9 will get you downtown (¥200), and from there it's easy to get around on foot. The **Kanazawa Loop Bus** (www.hokutetsu.co.jp/en/en_round; 8:30am-6pm daily; adults ¥500, children ¥250) does a circuit around the city, starting from **Kanazawa Station.** One route moves clockwise, the other counterclockwise. It passes through the Nagamachi samurai district in the west, veers south to the Ninja Temple, and makes various stops in the area surrounding Kenroku-en in the heart of town and the teahouse district of Higashi Chaya-gai in the north.

CAR

There are numerous car rental agencies in the area surrounding Kanazawa Station. A good bet is **Toyota Rent-A-Car** (2-15-1 Honmachi; tel. 076/223-0100; https://rent.toyota.co.jp), located about 4 minutes' walk southeast of Kanazawa Station, next to **Hotel Nikko Kanazawa.** If you plan to venture into the countryside around Kanazawa—to the Noto Peninsula, for example—a car will be necessary.

Takayama

Takayama is an amiable mountain town that wears its history well. The streets of its charming old section—which runs along the murmuring Miyagawa river, crisscrossed by a series of traditional red bridges—are home to museums, crafts shops, eateries, and family-run inns. Shrines and temples, connected by a range of footpaths, make for an inviting stroll in the hills just beyond downtown. For such a small city, there's a surprisingly decent nightlife zone too.

Often called by its fuller name of Hida-Takayama (Hida being the name of the mountain range that runs through this region) Takayama's biggest claim to fame is the visually impressive **Takayama Matsuri,** a festival held in spring and autumn every year. Towering floats are paraded on wheels through the old part of town to the accompaniment of traditional music.

The city rose to prominence in the 17th century when it became known as a reliable source of high-grade timber—no small thing in a country where traditional architecture was entirely based on wood. This fostered a local culture replete with brilliant carpenters, who in turn brought great riches to the city, which was brought under the control of the shogunate in what was then Edo (modern-day Tokyo).

Today, the town's history and local character are well-preserved, and Takayama can be enjoyably explored on foot. However, the word is unfortunately out and tourists do flock to the town. But the magic remains. Either as an entry point into the Japan Alps or as a standalone destination, if you're going to make it to just one town in Central Honshu's vast mountainous interior, make it Takayama.

SIGHTS

★ SANMACHI SUJI
三町筋

10 minutes' walk east of JR Takayama Station on eastern bank of Miyagawa

Takayama's merchant class has long made a mint. Nowhere is this more evident than in the old quarter of Sanmachi Suji. This old business district is concentrated around three streets, namely, Sannomachi, Ninomachi and

Takayama

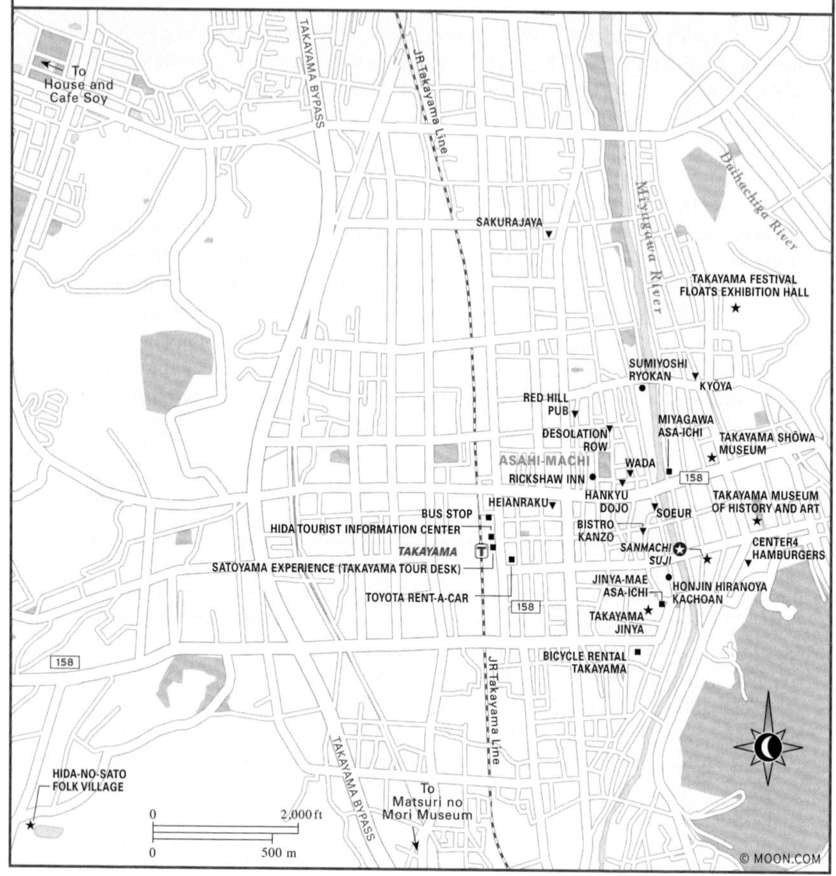

Ichinomachi. These three streets run east to west along the north side of the Miyagawa, a river coursing through the center of town that is crisscrossed by picturesque red bridges. The district has admittedly succumbed to full-blown, touristic euphoria and gets very crowded, but its charm remains intact.

To take in the ambience of this lovely old town, take a leisurely stroll along these streets and take in the lovely wooden gates and windows fronted by the narrow wooden slats characteristic of traditional Japanese architecture. Within this pedestrian dream you'll find a host of sake breweries, cafés, shops selling traditional wooden crafts, and lovely old homes. Note that most of the neighborhood businesses are open from 9am to 5pm on most days.

TAKAYAMA SHŌWA MUSEUM
高山昭和館

6 Shimōichino-machi; tel. 0577/33-7836; www.takayama-showakan.com; 9am-6pm daily; adults ¥800, children ¥500

One of the more colorful stops in the Sanmachi Suji area, the Takayama Shōwa Museum reveals a joyous glimpse of what life was like in Japan during the Shōwa Period

(1926-1989), with special attention given to the postwar years of the 1950s and 1960s. Western visitors may be surprised to see just how much some of the starlets, superheroes, fashion trends and household items in Japan bear resemblance to the era of the space race and Lucille Ball. The postwar zeitgeist was global.

Plastic figurines and metal toys, outsized radios, bicycles with long, curved (now-vintage) handlebars, posters of singers with perfectly quaffed hair who laid the foundation of what would become the mammoth J-Pop music biz: Curios hang from the ceiling, crowding shelves of faux barber and electronics shops alongside juke boxes, early television sets, and more. This museum gives you a fun glimpse into Japan's buoyant rise from the ashes of World War II when the nation had just begun to rebuild its sense of nationhood and there was widespread hope for a brighter future.

TAKAYAMA JINYA
高山陣屋

1-5 Hachiken-machi; tel. 0577/32-0643; www.pref.gifu.lg.jp/foreign-languages/English/tourism/takayama; 8:45am-5pm Mar.-Jul. and Sept.-Oct., 8:45am-6pm Aug.; 8:45am-4:30pm Nov.-Feb.; ¥430 adults, under 18 free

About five minutes' walk southwest of the Sanmachi Suji area, just across the Miyagawa river, this rambling one-story building is the last-standing prefectural office left over from the Edo period. Constructed in 1816, the building was used by the local government as recently as 1969. The well-preserved building is essentially empty but offers views onto a spacious garden. The kitchen and granary offer interesting perspectives on old food preparation and storage methods. On a darker note, exhibits in the interrogation room reveal the ways torture was used in feudal days to extract information from those unlucky enough to have been brought in for questioning. There's English-language signage throughout.

FESTIVALS

TAKAYAMA MATSURI
高山祭り

Takayama's old town, centered on Sanmachi Suji area; www.hida.jp/english/festivalsandevents/4000105.html; Apr. 14-15, Oct. 9-10; free

Considered one of Japan's three most visually stunning festivals, alongside Kyoto's Gion Matsuri and the Chichibu Yomatsuri, the Takayama Matsuri is a wonderful display of the town's brilliant knack for craftsmanship. Twice yearly, in spring and autumn, throngs gather in the heart of the old town to witness a dozen towering floats strutted through the streets. The spring half of the event, known as the Sannō Matsuri, is held in the southern section of the old town where the linked Hie (aka: Sannō) Shrine is located. The autumn edition, known as the Hachiman Matsuri, fills the streets a bit to the north, closer to the associated Hachiman Shrine.

The parades take place during the mornings and afternoons of all festival days. If the weather takes a sour turn, the floats are kept dry within their respective storehouses around town, where they can still be viewed. The biggest thrill comes in the evenings when the colorfully decked-out floats roll through town ridden by mechanical dolls. Floats are convoyed by locals dressed in traditional attire, who strum, sing, and hammer out heartfelt songs from the past. The festival is immensely popular, so it's wise to reserve accommodations three months or more in advance.

If you're not fortunate enough to be here during festival time, the **Takayama Festival Floats Exhibition Hall** (178 Sakura-machi; tel. 0577/32-5100; www.hidahachimangu.jp; 8:30am-5pm Mar.-Nov., 9am-4:30pm Dec.-Feb.; ¥820) displays a few of the floats, while the **Matsuri no Mori Museum** (1111 Chishima-machi; tel. 0577/37-1000; www.togeihida.co.jp; 9am-5pm daily; ¥1,000) offers an more in-depth look, though it's a detour from downtown.

三川屋本店

SPORTS AND RECREATION

SATOYAMA EXPERIENCE

Takayama tour desk (i-café Takayama, 1-22-2 Showamachi, Takayama), Hida-Furukawa branch (8-11 Ninomachi, Furukawachō); Takayama tour desk (tel. 0577/62-8180), Hida-Furukawa branch (tel. 0577/73-5715); https://satoyama-experience.com

For an authentic glimpse into the soul of the Hida region, you won't be disappointed by the well-regarded cultural and outdoor experiences provided by this excellent tour outfit staffed by friendly, English-speaking guides. Explore the surrounding countryside, from its towns to its natural beauty, by bicycle or on foot. You can even don snowshoes during winter, or join a cooking class or culinary tour. For details, check the website or stop at one of their inviting tour desks, located around the Takayama region.

SHOPPING

The area just west of the **Takayama Museum of History and Art,** starting from Sanmachi-dōri in the south up to Yasugawa-dōri two blocks to the north, has a glut of antique shops. This is a good place to search for a piece of lacquerware or something artfully made of wood. There are more great shops selling crafts old and new throughout the town.

Morning Markets

Two open-air morning markets are held in Takayama, each offering its own range of goods and flavor. These markets are a good place to mingle with local vendors, and to pick up a few locally made snacks, and perhaps a small token, such as one of the ubiquitous *saru-bobo* (baby monkey) folk-dolls.

JINYA-MAE ASA-ICHI
陣屋前朝市

1-5 Hachiken-machi; tel. 0577/32-3333; www.jinya-asaichi.jp; 6am-noon daily; 10 minutes' walk southeast of JR Takayama Station

At the Jinya-mae Asa-ichi, local produce is sold in front of the Takayama Jinya complex.

MIYAGAWA ASA-ICHI
宮川朝市

Shimosannomachi; tel. 0577/35-3145; www.asaichi.net; 7am-noon daily; 10 minutes' walk northeast of JR Takayama Station

The other, Miyagawa Asa-ichi, is largely focused on arts and crafts. This one is set up along the east bank of the Miyagawa, occupying the stretch between the bridges of Kaji-bashi in the south to Yayoi-bashi in the north.

FOOD

In Takayama you'll find a refreshingly vibrant restaurant scene, offering everything from countryside cooking to inventive fusion fare. Local favorites include Hida-gyū (local beef), barbecued, flipped as hamburgers, served on skewers, and packed into various steamed and fried casings. Another common element of local cooking is *sansai* (vegetables foraged in the nearby mountains). One of the more creative ways these local ingredients are prepared is summed up in *hoba-miso*, a dish in which vegetables, and sometimes beef, are mixed with a healthy portion of miso paste, then placed on a magnolia leaf and cooked over a charcoal brazier. *Mitarashi-dango,* or balls made of rice cake dipped in soy, put on skewers and slowly toasted, is sold at shops around town. Elsewhere, a number of European-influenced restaurants run by local chefs blur Japanese and Western cooking.

HEIANRAKU

6-7-2 Tenman-machi; tel. 0577/32-3078; www.facebook.com/heianraku.takayama; 11:30am-1pm and 5:30pm-8pm Wed.-Mon.; ¥740-1,500; 7 minutes' walk northeast of JR Takayama Station

This inviting, home-cooked restaurant offers a mix of Chinese, Japanese—including delicious *gyoza* (fried pork dumplings)—and vegetarian fare made with liberal helpings of locally foraged mountain vegetables. There's enough space for about a dozen at a time, with

1: traditional architecture in Sanmachi Suji
2: decorative festival float **3:** crowd at Takayama Matsuri

seating on tatami mats and at the counter. The staff give a warm welcome, and an English menu makes ordering a cinch. A great spot for either lunch or dinner.

CENTER4 HAMBURGERS

94 Kamiichino-machi; tel. 0577/36-4527; http://tiger-center4.com; 11am-2:30pm and 6pm-9:30pm Thurs.-Tues.; ¥760-1,340

This fantastic hamburger joint is overflowing with nostalgic bric-a-brac and loads of charm. The local couple who run it serve excellent burgers made from Hida-gyū, as the prized local beef is known, with a generous range toppings. There's even liver pâté. The menu also includes sandwiches (BLT, club, vegetarian), salads, clam chowder, and delicious milk shakes. Recommended.

★ KYŌYA

1-77 Oshin-machi; tel. 0577/34-7660; www.kyoya-hida.jp; 11am-9:30pm Wed.-Mon.; dishes from ¥450, set meals ¥1,200, full-courses from ¥3,500; about 15 minutes' walk northeast of JR Takayama Station

This cozy restaurant's all-wood interior, vaulted ceiling, and mix of rustic tables and tatami seating conjure a farmhouse vibe. The focus here is on local favorites like tender Hida-gyū beef and vegetables barbecued at the table, and *hoba-miso* (vegetables such as leeks and shiitake mushrooms mixed with miso paste and grilled on a magnolia leaf). This restaurant provides charming ambience, wonderful service, and fabulous food at a reasonable price. It sits next to a river on the north side of town. Look for the white building with a traditional roofline beside a bridge. Barrels of sake and bags of rice are perched above the entrance.

BISTRO KANZO

46 Uramachi; tel. 0577/34-2363; www.bistro-kanzo.com; 11:30am-2pm and 5pm-9pm Thurs.-Tues.; lunch ¥1,500-6,000, dinner ¥3,900-8,800

This chic bistro in the heart of downtown puts a French spin on local ingredients. Tender slabs of Hida-gyū feature prominently, alongside a range of seafood and beautiful desserts. The chef at the helm has a knack for presentation, routinely serving food that looks as artistic as it is delicious. The staff are friendly and helpful, and the prices are surprisingly reasonable in light of the caliber of the top-notch fare. English menu available. Reserve a few days or more in advance.

★ SAKURAJAYA

3-8-14 Sowamachi; tel. 0577/57-7565; 11:30am-2pm and 6pm-10pm Thurs.-Tues.; average dinner ¥4,000-5,000; about 20 minutes' walk north of JR Takayama Station on the west side of the Miyagawa

Serving up an intriguing fusion of German and Japanese food, this restaurant sits in a quiet residential area in the north of town. The menu reflects the chef and owner's long sojourn in Europe, combined with his love of using locally sourced ingredients. The menu includes fried chicken salad, duck sashimi, fried tofu, corn and mushroom tempura, roast Hida-gyū, baguette, and fried waffle-cut potatoes. Simply put, it's one of the most unique places to dine in town. Reserve a few days ahead and request a seat at the bar to watch the master at work. English menu available.

WADA

23 Asahi-machi; tel. 0577/33-4850; 5pm-1am Mon.-Thurs. and Sun., 5pm-2am Fri.-Sat.; dishes ¥370-600, ¥3,000 average per person; 10 minutes on foot, northeast of JR Takayama Station on the west side of the Miyagawa

Come to this atmospheric local haunt if you'd like to veer off the tourist trail. You'll find dark wood beams, diners washing skewers of fried goodness down with beer, and friendly chefs shouting back and forth behind the counter. The menu is delicious and varied: grilled meat on sticks, sashimi, tempura, tofu dishes, grilled eggplant basted in miso paste, and much more. There's an extensive drinks menu too. Although it's largely off the radar for foreign visitors, some staff speak English and there's an English menu too. Highly recommended.

SOEUR

2-35 Honmachi; tel. 0577/35-2001; https://soeur.hida-ch.com; 10:30am-6:30pm Wed.-Mon.; from ¥450; 10 minutes' walk east of JR Takayama Station, just west of the Miyagawa as you head toward the Sanmachi Suji area

This bright riverside café serves tasty baked goods, sandwiches, coffee and a range of teas. Its back wall is a floor-to-ceiling window overlooking the Miyagawa, with the old town across the river. It's got a relaxing jazz soundtrack and free Wi-Fi too. A good spot for a pit stop or light lunch.

BARS AND NIGHTLIFE

For a small town, Takayama has a surprising number of lively little watering holes. Most of the after-hours action takes place in the **Asahi-machi** neighborhood, about 10 minutes' walk northeast of JR Takayama Station and west of the Miyagawa.

RED HILL PUB

2-4 Sowachō; tel. 0577/33-8139; https://redhilltakayama.wordpress.com; 7pm-midnight daily; just over 10 minutes' walk northeast of Takayama Station, on the west side of the Miyagawa

This chilled-out, low-lit, slightly bohemian bar brims with funky decor. Run by a cheerful, English-speaking host with great taste in music, the space is a magnet for friendly locals and travelers alike. Alongside bar standards, including good cocktails, there's an eclectic range of tasty nibbles.

DESOLATION ROW

30 Asahi-machi; 090/8077-5699; 8pm-2pm daily; 2 minutes' walk east of Red Hill Pub

This bar is another great hideout. Upon entering, it's immediately clear where the owner's musical tastes lie. Rows of CDs and vinyl line the wall behind the bar, alongside a portrait of Bob Dylan, Beatles album jackets, and other classic-rock paraphernalia. The bar is well-stocked, including a good range of whiskies.

HANKYU DOJO

11 Asahi-machi; tel. 090/1234-5959; www.hankyudojo.com; 7pm-10pm daily

There's nothing quite like firing some arrows when you're fresh off a pub crawl. This little archery range routinely has tipsy Robin Hood wannabes lining up for a chance to try for a bullseye. The jovial staff gives a crash course to the novice archers. Safety first. A quiver of 10 arrows will set you back ¥300.

ACCOMMODATIONS

Under ¥10,000

SUMIYOSHI RYOKAN

4-21 Hommachi; tel. 050/3160-9558; http://sumiyoshi-ryokan.com; ¥6,000 d with shared bath (¥10,000 with two meals), ¥9,000 d with private bath (¥13,000 with two meals); about 15 minutes' walk northeast of JR Takayama Station

Packed with curios, this riverside *ryokan* oozes Meiji-era charm and boasts a prime location on the west bank of the Miyagawa, a stone's throw from the old town. All rooms have tatami floors and a liberal dose of antique charm. The kind owners are eager to please and serve excellent meals for an additional charge. One room has an en-suite bathroom, while the others share an appealing bath. Recommended.

RICKSHAW INN

54 Suehiro-machi; tel. 0577/32-2890; www.rickshawinn.com; ¥4,200 single with shared bathroom, ¥8,000 twin with shared bathroom, ¥11,900 twin with private bathroom, breakfast ¥500; 10 minutes' walk northeast of Takayama Station at the southern end of the entertainment district

This popular inn offers a range of room styles, from Western with en-suite bathrooms to tatami suites with shared or private baths. The helpful owners speak English and are happy to share their local expertise. There's an appealing shared lounge and kitchen, as well as laundry facilities. One of the larger rooms has a private kitchenette, while another sleeping up to six has a private lounge.

Folk Villages of Central Honshu

Not far from Takayama, you can visit villages filled with homes built in the *gassho-zukuri* style, which roughly translates to "built like hands joined in prayer." The Shirakawa-gō region and Gokoyama both boast UNESO World Heritage for their communities of traditional houses, some of which are more than 250 years old.

One of the most memorable overnight stays on offer in Japan can be had at one of the *gasshō-zukuri* farmhouses found throughout these picturesque villages. These rooms fill up fast, so it's best to be flexible and book as far in advance as you can. Check out the **Japan Guest Houses** website (www.japaneseguesthouses.com) and the website of the **Shirakawa-gō Tourist Association** (https://Shirakawa-gō.gr.jp/en/staytypes/gassho), which offer reservation services.

If you don't have time to spare an overnight stay, the **Hida-no-Sato Folk Village** (1-590 Kamiokamoto-machi, Takayama; 0577/34-4711; www.hidanosato-tpo.jp; 8:30am-5pm daily; ¥700) is only a slight detour from downtown Takayama. About 30 minutes' walk west of Takayama Station, this open-air grouping of some 30 buildings—from houses to storehouses and logging huts—dates to the Edo period but were moved from the nearby Shirakawa-gō region to their current location in 1971.

SHIRAKAWA-GŌ 白川郷

In **Ogimachi**, a community of about 600 residents, you'll find 114 thatched-roof farmhouses, many of them open to the public. If you want to stay here, good picks include the nicely decorated **Furusato** (588 Ogimachi; tel. 057/696-1033; ¥17,600 pp with two meals), run by an English-speaking owner; the expansive, riverside **Magōemon** (360 Ogimachi; tel. 057/696-1167; ¥13,000 pp with two meals); and **Kōemon** (456 Ogimachi; tel. 057/696-1446; ¥10,000 pp with meals), an old-school gem run by a helpful owner who speaks English. If you work up an appetite, **Irori** (374-1 Ogimachi; 057696-1737; 11am-3pm daily; ¥1,300) serves local specialties like fried tofu, as well as soba and udon set meals.

¥10,000-20,000

HOUSE AND CAFÉ SOY

365 Kamigiri-machi; tel. 0577/62-9005; www.hidatakayama-soy.com; ¥17,140 d; about 15 minutes' drive north of JR Takayama Station

This beautiful, family-run inn is set in a century-old country home. Fully up-to-date creature comforts have been added while maintaining the original aesthetic, wood beams and all. There are three spacious rooms: two with tatami floors, futons, and detached, private toilet and shower; the other with a wooden floor, beds, a private workspace, and a private bathroom. The first floor has an inviting lounge with large windows, plenty of cushy chairs and a fireplace. There's also an on-site café, serving drinks (from ¥550) and lunches (from ¥1,000). A great breakfast is included (either Western or Japanese). The warm hosts speak English and bend over backwards to make your stay as comfortable as possible. Car pickup from JR Takayama Station available on advance request. There's also a bus stop nearby. Recommended.

¥30,000-40,000

HONJIN HIRANOYA KACHOAN

1-34 Hon-machi; tel. 0577/34-1234; www.honjinhiranoyakachoan.jp; from ¥18,360 pp with two meals

This elegant, high-end *ryokan* is an excellent choice for a serious splurge. There are phenomenal meals, 28 immaculate traditional rooms with plush private bathrooms as well as shared gender-separated *onsen* baths, wonderfully attentive English-speaking staff who glide through the corridors in kimonos, and car pickup from the station, which is only about 10 minutes away on foot. Just slip into one of the 800 *yukatas* on offer and luxuriate for a night or two. Nearby, the same

The best way to reach Ogimachi is by driving yourself. Take the Tokai-Hokuriku expressway from Takayama until you reach Ogimachi. roughly 45 minutes one way. Alternatively, **Nōhi Bus** (tel. 0577/32-1688; www.nouhibus.co.jp) offers daily trips between Takayama and Ogimachi (¥2,470 one way, ¥4,420 round-trip), and Kanazawa and Ogimachi (1.5 hours; ¥1,850 one way, ¥3,290 round-trip).

GOKAYAMA 五箇山

Though Gokoyama is harder to reach, the isolated villages here, especially **Suganuma** (**菅沼**) and **Ainokura** (**相倉**) are incredibly atmospheric. The nine farmhouses of Suganuma rise from the verdant landscape like a mirage from a few centuries back. Twenty *gasshō-zukuri* farmhouses make up Ainokura, some of them converted into museums and inns.

To sleep in Ainokura, try **Goyomon** (438 Ainokura; tel. 0763/66-2154; www.goyomon.burari.biz; ¥5,000 pp for room only, ¥8,800 pp with two meals), a friendly family-run place; **Yomoshirō** (395 Ainokura; tel. 0763/66-2377; ¥9,600 pp with two meals), a four-room affair run by a friendly owner with a penchant for playing a percussion instrument called the *sasara,* commonly used in folk music; and **Nakaya** (231 Ainokura; tel. 0763/66-2555; www1.tst.ne.jp/snakaya/index.html; ¥9,800 pp with two meals), where guests dine around a cozy *irori* (sunken, open fireplace).

To reach the Gokayama area from Takayama, take the Tokai-Hokuriku expressway to the Gokayama exit, from which Suganuma can be reached in just a few minutes; Ainokura is an additional 15-minute drive. Alternatively, if you're first stopping at Ogimachi, take the more scenic route, 156 north to Gokayama. This road will first bring you to Suganuma, roughly 15 km (9 mi) north of Ogimachi, followed by Ainokura, another 9 km (6 mi) north of Suganuma. It's also possible to reach Ainokura by **bus** from Ogimachi four times daily (45 minutes; ¥1,300).

ryokan also runs the less pricy, though also striking, **Bekkan Annexe** (www.honjinhiranoya.co.jp). Check the website for details.

INFORMATION AND SERVICES

Upon exiting Takayama Station, the **Hida tourist information center** (5-51 Hanasatomachi; tel. 0577/32-5328; www.hida.jp; 8:30am-7pm Apr.-Nov., 8:30am-5:30pm Dec.-Mar.) will be sitting right in front of you. Here, you'll find local maps and generous English-language information on lodgings, transport, food, and more. English-speaking staff with deep local expertise are ready to help. For information about the greater Hida region online, go to www.hida-kankou.jp.

TRANSPORTATION

Getting There

TRAIN

Sitting at the west side of town, **Takayama Station** is served by the JR Takayama line, which runs south to **Nagoya** (2 hours 45 minutes; ¥6,230) and north to **Toyama** (1 hour 30 minutes; ¥3,560). Depending on where you're coming from, you can approach from either direction, with Nagoya linked to **Kyoto** and **Osaka** to the west and **Tokyo** to the east, and Toyama being directly linked by the (almost) brand-spanking-new Hokuriku *shinkansen* line to Tokyo in the east.

BUS

Nōhi Bus (www.nouhibus.co.jp; tel. 0577/32-1688) operates from a highway **bus terminal** next to Takayama Station. Buses run to and from Shinjuku Station in **Tokyo** (5 hours 30 minutes; ¥6,690), **Matsumoto** (2 hours 30

1
2
3
奉納
保存地区です。
を禁止します。
国指定史
重要伝統
千社札等

minutes; ¥3,190), **Kanazawa** (two hours 15 minutes; ¥3,600), **Nagoya** (2 hours 30 minutes; ¥2,980), **Kyoto** (4 hours 15 minutes; ¥4,200), and **Osaka** (5 hours 30 minutes; ¥4,700), among others.

Getting Around

Takayama is highly **walkable,** with the downtown area surrounding Sanmachi Suji about 10 minutes east of JR Takayama Station on foot.

BICYCLE

If you'd prefer to pedal your way around town, **Bicycle Rental Takayama** (1-77 Hachiken-machi; tel. 080/4771-7562; http://craftharvest.html.xdomain.jp; 8am-6pm daily; ¥500 half-day, ¥800 full day) offers well-maintained bikes and is run by friendly staff who are happy to answer questions. It's located about 10 minutes southeast of Takayama Station, or 3 minutes on foot south of Takayama Jinya at the south edge of the old part of town.

CAR

If you plan to venture farther into the countryside and don't want to bother with buses, there's a **Toyota Rent-A-Car** across the street from Takayama Station (5-20 Hanasato-machi; tel. 0577/36-6110; www.trl-gifu.co.jp; 8am-8pm daily).

Matsumoto 松本

The attractive town of Matsumoto is most famous for its iconic black castle. But wander away from the moat into downtown and you'll soon sense an air of sophistication. **Nawate-dōri** and **Nakamachi** are pleasant streets for a stroll, with classic shopfronts that have been reborn in the modern age as trendy cafés, eateries, galleries, and shops selling various crafts. There are also a few worthwhile art museums.

But the city's real draw is its access to the mountains. The old castle town is set in a valley surrounded by some of the highest peaks in the Japan Alps, a few of which are more than 3,000 meters (9,842 feet) high. Stepping off the train at Matsumoto Station, the air feels different—fresh, vital—and the mountains beckon. The city makes for a great jumping-off point for a jaunt into the Northern Alps, with easy access to Kamikōchi; Shin-Hotaka-no-Yu, which is easily reached en route to Takayama; and farther north, the Tateyama-Kurobe Alpine Route.

1: Shirakawa-gō **2:** a small local shrine in Ainokura **3:** Gokayama

SIGHTS

★ Matsumoto-jō
松本城

4-1 Marunōchi; tel. 0263/32-9202; www.matsumoto-castle.jp; 8:30am-5pm daily, until 6pm during Ō-bon and Golden Week holidays, last admission 30 minutes before closing; adults ¥610, children ¥420; walk 15 minutes northeast of Matsumoto Station, or take northern course of "Town Sneaker" bus to Matsumoto-jō bus stop from Matsumoto Station

Matsumoto-jō is among Japan's most stunning castles. Japan's oldest wooden castle has been given the status of National Treasure. Set on an expansive plain in the heart of Matsumoto, the imposing black fortress—its color inspiring the nickname Karasujō, or "Crow Castle"—exudes stateliness. The main keep is accompanied by three turrets, along with a freshly renovated pavilion. Built in stages, the complex as it stands today was largely completed by 1635.

Defensive flourishes include small windows for the arrows of archers to fly through and openings in the floor through which stones could be dropped on invaders. The original wooden exterior of the castle extends throughout six floors, with stunning panoramas of Matsumoto and the surrounding mountains to be had from the top level of the keep. If you happen to be in the city in mid-April, a profusion of cherry trees around the castle bloom, their pink petals contrasting brilliantly with the black paneling of the castle's exterior.

Free guided English-language tours of the castle are provided by the **Alps Language Service Association** (www.npo-alsa.com/home-en). Reserve on the website at least two weeks in advance.

Matsumoto City Museum of Art
松本市美術館

4-2-22 Chūō; tel. 0263/39-7400; www.matsumoto-artmuse.jp; 9am-5pm Tues.-Sun., closed Tues. if Mon. is holiday; adults ¥410, university and high school students ¥200; 15 minutes' walk east of Matsumoto Station

Less than 10 minutes' walk southeast of the Nakamachi shopping district, you'll find the Matsumoto City Museum of Art. This stylish exhibition space doesn't hide the fact that Matsumoto is the hometown of internationally renowned avant-garde artist Yayoi Kusama, famed for her infinity-inspired mirror installations and iconic polka-dotted dreamscapes. One section of the museum is dedicated specifically to her work, but Kusama's work is not the only thing on show. Other sections of the museum host revolving exhibitions, with an inclination toward domestic artists either with ties to or inspiration from Matsumoto and around.

FESTIVALS

MATSUMOTO-JŌ TAIKO MATSURI
松本城太鼓祭り

Matsumoto-jō grounds; last weekend of July; free

During the last weekend of July every year, some of Japan's best *taiko,* or traditional drum, troupes converge on Matsumoto to beat hearty rhythms with hefty batons. Their high-energy performances against the stunning backdrop of one of Japan's most pristine original castles make for an impressive introduction to Japan's rich tradition of percussion.

MATSUMOTO BONBON
松本ぼんぼん

Downtown Matsumoto; first Sat. in Aug.; free

At the annual Bonbon festival, some 25,000 residents suit up in traditional outfits and gleefully boogie through the streets of downtown Matsumoto. Feel free to start the day as

Matsumoto-jō

a spectator, but be prepared to cut loose and join the dance as the evening wears on. The action begins around 5pm.

TAKIGI NOH MATSURI
薪能祭り

Matsumoto-jō grounds; tel. 0263/32-2902; 5pm-8pm Aug. 8; free

Although usually performed on a spartan, indoor stage made of cypress, a special *Noh* performance is held once every August in Matsumoto-jō's inner garden. Starting before dusk, the first part of the performance is visible by daylight. After sunset, the stage is illuminated by the soft glow of lanterns, adding to the magic. The content of the dialog—sung and spoken in rarefied, archaic language—will be lost on both foreign and (most) Japanese audience members. But the air is alive with myth. Further, the slapstick interludes known as *kyogen* ("crazy talk") that break up the sections of heady *Noh* provide the same sort of relief offered to today's audiences as they did in feudal days.

FOOD

★ KOBAYASHI SOBA

3-3-20 Ōte; tel. 0263/32-1298; www.kobayashi-soba.co.jp; 11am-8pm daily; soba ¥1,000-2,500, set meals ¥2,200-7,700; just off the Nawate-dōri shopping street

This fantastic soba restaurant boasts toppings like burdock root, mountain vegetables, herring, and even *basashi* (horse sashimi). The *kamo* (duck with warm dipping sauce) option is recommended. After placing your order, you'll receive an elegant piece of tableware with spring onion, a fresh stick of wasabi, and daikon. Use the grater to shred the wasabi and daikon and wait for your noodles to arrive. After eating, try a cup of *soba yu*, which is nutrient-dense water in which soba noodles have been boiled. You'll find the restaurant in a classy traditional building with modern accents beside Yohashira Shrine. Recommended.

ITOYA

2-10-16 Chūō; tel. 0263/32-3826; http://nakamachi-street.com/shop/itouya; 5:30pm-11pm Wed.-Sat., 5:30pm-10pm Sun.; dishes ¥300-1,500

This small *izakaya* sits amid the old storehouses on historic Nakamachi Street on the south side of the river. The menu offers a good range of oden—vegetables, fish cakes, tofu, and eggs boiled in a soy and kelp-infused dashi broth—and small dishes made with locally sourced ingredients like mushrooms and vegetables foraged in the nearby mountains. The warm, kimono-clad host speaks some English and knows her *sake*. English menu available. All guests dine at a 10-seat wooden countertop.

PIZZA VERDE MATSUMOTO

4-8-22 Ōte; tel. 0263/87-1617; http://verde-matsumoto.jp; 11:30am-2pm and 5:30pm-10pm Tues.-Sun.; lunch from ¥1,000, pizza ¥1,000-1,680, dinner courses ¥2,500-3,500; about 8 minutes' walk southeast of the grounds of Matsumoto-jō

Awash in soccer memorabilia, this pizzeria serves fresh pies straight from a large black oven. All ingredients are high-quality, from the buffalo mozzarella and cherry tomatoes to ham and vegetables. The all-wood interior and friendly staff provide a warm welcome. There are a few tables and a countertop that seats eight people. English menu available. A great choice if you'd like a break from Japanese cuisine.

MENSHŌ SAKURA

1-20-26 Chūō; 0263/34-1050; 11:30am-3pm and 5:30-10pm daily; ramen from ¥850; about 10 minutes' walk northeast of JR Matsumoto Station

If you're a fan of ramen served in a hearty miso broth, you'll love this spot. The *gyoza* (fried pork dumplings) are also excellent—try them with chopped spring onion, chili, and mayo for a refreshing twist. It gets busy during peak hours, sometimes attracting a queue. Look for the charming white townhouse across the street from the Richmond Hotel.

DOON SHOKUDO INDOYAMA

4-6-18 Ōte; 0263/34-3103; www.facebook.com/Doon-shokudo-indoyama-460214724171580; 11am-7:30pm Mon.-Sat.; average ¥1,200; about 10 minutes' stroll east of Matsumoto-jō

This cozy, family-run restaurant does a few curries—vegetarian and meat (chicken, keema)—and does them exceedingly well. Owners Ashish and his Japanese wife are exceptionally welcoming. The bargain-priced food tastes home-cooked, which makes sense considering Ashish learned to cook from his mother in Dehradun. Recommended.

THE STORYHOUSE CAFÉ

1-5-29 Josei; 080/4355-6283; www.facebook.com/thestoryhousecafe; 8am-4:30pm daily; drinks from ¥250, food from ¥500; 8 minutes' walk west of Matsumoto-jō

This charming café, run by friendly, bilingual owners, serves great coffee, desserts, baked goods, light lunches (including good bagel sandwiches), and even a couple vegan options. Besides a few tables, there's a comfy sofa and a few musical instruments, and even a kid's area, making it a good choice if you're traveling with children. This is a solid spot for breakfast, a pit-stop, or a light lunch.

ACCOMMODATIONS

Under ¥10,000

NUNOYA RYOKAN

3-5-7 Chūō; 0263/32-0545; www.mcci.or.jp/www/nunoya; ¥4,500 pp

Housed in a well-preserved storehouse just off the atmospheric Nakamachi Street, this classic *ryokan,* built in the 1920s, has eight well-appointed tatami rooms—tastefully furnished with antique furniture and the odd scroll painting or tea bowl—a shared bath, kitchen, and lounge. The cheerful, English-speaking host is happy to help with making restaurant reservations or recommendations around town. It's within walking distance of most of the town's major sights and is surrounded by good food options. Note that no meals are served. Also, you'll have to go to a nearby café for a Wi-Fi connection.

MARUMO

3 Chōme-3-10 Chūō; tel. 0263/32-0115; www.avis.ne.jp/~marumo/index-j.html; ¥5,000 single, ¥10,000 d, breakfast ¥1,000

This aged, Meiji period *ryokan,* neighboring the Nunoya and set in a white storehouse, sits beside the river on Nakamachi Street. You'll find private tatami rooms with shared baths, a café on-site serving good breakfasts and coffee throughout the day, a compact private bamboo garden, and dark wood throughout. It's in a great location and has plenty of ambience.

¥10,000-20,000

BUENA VISTA

1-2-1 Honjō; tel. 0263/37-0111; www.buena-vista.co.jp; ¥11,400 d with breakfast; 10 minutes' walk southeast of JR Matsumoto Station

This nicely refurbished hotel offers clean, well-appointed rooms with inviting decor, many of which boast stellar views of town and the mountains beyond. Amiable staff are happy to help guests navigate the city. There's a good breakfast buffet served with great views from the 14th floor, and a smattering of other on-site restaurants serving French, Chinese, and Japanese cuisine. Opt for an executive room for access to a private lounge with complimentary drinks and snacks. Shuttle service available on request.

HOTEL KAGETSU

4-8-9 Ōte; tel. 0263/32-0114; www.hotel-kagetsu.jp; ¥16,270 d (without breakfast), ¥20,240 d with breakfast; 5 minutes' walk east of the castle

This classy hotel with a slightly European touch is tucked down a nice quiet street. There's an on-site café and restaurant serving good Western fare, an indoor gender-separated *onsen,* clean and spacious (if mildly dated) en-suite rooms with dark-wood furnishings—both Western and tatami. Extras include a blue-tooth speaker and handy phone. Shuttle service from JR Matsumoto Station is available on request.

MARUNOUCHI HOTEL

3-5-15 Ōte; tel. 0263/35-4500; www.matsumoto-marunouchi.com; ¥15,000 d; 5 minutes' walk south of the castle

Located in a lively part of downtown surrounded by restaurants, this smart modern hotel offers chic, spotless rooms, some of which (the suites) are a bit more spacious than the norm for Japan. The stylish en-suite bathrooms are well-appointed. Staff are helpful and there's a concierge to help with local tips and making dinner reservations. There's a good breakfast buffet. For the quality, the price is a bargain.

INFORMATION AND SERVICES

You'll find the excellent **Matsumoto Tourist Information Center** (1-1-1 Fukashi; tel. 0263/32-2814; 9am-5:45pm daily) in Matsumoto Station. It stocks ample information in English and is run by staff who speak English and are eager to help. There's another branch a few minutes' walk south of Matsumoto-jō on Daimyō-chō-dōri (3-8-13 Ōte; tel. 0263/39-7176; 9am-5:45pm daily). Online, visit https://visitmatsumoto.com for a good introduction to the town and surrounding area.

TRANSPORTATION

Getting There

TRAIN

While it's not served by the *shinkansen*, **JR Matsumoto Station** can be reached directly by limited express train from Shinjuku Station in **Tokyo** (2 hours 30 minutes; ¥6,500), **Nagoya** (2 hours; ¥6,230), and **Nagano** (50 minutes; ¥3,040). To come from Kanazawa, you'll need to first take the *shinkansen* to Nagano, then transfer to the limited express. And from **Kyoto,** you'll need to make the journey to Nagoya, then change to the limited express.

BUS

Underneath the ESPA building just across the street from Matsumoto Station's east side is the **Matsumoto Bus Terminal** (1-2-30 Fukashi; tel. 0263/32-0910). This is the hub that links Matsumoto to a few other cities around Honshu. **Tokyo, Nagoya,** and **Osaka** are served by **Alpico** (www.alpico.co.jp), while **Nōhi Bus** (www.nouhibus.co.jp) shuttles between Matsumoto and **Takayama.**

AIR

Flights arrive daily from **Fukuoka** and **Sapporo** to Matsumoto's **Shinshū Matsumoto Airport** (tel. 0263/57-8818; www.matsumoto-airport.co.jp). All arriving passengers have the option to take a bus to Matsumoto, about 10 km (6 mi) north of the airport (25 minutes; ¥600).

Getting Around

Once you're in the downtown and castle area, getting around Matsumoto **on foot** is a breeze. Free **bicycles** are available at eight locations around town. Inquire at the Tourist Information Center for more details. Another option is the **Town Sneaker minibus system** (https://visitmatsumoto.com/en/guide/buses#townsneaker; ¥200 per ride, ¥500 one-day pass). The buses follow four circuits around town, starting from the Matsumoto Bus Terminal, opposite Matsumoto Station's east (Castle) exit in the ESPA complex.

Around Matsumoto

Roughly between the towns of Takayama and Matsumoto, the free, open-air bath of **Shin-Hotaka-no-Yu** is one of the best hidden, and most otherworldly spots for a soak in Japan. On the opposite side of the mountain range that rises to the east of the legendary pool, the magnificent **Kamikōchi** region offers some of the best hiking and vistas in all Japan.

KAMIKŌCHI
上高地

Kamikōchi is Japan's answer to the Yosemite Valley or Patagonia. At an elevation of about 1,500 meters (4,921 feet), this highland plateau extends about 15 km (9.3 mi) through the Azusa River Valley, a landscape of soaring peaks, pristine rivers, expansive marshes, crystal-clear lakes, ponds, and primordial forests teeming with deer, foxes, troops of monkeys, and the occasional bear. Notable peaks surrounding the valley include the volcanic Yake-dake (2,455 meters/8,054 feet) and Oku-Hotaka-dake (3,190 meters/10,465 feet), the highest in all the Northern Alps.

In many ways, Kamikōchi is the spiritual and historical heart of Japanese mountaineering. Victorian archaeologist and Renaissance man William Gowland (1842-1922) first called these mountains the "Japanese Alps." Reverend Walter Weston (1861-1940), an intrepid British missionary, published his journal *Mountaineering and Exploration in the Japanese Alps,* documenting his explorations of the area and drumming up Japanese interest in exploring their rich alpine heritage.

Kamikōchi is open from late April through mid-November, though snowshoeing is possible in winter. Peak times are mid-July through the end of August, and October, when the leaves blaze orange, red, and copper. To avoid the rush, try to come mid-week or plan to stay overnight in the valley so you have a chance to explore the area before and after the day-trippers descend. The average temperature in the Kamikōchi area is about 5°C (9°F) cooler than outside the valley. You'll thank yourself for bringing a jacket, even in summer.

★ Hiking

Kamikōchi has something for everyone. Leisurely walkers flock to the trail from **Taishō-ike,** a pond in the southwest, to **Myōjin-bashi,** a bridge in the northeast, often starting at Kappa-Bashi, the iconic bridge at the center of the valley. From this relatively flat base trail, it's possible to access a more challenging paths, such as **Yake-dake.**

There are many options for multiday treks that are downright perilous, such as the **Daikiretto** traverse, which takes in **Yariga-take** and **Hotaka-dake** along the way. Both of these peaks make for good standalone treks, although they are flooded with foot traffic during high season. Another extended journey of note is a five-day expedition that leads from Kamikōchi all the way to **Murodō,** the highest point of the Tateyama-Kurobe Alpine Route.

The hikes listed here are among the most accessible and enjoyable. If you're keen for a multiday hike, it's best to speak with someone at the **Kamikōchi Tourist Information Center** and think about hiring a guide at the **Kamikōchi Visitor Center.** The official website of the **Chūbu-Sangaku National Park** (https://alpinewonderland.com) provides extensive information about various guided tours. There are snowshoeing tours in winter (half day, 8am-noon ¥6,800 per person; full day, 8am-4:30pm, ¥9,000 per person), when it's otherwise not feasible to enter the valley.

KAPPA-BASHI TO TOKUSAWA

Distance: 13.4 km (8.3 mi) round-trip

Time: 4 hours round-trip

Information and maps: Kamikōchi Tourist Information

Hida Mountains

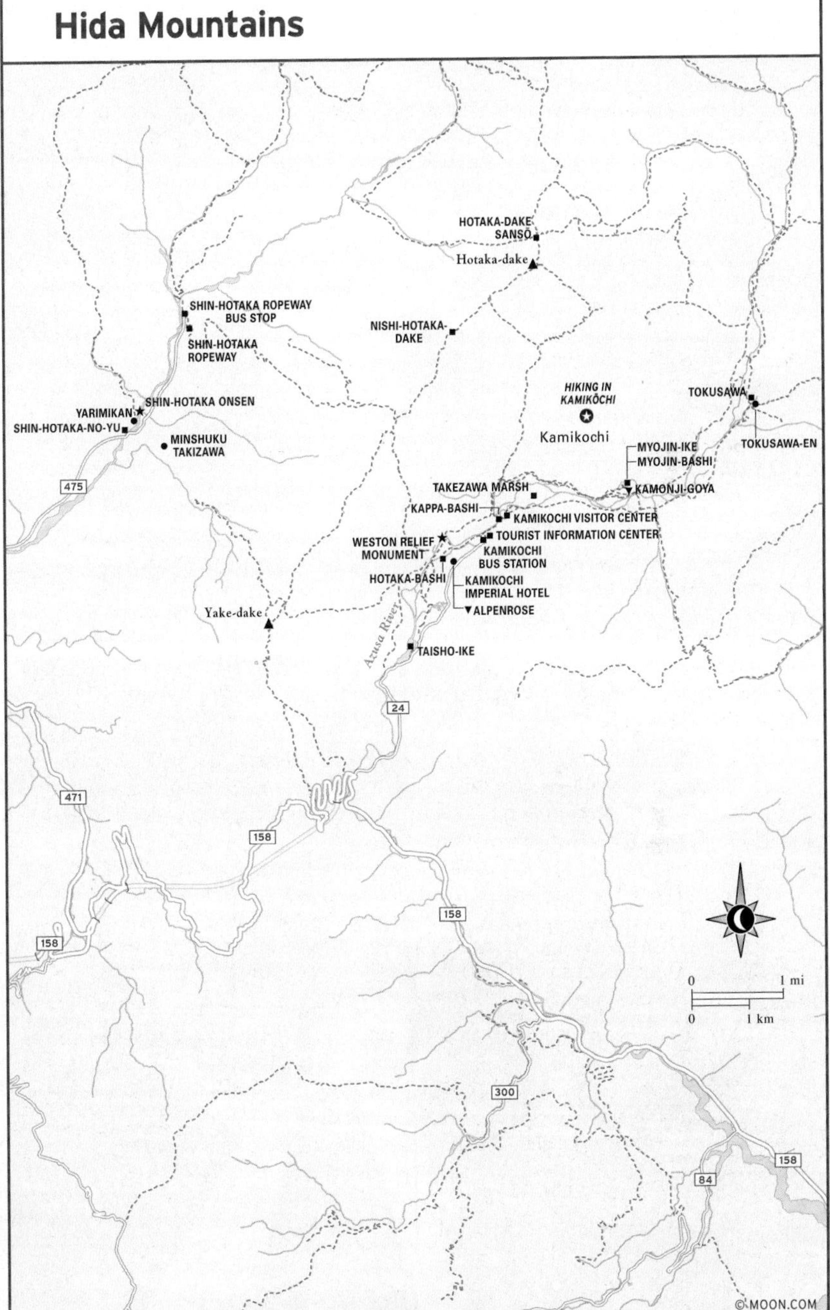

Center (tel. 0260/95-2433; 8am-5pm daily; www.kamikochi.or.jp)

Trailhead: just east of Kappa-bashi

This easy day hike (1,500-meter/4,921-foot elevation gain) begins at **Kappa-bashi** and runs east along the Azusa River. It's possible to hike along either bank of the Azusa River. The right bank leads past lovely views of Takezawa Marsh. From the marsh, continue walking east along the right bank of the river, until you reach the **Myōjin-bashi** bridge (1 hour from Kappa-bashi). Next to this bridge you'll find the tranquil pond, **Myōjin-ike** and the shrine **Hotaka-jinja** (¥300). Cross the bridge to the left bank of the river and continue walking east until you reach **Tokusawa** (1 hour from Myōjin-bashi), a meadow surrounded by towering elms with the eastern face of Mae-Hotaka-dake looming in the background.

This open space makes for a good place to stay overnight, either in the campground or lodge of **Tokusawa-en,** or to turn around, backtracking along the river. If you're keen to forge deeper into the Northern Alps, trailheads leading to more arduous hikes dot the area. Inquire at the Kamikōchi Tourist Information Center for recommendations.

KAPPA-BASHI TO TAISHŌ-IKE

Distance: 6 km (4 mi) round-trip

Time: 1.5 hours round-trip

Information and maps: Kamikōchi Tourist Information Center (tel. 0260/95-2433; 8am-5pm daily; www.kamikochi.or.jp)

Trailhead: just east of Kappa-bashi

For a shorter hike (1,500-meter/4,921-foot elevation gain), starting from Kappa-bashi, head west instead of east. Walk along the right bank of the river, passing the **Weston Relief monument** (15 minutes from Kappa-bashi), finally arriving at **Taishō-ike** (40 minutes from Kappa-bashi). This placid pool was created when neighboring volcano Yake-dake erupted in 1915, blocking the Azusa River. Even today, rotted trees remain rooted in the soil that now forms the bottom of the pond.

For a more strenuous hike, you can walk to the top of nearby volcano Yake-dake (2,455 meters/8,054 feet; 13 km/8 mi round-trip from Hotaka-bashi, 5.5. hours round-trip). From the Weston Relief, you'll reach Hotaka-bashi (about 20 minutes' walk), where you'll follow a paved road and veer left. You'll come to the trailhead for Yake-dake after about 10 minutes.

KAMIKŌCHI TO SHIN-HOTAKA

Distance: 9 km (4.3 mi)

Time: 4 hours one way

Information and maps: Kamikōchi Tourist Information Center (tel. 0260/95-2433; 8am-5pm daily; www.kamikōchi.or.jp)

Trailhead: Next to Hotaka-bashi (35 minutes' walk from Kappa-bashi)

It's possible to hike from Kamikōchi to **Nishi-Hotaka-guchi** (2,156-meter/7,073-foot elevation gain), the upper terminus of the Shin-Hotaka Ropeway. This hike has stunning views throughout, and you have the option of taking the ropeway down the other side of the mountain to Shin-Hotaka Onsen, provided you arrange for your luggage to be sent there before setting off.

To make this trip, follow the same route you would to walk toward Taishō-ike, following the trailhead with a wooden gate located near **Hotaka-bashi;** it is clearly marked for **Nishi-hotaka-dake.** The first stretch is a slightly punishing climb until you reach the **Hotaka-dake Sansō** mountain hut after about 3 hours of plodding uphill. From this hut, push on for another hour to Nishi-Hotaka-guchi, the top station of the Shin-Hotaka Ropeway.

Food

KAMONJI-GOYA

tel. 0263/95-2418; www.kamonjigoya.wordpress.com; 8:30am-4pm daily; ¥500-1,600

Just beside the placid waters of Myōjin-ike, this historic, cabin-like restaurant whips up celebrated *iwana* (river trout) lunch sets. Caught nearby, the fish is then cooked over hot charcoal in an *irori* (sunken hearth). Diners sit at hefty wooden tables and benches,

1: Kappa-bashi **2:** hikers

☆ Walking Japan's Medieval Highway

The old Nakasendō (**中山道**) highway used to stretch from Kyoto to Edo. In the heart of the Kiso Valley is a preserved, 7.8-km (4.8-mi) stretch between the old post towns of Magome (**馬籠**) and Tsumago (**妻籠**). The trail, with its verdant mountain views, can still be traversed on foot in the same way that wanderers did during feudal times. Post towns were essentially pit stops for foot traffic on the highways running all around the country during the Edo period.

The well-marked trail can be walked in three hours moving at a steady pace, passing through small villages, waterfalls, lush cedar forests, and farmland. It's best to begin the journey in Magome and end in Tsumago, as this direction is more downhill, though the first leg of the hike suggests otherwise. A **bus** runs a few times daily between the two towns in both directions (30 minutes; ¥600), stopping at Magome Pass.

Before heading out, be sure to forward your luggage to your destination. Deposit your luggage at the **Tourist Information Center** in Magome (4300-1 Magome, Nakatsugawa; tel. 0573/69-2336; 8:30am-5pm daily) or Tsumago (2159-2 Azuma, Nagiso-machi; tel. 0264/57-3123; 8:30am-5pm daily) between 8:30am and 11:30am—any time from mid-March through November—and arrange with staff to send your bags on. You can pick them up on the other side of the trail any time after 1pm on the same day.

WALKING THE TRAIL

- Enjoy the smooth stone footpath that runs through the heart of **Magome,** and past the well-groomed greenery sprouting up beside the path and fronting the classic wooden shop fronts that are ubiquitous in the charming town.

- The clearest example of Magome's post-town past is its still-standing **Honjin** (**本陣**) (9am-5pm daily Apr.-Nov., 9am-4pm Dec.-Mar., closed Wed. Dec.-Feb.; ¥500), now known as the **Tōson Memorial Museum** (**藤村記念館**). This structure was once the main inn used by officials and dignitaries passing through in feudal times. In contrast is the **Wakihonjin Museum** (**馬籠脇本陣史料館**) (9am-5pm daily Mar. 2-Dec. 24; ¥300), which was where those from the middle and lower rungs of the social ladder were permitted to bed up.

- Stop at **Hillbilly Coffee Company** (4278 Magome, Nakatsugawa; www.facebook.com/iamhilbillycoffee; 8am-5pm daily; drinks from ¥500) to fuel up before you hit the medieval highway.

- As you leave Magome, you'll find yourself walking over cobblestones along some stretches of the hike and asphalt in others, as the path plods steadily uphill to Magome Pass (801 meters/2,628 feet), before gliding down toward **Tsumago.**

alfresco, tucking into the eatery's famed dish. The menu also includes a smattering of *oden* (vegetables and fish cake stewed in soy and kelp-infused broth), among other items.

ALPENROSE

Kamikōchi Imperial Hotel 1F, Azumino Kamikōchi; tel. 0263/95-2001; www.imperialhotel.co.jp/e/kamikochi/restaurant/alpenrose; lunch 11am-2:30pm daily; ¥2,000-3,000

This restaurant pays homage to the European mountaineering associations with the area. This is the casual culinary arm of the Kamikōchi Imperial Hotel, in which the restaurant is located, serving a delicious range of western dishes à la carte. The biggest hit is hashed beef, soft-cooked eggs, and a rice-stuffed omelet covered in the Imperial's signature demi-glace. Ingredients sourced from the nearby mountains figure heavily on the menu. Reservations are not accepted during lunchtime, and dinner (5:30pm-8pm daily; ¥8,000-10,000) is only available for hotel guests.

Accommodations

In addition to the following recommended options, Kamikōchi has an extensive list of places to stay (www.kamikochi.org/plan/

- Tsumago's ambience is thick with history: Cars are banned on the main road of the historic district during daylight hours, and there are no wires hanging overhead. Like in Mangome, the feudal **Honjin** (9am-5pm daily; ¥300, ¥700 combination ticket for Honjin, Wakihonjin, and Rekishi Shiryokan) and **Wakihonjin** (9am-5pm daily; ¥600, ¥700 combination ticket) remain in place.
- Assuming you've worked up an appetite, **Keiseian** (5438-1 Magome, Nakatsugawa; tel. 0573/69-2311; www.takenet.or.jp/~keiseian; 11:30am-2:30pm daily; from ¥900) is the place to drop in for soba. All noodles are made from scratch. Order the *tororo soba*, made with *yamaimo* (grated yam).

Nakasendō highway

SPENDING THE NIGHT

To fully appreciate the Nakasendō, stay overnight at a local *ryokan*. In Magome, try **Tajimaya** (4266 Magome, Nakatsugawa; tel. 0264/69-2048; www.kiso-tajimaya.com; from ¥9,200 pp with two meals). In Tsumago, **Ryokan Fujioto** (858-1 Tsumago Azuma, Nagiso-machi, Kiso-gun; tel. 0264/57-3009; www.tsumago-fujioto.jp; ¥12,500 pp with two meals) or ★ **Takimi No Ie** (4689-447 Tsumago Azuma, Nagiso; tel. 0264/58-2165; www.takiminoie.com; ¥29,400 pp with two meals) are recommended.

GETTING THERE

To reach Magome, head to Nakatsugawa, which is linked by the Shinano limited express to both Matsumoto (1 hour 15 minutes; ¥4,090) and Nagoya (50 minutes; ¥2,820) via Nakatsugawa Station on the JR Chūō line. From **Nakatsugawa Station,** hourly buses run to Magome (30 minutes; ¥560) from bus platform 3. Buses also shuttle from Magome and Tsumago five times per day (25 minutes; ¥600). To reach Tsumago from Nagoya (1 hour 20 minutes; ¥3,160), take the Shinano limited express to Nakatsugawa, then transfer to the JR Chūō local line for the last 20 minutes of the journey to JR Nagiso Station. From Matsumoto, take the JR Chūō local line directly to Nagiso (2 hours; ¥1,490). Once you've reached Nagiso Station, take a bus into Tsumago (10 minutes; ¥270).

accommodation), ranging from plush hotels and humble bed-and-breakfasts to beautiful campsites. During the warmer months, lodgings are known to book up, so reserve a few months ahead if possible And if your place of choice is full, don't fret; there's likely an appealing alternative.

TOKUSAWA-EN

tel. 0260/95-2508; www.tokusawaen.com; May-Oct.; camping ¥500, ¥12,000 dorm (with 2 meals), ¥16,500 private room (with 2 meals)

Kamikōchi's busier junctions feel like Tokyo's Shinjuku Station compared to this serene campsite and lodge found deeper within the park. You can camp or stay in one of the shared or private Japanese-style rooms at the appealing lodge. Filling meals are served in a large dining room. It's possible to rent a tent and bedding if you don't have your own, but you'll have to reserve in advance (¥7,500 for 3 to 4-person tent, ¥2,000 sleeping bag, ¥500 blanket, ¥400 sleeping mat).

KAMIKŌCHI IMPERIAL HOTEL

Azumino Kamikōchi; 0260/95-2001; www.imperialhotel.co.jp; ¥21,000 pp

In business since 1933, this sumptuous lodge

brilliantly fuses luxurious accents with the beautiful natural surroundings. The interior is reminiscent of a chalet in the Alps, and the cooking is fittingly European. All elements are stellar, from the impeccable service to the top-notch bar. If you've got the means, it's a good place to indulge. It's often booked up a year or more in advance. If you want to snag a room, make the attempt as early as the inkling strikes.

Information and Services

First things first, stop at the **Tourist Information Center** (tel. 0260/95-2433; 8am-5pm daily; www.kamikochi.or.jp) in the Kamikōchi bus station. Here you'll find the trusty English-language *Kamikōchi Pocket Guide*, which contains good maps of the area's trails. To glimpse the full extent of Kamikōchi's hiking possibilities, see the Trekking section of the Kamikōchi website (www.kamikochi.org/plan/trekking).

To pick up some English-language materials on the natural history, flora and fauna, and lay of the land, walk a bit past Kappabashi to the **Kamikōchi Visitor Center** (tel. 0260/95-2606; 8am-5pm daily). This is also a good place to link up with English-speaking nature and climbing guides, or join a guided hike (prices vary).

Transportation

Coming from Matsumoto Station, take the **Matsumoto Electric Railway** to Shin-Shimashima Station (30 minutes; ¥700). From there, **buses** run to Kamikōchi (1 hour 15 minutes; ¥2,100). **Direct buses** also run all the way from Matsumoto (2 hours; ¥2,700 one way, ¥4,800 return) or Takayama via Hirayu Onsen (www.nouhibus.co.jp/route_bus/kamikochi-line-en; 1 hour 25 minutes; ¥2,250).

Getting around with your own **car** is a wise move. However, it'll only get you as far as the village of Sawado, located next to National Route 158 en route to Naka-no-yu. You can **park** in a lot (¥600 per day), then take a **shuttle bus** for the remainder of the journey into the park (25 minutes; ¥1,000 one way, ¥1,800 return). If you can stomach the fare, a **taxi** costs upward of ¥4,000. Speaking of which, reserve your return bus fare as soon as you arrive so that you're not stranded as dusk falls, at which point a taxi will be your only option.

SHIN-HOTAKA ONSEN
新穂高温泉

One of five hamlets in the alpine, hot-springs retreat of Okuhida (deep Hida) Onsen-gō, Shin-Hotaka Onsen is a hidden village blessed with an abundance of *rotenburo* (outdoor baths). While the other four *onsen* towns—namely, Hirayu Onsen, Fukuji Onsen, Shin-Hirayu Onsen and Tochio Onsen—have their charms, Shin-Hotaka is the most remote and dramatic.

This realm of steamy pools and mountainside vistas is a destination for powder hounds and trekkers in need of a break from modern life. It's not cheap, but a night at one of the *ryokan* here will be among the most relaxing you'll ever have.

Alongside its abundance of hot springs, the town is known for the **Shin-Hotaka Ropeway,** which glides toward the nearby peak Nishi-Hotake-dake and offers breathtaking views. If you're prepared for the journey, it's possible to trundle from the cable car station on the summit of Nishi-Hotake-dake to Kamikōchi on the opposite side of the mountain in three hours.

Onsen

SHIN-HOTAKA-NO-YU
新穂高の湯

Okuhida Onsengō Kansaka; 0578/89-2614 (Okuhida Onsen-gō Sightseeing Information Center); 8am-9pm daily May-Oct.; free

This public riverside *rotenburo* (open-air bath) is in the awkward position of being visible from a nearby bridge. Moreover, it's a mixed-gender pool. But none of this stops adventurous *onsen* connoisseurs from stripping down and sinking in. If you're not shy, give it a try and you'll be rewarded. The sound of the river resonates in the bathing area, while pebbles covering the floor of the pool massage the soles of your feet. Mountains covered in spindly foliage rise from both riverbanks. Before you enter the pool, just be sure to enter through the correct-gendered changing room, and use a small privacy towel while walking outside the pool for courtesy's sake.

NAKAZAKI SANSOU OKUHIDA-NO-YU
中崎山荘 奥飛騨の湯

710 Okuhida Onsen-gō Kansaka; tel. 0578/89-2021; 8am-8pm daily; adults ¥800, children ¥400

This recently renovated complex is conveniently located a quick walk downhill from the Shin-Hotaka Ropeway. This makes it a particularly appealing option for those seeking a bath before or after zipping up the mountain. The mountainside view from the indoor pool is spectacular, and the milky waters are packed with minerals too. Unlike the exhibitionists' mecca of Shin-Hotaka-no-yu just downhill, the baths here are separated by sex and well-concealed from passersby; this is a good thing for privacy, but the view from the outdoor bath is slightly obscured as a result.

Sports and Recreation

SHIN-HOTAKA ROPEWAY
新穂高ロープウェイ

710-58 Okuhida Onsen-gō Kansaka; tel. 0578/89-2552; www.shinhotaka-ropeway.jp; 8:30am-4:30pm daily; ¥1,600 one way, ¥2,900 round-trip

The longest ropeway in Asia, Shin-Hotaka Ropeway, offers phenomenal views of the Northern Alps. As you climb up the Hotake Mountain Range, the verdant Okuhida Onsen-gō region ripples through the landscape below. You'll be transported in two double-decker cars more than 800 ear-popping meters (2,624 feet) up to a viewing platform at 2,156 meters (7,073 feet), where you'll be greeted with a sweeping panorama of the Northern Alps.

If you make this trip between late June and the end of September, a hiking trail will likely be open from this viewing deck. The well-marked trail allows hikers to descend about 1.5 hours to a mountain hut called Hotaka-dake Sansō, situated on the ridge. From there, you can continue trailing downward for another 2.5 hours to the nature lovers' utopia of **Kamikōchi,** a highland valley on the other side of the mountains (about 3 hours).

Accommodations

YARIMIKAN

587 Okuhida Onsen-gō Kansaka; tel. 0578/89-2808; www.yarimikan.com; ¥18,510 pp with two meals

This immaculate riverside inn has all the elements in place for a luxurious getaway. Set in an old, relocated manor house with its ambience intact, the inn has two indoor baths and a whopping eight open-air baths fringing the banks of the Kamata-gawa, (both gender-separated and mixed), a few of which can be reserved for private use. For staying guests, baths are open around the clock. They're open to day-trippers from 10am to 2pm (¥500). There are 16 rooms, including a mix of Japanese and Western. All rooms have a private toilet; one has a private indoor tub, and two have private outdoor tubs. Service is stellar and the *kaiseki* meals are sublime. Splurge-worthy.

MINSHUKU TAKIZAWA

261 Nakao, Okuhida Onsen-gō; tel. 0578/89-2705; www.okuhida.com; ¥25,920 d with two meals

This authentic *onsen-ryokan* offers spacious tatami rooms with en-suite toilets. There are four onsen baths—two indoors, two open-air—all of which are private. The gourmet meals are beautifully presented and taste a cut above what you'd expect for the price. The ever-helpful host Takizawa-san extends a warm greeting to all guests. Free shuttle pickup and drop-off at the Shin-Hotaka Ropeway—10 minutes' drive north—are available upon request.

Transportation

GETTING THERE

It's possible to reach this remote hot-spring from Takayama by **bus** (1 hour 30 minutes; ¥2,160), passing Hirayu Onsen on the way. Take the bus all the way to the last stop, Shin-Hotaka Ropeway. That said, this *onsen* is legitimately remote and having your own **car** is by far the best way to explore these parts.

Northern Japan Alps 北アルプス

The Japan Alps are, in fact, a cluster of ranges in the center of Honshu, namely, the Hida, Kiso, and Akaishi. The Hida range, also known as the Northern Alps, runs through Gunma, Nagano, Niigata, and Toyama prefectures; the Kiso is clustered in Nagano Prefecture; and Akaishi range sprawls across Nagano, Yamanashi, and Shizuoka. While they can't claim Mount Fuji, the Alps boast the bulk of Japan's highest peaks, with a number of summits above 3,000 meters (9,843 feet).

Among the Japanese, Nagano Prefecture (also home to Matsumoto in the south) is associated with mountains perhaps more than any other. It's known for its wealth of *onsen* resorts and world-class ski resorts. Japanese mountaineering began in Nagano, where Walter Weston, a British preacher and polymath, launched Japan's first alpine club in 1905. At peak times, trekkers crowd Nagano's most popular trails.

Slow and serene, **Nagano** is the capital of the mountainous prefecture. Today, most visitors either come to see the grand temple of **Zenkō-ji,** which offers lodging to pilgrims and adventurous travelers alike, or stop en route to one of the remote *onsen* villages or picturesque ski resorts located within driving distance.

Perhaps the most comfortable way to sample the stunning vistas this area offers, the **Tateyama-Kurobe Alpine Route** whisks visitors along a 90-km (56-mi) journey—beginning at the northern end of the Alps in Toyama prefecture and ends in Nagano—through breathtaking alpine landscapes via a mix of transport methods. Also in the far northern part of the Alps, the ski town of **Hakuba** is one of Japan's top winter sports destinations for serious powder hounds.

Note that though many accommodations have meals included, and there are few other options for food in the mountains. Anyone heading into the remoter parts of this region should stock up on food and drinks at a convenience store in Takayama, or wherever they're coming from, before reaching the area.

ZENKŌ-JI
善光寺

491 Motoyoshi-chō; tel. 026/234-3591; www.zenkoji.jp; about 1 hour before dawn-4:30pm Apr.-Oct., closes 4pm Dec.-Feb., 4:15pm Mar. and Nov.; grounds free, inner sanctum and history museum ¥500 adults, ¥200 students in grades 10-12, ¥50 students through 9th grade

Zenkō-ji, has been a beacon to seekers of all stripes since it was founded in the 7th-century. The temple's appeal is universal: belonging to no specific sect, it has for centuries accepted women both as participants and priests. The popularity of the temple in Nagano is evident from its position in the town, a 1.5-km (1-mi) straight shot from Nagano station.

Much of the temple's power emanates from a sacred statue, Ikkō-Sanzon Amida Nyorai, which remains hidden from even the emperor's gaze. This visage dates to 552 and is said to be the first Buddhist icon to reach Japan's shores. Although the original is never unveiled, a replica is brought forth every seven years and made public from April to mid-May in the **Gokaichō Matsuri.** The next showing is expected in 2022.

The current incarnation of the temple's main hall dates to 1707. You can enter the

Skiing in Central Honshu

Just the mention of skiing destinations like Nagano Prefecture conjures up images of world-class ski resorts, such as those that hosted the Winter Olympics. Listed here are some of the area's best ski resorts.

SHIGA KŌGEN

志賀高原

The Shiga Kōgen Ski Area (Hasuike, Yamanouchi; www.shigakogen-ski.com; 8:30am-4:30pm Dec.-Apr.; 1-day lift pass ¥5,000 adults, ¥4,200 seniors and students, ¥2,500 children) is massive, with a whopping 51 lifts and 80 runs, many of which were used in the 1998 Winter Olympics. Receiving 12 meters (39 feet) of snow every winter, 21 separate ski areas cater to all skill levels. The **Haisuke area** is a good bet if you're a beginner or traveling with kids. For a full range of resorts, search for Shiga Kōgen at www.snowjapan.com or www.powderhounds.com/Japan.aspx.

Nozawa Onsen Snow Resort

Shiga Kōgen Tourist Association is next to the Haisuke bus stop (7148 Hirao, Hasuike; tel. 0269/34-2404; www.shigakogen.gr.jp), run by helpful English-speaking staff. **Hotel Shirakabaso** (7148 Hasuike, Yamanouchi; tel. 0263/95-2131; www.shirakaba.co.jp; doubles from ¥25,300 with 2 meals) is a cozy *ryokan* with clean, simple rooms, both indoor and outdoor *onsen,* nutritious, filling meals, and ski equipment rentals.

NOZAWA ONSEN SNOW RESORT

野沢温泉スキー場

These ski slopes (7653 Toyosato, Nozawaonsen-mura, Shimotakai-gun; tel. 0269/85-3166; www.nozawaski.com; 8:30am-4:30pm Dec.-Apr.; 1-day lift ticket ¥4,800 adults, ¥2,200 children under 15, ¥3,700 seniors over 60) are a great alternative to the runs in the region's more widely known resorts. The legendary soft snow and ample *onsen* make it a wonderful place for powder lovers to get their fix and rest their weary bones. There are 21 lifts and runs catering to all ability levels. There's also a half-pipe if you're partial to a snowboard. Ample English-language information in print and on boards around town make your visit easier.

HAKUBA VALLEY

白馬渓谷

It's possible to access all 10 ski resorts round the valley with the **Hakuba Valley Ticket** (www.hakubavalley.com/en/ticket). A 1-day pass costs ¥6,000. Among the resorts, **Happō-One Ski Resort** (Kitaazumi-gun, Hakuba-mura; tel. 0261/72-2715; www.happo-one.jp ; Dec.-Apr.; 1-day lift ticket ¥5,200), **Hakuba 47 Winter Sports Park & Hakuba Goryū Ski Resort** (24196-47 Kamishiro, Hakuba-mura; tel. 0261/75-3533; www.hakuba47.co.jp; Dec.-Apr.; 1-day lift ticket ¥5,000); and **Hakuba Cortina Snow Resort** (12860-1 Chikuniotsu, Otari; tel. 0261/82-2236; www.hakubacortina.jp/ski; Dec.-Apr.; 1-day lift ticket ¥4,000) are standouts.

ornate building, which houses an elaborate altar, as well as a pitch-black subterranean corridor containing a key, affixed to a wall, that is said to bestow salvation on all those who manage to touch it. Also included in the cost of admission is a history museum housed in a pagoda behind the main hall with an array of statues depicting various Buddhas and boddhisattvas, as well as Buddha's legendary 100 of yore.

Accommodations

Given Zenkō-ji's history of openness, it's no surprise that the temple is surrounded by a large area of *shukubō*, or temple lodgings. There are 39 different such accommodations all clustered on the street in front of Zenkō-ji.

FUCHINOBO

462 Motoyoshi-chō; tel. 026/232-3669; https://fuchinobo.or.jp; ¥12,000 pp with two meals

A good bet is Fuchinobo, inside the Zenkō-ji grounds. Staying here allows you to slow down, eat vegetarian cuisine (*shōjin ryōri*) like a monk, and attend morning prayers. Information on *shukubō* in Nagano is sparse online, but Fuchinobo can be booked through the *ryokan* reservation website Japanese Guesthouses (www.japaneseguesthouses.com).

Information and Services

Stop by the **Nagano Tourist Information Center** (tel. 026/226-5626; http://en.nagano-cvb.or.jp; 9am-7pm daily Apr.-Oct., 9am-6pm daily Nov.-Mar.) in Nagano Station for maps and pamphlets on the town and the attractions that the surrounding mountains hold.

Online, head to www.go-nagano.net for great information on the town and prefecture as a whole.

Transportation

Nagano Station is a stop on the Hokuriku Shinkansen line, which links directly to **Tokyo** (1 hour 45 minutes; ¥8,400) and **Kanazawa** (1 hour 10 minutes; ¥9,160). **Matsumoto** is accessible by the Shinano limited express (50 minutes; ¥3,040), which also runs to **Nagoya** (3 hours; ¥7,530).

Buses run to and from a number of ski resorts and *onsen* towns, from Hakuba to Nozawa Onsen, as well as other hubs, such as Matsumoto, Tokyo, and Kyoto, all from the **Nagano BT Bus Stop** (178-2 Okadamachi, Nakagosho; tel. 026/228-1155; www.nagano-bt.co.jp), about 10 minutes' walk west of Nagano Station's Zenkō-ji exit on the clearly indicated thoroughfare Terminal-dōri.

If you want to rent a car—a good option for exploring the countryside—there's an **Eki Rent-a-Car** (tel. 026/227-8500; www.ekiren.co.jp) just to the left, outside the Zenkō-ji exit, and a **Toyota Rent-A-Car** (1275-12 Minami Ishidōchō, Minaminagano; tel. 026/228-0100; https://rent.toyota.co.jp) 6 minutes' walk northwest of the same exit.

NOZAWA ONSEN
野沢温泉

With 13 community-owned *onsen,* relief for sore muscles is ready at hand in the wistful village of Nozawa Onsen. Although its prime time is winter, when skiers flock to the nearby slopes, this small town is a good escape any time of year. Alongside the public pools, *ryokan* are also arrayed around town, each with its private *onsen*.

The best part is, the 13 community-owned baths dotting the village are all free (6am-11pm daily), although a small donation to help with maintenance is welcome. Just drop a few coins into the boxes mounted on the outside of each pool's door. Each has its own mineral fusion and temperature, with some so scalding that only hard-boiled veterans, mostly local, dare enter. For the best experience, wander the atmospheric lanes and try as many baths as you can.

Onsen

Ō-YU
大湯

9328 Toyosato; tel. 026/985-3155; donations

If you prefer to choose just one pool, make it Ō-yu, which can be found inside a lovely wooden building in the heart of town. Before you slip into any of the pools, gingerly check the temperature; some are alarmingly hot, ranging from 40°C (104°F) at the lower end of the scale, up to a scorching 90°C (194°F) for the daredevils out there.

Festivals

DŌSOJIN MATSURI (NOZAWA FIRE FESTIVAL)

道祖神祭り

Nozawa Onsen; https://nozawa-onsen.com/nozawa-fire-festival; Jan. 15; free

In Japan it's believed that the ages of 25 and 42 are unlucky for men. Since 1863, locals of the small village of Nozawa Onsen have been fending off evil spirits and asking for the growth and health of all first-born sons in incendiary fashion. Considered one of Japan's top three fire festivals, the proceedings in Nozawa Onsen resemble all-out war.

Every January 15, the 25- and 42-year-old men of the town fight with the rest of the village men in a literal flame battle. First, some 100 villagers build a towering wooden shrine, which, after being blessed by a Shinto priest, is defended at its base by the 25-year-olds, while the 42-year-olds guard the top. Encroaching hordes wielding torches descend on the structure with the goal of burning it to the ground. Throughout the event, participants and spectators alike are primed with a continuous flow of sake by—no joke—the local fire department. The defenders and attackers take the fight seriously. It's not uncommon to see participants whose faces are covered in soot and fresh wounds oozing blood.

The guardsmen have no real chance of successfully defending the tower: The 25-year-olds have nothing but pine boughs to swat at the flames, while the 42-year-olds "protect" the shrine by dropping a steady supply of kindling down to the base. Ultimately, the fire wins out and the structure is consumed in a blazing inferno. Bad luck purged, the village returns to its sleepy status quo. The festival has become a popular spectacle, so book accommodations a few months ahead.

Food

JUNTOS MEXICAN

9256-1 Toyosato; tel. 08/03434-1016; www.facebook.com/Juntosmexican; 4pm-11pm daily Dec.-mid Mar., mid Mar-early May and Nov. 6pm-11pm Tues.-Sun., 6pm-11pm weekends and public holidays Jul.-Aug., hours vary Sept.-Oct.; ¥1,500-3,000

Take a break from Japanese fare and get your taco fix at this implausibly located cantina. The menu includes very decent tacos, burritos, churros, margaritas, and more. Portions are modest and you'll pay a premium, but consider it the cost of eating Mexican grub in the remote mountains of Japan. Located about 4 minutes' walk west of Ō-yu. English menu available.

GENKI BURGER

9534 Toyosato; tel. 050/5532-7945; www.genkiburger.com; 7:30am-10pm daily Dec. 1-Mar. 17, noon-10pm daily Mar. 18-Apr. 1; ¥850-1,400

With its English menu and crowd-pleasing classics, there's no hiding the fact that this burger joint, situated about 1-minute walk southwest of Ō-yu, caters heavily to the foreign contingent. But sometimes only a burger will do. The menu is diverse with plenty of toppings—red cheddar cheese, avocado, egg, bacon, cream cheese, jalapenos, chunky mushrooms, and more—and the loaded fries (cheese, spring onion, and more) are hard to resist.

NAPPA CAFE

8661-1 Toyosato; tel. 080/1250-7878; http://nappa-cafe.com; lunch 10am-5pm (lunch served 11am-2pm) daily; 10am-5pm daily; ¥500-1,000

With walls plastered in retro-cute and cat-themed decor, this cozy spot, also known as 78 Cafe, is run by friendly owners. The menu includes excellent coffee and chai, and a range of dishes like curry, croquet monsieur, and salad, as well as desserts. About 2 minutes' walk north of Ō-yu. English menu available.

LIBUSHI

9347 Toyosato; tel. 080/6930-3992; http://libushi.com; 4pm-11pm daily Dec.-Apr., 4pm-11pm Fri.-Sun. May-Nov.; ¥650-1,200

This little artisan brewpub adjacent to Ō-yu serves a great range of beers from 10 taps. They brew in house with water flowing under the town and occasionally serve the odd rare beer from elsewhere. A good spot to unwind after a day on the slopes. They open sporadically during the warmer months, but call ahead before making the trip.

Accommodations

PEANUTS HOUSE KUMAKUMA

4403-1 Toyosato; tel. 090/2317-1660; http://p-kumakuma.sakura.ne.jp; ¥11,400 d with two meals

Located about 7 minutes' walk south of Ō-yu in the heart of town and 10 minutes' stroll to the main gondola that leads to the top of the slopes, this conveniently located guesthouse is a great pick. It offers clean Japanese-style rooms with a shared bathroom, tasty home-cooked breakfast, and (with two day's advanced reservation) dinner. The welcoming hosts speak some English, too.

KAIYA NOZAWA

9695-1 Toyosato; tel. 0269/85-3474; www.nozawaholidays.com/properties/kaiya; ¥6,500 dorms, ¥15,000 d with shared bathroom, ¥19,000 d with private bathroom, ¥22,000 studio apartment for two adults

This freshly renovated guesthouse has an appealing mix of stylish Western and Japanese-style rooms, one of which has a private bathroom. There's also a full studio apartment, with a kitchen, bathroom, and living space. There's a communal lounge with a fireplace that serves as a nice place to socialize in comfort on cold days. All rates include a hearty breakfast to fuel you up before a day on the slopes. The friendly staff, both Japanese and foreign, are happy to help. It's an 8-minute walk southwest of Ō-yu and only 5 minutes west of the slopes.

★ SUMIYOSHI-YA

8713 Toyosato; tel. 0269/85-2005; https://sumiyosiya.co.jp; ¥24,200 d pp with 2 meals

This historic *ryokan* offers a diverse selection of 15 rooms, ranging from wooden floors with beds to tatami-and-futon affairs. Of the rooms, four have bathtubs. All rooms have access to the *ryokan*'s stunning, gender-separated communal hot-springs pools, both outdoors and indoors. The indoor pools are graced with windows containing colorfully tinted panes. The meals are excellent, as is the service. Most staff speak some English. This inn offers the quintessential *onsen-ryokan* experience. Highly recommended.

Information and Services

For good intel on skiing or hot-spring baths, stop by the **Nozawa Onsen Visitor Center** (9780-4 Toyosato, Nozawaonsen-mura; tel. 0269/85-3155; http://nozawakanko.jp; 8:30am-5:30pm daily). The staff speak English and are glad to assist with reservations and recommendations. Note that the town's online tourism portal provides a contact form (https://booking.nozawakanko.jp) for visitors to request assistance with things like room reservations. Also see the local booking website **Stay Nozawa** (www.staynozawa.com).

Transportation

GETTING THERE

From **Tokyo,** take the Hokuriku *shinkansen* to Iiyama (1 hour 50 minutes; ¥8,830), then transfer to the Nozawa Onsen Liner bus and take that to the **Nozawa Onsen stop** (25 minutes, ¥600). From Nagano, you can take the JR Iiyama line to **Togari-Nozawa-Onsen Station** (1 hour; ¥710). From there, the center of Nozawa Onsen is a bus ride away (20 minutes; ¥310).

Alternatively, it's possible to take a bus directly from Nagano's bus terminal to Nozawa Onsen (1 hour 30 minutes; ¥1,400). If you're landing in Japan and plan to head to Nozawa Onsen just to hit the slopes, during ski season **"snow shuttle" buses** run directly from Narita and Haneda airport. See www.naganosnowshuttle.com for details.

HAKUBA
白馬

With a total of 10 ski resorts, **Hakuba** is a winter sports mecca spread across a valley in the heart of the Northern Alps's highest section, with many peaks in the area topping 3,000 meters (9,842 feet). In the warmer months, avid hikers flock to the area. Year round, a proliferation of *onsen* baths provide relaxation and relief for skiers' and hikers' sore muscles. With relatively easy access from both Tokyo and Kansai, Hakuba makes for an appealing escape for those with limited time to explore Japan's vast alpine riches.

Hiking

Thanks to its easy access to some of the Alps' loftiest peaks, Hakuba is a wonderland for hikers. Though it does get crowded, these trails are less full than those at Kamikōchi. Tsugaike Nature Park is a great option for those seeking a manageable walk in lovely surroundings. Summiting Shirouma-dake, however, is a real challenge.

You might also want to inquire about a guided expedition at **Evergreen Outdoor** (4377 Hokujō; outdoor center; tel. 0261/72-5150; www.evergreen-hakuba.com). They offer a ski school (Dec.-Mar.; from ¥9,000 per day) and backcountry outings (Apr.-Nov.; from ¥4,000 for half-day). Excursions include half-day tours and multiday expeditions for hiking (Apr.-Nov.), climbing (Apr.-Nov.), mountain biking (Apr.-Nov.), backcountry trekking (Apr.-Nov.), canoeing (with fireflies in July and August; Jun.-Sept.), canyoning (Jul.-Sept.), rafting (Apr.-Oct.), kayaking (May-Nov.), and snowshoeing (Dec.-Apr.).

TSUGAIKE NATURE PARK

Distance: 5.5 km (3.4 mi)

Time: 4 hours

Information and maps: June-Oct.; adults ¥300, children ¥250; www.tsugaike.gr.jp/english/trekking/shizenen

Trailhead: Tsugaike Ropeway (gondola, followed by a cable car)

If you're looking for a gorgeous hike that's not overly taxing, Tsugaike Nature Park is ideal, as you'll travel part of the way by gondola, (departs from the nearby Tsuhaike Kogen bus stop) and cable car along the aptly named Panorama Way (26 minutes one way; adults ¥3,600, children ¥2,050 round-trip). Traipse through a lush highland (elevation: 1,900 meters/6,233 feet), surrounded by soaring peaks and dotted by large patches of clinging snow until early summer, and wildflowers from mid-June to mid-August. Starting in mid-September, the leaves blaze with autumn colors. When you reach the observation platform, you'll see Shirouma-dake glistening in the distance.

Daytime temperatures are warm but dip at night. Take a fleece jacket, a sturdy pair of shoes, a hat, and sunglasses. With a hiking time of about 4 hours, it's not necessary to carry too much—just water and a few snacks. Because most of the trail is wooden boardwalk, this route is a particularly good option if you're traveling with kids or simply want to enjoy the views in comfort. The "Getting Here" section of the park's website provides clear instructions on how to reach the park from both Shinjuku Station in Tokyo or Nagano Station.

SHIROUMA-DAKE

Distance: 7.4 km (4.6 mi)

Time: 5 hours to summit

Information and maps: June-Nov.; free; www.japan-guide.com/blog/peaks/170904.html

Trailhead: beside Sarukuraso Lodge (Hokujō, Kitaazumi-gun, tel. 0261/72-4709)

The best hike in the Hakuba region is Shirouma-dake (White Horse Peak), the area's tallest peak at 2,932 meters (9,619 feet), with a 1,700-meter (5,577-foot) elevation gain; it's one of Japan's only peaks that has snowfields year-round. There are wildflowers blooming in summer and

Hakuba

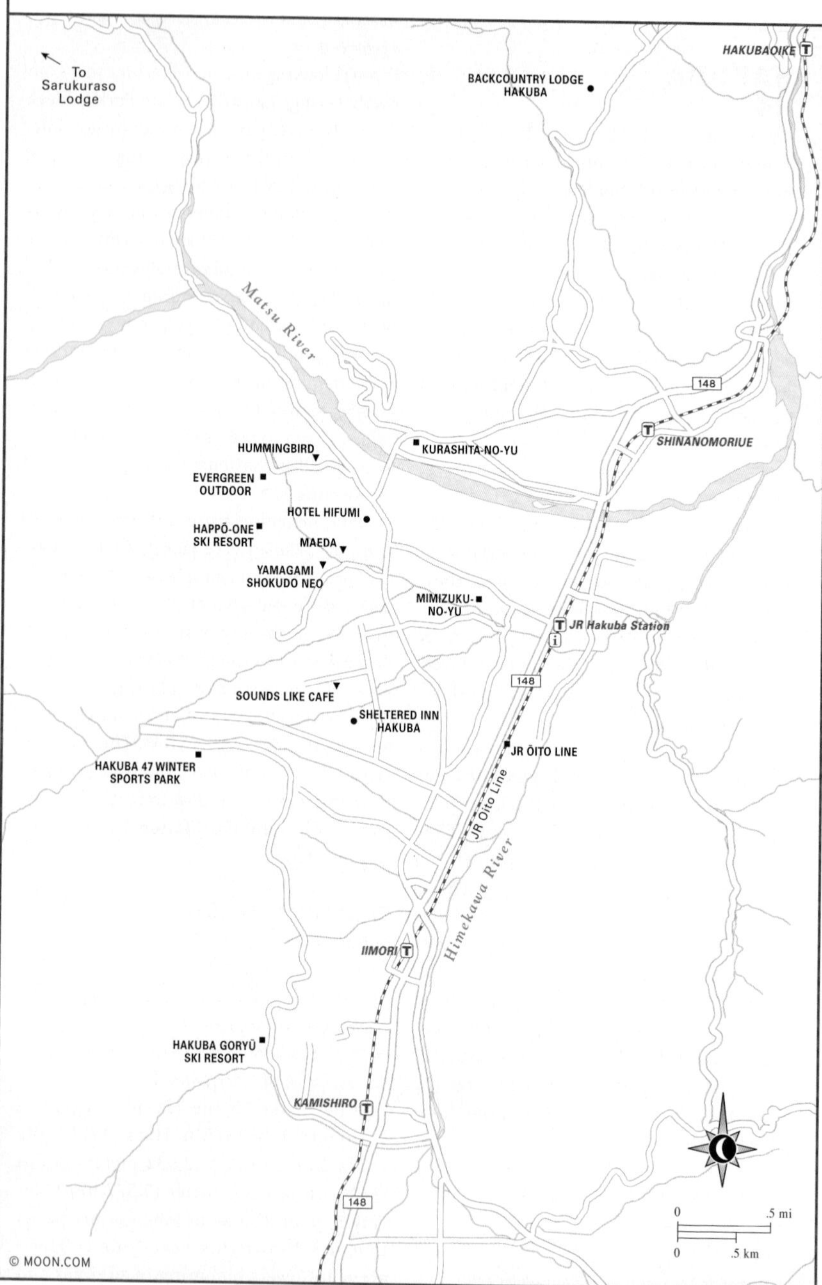
To Sarukuraso Lodge
BACKCOUNTRY LODGE HAKUBA
HAKUBAOIKE
Matsu River
148
SHINANOMORIUE
KURASHITA-NO-YU
HUMMINGBIRD
EVERGREEN OUTDOOR
HOTEL HIFUMI
HAPPŌ-ONE SKI RESORT
MAEDA
YAMAGAMI SHOKUDO NEO
MIMIZUKU-NO-YU
JR Hakuba Station
SOUNDS LIKE CAFE
SHELTERED INN HAKUBA
HAKUBA 47 WINTER SPORTS PARK
JR ŌITO LINE
JR Ōito Line
Himekawa River
IIMORI
HAKUBA GORYŪ SKI RESORT
KAMISHIRO
0 .5 mi
0 .5 km

breathtaking vistas from every angle, but don't underestimate the terrain: the mountain is notorious for landslides and falling boulders. It's best not to attempt summiting Shirouma-dake in squally weather or spring, when avalanches are common. The best time to make the hike is from June to October. Before setting off, share your trekking plan with Sarukura Lodge, which can be reached by car or bus from JR Hakuba Station in 20-30 minutes. If taking a bus, catch the one bound for Sarukura and get off at the last stop (¥1,000).

Wear full-blown hiking boots and waterproof clothing if the forecast says rain. If conditions are clear, a fleece top or medium-weight coat will do. Buy a pair of cheap crampons at the lodge so you're well prepared for the snowfield, and bring plenty of water and food. A hat and sunglasses are a good call, too.

The ascent starts on a gravel road, which runs past an artificial waterfall before phasing into a more traditional trail. When you reach two mountain huts and a neighboring campground, you'll know that you're about to enter the **Daisekkei** (Great Snowfield). This is the place to get serious. Put on your crampons, don a helmet (if you have one), and start to make your way upward, through the immense valley of snow. The bulk of the hike takes place in this snowy section of the mountain.

You'll know you're about to reach the summit when you exit the snowy expanse and come to **Hakuba Sansō Lodge** (tel. 0261/72-2002; www.hakuba-sanso.co.jp; ¥10,000 adults, ¥7,000 children 12 and up; ¥2,000 children under 12, prices are per person with 2 meals), beside a campground. The unfortunate reality is that conditions atop Shirouma-dake tend to be cloudy. But if it happens to be clear, the views are stunning. It's possible to stay the night at the mountain lodge and witness the glorious sunrise the next morning.

On your descent from Hakuba Yarigatake, after about 1.5 hours of lumbering downhill, you'll come to **Hakuba Yari Onsen** (¥1,000). This hot spring bath is among the highest in all the land at 2,100 meters (6,889 feet), and the views from its outdoor pool are just as dramatic as you'd imagine. After enjoying a soak, it's another 2-4 hours to complete the loop and reach the Sarukura Lodge trailhead.

Onsen

The entire Hakuba Valley is brimming with

trekking in Hakuba

Tateyama-Kurobe Alpine Route

Tateyama Ropeway

From spring through autumn, the Tateyama-Kurobe Alpine Route (www.alpen-route.com/en) offers a far-reaching tour of the Northern Alps. From mid-April through November, it's possible to traverse 90 km (56 mi) of mountainous terrain via railway, cable car, bus, or ropeway, or even on foot. The route begins in Toyama City, Toyama, and ends in the small town of Omachi in Nagano Prefecture.

Along the way you'll take in soaring mountains, Japan's highest dam, and resplendent highland meadows. Depending on the time of year, you'll also have the chance to see wildflowers in bloom, blazing foliage, and 20-meter (66-foot) walls of snow that linger long past winter.

GETTING THERE

The easiest access points for the Tateyama-Kurobe Alpine Route include **Toyama,** which is accessible from Tokyo via the JR Hokuriku *shinkansen* (2.5 hours; ¥12,500), **Nagano** (1 hour 40 minutes; ¥8,000 from Tokyo), and **Shinano-Omachi,** which is easily accessed by the JR Oito Line from Matsumoto (1 hour), with the total trip from Tokyo lasting about 3.5 hours (¥7,500). It's possible to start the route from either side, to complete a one-way or return trip, or even to see just a portion of the route. To get a full sense of the various options, check the official website. Making the trip one-way takes 6 hours or more, so start early in the day, or you can stay overnight somewhere along the way. It costs ¥10,850 one way, or ¥18,260 round-trip.

PLANNING AHEAD

The **Tateyama Option Ticket** is a discount ticket (http://jrtateyama.com/e; ¥9,000 one way) for foreign tourists only, which starts in Nagano, linking to the eastern end of the route (Ogizawa) by bus, and ultimately ends in Toyama. It's possible to purchase this ticket—which must be bought at least one day in advance and is valid for five days following purchase—at the JR green ticket counters at the major JR stations of Tokyo, Shinjuku, Osaka, Kyoto, and Nagano, among others.

Almost as important as arranging the ticket for the route itself, be sure to arrange for your **luggage** to be forwarded to your next destination. This is practically a necessity given the frequent stops and starts, and the amount of walking that's involved in completing the route. To learn more about how to set this up, go to www.alpen-route.com/en/transport_new/baggage.html.

Be forewarned that this popular mountain route can get crowded during Golden Week (end of April through early May), as well as during various summer holidays and weekends during the height of autumn foliage. Numbered tickets are disbursed for certain legs of the route at these crowded times. The best way to stay out of human traffic jams is simply to avoid peak times.

onsen baths. You can find a comprehensive list on the Hakuba Tourism website (http://hakubatourism.jp/hotsprings). The following are two of the best and most accessible ones.

MIMIZUKU-NO-YU
みみずくの湯

5480-1 Kitajō Happo-guchi, Hakuba-mura; tel. 0261/72-6542; http://hakuba-happo-onsen.jp/mimizukunoyu; 10am-9:30pm daily, last entry 9pm;

adults ¥600, children ¥300; 12 minutes' walk or a few minutes' drive west of Hakuba Station

At this old-school *onsen,* located between Hakuba Station and the slopes of Happō-One, the baths are divided by gender and include both indoor and *rotenburo* (outdoor) options. It's open year-round and offers arguably the best views of the Alps of all the *onsen* around Hakuba. There's also a room with massage chairs if you feel like even more relaxation after exiting the bath.

KURASHITA-NO-YU

倉下の湯

9549-8 Hokujō, Hakuba-mura; tel. 0261/72-7989; www.kurashitanoyu.com; 10am-9:30pm daily Dec.-Mar.; adults ¥600, children ¥300; 30 minutes' walk west of Shinano-Moriue Station (one stop from Hakuba on Oito line)

Another *rotenburo* with good mountain views, Kurashita-no-yu is located about 40 minutes' walk northeast of Happō-One, making it a convenient option after a day on the slopes at Hakuba's biggest resort. Its interior is bare-bones and rustic, but the waters here are known to be among the most mineral-rich in Hakuba.

Food

HUMMINGBIRD

4715-1 Hokujō Wadano, Hakuba-mura; tel. 0261/72-7788; 6pm-9pm daily; ¥1,000-3,800; about 10 minutes' walk east of Evergreen Outdoor Center, or a few km northeast of Hakuba Happō-One resort

This cozy, family-run restaurant is set in a highly inviting home. The generous couple who run it serve a nicely varied menu with stews, meat loaf, and sauteed chicken, pork, and salmon. The ingredients are seasonal and crisp. It's a highly popular spot, so call ahead to book a table a day or more in advance to avoid disappointment.

MAEDA

5054 Hokujō, Hakuba-mura; tel. 0261/72-2295; 11am-9pm daily; ¥700-1,350; 30 minutes' walk west of Hakuba Station, on the eastern edge of the Happō-One resort

This family-run noodle shop is a good choice for lunch. Other items on the menu include tasty *karage* (fried chicken), tempura, and more. There are tables with chairs and a tatami-floor seating area. Cash only. It fills up sometimes during peak hours. If you arrive when it's busy, put your name in and wait. English menu available.

YAMAGAMI SHOKUDO NEO

4265 Hokujō Happo, Hakuba-mura; tel. 0261/72-8228; http://yamagami-hakuba.main.jp; 6pm-9pm daily; gyoza from ¥390, barbecue ¥420-3,900, noodles ¥750-1,800; 30 minutes' walk west of Hakuba Station, 2 minutes' walk south of Maeda

This joint serves *gyoza* (pan-fried pork dumplings), ramen, yakiniku (barbecue), and other hearty fare, best washed down with a mug of ice-cold beer. English menu available. It's laid-back at lunch time but fills up at dinner. Service is efficient, if slightly brusque. Reserve ahead to avoid being turned away or forced to wait. Situated Just east of the Happō One resort.

SOUNDS LIKE CAFÉ

3020-504 Hokujō, Hakuba-mura; tel. 0261/72-2040; www.sounds-like-cafe.com; 8am-5:30pm Sat.-Wed., last food order 5pm; breakfast from ¥900, lunch from ¥1,050, coffee from ¥350, dessert from ¥400; 30 minutes' walk southwest of Hakuba Station, with the Hakuba 47 ski area to the southwest and the Happō One resort to the northwest

This great little café serves fantastic coffee, cake, breakfast items (muffins, eggs benedict, and more), burgers, and sandwiches. Service is friendly and the all-wooden interior and laid-back atmosphere make it an inviting place to while away a few hours if you need a break from the slopes. Given its early closing hours, it's best chosen for breakfast or lunch.

Accommodations

Accommodations in Hakuba fill up fast and can be frustratingly hard to book. Thankfully, the choices are seemingly endless. For an extensive list of potential lodgings, check out the websites **Snowbeds**

Travel (www.skijapantravel.com) and **Destination Hakuba** (https://hakuba-travel.com).

SHELTERED INN HAKUBA

836-66 Hokujō, Hakuba-mura, Kitaazumi-gun; tel. 0261/85-2088; https://shelteredinnhakuba.com; ¥13,000 d with breakfast

This clean, cozy lodge is well-located close to restaurants and the slopes of both Happō-One and Hakuba 47. It's run by warm, genuine, foreign staff who know the area intimately and are happy to share their knowledge. All private rooms are nicely decorated and well-appointed, sharing four Western-style bathrooms, a kitchen, and an inviting lounge with cushy sofas and a large flat-screen TV. There are also laundry facilities on-site and complimentary Western breakfast (fruit, toast, cereal). Only operates during ski season. Recommended.

★ BACKCOUNTRY LODGE HAKUBA

14718-174 Hokujō, Hakuba-mura; tel. 050/3497-9595; http://backcountry-hakuba.com; ¥20,000 d

This stylish bed-and-breakfast wins massive points for hospitality. Nestled in a forest and run by a friendly American and Japanese couple, this inviting hideaway offers clean, airy rooms that are tastefully decorated. The hosts are happy to share their local wisdom and make great meals. There are two homey lounges—one with a fireplace—and various other nooks and crannies to relax in. It's located toward the north of the Hakuba Valley, between the Iwatake and Tsugaike ski areas. Free shuttle to and from JR Hakuba Station and Hakuba Happō Bus Center is available upon request. A fantastic base for exploring Hakuba.

HOTEL HIFUMI

4998 Happo, Hakuba-mura; tel. 0261/72-8411; http://www.hakubahifumi.jp; ¥21,500 d pp with two meals

This stylish *ryokan* has swank Japanese rooms with a mix of tatami and wooden floors, and various modern touches. Many of the rooms have private outdoor tubs. For those that don't, shared private tubs can be reserved hourly for free by staying guests. Two communal pools (indoor and outdoor) are accessible to both genders within specified hourly time slots. Japanese-style breakfast and exquisite *kaiseki* dinners are served. It's conveniently located near the Happō-One gondola. There are only 10 rooms, so reserve as far in advance as possible.

Information and Services

The tourism information center is located in front of JR Hakuba Station (tel. 0261/72-3000; 5am-7pm daily in summer, 8am-5pm daily from autumn until spring). Excellent online resources include the **Hakuba Tourism** website (http://hakubatourism.jp), the **Hakuba Valley** website (http://hakubavalley.com/en), and **Hakuba Connect** (www.hakuba-connect.com), which offer information on ski runs, restaurants, nightlife, and gondola schedules.

Transportation

The best way to reach **JR Hakuba Station,** at the heart of the valley, is aboard a limited express train on the JR Ōito line from JR Matsumoto Station (1 hour; limited express Azusa ¥2,140, limited express Shinano ¥3,040).

By bus, you'll have more options. **Alpico** (www.alpico.co.jp) runs shuttles between **Nagano** and Hakuba (1 hour 10 minutes; ¥1,600), and even links to Tokyo's Shinjuku Station Nishi-guchi (5 hours; ¥4,850).

And if your aim is to be gliding through fresh powder the day you touch down in Japan, there's a **"snow shuttle"** that runs to and from the slopes directly from the airports in both Narita and Haneda. See the website (www.naganosnowshuttle.com) for details.

Kyoto 京都

The ancient Japanese capital hardly needs an introduction. It provides the source material for the vision many hold of Japan: geisha, tea ceremony, and more than 1,400 temples and shrines. With more than 12 centuries of heritage, Kyoto is inarguably one of the world's most culturally rich cities. In many ways, it is traditional Japan boiled down to its essence, where its history, spiritual life, aesthetics, ambience, and culinary genius coalesce. It's the ideal complement to Tokyo for any first-time trip to the country.

Kyoto was Japan's capital for almost a millennium. Besides the Kamakura period (1185-1333), when the temporary feudal government moved its political base to Kamakura, the emperor ruled from Kyoto from 794 to 1868. The foundations of Japanese traditional

Highlights

Look for ★ to find recommended sights, activities, dining, and lodging.

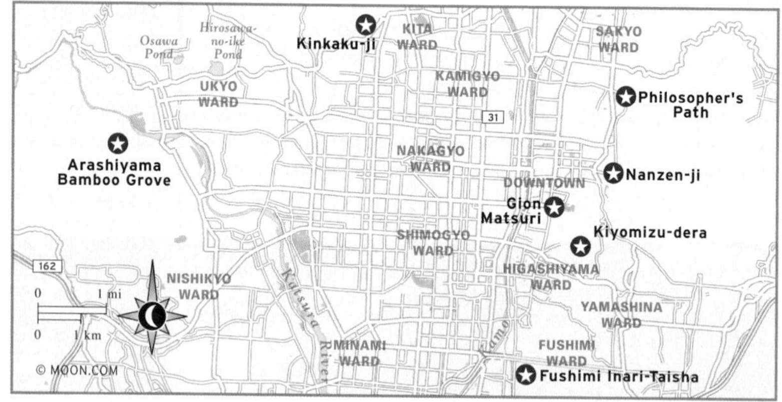

★ **Fushimi Inari-Taisha:** Kyoto's must-see Shinto shrine, the main complex is merely the prelude to a long mountain trail lined with 10,000 vivid *torii* gates (page 301).

★ **Kiyomizu-dera:** This temple sits imposingly atop a hill in the Southern Higashiyama district, affording sweeping views (page 307).

★ **Nanzen-ji:** One of Kyoto's grandest temples, it's surrounded by sub-temples, gardens, an aqueduct, and a hilly trail that leads to a sacred grotto (page 310).

★ **Philosopher's Path:** Seek tranquility with a stroll along this flower-lined pedestrian path, which stretches from Nyakuoji-bashi Bridge to the temple of Ginkaku-ji (page 311).

★ **Kinkaku-ji:** The upper two floors of this famed pavilion, once the retirement villa of shogun Yoshimitsu Ashikaga and now a temple of the Rinzai sect of Zen Buddhism, are gold-plated—an homage to the extravagance of Kyoto's aristocratic past (page 316).

★ **Arashiyama Bamboo Grove:** This magical bamboo grove stretches from the north gate of temple Tenryū-ji to Ōkōchi Sansō Villa (page 321).

★ **Gion Matsuri:** One of Japan's biggest festivals commemorates a purification ritual aimed at appeasing the gods of fire, earthquakes, and floods. Every July, this rite transforms Kyoto's streets into passageways for massive floats, pulled by locals donning colorful traditional attire (page 323).

culture and aesthetics were laid by the aristocracy in Kyoto during the Heian period (794-1185). During the Kamakura period, roughly coinciding with the arrival of Zen Buddhism from China in the early 13th century, an unlikely synergy between the warrior class of Kamakura and Zen monks of Kyoto, who shared values of austerity and self-restraint, allowed Zen to flourish and a new cultural firmament to take shape. Over its long history, Kyoto was struck by fires and wars, but was mercifully spared bombing raids during WWII due to its extraordinary historical and cultural value.

At its heart, Kyoto is a city of temples, particularly of Zen Buddhism. "Kyoto and Zen go together like love and Paris," wrote scholar and scribe John Dougill in the insightful and beautifully photographed *Zen Gardens and Temples of Kyoto.* Monks practice *zazen* (seated meditation) in rooms adorned with brushstrokes of flowing calligraphy, and paintings of misty landscapes and serpentine dragons. They eat elaborate vegetarian feasts (*shōjin ryōri*), and gaze at the simple lines and symbolically placed stones of enigmatic rock gardens. And even today, some unite inner and outer worlds by breathing life into the bamboo flute known as the shakuhachi, a calming instrument that draws one deeply into the present: the simple aim at the core of Zen.

It's easy to be overwhelmed by the sheer number of Buddhist temples—Zen and otherwise—arrayed throughout Kyoto. Highlights include the Zen temples of **Nanzen-ji** and **Gingaku-ji,** the famed rock garden of **Ryōan-ji,** the gold-plated **Kinkaku-ji** (Golden Pavilion) and **Kiyomizu-dera,** perched high above the city with stunning views. As for Shinto shrines, the one must-see is **Fushimi Inari-Taisha** with its hiking trail lined with more than 10,000 vivid *torii,* as the red gates seen at Shinto shrines are called. An equally striking sight is Arashiyama's magical **bamboo grove** on the outskirts of the city.

Beyond the city's temples and shrines, Kyoto is a gourmand's dream. Culinary arts are refined to painstaking levels, with the multicourse haute cuisine known as *kaiseki ryōri* at the pinnacle, often served in atmospheric *machiya* (narrow wooden townhouses known as "bedrooms for eels") scattered around the city's oldest districts. Kyoto is also home to Japan's heaviest concentration of traditional artisans. This is the best place to shop for calligraphy scrolls, goods made from *washi* (traditional hand-made Japanese paper), bamboo tea whisks, lacquerware, tea and sweets, textiles from kimono to *yukata* (lightweight summer kimono), and a variety of other accoutrements, from folding fans to the sorts of elegant hairpins worn by geisha.

ORIENTATION

Kyoto is laid out in a refreshingly simple grid pattern, and the main boulevards and small side streets are often mercifully named. This makes navigating the city easy.

A series of main thoroughfares run east-west through the city, numbered from north to south in ascending order (e.g., Ichijo for "First Avenue," Sanjo for "Third Avenue," etc.). The streets running north-south through the city and intersecting these broad east-west avenues are likewise often named (e.g., Kawaramachi-dōri, Senbon-dōri, etc.). The Kamo River also runs north-south through the city and serves as another geographic marker, with the culturally and historically rich neighborhoods of Gion and Higashiyama east of the river and downtown and the rest of Kyoto to the west.

Kyoto Station Area

Virtually all visitors to Kyoto will first arrive at Kyoto Station, located a 10-minute walk west of the Kamo River. Exiting this mammoth complex of glass and steel can be a jolt and a visceral reminder that Kyoto is a thoroughly modern city with a population of 1.5 million. The cityscape surrounding the station, located in the city's south-central side, is dotted by drab concrete structures, from shopping malls to electronics emporiums. Perhaps the purest embodiment of this is the visually jarring **Kyoto Tower,** located a brief

Kyoto

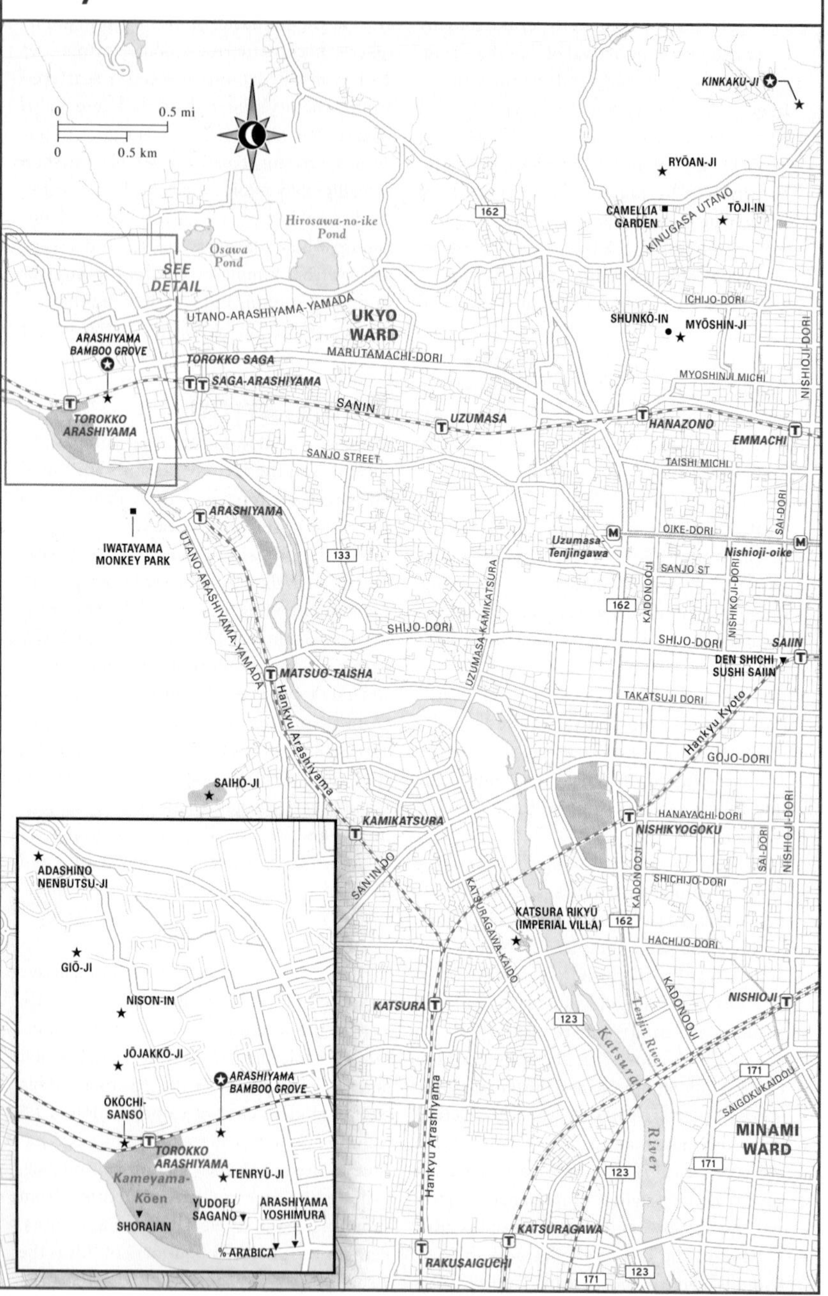

0
0.5 mi
0
0.5 km
KINKAKU-JI
RYŌAN-JI
162
CAMELLIA GARDEN
KINUGASA UTANO
TŌJI-IN
Hirosawa-no-ike Pond
Osawa Pond
SEE DETAIL
UTANO-ARASHIYAMA-YAMADA
UKYO WARD
ICHIJO-DORI
SHUNKŌ-IN
MYŌSHIN-JI
ARASHIYAMA BAMBOO GROVE
TOROKKO SAGA
MARUTAMACHI-DORI
SAGA-ARASHIYAMA
MYOSHINJI MICHI
NISHIOJI-DORI
SANIN
UZUMASA
HANAZONO
TOROKKO ARASHIYAMA
EMMACHI
SANJO STREET
TAISHI MICHI
ARASHIYAMA
SAI-DORI
IWATAYAMA MONKEY PARK
OIKE-DORI
Uzumasa-Tenjingawa
133
Nishioji-oike
UTANO-ARASHIYAMA-YAMADA
UZUMASA-KAMIKATSURA
SANJO ST
KADONOOJI
NISHIKOJI-DORI
162
SHIJO-DORI
SHIJO-DORI
SAIIN
DEN SHICHI SUSHI SAIIN
MATSUO-TAISHA
TAKATSUJI DORI
Hankyu Kyoto
Hankyu Arashiyama
GOJO-DORI
SAIHŌ-JI
HANAYACHI-DORI
NISHIKYOGOKU
KAMIKATSURA
SAN'IN DO
SHICHIJO-DORI
KATSURA RIKYŪ (IMPERIAL VILLA)
KATSURAGAWA-KAIDO
162
HACHIJO-DORI
KATSURA
NISHIOJI
123
Katsura River
Tenjin River
171
SAIGOKUKAIDOU
MINAMI WARD
123
171
KATSURAGAWA
RAKUSAIGUCHI
171
123
ADASHINO NENBUTSU-JI
GIŌ-JI
NISON-IN
JŌJAKKŌ-JI
ARASHIYAMA BAMBOO GROVE
ŌKŌCHI-SANSO
TOROKKO ARASHIYAMA
Kameyama-Kōen
TENRYŪ-JI
YUDOFU SAGANO
ARASHIYAMA YOSHIMURA
SHORAIAN
% ARABICA

KYOTO

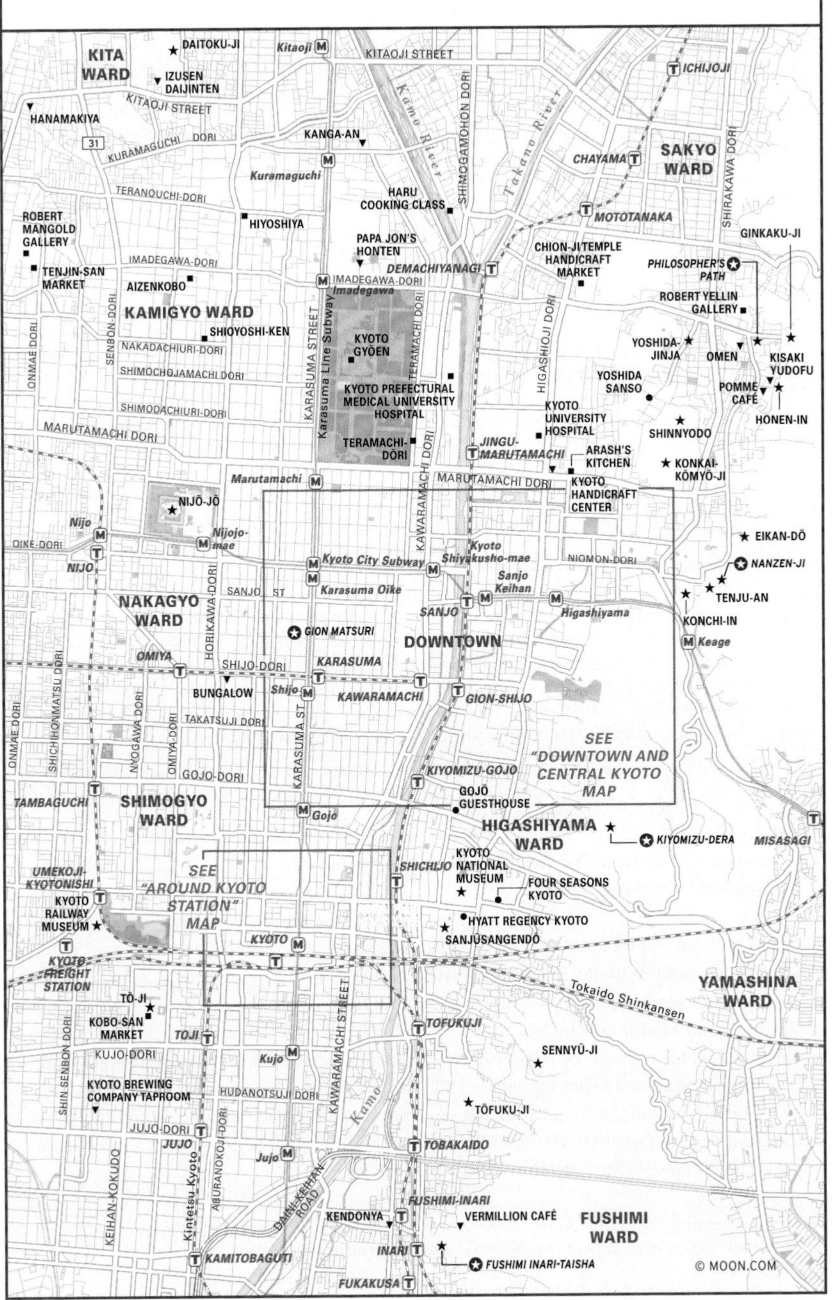
KITA WARD
DAITOKU-JI
IZUSEN DAIJINTEN
Kitaoji
KITAOJI STREET
HANAMAKIYA
31
KURAMAGUCHI DORI
KANGA-AN
Kuramaguchi
Kamo River
SHIMOGAMOHON DORI
Takano River
ICHIJOJI
CHAYAMA
SAKYO WARD
SHIRAKAWA DORI
TERANOUCHI-DORI
HARU COOKING CLASS
MOTOTANAKA
ROBERT MANGOLD GALLERY
HIYOSHIYA
PAPA JON'S HONTEN
GINKAKU-JI
CHION-JI TEMPLE HANDICRAFT MARKET
IMADEGAWA-DORI
TENJIN-SAN MARKET
AIZENKOBO
Imadegawa
DEMACHIYANAGI
PHILOSOPHER'S PATH
ROBERT YELLIN GALLERY
KAMIGYO WARD
Karasuma Line Subway
KARASUMA STREET
TERAMACHI DORI
HIGASHIOJI DORI
SHIOYOSHI-KEN
KYOTO GYOEN
YOSHIDA-JINJA
OMEN
KISAKI YUDOFU
ONMAE DORI
SENBON DORI
NAKADACHIURI-DORI
SHIMOCHOJAMACHI DORI
KYOTO PREFECTURAL MEDICAL UNIVERSITY HOSPITAL
YOSHIDA SANSO
POMME CAFÉ
SHIMODACHIURI-DORI
KYOTO UNIVERSITY HOSPITAL
HONEN-IN
SHINNYODO
MARUTAMACHI DORI
TERAMACHI-DŌRI
JINGU-MARUTAMACHI
ARASH'S KITCHEN
KONKAI-KŌMYŌ-JI
Marutamachi
KAWARAMACHI DORI
MARUTAMACHI DORI
KYOTO HANDICRAFT CENTER
NIJŌ-JŌ
Nijo
Nijojo-mae
EIKAN-DŌ
OIKE-DORI
NIJO
Kyoto City Subway
Kyoto Shiyakusho-mae
NIOMON-DORI
NANZEN-JI
Karasuma Oike
Sanjo Keihan
SANJO ST
TENJU-AN
NAKAGYO WARD
HORIKAWA-DORI
SANJO
Higashiyama
KONCHI-IN
GION MATSURI
DOWNTOWN
Keage
OMIYA
SHIJO-DORI
KARASUMA
SHICHIHONMATSU DORI
BUNGALOW
Shijo
KAWARAMACHI
GION-SHIJO
TAKATSUJI DORI
ONMAE DORI
MIBUGAWA DORI
OMIYA-DORI
KARASUMA ST
SEE "DOWNTOWN AND CENTRAL KYOTO MAP"
GOJO-DORI
KIYOMIZU-GOJO
TAMBAGUCHI
SHIMOGYO WARD
GOJŌ GUESTHOUSE
Gojo
HIGASHIYAMA WARD
KIYOMIZU-DERA
MISASAGI
SEE "AROUND KYOTO STATION" MAP
SHICHIJO
KYOTO NATIONAL MUSEUM
UMEKOJI-KYOTONISHI
FOUR SEASONS KYOTO
KYOTO RAILWAY MUSEUM
HYATT REGENCY KYOTO
SANJŪSANGENDŌ
KYOTO
KYOTO FREIGHT STATION
Tokaido Shinkansen
YAMASHINA WARD
KAWARAMACHI STREET
TŌ-JI
KOBO-SAN MARKET
TOJI
TOFUKUJI
SHIN SENBON DORI
KUJO-DORI
Kujo
SENNYŪ-JI
KYOTO BREWING COMPANY TAPROOM
HUDANOTSUJI DORI
Kamo
TŌFUKU-JI
JUJO-DORI
JUJO
TOBAKAIDO
Jujo
KEIHAN-KOKUDO
Kintetsu Kyoto
ABURANOKOJI-DORI
DAINI-KEIHAN ROAD
FUSHIMI-INARI
KENDONYA
VERMILLION CAFÉ
FUSHIMI WARD
INARI
KAMITOBAGUTI
FUSHIMI INARI-TAISHA
FUKAKUSA
© MOON.COM

Best Restaurants

★ **Ishibekoji Kamikura:** At this friendly *kaiseki* restaurant, the meal is as visually impressive as it is delicious (page 333).

★ **Kagizen Yoshifusa Kodaiji:** This cozy branch of an iconic traditional dessert café is a great spot to sample a traditional sweet with a cup of powdered green tea (page 334).

★ **Omen:** This udon shop is an ideal place to stop for lunch as you walk along the philosopher's path in one of the most tranquil parts of the city (page 334).

★ **Tōsuirō:** Enjoy exploring creative spins on tofu and *yuba* (tofu skin) at this atmospheric riverside restaurant (page 337).

★ **Café Bibliotic Hello!:** This chic café is a hip hideaway, ideal for a coffee break or light meal off the tourist trail, tucked down a quiet street in the center of downtown (page 338).

★ **Izusen Daijinten:** Sample Buddhism's unique culinary contribution to global food culture, *shōjin-ryōri*, at this idyllic restaurant situated in a temple complex (page 338).

★ **Shoraian:** Feast on a surprisingly affordable *kaiseki* spread in this lovely restaurant in the hills of Arashiyama, overlooking the Katsura River (page 338).

REGIONAL SPECIALTIES

Kaiseki ryōri is essentially Japanese fine dining. These elaborate, multi-course meals grew out of what were long ago simpler meals served after tea ceremonies. Dishes in a *kaiseki* meal are served in a very specific order, often beginning with an aperitif such as a small cup of *nihonshū* (rice wine) and a small appetizer, followed by soup, sashimi, individual dishes that are, respectively, boiled, grilled, deep-fried, steamed, and served in a vinegar-based sauce. This is generally followed by rice, pickled vegetables, and miso soup, and finally, a light dessert, which is often fresh fruit or ***wagashi*** (Japanese sweets), which are themselves another Kyoto specialty.

walk north of the station. There are also a few more attractive sights in the area, including the **Higashi Hongan-ji** temple complex.

Southeast Kyoto

Moving beyond the Kyoto Station area, the city's history remains preserved in bronze, bamboo, and wood, and tucked down atmospheric lanes around the edges of town. Beginning in Southeast Kyoto, located roughly 30 minutes' walk southeast of Kyoto Station, the major draw of this district is the spellbinding shrine complex of **Fushimi Inari-Taisha,** famed for its tunnel of vermillion *torii* gates that winds over a mountain trail. The splendid **Tofuku-ji** temple complex is also located in the area, about 10 minutes' walk north of Fushimi Inari-Taisha.

To access this rich district, take the JR Nara line from Kyoto Station to Tofukuji Station (for Tofuku-ji) or Inari Station (for Fushimi Inari-Taisha). It's also possible to walk from Kyoto Station to Tofuku-ji (25 minutes) or from Fushimi Inari-Taisha (40 minutes), or make either journey quicker by traveling on a bicycle.

Previous: Fushimi Inari-Taisha Shrine; Arashiyama Bamboo Grove; Gion Matsuri.

Best Accommodations

★ **Hotel Granvia:** This clean modern hotel, literally in the Kyoto Station building, wins big points for convenience (page 343).

★ **Yuzuya Ryokan:** This refined *ryokan* option in Northern Higashiyama occupies a prime location, right beside Yasaka-jinja and a short walk from downtown (page 344).

★ **Hotel The Celestine Kyoto Gion:** A phenomenal new modern hotel in a quiet pocket of Gion, this is a fantastic option at the higher end of the midrange hotels (page 344).

★ **Yoshida Sansō:** This discreet luxury *ryokan,* close to nature in a quiet part of northern Higashiyama near Ginkaku-ji, remains slightly off the radar (page 346).

★ **The Millennials Kyoto:** This sleek capsule hotel, with a shared lounge and workspace, is a great choice for young travelers on the go (page 346).

★ **Iori Machiya Stay Residence:** Rent a classic old *machiya* townhouse, with historic charm and modern creature comforts, in the heart of downtown (page 346).

★ **Ritz-Carlton Kyoto:** The Ritz offers a fantastic mix of luxury and convenience in the city center, with stellar amenities and a renowned *kaiseki* restaurant (page 348).

Southern Higashiyama

Heading north from there about 15 minutes on foot brings you to the southern edge of the large district of Higashiyama, which occupies most of the eastern half of the city. Southern Higashiyama's best-known sight is the crowd-pleasing temple complex of **Kiyomizu-dera.** Other notable spots in the area include the temple of **Sanjūsangen-dō,** which houses roughly 1,000 effigies of Kannon, Buddhism's goddess of mercy, and the huge complex of **Chion-in,** the head temple of the Jōdo school of Pure Land Buddhism.

The easiest way to reach the area is via the Karasuma subway line from Kyoto Station, exiting at Karasuma-Oike Station and transferring to the Tōzai line to Higashiyama Station. From here, the district spreads out to the south.

Gion

About 5 minutes' walk southwest of Chion-in leads to **Yasaka-jinja,** the important shrine presiding over the district of Gion, the city's main entertainment district, which lies along the eastern bank of the Kamo River and just west of the northern edge of Southern Higashiyama. This area originally developed into an entertainment hub to cater to the earthly needs of the pilgrims who came to visit the grand Yasaka-jinja, and today, it remains the best part of the city to observe the sensuous "floating world" of nighttime pleasures that have developed over the centuries. Think kabuki performances, geisha flitting over cobblestone streets, well-heeled guests tucking into multicourse feasts, and bars where hostesses carouse with loose-lipped businessmen.

To get to Gion, take the Keihan line to Gion-Shijō Station. The neighborhood of Gion surrounds the station.

Northern Higashiyama

Northern Higashiyama lies north of Gion and Southern Higashiyama. Major sights in this popular sightseeing district include the grand shrine of **Heian-jingū,** the wonderful temple complex of **Nanzen-ji, and** the vaunted **Philosopher's Path,** and at the northern edge of the district lie the beautiful temple grounds of **Ginkaku-ji.**

Starting at Kyoto Station, reach the area via the Karasuma subway line, transferring at Karasuma-Oike Station to the Tōzai line and exiting at either Higashiyama Station in the area's west, or Keage Station in the east, and walking north from either one.

Downtown and Central Kyoto

The vast swath of town north of Kyoto Station and along the western bank of the Kamo River, sitting opposite Gion and Northern Higashiyama, includes Downtown and Central Kyoto, which make up the central core of Kyoto. Like the Kyoto Station area, this part of town is very much part of the less aesthetically pleasing modern side of town. This large area's main sights include the dreamy cobblestone alleyway of **Ponto-chō** and the castle of **Nijō-jō.** Otherwise, this part of town is mainly a place to wine, dine and shop.

This area is highly walkable and can be reached from Kyoto Station by riding the Karasuma subway line to Shijo Station near the southwest corner of the downtown area, or to Karasuma-Oike Station in the neighborhood's northwest corner.

Northwest Kyoto

Moving west of Downtown and Central Kyoto, the district of Northwest Kyoto is another major sightseeing area, despite its slightly farther-flung position. A few standout sights in the area include the famously gilt temple of **Kinkaku-ji** and the iconic Zen temple of **Ryōan-ji,** known for its classic rock garden. Nearby, the less thronged temple complex of **Myōshin-ji** also begs to be explored.

To reach the area from Kyoto Station, take the JR San-in line to Hanazono Station, a short walk south of the temple of Myōshin-ji, from where it's possible to walk north to Ryōan-ji (25 minutes) and then Kinkaku-ji (20 minutes). If you're cycling, reach the area by following Karasuma-dōri north from Kyoto Station, passing the Kyoto Imperial Palace on your right and turning left on Imadegawa-dōri. Continue cycling west on this road for another 3.7 km (2.3 mi) to Ryōan-ji station. The area's main sights are spread out in the neighborhood north of here.

Arashiyama

In the far west of town, Arashiyama is, along with both Southern and Northern Higashiyama, among Kyoto's most crowded areas. Running through the heart of the district is the area's ethereal **bamboo grove,** with the temple of **Tenryū-ji** sitting near the bamboo grove's south end and the dreamy house and gardens of the **Ōkōchi-Sansō Villa** occupying a lofty spot above the area, affording great views of the city.

Arashiyama is located about 30 minutes by train from Kyoto Station, along the Katsura River and near the base of the Arashiyama mountain range. Take the JR Sagano/San-in line from Kyoto Station to Saga-Arashiyama Station, from where most the area's sights are about 10 minutes' walk to the southwest.

Around Kyoto

Around Kyoto there are a few appealing escapes from downtown in the mountains surrounding town. You'll find trails in the nearby mountains bordering the town to the east, north, and northwest, which run to atmospheric temples that only attract a fraction of the crowds seen in town. North of Downtown and Central Kyoto, a hiking trail will take you to the mountain temple of **Kurama-dera** and shrines of **Yuki-jinja** and **Kifune-jinja.** Nearby sits one of Kyoto's top *onsen*, **Kurama Onsen**. And in the mountains northwest of town, the village of Takao is home to the three temples of **Jingo-ji, Saimyo-ji,** and **Kozan-ji,** a UNESCO site.

PLANNING YOUR TIME

Like most of Japan, Kyoto is a highly seasonal destination. In spring (Mar.-May), an explosion of cherry blossoms bathes the city in a soft pink glow. In autumn (late Oct.-Nov.), foliage bursts into shades of red, orange, yellow, and brown—a photographer's dream.

TOP EXPERIENCE

Kyoto's Less Crowded Side

Kyoto's treasures are well-known—and extremely crowded. Its most popular temples host almost Disneyland-level throngs. The most famous sights are still amazing, crowds aside, but given how popular Kyoto has become, having genuinely good offbeat alternatives to escape the crowds is very important. Throughout this chapter, strategies for escaping crowds will be covered, but here are a few general suggestions.

The usual advice is, try to avoid coming to Kyoto during its peak seasons (late Mar.-early Apr. and Nov., and the O-bon holidays of mid-Aug.), and to **visit attractions at off-peak times**: before 8am or after 4pm on weekdays. Also keep in mind that some sights, including stand-outs like Fushimi Inari-Taisha and the Arashiyama Bamboo Grove are open **24/7.**

But it also pays to balance your itinerary with a mix of greatest hits and lesser-known gems. The city's most crowded spots include the spellbinding shrine of **Fushimi Inari-Taisha** in the southeast; the hilltop temple of **Kiyomizu-dera** and **Ginkaku-ji** in southern and northern Higashiyama, respectively; **Nijō-jō** in the city center; the famed rock garden of **Ryōan-ji** and gold-plated **Kinkaku-ji** in the northwest; and **Arashiyama's bamboo grove** in the far west. Luckily, most of these sites have stunning, less crowded options just a short walk away.

Finally, no matter where you are, dare to discover your own version of the city by simply veering a few blocks (or more!) off the beaten path. Charming shops, antique wooden townhouses, and local shrines well off the radar are the deeper pulse of the city as it lives today.

The off-seasons are the stuffy days of summer (June-Aug.)—note that June is on average the rainiest month of the year—and winter (Dec.-Feb.), which is cold and sometimes snowy but not overly harsh; lows range from 1-3°C (34-37°F), and highs hover around 9-11°C (48-52°F).

Be aware the city is besieged by the camera-wielding masses during *hanami* (cherry blossom viewing) season around the end of March and early April, and at the peak of *kōyō* in November, when autumn leaves reach their peak. If you don't mind sharing the city with large tour groups from the Asian mainland, and other international travelers, these times of year are popular for a reason.

Things have died down a bit by the second week of May, after an extended national holiday known as Golden Week passes, and in October, when the summer heat has passed but autumn foliage hasn't yet drawn massive crowds. If you don't mind sticky weather, June through August have long, glorious evenings that provide ideal conditions for strolling along the burbling Kamo River.

You'll ideally have two to five days to explore the city. However, even with only one day, you'll be able to see a handful of the city's key temples and shrines, which are clustered mainly around the southern Higashiyama area and west of the city in the famous district of Arashiyama.

Itinerary Ideas

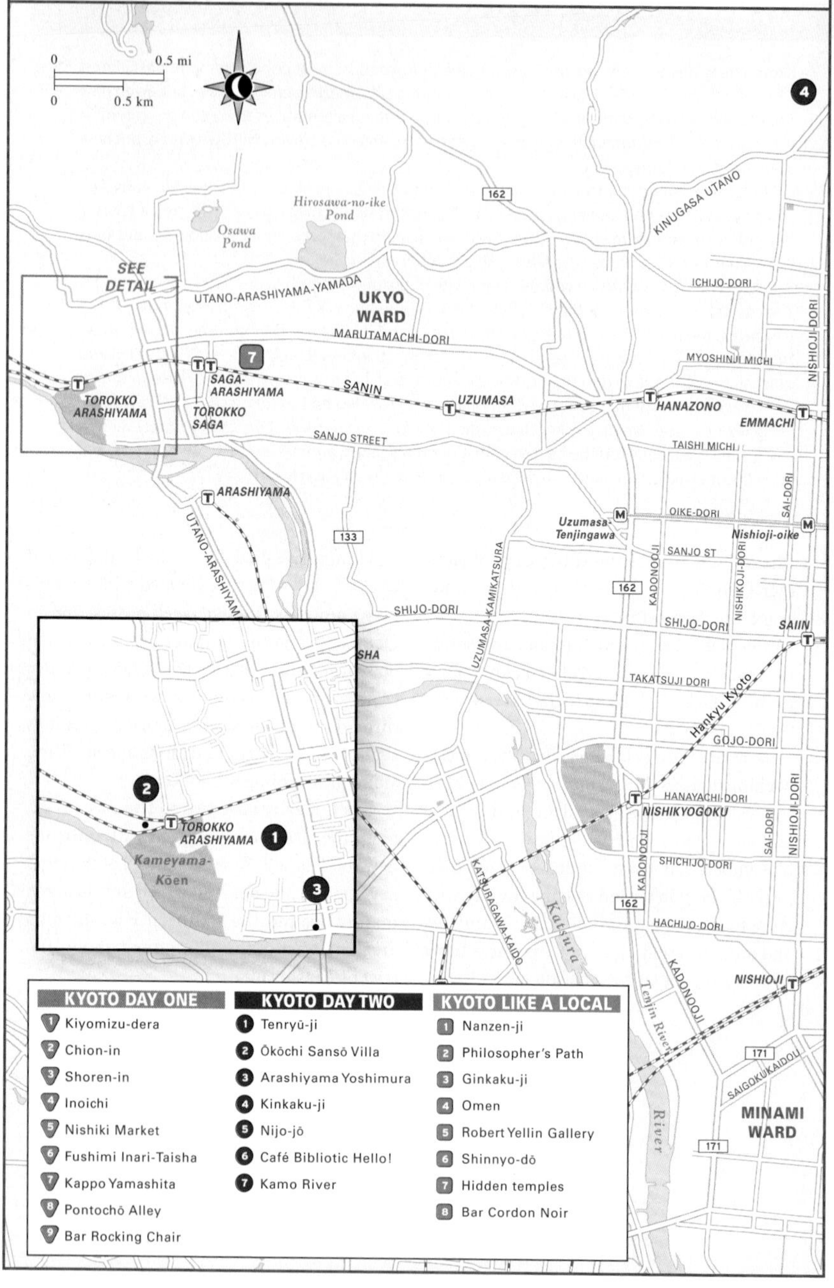

0 0.5 mi
0 0.5 km

4
162
KINUGASA UTANO
Hirosawa-no-ike Pond
Osawa Pond
SEE DETAIL
ICHIJO-DORI
UTANO-ARASHIYAMA-YAMADA
UKYO WARD
MARUTAMACHI-DORI
NISHIOJI-DORI
7
MYOSHINJI MICHI
SAGA-ARASHIYAMA
SANIN
TOROKKO ARASHIYAMA
TOROKKO SAGA
UZUMASA
HANAZONO
EMMACHI
SANJO STREET
TAISHI MICHI
ARASHIYAMA
SAI-DORI
OIKE-DORI
Uzumasa-Tenjingawa
Nishioji-oike
133
SANJO ST
UTANO-ARASHIYAMA
162
KADONOOJI
NISHIKOJI-DORI
UZUMASA-KAMIKATSURA
SHIJO-DORI
SHIJO-DORI
SAIIN
SHA
TAKATSUJI DORI
Hankyu Kyoto
GOJO-DORI
2
HANAYACHI-DORI
NISHIKYOGOKU
TOROKKO ARASHIYAMA
1
Kameyama-Kōen
3
SAI-DORI
NISHIOJI-DORI
SHICHIJO-DORI
KADONOOJI
KATSURAGAWA-KAIDO
162
HACHIJO-DORI
Katsura
KADONOOJI
NISHIOJI
Tenjin River
171
SAIGOKUKAIDOU
MINAMI WARD
171

KYOTO DAY ONE

1. Kiyomizu-dera
2. Chion-in
3. Shoren-in
4. Inoichi
5. Nishiki Market
6. Fushimi Inari-Taisha
7. Kappo Yamashita
8. Pontochō Alley
9. Bar Rocking Chair

KYOTO DAY TWO

1. Tenryū-ji
2. Ōkōchi Sansō Villa
3. Arashiyama Yoshimura
4. Kinkaku-ji
5. Nijo-jō
6. Café Bibliotic Hello!
7. Kamo River

KYOTO LIKE A LOCAL

1. Nanzen-ji
2. Philosopher's Path
3. Ginkaku-ji
4. Omen
5. Robert Yellin Gallery
6. Shinnyo-dō
7. Hidden temples
8. Bar Cordon Noir

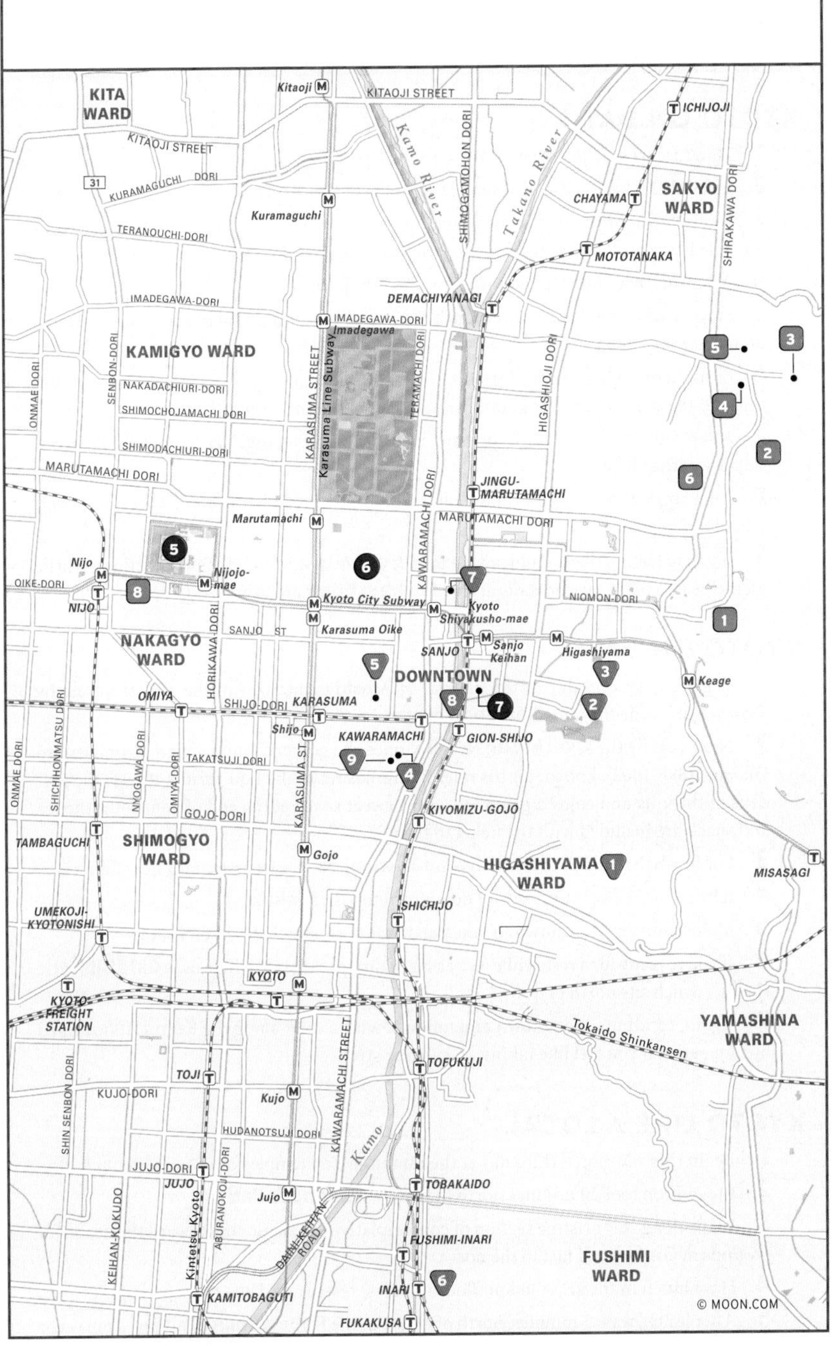
KITA WARD
KITAOJI STREET
Kitaoji
KITAOJI STREET
Kamo River
Takano River
SHIMOGAMOHON DORI
ICHIJOJI
31
KURAMAGUCHI DORI
Kuramaguchi
CHAYAMA
SAKYO WARD
SHIRAKAWA DORI
TERANOUCHI-DORI
MOTOTANAKA
IMADEGAWA-DORI
DEMACHIYANAGI
IMADEGAWA-DORI
Imadegawa
KAMIGYO WARD
SENBON-DORI
KARASUMA STREET
Karasuma Line Subway
TERAMACHI DORI
HIGASHIOJI DORI
NAKADACHIURI-DORI
SHIMOCHOJAMACHI DORI
ONMAE DORI
SHIMODACHIURI-DORI
MARUTAMACHI DORI
KAWARAMACHI DORI
JINGU-MARUTAMACHI
Marutamachi
MARUTAMACHI DORI
Nijo
Nijojo-mae
OIKE-DORI
NIJO
Kyoto City Subway
Kyoto Shiyakusho-mae
NIOMON-DORI
SANJO ST
Karasuma Oike
NAKAGYO WARD
HORIKAWA-DORI
SANJO
Sanjo Keihan
Higashiyama
DOWNTOWN
Keage
OMIYA
SHIJO-DORI
KARASUMA
Shijo
KAWARAMACHI
GION-SHIJO
SHICHIHONMATSU DORI
NYOGAWA DORI
OMIYA-DORI
TAKATSUJI DORI
ONMAE DORI
KARASUMA ST
KIYOMIZU-GOJO
GOJO-DORI
TAMBAGUCHI
SHIMOGYO WARD
Gojo
HIGASHIYAMA WARD
MISASAGI
UMEKOJI-KYOTONISHI
SHICHIJO
KYOTO
KYOTO FREIGHT STATION
KAWARAMACHI STREET
Tokaido Shinkansen
YAMASHINA WARD
TOFUKUJI
TOJI
SHIN SENBON DORI
KUJO-DORI
Kujo
HUDANOTSUJI DORI
Kamo
JUJO-DORI
JUJO
ABURANOKOJI-DORI
TOBAKAIDO
Jujo
KEIHAN-KOKUDO
Kintetsu Kyoto
DAINI-KEIHAN ROAD
FUSHIMI-INARI
FUSHIMI WARD
INARI
KAMITOBAGUTI
© MOON.COM
FUKAKUSA

Itinerary Ideas

KYOTO ON DAY 1

1 Plan to start at **Kiyomizu-dera,** arriving before 9am.

2 From there, head to the vast temple complex of **Chion-in.**

3 Next, stop at **Shoren-in,** a lovely temple 5 minutes' walk north of Chion-in, where it's possible to sip tea while gazing onto a garden.

4 After this, have lunch downtown at ramen shop **Inoichi.**

5 Stop by **Nishiki Market** after lunch if you feel like doing a bit of shopping for traditional culinary items.

6 From here, swing over to **Fushimi Inari-Taisha** and spend the afternoon walking through the atmospheric mountain path, lined with vermillion gates.

7 After your afternoon of exploration, rest until the evening. Try haute *kaiseki* fare at **Kappo Yamashita.**

8 After dinner, take a nighttime stroll through **Pontochō Alley,** soaking up the old-school ambience.

9 If you're feeling like a nightcap, go for a few drinks downtown. For something a little off the beaten path, the cocktails at **Bar Rocking Chair** are wonderful.

KYOTO ON DAY 2

1 Begin the second day in the district of Arashiyama, west of the city, stopping by **Tenryū-ji,** beside the famed **bamboo grove.**

2 Next stop by the **Ōkōchi Sansō Villa,** once the gorgeous home of an actor, Denjirō Ōkōchi (1898-1962), known for his roles in dramas set in the Edo period. Peruse the gardens of the villa and enjoy a green tea with a sweet snack at the end of your tour; the tea and snack are included with the ticket to the villa.

3 For lunch, backtrack to **Arashiyama Yoshimura,** a soba restaurant near Tenryū-ji.

4 Return to the northwest side of downtown to visit **Kinkaku-ji.**

5 Make your way downtown. If you feel up for it, stop by **Nijo-jō** en route.

6 If you're ready for a rest, while away a bit of time at the stylish hideaway **Café Bibliotic Hello!,** which sits north of downtown.

7 Again, eat dinner downtown and follow it with a walk along the **Kamo River,** lined by foot paths, if you feel like taking an evening stroll.

KYOTO LIKE A LOCAL

1 Begin this additional third day at the rambling Zen temple complex of **Nanzen-ji.**

2 Proceed on foot 20 minutes north to the **Philosopher's Path.**

3 Walk along this pristine section of contemplative canal, moving toward the beautiful grounds of **Ginkaku-ji** just to the north.

4 Have lunch in the area—udon (flour noodles) restaurant **Omen** is a good pick.

5 After lunch, walk 5 minutes' north of Omen to the **Robert Yellin Gallery,** a purveyor

of exquisite ceramics (*yakimono*). Be sure to call or email ahead to check if Robert will be there when you plan to visit.

6 Walk 15 minutes southwest of Robert's gallery to a quiet pocket of Northern Higashiyama. You'll discover off-the-beaten-path gems like the temples of **Shinnyo-dō** and **Konkai-Kōmyō-ji.**

7 From there, walk 20 minutes southwest to Higashiyama Station on the Tōzai subway line. Take the train to Nijō Station, then transfer to the JR Sagano line and ride to Saga-Arashiyama Station for a total trip of about 25 minutes (¥460). Walk 15 minutes northwest from Saga-Arashiyama Station to a cluster of **hidden temples** beyond the area's clogged bamboo grove. These quieter gems include Giō-ji, Nison-in and Jōjakkō-ji.

8 Have dinner either downtown or in Gion, and put a cap on the evening by sampling whisky at **Bar Cordon Noir.** Or see what's happening at Urbanguild, one of the city's more avant garde nightlife spots.

Sights

KYOTO STATION AREA

Aside from a few temples hiding inside this slice of decidedly modern Japan, Kyoto's treasures lie in the districts beyond. View the station area as a means to an end: the city's entry and exit point, and a place to handle logistics and shopping.

Kyoto Tower

京都タワー

Karasuma-dōri, Shichijo sagaru, Shimogyō-ku; tel. 075/361-3215; www.kyoto-tower.co.jp; 9am-9pm daily; ¥800 adults, ¥650 high school students, ¥550 elementary and junior high school students, ¥150 children over three; take JR lines to Kyoto Station, Karasuma central exit

Five minutes' walk north of Kyoto Station,

Tō-ji pagoda

Around Kyoto Station

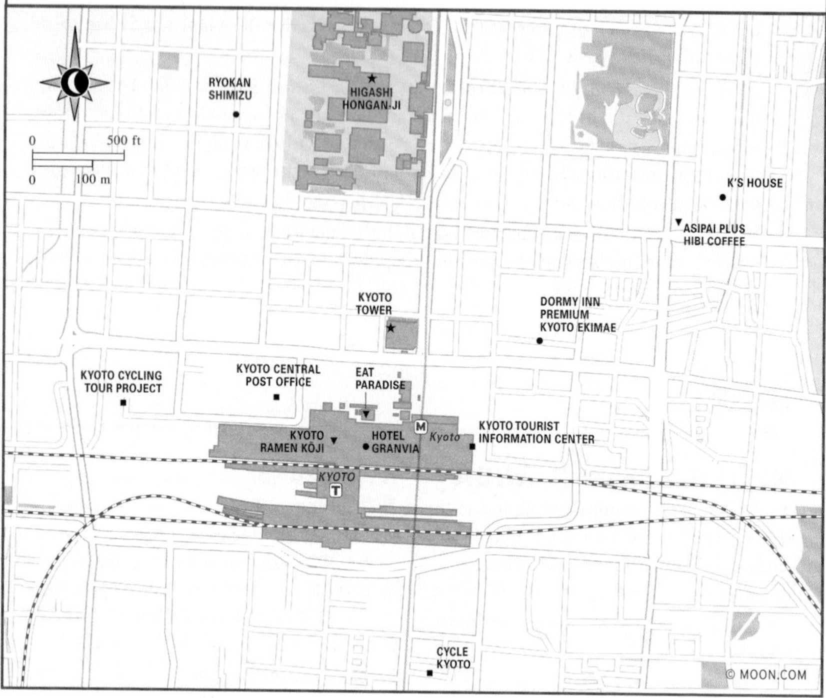

you'll encounter an eyesore of a monument that Japanologist and author Alex Kerr once called "a stake through the heart of the city." Behold, 131-meter (430-foot) Kyoto Tower, built in 1963. You'll want to move outward toward the more historic districts, but if you must stop by, it is true that there are great vistas from the viewing deck up top.

Higashi Hongan-ji
東本願寺

Karasuma-dōri, Shichijō-agaru, Shimogyō-ku; tel. 075/371-9181; www.higashihonganji.or.jp; 5:50am-5:30pm daily Mar.-Oct., 6:20am-4:30pm daily Nov.-Feb., free; walk 12 minutes north of Kyoto Station via the Karasuma central exit

A short walk north from Kyoto Tower, up the main north-south artery of Karashuma-dōri, you'll find a stunning sight that is thankfully much more in line with what you'd expect to see in Kyoto: Higashi Hongan-ji. The main hall of this temple is one of the largest wooden structures on the planet.

Unfortunately, you can't glimpse much beyond the facade of this complex, so the altars and artwork remain shrouded from view. But the buildings themselves still induce a sense of awe, with both their scale and their elaborate gold-plated flourishes. This vast temple complex is by far the most splendid glimpse of Kyoto's illustrious past in the area surrounding the station.

Kyoto Railway Museum
京都鉄道博物館

Kankiji-chō, Shimogyō-ku; tel. 0570/080-462; www.kyotorailwaymuseum.jp; 10am-5:30pm Thurs.-Tues.; ¥1,200 adults, ¥1,000 university and high school students, ¥500 junior high and elementary students, ¥200 children over three; walk 20 minutes west of

JR Kyoto Station, or take bus no. 205 or 208 from JR Kyoto Station to Umekoji-kōen-mae stop, or bus no. 104 or 110 to Umekōji-kōen/Kyoto Railway Museum-mae stop

If you're looking for a great rainy-day option, or you simply want a break from temple hopping, head to the Kyoto Railway Museum. A hit with kids and train lovers, this museum was formerly the Umekoji Steam Locomotive Museum. In 2016, it received a makeover and was reopened as the Kyoto Railway Museum, which traces train history from the steam engine all the way through to the bullet train. Old bullet-train models, commuter trains from days past, and even steam locomotives are on display and can be entered and explored. It's also possible to hop aboard a steam locomotive and go for a short ride (¥300 adults, ¥100 children).

Tō-ji

東寺

1 Kujō-chō, Minami-ku; tel. 075/691-3325; www.toji.or.jp; 8:30am-4:30pm Mar. 20-Apr. 17, 8:30am-5pm Apr. 18-Sept. 19, 8:30am-4pm Sept. 20-Mar. 19; grounds free, ¥500 kondo and kodo, ¥500 treasure hall, ¥800 pagoda (only 9am-4pm), kondo and kodo; take the Kintetsu line to Tō-ji Station, then walk 10 minutes west

Thanks to its towering pagoda, Tō-ji is one of the more visually prominent temples in the Kyoto Station area. Located southwest of the station, this wooden spire rises from a small sea of gloomy apartment blocks like a beacon of hope and a reminder that the heart of tradition still beats here too.

The best time to visit—perhaps the main reason—is its Kobo-san market, held on the 21st of every month. This is an excellent stop to add to your itinerary if you're keen to visit a flea market. Be sure to come early in the day, before goods have been picked over.

SOUTHEAST KYOTO

Southeast Kyoto is dense in noteworthy sights, and the area is slightly less crowded than Southern Higashiyama, to its north.

★ Fushimi Inari-Taisha

伏見稲荷大社

68 Yabunouchi-chō, Fukakusa, Fushimi-ku; tel. 075/561-1551; http://inari.jp; dawn to dusk daily; free; take the JR Nara Line to Inari Station, or the Keihan Railway line to Fushimi-Inari Station

If you only have time to visit one Shinto shrine during your stay in Kyoto, make it Fushimi Inari-Taisha. It is the head shrine for 40,000 shrines throughout Japan that are dedicated to Inari, the *kami* (god) of fertility, rice, sake, and prosperity.

Easily one of the most arresting sights in Kyoto, the bewitching complex spreads across a mountain, where more than 10,000 vermilion *torii* gates envelop a 4-km (2.5-mi) path through heavily wooded terrain. Hundreds of stone foxes with granary keys in their mouths stand watch over the complex, which consists of five shrines, numerous mausoleums, and altars where devotees leave open cartons of sake as offerings.

Ambling through the tunnel of red may feel ethereal, but the chief concerns of the shrine's deity are strongly rooted in the cares of the physical world. The site was originally dedicated to the gods of rice and sake when it was founded by the Hata family in AD 711. Its focus gradually shifted to commerce as farmers' clout waned and merchants' status increased. The black kanji characters etched deeply into the bright red beams of the seemingly endless rows of *torii* appear arcane. They are, in fact, the names of companies that have donated the gates to the shrine in the hope of achieving business success.

It's interesting to note that Japanese tradition deems the fox a mystical animal with the power to possess human beings by entering via the fingernails. Spiritual possession aside, if you're on the path as the sun begins to fall, the slightly eerie atmosphere may spook even the staunchest skeptic.

Tōfuku-ji

東福寺

15-778 Honmahi, Higashiyama-ku; tel. 075/561-0087; www.tofukuji.jp; 9am-4pm daily; grounds free,

奉納
1
2
3

Hōjō garden ¥400 adults and ¥300 junior high and elementary students, Tsūten-kyō and Kaizan-dō ¥400 adults and ¥300 junior high and elementary students; walk 7 minutes southeast from Tōfuku-ji Station, (JR Nara, Keihan lines)

A Zen enclave about 20 minutes' walk north of Fushimi Inari-Taisha is Tōfuku-ji, this fantastic temple complex is less crowded than you'd expect—except during autumn (especially Nov.) when its justly famous foliage pops with earth tones and fiery reds.

Surrounded by a wall, the temple grounds include the superb *Hōjō* garden. This carefully shaped landscape is an otherworldly expression of Zen, with mossy islands amid oceans of raked gravel, adroitly pruned shrubs, checkerboard patterns formed with natural elements, and misshapen stones suggesting imaginary mountains. This is a worthy stop and markedly less crowded than the great temples to the north in Higashiyama.

Sennyū-ji
泉涌寺

27 Yamanouchi-chō, Sennyū-ji, Higashiyama-ku; tel. 075/561-1551; www.mitera.org; 9am-5pm Mar.-Nov., 9am-4:30pm Dec.-Feb.; ¥500 adults, ¥300 junior high and elementary school students; walk 15 minutes southeast from Tōfuku-ji Station (JR Nara, Keihan lines)

After jostling through the camera-wielding masses at nearby Fushimi Inari-Taisha, this temple is a breath of fresh air. You may have the place all to yourself (or close to it). Uphill and well away from other tourists, about 5 minutes' walk northeast of Tōfuku-ji, it has a beautiful garden that is absolutely striking during autumn when the foliage turns.

Sennyu-ji gets its name (literally: "bubbling spring temple") from the freshwater spring flowing from its grounds. Situated at the foot of Mount Tsukinowa, this temple's illustrious history includes close ties to Japan's imperial family—hence its alternative name Mitera ("Imperial Temple"). A number of emperors' tombs sit within the walled-off mausoleum on the far side of the garden set deep into the grounds.

Inside the main Buddha hall (Butsu-den), reconstructed in 1668 and bearing architectural accents from China's Song Dynasty (960-1279), you'll find three golden Buddha effigies. Look up and marvel at the dramatic painting of a dragon, soaring overhead, left by the brushstrokes of the master Kanō Tanyū of the illustrious Kano School of painting. There's also a museum (entrance fee included in temple admission) on the grounds, where you'll find sacred texts, art and more on display.

SOUTHERN HIGASHIYAMA

The southern half of this district is the most jam-packed sightseeing area in all of Kyoto.

Sanjūsangen-dō
三十三間堂

657 Sanjusangendoma wari-cho, Higashiyama-ku; tel. 075/561-0467; http://sanjusangendo.jp; 8am-5pm daily Apr.-Nov. 15, 9am-4pm daily Nov. 16-Mar.; ¥600 adults, ¥400 high school and junior high school students, ¥300 children; from Kyoto Station, take Kyoto City Bus 100 or 206 to Sanjūsangen-dō-mae bus stop, or take Keihan line to Shichijō Station, exit 2, and walk 6 minutes southeast

Inside Sanjūsangen-dō you'll find a surreal sight: around 1,000 statues of Kannon, the Buddhist goddess of mercy, standing like etheric sentinels in row upon row. (Strictly speaking, Kannon is not a goddess, but a boddhisatva, or an enlightened one who has voluntarily delayed entering nirvana to save others trapped in the wheel of suffering, or life, death, and rebirth). At the center of these gold-plated beings is the thousand-armed Kannon, known as Senjū Kannon. While Sanjūsangen-dō is a highly recommended sight at any time of year, the fact that its treasures are all under a roof make it a great choice for a rainy day.

1: stone fox with granary key at Fushimi Inari-Taisha
2: Kyoto's Kiyomizu-dera **3:** Fushimi Inari-Taisha

Downtown Kyoto

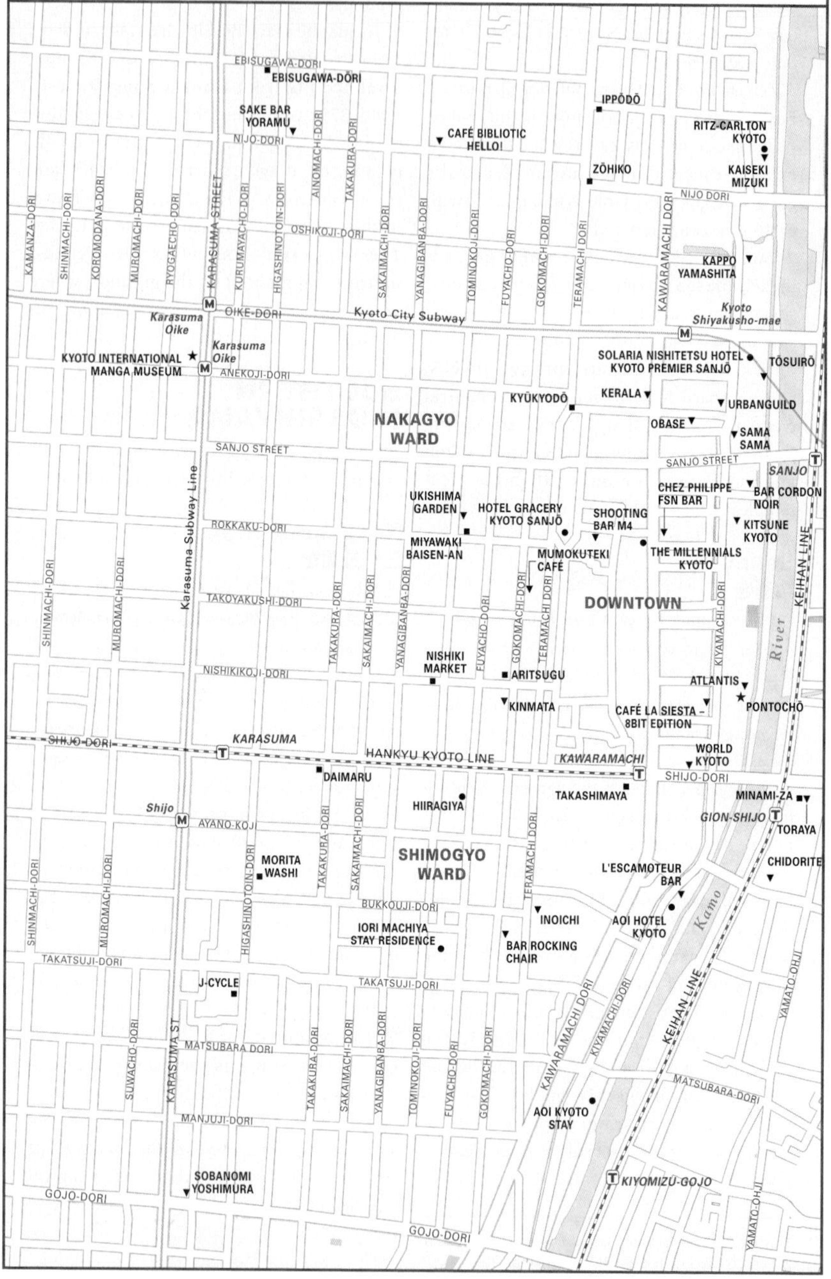

EBISUGAWA-DORI
EBISUGAWA-DŌRI
SAKE BAR YORAMU
NIJO-DORI
CAFÉ BIBLIOTIC HELLO!
IPPŌDŌ
RITZ-CARLTON KYOTO
KAISEKI MIZUKI
ZŌHIKO
NIJO DORI
OSHIKOJI-DORI
KAPPO YAMASHITA
KAMANZA-DORI
SHINMACHI-DORI
KOROMODANA-DORI
MUROMACHI-DORI
RYOGAECHO-DORI
KARASUMA STREET
KURUMAYACHO-DORI
HIGASHINOTOIN-DORI
AINOMACHI-DORI
TAKAKURA-DORI
SAKAIMACHI-DORI
YANAGIBANBA-DORI
TOMINOKOJI-DORI
FUYACHO-DORI
GOKOMACHI-DORI
TERAMACHI DORI
KAWARAMACHI DORI
Karasuma Oike
OIKE-DORI
Kyoto City Subway
Kyoto Shiyakusho-mae
KYOTO INTERNATIONAL MANGA MUSEUM
Karasuma Oike
ANEKOJI-DORI
SOLARIA NISHITETSU HOTEL KYOTO PREMIER SANJŌ
TŌSUIRŌ
KERALA
KYŪKYODŌ
URBANGUILD
NAKAGYO WARD
OBASE
SAMA SAMA
SANJO STREET
SANJO STREET
SANJO
CHEZ PHILIPPE
FSN BAR
BAR CORDON NOIR
UKISHIMA GARDEN
HOTEL GRACERY KYOTO SANJŌ
SHOOTING BAR M4
KITSUNE KYOTO
ROKKAKU-DORI
MIYAWAKI BAISEN-AN
MUMOKUTEKI CAFÉ
THE MILLENNIALS KYOTO
KEIHAN LINE
Karasuma Subway Line
SHINMACHI-DORI
MUROMACHI-DORI
TAKOYAKUSHI-DORI
DOWNTOWN
TAKAKURA-DORI
SAKAIMACHI-DORI
YANAGIBANBA-DORI
FUYACHO-DORI
GOKOMACHI-DORI
TERAMACHI DORI
KIYAMACHI-DORI
River
NISHIKI MARKET
ARITSUGU
NISHIKIKOJI-DORI
ATLANTIS
PONTOCHŌ
KINMATA
CAFÉ LA SIESTA – 8BIT EDITION
SHIJO-DORI
KARASUMA
HANKYU KYOTO LINE
KAWARAMACHI
WORLD KYOTO
SHIJO-DORI
DAIMARU
TAKASHIMAYA
MINAMI-ZA
HIIRAGIYA
Shijo
AYANO-KOJI
GION-SHIJO
TORAYA
SHIMOGYO WARD
MORITA WASHI
L'ESCAMOTEUR BAR
CHIDORITEI
SHINMACHI-DORI
MUROMACHI-DORI
HIGASHINOTOIN-DORI
TAKAKURA-DORI
SAKAIMACHI-DORI
TERAMACHI-DORI
BUKKOUJI-DORI
INOICHI
AOI HOTEL KYOTO
Kamo
IORI MACHIYA STAY RESIDENCE
BAR ROCKING CHAIR
TAKATSUJI-DORI
TAKATSUJI-DORI
J-CYCLE
KAWARAMACHI DORI
KIYAMACHI-DORI
KEIHAN LINE
YAMATO-OHJI
SUWACHO-DORI
KARASUMA ST
MATSUBARA DORI
TAKAKURA-DORI
SAKAIMACHI-DORI
YANAGIBANBA-DORI
TOMINOKOJI-DORI
FUYACHO-DORI
GOKOMACHI-DORI
MATSUBARA-DORI
AOI KYOTO STAY
MANJUJI-DORI
SOBANOMI YOSHIMURA
KIYOMIZU-GOJO
GOJO-DORI
GOJO-DORI
YAMATO-OHJI

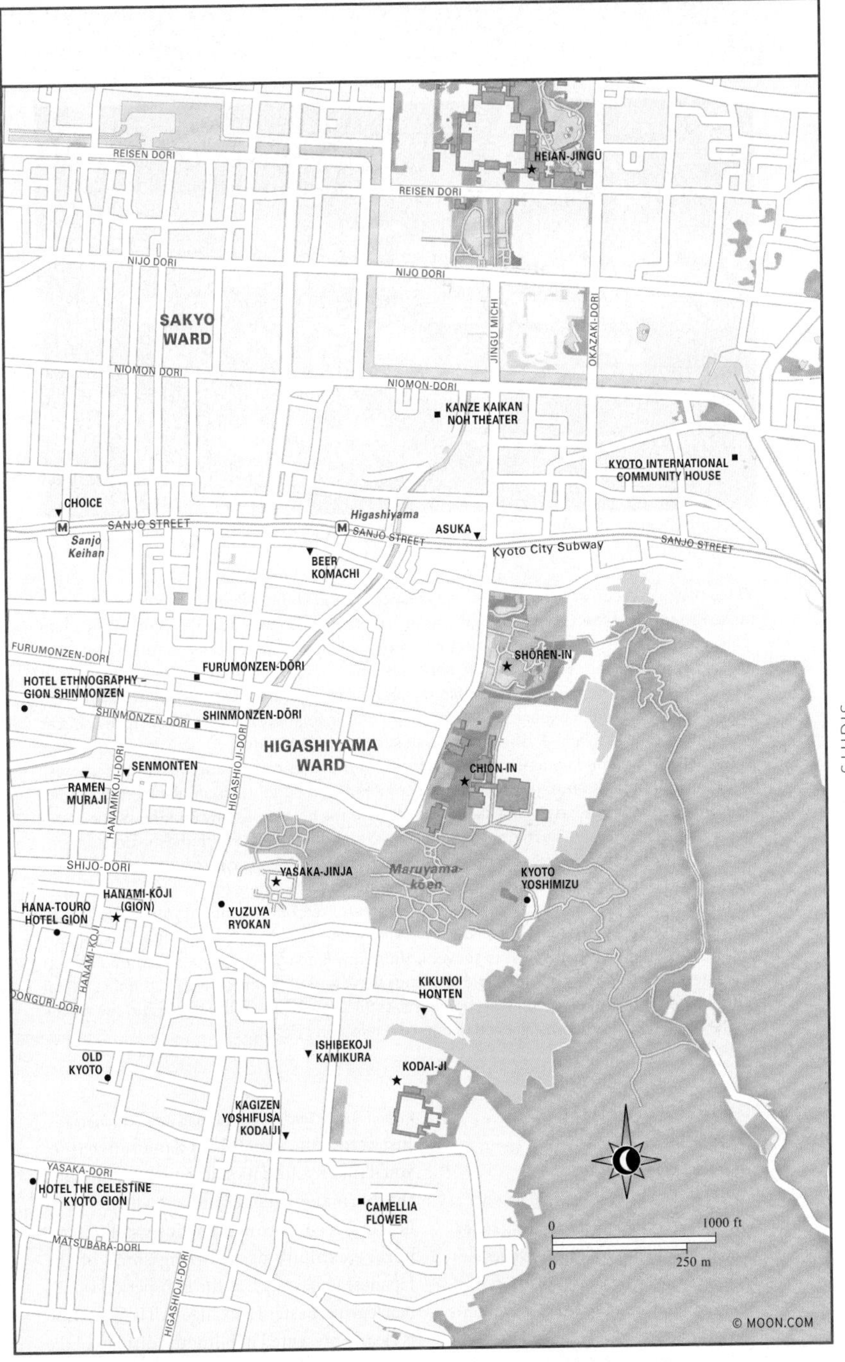

REISEN DORI
HEIAN-JINGŪ
REISEN DORI
NIJO DORI
NIJO DORI
SAKYO WARD
JINGU MICHI
OKAZAKI-DORI
NIOMON DORI
NIOMON-DORI
KANZE KAIKAN NOH THEATER
KYOTO INTERNATIONAL COMMUNITY HOUSE
CHOICE
Higashiyama
SANJO STREET
ASUKA
Sanjo Keihan
SANJO STREET
SANJO STREET
Kyoto City Subway
BEER KOMACHI
FURUMONZEN-DORI
SHŌREN-IN
FURUMONZEN-DŌRI
HOTEL ETHNOGRAPHY – GION SHINMONZEN
SHINMONZEN-DORI
SHINMONZEN-DŌRI
HIGASHIYAMA WARD
SENMONTEN
CHION-IN
RAMEN MURAJI
HANAMIKOJI-DORI
HIGASHIOJI-DORI
SHIJO-DORI
YASAKA-JINJA
Maruyama-kōen
KYOTO YOSHIMIZU
HANAMI-KŌJI (GION)
HANA-TOURO HOTEL GION
YUZUYA RYOKAN
HANAMI-KOJI
KIKUNOI HONTEN
DONGURI-DORI
ISHIBEKOJI KAMIKURA
OLD KYOTO
KODAI-JI
KAGIZEN YOSHIFUSA KODAIJI
YASAKA-DORI
HOTEL THE CELESTINE KYOTO GION
CAMELLIA FLOWER
0
1000 ft
0
250 m
MATSUBARA-DORI
HIGASHIOJI-DORI
© MOON.COM

Top Souvenirs: *Omamori*

omamori for sale

When you're in Japan in a crowd, discretely glance around at the cell phones, purses or bags of passengers around you. Chances are you'll notice colorful, hand-made pouches dangling by white woven cords. These pouches are amulets, or talismans, known as *omamori:* small ornaments that are sold at shrines and temples and are generally believed to bring protection or a run of good luck to the owner. They come in two main shapes. The rectangular ones contain words penned on thin strips of wood or paper inside. The others come in a variety of shapes, from foxes (sold at Inari shrines such as Kyoto's Fushimi Inari-Taisha) to bells and gourds.

The belief in *omamori* stems from the idea that Shinto charms contain a sprinkling of the power of a *kami* (god) that is housed in the shrine, combined with Buddhism's amulet culture, readily visible throughout other parts of Asia (for example, in the ubiquitous tiny Buddha statues seen swinging from the rear-view mirrors of Bangkok taxis). Although Shinto shrine maidens known as *miko* were once responsible for crafting *omamori,* today they are largely produced in factories and then blessed by priests upon arrival at shrines and temples where they're sold.

You don't need to be a devotee to respectfully buy and keep an *omamori.* If you choose to pick one up, just be sure you handle it with the same amount of respect you would any other religious object. While there's big business in souvenir shops hawking cutesy *omamori* featuring manga characters like Hello Kitty, some religious groups don't regard them as being authentic. A final note: whatever kind of *omamori* you choose, resist the urge to loosen the straps and see what's inside! Opening the pouch is believed to drain the talisman of its power.

Kyoto National Museum
京都国立博物館

527 Chaya-machi, Higashiyama-ku; tel. 075/525-2473; www.kyohaku.go.jp; 9:30am-6pm Tues.-Thurs. and Sun., 9:30am-8pm Fri.-Sat., closed following Tues. when Mon. is holiday; fee varies by exhibition; from Kyoto Station, take Kyoto City Bus 100 or 206 to Sanjūsangen-dō-mae bus stop, or take Keihan line to Shichijō Station and walk 10 minutes

Just across the street from Sanjūsangen-dō, you'll find Kyoto National Museum. Although the permanent collection is a little half-hearted, the museum often hosts stellar temporary exhibitions featuring some of the Japanese greats, such as the Edo-period woodblock print master Hiroshige. All information is clearly presented in bilingual displays. Like its neighbor Sanjūsangen-dō, the museum is also an excellent rainy-day option.

★ Kiyomizu-dera
清水寺

1-294 Kiyomizu, Higashiyama-ku; tel. 075/551-1234; www.kiyomizudera.or.jp; 6am-6pm daily with slight seasonal variation in closing times; ¥400 adults, ¥200 junior high and elementary students; from Kyoto Station, take Kyoto City Bus 100 or 206 to Gojō-zaka or Kiyomizu-michi bus stop, and walk 10 minutes from either stop

Perched above the sight-dense district of Southern Higashiyama, Kiyomizu-dera is one of Kyoto's most iconic temples. Look beyond the crowds and you'll see a fantastic temple that offers sweeping views of the city below.

Coming from Higashi Ōji-dōri, proceed up either Matsubara-dōri or the Chawan-zaka ("Teapot Lane"), via **Gōjō-zaka,** to the temple's main gate. Before entering the temple's main hall, keep your eyes open for **Zuigu-dō,** a separate hall on the temple's grounds that contains a hidden cave beneath it called the **Tainai-meguri.** The building itself is located to the left of the staircase leading up to the main temple. If you aren't sure you've come to the right place, simply ask someone to point you in the direction of the Tainai-meguri. After paying ¥100 and removing your shoes, make your way down the stairs and through the pitch-black grotto, navigating blind with only the help of a rope. This sacred subterranean space is believed to symbolize the womb of Daizuigu Bosatsu, a female bodhisattva believed to have the power to grant wishes. As you make your way through the space, allow your other senses to guide you. Inside, there's a stone that is said to have the power to grant any wish.

After making your wish, continue to **Jishu-jinja,** a matchmaking shrine where you may see young students trying their luck at walking 18 meters (59 feet) between two stone pillars in the shrine's grounds with their eyes closed. If successful, the feat is believed to bring about luck in romance. From here, wander the complex, exploring its various temples, subtemples, rituals, and faithful masses.

If you happen to be at Kiyomizu-dera when the cherry blossoms are in bloom—ill-advised if you can't stand crowds—the nighttime illumination of the trees surrounding the temple is spectacular.

Kōdai-ji
高台寺

526 Shimokawara-chō, Higashiyama-ku; tel. 075/561-9966; www.kodaiji.com/e_index.html; 9am-5:30pm daily; ¥600 adults, ¥250 high school and junior high school students, children free; walk 7 minutes east of Higashiyama Yasui bus stop (Kyoto City Bus 206)

This Rinzai sect temple features exemplary gardens (raked-gravel and landscape), the latter being famously beautiful during autumn. The main hall was once lacquered and graced with gilt designs, although the current incarnation is a simpler affair built in 1912. The grounds are illuminated in spring and autumn, conjuring a dreamy landscape (for details, visit www.kodaiji.com/e_illumi.html).

Originally built in 1606 in honor of Toyotoi Hideyoshi, one of Japan's three 'great unifiers', it also enshrines his wife Nene. Both are honored in a mausoleum that sits atop a hill behind the main temple complex. The temple's interior contains plenty of flamboyance thanks to the financial backing of Tokugawa Ieyasu, who followed Hideyoshi as the founder of the Tokugawa shogunate. There are also two teahouses on the grounds, reached via a path that runs through a bamboo grove. The construction of one of these teahouses was overseen by none other than Sen no Rikyū, creator of the tea ceremony.

It's located between Kiyomizu-dera, which lies about 20 minutes' walk south, and Yasaka-jinja, which sits 8 minutes' walk to the northwest. This temple is passed over by most tourists, making it a great place to go when exploring Southern Higashiyama.

Chion-in
知恩院

400 Rinka-chō, Higashiyama-ku; tel. 075/531-2111; www.chion-in.or.jp; 9am-4:30pm daily; outer grounds free, ¥500 adults, ¥250 junior high and elementary school students for all inner buildings and gardens; walk 10 minutes southeast from Higashiyama Station (Tōzai line), or take Kyoto City Bus 206 to Chion-in-mae bus stop, then walk 8 minutes east

Located just north of Yasaka-jinja and Maruyama-kōen, and about 8 minutes' walk north of Kōdai-ji, this massive temple is known as the "Vatican of Pure Land Buddhism." Besides being the head temple of the Jōdo sect of Pure Land Buddhism, the sheer scale of the complex is vaguely reminiscent of its Roman Catholic counterpart.

The sweeping front staircase was used in the film *The Last Samurai*. It also makes an appearance in *Lost in Translation*. There's very impressive joinery on display in the large Sanmon gate. With a height of 24 meters (78.7 feet) and a width of 50 meters (164 feet), it's the biggest wooden gate in the country. After passing through the gate, ascend the stairs to the temple's main grounds, centered on an expansive courtyard laced with stone paths.

It's free to enter the Miei-dō (main hall), which houses an effigy of Hōnen, the priest who founded the Jōdo sect, and the neighboring Amida-dō (Amida hall), in which you'll see a magnificent visage of the principle Buddha of the Amida Buddha ("Amida" is the Japanese version of the Sanskrit word for "Infinite Light"). Amida Buddha is the principle Buddha of the Pure Land sect, and is believed to have fashioned an afterlife paradise where anyone is welcome who faithfully chants Amida's name. You'll need to pay admission to venture farther inside.

Deeper within the temple precincts, alongside more buildings, you'll discover two gardens, **Yūzen-en** (9am-4pm daily; ¥300 adults, ¥150 children), a rock garden with a pond that sits southeast of the Sanmon gate, and **Hōjō-en** (9am-3:50pm; ¥400 adults, ¥200 children), a classic landscape garden dating to the mid-17th century that lies east of the temple's main hall. You can also pay to enter both gardens at a discounted rate (¥500 adults, ¥250 children).

Shōren-in
青蓮院

69-1 Sanjōbōchō, Awataguchi, Higashiyama-ku; tel. 075/561-2345; www.shorenin.com; 9am-5pm daily; ¥500 adults, ¥400 junior high and high school students, ¥200 elementary school students; walk 7 minutes southeast of Higashiyama Station (Tōzai line), or take Kyoto City Bus 5, 46 or 100 to Jingū-michi bus stop and walk 3 minutes south

This is a hidden gem in the truest sense: Now a temple, it was originally built as villa for an abbot of the Tendai School of Buddhism. The temple also had longstanding ties to the imperial family. An empress temporarily called it home in the 18th century after a fire.

The first building you'll enter brings you to the tatami-floored Kachoden (drawing room). Here, you'll find sliding doors with paintings of natural scenes and court life, opening onto an exquisite garden centered on a pond filled with colorful *koi* (carp). Wooden boardwalks link this bulding to other structures in the complex, including the Shijokodō, or compact main hall. Note that the two sacred paintings within the Shijokodō—a mandala (visual representation of the universe, according to Buddhist cosmology) and an image of Fudo Myō, a sword-wielding deity of wisdom enshrouded in flames—are usually veiled from public view.

After viewing the garden from within the drawing room, meander along the snaking path that laces through the garden. It passes by a lovely teahouse (¥1,000, includes green tea and sweet; only open select days throughout year; for details, go to www.shorenin.com/english/tea), a shrine and through an atmospheric bamboo grove. The grounds are lit up at night during spring and autumn (for details, go to www.shorenin.com/english/night). This is a recommended, largely crowd-free stop near Chion-in, from where it's about 5 minutes' walk north.

GION
祇園

To soak up the ambience of Kyoto's entertainment district, take a stroll down the cobblestone lane of **Hanami-kōji,** starting from the south side of Shijō-dōri, as dusk falls and the lanterns that hang in front of the wooden shopfronts flicker. Without an appointment to see a geisha performance or dine at one of the neighborhood's *kaiseki* restaurants, there's little in the way of casual entertainment here. You can enjoy the area by simply meandering through its lanes and breathing in the air of sophistication.

Yasaka-jinja
八坂神社

625 Gion-machi Kitagawa, Higashiyama-ku; tel. 075/561-6155; www.yasaka-jinja.or.jp; 24 hours; free; take the Keihan line to Gion-Shijō, exit 6, and walk 8 minutes east, or take Kyoto City Bus 206 to Gion bus stop and walk 1 minute east

In the heart of Gion, Yasaka-jinja is a grand shrine that is best known for hosting Kyoto's epic summerly Gion Matsuri. Despite its location in the heart of Kyoto's entertainment district, Yasaka-jinja stands as a dignified spiritual center. It's hard to miss the shrine, given its location in the heart of the southern half of Higashiyama, the city's most dense sightseeing district. It's equally tough to dispute the shrine's everyday spiritual vitality, evidenced by the steady flow of faithful who come for weddings, or to pray or make a New Year's Day request to the gods for a good year ahead. Religious proceedings aside, the shrine is a great place to stroll in serenity. It backs onto the excellent Maruyama-kōen, and at night it is lit by the soft glow of hanging lanterns.

NORTHERN HIGASHIYAMA

Northern Higashiyama has an abundance of spiritual sights, atmospheric strolling paths, and temple gardens. It's also more low-key and a bit less crowded.

Heian-jingū
平安神宮

97 Nishitennō-chō, Okazaki, Sakyō-ku; tel. 075/761-0221; www.heianjingu.or.jp; 6:30am-5:30pm daily Feb. 15-Mar. 14 and Oct., 6am-6pm daily Mar. 15-Sept. 30, 6am-5pm daily Nov. 1-Feb. 14; shrine grounds free, garden ¥600 adults, ¥300 children; from Kyoto Station, take Kyoto City Bus 5 to Okazaki-kōen/Bijutsukan bus stop and walk 8 minutes north, or take Tōzai subway line to Higashiyama Station, and walk 12 minutes northeast

Located in the heart of the Northern Higashiyama area, you'll find an imposing shrine known as Heian-jungū. This shrine, constructed in 1895 in honor of Kyoto's 1,100th birthday, is a replica—5/8 in scale—of the city's ancient Heian Palace, where the earliest emperors resided. The shrine is a good place to begin a journey through the culturally rich Northern Higashiyama neighborhood.

The approach to the shrine is unique in that the vermillion *torii* gate that marks its first entrance straddles and stands nearly 25 meters above the road that leads to the shrine, which sits within a park called Okazaki-kōen. After passing through the park area, you'll find the shrine at the northern end of Jingū-michi, a road that terminates where it meets Nijō-dōri, running east to west.

Inside the shrine's main three-doored gate, you'll find yourself in an expansive gravel-covered space that fronts the main hall of the shrine itself. Near the entrance, there are windows where amulets and talismans are being sold by shrine maidens, myriad hanging wooden plaques scrawled with visitors' wishes, and toward the back of the complex, locals entering and exiting the main alter to offer prayers.

Beyond the shrine's main building there's a garden that can be entered for a fee. Pay a visit to the shrine, but skip the garden, as better ones await nearby.

Geisha

If you find yourself in Kyoto's Gion district in the mid-evening, a geisha in training, known as a *maiko,* may float past. This district, which dates to the 16th century, remains one of the best places to spot one. These nostalgic entertainment quarters, called *hanamachi* (flower towns) are the traditional stomping grounds of the increasingly rare geisha (person of the arts), or *geiko* (child of the arts), as they're known in Kyoto.

Carried along by high-set *geta,* as her elevated wooden sandles are known, a *maiko* is easily recognized by her thick white makeup, charcoal-painted eyebrows, and deep-red lower lip. She is draped in an exquisite, flowery kimono tied with an elongated *obi* (belt) left to dangle from her waist as she walks.

TRAINING AND WORK

A common misconception is that geisha are prostitutes. Historically, some geisha would enter contractural relationships with wealthy patrons who would pay for their companionship, which would include a romantic dimension. The woman would often use the money earned to pay off her debt to her *okiya,* the matriarchal school where she spent five to six years acquiring her substantial talents: traditional dance, playing instruments such as the three-stringed *shamisen*, as well as singing and engaging in wide-ranging conversation.

Before World War II, some 80,000 geisha worked in *hanamachi* across Japan; today, a mere 1,000 work in this trade. In their heyday, geisha in training would enter an *okiya* as early as six years old. Today, the situation is more fluid, with geisha living where they want, dating whom they want and entering—at the earliest—at 15 (the age when compulsory education is completed in Japan).

IN KYOTO AND ELSEWHERE

To be entertained by geisha, you more or less need to know somebody. They mostly flit to and

★ Nanzen-ji
南禅寺

86 Fukuchi-chō, Nanzen-ji, Sakyō-ku; tel. 075/771-0365; www.nanzen.net; 8:40am-5pm Mar.-Nov., 8:40am-4:30pm Dec.-Feb.; grounds free, Hōjō garden ¥500 adults, ¥400 high school students, ¥300 junior high and elementary school students, San-mon gate viewing platform ¥500 adults, ¥400 high school students, junior high and elementary school students ¥300; take Tōzai subway line to Keage Station, then walk 12 minutes northeast

A personal favorite, Nanzen-ji is a magical temple complex that sprawls over a large area in Northern Higashiyama. Its grounds invite roaming and its paths lead up into the hills surrounding this lush site, transporting those who walk them to a hidden grotto and a smattering of subtemples with pristine gardens that most visitors to the site pass by. This 13th-century temple is the head temple of a strain of the Rinzai sect of Zen Buddhism

As you approach the temple grounds, take note of a couple of atmospheric, often missed subtemples: **Konchi-in** (86-12 Fukuchi-chō, Nanzen-ji, Sakyō-ku; tel. 075/771-3511; 8:30am-5pm daily Mar.-Nov., 8:30am-4:30pm daily Dec.-Feb.; ¥400 adults, ¥300 high school students, ¥200 junior high and elementary school students) and **Tenju-an** (86-8 Fukuchi-chō, Nanzen-ji, Sakyō-ku; tel. 075/771-0744; 9am-5pm daily Mar.-mid-Nov., 9am-4:30pm mid-Nov.-Feb.; ¥500 adults, ¥300 children). Both boast sublime gardens that are only visited by a fraction of the crowd streaming into Nanzen-ji. The entrance to Konchi-in is located on the right side of the road leading up to Nanzen-ji, about 40 meters (131 feet) before you come to the main gate to the Nanzen-ji complex. Proceed past the public restrooms on the right, and just beyond them, roughly parallel with the southern edge of Nanzen-ji's

geisha

from exclusive parties at secretive inns, high-end restaurants, and in members-only teahouses. The other option is attending a public performance, often staged to coincide with cherry blossom season and autumn foliage in Kyoto. Finally, if you spot one in the street, don't interrup her. She's a highly trained professional who is likely on her way to an appointment. The best places to catch a glimpse of a geisha or *maiko* in this candid way are **Kyoto** (Ponto-chō and Gion), **Tokyo** (Kagurazaka, Ginza, and Akasaka), and the city of **Kanazawa** on the Japan Sea side of Honshu.

lofty San-mon Gate, you'll see the entrance to Tenju-an.

After soaking up the calm ambience at these two subtemples, explore Nanzen-ji's grounds at a contemplative pace. Note the aqueduct running through the grounds—a Meiji Period (1868-1912) construction once used to transport goods and water between Kyoto and Lake Biwa northeast of the city. Facing the aqueduct from the temple's main grounds, up a stone staircase, is the subtemple **Nanzen-in** and its *Hōjō* garden. Follow the path leading uphill to the right, walking beside the canal as you go, for a great view of the city below.

If you cross under the canal from the main temple grounds and, instead, take a hard left, following the road beside the stream, you'll reach a stone stairway that leads into the hills. Walk to the top—about 200 meters (656 feet) behind the temple grounds—where you'll discover **Okuno-in,** a sacred space containing a waterfall and a hidden grotto.

★ Philosopher's Path
哲学の道

After taking a stroll along the Philosopher's Path in northeastern Kyoto, the inspiration for its name—Tetsugaku-no-michi in Japanese—will be evident. This walking path begins in the south from about 100 meters (328 feet) north of the temple of **Eikan-dō** and ends at the foot of the approach to **Ginkaku-ji** in the north, for a total distance of about 1.8 km (1.1 mi). Walking at a leisurely pace, this stroll will likely take about 30 minutes, not accounting for stops at sights along the way.

This pathway runs beside a canal that directs a gentle stream of water through one of the city's most tranquil neighborhoods, and is surrounded by a wide range of foliage, including cherry trees that burst with color

1
2
3
4

Northern Higashiyama's Less Crowded Side

While Northern Higashiyama's temples are not necessarily the most thronged in Kyoto, they do draw crowds. Thankfully, there's also a quieter side to the district, best seen on a hill known as Yoshidayama about 25 minutes' walk northwest of Nanzen-ji or 20 minutes' stroll west of the northern edge of the Philosopher's Path.

Three particular spots worth a visit in the area include the atmospheric temples of **Konkai-Kōmyō-ji** (121 Kurodani-chō, Sakyō-ku; tel. 075/771-2204; www.kurodani.jp/en; 9am-4pm daily; free), known for its atmospheric **Kurodani Garden,** and **Shinnyo-dō** (82 Shinnyo-chō, Jōdoji, Sakyō-ku; tel. 075/771-0915; https://shin-nyo-do.jp; 9am-4pm daily; grounds free, ¥500 main hall and inner garden, ¥1,000 during special periods of Mar. and Nov.-early Dec.). Both of these temples are brilliant places to see autumn foliage with a fraction of the crowds. Standing above them is the secluded hilltop shrine of **Yoshida-jinja** (30 Kaguraoka-chō, Yoshida, Sakyō-ku; tel. 075/771-3788; www.yoshidajinja.com; 9am-5pm daily; free). If you choose to visit this off-the-radar side of Northern Higashiyama, simply strolling through the grounds of all three (for free) will work its magic.

If you're coming from Nanzen-ji, start your exploration of the area at the most southern of the three sights, Konkai-Kōmyō-ji (popularly referred to as Kurodani), then walk a few minutes north to Shinnyo-dō and finish at Yoshida-jinja. Coming from Gingaku-ji, make your way first to Shinnyo-dō, then walk a few minutes south to Kurodani, before walking about 5 minutes northwest from there to Yoshida-jinja.

during *hanami* season. (Note that the path is thronged during springtime. Avoid visiting during daylight hours during the *hanami* rush. Instead, go after dusk when the trees are lit up for a few hours.)

Any time of year, the combination of the water and greenery make this path the ideal place for a contemplative stroll. This is exactly what Kyoto University philosophy professor Nishida Kitaro—who inspired the name of this path—did whenever he grew weary of trying to untangle some ontological Gordian Knot and craved to reconnect with his senses and the outside world.

The path winds through an area dotted with a host of atmospheric temples and shrines, some of them with stellar gardens. Rather than having a set agenda, I recommend ambling at your own pace and stopping at any that may catch your eye. In the spirit of its namesake, stroll the path with an open mind and see where your intuition leads.

1: Kyoto's Nanzen-ji **2:** Ginkaku-ji **3:** Heian-jingū **4:** Philosopher's Path

Ginkaku-ji
銀閣寺

2 Ginkaku-ji-chō, Sakyō-ku; tel. 075/771-5725; www.shokoku-ji.jp/en/ginkakuji/; 8:30am-5pm Mar.-Nov., 9am-4:30pm Dec.-Feb.; ¥500 adults, ¥300 junior high and elementary school students; take Kyoto City Bus 5 or 17 to Ginkaku-ji-michi bus stop, then walk 10 minutes east

Ginkaku-ji, or the "Silver Pavilion" is a stunning temple complex that boasts superb gardens and rambling halls. The temple, built in 1482, was originally the retirement villa of shogun Ashikaga Yoshimasa. Yoshimasa was the grandson of Ashikaga Yoshimitsu, who a few decades prior had built Kinkaku-ji (the Golden Pavilion) on the other side of town. It was repurposed into a Zen temple following Yoshimasa's death in 1490.

Located near the northern end of the Philosopher's Path, the grounds of Ginkaku-ji are classically Zen. On one hand, there's an intensely green, moss-covered garden. Contrasting this is a separate dry-gravel garden complete with a miniature representation of Mount Fuji and raked into geometric swirls.

A still pond surrounded by gnarled pine trees frames the beautiful main hall, which is decidedly more rustic than the temple's gold-plated counterpart, Kinkaku-ji, across town.

Simply exploring and taking in the grounds via a circular loop and meandering through the buildings' dark wooden corridors will make a visit to Ginkaku-ji worthwhile. But be sure to also walk the path that leads up a hill behind the complex, affording a sweeping vista of the grounds and the surrounding area below. For better or worse, Ginkaku-ji is one of Kyoto's most popular spots. Aim to visit either just as it opens, or within an hour of closing to avoid the picture-snapping masses.

Eikan-dō
永観堂

48 Eikandō-chō, Sakyō-ku; tel. 075/761-0007; www.eikando.or.jp; 9am-5pm (last entry 4pm) daily, special hours during evening in autumn; ¥600 adults, ¥400 children; walk 15 minutes northeast from Keage Station (Tōzai line), or walk 5 minutes east of Nanzenji-Eikandō-michi bus stop (Kyoto City Bus 5)

This tranquil Jōdo (Pure Lane) sect temple is 7 minutes' walk north from Nanzen-ji. It serves as the southern end of the Philosopher's Path and is famed for its autumn foliage, particularly its fiery maples. Originally the villa of a court noble during the Heian period (794-1185), it was converted into a temple originally known as Zenrin-ji. Its popularly used name of Eikan-dō is derived from an 11th-century priest named Eikan.

Its buildings, containing attractively painted sliding doors and linked by wooden walkways, sit beside a serene garden, crisscrossed by tiny streams that run into a pond with an island in the middle where a petite shrine stands. Standing above the grounds on a hill is the two-story Tahoto Pagoda, which has a square base and a rounded second level. Climb the stairs to this structure and enjoy views over the temple grounds and city beyond.

Note that the cost of entry is raised during autumn, when the grounds are illuminated at night (second half of Nov.; ¥1,000 daytime, ¥600 nighttime). Be forewarned: The crowds are intense when the leaves turn, particularly in November. During other times of year, however, the temple is an appealing escape from selfie-stick-toting masses who congregate at many of the other more otherwise famous temples around town.

the entrance to Nijō-jō

Hōnen-in
法然院

30 Goshonodan-chō, Shishigatani, Sakyō-ku; tel. 075/771-2420; www.honen-in.jp; 6am-4pm daily; free; take Kyoto City Bus 5 or 17 to Ginkaku-ji-michi bus stop, then walk 12 minutes southeast

A hushed temple founded in 1680 just off the Philosopher's Path, tucked away in a grove with lush grounds dotted by pools of water, Hōnen-in is about 10 minutes' walk south of jam-packed Ginkaku-ji. The thatched-roof entrance gate, blanketed in moss, is approached via a leafy path, creating a magical atmosphere. Upon entering, walk between two sculpted rectangular mounds of sand, over a pond, and past raked-gravel gardens to a hidden grotto. The main temple, which houses a black statue of Amida Buddha, can only be entered from April 1-7 and November 1-7. There's also a gallery on-site that hosts local art exhibitions. If you walk the Philosopher's Path, this is a highly worthwhile stop that is mercifully free of crowds.

DOWNTOWN AND CENTRAL KYOTO

Roughly in the geographical heart of the city, downtown is a convenient place to shop, eat, carouse in the evening, and sleep.

Ponto-chō
先斗町

If you've ever seen a photograph of a cobblestone alley in Kyoto—festooned with softly glowing red lanterns and flanked by dark wooden shopfronts with doors obscured by curtains—chances are the street in the image was Ponto-chō.

This pedestrian-only street is a sight in itself and evokes the quiet refinement of old Kyoto, perhaps better than any other lane in the city. Running along the west bank of the Kamo River, Ponto-chō extends from just south of Sanjō Station (Tōzai subway line, Keihan line) at its northern edge to bustling Shijō-dōri, near both Gion-Shijō Station (Keihan line) and Kawaramachi Station (Hankyū line) at its southern end.

For maximum impact, visit Ponto-chō after the sun sets, when the paper lanterns flicker and well-heeled patrons in their finery make their way into one of the alley's countless exclusive eateries and bars. Note that it's not impossible to wine and dine in Ponto-chō, but by and large, it's not the kind of area you should casually pop in. There are, however, some restaurants and bars that are accustomed to serving foreign customers where you'll be relieved to meet staff who speak English and find menus in English.

Nijō-jō
二条城

541 Nijōjō-chō, Nijō-dōri, Horikawa Nishi-iru, Nakagyō-ku; tel. 075/841-0096; http://nijo-jocastle.city.kyoto.lg.jp/?lang=en; 8:45am-5pm, last entry 4pm, Ninomaru Palace closed Tues. Dec.-Jan. and Jul.-Aug., also closed Dec. 26-Jan. 4; ¥620 adults, junior high school students and younger free for Nijō-jō only, ¥ 1,030 adults, ¥350 high and junior high school students, ¥200 elementary school students for Nijō-jō and Ninomaru Palace; take Tōzai line to Nijō-jō-mae Station, then walk 5 minutes

One of Kyoto's more eye-popping sights is its famed castle, Nijō-jō. This imposing compound—surrounded by stunning gardens and hemmed in by towering stone walls—is the city's most visible demonstration of the power that the military elite held over the emperor during the feudal Edo period (1603-1867).

Construction of the majestic complex began in 1603. It was intended to serve as the Kyoto home of the first shogun, Tokugawa Ieyasu and was completed 23 years later by Ieyasu's grandson Iemitsu, who also built a five-story keep. When the Edo period came to a close in 1867, and power was restored to the emperor, the castle was then used as an imperial palace for a time, until it was donated to the city. Today it stands at the center of the ancient capital, a stellar example of Japanese castle architecture and one of the city's most popular sites. Avoid going during the middle of the day when the site is flooded with visitors. Try to arrive just as it opens to beat the rush.

The castle can roughly be split into four sections: the outer walls and moats, two inner layers of defenses that encircle the complex—the Honmaru, or main ring of defense, and the secondary layer, or Ninomaru—and a smattering of attractive classical gardens. The Honmaru is not usually open to the public, but the Ninomaru area is.

Be sure to visit the **Ninomaru Palace.** Inside you'll discover some of the defensive tricks employed by the shoguns to subvert would be assassins, such as the legendary "nightingale floors" that squeaked in a way that vaguely resembles a bird call to warn of any attempted sneak attack. The palace is also covered in artistic flourishes, from floridly adorned ceilings to handsomely painted sliding doors, reflecting the opulent tastes of the shoguns. Outside the palace, be sure to meander through **Seiryū-en,** a beautiful landscape garden.

Kyoto International Manga Museum
京都国際マンガミュージアム

Karasuma-dōri, Oike-agaru, Nakagyō-ku; tel. 075/254-7414; www.kyotomm.jp/en; 10am-6pm Thurs.-Tues., closed Thurs. when Wed. is holiday; ¥800 adults, ¥300 junior high and high school students, ¥100 elementary school students; walk 3 minutes north from Karasuma Oike Station (Karasuma, Tōzai lines)

For hardcore manga fans, this place is pretty special. It's essentially a massive library of manga. It's housed in a former school building and boasts an impressive 300,000 individual volumes of manga, which can be freely read after paying the price of admission. There are also (mostly bilingual) exhibitions on the history of manga and how it's drawn. Story tellers known as *kamishibai*, who essentially read a story from a scroll of images, sporadically perform on-site too. Underscoring just how deep the roots of manga go into Japanese culture, the *kamishibai* tradition began long ago with monks who used drawings on scrolls to teach the basics of Buddhism to peasants who couldn't read. An essential stop for manga fans and a good rainy-day option for anyone.

NORTHWEST KYOTO

More out of the way than other areas of the city, Northwest Kyoto is nonetheless home to a handful of significant temples.

Ryōan-ji
龍安寺

13 Goryōnoshitamachi, Ryōan-ji, Ukyō-ku; tel. 075/463-2216; www.ryoanji.jp; 8am-5pm daily Mar.-Nov., 8:30am-4:30pm daily Dec.-Feb.; ¥500 adults, ¥300 junior high and elementary school students; from Sanjō Keihan Station (Tōzai line), take Kyoto City Bus 59 to Ryōan-ji-mae bus stop, or take Keifuku Kitano line from Arashiyama to Ryōan-ji-michi Staiton, then walk 9 minutes north

The raked gravel garden in the temple grounds of Ryōan-ji consists of 15 rocks placed just so. The garden is in many ways the pure embodiment of what most people think of when they hear the words "Zen garden." As with Ginkaku-ji, Ryōan-ji was once a villa, lived in by an aristocrat during the Heian period (794-1185). The site metamorphosed in 1450, becoming a temple of Zen Buddhism's Rinzai sect.

The origins of the temple's iconic rock garden are less clear. Though the precise meaning of the garden is an enigma, various stabs have been taken at theories on its meaning, from islands in the ocean to a mama tiger carrying her cubs across a pond to infinity. One interesting point: When viewed from any angle, one rock will always be concealed from view.

Aside from this spiritual statement made in gravel, the head priest's former quarters (*Hōjō*) and the old kitchen (*kuri*) still stand on the site. Take a peek at the compact gardens behind the *Hōjō,* as well as the beautifully painted sliding doors inside the *Hōjō's* tatami rooms.

To have a fighting chance of pondering the famed rock garden when it's not being mobbed by visitors, aim to arrive either just after the temple opens, or within an hour of closing.

★ Kinkaku-ji
金閣寺

1 Kinkaku-ji-chō, Kita-ku; tel. 075/461-0013; www.shokoku-ji.jp/en/kinkakuji/; 9am-5pm daily; ¥400 adults, ¥300 junior high and elementary school students; from Kyoto Station, take Kyoto City Bus 205 to Kinkaku-ji-mae bus stop, or take Kyoto City Bus 12 from Sanjō-Keihan Station (Tōzai line) to Kinkakuji-michi bus stop

Easily Kyoto's most recognizable temple, Kinkaku-ji cuts a striking profile, particularly on a sunny day. Its upper two stories are famously covered in gold, giving the site an ethereal glint and causing a mirage-like reflection to form in the pond surrounding its base. This Zen temple was originally built to serve as the villa of shogun Ashikaga Yoshimitsu, whose grandson built Ginkaku-ji in the northeast of town. The site was converted into a temple in 1408 upon Yoshimitsu's death.

Surrounded by greenery and fronted by a pond, Kinkaku-ji's design reflects the opulent Kitayama aristocratic culture at its height. The first floor was built in the style of a Heian-period palace—pillars made of timber, plaster walls painted white. The second floor is in the style of a samurai residence with statues of Kannon, the Buddhist goddess of compassion, and Four Heavenly Kings, mythological guardians of the four cardinal directions. The third floor is designed like a Zen Hall in the Chinese style. The roof is topped by a phoenix made of, yes, gold.

The grounds also include the former head priest's residence, or *Hōjō,* which can only be seen from outside, and a series of gardens that remain as they were when Yoshimitsu once strolled through them. If you see other visitors tossing ¥1 coins onto a statue—with a small fortune on the ground surrounding it—this is your chance to try to toss a few of your own. If you can throw a coin directly into the statue's lap, you'll be blessed with good luck.

As you exit the grounds, you'll pass a teahouse, some shops selling trinkets, and a small subtemple that contains a statue of one of the Five Wisdom Kings that is believed to have maybe been carved by Kobo Daishi (774-835), a monk and scholar of legendary proportions, and founder of the Shingon school of Buddhism.

As with many of Kyoto's top sights, it's worth trying to avoid going at the most popular times: midday any day of the week, and all day on weekends. Opening time on Monday or Tuesday mornings is a good time to visit.

Myōshin-ji
妙心寺

64 Myōshin-ji-chō, Hanazono, Ukyō-ku; tel. 075/461-5226; www.myoshinji.or.jp/english; 9:10am-11:40am (entry permitted every 20 minutes),

Kinkaku-ji

Northwest Kyoto's Less Crowded Side

Check out these two temples if you want to get away from the crowds:

NINNA-JI
仁和寺

33 Omurōuchi, Ukyō-ku; tel. 075/461-1155; www.ninnaji.or.jp; 9am-5pm daily Mar.-Nov., 9am-4:30pm daily Dec.-Feb.; grounds free, admission to Goten ¥500 adults, ¥300 junior high and elementary school students; take Kyoto City Bus 59 from Sanjō Keihan Station (Tōzai line), or take Keifuku Kitano line from Arashiyama to Omuro-Ninna-ji Station, then walk 6 minutes north

A 15-minutes walk northwest of Myōshin-ji, this ancient temple (founded in 888) at the base of the mountains north of town is also off the radar. It's a good place to escape the crowds of Ryōan-ji and Kinkaku-ji. A UNESCO World Heritage site with a handsome five-story pagoda, its gardens are perfectly suited to a meditative ramble.

Be sure to visit the **Goten,** where the head priest once resided. Surrounding this building on the southeastern corner of the compound are idyllic gardens centered on ponds, bridges, a variety of trees and shrubs, and raked gravel. A good place to go in the northwest of town if you want to have somewhere to yourself or very close to it.

Note that around mid-April the late-blooming Omuro cherry tree blossoms and fills the temple's grounds with pink. This is the one time when the temple fills with visitors. Admission during this time increases to ¥600.

TŌJI-IN
等持院

63 Tōji-in Kita-machi, Kita-ku; tel. 075/461-5786; 9am-5pm daily; ¥500; take Keifuku Kitano line from Arashiyama to Tōji-in Station, then walk 5 minutes north

About 20 minutes' walk east of Ninna-ji, this temple is another good off-the-radar option. Founded by Shogun Ashikaga Takauji in 1341, with the present structures dating to 1818, the real star at this temple is its garden. The serene space contains two notable ponds: one shaped like the character for the word *shin* or *kokoro* (心), which means "heart" or "mind," and one that resembles a lotus blossom. There's also a superb teahouse on-site that was built in 1457, brilliantly exhibiting the *wabi-sabi* (shabby-chic plus Zen) aesthetic of the tea ceremony.

12:30pm (entry permitted once), 1pm-4:40pm (entry permitted every 20 minutes) daily, closed sporadically; ¥700 adults, ¥400 junior high and elementary school students; walk 6 minutes northeast of Hanazono Station (JR Sagano San-in line), or take Kyoto City Bus 62, 63, 65 or 66 from Sanjō Keihan Station (Tōzai line) to Myōshin-ji-mae bus stop, then walk 3 minutes north

This sprawling Zen Buddhist complex of the Rinzai sect is just south of Myōshin-ji Station on the Kitano line. Besides the main temple of Myōshin-ji, the grounds are peppered with subtemples as well as a wonderful garden (at **Taizo-in**). Myōshin-ji is also notable for its *zazen* (seated meditation) classes (for prices and times, go to www.myoshinji.or.jp/english/zen/info.html).

The temple complex was founded in 1337, originally as a villa for an abdicated emperor, and was later converted into a temple. Throughout the compound as it stands today, there are nearly 50 subtemples, most of which are closed to the public with four open year-round. The bulk of the major structures are grouped around the southern gate. Whether you enter from the north or south, wandering through the lanes that thread through the compound will leave you feeling enchanted.

Within the temple of Myōshin-ji itself, stop by **Hattō Hall,** where a huge painting of a dragon is emblazoned across its ceiling.

Note that this building can only be entered on a guided tour (30 minutes, Japanese language only). Other buildings that can be entered in the compound include Taizo-in (9am-5pm; ¥500), a subtemple renowned for its stunning garden centered on a pond. The landscape garden at this subtemple was actually created in the mid-1960s, despite its classic appearance. Its rock garden, however, dates to the 15th century.

Two other subtemples within the complex that can be entered by the public are **Keishunin** (9am-5pm; ¥400), which has some alluring stroll gardens, and **Daishinin** (9am-5pm; ¥300) where you'll find a meditative rock garden.

Daitoku-ji
大徳寺

53 Daitoku-ji-chō, Murasakino, Kita-ku; tel. 075/491-0019; http://zen.rinnou.net/head_temples/07daitoku.html; main temple and grounds 24 hours, subtemples various hours; free to enter complex, subtemples charge separate admission fees; walk 20 minutes west of Kitaōji Station (Karasuma line)

In some ways similar to Myōshin-ji, this sprawling, walled temple compound is one of Kyoto's prime Zen centers. This oasis of calm has some of the best rock gardens in Kyoto, minus the throngs of Ryōan-ji. Daitoku-ji is also home to **Izusen Daijinten,** a restaurant on the temple's grounds that is the best place to dine like a monk in Kyoto.

Enter through the main gate, located at the east side of the complex, then proceed to explore four subtemples with gardens that consistently work their magic: **Ryōgen-in** (9am-4:30pm daily; ¥300), **Zuihō-in** (9am-5pm daily; ¥500), **Kōtō-in** (9am-4:30pm; ¥400) and **Daisen-in** (9am-5pm daily; ¥400). Note that Daitoku-ji itself, after which the entire compound is named, cannot be entered by the public.

Check out Ryōgen-in's raked-gravel garden (claimed to be Japan's smallest garden) and moss garden, and don't miss Zuihō-in's stunning rock garden, designed in the 1960s by garden designer Shigemori Mirei. This is a fantastic alternative to the popular Ryōan-ji. Kōtō-in's inner temple grounds are home a garden and a humble tea room designed by Sen no Rikyū, founder of the tea ceremony. Daisen-in boasts two spectacular dry landscape gardens considered to be among Japan's most iconic examples of this this quintessential element of Zen culture, but be forewarned that there's a very strict no-photography policy.

ARASHIYAMA
嵐山

West of Kyoto proper, the Arashiyama area is dense with sights, centered around the atmospheric **Arashiyama Bamboo Grove.** The main thoroughfare running through the Arashiyama area is a quintessential tourist trap; move through it and make a beeline for the treasures beyond.

Tenryū-ji
天龍寺

68 Susukinobaba-chō, Saga Tenryū-ji, Ukyo-ku; tel. 075/881-1235; www.tenryuji.com; 8:30am-5:30pm daily Mar. 21-Oct.20, 8:30am-5pm daily Oct. 21-Mar. 20; Hōjō garden ¥500 adults and high school students, ¥300 junior high and elementary school students, garden and buildings ¥800 adults and high school students, ¥600 junior high and elementary school students; use Saga-Arashiyama Station (JR Sagano line, 13-minute walk west), or a separate Arashiyama Station (Hankyū line, 15-minute walk northwest)

The best place to begin your exploration of Arashiyama is at the main act: Tenryū-ji. This important temple—the base of the Rinzai school of Zen Buddhism—has a wonderful garden beside the area's famed bamboo grove, which serves as a stunning example of the old Chinese gardening principle of drawing on "borrowed scenery."

This temple was built 1339-1345 by shogun Ashikaga Takauji (1305-1358), constructed in a ploy to appease the angry spirit of Emperor Go-Daigo. Takauji had once been Go-Daigo's ally, but later turned on him in his attempt to

Arashiyama's Less Crowded Side

Although it may be hard to believe after a trip to the bamboo grove, a few pockets of Arashiyama remain surprisingly uncrowded. Unlike other districts, where there may be 2-3 less-crowded temples near the heavy hitters, Arashiyama is peppered with several smaller atmospheric temples, as well as a lovely park.

The simplest way to explore the area's lesser-known temples is to turn right at the T-junction at the western end of the path that leads through the area's thronged bamboo grove, near the entrance to Ōkōchi-Sansō. From there, walk straight ahead and pass the pond on your left. From here, it's possible to take a lovely 25-minute walk (one way) starting from the T-junction, passing through a rural area of rice paddies and residences where you'll find some enchanting smaller temples well away from the crowds. You'll come to the following temples, in this north-south order:

- **Jōjakkō-ji** (3 Saga Ogurayama, Ukyō-ku; tel. 075/861-0435; www.jojakko-ji.or.jp; 9am-5pm daily; ¥500): This discreet temple is a good place to come if you're hungry for some peace and quiet. Its mossy grounds contain a pagoda and lots of trees.
- **Nison-in** (27 Monzenchōjin-chō, Saga Nison-in, Ukyō-ku; tel. 075/861-0687; http://nisonin.jp; 9am-4:30pm daily; ¥300 adults, ages 12 and under free): About 3 minutes' walk north of Jōjakkō-ji, Nison-in offers a similar experience. Entering its grounds has a calming effect and can be strolled leisurely.
- **Giō-ji** (32 Kozaka-chō, Saga Toriimoto, Ukyō-ku; tel. 075/861-3574; www.giouji.or.jp; 9am-5pm daily; ¥300 adults, ¥100 high school, junior high and elementary students): A 4-minute walk north from Nison-in, Giō-ji has a petite main hall topped by a thatched roof and a moss garden with grotto on its grounds. If you're going to pay admission to one of these temples, make it this one.
- **Adashino Nenbutsu-ji** (17 Adashino-chō, Sagatoriimoto, Ukyō-ku; tel. 075/861-2221; www.nenbutsuji.jp; 9am-4:30pm Mar.-Nov., 9am-3:30pm Dec.-Feb.; ¥500 adults, ¥400 high school and junior high school students, elementary school students and younger free): This temple has some 8,000 stone effigies commemorating those who have died without any surviving kin. From here, it's a 40-minute walk southeast back to Arashiyama Station on the Keifuku line.

Arashiyama's quieter options are not limited to temples. There's also **Kameyama-kōen,** a quiet park set on a hilltop on the northern bank of the Hozugawa river, which runs through Arashiyama. To reach it, just turn left—rather than right—at the T-junction at the western end of the path that leads through the famed bamboo grove, then walk uphill. Besides being a calm setting that offers beautiful views of the river below, the park is often host to troupes of monkeys.

gain control of Japan. The original complex contained as many as 150 buildings, which have been ravaged by fire many times through the centuries. The structures that stand today were built during the Meiji period.

The garden, however, remains largely as it was when it was first designed by famed garden master Muso Soseki (1275-1331), the first head priest of the temple. Centered on an expansive pond surrounded by manicured pines and misshapen rocks, a bamboo-covered slope rises into the distance. The story goes that the garden was meant to reflect a Chinese myth about a koi (carp) that made its way up a waterfall and transformed into a dragon. Stones rising from the pond, which teems with koi, stretch up a hill strewn with large stones, said to resemble the legendary waterfall.

Begin your tour of the temple by slipping off your shoes and exploring the interior of the main hall, or *Hōjō* (9am-5pm daily Mar. 21-Oct. 20, 9am-4:30pm daily Oct. 21-Mar. 20; ¥500), and then meander through the garden. Allow yourself to drift toward the north gate of the temple complex, which deposits you right in the thick of the area's iconic bamboo grove, one of the city's most famous sights.

★ Arashiyama Bamboo Grove
嵯峨野の竹林

Arashiyama, Ukyō-ku; 24 hours; free; take JR Sagano (San-in) line to Saga-Arashiyama Station, then walk 10 minutes west, or take Hankyū line to Arashiyama Station, then walk 17 minutes northwest

Strolling through the Arashiyama Bamboo Grove feels like passing into another realm. The shoots reach skyward and extend deeply in all directions with no other competing forms of vegetation in view.

Gaze in either direction and imagine two martial artists lithely leaping between the supple sprouts—the largest being up to 40 meters (131 feet) in height and 35 cm (18 in) in diameter—evoking the famous scene from kung-fu flick *Crouching Tiger, Hidden Dragon*. The real magic of this grove must be experienced first-hand. It doesn't always fully translate to photographs. There is an almost eerie glow to the light in this singular forest, which takes on an increasingly ethereal glow as dusk begins to fall.

I recommend entering this enchanted realm after first exploring Tenryū-ji. You'll find yourself in the midst of the bamboo as soon as you pass through the north gate of the temple. Once you pass through the gate, turn left and simply walk straight up the mountain path. The grove works its magic most intensely as you reach its final section, which terminates at the entrance to the alluring **Ōkōchi-Sansō** villa.

Ōkōchi-Sansō
大河内山荘

8 Tabuchiyama-chō, Saga Ogurayama, Ukyō-ku; tel. 075/872-2233; 9am-5pm daily; ¥1,000 adults and high school students, ¥500 junior high and elementary school students; take Hankyū line to Arashiyama Station and walk 25 minutes northwest, or take JR Sagano line to Saga-Arashiyama Station, then walk 17 minutes west

On the far side of the bamboo forest, you'll discover the highlight of Arashiyama: a dreamy mountaintop villa known as Ōkōchi-Sansō. Like many of Kyoto's beautiful places, Ōkōchi-Sansō was once the home of a figure of ample means, namely the movie star Ōkōchi Denjirō (1898-1962), famous for his roles in dramas set during the Edo period.

When you reach the top of the famed bamboo grove, forge ahead to the ticket window at the start of a footpath leading up a slope before making your way toward the magnificent

Arashiyama Bamboo Grove

Application Required

Saihō-ji's Moss Temple

There are two notable sights in Kyoto, Saihō-ji and the Katsura Rikyū, that require a bit more planning to visit, including an advance application and appointed visitation times. But for hardcore garden fans, both are worth seeing, and the application and rigid timing of a visit means crowds will be minimized by default. Visitors to both sights must be at least 12 years old.

SAIHŌ-JI
西芳寺

56 Matsuo Jingatani-chō, Nishikyō-ku; tel. 075/391-3631; http://saihoji-kokedera.com; by appointment; ¥3,000; walk 2 minutes Kokedera Suzumushidera bus stop (from Kyoto Station, take Kyoto City Bus 73), or take Kyoto City Bus 63 or 73 from Arashiyama to Kokedera Suzumushidera bus stop

This atmospheric temple, popularly known as **Kokedera** ("Moss Temple") is famed, as this name suggests, for its lush moss garden. The entire complex is awash in emerald hues from some 120 varieties of moss. Before proceeding to the garden, all guests must first chant and write out a sutra (Buddhist scripture). Just follow the lead of the monk and the brush strokes of Japanese visitors seated around you. Be forewarned that the writing desks are low to the ground.

All visits must be booked in advance—at least 7 working days—either via post or through an online service that is not affiliated with the temple. The effort is worth it for those who plan the trip well. Go to http://saihoji-kokedera.com/en/reservation.html for detailed application instructions. For an online reservation service that will charge a fee, check out www.govoyagin.com/activities/japan-kyoto-tour-saiho-ji-moss-temple-a-unesco-world-heritage-site/8017.

KATSURA RIKYŪ (IMPERIAL VILLA)
桂離宮

Katsura-Misono, Nishikyō-ku; tel. 075/211-1215; http://sankan.kunaicho.go.jp/english/guide/katsura.html; by appointment (tours offered hourly 9am-4pm Tues.-Sun., not offered Tues. if Mon. is holiday); ¥1,000 ages 18 and up, ages 12-17 free; walk 15 minutes northeast from Katsura Station (Hankyū line)

This villa was built on a plot of land in the Katsura area gifted by Shogun Toyotomi Hideyoshi, one of Japan's "three great unifiers," to a prince named Hachijō Toshihito. It's a stellar example of traditional villa architecture, and it boasts four teahouses, paired with an exquisite garden. Visiting requires joining a 40-minute tour (English audio guides available; English tours offered at 10am, 11am, 2pm, and 3pm), held several times daily (except Mon.), which leads through the grounds, looping around the pond at the center of the stroll garden. Buildings can't be entered and photos can only be shot from certain places.

To reserve a spot on one of the tours, you must apply in person—be sure to take your passport—at the **Imperial Household Office** (tel. 075/211-1215; 8:40am-5pm Tues.-Sun., closed Tues. if Mon. is holiday), located inside **Kyoto Gyōen.** There are also limited places up for grabs on the Imperial Household Agency's website (http://sankan.kunaicho.go.jp/order/index_EN.html), but they tend to be taken fast.

garden above. Simply follow the arrows indicating the order in which to explore the grounds, winding through dense tunnels of foliage and past a swath of earth overtaken by a verdant blanket of moss, revealing glimpses of downtown Kyoto spreading out in the distance below, as well as a mystical mountain vista seen from the other side of the peak. Try to spot the distant temple.

As you move through the grounds, also take time to savor the beautiful villa itself—built in a traditional Japanese residential style—as well as a serene teahouse oozing rustic charm. You can't enter either of these structures, but you can take a break at a modern teahouse that you come to at the end of the walking route. Here, hand over your entrance ticket to the kindly staff in exchange for a sweet and a warm cup of *matcha*.

If you'd prefer to skip the complicated procedures involved with applying to see some of the city's more exclusive sights—the Katsura Rikyū Imperial Villa and Saihō-ji's moss garden come to mind—just make a trip to Ōkōchi-Sansō, which offers similar views, instead.

This site is a bit of a walk from the nearest station, but that's part of the fun, as it means ambling through the area's iconic bamboo forest.

Entertainment and Events

PERFORMING ARTS

MINAMI-ZA

Shijō-Ōhashi, Higashiyama-ku; tel. 075/561-0160; www.kabukiweb.net/theatres/minamiza; performances from ¥5,000; take the Keihan line to Gion-Shijō Station, exit 6

The premier theater to see a kabuki performance in Kyoto is Minami-za. Located at the corner of Kawabata-dōri and Shijō-dōri, the theater is set in an imposing building. If kabuki intrigues you, it's possible to sit in for a few acts, rather than watch an entire play, which can last upward of four hours. English audio guides available.

KANZE KAIKAN NOH THEATER

44 Enshoji-chō, Okazaki, Sakyō-ku; tel. 075/771-6114; www.kyoto-kanze.jp; performances from ¥2,000; take the Tōzai subway line to Higashiyama Station, exit 1

The other form of traditional theater with a presence in Kyoto is the more refined—and enigmatic—*Noh*. The best place to watch this slow-paced, restrained artform is at the Kanze Kaikan Noh Theater. Performances on the stunning cedar-wood marvel of a stage are mainly held on holidays and weekends.

FESTIVALS

★ GION MATSURI

Gion; www.gionmatsuri.jp/manu/manual.html; throughout July; free

One of Japan's most iconic festivals, Kyoto's Gion Matsuri takes place during the sweltering month of July each year. It is rounded off with a parade of truly astounding floats pushed through the streets of Gion by revelers in traditional garb. The festival centers on the shrine of Yasaka-jinja.

The floats, known as *omikoshi,* are up to 25 meters (82 feet) tall and weigh up to 10 tonnes (12 tons). Up to 30 of them slowly proceed along Shijō-dōri, representing individual neighborhoods scattered around the city.

The festival dates back to the 9th century, when it was born as a purification ritual to appease what were believed to be the angry gods responsible for fires, earthquakes, floods, pestilence, and plague. In 869, Emperor Seiwa ordered a mass prayer and ritual at Yasaka-jinja to appease the god of the shrine. It was officially made an annual event in 970. By the Edo period, extravagant touches added by the merchant class had made it an occasion devoted to the peacocking of wealth.

Today, the festival culminates July 14-17, when Kyoto's city center is blocked off to traffic and residents mill about in *yukata*, drinking beer and nibbling on grub from food stalls. The city is decorated with flowers and flags, and lit by hanging lanterns. The *yamaboko junkō* (grand procession of floats) occurs July 17 and 24. The city's accommodations are booked well in advance of the festival, so book as far ahead as possible.

DAIMON-JI GOZAN OKURIBI

Five mountains surrounding city (viewable from downtown); Aug. 16; free

Another iconic Kyoto summer festival, the Daimon-ji Gozan Okuribi, begins at 8pm on August 16 every year, an occasion to bid farewell to deceased spirits believed to visit the living during the holiday of O-bon, celebrated in mid-August in Kyoto. Blazing fires in the shape of Chinese characters are lit and left to burn for about 40 minutes on the slopes of five mountains surrounding the city. The most famous one burns atop Daimon-ji-yama, a mountain looming over the northeastern side of the city. The best spot to view the blaze is from the Kamo River, between Sanjō-dōri in the south and Imadegawa-dōri in the north (best accessed via Sanjō Station, Tōzai subway line).

Sports and Recreation

PARKS

Kyoto is home to some serenely beautiful parks. Whether you're in the city during *hanami* season, want to spot wildlife, or simply want to have a picnic, there are plenty of good options.

MARUYAMA-KŌEN

Maruyama-chō, Higashiyama-ku; tel. 075/222-3586; 24 hours; free; from Kyoto Station, take Kyoto City Bus 100 or 206 to Gion bus stop and walk 5 minutes, or take the Keihan line to Gion-Shijō Station, exit 1, and walk 10 minutes

Perhaps the city's most popular park is Maruyama-kōen. Smack in the middle of Higashiyama, behind Yasaka-jinja, this park

Gion Matsuri float

Hanami (Cherry Blossom Viewing)

hanami viewing from the water

Japan's love of the seasons is most apparent in the cherry blossom-viewing (*hanami*) madness that sweeps through the nation every spring. Televised forecasts will feature blooms when they first spring to life in Okinawa as early as mid-January, before rippling northward and finishing off in Hokkaido in May. People from all walks of life head to local parks brandishing food and booze, or scout out more pristine locations armed with GPS-driven smart-phone apps revealing the best spots to revel under the pink petals.

HISTORY OF *HANAMI*

The roots of *hanami* are centuries deep. Look back far enough and you'll discover that the seeds of the tradition came from China's Tang Dynasty (AD 618-907), when appreciation of beauty including flowers was widespread. This cultural influence reached Japan during the Nara Period (710-794), with blossom viewing exploding in popularity during the Heian period (794-1185), when Emperor Saga (809-823) began throwing parties under the blossoms within court circles. The word *hanami* (literally: flower viewing) became synonymous with gazing at cherry blossoms after its use in Lady Murasaki Shikibu's 11th-century novel *The Tale of Genji*. By the Edo period, the celebration of and symbolism attached to the humble *sakura* (cherry tree) blossom had trickled down to commoners, for whom it remains an annual rite today.

KYOTO'S BEST *HANAMI* SPOTS

Japan is replete with dazzling *hanami* destinations, with Kyoto near the top of the list. By far, the most popular spot to spread out a tarp and have a boozy picnic is **Maruyama-kōen.** For slightly thinner crowds, try the banks of the **Kamo River** (beginning from Imadegawa-dōri and running north), the **Kyoto Imperial Palace** grounds, and the surprisingly peaceful **Kyoto Botanical Gardens** (Shimogamohangi-chō, Sakyō-ku; tel. 075/701-0141; www.pref.kyoto.jp/plant/; gardens 9am-5pm (last entry 4pm) daily, conservatory 10am-4pm (last entry 3:30pm); adults ¥200, high school students ¥150, elementary and junior high school students ¥80, additional ¥200 for conservatory; take Karasuma subway line to Kitayama Station, exit 3). For a phenomenal after-dark show, if you don't mind sharing the view with intense crowds, visit **Kiyomizu-dera**'s grounds where a profusion of *sakura* are lit up in the evenings. If you don't mind going slightly out of the way, **Shinnyo-dō,** a temple located about 20 minutes' walk southwest of Ginkaku-ji, boasts prominent cherry trees that are not thronged by tourists.

features a pond, burbling brooks, and an array of cherry trees. During *hanami* season, it's utterly thronged. During the rest of the year, it's an ideal place for a picnic or stroll.

KYOTO GYŌEN

Kyoto Gyoen, Kamigyō-ku; tel. 075/211-6348; 24 hours; free; take Karasuma subway line to Imadegawa Station or Marutamachi Station

Kyoto Gyōen is another downtown oasis. Set in the center of town, it occupies the grounds of the former **Kyoto Imperial Palace.** The sprawling grounds occupy the geographic heart of the city. Like Maruyama-kōen, it's also a famed *hanami* spot, renowned for its beautiful collection of weeping cherry trees. It's a great place to meander on foot or sit down for a picnic with the former imperial palace looming beyond.

IWATAYAMA MONKEY PARK

8 Genrokuzan-chō, Arashiyama, Ukyō-ku; tel. 075/872-0950; www.monkeypark.jp/Englishpage.html; 9am-5pm mid-Mar.-Sept., 9am-4:30pm Oct.-mid-Mar., last entry 30 minutes before closing; ¥550 ages 16 and over, ¥250 ages 15 and under; take JR Sagano line to Saga-Arashiyama Station, or Hankyū line to Arashiyama (transfer at Katsura Station)

For something wilder, there's Iwatayama Monkey Park in the west of the city. While it's certainly not a completely natural jungle out there, the Japanese macaques on this site in Arashiyama are essentially just going about their business. This is a good place to observe them close up. They're free to play and jump about, while the humans are enclosed.

KAMEYAMA-KŌEN

Saga Kamenō-chō, Ukyō-ku; tel. 075/701-0101; 24 hours; free; use Saga Arashiyama Station (JR Sagano line), or a separate Arashiyama Station (Hankyū line)

Across the Katsura River from the Iwatayama Monkey Park, this oasis of calm offers a refreshing escape from the crowds of the area. While there aren't as many as you'll see at Iwatayama, monkeys do hang around here too. There are also sweeping views of the river gorge and much of Arashiyama below. To reach the park, simply turn left and walk uphill when you reach the T junction at the western end of Arashiyama's famed bamboo grove.

CYCLING

CYCLE KYOTO

7 Higashikujō, Nishi Sannōchō, Minami-ku; tel. 090/9165-7168; www.cyclekyoto.net; tours ¥7,000-12,000 per person; 3 minutes' walk south of Kyoto Station Hachijō East Exit

Kyoto is an extremely good city for cycling. While you may prefer to explore on your own, there are also some great cycling tours available. The most reputable agency is Cycle Kyoto. Alongside group tours of the city's north and south, it's also possible to arrange family tours (¥40,000), private tours (¥45,000-85,000) and custom tours (price varies; inquire for details).

KYOTO CYCLING TOUR PROJECT

552-13 Higashi-Aburanokoji-chō, Aburanokoji-dōri, Shiokoji sagaru; tel. 075/354-3636; www.kctp.net; 9am-6pm; from ¥1,000 for standard bicycles; 5 minutes' walk west of Kyoto Station central exit, on the north side of the station

The most reliable rental shop in town is Kyoto Cycling Tour Project, which rents a variety of bicycles, including mountain bikes, city bikes, children's bikes, and more. Call the head office, where the staff speak English, to inquire about bicycle availability. It's possible to pick up a bike there, ride around for the day, and leave it at one of the outfit's five terminals spread around the city at the end of your ride.

HIKING

KURAMA TO KIBUNE HIKE

Hiking Distance: 5.2 km (3.2 mi) one way
Time: 1.5 hours one way
Information and maps: www.insidekyoto.com/kurama-to-kibune-hike; https://patrickcolgan.net/2017/01/15/hike-kibune-kurama;
Trailhead: Kurama Station

This route is easy to access and is set in the mountains north of town. The combination of spirituality and a stunning natural setting imbue this hike up and over Mount Kurama, between two mountain hamlets, with a visceral power. Reached by train (about 30 minutes from downtown), the villages of Kurama and Kibune are well away from the masses; it's possible to walk between them in about 1.5 hours. To reach the starting point fo the hike, Kurama Station, hop on the Eizan line at Demachiyanagi Station, which is the northern terminus of the Keihan line, then ride to Kurama Station (30 minutes; ¥420).

To get started, exit Kurama Station and walk by the large statue depicting the bright-red noggin of the mythical, improbably long-nosed Tengu (a prominent creature in Japanese folklore). Turn left onto Kurama's main thoroughfare, which leads to a set of stairs. Climb them and follow the path, which leads up Mount Kurama, for about 10 minutes. You'll recognize the first sight of note, **Yuki-jinja** (1073 Kuramahon-machi, Sakyō-ku; tel. 075/741-1670; www.yukijinjya.jp; 24 hours; free) by the giant cedar tree at its entrance (instead of a vermillion *torii* gate). This is the guardian shrine of Kurama village.

Push on from Yuki-jinja and after about 5 more minutes of walking you'll come to the temple of **Kurama-dera,** (1074 Kurama Honmachi, Sakyō-ku; tel. 075/741-2003; www.kuramadera.or.jp; 9am-4:30pm daily; free) which stands near the top of Mount Kurama. From here, the trail to Kibune is pretty clearly marked. Once you make it to Kibune, the one must-visit sight is **Kifune-jinja,** (180 Kuramakibune-chō, Sakyō-ku; tel. 075/741-2016; http://kifunejinja.jp; 9am-5pm daily; free), a shrine approached via an ethereal stone staircase flanked by red lanterns.

From Kibune, you can either return to Kurama Station or simply board the train at Kibuneguchi Station, which is also a stop on the Eizan line and also runs to Demachiyanagi Station on the northern edge of the city, where you can transfer to the Keihan line and make your way downtown from there.

There's also a fantastic mountain *onsen* with both indoor and outdoor pools at **Kurama Onsen** (520 Kuramahonmachi, Sakyō-ku; tel. 075/741-2131; www.kurama-onsen.co.jp; 10:30am-9pm, last admission 8:20pm; ¥2,500 adults, ¥1,600 ages 4-12 for full use of facilities; ¥1,000 adults, ¥700 ages 4-12 for open-air baths only). Note that it's also possible to walk this route in reverse if you'd like to take a dip in the hot spring baths of Kurama Onsen after a hike. Kurama Onsen is about 12 minutes' walk north of Kurama Station, set beside the burbling Anba River. There's also Japanese fare served on-site at the *onsen's* restaurant (www.kurama-onsen.co.jp/plan01_e/index.html).

TAKAO TO HOZUKYŌ STATION HIKE

Hiking Distance: 11 km (6.8 mi) one way

Time: 6 hours one way

Information and maps: www.insidekyoto.com/takao-hozukyo-hike-via-kiyotaki-kuya-no-taki-waterfall; https://tales-of-trails.com/2018/10/24/hiking-from-takao-to-hozukyo

Trailhead: Village of Takao

Reached from downtown by bus (about 50 minutes), this village in the mountains has three fantastic temples, namely, **Jingo-ji,** a sprawling temple complex that's dotted by pagodas and that serves as a place to carry out the ritual of Kawarake-nage, in which you can throw clay shards known as *kawarake* to dispel unwanted karma. You'll also come across **Saimyō-ji,** a hidden temple with an enchanted little grotto behind it; and the most famous but actually least essential **Kozan-ji,** a temple and UNESCO site, which can be skipped.

A trip to Takao can also include a hike—in this case down to Hozukyo Station, following the Kiyotaki River along the way, on the JR Sagano-San-in line, which runs directly to Kyoto Station in about 25 minutes. To reach Takao, you have two options. From Kyoto Station, find the JR3 bus stopping point and take the bus bound for either Toganoo or Shūzan. You'll need to get off at Yamashirotakao bus stop (50 minutes; ¥500). Alternatively, take bus Kyoto City Bus

8 from Nijō Station to Takao bus stop (40 minutes; ¥500).

Once you're in the village, begin the hike by descending to the Kiyotaki River. There's a sign near the bus stop that points the way to the hiking course and Jingo-ji. But first, visit Saimyō-ji, before walking about 10 minutes west along the Kiyotaki River until you reach the grueling set of stairs that leads up to Jingo-ji. Once you've finally reached the temple, be sure to throw some of the discs made of clay known as *kawarake* (¥100 for 2) into the valley below to release any bad karma you may be carrying around.

Leaving Jingo-ji, walk about 50 minutes southward along the Kiyotaki River until you reach Kiyotaki village. Continue southward, following the Kiyotaki River until it joins the larger Hozu River. The last stretch of the hike involves following the Hozu River until you reach Hozukyō Station, from where you can return directly to Kyoto Station on the JR Sagano line (¥240).

COOKING CLASSES

HARU COOKING CLASS

166-32 Shimogamo Miyazaki-chō, Sakyō-ku; www.kyoto-cooking-class.com; classes start from 2pm; from ¥6,900; walk 9 minutes northwest of Demachiyanagi Station (Eizan, Keihan Main lines)

At Haru Cooking Class, you can join bilingual cooking instructor and Kyoto food insider Taro at his home in the north of the city. Taro is well versed in both vegetarian and non-vegetarian cuisine, and he offers guided tours of the rambling realm of local food that is Nishiki Market. Lessons typically last up to four hours.

Shopping

KYOTO STATION AREA

Flea Markets

KOBO-SAN MARKET

1 Kujō-chō, Minami-ku; tel. 075/691-3325; www.toji.or.jp; 8:30am-5:30pm Mar. 20-Sept. 19, last entry 5pm; 8:30am-4:30pm Sept. 20-Mar. 19, last entry 4pm; free; take the Kintetsu line to Tō-ji Station, then walk 8 minutes west

On the 21st of every month, a great flea market known as the Kobo-san Market is held at the temple of Tō-ji, southwest of JR Kyoto Station. Go in the morning before the good stuff is picked over.

NORTHERN HIGASHIYAMA

In the heart of Gion, the two parallel streets of **Furumonzen-dōri** and **Shinmonzen-dōri** are chock-full of businesses selling traditional Japanese art. You'll find landscape paintings, Buddhist sculptures, teapots and implements, and scrolls. Note that it's a fairly pricey area to shop, but if you mean business and could potentially buy something, the sellers welcome foreign customers. To get to these two streets, take the Tōzai subway line or Keihan line to Sanjō Keihan Station, exit 2.

Flea Markets

CHION-JI TEMPLE HANDICRAFT MARKET

103 Tanaka Monzen-chō, Sakyō-ku; www.tedukuri-ichi.com/hyakumanben; 8am-4pm; free; take the Keihan line to Demachiyanagi Station, then walk 8 minutes east

On the 15th of every month, a great place to shop for souvenirs is the Chion-ji Temple Handicraft Market. The market is fun, lively, and well-stocked with locally made goods. Show up early before the masses pour in.

Traditional Goods and Souvenirs

KYOTO HANDICRAFT CENTER

21 Shōgoin Entomi-chō, Sakyō-ku; tel. 075/761-8001; www.kyotohandicraftcenter.com; 10am-7pm daily;

take Kyoto City Bus 206 to Kumano-jinja-mae bus stop, or take Keihan line to Jingu Marutamachi Station

Kyoto Handicraft Center is the best one-stop souvenir shop in the city. *Yukata,* ceramics, accessories, jewelry, woodblock prints, and more are available.

Ceramics

ROBERT YELLIN GALLERY

Ginkakuji-mae-chō 39, Sakyō-ku; tel. 075/708-5581; http://japanesepottery.com; take Kyoto City Bus 5 or 17 to Ginkaku-ji-michi bus stop

A stone's throw from Ginkaku-ji, you'll find one of Kyoto's best ceramics shops: the Robert Yellin Gallery. The gallery is set in a beautiful traditional home, complete with a landscape garden. Yellin is an American expat based in Kyoto who has a masterful grasp on the Japanese *yakimono* (ceramics; literally "fired thing") tradition, and has amassed an eye-popping collection to prove it. To avoid sticker shock, have a look at the online gallery on the official website to get a sense of how much a quality piece can potentially cost. Note that there are no official hours, but Robert is a friendly host who welcomes visitors. Your best bet is to call or email ahead and confirm he's not not out with clients or visiting kilns when you plan to visit. Otherwise, knock on the door if the gate is open and he'll be happy to greet you if he's there. Have a look at the access map, available on the website, as the gallery is a little tricky to find on a first visit.

DOWNTOWN AND CENTRAL KYOTO

Shopping Districts

NISHIKI MARKET

www.kyoto-nishiki.or.jp; 9am-5pm daily

One block to the north of Shijō-dōri, and running parallel to the busy thoroughfare, Nishiki Market is an extensive smorgasbord of local edibles. Whether you aim to buy something or not, the covered pedestrian thoroughfare is a sight to behold. To get there, take the Hankyū line to Kawaramachi Station or Karasuma Station, or the Karasuma line to Shijō Station.

EBISUGAWA-DŌRI

take the Karasuma subway line to Muratamachi Station

This street two blocks south of Marutamachi-dōri that runs westward from Teramachi-dōri is the best place in the city to pick up a piece of antique furniture, such as a *tansu* (antique chest).

Nishiki Market

TERAMACHI-DŌRI

about 10 minutes' walk east of Muratamachi Station

Another great shopping street for old Japanese items, Teramachi-dōri is the street you'll come to when you reach the eastern end of Ebisugawa-dōri, or. It's heaving with shops selling Japanese antiques, tea ceremony implements, painted scrolls, and more. Consider coming to Teramachi-dōri after a stroll to Ebisugawa-dōri.

Department Stores

You'll find two grand department stores downtown: **Daimaru** (79 Tachiuri Nishimachi, Shijō-dōri, Takakura Nishi-iru, Shimogyō-ku; tel. 075/211-8111; www.daimaru.co.jp; 10am-8pm daily) and **Takashimaya** (52 Shinchō, Shijō-dōri, Kawaramachi Nishi-iru, Shimogyō-ku; tel. 075/221-8811; www.takashimaya.co.jp; 10am-8pm daily). Both have a staggering selection of international brands and offer world-class service, along with stellar food floors in their basements. Stop by either one to browse and discover how big the concept of a "department store" is in Japan. To get downtown, take the Hankyū line to Karasuma Station, or the Karasuma subway line to Shijō Station. Both stores are within walking distance from there.

Traditional Goods and Souvenirs

KYŪKYODŌ

520 Shimohonnōjimae-chō, Teramachi-dōri, Aneyakōji-agaru, Nakagyō-ku; tel. 075/231-0510; www.kyukyodo.co.jp; 10am-6pm Mon.-Sat.; take the Tōzai subway line to Kyoto-Shiyakusho-mae Station

For the best place to buy incense—in its various forms—an item with great history in the city's myriad Buddhist temples, head to Kyūkyodō.

MORITA WASHI

1F Kajinoha Building, 298 Ogisakaya-chō, Higashinotoin-dōri, Bukkoji-agaru, Shimogyō-ku; tel. 075/341-1419; www.wagami.jp; 9:30am-5:30pm Mon.-Fri., 9:30am-4:30pm Sat.; take the Karasuma subway line to Shijō Station, or the Hankyū line to Karasuma Station

To see the surprising range of creative applications of traditionally handmade paper—a craft with deep roots in Kyoto—the best place in the city is Morita Washi.

MIYAWAKI BAISEN-AN

80-3 Daikoku-chō, Rokkaku-dōri, Tominokōji, Higashi-iru, Nakagyō-ku; tel. 075/221-0181; www.baisenan.co.jp ; 9am-6pm daily; take the Kurasuma or Tōzai subway line to Karasuma-Oike Station

Another traditional item that says "Kyoto" is the folding fan. For a superb selection, go to Miyawaki Baisen-an. This fan specialist has been in business since 1823.

AIZEN KŌBŌ

215 Yoko Ōmiya-chō, Nakasuji-dōri, Ōmiya Nishi-iru, Kamigyō-ku; tel. 075/441-0355; www.aizenkobo.jp; 10am-5:30pm Mon.-Fri., 10am-4pm Sat.-Sun.; take the Karasuma subway line to Imadegawa Station

Aizen Kōbō is a family-owned shop selling only textiles dyed with indigo. Located near the old textiles district of Nishijin, the shop sells a wide range of elegant garments made of silk and cotton.

HIYOSHIYA

546 Dodo-chō, Horikawa Teranouchi-higashi-iru, Kamigyō-ku; tel. 075/441-6644; http://wagasa.com; 9:30am-5pm Tues.-Sun.; take the Karasuma subway line to Imadegawa Station

Hiyoshiya is a family-owned shop that makes traditional wooden parasols with exquisite designs. They're more art pieces than functional umbrellas. They also create custom lampshades using the same technique.

Kitchenware and Food

ARITSUGU

tel. 075/221-1091; www.kyoto-nishiki.or.jp/stores/aritsugu; 9am-5:30pm daily

The best place to buy traditional Japanese kitchen knives, Aritsugu, is housed in Nishiki Market.

ZŌHIKO

719-1 Yohojimae-chō, Teramachi-dōri, Nijō-agaru, Nishigawa, Nakagyō-ku; tel. 075/229-6625; www.zohiko.co.jp; 10am-6pm daily; take the Tōzai subway line to Kyoto Shiyakusho-mae Station

If you dine at a *kaiseki* restaurant, something that will leap out at you as much as the flavor is the visual power of the feast. Lacquerware is a major reason for this. To see an excellent selection of this classic Japanese craft, go to Zōhiko. This restaurant sometimes closes on random days, so be sure to call ahead.

IPPŌDŌ

Teramachi-dōri, Nijō-agaru, Nakagyō-ku; tel. 075/211-4018; www.ippodo-tea.co.jp; 9am-6pm daily; take the Tōzai subway line to Kyoto Shiyakusho-mae Station

After sampling some of the different brews available at any number of the city's teahouses, you might be tempted to take home some high-grade tea. Ippōdō has the best selection of teas in the city.

SHIOYOSHI-KEN

218 Hidatono-chō, Kuromon-dōri, Nakadachiuri-agaru, Kamigyō-ku; tel. 075/441-0803; www.kyogashi.com; 9am-5:30pm Mon.-Sat.; take the Karasuma subway line to Imadegawa Station

If you want some sweets to go with the tea, Shioyoshi-ken is a historic shop that has a great selection of traditional Kyoto sweets.

NORTHWEST KYOTO

Flea Markets

TENJIN-SAN MARKET

Bakuro-chō, Kamigyō-ku; tel. 075/461-0005; http://kitanotenmangu.or.jp; 5am-6pm Apr.-Oct., 5:30am-5:30pm Nov.-Mar.; take Kyoto City Bus 50 or 101 to Kitano-Tenmangū-mae bus stop

On the 25th of every month, Kitano-Tenmangū shrine in the north of the city holds the Tenjin-san Market. While there are plenty of merchants hawking touristy tripe, there are also some genuinely good finds. Wandering the beautiful shrine grounds in search of them is part of the fun.

Antiques

ROBERT MANGOLD GALLERY

817-2 Kannon-ji Monzen-chō, Kamigyō-ku; tel. 075/201-3497; www.the-kura.com; open by appointment only; take Kyoto City Bus 50 or 101 to Kitano-Tenmangū-mae bus stop

If you have the money to spend and are keen to see a stunning collection of Japanese antiquities and traditional art, consider a visit to the Robert Mangold Gallery. Everything from artifacts of the Jomon Period (14,000-300 BC) to samurai armor can be found here.

Food

KYOTO STATION AREA

Ramen

KYOTO RAMEN KŌJI

10F Kyoto Station Building, Higashi Shiokoji-chō, Shiokoji-sagaru, Shimogyō-ku; tel. 075/361-4401; www.kyoto-ramen-koji.com; 11am-10pm daily; ¥1,000

If you're in or near Kyoto Station and need a quick, cheap meal on the go, Kyoto Ramen Kōji is a good bet. There are eight styles from all corners of Japan in one place. To reach this noodle zone (literally: "Kyoto Ramen Street"), turn so that you're facing north toward Kyoto Tower while you're under Kyoto Station's main soaring atrium. Look to your left and you'll see a number of escalators. Follow them until you get to the 10th floor. Once you've reached this lofty perch, turn left and you'll see the hall of ramen before you.

Cafés and Light Bites

EAT PARADISE

11F Kyoto Station Building, Higashi Shiokoji-chō, Shiokoji-sagaru, Shimogyō-ku; tel. 075/352-1111; 11am-10pm daily; ¥1,500

If you're not a noodle afficionado, don't fret. There's also a food court with more

TOP EXPERIENCE

Kaiseki Ryōri

Kaiseki ryōri is one of the world's most aesthetically sophisticated and beautiful cuisines. This rarefied style of cooking is a gestalt of everything Japan does right in the kitchen, from selecting the very best exquisitely fresh seasonal ingredients to preparing a stunning multicourse feast, artfully presented in elegant tablewear, in cozy yet refined settings.

autumnal *kaiseki* cuisine

Kyoto is at the center of the *kaiseki* tradition, being the place of its origin. *Kaiseki* cuisine initially emerged as a complement to the older tea ceremony, and was meant to be served as the meal before the bitter green brew was quaffed. A typical *kaiseki* meal consists of five or more dishes, beginning with sashimi and both grilled and steamed fish or vegetables. Next comes a soup and rice dish, with a light dessert to round out the meal. The preparation methods used in *kaiseki* cooking differ significantly from, say, gourmet French fare. Rather than adding new layers of taste with seasoning or sauce, *kaiseki* chefs are masters of letting the natural flavors of the ingredients speak for themselves.

Beyond the food itself, a staunch emphasis on hospitality (*omotenashi*) and the aesthetic dimension of the meal—involving gorgeous ceramic tablewear and careful placement of individual courses—are meant to elevate a *kaiseki* meal to a multisensory experience. Unsurprisingly, this doesn't come cheap. Depending on the restaurant, expect to pay more than ¥20,000 for a full *kaiseki* meal. If you're serious about food and want to experience the higher end of Japan's menu, plan on budgeting for this splurge once on your journey, whether you dine in an old townhouse in Kyoto, a sleek modern restaurant in Tokyo, or a rural inn overlooking a stream or a garden. Top picks include:

- **Ishibekoji Kamikura,** a stalwart in the heart of the fabled Gion district (page 333).
- **Kappo Yamashita,** a laid-back restaurant with casual countertop seating in front of a kitchen run by gregarious chefs (page 335).
- **Shoraian,** in Arashiyama, an atmospheric restaurant that has a tofu-focused menu and is housed in a formerly private residence overlooking a river (page 338).

Note that reservations must be made at least a few weeks or a month ahead for any *kaiseki* meal.

variety on the 11th floor of Kyoto Station: Eat Paradise. The restaurants here, ranging from Japanese (tempura, *tonkatsu*) to Italian, are appropriate when you're in the mood for a proper meal before hopping on the *shinkansen* or striking out for a day of sightseeing. To reach this food court, simply take the escalators one floor higher than where Kyoto Ramen Kōji is located and walk to the left until you reach the restaurants. Many restaurants here have English-language menus. Just pick the one that strikes your fancy.

ASIPAI PLUS HIBI COFFEE

460 Zaimoku-chō, Shichijō-dōri/Kawaramachi Higashi-iru, Shimogyō-ku; tel. 075/276-3526; http://hibicoffee.strikingly.com; Hibi Coffee 8am-7pm daily, Asipai 11:30am-3pm and 6pm-9pm; ¥1,000-2,000; take the Keihan line to Shichijō Station, then walk 4 minutes, or walk north from JR Kyoto Station for 10 minutes

Two unlikely businesses have joined forces under one roof, and their combined offerings—curry and coffee—surprisingly add up to a winner. The curries—shrimp, chicken, pork, and vegetarian, served with saffron rice—are flavorful and the coffee is artisanal, paired well with a piece of cake. Free Wi-Fi is available too.

SOUTHEAST KYOTO

Udon

KENDONYA

41 Fukakusa, Ichinotsubochō, Fushimi-ku; tel. 075/641-1330; https://kendonya.com; 11am-6pm Thurs.-Tues., random closing one day per month; ¥1,000; take the JR Nara line to Inari Station, then walk 4 minutes

Kendonya is a worthwhile udon (flour noodle) restaurant about 5 minutes' walk from Fushimi Inari-Taisha. The shop serves a form of chewy, al dente udon known as *koshi*, placed in a flavorsome soup. The staff are bubbly, creating a welcoming atmosphere.

Cafés and Light Bites

VERMILLION CAFÉ

5-31 Kaidoguchi-cho Fukakusa, Fushimi-ku; tel. 075/644-7989; www.vermillioncafe.com; 9am-5pm daily; ¥1,000; take the JR Nara line to Inari Station, then walk 9 minutes

A stone's throw from the army of fox statues and tunnel of vermillion *torii* gates snaking through the mountain where Fushimi Inari-Taisha stands, you'll find the aptly named Vermillion Café. This cozy café is located in the shrine area's backstreets and has a terrace overlooking a pond on the shrine's sprawling grounds. Excellent coffee and tasty baked goods are prepared on-site. This café is recommended for a great pit stop or a sit-down lunch.

SOUTHERN HIGASHIYAMA

Kaiseki

KIKUNOI HONTEN

459 Shimokawara-chō, Yasakatoriimae-sagaru, Higashiyama-ku; tel. 075/561-0015; http://kikunoi.jp; noon-1pm and 5pm-8pm; lunch ¥10,000 and up, dinner ¥20,000 and up; take the Keihan line to Gion-Shijō Station, then walk 13 minutes

For a stunning example of what a *kaiseki* feast can be, you won't be disappointed at Kikunoi Honten. Serving refined fare since it opened in 1912, Kikunoi is now being run by Yoshihiro Murata, a member of the third generation in a lineage of devoted chefs. Located near Maruyama-kōen in the heart of Gion, Kyoto's historic entertainment quarter, this restaurant changes its menu and the decor with the seasons. To get a spot at the table, speak with the staff or concierge of your accommodations at least three days prior.

★ ISHIBEKOJI KAMIKURA

463-12 Shimokawaracho Higashiyama-ku; tel. 075/748-1841; 6pm-9pm daily; ¥15,000 and up; take the Keihan line to Gion-Shijō Station or the Hankyū line to Kawaramachi Station, then walk 10 minutes

Another *ryotei*-style (traditional luxury) restaurant that delivers a masterful *kaiseki* experience in the Gion area is Ishibekoji Kamikura. Sit at the counter and watch chef Yoshiko Yano work culinary magic before your eyes. The food here—while exquisite just as it is at Kikunoi Honten—is renowned as being visually stunning as well. For maximum taste and color, try the "Omukai" seafood course.

Sushi

CHIDORITEI

203 Rokken-chō, Donguri-dori Yamato-oji Nishi-iru, Higashiyama-ku; tel. 075/561-1907; www7b.biglobe.ne.jp/~chidoritei/index.html; 11am-8pm Fri.-Wed.; ¥2,000; take the Keihan line to Gion-Shijō Station, then walk 4 minutes

Being landlocked, Kyoto isn't particularly known for sushi, but the city is known to serve a kind of sushi based on seasoned and marinated mackerel. The best place to try this is Chidoritei. This cozy family-run joint also serves good assorted *chirashi* bowls (sashimi over rice) and eel.

Cafés and Light Bites

★ KAGIZEN YOSHIFUSA KODAIJI

Kōdai-ji Omote-mon-mae Agaru, Higashi-yama-ku; tel. 075/525-0011; www.kagizen.co.jp; 9am-6pm Thurs.-Tues.; ¥1,000; take the Keihan line to Gion-Shijō Station or the Hankyū line to Kawaramachi Station, then walk 13 minutes

Any traveler with a sweet tooth take note: Kagizen Yoshifusa Kodaiji is one of the city's most venerated traditional dessert cafés. The shop's most popular branch is right on Shijō-dōri in the heart of Gion. I prefer the Kōdai-ji branch in Southern Higashiyama; it's a calm place to sample traditional sweets, such as azuki red bean paste stuffed pastries and arrowroot noodles dipped in black sugar, washed down with bitter, green-powdered *matcha* tea. This location is close enough to the bustling shopping streets leading uphill toward Kiyomizu-dera without being in the thick of it.

NORTHERN HIGASHIYAMA

Japanese

ASUKA

144 Nishi-machi, Jingumichi-nishi-iru, Higashiyama-ku; tel. 075/751-1941; 11am-11pm Tues.-Sun.; ¥1,000; take the Tōzai subway line to Higashiyama Station, exit 1, then walk 2 minutes

For good, simple Japanese rice and noodle dishes, Asuka is a trusty spot for a casual lunch or dinner when you're traipsing between Higashiyama's temples. The staff are friendly and the prices fair. English menu available.

SENMONTEN

380-3 Kiyomoto-chō, Higashi-gawa, Hanamikoji Shimbashi kudaru, Higashiyama-ku; tel. 075/531-2733; 6pm-2am Mon.-Sat.; ¥1,000; take the Keihan line to Gion-Shijō Station, then walk 7 minutes

Fried dumplings (*gyoza*) and beer: If this sounds good and you're not overly concerned about caloric intake or a balanced diet, you can't go wrong with Senmonten. There's nothing else on the menu, and that's fine. The *gyoza,* served in batches of 20, are crispy outside and stuffed with juicy pork and scallions.

Ramen

RAMEN MURAJI

373-3 Kiyomotocho, Higashiyama-ku; tel. 075/744-1144; https://ramen-muraji.jp; 11:30am-3pm and 5pm-10pm dinner Mon.-Sat., 11:30am-8pm Sun. and public holidays; ¥850; take the Keihan line to Gion-Shijō Station, then walk 5 minutes

Ramen Muraji serves a mean bowl of ramen in a creamy broth made from chicken bones, left to boil for hours on end and then tossed with bamboo strips and chicken. Add an egg from the side menu to make the bowl more filling. The restaurant is housed in a classic *machiya*-style building that's been tastefully spruced up and decorated. The entrance is tucked down a cobblestone alley in Gion next to a canal. There's unfortunately no English sign. Keep an eye out for white curtains in front of the entrance. English-language menu available.

Udon

★ OMEN

74 Jōdo-ji, Ishibashi-chō, Sakyō-ku; tel. 075/771-8994; www.omen.co.jp; 11am-9pm daily; ¥1,200; take Kyoto City Bus no. 5 to Ginkakuji-michi

The formula is simple at Omen. A generous portion of seven varieties of vegetables are served along with white wheat-flour noodles (udon)—either hot or cold—with soup and a liberal hit of sesame (to be used as seasoning) on the side. Mix the vegetables into the soup and dunk the noodles. Delicious. This is a great choice for a meal when you're in the vicinity of Ginkaku-ji. You'll have a choice of sitting either at the counter, at a separate table, or on a tatami floor.

Vegetarian

KISAKI YUDOFU

19-173 Jyodoji Minamida-chō, Sakyō-ku; tel. 075/751-7406; http://kyotokisaki.web.fc2.com;

11am-9pm Thurs.-Tues., open Wed. when it falls on holiday, last order 7:30pm; ¥2,500; take Kyoto City Bus no. 32 to Minamida-chō bus stop, then walk 3 minutes

Kisaki Yudofu is a great place for a healthy lunch when you're near the Philosopher's Path. Set meals come with various iterations of tofu and *yuba*, such as dipped in batter and fried as tempura, served with pickled vegetables, or seasoned with sesame. This is a good place for a solid vegetarian meal.

CHOICE

1F Suzuki Keiseigeka Bld., 89-1 Ohashi-cho, Higashiyama-ku; tel. 075/762-1233; http://choice-hs.net; 9am-9pm Fri.-Wed.; ¥1,200; take the Tōzai subway line to Sanjō Keihan Station, then walk 1 minute

On the other end of the spectrum from Senmonten is this restaurant with a decidedly healthier menu. Choice was opened by a doctor who has put a Japanese spin on a range of vegetarian, vegan, and even gluten-free dishes. There are excellent veggie burgers, salads, brown rice, pickled vegetables, smoothies and more. It's a stellar choice for vegetarians, vegans, and people with gluten intolerance.

International

ARASH'S KITCHEN

16-4 Shogoin Sannochō, Sakyo-ku; tel. 075/746-4769; www.arashskitchen.net; 11am-3pm and 5pm-11pm daily, a la carte from ¥300, dinner ¥3,000; take the Keihan line to Jingu-Marutamachi Station, then walk 8 minutes

For a break from Japanese food, try Arash's Kitchen. This Persian restaurant—with a bit of Indian thrown in—isn't much to look at, but it's popular. Staff are friendly, offerings are tasty, and there are occasional belly dance performances. Book a day ahead as it fills up.

Cafés and Light Bites

POMME CAFÉ

144 Jodoji Shimominamida-chō, Sakyo-ku; tel. 075/771-9692; 1am-6pm Thurs.-Mon.; ¥1,000

Another great option for a lunch near the Philosopher's Path is Pomme Café. This welcoming spot is run by a friendly proprietor who sells baked goods, coffee, and other drinks. It's not so much a place for a meal, but it makes for a terrific pit stop as you explore the area.

DOWNTOWN AND CENTRAL KYOTO

Kaiseki

KAPPO YAMASHITA

491-3 Kami Korikicho, tel. Nakagyo-ku; tel. 075/256-4506; 11:30am-1:30pm and 4pm-10pm Tues.-Sun.; lunch from ¥8,000; dinner from ¥15,000; take the Tōzai line to Kyoto Shiyakusho-mae Station, then walk 3 minutes

In a culinary tradition as focused on refinement as *kaiseki*, Kappo Yamashita stands out for its down-to-earth atmosphere. The chefs here are known to be friendly and even engage in banter with customers who sit at the counter—*kappo* means "counter style"—to watch them at work chopping, peeling, searing, broiling, and more. The staff are also happy to field questions about the menu.

KAISEKI MIZUKI

Kamogawa Nijo-Ohashi Hotori, Nakagyo-ku; tel. 075/746-5555; www.ritzcarlton.com/en/hotels/japan/kyoto/dining/kaiseki-mizuki; 11:30-2:30pm and 5:30pm-9:30pm daily; lunch from ¥6,000, dinner from ¥13,000; take the Hankyū line to Kawaramachi Station, then walk 6 minutes

Kaiseki Mizuki is a *kaiseki* option housed in the decidedly modern, luxurious settings of the Ritz-Carlton Kyoto; the atmosphere is sleek, in an elegant dining room with tableware made by artists. The innovative chefs aim to hit the principles of *go-mi* (five flavors), *go-shyoku* (five colors), and *go-ho* (five cooking methods).

Sushi

DEN SHICHI SUSHI SAIIN

Saiin, 4-1 Tatsumi-chō, Saiin, Ukyō-ku ; tel. 075/323-0700; 11:30am-2pm and 5pm-10pm Tues.-Sun.; ¥2,000; take the Hankyū line to Saiin Station, then walk 3 minutes

A place to get a sushi fix a bit west of

downtown is Den Shichi Sushi Saiin. Enter to a hearty "welcome" from the chefs, who are busy carving behind the counter, where patrons sit. The quality is high and prices are reasonable, frequently attracting a queue. Try to show up early to avoid the rush. Showing up late means options may have already been picked over.

Ramen

INOICHI

1F, Ebisuterasu, 528, Ebisunocho, Shimogyo-ku; tel. 075/353-7413; 11:30am-2pm and 5:30pm-10pm Tues.-Sun.; ¥1,200; take the Hankyū line to Kawaramachi Station, then walk 6 minutes

Inoichi serves ramen with white (lighter) or black (fuller) soy sauce for your broth. Bamboo shoots and a delicious "red egg" that has been marinated in soy sauce fill out the bowl, with the light yet robustly flavored broth being made with a mix of dried fish and kelp. If you don't mind waiting in the line that often forms outside, there's an English menu, so you can sort out your order while you wait.

Soba

SOBANOMI YOSHIMURA

420 Matsuyacho, Shimogyo-ku; tel. 075/353-0114; www.yoshimura-gr.com/sobanomi; 11am-3pm and 5:30pm-10:30pm daily; ¥1,500; take the Karasuma subway line to Gojō Station, exit 1, and walk 1 minute

Sobanomi Yoshimura makes good soba with a side menu featuring items like tempura vegetables, prawns and more. Watch the chefs prepare your food—including making the noodles from scratch—as you wait. Friendly staff and a welcoming atmosphere help make this a good place for lunch.

Vegetarian

MUMOKUTEKI CAFÉ

2F Human Forum Building, 351 Iseya-chō, Gokomochi-dori-Rokkaku-sagaru, Nakagyo-ku; tel. 075/213-7733; http://mumokuteki.com; 11:30am-10pm daily; from ¥1,000; take the Hankyū line to Kawaramachi Station, then walk 6 minutes

If you're downtown and in search of a vegetarian or vegan restaurant, head to the airy, elegant Mumokuteki Café without delay. There's a clearly labeled menu (English available) that breaks down the ingredients in each dish. Options include set meals, a salad bar, and a good selection of items that can be ordered a la carte. Avoid the lunch rush by coming early or mid-afternoon.

soba and tempura

KANGA-AN

278 Shingoryoguchi-chō, Karasuma-dōri, Kuramaguchi-Higahiiru, Kita-ku; tel. 075/256-2480; www.kangaan.jp; noon-1pm and 5pm-7pm daily; courses from ¥5,000; take Karasuma subway line to Kuramaguchi Station, then walk 4 minutes

To sample bona fide *shōjin-ryōri,* you have to go to a temple. Brought from China to Japan by the founder of Zen Buddhism, Dogen, *shōjin-ryōri* forgoes all meat, dairy, and even flavorful ingredients like garlic, onions, and spices. Arguably the best place to dine like a monk is the temple of Kanga-an in the city's north-central area. Diners are seated in private dining rooms divided by sliding paper doors and presented with a spread that is as aesthetically pleasing as it is healthy. Don't expect to be knocked out by flavor. Admire the delicacy instead. After your meal, move over to the bar next door to imbibe a cocktail in a pensive Zen-like state, looking out at the garden. Reserve two to three days in advance.

★ TŌSUIRŌ

517-3 Kamiosaka-chō, Sanjō-agaru, Nakagyo-ku; tel. 075/251-1600; http://tousuiro.com; 11:30am-2pm and 5pm-9:30pm Mon.-Sat., noon-8:30pm Sun.; lunch from about ¥4,000, dinner from about ¥5,000; take the Hankyū line to Kawaramachi Station, then walk 3 minutes

Tōsuirō is a great place to explore the wonders of tofu and *yuba*—and surprising wonders they are. Multicourse meals consist of small variations in cooking method. Assorted sashimi brings a different element to the table. When the weather is warm, book ahead to get a seat on the veranda overlooking the Kamo River—a quintessential Kyoto experience.

International

KERALA

2F KUS Building, Kawaramachi Sanjo agaru, Nakagyo-ku; tel. 075/251-0141; 11:30am-2pm and 5pm-9pm; lunch ¥1,200, dinner ¥2,000; take the Tōzai line to Kyoto Shiyakusho-mae Station, then walk 2 minutes, or take Keihan line to Sanjō Station, exit 6, then walk 5 minutes

As you eat your way through numerous rice, noodle, tofu, and fish-based meals, you might start to crave something different. Kerala, located downtown, offers a nice alternative. This shop serves excellent curries, tandoori dishes, biryanis and more. The menu is mostly north Indian, despite having a southern name. The dining room is small, and the focus is on the food.

SAMA SAMA

532-16 Kamiosakachō, Nakagyo-ku; tel. 075/241-4100; 6pm-2am Tues.-Sun.; ¥200 cover charge, dishes from ¥850; take the Keihan line to Sanjō Station, then walk 4 minutes

Another non-Japanese choice to spice things up is Sama Sama. The kitchen at this cozy Indonesian restaurant and bar whips up a diverse menu of omelets, and rice dishes with lots of chicken and fish. The Balinese owner is friendly and makes guests comfortable with a bit of conversation. Guests sit on floor cushions, creating a very laid-back atmosphere.

OBASE

534-39 Ebisucho, Kawaramachi Sanjo-Agaru, Nakagyo-Ku; tel. 075/211-6918; http://obasse.com; noon-1:30pm and 6pm-9:30pm Thurs.-Tues., random closing two days per month; lunch course ¥4,800, dinner course ¥9,000; take the Tōzai line to Kyoto Shiyakusho-mae Station, then walk 4 minutes

An Italian restaurant set in a renewed *machiya* townhouse, with counter seating on the first floor and tables on the second, Obase serves quality set-course meals with a Japanese twist. All vegetables are locally sourced and the friendly chefs choose dishes for you. Trust them—they know best. English menu available. Make a reservation a day or more ahead to be safe.

Cafés and Light Bites

PAPA JON'S HONTEN

642-4 Shokokuji-chō, Karasuma-dōri, Kamidachiuri higashi-iru, Kamigyō-ku; tel. 075/415-2655; http://www.papajons.net; 10am-9pm daily; lunch from ¥850, dessert from ¥350; take the Kurasuma subway line to Imadegawa Station, then walk 3 minutes

If you're near Imadegawa Station north of Kyoto Imperial Palace Park, Papa Jon's Honten is a good place for lunch—curry, quiche, sandwiches—or a coffee break with a slice of their famed cheesecake.

★ CAFÉ BIBLIOTIC HELLO!

650 Seimei-cho, Yanaginobanba-higashi-iru, Nijo-dori, Nakagyo-ku; tel. 075/231-8625; http://cafe-hello.jp; 11:30am-11pm daily; from ¥1,000; take the Tōzai and Karasuma subway lines to Karasuma Oike Station, exit 1, then walk 8 minutes

A spot that wins serious points for atmosphere—excellent lighting, exposed-brick walls lined with books, a globe lit from within—is the awesomely named Café Bibliotic Hello!. It's an appealing place to while away a few hours over a coffee, smoothie, or light meal with a book or laptop in hip surroundings. Just look for the red-brick exterior fronted by large banana plants.

TORAYA

415 Hirohashidono-chō, Ichijo-kado, Karasuma-dōri, Kamigyō-ku; tel. 075/561-5878; https://global.toraya-group.co.jp; 10am-7pm, closed on irregular days; from ¥1,000; take the Keihan line to Gion-shijō Station, exit 6, then walk 1 minute

Located in Gion, Toraya is an elegant place to sample a traditional sweet (think: sauce made from black sesame, rice cake stuffed with red bean paste) and a cup of *matcha* green tea—in summer, try it iced.

NORTHWEST KYOTO

Soba

HANAMAKIYA

17-2 Kinugasa Gochonouchi-chō, Kita-ku; tel. 075/464-4499; https://hanamakiya.gorp.jp; ¥1,000; a few minutes' walk east of Kinkaku-ji's grounds

There is a surprising dearth of restaurants around Kinkaku-ji, but thankfully there's Hanamakiya. Come here for a quick, filling lunch at a good value.

Vegetarian

★ IZUSEN DAIJIINTEN

4 Daitoku-chō, Murasakino, Kita-ku; tel. 075/491-6665; http://kyoto-izusen.com; 11am-4pm daily; from ¥3,500; from Kyoto Station, take Kyoto City Bus no. 204, 205, or 206 to Daitoku-ji bus stop, then walk a few minutes

On the grounds of the atmospheric **Daitoku-ji** temple complex, Izusen Daijiinten offers one of Kyoto's best *shōjin-ryōri* experiences. Great Buddhist vegan fare is served in a series of dishes that just keep coming, one after the other. Aside from being surprisingly diverse in flavor—pleasing even non-vegans—the dishes are beautiful to look at, too. There's a garden attached to the restaurant where you can sit in good weather. Be sure to wander the vast temple grounds after you eat—a highly recommended experience.

ARASHIYAMA

Kaiseki

★ SHORAIAN

Sagameno-chō, Ukyō-ku; tel. 075/861-0123; www.shoraian.com; 11am-5pm Mon.-Thurs., 11am-8pm Fri.-Sun.; lunch from ¥3,800, dinner from ¥6,300; take the Hankyū line to Arashiyama and walk 20 minutes, or the JR Sagano line to Saga-Arashiyama Station and walk 25 minutes

For a unique *kaiseki* experience in a more natural setting, try Shoraian. Set in the hills of Arashiyama, overlooking the Katsura River, the restaurant is housed in an old private residence. Climb a stone stairway through the forest, then go inside and sit down on a tatami floor. The service is outstanding, making guests feel like they're dining at someone's home. The menu consists of set courses that are heavily tofu-based and surprisingly affordable by *kaiseki* standards. Reserve a month ahead to ensure a spot. Its location outside the city and its affordability make this a superb introduction to *kaiseki.*

Tea Ceremony

a tea ceremony

Tea has been imbibed on the archipelago since the 8th century, when it arrived from China. During the 14th and 15th centuries, tea drinking was infused with Zen sensibilities, and a detailed set of movements and social protocols began to grow around the simple act. These behaviors gradually became what we know today as the *sadō* or *cha-no-yu* (the way of tea), which is fully expressed in the act of the tea ceremony, or *chaji,* itself.

SETTING

Alongside the ritual itself, the *wabi-sabi* (*wabi* meaning "rustic," *sabi* meaning "worn" or "aging") aesthetic sense—a concept that is quintessentially Japanese—is heavily present in the setting and tools used in the tea ceremony. Traditionally reached via a stone path, a teahouse is a tiny, weathered structure, topped by a thatched roof. The traditional squat entrance is intended to strip all incomers of social rank, implying all should join the ceremony as equals. Inside, are only the bare essentials: tatami-mat floors, paper *shoji* screens fronting windows onto scenes of nature, and often a garden. The proximity to nature is accentuated by natural materials—wood and paper—in the structure itself. This link is strengthened by the use of utensils with seasonally appropriate designs and flower arrangements. Coarse ceramic cups, saucers, and pots are used; their blemishes are celebrated rather than seen as drawbacks.

ETIQUETTE

Though there are minute movements and gestures, as well as common topics of conversation, prescribed for both hosts and guests in a tea ceremony, just be sure to cover the basics: remove your shoes before entering the teahouse, resist being overly chatty but do compliment the decor and utensils, and do your best to sit with your legs underneath you—or at least cross-legged—rather than sprawling out on the tatami. The traditional way to drink it is in three long sips, holding the bowl with your left hand underneath and right hand steadying it on the side.

WHERE TO GO

While a full-scale tea ceremony lasts up to four hours—from the preceding *kaiseki* feast to the ceremony itself—it's possible to experience a shortened version that simply consists of drinking one kind of *matcha* accompanied by a small sweet. To experience this Zen ritual in Kyoto in a relaxed yet refined setting, try **Camellia,** which has two locations:

- **Camellia Flower** (349-12 Masuya-chō, Higashiyama-ku; tel. 075/525-3238; www.tea-kyoto.com/experience/flower; 10am-6pm daily; shared tea ceremony ¥3,000 adults, ¥1,500 children ages 7-12, private tea ceremony ¥6,000 all ages for group of 2 or more): The bilingual woman who performs the 45-minute ceremonies here is informative and has a knack for putting guests at ease.

- **Camellia Garden** (18 Ryōan-ji Ikenoshita-chō, Ukyō-ku; tel. 070/5656-7808; www.tea-kyoto.com/experience/garden; 11am-6pm Mon.-Sat.; ¥8,000 per person for group of 2 or more, free for children under 6 years old): Set in an old house with a lovely garden, this branch is also run by a charming bilingual woman with a masterful grasp on the art of tea. The dreamy setting and slightly longer time given for each session (1 hour) justifies the slightly higher price tag. Book a spot on the website, which has a full booking calendar, for either location.

Soba

ARASHIYAMA YOSHIMURA

3 Saga-Tenryū-ji Susukinobaba-chō, Ukyō-ku; tel. 075/863-5700; http://yoshimura-gr.com; 11am-5pm daily; from ¥1,000; take the Hankyū line to Arashiyama station and walk 15 minutes

Arashiyama Yoshimura is a local soba shop that sells soba (hot or cold) lunch sets with various side dishes. Located a few minutes' walk from the temple of Tenryū-ji, this popular restaurant has a nice view of the Hozu River, rushing by outside. This is a good pick for a lunch before setting off on foot to explore the sights of the area. Note that it often attracts a queue, so try to avoid peak hours if you don't like to wait.

Vegetarian

YUDOFU SAGANO

45 Sagatenryūji, Susukinobaba-chō; tel. 075/871-6946; www.kyoto-sagano.jp; tel. 075/871-6946; 11am-7pm daily; courses from ¥3,000; take the JR Sagano line to Saga-Arashiyama Station and walk 15 minutes

For a more casual tofu-based meal, another option in Arashiyama is Yudofu Sagano. The specialty here is simmered pieces of hot tofu known as *yudo*, served with side dishes of mountain vegetables, tempura, and more.

Cafés and Light Bites

%ARABICA

3-47, Sagatenryuji Susukinobabacho, Ukyo-ku; tel. 075/748-0057; https://arabica.coffee, 8am-6pm daily; from ¥500; take the Hankyū line to Arashiyama station and walk 15 minutes

Just down the road from Arashiyama Yoshimura, you'll find %Arabica. This hip café, overlooking the Hozu River, serves artisanal coffee and makes for an ideal pit stop before or after exploring the area's sights. There's not much in the way of seating, but the area makes takeaway an appealing alternative.

Bars and Nightlife

If you'd like to get acquainted with the city's breweries, check out **Kampai Sake Tours** (tel. 080/7045-8365; https://kampaisake-tours.com/tour/kyoto-sake; 3 hours; 2pm-5pm Wed.-Sun.; ¥8,500).

SOUTHERN HIGASHIYAMA

BEER KOMACHI

444 Hachiken-chō, Higashiyama-ku; tel. 075/746-6152; www.beerkomachi.com; 5pm-11pm Mon. and Wed.-Fri., 3pm-11pm Sat.-Sun.; take the Tōzai subway line to Higashiyama Station

Beer Komachi is a friendly, laid-back spot to sample a range of Japan's craft beer offerings, with usually around seven types on tap. This spot also serves good nibbles, from beer-battered chicken to deep-fried blowfish.

NORTHERN HIGASHIYAMA

CLUB METRO

B1F Ebisu Building, 82 Shimotsutsumichō, Kawabata-dōri, Marutamachi-sagaru, Sakyō-ku; tel. 075/752-4765; www.metro.ne.jp; 8pm-3am daily; take the Keihan line to Jingū-Marutamachi Station

Club Metro is a longstanding venue with a penchant for catering to a wide range of musical tastes, from big-name DJs to indie rockers and even art exhibitions. With space for about 250 people, the space has an intimate feel. Events change nightly, so check the calendar online before making the trip.

DOWNTOWN AND CENTRAL KYOTO

SAKE BAR YORAMU

35-1 Matsuya-chō, Nijō-dōri, Higashinotoin, Higashi-iru, Nakagyō-ku; tel. 075/213-1512; www.sakebar-yoramu.com; 6pm-midnight Wed.-Sat.; from

¥1,600; take the Tōzai or Karasuma subway line to Karasuma-Oike Station

Make your way to Sake Bar Yoramu for a great introduction and sake tasting course. Owned by an Israeli sake enthusiast, the bar is a cramped but friendly spot to glean a bit more insight into the joys of Japan's most iconic drink.

L'ESCAMOTEUR BAR

138-9 Saito-chō, Saiseki-dōri, Shijō-sagaru, Shimogyō-ku; tel. 075/708-8511; 8pm-2am Tues.-Sun.; take the Keihan line to Gion-Shijō Station, or the Hankyū line to Kawaramachi Station

For a cocktail, L'Escamoteur Bar is a known quantity. Bartenders wearing bowler hats and bow ties mix great cocktails, some of which are meant to look like magic potions. This fun and friendly bar is strewn with curios and has an air of enchantment.

BAR CORDON NOIR

3F Matsushimaya Building, 121 Ishiya-chō, Nakagyō-ku; tel. 075/212-3288; 7pm-3am daily; cover charge ¥540; take the Tōzai subway line to Sanjō Station

Whisky aficionados, take note of Bar Cordon Noir. Although it's not cheap, the range of bottles here is truly impressive, with most of them either limited-edition or aged at least 17 years. The bartenders are friendly and highly knowledgeable, and cigars are sold. The room seats around 25.

CHEZ PHILIPPE FSN BAR

3F Rokkaku Terrace Building, Kawaramachi-dōri Rokkaku, Higashi-iru; tel. 090/5064-0642; 7pm-1am Tues.-Sun.; take the Tōzai subway line to Sanjō Station

Chez Philippe FSN Bar is run by local legend and French owner, Philippe. Live bands jam, and patrons play *go* (a strategic Japanese board game some consider more complex than chess) and mingle. The drinks are good and the crowd is friendly. This spot is highly recommended if you want a social evening out.

ATLANTIS

161 Matsumoto-chō, Ponto-chō-Shijō-agaru, Nakagyō-ku; tel. 075/241-1621; 6pm-2am Mon.-Sat., 6pm-1am Sun.; take the Hankyū line to Kawaramachi Station

A fashionable bar next to the Kamo River, Atlantis is a place to see and be seen. Located down Ponto-chō, it has a terrace overlooking the river. This is a great spot to go on a summer night. Note that outdoor seating is only offered during the months of May through September.

CAFÉ LA SIESTA - 8BIT EDITION

1F Reiho Kaikan, 366 Kamiya-chō, Nishi-kiyamachi-dōri, Shijō-agaru, Nakagyō-ku; tel. 075/634-5570; http://cafelasiesta.com; 7pm-4am Wed.-Mon.; take the Keihan line to Gion-Shijō Station, or the Hankyū line to Kawaramachi Station

Bring out your inner geek and enjoy playing some retro video games with drinks at Café La Siesta - 8bit Edition. Friendly staff and quality food and drinks make it a sure win for a fun, quirky night out.

BARCODE

3F Reiho Kaikan, 366 Kamiya-chō, Nishiyamachi-dōri, Shijō-agaru, Nakagyō-ku; tel. 075/221-7333; 8pm-5am daily; take the Keihan line to Gion-Shijō Station, or the Hankyū line to Kawaramachi Station

Feel like crooning? In the same building as Café La Siesta - 8bit Edition, Barcode is a fun place for a night of karaoke, which can be done for free with a machine and mics brought straight to your table. Sometimes this bar hosts international parties, which draw a diverse crowd.

URBANGUILD

3F New Kyoto Building, 181-2 Kiyamachi, Sanjō-shita, Nakagyō-ku; tel. 075/212-1125; www.urbanguild.net; 6:30pm-1am daily; fee varies by event; take the Tōzai subway line to Sanjō Station

Urbanguild is the best place to catch a glimpse of Kyoto's underground scene. A bit of decay and a DIY spirit are on display, with an antique chandelier and furniture made from recovered wood. Think punk, avant-garde theater, noise and experimental electronic music. Check the website's events page to see what's on and the cover charge.

BUNGALOW

15 Kashiwaya-chō, Shijō-dōri, Shimoji-ku, Nakagyō-ku; tel. 075/256-8205; www.bungalow.jp; noon-10pm Mon.-Sat.; take the Hankyū line to Ōmiya Station

Bungalow is a great downtown bar on two floors, serving a nice range of up to 10 domestic craft beers. Set in a minimal industrial-chic building, the bar also offers great organic food.

BAR ROCKING CHAIR

434-2 Tachibana-chō, Bukkoji-sagaru, Gokomachi-dōri, Shimogyō-ku; tel. 075/496-8679; www.bar-rockingchair.jp; 5pm-2am Wed.-Mon., 5pm-midnight Sun.; take the Hankyū line to Kawaramachi Station

Bar Rocking Chair is a serious cocktail den. Bartender and owner Kenji Tsubokura is a renowned mixologist who uses homegrown ingredients in his flavorsome creations. This is a great pick for laid-back drinks in a classy, though not stuffy, atmosphere.

SHOOTING BAR M4

3F TN Building, 452 Matsugae-chō, Nakagyō-ku; tel. 080/5350-0556; https://m4-kyoto.jimdo.com; 5pm-midnight daily; take the Tōzai subway line to Sanjō Station

At Shooting Bar M4, you'll find friendly staff, affordable drinks, and a BB gun shooting range. What more can you ask for?

KITSUNE KYOTO

179 Zaimoku-chō, Kiyamachi-dōri, Sanjō-sagaru, Nakagyō-ku; tel. 075/255-0421; https://kitsune-kyoto.com; 10pm-4am Sun.-Thurs., 9pm-5am Fri.-Sat.; ¥1,000 (includes 1 drink) before 11pm/¥2,000 (includes 1 drink) after 11pm for men, free for women Sun.-Thurs.; ¥1,000 (includes 1 drink) before 10pm/¥2,500 (includes 1 drink) men, free before 9pm/¥1,500 (includes 1 drink) for women Fri.; ¥1,500 (includes 1 drink) before 10pm/¥3,000 (includes 1 drink) after 10pm for men, ¥1,000 (includes 2 drinks) before 10pm/¥2,000 (includes 1 drink) after 10pm for women Sat.; take the Tōzai subway line to Sanjō Station

Kitsune Kyoto is a thumping nightlife venue with a solid sound system and space for up to 800 on its two floors. The focus is on electronic music, and the club often books heavy-hitter DJs.

WORLD KYOTO

B1F-B2F Imagium Building, 97 Shinmachi, Nishi-kiyamachi-dōri, Shijō-agaru, Shimogyō-ku; tel. 075/213-4119; http://world-kyoto.com; 8pm-4am Mon.-Thurs., 8pm-5am Fri.-Sat.; ¥2,000 (includes 1 drink) men, ¥1,000 (includes 1 drink) women Sun.-Thurs.; ¥3,000 (includes 1 drink) men, ¥2,000 (includes 1 drink) women Fri.-Sat.; take the Keihan line to Gion-Shijō Station, or the Hankyū line to Kawaramachi Station

World Kyoto is a large, cavernous club that hosts DJs from all corners of the earth. Techno, house, and various electronic sounds reverberate through this subterranean soundscape, which is hopping on weekends. The stone arches hint at the space's previous function as an Italian restaurant.

Accommodations

KYOTO STATION AREA

Under ¥10,000

K'S HOUSE

418 Naya-chō, Dotemachi-dōri, Shichijō-agaru, Shimogyō-ku; tel. 075/342-2444; https://kshouse.jp; ¥5,000 private twin room with bunk bed and shared bathroom, ¥6,000 private room with double bed and shared bathroom; walk 15 minutes from JR Kyoto Station's Karasuma central gate

K's House has gained a reputation as being a dependable, fun hostel, particularly for young travelers who want to mingle. Rooms range from dorms with bunk beds to small private spaces. All the basics of any guesthouse are in place: Wi-Fi, laundry, and bilingual staff who are happy to help guests arrange various travel logistics.

¥10,000-20,000

RYOKAN SHIMIZU

644 Kagiya-cho, Shichijō-dōri, Wakamiya agaru, Shimogyō-ku; tel. 075/371-5538; www.kyoto-shimizu.net; ¥13,000 d with private bath; walk about 5 minutes from JR Kyoto Station's Karasuma central gate

Ryokan Shimizu is a great budget *ryokan*. There are no luxurious meals or landscape garden views, but the rooms are clean, and both English-speaking staff and friendly fellow travelers are happy to swap information. If you're content sleeping in a futon on a tatami floor, and proximity to Kyoto Station is important to you, this hotel is a good bet. Bicycle rentals available (¥700 per day). Note that there is a midnight curfew.

¥30,000-40,000

DORMY INN PREMIUM KYOTO EKIMAE

558-8 Higashishiokōji-chō, Shimogyō-ku; tel. 075/371-5489; https://renewal.hotespa.net/dormyinn; ¥30,200 d; walk 5 minutes from JR Kyoto Station's Karasuma central exit

Dormy Inn Premium Kyoto Ekimae is a no-frills budget hotel option a short walk from Kyoto Station. This is essentially a business hotel with a few added flourishes: free breakfast, a late-night restaurant, and a bath on the rooftop.

★ HOTEL GRANVIA

JR Kyoto Station, Central Exit, Karasuma-dōri, Shiokōji-sagaru, Shimogyō-ku; tel. 075/344-8888; www.granviakyoto.com; ¥35,000 d

Hotel Granvia has well-appointed rooms with chic decor. The hotel is literally in the JR Kyoto Station building, offering direct access to transport links. The views over the city (or train tracks) are notable too.

SOUTHERN HIGASHIYAMA

Under ¥10,000

GOJŌ GUESTHOUSE

3-396-2 Gojōbashi Higashi, Higashiyama-ku; tel. 075/525-2299; http://gojo-guest-house.com; ¥2,000 dorm, ¥5,500 twin; take the Keihan line to Kiyomizu-Gojō

With its English-speaking staff, Gojō Guesthouse is a good budget option and is popular among backpackers. It is situated near the ever-popular Kiyomizu-dera, and set in a century-old *ryokan* building. The rooms are a mix of dorms and petite private rooms for up to three. All rooms share a bathroom and toilet.

Over 40,000

HYATT REGENCY KYOTO

664-2 Sanjūsangen-dō-mawari, Higashiyama-ku; tel. 075/541-1234; www.kyoto.regency.hyatt.com; ¥55,700 d; take the Keihan line to Shichijō Station, then walk 5 minutes

The Hyatt Regency Kyoto is a fantastic hotel with luxury trimmings at a relatively reasonable price. Located in the southern edge of Higashiyama, the hotel boasts good food options, from sushi to spaghetti, as well as helpful staff and chic spacious rooms, each with room service only a touch screen away.

FOUR SEASONS KYOTO

445-3 Maekawa-chō, Myohoin, Higashiyama-ku; tel. 075/541-8288; www.fourseasons.com/kyoto; ¥127,800 d; roughly 10 minutes' taxi ride from JR Kyoto Station

For a phenomenal luxury experience in the heart of Kyoto's most important sightseeing district, it's hard to outdo Four Seasons Kyoto. Elegant rooms with Japanese accents (paper lamps, painted screens) boast marble bathrooms with large tubs and views overlooking a gorgeous garden centered around a serene pond. There's excellent on-site dining too. The hotel's staff are warm and helpful, and it's all located a short walk from key sights such as Sanjūsangen-dō.

★ YUZUYA RYOKAN

Yasaka-jinja Minami-tonari, Gion-machi, Higashiyama-ku; tel. 075/533-6369; http://yuzuyaryokan.com; from ¥50,000; take the Keihan line to Gion-Shijō, then walk 10 minutes from exit 6

Yuzuya Ryokan is a sophisticated *ryokan* located right on Higashiōji-dōri, a stone's throw from Yasaka-jinja. The inn, discretely tucked away up a stairway right off the main drag, oozes refinement once you step inside. There's a charming garden for a relaxing stroll, excellent meals, wooden tubs in the rooms, and highly attuned staff. It's also very convenient, with downtown a mere 10-minute walk away and the sights of Southern Higashiyama arrayed all around it.

NORTHERN HIGASHIYAMA

¥10,000-20,000

KYOTO YOSHIMIZU

Maruyama-kōen, Bentendoue, Higashiyama-ku; tel. 075/551-3995; http://yoshimizu.com; ¥15,000 d; a 10-minute walk from the Gion bus stop

Set in the back of Maruyama-kōen, Kyoto Yoshimizu scores points for being amid nature, while also being within easy reach of the city. The inn is set in a traditional-style *ryokan* building but has both western-style and Japanese-style rooms. Breakfast is included.

HOTEL ETHNOGRAPHY - GION SHINMONZEN

219-2 Nishinochō, Shinmonzen, Yamato Ōji Hirashi-iru, Higashiyama-ku; tel. 075/708-7858; www.hotel-ethnography.com; rooms from ¥17,000; take the Keihan line to Gion-Shijō Station, then walk 6 minutes from exit 7

Hotel Ethnography - Gion Shinmonzen is a boutique hotel in Gion, a short walk from the east bank of the Kamo River. The interior is minimalist with tasteful Japanese accents, including arts and crafts made by local artisans. Some rooms even look out onto private gardens. Friendly English-speaking staff are on call to help you navigate the city and make arrangements for restaurants and activities. Fantastic value.

¥30,000-40,000

HANA-TOURO HOTEL GION

555 Komatsuchō, Higashiyama-ku; tel. 075/525-8100; doubles from ¥38,000; take the Keihan line to Gion-Shijō Station, then walk 5 minutes from exit 6

Hana-Touro Hotel Gion is a sleek, new boutique hotel smack in the middle of Kyoto's old geisha quarter of Gion. The rooms are modern, stylish, and clean, with balconies and wooden bathtubs. There's a rooftop terrace and a restaurant serving Japanese fare, and the front desk can assist with anything from attending geisha performances to renting bikes and kimonos.

★ HOTEL THE CELESTINE KYOTO GION

572 Komatsu-chō, Yasaka-dōri, Higashiōji-nishi-iru, Higashiyama-ku; tel. 075/532-3111; www.celestinehotels.jp; doubles from ¥33,580; take the Keihan line to Gion-Shijō Station, then walk 10 minutes from exit 1

Hotel The Celestine Kyoto Gion is brand-new and sits in a sweet spot right in the heart of Gion. If you're seeking an excellent

TOP EXPERIENCE

Staying in a *Ryokan*

A stay in a traditional Japanese inn (*ryokan*) offers the chance to experience many elements of Japanese hospitality and comfort—spare traditional interiors, sleeping in a futon on a tatami-mat floor, haute dining in your room—under one roof. Before the modern era, *ryokan* served as stopover points for anyone traversing the Tokaido Highway that once ran between the feudal capital of Edo (modern-day Tokyo) and the ancient capital of Kyoto. Many associate *ryokan* with the countryside, but fantastic *ryokan* are also found in virtually every city and town in the country.

WHAT TO EXPECT

Today, *ryokan* vary significantly, from modest family-run countryside pensions to luxe getaways. Some core elements shared by ryokan across the spectrum include simple **tatami-mat floors,** both private and shared ***onsen* baths,** and **excellent meals** delivered twice daily to your room, from breakfast (Japanese or Western, depending on the inn) to *kaiseki* spreads for dinner. (Some more modest digs serve meals in common dining areas.) Furniture will likely be simple: a low wooden table with legless chair or floor-cushions to sit on, a futon instead of a bed for sleeping (usually laid out as you eat dinner).

Perhaps what stands out most is the **relaxed pace** and impeccable ***omotenashi*** (hospitality) at the heart of a ryokan stay. Upon entering, slip off your shoes and ease into the slippers provided. In your room, be sure to take off your slippers before entering any tatami-mat area, where only socks or barefoot are acceptable etiquette. Ditch your day clothes in favor of a much more comfortable *yukata*.

Although it's by no means necessary or expected, upon leaving, nudge an envelope with a **cash tip** to the staff if their service impresses you. Tipping isn't customary in Japan, but *ryokan* are an exception due to the exceptional hospitality they often provide.

HOW TO CHOOSE A *RYOKAN*

Some factors to consider when choosing a *ryokan* to stay in will include whether the rooms have en-suite bathrooms or not, whether the inn has an *onsen*, whether you'd be sleeping on a futon or a bed, and what kind of food options will be included in your stay. Both **Japanese Guest Houses** (www.japaneseguesthouses.com) and **JAPANiCAN** (www.japanican.com) are excellent English-language *ryokan* portals that make browsing and reserving *ryokan* smooth and enjoyable.

option at the higher end of the midrange, and convenience is a priority, this hotel is highly recommended. En-suite bathrooms are complemented by gender-separated public baths, and an on-site restaurant whips up Japanese and western offerings. The rooms are sleek and amply sized, and the hotel's location is excellent.

OLD KYOTO

536-12 Komatsu-chō, Higashiyama-ku; tel. 075/533-7775; www.oldkyoto.com; from ¥32,000 per night, minimum 5-night stay; take the Keihan line to Gion-Shijō Station exit one and walk 10 minutes

There are three charming *machiya* in the southeastern corner of Gion run by an aesthetically minded restoration organization called Old Kyoto. Up to four people can occupy the Gion House, Indigo House, or Amber House at any one time, with a requirement of at least five nights' stay. Spruced up retro Japanese-style interiors are complemented by fully modernized creature comforts, including decked-out kitchens and laundry facilities. Considering the space and amenities, as well as the charm and location, these homes are excellent, affordable alternatives to the city's hotels.

★ YOSHIDA SANSŌ

59-1 Yoshida Shimōji-chō, Sakyō-ku; tel. 075/771-6125; www.yoshida-Sansō.com; from ¥32,125 per person with breakfast; take a taxi from Kyoto Station (20 minutes), or Kyoto City Bus no. 5 to Ginkaku-ji Michi bus stop and walk 15 minutes

Yoshida Sansō has a whiff of secrecy, as well as history, about it. Located in a quiet corner of the city near Ginkaku-ji, on the summit of Mount Yoshida, this classic old *ryokan* was originally built during the Shōwa Period (1926-1989)—seen in the architectural blend revealing inspiration from both East and West—to serve as the home of a prince, Higashi-Fushimi, who was the uncle of Japanese Emperor Akihito. There's an atmosphere of elegant wear on the surfaces of this hideaway. A short walk from Northern Higashiyama's temple circuit, as well as a network of hiking trails, Yoshida Sansō is a *ryokan* set apart.

DOWNTOWN AND CENTRAL KYOTO

Under ¥10,000

★ THE MILLENNIALS KYOTO

235 Yamazaki-chō, Nakagyō-ku; tel. 075/212-6887; www.themillennials.jp; ¥2,800 single capsule, ¥5,300 double capsule; take the Tōzai subway line to Sanjō Station, then walk 7 minutes from exit 6

The Millennials Kyoto is a hip "smart pod" (capsule hotel) aimed, as the name suggests, for young professionals on the go. Each "pod," just big enough to crawl in and comfortably crash, has a plug and USB socket, and its own iPod touch. There's a shared lounge, a shared workspace, and amenities including free Wi-Fi, free breakfast and coffee, and even free beer. Restrooms, showers, laundry facilities, and lavatories are all shared. If you're looking to mingle and don't mind sleeping in a capsule, this is a stylish option in a central location.

¥10,000-20,000

HOTEL GRACERY KYOTO SANJŌ

406 Sakurano-chō, Shinkyogoku-dōri, Sanjō Sagaru, Nakagyō-ku; tel. 075/222-1111; http://kyoto.gracery.com; rooms from ¥10,00; take the Tōzai subway line to Sanjō Station, then walk 9 minutes from exit 6

Hotel Gracery Kyoto Sanjō offers simple, well-designed, clean rooms, stocked with basic toiletries and bath amenities. Coin laundry, optional breakfast, and 24-hour luggage storage are among the many other extras. In the heart of downtown, with Gion only 15 minutes' walk away, the location is convenient too.

¥20,000-40,000

AOI HOTEL KYOTO

reception at 145-1 Tenno-chō, Shimogyō-ku; tel. 075/354-7770; ¥36,000 d; take the Hankyū line to Kawaramachi station or the Keihan line to Gion-Shijō Station, then walk 5 minutes from either

Aoi Hotel Kyoto is a great value. It has an excellent concierge service, and spacious rooms that are more akin to small studio apartments than to hotel rooms, with Japanese flourishes, including painted screens and flower arrangements. The hotel is right next to the Kamo River in the heart of downtown, within walking distance of heaps of good food options, nightlife, and a number of sights. Each room has ample amenities, including its own washer and dryer.

★ IORI MACHIYA STAY RESIDENCE

various locations downtown; tel. 075/352-0211; www.kyoto-machiya.com; from ¥21,000; address provided upon reservation

Iori Machiya Stay Residence offers the greatest range of *machiya* accommodations in Kyoto. An impressive 11 homes scattered around the downtown area, near the Kamo River's west bank, have been renovated to have all creature comforts, while retaining their original aesthetic character, with tatami floors, paper lanterns, alcoves housing scrolls and flower arrangements, and calligraphy.

Some of the properties even boast private terraces overlooking the river. Alongside beautifully restored digs in the heart of downtown, a concierge service is also on call, and is happy to answer any questions as well as arrange any number of experiences, from fine dining to the arts.

SOLARIA NISHITETSU HOTEL KYOTO PREMIER SANJŌ

509 Kamiosaka-chō, Kiyamachi-dōri Sanjō-agaru, Nakagyō-ku; tel. 075/708-5757; http://solaria-kyoto.nishitetsu-hotels.com; ¥24,000 d; take the Tōzai subway line to Kyoto Shiyakusho-Mae Station, then walk 2 minutes

Solaria Nishitetsu Hotel Kyoto Premier Sanjō opened in 2016 and is one of the city's best values. With a boutique feel, the property is smack in the middle of downtown, right next to the Kamo River. It commands stellar views of the river as well as the Higashiyama Mountains looming to the east. Rooms are well appointed, surprisingly chic for the price and quiet. The staff are friendly and speak English. A solid balance at a reasonable price.

Over ¥40,0000

KINMATA

Gokomachi, Shijō-agaru, Nakagyō-ku; tel. 075/221-1039; www.kinmata.com; ¥50,000 with 2 meals; take the Hankyū line to Kawaramachi Station, then walk 5 minutes

Founded in 1801, this institution is both a high-end ryokan with 7 Japanese-style rooms and a bastion of *kaiseki* dining (lunch ¥6,000-16,000, dinner ¥13,000-35,000). The ryokan rooms look the part: wooden interiors, opening onto an inner garden, tatami floors and screens made of reed and paper. The restaurant is overseen by chef Haraju Ukai, a seventh-generation culinary wizard. Classic, old-school and exquisite.

AOI KYOTO STAY

reception at 145-1 Tenno-chō, Shimogyō-ku; tel. 075/354-7770; www.kyoto-stay.jp; about ¥60,000 per night in each house; take the Hankyū line to Kawaramachi station, then walk 7 minutes, or take the Keihan line to Gion-Shijō Station and walk 5 minutes

Run by the same folks who operate Aoi Hotel Kyoto, Aoi Kyoto Stay follows a similar concept, but extends it to the level of a house. Six phenomenal homes—most of them built

stay at Kyoto's Iori Machiya

in Kyoto's ubiquitous *machiya* townhouse style—dot the eastern side of the downtown area near Ponto-chō and the western bank of the Kamo River. Plush beds, heated floors, luxurious bathrooms, and tasteful Japanese decor give each residence an air of sophistication with an equal measure of comfort. If you want to stay downtown and price is no object, renting one of these homes will not disappoint.

HIIRAGIYA

Nakahakusan-chō, Fuyachō, Aneyakōji-agaru, Nakagyō-ku; tel. 075/221-1136; www.hiiragiya.co.jp; from ¥60,000; take the Tōzai subway line to Kyoto Shiyakusho-mae Station exit 8, then walk 5 minutes

While the vaunted Tawaraya *ryokan* across the road may be steeped in more mystique, the Hiiragiya is on par with its renowned neighbor and is, relatively speaking, easier to book. From the outside, the inn looks exactly like you'd expect: earthen walls separate it from the street, with foliage poking over the top and black tiles on the roof. Inside, hushed tatami-mat rooms with sliding paper doors look onto private landscape gardens. Exquisite *kaisek ryori* meals are de rigueur, as is impeccable service. In a surprise twist, there is not only an old classic wing, but also a shiny modern one, offering a range of room types. Unlike at many of Kyoto's elite *ryokan,* is the staff here is accustomed to hosting visitors from abroad. To book a room, you'll need to submit a request online (in English) through the official website.

★ RITZ-CARLTON KYOTO

543 Hokoden-chō, Nijō-Ōhashi-hotori, Nakagyō-ku; tel. 075/746-5555; www.ritzcarlton.com; from ¥95,000; take the Tōzai subway line to Kyoto Shiyakusho-mae Station, then walk 10 minutes

For an ideal balance of extravagance and convenience, the Ritz-Carlton Kyoto reigns supreme. It's right next to the western bank of the Kamo River, in the center of the city, a bit north of the major artery of Nijō-dōri. It comes with all the sumptuous amenities you'd expect from this global luxury juggernaut. It also houses a fantastic *kaiseki ryori* restaurant. Perhaps its biggest trait worthy of mention is that it blends in seamlessly with Kyoto's low-rise skyline.

NORTHWEST KYOTO

Under ¥10,000

SHUNKŌ-IN

42 Myōshinji-chō, Hanazono, Ukyō-ku; tel. 075/462-5488; www.shunkoin.com; ¥8,800 s, ¥7,500 d, ¥6,000 triple pp; take the JR Sagano line to Hanazono Station, then walk 13 minutes

Shunkō-in offers the chance not only to just see Kyoto's magnificent temples, but also to actually sleep in one—well, at least in lodgings on its grounds. Bicycles and Wi-Fi are free, and the head priest speaks English, giving guests a chance to ask whatever they want to know about Zen.

Information and Services

TOURIST INFORMATION

ONLINE RESOURCES

Kyoto Travel Guide (www.kyoto.travel) is a great English-language resource online. The site introduces Kyoto's cuisine, culture, sights, neighborhoods, travel agents, and more. The **Deep Kyoto** (www.deepkyoto.com) blog unearths some of the city's hidden gems, from cafés to art exhibits.

KYOTO TOURIST INFORMATION CENTER

2F Kyoto Station Building; tel. 075/343-0548; 8:30am-7pm daily

Your first port of call in Kyoto is the Kyoto Tourist Information Center, located on the second floor of Kyoto Station next to the entrance to Isetan department store. This is the best place in the city to pick up English-language materials, from pamphlets on the city's main attractions to maps of the city's extensive bus routes and guided walks through key neighborhoods. Be sure to pick up a copy of the **Kyoto Visitor's Guide** (www.kyotoguide.com). This small booklet gives a good rundown of the city's sights, events, restaurants, and lodgings in the city. Its English-language website is likewise a great resource.

KYOTO INTERNATIONAL FOUNDATION

2-1 Torii-chō, Awataguchi, Sakyō-ku; tel. 075/752-3010; www.kcif.or.jp; 9am-9pm, Tues.-Sun.

Kyoto International Foundation is located about five minutes' walk from Keage Station (exit 2) on the Tōzai subway line in northern Higashiyama, a stone's throw from the sprawling temple realm of Nanzen-ji. This one-stop shop offers a host of informational services for foreign visitors, including a library stocked with international periodicals, Internet access (¥200 for 30 minutes), a comfortable lounge, and a message board where people post accommodations information, calls for language exchange partners, flyers offering goods for sale, and more. Various classes on traditional arts, such as tea ceremony and calligraphy, are often hosted at the complex, too.

POSTAL SERVICES

KYOTO CENTRAL POST OFFICE

843-12 Higashishiokoji-chō, Shimogyō-ku; tel. 075/365-2471; 9am-9pm Mon.-Fri., 9am-7pm Sat.-Sun.

Kyoto Central Post Office is located just outside Kyoto Station's main exit on the north side. As soon as you leave the station, it will be the sixth-floor building fronted by rows of windows to the left.

PHARMACIES AND MEDICAL SERVICES

Pharmacies (*yakyoku*) are plentiful; simply look for the internationally recognizable red cross symbol out front. Call **AMDA International Medical Information Center**'s Osaka branch (tel. 050/3598-7574; http://eng.amda-imic.com; 9am-5pm Mon.-Fri.) for medical advice in the Kansai region, including Kyoto. The English-speaking operators are happy to help you navigate the Japanese medical system, referring you to doctors, hospitals, and so on.

KYOTO UNIVERSITY HOSPITAL

54 Shōgoin Kawahara-chō, Sakyō-ku; tel. 075/751-3111; www.kuhp.kyoto-u.ac.jp; 8:15am-11am Mon.-Fri. reception

If you need to visit a hospital, your best bet is Kyoto University Hospital, located just east of the Kamo River in northern Higashiyama. English-speaking assistance and quality of care are ensured here.

KYOTO PREFECTURAL MEDICAL UNIVERSITY HOSPITAL

Kawaramachi-Hirokoji, Kajii-chō, Kamigyō-ku; tel. 075/251-5111; http://www.kpu-m.ac.jp; 9am-3pm reception Mon.-Fri.

Another reliable hospital is Kyoto Prefectural Medical University Hospital, located just west of the Kamo River next to Kyoto Imperial Palace, or about 15 minutes' walk west of Kyoto University Hospital. The hospital offers English interpretation services from 9am-3pm on weekdays.

Transportation

GETTING THERE

If you're traveling to Kyoto from within Japan, the *shinkansen* (bullet train) is your best bet, particularly if you have a JR Pass. If you're coming from overseas and Kyoto is your first or only stop, there are also three airports within relatively easy reach, although none of them are actually in the city.

Air

The nearest flight hub to Kyoto is **Osaka International Airport** (tel. 06/6856-6781; www.osaka-airport.co.jp; information center 6:30am-9:30pm), also known as Itami Airport. Located roughly 50 minutes from the city by limousine bus, this hub is primarily a stop on domestic routes. But if you see a good flight deal that connects to the airport from another international airport in the country, don't hesitate. Some airlines offer connecting flights via Tokyo's Narita Airport.

Osaka Airport Transport (tel. 06/6844-1124; www.okkbus.co.jp; 55 minutes; ¥1,340) offers limousine bus services from the airport to Kyoto and vice versa. Tickets can be purchased from machines outside the arrivals area. **MK Taxi Sky Gate Shuttle** (tel. 075/778-5489; www.mk-group.co.jp; ¥3,000) will bring you directly to your lodgings. The downside is that you'll have to share the journey with others staying elsewhere, so you may have a long ride if your stop is later in the route.

If connecting from Tokyo sounds like too much trouble, you can also fly directly to Osaka's **Kansai International Airport** (tel. 072/455-2500; http://kansai-airport.net). You can access Kyoto via express train in about 80 minutes via the **JR Haruka Airport Express** (¥3,430). Note that this route is covered by the JR Pass. As with Osaka International Airport, Kansai International Airport is also serviced by Osaka Airport Transport (90 minutes; ¥2,600) and MK Taxi Sky Gate Shuttle (¥4,300).

Finally, if you have a JR Pass and don't mind traveling by bullet train upon arrival, you can even consider flying into **Central Japan International Airport** (tel. 0569/38-1195; www.centrair.jp; 6:40am-10pm telephone center) in Nagoya. Although the distance between the two cities is 129 km (80 mi), the journey by bullet train from Nagoya to Kyoto—covered by the JR pass—is a mere 35 minutes (¥5,800).

Bus

Operators run buses during the daytime and overnight between **Tokyo** and Kyoto. The trip takes 7-8 hours one way. One of the best-known operators is **Willer Express** (http://willerexpress.com), which offers fares from ¥4,000. Compare fares and book bus tickets via the Willer Express website, **Japan Bus Online** (https://japanbusonline.com), or **Kosoku Bus** (www.kosokubus.com).

Train

By far, the easiest way to reach Kyoto from Japan's other major transport hubs is the *shinkansen* (bullet train). From Tokyo, **Nozomi trains** (140 minutes; ¥14,000 reserved seat) and **Hikari trains** (160 minutes; ¥13,500 reserved seat) make the journey. Note that the JR Pass only covers journeys made on the Hikari *shinkansen*, as well as the slower Kodama *shinkansen*.

If you're coming from **Osaka**, the Hikari *shinkansen*, covered by the JR Pass, will take you from Shin-Osaka Station to Kyoto Station in a mere 14 minutes (¥3,070 reserved seat). Another option covered by the JR Pass is the **JR Kyoto line**, which links the more conveniently located Osaka Station to Kyoto Station (30 minutes; ¥560). There are also non-JR lines (not covered by the JR Pass) running between Osaka and stations deeper in Kyoto's downtown area. One such line is the **Hankyū Kyoto line**, which links Osaka's Umeda Station, a major hub near Osaka Station in the city's north, with stations in Kyoto's downtown area such as **Karasuma** and **Kawaramachi** (about 40 minutes; ¥400). Finally, the Keihan Main line links Yodoyabashi Station in the center of Osaka to stations in downtown Kyoto, such as Gion-Shijō and Sanjō (about 50 minutes; ¥410).

From Kobe, take the *shinkansen* (30 minutes; ¥3,650 reserved seat), which departs from Shin-Kobe Station, covered by the JR Pass. A second option is the **Hankyu Kyoto/Kobe line**, which links Kobe-Sannomiya Station and Karasuma Station in downtown Kyoto with a transfer at Juso Station (70 minutes; ¥620).

Car

It rarely makes sense to drive to Kyoto unless you happen to be traveling through Japan by car already and it's your only means of transport in the country. The toll fees are not particularly cheap, reaching about ¥10,000 one-way. If you do happen to arrive in Kyoto in a rental car, visit www.parkme.com/kyoto-jp-parking to search for available parking space, rates, and more. Do not attempt to park along any random stretch of road, or in the lot of a business where you are not a paying customer, no matter how free a given space may look. Doing so could result in a fine.

GETTING AROUND

Some elements of Kyoto's public transport network leave a bit to be desired: Only two subway lines run beneath the city. But above-ground trains also connect disparate parts of town, and Kyoto's easily navigable streets are ideally suited for getting around by bus, taxi, or better yet, on a bicycle or your own two feet.

As with anywhere in Japan, prepaid IC cards bought from ticket machines in both JR and non-JR railways stations (Suica cards, Pasmo cards, etc.) can be used across various transport networks in the city, from buses to the subway system. The local IC card variant purchased through JR stations in Kyoto is the Icoca.

The city's streets can become awash in traffic, and jams are frequent during *hanami* season in late March and early April, as well as during the height of the *kōyō* (autumn leaves) season in November. Stick to subways and trains, or get around on a bicycle or on foot during these times to avoid getting stuck in a jam.

Bus

Originating from Kyoto Station, the green-striped **Kyoto City Bus** and red-striped **Kyoto Bus** companies serve different sections of the city. The bus system can be difficult to navigate, but it does have an extended reach, so buses can be useful when you need to reach sights that are not easily accessed by subway or train, are too far to reach by bicycle, or are too expensive to go by taxi.

Northwest Kyoto—home to sights like Ryōan-ji and Kinkaku-ji—is one part of the city that may call for a journey by bus. Likewise, sights dotting the area around Gingaku-ji in northern Higashiyama are also best served by bus. That said, even these parts of town can be reached by train if you're willing to walk anywhere from 10-30 minutes from the nearest station.

If you don't mind spending a bit of time puzzling out timetables and routes and you plan to use the bus system a lot, it's worth investing in a special bus pass (¥600 adults, ¥300 children), sold at the **Kyoto City Bus & Subway Information Center** (tel. 075/371-4474; 7:30am-7:30pm), found just outside the central exit of Kyoto Station. Activate your pass by inserting it into the slot in the payment machine next to the driver's seat of all buses as you exit. The one-day bus pass covers unlimited rides on both Kyoto City Bus and Kyoto Bus routes for a day. If you plan to get around by bus, remember to pick up an English-language bus map (Bus Navi: Kyoto City Bus Sightseeing Map) at the Kyoto Bus Information Center or at any tourist information center around town.

To take a single journey, enter through the back door and pay upon exiting via the front of the bus. Fares within the city are generally a flat ¥230 (¥120 children ages 6-12, children under 6 free), but go up for longer distances. Fares can be paid either with coins or any one of the types of IC cards available in Japan.

As its name suggests, the **K'Loop** (tel. 075/661-1234; http://kloop.jp; ¥1,000 adults one-day, ¥500 children one-day, 9am-6pm Mon.-Fri. call center) sightseeing bus makes a loop around the city, hitting a number of highlights (Kiyomizu-dera, Ginkaku-ji, Kinkaku-ji, Nijō-jō, etc.).

Subway

Kyoto has an efficient if limited subway system, with the **Karasuma line** running north-south and the **Tōzai line** running east-west. The Karasuma line is named after the city's main north-south artery, Karasuma-dōri, under which the subway runs. This line passes through key stations downtown like Shijō and Karasuma-Oike. Sights near the Karasuma line include Daitoku-ji and Kyoto Imperial Palace. At Karasuma-Oike, you'll find the Karasuma line's junction with the Tōzai line, which brings you within easy reach of Nijō-jō in the west, and Gion and southern Higashiyama in the east.

Single journeys on the subway start from ¥210. One-day unlimited subway passes (¥600 adults, ¥300 children) are sold at subway station ticket windows and through ticket machines. The Kyoto Subway & Bus Pass allows you to hop on both subway lines and buses an unlimited number of times for one day (¥900 adults, ¥450 children) or two days (¥1,700 adults, ¥850 children). You can pick up one of these passes at the Kyoto City Bus & Subway Information Center, at any commuter pass sales counter, or at the ticket window of any subway station. This pass doesn't cover rides on any of the above-ground train lines.

Train

Trains run by JR and a number of private operators serve Kyoto. The subway and bus systems provide more direct access to various sights and corners of the city, but a few areas—particularly the southeast around Tōfoku-ji and Fushimi Inari-Taisha (**JR Nara line**), and the sight-rich area of Arashiyama in the west (Sagano line)—are conveniently reached by train. The **Keifuku line** (aka **Randen line**) is essentially a sightseeing train that links Arashiyama in the west to the area in the city's northwest near Kinkaku-ji and Ryōan-ji.

Bicycle

Kyoto feels tailor-made for cycling. Its mostly flat, grid-pattern streets and the path-lined Kamo River burbling through the eastern half of town beg to be explored by bicycle. Many major sights do have designated bicycle parking lots. Orderly traffic and a glut of bicycle rental shops make this an even more appealing proposition.

Before hiring a bicycle from a specialized rental shop, check to see if your accommodation happens to provide bike rentals for guests. Daily rentals typically cost ¥1,000-1,500 for standard city bikes, while paying around ¥2,000 will often get you an electrically assisted one, which can come in handy if you plan to go into any of the hillier districts dotting the eastern edges of town.

A few more thoughts to consider before pedaling through Kyoto's streets: It's illegal to park your bike in a spot that is not specifically a bicycle parking area. Illegally parked bicycles are routinely picked up in city-run sweeps. If your bicycle is gone after you've left it on a stretch of sidewalk outside a café or leaning against some random building, it's quite likely been impounded. If you experience this unfortunate fate, look for a paper affixed somewhere near where you parked your bicycle and use the map on it to make your way to where it's being kept. You'll typically pay a ¥2,000 fine to get your bike back.

To avoid this fate, stick to parking your bike only in specifically designated bicycle lots outside major sights, train or bus stations. Or, leave it at one of the large parking lots found around town. A good example is the **Kyoto Wings** lot, found north of Daimaru department store in the heart of downtown, near the intersection of Takoyakushi-dōri and Higashinotoin-dōri. You can leave your bike here for ¥150 per day. For an extensive list of bicycle parking lots, which will keep you on the right side of the law, view the map at the bottom of this page: www.cyclekyoto.com/bicycle-parking.

Be aware that there are certain stretches of downtown Kyoto where it's illegal to ride a bicycle. For a detailed breakdown of exactly where you should not ride a bicycle, go to www.cyclekyoto.com/areas-to-avoid.

Taxi

Taking taxis is normally not advisable for those on a budget in Japan. Kyoto bucks this trend. The city is blessed with an overabundance of taxis, and the relatively short distances between sights ensures that most fares won't climb much above a few thousand yen.

Thanks to Kyoto's thriving tourism industry, most drivers speak a smattering of English. There are now foreigner-friendly taxis plying the avenues of Kyoto with English-speaking drivers. There's a stand in front of the **Kyoto Century Hotel,** just outside Kyoto Station's central exit, to the right, specifically reserved for these English-friendly cabs.

Kansai 関西

Japan, in a sense, is bipolar. Its modern heart is, without a doubt, in Tokyo. Go deeper into the past, however, and Kansai is the cultural birthplace of the nation, from which the very notion of Japanese-ness emerged. This dichotomy is felt in daily life, with reality TV shows and books expounding on subtle differences in customs between the politically, economically, and pop-culturally mightier pole of Kantō (Greater Tokyo) and the historically rich region of Kansai a few hours by *shinkansen* (bullet train) to the west.

Kansai extends roughly from Hyogo Prefecture in the west and Mie Prefecture in the east to Lake Biwa and the Japan Sea Coast of Kyoto Prefecture in the north. While Kyoto is technically part of Kansai, the nearby cities of Osaka, Kobe, and Nara make up the region's core, and

Highlights

Look for ★ to find recommended sights, activities, dining, and lodging.

★ **Dōtombori:** Eat yourself into a state of ruin on this famed food street, where fried, fatty, carbohydrate-laden goodies are sold by the plate, bowl, and skewer (page 377).

★ **Tōdai-ji:** The Buddhist temple known as Tōdai-ji, one of the largest wooden structures in the world, contains an awe inspiring 15-meter (49-foot) bronze statue of Buddha (page 385).

★ **Nightlife in Kobe:** Experience this city's sophisticated and historic nightlife scene at one of its renowned jazz haunts (page 394).

★ **Kinosaki Onsen:** Don a *yukata,* swap your shoes for wooden clogs, and relax in this picturesque seaside town where it's possible to have the quintessential *onsen* experience (page 397).

★ **Himeji-jō:** This soaring white fortress is an architectural reminder of a time when Japan was under the rule of ruthless feudal lords (page 399).

★ **Kōya-san:** Many of the Buddhist temples sprawling across this sacred mountain in Wakayama Prefecture accept overnight guests (page 401).

★ **Ise-Jingū:** This majestic shrine, ritually dismantled and rebuilt every two decades for centuries, is Shinto's holiest site (page 406).

Kansai

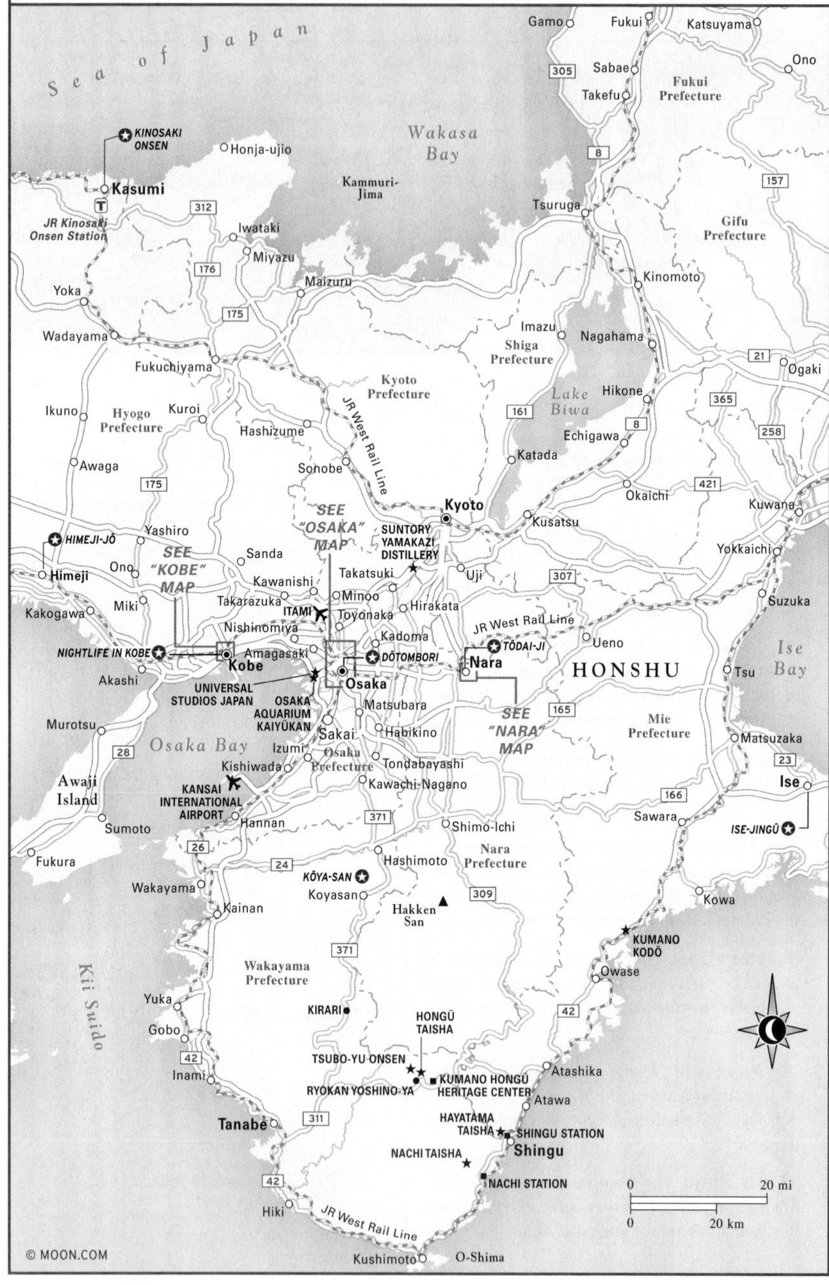

Sea of Japan
Wakasa Bay
Kammuri-Jima
KINOSAKI ONSEN
Kasumi
JR Kinosaki Onsen Station
Honja-ujio
Iwataki
Miyazu
Maizuru
Yoka
Wadayama
Fukuchiyama
Ikuno
Hyogo Prefecture
Kuroi
Hashizume
Awaga
Sonobe
JR West Rail Line
Kyoto Prefecture
Gamo
Fukui
Katsuyama
Ono
Sabae
Takefu
Fukui Prefecture
Tsuruga
Gifu Prefecture
Kinomoto
Imazu
Nagahama
Shiga Prefecture
Ogaki
Lake Biwa
Hikone
Echigawa
Katada
Okaichi
Kuwana
Kyoto
Kusatsu
SEE "OSAKA" MAP
SUNTORY YAMAKAZI DISTILLERY
HIMEJI-JŌ
Himeji
Yashiro
Sanda
Ono
SEE "KOBE" MAP
Kawanishi
Takatsuki
Uji
Yokkaichi
Kakogawa
Miki
Takarazuka
Minoo
ITAMI
Toyonaka
Hirakata
Suzuka
Nishinomiya
JR West Rail Line
NIGHTLIFE IN KOBE
Kobe
Amagasaki
Kadoma
DŌTOMBORI
TŌDAI-JI
Nara
Ueno
Ise Bay
Akashi
UNIVERSAL STUDIOS JAPAN
Osaka
HONSHU
Tsu
OSAKA AQUARIUM KAIYŪKAN
Matsubara
SEE "NARA" MAP
Murotsu
Sakai
Habikino
Mie Prefecture
Osaka Bay
Izumi
Osaka Prefecture
Matsuzaka
Kishiwada
Tondabayashi
Awaji Island
KANSAI INTERNATIONAL AIRPORT
Kawachi-Nagano
Ise
Hannan
Sawara
Sumoto
Shimo-Ichi
ISE-JINGŪ
Fukura
Nara Prefecture
Hashimoto
KŌYA-SAN
Wakayama
Koyasan
Kowa
Hakken San
Kainan
KUMANO KODŌ
Owase
Wakayama Prefecture
Kii Suido
Yuka
KIRARI
HONGŪ TAISHA
Gobo
TSUBO-YU ONSEN
Atashika
Inami
RYOKAN YOSHINO-YA
KUMANO HONGŪ HERITAGE CENTER
Atawa
Tanabe
HAYATAMA TAISHA
SHINGU STATION
Shingu
NACHI TAISHA
NACHI STATION
Hiki
JR West Rail Line
Kushimoto
O-Shima
0
20 mi
0
20 km
305
8
157
312
176
175
21
365
161
8
258
421
175
307
165
28
23
166
371
26
24
309
371
42
42
311
42

Best Restaurants

★ **Takotako King Honten:** Munch on fried balls of dough stuffed with bits of octopus meat at this boisterous bar-cum-*takoyaki* shop in Osaka (page 377).

★ **Momen:** Experience the haute side of Osaka's food scene, and the laid-back side of the *kaiseki ryōri* tradition, at this phenomenal countertop *kappō ryōri* restaurant (page 377).

★ **Ajinoya:** Come to this restaurant, just off the tourist trail, to sample Osaka's savory pancake dish known as *okonomiyaki* (page 378).

★ **Ganso Kushikatsu Daruma Honten:** Discover the joys of nibbling just about any food item you can fathom skewered on a stick, breaded and deep-fried at this greasy-spoon, Osaka-favorite *kushikatsu* restaurant (page 378).

★ **Steak Aoyama:** Find out what all the fuss is about surrounding Kobe beef at this intimate, friendly, family-owned steak restaurant, serving melt-in-your-mouth wagyu since 1963 (page 393).

REGIONAL SPECIALITIES

In Osaka, you'll find ***okonomiyaki,*** a savory pancake stuffed with cabbage, meat, and seafood and sprinkled with green onion; ***takoyaki,*** essentially a savory fried spherical donut containing hunks of octopus; and ***kushikatsu,*** or skewers of meat and vegetables that have been battered and deep-fried. Nearby, the port city of Kobe is known worldwide for the quality of its highly marbled beef, popularly known as ***wagyū,*** a term that refers to all forms of Japanese beef.

are all within a short train ride of the ancient capital. If you don't plan to visit Tokyo, taking a short jaunt (or a few) around the area will add a dash of zest to the rarefied offerings of Kyoto.

The urban nucleus of the region, Osaka is a garish, boisterous alternative to Tokyo, on a smaller scale. The city is famous for its decadent dishes, such as *takoyaki* (fried octopus dumplings) and *okonomiyaki,* a savory pancake stuffed with cabbage, meat, or seafood, and topped with all manner of sauces, fish flakes, mayonnaise, and more.

To the west of Osaka, about 30 minutes by train, Kobe is a sophisticated city set between green hills and the Inland Sea. Thin on sights, Kobe's cityscape is notably more pleasing to the eye than Osaka's, and invites visitors to become urban explorers. Farther west still from Kobe, the city of Himeji is home to what is perhaps Japan's most recognizable castle, the soaring white fortress of Himeji-jō.

Looking further into to the region's past, turn to Nara, Japan's first permanent capital. A half-hour express train ride south of Kyoto and about an hour east of Osaka by train, Nara's main draw is Nara-koen, a large park inhabited by some 1,200 deer and home to Todai-ji, a wooden temple with an awe-inspiring statue of Buddha.

Equally (if not more) impressive reminders of Kansai's spiritual roots are found in the Kii Peninsula, south of Osaka. Here, the mountaintop of Kōya-san is a repository of Buddhist temples, brimming with on-site temple lodgings. In the southern heart of the peninsula, the millenium-old pilgrimage route known as the Kumano Kodō runs over dramatically mountainous terrain. And in the eastern part

Previous: Ise-jingū; rock garden at Kōya-san; Himeji castle.

Best Accommodations

★ **Intercontinental Osaka:** Perhaps Osaka's best hotel, the Intercontinental is top-notch in all respects, from the views and dining to its prime location (page 380).

★ **Nara Hotel:** Luminaries like Albert Einstein and the Dalai Lama have slept at this historic property and wandered through its enchanting grounds (page 390).

★ **Oriental Hotel:** One of Japan's first hotels, this rebuilt waterfront tower offers a first-rate experience and stunning views of Kobe's appealing cityscape (page 395).

★ **Morizuya:** Kinosaki Onsen is the most appealing place in Kansai to take a dip in a hot spring, and this family-owned *ryokan* is the best place to stay after soaking in one of the town's seven public baths (page 399).

★ **Ekō-in:** Get a taste of the monk's life at Kōya-san first-hand at this excellent temple lodging, located a brief stroll from the magical Okuno-in cemetery (page 403).

of the peninsula, you'll find Shinto's holiest of holies, Ise-Jingu, dating to the 3rd century.

After taking all this in, you may need a breather. Kinosaki Onsen, on the Japan Sea side of Hyogo Prefecture, about 2.5 hours north of Himeji and Kobe by train (and 3 hours from Osaka), is an ideal place to drop your cares and sink into the waters of a hot spring bath.

ORIENTATION

With the mountainous region of Central Honshu to the east, Western Honshu to the west, and the island of Shikoku to the southwest, Kansai accounts for a large part of the western core of Honshu. There's very much a Kansai versus Kanto (Greater Tokyo) rivalry in Japan (think New York versus Los Angeles), with Kansai denizens—of whom there are about 22 million—known for their fierce local pride.

On the eastern edge of Kansai is **Mie Prefecture,** home to Japan's holiest site, Ise-Jingu, in the small seaside town of the shrine's namesake. Ise Bay lies to the east, with the Pacific hemming in Mie's south. **Shiga Prefecture,** home to Japan's largest lake, Biwa-ko, lies just north of Mie, while landlocked **Nara Prefecture,** home to Japan's ancient capital of the same name, lies to Mie's west.

Moving southwest from Nara, **Wakayama Prefecture** is home to the mountaintop Buddhist center of Koya-san, the mystical Kumano Kodō pilgrimage route, and beautifully rugged southern and western coastlines. Just north of Wakayama is Osaka Prefecture, home to the eponymous, food-obsessed city and undoubtedly the region's modern heart.

Softening things, timeworn Kyoto sits just north of **Osaka,** with **Nara** to its southeast and **Shiga** to its east, on the opposite shore of Biwa-ko. Finally, west of Kyoto and Osaka is **Hyogo Prefecture;** Its largest urban center is **Kobe.** A brief train ride west of Kobe, **Himeji** is home to Japan's most recognizable castle, the majestic white fortress of Himeji-jo. And on Hyogo's northern coast, beside the Sea of Japan, is **Kinosaki Onsen,** one of Japan's most idyllic hot-spring towns.

PLANNING YOUR TIME

Most destinations in Kansai are best viewed as add-ons to Kyoto, given their proximity to the ancient capital. Otherwise, consider spending a few nights in the region if a particular city, or historical or cultural spot interests you and you're going to be in Japan for two weeks or more.

Plan to spend anywhere from a half day to two days in each of Kansai's main hubs. **Osaka** and **Nara** are best as a day trip, or you could visit Osaka just for dinner and drinks. Osaka, in the middle of the other main destinations, makes a good base for exploring the region.

Osaka, **Kobe**, and **Himeji** are conveniently clustered together, only about 30-40 minutes apart by train, making Kobe and Himeji pleasant day trips from Osaka; you could even see both in one long day. If you have more time, Kobe is a pleasing place to hunker down for a night, moving on to Himeji the next day. It's possible to zip up to **Kinosaki Onsen**, roughly 2.5 hours north of both Kobe and Himeji by train, for a half-day of R&R. But staying one night at one of the seaside inns with a hot springs bath will allow you to enjoy fuller immersion.

How long to spend on the spiritually loaded Kii Peninsula depends on the individual. **Kōya-san** deserves one night—staying in temple lodgings—with time to explore the misty mountainscape on foot. The **Kumano Kodō** region can be either a day trip, an overnight jaunt, or a much lengthier multiday trek. **Ise-Jingu**, on the eastern side of the peninsula, calls for a day of exploration. It's Shinto's holiest site, after all.

The most pleasant times of year to visit Kansai are in **spring** (Mar.-May), and **fall** (Oct.-Nov.). That said, **summer** (June-mid-Sept.) and **winter** (Dec.-Feb.) are not so extreme that it makes travel unwise. In the summer, be prepared to endure temperatures upward of 30°C (86°F) and patches of rainfall from mid-June through July; and in winter, lows of about 3-5°C (37-41°F) with the occasional dump of snow.

Itinerary Ideas

A WEEKEND IN OSAKA AND NARA

Day 1: Osaka

1 Before tromping through Osaka's array of colorful neighborhoods at street level, first behold the city's vastness from above with a trip to **Umeda Sky Building** in the city's Kita (north) side, which opens at 10am.

2 Walk to nearby ramen shop **Mitsuka Bose Kamoshi**, one of the best bowls of noodles in Osaka, for an early lunch before office workers descend on restaurants throughout the city.

3 Hop on the Midōsuji line at Umeda Station and ride south to **Shinsaibashi**, the northern gateway to the city's Minami (south) side. Grab a coffee at Lilo Coffee Roasters.

4 Walk south toward **Triangle Park** in the heart of youth culture mecca Amerika-mura. Spend your afternoon here and in the stylish nearby Horie district a couple of blocks southwest, people-watching and popping into shops.

5 Continue south to the Dōtombori-gawa canal. Walk along the river's northern bank until you reach **Ebisu-bashi**, the famous bridge at the heart of Dōtombori. Join the throngs taking selfies in front of the famous Glico "running man" billboard.

6 Cross the bridge and enter the famed **Dōtombori arcade** proper. As dusk sets, this strip becomes a surreal, neon-soaked realm. Also stop by **Hōzen-ji**, an enigmatic temple in the heart of a consumerist frenzy.

Osaka and Nara Itinerary Ideas

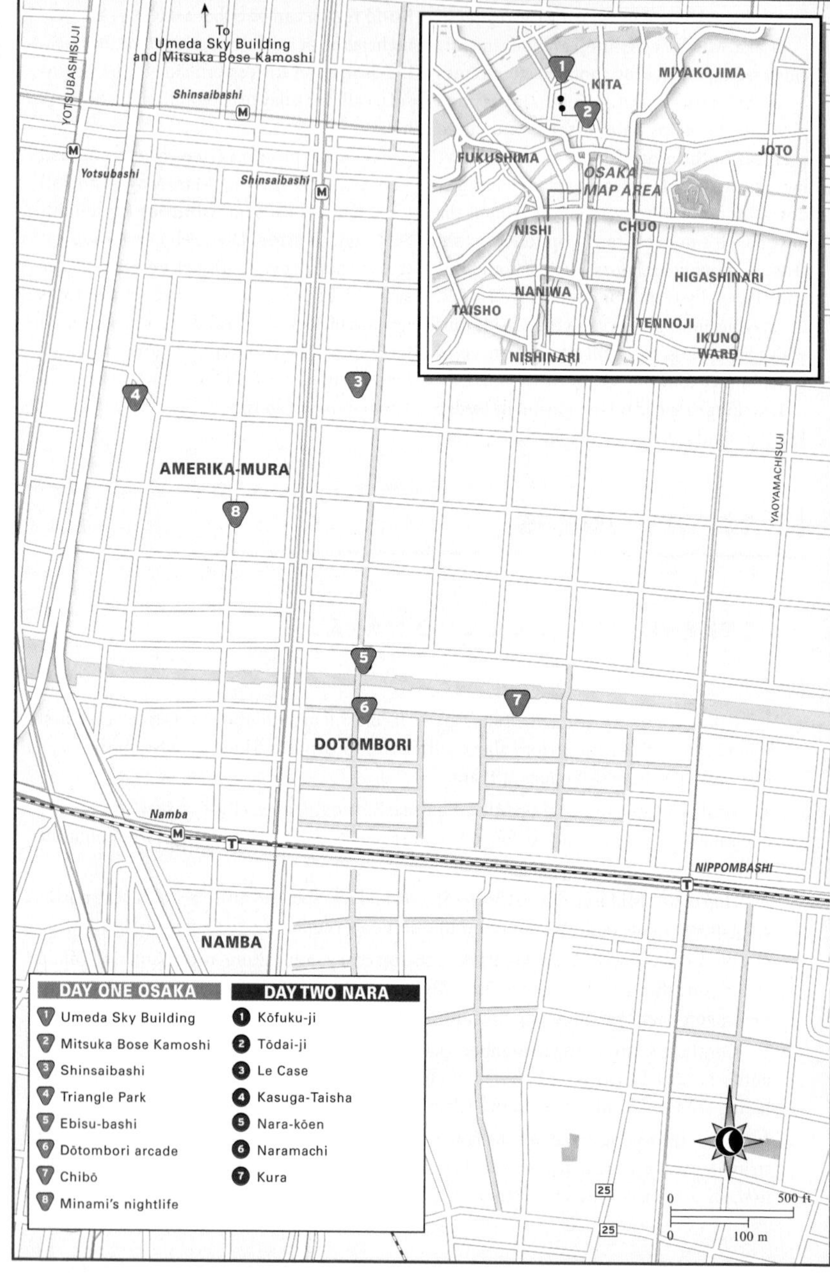

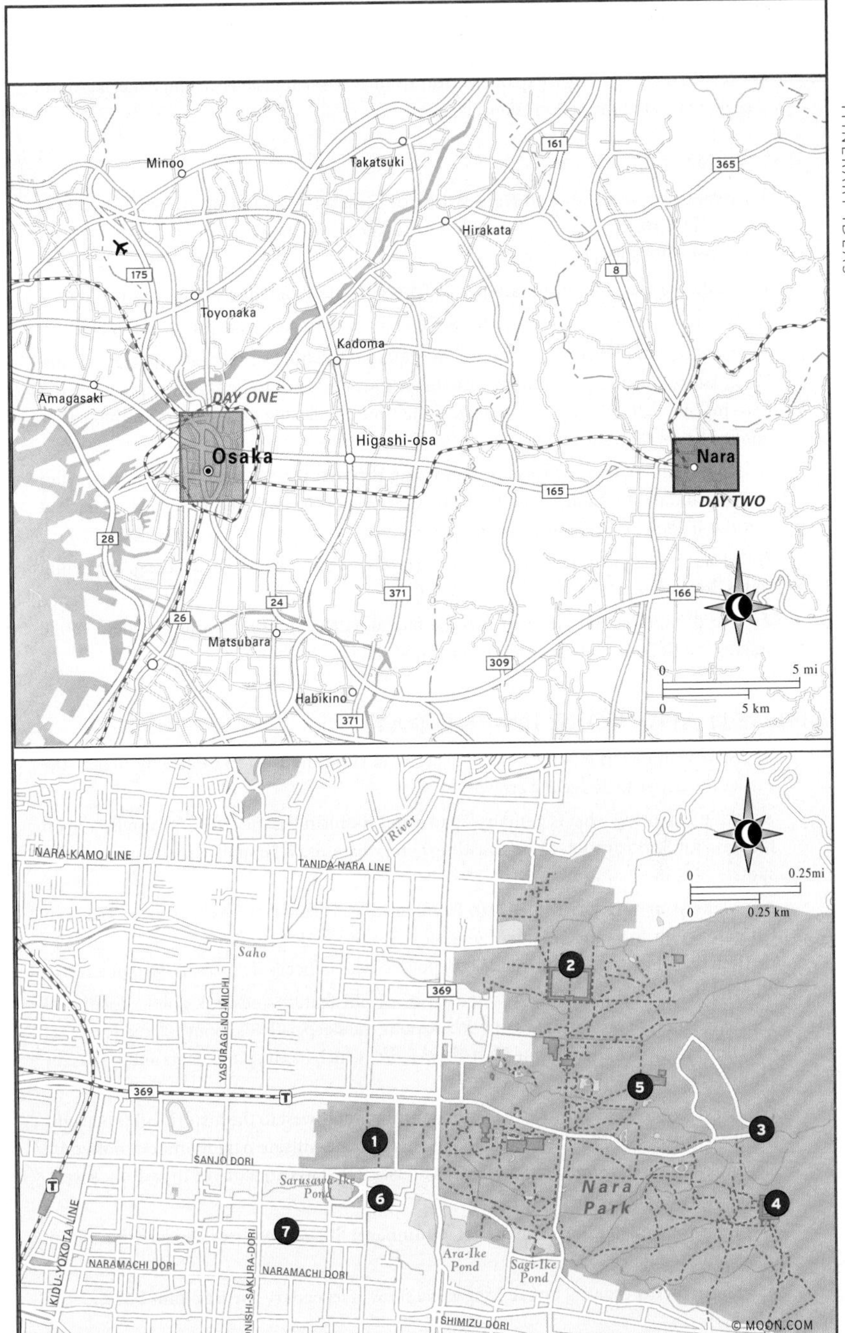
Minoo
Takatsuki
Hirakata
Toyonaka
Kadoma
Amagasaki
DAY ONE
Osaka
Higashi-osa
Nara
DAY TWO
Matsubara
Habikino
0 5 mi
0 5 km
NARA-KAMO LINE
TANIDA-NARA LINE
River
Saho
YASURAGI-NO-MICHI
SANJO DORI
Sarusawa-Ike Pond
Nara Park
KIDU-YOKOTA LINE
NARAMACHI DORI
KONISHI-SAKURA-DORI
Ara-Ike Pond
Sagi-Ike Pond
SHIMIZU DORI
0 0.25mi
0 0.25 km
© MOON.COM

7 Eat dinner in Dōtombori. Your choices are endless. *Okonomiyaki* is a very safe bet and an Osaka classic—try **Chibō.**

8 If you still have energy, explore **Minami's nightlife.** Shinsaibashi and Amerika-mura are where most of the action takes place.

Day 2: Nara

1 Aim to arrive at either JR Nara Station or Kintetsu-Nara Station around 10am. Take in views of **Kōfuku-ji,** a temple beside a pond known for its soaring pagoda, on your way to the beautiful garden Isui-en.

2 Walk northeast about 10 minutes to **Tōdai-ji,** one of Japan's most awesome sights.

3 Walk about 15 minutes south to **Le Case** for lunch. They serve great quiche.

4 Continue south from the restaurant to **Kasuga-Taisha,** Nara's most important shrine. Set in a forest teeming with deer, this shrine's grounds beg to be slowly explored. After entering the shrine's main hall, spend some time wandering on the surrounding paths, flanked by myriad stone lanterns.

5 Gradually make your way west, crossing through the center of **Nara-kōen.** After walking about 20 minutes, you'll exit the west side of the park and find yourself back at Kōfuku-ji; look for its looming pagoda.

6 Head south of Kōfuku-ji into the **Naramachi** neighborhood. Peruse the galleries and shops dotting the area.

7 For dinner, try the excellent *izakaya* fare at **Kura** before returning to where you're staying via JR Nara Station or Kintetsu-Nara Station.

HIMEJI AND KOBE IN ONE DAY

1 Start your day in Himeji, aiming to arrive at stunning **Himeji Castle** by 10am—the earlier the better to dodge the crowds.

2 After exploring what is perhaps Japan's most beautiful castle and its grounds, hop on the train for **Sannomiya,** Kobe's bustling core, where you'll be spoiled for choice of lunch spots.

3 Make your way down to **Kobe Earthquake Memorial Park,** passing through Chinatown on the way. This park gives a sense of the destruction caused by the 1995 earthquake. The seaside promenade is peppered with benches if you're in need of a rest.

4 Hop back on the train a few stops to Shin-Kobe Station and walk north. You'll find yourself at the foot of a forested slope. Walk along the steep path for about 400 meters (1,312 feet) until you reach the sublime **Nunobiki Falls,** which has inspired poets and artists for centuries.

5 Backtrack toward Shin-Kobe Station, walking southwest to the historic hilltop neighborhood of **Kitano-chō.** Amble through this upscale hillside neighborhood, dotted by elegant Western-style *ijinkan* ("foreigner's houses") that were once lived in by Kobe's well-heeled early foreign transplants.

6 Treat yourself to Kobe's famed beef for dinner at **Steak Aoyama.** Book a table online in advance.

7 Finish off the evening by catching a live show at legendary live jazz joint **Sone.**

Himeji and Kobe Itinerary Ideas

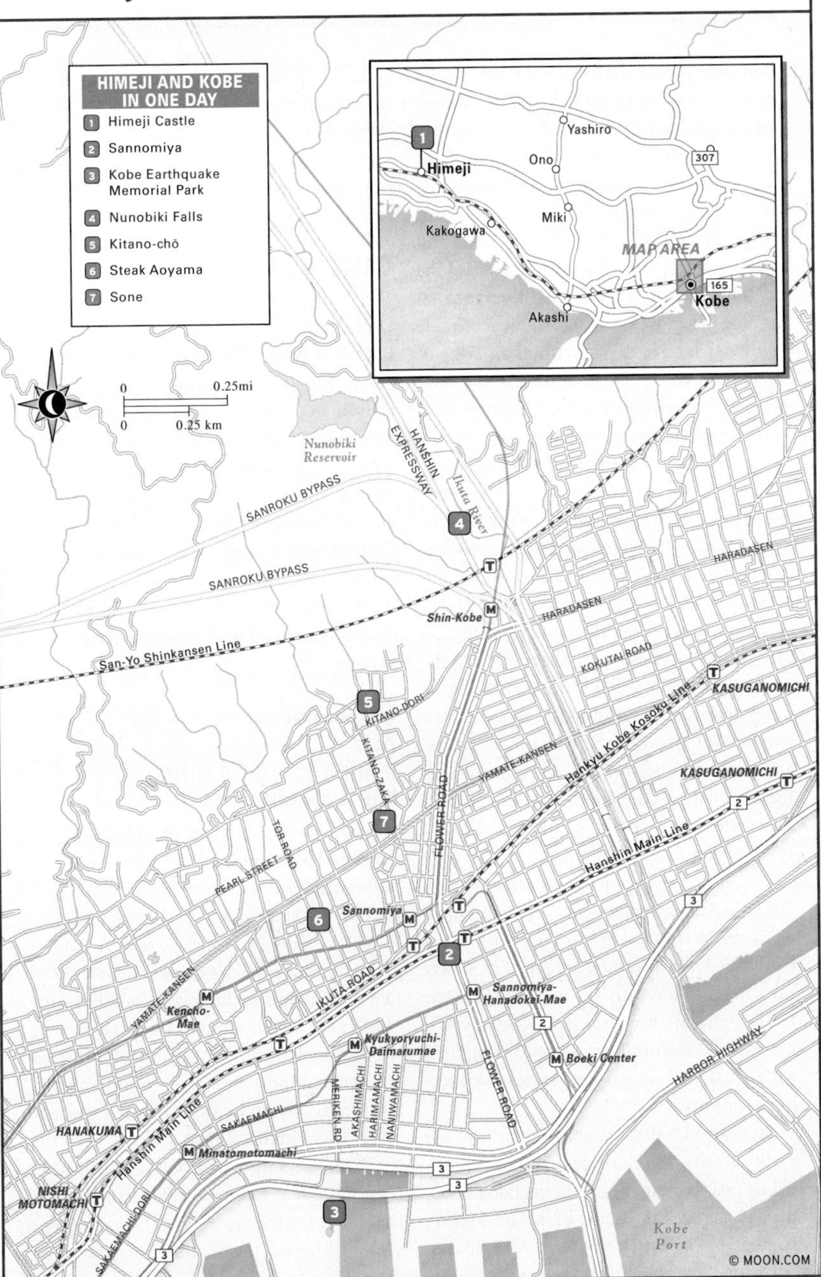

Osaka 大阪

A concrete jungle in the truest sense, Osaka can't claim to be beautiful. But it exerts a strange kind of magnetism, emanating from Osaka Castle in the center of town, vast shopping arcades and entertainment centers in the south, and the bay on the west side of town where you'll find Universal Studios Japan and a massive aquarium. The beating heart of the city is in the area surrounding the large canal running through Dōtombori on the south side of town, which is the domain of an army of street-food vendors, rowdy bars, and loudly dressed, disarmingly friendly locals who know how to have a good time.

Japan's third-largest city, Osaka is fundamentally a place of commerce that has been the region's economic core since the Edo period (1603-1868). Shunning pleasantries, the greeting shared by dyed-in-the-wool Osakans is "mōkari makka?" ("making any money?"). The cash does indeed flow into this bustling city, with Panasonic and Sharp among the commercial giants based here. Among its many monikers, Osaka has been called the City of Water and the City of 1,000 Bridges, alluding to the network of rivers crisscrossing the city that have long served as the circulatory system for shipping goods in and out of this vast commercial organism.

Despite its reputation as a place for earning, Osaka remains notably cheaper than Tokyo or Kyoto. In contrast to breaking the bank at a high-end sushi counter in Ginza or slowly savoring dish after dish in a rarefied *kaiseki* feast in a Kyoto townhouse, in Osaka you'll more likely be standing in a street eating fried balls of battered octopus on a stick while kicking back a beer.

Similarly, Osaka's entertainment is of the earthy variety. Since *rakugo* (humorous storytelling) was born in the city in the Edo period, the city has been the center of Japan's comedy scene, from slapstick to saucy. All told, the city's food, drinking dens, and earthy locals add up to a fun, colorful escape from Kyoto when the temples all start to look the same. Beyond this, Osaka is an exciting city in its own right and begs to be experienced by insatiable urban explorers and gourmands with a taste for the deep-fried side of life.

ORIENTATION

The easiest way to get the lay of the land in Osaka is to think of it on a north-south axis. Buttoned-down **Kita** (north) Osaka encompasses the vast business district of Umeda, as well as Osaka and Shin-Osaka stations. The fun, chaotic image most associated with Osaka comes from the flashy **Minami** (south) side of town. Here, the vast shopping and entertainment districts of **Shinsaibashi, Dōtombori, Namba,** and **Amerika-mura** exude a hedonistic air. Shops and cafés rule the daylight hours, while food, drink, and entertainment in all its forms take center stage at night.

SIGHTS

Kita

UMEDA SKY BUILDING
梅田スカイビル

1-1-88 Ōyodonaka, Kita-ku; tel. 06/6440-3855 (for Kuchu Teien); www.kuchu-teien.com; 9:30am-10:30pm daily, last entry 10pm; ¥1,500 adults, ¥700 children ages 4-12; 10 minutes' walk northwest from JR Osaka Station's north central gate, or 10 minutes walk west from Umeda Station

One of Osaka's most impressive buildings, the Umeda Sky Building was once declared to be the "triumphal arch of the future." Whether triumphal or not, the structure certainly has a futuristic layout, with a "floating garden" called the **Kuchu Teien** ("Garden in the Sky") on the 39th-41st floors, connected at both sides by two otherwise standing towers that shoot 173 meters (568 feet) skyward. For striking views of the mammoth cityscape on the north side of town, this is the place. There

Osaka

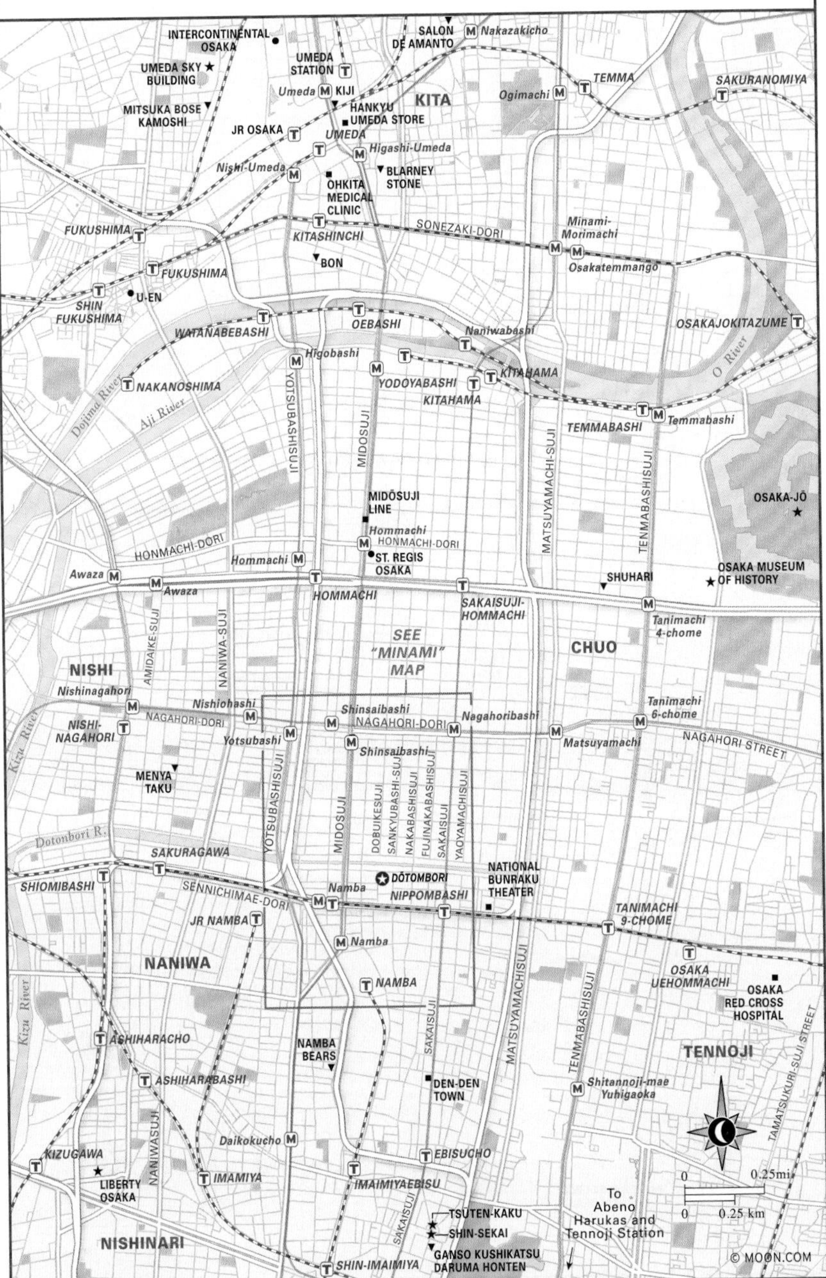
INTERCONTINENTAL OSAKA
UMEDA SKY BUILDING
MITSUKA BOSE KAMOSHI
SALON DE AMANTO
Nakazakicho
UMEDA STATION
Umeda
KIJI
HANKYU UMEDA STORE
KITA
TEMMA
SAKURANOMIYA
Ogimachi
JR OSAKA
UMEDA
Higashi-Umeda
Nishi-Umeda
BLARNEY STONE
OHKITA MEDICAL CLINIC
FUKUSHIMA
KITASHINCHI
SONEZAKI-DORI
Minami-Morimachi
Osakatemmangu
BON
FUKUSHIMA
U-EN
SHIN FUKUSHIMA
OEBASHI
WATANABEBASHI
Naniwabashi
OSAKAJOKITAZUME
Higobashi
KITAHAMA
O River
NAKANOSHIMA
YODOYABASHI
KITAHAMA
Dojima River
Aji River
Temmabashi
TEMMABASHI
YOTSUBASHISUJI
MIDOSUJI
MATSUYAMACHI-SUJI
TENMABASHISUJI
MIDŌSUJI LINE
OSAKA-JŌ
Hommachi
HONMACHI-DORI
HONMACHI-DORI
Hommachi
ST. REGIS OSAKA
OSAKA MUSEUM OF HISTORY
Awaza
Awaza
HOMMACHI
SHUHARI
SAKAISUJI-HOMMACHI
Tanimachi 4-chome
AMIDAIKE-SUJI
NANIWA-SUJI
SEE "MINAMI" MAP
CHUO
NISHI
Nishinagahori
Nishiohashi
Shinsaibashi
Tanimachi 6-chome
NISHI-NAGAHORI
NAGAHORI-DORI
NAGAHORI-DORI
Nagahoribashi
Yotsubashi
Matsuyamachi
NAGAHORI STREET
Kizu River
Shinsaibashi
MENYA TAKU
YOTSUBASHISUJI
MIDOSUJI
DOBUIKESUJI
SANKYUBASHI-SUJI
NAKABASHISUJI
FUJINAKABASHISUJI
SAKAISUJI
YAOYAMACHISUJI
Dotonbori R.
SAKURAGAWA
SHIOMIBASHI
DŌTOMBORI
NATIONAL BUNRAKU THEATER
SENNICHIMAE-DORI
Namba
NIPPOMBASHI
JR NAMBA
TANIMACHI 9-CHOME
Namba
NANIWA
OSAKA UEHOMMACHI
NAMBA
OSAKA RED CROSS HOSPITAL
Kizu River
ASHIHARACHO
NAMBA BEARS
SAKAISUJI
MATSUYAMACHISUJI
TENMABASHISUJI
TENNOJI
TAMATSUKURI-SUJI STREET
ASHIHARABASHI
DEN-DEN TOWN
Shitannoji-mae Yuhigaoka
Daikokucho
KIZUGAWA
EBISUCHO
NANIWASUJI
IMAMIYA
IMAIMIYAEBISU
LIBERTY OSAKA
0
0.25 mi
0
0.25 km
To Abeno Harukas and Tennoji Station
TSUTEN-KAKU
SHIN-SEKAI
SAKAISUJI
NISHINARI
GANSO KUSHIKATSU DARUMA HONTEN
SHIN-IMAIMIYA
© MOON.COM

Minami

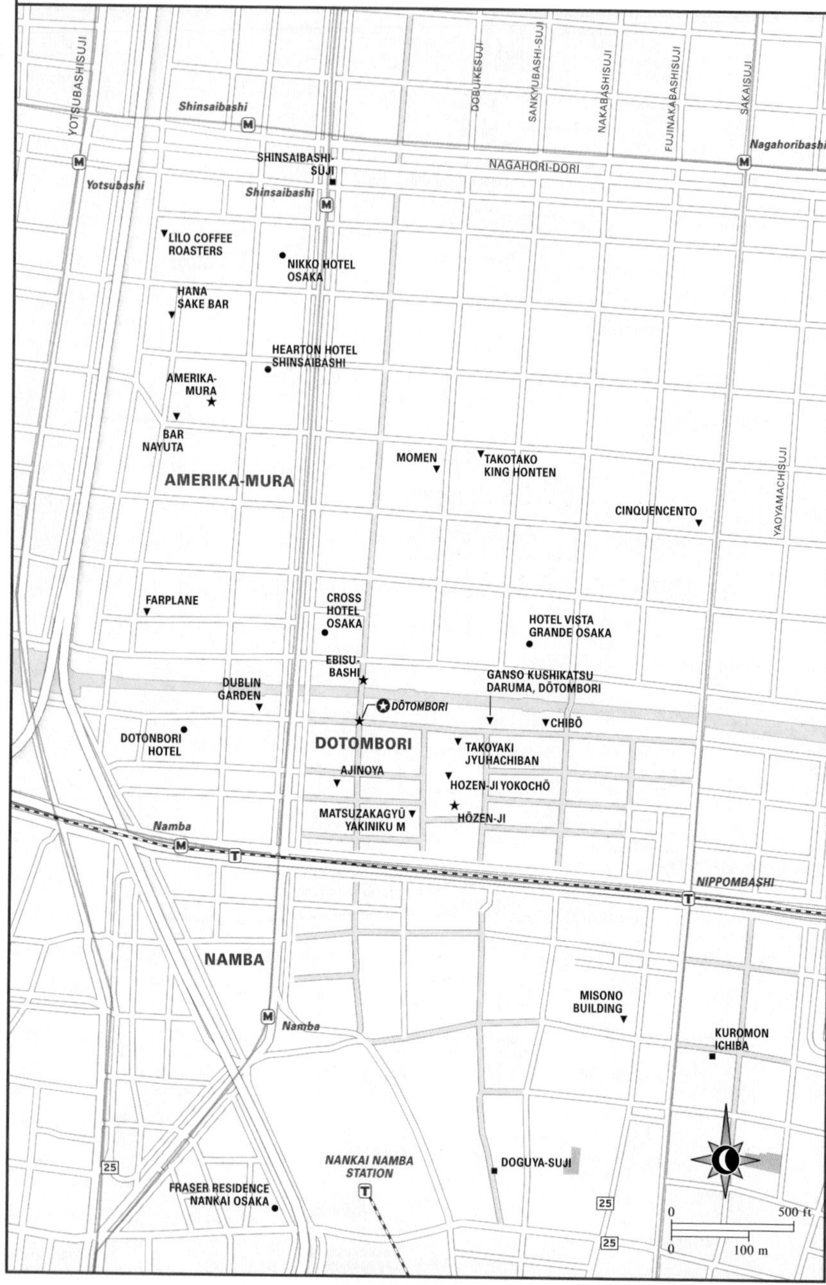

YOTSUBASHISUJI
Shinsaibashi
DOBUIKESUJI
SANKYUBASHI-SUJI
NAKABASHISUJI
FUJINAKABASHISUJI
SAKAISUJI
Nagahoribashi
NAGAHORI-DORI
SHINSAIBASHI-SUJI
Yotsubashi
Shinsaibashi
LILO COFFEE ROASTERS
NIKKO HOTEL OSAKA
HANA SAKE BAR
HEARTON HOTEL SHINSAIBASHI
AMERIKA-MURA
BAR NAYUTA
MOMEN
TAKOTAKO KING HONTEN
AMERIKA-MURA
CINQUENCENTO
YAOYAMACHISUJI
FARPLANE
CROSS HOTEL OSAKA
HOTEL VISTA GRANDE OSAKA
EBISU-BASHI
GANSO KUSHIKATSU DARUMA, DŌTOMBORI
DUBLIN GARDEN
DŌTOMBORI
CHIBŌ
DOTONBORI HOTEL
DOTOMBORI
TAKOYAKI JYUHACHIBAN
AJINOYA
HOZEN-JI YOKOCHŌ
MATSUZAKAGYŪ YAKINIKU M
HŌZEN-JI
Namba
NIPPOMBASHI
NAMBA
MISONO BUILDING
Namba
KUROMON ICHIBA
NANKAI NAMBA STATION
DOGUYA-SUJI
FRASER RESIDENCE NANKAI OSAKA
25
25
25
0
500 ft
0
100 m

is both an outdoor and an indoor observatory, which comes in handy during inclement weather. Come during the evening when the city becomes a vast sea of lights. Buy tickets to the Kuchu Teien on the ticket counter on the 39th floor. You can reach the building either aboveground or via a well-marked underground walkway.

OSAKA-JŌ
大坂城

1-1 Osaka-jō, Chūō-ku; tel. 06/6941-3044; www.osakacastle.net; 9am-5pm daily; grounds free, adults ¥600 or ¥900 combined with Osaka Museum of History, children under 15 free inside keep; take the Tanimachi or Chūō subway line to Tanimachi 4-Chōme Station, or the JR Loop line to Osaka-jō-kōen Station

The warlord Toyotomi Hideyoshi, Japan's great unifier of the 16th century, directed 100,000 laborers to construct his imposing castle, Osaka-jō. Even today, it looms over the eastern side of the city, dramatically illuminated at night.

Originally completed in 1583, the castle was soon after sacked by the forces of Tokugawa Ieyasu, the first shogun of the Tokugawa Shogunate, in 1614. Ieyasu simply rebuilt it block by block, ensuring its fortitude with even larger stones, each weighing up to 100 tonnes (110 tons), studding its wall. In 1931, citizens raised money to reconstruct the main tower. After being razed by bombing during World War II, the main structure was later refurbished in 1995. Thirteen structures from the 17th-century version built by Ieyasu remain in place. Even the concrete reproductions have enough visual oomph to make the castle one of Osaka's biggest draws.

The complex towers over a 106-hectare (262-acre) park that comes vividly alive in spring with the cherry blossoms. It's an excellent place to stroll or have a picnic. Inside the castle, there are displays with information about Osaka's history, the castle, and original builder Hideyoshi, on the lower floors; and on the top floor, there's an observation deck looking over the eastern side of the city.

Minami

Less a place to take in sights than a neighborhood to people-watch and gawk at seemingly endless shopping arcades bathed in neon lights, Minami rewards aimless strolling.

HŌZEN-JI
法善寺

1-2-16 Namba, Chūō-ku; tel. 06/6211-4152; http://

cherry blossoms at Osaka-jō

houzenji.jp; 24 hours; free; take the Midōsuji subway line to Namba Station, exit B-16

Walk two blocks south of the main culinary thoroughfare to a small atmospheric lane known as **Hozenji Yokochō,** where you'll find Hōzen-ji, a temple frequented by those working in the *mizu shōbai* ("water trade"), as the sensual realm of nightlife is known. Peek inside the temple to see the moss-encrusted statue of the esoteric Buddhist deity Fudō Myō-ō.

LIBERTY OSAKA (OSAKA HUMAN RIGHTS MUSEUM)
大阪人権博物館

3-6-36 Naniwa-nishi, Naniwa-ku; tel. 06/6561-5891; www.liberty.or.jp; 10am-4pm Wed.-Fri., 1pm-5pm Sat., closed fourth Fri. and Sat. each month; ¥500 adults, ¥300 high school students, ¥200 junior high and elementary school students; take Midōsuji JR Loop line to Imamiya Station, west exit

Liberty Osaka is a museum in Osaka's south that sheds light on a dark aspect of Japanese society. Similar to India, Japan had a rigid caste system in place throughout its feudal period, with *burakumin,* or outcasts, at the bottom. These outcasts were set apart due to their occupations being at odds with the tenets of Buddhism: undertakers, butchers, executioners, tanners, etc.

Although these classes were abolished in 1871, the sad reality is that discrimination against the descendents—often recognizable by surname—does persist in subtle undercurrents today. Alongside the *burakumin,* the museum also peers into the hardships faced by Japanese of Korean descent known as *Zainichi* and the history of sexual politics in Japan. English audio guide covering most displays available.

ABENO HARUKAS
あべのハルカス

1-1-43 Abenosuji, Abeno-ku; tel. 06/6621-0300; www.abenoharukas-300.jp; 9am-10pm daily; ¥1,500 adults, ¥1,200 ages 12-17, ¥700 ages 6-11, ¥500 ages 4-5; take Midōsuji, Tanimachi subway lines or JR Loop line to Tennoji Station, or take Kintetsu Minami Osaka line to Osaka-Abenobashi Station

A southern answer to the Umeda Sky Building in the city's north, the towering Abeno Harukas complex is Japan's tallest skyscraper at 300 meters (984 feet) and houses Osaka's highest observation deck, Harukas 300. Designed by Argentine-American architect Cesar Pelli of Petronas Towers fame, this hulking monolith in the southern hub of Tennoji is at the center of an urban renaissance sweeping through what was previously considered a dingy, dated side of town, giving the name Harukas ("clear up" or "brighten") added meaning. This is a good choice for jaw-dropping views of the urban sprawl if you're spending the bulk of your time on the south side of town.

Note that the lower portion of the vast complex houses the **Kintetsu department store** (B2-14th floor; https://abenoharukas.d-kintetsu.co.jp; 10am-8pm daily), Japan's largest, including three stories of restaurants (12th-14th floors; 10am-11pm daily).

Osaka Bay Area

OSAKA AQUARIUM KAIYŪKAN
海遊館

1-1-10 Kaigan-dōri, Minato-ku; tel. 06/6576-5501; www.kaiyukan.com; 10am-8pm daily; ¥2,300 adults, ¥1,200 ages 7-15, ¥600 ages 4-6, ages 3 and under free; take Chūō subway line to Osakako Station, then walk 8 minutes west

This excellent aquarium shows off the wildly diverse sea life of the Pacific Ring of Fire, from Antarctica and the Arctic to the Aleutian Islands, Monterey Bay in California, the Gulf of Panama, the Ecuadorian jungle, the Great Barrier Reef and more. One of the world's largest aquariums, its centerpiece is a massive tank that is large enough to accommodate a whale shark. Other residents of this impressive complex include bizarre jellyfish, penguins, manta rays, sea lions, coralfish, and many more.

1: Osaka Aquarium **2:** Tenjin Matsuri

1

2

Minami's Neighborhoods

DŌTOMBORI 道頓堀

This sprawling, mostly pedestrian area, named after the Dōtombori-gawa canal running through it, is the heart of Osaka's south side, where the bulk of the eating and partying takes place.

There are numerous bridges and walkways on the canal. The most famous is **Ebisu-bashi,** which offers the best vantage point of all the neon shimmering off the river, as well as the Glico electronic billboard featuring the iconic "running man." On the main thoroughfare running parallel to the canal on its south side, try to spot Kuidaore Taro, the statue of a drumming clown in a red and white striped suit. While this area is touristy, you owe it to yourself to indulge in some *takoyaki* or some other fried treat while perusing Osaka at its most brash.

To reach Dōtombori, take the Midōsuji subway line to Namba Station, exit 14. For maximum sensory impact, take the Midōsuji subway line to Shinsaibashi Station instead, then walk south along the Shinsaibashi-suji shopping arcade, which leads directly to Ebisu-bashi.

SHINSAIBASHI 心斎橋

Calm by day, this neighborhood along the north bank of the Dōtombori-gawa shows its real face when the sun sets and its warren of bars, hostess clubs, and restaurants comes to life. On any given evening, touts in flamboyant attire stand on their appointed corners, while hostesses in cocktail dresses stride briskly to clubs where they banter with businessmen using corporate expense accounts to cover lavishly priced drinks. Also roaming these streets are groups of 20-somethings on pub crawls and clubbers heading to the city's best music venues.

AMERIKA-MURA アメリカ村

An enclave of tattoo parlors, love hotels, and shops hawking everything from curios to street fashion occupies a number of blocks just west of the major above-ground traffic artery of Midōsuji, on the north side of the canal that runs through Dōtombori a handful of blocks to the south. The neighborhood takes its name from the brisk business selling US-made goods in this area in the postwar years.

There are no sights here, per se, but it's an interesting place to wander and see what flavor of the month the pierced, hair-dyed youth of Osaka are into. There are also lots of bars and restaurants dotting the area. Particularly at night, the central **Triangle Park** is a popular hangout spot. Behold the faux Statue of Liberty perched atop a drab apartment block.

SHIN-SEKAI 新世界

Farther to the south, get a sense of what the city imagined as the big, bright future around the turn of the 20th century. Shin-Sekai ("New World") is a rundown entertainment area dotted by gritty restaurants, garish pachinko parlors, dive bars, and old-timers playing mah-jongg. The centerpiece of the grizzled area is the 103-meter (338-foot) tall **Tsūten-kaku,** a retro steel tower bearing a heavy dose of neon. To make a visit worthwhile, it's best to go for dinner at one of the area's famed *kushikatsu* restaurants, though keep to the main area: to the west and south are a homeless encampment and a red-light district, respectively.

If you're coming to Shin-Sekai via JR, take the Loop Line to Shin-Imamiya Station. Tsūten-kaku is a 10-minute walk northeast of there. If you're taking the subway, hop on the Sakaisuji line found for Tengachaya and get off at Ebisucho, then walk about 3 minutes south to Tsūten-kaku. Or, if you're taking the Midōsuji line, go to Dobutsuen-mae, from where Tsūten-kaku is about 10 minutes' walk north.

TENNOJI 天王寺

About 15 minutes' walk southeast of Shin-Sekai, Tennoji Station has become a fashionable hub in what was previously a rather dated side of town. This is all thanks to the March 2014 opening of the mammoth Abeno Harukas tower, looming over the area around Tennoji Station. The tallest building in Japan, the observation deck atop this tower is a great alternative to the Umeda Sky Building if you're doing the bulk of your sightseeing on the south side of town, or if your aim is to get as high off the ground as possible.

ENTERTAINMENT AND EVENTS

Bunraku

If you're going to watch one traditional performance in Osaka, make it bunraku. This singular form of puppet theater involves fully visible puppeteers dressed all in black, controlling the nearly life-size puppets onstage. The art form, listed as UNESCO World Intangible Cultural Heritage, was not born in Osaka but has thrived more in the city than anywhere else. The outsized puppets depict tales set in the pleasure quarters of old, where dramas played out among merchants and members of the sensually loaded *mizushobai* (water trade).

NATIONAL BUNRAKU THEATER

1-12-10 Nipponbashi, Chūō-ku; tel. 06/6212-2531; www.ntj.jac.go.jp; from ¥2,400 for full performances, from ¥500 for single acts; take the Sakai-suji subway line to Nipponbashi, exit 7

To learn more about this unique form of theater, or to see a performance, go to the National Bunraku Theater. Similar to kabuki, the length of bunraku performances can test the endurance, with some clocking in at more than four hours. If that sounds like too much, non-reserved tickets for single acts are also available. If you want to sit through an entire play, reserve as far in advance as possible. Check the website for the performance schedule.

Festivals

TENJIN MATSURI
天神祭

Tenmangū shrine and Ō River; www.tenjinmatsuri.com; July 24-25; free

Along with Tokyo's Kanda Matsuri and Kyoto's Gion Matsuri, Osaka's Tenjin Matsuri is widely regarded as one of Japan's three blowout festivals. Taking place every July 24-25, practically all of the city participates in this massive festival—dedicated to Sugawara Michizane, the God of learning—which has a history that stretches back to the 10th century. The proceedings begin on the morning of the 24th at the shrine of Tenmangū (2-1-8 Tenjinbashi, Kita-ku; tel. 06/6353-0025; https://osakatemmangu.or.jp; take JR Gakkentoshi line to Osakatemmangu Station), located on the north side of town about 25 minutes' walk southeast of JR Osaka Station. Following a ritual and prayers for the city's peace and prosperity at Temmangū on the first day, the festival reaches a crescendo on the second day when (starting from around 3:30pm) locals wearing traditional garb pull opulent portable shrines the size of cars, known as *mikoshi,* from Tenmangū through the surrounding streets, then proceed to glide through the Ō River in swarms of boats. The evening ends with a huge fireworks show along the Ō River.

KISHIWADA DANJIRI MATSURI
岸和田だんじり祭

1-10 Miyamoto-chō, Kishidawashi; tel. 072/423-2121; https://osaka-info.jp/en/page/kishiwada-danjiri-festival; 6am-10pm Sat.-Sun. of third weekend in Sept.; free

In the Kishiwada Danjiri Matsuri, held on September's third weekend each year, scores of locals tug around 35 massive wooden floats called *danjiri,* weighing up to 3,000 kg (6,613 lbs), through the streets west of Kishiwada Station in far southern Osaka (reached via Nankai line from Namba Station in 25 minutes; ¥490). The floats, which resemble religious architecture, are ridden by revelers wearing white headbands and colorfully woven traditional threads. If you're in the city for the event, give the floats a wide berth; they can move at surprising speeds. The timing of the festival always falls on the weekend (Sat.-Sun.) preceeding a national holiday known as Respect for the Aged Day (third Mon. of Sept.). To see a map of the route that the floats typically take through the town's streets, visit www.city.kishiwada.osaka.jp/site/danjiri/danjiri-map.html.

SPORTS AND RECREATION

SPA WORLD

3-4-24 Ebisu-higashi, Naniwa-ku; tel. 06/6631-0001; www.spaworld.co.jp; 10am-8:45am daily, closing hours vary for some bathing areas; ¥1,200 adults, ¥1,000 age 12 and under Mon.-Fri./¥1,500 adults, ¥1,200 age 12 and under Sat.-Sun. for onsen and swimming areas; take Midōsuji, Sakai-suji subway lines to Dobutsuen-mae Station, or take Nankai, JR Loop lines to Shin-Imamiya Station

At the southern end of Shin-Sekai you'll find this rambling smorgasbord of bathing options. Supplied with water drawn from deep within the earth, there are floors for European- (4th floor, with towel) and Asian- (6th floor, nude) style bathing, which alternate monthly by gender (only women can access Asian zone, while only men can access European zone in even-numbered months). Beyond *onsen* (hot-spring) pools, there are areas for swimming (8th floor; ¥600 bathing suit rental), and for an additional fee (3rd floor; ¥800 adults Mon.-Fri./¥1,000 Sat.-Sun. and holidays) you can access 8 types of *ganban-yoku* (stone sauna) options in a range of styles from around the world, from the Turkish *hamam* to the Russian *banya*. There's also a kid's play area (additional ¥500) and a smattering of restaurants on site. If you arrive between midnight and 5am or extend your stay during this window of time, you'll be charged an additional ¥1,300.

SHOPPING

Kita

On the north (Kita) side of town, the shopping options are mostly concentrated in **Umeda**, where department stores and chains of every stripe abound.

NAKAZAKICHŌ

5 minutes' walk east of Hankyū-Umeda Station, or 5 minutes' walk west of Nakazakichō Station (Tanimachi subway line)

The hip, artsy enclave of Nakazakichō on the east side of the JR Kyoto line tracks is filled with indie boutiques, stylish cafés, and bars set in retro Shōwa period (1926-1989) buildings draped in vines that somehow managed to evade bombing during World War II. If you're keen to explore Osaka's off-the-radar hip side, note that many establishments don't open their doors until around noon. If you linger until the evening, alternative types congregate at the watering holes around the area.

The area rewards wandering, but if you'd like to have a starting point, check out **Green Pepe** (3-1-12 Nakazaki, Kita-ku; tel. 06/6359-5133; www.greenpepe3104.com; noon-7pm Wed.-Mon.), a quirky purveyor of vintage clothing and antique miscellany that is very in keeping with the ethos of the neighborhood.

HANKYU UMEDA STORE

8-7 Kakudachō, Kita-ku; tel. 06/6361-1381; www.hankyu-dept.co.jp/fl/english/honten; 10am-8pm Sun.-Thurs., 10am-9pm Fri.-Sat., 11am-10pm restaurant floors

This is the best department store in town. As the flagship of the Hankyū department store chain, this monument to high-end commerce is suitably chic both in its atmosphere and offerings. Alongside pricey, stylish attire and a seemingly endless range of goods for home and life, there's a cavernous basement food hall and two restaurant floors on the 12th-13th floors. It occupies the building above Umeda Hankyū Station.

Minami

Similar to the offerings on the north (Kita) side of town, the south (Minami) half is filled with shopping streets and markets that call for open-ended exploration rather than targeted visits to particular shops. Here are some of the shopping districts that reward sauntering.

SHINSAIBASHI-SUJI

East of Midōsuji, from Shinsaibashi Station in north to Dōtombori in the south; hours vary by shop; take Midōsuji subway line to Shinsaibashi Station, exit 5

This seemingly neverending covered walkway, situated east of and running parallel to

Osaka by Go-Kart

A curious phenomenon witnessed with increasing frequency in Japan in recent years has been people dressed up in cosplay outfits zipping through the streets in go-karts. If you want to experience this in Osaka, check out these companies, which also operate in Tokyo:

- **Akiba Kart Osaka:** 3-3-9 Nipponbashi, Naniwa-ku; tel. 080/9697-8605; https://osakakart.com/en; 10am-8pm daily; ¥9,000-11,000
- **Street Kart Osaka:** 3-1-10 Ōhiraki, Fukushima-ku; tel. 06/6131-5117; noon-10pm daily; https://kart.st/en/osaka.html; ¥9,000

It may be fun, but the dangers of sharing the roads with trucks, buses, and drivers of all stripes is real. A **passport** and an **international driver's permit** are mandatory.

the major north-south artery of Midōsuji, is lined with shops of every kind: groceries, cosmetics, bookstores, cheap threads, cafes. In truth, it's mostly notable for its bustle rather than its shops. Walk down it on your way from Shinsaibashi Station to Dōtombori to people watch and check the city's pulse.

AMERIKA-MURA AND HORIE

West of Midōsuji, from Shinsaibashi Station in north to Dōtombori in the south; http://americamura.jp/en; hours vary by shop; take Midōsuji subway line to Shinsaibashi Station, exit 7

A rough approximation to Tokyo's Harajuku, this maze of lanes brims with shops selling streetwear, vintage threads and hip-hop attire marketed to the city's fashion-conscious youth. Literally meaning "America-mura" (America Village), the neighborhood has been a mecca for the city's 20-somethings for decades. At the heart of the area is Sankakukōen (Triangle Park), a concrete space where trend-conscious youngsters gather when they're not picking through threads nearby. This is another district to meander through and follow your inspiration.

A few blocks southwest of Amerikamura, you'll enter a more mature, yet equally stylish neighborhood: Horie. Most of the boutiques in this area stock elegant attire and lifestyle goods produced in Japan. A good starting point is **Biotop** (1-16-1 Minamihorie, Nishi-ku; tel. 06/6531-8223; www.biotop.jp/osaka; 11am-11pm daily), a multistory shop with a café and greenhouse on the first floor, a garden on the roof, and a few floors of chic offerings from Japanese denim and bonsai trees to domestically fired ceramics. One minute's walk west of Biotop, the gallery-cum-fashion shop **Palette Art Alive** (1-19-1 Minamihorie, Nishi-ku; tel. 06/6586-9560; http://palette-art-alive.com; noon-8pm daily) serves as a showcase for the next generation of Japan's bleeding-edge fashion designers.

DOGUYA-SUJI

14-5 Nanbasennichimae, Chūō-ku; tel. 06/6633-1423; https://doguyasuji.or.jp; hours vary by shop; take Midōsuji subway line to Namba Station, exit E-3, or take Nakai line to Namba Station, south exit

This pedestrian emporium's name literally translates to "Kitchenware Street," which sums it up. Pick up things for the kitchen here, from cookery and sushi-shaped magnets for the fridge to high-grade knives. The shops are generally open daily from around 10am-6pm. The street runs north-south, parallel to Namba Station, which is a few minutes' walk west.

KUROMON ICHIBA

2-4-1 Nipponbashi, Chūō-ku; tel. 06/6631-0007; https://kuromon.com/jp; hours vary by shop; take Sakaisuji, Sen-Nichimae subway lines to Nippombashi Station, exit 10

About 6 minutes' walk east of Doguya-suji,

"Eat Yourself to Ruin"

deep-fried skewers

A stereotype exists across Japan that Osakans have a devil-may-care attitude toward indulging in earthly pleasures. Of all the seven deadly sins, gluttony, or at least something approaching it, tops the city's list. A jaunty attitude toward culinary excess has a long tradition in Osaka, which was historically referred to as "Japan's Kitchen." There's even a word for draining one's financial resources in the pursuit of scarfing down all the deep-fried goodies the city has to offer: *kuidaore* ("ku-ee-dao-rei"). After a night spent tipsily stumbling between rickety ramen stands and smoky yakitori (grilled, skewered chicken) joints, the risk of succumbing to *kuidaore* (literally: "eating oneself to ruin") becomes a distinct possibility. Here's a small sample of what you'll find:

- **Takoyaki:** Fried balls of dough stuffed with chunks of octopus tentacle.
- **Okonomiyaki:** Savory pancakes sizzling on an open griddle are stuffed with cabbage, meat, and seafood, and often topped with bonito flakes and mayonnaise.
- **Kushikatsu:** All manner of things on sticks—lotus root, sausage, eggplant, pork belly, mushroom—is dipped in panko, egg, and flour, then deep-fried in a vat of boiling oil until it's crispy on the outside.
- **Kaiten-zushi:** This is sushi delivered by conveyor belt.
- **Horumon:** This dish consists of discarded animal bits, including stomach, intestine, tripe, even uterus, grilled, thrown into stews or even deftly served raw.
- **Yaki-niku:** Thanks to its sizable Korean population concentrated in the neighborhood of Tsuruhashi, Osaka is also known for its Korean BBQ.
- **Kappō-ryōri:** In essence, this means *kaiseki* minus the fuss, with diners sitting directly at the counter to banter with the chef who serves up beautifully presented courses made from the finest seasonal ingredients.

you'll find Osaka's largest food market. This covered walkway contains some 170 shops hawking culinary items of every type, from skewers of grilled meat and noodles to fresh fruits, vegetables, and fish sourced by restaurants around town. If you'd like to sample something at the market, quaff a paper cup of rich, flavorsome (though unsweetened) soy milk from neighborhood tofu institution **Takahashi Shokuhin** (1-21-31 Nipponbashi, Chūō-ku; tel. 06/6641-4548; https://kuromon.com/en/takahashi-shokuhin; 8am-5pm Mon.-Sat.; ¥70). To reach this vendor, established in 1925, walk straight out of Nippombashi Station, exit 10, and take the first left. Takahashi Shokuhin will be on the right side of the first block of shops. From here, wander through the market, following your inspiration, and take in the atmosphere. The market is inundated with tourists from around 10am, so aim to visit by around 9am.

DEN-DEN TOWN

4-12 Nipponbashi, Naniwa-ku; tel. 06/6655-1717; www.denden-town.or.jp; hours vary by shop; take Sakaisuji, Sen-Nichimae subway lines to Nippombashi Station, exit 5, then walk 10 minutes south, or take Sakaisuji line to Ebisuchō Station, exit 2 or 5, then walk about 7 minutes north, or take Nakai line to Namba Station, south exit, then walk 9 minutes southeast

Roughly 10 minutes' walk south of both Doguya-suji and Kuromon-Ichiba lies a shopping district where you'll find gadgets and various accoutrements of geekdom. If you're visiting Tokyo, then a trip to Akihabara will more than have these things covered. But if you're only going to be in Osaka and want to peruse cameras, electronics, computer parts, and pop-cultural artifacts (manga zines, anime figurines, cosplay outfits, retro video games, and more), then this is your place.

FOOD

Kita

KIJI

9-20 Kakudachō, Kita-ku; tel. 06/6361-5804, 11:30am-9:30pm Mon.-Sat.; ¥1,500

For okonomiyaki on the north side of town, head to Kiji. This great *okonomiyaki* joint is set in the second floor of a building in the tightly packed Shinumeda Shokudogai restaurant district located between JR Osaka Station and Hankyū Umeda Station.

MITSUKA BOSE KAMOSHI

1-2-16 Ōyodominami, Kita-ku; tel. 06/6442-1005; https://mitsukabose.com; 11:30am-2:30pm and 6:30pm-11:30pm Tues.-Sat., 11:30am-2:30pm and 5:30pm-10pm Sun. and holidays; ¥1,000; take the JR line to JR Osaka Station's central north gate

In a city with a wealth of ramen options, Mitsuka Bose Kamoshi is the best spot to try the miso-based variety. Soup stock options include everything from squid ink to burnt miso. Its location right next to the Umeda Sky Building makes it an appealing option either before or after heading skyward. Note that this restaurant is on the **Osaka Ramen Route** (www.osakaramenroute.com), the fun brainchild of the Friends in Ramen (www.friendsinramen.com) blog. This stamp-collecting rally brings you to the city's best bowls of noodles and ends with a prize when you complete the circuit.

BON

1-3-15 Dojima; tel. 06/6344-0400; www.kitchen-dan.jp; 6pm-12:30am daily; from ¥15,000; take the Yotsuhashi-suji subway line or JR Tōzai line to Kitashinchi Station, exit 11-5

Deep-fried goodies on skewers (*kushikatsu*) await at Bon, an expert shop in Kita-Shinchi, just south of JR Osaka and Umeda stations. This is the place to go for this local favorite in a refined setting.

SHUHARI

1-3-20 Tokiwamachi, Chūō-ku; tel. 06/6944-8808; http://shuhari.main.jp; 11:30am-3pm and 5:30pm-11pm daily; from ¥1,000; take the Tanimachi subway line to Temmabashi Station, exit 2

If you've worked up an appetite after exploring Osaka-jō, Shuhari is a good spot for lunch. Located in Tanimachi 4-chōme near the park around Osaka-jō, this restaurant has a nice menu of soba sets served with tempura and fresh wasabi.

SALON DE AMANTO

1-7-26 Nakazakinishi, Kita-ku; tel. 06/6371-5840; http://amanto.jp; noon-10pm daily; ¥1,000; take Hankyū-Kobe, Hankyū-Kyoto, Hankyū-Takarazuka lines to Umeda-Hankyū Station, or take Tanimachi subway line to Nakazakichō Station

If you've got a soft spot for bohemian haunts, try this retro, DIY space in the hip, somewhat hidden district of Nakazakichō about 10 minutes' walk east of Umeda. Set in a building that dates to the 1880s, by day it provides caffeine hits and simple dishes like curry rice and chicken and egg on rice. By night, it turns into a bar that sometimes hosts music and art events in the evenings.

Minami

LILO COFFEE ROASTERS

1-1-10-28 Nishi-Shinsaibashi, Chūō-ku; tel. 06/6227-8666; https://coffee.liloinveve.com; 11am-11pm daily; ¥280-750; take Midōsuji subway line to Shinsaibashi Station, exit 8

With its cozy patio and streetside seating, and baristas who know their stuff, this narrow, minimalist café is the place to go for

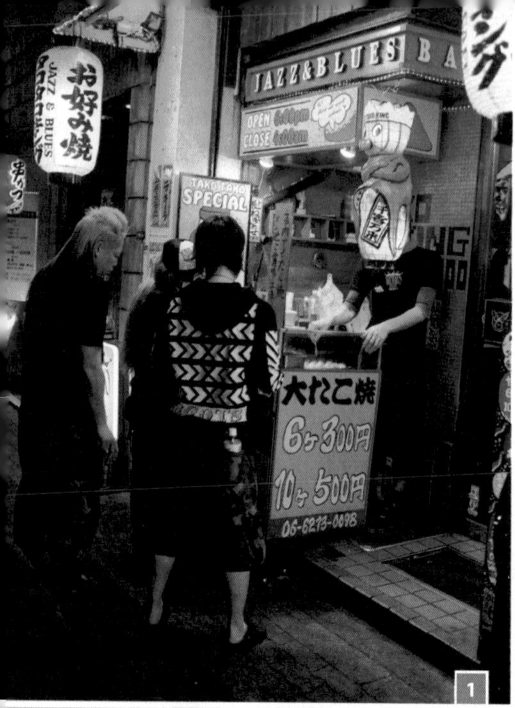
JAZZ&BLUES
お好み焼
TAKO TAKO SPECIAL
大たこ焼
6ヶ300円
10ヶ500円
06-6213-0098

1

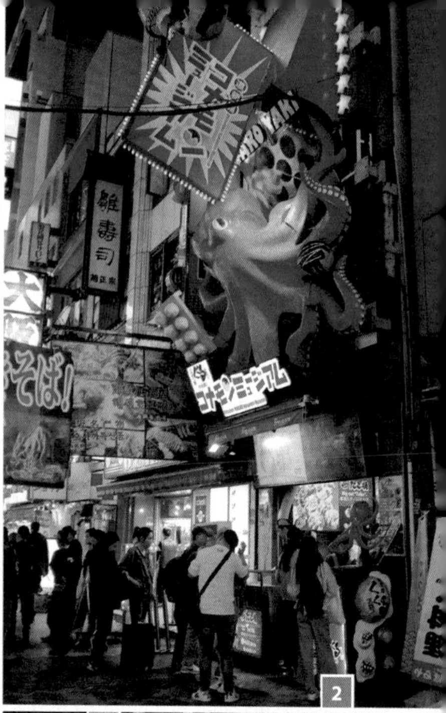
2

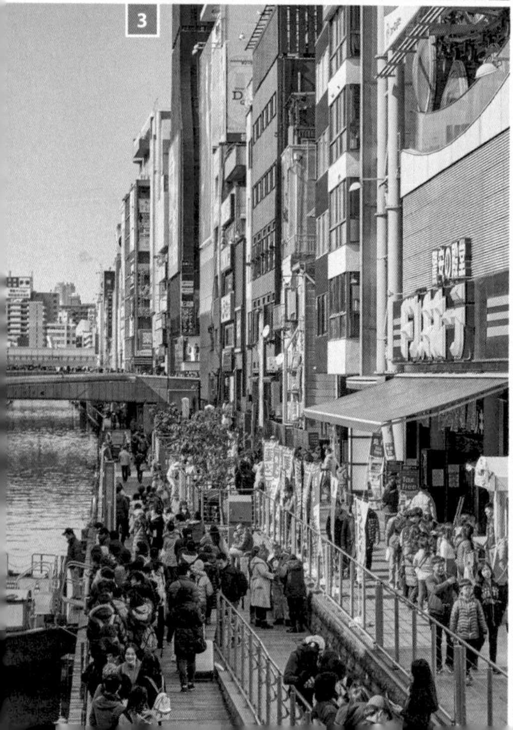
3

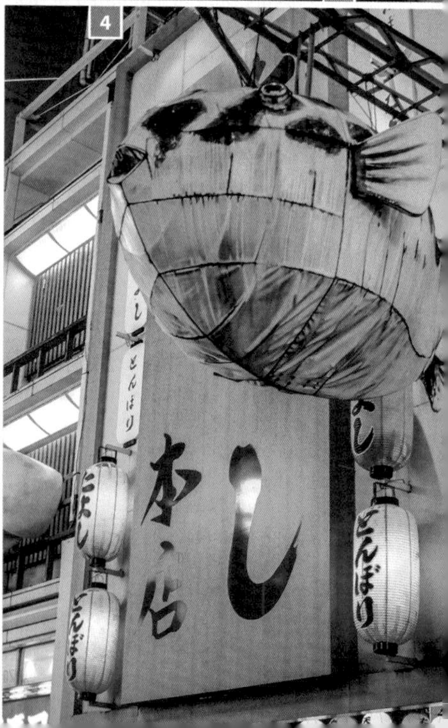
とんぼり
とんぼり

4

a proper cup of coffee to fuel your stroll through Amerika-mura. A variety of beans are on offer, from single-origin to blends, in a range of roasts. They also sell light nibbles like croissants and hot dogs and have a few beers on tap.

★ TAKOTAKO KING HONTEN

2-4-25 Higashishinsaibashi, Chūō-ku; tel. 06/6213-0098; https://takotakoking.com/honten.html; 6pm-4am daily; ¥300-900; take Midōsuji subway line to Shinsaibashi, exit 6

This is a great spot to indulge on one of Osaka's signature greasy-spoon dishes, *takoyaki* (fried balls of dough stuffed with octopus), away from the throngs of Dōtombori. This friendly local institution draws a crowd, especially on weekends, with its mix of affordable, delicious food made on the spot (*takoyaki, okonomiyaki,* and more), drinks, and lively ambience. There's both seating inside and on the sidewalk, and a takeout window. If this location is too crowded, there's an equally good branch 2 minutes' walk west on the same side of the same street (2-8-28 Higashishinsaibashi, Chūō-ku; tel. 06/6212-0079; https://takotakoking.com/honnishiten.html; 6pm-3am daily).

★ MOMEN

2-1-3 Shinsaibashi, Chūō-ku; tel. 06/6211-2793; 5pm-10pm Mon.-Sat.; from ¥15,000; take the Midōsuji subway line to Shinsaibashi Station, exit 6

If all the deep-fried fare begins to feel fatiguing, remember that Osaka does have a refined side. Momen is an excellent *kappo ryōri*—essentially *kaiseki* served more casually at a countertop—restaurant in Shinsaibashi, where patrons sit bantering with the chefs as they whip up seasonally inspired artistic creations with top-notch ingredients. The restaurant seats only nine, so reserve at least a few weeks in advance, if not earlier, to ensure a spot. Also note that the restaurant only accepts cash. It's not cheap, but it's an experience you will remember.

★ DŌTOMBORI

Eating along Osaka's Dōtombori canal is a quintessential part of a visit to the city. Although there are other purveyors of Osaka's signature dishes elsewhere in the city, there's something special about savoring them in this bright, bustling strip. Out of all the tacky signs demanding your attention (and yen), some of the shops really deliver on their promises.

For great *okonomiyaki* right next to the canal, try **Chibō** (1-5-5 Dōtombori, Chūō-ku; tel. 06/6212-2211; www.chibo.com; 11am-1am Mon.-Sat., 11am-midnight Sun.; from ¥900). There's often a queue, but it moves fast. For excellent *kushikatsu* right on the main strip just a few doors down from Chibō, head to **Ganso Kushikatsu Daruma, Dōtombori** (1-6-4 Dōtombori, Chūō-ku; tel. 06/6213-8101; www.kushikatu-daruma.com; 11:30am-10:30pm; single skewers from ¥110). For very decent *takoyaki* along the lively thoroughfare, try **Takoyaki Jyuhachiban** (-7-21 Dōtombori, Chūō-ku; tel. 06/6211-3118; ¥350 for six).

Eating along this neon-splashed canal is fundamental to any introduction to Osaka, but for some, the crowds and kitsch may be too much. If you prefer somewhere a little more subdued and authentic, there are loads of other great restaurants nearby. To get to the canal, take the Midōsuji subway line to Namba Station, exit 14.

MATSUZAKAGYŪ YAKINIKU M

1-1-19 Namba, Chūō-ku; tel. 06/6221-2917; www.matsusaka-projects.com; 5pm-midnight daily, noon-3pm Sat.-Sun.; dinner ¥5,000

Not far from Dōtombori but feeling like a world away, Matsuzakagyū Yakiniku M is a great place to dig into some *yakiniku* made with famed, high-grade Matsuzaka beef, which gives Kobe beef stiff competition. The joint gets crammed with patrons, but the

1: Takotako King **2:** one of Dōtombori's many *takoyaki* shops **3:** Dōtombori canal
4: fugu restaurant on Dōtombori

private dining booths and jazz soundtrack add an air of refinement. Most importantly, the food is delicious.

★ AJINOYA

1-7-16 Namba, Chūō-ku; tel. 06/6211-0713; http://ajinoya-okonomiyaki.com; noon-10:45pm Tues.-Fri., 11:30am-10:45pm Sat.-Sun.; lunch from ¥1,000, dinner from ¥2,000; take the Midōsuji subway line to Namba Station, exit 14

Just a few blocks south of Dōtombori, Ajinoya serves fantastic *okonomiyaki*. If the line for the nearby more touristy Chibō is discouragingly long, take heart. The service is speedy and the quality of the food is excellent.

★ GANSO KUSHIKATSU DARUMA HONTEN

2-3-9 Ebisu-Higashi, Naniwa-ku; tel. 06/6645-7056; www.kushikatsu-daruma.com; 11am-10:30pm daily; single skewers from ¥110; take the Midōsuji subway line to Dōbutsuen-mae, exit 5

If you prefer to eat *kushikatsu* right on Dōtombori, the Daruma shop there does a fine job. But to experience this dish in the gritty surroundings of its glorious origins, head farther south to Ganso Kushikatsu Daruma Honten. Set in the aged commercial development of Shin-Sekai, this shop claims to be where the dish originated.

BARS AND NIGHTLIFE

Osaka is a fun city at night, with most of the action taking place in the southern half of the city. Cocktail bars, dance clubs, and live music are abundant in the bustling streets of Shinsaibashi and Namba.

Kita

BLARNEY STONE

6F Sonezaki Center Bldg., 2-10-15 Sonezaki, Kita-ku; 5pm-1am Mon.-Thurs., 5pm-5am Fri.-Sat., 3:30pm-1am Sun; take the Midōsuji or Tanimachi subway line to Higshi Umeda Station, exit 7

Blarney Stone is a good spot in the northern half of the city to mix with expats and locals over a pint or two. This faux Irish pub is especially lively during the after-work hours.

Minami

DUBLIN GARDEN

2-1-5 Dōtombori, Chūō-ku; tel. 06/6213-1122; take the Sennichimae subway line to Namba Station, exit 1

If the weather is nice, the Dublin Garden is a great space to drink outdoors. You can grill your own meat while you're there too. There's an all-you-can-drink plan that lasts two hours. It's a great place to party with friends.

CINQUENCENTO

10-1-2 Higashi-Shinsaibashi, Chūō-ku; tel. 06/6213-6788; 8pm-5am daily; take the Sakai-suji subway line to Nipponbashi, exit 2

Cinquencento is a lively martini bar with a reasonably priced menu. It's a fun place to mingle with locals and expats before or after hitting the local clubs. Alongside Minoh's offerings, a handful of other Japanese microbrews flow from 10 taps.

BAR NAYUTA

1-6-17 Nishi-Shinsaibashi, Chūō-ku; tel. 06/6210-3615; http://bar-nayuta.com; 5pm-3am daily; take the Midōsuji subway line to Shinsaibashi Station, exit 7

For great cocktails in a classic speakeasy atmosphere, head to Bar Nayuta. The man behind the bar, Hiro, is a master mixologist who puts a unique spin on his drinks. This is an excellent choice if you're seeking a place with a whiff of refinement.

MISONO BUILDING

2-3-9 Sennichimae, Chūō-ku; hours vary; take the Sakai-suji subway line to Nipponbashi Station, exit 5

For adventurous nightlife connoisseurs with a penchant for drinking in slightly grittier surroundings, head to Ura Namba's iconic Misono Building. Protected from the tourist onslaught on the backside (*ura* in Japanese) of Namba, the second floor of this dilapidated building is crammed with old bars that stay open into the wee hours. Choose the quirky façade that most strikes your fancy, then bar hop from there.

TOP EXPERIENCE

Suntory Yamakazi Distillery and Japan's Award-Winning Whisky

whisky for sale in the Suntory Yamakazi Distillery gift shop

Japan's renowned spirit of craftsmanship, knack for detail, and fresh, flavorsome groundwater have all contributed to the country's success in the world of whisky. Afficionados also credit the nation's four seasons with adding extra layers of texture to barrel casks that sit aging for years.

Japan's first domestically distilled malt whisky was bottled in 1924 by at **Suntory Yamakazi Distillery** (5-2-1 Yamazaki, Shimamoto, Mishima District, Osaka Prefecture; tel. 075/962-1423; www.suntory.com/factory/yamazaki; 9:30am-5pm daily, sporadic closings) in Osaka Prefecture, between Osaka and Kyoto. To reach the distillery, take the JR Kyoto line to Yamazaki Station (30 minutes from Osaka Station, ¥460; 15 minutes from Kyoto Station, ¥220), then walk 10 minutes west.

Suntory's Yamazaki 12 Years single malt was the first Japanese whisky to take home a gold medal at the International Spirits Challenge in 2003. The success has snowballed from there, with Suntory's Hibiki taking the Best Blended Whisky in the World prize for the fourth time at the World Whiskies Awards in 2016. At the 2017 awards, Japan made the strongest showing of any country, snagging three prizes: World's Best Single Cask Single Malt, Chichibu Whisky Matsuri 2017; World's Best Blended, Hibiki 21 Year Old; and World's Best Grain, the Fuji-Gotemba Distillery Single Grain 25 Year Old Small Batch.

If you visit Suntory Yamakazi Distillery, you can simply walk through on your own for free, and there are bilingual exhibits at an on-site **museum** about the history of the label, plus you can sample the goods at a paid **tasting counter** (10am-4:30pm). Or, you can pay for a guided, behind-the-scenes **distillery tour** (80-100 minutes; ¥1,000-2,000) in English. Be sure to **reserve ahead;** go to www.suntory.com/factory/yamazaki/info for more information.

CIRCUS

2F 1-8-16 Nishi-Shinsaibashi; tel. 06/6241-3822; http://circus-osaka.com; 11pm-late Fri.-Sat. nights and special events; take the Midōsuji subway line to Shinsaibashi Station, exit 7

If you're seeking a club that takes its electronic music seriously, Circus is the best place in Osaka. The crowd goes more for the music than to see or be seen. An added bonus: the dance floor is non-smoking.

HANA SAKE BAR

1-8-4 Nishishinsaibashi, Chūō-ku; tel. 06/6484-7896; https://hanasakebar.com; 6pm-11:30pm Mon.-Thurs., 6pm-1am Fri.-Sat. and any day before holiday, 5pm-10:30pm Sun. and last day of consecutive holiday period; take Midōsuji subway line to Shinsaibashi Station, exit 8

Come to this welcoming spot in Amerika-mura to mingle with friendly locals and sip Japanese booze, from sake tasting sets to domestically distilled shochu and whisky. The interior is minimalist—concrete floor, white walls, wooden tables and countertop—and the owner is friendly, knowledgeable, and speaks good English.

FARPLANE

East Village Bldg. 3F, 2-8-19 Nishishinsaibashi, Chūō-ku; tel. 06/6211-6012; http://farplane.jp/bar; 8pm-late daily; cover charges vary for special events; take Midōsuji subway line to Shinsaibashi Station, exit 8

For something outré, the appropriatedly named Farplane cannot be beat. This fetish bar with velvet-draped ceilings, chandelliers, and edgy posters on the walls grew out of what was once a shop selling sexy attire. Today, the city's weirdos flock to the space, run by bartenders in kinky outfits. It hosts occasional events like the monthly Creamy Banana Burlesque show and its annual Farplane Night (http://farplane.jp/farplane-night). For a full event schedule (Japanese only), go to http://farplane.jp/category/event.

NAMBA BEARS

3-14-5 Namba-naka, Naniwa-ku; tel. 06/6649-5564; http://namba-bears.main.jp; take the Midōsuji subway line to Namba Station, exit 4

If your musical taste is more of the rock variety, Osaka's go-to live venue is Namba Bears. DIY in spirit, the compact, bare-bones space hosts indie bands and punk rockers, providing sustenance to the city's underground scene. Bring your own booze.

ACCOMMODATIONS

Kita

U-EN

2-9-23 Fukushima, Fukushima-ku; tel. 06/7503-4394; www.hostelosaka.com; ¥2,800 dorm bed, ¥6,600 d; take the Hanshin main line to Shin-Fukushima Station, exit 2

U-en is a stylish hostel set in an old, renovated townhouse in the north of town. There are both Japanese-style private rooms and dorm beds. Flashes of traditional design—tatami floors, paper-screen doors—give it just the right amount of style. This is a great choice if you're on a tight budget.

★ INTERCONTINENTAL OSAKA

3-60 Ofuka-chō, Kita-ku; tel. 06/6374-5700; www.ihg.com; ¥48,000 d; take the JR lines to Osaka Station or the Hankyū line to Umeda Station

A stone's throw from both JR Osaka Station and Umeda Station, the Intercontinental Osaka has all the amenities of a five-star hotel and is easily one of the city's best. This property is in an excellent location, with fantastic views and great restaurants on-site. Highly recommended.

Minami

HEARTON HOTEL SHINSAIBASHI

1-5-24 Nishishinsaibashi, Chūō-ku; tel. 06/6251-3711; www.hearton.co.jp; ¥12,000 d; take the Midōsuji subway line to Shinsaibashi Station, exit 7

Hearton Hotel Shinsaibashi is a good hotel with reasonable rates in the thick of things in Shinsaibashi. If you're interested in exploring Osaka's main nightlife zone and need a clean place to bed down for the night, this is a good choice.

CROSS HOTEL OSAKA

2-5-15 Shinsaibashisuji, Chūō-ku; tel. 06/6213-8281; www.crosshotel.com; ¥17,000 d; take the Midōsuji or Sennichimae subway line to Namba Station, exit 14

Cross Hotel Osaka is only a few minutes' walk from Dōtombori, Shinsaibashi, and Amerika-mura, putting street food, nightlife, and funky boutiques within easy reach. Rooms here are smart and clean, and the bathrooms are spacious compared to hotels in the same price range. It also has a bar and a few restaurants.

DOTONBORI HOTEL

2-3-25 Dōtombori, Chūō-ku; tel. 06/6213-9040; http://dotonbori-h.co.jp; ¥12,000 d; take the Sennichimae or Midōsuji subway line to Namba Station, exit 25

Beyond its quirky exterior fronted by pillars shaped like large human faces perched atop pairs of legs, Dotonbori Hotel is a solid, no-frills option in the center of Dōtombori. It's clean, modern, and convenient, and friendly staff are ready to help. This is a good pick for value, and a Japanese and Western-style breakfast buffet is available for an additional fee.

NIKKO HOTEL OSAKA

1-3-3 Nishishinsaibashi, Chūō-ku; tel. 06/6244-1111; www.hno.co.jp; ¥24,000 d; take the Midōsuji subway line to Shinsaibashi Station, exit 8

The Nikko Hotel Osaka is a great pick if you want to stay near the heart of the action in Minami with a whiff of luxury. The hotel's quality breakfast spread, on-site dining options, and clean stylish rooms put it a cut above the more budget-conscious options in the area. Its location directly above Shinsaibashi Station offers fantastic access to the attractions in the south part of the city.

ST. REGIS OSAKA

3-6-12 Honmachi, Chūō-ku; tel. 06/6258-3333; www.stregisosaka.co.jp; ¥27,000 d; take the Chūō subway line to Honmachi Station, exit 3

Starting from its 12th-floor lobby, St. Regis Osaka exudes chic design sense throughout its 160-room property. Located on the prestigious Midōsuji-dōri shopping artery, this classy hotel has an outdoor Japanese garden and haute restaurants on-site (French, Italian). This is an excellent pick if you want to travel in style.

FRASER RESIDENCE NANKAI OSAKA

1-17-11 Nambanaka, Naniwa-ku; tel. 06/6635-7111; https://osaka.frasershospitality.com; from ¥27,000; take the Namba Nankai line to Namba Nakai Station

If you prefer to feel "at home" in a hotel, check out Fraser Residence Nankai Osaka. Aside from being in the thick of the action in Namba, what sets Fraser Residence apart is that its rooms resemble apartments. This makes the hotel an especially appealing option for those who are traveling with kids or staying longer-term.

INFORMATION AND SERVICES

Tourist Information

For tourist information in the Kita (north) side of the city, head to **Tourist Information Osaka** (tel. 06/6131-4550; www.osaka-info.jp; 7am-11pm daily for tourist office, 9am-5:30pm daily for phone inquiries), located directly in front of the central ticket gates of JR Osaka Station.

In the Minami (south) of the city, **Tourist Information Namba** (tel. 06/6131-4550; www.osaka-info.jp; 9am-8pm daily for tourist office, 9am-5:30pm daily for phone inquiries) is outside Nakai Namba Station and Namba Station on the first floor near the ticket gates for the Midōsuji and Sennichimae subway lines. These city-run centers have a good selection of English-language maps, brochures, and friendly bilingual staff who are happy to help you handle trip logistics, including booking accommodations.

Wi-Fi Access

For information on how to connect to one of some 5,000 free Wi-Fi points around the city, see http://ofw-oer.com/en.

Medical Services

In the case of an emergency, the **Osaka Red Cross Hospital** has some English-speaking doctors on staff. (5-30 Fudegasaki-chō, Tennōji-ku; tel. 06/6774-5111; www.osaka-med.jrc.or.jp; 24 hours; Kintetsu line to Osaka-Uehonmachi Station, about 8 minutes' walk east of station)

For less urgent situations, English-speaking doctors can be consulted at **Ohkita Medical Clinic** (1-12-17 Umeda, Kita-ku; tel. 06/6344-0380; 10am-7pm Mon.-Fri, 10am-1pm Sat.; take JR lines to Osaka Station, south-central exit, 4 minutes' walk) and **Yasugi Clinic** (1-75 Ikedachō, Osaka-fu, tel. 06/6353-0505; http://yasugi-clinic.com; 9am-11:45am Mon., Wed.-Sat., 4:30pm-6:45pm Mon., Wed.-Fri.; Osaka loop line to Tenma Station, 6 minutes' walk). Both are on the north side of town.

Otherwise, the **Osaka Call Center** (http://ofw-oer.com/call/en; 24 hours) offers free English-language medical support, reachable directly through the website. To call, you must be connected to the internet.

Diplomatic Services

The **U.S. Consulate General Osaka** (2-11-5 Nishitenma, Kita-ku; tel. 06/6315-5900; https://jp.usembassy.gov; Midōsuji subway line to Yodoyabashi Station, exit 1) is open weekdays 9am-5pm.

TRANSPORTATION

Getting There

AIR

Osaka is served by two airports. The larger of the two is **Kansai International Airport** (www.kansai-airport.or.jp), or KIX, located about 50 km (31 mi) southwest of town. **Itami Airport** (http://osaka-airport.co.jp) is located about 12 km (7 mi) northwest of the city. Though Itami is sometimes referred to as "Osaka International Airport," it only hosts domestic flights.

To shuttle back and forth between KIX and downtown, you can choose between a few trains and an airport limousine service. The most convenient is the twice-hourly **Nankai Rapid Limited Express** train (7am-10pm daily; ¥1,430), or "Rapi:t," which takes you from the airport to Namba Nakai Station (40 minutes) in the heart the Namba district in the Minami (south) side of the city. Another train running twice an hour is the **JR Kansai Airport Express Haruka** (6:30am-10pm), which runs to both Tenno-ji (30 minutes; ¥1,710) on the south side of downtown, and Shin-Osaka (45 minutes; ¥2,330) in the north. While one of these trains is generally the best way to go, if you happen to arrive after the train services stop, there's a limousine service called **KATE** (www.kate.co.jp) that runs between KIX and Osaka Station (1 hour, depending on traffic; ¥1,550) that runs once hourly after midnight. Worst case, you can hail a taxi, although this isn't recommended as fares to Namba in the city's south start from ¥14,000 and climb as you go north.

Traveling between Itami and downtown is done either by **Osaka Airport Limousine** (www.okkbus.co.jp) or **Osaka Monorail.** The former runs to Osaka Station (25 minutes; ¥640) in the city's north and Osaka City Air Terminal (¥640, 35 minutes) in the southern hub of Namba. The latter runs to Senri-Chūō Station, where you can transfer to the Hankyū Senri line, which runs to Osaka Station, with connections to the rest of the city's train and subway lines.

TRAIN

Coming from Tokyo (3 hours; ¥14,140,) or Kyoto (15 minutes; ¥1,420) the **Tōkaidō-San'yō *shinkansen*** stops at **Shin-Osaka Station.** If you have a JR Pass, simply hop on.

Otherwise, take the **JR Kyoto line** from Osaka Station to Kyoto Station (30 minutes; ¥560), the **Hankyū Kyoto line** from Hankyū Umeda Station in Osaka's northern Umeda district to Kawaramachi Station (45 minutes, ¥400) in downtown Kyoto, or the **Keihan Main line** from Yodoyabashi Station in the center of Osaka (linked to the Midōsuji subway line) to Gion-Shijō (50 minutes; ¥410) and Sanjō (55 minutes; ¥410) stations in the heart of Kyoto.

BUS

If you don't mind taking the bus, it will save you a few thousand yen. **Willer Express** (www.willerexpress.com) has a center in the first floor of the east tower of the Umeda Sky Building (Tower East 1F, 1-1-88 Ōyodo-naka, Kita-ku; https://willerexpress.com/en/wbt-umeda; 7:30am-11pm daily, 7:30am-2pm on third Thurs. of month). Willer runs buses to and from Tokyo, Hiroshima, Hakata (Fukuoka), and beyond. Operating out of the JR Osaka Station Highway Bus Terminal, just outside JR Osaka Station's north-central concourse, **JR West Highway Bus** (www.nishinihonjrbus.co.jp) operates along similar routes.

BOAT

If you're feeling adventurous, a number of domestic ferry operators run to and from **Osaka Nankō Port** (2-1-10 Nakō-kita, Suminoe-ku; tel. 06/6613-1571) and Ehime Prefecture's Toyo Port on Shikoku (**Orange Ferry,** www.orange-ferry.co.jp; 8 hours; from ¥6,500) and Kyushu (**City Line,** www.cityline.co.jp; 12.5 hours to Kita-Kyushu; from ¥4,540; or **Ferry Sunflower,** www.ferry-sunflower.co.jp; 12 hours to Beppu; from ¥11,200; 16 hours to Kagoshima; from ¥13,500).

Getting Around

SUBWAY

Although Osaka does have an above-ground train network, its subway system is much more useful. Out of eight subway lines, you'll most likely only need the red-coded **Midōsuji line.** This line starts from Shin-Osaka in the north and runs southward through the business and entertainment zone of Umeda near Osaka Station, the entertainment districts of Shinsaibashi and Namba, and the relaxed southern hub of Tenno-ji. Trains depart every three to five minutes and run from early morning until around midnight, with single journeys costing from ¥180 to ¥370.

BICYCLE

Cycle Osaka (www.cycleosaka.com; tel. 080/6183-8765; 10am-6:30pm) offers full-size cross bikes (¥1,500 per day) and more compact folding bikes (¥1,500 per day). It's possible to rent a bike and explore on your own or join one of the company's tours. Book online a few days ahead to ensure you get a bike. The bilingual staff also lead illuminating tours through the city's varied neighborhoods, bazaars, and culinary zones.

Nara

Nara has a lot to be proud of. This small city of about 360,000 can rightly claim to be the birthplace of Japanese culture as we know it. Founded in 710 and initially named Heijōkyō, or "citadel of peace," the city was the first capital of Japan until 794, when the new nation's political center migrated to Kyoto. During its brief period as the nation's capital, religious, artistic, and architectural influences from China found fertile ground, and Japanese Buddhism emerged from the city.

Remnants of this eventful history are everywhere. Look no further than the myriad temples and gardens scattered throughout the city, particularly concentrated in the sprawling green space that is Nara-kōen where you'll find a throng of docile deer in search of a handout and the towering temple of Todai-ji, housing one of Japan's most iconic sights, the Great Buddha, a statue standing 16 meters (53 feet) tall.

Beyond the grounds of Nara-kōen, a cluster of temples in the west side of town are also a draw, including Horyū-ji, which contains the world's oldest wooden buildings. Head to **Naramachi,** a brief stroll from the city's main railway hubs, where Edo-period ambience oozes from the narrow roads lined by old, whitewashed wooden buildings that now house a variety of restaurants, cafés, shops, and galleries.

Nara

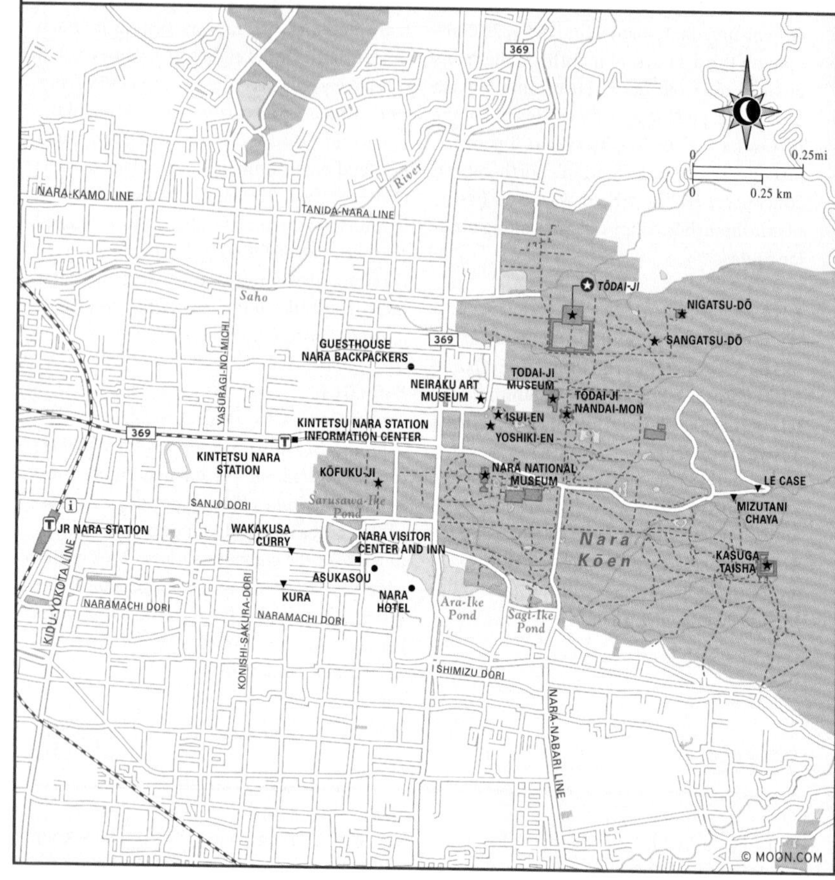

SIGHTS

Nara-kōen

奈良公園

http://nara-park.com; tel. 0742/22-0375; 24 hours; free; take the Kintetsu line to Kintetsu Nara Station, then walk 12 minutes east, or take JR Nara, Yamatoji, Sakurai lines to JR Nara Station, then walk 22 minutes east

Stretching from the eastern side of Naramachi and downtown Nara in the west to the hills at the eastern edge of town, Nara-kōen is an expansive leafy space dotted with important religious sites and crisscrossed by paths ideal for ambling and ponds full of colorful *koi* (carp). It's a wonderful place to stroll and is home to a number of impressive cultural properties harkening back to the beginnings of Japan.

The prized citizens of this green expanse are around 1,500 semi-wild deer, believed to be couriers of the gods in Shinto. Today they are doted on by visitors who feed them with deer crackers (*shika senbei,* ¥150), sold in the park. Forget Bambi—the deer here can become surprisingly aggressive in their quest for crackers. Don't be surprised if you're besieged as soon as you open a pack. It's best not to allow small children to feed them.

Kōfuku-ji
興福寺

48 Noborioji-chō; tel. 0742/22-7755; www.kohfukuji.com; 9am-5pm, last entry 4:45pm; grounds free, ¥600 treasure hall; take the Kintetsu line to Kintetsu Nara Station, then walk 5 minutes

Begin your exploration of Nara-kōen's Buddhist treasures at Kōfuku-ji, an illustrious temple complex with a lofty pagoda in the west side of the park.

Built in 669, it was relocated to Nara-kōen when the fledgling nation's capital moved to Nara in 710. In its heyday, some 175 structures dotted the grounds. Over the centuries, many of the buildings succumbed to fires and fighting between rivaling factions of the Fujiwara clan's temple-raised warrior monks, or between the Fujiwara clan and the invading Taira clan. Although Shogun Minamoto Yoritomo (1147-1199) had the complex rebuilt, many of its structures succumbed to fire again in 1717.

Though the treasure hall does house some compelling Buddhist images, I recommend just strolling through the grounds and taking in the atmosphere for free.

Nara National Museum
奈良国立博物館

50 Noboriōji-chō; tel. 050/5542-8600; www.narahaku.go.jp; 9:30am-5pm Tues.-Sun.; ¥520 for permanent collection; take the Kintetsu line to Kintetsu Nara Station, then walk 15 minutes

Just east of Kōfuku-ji, you'll find the excellent Nara National Museum. Its collection includes a wide array of Buddhist statuary, paintings, calligraphy, and other art, stretching from the 7th century to the Edo period, with quality English signage throughout. Pay ¥500 for the informative illustrated guide "Viewing Buddhist Sculptures," which will help you understand the symbolism in Buddhist art.

Kasuga-Taisha
春日大社

160 Kasugano-chō; tel. 0742/22-7788; www.kasugataisha.or.jp; 6am-6pm Apr.-Sept.; 6:30am-5pm Oct.-Mar.; free; take the Kintetsu line to Kintetsu Nara Station, then walk 25 minutes

In the southesast corner of Nara-kōen, Kasuga-Taisha is the most important Shinto shrine in the city. There's a *honden* (main hall) and a *haiden* (prayer hall), but the real magic is found by meandering along the paths on the shrine's grounds and exploring its subshrines. This is one of the most worthwhile stops in the park.

Since the Great Tohoku Earthquake struck the northeastern coast of Honshu in March 2011, a group of priests has been leading the faithful in morning prayers each day for the protection and peace of Japan. To witness this ceremony, which is open to the public, head to the *Naoraiden* (Ceremonial Hall) at 8:50am.

★ Tōdai-ji
東大寺

406-1 Zōshi-chō; tel. 0742/22-5511; www.todaiji.or.jp; 7:30am-5:30pm Apr.-Oct., 8am-4:30pm Nov.-Mar.; ¥500 for Daibutsu-den, ¥800 Tōdai-ji Museum; take the Kintetsu line to Kintetsu Nara Station, then walk 20 minutes

Northwest of Kasuga-Taisha, Tōdai-ji is the centerpiece of Nara-kōen. This magnificent wooden temple houses the giant bronze Daibutsu statue. If you're only going to see one sight in Nara, make it Tōdai-ji's Great Buddha.

Emperor Shomu (701-758) directed the building of the temple for the sole purpose of hosting the towering bronze Vairocana, the cosmic Buddha from whom all worlds and beings are believed to emanate. Shomu held a ceremony for the unveiling of the statue; gifts from visiting monks from China and India are on display in the Nara National Museum today. The original structure was set ablaze during the wars that ultimately brought the Heian Period to a close in 1185.

Approach the temple via the **Tōdai-ji Nandai-mon,** or Great South Gate, flanked by two fierce, muscular statues of Niō, a divine Buddhist guardian. These dramatic

奈良鹿愛護会
鹿せんべい
¥150
1

2

wooden sentinels stand 8 meters (26 feet) tall.

About 200 meters (656 feet) to the north is the **Daibutsu-den** (Great Buddha Hall), the world's largest wooden building and the home of the Daibutsu statue. Despite measuring 57 meters (187 feet) in width, 50 meters (164 feet) in depth, and 48 meters (157 feet) in height, the current structure, built in 1709, is only two-thirds the size of the original. The octagonal bronze lantern in front of the main hall dates to the 8th century. The spectacular Daibutsu statue weighs 500 tonnes (550 tons)—103 kg (290 lbs) of it gold—stands 16 meters (53 feet) tall, and exudes an uncanny sense of calm.

After basking in the presence of the Great Buddha, ascend a staircase to **Nigatsu-dō,** a subtemple atop a hill about 300 meters (984 feet) east of Tōdai-ji. The interior of this small structure is only glimpsed by elite priests, but you will be able to take in the stunning views over Nara from the veranda. Two minutes south, the oldest structure in the Tōdai-ji complex, **Sangatsu-dō,** houses a towering Kannon statue and more than a dozen other figures from the Nara Period.

Isui-en and Yoshiki-en
依水園, 吉城園

74 Suimon-chō; tel. 0742/25-0781; https://isuien.or.jp; 9:30am-4:30pm daily, last entry 4pm; ¥900; take the Kintetsu line to Kintetsu Nara Station, then walk 15 minutes

Isui-en has all the makings of an ideal landscape garden: abundant flowering plants and trees, a pond, and winding pathways. Access to the neighboring **Neiraku Art Museum,** which houses a collection of bronzes and ceramics from China and Korea, is included in the garden's admission fee. If you're taken enough by the scene to appreciate it while sitting on a tatami floor, there's a teahouse (cup of green tea and a sweet, ¥850). The view of Nara National Museum and Tōdai-ji to the south is worth the cost of admission. Foreigners get in free to the garden next door, Yoshiki-en.

1: a woman selling snacks for the deer at Nara Park
2: Tōdai-ji

FESTIVALS

WAKAKUSAYAMA YAMAYAKI
若草山山焼き

At the base of Mount Wakakusayama, next to Nara-kōen; http://nara-park.com/yamayaki-en; around 5pm-evening fourth Sat. of Jan.; walk about 15 minutes east of Todai-ji and Kasuga-Taisha

On the fourth Saturday of each January, fireworks are launched in town, then the slope of Mount Wakakusayama is lit ablaze in this fiery festival. The action heats up from about 5pm when a procession of locals lights their torches at a shrine in town, then proceed to the foot of Mount Wakakusayama to set the peak on fire. The festival has been going for centuries, though its origins remain a mystery.

SHUNI-E
修二会

Nigatsu-dō; from sunset on March 1-14; walk 10 minutes' west uphill from Todai-ji's main temple complex

This festival sees monks stand along the veranda of Nigatsu-dō, a subtemple of Todai-ji, from where they fling embers from around 10 huge flaming bundles of kindling onto a crowd of onlookers below. This is a 1,250-year-old ritual intended to spiritually cleanse the repentant recipients of the raining cinders. The ritual begins on each day of the period at around 6:30pm. Aim to arrive a few hours early if you want a good spot from which to receive the purifying sparks. On the 12th and 13th nights, around 1:30am-2:30am, priests ceremonially draw curative water (*omizutori*, or drawing water), said to only fill a nearby well at that time every year. Following the water drawing, a ritual known as Dattan is performed until about 3:30am inside Nigatsu-dō, involving the waving of torches, ringing of bells, and playing of horns.

FOOD

LE CASE

158 Kasugano-chō; tel. 0742/26-8707; http://quicheteria-lecase.com; 11:30am-5pm Wed.-Mon., last order 4pm, closed last Mon. every month; from ¥1,250; take the Kintetsu line to Kintetsu Nara Station, then walk 25 minutes

A great choice for a meal while you're tramping between Nara-kōen's sights is Le Case. This eatery between Todai-ji and Kasuga-Taisha serves French fare, including quiche (its speciality), as well as cheesecake. Given the dearth of restaurants in this part of town, this is highly recommended if you're hungry in the park.

MIZUTANI CHAYA

30 Kasugano-chō; tel. 0742/22-0627; www.mizuyachaya.com; 10am-4pm daily; from ¥580; take the Kintetsu line to Kintetsu Nara Station, then walk 25 minutes

Charming Mizutani Chaya is housed in a thatched-roof building and set in a grove of trees between Kasuga-Taisha and Nigatsu-dō, the hillside sub-temple of Tōdai-ji. Alongside teahouse staples, the restaurant also serves rice dishes and bowls of udon with various toppings. It's nice, simple food with a classic ambience.

KURA

16 Komyoin-chō; tel. 0742/22-8771; 5pm-10pm daily; dinner from ¥4,000; take the Kintetsu line to Kintetsu Nara Station, then walk 8 minutes

In the old-school section of downtown known as Naramachi, Kura is an *izakaya* that serves good food, from yakitori to fried pork cutlets and *oden* (vegetables and fishcake left simmered in broth and served with spicy mustard). Given that booze is a vital component here, this place may be best suited to dinner rather than lunch. Set in a white-walled building, the interior is composed of aged wood with a wrap-around countertop. At first glance, it may look slightly intimidating, but step inside and the friendly staff will offer an English-language menu.

WAKAKUSA CURRY

38-1 Mochiidonochō; tel. 0742/24-8022; www.wakakusacurry.jp; 11am-8pm, last order 7:30pm Thurs.-Tues.; ¥700-1,280

This curry joint in the midst of Naramachi serves tasty curry and rice, from chicken and lamb curry to vegetarian and more. There are plenty of toppings, from cheese to breaded and fried pork cultets. You can choose your spice level (0-25), too. A great place for lunch before or after traipsing through Nara-kōen.

ACCOMMODATIONS

GUESTHOUSE NARA BACKPACKERS

31 Yurugichō; tel. 0742/22-4557; www.nara-backpackers.com; ¥2,400 dorm rooms, private rooms ¥3,800 pp; take the Kintetsu line to Kintetsu Nara Station, exit 1

Guesthouse Nara Backpackers is perhaps Nara's best budget accommodation option. Set in the 90-year-old former home of a tea master, this hostel has many original design flourishes intact, such as its original glass windows, and some of the rooms look out onto a garden. Rooms range from mixed dorms and female-only dorms to a range of private rooms. There's also a shared lounge and kitchen (7am-11pm). The hostel does not accept guests younger than 10 years old. All guests share a common bath where towels can be rented and toiletries can be bought. Rental bikes are also on offer. Room rates drop with longer stays.

ASUKASOU

1113-3 Takabatake-chō; tel. 0742/26-2538; www.asukasou.com; ¥35,000; take the Kintetsu line to Kintetsu Nara Station, exit 2

For ease of access to the main sights of Nara-kōen, Asukasou is a great pick. Located in Naramachi just a few minutes' walk from the southwest corner of Nara-kōen, there's a Japanese restaurant on-site and a rooftop, open-air *onsen* bath that can be reserved. Some rooms have futons on tatami floors while others have beds.

Exploring West of Nara

As if the impressive structures around Nara-kōen weren't enough, a cluster of temples of great historical import sits just southwest of town. With roots stretching back to the 7th and 8th centuries, when Buddhism was just being transplanted to Japanese soil, three particular temples are treasure troves of exquisite Buddhist art. Explore these gems if you have extra time in Nara and want to dodge crowds. You can visit all three temples in a half-day trip; begin with Hōryū-ji, then proceed north to Yakushi-ji and Tōshōdai-ji.

HŌRYŪ-JI 法隆寺

1-1 Hōryūji Sannai, Ikaruga-chō; tel. 0745/75-2555; www.horyuji.or.jp; 8am-5pm late Feb.-early Nov., 8am-4:30pm early Nov.-late Feb.; adults ¥1,500, ages 12 and under ¥750

Both the most historically important and visually arresting, this sprawling complex was founded in 607 by Prince Shotoku (574-622), who is credited with drafting Japan's first constitution. The temple's Chūmon (Central Gate) is flanked by Japan's oldest effigies of Kongo Rikishi, the fearsome pair of deities with rippling muscles seen at temples throughout Japan. In fact, some of the original structures on the complex are among the world's oldest surviving wooden constructions. The recently built Gallery of Temple Treasures houses a vast wealth of paintings, relics, statues, and more, and the Yumendono (Hall of Dreams) houses a gilt-wooden life-sized effigy of Prince Shotoku, amid other treatsures. This only scratches the surface of the wealth found at Hōryū-ji. For a comprehensive summary, pick up an English guide to the complex when you arrive.

From JR Nara Station, take the Yamatoji line to Hōryū-ji Station (12 minutes; ¥220), then hop on bus 72 (8 minutes; ¥190) to Hōryū-ji Sandō, or simply walk north from Hōryū-ji Station for 20 minutes. To return to Nara, take bus 97 from Hōryū-ji-mae bus stop.

YAKUSHI-JI 薬師寺

457 Nishinokyocho; tel. 0742/33-6001; www.nara-yakushiji.com; 8:30am-5pm daily; adults ¥1,600, high school and junior high students ¥1,200, elementary school students ¥300

The temple of Yakushi-ji is likewise one of the oldest temples in Japan, having been built by Emperor Tenmu in 680 in hopes for the healing of his sick wife. The temple's sole surviving original structure is the East Pagoda, which is under renovation and enclosed by scaffolding until April 2020. The rest of the buildings date to the 13th century or are modern reconstructions, but the real treasures are found within them.

To reach Yakushi-ji from Hōryū-ji, take bus 97 from Hōryū-ji-mae (bus stand 2) to Yakushi-ji Higashiguchi (40 minutes). If you're coming directly from Kintetsu Nara Station, take the Kintetsu Nara line to Yamato-Saidaiji Station, then transfer to the Kintetsu Kashihara line and ride until Nishinokyō Station (25 minutes; ¥260). The temple is about 1 minute's walk southeast from there.

TŌSHŌDAI-JI 唐招提寺

13-46 Gojōchō, Nara; tel. 0742/33-7900; www.toshodaiji.jp; 8:30am-5pm, last entry 4:30pm daily; adults ¥600, children ¥200

Walk north from Yakushi-ji for about 10 minutes to reach Tōshōdai-ji, the youngest of the three temples, having been constructed in 759 by a visiting Chinese priest named Ganjin (Jian Zhen). Today, a wooden statue of the roving priest is brought before the public in the temple's Miedō (Founder's Hall) for a few days in early June, to commemorate the date of Ganjin's death on June 6. At any time of year, however, you can glimpse the 5-meter-tall (16-foot) effigy of Kannon (Goddess of Mercy), complete with what are said to be 1,000 arms, towering within the main hall, or Kondō. The grounds are also laced with leafy footpaths.

To directly reach Tōshōdai-ji from Kintetsu Nara Station, take the Kintetsu Nara line to Nishinokyō Station (15 minutes; ¥260), then walk 500 meters (1,640 ft) north. Alternatively, take bus 78 from JR Nara Station (bus stand 6; 20 minutes; ¥260) or Kintetsu Nara Station (bus stand 8; 20 minutes; ¥260) to the Tōshōdai-ji bus stop. When returning to Nara, you must depart from the Tōshōdai-ji Higashiguchi bus stop on bus 77 or 97.

★ NARA HOTEL

1096 Takabatake-chō; tel. 0742/26-3300; www.narahotel.co.jp; ¥35,000 d; take the Kintetsu line to Kintetsu Nara Station, exit 2

If you like the idea of staying in a truly historic hotel and don't mind parting ways with hard-earned cash, try the Nara Hotel. In business since 1909, this hotel's distinctive architecture is a fusion of Japanese and Western design. The rooms are expansive, the service top-notch, the grounds immaculate, and on-site dining is first-rate. Even the Dalai Lama and Albert Einstein bedded down at Nara Hotel when they passed through.

INFORMATION AND SERVICES

There are a few good tourist information centers with abundant English-language materials near both the main JR and Kintetsu stations. The **JR Nara Station Information Center** (tel. 0742/27-2223; www.narashikanko.or.jp; 9am-9pm daily) is just outside the east exit of JR Nara Station, while **Kintetsu Nara Station Information Center** (tel. 0742/24-4858; 9am-6pm daily) is near exit 3 of Kintetsu Nara Station. Closer to Nara-kōen, there's also the **Nara Visitor Center and Inn** (3 Iken-chō; tel. 0742/81-7461; www.sarusawa.nara.jp; 8am-9pm daily), which stocks ample information and even hosts cultural events sometimes. Friendly staff will be happy to answer questions at this center, which is attached to the Sarusawa Inn.

TRANSPORTATION

Getting There

To reach **JR Nara Station** from Osaka, take the JR Kansai line from Namba Station (45 minutes; ¥540) in the south side of Osaka. Also from Namba Station, you can take the Kintetsu Nara line to **Kintetsu Nara Station** (40 minutes; ¥560).

It's also possible to arrive in Nara directly from both of Kansai's main regional airports. From **Kansai International Airport** (KIX), there's an hourly limousine run by **Nara Kōtsū** (www.narakotsu.co.jp). The ride takes 90 minutes and costs ¥2,050. Hourly Nara Kōtsū buses also make the 1-hour journey from Osaka Itami Airport (¥1,480).

Getting Around

The easiest way to get around much of Nara is **on foot,** but there are two **buses** that run in a loop around the main sights in and surrounding Nara-kōen, with bus 1 running counterclockwise and bus 2 running clockwise (¥210 flat fee for single journey).

Kobe 神戸

Kobe ("God's Door") is situated on a slope that leads from the peak of Mount Rokko, looming to the north of the city, down toward the bay on the Inland Sea, where small islands are dotted by forests and fishing hamlets. Kobe has long been an important maritime center, having opened up to foreign trade during the Meiji Restoration (1868-1912). Beyond trade, the city became a conduit to the world beyond and was the first place in Japan to have a cinema or host jazz musicians. In a word, Kobe is cosmopolitan.

Mirroring its larger sibling near Tokyo, Yokohama, the city's mercantile past also led to the creation of a bustling Chinatown centered in the area of Nankinmachi (named after the city of Nanjing). Victorian architecture is still on display in the affluent neighborhood of Kitano-chō, once home to many members of the city's foreign traders and diplomats. The modern hub of **Sannomiya,** a short walk downhill toward

Kobe

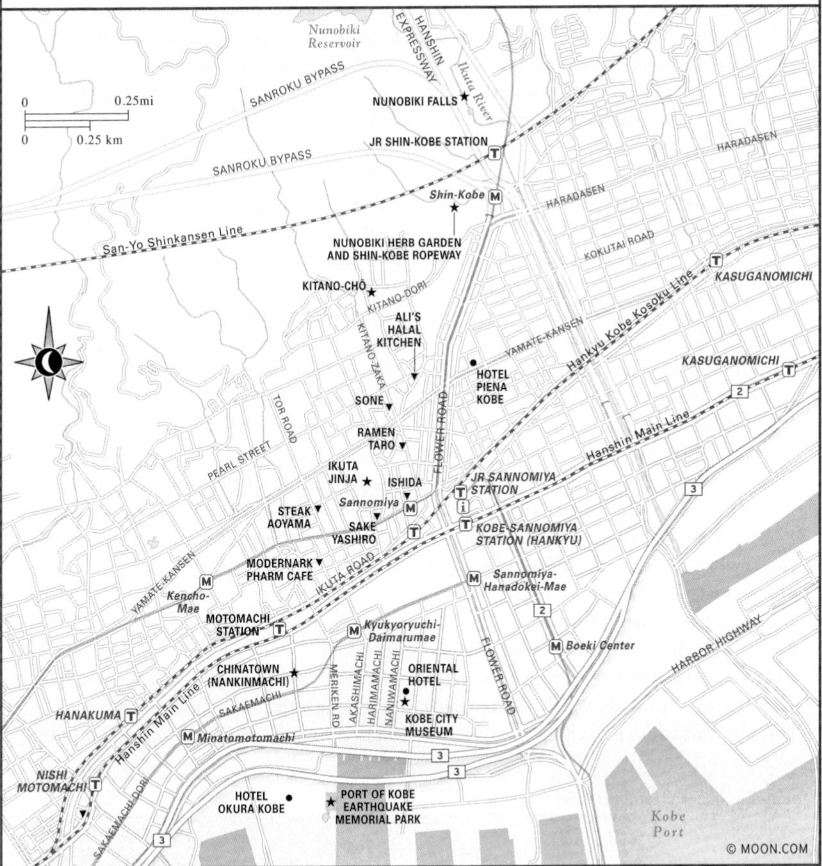

the bay, is the city's modern heart. Excellent restaurants, and ample shopping and nightlife with a nice buzz are the draws of this neighborhood.

Though all indicators suggest that Kobe is thriving, in January 1995 the city was hit by a 6.9-magnitude quake that left 6,400 dead, 40,000 injured, and 100,000 homes along with much of the infrastructure in ruins. Thankfully, the city bounced back and its streets hum with life. The city still retains its global orientation with an expat population of around 50,000 and a host of multinational firms based in the city, particularly concentrated on manmade Rokko Island.

With many of Kobe's desirable neighborhoods within walking distance of each other, the city is an ideal place to stroll in search of a good café, a well-made meal, or perhaps a drink, while taking in views of the seaside in the distance.

SIGHTS

Light on sights, Kobe is more of a place for a stroll. Be sure to spend some time in **Kitano-chō,** filled with the charming 19th-century Western-style brick residences of diplomats and merchants. Its atmospheric streets wind past cafés and bistros, and shops selling art, crafts, and fashion. The kitschy shops and food offerings of Kobe's **Chinatown** (Nankinmachi), illuminated by red lanterns at night, can seem a bit tired and overpriced, but it's a fun place to wander.

Nunobiki Herb Garden and Shin-Kobe Ropeway

布引ハーブ園, 神戸布引ロープウェー

1-4-3 Kitanochō, Chūō-ku; tel. 078/271-1160; www.kobeherb.com; herb garden only ¥200, Kobe Nunobiki Ropeway ¥950 one-way/¥1,500 round-trip, both including herb garden admission; take Seishin-Yamate line to Shin-Kobe Station

Not far from Shin-Kobe Station, a stone path leads 400 meters (1,312 feet) up a mountain where you'll find the strikingly pristine Nunobiki Falls, the serene Nunobiki Herb Garden, and zipping over it all, the Shin-Kobe Ropeway. You can either walk or ride the ropeway to the top and return down either way, too. The first leg of a walk up the mountain leads to **Nunobiki Falls** (24 hours; free; about 20 minutes from the bottom). Long the object of reverence and artistic inspiration, the falls vividly illustrate just how close to nature Kobe is.

Another 20 minutes' walk uphill from the falls is the **Nunobiki Herb Garden** (10am-5pm Mon.-Fri., 10am-8:30pm Sat.-Sun. and holidays, only viewing platform is open after 5pm). This sculpted green space has lavender fields, glasshouses full of tropical blossoms, a café, and viewing platform. The top station of the **Shin-Kobe Ropeway** (9:30am-5:15pm Mon.-Fri. and 9:30am-8:30pm Sat.-Sun. and holidays Mar. 20-Jul. 19 and Sept. 1-Nov. 30, 9:30am-8:30pm daily Jul. 20-Aug. 31, 9:30am-5pm daily Dec. 1-Mar. 19) lies just beyond the upper entrance to the herb garden, which is roughly 30 minutes' walk uphill from the lower entrance to the garden.You can access the trail that leads to Nunobiki Falls and beyond by exiting from the ground floor of Shin-Kobe Station, turning left, and walking beneath the station to the beginning of the path. To access the lower station of the Shin-Kobe Ropeway, walk about 10 minutes' southwest of Shin-Kobe Station.

Ikuta Jinja

生田神社

1-2-1 Shimo-Yamate-dōri; tel. 078/321-3851; 7am-dusk daily; free; take the JR line to Sannomiya Station

Ikuta Jinja is a surprisingly old shrine in the

Kobe Earthquake Memorial Park

heart of Kobe's sleek Sannomiya area. It's remained standing through generations of war from the earliest days of the nation, World War II bombing raids, and even more recently, the 1995 earthquake that reduced much of the city to rubble. Some dating puts the shrine's age at up to 18 centuries. Less a spectacular sight than it is a pocket of calm in the midst of the bustle; it's a nice place for a breather as you walk through downtown.

Kobe City Museum
神戸市立博物館

24 Kyōmachi; tel. 078/391-0035; www.city.kobe.lg.jp/culture/culture/institution/museum; 10am-5pm Tues.-Sun.; ¥200, up to ¥1,000 special exhibits; take the JR line to Sannomiya Station

Housed in a Greek revival-style building dating from the pre-World War II years, the Kobe City Museum does a good job of documenting the history of the city's interactions with the west. The displays incorporate art and relics from the 19th century on, revealing the ways that western culture gradually became part of the fabric of the city, from fashion to technology. An interesting example of this cross-cultural exchange is seen in the "Southern Barbarian" school of art, which emerged after Jesuit missionaries began to train Japanese artists in painting techniques from the West. There's sufficient English-language signage throughout.

Port of Kobe Earthquake Memorial Park
神戸港震災メモリアルパーク

24 hours; free; take the Kaigan subway line to Minato Motomachi, or the JR or Hanshin line to Motomachi Station

If you make the trek to the harbor area, stop by the Port of Kobe Earthquake Memorial Park. Here you'll see a cluster of displays, with a video in English retelling the fateful events of the morning of January 17, 1995, when the 6.9-magnitude Great Hanshin Earthquake rocked the city, killing 6,000 and knocking down some 300,000 buildings. The most telling display is a section of the harbor left as it was immediately following the quake: the concrete tilted and partly submerged in water, with lampposts pointing in unnatural angles.

FOOD

★ STEAK AOYAMA

2-14-5 Nakayamate-dōri, Chūō-ku; tel. 078/391-4858; www.steakaoyama.com; noon-2:30pm and 5pm-9pm Thurs.-Tues.; lunch from ¥1,600, dinner from ¥2,700; take the Hankyu Kobe line, JR Tokaido line, or Seishin Yamate subway line to Sannomiya Station, east exit 3

For an affordable Kobe beef experience, you can't go wrong with Steak Aoyama. This family-owned restaurant, serving succulent slabs of meat since 1963, is the stuff of local culinary legend. Its masterful chef makes pleasant conversation with guests without resorting to cheesy teppanyaki grill sideshows. Set meals come with soup, locally prepped vegetables, tofu, and dessert, all complemented by a great wine selection. To snag one of the eight seats offered in four rounds of meals per day, book at least a month, if not two, in advance via phone or the restaurant's Facebook page.

GARDEN RESTAURANT FUSHA

1 Karasuharachō; tel. 078/511-2400; www5e.biglobe.ne.jp/~donqui/index.htm; 11:30am-2pm lunch, 2pm-5:30pm café time, 5:30pm-9:30pm dinner, last order 8pm, lunch from ¥2,350, café time from ¥480, dinner from ¥3,800

With sweeping views of the city below, Garden Restaurant Fusha serves good Western dishes with a French twist. This restaurant is about 15 minutes' taxi ride from Sannomiya Station—a bit out of the way. To make the journey worth your time, plan to savor a slow meal—preferably dinner—as you look out over the twinkling lights of the city. To ensure great views, book ahead a day or more in advance.

MODERNARK PHARM CAFE

3-11-15 Kitanagasadōri; tel. 078/391-3060; http://modernark-cafe.chronicle.co.jp; 11:30am-10pm daily;

food from ¥950, drinks from ¥500; take the JR Tōkaidō line or Hanshin main line to Motomachi Station

Kobe also has a good range of healthier food options. For quality vegetarian fare in a laid-back café, Modernark Pharm Cafe is a good bet. The menu includes a vegetarian platter, bean burrito, various baked goods, organic beers, teas, juices, coffee, and more. Located north of Motomachi Station in the heart of downtown.

ISHIDA

Konan Asset Sanmei Bldg. 3F, 1-21-2 Kitanagasadōri, Chūō-ku; tel. 078/599-7779; www.kobe-ishidaya.com; lunch 11:30am-3pm, dinner 5pm-10pm Wed.-Mon.; lunch ¥6,980-12,000, dinner ¥9,420-24,100; take JR Kobe, Hankyū-Kobe, Hanshin Main, Port Island lines to Sannomiya Station

This famed shop serves indulgent courses centered on the city's lauded beef, which literally melts in your mouth. The atmosphere is refined, the service is brilliant, and all guests have a front-row seat to watch the chefs in action. Both lunch and dinner courses come with an appetizer, soup, salad, bread or rice, a seasonal vegetable medley, dessert, and coffee or tea. English menu available. Note that there are four branches in Kobe, which all have the same menu. Reserve a few weeks in advance to be safe (https://kobebeef-ishida.com/reservation).

ALI'S HALAL KITCHEN

1-20-14 Nakayamatedōri, Chūō-ku; tel. 078/891-3322; www.aliskitchen.jp; lunch 11am-3pm, dinner 5pm-10pm daily; lunch ¥750-1,500, dinner ¥2,500-5,000; take JR Kobe, Hankyū-Kobe, Hanshin Main, Port Island lines to Sannomiya Station

The owner and chef at this cozy halal spot whips up excellent Pakistani and north Indian food, from tandoori prawn to mutton masala to biryani. There's also a nice range of middle eastern fare, such as fattoush, a type of Lebanese salad containing cucumbers and tomatoes, and kabsa (basmati rice with a mix of meat and veg). A great pick if you're feeling like something different.

★ BARS AND NIGHTLIFE

When it comes to nightlife, Kobe is best known for its jazz haunts. The city is also home to a thriving sake brewing district with some 40 breweries. If you'd like to get acquainted with the city's breweries and do a fair bit of tasting during daylight hours, before a night of jazz perhaps, check out **Kampai Sake Tours** (tel. 080/7045-8365; https://kampaisaketours.com/tour/sake-kobe; 3.5 hours; 1:30pm-5pm Tues.-Sun.; ¥7,700).

SONE

1-24-10 Nakayamate-dōri, Chūō-ku; tel. 078/221-2055; http://kobe-sone.com; 5pm-midnight; ¥1,140 cover, meals from ¥2,500; take the Hankyu Kobe line, JR Tokaido line, or Seishin Yamate subway line to Sannomiya Station, east exit 8

Kobe has a long association with jazz, and Sone is the best place to experience the rhythm of the city. This live house—pronounced "so-nay"—has been hosting gigs for the musically discerning since it held its first spontaneous jam session in 1969. Even today, the venue gets hopping during its four nightly performances and is regarded as Kobe's preeminent jazz den. Recommended for serious jazz aficianados. Performances start at 6:50pm.

JAM JAM

B1, 1-7-2 Motomachi; tel. 078/331-0876; www.facebook.com/jamjam.jazz.kobe; noon-11pm daily, closed first and third Mon. of month; take JR Kobe, Hanshin lines to Motomachi Station

This subterannean jazz bar has a phenomenal sound system and two separate seating areas: one for those who want to listen in peace, and another for those who want to talk quietly. The drinks are good and the soundtrack sets a perfectly laid-back mood. Enjoy the tunes and note that no song requests are taken.

SAKE YASHIRO

Fujiya Bldg. 1F, 1-1-5 Shimoyamate-dōri, Chūō-ku; tel. 078/334-7339; 4pm-11:30pm daily; take the Hankyu Kobe line, JR Tokaido line, or Seishin Yamate subway line to Sannomiya Station

Kobe's Nada district in the east part of

the city is one of Japan's biggest producers of sake (rice wine), supplying about one-third of the country's stock. A great place to sip some of the sakes made in Kobe is at the laid-back bar of Sake Yashiro, a stone's throw from Ikuta-Jinja. The bar's extensive, seasonal menu includes nibbles as well as 90-plus varieties of sake from around Japan, with about half of them coming from Kobe. This is a great place for an introduction to the world of sake.

KOBE JAZZ STREET FESTIVAL

Various locations around town, starting from north side of Hankyū-Kobe Sannomiya Station; www.kobejazzstreet.gr.jp; noon-5pm on Sat.-Sun. during first half of Oct.; ¥4,600 1-day pass, ¥8,700 2-day pass

True to its cosmopolitan roots, Kobe is said to be the birthplace of Japan's first jazz group, the Laughing Stars, which formed in the city in 1923. After World War II, jazz giants like Louis Armstrong and Duke Ellington also jammed in the emergent jazz hub. Given its importance as a commercial port, Kobe's already international district of Kitano was fertile ground for a postwar jazz explosion. Today, the heart of the city's jazz scene still beats strong. Check the website for dates and times.

ACCOMMODATIONS

HOTEL PIENA KOBE

4-20-5 Ninomiyachō, Chūō-ku; tel. 078/241-1010; www.piena.co.jp; ¥13,000 d; take the Hankyu Kobe line, JR Tokaido line, or Seishin Yamate subway line to Sannomiya Station

If you're looking for a clean, centrally located hotel in the midrange budget range, Hotel Piena Kobe is a cut above. Although they look slightly tired, the Western-style rooms are a good size compared to many mid-level hotels in the city and have touches of chic design. There's a good breakfast buffet, too.

HOTEL OKURA KOBE

2-1 Hatoba-chō, Chūō-ku; tel. 078/333-0111; www.kobe.hotelokura.co.jp; ¥25,000 d

For something a bit more luxurious, the Hotel Okura Kobe is a one of Kobe's best. Situated beside Meriken Park, the rooms in this 35-story tower are well-equipped and comfortable, with many boasting great views of the city and harbor. Staff are helpful and the dining room serves a good breakfast, too. The hotel shuttles guests from Kobe Sannomiya Station by bus for free.

★ ORIENTAL HOTEL

25 Kyōmachi, Chūō-ku; tel. 078/326-1500; www.orientalhotel.jp; ¥39,000 d; take the Hankyu Kobe line, JR Tokaido line, or Seishin Yamate subway line to Sannomiya Station

The Oriental Hotel is a graceful property closely linked to Kobe's cosmopolitan past. Although it was rebuilt following the Great Hanshin Earthquake of 1995, the hotel still retains a sense of history as one of Japan's first hotels, having originally opened in 1870. Friendly, bilingual staff, well-appointed rooms with plush furnishings and great views, and elegant on-site dining make it one of the best places to stay in the city. Room rates appear steep on the hotel's website, but look at various booking sites and you may find a good deal.

INFORMATION AND SERVICES

For a range of English-language maps and other information on the city, as well as the "Kobe Welcome Coupon" booklet—which offers discounts for museums, transport, and various activities around the city—the best place to stop is the **Kobe Information Center** (8 Kumoi-dōri, Chūō-ku; tel. 078/322-0220; http://hello-kobe.com; 9am-7pm daily). English-speaking staff are on hand to help with recommendations and bookings. The office is just outside the east exit of JR Sannomiya Station. If you enter Kobe via *shinkansen*, there's also a smaller counter with English-speaking staff and a modest selection of resources in front of the main *shinkansen* ticket gate of JR Shin-Kobe Station.

Kobe Beef

Kobe beef

Rare indeed does a slab of meat have such a household name that simply uttering it, anywhere from New York to Paris, will invoke an air of reverence. Even rarer is a cut of beef so famous that it's more recognizable to many than the city after which it is named. Such is the power of Kobe beef. A taste will convince the hardest skeptic: beyond well-marbled, it has fat so soft that it actually melts in your mouth.

The legendary quality of Japanese beef can be traced back to the 1880s when several European cattle breeds were brought to Japan and mixed with breeds native to the islands. Four strains emerged that remain the backbone of Japan's beef industry even today. While Kobe beef is indeed delicious, there are equally great strains of beef in Matsusaka, Mie Prefecture, northwest of Ise; Sendai and Hokkaido up north; and Miyazaki, down south in Kyushu. A mere 3,000 head of a breed of Tajima cattle, as the famed breed raised in Hyōgo Prefecture is known, are officially recognized as the source of bona fide Kobe beef. These legendary cows are fattened up on a choice diet of grass, dried pasture forage, and supplements, and even occasionally massaged (true), although their troughs are not filled with beer, nor are the bovines serenated with classical music (false).

To taste what all the fuss is about, there's no better way than eating it in the place of its origin. Try **Steak Aoyama** (page 393) or **Ishida** (page 394). A small cut at the cheap end of the scale will set you back around ¥7,000, while choicer steaks cost upward of ¥20,000; you may find more reasonable prices during lunchtime—typically from around ¥2,000 at the cheaper end.

TRANSPORTATION

Getting There

AIR

Arriving via **Kansai International Airport,** the **limousine bus** is more comfortable than the longer train journey via Osaka. The bus journey (75 minutes; ¥2,000) ends right at **Sannomiya Station** in the heart of downtown Kobe. Buy bus tickets on the spot at the airport; just follow the signs for the bus limousine in the arrivals hall.

If you're flying into **Osaka Itami Airport,** the **limousine bus** is also the way to go. This ride, which goes to Sannomiya Station, takes 40 minutes and costs ¥1,050 per person. From the smaller **Kobe Airport,** which only handles domestic flights, take the **Portliner** (18 minutes; ¥330), which goes straight to

Sannomiya Station. Buy tickets on-site in the arrivals hall in both airports.

TRAIN

If you're traveling to Kobe via *shinkansen*—whether on the Sanyō or Tōkaidō line—you'll arrive at **Shin-Kobe Station,** slightly north of downtown. Transfer to the Seishin-Yamate line to travel south from Shin-Kobe Station to the more central **Sannomiya Station** (8 minutes; ¥210).

Coming from Osaka Station, you can easily arrive at Sannomiya Station in less than 30 minutes. If you're using a JR Pass, take the JR Kobe Line (22 minutes; ¥410 without JR Pass). Another option is the private Hankyū Kobe line, which runs from Hankyū Umeda Station in Osaka to **Hankyū Kobe-Sannomiya Station** (28 minutes, ¥320).

From Kyoto, you'll need first to travel to Osaka and change trains to either the JR Kobe line at Osaka Station, or the Hankyū Kobe line at Umeda Station.

BUS

Like Osaka, Kobe can be reached from a number of stations in Tokyo or Yokohama on a highway bus. The trip takes about 8.5 hours and fares start from ¥5,400. Check **Willer Express** (http://willerexpress.com) for details.

Getting Around

Kobe's relatively small scale comes with the bonus of short walk-times between most places and the nearest train station, making its **train network** the easiest way to get around. It's only about a 25-minute walk between Kitanochō in the north and Chinatown in the south. There are also three above-ground lines and two subway lines running through the city.

Starting from Sannomiya Station in the east, the **JR, Hanshin,** and **Hankyū lines** run westward across the city. The Seishin-Yamate subway line runs north from **Sannomiya Station** to **Shin-Kobe Station,** and from there all the way up to **Tanigami Station.** The Kaigan subway line runs from ***Sannomiya-Hanadokeimae*** Station southward through downtown toward the bay, where a handful of other stations are located.

There's also the **City Loop bus** (https://kobecityloop.jp; ¥260 adults, ¥130 children under 12 for single ride; ¥660 adults, ¥330 children under 12 for one-day pass). The green buses with a retro flair do a lap around the city's most touristed areas, including Sannomiya, Meriken Park, Harborland, and Kitanochō. The easiest place to hop onto one of these buses is at the stop on the north side of Sannomiya Station. Pay for a single journey at the machine next to the driver's seat as you exit the bus. If you plan to use a one-day pass, buy one at the **Kobe Information Center** outside JR Sannomiya Station's east exit.

Around Kobe

★ KINOSAKI ONSEN
城崎温泉

Conjure it in your mind's eye: *ryokan* guests amble slowly through quaint streets wearing *yukata* (summer kimono) and geta (wooden clogs). Seven onsen baths are spread around town, offering variety to the ones inside the numerous inns. And local restaurants steeped in history serve seafood caught just off the coast. Welcome to Kinosaki Onsen.

This charming town on the Japan Sea coast of Hyogo Prefecture, a few hours by train north of Himeji and Kobe, is a good place to have the quintessential *onsen* experience. Set along a river lined by willow trees, Kinosaki has been one of the best places in Kansai to step into hot water since hot springs were first discovered in the area in the 8th century. Of its seven main *onsen* baths, take a dip in **Sato-no-yu**

1

2

(1pm-9pm Tues.-Sun.; last entry 8:40pm; ¥800), located next to JR Kinosaki Onsen Station, and **Gosho-no-yu** (Yunosato-dōri; 7am-11pm, last entry 10:30pm, closed every first and third Thurs.; ¥800), located in the heart of town on Yunosato-dōri. Sato-no-yu is all about fun, with its walk-in refrigerated "penguin sauna" and its Arabian-themed sauna. The latter resembles Kyoto's Imperial Palace.

Accommodations

★ MORIZUYA

417 Yushima; tel. 0796/32-2106; www.morizuya.com; ¥35,000 d with 2 meals

If you choose to stay overnight in Kinosaki Onsen, Morizuya, is a great, family-owned *ryokan* in the center of town, within walking distance of all seven bathhouses. The inn has Japanese-style rooms with shared bathrooms and its own smaller *onsen* facilities; it also serves *kaiseki* meals and picks up guests at JR Kinosaki Onsen station.

ONISHIYA SUISHOEN

1256 Momoshima; tel. 0796/32-4571; www.suisyou.com; from ¥15,000 without meals, from ¥36,000 with meals

Kinosaki Onsen Onishiya Suishoen has cozy rooms, indoor and outdoor baths, and both Japanese (with provate baths) and Western rooms (sans private bath). The *onsen* is located a bit outside town, but the hotel picks up guests from the main train station and shuttles guests to the seven *onsen* around town in a taxi.

OYADO HAYAKAWA

770 Yushima; tel. 0796/32-2221; ¥17,600

Oyado Hayakawa is a good midrange option in the center of town. It has spacious comfortable rooms and a friendly, attentive couple of English-speaking hosts. There are indoor, gender-separated onsen baths on site. All rooms have their own toilet and wash basin, although bathing facilities are shared. Some upgraded rooms have private baths, too. No meals are served.

1: hot spring with a view 2: Kinosaki Onsen at night

Transportation

To reach Kinosaki Onsen from JR Osaka Station, take the Konotori limited express train (2 hours 45 minutes; ¥5,400, reservation required). From JR Kobe Station, take the Hamakaze 3 limited express train (2 hours 20 minutes; ¥5,070). From JR Kyoto Station, take the Kinosaki 7 limited express train (2 hours 25 minutes; ¥4,640).

★ HIMEJI-JŌ
姫路城

68 Honmachi; 9am-5pm Sept.-Apr., 9am-6pm May-Aug., last entry one hour before closing; ¥1,000 adults, ¥300 children

In the sleepy city of Himeji, home to some 500,000 people, you'll find the most stellar surviving example of a castle in all of Japan. "White Heron Castle," as it is also known, describes well Himeji-jō. Refined and nearly unconquerable, this luminous white fortress atop a hill is hands-down the most stunning citadel in Japan. Aside from being a brilliant example of Japanese castle architecture, it is one of the few original structures left intact—a miracle in itself, considering that Himeji was nearly bombed to smithereens during World War II.

Built by warlord Toyotomi Hideyoshi in 1581, the trusty stronghold was expanded in the 16th century by Ikeda Terumasa, shogun Tokugawa Ieyasu's son-in-law. It served as the home and fortress of almost 50 lords until 1868 when the Meiji Restoration brought Japan's feudal era to an end and ushered in the modern age. Renovated in 2015, it looks as good as new.

The castle's main five-story keep and a few smaller keeps are all surrounded by moats and stone walls featuring defensive openings for arrows, bullets, boiling oil, or water to be sent the enemy's way. Between the castle's various buildings, well-landscaped grounds full of flowering plants and well-sculpted trees also make for an appealing stroll.

1

2

If you have time and want to extend your time in Himeji by an hour or two, cross the castle's western moat and enter **Kōkō-en** (9am-6pm May-Aug., 9am-5pm Sept.-Apr.; ¥300 adults, ¥150 children, ¥1,040 adults, ¥360 children with Himeji-jō combination ticket). These reconstructed samurai homes and gardens are thick with feudal-period ambience—a recommended addition to your exploration of the castle.

Transportation

Visiting Himeji Castle is best approached as a jaunt from nearby Kobe, Osaka, Nara, or Kyoto, or as a stop on a longer westward journey to Okayama or Hiroshima aboard the San'yō *shinkansen.*

Himeji Station is a straight shot on the JR Tōkaidō line from **Kobe** (40 minutes; ¥970). It's also possible to take the same train from **Kyoto Station** as a special rapid express train bound for Banshuako Station (90 minutes; ¥2,270), or as a special rapid express train from **Osaka Station** (1 hour; ¥1,490).

To reach the castle, exit the north side of JR Himeji Station and **walk** 25 minutes north along Ōtemae-dōri. Alternatively, rent a **bicycle** from the station's tourist information center.

Kii Peninsula 紀伊半島

Stretching across southern Kansai is a wild, spiritually rich swath of terrain—the Kii Peninsula, Honshu's largest. At its heart, the mystical Buddhist center of Kōya-san sprawls across a mountaintop, south of which a series of pilgrimage routes known collectively as the Kumano Kodō connects a circuit of shrines set in dense alpine forest. To the east in neighboring Mie Prefecture is Ise-Jingu, a relatively unadorned spiritual mecca of vast importance; it is considered the holiest site in all of Shinto. Visiting the Kii Peninsula region will give you a nature fix as well as a spiritual one: an antidote to the concrete urban centers to the north.

★ KŌYA-SAN
高野山

Moss-encrusted lanterns, misty forest, and a host of storied temples and mausoleums await at Kōya-san, one of the holiest, most atmospheric places in Japanese Buddhism. Established by Kobo Daishi (aka Kukai, 774-835) as the headquarters of the still vital sect of esoteric Shingon Buddhism in 826, this dense network of monasteries sits beside a mystically charged graveyard, towering cedar trees, and myriad statues of red-bibbed *jizō* (guardian of children and travelers) sprawling across a verdant plateau at an elevation of about 1,005 meters (3,300 feet), deep in the mountains of Wakayama Prefecture.

To experience the full power of Kōya-san, plan to stay for one night. Aim to arrive in the early or mid-afternoon, check into your lodging, and then after dinner, head to the cemetery of Okuno-in at nighttime to the sound of crickets—or cicadas in summer—with only the soft glow of stone lanterns lining the path. The effect is magical. Strike off early the next morning to explore Okuno-in again—this time as the rays of the sun gently infuse the forest with soft light in the often-misty morning. The earlier and closer to dawn the better. After this, return to the town section of Kōya-san. Here, visit the Danjō Garan temple complex, including stops at Kongobu-ji and Tokugawa Ieyasu's mausoleum in town.

Sights

DANJŌ GARAN
壇上伽藍

8:30am-5pm daily; ¥200 admission to each structure

Kōya-san is roughly divided into the Danjō

1: Himeji Castle 2: Kōyan-san

1
2

Garan temple precinct (with eight temples and pagodas in all), the surrounding small town dotted by temples and temple residences (*shokubo*) in the west, and the heavily forested cemetery of **Okuno-in** (24 hours; free) in the east. Its immense cultural value has landed it firmly on UNESCO's World Heritage list.

KONGŌBU-JI
金剛峯寺

132 Kōya-san; tel. 0736/56-2011; ¥500

Highlights of the western section include the temple complex of Kongōbu-ji, the HQ of the Shingon Buddhist sect known for its range of beautifully painted, sliding *fusama* doors. Also among the sights on the western half of town are the various structures of the Danjō Garan complex, as well as the **mausoleum of the clan of Tokugawa Ieyasu** (682 Kōya-san; tel. 0736/56-2011; 8:30am-5pm daily; ¥200), founder of the Tokugawa shogunate.

MAUSOLEUM OF KŪKAI
弘法大師御廟

24 hours; free

The main draw of the Okuno-in area is the mausoleum of Kūkai, standing grandly in the back of a deep forest of enormous cedar trees and dotted by some 100,000 gravestones and stone lanterns. Also of interest in the cemetery is the mausoleum of warlord Toyotomi Hideyoshi (1537-1598), the brilliant general and samurai who played a prominent role in unifying Japan. The mausoleum of Kukai is more accurately a temple. Its ceiling is lined with seemingly infinite rows of suspended lanterns. Around the backside of the mausoleum, incense wafts from sticks planted in large bronze cauldrons, and chanting pilgrims wear conical straw hats and carry walking sticks.

Accommodations

One of the best ways to see behind the scenes of temple life in Japan is by staying at one of the mountain monastery's 53 temple lodgings, known as *shukubō*. It's similar to the experience of staying at a *ryokan*, but at breakfast and dinner, guests are served *shōjin-ryōri*, a refined form of strictly vegetarian cuisine eaten by monks, consisting of elements like rice, soup, vegetable tempura, pickled greens, tofu, tea, and perhaps a single cherry for a light finishing note. You also have the chance to rise at dawn to meditate, transcribe a sutra, chant, help spruce up the grounds, or witness a *goma* (fire ceremony), in which a monk tosses grains, oil, incense, flowers, water, and rice into a fire, suggesting the transformation of ignorance to wisdom.

★ EKŌ-IN

497 Kōya-san; tel. 0736/56-2514; www.ekoin.jp; ¥10,000 pp with meals

This well-loved temple lodging is a short walk west of Okuno-in, making it a prime spot for exploring Kōya-san. Known for its interesting nighttime tours of the sprawling cemetery, the inn also has clean, well-maintained rooms—some with private bath, others shared—and the English-speaking monks who run the operation are gracious hosts. There's a lovely garden on site and a shared *onsen* bath (sex separated), and guided meditation sessions are on offer.

KŌYA-SAN GUEST HOUSE KOKUU

49-43 Kōya-san; tel. 0736/26-7216; http://koyasanguesthouse.com; ¥3,500 for capsule, ¥6,000 for double bed in private room for one person, ¥9,000 for double bed in private room for two people

Kōya-san Guest House Kokuu is a budget-conscious yet stylish hostel with both capsules and private rooms. It's located about 6 minutes' walk from Okuno-in. While there is food on offer, it's not *shōjin-ryōri* (monk's vegetarian fare). Instead, it's Western breakfast and curry from India and Thailand for dinner. The helpful hosts are friendly and speak English.

1: path through Okuno-in **2:** *shōjin-ryōri* at Joki-in

TOP EXPERIENCE

Kumano Kodō 熊野古道

If Kōya-san is the Buddhist heart of the Kii Peninsula, the pilgrimage circuit known as Kumano Kodō that runs through the rugged south of the region is its Shinto sibling. For more than a millenium, pilgrims, emperors, and priests have flocked to the region. The religious roots of these four pilgrimage routes, together designated a UNESCO World Heritage Site, are a syncretic blend of Japan's two main faiths. This ease with mystic mixing gives the Kumano Kodō region a revered status among followers of the syncretic spiritual path known as Shugendō, followed by mountain-traipsing monks known as the *yamabushi*.

Although the Kumano Kodō covers a vast region of sub-shrines and hallowed terrain, for a more casual visitor there are three main shrines, referred to as the **Kumano Sanzan.** The best point of entry into the Kumano Kodō region is the town of **Tanabe,** located in southwestern Wakayama Prefecture (2 hours 15 minutes on the JR Kinokuni line from Shin-Osaka Station to Kii-Tanabe station; ¥4,750). Reaching the bulk of the sights requires taking a bus from Tanabe to **Hongū** (bus stop 2; 2 hours; ¥2,060), though a rental car is another good option. (**JR Rent-a-Car** just outside Kii-Tanabe Station, 1-24 Minato, Tanabe-shi; tel. 0739-26-0939; www.ekiren.co.jp; 9am-6pm daily).

- At the nexus of the four paths of the Kumano Kodō is **Hongū Taisha** (**本宮大社**, tel. 0735/42-0009; www.hongutaisha.jp; shrine office 8am-5pm daily, treasure hall 9am-4pm daily; grounds free, treasure hall for adults ¥300, ages 12-15 ¥100), located deep in the mountains of the peninsula atop a verdant, rocky spine. Tanabe to Hongū (bus stop 2, 2 hours; ¥2,060) also passes through the main *onsen* towns of the area, including Yunomine. To reach Hongū Taisha, get off at the Hongu Taisha-mae Bus Stop; it's a short walk from there.
- To the southeast, **Nachi Taisha** (**那智大社**, tel. 0735/55-0321; www.kumanonachitaisha.or.jp; shrine office 6am-4:30pm, treasure hall 8:30am-4:30pm daily; grounds free, treasure hall for adults ¥300, ages 6-15 ¥200) sits in front of Nachi-no-taki, a picturesque waterfall that inspired the building of the shrine, where the Pacific is also in sight. The Nachi area can be reached by bus from Nachi Station (20 minutes; ¥480), accessed from Kii-Tanabe Station via the Kinokuni line bound for Shingū (2 hours 20 minutes; ¥1,660) and from Hongū by bus. Just take the bus

FUDO-IN

456 Kōya-san; tel. 0736/56-2414, https://fudouin.or.jp; ¥15,000

In the center of town, Fudo-in is an excellent pick with spacious rooms. It's roughly in the middle between Okuno-in in the east and Kongōbu-ji in the west. The temple's biggest draw is its position away from the road, which makes it an exceptionally quiet place. The grounds are beautiful and the monks on staff are eager to serve guests.

JOKI-IN

365 Kōya-san; tel. 0736/56-2321; www.jo-kiin.com; ¥12,000 pp

On the west side, close to Kongōbu-ji, Joki-in is a great low-key *shukubō* run by friendly English-speaking staff. It has both private and shared rooms, and is conveniently located between Kongōbu-ji and Danjō Garan. The dinners are served privately to the rooms, while breakfast is eaten communally. This is a good choice if your aim is to avoid the more crowded *shukubō* around town.

Information and Services

For maps, pamphlets, English-language advice, and audio guides stop by the **Kōya-san Shukubō Assocation** (600 Kōya-san, Kōya-chō; tel. 0736/56-2616; http://shukubo.net; 8:30am-5pm Mar.-Dec., 9am-5pm Jan.-Feb). It's located next to the bus stop for Senjūin-bashi. As its name suggests, the center deals directly with temple lodgings (*shukubō*) and

until Daimon-zaka bus stop and make your way up the hill just off the road, walking along a path lined with towering trees. Ask the bus driver to point you in the right direction just to be safe.

- On the eastern coast of Wakayama Prefecture, north of Nachi Taisha, is **Hayatama Taisha** (**速玉大社**, tel. 0735/22-2533; http://kumanohayatama.jp), the terminus of the pilgrimage route. This prehistoric shrine is said to house the *kami* (god) who oversees the rhythms of nature and all lifeforms. Either take a bus from Hongū or take the JR Kinokuni line from either Shin-Osaka Station (4 hours; ¥6,690) or from Nagoya (3 hours 30 minutes; ¥6,870).

It's possible to access one or all of these three main shrines via a combination of bus and train, but the more orthodox (and adventurous) may prefer to see a section of the trails on foot. The most popular trail is the **Nakahechi route** (56 km/35 mi). To trod a more manageable version of this well-worn pilgrim's path, take the bus bound for Ryūjin from Kii-Tanabe Station and ride until the Hosshinmon-oji bus stop. This stop is near a sub-shrine that serves as the entrance to the path that leads to the holiest of the three main shrines, Hongū Taisha.

The path continues along the river, leading out of the shrine grounds to **Yunomine Onsen** (**湯の峰温泉**), a wonderful place to soak in a hot bath and stay for a night. Some standout places to bathe and rest include **Tsubo-yu Onsen** (6am-10pm daily, last entry 9:30pm; ¥770), **Yunomine Sentō** (6am-10pm daily; ¥260), and **Ryokan Yoshino-ya** (359 Yunomine; tel. 073/542-0101; www.yunomine.com; ¥6,090 pp without meals, from ¥9,500 pp with meals, ¥1,080 surcharge for room with private bathroom, ¥1,060 surcharge with meals).

MORE INFORMATION

Compared to tourism boards throughout most of rural Japan, the **Tanabe City Kumano Tourism Bureau** (1-20 Minato, Tanabe-shi; tel. 0739/34-5599; www.tb-kumano.jp; 9am-5pm Mon.-Fri.), located on the second floor of JR Kii-Tanabe Station on the Kisei line, goes above and beyond the call of duty to help foreign visitors, as does the **Kumano Hongū Heritage Center** (100-1 Hongū; tel.0735/42-0751; 9am-5pm daily; free), which doubles as a museum.

can help with reserving rooms and meals if you inquire ahead of your arrival. They also rent bicycles should you want to get around on two wheels.

Transportation

The easiest way to reach Kōya-san by **train** is by taking the Nakai line from Namba Station in Osaka (one hour 45 minutes, ¥1,260). Note that you may need to change trains at Hashimoto Station, depending on the particular train you board. Disembark at **Gokuraku-bashi Station** and take the **cable car** five minutes to the top of Kōya-san, the mountain itself. The ¥390 charge for the cable car ride is covered in the cost of the train ticket.

Exiting the lift, buses will be waiting to whisk you into town, about 2.5 km (1.5 mi) away. Once you're in town, all sights of note are within a radius of about 4 km (2.5 mi), making the area an appealing place to discover **on foot.** There are also **buses** that shuttle to and from the main sights. You can also save a little money by traveling to Kōya-san via the JR line, but the route involves multiple transfers.

If you want to get there quickly and you don't mind spending a little extra for the limited express (*tokkyū*) train, note that the **Kōya-san World Heritage Ticket** (www.nankaikoya.jp/en/stations/ticket.html; ¥3,400) offers discounts on some of Kōya-san's sights, and on round-trip travel to and from Osaka. If you opt for the limited express train, which costs ¥2,040 one way, then it's a no-brainer to get this special ticket. Pick one up in advance at the ticket counter in Namba Station.

ISE
伊勢

Arriving in Ise, you could be forgiven for having the impression that the town—home to Shinto's holiest of holies—is a bit mundane. Truth be told, it is. However, proceed to the dense cedar groves where the Gekū (outer) and Naikū (inner) shrines await, and the subtly spiritual atmosphere becomes palpable.

Sights

★ ISE-JINGŪ
伊勢神宮

free

The holiest shrine in all of Shinto, Ise-jingū has been reborn repeatedly over the millennia. It is ancient, yet continuously renewed, as it is symbolically torn down and rebuilt every 20 years using cypress wood felled in the Kiso Mountains of Japan's Central Alps. This ancient rite was last conducted in 2013, the 62nd time. The leftover wood from each previous version of the shrine is whisked away to be used at other shrines around the country. While the exteriors of the shrine buildings can be at least partly glimpsed from the outside, the inner precincts are only accessible to the emperor and a handful of elite priests.

Above all else, Ise-jingū is a stronghold of secrets. Housed in the innermost section of the sacred complex is a bronze mirror believed to have been given to the emperor by the sun goddess Amaterasu-Omikami herself, from whom the Japanese imperial line is said to have emerged. This sacred object—one of the three Imperial regalia, along with sacred beads housed in Tokyo's Imperial Palace and the sacred sword held in Nagoya's Atsuta-jingū—has been shrouded in a thick layer of cloth since the 3rd century and has never even been seen by the emperor himself.

Despite this layer of secrecy, visiting Ise-jingū is a powerful experience. The shrine is divided into **Gekū** (Outer; free) and **Naikū** (Inner; sunrise-sunset; free) areas. Spaced 6 km (4 mi) apart, the two parts of the complex are set amid thickly forested hills crisscrossed by gently running streams. Gekū, which is approached via a path lined by immense cryptomeria trees and three immense *torii* gates, is dedicated to Toyouke-Omikami (goddess of the harvest, hearth, and home). Naikū, which is approached by crossing the Isuzu-gawa by walking over the Uji-bashi bridge, is presided over by Amaterasu, mythical progenitor of the Imperial family. The shrine buildings themselves are relatively humble in appearance, akin to ancient granaries, with decorative beams extending from the highest point of the thatched rooftops. The inner precincts are hidden from view by wooden fences.

SENGŪKAN
せんぐう館

126-1 Toyokawa-chō; tel. 0596/22-6263; 9am-4:30pm daily; closed fourth Tues. every month; ¥300

For a good breakdown of the ceremonial rebuilding of the shrine that takes place every 20 years, be sure to stop by the Sengūkan. This museum on the grounds of the Gekū contains visual displays depicting the process of shrine renewal, as well as a model of the Gekū's premises at a 1:20 scale. There's also a life-size replica of the Goshōden to satisfy the curiosity of visitors who are barred from entering the real one.

Note that photography and smoking are strictly banned in the inner precincts of the shrine. Further, there's no need to dress formally, but wear something neat when you visit the shrine. To make the most of your trip, be sure to pick up the English-language booklet and map available at the small information booth next to the entrance of both Gekū and Naikū.

1: outer shrine path, Ise-jingū **2:** inner shrine area, Ise-jingū

1

2

Food and Accommodations

The town becomes very sleepy at night, which could be good or bad, depending on what you're seeking. If this appeals to you, spending one night in Ise can be a good way to catch your breath.

BUTASUTE GEKUMAETEN

1-1-33 Iwabuchi; tel. 050/3467-5077; https://butasutegekumae.gorp.jp; lunch 11am-3pm, dinner 5pm-8pm Fri.-Wed.; ¥1,000-3,750

Gyūdon (beef atop rice) is the specialty here. Portions are good and the quality of beef is high. They also sell menchi katsu (croquette filled with minced beef), which are ideal for a bite on the go. This location is 7 minutes' walk southwest of Iseshi Station, heading toward Gekū. There's another branch near **Naikū** (52 Ujinakanokiri-chō; tel. 0596/23-8802; 11am-6pm Apr.-Sept., 11am-5pm Oct.-Mar.), which tends to get more crowded.

AKAFUKU

26 Ujinakanokiri-chō; tel. 0596/22-7000; www.akafuku.co.jp/store/5139; 5am-5pm daily; ¥290-550

With 300 years of history, the *akafuku mocha* (pounded-rice cake covered in red bean paste) served here is famous. This is the main branch of the shop, and it's conveniently located near Shinbashi bridge in the heart of a shopping district known as Oharai-machi near Naikū.

ISE GUESTHOUSE KAZAMI

1-6-36 Fukiage, Ise; tel. 0596/63-9170; www.ise-guesthouse.com; mixed dorms ¥4,200, private room singles ¥9,000, ¥10,000 d

Freshly reopened after extensive renovations in autumn 2018, with exposed timber throughout, an indoor atrium, and clean, cozy rooms, this is Ise's best budget place in town. There's a shared lounge, kitchen, and laundry facilities. All rooms share a bathroom, too. The guesthouse is a social place and occasionally hosts music events. It's only a few minutes walk south of Iseshi Station. Bicycle rentals available (¥500 per day).

HOSHIDEKAN

2-15-2 Kawasaki; tel. 0596/28-2377; www.hoshidekan.jp; ¥6,300 s, ¥12,500 d with breakfast

For something on the quiet northern side of Iseshi Station, away from the tourists, this spacious *ryokan* with a leafy courtyard at its core is a good pick. There are 10 Japanese-style rooms that share bathroom and toilet facilities. The staff are helpful and speak English. Bicycle rentals available (¥300 per day). It's 15 minutes' walk northeast of Iseshi Station.

Information and Services

Before exploring the shrines of Ise, stop by either the **Ise Tourist Information Center** (tel. 0596/65-6091; 9am-5:30pm daily) located inside Ise-shi Station, or the **branch** (14-6 Honmachi, Ise-shi; tel. 0596/23-3323; 8:30am-5pm daily) located just across the street from the Gekū, or outer shrine. You'll find good English-language maps and brochures about the area's attractions. English speaking staff will answer questions and can make recommendations for accommodations and restaurants in the area.

Transportation

Begin your journey to Ise by taking either the JR or Kintetsu line from either Nagoya, Kyoto, Osaka, or Nara to **Iseshi Station,** about 10 minutes' walk from the outer shrine. The closest option from among these four is the Kintetsu line limited express (*tokkyū*) from Nagoya (1.5 hrs; ¥2,770). If you have a JR pass and you're coming from either Kyoto or Osaka, it's easiest to take the *shinkansen* to Nagoya, then travel from there.

If you don't have a JR pass and you're coming from **Kyoto,** take an express (*kyūkō*) train on the the Kintetsu line to Yamatoyagi, then transfer to the limited express to Iseshi Station (2 hrs. 20 min.; ¥3,330). To arrive via **Osaka** without a JR Pass, take the Osaka Loop line bound for Tennoji to Tsuruhashi Station, then transfer to the Kintetsu line, preferably paying the additional fee for the limited express, which will get you to Iseshi Station (2 hours 15 min.; ¥3,300).

Begin your exploration at Gekū by **walking** 10 minutes from Iseshi Station down the main avenue of Gekū-sandō, which leads directly to the Outer shrine's entrance. Proceed to the Goshōden, or main hall, about 10 minutes past the shrine's entrance. To reach Naikū, hop on the bus from the stop in front of Gekū (20 minutes; ¥410). Alternatively, ride bus 51 or 55 to Naikū-mae bus stop from bus stop 11 just south of the south exit of Iseshi Station, or simply hail a taxi from Iseshi Station (about ¥2,000). Return to Iseshi Station from Naikū by bus from bus stop 2 near Naikū.

Western Honshu

Long ago, Western Honshu—also known as Chūgoku ("middle country")—was the geographical heartland of the nascent Japanese nation. Evidence of the region's early residents is strewn throughout 1st-century burial sites found along its northern and southern coasts. In ancient times, the imperial family was based in Kyoto to the east. The large island of Kyūshū defined the western edge, and anything east of Kyoto was terra incognita. Tokyo was not yet a dream.

This region is defined by its San'yō (southern) and San'in (northern) coasts. Making a circuit around the coasts dramatically illustrates Japan's most fundamental dichotomy: While the northern San'in side is quieter and more overtly steeped in tradition, the faster-paced southern

Highlights

Look for ★ to find recommended sights, activities, dining, and lodging.

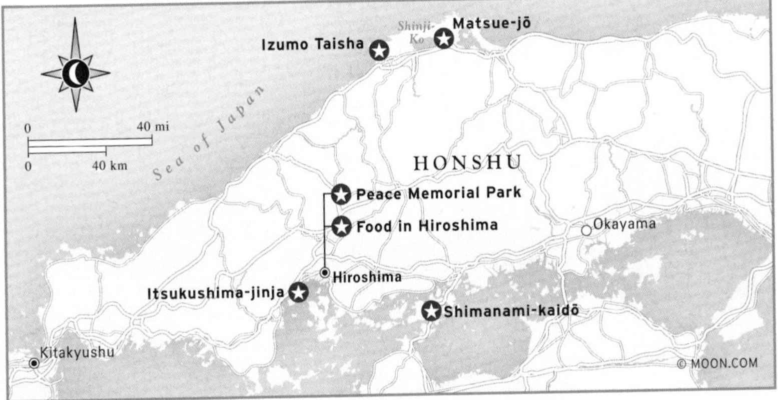

★ **Peace Memorial Park:** Pay your respects to Hiroshima's harrowing past with a visit to its sobering collection of A-bomb monuments (page 416).

★ **Food in Hiroshima:** While most associate Osaka with the savory pancake known as *okonomiyaki*, enjoy discovering Hiroshima's fried-noodle-infused spin on the dish (page 421).

★ **Itsukushima-jinja:** Take in one of Japan's quintessential views, the "floating" vermillion *torii* gate of Miyajima (page 426).

★ **Shimanami-kaidō:** Cross the sparkling Inland Sea by bicycle, following a series of bridges over a string of isles between Honshu and Shikoku (page 432).

★ **Matsue-jō:** Explore one of Japan's most atmospheric, original castles, surrounded by an imposing moat (page 440).

★ **Izumo Taisha:** Visit this grand shrine, to which all kami (gods) retreat for a divine council during the 10th lunar month every year (page 443).

Western Honshu

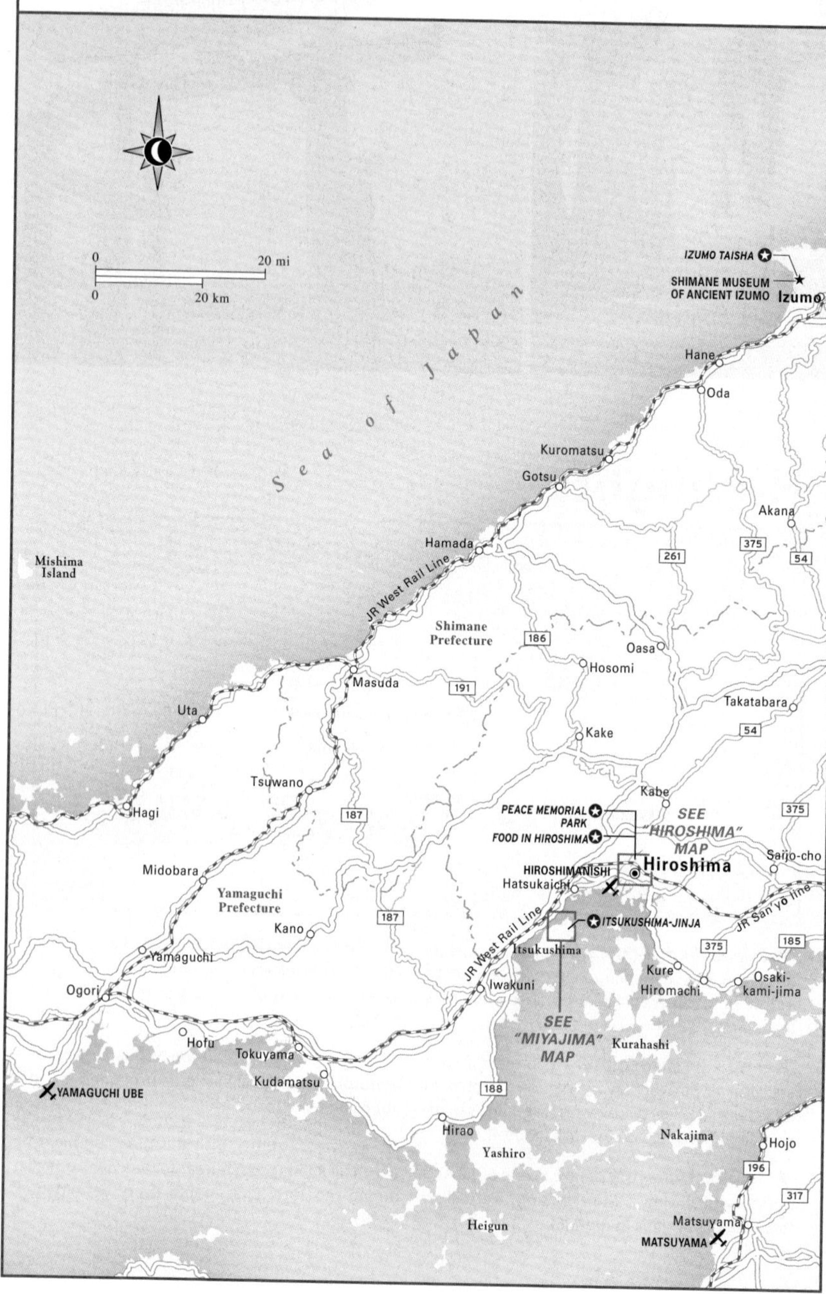

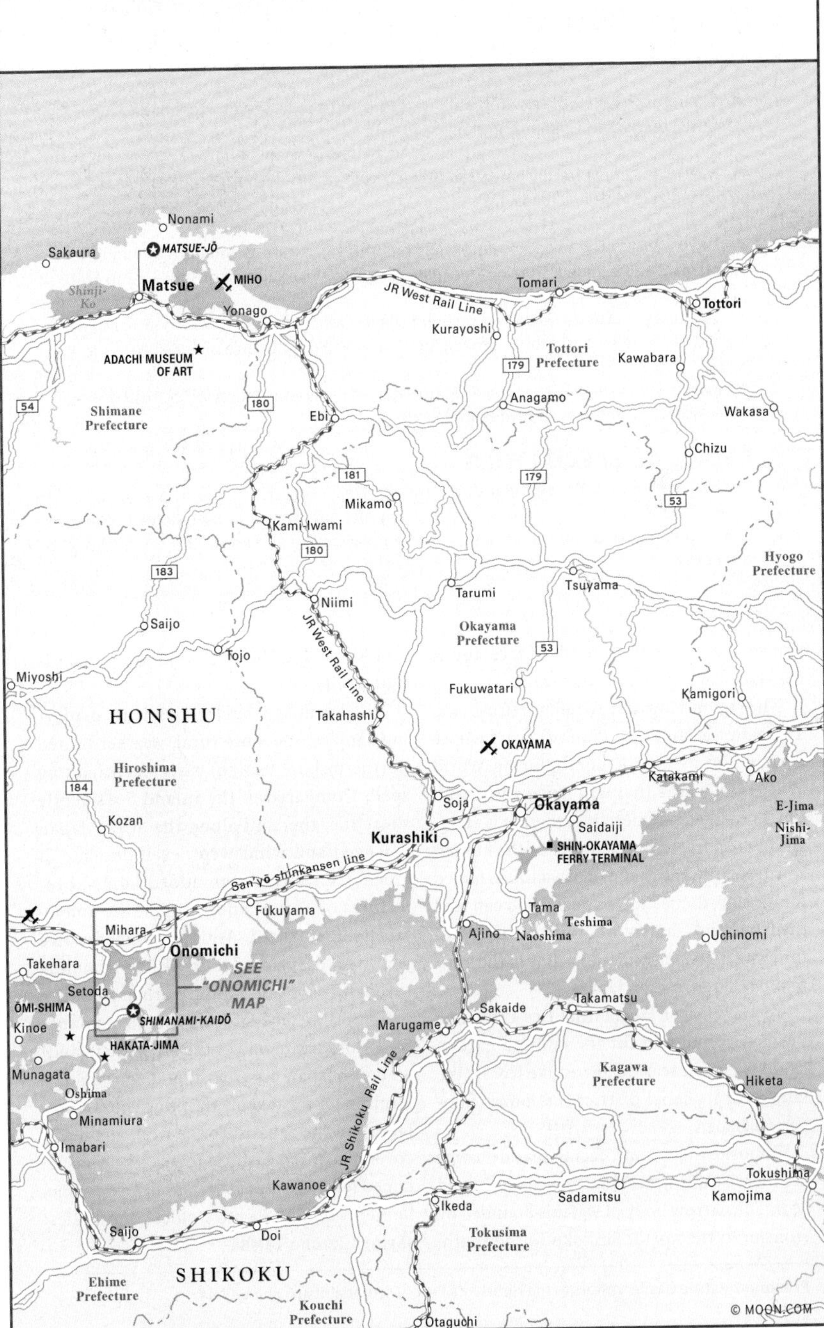
Nonami
MATSUE-JŌ
Sakaura
Shinji-Ko
Matsue
MIHO
Yonago
ADACHI MUSEUM OF ART
JR West Rail Line
Tomari
Tottori
Kurayoshi
Tottori Prefecture
179
Kawabara
54
180
Shimane Prefecture
Anagamo
Ebi
Wakasa
Chizu
181
179
Mikamo
53
Kami-Iwami
180
Hyogo Prefecture
183
Tarumi
Tsuyama
Niimi
Saijo
Okayama Prefecture
53
Tojo
JR West Rail Line
Miyoshi
Fukuwatari
Kamigori
HONSHU
Takahashi
OKAYAMA
Hiroshima Prefecture
Katakami
Ako
184
Soja
Okayama
E-Jima
Kozan
Saidaiji
Nishi-Jima
Kurashiki
SHIN-OKAYAMA FERRY TERMINAL
San'yō shinkansen line
Fukuyama
Tama
Teshima
Mihara
Ajino
Naoshima
Uchinomi
Onomichi
Takehara
SEE "ONOMICHI" MAP
Setoda
ŌMI-SHIMA
SHIMANAMI-KAIDŌ
Takamatsu
Sakaide
Kinoe
Marugame
HAKATA-JIMA
Munagata
Kagawa Prefecture
Oshima
Hiketa
Minamiura
JR Shikoku Rail Line
Imabari
Tokushima
Kawanoe
Sadamitsu
Kamojima
Ikeda
Saijo
Doi
Tokusima Prefecture
SHIKOKU
Ehime Prefecture
Kouchi Prefecture
Otaguchi

Best Restaurants

★ **Okonomiyaki Lopez:** This hallowed Hiroshima joint serves *okonomiyaki* made by a masterful, gregarious Guatemalan chef (page 421).

★ **Kakiya:** Sample freshly harvested oysters, from raw to deep fried, in this chic restaurant on picturesque Miyajima (page 428).

★ **Cafe Lente:** Eat a healthy, simple lunch at this smart café as you gaze through floor-to-ceiling glass at the famed "floating" *torii* gate of Itsukushima-jinja just offshore (page 428).

★ **Takadaya:** Dine on skewers of grilled chicken, washed down with your booze of choice, at this old-fashioned yakitori shop in the delightfully nostalgic old town of Kurashiki (page 434).

★ **Kawa-kyō:** This local hot spot in Matsue serves the "seven delicacies" of nearby Shinji-ko, a brackish lake brimming with aquatic life (page 441).

REGIONAL SPECIALITIES

Hiroshima is known for its own take on ***okonomiyaki,*** in which the savory pancake dish more commonly associated with Osaka is topped with ***yaki-soba*** (fried soba) noodles and also contains fried egg. Hiroshima and the surrounding seascape is also known for the quality of its **oysters.**

San'yō coast presents a modern face and is conveniently served by bullet train.

The region's top destination is Hiroshima, a city on the southern (San'yō) coast whose destruction by atomic bomb during World War II left a scar that will never fully heal. But its energetic modern incarnation is an inspiring testament to the power of the human spirit. Nearby, the island of Miyajima is famed for its semi-domesticated deer—you can feed them by hand—and most of all, the "floating" *torii* gate of Itsukushima-jinja, one of the most photogenic shrines in Japan.

To the east of Hiroshima lies Okayama Prefecture, known for its sublime garden Kōraku-en and seaside towns like Kurashiki, famed for its canal district that oozes Edo-period charm.

Opposite these south-facing seaside towns lies the wistfully beautiful Seto Naikai (Inland Sea). The narrow body of water is bounded by Honshu to the north, Shikoku to the south, and Kyushu to the west, and is entered via four straits.

While most travelers stick to exploring Sany'yō, the more rural, weather-beaten northern shore (San'in) casts an enchanting spell. Compared to the Inland Sea's gentle shoreline, the land along the Sea of Japan is jagged and windswept, even desolate in a beautiful way. As an added bonus, prefectures of Tottori and Shimane are among Japan's least visited. At times, you'll feel like you've got the place to yourself after trundling through Tokyo and Kansai's urban sprawl.

The 50-meter-high (164-foot) sand dunes of Tottori create one of the most alien landscapes in Japan. Approaching them, you'd be forgiven for mistakenly thinking you'd stumbled onto the Sahara. To the west, you'll discover charming historic towns like Matsue, famed for its lovely castle, and nearby Izumo, home to one of Shinto's oldest and holiest shrines, Izumo Taisha.

Previous: Matsue Castle; visitors to the Hiroshima Peace Memorial; Itsukushima-jinja

Best Accommodations

★ **World Friendship Center:** This welcoming B&B, run by friendly American hosts, is an ideal place to make sense of your time in Hiroshima, from its tragic past to its dynamic present (page 423).

★ **Iwasō Ryokan:** This historic *ryokan* in Miyajima is surrounded by maple trees that become a kaleidoscope of color in fall (page 429).

★ **Guesthouse Yuurin-an:** Set in a nicely renovated historic home, this friendly inn is an ideal base for an overnight stay in Kurashiki if your aim is to mingle in a cozy, communal setting (page 435).

★ **Ryokan Kurashiki:** With top-end meals and plush rooms, this old-school *ryokan* is the best place to stay in Kurashiki's atmospheric old town (page 435).

★ **Minamikan:** Enjoy Matsue in style at this swish *ryokan* with a mix of traditional and modern rooms, many with lakeside views of Shinji-ko (page 442).

ORIENTATION

Bordering Kansai to the east, Kyūshū to the west, and Shikoku to the south, the lay of the land in Western Honshu is most easily grasped when divided between its more heavily populated southern coast (**San'yō,** or "sunny side of the mountains"), bordering the Inland Sea, and the rural northern coast (**San'in,** or "in the shadow of the mountains"), facing the frothy **Sea of Japan.** These coasts are separated by the **Chūgoku Mountains,** which run east-west across the region.

San'yō
山陽

Approaching from elsewhere in Honshu, which means coming from the east by default, the first place most travelers come to in Western Honshu is the city of **Okayama,** capital of Okayama Prefecture. This amiable city is a *shinkansen* (bullet train) stop only 25 minutes' ride west of Himeji and Kobe (35 minutes). Also in Okayama Prefecture is the historic town of **Kurashiki,** known for its charming canals, about 20 km (12.4 mi) west of Okayama.

Moving west, Hiroshima Prefecture is next door. From Kurashiki, the first town of note you'll come to here is the idyllic port town of **Onomichi,** roughly 70 km (43.5 mi) west of Kurashiki. This is the starting point on the Honshu side of the series of bridges leading over the Inland Sea known as the **Shimanami-kaidō.** Another 90 km (56 mi) west of Onomichi brings you to the city of **Hiroshima,** which is undoubtedly the region's urban nucleus. About 25 km (15.5 mi) southwest of the city proper, the island of Itsukushima (aka **Miyajima**), famed for its "floating" *torii* gate of the idyllic seaside shrine of Itsukushima-jinja, lies just off the coast in the shimmering Inland Sea.

San'in
山陰

On the northern San'in coast, facing the Sea of Japan, the easternmost prefecture is **Tottori,** roughly 70 km (43.5 mi) west of Kinosaki Onsen on the northern coast of Hyōgo Prefecture, which defines the western edge of the neighboring region of Kansai. This sparsely populated prefecture is best known for its dramatically undulating coastal sand dunes next to its eponymous capital city.

Lying to the west of Tottori is historically rich and spiritually charged **Shimane**

Prefecture. Its prime center is the old castle town of **Matsue,** about 120 km (74.6 mi) west of the sand dunes and capital city of Tottori. Another 35 km (21.7 mi) west of there, the town of **Izumo** is home to Izumo Taisha, one of the holiest shrines in Shinto.

PLANNING YOUR TIME

Western Honshu is often the culmination of a trip that begins in Kanto or Kansai, starting in Tokyo, passing through Kyoto, and ending in Hiroshima and Miyajima. For a trip focused on Hiroshima and Miyajima, you'll just need **a few days.**

If you plan to spend more time in the region, aim to visit Okayama's Kōraku-en and Kurashiki on the San'yō side. On the San'in side, prioritize Matsue and Izumo. Note that navigating the San'in side with public transport takes a little extra coordination and planning; tour this area in a **rental car** if possible.

San'yō is one of the sunniest parts of Japan. **Summers** (June-Sept.) are hot and humid, with the rainy season rolling in throughout June and July. Temperatures drop in **winter** (Dec.-Feb.) to as low as 2°C (36°F), but rarely dip below freezing.

San'in has similar weather throughout most of the year, with the exception of **winter,** when snow covers the landscape and temperatures can fall to freezing. During **summer,** the northern coast is cooled (somewhat) by a sea breeze that comes in from the Sea of Japan. This can bring much-needed relief on some of summer's hottest days.

The best time to visit either coast is April to May or October to November, when **cherry blossoms** and **fall foliage,** respectively, add a splash of color to the landscape. Be sure to book accommodations well in advance if you plan to travel during either one of these peak seasons.

Hiroshima 広島

To fully experience Hiroshima, you must take in its past and present in equal measure. When you make the somber trip to Peace Memorial Park, fully give your attention to its call for a world without atomic weaponry. Feel the weight of the unimaginable destruction that occurred here on August 6, 1945.

As you leave the park, however, prepare to switch gears. While history must be honored and the Peace Park should be at the top of any itinerary for a visit to the city, Hiroshima's modern downtown is a revelation. Friendly locals, broad leafy avenues, a buzzing restaurant scene, and lively nightlife beckon you to enjoy the city as it lives and breathes today. Some of Hiroshima's sights have also been rebuilt and revitalized following the bombing, including its castle and the Shukkeien landscape garden.

To properly take all this in, avoid treating Hiroshima like a whistle-stop. Instead, plan to stay for a night. Few cities in the world offer such a poignant message on the strength of the human spirit to overcome tragedy and bring about rebirth.

SIGHTS

★ Peace Memorial Park
広島平和記念公園

1-1 Nakajimachō, Naka-ku; www.city.hiroshima.lg.jp/www/contents/1483699383190/index.html; 24 hours; free; from Hiroshima Station, take tram line 2 or 6 to Genbaku-Domu Mae (15 minutes, ¥180 one way)

The park that contains all of these memorials of the atomic bombing of Hiroshima occupies a sprawling 12-hectare (30-acre) green space that was once the city's commercial and political hub—precisely the reason that the area was targeted in the bombing. The city waited four years, and declared that the area would become the home of a number of peace memorials and museums rather than redeveloped.

Begin your exploration of Peace

Hiroshima

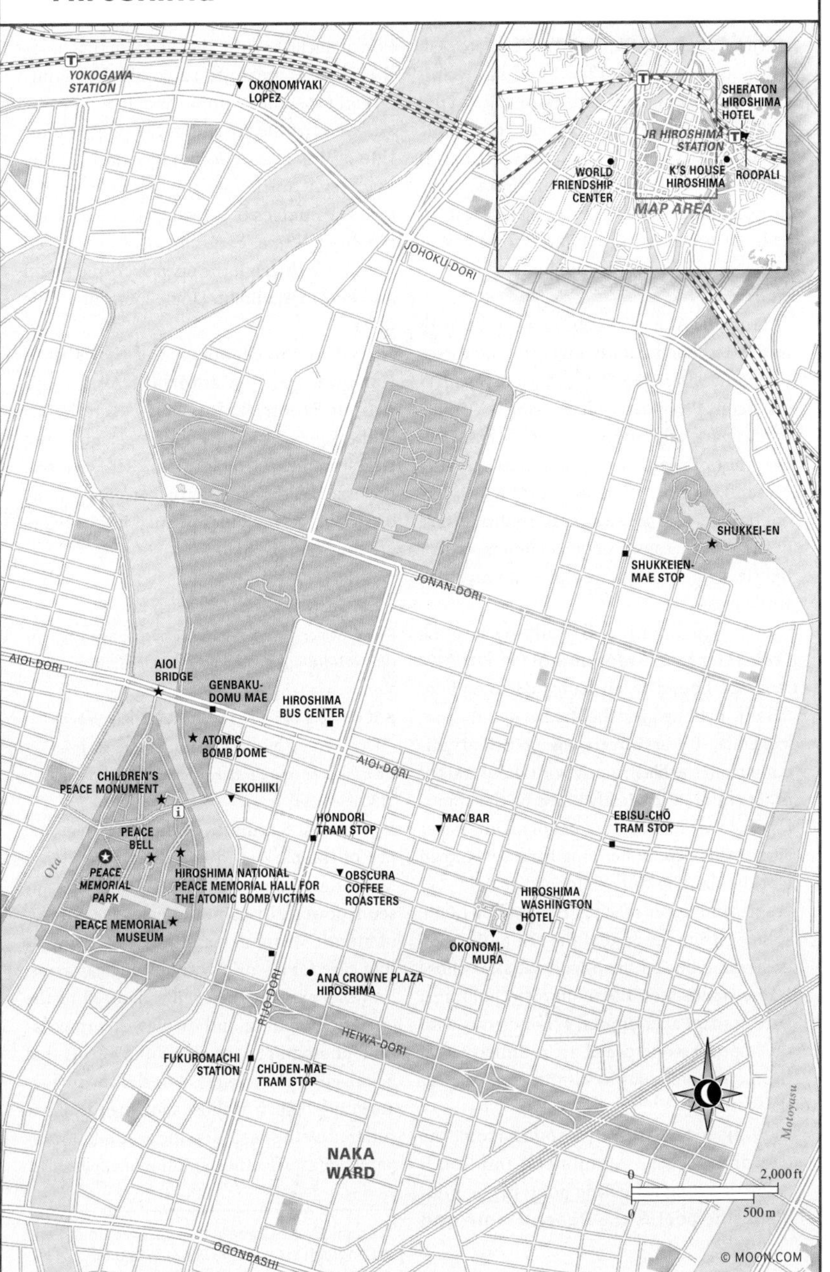
YOKOGAWA STATION
OKONOMIYAKI LOPEZ
SHERATON HIROSHIMA HOTEL
JR HIROSHIMA STATION
WORLD FRIENDSHIP CENTER
K'S HOUSE HIROSHIMA
ROOPALI
MAP AREA
JOHOKU-DORI
SHUKKEI-EN
SHUKKEIEN-MAE STOP
JONAN-DORI
AIOI-DORI
AIOI BRIDGE
GENBAKU-DOMU MAE
HIROSHIMA BUS CENTER
ATOMIC BOMB DOME
AIOI-DORI
CHILDREN'S PEACE MONUMENT
EKOHIIKI
HONDORI TRAM STOP
MAC BAR
EBISU-CHŌ TRAM STOP
PEACE BELL
Ota
PEACE MEMORIAL PARK
HIROSHIMA NATIONAL PEACE MEMORIAL HALL FOR THE ATOMIC BOMB VICTIMS
OBSCURA COFFEE ROASTERS
HIROSHIMA WASHINGTON HOTEL
PEACE MEMORIAL MUSEUM
OKONOMI-MURA
ANA CROWNE PLAZA HIROSHIMA
RIJO-DORI
HEIWA-DORI
FUKUROMACHI STATION
CHŪDEN-MAE TRAM STOP
Motoyasu
NAKA WARD
0
2,000 ft
0
500 m
OGONBASHI
© MOON.COM

Memorial Park at the **Atomic Bomb Dome** (Hiroshima Peace Memorial), Hiroshima's most famous sight. The blackened architectural shell stands beside the Motoyasu River, as one of only a few buildings to miraculously remain standing despite being within 2 km (1.2 mi) of the blast. The iconic skeleton was once a much larger, handsome red-brick building that housed the Prefectural Industrial Promotion Hall. In order to preserve its architectural integrity, the UNESCO World Heritage Site cannot be entered.

From the Atomic Bomb Dome, walk north to the T-shaped Aioi Bridge, which crosses the point where the Ota and Motoyasu rivers merge. From here, enter on the north side of the park and approach the **Peace Bell** (24 hours; free), cast by national treasure Masahiko Katori. Note the world map without borders emblazoned on the outer surface of the bell. In a spirit of quiet contemplation, lightly strike the bell and offer a prayer for world peace.

After ringing the bell, walk south to the **Children's Peace Monument** (tel. 082/242-7831; 24 hours; free) dedicated to Sadako Sasaki, a young girl who died at age 12 from leukemia, 10 years after being exposed to radiation from the blast, along with thousands of other children tragically killed by the bombing. Sadako's harrowing story of folding paper cranes throughout her long illness is known worldwide. She only managed to fold 644 cranes and never reached her goal of 1,000, so her classmates folded the remaining 356 cranes and buried them with Sadako, whose statue stands atop the monument holding a wire crane. Paper cranes, synonymous with the hope for world peace, are routinely left at the monument today by visitors from all over the world.

Walk a few minutes south from the Children's Peace Monument and you'll come to a long reflecting pool. In the middle of the pool is the **Peace Flame and Cenotaph for Atomic Bomb Victims,** which was lit on August 1, 1964, and will continue to burn until the worldwide abolition of nuclear arms. The platform that holds the flame is meant to resemble two hands brought together with open palms pointing skyward. At the far end of the pool, the inside of this moving cenotaph, designed by Pritzker-winning architect Kenzo Tange, bears the names of all who perished in the bombing. Names continue to be added even now. Gaze through the open arch and you'll see the Atomic Bomb Dome looming in the distance.

East of the cenotaph, the **Hiroshima National Peace Memorial Hall for the Atomic Bomb Victims** honors the victims of the bomb. Inside the building, a glass and steel structure resembles a clock set to 8:15am, the time that the explosion occurred. Portraits of victims and tributes penned by survivors are shown in the hall.

PEACE MEMORIAL MUSEUM

Peace Memorial Park, 1-2 Nakajimachō, Naka-ku,; 082/241-4004; http://hpmmuseum.jp; 8:30am-6pm Mar.-Jul and Sept.-Nov., 8:30am-7pm Aug., 8:30am-5pm Dec.-Feb.; adults ¥200, high school students ¥100, junior high and younger free; take tram line 2 or 6 to Genbaku-Domu Mae (15 minutes, ¥180 one way)

Walk about 3 minutes to the southeast corner of the park, and you'll find the Peace Memorial Museum. Opened in 1955, the museum powerfully communicates the horrors of atomic weaponry and makes a compelling case for a world without nuclear arms. Exhibits explain the events that led to the horrific bombing and display documentation, photographs, and personal effects that belonged to the victims. Some of the images are graphic, such as those showing the burns suffered by the people on the ground. Be prepared for an affecting, emotional experience.

1: Atomic Bomb Dome in the Peace Memorial Park
2: Cenotaph **3:** Children's Peace Memorial
4: students ringing the Peace Bell

1
2
3
4

August 6, 1945

At 8:15am, on August 6, 1945, just as Hiroshima hummed to life on what would have seemed like an ordinary day, a rotund capsule named *Little Boy* dropped over the city from a US bomber plane called the *Enola Gay*, triggering an event of horrific magnitude never seen before or since. In an instant, a blinding, incinerating flash consumed the sky and half the city was flattened. The other half soon went up in flames.

Thousands upon thousands died in an instant, while thousands of brutally charred victims sought relief by throwing themselves into the Motoyasu River, swelling the waterway with hundreds of corpses. Those who survived the first wave of horrors would soon contend with lethal drops of "black rain," pregnant with radioactive fallout. All told, some 140,000 died in the world's first nuclear bomb attack.

Hiroshima had the unfortunate distinction of being an ideal target for the bomb. For starters, the US military sought a city with a downtown core that measured more than 4.5 km (3 mi) around. Hiroshima was on a short list that also included Niigata, Kokura, and Nagasaki. Hiroshima's grim fate was sealed partly due to the fact that US forces did not think any American prisoners of war were being kept in the city.

On that fateful morning, the skies were clear. The bombers used the T-shaped Aioi Bridge, which crosses the Ota and Motoyasu rivers, as their target. This bridge stands—rebuilt and now bustling with traffic like the rest of the city—just north of the Atomic Bomb Dome in Peace Memorial Park, near the hypocenter of the blast.

On each anniversary of the city's decimation, around 50,000 people fill Peace Memorial Park to commemorate those who died that day. Alongside locals and travelers, foreign dignitaries and ambassadors amass to hear speeches by Japan's top officials, offering pleas for world peace.

The day's proceedings begin at 8:15am, when temple bells chime, sirens wail, and all citizens observe a somber moment of silence to honor those who perished in the blast and its aftermath. The solemnity is softened in the evening when 10,000 floating lanterns are released onto the Motoyasu River. Seeing myriad floating lights, gently flowing past the Atomic Bomb Dome, is an undeniably haunting, ethereal sight.

Shukkei-en
縮景園

2-11 Kaminoborichō, Naka-ku; tel. 082/221-3620; http://shukkeien.jp; 9am-6pm Apr.-Sept., 9am-5pm Oct.-Mar.; adults ¥260, high school students ¥150, junior high and elementary school students ¥100; from Hiroshima Station, take tram line 9 to Shukkeien-mae stop (15 minutes, ¥180) or, walk 8 minutes northwest to the garden from JR Hiroshima Station

Shukkei-en, which roughly translates to "contracted view garden," lives up to its name, emulating peaks, woodlands, islands, and valleys in miniature form. Paths wind through these natural scenes with ease, just as Lord Asano Nagaakira had in mind when he appointed tea master Ueda Soko to create a green escape for him in 1620. The garden was all but flattened in 1945, but some vegetation miraculously flourished the year after the bombing, and the natural space was eventually revived. Today, its striking layout, with a variety of alluring footpaths, plum and cherry blossoms, teahouses, and island-studded pond, make it one of the city's most lovely spots.

FESTIVALS

TŌKASAN YUKATA FESTIVAL
とうかさん大祭

Chūō-dōri and around; www.toukasan.jp; noon-11pm for three days starting first Fri. of June; free

The streets of downtown fill with denizens in *yukata* (lightweight cotton kimonos) during this lively annual festival. Expect to see *yatai* (street food stalls), games (think fish scooping and shooting at targets with airsoft guns), dancing, beating on *taiko* drums, and more.

★ FOOD

The two most popular items on Hiroshima's menu are oysters hauled in from the bay and the local style of *okonomiyaki* (a savory cross between a pancake and an omelet), loaded with cabbage, seafood, meat, soba noodles, bean sprouts, and a slathering of mayonnaise, bonito flakes, sweet sauces, and other condiments. If you aim to try one local dish in Hiroshima, make it *okonomiyaki.*

OKONOMI-MURA

5-13 Shintenchi, Naka-ku; tel. 082/241-2210; www.okonomimura.jp; 11am-2am daily; from ¥800-1,300; take tram lines 1, 2, or 6 to the Ebisu-chō tram stop, then walk 6 minutes southwest

It's firmly on the tourist track, but this is a great place to enter the world of *okonomiyaki.* Some 25 stalls serve up the city's signature dish in this cramped, boisterous "Okonomiyaki Village" spread across the second through fourth floors of the building. Situated within a bar district, this place hops late at night, but it's good any time of day. Among the glut of purveyors, Hasshō on the second floor stands out, but follow your inspiration and you'll likely be satisfied wherever you choose.

★ OKONOMIYAKI LOPEZ

1-7-13 Kusunoki-chō, Nishi-ku; tel. 082/232-5277; 11:30am-2pm Tues. and Fri., 4:30pm-11pm Mon.-Fri.; from ¥650; take the JR San'yō line to Yokogawa, then walk 6 minutes east

This *okonomiyaki* joint is a Hiroshima institution run by Guatemalan-born chef Fernando Lopez and his Japanese wife Makiko. Lopez has lived in the city for more than two decades and learned from the *okonomiyaki* maestro Ogawa Hiroki. The friendly husband-wife team exude warmth, engaging in lighthearted conversation while adroitly flipping *okonomiyaki*; their food is among the best *okonomiyaki* in a city crazy about the dish. Portions are generous, too.

EKOHIIKI

1-7-20 Ōte-machi, Naka-ku; tel. 082/545-3655; http://ekohiiki.com; 11:30am-2pm and 5pm-11pm Tues.-Sun.; plates from ¥580-1,500, set meals ¥800-2,000; take the Astram line or tram line 1, 3, or 7 to Hondori tram stop, then walk 3 minutes west

This restaurant just east of Peace Memorial Park is a great place to sample the city's famed oysters. The consistently plump, juicy oysters are prepared any way you like: raw, grilled, deep-fried, and more. There's also a good range of side dishes, from chicken wings to

okonomiyaki, Hiroshima style

sashimi, and a diverse alcohol selection, too. Service is friendly, and there's a good English-language menu.

OKKUNDO

Sansan Bldg. 3-3-3 Otemachi, Naka-ku; tel. 082/246-1377; www.powerland.co.jp; 11am-11pm daily; ¥520-1,060; take tram line 1, 3, or 7 to Chūden-mae tram stop, then walk 4 minutes northwest

Serving up generous helpings of *mazemen*—flavorful noodles mixed with a light sauce topped with soft-boiled egg, leek, roast pork and more—this shop is a good option if you've had your fill of *okonomiyaki* and seafood. There's also a good side menu of items like *gyoza* (fried dumplings) and onion rings, too. It feels like a hole in the wall, but the service is friendly.

ROOPALI

14-32 Wakakusachō, Higashi-ku; tel. 082/264-1333; www.roopali.jp; 11am-2:30pm and 5pm-9:30pm daily; lunch ¥720-1,300, dinner a la carte ¥1,200-2,000, set meals ¥1,880-3,500; 6 minutes' walk east of JR Hiroshima Station's north exit

A meal at this Indian restaurant is a good way to spice things up. The menu includes a good range of curries and its lunch sets are very good value. Its bright decor and sign bearing the visages of Krishna and Ganesh make it easy to spot.

OBSCURA COFFEE ROASTERS

3-28 Fukuro-machi, Naka-ku; tel. 082/249-7543; https://obscura-coffee.com; 9am-8pm daily, closed third Wed. every month; ¥290-570; take the Astram line or tram line 1, 3, or 7 to Hondori tram stop, then walk 2 minutes southeast

Originally launched in Tokyo, this café chain was founded by three coffee lovers from Hiroshima. For a quick pick-me-up or pastry, to be enjoyed in the café or taken away, this artisanal cafe is a great bet. The minimalist interior is offset by rugs and wooden furniture. If you're seeking a calm break, it fits the bill nicely, but might not be the place to go with young kids.

BARS AND NIGHTLIFE

MAC BAR

Borabora Bldg. 3F, 3-4 Tatemachi, Naka-ku; tel. 082/243-0343; www.facebook.com/pages/Mac-Bar/845730498970349; 6pm-late daily; take tram 1, 2, 6, or 9 to Tatemachi tram stop, then walk 2 minutes southwest

If you like classic rock and want a mellow evening out with a 40s and up crowd, this is your place. Tucked away in a nondescript building, this is the third incarnation of this local institution, which has been in business for more than four decades. With its remarkable CD collection and solid sound system, it's a laid-back spot for a drink.

BAR ALEGRE

Cony Bldg. 3F, 1-32 Horikawa-chō, Naka-ku; tel. 082/545-5295; www.bar-alegre.jp; 7pm-2:30am Mon.-Sat.; ¥500 cover charge; take tram 1, 2, or 6 to Ebisu-chō tram stop, then walk 3 minutes south

The talented mixologists at this cozy bar make serious craft cocktails. The bar is well-stocked and the atmosphere evokes a speakeasy. It's a great place to go if you want something sophisticated but not fussy.

ENJOINT BAR COVER

Hakubishi Daigo Bldg. 2F, 7-6 Nagarekawa, Naka-ku; tel. 082/249-3917; https://enjointbar.wixsite.com/cover; 10pm-5am Wed.-Sun.; take tram line 1, 2, or 6 to Ebisu-chō tram stop, then walk 7 minutes south

This bar has a pretty serious sound system for its size, with DJs spinning house, reggae, and other dance-friendly genres on Friday and Saturday nights. This is a good choice for a lively weekend night out.

MOLLY MALONE'S

Teigeki Bldg. 4F, Naka-ku; tel. 082/244-2554; www.mollymalones.jp; 5pm-1am Tues.-Thurs., 5pm-2am Fri., 11:30am-2am Sat., 11:30am-midnight Sun.; take tram line 1, 2, or 6 to Ebisu-chō tram stop, then walk 4 minutes southwest

This Irish pub has all the right fixings: Guinness, Kilkenny, Bass ale on tap; fish and chips, and roast. It's no surprise it's garnered a strong following. This is a good place to meet and mingle with locals and expats alike.

ACCOMMODATIONS

K'S HOUSE HIROSHIMA

1-8-9 Matoba-chō, Minami-ku; tel. 082/568-7244; https://kshouse.jp; dorms from ¥2,000, double with en-suite bath ¥2,680-6,450; take tram line 1, 2, 5, or 6 to the Matobachō tram stop, then walk 2 minutes southwest, or walk 8 minutes south of Hiroshima Station

Located an 8-minute walk southwest of Hiroshima Station, this hostel has mixed dorm rooms, private tatami rooms, and rooms for two. All rooms share a bathroom, lounge, kitchen, and laundry facilities. This is a good place to meet fellow travelers and exchange tips, and it's an affordable, convenient home base.

★ WORLD FRIENDSHIP CENTER

8-10 Higashi Kan-on, Nishi-ku; tel. 082/503-3191; http://wfchiroshima.com; ¥4,200 pp; take tram line 2 or 3 to Koami-chō tram stop, then walk 7 minutes southwest

This no-frills guesthouse, owned by an American couple, is a good place for those interested in peace activism to engage directly with those affected by the A-bomb. Besides providing good, clean, and private tatami rooms, with a shared bathroom and breakfast, you'll have the opportunity to talk with survivors of the attack. The friendly hosts also impart generous local knowledge to all guests.

HIROSHIMA WASHINGTON HOTEL

2-7 Shintenchi, Naka-ku; tel. 082/553-2222; https://washington-hotels.jp/hiroshima/; ¥18,900 d; take tram line 1, 2, 6, or 9 to Hatchobori tram stop, then walk 4 minutes south

This clean, well-appointed business hotel is a great value. Its decor and ambience are a cut above what you'd expect for the price. The location is convenient, too, right in the middle of downtown and roughly equidistant to Peace Memorial Park and JR Hiroshima Station.

ANA CROWNE PLAZA HIROSHIMA

7-20 Naka-machi, Naka-ku; tel. 082/241-1111; www.anacrowneplaza-hiroshima.jp; ¥19,500 d; take tram line 1, 3, or 7 to Fukuromachi tram stop, then walk 2 minutes southeast

This hotel in the heart of downtown, just east of Peace Memorial Park, has bright, airy rooms and a friendly staff. The bathrooms are spacious and well-stocked, and an optional continental breakfast is served. This is a solid midrange option close to the city's main sights.

SHERATON HIROSHIMA HOTEL

12-1 Wakakusa-chō, Higashi-ku; tel. 082/262-7111; www.marriott.com/hotels/travel/hijsi-sheraton-grand-hiroshima-hotel; ¥30,380 d; take any JR line that runs to Hiroshima Station, then walk 2 minutes east

If you're willing to spend a bit more, this luxurious hotel is conveniently located right outside the north exit of the main station. Rooms are notably larger than the norm in Japan and very well-appointed, and staff are cheerful and eager to please. There's a breakfast buffet (¥2,750 per person) and a Japanese restaurant on-site. Recommended.

INFORMATION AND SERVICES

You can pick up English-language information and get recommendations from one of three **tourist information centers** in Hiroshima Station. The first one sits next to the ticket gate for *shinkansen* (bullet train) arrivals and departures at the north side of the station (6am-midnight daily; tel. 082/263-5120). Another information counter sits next to the north exit (8:30am-6:30pm daily; no phone), while another sits beside the south exit (9am-6pm daily; no phone).

For information online, from restaurant and nightlife listings to transportation breakdowns, check out the helpful websites **Visit Hiroshima** (http://visithiroshima.net) and **Hiroshima Navi** (www.hiroshima-navi.or.jp), or the webzine **Get Hiroshima** (www.gethiroshima.com), run by expats.

TRANSPORTATION

Getting There

Sitting on the east side of downtown, **Hiroshima Station** is served by the *shinkansen,* running to and from **Tokyo** (4 hours; ¥19,080), **Shin-Osaka** (1 hour, 30 minutes; ¥10,440), and **Kyoto** (1 hour, 40 minutes; ¥11,410) in the east, and **Fukuoka** (Hakata Station; 1 hour; ¥9,150) in the west. Local trains on the JR San'yō line also stop at the station, with the train route beginning from Himeji in the east and plodding westward to Shimonoseki on Honshu's far western fringe.

Both international and domestic flights serve **Hiroshima Airport** (tel. 082/231-5171; www.hij.airport.jp), about 45 km (28 mi) east of downtown. Overseas routes include Dalian and Shanghai in China, as well as Hong Kong, Taipei, and Seoul, while domestic links include Okinawa and Sendai. **Shuttle buses** connect the airport to Hiroshima Station (45 minutes; 8:20am-9:40pm from the airport to downtown, 6am-7:20pm from Hiroshima Station to airport; ¥1,340). If you've got a JR rail pass, it will most likely prove more effective to travel to Hiroshima by train, unless you're coming from overseas or somewhere particularly far-flung within Japan, such as Okinawa.

Hiroshima is well-connected by highways, with buses making the journey to the city from all around Japan. Some buses use **Hiroshima Bus Center** (6-27 Motomachi; www.h-buscenter.com), accessed via the third floor of the Sogō Department Store in the heart of downtown.

Servicing Matsuyama (ferry: 2 hours, 30 minutes; adults ¥3,600, children ¥1,800; hydrofoil: 1 hour 15 minutes; adults ¥7,100, children ¥3,550), operator **Setonaikai Kisen Ferry** (tel. 082/253-1212; www.setonaikaikisen.co.jp) travels in and out of **Hiroshima Port Ujina Terminal** (1-13-26 Ujinakaigan, Minami-ku; tel. 082/253-6907). Boats running to and from Miyajima (30 minutes, ¥1,850) also serve this port, which is located south of downtown and accessible by Ujina-bound tram lines 1, 3, and 5 (all ¥160).

Getting Around

Hiroshima's scale makes it ideal to explore **on foot.** That said, some sights are just far enough that you may want to hop on the city's efficient tram network, avail yourself of a tour bus, or pedal around on a bike.

Hiroshima is well-served by the handy **Hiroden tram network** (www.hiroden.co.jp; single ride ¥160, one-day pass ¥640, one-day pass with Matsudai ferry to Miyajima ¥840). Trams 2 and 6 are particularly useful, linking to Peace Memorial Park and around. To take a single ride, board from the back and deposit your fare in the machine beside the driver's seat when you exit from the front. Passes can be bought at the tram terminal in Hiroshima Station. Note that the ferry to Miyajima, covered by the special one-day pass, is different from the one that departs from Hiroshima Port.

The city's *meipurū-pu* **Sightseeing Loop Bus** (www.chugoku-jrbus.co.jp; single ride ¥200, one-day pass ¥400) traces two color-coded routes (orange and green) around town, both starting from the north side of the station near the *shinkansen* concourse. The orange route passes by the Shukkei-en landscape garden, the castle, and some museums, while the green bus takes in temples dotting the north side of town. Both link to Peace Memorial Park and around. JR pass holders can ride both buses for free.

If you'd like to **cycle** around town, staying in an accommodation that offers cycle rentals is your best bet. The city does have a bicycle rental system, with 20-plus cycleports around town, but it's a little complicated to operate. If you'd like to try, head to the HQ of **Peacecle** ("peace" + "cycle," 2-29 Koyobashi-chō; tel. 082/568-5760; www.docomo-cycle.jp.hiroshima).

Miyajima

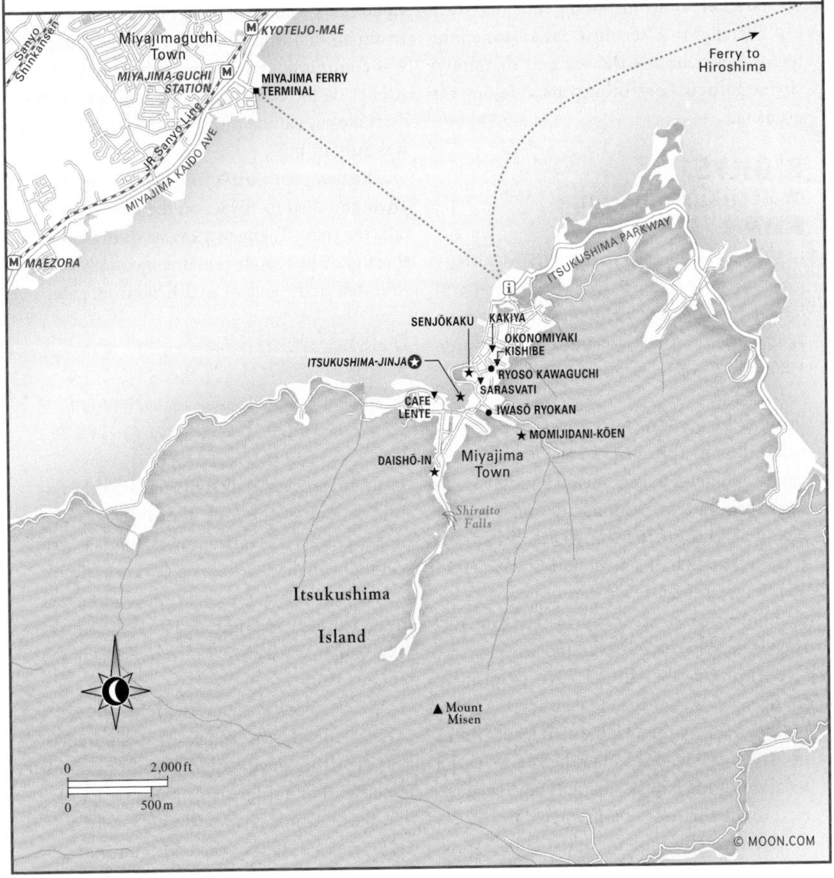

Sanyo Shinkansen
Miyajimaguchi Town
KYOTEIJO-MAE
MIYAJIMA-GUCHI STATION
MIYAJIMA FERRY TERMINAL
Ferry to Hiroshima
JR Sanyo Line
MIYAJIMA KAIDO AVE
MAEZORA
ITSUKUSHIMA PARKWAY
SENJŌKAKU
KAKIYA
OKONOMIYAKI KISHIBE
ITSUKUSHIMA-JINJA
RYOSO KAWAGUCHI
SARASVATI
CAFE LENTE
IWASŌ RYOKAN
MOMIJIDANI-KŌEN
DAISHŌ-IN
Miyajima Town
Shiraito Falls
Itsukushima Island
Mount Misen
0 2,000 ft
0 500 m
© MOON.COM

Miyajima

The island of Miyajima (officially named Itsukushima) may not be a household name in the West, but the scene of the vermillion *torii* gate rising directly from the sea at the shrine of Itsukushima-jinja is widely hailed as one of Japan's three best views. Beyond this famously "floating" shrine gate, the island is defined by low-lying mountains dotted by temples and laced with good walking trails up Mount Misen, where you'll find a cluster of temples and shrines.

Similar to Nara Kōen, Miyajima is also known for its population of alarmingly tame deer, whose heads are topped with tiny horns. Don't be surprised if they walk right up to you, and don't feed them unless you want to be mobbed.

Miyajima is easily visited on a day trip

from Hiroshima, less than an hour away. But if you'd like to avoid the crowds and soak up its ethereal atmosphere, consider staying overnight. After dusk falls, stone lanterns flicker beside the sea and the famed shrine gate cuts a striking profile during the evening.

SIGHTS

★ Itsukushima-jinja

厳島神社

1-1 Miyajima-chō, Hatsukaichi; tel. 0829/44-2020; www.itsukushimajinja.jp; 6:30am-5:30pm Jan.-Nov., 6:30am-5pm Dec.; adults ¥300, high school students ¥200, junior high and elementary school students ¥100; walk 10 minutes southwest from Itsukushima ferry terminal

Fringed by verdant hills and tucked into a small inlet of the Inland Sea, in which it is partly submerged, this shrine and its "floating" *torii* gate are among the most recognizable Shinto shrine complexes. Structures include a main hall, prayer hall, and *Noh* theater stage, linked by a series of boardwalks. Camphor-tree wood, known to keep from rotting, is used in the construction.

Although the shrine was originally founded as early as the 6th century, it was rebuilt in 1168 by then Heike clan leader Taira no Kiyomori, who selected the site to be the location of his family shrine. The *Noh* stage next to the shrine was constructed in 1680.

The shrine's peculiar construction can be attributed to the belief that the island is hallowed ground. Traditionally, only the priestly class were permitted on the island and were required to approach by boat.

To see the shrine and its famed gate "floating," arrive at high tide. Inquire at the ferry terminal for a tide forecast. If you stick around for sunset, the gate and shrine are lit up until 11pm: a magical sight best appreciated on a leisurely walk, preferably from your local *ryokan* during an overnight stay on the holy island.

The sprawling shrine complex of **Senjōkaku** (8:30am-4:30pm daily; adults ¥100, junior high and elementary school students ¥50) (the name means "hall of 1,000 mats") stands atop a hill just north of Itsukushima-jinja. Built in 1587, the shrine was commissioned by Toyotomi Hideyoshi. Alongside the complex, which is also known as Hōkoku, stands a five-story pagoda that was built in 1407.

The complex wasn't finished by the time Toyotomi died in 1598, and the next ruler to take the reins, Tokugawa Ieyasu, didn't follow through. The temple remains incomplete, as reflected in the lack of an official front gate.

Daishō-in

大聖院

210 Miyajima-chō, Hatsukaichi; tel. 0829/44-0111; https://daisho-in.com; 8am-5pm daily; free; walk 20 minutes southwest from Itsukushima ferry terminal

About 10 minutes' walk south of Itsukushima-jinja, sitting at the foot of heavily wooded Mount Misen, this intriguing temple is worth seeing if you plan to hike up or down Mount Misen. It is, in fact, one of the most important in the Shingon sect, founded by Kōbō Daishi (aka Kūkai), who called for the building of the temple in 806.

At the temple, you can see prayer wheels; a cave festooned with lanterns that feature images depicting the 88 pilgrimage stops of the famed Shikoku pilgrimage; 500 statues of a disciple of Amida Nyorai (Buddha of Infinite Light) named Rakan, each with an individual facial expression; an 11-headed effigy of Kannon (Goddess of Mercy); a mandala sand painting done by visiting Tibetan monks; and more.

To accelerate your own Buddhist scholarship, reach out and spin the prayer wheels bearing the inscriptions of sutras (scriptures) as you walk up the temple's main staircase. This action is said to equate to reading the content of the sutras emblazoned on each prayer wheel, and receiving the blessing contained therein.

1: prayer wheels at Daishō-in **2:** Momijidani-kōen **3:** Itsukushima-jinja

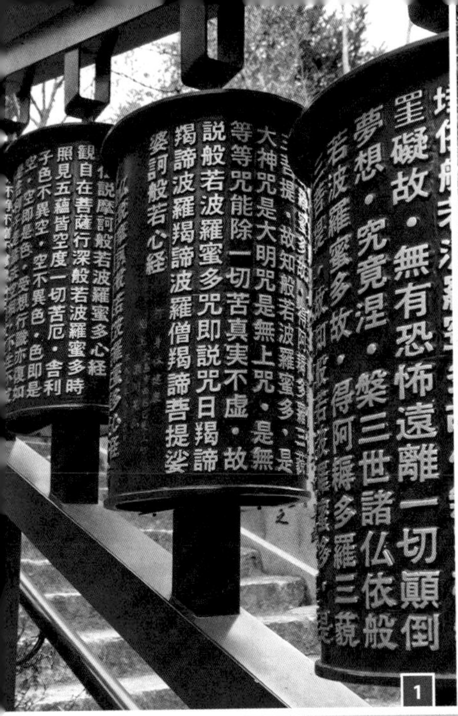

説摩訶般若波羅蜜多心経
観自在菩薩行深般若波羅蜜多時
照見五蘊皆空度一切苦厄・舎利
子色不異空・空不異色・色即是
菩提・故知般若波羅蜜多・是
大神咒是大明咒是無上咒・是無
等等咒能除一切苦真実不虚・故
説般若波羅蜜多咒即説咒日羯諦
羯諦波羅羯諦波羅僧羯諦菩提娑
婆訶般若心経
罣礙故・無有恐怖遠離一切顛倒
夢想・究竟涅槃三世諸仏依般
若波羅蜜多故得阿耨多羅三藐

1

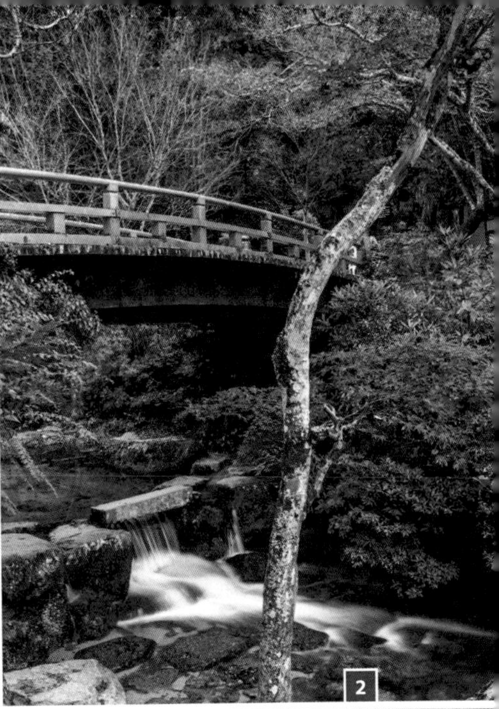
2

3
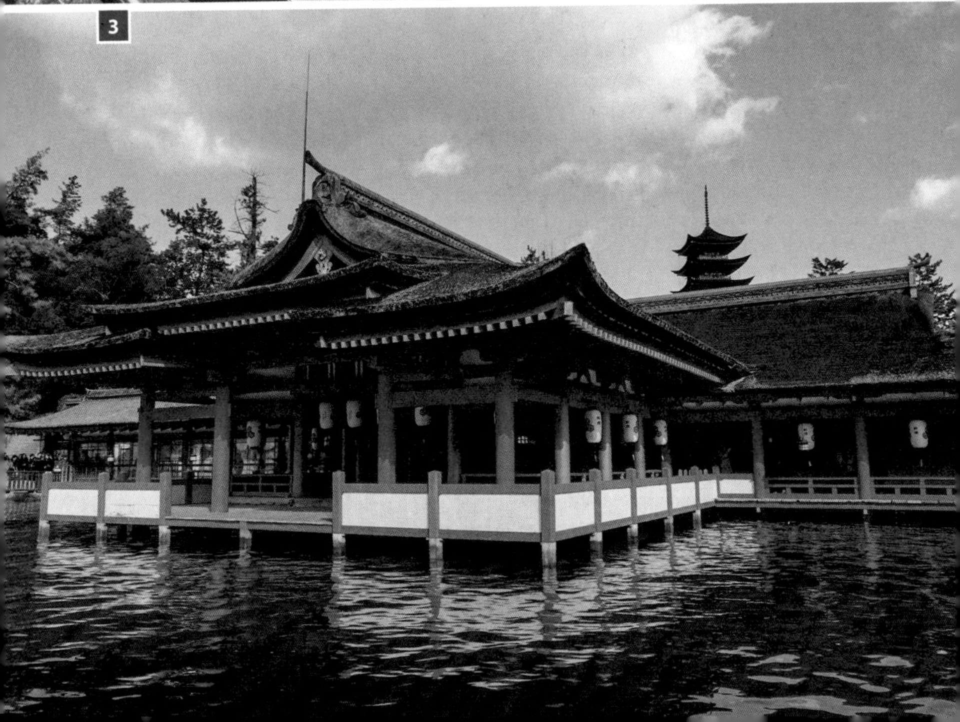

HIKING

MOUNT MISEN AND MOMIJIDANI-KŌEN

Momijidani-kōen sits at the foot of Mount Misen, the island's highest peak at 535 meters (1,755 feet). It's justly known for its autumn foliage. Bisected by a stream, spanned by arched bridges and lined by stone lanterns, with tame deer roaming freely, it's near the ropeway that takes you within a 30-minute walk of the summit.

Mount Misen offers phenomenal views of the Inland Sea, stretching to Hiroshima and even as far away as Shikoku on cloudless days. You can hike to the top, passing through thick forest, where a temple marks the spot where Kūkai meditated for 100 days. A flame housed at the **Reikadō** (Hall of the Spiritual Flame) was lit by Kūkai and has been continuously burning for 1,200 years. The Peace Flame at Hiroshima's Peace Park was lit with this fire.

To reach the summit of Moun Misen, you can hike one of three trails. If you'd rather not work up a sweat, simply hop on the **Miyajima Ropeway** to the top (www.miyajima-ropeway.info; 9am-5pm daily; adults ¥1,000 one way/¥1,800 round trip, children ¥500 one way/¥900 round trip). The lower ropeway station is about 10 minutes' walk from Momijidani-kōen, from where the ride to the upper station takes about 15 minutes. From there, it's another 30-minute hike uphill to the summit. If you've got time, for the best experience, opt to trundle up the verdant peak on foot.

If you want to hike to the top instead of riding the ropeway, the Miyajima Tourist Association has online information in English. Check out www.miyajima.or.jp/english/course/course_tozan3.html for descriptions of each hike, and www.miyajima.or.jp/english/map/map_misen.html for a map.

FOOD

★ KAKIYA

539 Miyajima-chō, Hatsukaichi-shi; tel. 0829/44-2747; www.kaki-ya.jp; 10am-6pm daily; ¥1,200-3,000; 5 minutes' walk northeast of Itsukushima-jinja

If you haven't already sampled oysters in Hiroshima, or if you want more, this is a great spot to try them in their various guises (deep-fried, raw, grilled), in the heart of the island's small town.

OKONOMIYAKI KISHIBE

483-2 Miyajima-chō, Hatsukaichi-shi; tel. 0829/44-0002; 5pm-9pm Fri.-Wed.; ¥650-1,250; walk 4 minutes northeast of Itsukushima-jinja

Like oysters, *okonomiyaki* is as good on the island as it is on the neighboring mainland. If you haven't had your fill in Hiroshima, this mom-and-pop shop serves Hiroshima-style *okonomiyaki* as well as ramen. This is a good place for a homey meal.

SARASVATI

407 Miyajimacho, Hatsukaichi; tel. 0829/44-2266; https://itsuki-miyajima.com/shop/sarasvati; 8:30am-7pm daily; drinks from ¥350; sandwich sets ¥950; 2 minutes' walk east of Itsukushima-jinja

This stylish café a stone's throw from the shrine serves great coffee, tea, and desserts. It's located in the midst of the tourist buzz, but is a good place to escape the crowds.

★ CAFE LENTE

1167-3 Kitaonishi-chō, Miyajimachō; tel. 0829/44-1204; 11am-6pm daily; drinks from ¥500, dishes from ¥800; 7 minutes' walk west of Itsukushima-jinja

This is a chic little oasis with nearly floor-to-ceiling windows that offer great views of the pine-studded shore and iconic floating *torii* gate beyond. They serve good coffee, tea, desserts, and a smattering of light, healthy meals.

ACCOMMODATIONS

Staying overnight on Miyajima is a great way to experience the island's subtle charms that are often missed amid the crowds of day-trippers. If you have the time and budget, there are some wonderful traditional lodgings tucked away in the island's small village.

RYOSO KAWAGUCHI

469 Miyajimacho, Hatsukaichi; tel. 0829/44-0018; http://ryoso-kawaguchi.jp; rooms from ¥6,500 pp, dinner from ¥1,000 pp, dinner from ¥5,000 pp; 3 minutes' walk east of Itsukushima-jinja

This welcoming inn, tucked away in the heart of the village east of the shrine, is a great midrange pick. The guesthouse itself is quite old, but well-maintained, with private rooms sharing two private *onsen* (hot spring) tubs (one for couples, one for singles). The host is warm and helpful, and the meals (breakfast and dinner) are tasty and filling. Recommended.

★ IWASŌ RYOKAN

345-1 Minamimachi, Miyajimacho, Hatsukaichi; tel. 0829/44-2233; www.iwaso.com; ¥22,000-28,000 pp with breakfast and dinner; 4 minutes' walk southeast of Itsukushima-jinja, heading toward Momijidani-kōen

This renowned, high-end *ryokan* has history and a magical ambience. In business since 1854, the property is divided into three wings with a handful of cottages. Some rooms use a shared bathroom. All rooms have access to a shared *onsen*. Two lavish meals are served daily to the exquisite tatami rooms. It's located about 15 minutes' walk east of the Miyajima-sanbashi Pier. There's also an optional courtesy shuttle bus pickup from the pier. You'll have to reserve six months or more in advance to snag a room in autumn, when the leafy gorge behind the property explodes with red, orange, and yellow.

INFORMATION AND SERVICES

For English information on Miyajima, stop by the **tourist information booth** in the island's ferry terminal (tel. 0829/44-2011; http://visit-miyajima-japan.com; 9am-6pm daily).

TRANSPORTATION

Miyajima is accessible by ferry from **Miyajima-guchi station,** a stop on the JR San'yō line, about 20 km (12 mi) southwest of Hiroshima (30 minutes, ¥410). From Miyajima-guchi's **ferry terminal,** two companies operate ferries to and from Miyajima: **JR** (tel. 0829/56-2045; www.jr-miyajimaferry.co.jp; departures from Miyajima-guchi 6:25am-10:42pm daily) and **Matsudai** (tel. 0829/44-2171; www.miyajima-matsudai.co.jp; departures from Miyajima-guchi 7:15am-8:35pm daily). Note that while both operators charge the same fare (10 minutes, ¥180 one way), you can ride the JR ferry for free if you have a JR pass.

If you'd like to zip straight to the island from Hiroshima's core in about 30 minutes, serving Hiroshima's Ujina Port is hydrofoil operator **Setonaikai Kisen** (tel. 082/253-1212; www.setonaikaikisen.co.jp; departures from Ujina Port 9:25am-4:25pm Mon.-Fri., 8:25am-4:25pm Sat.-Sun.; ¥1,850 one way). Ujina Port can be reached from downtown via tram numbers 3 and 5 (20 minutes, ¥160).

Aqua Net Ferry (tel. 082/240-5955; www.aqua-net-h.co.jp; departures from Peace Memorial Park 8:30am-5:10pm daily) whisks away passengers directly from Peace Memorial Park (45 minutes; ¥2,000 one way, ¥3,600 return). You'll find the dock on the opposite side of the Ōta-gawa river from the Peace Memorial Park.

While taxis do trundle through the island's quiet lanes, plan to explore Miyajima on foot. All sights of interest are within a comfortable stroll from each other.

East Along the Inland Sea

ONOMICHI
尾道

This seaside town is full of retro storefronts, traditional homes, and aging fishing boats floating in the harbor. A vintage shopping arcade houses a mélange of old and new: classic *kissaten* (old-fashion coffee shops), bakeries, trendy fashion boutiques, and art galleries. In temple-studded neighborhoods spread across the slopes behind the town, an army of cats makes itself at home. Many films and TV dramas have been shot in Onomichi, which has also produced its fair share of auteurs.

To take in the spiritual side of the town, there is a temple walk. If you're of a more literary bent, there's also a path marked by poetry-inscribed stones that intersects the temple walk and pays homage to literary figures who were inspired by the town, haiku master Matsuo Bashō among them. Onomichi also serves as the starting point of the Shimanami Kaidō, a 60-km (37-mi) series of bridges across the Inland Sea that links Honshu and Shikoku. This scenic journey can be made by car or bicycle and traverses a string of rural islands en route.

Hiking

TEMPLE WALK

Distance: 2.5 km (1.6 mi)

Time: 1-3 hrs (depending on time spent at temples)

Information and maps: Tourist Information center (1-1 Higashigosho-chō)

Start: north of first bridge that goes over train tracks east of Onomichi Station

This famed walking route leads to 25 temples, which were built using donations from well-heeled merchants during the town's heyday as a major port city. Aside from including some spectacular architecture, the walk offers stunning views of the Inland Sea and rustic townscapes. You'll walk up and down steps and slopes, and through residential areas. The temples range from petite and deserted to vast complexes.

Senkō-ji (15-1 Higashi, Tsuchido-chō; tel. 0848/23-2310; www.senkouji.jp), said to have been built by Kōbō Daishi (aka Kūkai) in 806, is the most iconic temple. This complex sits below a park that is reachable by ropeway and offers fantastic views of the city and sea below. Another notable temple is **Jodo-ji,** the last one on the walk; it is said to have been built in the early 7th century, making it the oldest on the route. The temple has a two-story pagoda and lovely garden, both of which are officially designated National Treasures by the Agency for Cultural Affairs. If you prefer to go straight to the town's highest viewing platform without breaking a sweat, hop on the **Senkō-ji Mountain Ropeway** (tel. 084/822-4900; http://onomichibus.jp/ropeway; 9am-5:15pm daily; ¥320 one way, ¥500 return) to **Senkō-ji-kōen,** the park located above the temple of the same name. The bottom station of the ropeway is about 20 minutes' walk northeast of Onomichi Station. The easiest way to approach the trek is with an English-language map from the tourist information center in hand.

Food

YASUHIRO

1-10-12 Tsuchido; tel. 0848/22-5639; https://yasuhiro.co4.jp; 11:30am-2pm and 5pm-9pm (last order 8:30pm) Tues.-Sun., closed on Tues. if Mon. is a holiday; lunch sets from ¥1,650, dinner courses from ¥5,400; walk 6 minutes east of Onomichi Station

This mom-and-pop sushi shop near the waterfront has been in business for upward of five decades. The menu includes a good range of rice bowls, sushi platters, tempura, set meals, and more. The quality of the fish used has garnered a loyal following. Lunchtime prices are more affordable. There's a good English-language menu on the website.

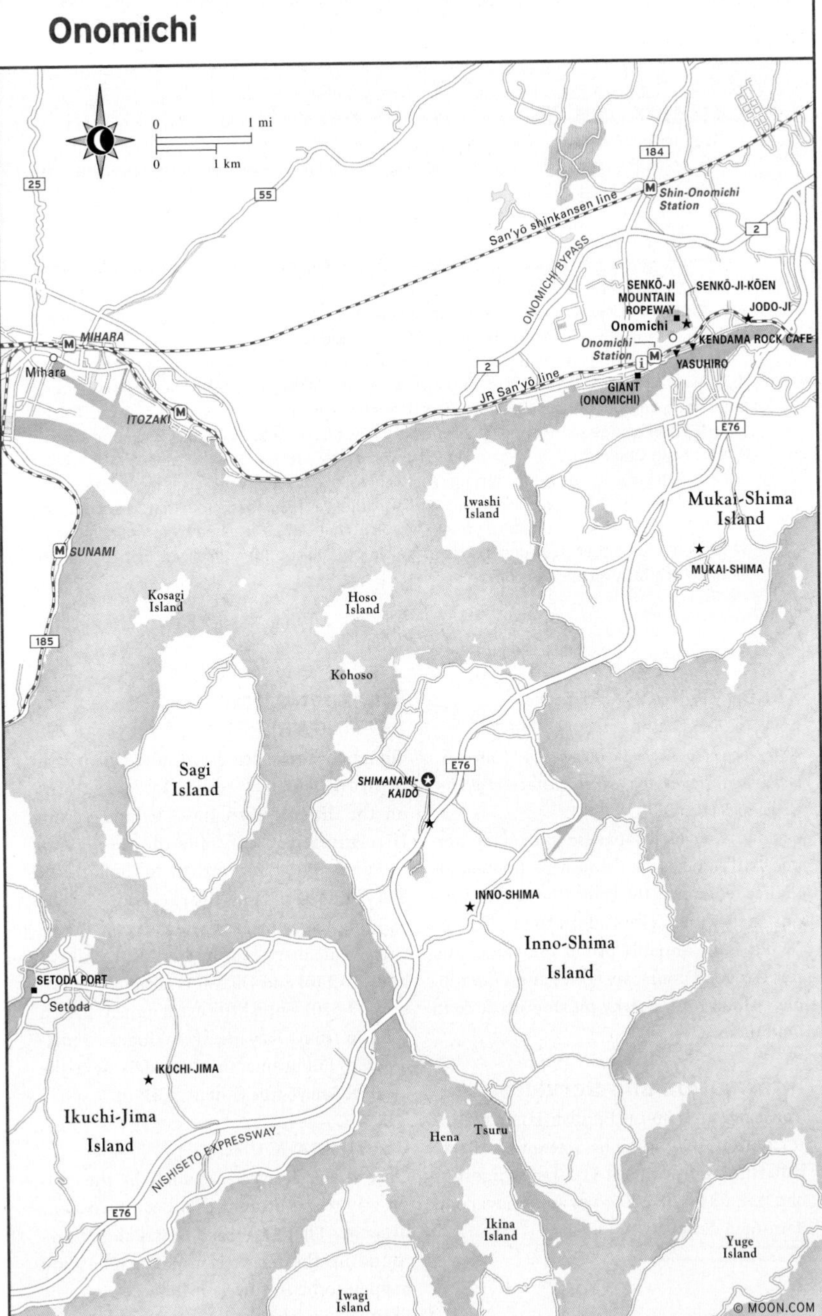

Onomichi
0
1 mi
0
1 km
25
55
184
Shin-Onomichi Station
San'yō shinkansen line
2
ONOMICHI BYPASS
SENKŌ-JI MOUNTAIN ROPEWAY
SENKŌ-JI-KŌEN
JODO-JI
Onomichi
Onomichi Station
KENDAMA ROCK CAFE
YASUHIRO
GIANT (ONOMICHI)
JR San'yō line
MIHARA
Mihara
ITOZAKI
E76
Iwashi Island
Mukai-Shima Island
MUKAI-SHIMA
SUNAMI
Kosagi Island
Hoso Island
185
Kohoso
Sagi Island
SHIMANAMI-KAIDŌ
INNO-SHIMA
Inno-Shima Island
SETODA PORT
Setoda
IKUCHI-JIMA
Ikuchi-Jima Island
NISHISETO EXPRESSWAY
Hena
Tsuru
Ikina Island
Yuge Island
Iwagi Island
© MOON.COM

☆ Cycling Across the Inland Sea

Extending southward from near Onomichi's ferry terminal, a route known as the **Shimanami-kaidō** (**しまなみ海道**, Shimanami Sea Route) links six picturesque islands via nine massive bridges, terminating in the town of Imabari in northwest Shikoku's Ehime Prefecture. The roadway takes in sublime stretches of the Inland Sea. A breathtaking way to enjoy this route, when the weather cooperates, is by bicycle.

THE ROUTE

The islands crossed, from north to south, are **Mukai-shima, Inno-shima, Ikuchi-jima, Ōmi-shima, Hakata-jima,** and **Oshima.** The bridges that link them are engineering marvels. Tolls for cyclists have been waived on the bridges for some time, although there's a chance they could be in effect in the future (up to ¥200 per bridge).

There's no "right" way to travel this route, although the recommended course is well marked. If you want to cycle all the way from Onomichi to Imabari (**今治**), the 70km (43mi) trip takes about eight hours without pit stops. Many cyclists prefer to spend a night on one of the islands, Ikuchi-jima (**生口島**) being a prime spot. Others go part-way, then take the ferry back to Onomichi.

Starting in Onomichi, you'll first need to hop on a **ferry** to nearby Mukai-shima (¥70-110 per person with bicycle). The bridge linking Onomichi to Mukai-shima doesn't allow pedestrians or cyclists. From Mukai-shima, you're free to pedal all the way to Imabari. Note that **Setoda Port** on Ikuchi-jima is the island farthest from Onomichi that can be reached by ferry (40 minutes; ¥1,200; boats depart every hour or two); this is an important consideration if you plan to return to Onomichi by ferry on the same day.

KENDAMA ROCK CAFE

1-17-13 Tsuchido, Onomichi; tel. 0848/24-8180; www.kendamarock.com; 11am-6pm daily; drinks and desserts from ¥500; walk 11 minutes east of Onomichi Station

Kendama, a classic Japanese spin on the cup-and-ball game, is the theme here. Rows of the kit needed to play the game (the *ken*) in various shapes and colors adorn the walls. The owner is an amiable pro at the game, and serves a good pour-over coffee and a few nibbles. Good for a quirky pit stop if you're in Onomichi.

Information and Services

You can stock up on English-language information at Onomichi Station's **tourist information counter** (1-1 Higashigoshochō, tel. 0848/20-0005; www.ononavi.com; 9am-6pm daily).

Transportation

GETTING THERE

Onomichi's core centers around **Onomichi Station,** which is served by local trains on the **JR Sany'yō line.** Coming from Hiroshima, you can take the *shinkansen* to Fukuyama, then transfer to the local JR San'yō line bound for Mihara (1 hour; ¥5,280). Coming from the east, you can take the JR San'yō line directly from both Kurashiki (1 hour; ¥1,140) and Okayama (1 hour 20 minutes; ¥1,320). For a little extra money, hasten the trip from Okayama by taking the *shinkansen* to Fukuyama, then transferring to the local JR San'yō line (1 hour; ¥3,370).

GETTING AROUND

Once you've arrived in Onomichi, the easiest way to get around is either **on foot** or **bicycle.** There are bike rental shops surrounding the ferry terminal. And if you happen to be in town on the weekend, the **Skip Line** is a bus route that runs clockwise

RENTALS AND INFORMATION

You can rent a bicycle and pick up a map of the route at a variety of **bicycle terminals** in Onomichi and on some of the islands (¥1,000 per day, plus ¥1,000 deposit, refundable if bicycle is returned to same terminal). Reserving a bicycle online (http://shimanami-cycle.or.jp/rental/english) is recommended during high season. If you prefer a fancier steed and don't mind paying a premium, **Giant** (https://bicyclerental.jp/en/; from ¥4,000 per day) has rental outlets in both Onomichi and Imabari.

You can leave your luggage in a locker at most bicycle terminals if you plan to do a return trip. If you plan to forge onward, a popular luggage forwarding service is **Kuro Neko** (www.kuronekoyamato.co.jp; from ¥1,000), which sends packages overnight to and from select convenience stores. Catering specifically to the Shimanami-kaidō, **Sagawa Express** (www.sagawa-exp.co.jp/stc/english/) allows you to send luggage between participating hotels in both Onomichi and Imabari.

view of the Inland Sea near the start of Shimanami-kaidō

For general information on the route, including a downloadable English map, visit www.go-shimanami.jp. The friendly **tourist information office** in Onomichi can also provide any information you need.

through the heart of town, starting from Onomichi Station. Buses leave every 30 minutes (single ride ¥140, 1-day pass ¥500; 9:30am-4:30pm Sat.-Sun.).

KURASHIKI
倉敷

About an hour west of Okayama by train, the Bikan historical district in the town of Kurashiki looks like it was designed for a leisurely stroll. The "Kura" in Kurashiki ("storehouse") relates to the fact that the town was replete with storehouses full of rice during the Edo period (1603-1868). The charming canal that runs through the center of downtown Kurashiki was one of the arteries used to transport rice to port.

The quaint townscape left over from the town's affluent heyday has attracted a bustling tourist trade. The most scenic part of the canal district is the **Bikan Historical Quarter,** spanned by stone bridges and fringed by hanging willow branches. Starting at the canal's northern end at the **Ōhara Museum of Art,** slowly amble beside the canal and take in the old-world ambience conjured by the white-plaster storefronts and black-tile roofs. A number of small museums with collections of folk crafts and old-fashioned toys are housed in some of the district's old storehouses, along with cafés, restaurants, and boutiques. Also atmospheric is Kurashiki's **Ivy Square,** a former spinning mill whose ivy-covered brick buildings now house restaurants, small museums, and a hotel.

The Bikan neighborhood is located about 10 minutes' walk southeast of JR Kurashiki Station. Though the town can easily be seen in a day, it can get packed in the afternoon. To experience its subtler magic, try to stay for one night at one of the town's many charming *ryokan*. After the tourists depart, take a long stroll along the canal and you'll be mesmerized by the soft light from the street lamps dancing in the water. A caveat: If you choose to visit Kurashiki, avoid arriving on a Monday, when many of the town's shops close.

Sights

ŌHARA MUSEUM OF ART
大原美術館

1-1-15 Chūō; tel. 086/422-0005; www.ohara.or.jp; 9am-5pm Tues.-Sun., last admission 4:30pm; ¥1,300 adults, ¥800 university students, high/junior high/ elementary school students ¥500; walk 12 minutes southeast of Kurashiki Station

If you've traveled in Paris or visited some of New York's fantastic museums of Western art, this charming complex in Kurashiki may slightly underwhelm. But this was the first museum in Japan dedicated to Western art, founded in 1930. Local textile tycoon Ōhara Magosaburō (1880-1943) and local artist Kojima Torajirō (1881-1929) teamed up to assemble a collection of works by artists including Picasso, Gauguin, Modigliani, Matisse, Rodin, El Greco, Pollock, Warhol, and more. Even a canvas containing some of Monet's immortal water lilies resides here, apparently purchased directly from the French Impressionist himself. The Western art is concentrated in the Main Gallery. The museum is spread across three buildings that sit side-by-side along the canal.

For a change of pace, two buildings adjacent to the Main Gallery house the museum's Craft Art Gallery, which displays Japanese works from woodblock prints to pottery, while the Asiatic Art Gallery exhibits antiquities from China and from countries as far away as Egypt.

Food

★ TAKADAYA

11-36 Hon-machi; tel. 086/425-9262; www3.kct.ne.jp/~takataya_ikunoya/index.htm; 5pm-10pm Tues.-Sun.; skewers ¥120-420, courses ¥1,000-2,000; walk 15 minutes southeast of Kurashiki Station

This cozy restaurant oozes retro charm. The outside is appropriately storehouse-chic, while its interior is mostly dark wood, with slightly dim lighting and plenty of crumbling beer posters. The menu includes all forms of meat on skewers, alongside varied side dishes of vegetables, tofu, rice, and more. There's a good list of cocktails on offer as well. There's seating at tables, in tatami rooms, and at the counter. English menu available. Look for the blue *noren* (curtain). It's about 4 minutes' walk from Ōhara Museum of Art. Recommended.

MIYAKE SHOTEN

3-11 Hon-machi; tel. 086/426-4600; www.miyakeshouten.com; 11:30am-5pm Mon.-Fri., 11am-8pm Sat., 8:30am-5pm Sun. Dec.-Feb.; 11:30am-5:30pm Mon.-Fri., 11am-8pm Sat., 8:30am-5:30pm Sun. Mar.-Jun. and Oct.-Nov.; 11:30am-6pm Mon.-Fri., 11am-8pm Sat., 8:30am-6pm Sun. Jul.-Sept.; set meals ¥900-1,450, desserts ¥500-950; walk 13 minutes southeast of Kurashiki Station

This shop serves one main dish and does it well: Japanese-style vegetable curry over brown rice. The set meals include side dishes of pickled vegetables. The menu also includes coffee and desserts. The ambience is cozy and classic: wood beams and furniture, *fusama* (sliding doors), and a mixture of seating at tables and on the floor. It's tucked behind a classic storefront with a white *noren* bearing the restaurant's name. This is a good spot for a healthy lunch, situated on a street running parallel to the canal.

KURASHIKI COFFEE-KAN

4-1 Hon-machi; tel. 086/424-5516; www.kurashiki-coffeekan.com; 10am-5pm daily; ¥570-980; walk 13 minutes southeast of Kurashiki Station

In this 19th-century building with a warm interior—exposed brick, dark-wood countertop, exposed wooden beams—the brew is high-grade, with prices to match. The menu only includes coffee, both hot and iced, so this is just a spot to take a quiet break from the crowds. When the weather's nice, there's an atmospheric inner courtyard with outdoor seating. Look for the arched doorway, fronted by a red iron gate facing the canal.

Accommodations

★ GUESTHOUSE YUURIN-AN

2-15 Hon-machi; tel. 086/426-1180; www.u-rin.com; dorms ¥3,850, private rooms ¥4,600 pp (2- to 3-person occupancy)

If you're interested in meeting fellow travelers and interacting with friendly, welcoming hosts, this is your place. Housed in a century-old home in the heart of the historic district, a stone's throw from the canal, this charming guesthouse offers a mix of dorm and private rooms, with communal bathrooms. Just the right degree of renovation has left the original house intact, meaning rooms are separated by sliding doors (the communal vibe is real). The lounge, which serves drinks and simple but tasty fare, is a nice place to unwind and mingle.

★ RYOKAN KURASHIKI

4-1 Honmachi; tel. 086/422-0730; www.ryokan-kurashiki.jp; ¥36,000 pp with 2 meals

Right next to Kurashiki Coffee-kan, this luxurious timepiece is the finest accommodation in town. The buildings were once storehouses for sugar and rice. Each room has a Western-style bedroom, private bathroom, tatami-floor lounge, plus tastefully chosen artwork, calligraphy, flower arrangements and antique furniture. The kimono-clad staff are supremely attentive and speak some English. Meals served are of the haute *kaiseki* (multi-course) variety, featuring locally caught seafood and seasonal ingredients. If you want to splurge, this is the best place to do so in Kurashiki.

Information and Services

There's a tourist information center is just outside Kurashiki Station inside Kurashiki City Plaza (1-7-2 Achi; tel. 086/424-1220; 9am-6pm daily). Alternatively, head to the information center housed in a Meiji-period building beside the canal in the heart of the historic district (1-4-8 Chūō; tel. 086/422-0542; 9am-6pm daily). You can also visit the town's **Kurashiki Sightseeing Web** (www.kurashiki-tabi.jp), which provides information on what to see and where to shop, eat, and sleep.

Transportation

Kurashiki Station is on the JR San'yō line, southwest of Okayama Station (15 minutes, ¥320) and east of Onomichi (one hour, ¥1,140). About 10 km (6.2 mi) southwest of Kurashiki Station is **Shin-Kurashiki,** a stop on the *shinkansen* line that is directly accessible from **Hiroshima** to the west (1 hour 15 minutes, ¥5,270), among other stations on the San'yō *shinkansen* line, from **Shin-Osaka** in the east to Hakata (Fukuoka) at the western end of the line. The JR San'yō local line links Shin-Kurashiki and Kurashiki stations (10 minutes, ¥200).

Once you're in Kurashiki, exploring the town **on foot** is the only way to go. The narrow back lanes and lazy canal call for sauntering.

OKAYAMA
岡山

Okayama is a compact city with friendly denizens and a mostly sunny sky. The city is most famous for its landscape garden Kōraku-en.

Though Okayama can be seen in a day, it's a pleasant place to spend the night. The area near the city's main train station begins to stir and a nice buzz infuses the air in the evening. More often than not, it's best approached as a brief stop and a convenient transport hub, serving as both a *shinkansen* stop and the station to transfer to the only railway line that links Honshu to Shikoku.

Sights

KŌRAKU-EN
後楽園

1-5 Kōraku-en, Kita-ku; tel. 086/272-1148; https://okayama-korakuen.jp; 7:30am-6pm Mar. 20-Sept. 30 (last admission 5:45pm), 8am-5pm Oct. 1-Mar.19 (last admission 4:45pm); ages 15 and over ¥400, ¥560 for combined admission to castle, under age 15 free

Long considered one of Japan's top three gardens, alongside Mito's Kairaku-en and Kanazawa's Kenroku-en, Kōraku-en straddles

the Asahi River. It was originally built in 1700 by local lord Ikeda Tsunamasa, whose former home, **Okayama Castle** (2-3-1 Marunouchi; 086/225-2096; https://okayama-kanko.net/ujo; 9am-5:30pm daily; ¥300 adults; ¥120 children 6-14 years old), sits beside the lush landscape garden. This black fortress, nicknamed "crow castle," has accents of white and golden fish ornaments curling upward on the corners of its eaves. If you're most interested in seeing it from the outside, the view from the garden suffices.

The garden was opened to the public in 1884, following the dawn of the Meiji era. Although floods in 1934 and World War II bombing marred the grounds, they have been returned to their former state. A large central pond contains a teahouse on pillars. Groves of plum, cherry, apricot, and maple trees and a tea field draw the eye, while shrines and a *Noh* stage add a dose of culture. There's a crane aviary, too. Cherry blossom season in spring and the coming of autumn foliage are popular times to visit the grounds, but they're expansive enough never to feel thronged.

The garden is about 25-30 minutes' walk northeast of Okayama Station. You can also take the Higashiyama tram line to Shiroshita stop (10 minutes; ¥100), from where the castle is about 10 minutes' walk east and the garden's main gate is 10 minutes' walk northeast (via the large bridge). Alternatively, catch the bus that runs several times hourly from Okayama Station bus stop 1 to Kōrakuen-mae bus stop (15 minutes, ¥100), which puts you directly in front of the garden's main gate. Enter via the main entrance, located near the **Okayama Prefectural Museum,** or via the south entrance, near Okayama Castle.

1: Kōraku-en **2:** golden fish sculpture on Okayama Castle's roof

Food

OKABE

1-10-1 Omote-chō; tel. 086/222-1404; http://tofudokoro-okabe.com/shokujidokoro; 11:30am-2pm Mon.-Wed. and Fri.-Sat.; ¥880-970; take the Higashiyama tram line to Kencho-dōri tram stop, then walk 4 minutes northwest

This homey tofu-focused lunch spot is a good option before or after visiting Kōraku-en. There are just three set meals on offer: deep-fried tofu, tofu skin over rice, and the assorted Okabe original set. The food is reasonably priced and tasty. Note that the food is not vegan, as some fish stock is used in the food preparation. English-language menu with pictures is available.

ICHIRIN SHUZO

2-16 Honmachi, Kita-ku; tel. 086/231-0690; www.ichirinshuzo.com; 5pm-midnight Mon.-Sat.; ¥285-1,142 per dish, courses ¥3,000-4,000; 3 minutes' walk east of Okayama Station

This seafood *izakaya* (pub that serves food) is a popular spot serving creative seafood concoctions and more, from fermented soybeans atop squid sashimi to salted mackerel and black pepper-infused pork spare ribs. It gets busy, especially on the weekends, so reserve ahead to be safe.

TORIYOSHI

5-8 Honmachi, Kita-ku; tel. 086/233-1969; 4pm-midnight daily; ¥250-850 per plate; walk 3 minutes east of Okayama Station

Across the street from Ichirin Shuzo, this boisterous *izakaya* is a great place to drink and eat with locals. The menu includes staples like yakitori (grilled chicken on skewers), side salads, grilled fish, sashimi, and more. Come here if you want to supplement your dinner with a steady flow of booze (beer, sake, whisky soda, etc.) and mingle with friendly locals. English menu available.

Peach Boy Momotarō

Momotarō characters on a manhole

The Kibi Plain is said to be where Momotarō, one of Japan's most beloved folk heroes, sprang from a peach, then grew up to save his homeland from marauding ogres. Momotarō—literally: Peach Tarō—holds special status in Japan's rich mythology, along with other heroes and monsters from Astro Boy to Godzilla. You won't have to look far in Okayama Prefecture or Kagawa Prefecture on Shikoku—both considered the peach boy's old stomping grounds—to see his cherubic face plastered on buses, billboards, and manhole covers.

Our hero was said to have been discovered by chance when the peach in which he descended to earth was plucked from a river by a childless, elderly woman, who was washing clothes as the fruit bobbed by. When she and her husband went to eat the fruit, out popped Momotarō. After the kindly older couple raised the boy, he embarked on his hero's journey by venturing to a faraway island to fight a band of three-eyed ogres that plundered the locals' wealth and even ate villagers. Along the way, Momotarō teamed up with a dog who could talk, a pheasant, and a monkey. Together, the motley crew routed the ogres in their lair on a distant isle. They reclaimed the loot previously stolen by the demons and took the chief ogre hostage. Everyone lived happily ever after.

J'S EN

2-10-11 Hokan-cho, Kita-ku; tel. 086/251-0088; http://js-kitchen.jp; 11:30am-2pm lunch, 5pm-10pm dinner daily; lunch sets ¥1,000-2,200, dinner ¥4,000-5,000; walk 10 minutes northwest of Okayama Station

This friendly Korean BBQ (*yakiniku*) joint is an excellent place to sample Okayama beef. The meat is balanced by a healthy range of salads, cabbage, soups, and more. The welcoming staff go out of their way to help you, too. Reserve a day in advance if you can.

Accommodations

If you plan to travel to various towns around Okayama, such as Kurashiki, the city of Okayama itself makes a good base.

TORII-KUGURU GUESTHOUSE AND LOUNGE

4-7-15 Hōkan-chō, Kita-ku; tel. 086/250-2629; http://toriikuguru.com; dorms (mixed and female-only) ¥3,240, private singles ¥4,860, private doubles ¥7,020; walk 13 minutes northwest of Okayama Station

This laid-back, welcoming guesthouse, in an old-school shopping district on the quieter side of town, is a great option for those traveling on a tight budget. The interior is clean and bright with wood floors, tasteful lighting, and shared bathrooms. Uniquely, the guesthouse is situated in Nawate, a petite complex that also includes a lounge and bar. You'll know you've found it when you reach the *torii* gate kept from a shrine that once stood on the plot next to the reception desk.

KŌRAKU HOTEL

5-1 Heiwachō, Kita-ku; tel. 086/221-7111; https://hotel.kooraku.co.jp; ¥15,000 room only, ¥17,000 with breakfast; walk 5 minutes east of Okayama Station

This clean, bright midrange hotel has airy, modern rooms with well-appointed bathrooms. The common areas are stylish with a boutique vibe, and there's a restaurant serving Japanese fare on the second floor.

Breakfast plan optional. This is a good mid-priced option in the heart of the entertainment district.

ANA CROWNE PLAZA OKAYAMA

15-1 Ekimoto-machi, Kita-ku; tel. 086/898-1111; www.anacpokayama.com; ¥15,750 room only

This upper-range business hotel just outside the west side of Okayama Station is a great value. The plush rooms are spacious and tastefully decorated. There are three restaurants and a bar with striking views over the city. If you've got the means, book one of the south-facing premium rooms for the best views and the added space.

Information and Services

Keeping with the theme of the region's favorite folk hero, the **Momotarō Tourist Information Center** (tel. 086/222-2912; www.okayama-kanko.net; 9am-8pm daily) is situated near the east exit of bustling Okayama Station, in the underground shopping complex. Staff speak some English. This is the best place to pick up information on the city and surroundings. Online, the official **Explore Okayama** website (www.okayama-japan.jp/en) is a useful resource, too.

Transportation

GETTING THERE

Its position on the *shinkansen* line and local JR San'yō line makes Okayama easily accessible by **rail.** Coming from the east, a number of major hubs are accessible via *shinkansen:* **Osaka** (50 minutes, ¥6,020), **Kyoto** (1 hour, ¥7,850), and **Tokyo** (3 hours 30 minutes, ¥17,340). Lying to the west is **Hiroshima** (40 minutes, ¥6,230).

It's also possible to make the leap across the Inland Sea by rail. Okayama is connected to **Takamatsu** on Shikoku (1 hour, ¥2,030) via the JR Marine Liner, and to **Tokushima** (2 hours, ¥5,200) via the Uzushio limited express train.

GETTING AROUND

Okayama is a very **walkable** city. That said, Kōrakuen is about 20 minutes on foot from the main station. To cut your walking time to a manageable level, hop on the city's efficient **tram network** (all rides within downtown ¥100). The Higashiyama line runs all the way up the main thoroughfare of Momotarō-dōri to the gently flowing Asahi-gawa near both the garden and castle.

Another good way to get around is on two wheels. There are many **bicycle** rental shops scattered around the east side of the station. Try **Eki Rinkun** (1-1 Ekimotomachi; tel. 086/223-7081; 7am-9:45pm daily; ¥350 per day).

If you plan to venture into the surrounding countryside, renting a **car** may be the best bet, depending on how far you plan to go. A safe choice is **Toyota Rent-a-Car** (11-10 Ekimotomachi; tel. 086/254-0100; www.rent.toyota.co.jp; 7am-9pm daily).

San'in

MATSUE
松江

Nicknamed the "water city," Matsue is sandwiched between the salt-lake of Nakaumi in the east and Shinji-ko in the west, with the river Ōhashi-gawa running between these two lakes and bisecting the city into northern and southern districts.

The bulk of compact Matsue's sights are located on the north bank of the Ōhashi-gawa. There, you'll find a pristine original black castle and the former **samurai quarter,** lined by a number of well-preserved samurai residences, hidden behind white plaster and wood-paneled walls.

Matsue can easily be seen in a day. It also serves as a good base for exploring regional attractions like the grand shrine of Izumo

Taisha and the Adachi Museum of Art, with its superb landscape garden. If you plan to explore the town and the surrounding area, plan to stay for a night or two.

Sights

★ MATSUE-JŌ
松江城

1-5 Tono-machi; tel. 0852/21-4030; www.matsue-castle.jp; 7am-7:30pm Apr.-Sept., 8:30am-5pm Oct.-Mar.; adults ¥680 (¥330 with foreign passport), junior high and elementary school students ¥290; walk 30 minutes north of Matsue Station, or take the Lake Line bus from Matsue Station to Ōte-mae bus stop (10 minutes; ¥200)

This black castle, constructed with pine timber in 1611, is one of Japan's most atmospheric and well preserved. Local lord Yoshiharu Horio (1542-1611) had the fortress built in 1611. Sitting atop a hill overlooking Matsue, the groaning main tower stands 30 meters (98 feet) tall, second in height among Japan's 12 remaining original castles.

Matsue-jō miraculously withstood the Edo period (1603-1868), the anti-feudal wave of dismantling that ensued following the Meiji Restoration (1868), as well as centuries of earthquakes and fire. Walk through the subdued, pine-studded grounds, across its moat and through its heavily fortified outer walls, and feel the subtle air of mystery surrounding the darkened citadel as you approach it. The requisite display of samurai armor and weaponry is exhibited on the first few floors. Each level reveals more expansive vistas of Matsue and the surrounding countryside, extending as far as Mount Daisen on clear days. If you're visiting Matsue, the castle is a must-see.

To reach the castle, walk 30 minutes northwest of JR Matsue Station, crossing the Ōhashi River on the way. Alternatively, take the Lakeline bus from terminal seven in front of Matsue Station to the Ōte-mae bus stop (13 minutes, ¥150 one way).

ADACHI MUSEUM OF ART
足立美術館

320 Furukawachō, Yasugi; tel. 0854/28-7111; www.adachi-museum.or.jp; 9am-5:30pm Apr.-Sept., 9am-5pm Oct.-Mar.; adults ¥2,300, university students ¥1,800, high school students ¥1,000, junior high and elementary school students ¥500; from Matsue Station, take JR San'in line to Yasugi Station (25 minutes; ¥410), then take museum shuttle bus (20 minutes; free)

Truth be told, the main draw of this museum

Matsue-jō

is not so much its art collection, amassed by local businessman Adachi Zenkō (1899-1991), but its sublime gardens. The museum's collection of more than 1,000 paintings by 20th-century Japanese artists, including Yokoyama Taikan (1868-1958), a painter who played a seminal role in establishing the modern Nihonga movement. Founded in 1980 and located 20 km (12.4 mi) east of Matsue in the town of Yasugi (one hour from Matsue by train), the museum claims the top slot year after year in polls on Japan's top gardens.

Adachi is divided into six separate gardens, each one as fastidiously laid out as the next. Every element is perfectly in its place, from the patterns raked into gravel to the seemingly (though not actually) random placement of orbed shrubs and mountains rising up beyond the garden.

Unlike most formal gardens, this one can only be appreciated from afar. Following an indoor trail of sorts, you pass through passageways walled only by glass on one or both sides, taking in views of the Moss Garden, the Dry Landscape Garden, the Kikaku Waterfall, the Garden of Juryū-an, the Pond Garden, and the White Gravel and Pine Garden. As you proceed through the museum's various stages, you'll take in views of Japanese art dating from the 1870s until today.

Most people visit the museum and its gardens on a day trip from Matsue. Regardless of whether you're stopping in the old castle town to the west, Adachi's collection and remarkable landscape are worth the trip. To reach the museum from Matsue Station, take the JR San'in line to Yasugi Station (about 30 minutes, ¥410). From there, take the free museum shuttle bus that departs from the station twice hourly (20 minutes).

Food

YAKUMO-AN

308 Kitahori-chō; tel. 0852/22-2400; www.yakumoan.jp; 10am-3pm daily; ¥700-1,150

Just beyond the moat on the north side of the castle, next to the Buke Yashiki samurai house, this soba joint serves good set lunches. With its garden and pond filled with colorful carp, the historic building reflects the atmospheric surroundings. Service is good and friendly. There's no English menu, but pictures give a clear indicator of what you're ordering. The *kamo* (duck) soup is delicious. Also on the menu, *warigo* includes three stacked lacquer bowls of soba, into which you pour *dashi* (soup stock), then add seaweed flecks. A queue often forms during the lunch rush, but it moves relatively fast.

★ KAWA-KYŌ

65 Suetsugu Hon-machi; tel. 0852/22-1312; 6pm-10:30pm Mon.-Sat.; ¥800-1,575; walk 20 minutes north of JR Matsue Station

This friendly, family-run restaurant serves up the touted "seven delicacies" of nearby lake Shinji-ko. Among these dishes are a standout called *hosho-yaki,* a style of cooking *suzuki* (sea bass) by swathing it in *washi* (traditional paper) and slow-baking it over heated coals, and broiled *unagi* (freshwater eel) that's been basted in soy sauce. The daughter of the charming family speaks English well. This is a great place to pair your meal with locally produced sake, too. Reserve at least a few days in advance. Highly recommended.

CAFE BAR E.A.D

36 Suetsugu Hon-machi; tel. 0852/28-3130; 9pm-1am Wed.-Mon.; www.facebook.com/eadcafe; ¥300-900 per dish; around the corner from Kawa-kyō

Sitting beside the Ōhashi River, near the eastern edge of Shinji-ko, this café and bar is a good place to eat a casual late-night dinner or unwind over a few drinks. When it's warm, you can also kick back on the rooftop terrace, where the restaurant sometimes holds BBQs and concerts. The food menu includes good pizza and curry with rice.

Accommodations

RYOKAN TERAZUYA

60-3 Tenjin-machi; tel. 0852/21-3480; www.mable.ne.jp/~terazuya; room only ¥4,600 pp, room with breakfast ¥5,300 pp, room with breakfast and dinner ¥9,100 pp; walk 10 minutes southwest of Matsue Station

This inviting family-run *ryokan* is a great option if you're traveling on a budget. The simple, clean tatami rooms all have futons instead of beds, air-conditioning, a shared bathroom. The friendly couple who run the inn speak a smattering of English. Note that there's a curfew of 10pm. If you can accept this doors-closing policy and work with the shared bathroom, it's an excellent place to stay. The owners provide complimentary pickup from the train station.

★ MINAMIKAN

14 Suetsugu Hon-machi; tel; 0852/21-5131; www.minami-g.co.jp/minamikan; ¥45,000 d with two meals; walk 17 minutes from Matsue Station

This plush *ryokan* is Matsue's best hotel. In business for well over a century and renovated in 2007, the lavish property sits at the eastern edge of Shinji-ko, which it overlooks. The aesthetic is distinctly classical, from the beautiful garden of white gravel dotted by stone lanterns and pine trees to the tatami rooms of varying grades (and prices): some more Western, others strictly classic. The simpler rooms are tatami-mat affairs. At the upper end, rooms come with en-suite cypress *onsen* bathtubs fronted by lake-facing windows. The entire property is non-smoking. It's located a stone's throw from the popular local restaurant Kawa-kyō.

Information and Services

There's a friendly **tourist information center** just in front of the north exit of Matsue Station (665 Asahi-machi; tel. 0852/21-4034; www.kankou-matsue.jp; 9am-6pm daily). English speaking staff are happy to give advice on sights and transportation. There's free Wi-Fi on-site.

For a good online guide to Matsue and to Shimane Prefecture as a whole—encompassing Izumo and the Oki Islands—visit Shimane's helpful English website at www.kankou-shimane.com/en.

Transportation

GETTING THERE

Matsue is best reached by **train.** The closest *shinkansen* stop is actually on the opposite San'yō coast in **Okayama,** which is where you should head if you're approaching from anywhere to the east (Kyoto, Osaka, and beyond) or from the west (Hiroshima, Hakata). You can reach Matsue from Okayama Station via the **Yakumo limited express train** (2 hours 40 minutes, ¥6,030), or by **local train** via Yonago, taking the JR Hakubi line from Okayama to Yonago and then transferring to the JR San'in line, which you'll ride until Matsue (5 hours, ¥3,350). Given the time it takes to travel by local train, the limited express, covered by the JR pass, is an attractive option.

Matsue Station is on the JR San'in line, which runs from Tottori in the east, continuing west along the Sea of Japan coast. From Tottori, which lies to the east of Matsue, take the JR San'in line all the way (3 hours 15 minutes, ¥2,270), transferring at Yonago to the next stretch of the line bound for Nishi-Izumo. You can cut the time required for this journey by hopping on the **Super Matsukaze limited express,** which goes directly from Tottori to Matsue (1 hour 30 minutes, ¥4,620). Coming from Izumo in the west, take either the local JR San'in line (40 minutes, ¥580) or the Yakumo limited express (25 minutes, ¥1,850) from Izumo-shi Station to Matsue Station. The limited express trains are good options for holders of the JR pass.

Taking the train is the most comfortable, efficient way of reaching Matsue, but there is a **bus terminal** next to Matsue Station. Visit the website of the **Chūgoku JR Bus Company** (www.chugoku-jrbus.co.jp) for detailed routes, timetables, and fares.

GETTING AROUND

Matsue is a very **walkable** city. It's about 30 minutes on foot from Matsue Station to the castle.

The **Lakeside Line** bus follows a circuit around town, stopping at the castle and neighboring samurai quarter (www.visit-matsue.com/info/moving; 8:40am-6:48pm daily Mar.-Nov., 8:40am-4:58pm Dec.-Feb.; single ride ¥200, day pass ¥500). Buses depart every 20 minutes, and riding the full route takes about 50 minutes.

Another great way to explore Matsue is on two wheels. **Bicycle rentals** are available outside both Matsue Station and Matsue Shinji-ko Onsen Station. A good bet is **Eki Rent-a-Cycle** (483-5 Asahi-machi; tel. 0852/23-8880; 9am-5pm daily), located just outside the south exit of Matsue Station. Just around the corner you'll find **Times Car Rental** (466-1 Asahi-machi; tel. 0852/24-4534; https://rental.timescar.jp/shimane/shop/3201; 8am-7pm), which also rents bicycles. Note that both of these outfits rent cars, too, in case you want to venture farther afield.

IZUMO
出雲

The charming town of Izumo, located about a half-hour train ride west of Matsue on the pastoral San'in coast, is primarily known for its myth-infused grand shrine, Izumo Taisha. After Ise Jingu, Izumo Taisha is Shinto's second holiest shrine and is believed to be its oldest. The main deity enshrined at this sprawling complex is the god of marriage and relationships, Ōkuninushi. Beside the shrine, the Shimane Museum of Ancient Izumo illuminates the region's primeval past, as well as the construction and gradual evolution of this monumentally important shrine. With its compact size, Izumo is an easy day trip from Matsue.

Sights

★ IZUMO TAISHA
出雲大社

195 Kizukihigashi, Taisha-chō; tel. 0853/53-3100; www.izumooyashiro.or.jp; 8:30am-5pm daily; free; walk 5 minutes north of Izumotaisha-mae Station (Ichibata Densa-Taisha line)

Izumo Taisha is Japan's oldest Shinto shrine, and second only to Ise-Jingu in cultural importance. Its history stretches back so far into antiquity that the founding of the shrine is almost indistinguishable from the beginnings of Japan itself. It's mentioned in the 8th-century *Kojiki,* Japan's earliest

Izumo Taisha

penned chronicle, which tells us that it dates at least as far back as the early part of that century.

The setting is lovely, with verdant mountains hovering in the background just beyond the grounds. On the approach to the shrine, walk along either side of a long avenue lined by pine trees, but whatever you do, don't walk in the middle: This walkway is reserved for the gods.

The main hall, constructed in 1744, is 23.8 meters (78 feet) tall. Until that time, it was rebuilt semi-regularly, much like Ise-Jingu still is today. In ancient times, it was the largest wooden structure in Japan, but was scaled down by half with each successive rebuilding, starting in the 13th century. At its highest point, the main hall was said to have been as tall as 48 meters (157.5 feet). The main hall's most distinguishing feature today is the 7.6-meter-long (25-foot), five-ton *shimenawa* (braided straw rope) festooned above the main entrance. As in the shrine's counterpart in Ise, it's forbidden for commoners to enter the inner sanctum, which sits tucked away behind towering fences.

The shrine's principle deity is Ōkuninushi ("Great Land Master"), the god of marriage and fortune, and legend tells us, the creator of Japan's geographical contours and onetime ruler of Izumo. Worshippers visiting the shrine clap their hands four times instead of two, as is customary in Shinto, when summoning Ōkuninushi. Two claps are reserved for themselves, and the other two for their hoped-for or current partner. In addition to praying for success in marriage, if you can manage to chuck a ¥5 piece and lodge it into the mammoth rope overhanging the entrance—no small feat—it's said that you'll be blessed with good fortune and your marriage will be relatively smooth sailing. It's worth a shot!

The shrine is located more than 9 km (5.6 mi) northwest of Izumo-shi Station. To reach the shrine, catch a bus in front of Izumo-shi Station at stop number one (25 minutes ¥520 one way). Buses leave about twice hourly. Alternatively, take the local Ichibata railway line from Izumo-shi Station to Izumo Taisa-mae Station (20 minutes, ¥490 one way). The shrine is about 10 minutes' walk north of there.

SHIMANE MUSEUM OF ANCIENT IZUMO
島根県立古代出雲歴史博物館

99-4 Kizukihigashi, Taisha-chō; tel. 0853/53-8600; www.izm.ed.jp; 9am-6pm Mar.-Oct., 9am-5pm Nov.-Feb., closed third Tues. of month; adults ¥300, university students ¥200, high/junior high/elementary school students ¥100; walk 10 minutes north of Izumo Taisha-mae Station (Ichibata Densa-Taisha line)

Sitting on the right side of the main gate to Izumo Taisha, this museum illuminates Izumo's rich history. Bronze bells and swords unearthed in the area date back to the Yayoi period (300 BC-AD 300). The focus of the museum, however, is on the shrine: its evolution over time and the myths attached to it, including the great annual Kamiari Festival, in which Japan's 8 million deities meet in Izumo for a week during the 10th lunar month.

One relic of note is a gigantic pillar that measures a full meter (3.3 feet) in circumference. The discovery of pillars of such mammoth proportions, among other evidence, has led to speculation that the main hall may have been as tall as 48 meters (157.5 feet) at its peak. Models illustrate how this top-heavy construction might have looked. From the displays, it's easy to see why it is said to have collapsed under its own weight five times between the 11th and 13th centuries.

Festivals

KAMIARI-SAI
神在祭

Seven days (11-17) of the 10th lunar month

According to legend, Ōkuninushi relinquished control of Izumo to the lineage of Amaterasu (sun goddess) in exchange for the founding of a grand shrine for him. Every year during the 10th lunar month, which is

Tottori Sand Dunes

Tottori is Japan's most sparsely populated prefecture, a tiny sliver of land populated by warm-hearted locals with a singular claim to fame: massive hills of sand. Running along 16 km (10 mi) of coastline just north of the capital city of the same name, the *sakyu* (dunes) sprawl across more than 30 square km (12 square mi). The dunes are part of the San'in Kaigan National Park, a wild stretch of shoreline that runs from the city of Tottori in the west to Kyōtango in Kyoto Prefecture in the east.

This unlikely simulacrum of the Sahara is located about 5 km (3.1 mi) north of town. The massive dunes were created over millennia, as sands from the **Sendaigawa River** were pushed out to sea, only to be brought back to shore by the **Sea of Japan**'s currents. This process of redistribution is ongoing, and the coast of Tottori is always in flux. You can either gaze seaward from atop the dunes or walk along the beachfront. Tour providers in the sand dunes' area offer everything from paragliding and sandboarding to yoga sessions on the dunes and cycling with bikes with special tires that don't get bogged down in the terrain. In the Uradome area, you'll also find sea kayaking outfits. To learn more about the activities available, visit Tottori's **tourist information portal** (www.tottori-tour.jp/en).

Near the east side of the dunes, the **Tottori Sand Museum** (2083-17 Yūyama, Fukube-chō; tel. 0857/20-2231; www.sand-museum.jp; ¥600) houses massive, intricate sand sculptures, based on a central theme, created by artists from all corners of the world. Be sure to check the museum's website to confirm whether it's open during your planned visit. It's located at the eastern edge of the dunes near the intersection of routes 265 and 319.

TRANSPORTATION

Buses from **Tottori Station** run to the **Sakyū Center,** a worn complex atop the dunes with an observation deck and a tacky souvenir shop. From here you can gaze seaward from on high, then either walk down to the beachfront or take a chairlift down. Alternatively, you can take a bus to **Sakyū Kaikan,** which will put you right next to the eastern side of the dunes.

usually November, all 8 million gods and goddesses convene in Izumo to determine the fates of mortals during the year to come. This month is called Kamiarizuki ("month with gods") in Izumo, but Kannazuki ("month without gods") throughout the rest of Japan. The shrine hosts the annual Kamiari Festival during that week. When the gods crowd into Izumo, they stay in the two long buildings that sit along both sides of the complex.

The proceedings are marked with bonfires on the beach and other rituals. During this special month, Izumo Taisha becomes a special place of pilgrimage for marriage-hopefuls. If you're already attached, however, be careful not to come together; it's said that Okuninushi is displeased by those who show up with their partner without first consulting him. As fun as a joint trip to the shrine during Kannazuki may sound, don't tempt fate!

Food

ARAKIYA

409-2 Kizuki-higashi, Taisha-chō; tel. 0853/53-2352; www.izumo-kankou.gr.jp/1640; 11am-5pm Thurs.-Tues., closed Thurs. if Wed. falls on holiday; set meals ¥810-1,490; walk 5 minutes south of Izumo Taisha bus stop, or 10 minutes northwest of Izumo Taisha-mae Station on the Ichibata Densha-Taisha railway line

Housed in a traditional building, this restaurant serves great soba *warigo* style, stacked in three lacquerware boxes. Just pour the soup stock over the noodles and add the seaweed flakes, grated daikon, and chopped green onions. The *kamo* (duck) option is also delicious. A picture menu makes ordering easy. While it has a solid local following and sometimes attracts a slight queue, this restaurant is outside the more bustling tourist zone.

TONKI

1266-2 Tsukane, Imaichi-chō; tel. 0853/21-4395; 5pm-11pm daily; ¥1,100-1,700 set meals; walk 8 minutes north of Izumo-shi Station

This restaurant has the broad menu of an *izakaya,* but is known for its *tonkatsu* (fried, breaded pork cutlet). The easiest thing to do is order a *tonkatsu teishoku* (set meal). There's no English menu, but there are photos. Of the seven types of pork to choose from, the main two worth trying are *hire* (lean, tenderloin) and *rousu* (fatty, loin). If you feel like something else, the menu extends to sashimi, various grilled meat dishes, and other nibbles.

Information and Services

If you're arriving via Izumo-shi Station, stop by the **tourist information office** located in the station (tel. 0853/53-2298; 8:30am-7:30pm daily). Near Izumo Taisha-mae Station, proceed a few minutes north along the main road that leads to the shrine grounds and you'll find a helpful **tourist information center** on the right side of the street (780-4 Kizuki-minami; tel. 0853/53-2298; 9am-5pm daily).

Online, the **Visit Izumo** website (www.izumo-kankou.gr.jp/english) provides plenty of good local intel, from a primer on the region's history and sights off the beaten path to a list of eateries in town.

If you reserve ahead by at least one week, it's possible to arrange for an English-speaking guide to show you around the shrine. For more details, send an email to **Good Will English Guide in Izumo (GoEn)** at izumo-goen@gmail.com.

Transportation

To reach Izumo Taisha from nearby **Matsue,** you can take the JR San'in line from Matsue Station to **Izumo-shi Station** (40 minutes; ¥580), then transfer to the old-school Ichibata line and ride until **Izumo Taisha-mae Station** (20 minutes; ¥490).

Alternatively, you can hop on a **local bus** from Matsue Station to **Matsue Shinji-ko Onsen Station,** which sits at the northeast corner of lake Shinji-ko. From there, you can hop on the Ichibata line and ride directly to Izumo Taisha-mae Station (1 hour, ¥810).

From Izumo Taisha-mae Station, the grounds of Izumo Taisha are about 10 minutes' **walk** north.

Tohoku 東北

Tohoku is old Japan at its best, a land where treasures lie hidden in a rugged landscape of windswept coastline, primeval forests, and impenetrable mountain ranges. The region's climate fluctuates between sweltering summers and severe winters, when some of the heaviest snowfalls on earth, carried by harsh Siberian winds, pile up on the western side of Tohoku's colossal rocky spine.

A wellspring of myth, Tohoku is a place where aquatic monsters await those who stray too close to rural riverbanks, demons visit village homes to frighten children into good behavior every New Year, and shapeshifting fox spirits morph into femme fatales.

Once known as Michinoku (The Interior Road), the region was vividly described by the wandering haiku poet Matsuo Bashō

Highlights

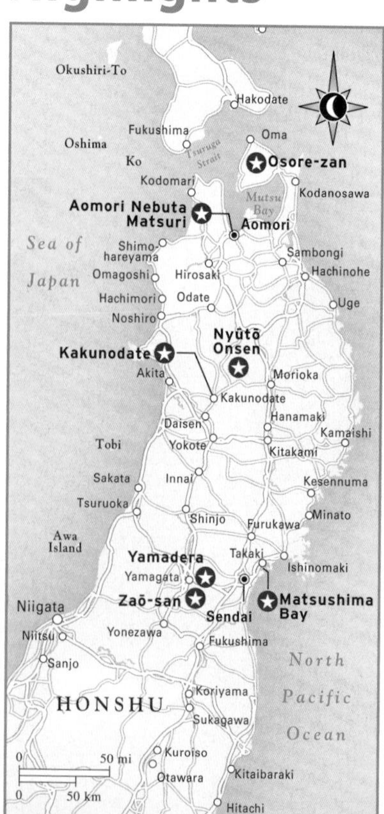

Look for ★ to find recommended sights, activities, dining, and lodging.

★ **Matsushima Bay:** This rugged bay, immortalized by haiku poet Matsuo Bashō during his 17th-century pilgrimage across the region, is dotted by 260 pine-tree-covered islands (page 458).

★ **Yamadera:** Pilgrims who make the steep hike up 1,015 stone steps to this Buddhist temple complex clinging to a mountainside are rewarded with breathtaking views (page 460).

★ **Zaō-san:** This volcano is host to some of Japan's best skiing, and is famed for its "snow monsters" (page 463).

★ **Nyūtō Onsen:** This cluster of rustic hot springs resorts evokes romantic visions of Japan from a bygone era (page 474).

★ **Kakunodate:** This charming town has perhaps the best-preserved samurai heritage in all of Japan (page 475).

★ **Aomori Nebuta Matsuri:** This legendary festival, held every August, features dancers and illuminated floats in Aomori's streets (page 480).

★ **Osore-zan:** "Mount Dread," believed to mark the entrance to Buddhist Hell, is a windswept volcanic landscape at Honshu's northern edge (page 482).

Tohoku

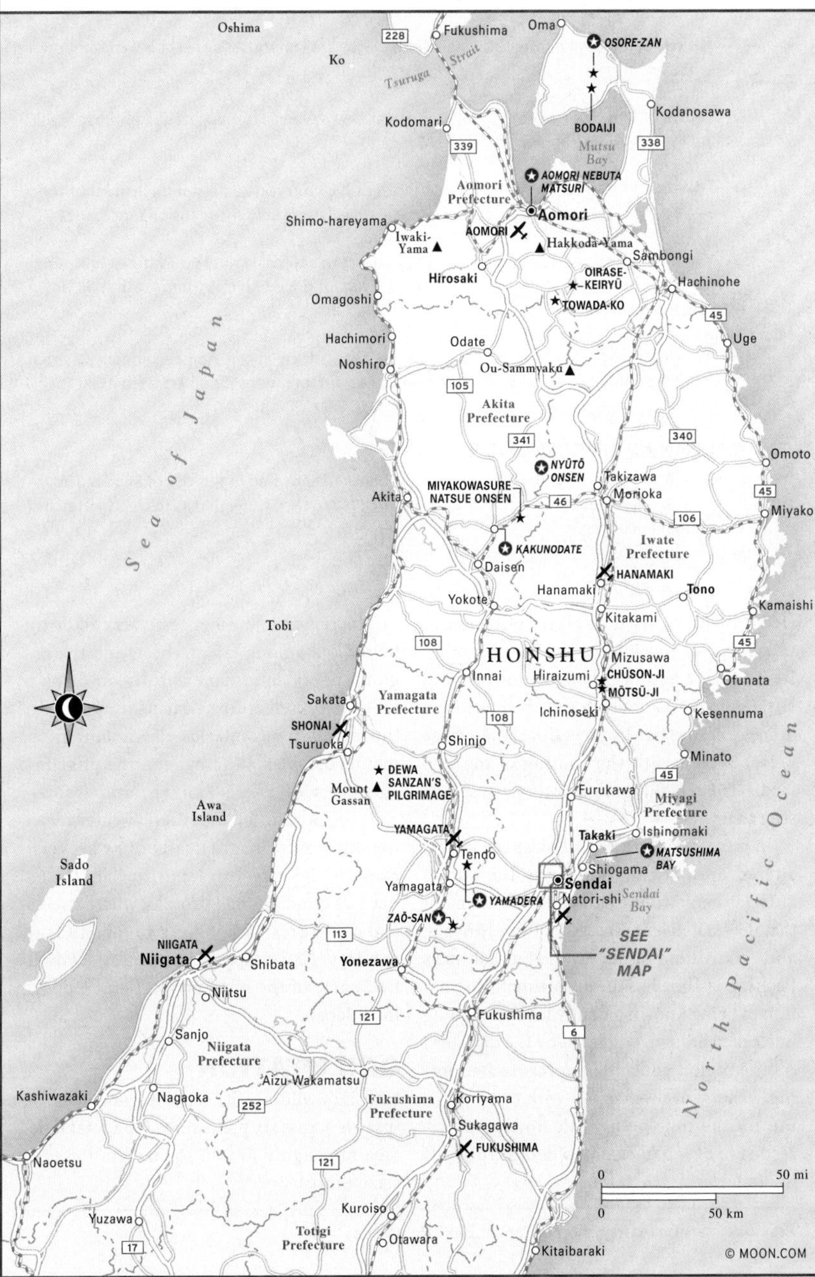
Oshima
Ko
Tsuruga Strait
Fukushima
Oma
OSORE-ZAN
BODAIJI
Kodanosawa
Mutsu Bay
Kodomari
Aomori Prefecture
AOMORI NEBUTA MATSURI
Aomori
Shimo-hareyama
Iwaki-Yama
AOMORI
Hakkoda-Yama
Sambongi
Hirosaki
OIRASE-KEIRYŪ
TOWADA-KO
Hachinohe
Omagoshi
Hachimori
Uge
Odate
Noshiro
Ou-Sammyaku
Sea of Japan
Akita Prefecture
Omoto
NYŪTŌ ONSEN
Takizawa
Morioka
MIYAKOWASURE NATSUE ONSEN
Akita
Miyako
KAKUNODATE
Iwate Prefecture
Daisen
HANAMAKI
Hanamaki
Tono
Yokote
Kitakami
Kamaishi
Tobi
HONSHU
Mizusawa
Innai
Hiraizumi
CHŪSON-JI
MŌTSŪ-JI
Ofunata
Sakata
Yamagata Prefecture
Ichinoseki
Kesennuma
SHONAI
Tsuruoka
Shinjo
Minato
DEWA SANZAN'S PILGRIMAGE
Mount Gassan
Furukawa
Awa Island
Miyagi Prefecture
YAMAGATA
Takaki
Ishinomaki
Tendo
MATSUSHIMA BAY
Shiogama
Sado Island
Yamagata
Sendai
YAMADERA
Natori-shi
Sendai Bay
ZAŌ-SAN
North Pacific Ocean
NIIGATA
Niigata
Shibata
Yonezawa
SEE "SENDAI" MAP
Niitsu
Fukushima
Sanjo
Niigata Prefecture
Aizu-Wakamatsu
Kashiwazaki
Nagaoka
Fukushima Prefecture
Koriyama
Sukagawa
FUKUSHIMA
Naoetsu
0
50 mi
0
50 km
Kuroiso
Yuzawa
Totigi Prefecture
Otawara
Kitaibaraki
228
339
338
45
105
340
341
46
106
108
113
121
6
252
17
© MOON.COM

Best Restaurants

★ **Kaku:** Sample *gyūtan* (beef tongue), Sendai's most famous dish, at this local hot spot (page 456).

★ **Saikan:** Along with sleeping in a temple at Dewa Sanzan, go vegetarian and eat highly refined monk's cuisine known as *shōjin-ryōri* (page 468).

★ **Tonoya Yo:** Go seasonal and local at this stylish countryside eatery in the hamlet of Tōno where a young local chef whips up delicious, creative *kaiseki*-influenced fusion fare (page 471).

★ **Kadare Yokochō:** Squeeze in beside locals at this Hirosaki hot spot, where eight separate eateries serve everything from curry to skewers of grilled chicken, and wash it all down with beer (page 479).

★ **Tsugaru Joppari Isariya Sakaba:** Go deeply local at this Aomori hideout where a master of the three-stringed Tsugaru *jamisen* shreds out folk tunes for diners each night (page 480).

REGIONAL SPECIALTIES

Tohoku classics include ***gyūtan*** (grilled beef tongue), renowned in the city of Sendai. The region is also renowned for the quality of its ***nihonshū,*** or rice wine, thanks to clean water and an abundant rice crop.

(1644-1694) in his immortal collection of verse, *The Narrow Road to the Deep North*. In Bashō's day, a number of mighty towns, from Hiraizumi to Kakunodate and Hirosaki, were home to castles run by powerful clans, whose power waned with the coming of modern Japan. The remains of this history can still be seen today.

In more recent times, Tohoku's image was altered dramatically following the March 2011 9.0-magnitude earthquake and tsunami that devastated large swaths of Iwate, Miyagi, and Fukushima prefectures. (Fukushima's Pacific coastline has the unfortunate distinction of being known globally for the ongoing nuclear meltdown triggered by the disaster.) As the region continues to regain its footing, visitors are welcomed with open arms. But for the time being, this underappreciated side of Japan remains delightfully off the radar.

The region's summer festivals can fairly be ranked among Japan's best, and the region's poetic landscape is fully on display in Miyagi Prefecture's Matsushima Bay. In the mountainous interior, the mountaintop temple complex at Yamadera, the pilgrimage route of Dewa Sanzan, and Osorezan, believed to be an ethereal gateway to the other side, magnetically draw seekers. Running through this landscape are towns like Kakunodate and Hirosaki, where streets and structures harken back to Japan's feudal days. And deep in alpine forests, you'll find some of the most magical *onsen* pools in all Japan.

ORIENTATION

Honshu's wild north, Tohoku ("northeast"), sprawls across six prefectures for a total land area of roughly 67,000 square km (26,000 square mi).

Previous: Matsushima Bay; snow on Mount Zaō; Kakunodate

Best Accommodations

★ **Miyamaso Takamiya:** This four-century-old *ryokan* has it all: curative *onsen* baths, haute cuisine, and easy access to spectacular ski slopes (page 466).

★ **Kuranoya:** Discover the laidback charms of Tōno that lured the amiable owners away from Tokyo's rat race to start this charming countryside inn (page 471).

★ **Tsurunoyu Onsen:** This rustic *ryokan* in the Nyūtō Onsen area, known for its milky waters, is home to one of the most picture-perfect *onsen* pools in all of Japan (page 474).

★ **Taenoyu:** With chic, *tatami*-mat rooms and an outdoor *onsen* bath facing a waterfall enshrouded by forested hills, this hot-spring retreat in the Nyūtō Onsen area is an ideal escape from the workaday world (page 474).

★ **Ishiba Ryokan:** With a few centuries of history behind it, this welcoming inn looks onto a serene garden, with Hirosaki Castle just a brief stroll away (page 482).

Miyagi Prefecture is the gateway to Tohoku for many travelers; it contains Tohoku's largest city, **Sendai,** which can be reached from Tokyo in around 90 minutes by *shinkansen,* and **Matsushima Bay**. Moving west, **Yamagata Prefecture**, where you can find the temple complex of **Yamadera** and the holy mountains of **Dewa Sanzan,** borders the Sea of Japan. **Zaō-san,** a picturesque volcano, straddles the border of Miyagi and Yamagata prefectures.

Tohoku's dramatic Sanriku coastline begins along Miyagi's Pacific coastline and stretches northward into **Iwate Prefecture**, which is home to **Hiraizumi** and **Tōno.** Moving west, on the Sea of Japan side, the pastoral landscape of **Akita Prefecture** is known for its summer festivals, *onsen,* and rice. **Morioka,** the capital of Iwate Prefecture with a population just shy of 300,000, is a straight shot on the *shinkansen,* 2.5 hours north of Tokyo. This is less a sightseeing destination than a transit hub, and you'll likely pass through it in order to access Iwate and Akita's stunning natural beauty.

North of Iwate, weather-beaten coastline of **Aomori Prefecture** extends from the Pacific in the east, to the Tsugaru Strait in the north, dividing Honshu from Hokkaido, with the Sea of Japan lying to the west. Aomori is known for its ancient castle town of **Hirosaki, festivals** in Aomori city and Akita, and the volcanic landscape of **Osore-zan.**

PLANNING YOUR TIME

Given the effort required to reach some of Tohoku's most magical spots, it's best to set aside a fair amount of time to truly experience them. But if you're keen to explore one of Japan's least visited, most rewarding regions, plan to spend anywhere from **three days** to **a week or more** discovering the secrets of Honshu's deep north. A foray into Tohoku works best as a multiday excursion from Tokyo, a leg of a journey to or from Hokkaido, or as a stand-alone trip.

Tohoku's largest city, **Sendai,** serves as a good base to for day trips to **Matsushima Bay** and **Yamadera.** The **Zaō Onsen** area offers excellent skiing in winter, hiking in the warmer months, and *onsen* resorts year-round. In neighboring Yamagata Prefecture, the three holy mountains of **Dewa Sanzan** make for a great day hike.

Back on the Tohoku *shinkansen* (bullet train), the historically rich towns of **Hiraizumi, Tōno,** coastal **Miyako,** *onsen* town **Tazawa-ko,** and samurai town **Kakunodate** can all be explored in about a day each, though you might be tempted to stay a night or two if you feel like slowing down and enjoying the countryside.

Aomori Prefecture rewards those intrepid enough to forge into Tohoku's northern edge, with the ancient castle town of **Hirosaki** and the desolately beautiful volcanic landscape of **Osore-zan** beckoning seekers of the mysteries of the afterlife.

Visiting Tohoku involves considerable **train travel.** Two *shinkansen* lines link Tokyo to the region. The **Tohoku line** runs northeast to Sendai before continuing on to Morioka, Hachinohe, and Shin-Aomori. Separate regional *shinkansen* lines provide direct access to Yamagata and Akita. Local train lines also branch off the *shinkansen* tracks to provide links to regional towns such as Tōno, Hirosaki, and beyond.

If you'll be driving in the region, it's worth looking into the **Tohoku Express Pass** (www.go-etc.jp/english/expressway/index.html), which allows for unlimited use of Tohoku's expressways. Having your own wheels comes in handy if you're visiting particularly remote areas, such as Dewa Sanzan, Nyūtō Onsen, or Osore-zan, where public transport links are limited. However, if you're sticking to the region's cities and many of its smaller towns, opt to travel by train.

More so than in most parts of Japan, time of year is key in Tohoku, which is most magical during **winter,** when skiers shred through some of the world's best snow before retiring to secluded hot springs. In **summer,** Tohoku's mountains are crisscrossed by excellent hiking trails, and in its cities and towns, festivals reveal the region's wild side. Though the region is delightfully off the tourist track for much of the year, popular *onsen* resorts book up fast in winter, as do hotels during popular summer festivals. Also bear in mind that winter is so extreme in some parts of Tohoku that entire areas, including parts of Dewa Sanzan and much of the Shimokita Peninsula, are inaccessible from roughly December through March.

Sendai 仙台

Sendai is Tohoku's largest metropolis and the capital of Miyagi Prefecture, with a population of more than 1 million. This city may have an urban sheen, but dig deeper and you'll discover a rural core and welcoming people. A smile and openness go a long way here.

Sendai is laid out in a grid, with numerous tree-lined boulevards and abundant parks, earning it the nickname "City of Trees." Its history is deeply entwined with the once great Date clan, and Sendai still bears the fingerprints of its founder, the dynamic feudal lord Date Masamune (aka the "one-eyed dragon"). His fearsome nickname refers to the story that he plucked out his own right eye after being struck by smallpox as a youth.

Tohoku thrived for some 270 years, with the Date clan at the helm, but its influence waned following the Meiji Restoration. Mostly razed in World War II bombing raids, Sendai has few historical sites today, though the ruins of Aoba Castle are worth visiting. More recently, the city was front and center when the devastating earthquake and tsunami struck the east coast of northern Honshu in March 2011, but Sendai is miraculously back on its feet. Public transport networks, which took a heavy blow, are all back in working order and there are no visible signs of the disaster in the city center.

The best time to visit Sendai is early August during the famous annual **Tanabata Matsuri.** The city's locals, and throngs of visitors, amass downtown to wander through

Sendai

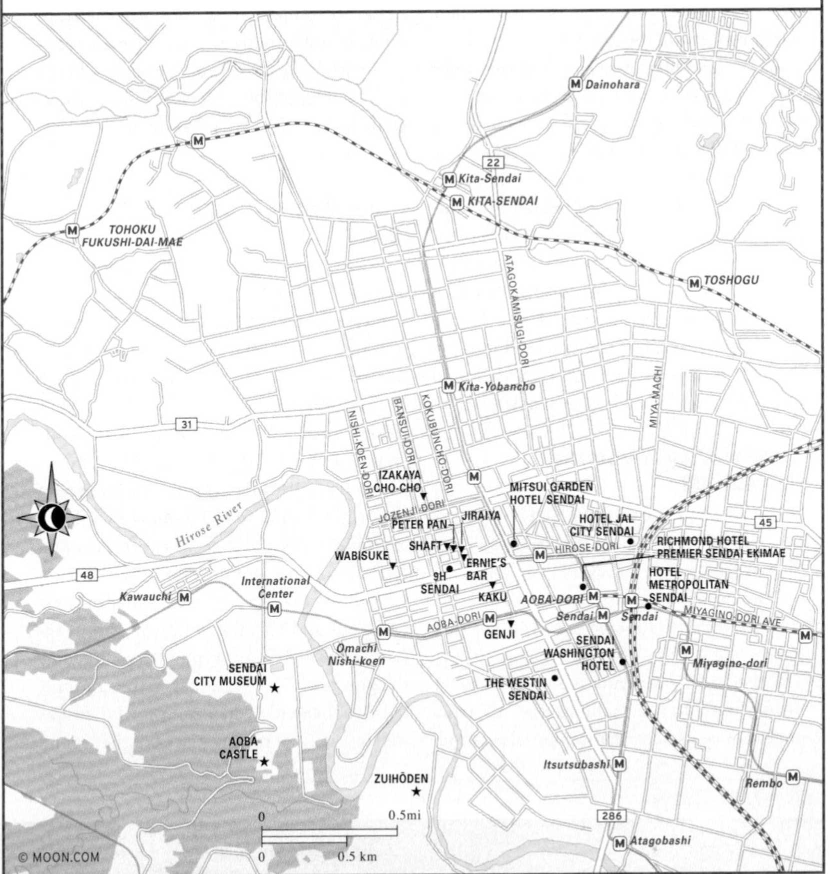

covered shopping streets overhung with huge colorful streamers, write their wishes on strips of paper, and make merry in the streets. In September, the city sees world-class jazz musicians occupy various stages around town to jam in the **Jozenji Streetjazz Festival.** Whatever time of year you find yourself in Sendai, it's a convenient base for making trips elsewhere in the region. Make sure to eat grilled *gyūtan* (beef tongue), the local dish. If you're in town for a night, be sure to stroll through the city's entertainment district, Kokubunchō, the largest nightlife zone between Tokyo and Sapporo.

SIGHTS

Aoba Castle

青葉城

Kawauchi, Aoba-ku; tel. 022/214-8544; www.sendaimiyagidc.jp; 9am-5pm Apr.-Oct., 9am-4pm Nov.-Mar., closed on days after national holidays; ¥700; from Sendai Station, take the Loople Sendai bus (¥260) to bus stop 6 (castle grounds)

Although the ruins of its outer walls and a lone guard tower are the only remains of the mighty fortress that once served as the early 17th-century headquarters of Date Masamune, a visit to Mount Aoba and Aoba Castle offers sweeping views of the cityscape below.

Built in 1600, the stronghold that once loomed above Sendai was ravaged by fire in 1882 and further decimated by bombing toward the end of World War II. Alongside the remnants, a statue of Date dynamically mounted on a horse and kitted out in armor proudly stands on the grounds. If Date's helmet looks familiar, it's likely because it inspired Darth Vader's helmet in *Star Wars*.

Within the grounds you'll also find a museum that recaps the citadel's glory days through models, artifacts, and a brief film in Japanese (English headsets available).

Sendai City Museum
仙台市博物館

26 Kawauchi, Aoba-ku; tel. 022/225-3074; www.city.sendai.jp/museu; 9am-4:45pm Tues.-Sun.; ¥460 adults, ¥230 high school students, ¥110 elementary and junior high school students; from Sendai Station, take the Loople Sendai bus (¥260) to bus stop 5

The Sendai City Museum is a good place for history buffs to get a samurai fix. An array of gear once used by the warrior class, from helmets and armor to weaponry—much of it donated by the Date family—fills this well-designed complex. In addition to the trappings of war, the collection also includes Edo-period costumes and artwork. There's even an interactive section for kids. If you're going to Aoba Castle, it's a pleasant 15-minute walk to the museum.

Zuihōden
瑞鳳殿

23-2 Otamayashita, Aoba-ku; tel. 022/262-6250; www.zuihoden.com; 9am-4:30pm Feb.-Nov., 9am-4pm Dec.-Jan.; ¥550 adults, ¥400 high school students, ¥200 elementary and junior high school students; from Sendai Station, take the Loople Sendai bus (¥260) to bus stop 4

Razed during World War II, the reconstructed mausoleum of Date Masamune, Zuihōden, faithfully captures the essence of the original, built in 1637, and is a textbook example of the florid architectural characteristics of the Momoyama period (1568-1600), overloaded with red, blue, orange, and gold and carvings of birds and dragons. Date's elaborate crypt is surrounded by the graves of Date's retainers (who committed ritual suicide when their lord died), as well as the final resting places of the second

detail of Zuihōden

and third lords in the Date line. It's about a 25-minute walk from the Sendai City Museum.

FESTIVALS

TANABATA MATSURI
七夕まつり

various locations downtown; www.sendaitanabata.com/en; 11am-9pm Aug. 6-8; free

It's all about love at the Tanabata Matsuri (Star Festival), one of Tohoku's biggest summer festivals. The festival revolves around the story of two star-crossed lovers, Princess Orihime (embodied by the star Vega) and the simple country boy Hikoboshi (embodied by Altair). The festival marks the time they are able to meet once a year, barring the interference of clouds.

Sendai's version of the event on August 6-8 elevates the pageantry to an art. Kicking off the festivities on the evening of August 5 (from 7pm), upward of 15,000 fireworks are launched in Nishi-kōen, next to the bank of the Hirose River on the west side of town. On the following day, streamers inscribed with flowery verses are hung from doors, flapping in the breeze. Large multihued balls, filled with spices and herbs, hang from the ceilings of covered pedestrian arcades, warding off demons. The streets fill with sentimental revelers who are encouraged to (literally) wish upon a star by writing out their desires on paper strips known as *tanzaku,* which are then affixed to bamboo strewn throughout the city, and to freely reveal their bottled-up feelings.

JOZENJI STREETJAZZ FESTIVAL
定禅寺ストリートジャズフェスティバル

various locations downtown; www.j-streetjazz.com; second weekend of Sept., hours vary by performance; free

Buskers from across Japan jam in Sendai's downtown, drawing hundreds of thousands to the city center for this impressively free festival. Performances take place in the downtown area in parks, shopping arcades, and beyond, rain or shine. If jazz isn't your thing, there are also performances of other musical genres, from Latin and pop to rock and gospel. The festival is very popular, so you'll have to book your accommodation far in advance (six months or more to be safe).

FOOD

ISSHIN

B1F Jozenji Hills, 3-3-1 Kokubunchō, Aoba-ku; tel. 022/261-9889; 5pm-midnight Mon.-Sat.; ¥8,000; take Nanboku line to Kotodaikoen Station, exit 2

Isshin is famed across Japan among a certain kind of *izakaya* (pub) buff for its meticulous attention to getting food just right. The menu makes good use of local, seasonal ingredients. Complementing the food is an impressive sake menu, which mainly stocks labels from Miyagi Prefecture. Be aware that there is a ¥1,500 entrance fee, but the dish that comes with the fee is almost meal-size.

GENJI

2-4-8 Ichibancho, Aoba-ku; tel. 022/222-8485; 5pm-11pm Mon.-Sat., ¥2,500; take Tozai line to Aoba-dōri Ichibancho Station, exit 1

For a classic greasy-spoon *izakaya,* look no further than Genji. This small dark tavern is tucked down a side street and gets rowdy, thanks in part to its loyal following and the seating arrangement that hugs the counter. The menu is a good mix of Japanese-style pub food—small plates of sashimi, *oden* (boiled eggs, fishcakes, daikon in a soy-flavored broth)—and plenty of sake and beer.

JIRAIYA

2-1-15 Kokubun-chō, Aoba-ku; tel. 022/261-2164; www.jiraiya.com; 5pm-11:30pm Mon.-Sat., 5pm-10:30pm Sun.; ¥2,500; take Nanboku line to Kotodaikoen Station, south exit 2

Jiraiya has a reputation for serving the fresh local catch, grilled over an open fire, and pairing it well with local sake. The specialty is *kinki* (deep water rockfish), skewered whole on a stick and finished off with soup made from the fish's head and bones. Look for the oversized red paper lantern. Reserve a day in advance on weekends.

IZAKAYA CHO-CHO

1F Terrace House, Jozenji, 3-4-27 Kokubunchō, Aoba-ku; tel. 022/395-9150; http://cho-cho.net; 5pm-midnight Sun.-Thurs., 5pm-1am Fri.-Sat.; ¥4,500; take Nanboku line to Kotodaikoen Station, south exit 2

Izakaya Cho-cho has friendly servers who are happy to help you navigate the menu of grilled chicken, fish, sashimi, and heaps of small vegetable dishes, all cooked over an open fire. All varieties of sake, largely including Miyagi-based breweries, are affordably priced at only ¥490 per glass. Reserve a day in advance on weekends.

★ KAKU

3-8-14 Ichibanchō, Aoba-ku; tel. 022/268-7067; http://gyutankaku.in; 11:30am-2:30pm and 5pm-10:30pm Mon.-Sat.; ¥1,700; take Nanboku line to Kotodaikoen Station, south exit 2

Sendai's most famous dish is its *gyūtan*. Ask any local where to go and they'll vote for Kaku, where you can get boiled and grilled beef tongue, served with oxtail soup and crispy pickled cucumbers and cabbage. The menu has photos that make it easy to choose, despite the lack of English. The dish goes well with beer or sake. Note that the restaurant allows smoking.

WABISUKE

6-16 Tachimachi, Aoba-ku; tel. 022/217-8455; 5pm-midnight Mon.-Thurs., 5pm-11pm Sat.; ¥4,500; take Tozai line to Ochonishikoen Station, east exit 1

One more dish that Sendai can claim as its own is *seri nabe,* a style of hot pot that combines duck, tofu, greens, mushrooms, and herbs in a light soup stock made from kelp and bonito flakes. Wabisuke does it best. The flavors are rich but subtle. Traditionally a winter dish, *seri nabe* can be eaten any time of year thanks to its light soup stock.

BARS AND NIGHTLIFE

Sendai is home to Tohoku's biggest entertainment zone, with the bulk of the action taking place in the neon-soaked district of Kokubun-chō, home to a few thousand bars and eateries. This grid of streets, which can become quite raucous on weekends, extends roughly from the streets of Hirose-dōri in the south to Jozenji-dōri in the north. Look past the glut of "pink" establishments and you'll find a few good spots for an evening out.

PETER PAN

2-6-1 Kokubun-chō, Aoba-ku; tel. 022/264-1742; http://peterpan-rock.com; 3pm-10pm Tues.-Thurs. and Sun., 3pm-midnight Fri.-Sat.; ¥500 cover charge after 6pm; take Nanboku line to Hirose-dōri Station, west exit 5

Cafe by day, rock 'n' roll bar by night, this welcoming spot is manned by a father-son duo who delight patrons with the diverse assortment of vinyl, ranging from classic rock to alternative.

ERNIE'S BAR

2-1-11 Kokubun-chō, Aoba-ku; tel. 022/265-2118; https://erniesbar-sendai.com; 6pm-5am daily; take Nanboku line to Hirose-dōri Station, west exit 5

This cozy bar attracts a mix of locals, travelers, and expats. Sports events are broadcast on TVs, and there's a dartboard and a buoyant soundtrack of funk, jazz, and more to keep the atmosphere friendly and light.

SHAFT

Sankei 18 Bldg. 1F, 2-7-22 Kokubunchō, Aoba-ku; tel. 022/722-5651; www.clubshaft.com; hours vary by event; cover charge varies by event; take Nanboku line to Hirose-dōri Station, west exit 2

This intimate nightclub has a good sound system, affordable drinks, and draws a young, friendly crowd. Events range from techno DJs to live digeridoo sessions. Check the website to see what's on before making the trip.

ACCOMMODATIONS

MITSUI GARDEN HOTEL SENDAI

2-4-6 Honcho, Aoba-ku; tel. 022/214-1131; www.gardenhotels.co.jp; ¥8,000 d; take Nanboku line to Hirose-dōri Station, west exit 1

Like many hotels in Sendai, the Mitsui Garden Hotel Sendai is a great value. The reception desk is on the seventh floor and the rooms all have large picture windows offering views of the streets below. The rooms are compact but well-appointed and the free Wi-Fi is strong. For a short stay, this hotel has everything you need.

HOTEL METROPOLITAN SENDAI

1-1-1 Chūō, Aoba-ku; tel. 022/268-2525; https://east-sendai.metropolitan.jp; ¥16,000 d room only, ¥20,000 with breakfast

The stylish Hotel Metropolitan Sendai has a whiff of sophistication. The breakfast is made using locally sourced ingredients and served in a dining room with a great view of the city. But the main selling point is the fact that it's directly connected to JR Sendai Station.

RICHMOND HOTEL PREMIER SENDAI EKIMAE

5F Toho Bldg., 2-1-1 Chuo, Aoba-ku; tel. 022/716-2855; http://sendai-ekimae.richmondhotel.jp; ¥12,000 d; from JR Sendai Station, take north exit 4

Richmond Hotel Premier Sendai Ekimae is only three minutes' walk from JR Sendai Station, so it's hard to beat for convenience. The hotel offers clean well-lit rooms and comfy mattresses. Breakfast is included.

SENDAI WASHINGTON HOTEL

4-10-8 Chuo, Aoba-ku; tel. 022/745-2222; http://sendai.washington-hotels.jp; ¥13,000 d; from JR Sendai Station, take west exit 1

The Sendai Washington Hotel, just southwest of the station, offers reasonably priced rooms and convenience. It also has a restaurant serving a menu based around local ingredients.

THE WESTIN SENDAI

1-9-1 Ichibancho, Aoba-ku; tel. 022/722-1234; www.westin.com; ¥17,000 d; take Tozai line to Aoba-dōri Ichibancho Station, south exit 1

For a five-star experience without a five-star price tag, stay at the Westin Sendai. You'll find chic rooms, good dining, and stellar views of the city and surroundings.

INFORMATION AND SERVICES

For English-language maps and sightseeing information, head to the **Sendai City Information Center** (tel. 022/222-4069; www.sentabi.jp; 8:30am-7pm), located on the second floor of JR Sendai Station.

TRANSPORTATION

Getting There

From **Tokyo,** the **JR Tohoku** *shinkansen* runs to Sendai in about 2 hours (¥11,200 or included with JR pass). Coming from the north, the next major hub on the train is **Morioka,** a 40-minute ride on the JR Tohoku *shinkansen* (¥6,670).

Sendai also has a domestic airport, which connects to Tokyo, Sapporo, Osaka, Nagoya, and Hiroshima, among other cities. To reach **JR Sendai Station** from **Sendai Airport** (022/382-0080; www.sendai-airport.co.jp), take the **Sendai Kūkō Access line,** which departs three times hourly (30 minutes; ¥650).

Taiheyo Ferry (tel. 022/263-9877; www.taiheiyo-ferry.co.jp) also runs between **Nagoya** and Sendai, and between Sendai and **Tomakomai,** near Shikotsu-ko in Hokkaido, up north. Check the website for timetables and fares.

Finally, if you have rented a **car,** the **Tohoku Expressway** links Tokyo and Sendai before continuing north through Morioka and Aomori. If you prefer to take a **bus,** check out **Willer Express** (tel. 050/5805-0383; http://willerexpress.com), which has buses running from Tokyo to Sendai in 5.5 hours from about ¥2,500.

Rebuilding After the 2011 Earthquake and Tsunami

On March 11, 2011, at 2:46pm, a 9.0-magnitude earthquake struck from under the Pacific off the eastern coast of Tohoku. The fourth most powerful quake in recorded history, it could even be felt in Osaka.

Much greater destruction was left by the tsunami that followed. Some 30 minutes after the rumbling subsided, a succession of waves up to 15 meters (50 feet) high thundered into the coastlines of Fukushima, Miyagi, and Iwate prefectures, wiping out entire communities, tossing fishing boats around like toys, and taking more than 15,000 lives, with a few thousand more unaccounted for. Estimates say as many as 470,000 became refugees following the disaster. In a word, the human cost was immense. Economically, the damage amounted to a staggering estimated $300 billion.

Although the process of recovery was relatively speedy in Sendai, where everything feels very much like business as usual, the pace of renewal in the surrounding coastal region lags as small seaside communities continue to rebuild seven years on. And of course, there is the ongoing crisis triggered by the meltdown of the Fukushima Dai-ichi nuclear power plant. A 20-km (12-mi) exclusion zone surrounds the plant, and cleanup efforts, involving the removal and disposal of extremely radioactive spent nuclear fuel, will last indefinitely. The upshot of this catastrophe is that the Japanese are more engaged in the nuclear debate than ever before, and the push toward green energy solutions is gaining traction.

Getting Around

Sendai does have one **subway** line, running north to south, with tickets costing ¥200-350. It might be useful for reaching your hotel, but it doesn't have stations close to any tourist sites.

A more useful mode of transport within the city is the **Loople Sendai** (http://loople-sendai.jp) bus, which runs in a clockwise loop around town. Among its stops are Zuihoden, Sendai City Museum, and Aoba Castle. The loop takes an hour and leaves Sendai Station every 20-30 minutes (9am-4pm; one-day pass ¥600, single ticket ¥260).

Around Sendai

★ MATSUSHIMA BAY
松島湾

Matsushima; https://visitmiyagi.com/areas/matsushima-bay; from Sendai Station, take Senseki line to Matsushima-Kaigan Station, then walk 6 minutes northeast to Matsushima Pier, or take Senseki line to Hon-Shiogama Station, then walk 10 minutes east to Shiogama Pier

Few places in Japan have as many historical associations with beauty as Matsushima Bay, considered one of Japan's three most scenic spots, along with Miyajima and Amanohashidate. Famously celebrated in the poetry of haiku master Matsuo Bashō, who was said to be left speechless by the scene in 1689, this misty stretch of water is dotted with some 260 tiny islands topped by twisted pine trees. These same islands, centuries later, shielded the communities along the bay from the brunt of the destruction caused by the March 2011 earthquake and tsunami that ravaged large swathes of Tohoku's coast.

Seen from above, the bay resembles a miniature landscape garden, its islands appearing as well-placed rocks or clusters of shrubs on an oceanic backdrop. Many of these small spits of land are ascribed personalities and special properties. It may be a stretch, but the tiny rock formation of Niojima is said to look like a sculpture of a Deva King. Sagijima (Heron

Island) is said to look like the bird of its namesake taking flight. Kabutojima appears to be the helmet of a warrior floating above the waters. And passing through the tiny opening, known as Chomei-ana, at the bottom of a craggy islet is said to bring longevity.

A number of architectural gems also surround the bay, thanks in part to the efforts of feudal lord Date Masamune. If you have time, plan to spend a few hours at these sights before or after your cruise.

Sights

ZUIGAN-JI

瑞巌寺

91 Aza-Chōnai; tel. 022/354-2023; www.zuiganji.or.jp; 8am-5pm Apr.-Sept., closes 30-90 minutes earlier in Oct.-Mar.; ¥700 adults, ¥400 children 15 years and under; take the Senseki line to Matsushima-Kaigan Station, then walk 8 minutes north

Established as a sanctuary for meditation in 828 AD by a priest named Jikaku Daishi (aka Ennin) of the Tendai sect, Zuigan-ji was transformed into a Zen temple during the militaristic Kamakura Period (1192-1333). Date Masamune ordered the complex to be rebuilt in 1606, hiring an army of artists and craftsmen for the job, which took four years to finish.

Designated a national treasure, Zuigan-ji is one of Tohoku's best Zen Buddhist temples. Approach the main hall via a cedar-lined path. Inside, you'll discover that Zuigan-ji has some unique features, among them a watchtower and nightingale floors, which a make chirping sound akin to the bird after which they are named to alert of any stealthily approaching enemy. These floors, known as *uguisubari* ("bush warbler guard watch"), are often found in castles that were once resided in by lords weary of the potential threat of stealthy ninja invaders. These wooden surfaces produce their trademark acoustic effect via nails underneath the floorboards that scrape against strategically placed metal clamps when they are walked on. The fine examples of Edo-period religious architecture that make up this complex were recently renovated. English-speaking guides are on-site on the first, third, and fourth Sunday each month from 10am to 3pm.

ENTSŪ-IN

円通院

67 Aza-Chōnai; tel. 022/354-3206; www.entuuin.or.jp; 8:30am-5pm Apr.-Nov., 9am-4pm Dec.-Mar.; ¥300; take the Senseki line to Matsushima-Kaigan Station

Next to Zuigan-ji and about six minutes' walk north from Matsushima Kaigan Station, Entsū-in was constructed in 1646 as the

view over Matsushima Bay

mausoleum of Date Mitsumune, the son of lord Date Terumune, who died at the young age of 19. The temple may not be as famous as its neighbor, but its gardens, which include a mossy landscape garden with a heart-shaped pond and a cedar grove, make it rewarding to visit.

Although the temple is dedicated to Kannon, the Buddhist goddess of mercy, there are a slew of peculiar icons peppered throughout the mausoleum, such as crosses, hearts, spades, diamonds, and clubs, and the first known depiction in Japanese art of a rose. These notably Western flourishes are no surprise, as the Date clan was known to have a keen interest in Christianity and the West.

GODAI-DŌ
五大堂

111 Aza-Chōnai; tel. 022/354-2023; www.zuiganji.or.jp/keidai/godaidou.html; 8am-5pm daily; free; walk 1 minute northeast of Matsushima Pier

An icon of Matsushima Bay, this compact temple stands on a tiny island next to Matsushima Pier, reached from the mainland via two bridges. Originally built in 807, the current structure is a reconstruction built in 1604 by Date Masamune, the prominent lord who once wielded great power from his base in Sendai. Inside the hall there are a collection of statues only unveiled to the outside world once every 33 years—the next showing won't be until 2039. What you can see are the 12 animals of the Chinese zodiac etched into the temple's outside walls. The main draw of making a stop at this landmark, however, is the lovely views of the bay from its grounds.

Boat Tours

It's possible to see Matsushima by boat. **Ferries** run by several operators depart on the hour (10am-4pm daily, until 3pm in winter; one-way ¥1,500 adults, ¥750 elementary school students) from **Matsushima Pier** (98-1 Chōnai; tel. 022/354-2233; www.matsushima.or.jp; walk 7 minutes northeast from Matsushima-kaigan Station) and **Shiogama Pier** (1-4-1 Minatomachi, Shiogama; tel. 022/361-1500; http://shiogama.co.jp/marinegate; walk 10 minutes east of Hon-Shiogama Station). From April through October, boats also run from Matsushima Pier into the quieter side of the bay known as **Oku-Matsushima.** These longer tours last more than 1.5 hours and cost ¥2,900.

Information and Services

Before starting your exploration of the bay, make a quick stop at the **Tourist Information Center** (022/354-2263; www.matsushima-kanko.com; 9:30am-4:30pm Mon.-Fri.; 8:30am-5pm Sat.-Sun.) inside Matsushima-kaigan Station. Here you can find any English-language information to help you make the most of your time and pointers on how to access the less touristed parts of the bay.

Transportation

From **Sendai,** take the **JR Senseki** line from JR Sendai Station to **Matsushima-kaigan Station** (40 minutes; ¥410) or to **Hon-Shiogama Station** (30 minutes; ¥320); cruises depart from both **Matsushima Pier** and **Shiogama Pier,** respectively.

To drive from Sendai, take the **Sanriku Expressway,** which links to Matsushima. If you'll be driving in the region, it's worth looking into the **Tohoku Express Pass** (www.go-etc.jp/english/expressway/index.html), which allows for unlimited use of Tohoku's expressways.

★ YAMADERA
山寺

Yamadera ("Mountain Temple") is one of the most scenic religious sites in all of Japan.

1: statue in the snow at Yamadera **2:** Buddha
3: Kaisan-dō and Nokyo-dō

1

2

3

The largest temple complex of the Tendai Buddhist sect in Tohoku, it is located in a more dramatic spot, clinging to a series of ledges on the face of verdant Mount Hoju. Ascending a steep, stone staircase through an enchanted forest dotted by Buddhist statues and stone lanterns, you're rewarded with stunning views of a river valley below and mountains in every direction, as far as the eye can see. If you're only going to visit one temple in Tohoku, make it this one.

Sights

RISSHAKU-JI

立石寺

Yamadera 4456-1; tel. 023/695-2843; www.rissyakuji.jp; 8am-5pm daily; ¥300 adults, ¥200 children

Although colloquially known as Yamadera, the official name of this ancient, atmospheric temple is Risshaku-ji. The journey to this lofty cluster of pavilions and temples—more than 30 structures in all—makes you feel like you've been transported to another realm.

Eminent Buddhist priest Jikaku Daishi, popularly known as Ennin, led an expedition to bring the light of Buddhism to the north in 860, carrying a sacred flame that still burns today in **Konpon Chūdō,** Yamadera's main hall at the base of Mount Hoju. This is the oldest surviving structure in the complex, rebuilt numerous times over the centuries. Only the temple at Mount Hiei in Kyoto is more important to the Tendai sect of Buddhism.

Veering to the left of Konpon Chūdō, you'll pass a statue of Bashō. Across from the statue, on the other side of the path, is a small **treasure hall** (tel. 023/695-2002; 9am-5pm Apr.-Nov.; ¥200 adults, ¥100 children), built in 1976 to house some of the temple's holiest artifacts.

The vertical journey to the lofty temples for which the complex is best known begins at the **San-mon** gate, where you pay an admission fee to enter the bulk of the complex. From this point, you must climb 1,015 stone steps; the hike takes about 30 minutes. Buddhist statues dot the hills and a multitude of weathered stone lanterns line the path.

You'll know you're nearing the top when you come to the 19th-century **Nio-mon** gate, a relatively recent addition to the complex. Up another short staircase, you'll see a slew of temples clinging to craggy outcrops of rock and superb views of the landscape below. The large temple straight ahead is **Okuno-in,** in front of which is one of the largest stone lanterns in all of Japan. A path veering to the left leads you to **Kaisan-dō,** Ennin's mausoleum, and just to its left, **Nokyo-dō,** a tiny pavilion once used for copying sutras, or Buddhist scripture, coated in red lacquer hanging onto the edge of a cliff.

For maximum impact, proceed to **Godai-dō,** a sheltered wooden terrace built in the 17th century and suspended from a cliff that offers a panoramic vista of the small hamlet below, pierced by a river, and endless rows of peaks beyond.

Transportation

GETTING THERE

If you're coming from **Sendai** in the east, take the **JR Senzan** line for about an hour (¥840) to **Yamadera Station.** If you're coming from **Yamagata** in the west, you'll also take the JR Senzan line for about 20 minutes (¥240).

GETTING AROUND

The base of the mountain is five minutes' **walk** from the train station. Take note of the **public restroom** on the right side of the road leading toward the river after you exit the station. There aren't any bathroom facilities once you reach the temple complex on the mountain. Cross the river that runs through the town in front of the station, then turn right at the T-intersection. The trail that leads to Risshaku-ji is on the left-side of that road.

★ ZAŌ-SAN
蔵王山

Zaō-san (Mount Zaō) is a picturesque volcano that straddles the border of Yamagata and Miyagi prefecture, offering the ideal setting for a range of outdoor activities year-round. In winter, Zaō Onsen Ski Resort, famed for its frozen, powder-encrusted trees playfully known as "snow monsters," draws serious powder hounds to its slopes. In summer, Okama Crater at the mountain's summit is a fantastic trekking destination. And at any time of the year, the village of Zaō Onsen beckons visitors to its ancient sulfuric *onsen* baths, which offer an ideal place to escape from the frantic modern world and relax in nature.

Hiking

Zaō-san is laced with hiking trails, ranging from 30-minute strolls to half-day journeys. The most popular route involves traipsing across the summit and taking in stellar views of the Okama Crater. Go online for a basic map of Zaō-san's trails, as they connect to the Zaō Ropeway (229-3 Zaō Onsen; tel. 023/694-9518; http://zaoropeway.co.jp). The ropeway puts the summit a simple, pleasurable ride away.

There are two main stretches of the ropeway: The **Zaō Sanroku Line** (8:30am-5pm daily Apr.-mid-Dec., 8:15am-4:45pm mid-Dec.-Mar.; ¥800 one way or ¥1,500 round trip for adults, ¥400 one way or ¥800 round trip for children), which starts at **Zaō Sanroku Station** (855 meters/2,805 feet) is located about 10 minutes' walk southeast of the Zaō Onsen Bus Terminal and ends at **Juhyō Kogen Station** (1,331 meters/4,367 feet). And the **Sanchō Line** (8:30am-5pm Apr.-Dec. 10; 8:30am-4:30pm Dec. 11-Mar.; ¥1,500 one way or ¥2,800 round trip adults, ¥800 one way or ¥1,400 round trip children) starts from **Juhyō Kogen Station** and glides up to **Jizō Sanchō Station** (1,661 meters/5,449 feet), from which most hikers begin their exploration on foot of the mountain.

OKAMA
御釜

Distance: 2.2 km (1.4 mi) one-way to Kumano-dake; 4 km (2.5 mi), one-way to Kattadake
Time: 1 hour to Kumano-dake; 90 minutes to Kattadake
Information and maps: Zaō Onsen bus terminal (http://zaoropeway.co.jp)
Trailhead: Zaō Jizō Sanchō Station (upper terminus of Zaō Ropeway)

At 1,841 meters high, Zaō-san is one of the loftier peaks in Tohoku. At its center, the indigo-blue **Okama** is a crater lake named for its affinity with a pot. The cooking analogy is apt: Zaō-san is a recently active volcano. Exercise caution and check on conditions before attempting to make the trek to its summit.

Although the area surrounding the crater is closed in winter, it makes for a spectacular hike during the warmer months. You can begin a hike to the mountain's summit by riding the ropeway to its top station and then walking the rest of the way.

After taking the Zaō Ropeway to the terminus at **Zaō Jizō Sanchō Station**, follow the path that leads to the right, southeastward toward **Jizō-san** (1,736 meters/5,695 feet), the mountain's third highest peak, and **Kumano-dake**, the highest at 1,841 meters (6,040 feet).

To reach Kumano-dake, you'll need to walk for about an hour over fairly rocky terrain. Along the way, you'll pass Buddhist statuary discretely dotting the landscape, which becomes increasingly volcanic as you approach the top; there you'll enjoy fantastic views of Okama Crater lying to the southeast. From there, you can press on for another 40 minutes or so to **Katta-dake** (1,758 meters/5,768 feet), Zaō-san's second highest peak looming beyond the southern edge of the cobalt waters of Okama Crater.

Skiing

ZAŌ ONSEN SKI RESORT

tel. 023/647-2266; www.zao-spa.or.jp; ¥3,000-5,000 one-day lift ticket (price varies by season)

One of the best places to ski in Japan, the Zaō Onsen Ski Resort is famed for its *juhyo*, trees

1

2

encased in ice and snow that are known as "snow monsters." At the upper reaches of this ski resort, you can ski and snowboard past these "beasts," which often seem to take on lives of their own. The best time to see them is mid-February through early-March, when things are fully frozen.

The snow here is soft, deep, and powdery, making it optimum for skiers. Snowboarders also flock to the resort, but there are many places where the runs temporarily plateau, which can be a tad frustrating for those on boards.

Starting from the top of the resort, the run down the mountain is 10 km (6 mi) long. More than 30 ski lifts, as well as a series of gondolas and ropeways, help people move between runs, which include a large number of beginner and intermediate courses, as well as a few daunting runs for those who are more experienced. Stunning vistas of Yamagata's surrounding mountains, extending in every direction, enhance the experience, as does the proximity to Zaō Onsen near the bottom of the ski area.

Onsen

This hot spring village, 880 meters up the face of Mount Zaō, provides the ideal place to rest and unwind after a day of hiking through alpine terrain in the warmer months or skiing in winter. Its *onsen* baths are highly acidic, with PH levels approaching 1; this is evident from the pungent scent of sulfur wafting through the air. There are old-school communal tubs and a range of more modern pools to choose from.

Some old-school options include **Shinzaemon-no-yu** (905 Zaō Onsen, Kawamae; tel. 023/693-1212; 10am-6:30pm Mon.-Fri., 10am-9:30pm Sat.-Sun.; ¥700). Note that it closes sporadically on Wednesday, generally once a month. **Kawarayu Public Bath** (6am-10pm daily; ¥200) is another public bath that's worth a trip, which is good in that it's open daily and is the cheapest of the lot. There's also a fantastic large gender-separated outdoor bath, **Zaō Onsen Dai-rotemburo** (tel. 023/694-9417; 6am-7pm May-Oct., 6am-6pm late-Apr.-mid-Nov.; ¥550), which sits beside a mountain river. If you're in Zaō during the right time of year, this is the best pool in town, but it's unfortunately closed late November to mid-April.

1: Okama crater lake on Mount Zaō
2: Mount Zaō skiing

Food

ROBATA

42-5 Zaō Onsen; tel. 023/694-9565; 11am-11pm Fri.-Wed.; ¥2,000; from JR Yamagata Station, take bus to Zaō Onsen bus stop; from there, it's a 3-minute walk

Serving Genghis Khan (Mongolian barbecue) Robata is a hit in Zaō Onsen, particularly in winter. Customers grill lamb, pumpkins, cabbage, and sundry other veggies on hot plates at the table.

HOT DINER SUNPAL

tel. 023/694-9055; www.sunrise-zao.com/#restaurant; 9am-4pm; ¥1,000

Hot Diner Sunpal serves hearty fare closer to the ski slopes. Here you can load up on Korean barbeque or *bibimbap* (rice mixed with egg, meat, vegetables, and more) for lunch or after a long day on the slopes. The food is reasonably priced and filling. The restaurant is at the foot of the ski slopes, next to the Snow Freak Sunrise hotel, which is operated by the same owners.

SANGOROGOYA

Zaō Onsen Chuo Kogen Gerende; tel. 023/694-9330; http://sangoro.co.jp; ¥1,000; from JR Yamagata Station, take bus to Zaō Onsen bus stop; from there, walk to the center of the Zaō Onsen village area

If you're feeling like a lighter mix of Japanese and Western-style classics, head for Sangorogoya. The menu ranges from pizza and clam chowder to curry and *udon* noodles. The cozy interior revolves around a circular counter with a fireplace in the center.

Accommodations

FREAK SUNRISE

832 Zaō Onsen; tel. 023/694-9055; www.sunrise-zao.com/#hotel; ¥7,000

For a no-frills guesthouse that sits literally right at the bottom of a ski run, a few minutes' walk from a ski lift, Snow Freak Sunrise is good if you're on a tight budget and don't mind sharing a bathroom or sleeping on a futon. The owner is a very laid-back, friendly guy who speaks English and is happy to assist you with getting settled in and renting skis.

MEITOYA SOU

48 Zaō Onsen; 023/666-6531; www.meitoya.com; ¥15,000 with breakfast; from JR Yamagata Station, take bus to Zaō Onsen bus stop; from there, walk to the center of the Zaō Onsen village area

Meitoya Sou is a traditional Japanese-style inn that was remodeled in 2017. The rooms are a combination of Japanese and Western-style. Each has a private toilet and basin, but only some have private full bathrooms. There is an indoor and outdoor *onsen* bath. Japanese-style breakfast is available.

★ MIYAMASO TAKAMIYA

54 Zaō Onsen; tel. 023/694-9333; www.zao.co.jp/takamiya; ¥35,000; from JR Yamagata Station, take bus to Zaō Onsen bus stop; from there, walk to the center of the Zaō Onsen village area

Established in 1716, Miyamaso Takamiya wears its history well. The hotel has even hosted the imperial family. With nine indoor and outdoor *onsen* baths, and a restaurant serving *kaiseki* (traditional multicourse meals) with famous Yamagata beef, guests don't want for much. It's a 10-minute walk to the ropeway station. Dark wood, soft lighting, and Japanese-style rooms with tatami floors complete the picture.

Information and Services

There's a **Tourist Information Center** (708-1 Zaō Onsen; tel. 023/694-9328; www.zao-spa.or.jp) in the Zaō Onsen bus terminal, where you can pick up English-language information about the ski resort and *onsen* options.

Transportation

From **Tokyo,** take the **Yamagata** *shinkansen* to Yamagata Station (2.5 hours; ¥11,000). From **Sendai,** take the **JR Senzan** line to JR Yamagata Station (1.5 hours; ¥1,140 one way); trains depart hourly. From there, you can reach Zaō Onsen via a **bus** that departs hourly (30 minutes; ¥1,000) from bus stand #1. The train ride is covered by the JR Pass, but the bus is not.

During the ski season, you can travel by highway bus from the **JR Shinjuku Station Highway Bus Terminal** (http://shinjuku-busterminal.co.jp; 6am-11:30pm daily) in **Tokyo.** The bus ticket office is located near the JR Shinjuku Station New South Exit. The overnight trip takes about 8 hours and costs ¥4,500 (¥8,000 round trip). The trip back to Tokyo runs during the day. Similarly, a round-trip bus travels once a day between **Sendai** and Zaō Onsen during ski season. The trip takes a little over an hour and a half (¥1,600). Inquire at the ticket window in **JR Sendai Station** for details.

In addition to the **Zaō Sanroku Line,** there's also the separate, less extensive **Zaō Chūō Ropeway** (940-1 Zaō Onsen; tel. 023/694-9168; http://zaochuoropeway.co.jp; 8:30am-5pm Apr.-Oct., 8:30am-4pm Nov.-Dec. 20; ¥800 one way, ¥1,500 round trip adults; ¥400 one way, ¥750 round trip children). This line runs from **Onsen Station** in the heart of Zaō Onsen's town area to **Torikabuto Station** (1,387 meters/4,550 feet), set atop the neighboring peak of Torikabuto.

HIRAIZUMI
平泉

Once the northern foothold of the mighty Fujiwara clan, Japan's most powerful family during the Heian Period (794-1185), Hiraizumi briefly rivaled Kyoto in cultural and mercantile prowess, thanks to its thriving trade in gold bullion. During its heyday, Hiraizumi was a boomtown where wayward children of noble birth and insubordinate military types were sent to keep the rough-and-tumble northern wilds under control.

Over the course of the 12th century, the Fujiwara lords poured vast wealth into building an array of villas, pagodas, and shrines around the city in an attempt to create a Buddhist paradise on earth. But Hiraizumi's time in the sun was short-lived. The great northern center would ultimately succumb to treachery and court intrigue. Today, a few reminders of its former greatness are on display in gold, wood, and stone, earning the town's sites UNESCO World Heritage status in 2011, including the captivating **Chūson-ji** temple complex, famed for the entirely gilt interior of its main hall, and the transcendent garden behind the temple of **Mōtsū-ji.**

Any trip to Hiraizumi is incomplete without making a detour east of town to **Geibi-kei (Geibi Gorge).** Here you can drift down river on a boat steered by a good-natured boatman who regales passengers with traditional songs and tales. It's all in Japanese, but it's good fun. If you happen to be in town during the first five days of May, the **Fujiwara Spring Festival** features locals dressed in period costume, a parade, and *Noh* theater performances on Chūson-ji's classic outdoor stage.

Sights

CHŪSON-JI

中尊寺

202 Koromonoseki; tel. 0191/46-2211; www.chusonji.or.jp; 8:30am-5pm Mar.-Oct., 8:30am-4:30pm Nov.-Feb.; ¥800 adults, ¥500 high school students, ¥300 junior high school students, ¥200 elementary school students; from Hiraizumi Station, take regular bus from bus stand 1 (5 minutes), Hiraizumi Loop Bus (20-30 minutes), or walk about 20 minutes northwest

The approach to the stunning temple Chūson-ji leads you along a path set in a thick cedar forest. Founded in 850 by the wandering priest Ennin, who also founded Risshaku-ji at Yamadera, the complex grew to include dozens of buildings and flourishes thanks to investment by the Fujiwara clan in the 12th century. In 1337, the temple was sadly ravaged by a fire that destroyed all but two buildings, the **Konjiki-dō** ("Golden Pavilion") and **Kyōzō**, or sutra repository.

The first building you encounter on your way into this rambling complex is the main hall. Toward the back of the path you'll also encounter an outdoor *Noh* stage. The Konjiki-dō is by far the most famous building in Hiraizumi, or in Tohoku for that matter. From the outside, you see a white shell of a building. But step inside and you'll be dazzled by a mausoleum, built in 1124, entirely covered in gold. This extravagant building enshrines four generations of the Fujiwara clan and actually contains the mummies of its first three lords. Behind the Konjiki-dō, you'll also find the Kyōzō sutra hall, which was actually built 16 years before the Konjiki-dō.

For a sense of Hiraizumi's former glory, follow the path next to the entry to Konjiki-dō until you'll reach the **Sankōzō.** This treasure hall features fans, jewelry, garments, Buddhist statuary, sacred scrolls and other personal effects from the Fuijiwara clan.

MŌTSŪ-JI

毛越寺

58 Osawa; tel. 0191/46-2331; www.motsuji.or.jp; 8:30am-5pm Mar. 5-Nov. 4, 8:30am-4:30pm Nov. 5-Mar. 4; ¥500 adults, ¥300 high school students, ¥100 junior high and elementary school students; from Hiraizumi Station, take Hiraizumi Loop Bus (3 minutes) or walk 10 minutes west

After Chūson-ji, if you see only one more temple during your time in Hiraizumi, head to Mōtsū-ji. Like its gilt cousin, this temple was also founded by Ennin. Alas, Mōtsū-ji suffered a similar fate to its once opulent neighbor, succumbing to a succession of sieges and fires. Thankfully, not all was lost.

A few structures remain, including a treasure hall that's worth a look. As you walk through the site, signposts indicate where

TOP EXPERIENCE

Dewa Sanzan's *Yamabushi* Pilgrimage

Dewa Sanzan, or "Three Mountains of Dewa," is an ancient pilgrimage destination deep in the mountains of Yamagata Prefecture. These three mountains became known among spiritual seekers 1,400 years ago when Prince Hachiko declared them a sacred site.

Dewa Sanzan is at the core of a syncretic folk religion that blends Buddhism and Shinto known as Shugendō. Those who are adept in Shugendō, known as *yamabushi,* roam and live off the land, seeking enlightenment through long journeys on foot. Only a small fraction of practicing *yamabushi* today are full-fledged monks, but there is a growing trend toward weekend warriors who head for the mountains when they've got the chance and even suit up in full kit: straw sandals, rosary beads, and robes. Headgear ranges from conical to pillbox-shaped, meant to double as protection and a cup for drinking. Some wield flutes, small hand-drums, or an iconic conch-shell trumpet.

Haguro-san (**羽黒山**), **Gassan** (**月山**), and **Yudono-san** (**湯殿山**) represent birth, death, and rebirth, respectively, and are meant to be traveled in that order. These mountains can be visited individually, but if you plan to hike the entire circuit, allow a minimum of two days and nights, and book all accommodations before reaching Tsuruoka.

WHERE TO STAY

If you want to stay overnight, bare-bones ★ **Saikan** (7 Tōge; tel. 0235/62-2357; ¥8,000), a small annex of the shrine atop Haguro-san, offers *shukubō* (temple lodging) with tatami floor and futon and a lunch served Buddhist style: vegetarian fare known as *shōjin ryōri* featuring locally foraged vegetables. Book a few months in advance for an undeniably singular experience. If Saikan is all booked up, try **Daishinbo** (95 Tōge; tel. 0235/62-2372; ¥9,000), another fantastic temple lodging on Haguro-san. This 350-year-old inn has a public bath, a lovely garden, and meals of *shōjin ryōri* are served here, too.

INFORMATION AND SAFETY

A number of tour operators give you the chance to sample this unique way of life. **Contact**

temple structures once stood. Mōtsū-ji's magic is revealed when you stroll through its garden, one of Japan's last remaining Pure Land gardens. This style of landscaping, aimed at manifesting an earthly vision of Buddhist paradise, was popular during the Heian Period. The garden is meant to evoke a sense of expansiveness and beauty: a hint at something beyond.

Sports and Recreation

GEIBI-KEI (GEIBI GORGE)

猊鼻渓

467 Nagasaka Azamachi, Higashiyama-chō, Ichinoseki-shi; tel. 0191/47-2341; www.geibikei.co.jp; 8:30am-4:30pm Apr.-Aug., 8:30am-4pm Sept.-Oct., 9am-3pm Nov.-Mar.; adults ¥1,600, elementary school students ¥860, ages 3 and older ¥200; from Hiraizumi Station, take JR Tohoku line to Ichinoseki, then transfer to JR Ofunato line and ride to Geibikei Station (55 minutes; ¥580); or, take bus from Hiraizumi Station (35 minutes; 4 daily Apr.-Nov.; ¥500)

Flat-bottomed boats glide about 2 km (1.2 mi) down the lazy Satetsu River in this picturesque gorge, located about 15 km (9.3 mi) east of Hiraizumi. Limestone cliffs more than 50 meters (164 feet) tall bound the gorge, which is named after a rock formation resembling the nose of a lion. The gorge is particularly beautiful during autumn. During winter, passengers are kept relatively warm by sitting around *kotatsu* (low heated tables) on the crafts.

The boats, operated by bargepole,

Yamabushido (https://yamabushido.jp), **Travel Tohoku** (www.traveltohoku.co.jp), or **Oku Japan** (www.okujapan.com) to learn more.

Some practicalities: Travel in the area around Dewa Sanzan is treacherous during winter. To avoid unnecessary complications, it's best to visit between April and October. Wear sturdy hiking boots and waterproof outerwear (pants, jacket). Pack a bit more food and water than you may expect to need, bug spray, and a bear bell. Before venturing to any of the three mountains, it's best to stop at Tsuruoka's **Tourist Information Center** (1-34 Suehiro-machi; tel. 0235/25-7678; 10am-5pm daily), right outside Tsuruoka JR Station.

Dewa Sanzan

GETTING THERE

Dewa Sanzan is reached via **Tsuruoka station.** From **Tokyo,** take the JR Joetsu *shinkansen* to **Niigata** (2 hours, ¥10,570), then transfer to the limited express to Tsuruoka, (2 hours, ¥4,450). This whole trip is covered by the JR Pass.

Shonai Kutsu (http://www.shonaikotsu.jp) runs overnight buses between Tokyo and Tsuruoka. (one way 8 hours, ¥7,540; round trip ¥13,570). Once in Tsuruoka, **buses** run from JR Tsuruoka Station to Haguro-san's base (40 minutes, ¥820) and summit (one hour, ¥1,190), or to the eighth station of Gas-san (¥1,580). Services to Gas-san run July-August, and on weekends only until mid-September. Yudono-san is not accessible via public transport.

You can also **rent a car** in Tsuruoka and drive; inquire at the Tourist Information Center next to JR Tsuruoka Station about rental car options, which are readily available in town.

accommodate up to a few dozen passengers. The boat also stops so passengers can walk for about 20 minutes deeper into the gorge for a glimpse of the rock resembling a lion's snout. While you're on shore, you can also pay ¥100 for five "lucky stones" known as *undama*, signifying various themes (love, money, health, etc.), which you can attempt to throw into a hole in the rock beside the lion's nose. If your aim is good, it's said that you'll be blessed in the area of life signified by the stone you've thrown. On the way back to the port, the boatman regales the passengers with a folk song, which can be hauntingly beautiful as it echoes through the chasm. The full experience lasts about 90 minutes.

Festivals

FUJIWARA FESTIVAL (藤原まつり)

Hiraizumi town center, Chūson-ji; contact tourist information center for details; May 1-5, Nov. 1-3; free

Once in spring and again in fall, Hiraizumi hosts a festival that brings back to life the town's glory days in the Heian period (794-1185). The festival takes its name after the Fujiwara clan, which was at the helm when Hiraizumi rose to prominence.

The spring edition of the festival reaches its climax May 3 when a procession of locals in period garb parades through downtown. This spectacle commemorates an event in the town's past when Minamoto no Yoshitsune, brother of Minamoto

Ghosts and Ghouls of Tōno

Set amid rice paddies and encircled by verdant undulating mountains, **Tōno (遠野)** is a hamlet in the heart of Iwate Prefecture with deep ties to Japanese folklore. Featured in *Legends of Tōno*, a collection of mythical tales released in 1910 by Yanagita Kunio, the town's most famous residents are supernatural, with the troll-like river-dwelling *kappa*, believed to snatch children who stray too close to the water, atop the list.

Start your journey into another time at the **Tōno Municipal Museum** (3-9 Higashidate-chō; tel. 0198/62-2340; 9am-5pm daily; ¥310), which offers an overview of Yanagita's tome and features displays on village life from centuries past. Nearby, you'll also find **Tōno Folktale Museum** (2-11 Chūō-dōri; tel. 0198/62-7887; www.city.tono.iwate.jp/index.cfm/48,23855,166,html; 9am-5pm daily; ¥310), which is housed in the former *ryokan* where Yanagita penned his work. But the real fun begins when you venture into the countryside, preferably on a bicycle, to discover spots give you a backdrop to imagine Tōno's mythology and history.

First, rent a bicycle at the **Tourist Information Center** (across the street from Tōno Station; tel. 0198/62-1333; www.tonojikan.jp; 9am-5pm Mon.-Fri.; bicycles ¥1,000 per day), which also stocks English-language maps of the area. Helpful staff can also tell you about the combination ticket (¥1,170), or **Shinai Kanko Kyotsuken,** which allows you to enter five sites of your choice. Set off on your journey, and don't miss these spots:

- **Denshōen** (6-5-1 Tsuchibuchi; tel. 0198/62-8655; www.densyoen.jp; 9am-5pm daily Apr.-Dec., 9am-4pm daily Jan.-Mar.; ¥320 adults, ¥220 children ages 7-18) is a folk village that offers glimpses into the legends, crafts, and traditional skills of the area. It features some 1,000 Oshira-sama dolls, made from mulberry wood and traditionally worshipped as agricultural spirits. There's also a soba restaurant on-site.
- **Jōken-ji** (7-50 Tsuchibuchi, Tsuchibuchi-chō; tel. 0198/62-1333; open 24/7; free) is associated with the *kappa*, the legendary river-dwelling monster. Note the stone *kappa* guardian dog statue located on the left side of the temple grounds. Behind the temple, you'll find the **Kappabuchi pool,** believed to be the home of the river spirit.
- **Fukusen-ji** (Matsuzaki-chō Komagi; tel. 0198/62-3822; 8am-5pm daily Apr.-Dec.; ¥300 adults,

Yoritomo, founder of the Kamakura Shogunate (1185-1333), fled to Hiraizumi from Kyoto in search of asylum in the mid-12th century after his father was killed in battle by the Taira clan. Although the Taira clan let Yoshitsune live if he vowed to become a monk, he instead pledged to avenge his father's death. In Hiraizumi, Fujiwara clan leader Hidehira took such a liking to Yoshitsune that he took him in as a son. The role of Yoshitsune is always played by a fresh, young heartthrob each year, ensuring the attendance of a gaggle of female admirers. Various games, dances and a memorial service to honor the Fujiwara clan also take place during the festival.

In autumn, the Fujiwara lords are again honored. There's also a parade of children in kimono, a *Noh* play on the stage at Chūson-ji, and various traditional dances. Another draw coinciding with the autumn edition of the festival is the brilliant foliage that will have reached the town and its surroundings by then.

Food and Accommodations

CAFE SEKIMIYA

36-1 Suzusawa; tel. 0191/34-4030; lunch 11:30am-2:30pm Mon.-Sat., dinner 5:30pm-9pm Mon.-Sat., closed third Mon. of month; lunch ¥1,000-2,000, dinner ¥3,000-5,000; walk 7 minutes northwest of Hiraizumi Station

This cozy café serves well-rounded Western meals, from soup and quiche to pasta and grilled fish and meat dishes. The stylish

¥250 junior high and high school students, ¥200 elementary school students) sprawls over a verdant mountain slope. A number of substantial halls are featured, along with a five-story pagoda, and Japan's largest wooden sculpture of Kannon, the goddess of mercy.

There's also a **JR Rent-a-Car** (5-8 Shinkokuchō; tel. 0198/63-2515; www.ekiren.co.jp; 8:30am-5pm daily; ¥5,940-¥14,580 per day) office across the street from the station.

FOOD AND ACCOMMODATIONS

- **Tōno Brewing Taproom** (10-15 Chūō-dōri; tel. 0198/66-3990; http://tonobrewing.com; hours vary, check website for monthly schedule; from ¥550): Alongside great brews, they serve tasty nibbles such as curry rice dishes, sausages, fried chicken, salads, and more.
- ★ **Tonoya Yo** (2-14 Zaimokuchō; tel. 0198/62-7557; http://tonoya-yo.com; courses ¥4,000-14,000): This restaurant and B&B, located 8 minutes' walk from Tōno Station's north side, is run by a Tōno native named Yotaro whose adroitness in the kitchen shines through in his highly polished meals infused with the spirit of *kaiseki*. Reserves at least two days in advance. You can also rent out the Tonoya Yo storehouse for up to seven people (5-7 guests ¥16,000 pp; includes 2 meals).
- ★ **Kuranoya** (3-145-136 Kokoji, Matsuzaki-chō; tel. 0198/60-1360; www.kuranoya-tono.com; ¥6,800 s, ¥12,600 d): This wonderful B&B is run by a warm English-speaking couple. The Japanese-style rooms are clean and comfortable, with either a bathtub or shower, and the delicious home-cooked meals are made with local, seasonal ingredients (breakfast included for all rates, dinner ¥1,000).

GETTING THERE

Take the **JR Tohoku** *shinkansen* to Shin-Hanamaki Station from **Tokyo** (3 hours, ¥13,870) or from **Sendai** (1 hour, ¥5,810). From there, change to the local **JR Kamaishi** line (45 minutes, ¥1,280). From **Hiraizumi,** take the JR Tohoku line to Hanamaki (45 minutes), then transfer to the JR Kamaishi line (1 hour, ¥1,660).

interior is nicely lit with dark wood furniture, doors, and beams.

SOBADOKORO YOSHIIE

43 Koromonoseki; tel. 0191/46-4369; 10:30am-3pm daily; from ¥800; walk about 22 minutes northwest of Hiraizumi Station

Set in an old-school building, this soba restaurant serves buckwheat noodles in various guises (cold, in hot soup, or in disconcerting quantities of tiny bowlfuls as *wanko-soba*). All meals come with a nice spread of vegetable side dishes, chopped green onions, and dipping sauce (for noodles not served in soup). A good choice if you've worked up an appetite either before or after visiting Chūson-ji, which is about 3 minutes' walk uphill to the north.

MINPAKU HIRAIZUMI

117-17 Hiraizumi Shirayama; tel. 090/267-7889; walk 7 minutes west of Hiraizumi Station; ¥6,000 pp with breakfast

This inviting B&B has two nicely appointed tatami-mat rooms, a hot tub, and a comfortable lounge area. It's run by a warm elder couple who whip up a nice Japanese-style breakfast for guests. It's located between Hiraizumi Station and Mōtsū-ji.

Information and Services

Hiraizumi is rich in options. To dig deeper, check out the website of the **Hiraizumi Tourism Association** (www.hiraizumi.or.jp). Once you're in town, stop by the **Tourist Information Center** (61-7 Izumiya;

tel. 019/146-2110; 8:30am-5pm daily) right outside JR Hiraizumi Station.

And for an English-language crash course on Hiraizumi's complex history, stop by the free **Hiraizumi Cultural Heritage Center** (44 Hanadate; tel. 0191/46-4012; 9am-5pm daily). This complex does a good job of visually illustrating the town's past through a number of exhibits and artifacts. It's about 15 minutes' walk northwest of Hiraizumi Station on the way to Chūson-ji.

Transportation

GETTING THERE

If you begin this journey from **Sendai,** take the **JR Tohoku *shinkansen*** to Ichinoseki, then transfer to the **JR Tohoku Main Line** for the remainder of the trip (40 minutes; ¥4,020). Or, take the local JR Tohoku line (1 hour 15 minutes; ¥1,670) directly to Hiraizumi.

Coming from **Tokyo,** take the JR Tohoku *shinkansen* to Ichinoseki Station (2 to 2.5 hours; ¥13,000). From Ichinoseki, transfer to the JR Tohoku Main Line, which links to Hiraizumi (8 minutes; ¥200). The entire trip is covered with a JR Pass.

From **Morioka** in the north, take the JR Tohoku *shinkansen* to Kitakami (20 minutes). Then transfer to the JR Tohoku line and ride the rest of the way to Hiraizumi (30 minutes). The entire trip costs ¥3,950. The local JR Tohoku line also makes the journey (1.5 hours; ¥1,490).

If you're driving, the **Tohoku Expressway** runs from Tokyo and Sendai in the south, through Hiraizumi, up to Morioka and Aomori in the north.

GETTING AROUND

The bulk of Hiraizumi's sights, including Mōtsū-ji and Chūson-ji, can be reached by riding the **Hiraizumi "Run Run" Loop Bus.** It departs from **Hiraizumi Station,** makes a loop around town in 15-30 minutes, then returns to Hiraziumi Station. A ride to a single destination costs ¥150, and an unlimited day pass is ¥400.

TAZAWA-KO
田沢湖

Japan's deepest lake (423 m/1,388 ft) and the 17th deepest worldwide, Tazawa-ko is hemmed in by largely untouched shores and surrounded by mountains. In many ways, it is the quintessential alpine lake, complete with sapphire-blue waters, rustic hamlets, and its very own folklore.

Sports and Recreation

BOAT TOURS

Tours of the lake are offered four times daily (late Apr.-late Nov.; ¥1,200) from the **Shirahama Beach boat pier,** which is located on the eastern side of the lake near the **Tazawa-kohan bus stop**.

BIKING

With 20 km (12 mi) of shoreline to explore, the lake is ideally seen by bicycle. There is a **bicycle rental shop** (¥400 per hour) near the **Tazawa-kohan bus stop** on the eastern side of the lake.

Start from Tazawa-kohan and circle the lake going clockwise. You'll pass through a dense tree canopy after about 15 minutes of cycling, before going through rice fields with trails branching off and into the mountains beyond. You'll reach a village with thatched-roof houses, and then come to **Goza-no-Ishi Jinja,** a shrine once frequented by local lords in feudal times, on the lake's north side.

Getting There

The *shinkansen* runs to **Tazawa-ko Station** from **Tokyo** (3 hours; ¥16,470) and from **Sendai** (1.5 hours; ¥8,360). A visit to Tazawa-ko is easy to add on to a trip to **Nyūtō Onsen** since you catch the local bus to the *onsen* area from Tazawa-ko Station (50 minutes; ¥820).

1: Tsurunoyu Onsen in fall **2:** torii at Tazawa-kō
3: Nyūtō Onsen's mixed-sex outdoor bath

1

2

3

★ NYŪTŌ ONSEN
乳頭温泉

Nyūtō Onsen ("nipple hot spring") is a cluster of *onsen ryokan* tucked away in the mountains of Akita Prefecture. The suggestive name was inspired by the cloudy tint of the water running under the ground in the area, said to resemble, ahem, milk, as well as the shapes of the surrounding hills. There are eight *ryokan* here, many of them quite old. The baths are not the private property of the inns; rather, non-overnight guests are permitted to use them during select hours for a fee. One unique aspect of the baths around Nyūtō Onsen is that mixed bathing is permitted in many of them—with privacy towel, of course—although gender-segregated baths are also available.

Onsen and Accommodations

★ TSURUNOYU ONSEN

50 Kokuyurin, Sendatsui-zawa; tel. 0187/46-2139; www.tsurunoyu.com; ¥9,830-19,950 pp with meals, ¥1,100 heating fee charged during winter

Tsurunoyu Onsen is the oldest *ryokan* of the lot, with some of the rooms in its atmospheric corridors dating to the Edo period. Non-staying guests are permitted to use the baths as well for a limited time each week (10am-3pm Tues.-Sun.; ¥600). Gender-separated baths are available indoors, but this *onsen* is best known for its mixed outdoor baths. The setting includes a milky-white pool surrounded by trees on one side, with a wooden roof propped up by roughly hewn timber beams to the other side where the hotel stands. Inside the inn, guests eat, lounge, and stroll wearing *yukata* at all hours. The rooms are as classic as you would hope—that is, dark wood, tatami floors. The easiest way to reserve is via phone, although this requires having someone help who can speak Japanese. To reserve online, visit www.travelarrangejapan.com/Accommodations/tsurunoyu-onsen.

To reach Tsurunoyu, get off at the **Arupa Komakusa bus stop,** 35 minutes on the bus from **Tazawa-ko Station** (¥620), to be picked up by the staff of the inn. Be sure to prearrange the time of your arrival, as this service is offered by appointment only.

★ TAENOYU

2-1 Komagatake; tel. 0187/46-2740; www.taenoyu.com; ¥13,070-21,400 with 2 meals; 10am-3pm Wed.-Mon., ¥800 for non-staying guests

In the style of an infinity pool with a rushing waterfall framed by forested hills in the backdrop, the mixed-sex *rotemburo* (outdoor bath) here may have the most dramatic view of all seven *ryokan* in the area. The facilities are perhaps the most up-to-date of all the hotels here, with thoroughly modern rooms and great indoor baths, including some that can be reserved for private use and others that are divided by sex. There's a dining area where breakfast and afternoon tea are served, and a separate space for dinner, which is a multicourse affair made with locally sourced ingredients and washed down with *sake* brewed in Akita. Some rooms have private baths, others shared. To reach Taenoyu, take the bus from **Tazawa-ko Station** until **Taenoyu-mae bus stop** (50 minutes; ¥820).

KUROYU ONSEN

2-1 Kuroyu-zawa; tel. 0187/46-2214; www.kuroyu.com; ¥11,500-23,000 pp with meals; 9am-4pm daily May-mid Nov., ¥600 for non-staying guests

Another *ryokan* in the area with an alluring rustic charm is Kuroyu Onsen. The Japanese-style rooms are slightly less impressive than Tsurunoyu, with many having shared bathrooms. Its strength is its setting, beside a river with forest views. This property also offers a number of indoor and outdoor baths—both mixed and gender-separated—and the water at Kuroyu is reputed to contain healing properties. To reach Kuroyu, take the bus from **Tazawa-ko Station** until the **Nyūtō Onsen bus stop** (50 minutes; ¥820). Then, walk 15 minutes up the road that branches off to the right from the road where you exit the bus. Kuroyu also offers pickup service from Nyūtō Onsen bus stop for staying guests if arranged beforehand.

Information and Services

To learn more about Nyūtō Onsen, including its collection of seven alluring *ryokan*, visit http://ryokan.glocal-promotion.com. Also, there's a pass that gives staying guests unlimited access to the baths at all seven *ryokan*. You can pick up this pass, known as the **Yumeguri Pass** (https://glocalpromo.wixsite.com/nyutoonsen-extrainfo/hot-spring-pass; ¥1,800), at the help desk of any of the area's *ryokan*.

Transportation

GETTING THERE

Local **buses** run hourly to the Nyūtō Onsen area from **Tazawa-ko Station,** accessible by *shinkansen* from **Tokyo** (3 hours; ¥16,470) and **Sendai** (1.5 hours; ¥8,360). The one-way bus trip takes about 50 minutes (¥840). Note that the bus does not stop directly at the entrance to Tsurunoyu, Kuroyu, or Taenoyu.

GETTING AROUND

For non-staying guests, once you're in the Nyūtō Onsen area, the **Yumeguri-go shuttle bus** travels between each *ryokan* roughly once every two hours. Guests who are staying overnight at one of the area's *ryokan* can purchase a **Yumeguri Pass** (¥1,800 for unlimited rides on this shuttle bus and unlimited access to all of the area's baths). Non-staying guests can buy a one-day shuttle bus pass, known as the **Yumeguri Map** (¥600), but they must pay for admission to each bath separately. The Yumeguri Map can be purchased at the **Tazawa-ko Tourist Information Center** (68 Osaka, Tazawa-ko Obonai; tel. 0187/43-2111; 8:30am-5:15pm daily) or any other bus stop along the route into Nyūtō Onsen, including **Kyukamura-mae bus stop.**

If you're able to drive, **renting a car** in Tazawa-ko or Kakunodate or will allow easier access to any of the area's *onsen* resorts, all of which have free parking lots.

★ KAKUNODATE (角館)

Kakunodate is an archetypal samurai town. The castle may have vanished during the early days of the Edo period, but a cluster of samurai residences, among the best preserved in all of Japan, remain.

Founded in 1620 by Ashina Yoshikatsu of the Satake clan, this charming town evokes the past, most notably in its samurai district, or *buke yashiki*, located about 20 minutes' walk from **Kakunodate Station.**

Kakunodate

Gated homes, craft shops, and wooden storehouses line these streets, which ooze ambience, inspiring the nickname "Little Kyoto." Of the six residences open to the public, two stand out: the rambling, atmospheric **Aoyagi House,** where you'll find the **Aoyagi Samurai Manor Museum** (3 Omotemachi; tel. 0187/54-3257; www.samuraiworld.com; 9am-5pm daily, until 4:30pm in winter; ¥500 adults, ¥300 junior high and high school students, ¥200 elementary students); and **Ishiguro House** (1 Omotemachi; tel. 0187/55-1496; 9am-5pm daily, ¥500 adults, ¥300 children), with its striking garden and finely preserved stockroom.

South of the samurai residences and about 15 minutes' walk from Kakunodate Station, you'll also discover an old merchant's district with a few atmospheric storehouses still intact. it's worth visiting **Andō Jozo Miso** (27 Shimo-Shinmachi; tel. 0187/53-2008; 11am-5pm daily; free), a nicely preserved brick storehouse built in 1891. This brewery has been producing miso and soy sauce since the 18th century, and it shows. Sample some of their delicately flavored pickled vegetables or sip on miso soup in the café.

If you find yourself in Kakunodate during cherry blossom season, which runs from late April to early May, consider yourself blessed. This is one of Tohoku's most stunning spots to view the pink blossoms. The town boasts some 300 weeping cherry trees, of which more than 150 are designated National Natural Treasures.

Information and Services

Just in front of the Kakunodate Station you'll find the **Tourist Information Center** (394-2 Kamisugasawa; tel. 0187/54-2700; 9am-6pm daily), stocking plenty of English-language information on the town's historic riches. Inquire here about bicycle rentals, too.

Transportation

The *shinkansen* runs to **Kakunodate Station** from **Tokyo** (3 hours; ¥17,150) and from **Sendai** (1.75 hours; ¥9,120). From **Tazawa-ko,** continuing to Kakunodate is simple. Hop on the Tazawa-ko local train line from Tazawa-ko Station to Kakunodate Station (25 minutes; ¥320; or 15 minutes, ¥1,390 by *shinkansen*). Trips from the Nyūtō Onsen area require going back to Tazawa-ko.

Aomori Prefecture 青森県

Until recently, Honshu's northernmost prefecture, Aomori, was a wild and enigmatic land. Its interior is split down the middle by the soaring Ōu Mountains, while the rugged Tsugaru Peninsula in the northwest and the windswept Shimokita Peninsula in the northeast surround Mutsu Bay as they jut into the storm-torn Tsugaru Strait that separates Honshu from Hokkaido to the north.

Today, Aomori is a proud and lively port city, acting as the prefecture's capital from where it sits on the southern shore of Mutsu Bay. Although the city doesn't have as many sights as Hirosaki, it hosts one of Japan's greatest summertime festivals, the Nebuta Matsuri, in which towering illuminated floats depicting figures and myths are transported through streets packed with revelers.

South of Aomori and east of Hirosaki, the deep, dark-blue waters of lake Towada-ko and stunning nearby Oirase-keiryū gorge are good reasons to go inland. To glimpse the old Aomori, shrouded in mystery, head for Osore-zan deep in the heart of the Shimokita Peninsula in the prefecture's faraway northeast. Here, the world's northernmost wild monkeys stay warm in *onsen* pools, and blind mediums at Osore-zan (Mount Dread) make contact with the dead.

HIROSAKI
弘前

The name Hirosaki evokes many images and ideas, from the popular belief that it's home to some of Japan's most beautiful women to its splendid cherry blossoms. This old castle town was once the cultural and political heart of the Tsugaru region, as the western half of Aomori Prefecture was known during the Edo period. Navigating the maze-like streets that wind slowly toward the castle grounds provides a visceral reminder of the town's former political importance. One is forced to weave patiently through the former samurai quarter in the same muddled way laid out by the city's creators to slow down advancing enemy troops.

Partly thanks to the fact that Hirosaki was spared the firebombing raids that leveled so many Japanese cities in World War II, today the city feels a little neglected in parts, but its large number of Edo-period buildings, the castle, and the lovely surrounding countryside add up to a beautiful provincial city worth exploring for a day, preferably by bicycle.

Sights

HIROSAKI CASTLE
弘前城

1 Shimoshiroganechō; tel. 0172/33-8739; 9am-5pm daily Apr. 1-Nov. 23; ¥310; from JR Hirosaki Station, take Dotemachi Loop Bus to Shiyakusho-mae bus stop

Set in **Hirosaki-kōen** (www.hirosakipark.jp), a lovely park west of Hirosaki Station, Hirosaki Castle is on the petite side, but what remains is genuine. Originally built in 1611 by Lord Tamenobu Tsugaru, the first iteration of the castle was slightly grander, with a five-story keep that burned to the ground after it was struck by lightning in 1627. The three-story keep standing today was constructed in 1810. Elsewhere, three moats, a smattering of turrets, and some gates—the Kamenoko-mon on the north side being a fine example—were either rebuilt or remain from the original structure.

While the castle is an attractive sight, the real stars of the park are 2,500 stunning cherry trees. In late April and early May, a profusion of pink petals form canopies and tunnels, and delicately float on the waters of the moats, creating one of Japan's most famous *hanami* spots. It makes sense to start your tour of Hirosaki in this park as the bulk of the city's sights can be reached on foot from here.

NEPUTA MURA
ねぷた村

61 Kamenokomachi; tel. 0172/39-1511; www.neputamura.com; 9am-5pm daily; ¥550 adults, ¥350 children; from JR Hirosaki Station, take Dotemachi Loop Bus to Bunka Center bus stop

Located near the northeast corner of Hirosaki-kōen, Neputa Mura, or Neputa Village, is a good place to get a sense of Hirosaki's local culture, particularly the iconic summer festival known as the **Neputa Matsuri,** held in Hirosaki and Aomori. Inside the dimly lit museum you'll find towering floats, lit from within and covered by paintings of fearsome warriors, striking women, mythological figures, and more. If you're unable to attend the real festival, getting up close to these stunning floats is the next best thing.

There are also displays and exhibitions on local arts and crafts, such as making wooden *kokeshi* dolls, as well as performances on the Tsugaru shamisen, a three-stringed instrument that emits a twang when plucked, often at blazing speeds; and sporadic demonstrations of a beat-down on a rotund *taiko* drum.

FUJITA MEMORIAL JAPANESE GARDEN
藤田記念庭園

8-1 Kamishirogane; tel. 0172/37-5525; 9am-5pm Tue.-Sun. Apr.-Nov.; ¥310 adults, ¥100 children; from JR Hirosaki Station, take Dotemachi Loop Bus to Shiyakusho-mae bus stop and walk 5 minutes

Planted and pruned from 1919, Fujita Memorial Japanese Garden is a fine example of a classic Japanese landscape garden. Besides an exquisitely manicured green space, complete with a zigzagging wooden bridge, stone

1
2
FAMILIA
六十九年賞
波切
不動
16
ワーキン
日本通運
NIPPON EXPRESS
OLYMPUS
青森オリンパス株式会社

lanterns, and a pond, the grounds contain a tea ceremony house and the family house of local businessman Fujita Kenichi, after whom the garden is named. The Western-style manor has been turned into a tearoom, which makes for a good pit stop. Located near the southwest corner of Hirosaki-kōen.

CHŌSHŌ-JI
長勝寺

1-23-8 Nishi-Shigemori; tel. 0172/32-0813; 9am-4pm; ¥300; from JR Hirosaki Station, take Tamenobu-go bus to Shigemori-machi Chōshō-ji Iriguchi bus stop

Walk 15 minutes southwest of Fujita Memorial Japanese Garden and you'll be in the heart of a district known as **Zenringai,** which boasts 33 temples representing every stripe of Zen. As a starting point, head to Chōshō-ji, a groaning wooden structure on a hilltop that sits behind an opulent gate standing 16 meters (53 feet) tall. Built in 1629, the temple contains a convincing statue of Lord Tametsugu Tsugaru and a hall housing an army of wooden sculpture depicting Buddha's 500 disciples. Look out for views of Iwaki-san, a snowcapped Mount Fuji for the north, looming in the distance.

After leaving Chōshō-ji, carry on wandering and enter the grounds or buildings of any temple or graveyard that catches your eye. Very likely, you will make some amazing discoveries.

Festivals

HIROSAKI NEPUTA MATSURI
ねぷた祭

Around Hirosaki Castle, Dotemachi shopping street, around Hirosaki Station; tel. 0172/37-5501; www.hirosaki-kanko.or.jp/en/edit.html?id=edit11; from 7pm Aug. 1-6, from 10am on Aug. 7; free

Some 80 fan-shaped floats featuring scowling samurai, fair maidens, and mythological figures are paraded through town alongside locals dressed in traditional attire who beat massive *taiko* drums and play bamboo flutes. Hirosaki's Neputa Matsuri is intimately connected to the larger **Aomori Nebuta Matsuri,** held around the same time in Aomori city. The intensity of the festival in Aomori city is associated with preparing for battle. By contrast, the more low-key festival in Hirosaki is said to mark the victors' return from combat, with some of the art on the floats showing grizzly skirmish scenes.

HIROSAKI CASTLE SNOW LANTERN FESTIVAL
弘前城雪燈籠祭

Hirosaki-kōen; www.hirosaki-kanko.or.jp/en/edit.html?id=snow%20lantern%20festival; 9am-9pm, illumination from 4:30pm, second Fri. of Feb. through following Mon.; free

In an event that is locally known as the **Hirosaki Yuki-doro Matsuri,** the town's denizens make good use of the heavy dump of snow their town receives each winter. In early February, the town builds some 200 hundred lanterns and 300 tiny igloos, illuminated from within by candlelight, from snow throughout the park surrounding Hirosaki Castle. It's hard to deny the magic of the wintery scene.

Food

AIYA

2-7-3 Tomita; tel. 0172/32-1529; 5pm-11pm daily; ¥3,000; walk 15 minutes west from JR Hirosaki Station

If you find yourself in Hirosaki at dinnertime, head to Aiya. At 7pm and 9pm every night, there is a thrilling jam session on the Tsugaru *jamisen,* a three-stringed instrument with deep historical and soulful ties to the Hirosaki region. The musicians, who play with great dexterity and speed, are members of the family that owns and runs the restaurant. Sometimes multiple generations take to the stage in one evening.

★ KADARE YOKOCHŌ

2-1 Hyakkoku-machi; tel. 0172/38-2256; http://kadare.info; 3pm-11pm daily

There are eight small eateries on the first floor of this building, akin to an indoor culinary

1: cherry blossoms at Hirosaki Castle **2:** Nebuta Matsuri festival float

Festivals of the North

Going to a traditional Japanese festival is a great way to get a taste of local life, and the Tohoku region hosts some of the best. **Sendai's Tanabata Matsuri** (page 455) is a huge affair, as are Aomori's Nebuta Matsuri and Akita's Kantō Matsuri. If you want experience the revelry, plan an early-August trip to Tohoku.

TOP EXPERIENCE

★ AOMORI NEBUTA MATSURI
ねぶた祭

various locations in downtown Aomori; www.nebuta.or.jp; Aug. 2-7; sidewalk seating free, reserved seating ¥3,000, on sale from about one month before festival

Every August in Aomori city, reaching a crescendo the night of August 5, locals parade large, luminous papier-mâché lanterns through heaving streets. The ornate floats depict samurai warriors, mythical figures, animals, and more. Revelers fill the streets wearing colorful, lightweight summer kimonos (*yukata*), nibbling on summer fare—yakitori, grilled corn—and downing beers. It's easily one of Japan's best festivals and attracts people from across the country.

No one really knows how the Nebuta Matsuri came about. Some point to the account of Sakanoue-no-Tamuramaro, a 9th-century warrior and imperial commander who led troops in a campaign to conquer the far north. According to legend, Tamuramaro placed massive lanterns, similar to those mimicked in the Nebuta Matsuri today, as bait to draw curious enemy combatants to the imperial camp.

Aomori Nebuta Matsuri float

Food and Accommodations

To stay in Aomori during the festival, book accommodations six months in advance.

- ★ **Tsugaru Joppari Isariya Sakaba** (2-5-14 Honchō; tel. 017/722-3443; http://marutomisuisan.jpn.com/isariya-tugaru; 5pm-midnight daily; dishes ¥590-1,890; walk 15 minutes southeast of Aomori Station): Come here for the atmospheric room, delicious food, and sake brewed in Aomori. At 7pm nightly, a musician in traditional garb strums a banjo-like *jamisen* and sings folk songs. Book a few days in advance to be sure you get a seat.
- **Cafe Marron** (2-6-7 Yasukata; tel. 017/722-4575; 7am-8pm Thurs.-Tues.; drinks from ¥400, dishes ¥250-880): This old-school café, infused with 1950s ambience, serves good coffee and reasonably priced bites and desserts.
- **Hotel JAL City Aomori** (2-4-12 Yasukata; tel. 017/732-2580; www.aomori-jalcity.co.jp; ¥13,000 d with breakfast): This business hotel with clean, stylish rooms is located 7 minutes' walk east of Aomori Station and offers a Japanese-style breakfast buffet.
- **Richmond Hotel** (1-6-6 Nagashima; tel. 017/732-7655; https://richmondhotel.jp/aomori; ¥16,600 d with breakfast): This clean, modern hotel offers simple, well-appointed rooms. It's a 15 minute-walk southeast from Aomori Station, making it a good choice if you're driving.

Getting There

To reach Aomori take the JR Tohoku *shinkansen* (Hayabusa train; seat reservation required) to Shin-Aomori Station from **Tokyo** (3.5 hours; ¥17,150) or **Sendai** (1.5 hours, ¥11,420), then transfer to the JR Ou line and make the short journey to **Aomori Station** (6 minutes; ¥190), which is the gateway to downtown. Coming from **Hirosaki,** you can take the JR Ou line (50 minutes; ¥670) directly to Aomori Station.

Kantō Matsuri

KANTŌ MATSURI
竿燈祭

various locations around Akita city; www.kantou.gr.jp/english; daytime performances around town from 3pm, nighttime parades 7:25pm-9pm on Aug. 3-6; street seating free, reserved seating ¥2,100-3,000 pp

The Kantō ("pole lantern") festival is among Japan's most visually impressive spectacles. Daytime events are held around town, but the real buzz surrounds the nighttime performances that take place along a 1-km (0.6-mi) stretch of the Chūō-dōri thoroughfare.

As dusk falls, some 230 bamboo poles are hoisted aloft by Akita citizens, young and old, to the sound of flutes, shouts, and *taiko* drums. Topped with up to 46 lanterns sacred offerings of intricately cut white paper known as *gohei*, the poles measure upward of 15 meters (49 feet) long and weigh 50 kg (110 lbs) or more. Each participant balances the towering pole on his or her palm, shoulder, lower back, and even forehead, as prayers for a good harvest are chanted to the heavens.

Food and Accommodations

As for accommodation during the festival, book three months or more in advance.

- **Sato Yosuke** (2-6-1 Naka-dōri; tel. 018/834-1720; www.sato-yoske.co.jp/shop/akita; 11am-9pm daily; ¥780-1,620: A tasty restaurant serving *udon* noodle sets (with sides of tempura and more), located in the basement-level food court of the Seibu Department Store a few minutes' walk west of Akita Station.
- **Mugendo** (2-4-12 Naka-dōri; tel. 018/825-0800; https://mugendo-ekimae.gorp.jp; lunch 11am-2pm, dinner 5pm-10pm, last order 9:30pm; ¥640-1,300, dinner courses ¥3,000-5,000: This chic restaurant, a few minutes' walk west of the station, serves a range of Japanese cuisine.
- **Hotel Metropolitan Akita** (7-2-1 Naka-dōri; tel. 018/831-2222; www.metro-akita.jp/301.html; ¥23,000 d, breakfast ¥1,600): This hotel offers clean, modern, if no-frills rooms, and scores big points for convenience with its location right beside Akita Station.
- **Castle Hotel** (1-3-5 Naka-dōri; tel. 018/834-1141; www.castle-hotel.jp; doubles ¥12,400 with breakfast): Some of its airy, recently renovated rooms overlook Senshu Park, above which the city's castle—now in ruins—once stood. A 10-minute walk west of Akita Station.

Getting There

To reach Akita, if you're coming from **Tokyo,** JR Akita *shinkansen* trains depart hourly and run directly to **Akita Station** (3 hours 45 minutes; ¥17,460; seat reservation required). You can also catch the *shinkansen* from **Sendai** (2.5 hours; ¥10,560). Coming from **Hirosaki,** take the **Tsugaru limited express train** (2 hours; ¥4,250).

alley. Food ranges from Indian and yakitori to crepes and some excellent grilled seafood. You can sit anywhere in the space and freely order from any of the restaurants. Most of the shops have an English-language menu. The restaurants effectively function as bars, making it a great place to dine, carouse with locals, and maybe make some new friends.

Accommodations

DORMY INN HIROSAKI

71-1 Hon-machi; tel. 0172/37-5489; www.hotespa.net/hotels/hirosaki; ¥10,500 d

Reasonably priced, clean, decent-sized rooms, very helpful staff, and both an indoor and open-air *onsen* bath on the rooftop make this a good budget option. Bowls of ramen are served free of charge to guests at night (9pm-11pm daily). It's a bit far from the station on foot (25 minutes' walk west), but the hotel provides a free shuttle bus. It's about 10 minutes' walk southeast of the Hirosaki Castle grounds, with most of the town's other attractions also within walking distance.

★ ISHIBA RYOKAN

55 Mototera-machi; tel. 0172/32-9118; www.ishibaryokan.com; ¥5,400 pp with shared bath/toilet, ¥6,500 pp with ensuite bath/toilet, breakfast ¥950-1,400

This charming inn is set in an old, creaky building with lots of dark wood dating to the 1800s. It has clean, expansive tatami rooms, and the older couple who own and run the place are friendly and eager to assist. Its location, only a few minutes' walk east of Hirosaki Castle's grounds, is hard to beat for access to exploring the historic side of town. Perhaps its biggest draw is the calming garden seen from most of the rooms. Pickup from Hirosaki Station is possible with advanced request. Rental bicycles are also available.

Information and Services

When you arrive at JR Hirosaki Station, head straight for the ground-floor **Hirosaki City Tourist Information Center** (tel. 0172/26-3600; 8:45am-6pm daily). Bicycles can be rented here.

If you need some help with coordinating logistics for a journey farther afield in Aomori, the **Hirosaki Municipal Tourist Center** (2-1 Shimoshirogane-machi; tel. 0172/37-5501; www.en-hirosaki.com; 9am-6pm) is the ideal place. Offering heaps of English-language maps and pamphlets, friendly English-speaking staff are there to help you with hotel arrangements, bicycle or car rentals, or any other question or concern you may have about your travels in the prefecture.

Transportation

GETTING THERE

To reach Hirosaki, take the **JR Ōu** line from **Aomori** (45 minutes; ¥670). If you're traveling from anywhere south of Aomori—**Morioka, Sendai, Tokyo,** and so on—you'll first need to make the trip to Shin-Aomori Station via the **JR Tohoku** *shinkansen,* then transfer to the JR Ōu line for the remainder of the trip.

If you happen to be coming from **Hokkaido,** note that eight ferries run daily between Hakodate in southern Hokkaido and Aomori (4 hours; from ¥2,200). For details, ask at the ticket counter in the **Tsugaru Kaikyō Ferry Hakodate Terminal** (3-19-2 Minato-chō; tel. 0138/43-4545; www.tsugaru-kaikyo.co.jp/terminal/hakodate), where the ferries depart on the Hokkaido side.

Thanks to the Seikan Tunnel, which runs under the Tsugaru Strait, separating Honshu from **Hokkaido,** it's also possible to take the Hokkaido *shinkansen* from Shin-Hakodate-Hokuto Station to Shin-Aomori (1 hour and 45 minutes; ¥8,300). From Shin-Aomori, transfer to the JR Ōu line, which runs directly to Hirosaki.

★ OSORE-ZAN (MOUNT DREAD)

恐山

One of Japan's three most sacred peaks, along with Kōya-san in Wakayama Prefecture and Hie-zan in Kyoto, Osore-zan is the northernmost of the lot, looming over the remote Shimokita Peninsula in the north of Aomori Prefecture. The mountain was discovered more than a millennium ago by a Buddhist priest seeking a hallowed peak bearing a likeness to the otherworldly realm of purgatory as envisioned by Buddhism.

The name Osore-zan literally means "Mount Fear." This is appropriate, given that it's believed to be sacred to the spirits of the dead. The desolate landscape does a good job of evoking dread, with signs of volcanic activity bubbling to the surface of the gray, windswept terrain. Jets of steam and hot water routinely spout from openings in the earth, and throughout the mountain there is a thick odor of sulfur.

Sights

BODAI-JI
菩提寺

3-2 Usoriyama, Tanabu, Mutsu-shi; tel. 0175/22-3825; http://kankousan.com/kankou/aomori/osorezan; 6am-6pm daily May-Oct.; ¥500

Similar to the three holy mountains of Dewa-Sanzan, Osore-zan is laden with Buddhist symbolism and is said to feature elements of the realm souls must pass through en route to the afterlife. At the peak of the mountain you'll find Bodai-ji, a temple with a clear focus on Jizō, the guardian of children. Near this holy place is Usori-ko—a lake with excessively blue water due to its toxically high sulfur content, which is believed to embody the Sanzu no Kawa, a mythical river akin to the ancient Greeks' River Styx that must be crossed to reach the afterlife.

It is believed that the souls of unborn infants and dead youngsters stack pebbles on the bottom of this "river" to help them walk across it, but demons seek to topple the stone piles to divert the souls of the young from reaching paradise. Thankfully, ever-present guardian Jizō—represented in the stone statues seen throughout the mountain—watch over these souls and keep the evil spirits at bay. Colorful toy pinwheels and piles of stones are laid throughout the landscape by parents whose children have passed on, in the hopes of assisting them in crossing. Feel free to add more stones to any of the piles to help the souls make their way.

After making the journey to this far-flung holy spot, feel free to avail yourself of the rustic hot springs found on the temple grounds.

Osore-zan

Festivals

OSORE-ZAN TAISAI

恐山大祭

Bodai-ji; www.en-aomori.com/culture-043.html; Jul. 20-24, Oct. 9-11

It's no surprise that Osore-zan is believed to be an ideal space to commune with the dead. People keen to reach the other side flock to the mountain for the Osore-zan Taisai festival at Bodai-ji twice yearly—July 20-24 and October 9-11—when the mountain becomes a gathering point for blind mediums called *Itako* who ritually purify themselves for three months prior. During the two days on the mountain, these highly trained spiritual messengers, seen toting mulberry-wood dolls believed to serve as conductors for sending and receiving psychic communiques, enter deeply into the trance state needed to do their job. Smaller numbers of *Itako* can sometimes be found on the mountain at other times of the year.

Information and Services

There's a small **Tourist Information Center** (4-3 Shimokita-machi, Mutsu-shi; tel. 0175/34-9095; www.mutsu-kanko.jp/en/info_center.html; 9am-7pm daily) beside Shimokita Station where you can pick up pamphlets and maps and inquire about bus schedules.

Transportation

GETTING THERE

Osore-zan is admittedly a difficult place to reach. Its remoteness is part of its appeal, but it definitely takes some planning to pull off a trip here without headache. While it's certainly possible to reach Osore-zan using public transportation, if you're coming from Aomori or Hirosaki and you're able to **drive,** this is by far the smoothest option. The drive from **Aomori** takes 2 hours (115 km/72 mi); the drive from **Hirosaki** takes about 2 hours 45 minutes (160 km/99 mi).

If driving isn't an option, allow lots of time to arrive and be sure to have all of the transfers between different train lines, buses, and so on very clearly mapped out before setting off. Coming from **Aomori,** take the Aoimori Railway (not to be confused with "Aomori") and ride 45 minutes to **Noheji** (¥1,040). If you're coming from **Hirosaki,** take the JR Ōu line to Aomori, then transfer to the Aoimori Railway and take it until Noheji (1.5 hours; ¥1,710).

Once you've reached Noheji, transfer to the **JR Ōminato line** and ride about 50 minutes to Shimokita Station (¥1,140). Now you're finally deep in the Shimokita Peninsula, where you'll find the elusive Osore-zan. Exit Shimokita Station and move next to the **Mutsu Bus Terminal,** about 3 km (2 mi) northeast of Shimokita Station. From here, catch the bus to Osore-zan (45 minutes; ¥810). Four or five buses depart Mutsu Bus Terminal from bus stand #1 daily May-October. Buses don't run to Osore-zan November-April due to inclement weather.

Hokkaido 北海道

Relaxed people, wide-open spaces, and an abundance of nature characterize Japan's northernmost main island of Hokkaido, which, despite being Japan's largest prefecture, only accounts for 5 percent of its population. In many ways, Hokkaido is Japan's final frontier. Those who are drawn to the island come largely seeking adventure.

The last major island in the country to be developed, Hokkaido has a history that in some ways mirrors that of the American West, complete with 19th-century settlers intent on blazing new trails. Also calling to mind North America's Wild West, Hokkaido is home to Japan's original inhabitants, the Ainu, whose customs and culture were sadly pushed to the fringes by the encroachment of modern life.

Highlights

Look for ★ to find recommended sights, activities, dining, and lodging.

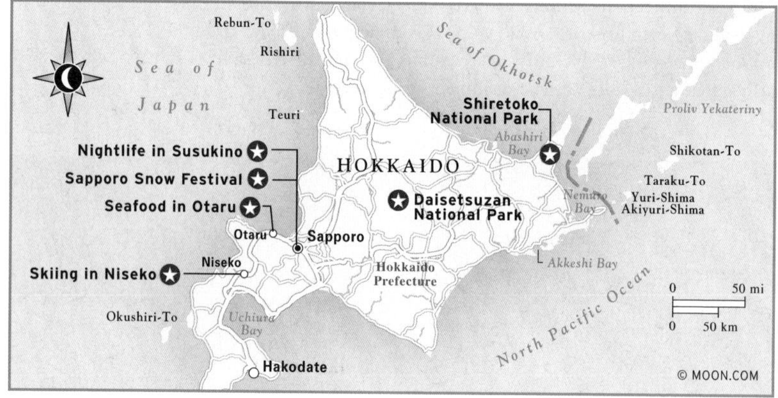

★ **Sapporo Snow Festival:** Teams of artists carve intricate statues in ice and build massive snow sculptures as large as buildings, drawing thousands of visitors to Sapporo every February (page 499).

★ **Nightlife in Susukino:** This Sapporo neighborhood boasts 4,000 bars, restaurants, and clubs, making it the largest nightlife zone north of the capital and one of the biggest in all of Japan (page 502).

★ **Seafood in Otaru:** The picturesque port of Otaru, historically a center for herring fishing, remains a major destination for seafood lovers (page 509).

★ **Skiing in Niseko:** The best places to ski in Hokkaido, Niseko's four resorts are a known quantity among devoted powder hounds worldwide (page 510).

★ **Daisetsuzan National Park:** Options for hiking and *onsen* abound in Japan's largest national park (page 524).

★ **Shiretoko National Park:** This vast wilderness and UNESCO World Heritage Site is known by the Ainu as "the end of the world" (page 536).

Hokkaido

Today, most of Hokkaido remains as wild as ever. The architecture seen in its scant cities and towns reveals an urban history that is decidedly modern compared to the rest of the nation. This is not the Japan of grand temple complexes or ancient Shinto rites. Here, the cultural markers were largely set from the 19th century on.

Most visitors access the island via the port town of Hakodate by train or through Sapporo by plane. In Sapporo, travelers eat their way through the city's hearty food scene and explore the lively nightlife of the Susukino area. In winter, the impressive Sapporo Snow Festival also draws a crowd. Craft beer flows from taps in the nearby cities of Hakodate, which charms guests with its 19th-century ambience, and Otaru, known for fresh seafood.

Beyond the urbanized southwest, visitors are drawn to Hokkaido's *onsen* (hot spring baths) and expansive national parks. In the

Previous: Mount Akadake, Daisetsuzan National Park; seafood at an Otaru market; a ski run in Hokkaido

Best Restaurants

★ **Shingen:** Eat noodles like a local at this vaunted Sapporo ramen shop (page 500).

★ **Suage+:** Discover soup curry, a dish loaded with meat, vegetables, and a spicy kick uncommon in the world of Japanese cuisine (page 500).

★ **Daruma:** Grill lamb and vegetables on your own griddle and get a taste of the culinary phenomenon known as Genghis Khan (page 500).

★ **Sushi Yoshi:** Taste the fruits of the sea over a bowl of rice at this outstanding sushi spot (page 509).

★ **Poronno:** Get a taste for Ainu cuisine near the shores of far-flung Lake Akan (page 533).

REGIONAL SPECIALTIES

Hokkaido is particularly known for its **seafood,** with crab being king, and the towns of Otaru and Hakodate being standouts. Among Hokkaido's other iconic cold-weather dishes is Mongolian barbecue, locally known as **Genghis Khan.** This DIY meal, ubiquitous in Sapporo, consists of lamb and onion cooked on dome-shaped grills resembling a battle helmet. Other Sapporo specialties include **miso ramen,** served in a flavorsome miso-based broth, and **soup curry,** a curry-flavored soup packed with tender meat (commonly pork or chicken) and loads of vegetables (paprika, eggplant, lotus root, pumpkin, etc.).

warmer months, when wildflowers erupt in vivid colors across much of the island, this region offers fantastic hiking opportunities. And during the island's long, snowy winters, ski resorts beckon powder lovers. Brown bears, red-crowned cranes, and abundant marine life along the coast also make the island an excellent choice for wildlife enthusiasts.

For a truly unique cultural experience, head to the Lake Akan area in the remote northeast. This region is home to a sizable number of Japan's indigenous Ainu people who have managed to preserve their traditional ways.

ORIENTATION

Japan's northernmost main island, with Russia's far east looming to the north, Hokkaido is vast by Japanese standards at 83,423 sq km (32,210 sq mi), making it the country's second largest island after Honshu. It doesn't lend itself to cleanly delineated regions per se, but Hokkaido can roughly be divided into four main zones: Southern Hokkaido, Central Hokkaido, Eastern Hokkaido, and remote Northern Hokkaido.

On the smallest region of the island, the main city in **Southern Hokkaido** is **Hakodate.** This is the first port of call for those traveling to the island from Honshu, which lies to the south across the Tsugaru Strait, by *shinkansen* (bullet train) or ferry.

Moving just north of Southern Hokkaido, the **Central Hokkaido** region is by far the island's most populated and influential (politically and economically) today. This is largely thanks to the presence of **Sapporo,** the island's capital, as well as its largest (and Japan's fifth largest) metropolis. The port town of **Otaru,** 35 km (22 mi) northwest of Sapporo, is one of the other main towns of the region. The interior of the region is also home to **Shikotsu-Tōya National Park,** a wonderland of lakes and volcanoes, the famed hot-spring village of **Noboribetsu Onsen,** and the standout ski resorts of **Niseko** and **Rusutsu,** which sit only about 20 km (12 mi) apart.

Best Accommodations

★ **Aya Niseko:** If money is no object, you can't go wrong by staying at one of these private apartments next to Niseko's slopes (page 512).

★ **Daisetsuzan Shirakaba-sō:** This large wooden lodge with open-air *onsen* puts you smack in the middle of Hokkaido's wild interior (page 527).

★ **Art Inn:** This unique art hotel is near the shores of Kussharo-ko (page 533).

★ **Hotel Kifu Club Shiretoko:** This chic property on the remote Shiretoko Peninsula offers rooms that face the windswept coast of the Sea of Okhotsk (page 539).

★ **Maruzen Pension Rera Mosir:** An adventurous mountain guide runs this clean, modern inn sitting at the edge of Rishiri Island's wild interior (page 541).

East of greater Sapporo is Hokkaido's second largest city, Asahikawa, which sits on the western edge of the vast **Daisetsuzan National Park.** Located essentially in the geographic center of the island, this massive swathe of nature is Japan's largest national park. Also in the island's heartland are the towns of **Biei** and **Furano,** which are awash in wildflowers in summer.

Heading eastward from Daisetsuzan, **Eastern Hokkaido** contains a hearty mix of salty fishing towns, and more than a hint of the pioneer spirit persists. This part of the island boasts **Akan National Park.** The region surrounding Akan National Park is where the fading Ainu culture has survived the longest. Roughly 50 km (31 mi) south of the Akan area, the **Kushiro Wetlands** (part of Kushiro-Shitsugen National Park) are famous for their thriving population of red-crested cranes.

Finally, the remotest region of them all is **Northern Hokkaido,** where towns are few and far between. In the far northeast, more than 200 km (124 mi) northeast of Daisetsuzan, **Shiretoko National Park** is a UNESCO World Natural Heritage Site and veritable showcase of biodiversity. Moving to the far northern reaches of the island, the Sea of Japan lies to the west, while the Okhotsk Sea spreads eastward. The main town here is Wakkanai. The beautiful islands of **Rishiri** and **Rebun,** gorgeous hiking spots in the warmer months for those who *really* want to get away from it all, lie about 60 km (37 mi) west of this town, from where they can be reached by ferry. The northernmost point of Japan is at Cape Sōya, about 40 minutes' drive northeast of downtown Wakkanai. North of here looms the southern tip of the Russian island of Sakhalin.

PLANNING YOUR TIME

Given its far-flung position as Japan's northernmost main island, Hokkaido is best approached either as a stand-alone destination, or as a nature-focused counterbalance to the vast sprawl of urban Japan. Another big factor in planning a trip to Hokkaido is season. Hokkaido's ample ski slopes, from **Niseko** to **Rusutsu** and **Furano,** are among the best in the world, which means they can become alarmingly crowded during the height of **winter.** Book accommodations to any ski or *onsen* resorts several months in advance.

In **summer,** the island's climate is pleasantly mild and dodges the typhoons that sweep across the rest of the country. Though traveling to the more remote national parks on the island can be tricky during winter, these unspoiled stretches of wilderness become a paradise for hikers during the warmer

Visiting Russia

It's possible to visit Russia from Hokkaido. The **Hokkaido Sakhalin Line** (tel. 0162/22-2550; http://hs-line.com) operates ferries twice a week August-mid-September (4.5 hours, ¥18,000 one way, ¥36,000 round trip) between **Wakkanai** and the port of **Korsakov** on Sakhalin.

You'll need to arrange this trip through a travel agent, which will also help with the visa paperwork. Sapporo-based agent **Nomad** (Minami 2 jō Nishi 6-8 Chūō-ku, Sapporo; tel. 011/200-8840; www.hokkaido-nomad.co.jp, infoship@hs-line.com; 9am-6pm Mon.-Fri.) can help get everything in order.

months. As an added bonus, they are among Japan's least crowded outdoor zones. Though it's cooler than the rest of Japan, weather in Hokkaido is also pleasant in the relative low seasons of **spring** and **fall.**

Bearing in mind the importance of timing, the vast distances between most of the island's main attractions means that there are few day-trip destinations. Most places call for an **overnight stay,** or at the very least, a well-planned stop with the next leg of the journey pre-arranged. Beginning at the far south of the island, the port city of **Hakodate** is a good entry point to Hokkaido if you're traveling by train, as it's connected to Aomori via the undersea Seikan Tunnel (54 km/33 mi).

If you're flying into Hokkaido, **Sapporo** will most likely be your entry point. Plan to spend a night or two here before heading elsewhere. To the west, **Otaru** is a good day trip from Sapporo. To the south, the surprisingly accessible **Shikotsu-Tōya National Park** and nearby **Noboribetsu Onsen** both work well for either a day trip or an overnight stay, depending on how much time you want to spend outdoors.

During winter, the buzzing ski resorts of **Niseko** and **Rusutsu,** both located southwest of Sapporo, and **Furano** in **Daisetsuzan National Park** at the island's center, are all excellent destinations for avid powder hounds. And in summer, given the distances between points such as Daisetsuzan National Park in the island's center, **Kushiro and Akan National Park** in the southeast, and **Shiretoko National Park** in the northeast, you won't want to spend less than a few nights in any of these remote corners of the island. In a country known for its tightly packed urban areas, you'll relish the chance to unplug, breathe in the fresh air, and bask in Hokkaido's wide-open spaces.

Using public transportation in Hokkaido can be tedious due to infrequent bus departures, sporadic train schedules, and large swathes of the island not being close to any rail network. If you plan to venture beyond the urban centers (Hakodate, Sapporo, Otaru, etc.), consider **renting a car** before striking off to remote locales such as Daisetsuzan National Park or Shiretoko National Park. Hokkaido's country roads are refreshingly spacious and often straight for long stretches with sparse traffic. This will make exploring the island much more enjoyable and will free you up to experience its natural splendor on your own terms.

A few **caveats:** Gas stations and convenience stores—ubiquitous in urban Japan—are scant in many parts of the island, and cell phone reception is often weak or nonexistent once you get away from it all. So be sure to fill your gas tank to the max and don't waste an opportunity to refuel or stock up on food or drinks. In addition, it's not advisable to drive in winter, when the roads are almost universally iced over and when whiteouts can and do occur when sudden blizzards strike. It's best to stick to public transport during the island's long winters. Finally, wildlife is profuse in the rugged interior. Resist the urge to speed on the open road, even if there are no other cars in sight, lest a fox or deer suddenly crosses your path.

Itinerary Ideas

SAPPORO AND OTARU

Day 1

1 Begin the day in Sapporo with a morning visit to **Hokkaido Jingū.** Although quite young by Shinto standards, this grand shrine is perhaps the island's most significant religious structure.

2 Head downtown for lunch and try one of Sapporo's renowned dishes, such as miso ramen at **Shingen.** Aim to arrive a bit ahead of opening time to avoid a queue.

3 To walk off some of your lunch, amble north toward the city's expansive central park, **Ōdōri Kōen.** This green stretch is a good place to people watch, soak up Sapporo's vibrant downtown, and behold Sapporo TV Tower. On your way to the park, be sure to stop by Baristart Coffee for a post-lunch caffeine hit to go.

4 Walk north about 7 minutes until you reach the **Former Hokkaido Government Office** and the history museum now housed there. This red-brick building is a classic example of the structures that popped up during Hokkaido's development in the 19th century, the start of the modern era.

5 To supplement the history lesson gleaned in the museum, walk about 10 minutes west to the **Hokkaido University Botanical Garden,** a 14-hectare (34-acre) green expanse, lined with hiking trails and plenty of places to sit.

6 Before sunset, make your way to **Mount Moiwa** in the southwest of town. Take the ropeway and cable car to the top of the peak and watch as the city lights twinkle.

7 Return downtown for dinner. **Daruma** is a good pick for Genghis Khan (Mongolian barbecue), a hearty option that's pure Sapporo.

8 If you've got the energy, explore the sprawling nightlife district of **Susukino.** Whether you're in the mood for jazz, cocktails, or a club, there's a venue that will fit the bill.

Day 2

Start your day by taking the train 40 minutes west to the port town of **Otaru.** If you had a big night in Susukino, it's fine to start in the mid- to late morning. Atmospheric Otaru lends itself to leisurely exploration.

1 Upon arriving in the town, walk down its long main central boulevard toward the ocean. Your first stop is the Otaru Canal and its row of atmospheric 19th-century warehouses. The **Otaru City Museum,** which sits beside the canal, gives a sense of Otaru's past as an important fishing hub.

2 Walk a few minutes west of the canal's south end and you'll find yourself on **Nichigin-dōri,** once known as the Wall Street of northern Japan. Admire the stately facades of the stone buildings, particularly the old Bank of Japan building.

3 For lunch, **Sushi Yoshi** is just a short walk south. Amid Otaru's stiff competition, this sushi shop is known for its quality. Plan to arrive a bit before opening to avoid the lines.

Sapporo and Otaru Itinerary Ideas

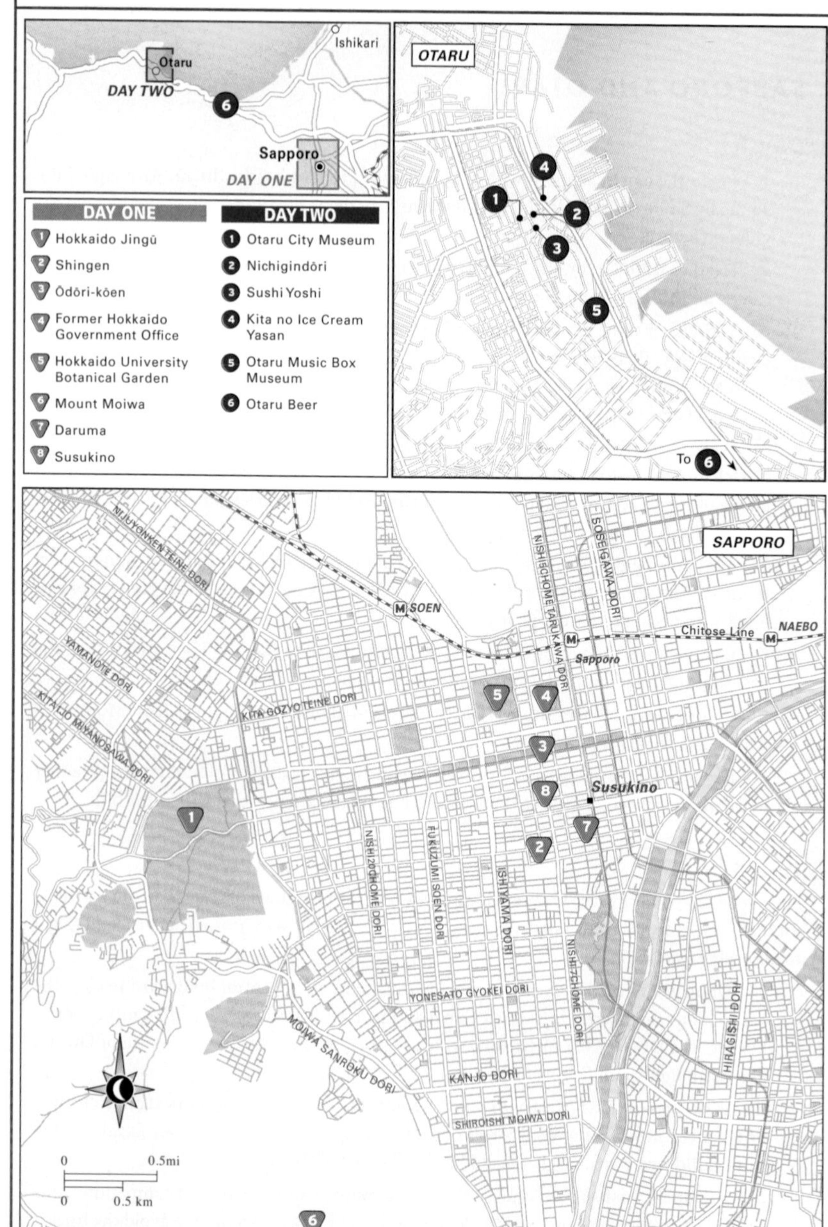

One Day in Hakodate

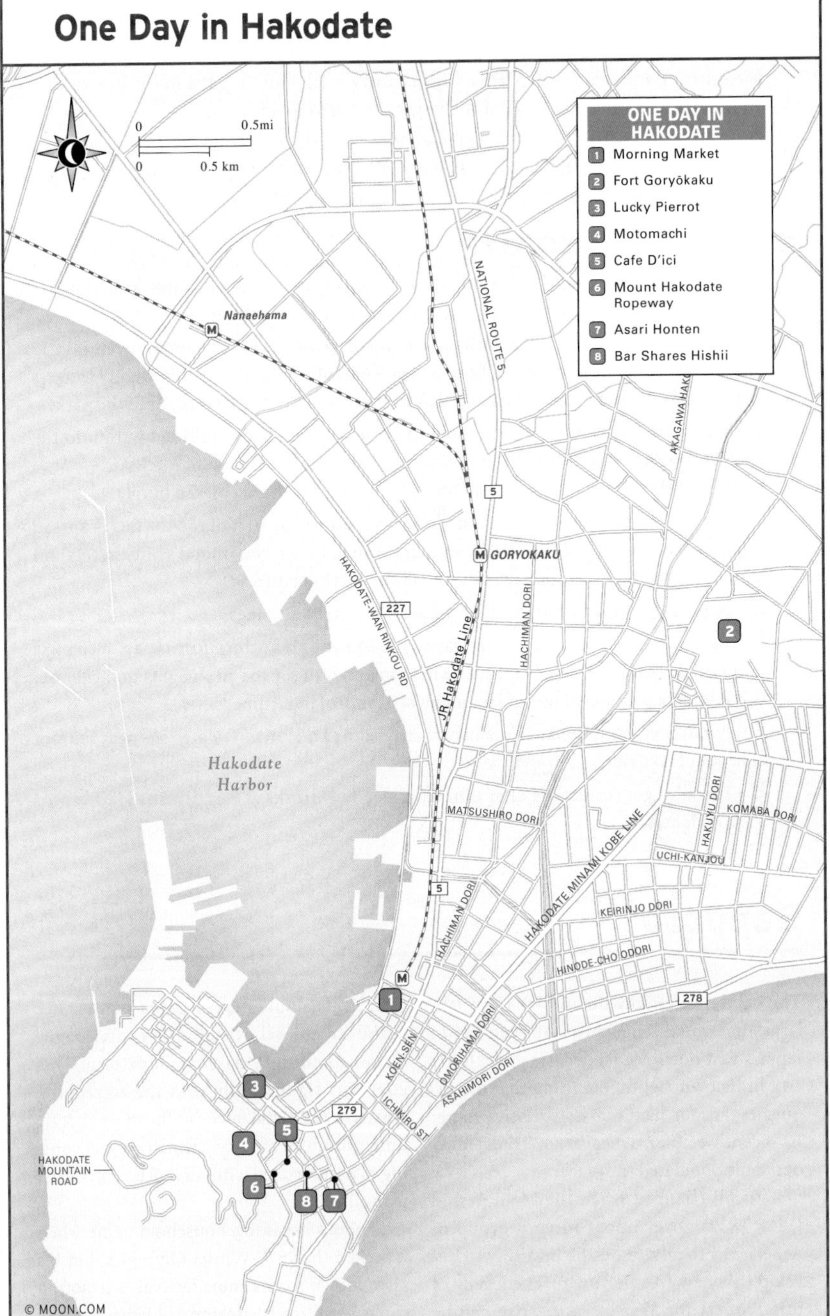

4 For dessert, stop at the legendary **Kita no Ice Cream Yasan,** known for its mix of traditional to downright funky flavors, like pumpkin and squid ink.

5 Ice cream in hand, walk about 15 minutes southeast toward the **Otaru Music Box Museum,** set in another evocative 19th-century brick building. If a music box catches your fancy, you can likely buy it if you've got the yen to spare.

6 End your day trip canal-side at **Otaru Beer,** a distinctive local brewery housed in a classic warehouse next to the water. If you stay until sunset, enjoy a stroll and take photos along the water's edge as the light softens before returning to Sapporo.

ONE DAY IN HAKODATE

1 Begin your exploration of Hakodate at the city's lively **morning market.** If you're feeling hungry, some of the stalls whip up a good seafood breakfast.

2 Hop on the tram and ride until the Goryōkaku-kōen-mae stop. From here, walk 15 minutes north to the star-shaped **Fort Goryōkaku.** To fully admire this mighty fortress and its park, go to the top of the Goryōkaku Tower at the southwest corner of the park.

3 For lunch, make your way to the other side of town, backtracking by tram to the Suehirochō stop. Then walk 5 minutes southeast to the main shop of **Lucky Pierrot,** a local institution known across Japan for its Chinese-influenced chicken burger.

4 After fueling up, walk to Hakodate's nearby historic district of **Motomachi,** spread across the foot of Mount Hakodate. Wander through the neighborhood's hilly streets and admire its wealth of well-preserved 19th-century architecture.

5 Make a pit stop at **Cafe D'ici** for some great coffee and cakes.

6 Before the sun sets, make your way to the **Mount Hakodate Ropeway,** just a few minutes' walk from Cafe D'ici. Ride to the top and wait for the city's lights to flicker on; this is widely considered one of Japan's most beautiful nighttime views.

7 For dinner, try *yakiniku* (Korean barbecue) at **Asari Honten,** which sits near the foot of Mount Hakodate.

8 If you've got the energy after dinner, grab a few drinks at **Bar Shares Hishii** near Mount Hakodate.

Sapporo 札幌

The capital of Hokkaido and Japan's fifth-largest metropolis, Sapporo is the gateway to Japan's vast northern wilderness and a lively city in its own right. One thing that distinguishes this northern hub is its relative youth. As recently as 1857, a meager seven adventurous souls populated the place.

This all changed when the Meiji period (1868-1912) government hired a group of Americans to advise on the best way to develop this new frontier town. The legacy of this request for Western expertise can be seen in its abundance of green spaces, and at the street level, with the city's thoroughfares laid out in a classic grid pattern. This contrasts significantly with the zigzagging streets of old castle towns or the more chaotic underpinnings of Tokyo, which grew according to human need without much centralized planning.

Sapporo became a household name when it hosted the 1972 Winter Olympics, but it's also known for its snow festival. Attracting some 2 million visitors every February, the

city creates impressively sculpted works of art in ice and snow—some of them the size of buildings. The climate has also played a significant role in the development of Sapporo's culinary heritage, mostly comprising hearty dishes such as heavy miso-based ramen, and the local invention of soup curry, and "Genghis Khan" grilled lamb and seafood. And, of course, there's Sapporo beer. Sprawling Susukino is the country's largest nightlife district north of Tokyo.

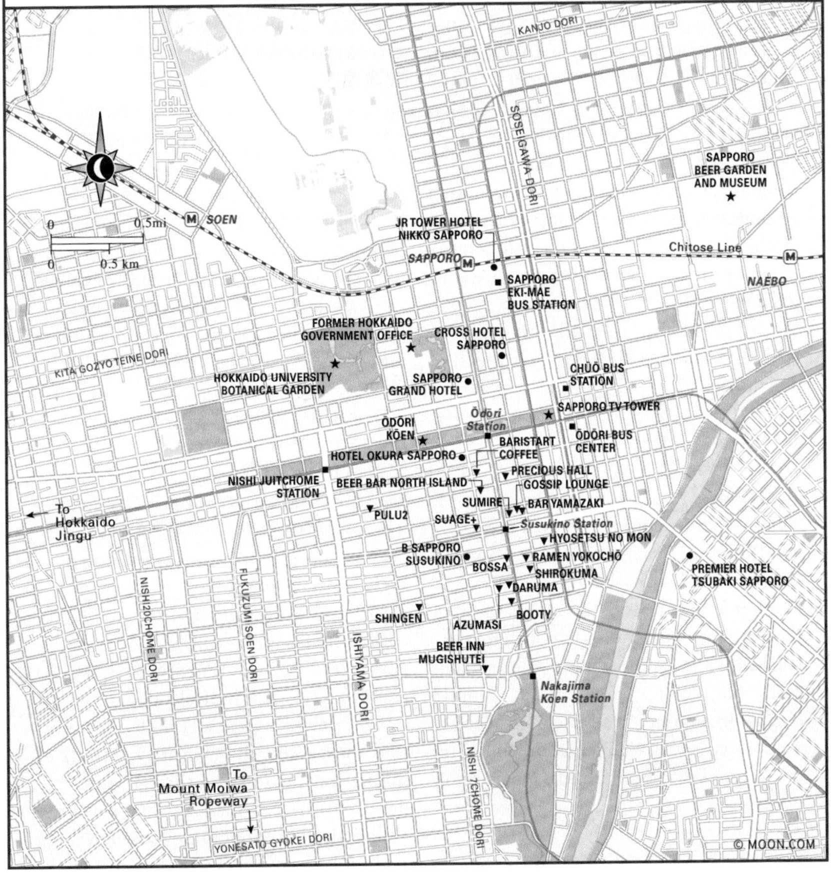

Whether you make an overnight stop on your way to Hokkaido's pristine backcountry, or explore the city on its own, plan to spend a day or two enjoying Sapporo's varied offerings.

ORIENTATION

Sapporo is the easiest city to navigate in Japan, thanks to its **grid layout** and **numbered blocks.** Ōdōri Kōen, which separates the city roughly into **northern** and **southern** halves, is the point from which every address is numbered. For example, the Old Hokkaido Government Office is located at "3 Kita 6 jō Nishi," with "Kita" being north and "jō Nishi" being "block 6." This means it is located three blocks to the north and six to the west from the eastern edge of Ōdōri Kōen.

With this general note about addresses in mind, in simple terms, **Sapporo Station** is at the north end of downtown, **Ōdōri Kōen,** which runs east-west, is about 10 minutes' walk south of there; **Nijō fish market** is about 5 minutes' walk south of the park's eastern edge; and the rambling nightlife zone of **Susukino** begins from around a 10-minute walk south of Ōdōri Kōen, or 10 minutes' walk southwest of the fishmongers of Nijō market. A handful of sites are scattered around the outskirts of town, such as **Mount Moiwa** in the southwest corner of town and **Moerenuma Park** northeast of downtown.

SIGHTS

Ōdōri Kōen

大通公園

This stretch of centrally located green is a good place to orient yourself in Sapporo. Well-groomed lawns, benches, flowers, and fountains create a bubble of calm in the middle of downtown. Dividing the city into north and south, the park is a block wide and runs east to west for 1.5 km (1 mi), spanning 13 blocks. In summer, it's a pleasant place to rendezvous or have a picnic; in winter, it's the primary site of the famed Sapporo Snow Festival.

Sapporo TV Tower

さっぽろテレビ塔

Ōdōri-nishi 1-chōme, Chūō-ku; www.tv-tower.co.jp; 9am-10pm daily; ¥720; take any of Sapporo's 3 subway lines to Ōdōri Station

At the eastern side of the park is Sapporo TV Tower. The hulking red structure rises almost 150 meters above the park below and is similar in appearance, and spirit, to Tokyo Tower, which some consider a blot on the landscape. Aesthetics aside, the tower does offer good views of the cityscape and surrounding mountains from its 90-meter-high (295-foot) observation deck. With Sapporo Station to the north and the dining, culinary, and nightlife hub of Susukino to the south, the city radiates from here.

Former Hokkaido Government Office

北海道庁

Kita 3 Jō Nishi 6-chōme, Chūō-ku; tel. 011/204-5019; 8:45am-6pm daily; free; take any of Sapporo's 3 subway lines to Sapporo Station, exit 10, or walk 7 minutes north of Ōdōri Kōen

The Former Hokkaido Government Office building is worth a quick stop, too. Its stunning red-brick edifice is a prime example of the American neo-baroque style that flourished in the late 19th century; it includes a museum exploring Hokkaido's history.

Hokkaido University Botanical Garden

北海道大学植物園

Kita 3 Jō Nishi 8-chōme, Chūō-ku; tel. 011/221-0066; www.hokudai.ac.jp/fsc/bg; 9am-4pm Tue.-Sun.; ¥420 summer, ¥120 winter and greenhouse only; take JR line to Sapporo Station, west exit (10-minute walk), or take Tozai subway line to Nishi-Juitchome Station, exit 4 (7-minute walk)

Just west of the Former Hokkaido Government Office, the Hokkaido University Botanical Garden offers a 14-hectare (34-acre) leafy escape from the city with a network of hiking trails that weave through the remnants of the forest that once blanketed the wild plain that Sapporo now occupies. It's pleasantly devoid of crowds on most weekdays. This is a great place for a relaxing yet informative amble.

Hokkaido Jingū

北海道神宮

474 Miyagaoka, Chūō-ku; tel. 011/611-0261; www.hokkaidojingu.or.jp; open 24/7; free; take Tozai subway line to Maruyama-kōen Station, exit 3

Japanese religion crept onto the island relatively recently. Hokkaido Jingū, found in a heavily wooded area within the city limits, is

1: Hokkaido Jingū **2:** flight at the Sapporo Beer Museum **3:** Sapporo Brewery

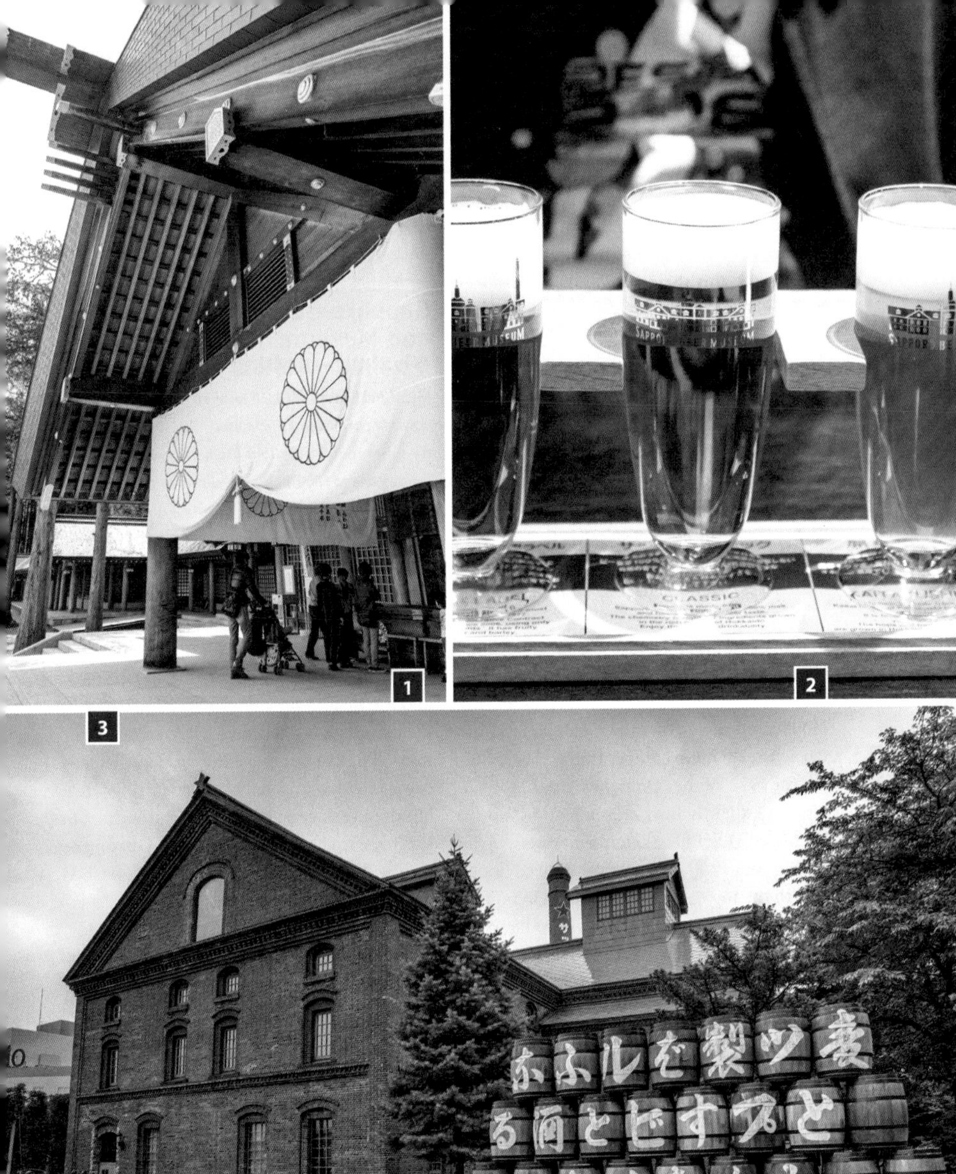
1
2
CLASSIC
3

one of the most prominent shrines in the prefecture. Feel the noise of the city fade as you walk deeper into the sylvan space. The cobblestone paths, dragon-shaped water spouts, imperial insignia, and hefty timber beams comprising the handsome inner sanctum may look stately and old. But compared with similar structures to the south, in the Shinto heartlands, this shrine is young, having been built *only* in 1869.

Sapporo Winter Sports Museum
札幌ウインタースポーツミュージアム

1274 Miyano-mori, Chūō-ku; tel. 011/641-8585; www.sapporowintersportsmuseum.com; 9am-6pm May-Oct., 9:30am-5pm Nov.-Apr.; ¥600; take Tozai line to Maruyama-kōen Station, exit 2; then take bus no. 14 (twice hourly) to Ōkurayama-kyōgijō-iriguchi bus stop and walk 2 minutes northwest to the stadium on the hill

With a rundown of Japan's triumphs in winter Olympic history, the Sapporo Winter Sports Museum turns out to be surprisingly fun. Housed west of downtown in the stadium where the ski jump competition was held during the 1972 Winter Olympics, this highly interactive, slightly zany museum allows you to simulate an Olympic ski jump on screen. After testing your skills on the computerized slopes, ride to the top of the jump where Olympians really did risk life and limb while the world watched.

Mount Moiwa Ropeway
藻岩山ロープウェイ

5-3-7 Fushimi, Chūō-ku; tel. 011/561-8177; www.sapporo-dc.co.jp; 10:30am-10pm Apr.-Nov., 11am-10pm Dec.-Mar.; ¥1,700 round-trip for ropeway and cable car, ¥1,100 round-trip for ropeway only, ¥600 round-trip for mini cable car only; from Susukino, take the streetcar to Ropeway Iriguchi station (25 minutes), then walk 5 minutes to the Mount Moiwa Ropeway

The Sapporo TV Tower may provide a good vista of Sapporo's downtown from up close. But for a more sweeping glimpse of the cityscape, head to Mount Moiwa at the southwestern corner of town. Ride the Mount Moiwa Ropeway over the gentle verdant slope of this mountain within the metropolis. The ropeway transports you three-quarters of the way up, where you transfer to a miniature cable car that takes you to an observation deck with stunning views of the city, particularly at dusk when the lights flicker.

Sapporo Beer Garden and Museum
サッポロビール博物館

Kita 7 Jō Higashi, 9-1-1, Higashi-ku; tel. 011/748-1876; www.sapporoholdings.jp; museum 10:30am-6pm daily, beer garden 11:30am-10pm daily; take Tōhō subway line to Higashi-Kuyakusho-mae station exit 4, then walk 10 minutes south

Sapporo is synonymous with beer. See where this association all began at the Sapporo Beer Garden and Museum, located east of Sapporo Station. Housed in a historic brick building with ivy creeping up its sides, the museum depicts the beer-making process and the history of Sapporo beer's rise within the country's brewed ranks. A free one-hour tour—English-language headsets available—caps off with a reasonably priced tasting, a few hundred yen per beer. The beer garden next to the museum has four restaurants. Opt for the classic: "Genghis Khan" grilled lamb, washed down with the hometown tipple.

Moerenuma Park
モエレ沼公園

1-1 Moerenuma-kōen, Higashi-ku; tel. 011/790-1231; http://moerenumapark.jp; 7am-10pm daily; free; take Tōhō subway line to Kanjodōri-higashi Station, then local bus number 69 or 79 to the Moernuma Kōen Higashi-guchi bus stop (the only park exit open year-round) (25 minutes, ¥210, 2 buses hourly)

Moerenuma Park is on the outskirts of town, but if you've got time it's worth the trip. Roughly 5 km (3 miles) around, the park's wide open green spaces are dotted by hulking geometric sculptures imagined by the brilliant late Japanese-American sculptor, artist, and landscape architect Isamu Noguchi. The Sapporo government asked Noguchi to dream up a park to build on the grounds, which were formerly a landfill. Strolling through the park is like stepping into Noguchi's mindscape. Noguchi died in 1988 before the park could be completed, but his vision was actualized after his passing and the park opened in 2005.

FESTIVALS

★ SAPPORO SNOW FESTIVAL
さっぽろ雪まつり

www.snowfes.com; early Feb.; free

During the Sapporo Snow Festival, intricate, sometimes towering sculptures made from snow and ice populate Sapporo's Ōdōri Kōen, the streets of Susukino, and Tsudome, a large event space on the outskirts of the city. Teams from around the globe come to try their hands at creating elemental effigies of characters and entities ranging from outsized anime characters and fish to dragons and mermaids. If you show up during the first week of the festival, before the Susukino and Ōdōri Kōen sites open, you can watch artists dressed like construction workers wield industrial-grade saws, hammers, and chisels, which they use to chip away ice and hammer out minute details in nimbly poised mermaids and skulking tigers.

Pop idols perform for massive crowds on stages made of piled-up snow. Vendors sell roast corn, potatoes drenched in butter, sausages, beer, and hot cocoa, as well as a sampling of regional specialties from around Japan. Crowds gleefully mill about the city or sit under large outdoor heaters, contentedly nursing hot wine in routinely below-freezing temperatures. Snowboarders do competitive jumps from a massive snow ramp built in the center of Ōdōri Kōen. There are snow slides with rentable sleds and small ice skating rinks too. Given the large crowds—a few million come each year—nightlife gets rowdy, which is a good or bad thing, depending on your perspective.

Given the festival's wild popularity, it's wise to book accommodation at least three months in advance if you plan to make the trip.

FOOD

Ramen

RAMEN YOKOCHŌ

Minami 5 Jō Nishi 3-6, Chūō-ku; www.ganso-yokocho.com; 11:30am-3am; ¥1,000; take Nanboku subway line to Susukino Station, exit 5

In a city as obsessed with ramen as Sapporo, it's hard to know where to begin. For an introduction, make your way to Ramen Yokochō. This narrow, covered alleyway is brimming with options, from noodles tossed in a heavy

glass pyramid in Moerenuma Park

miso-based soup to lighter salt-based broths. It's hard to go wrong with any shop here. If photos don't pull you into a particular one, just opt for one with a healthy number of customers and step in. When searching for the alley, look for the sign over the entrance emblazoned with red and green neon Japanese characters.

SUMIRE

Minami 3 Jō Nishi 3-9-2; tel. 011/200-4567; www.sumireya.com; 5pm-2am Mon.-Sat., 5pm-midnight Sun.; ¥1,000; take Nanboku subway line to Susukino Station, exit 5

A great stand-alone ramen shop just a few blocks north (4 minutes' walk) from Ramen Yokochō is Sumire. This second-floor shop feels slightly more spruced up inside than the old-school shops of Ramen Yokochō. Along with your noodles, at Sumire you can expect perfectly boiled eggs and thick strips of pork floating in an incredibly fragrant soup. It's a great choice after a night out drinking in Susukino. Be forewarned that the soup is quite salty. Calling it rich is an understatement.

★ SHINGEN

Minami 6 Jō Nishi 8-8-2, Chūō-ku; tel. 011/530-5002; 11:30am-1am daily; ¥1,000; take Nanboku subway line to Susukino Station, exit 5

An excellent ramen joint in the Susukino area frequented by locals is Shingen. Around a dozen seats line the countertop at this greasy spoon, which is a wonderful place to get a real taste of Sapporo. Shingen excels in delivering rich creamy soup that manages to retain subtle flavors without being overwhelmed by salt or oil—a tricky balance for miso ramen. The waits here can be a little daunting at peak times; try to come mid-afternoon or late at night. If there's a queue, don't fret too much. It tends to move quickly.

Soup Curry

★ SUAGE+

Miyako Shimatsu Bldg. 2F, Minami 4 Jō Nishi 5-chōme, Chūō-ku; tel. 011/233-2911; 11:30am-10:30pm Mon.-Sat., 11:30am-10pm Sun.; ¥1,200; take Nanboku subway line to Susukino Station, exit 5

Along with ramen, soup curry, served with a side of rice, is another classic Sapporo dish. Suage+ is a popular spot with an interior reminiscent of a wine bar more than a soup curry shop. In Susukino, the shop uses great ingredients such as huge *maitake* mushrooms, chicken, and lavender pork. You can choose your spice level. Try cheese as a topping for your rice.

PULU2

Minami 2 Jō Nishi 9-chōme, Chūō-ku; tel. 011/272-1190; 11am-8pm daily; ¥1,000; take Tōzai subway line to Nishi Juitchome Station, exit 2

If you want your soup curry with a side of reggae, head for Pulu2 Set in a basement with reggae piped through a solid sound system, Jamaican flags and Peter Tosh posters adorn the walls, while in the open kitchen the master and owner can be seen at work whipping up a mean curry. Dishes have large chunks of vegetables, chicken, or lamb, and spiciness levels from zero to 100. After eating a 20, I shudder to think what anything above 50 would taste like. It's a little out of the way, but is well off the tourist trail.

Genghis Khan

★ DARUMA

Minami 5 Jō Nishi 4-chōme, Chūō-ku; tel. 011/552-6013; http://best.miru-kuru.com/daruma/sm; 5pm-3am daily; ¥3,000; take Nanboku subway line to Susukino Station, exit 5

Although slightly touristy and crowded, Daruma is the quintessential Genghis Khan (Mongolian barbecue) restaurant. Thin cuts of lamb and copious onions sizzle and

---

1: Sapporo Snow Festival **2:** soup curry at Suage+ **3:** Ghengis Khan Mongolian barbecue **4:** Susukino district at night

1
2
3
4
SUPER
"DRY"
Asahi
docomo
アイフル
マルハン
すすきのビル
KIRIN
Coca-Cola

splatter from atop the dome-shaped skillets arrayed around the counter, where about 15 diners sit enveloped in cooking smoke. A small menu of side items includes kimchi, seaweed, and rice.

SHIROKUMA

Minami 6 Jō Nishi 3-chōme, Chūō-ku; tel. 011/552-4690; www.nisso.gr.jp/shirokuma; 6pm-1am Mon.-Wed., 6pm-1:30am Thurs.-Sat.; ¥4,000; take Nanboku subway line to Susukino Station, exit 5

An equally good Mongolian barbecue joint is Shirokuma. While all of the Genghis Khan options around town amass queues, this one is decidedly more local and somewhat less of a crowd magnet than Daruma. Aside from a slightly more extensive side menu, the equation is similar here: take a seat at the counter and start grilling.

Seafood

AZUMASI

Minami 6 Jō Nishi 4-4-1, Chūō-ku; tel. 011/513-7800; 6pm-3am daily; ¥3,000; take Nanboku subway line to Susukino Station, exit 5

Azumasi is a cozy oyster bar with a trendy interior with both counter and floor seating. Friendly owners and stylish patrons help make this a good place for oysters and sake in the heart of Susukino.

HYOSETSU NO MON

Minami 5 Jō Nishi 2-chōme, Chūō-ku; tel. 011/521-3046; www.hyousetsu.co.jp.e.em.hp.transer.com; 11am-11pm daily; ¥3,000 lunch, ¥8,000 dinner; take Nanboku subway line to Susukino Station, exit 5

Hyosetsu no Mon is a fantastic choice for sampling some of Hokkaido's excellent crab. Established in 1964, the shop serves a wide range of crab dishes: *shabu shabu* (hot pot), sashimi, sushi, tempura, *chawanmushi* (savory egg custard), and more. A great choice is the king crab *shabu shabu,* packed with vegetables. As the pot boils, the broth is infused with rich flavors of the meat.

Café

BARISTART COFFEE

Minami 1 Jō Nishi 4-8, Chūō-ku; www.baristartcoffee.com; 9am-7pm daily; ¥500; take Tōzai or Nanboku subway line to Ōdōri Station, exit 2

The artistes at Baristart Coffee not only make great artisan brew, they use incredibly rich milk sourced from Hokkaido farms in all of their dairy-infused options. Try their excellent latte.

BARS AND NIGHTLIFE

★ Susukino

As if Sapporo's deep connection with beer brewing wasn't already enough party cred, its Susukino district is the nation's largest nightlife zone north of Tokyo. All told, some 4,000 bars, dance clubs, jazz joints, and host and hostess clubs vie for the attention of sometimes raucous clientele. Aside from a copious amount of beer on tap, there are also world-class cocktail lounges and a handful of underground clubs with top-notch sound systems.

BEER BAR NORTH ISLAND

Large Country Bldg. 10F, Nishi 4-chōme, Minami 2 jo, Chūō-ku; tel. 011/251-8820; 6pm-midnight Mon.-Sat. 6pm-midnight, Sun. 3pm-10pm

A night out in Sapporo really begins at Beer Bar North Island, located southeast of Ōdōri Kōen, across from the Nijō fish market.

GOSSIP LOUNGE

Minami 3 Jō Nishi 3-chōme; tel. 011/206-1331; 8pm-6am daily; take Nanboku subway line to Susukino Station, exit 2

Another good spot to start a night in Susukino is Gossip Lounge. The friendly English-speaking staff here are knowledgeable of the neighborhood and aren't shy about recommending various places. The good thing is that you get what you pay for here. The bar works on a token system: Pay ¥1,600 for five tokens, which are then used for decent mixed drinks that cost 1-3 tokens each. The bar is centrally located, which makes it an ideal starting point for a night out.

BAR YAMAZAKI

4F Katsumi Bldg., Minami 3 Jō Nishi 3-chōme, Chūō-ku; tel. 011/221-7363; www.bar-yamazaki.com; 6pm-12:30am Mon.-Sat.; take Nanboku subway line to Susukino Station, exit 1

Bar Yamazaki is a classic cocktail lounge with a famously innovative former master, Tatsuro Yamazaki, who sadly passed in November 2016 at the ripe old age of 96. The bar has an appealing dark wood interior, softly lit by elegant old-fashioned lamps. Plush chairs line the bar and there are comfortable private booths. The menu features some 200 cocktails, among them an array of award-winning original concoctions, including the "Sapporo," which snagged a prize at the Amaretto Di Saronna Cocktail Competition in Italy. The quality cocktails and service do come at a price, however: There's a ¥1,000 seating charge and a 10 percent service charge.

BOSSA

2F Silver Bldg., Minami 3 Jō Nishi 4-chōme, Chūō-ku; tel. 011/271-5410; www.bossa.tv; 11am-1am; take Nanboku subway line to Susukino Station

For a bar with an equally classy, yet more vivacious atmosphere, try Bossa. Café by day and lively bar by night, this excellent jazz joint opened in 1971 and boasts a seriously good sound system. The owner has some 9,000 vinyl records and 6,000 CDs. Posters of jazz greats adorn the walls, and potted plants give the all-wood interior a relaxed, cozy vibe. Customers chat and laugh freely with an excellent jazz soundtrack. Check out the "Milky Way" section of the menu, which includes a number of dairy-based cocktails that use locally sourced milk. There's also an all-you-can-drink option for ¥1,850.

BOOTY

Minami 7 Jō Nishi 4-chōme, Chūō; tel. 011/521-2336; www.booty-disco.com; 8pm-early morning Fri.-Sat.; take Nanboku subway line to Susukino Station

For a decidedly rowdier experience, head to Booty. This weekend-only party hot spot has an *izakaya* (pub) on one floor and a club with a dance floor on another. The music leans hip-hop, reggae, and R&B. Thanks to its lack of cover charge, it gets bumping.

PRECIOUS HALL

B1 Parade Bldg., Minami 2 Jō Nishi 3-13; tel. 011/513-2221; www.precioushall.com; hours vary by event; take Tōzai or Nanboku subway lines to Ōdōri Kōen Station, exit 2

Though technically north of Susukino, Precious Hall throws great house and techno events with a bit of an underground edge. This place is known for its spectacular sound system and clued-in crowd, but nights here can admittedly be hit or miss, largely depending on the event. Check the schedule on the website before making the trip.

BEER INN MUGISHUTEI

Minami 9 Jō Nishi 5-chōme, Chūō-ku; tel. 011/512-4774; www.mugishutei.com; 7pm-3am daily; take Nanboku subway line to Nakajima Kōen Station, exit 2

If your idea of a good night is to drink your way through as many obscure varieties of beer as you can fathom in a mellow setting, Beer Inn Mugishutei, just might blow your mind. Located in a quiet corner of southern Susukino, this underground beer mecca offers more than 300 types of beer from all around the globe. Rows upon rows of vintage cans line the walls. The atmosphere is no-frills—darts, foosball, and some old wooden tables—but the beer is the point. One caveat: There's a ¥900 "charm charge." If this doesn't put you off, you'll be hard pressed to find another spot offering this many types of beer.

ACCOMMODATIONS

¥10,000-20,000

B SAPPORO SUSUKINO

Minami 5 Jō Nishi 6-14-1; tel. 011/562-1122; http://sapporo-susukino.theb-hotels.com; ¥10,500 d; take Nanboku subway line to Susukino Station, exit 5

The B Sapporo Susukino is a boutique hotel offering petite but stylish rooms at reasonable rates. This new hotel is five minutes' walk from Susukino station, in the heart of the action. Free Wi-Fi, a mobile phone equipped with SIM for each room, and breakfast buffet are included.

HOTEL OKURA SAPPORO

Minami 1 Jō Nishi 5-chōme; tel. 011/221-2333; www.okura-nikko.com; ¥12,000 d; take Tōzai or Nanboku subway line to Ōdōri Kōen Station, exit 3

Hotel Okura Sapporo is a highly regarded brand in Japan, and in Sapporo, this usually pricy option is accessible for a very reasonable rate. Chic modern design throughout the hotel, good dining options (Chinese, Japanese, continental), a great location, and friendly customer service make it an appealing choice.

CROSS HOTEL SAPPORO

Kita 2 Jō Nishi 2-23, Chūō-ku; tel. 011/272-0010; www.crosshotel.com; ¥15,000 d; take JR lines to Sapporo Station

The Cross Hotel Sapporo is a great hotel in an excellent location that offers a lot for its price tag. The clean, modern rooms are furnished with a designer's touch—with choices of natural, urban and hip decor—and are generously sized. There's a large public bath on the top floor with great views of the city below. The excellent breakfast fuses European cooking with local ingredients. The friendly staff speak English.

PREMIER HOTEL TSUBAKI SAPPORO

Toyohira 4 Jō 1-1-1, Toyohira-ku; tel. 011/821-1111; https://tsubaki.premierhotel-group.com; ¥18,000 d; take Tōzai subway line to Kikusui Station, exit 2

Premier Hotel Tsubaki Sapporo has a dash of old-world charm. Plush furniture, muted golden drapes, and well-appointed genuinely spacious rooms (36 square meters/387 square feet and up). It's slightly outside the middle of town—about 15 minutes' walk from Susukino—but if you like to get a little bit away from the bustle, this is an excellent choice. There's also a good breakfast spread in a bright dining room. The concierge and other staff speak English and are eager to help with trip preparation.

¥20,000-30,000

SAPPORO GRAND HOTEL

Kita 5 Jō Nishi 2-5, Chūō-ku; tel. 011/251-2222; www.jrhotels.co.jp/tower/english; ¥34,000 d; take JR lines to Sapporo Station

The Sapporo Grand Hotel has been welcoming guests since 1934; it was the city's first European-style hotel. Today, attendants in

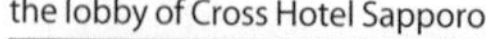

the lobby of Cross Hotel Sapporo

white gloves and attentive staff make all guests feel as if they're visiting dignitaries. There are swanky bars and a range of restaurant options, and smart, understated elegance infuses the rooms. If you've got a little extra to spend, this is a great choice.

¥30,000-40,000

JR TOWER HOTEL NIKKO SAPPORO

8-2-36 Ōdōri Nishi, Chūō-ku; tel. 011/251-2222; www.okura-nikko.com; ¥33,000 d; take JR lines to Sapporo Station

JR Tower Hotel Nikko Sapporo offers the best vistas of any hotel in the city. Luxurious rooms, a bar, restaurants (Western and Japanese), and a spa complete the package. As it's connected directly to JR Sapporo Station, it's highly convenient to boot.

INFORMATION AND SERVICES

HOKKAIDO-SAPPORO TOURIST INFORMATION CENTER

JR Sapporo West Concourse, Kita 6 jō Nishi 4, Kita-ku; tel. 011/213-5088; www.welcome.city.sapporo.jp; 8:30am-8pm daily

Sapporo has heaps of resources for visitors to the city. Coming from JR Sapporo Station, head to the Hokkaido-Sapporo Tourist Information Center. This is the best place in the city to ask questions ahead of any foray into the backcountry, or any exploration of Sapporo itself. Along with offering maps, bus schedules, leaflets, and more, the English-speaking staff are knowledgeable helpful. It's connected to the JR General Information Center on the ground floor of the Hokkaido-Sapporo Food and Tourism Information Building.

SAPPORO INTERNATIONAL COMMUNICATION PLAZA

3F MN Building, Kita 1 jō Nishi 3, Chūō-ku; tel. 011/211-3678; www.plaza-sapporo.or.jp; 9am-5:30pm Mon.-Sat.

Across the street from the Sapporo Clock Tower, at the Sapporo International Communication Plaza, you'll meet approachable staff offering bilingual support aimed specifically at foreign visitors. Alongside a good supply of English-language pamphlets and maps, free Wi-Fi is available.

SAPPORO CITY CALL CENTER

tel. 011/222-4894; 8am-9pm daily

For help over the phone, the Sapporo City Call Center is a hotline offering English-language assistance.

TRANSPORTATION

Getting There

AIR

There are dozens of flights daily to and from Tokyo and Sapporo. Both major Japanese carriers and smaller budget airlines cover the route between **Haneda Airport** and **Narita Airport** in Tokyo, and Sapporo's **New Chitose Airport** (www.new-chitose-airpot.jp). Other airports servicing routes to and from Sapporo include **Nagoya, Osaka,** and **Hiroshima,** among others. The journey takes about an hour and a half from Tokyo, with one-way flights ranging from less than ¥10,000 to upwards of ¥40,000.

Rapid trains run regularly to Sapporo from New Chitose Airport (35 minutes; ¥1,590). There's a second airport in the city, **Okadama,** but flights to this smaller hub are limited. If you fly there, you can reach downtown via a **shuttle bus** that runs between the airport and **Sakaemachi** subway station (5 minutes; ¥210), from which the rest of the city is within easy reach.

TRAIN

It's also possible to take the train to Sapporo from Tokyo. Board the **Tohoku/Hokkaido** *shinkansen* in Tokyo and ride until Shin-Hakodate-Hokuto (4.5 hours; ¥22,890). From there, transfer to the **Hokuto limited express train** to Sapporo (3.5 hours; ¥8,830). Although this is hardly economical or efficient, this journey can still make sense if you have a JR Pass, which covers the whole trip. It also makes sense if you're traveling through Tohoku en route to Hokkaido. Note that a seat reservation is required for the Hayabusa *shinkansen* running from Tokyo to Shin-Hakodate-Hokuto.

BUS

If you're coming to Sapporo from within Hokkaido, chances are there's a bus route that will work just as well as taking a train. There are a number of expressway bus operators on the island, running routes to Sapporo's main bus hubs: **Sapporo Ekimae Bus Station,** the busiest terminal in the city near JR Sapporo Station; **Chūō Bus Station,** northeast of Sapporo TV Tower; and to the southeast of Sapporo TV Tower, **Ōdōri Bus Center.** Some of the destinations in Hokkaido with bus routes linking to Sapporo include **Niseko** (3 hours; ¥2,300), **Noboribetsu Onsen** (2 hours; ¥2,100), **Tōya-ko Onsen** (3 hours; ¥2,700), **Furano** (3 hours; ¥2,100), **Asahikawa** (2 hours; ¥2,000), and **Wakkanai** (6 hours; ¥6,000).

Getting Around

Thanks to its grid layout and numbered blocks, Sapporo is very easy to navigate.

There's a trusty **subway** system with three lines (from ¥200), buses run by **JR Hokkaido Bus** (covered by the JR Pass), and a few other operators not covered by the pass, a **tram** that does a loop around the Ōdōri Kōen area and Susukino in the south (¥170 fare for all destinations; enter from the rear of the tram and pay upon leaving through the front), and of course, **taxis,** which are similar to Tokyo in price, although fares vary based on the size of the vehicle and the operator. Typically, taxis start around ¥670, plus ¥265 for each additional kilometer.

There are a variety of one-day transportation passes for traversing the city. The **subway card,** which allows unlimited use of the city's three subway lines for one calendar day (¥830 adults, ¥420 children), can be purchased at ticket machines. The **Sapica IC card,** also purchased at ticket machines in subway stations, allows you to top it up and use it interchangeably on the subway, and on some (but not all) city buses and trams. The Sapica card is unique in that each swipe allows you to gain 10 percent points that are applied toward future trips. Note that this card cannot be used beyond the Sapporo area. To travel beyond Sapporo, you'll need a **Kitaca card.** To read more on all the various passes and more on transportation in the Sapporo region, see www.sapporo.travel/learn/transportation/sapporo.

Around Sapporo

OTARU
小樽

Otaru is a town on the ocean with a picturesque harbor, nostalgic pockets of history and loads of charm. Located 30-45 minutes west of Sapporo by train, the former herring center makes for a great day trip or a worthwhile stop when traveling between Niseko and Sapporo. Old-fashioned lanterns line its streets, as do classic European-style buildings. Chic new restaurants, bars, cafés, and shops selling beautifully blown glassware, for which the city is famed, are set in stately brick buildings and old ivy-covered warehouses.

Otaru's history is deeply associated with fishing, as seen in the cluster of large warehouses along its scenic canal, and in its old herring mansions where the city's rich fishing merchants once lived and worked. It's no surprise that the town's port was the terminus of Hokkaido's first railway, linking it to Sapporo. Its mercantile history is also displayed in the elegant brick façades gracing old structures around Nichigin-dōri, dubbed "Wall Street of the North" in its heyday from the late Taisho to early Showa periods (1920s-1930s).

Today, the legacy of this industrious past is evident throughout Otaru, which is just the right size to explore on a day trip.

Sights

OTARU CANAL

小樽運河

Along this famed stretch of water, lined by gas streetlamps, you'll find a row of alluring stone warehouses where a number of companies once did brisk business in shipping and trade. Finished in 1923, the canal fell into disuse when the city upgraded its docks so that ships could directly unload their cargo. In the 1970s, citizens turned the much-romanticized waterway into a road. Thankfully, the canal was saved. Since then, beer halls, eateries, dessert shops, and museums have opened in these charming buildings, evocative reminders of Otaru's past.

OTARU CITY MUSEUM

小樽市総合博物館

2-1-20 Iornai; tel. 0134/22-1258; 9:30am-5pm Wed.-Mon.; ¥400; from JR Otaru Station, walk 10 minutes down Chūō-dōri

Next to the canal, you'll find one branch, the Canal Building (Ungakan), of the Otaru City Museum. Set in a renovated late-19th-century warehouse, this museum explores the natural and cultural history of Hokkaido and Otaru: the crucial role that herring fishing once played for the town, Ainu artifacts, and literary depictions of the city. An English-language guide is available at the front desk. There is another branch of this museum, highlighting the city's railways, but it's a bit out of the way.

NICHIGIN-DŌRI

日銀道り

From JR Otaru Station, walk 10 minutes

As you walk southeast along Otaru Canal, turn right on Nichigin-dōri, once known as northern Japan's Wall Street. Otaru was also a financial hub in its prime. The graceful façades of many buildings along the street recall that legacy, but none more so than the brick architectural gem that once housed Otaru's original branch of the **Bank of Japan** (1-11-16 Ironai; tel. 0134/21-1111; 9:30am-5pm Thurs.-Tues. Apr.-Nov., 10am-5pm Thurs.-Tues. Dec.-Mar.; free).

Built in 1912, the impressive office block also features owl cornerstones, a nod to Ainu tradition, which considers the bird a divine guardian. Inside, you'll find a free museum that explores Otaru's history as a crucial financial node during Japan's modernization.

MUSIC BOX MUSEUM

小樽オルゴール堂本館

4-1 Sumiyoshi-chō; tel. 0134/21-3101; www.otaru-orgel.co.jp; 9am-6pm daily; free; from JR Minami-Otaru Station, walk 7 minutes, or from the canal it's a 15-minute walk

One more museum worth visiting in Otaru is the Music Box Museum. Located at Marchen Crossroads, a historic intersection reached by walking 15 minutes southeast of the canal along Sakaimachi-dōri, the Music Box Museum is housed in an enchanting stone building, finished in 1912 and fronted by a Victorian-style steam clock, a gift from the city of Vancouver. Inside, you'll be bowled over by thousands of music boxes dating from the Renaissance onward. The museum also has three other locations dotting the area with a whopping 25,000 music boxes on display.

This is a shop as much as a museum. Be prepared to part with some yen if you see a box you like. If you'd like to try your hand at designing one of your own, workshops are offered too.

Festivals

OTARU SNOW LIGHT PATH FESTIVAL

小樽雪あかりの路

Otaru canal, various other locations around town; http://yukiakarinomichi.org; 5pm-9pm daily for 10 days in mid-Feb.; free

Similar to Sapporo, the town has a magic of its own in winter, when candles softly flicker within lanterns made from snow, lining the town's famed canal and tucked into various

1

2

3

nooks and crannies around the city. All told, some 100,000 candles are lit in Otaru during this festival. It's an intimate, laid-back alternative to Sapporo's jam-packed snow festival.

★ Food

AJIDOKORO TAKEDA

3-10-16 Inaho; tel. 0134/22-9652; www.otaru-takeda.com; 8am-6pm; ¥2,000

While Otaru's herring days may have faded, the city is still renowned for its fresh catch. To get a real taste of the kind of market where the town's sushi chefs source their ingredients, head to Sankaku Market, located just northeast of JR Otaru Station in a roofed alleyway. Amid all the stalls at Sankaku with squid arrayed on ice, massive king crabs in tanks and salmon roe ready to be placed atop bowls of rice, there's one that stands out: Ajidokoro Takeda. This mom-and-pop eatery is operated by the same people who run the Takeda Fish Store across the aisle. Try the *sanshoku don*, a bowl of rice covered with three types of impressively fresh seafood. If you're there during lunch hours, a wonderful bowl of crab soup comes with it (or any other lunch item). Compared with seafood spreads at larger fish markets, this is a steal. Look for the yellow sign.

SUSHIYA KŌDAI

1-4-15 Inaho; tel. 080/6073-6635; 6pm until close Thurs.-Mon.; ¥4,000

A different kind of seafood experience awaits at Sushiya Kōdai. Here, you stand while you eat. The chef here studied under a master at Ise Sushi, another Otaru sushi mecca. Sushiya Kōdai is down a small alley of 13 restaurants called **Otaru Yataimaura Renga Yokochō,** located 7 minutes' walk from JR Otaru Station. The *ikura* (salmon roe) is worthy of note.

★ SUSHI YOSHI

1-10-9 Ironai; tel. 0134/23-1256; 11:30am-3:30pm and 5:30pm-9:45pm daily; ¥5,000 lunch, ¥8,000 dinner

A great option with a neighborhood vibe, four minutes' walk east of Sushiya Kōdai, Sushi Yoshi doesn't disappoint. The shop is known for its eel and sea urchin *nigiri* (sashimi over vinegared rice), as well as its *tokusei kaisen don*, a bowl of rice topped with assorted fruits of the sea. If you're feeling adventurous, try monkfish liver, left to marinate in saltwater for a half-day then steamed and dipped in a citrusy sauce infused with ginger, seaweed, chili and shredded radish.

KITA NO ICE CREAM

1-2-18 Ironai; tel. 0134/23-8983; 9:30am-6pm daily; ¥300-700

Although touristy, the sheer number of obscure—even off-putting—flavors (sea urchin or squid ink, anyone?) make this little ice cream parlor worth a stop. There are also plenty of safer options like vanilla and chocolate, as well as some slightly more offbeat ones (*matcha* and sake). It's set in an old stone building and has a dated wooden interior that's sure to invoke a sense of nostalgia.

Bars and Nightlife

OTARU BEER

5-4 Minatomachi; tel. 0134/21-2323; https://otarubeer.com/jp; 11am-11pm daily

While strolling along Otaru's canal, pick the door to Otaru warehouse No. 1, or Otaru Beer Sōko No. 1, the first warehouse you'll come to after approaching the canal from JR Otaru Station via Chūō-dōri. This is the base of Otaru Beer, brewed on-site.

The founder of this craft beer operation is one of Otaru's few German residents, Braumeister Johannes Braun, who follows the centuries-old German Beer Purity Law, which strictly regulates the ingredients used to brew. Appropriately, the menu also includes a range of German fare, and good pizza too. Smoking is allowed inside, so if you can put up with that, this is a great spot for either pre-dinner drinks or a dinner complemented by this good local craft brew.

1: Otaru Snow Light Path Festival **2:** Music Box Museum **3:** historic canal and warehouse in Otaru

Information and Services

OTARU STATION TOURIST INFORMATION CENTER

2-22-15 Inaho; tel. 0134/29-1333; 9am-6pm daily

The Otaru Station Tourist Information Center has English-language maps and other resources.

CANAL PLAZA TOURIST INFORMATION CENTER

2-1-20 Ironai; 9am-6pm daily; tel. 0134/33-1661

There are also English-language maps in the Canal Plaza Tourist Information Center, located in an ageing warehouse beside the canal in a building called the Canal Plaza.

Getting There

From **Sapporo,** take the **JR Hakodate** (50 minutes; ¥640), departing once hourly. Coming from **Niseko,** the JR Hakodate line also runs to Sapporo in just under two hours (¥1,450).

SHIN NIHONKAI FERRY

Otaru terminal; tel. 0134/22-6191; www.snf.jp

A number of ferries operated by **Shin Nihonkai Ferry** run between Otaru and cities on Honshu, including **Akita, Niigata, Tsuruga** (Fukui Prefecture), and **Maizuru** (Kyoto-fu). Check the website for details on route and fares. Note that reservations must be made between two months and 10 days before embarking.

NISEKO
ニセコ

With an average snowfall of 15 meters (49 feet) annually, just under 50 km (31 mi) of ski runs weaving through 800 hectares (1,977 acres) of powdery terrain, and four interlinked resorts occupying the eastern slopes of Mount Niseko Annupuri, it's no surprise that Niseko is the most high-profile place for powder hounds in Japan. And with snowcapped Fuji look-alike Yotei-zan looming in the foreground, the views from the slopes are spectacularly dramatic.

Another point that sets Niseko apart is that it's the most foreign-friendly of Japan's major resorts. English is readily spoken, menus are easy to navigate, and the shelves at local shops are lined with a bounty of goods from overseas. Moreover, the foreign snowboarders and skiers have developed a community around the mountain, giving Niseko vibrant nightlife and excellent dining options.

Runs include well-groomed courses for beginners and intermediates, as well as off-piste and backcountry runs for those seeking more of a challenge. It's possible to buy a pass for individual resorts or to access them all. And after a long day on the slopes, there are some 25 *onsen* in the area to soothe your aching muscles. The area is quite crowded December through February, but discount hotel rates and less crowded slopes await anyone who comes toward the end of the season in March or April.

★ Skiing

NISEKO UNITED

www.niseko.ne.jp; 8am-8:30pm late-Nov.-Apr.; ¥6,300 8 hours, ¥7,400 full day

By far the most effective way to make the most of a trip to Niseko is by shelling out the yen required for a pass coined Niseko United, which allows you to access the runs connected to four resorts at the foot of the mountain. Moving clockwise southward around the mountain, these resort areas include **Niseko HANAZONO, Grand Hirafu, Niseko Village,** and **Niseko Annupuri.** Individual resort passes range from around ¥4,000 for a half day to around ¥5,000 for a full day, so shelling out a few thousand yen more for the United pass is well worth it.

The pass, which can be purchased for a single day or multiple days, allows you to use 18 lifts and 60 runs, and ride shuttle buses between the resorts, which comes in handy, considering the resorts are 5-10 km (3-6 mi) apart. Equipment rental shops are ubiquitous at all four resorts, as are English-speaking staff. Top-notch gear rented at reasonable prices is the norm.

Among these four resort areas, Hirafu is

by far the biggest and most popular. Food and nightlife options abound, and English is readily spoken. HANAZONO is an extension of Hirafu on the eastern side of the mountain. Slightly upscale Niseko Village is the second largest, with a few large resort hotels and some of the steepest runs, but it has only a smattering of restaurants and bars. Annupuri is low-key, has less crowded (and less steep) runs and only a handful of guesthouses for accommodation. There is another fifth resort west of Annupuri called **Moiwa,** which is much less crowded because it is not covered by the United Niseko pass. Moiwa is an attractive option for beginners, as its runs are much less intense.

Onsen

Onsen options are plentiful in Niseko. Many hotels in Niseko have *onsen* on their premises. If you'd like to find a hot springs bath and your hotel doesn't have one, there are plenty of other options, most of which charge ¥500 to ¥1,000 per person. This list barely scratches the surface of Niseko's extensive *onsen* options. If there's no *onsen* where you are staying, your hotel's front desk will likely have no shortage of recommendations for a great *onsen* nearby.

NISEKO PRINCE HOTEL HIRAFU-TEI

204 Yamada, Kutchan-chō; tel. 0136/23-2239; http://hirafutei.info; 7am-10:30am and 1pm-10pm; ¥1,000 adults, ¥600 children aged 4-12

In Hirafu, a good option is the Niseko Prince Hotel Hirafu-tei, a huge complex with gender-separated bathing areas. A selling point is its views of Mount Yotei and Mount Annupuri.

HILTON NISEKO VILLAGE

Abuta-gun, Niseko-chō; tel. 0136/44-1111; 1pm-9pm; ¥1,000 adults, ¥500 children ages 6-12

In the Niseko Village area, try the Hilton Niseko Village. The facilities here are luxurious and include a stone outdoor tub facing a koi pond, with Mount Yotei gleaming in the distance.

IKOI NO YUYADO IROHA

477 Niseko, Abuta-gun; tel. 0136/58-3111; www.niseko-iroha.com; noon-10pm, last entry 9pm; ¥800 adults, ¥400 children ages 6-12

In the Annupuri area, Ikoi no Yuyado Iroha is a good option. The water here is said to be great for the skin.

Niseko ski village

Accommodations

NISEKO NORTHERN RESORT ANNUPURI

480-1 Aza Niseko; tel. 0136/58-3311; www.niseko-northern.com; ¥15,000 d

Niseko Northern Resort Annupuri is located on the quieter side of the mountain from Grand Hirafu in Annupuri. There is an indoor and outdoor *onsen,* a sauna, and even a library stocked with books in both English and Japanese. For both breakfast and dinner, there's an excellent buffet, and for the evenings, a supremely cozy bar with Scandinavian design accents where you can unwind.

HOTEL NISEKO ALPEN

204 Yamada, Kutchan-chō; tel. 0136/22-1105; www.hotel-nisekoalpen.jp/en; ¥18,000 d

Hotel Niseko Alpen is situated conveniently near the lifts for the slopes of Grand Hirafu. You'll find well-appointed, bright Western-style and Japanese-style rooms, an *onsen*, an indoor pool and a sumptuous buffet prepared with local ingredients. Bilingual staff are ready to help with anything that may arise during your stay.

HILTON NISEKO VILLAGE

Onsen Higashiyama; tel. 0136/44-1111; www.niseko-village.com/en/stay/hilton-niseko-village.html; ¥40,000 d

The Hilton Niseko Village is another great choice for convenience. The cable car actually emerges from the hotel, which is ski-in, ski-out in the truest sense. There are indoor and outdoor *onsen* baths, stunning views of Yotei-zan looming in the distance, and excellent buffets for both breakfast and dinner.

★ AYA NISEKO

195-1 Yamada, Kutchan-chō; tel. 0136/23-1280; www.ayaniseko.com; from ¥63,500 for 1-bedroom suite

One of Niseki's best-located properties, these private apartments are roomy, stylish (contemporary Japanese aesthetic), and well-appointed (full bath, laundry facilities, etc.). The bilingual staff extend a warm welcome and are ready to help. The property is near the base of the Hirafu ski slopes and close to extensive restaurant options. The condominiums have one-three bedrooms, making them a great choice for large groups or families. There are also *onsen* on site (both private and sex-separated shared baths), and even a gym and gallery.

Information and Services

EXPLORE NISEKO

190-13 Yamada, Kutchan-chō; tel. 050/5309-6905; www.explore-niseko.com; 9am-6pm daily

Near the slopes of Hirafu, this sleek, independently owned one-stop shop offers help with bookings and stocks a wealth of maps and brochures in English.

NISEKO HIRAIFU WELCOME CENTER

204 Yamada, Kutchan-chō; tel. 0136/22-0109; www.grand-hirafu.jp; 8:30am-9pm daily

In the bustling resort of Grand Hiraifu, there's also the Niseko Hiraifu Welcome Center, which also offers plenty of English-language information.

MICHI NO EKI NISEKO VIEW PLAZA

77-10 Motomachi, Abuta-gun; tel. 0136/44-2420; www.hokkaido-michinoeki.jp; 9am-6pm daily

Near Kutchan Station is the Michi no Eki Niseko View Plaza, located on Route 66 near Niseko. This center offers help with hotel bookings, free Wi-Fi, a slew of information in English on happenings in Niseko, maps, and more.

Transportation

GETTING THERE

Niseko is sprawled out around the small town of **Kutchan,** 2.5-4 hours' drive from **Sapporo** and **New Chitose Airport.** During the ski season (Dec.-Mar.), several daily buses operated by **Chūō Bus** (tel. 011/231-0500; www.chuo-bus.co.jp) run between both Sapporo and the airport, and the three main resorts that comprise Niseko: Hirafu, Niseko Village, and Annupuri, from

Beyond Niseko: More Skiing in Hokkaido

Though Niseko is Hokkaido's crown jewel for skiers, there are several other less crowded options, along with one practically within Sapporo's city limits.

RUSUTSU

Located 30 km (18.6 mi) southeast of Niseko, Rusutsu Resort (13 Izumi-kawa, Rusutsu; tel. 0136/46-3111; www.hokkaido-rusutsu.com; 9am-5pm day, 4pm-9pm night, late-Nov.-early-Apr.; ¥5,900 adults, ¥3,000 children ages 4-12) is a much less crowded alternative to Niseko. There are fewer options for restaurants or nightlife, but the slopes are notably less packed.

To keep things simple, you can either approach Rusutsu (**留寿都**) as a day trip from Niseko or opt to stay at the family-friendly **Resort Resort Hotel** (13 Izumi-kawa, Rusutsu; tel. 0136/46-3111; www.hokkaido-rusutsu.com; ¥47,800 d with two meals). This sprawling complex is directly attached to Rusutsu Resort and has all amenities you'll need, including restaurants, under one roof. For something independently owned, the **Villa Rusutsu** (55 Izumi-kawa, Rusutsu; tel. 0136/46-2830; www.villarusutsu.com; ¥40,000 d with breakfast, 4-night minimum stay required during much of peak season) is a classic ski lodge with brilliant rooms, a hot tub, sauna, restaurant, and more.

To reach Rusutsu from Niseko, drive along **Route 230** toward Tōya-ko (30 minutes).

FURANO

Another less crowded option is Furano Ski Area (www.snowfurano.com; 8:30-5pm day, 5pm-8pm night, late Nov.-Apr.; ¥4,800 half day, ¥5,500 full day, ¥1,600 night), one of Hokkaido's best. With 11 lifts, the runs are geared primarily toward newbies and intermediates, but there's enough to keep more advanced skiers and snowboarders happy, too.

For accommodations, **Alpine Backpackers** (14-6 Kitanomine-chō; tel. 0167/22-1311; www.alpn.co.jp/furano/accomodation/backpakers.txt.html; dorms ¥2,800, twins ¥5,600) is a solid budget option near the slopes with a shared kitchen and cafe on-site; and **Furano Fresh Powder** (14-26 Kitanomine-chō; tel. 0167/23-4738; www.freshpowder.com; studio from ¥28,750) offers six well-appointed private apartments, from a studio up to a five-bedroom chalet, each with private, self-contained kitchens, bathroom facilities, and more.

To reach Furano (**富良野**) from Sapporo, take the limited express Kamui or Lilac train to Asahikawa, then transfer to the JR Furano line (3 hours; ¥5,990). **Hokkaido Chūō Bus** (tel. 011/231-0500, www.chuo-bus.co.jp) also operates several daily buses between Sapporo and Furano (three hours, ¥2,260). Seats cannot be reserved for these buses.

SAPPORO TEINE

For sheer convenience, Sapporo Teine (**サッポロテイネ**, 593 Teinehon-chō, Teine-ku; tel. 011/682-6000; https://sapporo-teine.com; 1-day pass for adults ¥5,400, children (age 14-18) ¥4,400, children (age 4-12) ¥2,800) right outside Sapporo is unbeatable. Only about 15 km (9.3 mi) west of the city, this fully equipped ski resort has a beginner-friendly area (Olympia Zone) and the more advanced Highland Zone.

The easiest way to access the slopes is by taking the train on the JR Hakodate line from Sapporo Station to **Teine Station** (15 minutes; ¥260), then transferring to a shuttle bus (15 minutes, ¥370 for Olympia Zone; 30 minutes, ¥390 for Highland Zone). There are a variety of special combo tickets covering transport from downtown by bus and lift fare and more. Check the English-language website to suss out all possible options.

the morning hours until the early afternoon (¥2,600 one way, ¥4,500 round-trip).

There are also local and rapid trains on the **JR Hakodate** line that run every hour and a half or so between JR Sapporo Station and **Kutchan Station** (2 hours; ¥1,840), the Niseko area's main hub. Note that in Otaru you'll have to transfer to the JR Hakodate line bound for Niseko. This ride is covered by the JR Pass. From Kutchan Station, buses depart every few hours to **Hirafu** (15 minutes) and less frequently to **Niseko Village** (30 minutes) and **Annupuri** (45 minutes). Many hotels offer to pick up guests at the closest of these stations. If you don't have a hotel pickup arranged, continue on to **JR Niseko Station** by transferring at Kutchan Station to the JR Hakodate line train bound for Oshamambe, another 15 minutes beyond Kutchan. You'll have better luck here catching a **taxi** at JR Niseko Station than you would at JR Hirafu Station. Weighing all factors, it's easier to reach any of Niseko's resorts by bus from Sapporo or New Chitose Airport. Plan ahead accordingly and reserve a seat well in advance, as skiers flock to the resort in winter.

Outside of the ski season, public transport in Niseko is very limited. You'll want to have your own wheels to reach the region via Route 5, which loops from Sapporo around the coast near Otaru, before turning toward the mountains to the south and inland where Niseko is located.

GETTING AROUND

With a **Niseko United pass,** you'll not only be able to access the slopes at the four resorts covered, you'll also be able to ride between them freely aboard a **shuttle bus.**

SHIKOTSU-TŌYA NATIONAL PARK
支笏洞爺国立公園

A few hours' drive south of Sapporo, Shikotsu-Tōya National Park is one of the more accessible of Hokkaido's outdoor escapes. The park has five distinct areas, but its two focal points are the lakes it is named after: **Tōya-ko** and **Shikotsu-ko.** Hiking trails weave through the densely forested mountains surrounding this pair of sparkling caldera lakes. Elsewhere, volcanoes and *onsen* add a geothermal element.

Shikotsu-ko, due south of Sapporo, is set in a rugged volcanic landscape, flanked by the peaks of Eniwa-dake, Fuppushi-dake, and Tarumae-zan. It is the second deepest lake in the country at 265 meters (869 feet) deep. It's best explored only if you have a car, as public transport in the immediate area is limited. Excellent hiking awaits at Tarumae-zan on the lake's southern shore. If you're keen to camp, you're in luck—Shikotsu-ko has a number of well-appointed campsites. More civilized digs are found at *ryokan* around the lake's northern and eastern shores.

Tōya-ko has the added benefit of more infrastructure. Ascend to the summit of Usu-zan on the lake's southern side either on foot or via ropeway to survey the gorgeous surroundings. Nearby is Japan's youngest volcano, Shōwa-shinzan, which literally popped out of the ground on farmland in 1944 and has been hiccupping fumes since. While it's quieted down in recent years, Usu-zan is also active. It last spewed ash across the area in 2000. On the lake's southern shore, Tōya-ko Onsen has a slew of *onsen* resorts, from bare bones to luxury affairs.

Yotei-zan, the mountain between the ski areas of Niseko and Rusutsu, is another one of the park's five main areas, as are the *onsen* towns of Jozankei and Hokkaido's most celebrated hot-springs resort, **Noboribetsu**. This national park is a good pick if your time is limited.

Sights

Hiking is the major draw in the areas around both Shikotsu-ko and Tōya-ko. Near Tōya-ko there are a few sights as well.

1: camping at Lake Shikotsu **2:** walking trail near Noboribetsu Onsen **3:** Shikotsu-Tōya National Park

MSR
1
2
3

VOLCANO SCIENCE MUSEUM
洞爺湖ビジターセンター 火山科学館

142-5 Tōya-ko Onsen; tel. 0142/75-2555; www.toyako-vc.jp/en/volcano; 9am-5pm daily; ¥600 adults, ¥300 children under 15; from the Tōya-ko bus terminal, walk 5 minutes west

At the Volcano Science Museum, you can experience a simulated eruption from the comfort of a theater and peruse educational displays on how volcanoes form, what causes them to erupt, and what kind of damage they're capable of doing. The museum is housed in the same building as the **Tōya-ko Visitor Center.**

USU-ZAN ROPEWAY
有珠山ロープウェイ

184-5 Aza Showa Shinzan, Sobetsu-chō; tel. 0142/75-2401; www.wakasaresort.com; 9am-4pm daily; ¥1,500 adults round-trip, ¥750 elementary school students round-trip; from Tōya-ko Onsen, drive 10 minutes, take a taxi (about ¥2,000 one way), or catch a bus (15 minutes, ¥340 one way) to the village of Kazan-mura near the base of Shōwa-shinzan where the ropeway starts

After your education at the Volcano Science Museum, it's time to see volcanic activity in the real world. Make your way to the Usu-zan Ropeway, roughly 12 minutes' drive southeast of the museum. Usu-zan has erupted four times over the past century; most recently in 2000.

If you're willing to proceed with that slightly disconcerting information in mind, hop aboard the ropeway, which whisks you near the summit of the volcano to a viewing platform that offers stunning views of Tōya-ko and the neighboring mountain Shōwa-shinzan. Walk to a neighboring platform to peer into a crater that formed during an eruption in 1977. Note that the ropeway is open longer in summer and closes for a few weeks in winter for maintenance. Also, the bus from Tōya-ko Onsen only departs once every two hours and is not in operation from early November until late April. Check the website before making the trip.

Hiking

TARUMAE-ZAN

Distance: 6.8 km (4.2 mi)
Time: 2.5-3 hours
Information and maps: Shikotsu-ko Visitor Center; https://hokkaidowilds.org/hiking/mt-tarumae
Trailhead: Seventh station (elevation of 650 meters; 2,132 feet), reached by gravel road linking northeast side of mountain to Route 141

Of the myriad mountains surrounding Shikotsu-ko, Tarumae-zan (1,041 meters/3,415 feet) stands out. One of the most active volcanoes in the country, it erupted as recently as 1981. It's a relatively easy ascent from the seventh station. Each station is essentially a waypoint. Depending on the popularity of a given route, these spots will sometimes provide basic amenities. Just as often, there will be a few primitive benches and a signpost indicating the elevation and distance to go until the end of the trail. Good views await of Shikotsu-ko, the barren landscape within the crater, and the Hidaka range and dormant volcano Yotei-san looming in the distance. You can then walk around the crater in about an hour, although entering it is not possible due to the presence of poisonous gases.

As for reaching the mountain, it's really not feasible without a rental car. If you have one, about 70 percent of the peak will be within reach. From the small town of Shikotsu Kohan on the lake's eastern shore, it's roughly a 45-minute drive on Route 141 to the trailhead at Nango-mae. Pick up a map and ask any questions you may have at the Shikotsu-ko Visitor Center.

FUPPUSHI-DAKE

Distance: 8 km (5 mi)
Time: 5 hours (from Tarumae-zan trailhead)
Information and maps: Shikotsu-ko Visitor Center
Trailhead: Seventh Station (same as Tarumae-zan)

Note that the trailhead for Tarumae-zan is also the starting point for a longer, more grueling hike up neighboring peak Fuppushi-dake (1,102 meters/3,615 feet), a good challenge for intermediate to advanced hikers.

This hike is extremely steep in parts and can become treacherous in winter when there is a real risk of avalanche. It takes about six hours up and back and is known to be an area where bear activity is notable. Exercise caution by wearing a bear bell. Pick up a map and get information about reaching the trailhead at the Shikotsu-ko Visitor Center.

USU-ZAN WEST CRATERS

Distance: 2.2 km (1.4 mi)
Time: 40 minutes
Information and maps: Tōya-ko Visitor Center; www.toya-usu-geopark.org/english/trail
Trailhead: Tōya-ko Visitor Center

Around Tōya-ko, the Usu-zan West Craters (729 meters/2,391 feet) make for a great hike. Usu-zan erupted twice in 2000, creating some 60 new craters on its western slopes. Smoke billowed skyward, and nearby buildings and infrastructure were destroyed by the explosion. The ruins that still dot the devastated area can be explored on foot through a series of hiking trails. The easiest to access is the **Kompirayama Walking Trail** (7am-6pm mid-Apr.-early Nov., until 5pm Oct.-early Nov.; free), which starts from the Tōya-ko Visitor Center in Tōya-ko Onsen. The 40-minute walk leads through a post-apocalyptic scene of apartment buildings, bridges, roads, and a public bath house laid waste by the blast. It's a sobering illustration of nature's destructive power.

Noboribetsu Onsen

Noboribetsu Onsen (**登別温泉**), located near the coast at the southern edge of Shikotsu-Tōya National Park, is by far Hokkaido's most famed hot-spring retreat. The waters coursing beneath this *onsen* village, a known quantity since it was promoted as a place for injured troops to recover after the Russo-Japanese War (1904-1905), emerge from the colorfully named **Jigoku-dani,** or Hell Valley, located just above town. This valley does indeed invoke images of a barren inferno, minus the flames. Steam wafts from vents, streams are laced with heavy concentrations of sulfur (which permeates the air with its stench), and hissing sounds escape with each blast of heat.

In town, the hot springs options are extensive. Most hotels allow for day-guests to use the baths during select hours for ¥700-2,000.

DAIICHI TAKIMOTOKAN

55 Noboribetsu Onsen-chō; tel. 0143/84-2111; www.takimotokan.co.jp; 9am-9pm, entry until 6pm; ¥2,000 for non-staying guests

The best in town is Daiichi Takimotokan. The highly curative waters in the numerous baths at this resort come from seven different springs, each with its own minerals and level of acidity. Set in bright, airy facilities, the baths are some of the best modern-style *onsen* pools in all of Japan.

SAGIRIYU PUBLIC BATH

60 Noboribetsu Onsen-chō; tel. 0143/84-2050; http://sagiriyu-noboribetsu.com; 7am-9pm Nov.-Mar., 7am-10pm Apr.-Oct.; ¥420 adults, ¥180 children

And if you want to take a dip without spending too much, the Sagiriyu Public Bath does the trick. This is Noboribetsu's only public bath house, and unsurprisingly, it's offerings aren't as luxurious as what you'll find in the hotels around town. But the baths are still bright and nicely designed. Three pools are filled with two types of water, and there's a sauna too.

Accommodations

KASHOUTEI HANAYA

134 Noboribetsu Onsen-chō; tel. 0143/84-2521; www.kashoutei-hanaya.co.jp; ¥26,300 d with 2 meals

This friendly, modern *ryokan* has ample Japanese and Western-style rooms overlooking the Oyunuma River. The *kaiseki* meals are excellent, and the shared, sex-separated baths (both indoor and open-air) are inviting. It's well-located about 7 minutes' walk south of the Noboribetsu Onsen bus station.

HANAYURA

100 Noboribetsu Onsen-chō; tel. 0143/84-2322; www.hanayura.com; 2 d with 2 meals ¥30,000,

doubles with private onsen bath and 2 meals ¥36,000
This luxury *ryokan* has spacious Japanese-style rooms, with some Japanese-Western hybrids too, some of which have private *onsen* tubs. There are also shared indoor and outdoor pools (sex-separated). Seafood-heavy *kaiseki* meals made with highly seasonal ingredients are served in private dining rooms in the on-site restaurant for both breakfast and dinner. It's located about 8 minutes north of the main Noboribetsu Onsen bus terminal next to the Kusurisanbetsu River.

Information and Services

SHIKOTSU-KO VISITOR CENTER

Shikotsu-ko Onsen; tel. 0123/25-2404; 9am-4:30pm Wed.-Mon. Dec.-Mar., 9am-5:30pm daily Apr.-Nov.
The Shikotsu-ko Visitor Center displays wildlife exhibits that give a good introduction to the flora and fauna of the area. It is also the place to go for maps and information on getting around.

TŌYA-KO VISITOR CENTER

142-5 Tōya-ko Onsen; tel. 0142/75-2555; 9am-5pm daily
In Tōya-ko, the Tōya-ko Visitor Center is connected to the Volcano Science museum.

TŌYA-KO TOURIST INFORMATION CENTER

142 Tōya-ko Onsen; tel. 0142/75-2446; 9am-5pm daily
The Tōya-ko Tourist Information Center is housed in the Tōya-ko bus terminal. Both provide ample English-language maps and information about the surrounding area.

NOBORIBETSU PARK SERVICE CENTER

Noboribetsu Onsen-chō; tel. 0143/84-3311; 9am-6pm daily
Finally, the Noboribetsu Park Service Center, located near the trailhead to Jigoku-dani and some other good nature hikes, is a good place to learn the lay of this volcanically active land with its wide selection of English-language maps and pamphlets.

Transportation

GETTING THERE

Having a **car** is all but essential for making a trip to Shikotsu-Tōya National Park worthwhile. Aside from a dearth of public transport servicing the park, there are no public transport links between Shikotsu-ko and Tōya-ko.

Starting with Shikotsu-ko, the lake is about 40 minutes' drive from **Shin-Chitose Airport,** 80 minutes' drive from **Sapporo,** and roughly an hour east of **Tōya-ko.** That said, there are four to six daily **buses** departing from Shin-Chitose Airport to the small town of Shikotsu Kohan on the eastern shore of the lake (1 hour; ¥1,030 one way), or from Chitose Station to Shikotsu Kohan (45 minutes; ¥930 one way). The problem with taking a bus to the lake is that many of the activities and sights around the lake, such as the trailhead to Tarumae-zan, are only accessible by private transport.

The best entry point to Tōya-ko is Tōya-ko Onsen, a small town on the southwest corner of the lake. The **Tōya-ko Onsen bus terminal** is linked to **JR Tōya Station** on the JR Muroran line, which in turn connects to **Hakodate** to the south (2 hours; ¥5,490), **Sapporo** to the north (2 hours; ¥5,920) and **Noboribetsu** (40 minutes; ¥2,720). To go from JR Tōya Station to Tōya-ko Onsen, take the local bus (15 minutes; ¥330), which also stops close to Usu-zan West Crater en route.

Noboribetsu Onsen is about 15 minutes' bus ride (¥340) from JR Noboribetsu Station, located on the coast just south of the hot-spring village on the JR Muroran line. This train line also links JR Noboribetsu Station to Hakodate (2.5 hours; ¥6,980), Sapporo (1 hour 15 minutes; ¥4,480), and JR Tōya Station (35 minutes; ¥2,720). Note that buses run between Noboribetsu Onsen and JR Noboribetsu Station once or twice an hour. In a pinch, a **taxi** ride from JR Noboribetsu Station to Noboribetsu Onsen costs up to about ¥2,500.

Hakodate

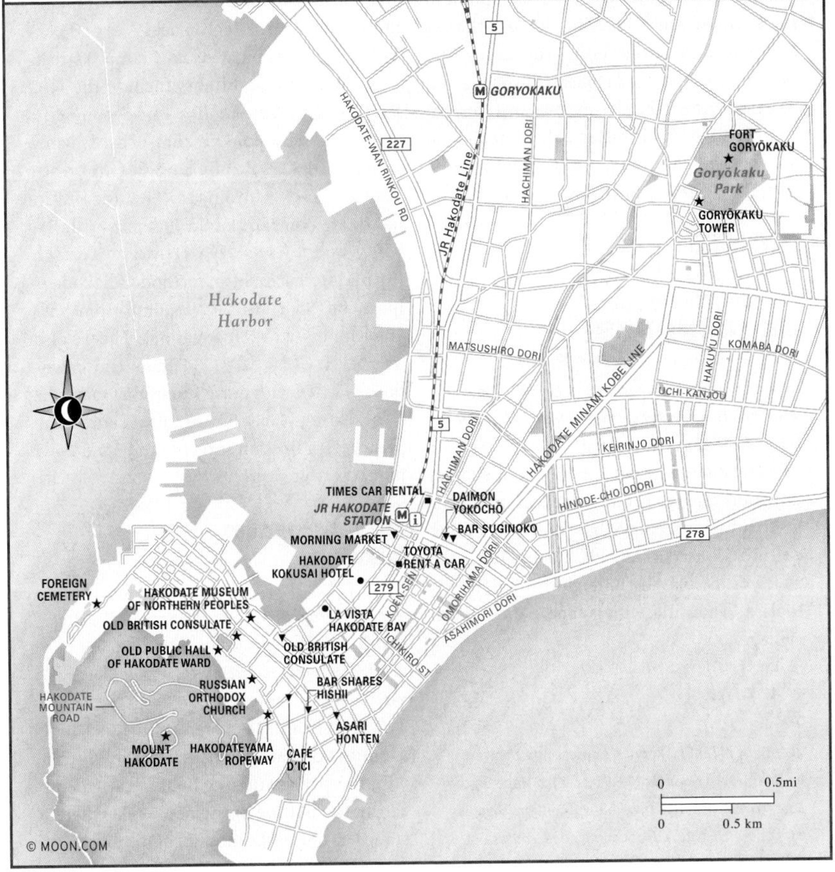

GORYOKAKU
HAKODATE-WAN RINKOU RD
227
5
JR Hakodate Line
HACHIMAN DORI
FORT GORYŌKAKU
Goryōkaku Park
GORYŌKAKU TOWER
Hakodate Harbor
MATSUSHIRO DORI
HAKUYU DORI
KOMABA DORI
UCHI-KANJOU
HAKODATE MINAMI KOBE LINE
KEIRINJO DORI
HINODE-CHO ODORI
278
TIMES CAR RENTAL
JR HAKODATE STATION
DAIMON YOKOCHŌ
BAR SUGINOKO
MORNING MARKET
TOYOTA RENT A CAR
HAKODATE KOKUSAI HOTEL
279
KOEN SEN
OMORIHAMA DORI
ASAHIMORI DORI
FOREIGN CEMETERY
HAKODATE MUSEUM OF NORTHERN PEOPLES
LA VISTA HAKODATE BAY
OLD BRITISH CONSULATE
OLD PUBLIC HALL OF HAKODATE WARD
OLD BRITISH CONSULATE
ICHIKIRO ST
RUSSIAN ORTHODOX CHURCH
BAR SHARES HISHII
HAKODATE MOUNTAIN ROAD
ASARI HONTEN
MOUNT HAKODATE
HAKODATEYAMA ROPEWAY
CAFÉ D'ICI
0 0.5mi
0 0.5 km

Hakodate

Located at Hokkaido's southern tip, Hakodate is the third-largest city in the prefecture and represents a spectacular fusion of what the island has to offer. The harbor was one of the first in Japan to welcome foreign trade after the 1854 signing of the Treaty of Kanagawa, which ended Japan's centuries-long policy of self-isolation.

Once the city flung open its doors in the mid- to late 1800s, a flood of Western influences poured in, from western Europe, Russia, and beyond. This is most evident in the city's hilly Motomachi district where you'll find a Russian orthodox church, elegant brick façades, Western-style mansions, and a star-shaped citadel with an Occidental touch that is now a fabulous cherry blossom viewing spot. There are also bustling markets, some of the country's best fresh-caught seafood, and one of the most stunning nightscapes, seen from atop Mount Hakodate, of any city in Japan.

Hakodate is an ideal entry or exit point to the island if you're traveling by rail, thanks to the opening of the Seikan Tunnel in 2016, linking Hokkaido and Honshu. If you plan on passing through the city, make it an overnight stop. You'll be glad you have the time to soak up what this charming, historic, and visually appealing gateway town has to offer.

SIGHTS

Hakodate Museum of Northern Peoples

函館市北方民族資料館

21-7 Suehirō-chō; tel. 0138/22-4128; www.zaidan-hakodate.com/hoppominzoku; 9am-7pm daily; ¥300 adults, ¥150 students and children; from JR Hakodate Station, take city tram no. 5 to Suehirō-chō

The Hakodate Museum of Northern Peoples is a good place to get an introduction to this fascinating group and their sadly dwindling culture. Housed in an old bank building, the relics on display include clothing, jewelry, tools, and housing, with Japanese and English signage.

Motomachi

元町

at foot of Mount Hakodate, bordered on the west by Motoi-zaka slope and Nijukken-zaka slope on the east; www.hakodate.travel/en/wp-content/themes/thakodate/th_top7/pdf/recommended_routes.pdf; from JR Hakodate Station, take tram no. 5 to Suehirō-chō, then walk up the hill

During the mid-1800s, foreign traders flooded into Hakodate, and the Motomachi district near the foot of Mount Hakodate is where they congregated. In many ways, this hilly area is strikingly similar to the neighborhood of the same name in Yokohama and Kobe's Kitano-chō, both of which were also hubs of foreign activity in the decades after Japan opened itself to foreign trade in 1854. Today, Motomachi is strewn with the architectural legacy of this tumultuous period of change. The entire neighborhood is a time capsule, with narrow cobblestone lanes and western-style mansions, and beautiful views of the bay. The most prominent street in the area is the **Hachiman-zaka slope,** roughly in the center of the Motomachi area and perhaps Hakodate's most visually famous street.

Some of the highlights include the **Old British Consulate** (33-14 Motomachi; www.hakodate-kankou.com/british; 9am-7pm; ¥300), **Old Public Hall of Hakodate Ward** (11-13 Motomachi; www.zaidan-hakodate.com/koukaido; 9am-7pm daily; ¥300) and a **Russian Orthodox Church** (3-13 Motomachi; http://orthodox-hakodate.jp; 10am-5pm Mon.-Fri., 10am-4pm Sat., 1pm-4pm Sun.; ¥200 donation). There's also a **Foreign Cemetery** (23 Funamichō; dawn-dusk), dotted with grave stones that mark the final resting places of American sailors and preachers, a Russian surgeon, and other early pioneers from overseas.

Mount Hakodate

函館山

https://334.co.jp/eng; to reach the ropeway, take tram no. 5 from JR Hakodate Station to Jujigai tram stop (5 minutes) and walk 10 minutes southwest, or take the Hakodate Bus from JR Hakodate Station (10 minutes) to the ropeway terminal

The view from 334-meter-high (1,095-foot) Mount Hakodate, particularly at nighttime with the city's twinkling lights clearly delineating the outline of the peninsula where it stands, is one of the most recognizable nightscapes in all of Japan. To make your way to the top, you have the option of riding a gondola via the **Hakodateyama Ropeway** (tel. 013/823-3105; www.334.co.jp; 10am-10pm late-Apr.-mid-Oct., 10am-9pm mid-Oct.-late-Apr.; one-way ¥780 adults and ¥390 children, round-trip ¥1,280 adults and ¥640 children), which departs from the Motomachi district; taking a bus for 30 minutes from JR Hakodate Station (twice hourly during evening hours, late-Apr.-mid-Nov.; ¥360), weaving and

1: Hakodate waterfront **2:** crabs and sea urchins for sale at Hakodate morning market **3:** cable car ropeway to Mount Hakodate

¥ 5500
毛ガニ(中)
¥ 250
1
2
3

stopping on the way up the mountain at various lookout points; or even hiking in the warmer months of May through October. From the top, enjoy the views from the free observation decks.

Goryōkaku Park
五稜郭

44 Goryōkaku-chō; tel. 0138/21-3456; 9am-6pm daily; free; take tram to Goryōkaku-kōen-mae stop, then walk 10 minutes north

Northeast of JR Hakodate Station lies a massive geometric spectacle with an interesting backstory. **Fort Goryōkaku** was the first citadel constructed in Japan that mimicks military strongholds found in the West. Built in 1864 in the shape of a star, the fort was meant to defend Hakodate from potential encroachment from abroad, specifically Russia. Its five-sided design was designed to create a deadly gauntlet for an invading army that would be fired at from both sides. Rather than defending from a foreign enemy, the fort instead became the site of a civil war when Meiji imperial forces fought troops loyal to the shogunate, then in its death throes.

When its martial relevance faded, the site was instead turned into a free public park in the 1910s. The fort is gone, but its uniquely shaped moat, brimming with lily pads, remains. The beautifully landscaped grounds are dotted by some 1,600 cherry trees, making for an excellent spot for a stroll or picnic, especially in early to mid-May when the pink petals are in full bloom. This is easily one of the best *hanami* spots (places to welcome spring and enjoy cherry blossoms) in Hokkaido.

GORYŌKAKU TOWER
五稜郭タワー

43-9 Goryōkaku-chō; tel. 0138/51-4785; www.goryokaku-tower.co.jp; 8am-7pm daily Apr. 21-Oct. 20, 9am-6pm Oct. 21-Apr. 20; ¥900 adults, ¥680 junior high and high school students, ¥450 elementary school students; from JR Hakodate Station, take the tram to the Goryōkaku-kōen-mae stop (10 minutes), then walk 10 minutes north

To glimpse the fort site from above, head to the nearby Goryōkaku Tower. This nearly 100-meter-tall tower stands just outside the moat at the southwest corner of the park.

FOOD

MORNING MARKET

Next to JR Hakodate Station; www.hakodate-asaichi.com; 5am-noon, from 6am in winter; walk 1 minute south of the station

Held next to JR Hakodate Station every morning, the Morning Market, or Asaichi, is a bustling bazaar of seafood, produce, and sundry dry goods. Paying a visit is a fun way to start your day and a good introduction to Hakodate. Walk among endless rows of stalls hawking squid, urchin, salmon roe, crabs, melons, and more, operated by earthy fishermen and kind aunties. Some of the stalls sell seafood breakfasts. If you show up before 8am, you may even catch a bit of auctioneering.

DAIMON YOKOCHŌ

7-5 Matsukaze-chō; tel. 0138/24-0033; www.hakodate-yatai.com; hours and prices vary by shop; walk 7 minutes east of Hakodate Station

Enter this network alleyways festooned with glowing paper lanterns in the evening and you'll find about 25 eateries. The offerings range from seafood and *okonomiyaki* to yakitori. This is a local hot spot, so follow your inspiration and you won't go wrong.

LUCKY PIERROT BAY AREA MAIN SHOP

23-18 Suehiro-chō; tel. 0138/26-2099; http://luckypierrot.jp/shop/bayarea; 10am-12:30am Mon.-Fri. and Sun., 10am-1:30am Sat.; burgers from ¥350; walk 4 minutes southeast of Suehiro-chō tram stop (line 5)

This eclectic local burger shop is an institution. Look past the quirky decor reminiscent of an old carnival—clown mascot, antique merry-go-round horse—and you'll find a menu of cheap, tasty burgers and sides. Its Chinese chicken burger has been voted Japan's best burger.

ASARI HONTEN

10-11 Horai-chō; tel. 0138/23-0421; 11am-9pm Thurs.-Tues.; courses ¥2,200-5,200; walk 1 minutes west of Horai-chō tram stop (line 2)

This old-school wooden building with private dining rooms where guests sit on tatami floors serves great *sukiyaki* (beef hot pot). A fantastic place for an intimate meal with plenty of small-town charm. Reserve at least a few days in advance if you plan to go. The restaurant has a reputation and is often full. English menu available.

CAFÉ D'ICI

22-9 Motomachi; tel. 0138/76-7476; 10:30am-7pm Fri.-Wed., closed 1st and 3rd Wed. every month; average ¥1,000; walk 6 minutes' southwest of Jujigai tram stop (lines 2, 5)

This small, inviting café, run by a charming local woman, serves great coffee and small nibbles (baked goods, desserts, small soup/salad sets). It's a great spot for a small bite or caffeine pit stop while strolling through Motomachi.

BARS AND NIGHTLIFE

BAR SUGINOKO

8-5 Matsukaze-chō; tel. 0138/23-4577; www5d.biglobe.ne.jp/~suginoko; 6:30pm-11pm Tues.-Sat.; walk 7 minutes east of Hakodate Station

Located right next to the eastern edge of the culinary alleyways of Daimon Yokochō, this storied bar is known for its friendly masters and signature rum highball, along with various cocktails meant to evoke the colors of Hokkaido (plenty of greens and blues). Seating spreads across two floors and includes comfy sofas and a line of swivel chairs at the bar.

BAR SHARES HISHII

27-1 Motomachi; tel. 0138/22-5584; www.bar-shares-hishii.info; 8pm-2am (last order 1:30am) Mon.-Sat.; cover charge ¥500; walk 5 minutes west of Horai-chō tram stop (line 2)

This dimly lit bar near the Mount Hakodate Ropeway in Motomachi has an impressive whisky and cocktail menu. The atmosphere exudes class, and the masters, in vest and tie, really know their way around the bar.

ACCOMMODATIONS

¥10,000-20,000

HAKODATE KOKUSAI HOTEL

5-10 Ōtemachi; tel. 0138/23-0591; www.hakodate-kokusai.jp; ¥15,000 d; from JR Hakodate Station, take Hakodate City Tram to Shiyakusho-mae stop

Hakodate Kokusai Hotel is elegant and sprawling with more than 300 rooms occupying three buildings set near the bay. Its restaurants serve Chinese, Western, and Japanese fare, and it has a lounge with great nighttime views. Its central location, seven minutes' walk from JR Hakodate Station, makes it a convenient home base while you're exploring the city. A 20-minute walk to the southwest leads to the Mount Hakodate Ropeway station, and a 20-minute ride aboard the Hakodate city tram leads to Goryokaku.

¥20,000-30,000

LA VISTA HAKODATE BAY

12-6 Toyokawa-chō; tel. 0138/23-6111; www.hotespa.net/hotels/lahakodate; ¥22,000 d; from JR Hakodate Station, take Hakodate City Tram to Uoichibadori stop

La Vista Hakodate Bay also sits on a prime spot, overlooking the bay. The atmospheric hotel has mood lighting, stylish dark-wood furniture, Western-style rooms with Japanese accents, and a wonderful *onsen* on the roof. Restaurants on-site whip up Chinese and Spanish cuisine, making heavy use of seafood brought in from the waters just offshore.

INFORMATION AND SERVICES

TOURIST INFORMATION CENTER

12-13 Wakamatsu-chō; tel. 0138/23-5440; www.hakodate.travel; 9am-7pm daily Apr.-Oct., 9am-5pm daily Nov.-Mar.

For good materials in English about the city's many attractions, look no further than the Tourist Information Center in JR Hakodate Station.

TRANSPORTATION

Getting There

From Sapporo, take the **limited express train** (Super Hokuto) south on the **JR Hakodate line,** (3.5 hours; ¥8,830) to **Hakodate Station.** Take the same line from **Niseko** to Hakodate as well (3.5 hours; ¥5,560), changing trains at Oshamambe.

Coming from **Shin-Aomori,** take the **JR Hokkaido** *shinkansen* (reservation required) until Shin-Hakodate-Hokuto (1 hour), then transfer to the Hakodate line for the remaining 15 minutes of the trip to JR Hakodate Station, for a total cost of ¥7,890.

Hakodate also has an international **airport,** with flights to cities such as Taipei and Seoul, and a number of airports within Japan. Buses run between the airport and JR Hakodate Station (20 minutes; ¥300).

Getting Around

Hakodate is easily navigable **on foot.** That said, **streetcars** are easy to catch and make for a fun ride (¥210-250). City **buses** are similarly priced (¥210-260). Go to the tourist information center in JR Hakodate Station to pick up a one-day bus pass (¥800), a one-day streetcar pass (¥600), or a combination pass that covers them both (¥1,000).

If you plan to drive through Hokkaido and are arriving via Hakodate, note that rental cars are easy to pick up in the city. Try **Nippon Rent-a-car** (22-5 Wakamatsu-chō; tel. 0138/22-0919; www.nrh.co.jp; 8am-6pm daily) just outside JR Hakodate Station, **Toyota Rent A Car** (19-2 Ōtemachi; tel. 0138/26-0100; https://rent.toyota.co.jp; 8am-8pm) five minutes' walk southwest of JR Hakodate Station, and **Times Car Rental** (22-7 Wakamatsu-chō; tel. 0138/27-4547; www.timescar-rental.com; 8am-8pm daily Apr.-Oct., 8am-7pm daily Nov.-Mar.) 4 minutes' walk southwest of the station.

Central Hokkaido

At the geographical core of the island, Hokkaido is brimming with the very elements the island is known for. In summer, trekkers flock to the alpine vastness of Daisetsuzan National Park, which is rugged enough to please ambitious hikers and has rustic *onsen* towns for post-hike R&R. And in winter, the mountains near Furano are covered with powder, becoming one of Japan's best ski resorts.

TOP EXPERIENCE

★ DAISETSUZAN NATIONAL PARK

大雪山国立公園

Daisetsuzan is the biggest national park in all of Japan. This swathe of untamed wilderness at the heart of the island covers 2,267 square km (875 square mi), an area larger than Tokyo. The park is the first place in the country to see its leaves turn fiery red, golden yellow, and earthy brown in autumn, and it's the first to be dusted with snow. It's home to a host of wildlife, from the indigenous Ezo deer to brown bears and the rabbit-like Japanese pika.

This vast unspoiled kingdom is a paradise for hikers, with a smattering of excellent day-hikes, such as Asahi-dake, and the grueling week-long affair known as the Daisetsuzan Grand Traverse, stretching from Asahi-dake in the north to the peak of Tokachi-dake in the south. A network of huts and places to camp facilitate your journey. If roughing it is not your style, there are also a few *onsen* resort towns home to cozy *ryokan* with steamy baths, such as **Asahidake Onsen** in the northwest, **Sōunkyō Onsen** in the northeast, and bare-bones **Tokachidake Onsen** in the southwest. Note that of these three transit points, only Sōunkyō Onsen has an ATM and a few restaurants. Asahidake Onsen and Tokachidake Onsen don't even have a convenience store.

So, pick up all your supplies before arriving in the park.

If traipsing through a landscape of steaming volcano craters, summer wildflowers, dense forests, and murmuring streams far from the hubbub of modern Japan appeals to you, Daisetsuzan has what you seek.

Hiking

June through September, Daisetsuzan is a hiker's paradise. The most popular area to begin any exploration of the park on foot is around the small hot-springs village of Asahidake Onsen. Here, you'll be at the base of the park's highest mountain, **Asahidake** (2,291 meters/7,516 feet), which makes for a great day hike. To see a map of the extensive trails snaking through the park at a glance, visit http://sounkyovc.net/data/pdfs/maps/route_all_en.pdf.

ASAHIDAKE ROPEWAY

Asahidake Onsen, Higashikawa-chō; tel. 0166/68-9111; http://asahidake.hokkaido.jp; 6am-5:30pm Jul.-mid-Oct., 9am-4pm mid-Oct.-Jun.; ¥2,900 round-trip or ¥1,800 one way Jun.-Oct. 20; ¥1,800 round-trip or ¥1,200 one way Oct. 21-May

To start the hike, first take the Asahidake Ropeway, located in the heart of the hot-spring village of Asahidake Onsen, to Sugatami (1,600 meters/5,249 feet). From here the ascent on foot begins. Arriving at the top of the ropeway, you'll be in a tundra zone, free of trees, with mountain flowers blooming in summer.

In truth, this list merely scratches the surface of the multitude of hiking options in the park, ranging from a few hours on foot to the epic trek known as the **Daisetsuzan Grand Traverse.** The traverse begins either from Asahidake Onsen or Sōunkyō Onsen and runs north-south through most of the length of the park, ending at the remote hot-spring village of Tokachidake Onsen. The total journey typically takes 5-7 days. If you're hankering for something more demanding, seek out more recommendations at one of the helpful information centers in Asahikawa Onsen or Sōunkyō Onsen, or contact **Hokkaido Nature Tours** (1-7 5-13 Ishiyama, Minami-ku, Sapporo; tel. 070/3540-6622; www.hokkaidonaturetours.com). They offer excellent tours in English, including the extremely grueling but equally rewarding Daisetsuzan Grand Traverse.

And for a fantastic online resource for Daisetsuzan and Hokkaido as a whole, visit the website of **Hokkaido Wilds** (https://

hikers ascending the Asahidake volcano in Daisetsuzan National Park

hokkaidowilds.org). For a certified bilingual guide with deep Hokkaido expertise, consider contacting **Jun Ishiguro** (www.explore-share.com/trip/hiking-hakuundake-kurodake-daisetsuzan), director of the Hokkaido Mountain Guides Association.

SUGATAMI-DAIRA

Distance: 2 km, 1.2 mi
Time: 1 hour
Information and maps: Asahidake Visitor Center
Trailhead: Sugatami (via Daisetsuzan Asahidake Ropeway)

From Sugatami, you have a few options. One is to walk the loop around Sugatami-daira, where you'll discover small bodies of water and vents releasing sulfur from the bowels of the earth.

ASAHIDAKE

Distance: 5.8 km, 3.6 mi
Time: 4-5 hours
Information and maps: Asahidake Visitor Center
Trailhead: Sugatami (via Daisetsuzan Asahidake Ropeway)

For something more challenging, after exiting the ropeway car at Sugatami, follow the trail sign indicating the path to the summit of Asahidake, which is roughly a five-hour return hike. This trail weaves through snowfields, flowery meadows, and boggy marshland. Views from the top of Asahidake, one of Japan's "100 famous mountains," are spectacular.

KURODAKE

Distance: 12 km (7.5 mi) from Asahidake Ropeway to Kurodake Ropeway
Time: 8 hours
Information and maps: Asahidake Visitor Center, Sōunkyō Visitor Center
Trailhead: Sugatami (if approaching from Asashidake side)

For a more involved hike that lasts 1-2 days and is only recommended for more experienced hikers, rather than returning from the summit of Asahidake, forge on to the neighboring summit of Kurodake (1,984 meters/6,509 feet). From there, you'll begin your descent toward the hot-spring town of Sōunkyō Onsen below (670 meters/2,198 feet). Begin this journey by walking to the seventh station of the mountain (1,520 meters/4,986 feet), where you'll find the upper station of a chair lift. This first jaunt takes 60-90 minutes. Take the chair lift (¥400 one way, ¥600 round-trip), which descends to the fifth station (1,300 meters/4,265 feet), where you'll find the upper station of the **Kurodake Ropeway** (tel. 0165/85-3031; www.rinyu.co.jp/modules/pico01; 6am-7pm Jun.-Aug., 8am-4pm Sept.-May; ¥1,100 one way, ¥1,950 round-trip). Hop aboard this ropeway and ride down to Sōunkyō Onsen below.

In total, traipsing from Asahidake Ropeway to the Kurodake Ropeway can take up to 8 hours, so prepare accordingly. This includes reviewing the timetable for each ropeway. If you plan to extend this to an overnight journey, there's a mountain hut about 10 minutes' hike from the summit of Kurodake, which you can stay in without a reservation (though it can get packed during high season). The hike can also be completed in reverse order.

Onsen

Hot-spring options in Daisetsuzan are plentiful, with the bulk of them being at hotels in the main entry points of Asahidake Onsen and Sōunkyō Onsen. These hot-spring villages, in the northwest and northeast of the park, respectively, have plenty of hotels offering bathing options for non-staying guests for about ¥1,000.

DAISETSUZAN SHIRAKABA-SŌ

Asahidake Onsen, Higashikawa-chō; tel. 0166/97-2246; http://shirakabasou-asahidake.com; 1pm-8pm daily; ¥800 day guests; towel rental ¥200

If you find yourself in Asahidake Onsen, Daisetsuzan Shirakabasou, located 6 minutes' walk southwest from the Asahidake Ropeway, is a good bathing option.

KURODAKE-NO-YU

Sōunkyō Onsen, Kamikawa-chō; tel. 01658/5-3333; www.sounkyo.com/kurodakenoyu.html; 10am-9pm daily May-Oct., 10am-9pm Wed. Nov.-Apr.; ¥600 adults, ¥300 children

In Sōunkyō Onsen, Kurodake-no-yu is a gender-separated public bath on the main drag in the middle of this slightly more developed town about 6 minutes' walk south of the Asahidake Ropeway. Alongside gender-separated indoor pools, there's an open-air bath on the third floor. The views in this bath aren't anything spectacular, but after a long day of hiking, its waters can't be beat.

Accommodations

★ DAISETSUZAN SHIRAKABA-SŌ

Asahidake Onsen; tel. 0166/97-2246; http://shirakabasou.com; dorms with 2 meals ¥7,890 pp, private rooms with 2 meals ¥8,940 pp

This outdoorsy wooden lodge about 6 minutes' walk southeast of the Asahidake Ropeway contains private tatami-mat rooms and one Western-style room, as well as dorms with bunkbeds—all using shared bathrooms. There's also a shared lounge and kitchen, a dining room, and a shop stocked with basics, from snacks to insect repellent and bear bells (8am-10pm daily). There's an open-air shared bath, which is free for guests. Be sure to check out the viewing deck, reached via a lofty spiral staircase. A great base for exploring the park from the Asahidake Onsen side.

SŌUNKYŌ YOUTH HOSTEL

Sōunkyō; tel. 080/2862-4080; www.sounkyo-hostel.com; dorms (sex-separated) ¥3,200 pp, private doubles ¥8,000

Located about 10 minutes' walk (uphill) southeast from Sōunkyō bus stop and 7 minutes east of the lower station of the Kurodake Ropeway, this medium-sized hostel has a mix of dorms with bunkbeds and a few private tatami-mat rooms, all of which share a bathroom. There's a communal lounge area and kitchen amply stocked with utensils and seasoning that can be freely used, but no meals are served. A convenient base in Sōunkyō.

Information and Services

ASAHIDAKE VISITOR CENTER

Asahidake Onsen, Higashikawa-chō; tel. 0166/97-2153; www.asahidake-vc-2291.jp; 9am-5pm daily

The Asahidake Visitor Center in Asahidake Onsen, a 1-minute walk south of the Asahidake Ropeway, is a great place to stock up on English maps and timetables, and ask for recommendations on trails and pre-hike preparations.

SŌUNKYŌ VISITOR CENTER

Sōunkyō, Kamikawa-chō; tel. 01658/9-4400; http://sounkyovc.net; 8am-5:30pm daily Jun.-Oct., 9am-5pm Tues.-Sun. Nov.-May

In Sōunkyō Onsen, head to the Sōunkyō Visitor Center for an abundance of English-language maps and pamphlets, helpful staff, and a variety of visual displays illustrating the flora, fauna, and terrain of the park.

Transportation

GETTING THERE

The easiest way to reach Asahidake Onsen in the park's northwest is via bus from JR Asahikawa Station (1.5 hours; ¥1,430), departing once every hour or two. To reach JR Asahikawa Station from JR Sapporo Station, take the limited express train (85 minutes; ¥4,810). It's also possible to drive to Asahidake Onsen from Asahikawa (via Route 1160) or Biei (via Route 213, then Route 1160) in roughly an hour.

To enter the park via Sōunkyō Onsen, take a bus from JR Asahikawa Station (2 hours; ¥2,100). Or, take the JR Sekihoku line from JR Asahikawa Station to JR Kamikawa Station (local train 1 hour and 15 minutes, ¥1,070; express train 40 minutes, ¥2,210), then take a bus departing once every hour or two to go the rest of the way to Sōunkyō Onsen (30 minutes; ¥870). If you're staying in Sōunkyō Onsen, ask if your hotel provides shuttle bus services to guests. Many of them offer pickup from Asahikawa. A few even go as far as Sapporo.

Summer Wildflowers

Similar to the cherry blossom craze that sweeps across Japan every spring, wildflowers of all hues blanket meadows and fields across Hokkaido in summer. Among Hokkaido's best spots to see wildflowers in summer are the fields around **Furano** (富良野) and **Bei** (美瑛), and on **Rebun Island** (page 540).

Here at Japan's northern edge, flowers bloom a bit later than in the south. Fields are awash in color from May to October. Lavender blankets the region in violet from late June through mid-August, and a host of other colorful flowers blanket entire fields from June through September. Among them are poppies, lupines, and rape blossoms in June; lilies in July; and salvias, sunflowers, and cosmos from August through September. The heavy flow of travelers to the area—a million per year by some estimates—attests to their beauty. Here are some of the best places to see summer wildflowers:

FURANO

- **Farm Tomita** (tel. 0167/39-3939; www.farm-tomita.co.jp; 9am-4:30pm daily Oct.-late Apr., 8:30am-6pm daily late Apr.-Sept.; free) is known for the striking contrast of its vivid purple fields against the Toakchi mountains in the background.
- **Lavender East** (www.farm-tomita.co.jp/en/east; 9am-4:30pm daily in July only; free) boasts 14 hectares (35 acres) of lavender—the largest field in the area. You can take a bus ride (¥200 adults, ¥100 children ages 4-12) through the extensive fields.
- **Flower Land Kamifurano** (tel. 0167/45-9480; http://flower-land.co.jp; 9am-5pm daily Apr.-May, 9am-6pm daily Jun.-Aug., 9am-5pm daily Sept.-Nov.; free) has a plethora of blossoms, too, and a bus tractor (¥500 adults, ¥300 children) can take you on a tour of the fields from June to mid-September.

Getting There and Around

To reach Furano from **Sapporo,** take the limited express **Kamui** or **Lilac** train to Asahikawa, then transfer to the **JR Furano** line, which runs first to Biei, then reaches Furano (3 hours; ¥5,990). If you've got a rental car, take the **Doo Expressway** between Sapporo and Mikasa to Furano (2 hours, ¥1,500 in tolls). **Hokkaido Chūō Bus** (tel. 011/231-0500; www.chuo-bus.co.jp) also operates several daily buses between Sapporo and Furano (three hours, ¥2,260). Seats cannot be reserved for these buses.

In town, the best way to get around is by bicycle, which you can rent at **Furano-Biei Tourism Center** (1-30 Hinode-machi in JR Furano Station; tel. 0167/23-3388; www.furanotourism.com; 9am-6pm daily).

You can shuttle between Furano and Biei on the **Furano-Biei Norokko train** (early June through late September on weekends, or daily from late June through mid-August). Starting

Eastern Hokkaido

Far from the more civilized towns and cities of southwestern Hokkaido, the eastern part of the island is a vast natural sanctuary. Akan National Park bears witness to the region's volcanic past with its three gorgeous caldera lakes, Akan-ko, Mashū-ko, and Kussharo-ko. Trails lining the region draw hikers in summer. Meanwhile, red-crowned cranes, representatives of longevity for the Japanese, congregate in the nearby Kushiro Wetlands, which can be explored by canoe. The region is also one of the best places to experience the culture of the Ainu, Japan's original inhabitants.

flower fields in Furano

from Furano, catch the train at a station called **Lavender-Batake Station,** 5 minutes' walk from Farm Tomita.

BIEI

- **Shikisai Hill** (tel. 0166/95-2758; www.shikisainooka.jp; 9am-5pm Apr.-May and Oct., 8:30am-6pm Jun.-Sept., 9am-4pm Dec.-Feb., 9am-4:30pm Mar; free), is a lovely slope that is blanketed in flowers and lined with trails.
- **Patchwork Road** is a splendid area about 3.5 km (2.2 mi) northwest of town named for the way that it appears from above—like an earth-tone quilt.

Getting There and Around

To reach Bei from **Sapporo,** take the limited express **Kamui** or **Lilac** train to Asahikawa, then transfer to the **JR Furano** (2 hours 15 minutes; ¥5,560). If you've got a rental car, take the **Doo Expressway** that runs between Sapporo and Asahikawa to reach Biei (2.5 hours; ¥3,500 in tolls).

In Biei, you can get around by bike, and the **Biei Tourist Information Office** (1-2 Biei-chō Honcho next to Biei Station; tel. 0166/92-4378; www.biei-hokkaido.jp; 8:30am-7pm daily May-Oct.; 8:30am-5pm daily Nov.-Apr.; ¥200 per hour) offers rentals.

KUSHIRO WETLANDS
釧路湿原

Near the southeastern corner of Hokkaido lies Japan's most extensive marshlands, the Kushiro Wetlands National Park. The main appeal of Kushiro, which comprises 60 percent of Japan's marshland (269 square km/104 square mi) is the chance to explore it from the water level in a canoe, and to see the red-crested white cranes that were narrowly saved from extinction over the past 90-plus years, largely thanks to efforts to preserve their habitat in this small corner of Hokkaido's vast wilderness.

Given the remoteness of the wetlands, it makes sense to combine your trip with Akan National Park.

Canoeing

The calm waterways of the Kushiro Wetlands

provide the ideal environment to glide along in a canoe. While there are several observation platforms around the Kushiro Wetlands, a far more powerful experience is seeing them with paddle in hand while floating in a canoe down the Kushiro River. A number of canoe rental shops can be found at lake **Toro-ko** on the eastern side of the park, accessed by taking the JR Senmo line train from JR Kushiro Station to JR Toro Station (30 minutes; ¥540).

TORO NATURE CENTER

86-17 Toro Kita, Shibecha; tel. 015/487-3100; www.dotoinfo.com/naturecenter; from ¥9,000 per person

Toro Nature Center is a good starting point for your canoe trip through the wetlands. They offer a vast range of options for canoe tours, from an hour and a half to nine hours.

Transportation

GETTING THERE

The best way to get to the Kushiro Wetlands is with a **rental car.** The infrequency and seasonality of public transportation are tough, but if public transport is your only option, read on.

The Kushiro Wetlands are best accessed via the port town of Kushiro, to the south. If you're coming from Sapporo, take the limited express train from JR Sapporo Station to **JR Kushiro Station** (4.5 hours; ¥9,370). From here, the JR Senmo line runs along the eastern edges of the park as it makes its way north to Abashiri, passing through **Kushiro Shitsugen Station** (20 minutes; ¥360) at the eastern side of the park on the way. Making it into the park's interior or western side requires a car.

Akan Bus Co. (tel. 0154/37-8651; www.akanbus.co.jp) offers guided tours from JR Kushiro Station to Kushiro Wetlands from mid-July through October.

GETTING AROUND

The only way to get around the Kushiro Wetlands easily is with a **rental car.** There are a cluster of car rental shops around the southern side of **JR Kushiro Station.**

AKAN NATIONAL PARK

阿寒国立公園

Due north from Kushiro Wetlands lies the lake-studded mountainous region of Akan National Park. The park has similar terrain to much of the island. Spread over 905 square km (349 square mi), the it's chock-full of volcanoes and timberlands, penetrated by hiking trails and rustic *onsen* to soak weary

Akan-ko

Crane Spotting

red-crowned cranes

With long legs, a slender bill, and a white body trimmed with black and a tuft of red feathers atop the head, the Japanese crane has long been regarded a potent symbol of longevity and happiness. According to legend, the red-crowned crane can live for as long as a millennium. Yet, by the early 20th century the graceful bird, so powerful a motif in Japanese culture, was thought to be extinct due to heavy hunting in the early 20th century.

A small population was thankfully discovered in the Kushiro Wetlands in 1924, after which the species was brought back from the brink through a heroic conservation effort. Today, more than 1,200 of the dignified birds breed, feed, squawk, dance, jump, and groom in the vast marshes around Kushiro. Hyperbole about their lifespan aside, they have been known to live up to 80 years in captivity. Besides having a long lifespan, the birds pair for life, making them a common allusion at weddings in Japan.

WHERE TO SEE CRANES

The Kushiro Wetlands offer the best chance to see the red-crusted crane. November to March is the best time to see these elegant creatures in the wild.

If you're in Kushiro during that period and have a rental car, drive to the **Tsurui-Ito Red-Crowned Crane Sanctuary** (Nakasetsuri Minami, Tsurui-mura; tel. 0154/64-2630; www.wbsj.org/en/tsurui; 9am-4:30pm Thurs.-Mon. Oct.-Mar.; free), which offers one of the least obstructed views of the birds in their natural habitat. There is also a Nature Center run by the **Japan Wild Bird Association** (www.wbsj.org) next to the sanctuary.

If you're relying on public transport and/or you're not visiting in winter, the **Kushiro City Red-Crowned Crane Natural Park** (112 Tsuruoka, Kushiro; tel. 0154/56-2219; http://kushiro-tancho.jp; 9am-6pm Apr.-Sept., 9am-4pm Oct.-Mar.; ¥470) also allows you to observe the birds coming and going as they please at this sanctuary that has played a crucial role in their return to health. Perhaps the most direct views of all are to be had from a canoe. The **Toro Nature Center** offers canoe tours down the Kushiro-gawa, a river that winds through the wetlands where cranes often gather.

muscles. Three caldera lakes, **Mashū-ko, Kussharo-ko,** and **Akan-ko** are the park's focal points. The town of **Akanko Onsen** on the lake's south shore is also a great place to see a traditional Ainu village and learn about the fascinating, sadly vanishing culture of Japan's first settlers.

Given the remoteness of Akan National Park, it makes sense to also visit Kushiro Wetlands if you make the trip.

Sights

AKAN KOHAN ECO-MUSEUM CENTER

1-1-1 Akan-ko Onsen, Akan-chō; tel. 0154/67-4100; http://en.kushiro-lakeakan.com; 9am-5pm daily; free

Marimo, the singular spherical species of algae that forms within Akan-ko, can be seen at the Akan Kohan Eco-Museum Center, located in the eastern side of Akan-ko Onsen.

AKAN-KO SIGHTSEEING CRUISE

4-5-8 Akan-ko Onsen, Akan-chō; tel. 0154/67-2511; www.akankisen.com; ¥1,900 adults, ¥990 children

The Akan-ko Sightseeing Cruise departs from Akan-ko Onsen, plying the waters of Akan-ko in an 18-km (11-mi) loop in 85 minutes. Along the way, the boat stops at a small research center where the balls of green bob in tanks. If it's sunny, the mossy orbs often come to the surface to bask in the light (photosynthesis). If it's cloudy or cold, they retreat. Akan-ko is one of the only places in the world where these little structures are known to form. It can take up to five centuries for one the size of a soccer ball to take shape.

AINU KOTAN

4-7-19 Akan-ko Onsen, Akan-chō; tel. 0154/67-2727; www.akanainu.jp

Back on land, the Ainu Kotan is a village where Ainu crafts, a museum, a restaurant, and a performance space are clustered together on one street at the western end of Akan-ko Onsen. Enter through a gate watched over by an imposing owl, the guardian spirit of the Ainu. Admittedly, the development is geared toward tourists, but it still offers a glimpse of real Ainu culture if you look past the souvenirs.

IKOR

4-7-84 Akan-ko Onsen, Akan-chō; tel. 0154/67-2727; www.akanainu.jp/en/about/ikoro; ¥1,080 for most performances

Aside from a variety of shops selling handmade accessories, folk art, leather goods, and woodcrafts, there is a notable theater called Ikor ("Treasure"), where traditional music, dance, puppet shows, and fire rituals are performed.

AINU LIVING MEMORIAL HALL PONCISE

4-7-20 Akan-ko Onsen, Akan-chō; tel. 0154/67-2727; 10am-9pm daily; free

This folklore museum sitting atop the hill at the end of the village's sole street, also gives a historical glimpse of daily life of the Ainu, including reconstructed traditional buildings recalling the old days. Fair warning: There are unfortunately a few pitiful displays of animals in cages—dogs and bears—in the village. This is sadly a common feature of many Ainu villages meant to draw tourists.

Hiking

There are great hiking and *onsen* options in Akan National Park. Before setting out on a hike, pick up an English-language map at one of the information centers listed below.

ME-AKANDAKE

Distance: 7.5 km (4.7 mi)

Time: 4-5 hours

Information and maps: Akan Kohan Eco-Museum Center; www.mountainsofhokkaido.com/hikes/meakan-dake

Trailhead: Me-Akan Onsen, about 15 minutes' drive southwest of Akan-ko Onsen via Route 241

There are some great hikes around Akan-ko, with the trail leading to the summit of Me-Akandake (1,499 meters/4,917 feet) atop the list. This active volcano is the park's highest peak and is another member of Japan's "100 famous mountains" club. The trail is suitably volcanic in nature, with sparse vegetation sprouting from loose soil, including alpine blossoms like rhododendrons and carnations. The vista from the top of the lake-studded landscape is stunning.

The best way to approach the hike is first to drive to **Me-Akan Onsen** (720 meters/2,362 feet). Once you've reached Me-Akan Onsen, the trailhead begins in a spruce forest where you'll begin your ascent to the summit before returning to Me-Akan Onsen via the Onneto Nature Trail. A caveat: Be safe and pick up a map at the Akan Kohan Eco-Museum Center before setting out. Moreover, check on the current trail conditions. Me-Akandake acts up sometimes, prompting temporary trail closure due to falling rocks.

MASHŪDAKE

Distance: 14.4 km (8.9 mi)

Time: 4-6 hours

Information and maps: Kawayu Eco-Museum Center; www.kawayu-eco-museum.com/english/wp-content/uploads/2017/03/mashu_english.pdf; https://japanhike.wordpress.com/2012/02/06/mt-mashu

Trailhead: Next to observation Deck Number 1 parking lot

If you want to take in epic views of the pristine lake of Mashū-ko, the best way is to ascend to the top of Mashūdake (857 meters/2,811 feet). The trailhead for this wonderful hike is found near **Observation Deck Number 1,** just off Route 52 beside the southwestern edge of the lake. The trail curls around roughly one-third of the lake until it reaches the summit of the peak looming over the western rim of the caldera. It's just over 7 km (4 mi) one way, passing through grassland and forest. On a cautionary note, the area is known for being home to a large number of *higuma* (brown bears). Be safe and carry a bear bell to keep the lumbering creatures at bay.

Food

★ PORONNO

4-7-8 Akan-ko Onsen, Akan-chō; tel. 0154/67-2159; 10am-9:30pm May-Oct., noon-8:30pm Nov.-Apr.; ¥1,500 lunch, ¥5,000 dinner

Be sure to have a meal at Poronno, located in the Ainu Kontan in Akan-ko Onsen. The eatery serves Ainu cuisine and eschews additives; instead, locally sourced items like venison set meals and ramen loaded with leeks pulled from local mountainsides are served.

Accommodations

★ ART INN

3-2-40 Kawayu Onsen, Teshikaga-chō; tel. 015/486-7773; www.artinn.asia; ¥16,000 d

This artist-run hotel, about 2.3 km (1.4 mi) east of Kussharo-ko in the town of Kawayu Onsen, ensures a quirky stay. There are three basic rooms with futons that guests can roll out as they please, and three galleries featuring left-field works by local artists. There's an open-air bath (private rental ¥3,000) available for each room. Some rooms have spacious balconies overlooking a river. All rooms have private restrooms. There's no food on-site, but the friendly staff speak limited English and can recommend eateries nearby.

ONSEN MINSHUKU YAMAGUCHI

5-3-2 Akanko Onsen, Akan-chō; tel. 0154/67-2555; www.tabi-hokkaido.co.jp/~yamaguchi/; private rooms ¥6,650 pp with 2 meals

This family-owned inn is a no-frills bargain base for exploring the Akan region. Its tatami rooms and shared bathroom and *onsen* tub are dated, but the owners are kind and its proximity to the Ainu Kotan and the shore of Akan-ko score it major points for convenience. Two basic, home-cooked Japanese meals are included.

The Ainu

Japan's indigenous people, the Ainu, have maintained a culture of woodcraft, song and dance, and elaborate fire rituals for about seven centuries. By now, they have largely assimilated into modern Japan, but the historical journey has been less than smooth.

Ainu tribal handcrafted bracelet

AINU CULTURE AND SPIRITUALITY

Of Caucasian descent with mysterious roots somewhere in Siberia, Ainu men traditionally grow long beards, while the women once tattooed designs on their hands and at the corners of their mouths. They wore clothes made of feathers and fibers derived from trees featuring an array of complex geometric patterns, vaguely evocative of Polynesian art. They once dwelled in rectangular huts topped by roofs of rush and reeds.

Ainu spirituality is deeply rooted in the natural world, with rivers, rocks, mountains, and animals ascribed divine essence. Even today, many place names connected to nature reveal Ainu roots, particularly in Hokkaido. Some theories suggest that even the Japanese name of Mount Fuji (Fuji-san) is derived from the Ainu word for "fire," combined with *san*, or "mountain" in Japanese. The Ainu hold the bear in particular esteem as nature's highest spirit, and see the owl as a guardian.

HISTORY OF DISCRIMINATION

Before the onset of modernity, they lived off the land as hunter-gatherers and fishers, gradually pushed northward by the encroachment of the Japanese. Things took a turn for the worse in 1899 with the passing of the Hokkaido Former Aborigines Protection Act, which outlawed their language and their right to hunt and fish, essentially banning all aspects of their culture.

Given small barren parcels of land, the Ainu were instructed to become farmers. Many hid their ancestry and sought to blend in. Throughout the mid-20th century, tourism to Hokkaido began to grow, which gave new income avenues to those who were content to perform cultural rituals for tourists, although many found this trend demeaning. Following significant social activism from the 1960s on, the Ainu received recognition of their right to practice their own culture in 1997 when the Hokkaido Former Aborigines Protection Act was repealed. The Ainu were officially recognized as Japan's indigenous people in 2009.

Though these are welcome changes, the fact remains that only about 24,000 Ainu survive, of whom only a few hundred have four Ainu grandparents.

VISIT AND LEARN MORE

If you're interested enough in Ainu ways to make a detour to explore their world more deeply, the **Nibutani Ainu Culture Museum** (55 Biratori-chō, Nibutani, Saru-gun; tel. 01457/2-2892; www.town.biratori.hokkaido.jp/biratori/nibutani; 9am-4:30pm daily, ¥400 adults, ¥150 children) may be the best living representation in Japan of their dwindling ways. Located in the district of Nibutani in the town of **Biratori,** about 110 km/68 mi (1 hour 40 minutes' drive) southeast of Sapporo, 80 percent of the town's inhabitants are of Ainu heritage. English-language information at this museum is profuse, and amiable researchers are on staff to answer any questions you may have.

Information and Services

AKAN KOHAN ECO-MUSEUM CENTER

1-1-1 Akan-chō; tel. 0154/67-4100; http://business4.plala.or.jp/akan-eco; 9am-5pm Wed.-Mon. Aug. 21-Jul. 31, 9am-6pm Aug. 1-20; free

In Akan-ko Onsen, stock up on maps and glean insight into local wildlife at the Akan Kohan Eco-Museum Center, located on the east side of town. You can see a few specimens in tanks of the mossy balls known as *marimo* taken from Akan-ko while you're at it.

KAWAYU ECO-MUSEUM CENTER

2-2-6 Kawayu Onsen; tel. 015/483-4100; www.kawayu-eco-museum.com; 8am-5pm Thurs.-Tues. Apr.-Oct., 9am-4pm Thurs.-Tues. Nov.-Mar.

In Kawayu Onsen, pick up information and ask questions at the Kawayu Eco-Museum Center. This visitor's center doubles as a museum that houses well-designed displays depicting the geologically volatile surroundings. It's also the starting point for a number of short nature trails.

Transportation

GETTING THERE

The best way to get around Akan National Park is with a **rental car.**

Reaching Akan National Park via public transportation is tricky. From JR Kushiro Station, four to five daily public **buses** run to Akan-ko (2 hours; ¥1,500). **Akan Bus Co.** (tel. 0154/37-8651; www.akanbus.co.jp) offers guided tours from JR Kushiro Station to Akan-ko and Mashū-ko from mid-July through October. The tours run from Kushiro to Abashiri, passing through Kawayu Onsen, Mashū-ko, and Akan-ko onsen along the way. Inquire for details. Reservations required. Buses also run between Akan-ko Onsen and Asahikawa, en route passing through Sōunkyō Onsen in Daisetsuzan National Park, for a journey of 4.5 hours (¥5,210).

If you're going directly to Kawayu Onsen, near Mashū-ko, it's possible to take the JR Senmo line from JR Kushiro Station, south of the park, to JR Kawayu Onsen Station (1.5 hours; ¥1,840). The JR Senmo line also runs from the northern port town of Abashiri to the west of Shiretoko National Park to JR Kawayu Onsen Station (1.5 hours; ¥1,640), or from Shiretoko-Shari, near the southwestern corner of Shiretoko National Park (1 hour, ¥930).

GETTING AROUND

When it comes to getting around Akan National Park, the only feasible option is having your own **car.** Drive between Akan-ko Onsen, located on **Route 240,** and Mashū-ko via **Route 241,** stopping in Sokodai to take in some gorgeous scenery as you go.

Northern Hokkaido

Japan's northern edge is a breathtaking wilderness, stretching as far as the eye can see until it drops into the ocean at Russia's southern edge. In the far east, UNESCO-listed Shiretoko National Park is home to hundreds of lumbering brown bears and the site of the southernmost drift ice floes in the world.

TOP EXPERIENCE

★ SHIRETOKO NATIONAL PARK
知床国立公園

The Shiretoko Peninsula, which juts more than 60 km (37 mi) into the Sea of Okhotsk in the island's faraway northeast, was once considered the edge of the earth by the Ainu. The very name Shiretoko National Park is adapted from the Ainu word "Sir etok," which means just that. The far-flung region is beautiful and untamed even by Hokkaido standards. So remote is Shiretoko that you can't even drive to its tip at Shiretoko Cape—roads stop roughly three-fourths of the way. One vista that can be seen by car is the **Shiretoko Pass** along Route 334, with views of **Rausu-dake** (1,660 meters/5,446 feet) from the small village of **Utoro** in the west, or **Rausu** in the east. Your only options from here are to hike vast distances or hop aboard one of the sightseeing boats that ply the peninsula's western coast.

The park is home to large populations of deer, foxes, and formidable brown bears that are a real and present danger for those venturing into its backcountry, with mountains blanketed in dense forest. During winter, some of the southernmost drift ice in the northern hemisphere forms off the peninsula's rugged western shore. The peninsula was named a UNESCO World Heritage Site in 2005 for its extraordinary wealth of biodiversity and the unique ways that its natural worlds interact on land and at sea.

It goes without saying that reaching and navigating this far-flung wonderland is a challenge. But those who make the journey reap ample rewards. If you want to see Hokkaido—and Japan—at its most wild, there is no better place than Shiretoko.

Rausu-dake

Boat Cruises

Sightseeing cruise boats depart from Utoro and Rausu from mid-April to mid-November. A ride aboard one of these boats is the best way to see the rugged, otherwise inaccessible coastline of weather-beaten cliffs, punctuated by cascading waterfalls, lounging sea lions, deer, foxes, and foraging brown bear mothers with their cubs. Alongside stunning views of the dramatic Shiretoko coast, these cruises also get up close and personal with the diverse marine life of the area, including orcas, whales, and dolphins. Keep your eyes on the skies too. In winter, Steller's sea eagles and white-tailed eagles soar overhead. In the warmer months, shearwaters, skuas, and horn-billed puffins descend to the water to feed and the occasional black-footed albatross appears.

SHIRETOKO NATURE CRUISE

27-1 Hon-chō, Rausu-chō; tel. 0153/87-4001; www.e-shiretoko.com; 7am-8pm daily; 1 hour ¥4,000 pp or 2.5 hours ¥10,000 pp in winter, 2.5 hours ¥8,000 pp in summer

Operating out of Rausu on the east coast, Shiretoko Nature Cruise offers excursions on smaller ships with open observation decks through the Nemuro Strait.

AURORA CRUISES

107 Utoro Higashi; tel. 0152/24-2147; https://ms-aurora.com/shiretoko/en; 9am-6pm daily late Jan.-Oct.; prices vary with season and route

On the west coast, Aurora offers cruises aboard larger ships with all the extras you'd expect—snack bar, indoor seating—from Utoro to Kamuiwakka Falls from late April to late October (1.5 hours; ¥3,100 adults, ¥1,550 elementary school students) and from Utoro to Cape Shiretoko (3 hours and 45 minutes; ¥6,500 adults, ¥3,250 elementary school students). Aurora also offers hourlong cruises from late January through early April through drift ice floes aboard an icebreaker, departing from the port of Abashiri (https://ms-aurora.com/abashiri/en; ¥3,300 adults, ¥1,650 elementary school students).

Hiking

Before doing any hiking, stop by the helpful **Shiretoko Nature Center.** Stock up on English-language maps and pamphlets, and ask any questions here before setting off on any wilderness journeys.

More seasoned mountaineers should look into the **Shiretoko Traverse.** This 25-km (15 mi) trek requires at least two full days; it starts at Rausu-dake in the south, heads north over the top of Io-zan, and ends at the warm cascade of Kamuiwakkayu Falls. There are four campsites along the way. The terrain is tough and the risks, including bears, are real. Stop by the Nature Center to inform staff of your plans and gather maps before striking out.

FUREPE WATERFALL

Distance: 2 km (1.2 mi)

Time: 20 minutes

Information and maps: Shiretoko Nature Center; http://center.shiretoko.or.jp/guide/furepe

Trailhead: Shiretoko Nature Center

If you don't intend to take longer hikes but would like to at least stroll through the landscape, weaving through fields that lead to dramatic cliffs along the way, the walk to Furepe Waterfall begins from the Shiretoko Nature Center. The walk only takes 20 minutes one way and is a good addition to a short itinerary focused on nature cruises or driving through the park. Don't expect booming falls. At about 100 meters (328 feet) high, Furepe is fed by ground water and at times only trickles into the Sea of Okhotsk. The trail's main selling points are the scenery that surrounds it on the way to the falls, and its accessibility.

SHIRETOKO GOKO LAKES

Distance: 0.8 km (0.5 mi) for elevated boardwalk; 3 km (1.9 mi) for hike around all five lakes

Time: 40 minutes for elevated boardwalk; 1.5 hours around all five lakes

Information and maps: Shiretoko Go-ko Field House; www.goko.go.jp/multilingual_eng

Trailhead: Shiretoko Go-ko Lakes Field House

This cluster of five petite alpine lakes formed by the eruption of neighboring Io-zan

(Sulphur Mountain) is set in a primordial forest, with the snow-streaked Shiretoko mountain range towering in the background. This region of the park's relative ease of access means that it can be inundated by hikers in the peak summer months. But crowds aside, this area boasts breathtaking scenery and a lush ecosystem.

You have the option to hike along a free, 800-meter elevated wooden platform that leads to the blandly named Lake 1 (open late Apr.- Nov.). The purpose of having this elevated path is to protect the delicate ecosystem. Or, you can also stay on the ground and walk a longer 3-km (2-mi) path that winds around all five lakes.

To hike the longer trail from late April to May 9 or between August 1 and October 20, you'll have to first register at the **Shiretoko Go-ko Lakes Field House** (tel. 0152/24-3323; 7:30am-6pm daily late Apr.-Oct. 20, from 8:30am Oct. 21-late Nov.), purchase a ticket (¥250) and patiently sit through a lecture on bear safety. For perspective, some 600 *higuma* (brown bears) roam the forests, mountains, and coasts of Shiretoko alone.

This process becomes more involved during peak bear season, (May 10-July 31). During this period, hikers are only allowed to take the longer trail as members of a tour group led by a licensed guide. It costs around ¥5,000 per person to join one of these tours, which accommodate up to 10 people. Tours last around three hours and depart from the field house roughly every 10 minutes. It's possible to join one of the tours on the same day if space allows, but register in advance online to be safe (www.goko.go.jp/fivelakes).

To reach the Shiretoko Go-ko Field House, drive about 5 km (3.1 mi) north of Utoro, following the main road that leads into the park, then veer left at the Shiretoko Nature Center. The Shiretoko Go-ko Lakes Field House will be at the end of the road. Parking costs ¥500 per car.

RAUSU-DAKE

Distance: 12 km (7.5 mi) round-trip

Time: 7-9 hours

Information and maps: Rausu Visitor Center; https://japanhike.wordpress.com/tag/shiretoko

Trailhead: Hotel Chinohate (near Iwaobetsu Hot Spring)

Another great hike at the southern edge of the park, smack in the middle of the peninsula, is Rausu-dake. The 1,660-meter (5,446-foot) peak stands amid the park's central north-south spine. Much of the snowcap melts from June to September, making it possible to walk to the summit in four to five hours. As elsewhere in Shiretoko, carry a bear bell on this hike. Brown bears are abundant in the Rausu-dake area.

Begin your ascent at the trailhead behind the now-closed Hotel Chinohate, located near Iwaobetsu Onsen, accessible from Route 93. From the top, you can simply return to Iwaobetsu Onsen. Alternatively, when you reach the three-way junction on your way back, follow the trail that leads down the opposite face toward Rausu, for roughly a three-hour descent. If you follow this trail, be sure to stop by **Kuma-no-yu**, a fantastically primitive, sex-separated outdoor *onsen* beside a sweltering river near the Rausu-side trailhead. Note that there is also a campsite near this ideal post-hike bath.

To access the trailhead with any reasonable level of convenience, you'll want to have a car. The trailhead is 4 km (2.5 mi) from the nearest bus stop (Iwaobetsu), which adds a significant leg to the journey if you're walking the whole way. Also, think twice before taking a taxi from Utoro, as fares for the drive to the trailhead can climb to a wince-inducing ¥7,000.

Onsen

KUMA-NO-YU

Yunosawa-chō, Rausu; tel. 0153/87-2126; 24 hours; free

Kuma-no-yu is an excellent outdoor *onsen*, with two pools separated by gender by a privacy fence. The pools sit beside a boiling river about 15 minutes' walk south of Rausu Onsen Campground (Yunosawa-chō, Rausu; tel. 0153/87-2126; www.rausu-town.jp/kankou/activity/activity.php), and near the trailhead to Rausu-dake on the Rausu side of the mountain. The bare-bones baths are the ideal place to submerge yourself in Shiretoko's back woods. Stop by the Rausu Visitor Center for information on reaching these rustic pools.

Accommodations

SHIRETOKO SERAI

41-5 Rebuncho, Rausu-chō; tel. 0153/85-8800; www.shiretokoserai.com; ¥10,pp d with 2 meals

On the Rausu (eastern) side of the peninsula, this midsized hotel has smart, well-appointed rooms with small but clean private baths and toilets. A Western-style breakfast buffet is served in the shared lounge, which functions as a bar in the evening. Lunch and dinner are also served from an à la carte menu to staying guests and visitors. The hotel also arranges a number of tours around the park with English-speaking guides (www.shiretokoserai.com/en/tour; prices vary by tour).

★ HOTEL KIFU CLUB SHIRETOKO

318 Utoro-higashi, Shari; tel. 0152/24-3541; www.kifuu.com; ¥13,200 pp with 2 meals

With a mix of Japanese- and Western-style rooms, as well as a private cabin—all facing the Sea of Okhotsk—this property is a stylish and comfortable place to stay on the western coast of the peninsula near Utoro. There's a shared indoor *onsen* bath (sex-separated) and a private open-air *onsen* pool looking out to sea. Japanese-style breakfast and dinner are served in a dining area next to a communal lounge with a fireplace. Just outside the lounge, a large wooden balcony faces the ocean.

Information and Services

SHIRETOKO NATURE CENTER

531 Iwaubetsu, Shari-chō; tel. 0152/24-2114; http://center.shiretoko.or.jp; 8am-5:30pm daily mid-Apr.-mid-Oct., 9am-4pm daily mid-Oct.-mid-Apr.

Your first port of call in Shiretoko is the Shiretoko Nature Center, located about 5 km (3 mi) north of Utoro on the main road leading into the park. Load up on English-language maps and brochures and ask the staff any pertinent questions about hikes or other activities you plan to do in the park.

RAUSU VISITOR CENTER

6-27 Yunosawa; 0153/87-2828; http://rausu-vc.jp; 9am-5pm Tues.-Sun. May-Oct., 10am-4pm Tues.-Sun. Nov.-Apr.

On the east coast, the Rausu Visitor Center also provides information and maps in English. It's located on Route 334, just west of town. Wildlife of the tamer sort is known to frequent the grounds behind the center, where you'll also find a geyser that spouts almost eight meters skyward once an hour.

Transportation

GETTING THERE

Infrequent **buses** or a **rental car** are the only means of transport in Shiretoko. Trains and buses running to and from the park are sporadic, so be prepared to exercise great patience if you plan to rely on public transport.

If you're approaching the park from the west, take the **JR Senmo** line from Abashiri Station to **Shiretoko-Shari Station** (45 minutes; ¥840), located roughly 40 km (25 mi) southwest of the park. Coming from the south, Shiretoko-Shari can be reached via the JR Senmo line from Kushiro (2.5 hours; ¥2,810). If you come all the way from Sapporo, via Kushiro, the entire journey takes about 6-7 hours (¥11,310).

From Shiretoko-Shari, public buses run to Utoro at the park's southwest edge (1 hour; ¥1,650). Buses continue on from Utoro to Shiretoko Go-ko (25 minutes; ¥690). From there, other buses run to Kamuiwakkayu Falls (¥1,300). Other buses run between Utoro and Rausu (55 minutes; ¥1,310), and from Rausu down to Kushiro (3.5 hours; ¥4,740). Generally speaking, none of the buses linking to the park operates outside of the months of May through October.

Note that the road leading from Shiretoko Go-ko to Kamuiwakkayu Falls is only open for buses running between these two points August 1-25 and September 15-24. Otherwise, having your own car is by far the best way to make it around the park. Given how much effort is involved in making the journey to Shiretoko, it pays to combine a trip here with a jaunt to Akan National Park and the Kushiro Wetlands to the south.

RISHIRI-REBUN-SAROBETSU NATIONAL PARK
利尻礼文サロベツ国立公園

Located off the far northern coast of the Hokkaido, near the rough-and-ready port town of Wakkanai, the islands of **Rebun** and **Rishiri** are the focus of Rishiri-Rebun-Sarobetsu National Park. In summer they are awash in wildflowers and travelers. Rebun is focused on meadows of wildflowers, while Rishiri, a giant volcano, draws those hungry for a challenge.

Rebun Island
礼文島

Located about 80 km (50 mi) west of Hokkaido's northernmost tip, Rebun is a long sliver of land defined by a rugged coastline of craggy cliffs and waterfalls, fishing hamlets, and a plethora of alpine flowers in summer.

For more of the island's hikes, visit www.rebun-island.jp/en/rebunnavienglish.pdf. For guided hikes with an English-speaking guide (from ¥20,000 for 2), check out www.rebun-guide.com/english.

HIKING TO REBUN-DAKE

Distance: 4.5 km/2.8 mi one way

Time: 4 hours round-trip

Information and maps: www.rebun-island.jp/en/trekking/index.html

Of the many trails winding around Rebun, the one that affords the best vistas of the island's topography leads to the top of Rebun-dake (490 meters/1,607 feet). To reach the trailhead, take the bus from Kafuka to Nairo. From the top, the island's gently rolling contours comes into focus.

HIKING TO SHIRETOKO

Distance: 7.1 km/4.4 mi one way

Time: 5 hours round-trip

Information and maps: www.rebun-island.jp/en/trekking/index.html

Another worthwhile hike takes you over the rounded southern end of the island, through meadows of wildflowers during summer, to **Momoiwa** ("Peach Rock"). From this rock at an elevation of 250 meters (820 feet), continue on to **Shiretoko,** at the island's far southern edge, marveling at the flowers blanketing the hills. From Shiretoko, sporadic buses run to **Kafuka,** where you can take the ferry back to **Wakkanai** on the main island. Check the bus schedule before starting the hike.

USUYUKI-NO-YU

961-1 Kafuka-mura; tel. 0163/86-2345; www.usuyuki.jp; noon-10pm daily; ¥600

After you've exhausted yourself traversing Rebun, stop at Usuyuki-no-yu. This *onsen* overlooks the ocean, a stone's throw from the ferry station in Kafuka.

PENSION U-NI-

Tonnai, Kaduka-mura; tel. 0163/86-1541; www.p-uni.burari.biz; ¥11,880 pp with 2 meals

For a spot to sleep, Pension U-ni- is a very welcoming, family-owned inn that exudes a heavy dose of charm. Inform the desk ahead of time and they will pick you up at the ferry terminal for free.

TOURIST INFORMATION CENTER

tel. 0163/86-2655; www.rebun-island.jp

On Rebun, head to the information center inside the Kafuka ferry terminal for maps and information on anything related to exploring the island, including accommodation. The center stays open until the last ferry leaves the port.

Rishiri Island
利尻島

Gazing east from Rebun's shores, you'll see Rishiri about 10 km (6 mi) to the south, towering like a scaled-down Mount Fuji, seeming to float on the ocean's surface. The round, lofty counterpart to flat Rebun, Rishiri's interior is dominated by Mount Rishiri, a dormant volcano.

HIKING RISHIRI-ZAN

Unlike Rebun, with a range of difficulty levels, hiking here revolves around summiting Rishiri-zan (10 hours round-trip), a grueling ascent of 1,500 meters (5,000 feet) to the peak. Climbing season is limited (June-Sept.) and the slog to the top is easy to underestimate. Should you need to take shelter for the night or during inclement weather, there's a no-frills **mountain hut** (no reservation needed), without running water, a bit above the eighth station (about 1,200 meters/4,000 feet). To climb the whole peak, the trailhead is located about 4 km (2.5 mi) inland from Oshidomari, the island's main ferry port. Ask about bus times and pick up a map at the island's tourist information center in Oshidomari. For guided hikes on Rishiri (from around ¥5,000), visit www.explore-share.com/hiking-trips/japan/rishiri-island.

RISHIRI FUJI ONSEN

227-7 Minato-machi, Oshidomari; tel. 0163/82-2388; 11am-9pm June-Aug., noon-9pm Sept.-May

The steamy pools of Rishiri Fuji Onsen are located on the main road that leads from Oshidomari to the Rishiri-zan trailhead.

★ MARUZEN PENSION RERA MOSIR

227-5 Sakaemachi, Oshidomari; tel. 0163/82-2295; www.maruzen.com/tic/oyado; ¥11,000 pp with 2 meals

Maruzen Pension Rera Mosir is the best place to stay overnight. This thoroughly modern B&B is surrounded by natural splendor, albeit slightly removed from the ferry terminal (a 20-minute walk). Contact the front desk ahead of your arrival to arrange a free pickup. The biggest draw of the inn, however, the owner: a mountaineer who knows the island's trails intimately, who is ready to answer questions and is happy to whisk guests to the trailhead for Rishiri-zan. Dinners and Japanese-style breakfasts are served in the dining room.

RISHIRIFUJI TOURIST INFORMATION CENTER

tel. 0163/82-2201; 8am-5:30pm mid-Apr.-mid-Oct.

On Rishiri, the Rishirifuji Tourist Information Center is the one-stop shop for all intel.

Getting There and Around

From Sapporo, take the **limited express** to Asahikawa, then transfer to a separate limited express train bound for Wakkanai (15.5 hours; ¥10,450), a port town on the northern tip of Hokkaido. It's also possible to **fly** from Sapporo to Wakkanai (¥12,000-25,000); the airport is linked downtown by bus (35 minutes; ¥600). From Wakkanai, **Heart Land Ferry** (tel. 011/233-8010; www.heartlandferry.jp) runs to both Rishiri's Oshidomari port (1 hour 45 minutes; from ¥2,500) 2-4 times daily and Rebun's Kafuka port (2 hours; from ¥2,800) 2-4 times daily.

On Rishiri, buses run in a loop around the island (¥2,200). The trip from **Kutsugata** on the west shore to Oshidomari, the site of the main ferry terminal, takes about 45 minutes (¥730). On Rebun, buses run from the main port at **Kafuka** on the eastern coast, north to **Sukoton-misaki** in the north (70 minutes; ¥1,250). They also run between Kafuka and **Shiretoko** in the south (15 minutes; ¥300). Inquire about bus schedules and routes at the ferry terminal on each island. If you plan to **drive** or **cycle,** rental shops abound near the ferry terminals. Rebun's hilly terrain is best explored by car, while the relatively flat road around Rishiri begs to be explored by bicycle.

Shikoku 四国

The smallest and least populated of Japan's

four main islands, Shikoku has always felt remote from the Japanese mainland. It's much easier to access now, thanks to a series of bridges linking Honshu with Shikoku's northern coast, but a sense of otherness pervades the island nonetheless. Its deep mountainous interior has limited public transportation, and its dramatic coastline rolls on seemingly without end.

The island's northern coast is bordered by one of the world's loveliest seascapes, the Seto Naikai (Inland Sea). This calm, blue expanse is often compared to Greece's majestic Aegean Sea. On the myriad spits of land that dot this placid body of water, the pace of life and salty locals invite you to experience Japan at its most laid-back. It is

Highlights

Look for ★ to find recommended sights, activities, dining, and lodging.

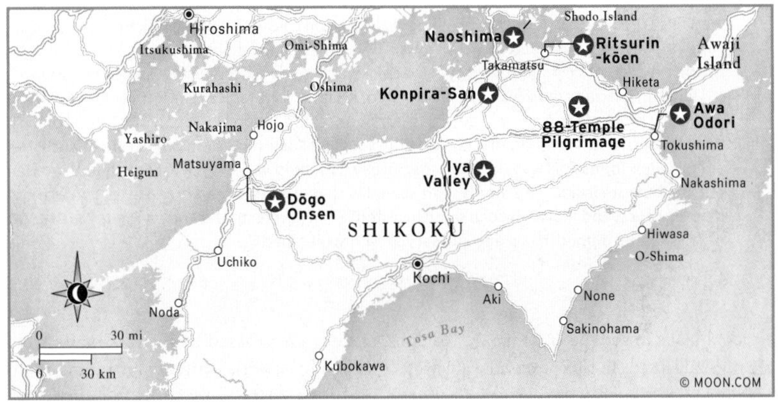

★ **Ritsurin-kōen:** Wander through tunnels of boughs and over arched bridges in this pine-studded garden wonderland (page 549).

★ **88-Temple Pilgrimage:** While walking the entire circuit is a Herculean task, traipsing at least some of the way that Kōbō Daishi once trod is an unforgettable experience, both earthy and enlightening (page 552).

★ **Konpira-san:** Climb the dizzying staircase of stone to the mountaintop shrine dedicated to the divine protector of mariners, basking in stunning vistas from the top (page 554).

★ **Naoshima:** Take a ferry to this idyllic island for its rustic charm and bohemian ethos as much as its collection of world-class art museums (page 558).

★ **Awa Odori:** Join the dancing throngs of merrymakers in *yukata* (lightweight kimonos) at Japan's penultimate summer festival in balmy Tokushima (page 566).

★ **Iya Valley:** Explore some of Japan's wildest terrain in this vertiginous valley crisscrossed by vine bridges and enveloped in mist (page 570).

★ **Dōgo Onsen:** Bathe in the antique *onsen* that helped inspire anime maestro Hayao Miyazaki's dreamy bathhouse of the gods, seen in his masterpiece *Spirited Away* (page 578).

Best Restaurants

★ **Ranmaru:** The juicy, flavorful chicken thighs served at this greasy-spoon favorite are slathered in a secret spice mix, cooked to crunchy perfection and ideally washed down with beer (page 551).

★ **Nikitatsu-an:** This classy restaurant is a wonderful place to pair the refined infusion brewed at the sake shop next door with a range of delectable dishes made with fresh, local ingredients (page 582).

★ **Daikokuya:** Try this restaurant's spin on local specialty *taimeshi*, plus the menu makes use of seasonal ingredients, and the noodles are great, too (page 582).

★ **Hirome Ichiba:** This buzzing, down-home Kōchi food court overflows with choices, and doubles as a favored watering hole during evenings and weekends (page 591).

★ **Myojinmaru:** Come to this relaxed eatery off the tourist trail to try the most beloved item on Kōchi's menu, katsuo tataki (seared bonito) (page 591).

REGIONAL SPECIALTIES

The island of Shikoku is known for the quality of its udon. The most famous variety is Kagawa Prefecture's ***sanuki* udon.** These wheat noodles are eaten cold with dipping sauce or in a hot soup. Toppings include grated daikon, green onion, bonito flakes, and more. Another Kagawa specialty is ***honetsuki-dori,*** a style of crispy, fried chicken intensely seasoned with salt and pepper.

The main specialty in Tokushima, just south of Kagawa, is its ramen. These noodles are served in a heavy broth made from soy sauce and pork bones, and topped with pork ribs, green onions, bean sprouts, and a raw egg that cooks in the soup. Shikoku's southern prefecture of Kōchi has a reputation for its ***katsuo*** (bonito), specifically its seared variety that is cooked until golden outside but rare inside. The dish is then served with ginger, leek, garlic, citrusy ponzu and soy dipping sauce, and more. Shikoku's northwestern Ehime Prefecture is known for its ***taimeshi,*** or red snapper dipped in raw egg and served with sweetened rice.

an ideal place to see the "real Japan." There are myriad islands in this peaceful waterway, among which the most easily accessible are Naoshima, Teshima, and Inujima. With ever-popular Naoshima as the torch bearer, these three "art islands" have added a creative dimension—world-class museums, local art projects, and more—to revitalize the quaint villages hugging their shores.

In the city of Tokushima, colorfully clad dancers bring the streets to life in the electrifying Awa Odori dance festival at the sweltering peak of summer each year. To the west, in the rugged Iya Valley, deep ravines are crossed by bridges made from thick vines, with white-water rapids rushing below. And nearby, hamlets cling to vanishing ways of life, now slowly being revived thanks to staunch preservation.

In balmy Kōchi Prefecture, sprawling east to west across the island's vast subtropical south, palm trees, citrus fruit, great beaches, fun-loving locals, and Shikoku's other rowdy dance festival, the Yosakoi Matsuri, form an intoxicating mix. And in western Ehime Prefecture, Matsuyama is home to a supurb castle and the vaunted Dōgo Onsen. From the northern coast of Ehime, it's possible to cycle

Previous: Ritsurin-kōen in winter; Awa Odori; Dōgo Onsen.

Best Accommodations

★ **Francoile:** This two-room bed-and-breakfast in a quiet village on the north side of Naoshima is an off-the-radar base from which to explore the famed "art island" (page 562).

★ **Benesse House:** Sleep amid the works of world-famous artists at Naoshima's luxury museum-cum-hotel, which offers sweeping views of the Inland Sea (page 563).

★ **Chiiori:** This thatched-roof home is a dreamlike escape from modernity on the steep slopes of the Iya Valley (page 575).

★ **Chaharu Hanare Dōgo Yumekura:** A stone's throw from the historic bathhouse of Dōgo Onsen, this chic, up-to-the-minute *ryokan* offers guests premium service, exquisite meals, and inviting en-suite baths (page 583).

★ **Kaiyu Inn:** Offering smart, spacious rooms, this far-flung inn is an idyllic getaway for surfers, snorkelers, and urban escapees who want to connect with the ocean (page 593).

in either direction across the Inland Sea, island hopping on two wheels all the way.

We have native son Kōbō Daishi (774-835), or Kūkai, founder of the sect of Shingon Buddhism, to thank for many of the 88 temples that comprise Shikoku's famed pilgrimage route, one of the world's great spiritual journeys. Stretching 1,400 km (870 mi), it takes about 40 days to walk, as countless pilgrims have done in the past. These days, many undertake the journey in the comfort of a bus or car. Completing even a section of the epic journey on your own two feet, however, unlocks its transformative power in a way that an air-conditioned vehicle never can.

ORIENTATION

Shikoku may be the smallest of Japan's four main islands, but it's not exactly bite-sized at 225 km (140 mi) long east to west, and anywhere from 50 km (31 mi) to 150 km (93 mi) wide. Honshu lies to the north, across the Inland Sea; and east, across the Kii Strait. Kyushu lies to the southwest, across the Bungo Strait.

Mountain ranges cut through the middle of the island on an east-west axis, with a thin band of terrain facing the Inland Sea on the north side and a larger south-facing swath gradually descending to the Pacific. Shikoku translates as "four provinces"; moving clockwise from Shikoku's northeast, **Kagawa Prefecture** is the most urbanized of these four prefectures, as well as the most connected to the rest of Japan. Just south of Kagawa, occupying the eastern-central section of the island, is **Tokushima Prefecture.** Tokushima is a great entry point to the island's wild interior, including the **Iya Valley** in the prefecture's far, remote west. Along the southern edge of Tokushima flows the Yoshino River, a white-water rafting mecca that also forms the northern border of **Kōchi Prefecture** (formerly Tosa).

Kōchi encompasses the southern half of the island, stretching from **Cape Muroto** in the southeastern corner to **Cape Ashizuri,** the island's farthest southern extremity in the far west. This thinly populated prefecture brims with thickly forested mountains and wild stretches of coast. The prefectural capital city, **Kōchi,** is a lively, subtropical town that sits in an alluvial plain blessed by mild winters and agricultural abundance. Rounding out the island, northwestern **Ehime Prefecture** (once called Iyo) borders Kōchi to the south and both Kagawa and Tokushima to the east. Its main city and

Shikoku

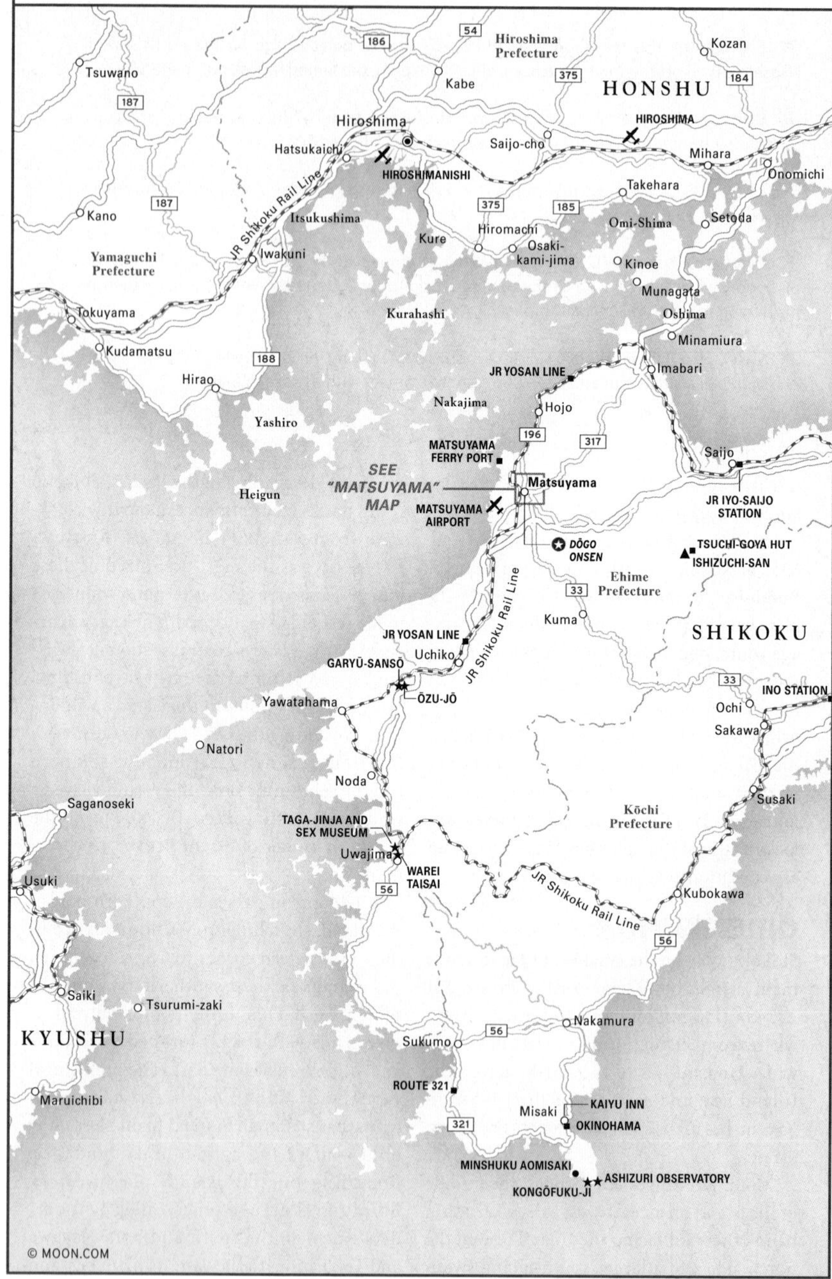

Hiroshima Prefecture
HONSHU
Tsuwano
Kabe
Kozan
Hiroshima
HIROSHIMA
Hatsukaichi
Saijo-cho
Mihara
HIROSHIMANISHI
Onomichi
Takehara
Kano
Itsukushima
JR Shikoku Rail Line
Hiromachi
Omi-Shima
Setoda
Kure
Osaki-kami-jima
Yamaguchi Prefecture
Iwakuni
Kinoe
Munagata
Tokuyama
Kurahashi
Oshima
Kudamatsu
Minamiura
JR YOSAN LINE
Imabari
Hirao
Nakajima
Hojo
Yashiro
MATSUYAMA FERRY PORT
Saijo
SEE "MATSUYAMA" MAP
Matsuyama
Heigun
MATSUYAMA AIRPORT
JR IYO-SAIJO STATION
DŌGO ONSEN
TSUCHI-GOYA HUT
ISHIZUCHI-SAN
Ehime Prefecture
JR Shikoku Rail Line
Kuma
SHIKOKU
JR YOSAN LINE
Uchiko
GARYŪ-SANSŌ
ŌZU-JŌ
INO STATION
Yawatahama
Ochi
Sakawa
Natori
Noda
Susaki
Saganoseki
Kōchi Prefecture
TAGA-JINJA AND SEX MUSEUM
Uwajima
WAREI TAISAI
Usuki
JR Shikoku Rail Line
Kubokawa
Saiki
Tsurumi-zaki
Nakamura
KYUSHU
Sukumo
ROUTE 321
Maruichibi
Misaki
KAIYU INN
OKINOHAMA
MINSHUKU AOMISAKI
ASHIZURI OBSERVATORY
KONGŌFUKU-JI
54
186
375
184
187
187
375
185
188
196
317
33
33
56
56
56
321

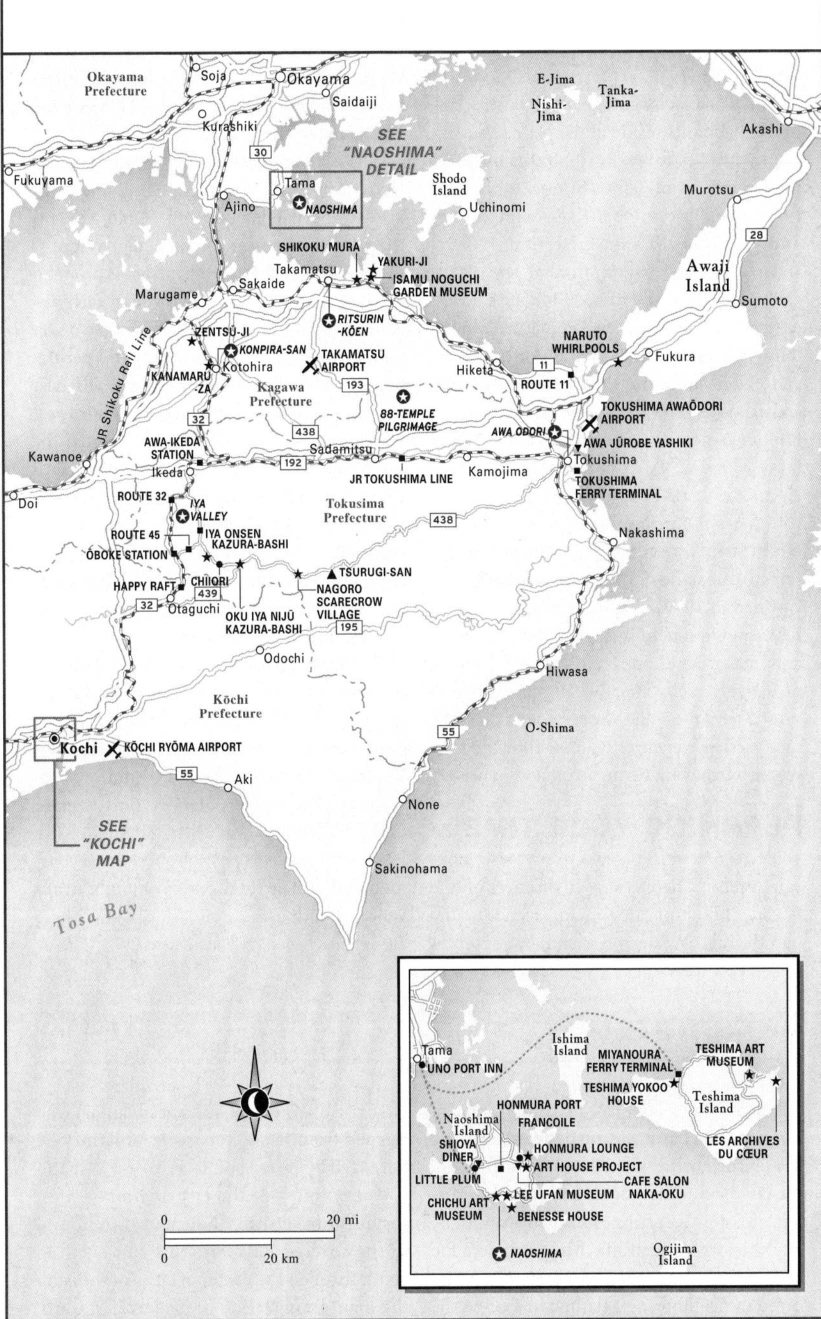
Okayama Prefecture
Soja
Okayama
Saidaiji
Kurashiki
Fukuyama
SEE "NAOSHIMA" DETAIL
Tama
NAOSHIMA
Ajino
Shodo Island
Uchinomi
E-Jima
Nishi-Jima
Tanka-Jima
Akashi
Murotsu
Awaji Island
Sumoto
SHIKOKU MURA
YAKURI-JI
ISAMU NOGUCHI GARDEN MUSEUM
Takamatsu
Sakaide
Marugame
RITSURIN -KŌEN
ZENTSŪ-JI
KONPIRA-SAN
Kotohira
KANAMARU -ZA
TAKAMATSU AIRPORT
Kagawa Prefecture
88-TEMPLE PILGRIMAGE
NARUTO WHIRLPOOLS
Fukura
Hiketa
ROUTE 11
TOKUSHIMA AWAŌDORI AIRPORT
AWA ODORI
AWA JŪROBE YASHIKI
Tokushima
TOKUSHIMA FERRY TERMINAL
JR Shikoku Rail Line
Kawanoe
AWA-IKEDA STATION
Ikeda
Sadamitsu
JR TOKUSHIMA LINE
Kamojima
Doi
ROUTE 32
IYA VALLEY
Tokusima Prefecture
ROUTE 45
IYA ONSEN KAZURA-BASHI
ŌBOKE STATION
HAPPY RAFT
CHIIORI
Otaguchi
OKU IYA NIJŪ KAZURA-BASHI
TSURUGI-SAN
NAGORO SCARECROW VILLAGE
Nakashima
Odochi
Hiwasa
Kōchi Prefecture
O-Shima
Kochi
KŌCHI RYŌMA AIRPORT
Aki
None
Sakinohama
SEE "KOCHI" MAP
Tosa Bay
0 20 mi
0 20 km
Tama
UNO PORT INN
Ishima Island
MIYANOURA FERRY TERMINAL
TESHIMA ART MUSEUM
TESHIMA YOKOO HOUSE
Teshima Island
LES ARCHIVES DU CŒUR
HONMURA PORT
Naoshima Island
FRANCOILE
SHIOYA DINER
HONMURA LOUNGE
ART HOUSE PROJECT
LITTLE PLUM
CAFE SALON NAKA-OKU
CHICHU ART MUSEUM
LEE UFAN MUSEUM
BENESSE HOUSE
NAOSHIMA
Ogijima Island

capital is **Matsuyama,** home to the famed **Dōgo Onsen,** Japan's first hot-spring inn. **Ishizuchi-san,** Shikoku's tallest mountain at 1,982 meters (6,503 feet), is also found in Ehime. The vast majority of Shikoku's 3.8 million inhabitants reside in the plains abutting the Inland Sea to the north, in the midsized urban centers of **Tokushima** (Tokushima Prefecture), **Takamatsu** (Kagawa Prefecture), and Matsuyama (Ehime Prefecture).

In 1988, the completion of the **Seto-Chūō Expressway** linked Shikoku's northeast coast to Okayama Prefecture via six long bridges crossable by train or car. A decade later came the **Kobe-Awaji-Naruto Expressway,** linking Kobe and Naruto on Shikoku's northeastern coast via the rather large island of Awaji-shima. This route includes the world's longest suspension bridge, the Akashi-Kaikyō Bridge. Finally, the **Nishiseto Expressway,** commonly referred to as the **Shimanami Kaidō,** was finished in 1999. This route bridged the gap between Onomichi in Hiroshima Prefecture and Imabari in Ehime Prefecture. Of the three great bridge networks, the Shimanami Kaidō stands out for being the only one that can be traversed by bicycle or on foot, allowing for a scenic journey that is an attraction in itself.

PLANNING YOUR TIME

When it comes to Shikoku's relative size, looks can deceive. There is a *lot* to discover on the island. Shikoku is an enticing accent to any trip through Western Honshu, but deserves deep exploration on its own. A jaunt through the **northern half** of the island calls for about five days. Plan to spend another 2-3 days, minimum, if you add **Kōchi** to your itinerary. One could easily spend 10-12 days on the island and still find more to discover.

The island is blessed with warmer weather than most of Honshu: a long, pleasant **spring,** hot muggy **summers,** and pleasant **autumns.** The island—particularly southwestern Ehime and all of Kōchi—is prone to **typhoons** in late summer through early autumn. Stay up-to-date on the weather if you plan to travel to the island during this period. Snow rarely falls outside the island's highest mountains during its relatively tame **winters.** Given the island's off-the-radar status for most travelers to Japan, it's a great place to relish seasonal delights like ***hanami*** (cherry blossom viewing) in spring (late March through early April) and **autumn leaves** from mid-October through November without jostling for elbow room, as often happens in Honshu's prime locations.

The most exciting time to visit Shikoku is undoubtedly during summer when the cities of Kōchi and Tokushima host two riotous dance festivals: the modern-dance-flavored **Yosakoi Matsuri** (Aug. 9-12), and my personal favorite *matsuri* of any type, the more traditional **Awa Odori Matsuri** (Aug. 12-15). Plan as far ahead as possible, because accommodations fill up three or more months in advance in both cities. Pound for pound, these are Japan's best dance festivals.

Takamatsu

Takamatsu is the laid-back maritime capital of Kagawa Prefecture. Sitting beside the Inland Sea on the northeastern corner of the island, the city is the first port of call for most visitors crossing over from Honshu by train. The city's history is eventfully checkered, from the battle of the Taira and Minamoto clans that raged in neighboring Yashima in 1185 to the later rise of Warlord Chikamasa Ikoma, who reigned from the hilltop castle, built in 1588 but razed by Allied bombs in World War II.

Today, most of the city's action—cafés, restaurants, fashion boutiques—is found in the covered walkways that run north to south through the center of city, southeast of the main train station in the north of town.

The only remains of the castle—uniquely positioned on the waterfront—include some moats and stray walls. The city's more lasting heritage is seen at its Ritsurin-kōen, a superb landscape garden known for its profusion of pine trees twisting every which way.

Although the city makes for a pleasant one-night stay, it's best viewed as a jumping-off point to Yashima, with its temples and intriguing museums; Naoshima, an island overtaken by the collective vision of artists; and Kotohira, home to Japan's first kabuki theater as well as one of its grandest shrines, Konpira-san.

SIGHTS

TOP EXPERIENCE

★ Ritsurin-kōen
栗林公園

1-20-16 Ritsurin-kōen; tel. 087/833-7411; www.my-kagawa.jp; dusk to dawn daily; ¥410

While Mito's Kairakuen, Kanazawa's Kenrokuen, and Okayama's Korakuen are considered the top three of Japan's landscape gardens, Ritsurin is of the same caliber. Planted, expanded, and pruned for more than a century by a succession of Takamatsu's feudal lords, this 750,000-square-meter (75-acre) green space—Japan's largest dedicated garden—deserves at least two hours of wandering; it is the city's one must-see attraction.

There are arched wooden bridges, almost 30,000 trees, long winding paths through tunnels of pine branches, artificial hills, teahouses, a manmade waterfall, and several lakes teeming with colorful *koi* (carp). Be sure also to stop by **Kikugestu-tei** (9am-4pm daily), a lovely teahouse perched beside the South Lake, for a green tea and a sweet. Buy a combination ticket at either entrance for the gardens and the teahouse.

Divided into south and north sections, the garden began to take shape in the mid-1620s at the hand of Takatoshi Ikoma, once the feudal lord of Sanuki (modern-day Kagawa). The grounds were inherited next by Yorishige Matsudaira, who was later appointed lord of the Takamatsu domain in 1642. The Matsudaira clan continued to expand the grounds until it finally reached its full dimensions in 1754. It served as the Matsudaira family's private escape until opening to the public in 1875, following the Meiji Restoration (1868). It was declared a National Treasure in 1953.

Located about 2.5 km (1.5 mi) south of JR

Ritsurin-kōen

Takamatsu Station, the garden can be reached on foot (35 minutes) or via taxi; travel south along Chūō-dōri until you reach the East Gate, which serves as the main entry point. Alternatively, you can take the JR line from Takamatsu Station to Ritsurin-kōen Kitaguchi Station, which is a short walk from the garden's North Gate (5 minutes; ¥210). These trains run two or three times hourly. Pick up an English-language map at either entrance and meander. English audio guides are also available for ¥200.

Shikoku Mura
四国村

91 Yashima-nakamachi; tel. 087/843-3111; www.shikokumura.or.jp; 8:30am-6pm Apr.-Oct., 8:30am-5:30pm Nov.-Mar.; ¥1,000; from JR Takamatsu Station, take the JR Kotoku line to Yashima Station (15 minutes, ¥220)

This open-air museum at the foot of the Yashima Plateau, east of downtown Takamatsu, features traditional thatched-roof homes from the island's interior mountainsides, storehouses, and cabins from fishing hamlets. Activities include workshops for making products like soy sauce and pressing sugarcane, and even a kabuki theater that periodically hosts plays. There's good English-language-signage throughout. The hillside grounds are worth checking out if you don't plan to venture deeper into the island's core, particularly the lush Iya Valley.

Isamu Noguchi Garden Museum
イサム・ノグチ庭園美術館

3-5-19 Murechō; tel. 087/870-1500; www.isamunoguchi.or.jp; 10am, 1pm, 3pm Tues., Thurs., and Sat. tours by appointment only; ¥2,160; from Takamatsu-Chikko Station, take the Kotoden Nagao line to Kawaramachi, then transfer to the Kotoden Shido line bound for Kotodenshido to Yakuri Station (40 minutes, ¥340), or from Yakuri Station, walk (25 minutes) or hop in a taxi (5 minutes, about ¥700)

This museum allows you to step into the whimsical, philosophical mind of the great Japanese-American modern artist, sculptor, landscape architect, and designer Isamu Noguchi (1904-1988). Although he was primarily based in the US, he spent long stints working at his Japan studio, located east of Takamatsu in the small town of Mure.

Noguchi fashioned everything from landscape gardens and large sculptures for corporate clients (IBM, HSBC) to furniture. The Noguchi Table he designed for the Herman Miller company in 1947 remains one of the most influential table designs of all time. Some of his other famous works include the Japanese garden in UNESCO's Paris headquarters and the bridges in Hiroshima's Peace Park.

The museum in Mure brilliantly displays Noguchi's diverse creative impulses through a variety of works and tools he used and in the surrounding grounds, where you'll find some 150 unfinished stone sculptures. A tour of the museum also includes a visit to his former home, a beautifully renovated Edo-period merchant's house.

To visit, you must make a reservation by phone or email at least one week in advance, though sometimes they can accommodate visitors on shorter notice. English-speaking guides are available.

Yakuri-ji
八栗寺

Temple: 3416 Mure, Mure-chō; tel. 087/845-9603; www.yakuriji.jp; 24 hours; free. Cable car: 3378-3 Mure, Mure-chō; tel. 087/845-2218; www.shikokucable.co.jp; 7:30am-5:15pm; ¥930 return, ¥460 one way

If you've made it all the way out to Isamu Noguchi's former residence, it behooves you to visit Yakuri-ji, temple number 85 on the island's pilgrimage circuit of 88. About 20 minutes' walk east of the great sculptor's old home brings you to the lower station of a cable car that whisks you 0.7 km (0.43 mi) up to the temple, set in a reclusive forest away from the crowds.

Founded in 754 by Chinese monk Chin'en-chen (known as Ganjin in Japan), this holy site stands not far from where the Heike and

Minamoto clans fought it out in the Battle of Gempei in 1185. Relics from that very skirmish are on display in a museum on the temple grounds.

FOOD

★ RANMARU

7-4 Daikumachi; tel. 050/3462-0595; 6pm-midnight daily; ¥880-1,100

Most people think of silky *sanuki udon* noodles at the mention of Kagawa. But the truth is, the prefecture is just crazed about chicken. Chicken served *sanuki* style, known as *honetsuki-dori* (fried bone-in chicken), involves slathering the chicken in copious amounts of garlic, oil, and salt and cooking it like a steak. The flavorful meat is surprisingly tough and requires the use of kitchen shears to scissor through it. It goes best with ice-cold beer. Ranmaru, a greasy spoon with a 1960s-era interior, is a lively local favorite for this hearty dish. There's often a queue, but a shorter one than at some of the other *sanuki* chicken joints in the area.

OFUKURO

1F Hamada Enterprise Bldg., 1-11-12 Kawaramachi; tel. 087/831-0822; 5pm-11:30pm Mon.-Sat.; dishes from ¥500

For something healthier with less salt and oil, Ofukuro is a great place to dig into a well-balanced set meal. You'll find various fish dishes, combined with a generous range of vegetable side dishes, a salad, and miso soup served with a variety of garnishes. This cozy restaurant, run by friendly staff, is located on a street lined with shops. If you have trouble finding it, just ask around, as it's a local favorite.

UDON HONJIN YAMADAYA SANUKI HONTEN

3186 Murecho Mure; tel. 087/845-6522; www.yamada-ya.com; 10am-8pm daily; ¥800-1,150

Near Shikoku Mura, the Isamu Noguchi Garden Museum or the temple of Yakuri-ji, is this excellent purveyor of *sanuki udon*. This thick style of noodle, made from wheat-flour and originating in the kitchen of Kagawa, is arguably Shikoku's most famous contribution to the nation's menu. Set in a historic mansion registered as a cultural property, this homey shop offers an experience as much as a meal. I recommend trying *udon* with crispy tempura (battered and fried vegetables and shrimp) or with pork (*niku udon*).

NIGHTLIFE

KING'S YAWD

1-2-2 Tokishin-machi; 087/837-2660; http://blog.livedoor.jp/kingsyawd; 6pm-3am Tues.-Sat.;

This chilled out bar serves jerk chicken and other Jamaican favorites to a reggae soundtrack. It's a friendly spot that draws a good mixed crowd. English menu available.

MUSIC INN GRANDFATHER'S

1-6-4 Tokiwachō; 087/837-5177; 6pm-2am Sun.-Thurs., until 3am Fri.-Sat.

This classy bar ticks all the right boxes: great sound system, extensive collection of vinyl records leaning heavily toward soul and funk, dimly lit cozy atmosphere, fantastic cocktails, and affable, urbane bartenders who exude just the right amount of effortless sophistication.

ACCOMMODATIONS

¥10,000-20,000

DAIWA ROYNET HOTEL TAKAMATSU

8-23 Marugamemachi; tel. 087/811-7855; www.daiwaroynet.jp/takamatsu; ¥10,400 d; take the Kotoden Nagao line or the Kotoden Kotohira line from Takamatsu Chikko Station, about 7 minutes' walk from JR Takamatsu Station, to Kawaramachi Station (5 minutes, ¥190), and the hotel is 7 minutes' walk from there

Located smack in the middle of the city's main shopping and entertainment zone, this modern hotel with pleasant service has well-appointed, compact rooms with free Wi-Fi throughout. A restaurant serving a western and Japanese-style breakfast is also available on-site, as are bicycle rentals and coin laundry facilities.

TOP EXPERIENCE

★ 88-Temple Pilgrimage Route

The journey of a Shikoku *henro* (pilgrim) is arduous. They must trek 1,400 km (870 mi) over mountains and along rugged coastline. All told, the quest to walk the loop clockwise around Shikoku takes around two months for most—around 25 km (15.5 mi) daily.

Legend has it that Kōbō Daishi (aka Kūkai), who founded the Shingon ("True Word") esoteric school of Buddhism, established the 1,200-year-old route. Each temple is said to symbolize a craving, or sin, thought to plague humankind. The motives for undertaking the journey are as varied as the pilgrims who make it, from atonement for past misdeeds to praying for health and success, all the way up to striving for enlightenment.

pilgrims on the *henro* typically wear white

A *henro* is traditionally outfitted in a white vest called a *hakui*, with a conical *sugegasa* hat of woven straw. Completing the getup are prayer beads strung around the wrists and a *zudabukuro* bag slung over the shoulder, used for toting candles, incense, and their *nōkyōchō* (book for collecting stamps at each temple). Another important item is the *kongozue* (wooden staff), which symbolizes Kūkai. It has a bell on top meant to deter wild animals and keep one in the present moment with its light jingle. The bottom end is respectfully washed at night, symbolically cleaning Kūkai's feet, and must never be etched with a knife or used when walking across a bridge, as Kūkai is said to have once slept under a bridge.

WALKING THE ROUTE

Today, those who drive, cycle, ride a bus, or take the train far outnumber the purists who complete the whole thing on foot. But for maximum impact, traditionalists swear by following the path laid out by devotees of the great Kūkai. For pilgrims with less time on their hands, it's perfectly acceptable to walk a short leg of the circuit. Here are a few popular options:

- **Near Tokushima:** Ryōzen-ji, Gokuraku-ji, Konsen-ji, Dainichi-ji, and Jizō-ji (Temples no. 1 through no. 5) (11 km/7 mi, 2.5 hours one way). Take the JR Kotoku line from Tokushima Station to Bandō Station (20 minutes; ¥260), then walk about 15 minutes to Ryōzen-ji.
- **Near Kōchi:** Chikurin-ji (no. 31), Zenjibu-ji (no. 32), and Sekkei-ji (no. 33) (16 km/10 mi, 4 hours one way). Take the My Yu Bus from JR Kōchi Station (25 minutes; ¥600 for day pass) to Chikurin-ji, situated on Godai-san, then walk from there.
- **Near Matsuyama:** Jōruri-ji (no. 46) through Enmyō-ji (no. 53) (27 km/17 mi, 6 hours one way). From Matsuyama City Station, take the Iyo Railway's Yokogawara line bound for Yokogawara to Takanoko Station (13 minutes; ¥260). From there, take a local bus bound for Tanba, getting off at the Jōruri-ji-mae bus stop.

However much of the circuit you undertake, wear cushy shoes meant for running or walking, and thick socks, and bring a first-aid kit. Plan to hike in April-May or October-November. Winter tends to be frigid, while summer is sweltering.

LEARN MORE

Good books for planning your journey include the **Shikoku Japan 88 Route Guide** (https://henro.co/route-guide-book), which can also be bought at Ryōzen-ji (no. 1), and the free e-book **Shikoku Pilgrimage: A Guide for Non-Japanese** (http://henro88map.com/pdf/Henro-ENG.pdf).

TAKAMATSU TOKYU REI HOTEL

9-9 Hyōgomachi; tel. 087/821-0109; www.tokyuhotels.co.jp/takamatsu-r; ¥15,300 d; on the main artery of Chūō-dōri, about 10 minutes' walk south of JR Takamatsu Station, or 15 minutes on foot from the city's ferry terminal

Another good, no-frills option in the heart of downtown, this hotel is located right next to a long, covered arcade filled with shops and eateries. As with most business hotels in town, the rooms are compact but clean, and there's free Wi-Fi and an on-site restaurant serving a mixed breakfast of both Japanese and western dishes.

¥20,000-30,000

JR HOTEL CLEMENT TAKAMATSU

1-1 Hamanochō; tel. 087/811-1111; www.jrclement.co.jp; doubles from ¥22,000

For convenience, it's hard to beat this hotel. It's located about five minutes' walk northeast of JR Takamatsu Station, just across the street from the city's ferry terminal. The modern rooms are airy, with views looking out over the harbor and the Inland Sea beyond. There are also chic bar and dining options on-site.

INFORMATION AND SERVICES

On the first floor of JR Takamatsu Station, you'll find a helpful **Tourist Information Center** (1-120, Hamanochō; tel. 087/826-0170; www.my-kagawa.jp/point/2486; 9am-8pm daily). English-speaking staff are there to field your questions or supply you with English-language material.

Another good resource is the Kagawa International Exchange Center, or **I-PAL Kagawa** (1-11-63 Banchō; tel. 087/837-5908; www.i-pal.or.jp; 9am-6pm Tues.-Sun.). This center, located in the northwestern corner of Chūō-kōen, about 15 minutes' walk south of Takamatsu Station, functions as a repository of English-language information, from books and periodicals to printed event listings. You can hop on a computer here and browse the Internet for up to 30 minutes if you need to.

Online, **Takamatsu Life** (http://takamatsulife.com) is a great local resource too. The website features listings of entertainment and events, local activities, and more.

TRANSPORTATION

Getting There

TRAIN

Most people arrive in Takamatsu by train. If you're coming from Honshu, it's possible to go directly to the city from **Okayama** (1 hour; ¥2,030). From within Shikoku, it's possible to take trains directly from **Matsuyama** (2.5 hours; ¥6,390), **Tokushima** (1 hour 5 minutes; ¥3,360), and **Kōchi** (2 hours 10 minutes; ¥5,630). As long as you're coming via a **JR line** from any of these cities, the JR Pass will cover the fare.

BUS

It's also possible to arrive in Takamatsu on a night bus from **Tokyo** (10 hours; ¥10,000 one way, ¥19,000 return). If you're coming from closer to the city, buses also run from **Kōbe, Osaka,** and a number of cities within **Shikoku.** Buses arrive and depart near **JR Takamatsu Station.** Check the website of the highway bus operator **Willer** (http://willerexpress.com) for full timetables and rates.

BOAT

If you'd rather enjoy views of the Inland Sea as you make your way to Shikoku, it's also possible to take a ferry from **Kōbe** (4 hours 30 minutes; ¥1,990 one-way, ¥3,790 return). Ferries coming from Kobe dock about a 10-minute shuttle bus ride to the east of JR Takamatsu Station at the **Jumbo Ferry Takamatsu** docks (5-12-1 Asahimachi; tel. 087/811-6688). For details, check the **Japan Ferry** website (https://ferry.co.jp). Another ferry network links Takamatsu to **Shodoshima** (1 hour). See the **Shikoku Ferry** website (www.shikokuferry.com) for details. Finally, **Shikoku Kisen** (www.shikokukisen.com) links Takamatsu to **Naoshima** (1 hour) and **Uno** in Okayama Prefecture (1 hour). Ferries coming from or going to Shodoshima, Naoshima, or Uno leave and arrive from **Sunport Ferry**

Port (8-22 Sunport; tel. 087/822-4383; www.shikokuferry.com), a short walk northeast of JR Takamatsu Station.

AIR

If you prefer to fly, there are daily flights to **Takamatsu Airport** (Konanchooka; tel. 087/814-3355; www.takamatsu-airport.com) from Tokyo's **Haneda** and **Narita** airports, as well as from **Naha,** Okinawa. Admittedly, flying to Takamatsu is not the most economical option. Although JAL (Japan Airlines) and ANA (All Nippon Airways) fly to Takamatsu from Tokyo, the budget carrier **Jetstar Japan** offers much cheaper deals. Internationally, there are limited flights between Takamatsu and regional cities like Seoul, Taipei, Shanghai, and Hong Kong. Note that Takamatsu Airport is located about 40 minutes from downtown, about 16 km (10 mi) south of the city. You can take a **bus** (¥760) or **taxi** (¥5,000) into downtown.

Getting Around

Once you're in the city, Takamatsu is laid out on a straightforward grid pattern. This makes the city easy to navigate. If you're moving within the downtown area, you can negotiate most of the city **on foot.**

TRAIN

To save on travel time, there's also a good local train network known as **Kotoden.** These trains run to the eastern suburb of Yashima and south to the town of Kotohira. The easiest place to hop on this line is at the **Takamatsu Chikkō Station,** located next to Tamamo-kōen about 4 minutes' walk east of JR Takamatsu Station. Meanwhile, the **JR Tokushima** line links Takamatsu and Tokushima. Unlike the Kotoden line, it has the added bonus of being covered by the JR Pass.

BUS

Although they're less convenient than the local train lines, city buses also run to sites such as Ritsurin-kōen and the suburb of Yashima to the east. You can catch the bus from outside **Takamatsu Chikkō Station** at the northern edge of Chūō-dōri.

BICYCLE

You can rent bicycles beneath **JR Takamatsu Station** (tel. 087/831-5383; 7am-10pm; ¥100 6 hours, ¥200 full day). Just ask at the tourist information counter in the train station. Before pedaling away, be sure you understand the **parking** system to avoid receiving any ¥1,500 fines. If you plan to travel mostly within the downtown area, renting a bicycle is the most economical—and fun—way to get around.

CAR

Finally, you can rent a car at **Toyota Rent-a-Car** (70-2 Hamanochō; tel. 087/851-0100; www.r-higashishikoku.jp; 8am-8pm daily). The ever-trusty car rental agency operates an office about 4 minutes' walk southeast of JR Takamatsu Station.

Around Takamatsu

★ KONPIRA-SAN
こんぴらさん

892-1 Kotohira-chō; tel. 0877/75-2121; 8:30am-4:30pm daily; Hōmutsu-kan ¥800, Shoin ¥800

Soon after exiting Kotohira's small main train station, signs of seafaring begin to rise up around you. A few minutes down the main street from the station's main exit, you'll come to a large wooden tower with a stone base and a giant lantern at its top. This was once Japan's tallest lighthouse.

In keeping with Kotohira's connections to

1: golden propeller at Konpira-san **2:** path to top of Konpira-san

1
奉納
2

Kōbō Daishi: Mountain Mystic and Renaissance Man

Kūkai, known posthumously as Kōbō Daishi (774-835), may be pound-for-pound the most important figure in the history of Japanese religion. Starting in 804, Kūkai embarked on a two-year journey into the heart of Buddhism's deepest teachings in China, where he studied the *Mavavairocana Tantra* Indian tantric text under the great sage Huiguo (746-805) at Xi Ming Temple. Kūkai returned to Japan having mastered Sanskrit and Chinese, calligraphy and poetry, and began wandering the wilds of Shikoku, ending amid the rocky cliffs of Cape Muroto in the far southeast of Kōchi Prefecture, where he is said to have reached enlightenment.

The Daishi ("Great Saint") went on to establish the **Shingon** ("True Word") sect of Buddhism, now centered in the mountaintop sanctuary of Kōya-san in Wakayama Prefecture, where Kūkai's legendary *vajra* (sacred mace) is said to have landed after he hurled it from China, and where his body is now entombed. Known as much for his cultural and social achievements as his mystical scholarship and insight, Kūkai was something of a Renaissance man. He penned works on religion and literature, composed poetry, collated the nation's first dictionary, founded Japan's first public schools, and even developed new irrigation techniques. Most significantly, he is said to have created Japan's two syllabaries, *hiragana* and *katakana*, which combined with *kanji*, or adopted and modified Chinese characters, make up Japan's modern-day written language. Some even credit him with discovering the element of mercury.

It is possible to visit Kūkai's birthplace in Shikoku, **Zentsū-ji** (3-3-1 Zentsūji-chō; tel. 0877/62-0111; www.zentsuji.com; always open; free), a brief trip north of Kotohira. It's home to a five-story pagoda and the Golden Hall—housing a statue of Amida Buddha, the main celestial Buddha of the Pure Land sect—and to the Mie-dō, said to be where Kūkai received his first bath.

seafaring, Konpira-san, or **Kotohira-gu** (**金刀比羅宮**), is not only one of Shinto's holiest sites, it's a shrine solely devoted to the protection of sailors. The complex sprawls up the slopes of Zozu-san (Elephant Head Mountain) on the western outskirts of town. Reaching the main shrine is no light matter. Walking up a path lined by a multitude of stone lanterns, you'll climb 785 steps before you reach the main hall, where you'll be rewarded with stunning views of the town and distant peaks on the horizon. On the way up, you'll pass several stop-off points where there are various sub-shrines and small museums exhibiting kabuki and *Noh* masks, painted screens, and other more peculiar items. Among them: a huge golden propeller, massive anchors, a white horse in a stable for the shrine's god to ride, and at the top, memorabilia from the high seas. In the Ema Hall, you'll find photos of commercial ships, battleships, and even spaceships and astronauts, extending the shrine's powers of protection into the interstellar orbit.

If the ascent sounds daunting but you're keen to make it to the main shrine without breaking a sweat, you can pay two bearers—parked at the base of the mountain—to transport you in a palanquin (¥5,300 up, ¥3,200 down, ¥6,800 round-trip) to the main hall. If you're a glutton for punishment and want to see the entire complex, push on for another 583 steps past the main hall until you reach the *Okusha* (inner shrine). However much of the path you plan to walk, be sure to wear comfortable footwear. The walk to the main hall takes about 45 minutes from the foot of the mountain, while the trek from there to the inner shrine is an additional 45 minutes one way.

You can arrive in Kotohira by either the JR line or Kotoden line. Coming from Takamatsu, the JR trains depart from JR Takamatsu Station once hourly (1 hour; ¥850 one way). Less frequent Shimanto limited express trains make the same journey (35 minutes; ¥2,000). JR Kotohira Station is located about 10 minutes' walk northeast of the heart of town, toward Konpira-san. From JR Kotohira Station, either walk 15 minutes to base of the steps that lead to the shrine, or call ahead (tel. 0877/73-2221) to reserve a spot on a bus that departs from in front of the station and drops off passengers about half-way to the main hall.

KANAMARU-ZA
金丸座

1241 Kotohira-chō; tel. 0877/73-3846; 9am-5pm daily; ¥500; walk about 15 minutes southwest of JR Kotohira Station. The theater is up a hilly road about 200 meters south of the path that leads to the approach to Konpira-san

Although Konpira-san is Kotohira's best known sight, this less visited kabuki theater is truthfully a more atmospheric discovery. Built in 1835, Kanamaru-za is Japan's oldest kabuki theater with all of its trappings intact. As you enter the venerable building, it feels like a trip back in time. There are lanterns adorning the walls and hanging from the ceilings, and a tatami-floor seating area for the audience. The stage is backed by a large painting of a thick, gnarly pine tree.

The best part is that you're allowed to roam freely through the complex. You can stand on the stage, poke around the backstage area, check out the dressing rooms, and even go beneath the stage to see the space where staff could turn the rotating stage from underneath. There are trapdoors through which actors can appear or disappear for dramatic effect.

A few times a year, the theater still holds performances. Information on these performances is hard to come by in English, but if you're keen to try to see a performance at Kanamaru-za, keep an eye on the nationwide kabuki listings compiled at www.kabuki21.com.

Naoshima and the Inland Sea

TOP EXPERIENCE

Naoshima, an island that has become a jewel of the Inland Sea (technically the Seto Inland Sea), combines beautiful natural surroundings, a fabulous design sense and a forward-looking spirit of artistic experimentation. Easily accessed from Takamatsu on Shikoku and from Uno on Honshu, Naoshima is a must-visit for any trip to the area.

Beyond offering a deep-dive into contemporary art, the island's communities are charming, authentic, slow-paced, and mellow, and the seaside views are stunning. The artistic development of Naoshima has set something larger in motion in the region. Nearby, the tiny islands of Teshima and Inujima are two more "art islands" that are brilliantly following Naoshima's lead.

These art-studded isles are the most famous in this glittering seascape. But venture a bit farther out to sea and you'll discover a constellation of quieter isles that radiate a distinct charm at once magnetic and subtle.

Once you're gliding through the blue-green expanse, the view from a ferry approaching any one of the thousands of alluring specks of land is archetypally maritime. Boats tethered to weather-beaten docks bob on gentle waves. Fishermen empty barnacle-encrusted fishing nets of their daily catch. Squid hang to dry on wires in the open-air like garments on clotheslines. In town, octogenarian aunties run corner stores and greasy-spoon restaurants, while stray cats prowl nearby for scraps.

Experiencing this slower, unsung side of Japan firsthand is the Inland Sea's greatest draw. The "art islands" of Naoshima, Teshima, and Iunjima are great entry points, and do offer a taste of this timeworn way of life. But you'll be amply rewarded with solitude and feel as if you've taken a trip back in time if you hop on a ferry bound for some of the sea's lesser-known gems. Among the countless rustic standouts are Shodoshima and the Kasaoka chain, centered on Shiraishi-jima and Manabe-shima.

★ NAOSHIMA
直島

Roughly 7.8 square km (3 square mi), with a population of around 3,300, this sublime isle is awash with art, mostly funded by the big pockets of the language-study and test-prep company Benesse Corporation as **Benesse Art Site Naoshima** (http://benesse-artsite.jp). Soichiro Fukutake, the chairman of Benesse, is a native of nearby Okayama and a keen patron of the arts. Since 1992, when the Benesse House Museum opened as a boutique hotel-cum-museum where guests are permitted to roam unfettered at night, Naoshima has been transformed from a dwindling fishing community into an immersive, world-class art hub. As the island's profile rose, other creatives came to launch cafés, bed-and-breakfasts, and restaurants.

The minimalist structures in this area that were created by Pritzker Prize-winning architect Tadao Ando, are works of art themselves, not to mention the outdoor sculptures dotting the landscape, and works by Jackson Pollock, Claude Monet, Jasper Johns, and David Hockney scattered around the island's museums.

If you time your visit carefully, you can visit Naoshima on a day trip. But if you have the funds, consider staying on the island for a night. After the legion of day-trippers depart, quiet falls across the island and Naoshima returns to its slower native rhythm. A caveat: Avoid visiting on Monday, when most museums are closed. If Monday happens to be a holiday, things close on Tuesday instead.

Sights

ART HOUSE PROJECT
家プロジェクト

Various locations in village of Honmura; http://benesse-artsite.jp/en/art/arthouse.html; 10am-4:30pm Tues.-Sun., closed Tues. when Mon. is holiday; ¥1,030 multi-site admission, ¥410 admission to single site; take a bus from Miyanoura Port to Honmura (¥100), or walk 3 minutes' west from Honmura pier

The Art House Project in the traditional community of Honmura, on the island's east side, presents a series of conceptual artworks incorporated into unassuming old structures dotting the village. Art lovers find these works by following a walking route like a treasure hunt, with map in hand. The traditional buildings in which they appear range from homes and workshops to a shrine and a temple. The works are eclectic: LED lights illuminating a pool of water inside a home, underground chambers in hillsides looking onto glass staircases emerging up through the surface of the earth, a two-story Statue of Liberty replica jutting up through a former dentist's home, and more.

Honmura is a good place to visit during the morning or early afternoon. That way, you can combine your art walk here with a stop at one of the area's homey cafés or restaurants, serving fresh, healthy nosh. For more information on the individual artists and their creations spread around the village, and to purchase a ticket to enter the various sites of the Art House Project, stop by the **Honmura Lounge** (850-2 Naoshima; tel. 087/840-8273; http://benesse-artsite.jp/en/art/arthouse.html; 10am-4:30pm Tues.-Sun., closed Tues. when Mon. is public holiday), located near the town's main bus stop.

BENESSE HOUSE MUSEUM
ベネッセハウス ミュージアム

tel. 087/892-3223; http://benesse-artsite.jp/stay/benessehouse; 8am-9pm daily; ¥1,030, age 15 and under free; take a bus from Miyanoura Port, via Honmura, to the Tsutsujiso bus stop (10 minutes, ¥100), which lies near the east side of Benesse House

This well-known complex doubles as museum and high-end accommodation. It's the jewel in Benesse Corporation's crown on Naoshima, designed by architectural giant

1: the Benesse House Museum **2:** sunset on Naoshima

1

2

Tadao Ando. The sprawling property on the south side of the island includes a museum, a building called the Oval, a park, and a beach.

Beyond art featured in the rooms and museum—David Hockney, Gerhard Richter, Hiroshi Sugimoto—the grounds are dotted by outdoor pieces that suit the surroundings, such as Yayoi Kusama's avant-garde take on a giant pumpkin that looks as if it's been plopped onto a pier. Guests can peruse the Museum's collection 24/7. The views over the Inland Sea from the hill outside the museum are phenomenal at any time of day, but the sunsets are especially stunning.

CHICHŪ ART MUSEUM
地中美術館

http://benesse-artsite.jp/en/art/chichu.html; 10am-6pm Mar.-Sept. Tues.-Sun., 10am-5pm Oct.-Feb. Tues.-Sun.; ¥2,060, age 15 and under free; take the bus from Miyanoura Port, via Honmura, to the Tsutsujiso bus stop (10 minutes, ¥100), and then either walk (30 minutes) or take the free shuttle bus (10 minutes); or walk east from Miyanoura Port (35 minutes) or cycle over (10 minutes)

This museum is a mind-bending, almost completely subterranean complex lit mostly by natural light filtered through skylights of various shapes and sizes. This is one of Naoshima's highlights, one of many structures designed by all-star architect Tadao Ando. Natural light changes throughout the day in a seamless dance with the artworks on display. The collection is not huge, but it includes heavy hitters like Claude Monet and Walter De Maria. On Friday and Saturday evenings, the "Open Sky Night Program" is held, in which the sunset can be viewed from within the subterranean space.

Buy a ticket in front of the museum's entrance. You must leave any luggage or cameras in one of the lockers provided at the ticket center. During the museum's peak times, each visitor is only allowed to enter the museum at a preordained time to prevent overcrowding.

Sports and Recreation

I LOVE 湯 ("I LOVE YU")

2252-2 Higashicho, Naoshima-chō; http://benesse-artsite.jp/en/art/naoshimasento.html; 1pm-9pm Tues.-Sun., closed Tues. if Mon. falls on public holiday; adults ¥650, children 2-15 ¥300, ages 2 and under free; 4 minutes' walk east of Miyanoura Port on the island's west side

For an experience beyond ogling art, why not bathe in it? I Love Yu (*Yu* meaning "hot water") is a funky *sento* (bath house) designed by artist Shinro Ohtake, whose quirky spin on the neighborhood bath is a natural fit on the island. In place of the de rigueur mural of Mount Fuji, you'll find a life-sized elephant walking overhead, white tiles emblazoned with blue undersea visions of divers; jelly fish, and octopuses on the walls; and a ceiling made of vividly stained glass.

Events

SETOUCHI TRIENNALE

https://setouchi-artfest.jp; 3-season passport to most art sites ¥4,800 adults, ¥3,000 16-18, under 15 free; single-season passport ¥4,000 adults, 2,500 16-18, under 15 free

This massive happening features performances (dance, music, drama) and visual spectacles. Taking place every three years on Naoshima and an array of other islands in the Inland Sea, the proceedings are generally broken into seasonal programs in spring, summer, and autumn. The website has thorough English-language information on everything from the event, the islands involved, ferry links, and more. If you intend to catch this world-famous arts and culture event, book your accommodation as far in advance as you can—six months ahead or more. If you have trouble landing a room, check out potential options around Takamatsu on Shikoku or Uno in Okayama Prefecture.

Quiet Getaways

Naoshima and the other creative hubs nearby on Inujima and Teshima are undeniably the most accessible—and consequently, crowded—places to experience this gorgeous swath of sea. Other islands beckon from just beyond the tourist trail for those who yearn to experience the Inland Sea's charm at a much more intimate level, less impacted by the encroachment of mass tourism. Here are a few of the best slivers of land to get a taste of this simpler way of life.

SHŌDO-SHIMA

小豆島

To sink deeply into the Inland Sea's island time and immerse yourself in the local rhythms, the climatically mild Shōdo-shima, east of Teshima, is a good starting point. Here you'll find olive groves, citrus trees, walking trails, soaring cliffs, and lovely seascapes. Visit www.town.shodoshima.lg.jp for information about activities on the island and detailed access information.

While a day trip to Shōdo-shima is possible, an overnight stay will allow you to fully soak up the laid-back pace. A great spot to do this is the **Sen Guesthouse** (687-15 Tanoura Otsu; tel. 0879/61-9980; www.senguesthouse.com; ¥12,000 d with shared bathrooms, dorms ¥3,400). Run by a friendly English-speaking couple, this property has a private beach, barbecue area, balcony with seaside views, a shared kitchen, and more. Another good pick option on the island is the **Shōdo-shima Olive Youth Hostel** (1072 Nishi-mura, Uchinomi-chō; tel. 0879/82-6161; www.jyh.gr.jp/shoudo; dorms ¥3,400).

KASAOKA ISLANDS

笠岡諸島

Farther west, the Kasaoka Islands also make for a great escape. Accessed from Kasaoka port, located about 45 minutes by local train on the JR San'yō line from Okayama (¥760) and 30 minutes from Kurashiki (¥500), two of the most charming islands are **Shiraishi-jima** (www.kasaoka-kankou.jp/en/island/shiraishijima) and **Manabe-shima** (www.kasaoka-kankou.jp/en/island/manabeshima/), one of Japan's famed "cat islands," where felines rule the roost.

Both islands make for a pleasant day trip, while the **Shiraishi Island International Villa** (tel. 086/256-2535; www.international-villa.or.jp; ¥3,500 pp) is a great place for a serene overnight stay. If you're on Shiraishi-jima during the warmer months, swing by the beachside **Moooo! Bar** (www.mooooobar.com; daily July-Aug., Sun. June and Sept.). It's a great place to sip a cocktail in the summer heat or watch as the sun dips below the horizon. For detailed access information on both islands, visit www.kasaoka-kankou.jp/en/access.

Food

CAFÉ SALON NAKA-OKU

1167 Honmura; tel. 087/892-3887; 11:30am-3pm and 5:30pm-9pm Wed.-Mon., some irregular closings; set lunches ¥650-800, ¥480-980 per dish

Much of Naoshima shuts down on Monday, giving this inviting café added cache. Its nicely aged wooden interior and home-cooked menu of classics like *karage* (fried chicken), *omuraisu* (omelette stuffed with fried rice), Japanese-style curry rice, and cakes, are a winning combination. There's also a good selection of booze if you want a drink in the evening. It's at the top of a hill on the backside of the village of Honmura, away from the bustle.

APRON

777 Naoshima-chō Ichien; tel. 087/892-3048; www.facebook.com/aproncafe.naoshima; 11am-4pm Tues.-Sun.; ¥1,100-1,580; near the Ando Museum down one of the footpaths that snake through inner Honmura

This bright, friendly café in the heart of Honmura is a great place for a healthy lunch. Stylish furniture, potted plants, art on the walls, and a chilled-out soundtrack create a relaxed vibe. The inventive lunch plates contain many small dishes: organic salads with fresh herbs, quiche packed with local produce, multigrain and black rice, cheese gratin, quinoa, vegetable curry, and scones made with cranberry and coconut.

SHIOYA DINER

2227 Naoshima; tel. 087/892-3290; 5pm-8:45pm (last order 8pm) Tues.-Sun.; ¥400-1,000; 4 minutes' walk inland from the port, around the corner from I Love Yu bathhouse

As advertised, this is a diner in the classic sense, and the retro decor and soundtrack straddling rockabilly and oldies reinforces this. Run by a friendly Japanese couple smitten by Americana, it's homey and funky, with just the right amount of kitsch. The menu includes comfort foods like chicken breast and mashed potatoes, tacos, hot dogs, burgers, and fries, plus there's beer on tap and Corona in the bottle. This is a great place to dine on the Miyanoura Port (west side) of the island, particularly if you're feeling like a break from Japanese fare.

Accommodations

If you can manage to snag a room on the island, be prepared for a surprisingly quiet night. The whole island closes down by around 7pm, save for a convenience store each in Honmura and Miyanoura, and a smattering of vending machines. That said, experiencing the island minus the tourist hordes is a revelation. You'll feel as if you could be on any one of the myriad sleepy isles dotting the Inland Sea.

Naoshima's lodgings are often fully booked. So be sure to conduct an exhaustive search (www.naoshima.net/stay). If the island's lodgings are full, aim to stay either on Honshu or Shikoku near either ferry port. It's simple to shuttle between Naoshima and Uno (Honshu) or Takamatsu (Shikoku) for a day trip or two.

LITTLE PLUM

2252-1 Miyanoura; tel. 087/892-3752; www.littleplum.net; dorms ¥3,000

These bare-bones but clean dorms are a good pick for budget travelers. Conveniently located near the small cluster of restaurants and the I Love Yu bathhouse in Miyanoura, there are two gender-separated dorm rooms, and one private room with two bunk beds that can accommodate a mixed group of up to four. There's a laid-back café of the same name attached (5pm-10pm Tues., 11am-10pm Wed.-Sun.), which serves simple set lunches like dry curry or fried chicken with rice, as well as drinks, desserts, and other dishes—pizza, salads, soups, etc.—a la carte. Bike rentals also available: a boon on an island where larger bicycle rental shops are routinely booked all day from the morning on.

UNO PORT INN

1-4-4 Chikko, Tamano; tel. 0863/21-2729; http://unoportinn.com; ¥11,800 d; take the JR Uno line to Uno Station, then walk 2 minutes west

With a cozy café on site serving nibbles and coffee, English-speaking staff, and petite, clean rooms (both Western and Japanese-style), this welcoming inn near the port on the Honshu side is a good place to stay for a night either before or after a trip to Naoshima. All rooms—each with a unique Japanese cinema-inspired theme—have a private bathroom, with most of them accessed through separate doors at the end of the hallway on each floor. Free Wi-Fi and laundry facilities are available.

★ FRANCOILE

953-2 Sonota, Naoshima-chō; tel. 090/4375-1979; www.francoile.com; ¥17,000 d

On the Honmura side, this bed-and-breakfast is a great place to stay for a night. There are just two rooms in this modern, well-decorated lodging on the backside of the village. Both rooms have good lighting, spacious private bathrooms and two twin beds. There's also a café (2pm-5pm Tues.-Thurs. and Sat.-Sun.) on the first floor serving good pour-over coffee and muffins. The place is run by a young Japanese couple with an amazing sense of hospitality, one of whom speaks great English.

With only two rooms, peace and quiet are a given. But it also means you'll need to reserve well in advance. Recommended.

★ BENESSE HOUSE

tel. 087/892-3223; http://benesse-artsite.jp/en/stay/benessehouse; ¥32,000 d

In the island's museum-studded south, this luxury property has rooms spanning four sites, all of which sit near the museum at the center of the Benesse art empire. All four complexes are paragons of the art gallery-cum-hotel concept. These include the beachside Benesse House Park and Beach, with its spa and library; the museum itself, which can be wandered by guests after hours; and the most-expensive Oval, which is perched on a hill above the museum and reached by monorail. The rooms are stylish yet minimal—televisions are notably absent—and feature artwork that belongs in the museum's private collection. If you have the means, this is the most luxurious, visually stunning accommodation on the island. Book as far in advance as you can.

Information and Services

Pick up one of the clearly marked English maps at the **Naoshima Tourism Association** (tel. 087/892-2299; 8:30am-6pm daily), an information desk in the lively Miyanoura ferry terminal on the west side of the island. If you arrive via Honmura port on the east side of the island, stop by the **Honmura Lounge & Archive** (850-2 Naoshima; tel. 087/840-8273; 10am-4:30pm Tues.-Sun.).

Transportation

GETTING THERE

You can reach Naoshima by **ferry** from both Honshu and Shikoku. Coming from **Takamatsu** (Shikoku), you can catch a ferry directly from Takamatsu Port (one hour; ¥520), a few minutes' walk from JR Takamatsu Station. If you're coming from **Okayama** (Honshu), you'll need to take the Marine Liner to Chayamachi, then transfer to the JR Uno Port line (50 minutes; ¥1,100) to Uno Port where you'll catch a ferry (20 minutes, ¥290).

GETTING AROUND

Your best options for getting around Naoshima are either by **bus** or **bicycle.** There's a convenient bus that runs from Miyanoura in the island's west, through Honmura on the east side, around to Benesse House and the Chichū Art Museum (all rides ¥100).

There are loads of bicycle **rental shops** around the port in Miyanoura, but be forewarned: the bicycles often run out very early in the day. If you want to rent a bicycle, plan on showing up at the port around 8:30am.

TESHIMA AND INUJIMA

The islands of Teshima and Inujima flesh out the **Benesse Art Site Naoshima** (http://benesse-artsite.jp). If you'd like to experience another "art island" without the mad rush of tourists that sometimes descend on Naoshima, a day trip to one of these adjacent islands will feel downright serene. Note that museums on Teshima and Inujima tend to close on Tuesday; be careful to coordinate the schedule correctly, remembering that nearby Naoshima all but shuts down on Monday.

Teshima

豊島

Of the two islands, Teshima is the larger and more popular, sitting between Shōdo-shima to the east and Naoshima to the west. The small green isle is dotted by fishing villages and swathed in citrus trees.

TESHIMA YOKOO HOUSE

豊島横尾館

2359 Teshimaieura; tel. 0879/68-3555; http://benesse-artsite.jp/en/art/teshima-yokoohouse.html; 10am-5pm Wed.-Mon. Mar.-Oct., 10am-4pm Fri.-Mon. Nov.-Feb.; ¥510

Built inside a traditional house near Ieura Port, the Teshima Yokoo House complex was designed by architect Nagayama Yuko. The house showcases works on life and death by the artist Yokoo Tadanori, after whom it is named. Outside, a classical Japanese rock garden strewn with multicolored rocks and mosaic tiles was built by locals. Inside, carp swim through a pond under a plexiglass floor. Inside an attached tower with mirrored floor and ceiling, the 14-meter-tall (46-foot) walls are plastered with nearly 1,000 waterfall postcards. Look up or down for a simulated glimpse of infinity. Even the bathrooms' chrome interiors create a disorienting effect.

TESHIMA ART MUSEUM
豊島美術館

607 Karato; tel. 0879/68-3555; http://benesse-artsite.jp/en/art/teshima-artmuseum.html; 10am-5pm Wed.-Mon. Mar.-Oct., 10am-4pm Fri.-Mon. Nov.-Feb.; ¥1,540

This mesmerizing, water droplet-shaped structure sits beside a rice terrace on a hill. A joint-collaboration by artist Naito Rei and architect Nishizawa Ryūe, this shell is punctuated by openings in the ceiling that reveal the sky and lush backdrop of the island's verdant topography. To enter, you must take off your shoes. Inside, look down and observe the captivating rivulets of water that periodically spring from the floor and dance around the space. This is a place to slow down and observe the beauty of the island itself, which is the true star of this exhibit. Attached, there's a glass-roofed café that maintains the same hours as the museum.

LES ARCHIVES DU CŒUR

2801-1 Karato, Teshima, Tonosho-chō; tel. 0879/68-3555; http://benesse-artsite.jp/en/art/boltanski.html; 10am-5pm Wed.-Mon. Mar.-Oct., 10am-4pm Fri.-Mon. Nov.-Feb.; ¥510

Come here to hear a singular archive of heartbeats recorded around the globe. Step into the special darkened room where thousands of heartbeats are piped through a mesmerizing sound system. You can also record, register, and get a CD of your own heartbeat for ¥1,540.

INFORMATION DESK

9am-5pm Wed.-Mon.; tel. 087/968-3135

On Teshima, you'll find English-language maps and other materials at the information desk in the Ieura port ferry terminal.

GETTING THERE AND AROUND

On Teshima the main ports are **Ieura** on the northwest shore and **Karato** in the northeast. Ferries run between Ieura and **Miyanoura** on Naoshima (22 minutes; ¥620) and **Uno** on Honshu (40 minutes; ¥770), and some

Teshima Art Museum

continue on to **Karato** (1 hour; ¥480). Ferries sailing from **Tonosho** on Shōdo-shima sail to both Karato (20 minutes; ¥770) and Ieura (35 minutes; ¥770). For a full ferry timetable to and from Teshima, and additional information on how to reach these ports, visit http://benesse-artsite.jp/en/access.

Once you've reached Teshima, sporadic **buses** (¥200) run between Ieura and Karato, stopping at some sights, including the Teshima Art Museum, along the way. Alternatively, and recommended, rent a **bicycle** at the port in Ieura (standard ¥500 per day; electric ¥1,000 four hours, ¥100 each additional hour). Given the hilliness of the island's terrain, it's worth paying a bit extra for an electrically powered bicycle.

Inujima
犬島

This diminutive island lies to the north of Naoshima and Teshima, closer to Okayama than the northern shore of Shikoku. Here you'll also find galleries with stunning seaside vistas, the Seirensho Art Museum and the Inujima Art House Project, akin to the one on Naoshima. Of the three art islands, Inujima is the smallest and has the fewest inhabitants. Unlike Teshima and Naoshima, Inujima lacks public transport and is best explored on foot.

SEIRENSHO ART MUSEUM
精錬所美術館

327-4 Inujima; tel. 086/947-1112; http://benesse-artsite.jp/en/art/seirensho.html; 10am-4:30pm Wed.-Mon. Mar.-Nov./Fri.-Mon. Dec.-Feb.; ¥2,060, including admission to Inujima Art House Project and Seaside Inujima Gallery

The top sight on Inujima, much less visited even than Teshima, is the dreamlike, highly interactive Seirensho Art Museum. Built around the shell of a former copper refinery, this museum explores environmental crises and the contradictory nature of modernization in Japan through the artwork of Yanagi Yukinori. Among the materials Yanagi used to create the works housed in the museum are the remnants of the house once lived in by Mishima Yukio, a controversial, conflicted literary figure who is widely considered one of the most important Japanese novelists of the 20th century. It's worth noting that the architect Sambuichi Hiroshi had the museum built according to strict eco-friendly standards, using locally sourced granite and waste left over from the process of smelting copper. Plan your lunchtime around your visit to the museum. The attached café serves great lunches made with ingredients sourced from the island.

INUJIMA ART HOUSE PROJECT

Various locations around island; tel. 086/947-1112; http://benesse-artsite.jp/en/art/inujima-arthouse.html; 10am-4:30pm (last entry 4pm) Wed.-Mon. Mar.-Nov./Fri.-Mon. Dec.-Feb.; ¥2,060 including admission to Seirensho Art Museum and Seaside Inujima Gallery

The island's 50 or so inhabitants have fully embraced the "art island" concept, which has overtaken the main village in the form of five "art houses" and a few installations. As with the Seirensho Art Museum, the island's past and locally available materials figure heavily in the works on display. A good example is Asai Yusuke's installation *Listen to the Voices of Yesterday Like the Voices of Ancient Times*, which is built on the spot where a stonecutter's home once stood, using stone and other materials collected around the island, juxtaposed with images of plants and animals reminiscent of ancient cave paintings scrawled across the ground where the house once stood.

INUJIMA TICKET CENTER

10am-4pm Wed.-Mon. Mar.-Nov., 10am-4pm Fri.-Mon. Dec.-Feb.

On Inujima, pick up English-language information at the Inujima Ticket Center.

GETTING THERE AND AROUND

Inujima's one main port is on the northeast corner of the island. Ferries connect the island to **Ieura** on Teshima (25 minutes; ¥1,200) and Okayama's **Hoden port** (10 minutes; ¥300). Three buses run between Okayama Station and near Hoden port (50 minutes; ¥750; daily during Setouchi Triennale, otherwise Sat. and Sun. only). For a full ferry timetable to and from Inujima, and additional information on how to reach these ports, visit http://benesse-artsite.jp/en/access.

Once on Inujima, it's possible to see all of its main sights in about three hours on foot.

Tokushima 徳島市

Located on the eastern coast of Shikoku, Tokushima is synonymous with the raucous Awa Odori dance festival that takes the affable city by storm each August. Dancing aside, the city is a fun place in its own right with a surprisingly lively nightlife district, Sakaemachi, and nice riverside promenades. Bizan-san, a mountain accessible by cable car, looms beyond the south side of the city, offering panoramic views. It's also possible to hop on a boat and cruise the city's extensive waterways. These include the Yoshino-gawa river delta—the end point of the longest river on Shikoku—and the Shinmachi-gawa, which crosses it.

All of these things can easily be seen in a day. Unless you're headed to the city's legendary summer shindig, plan to pass through, en route to the Iya Valley or Kōchi.

SIGHTS

Awa Odori Kaikan
阿波おどり会館

2-20 Shinmachibashi; tel. 088/611-1611; www.awaodori-kaikan.jp; 9am-5pm, closed second and fourth Wed. every month; ¥300; walk 12 minutes southwest of JR Tokushima Station

While there's no substitute for the real thing, if you visit Tokushima outside of festival time, this building contains a gift shop, a third-floor museum dedicated to the festival, and a hall that hosts dances by professional troupes several times daily. The most impressive performance is held at 8pm nightly. In keeping with the spirit of the festival, full participation is encouraged, so you may just end up learning how to do the city's signature dance.

Bizan Ropeway
眉山ロープウェイ

2-20 Shinmachibashi; tel. 088/652-3617; https://awaodori-kaikan.jp/bizan-ropeway; 9am-5:30pm Nov.-Mar., 9am-9pm Apr.-Oct.; ¥610 one way, ¥1,020 return; walk 12 minutes southwest of JR Tokushima Station

Alongside introducing the city's dance festival, the fifth floor of the Awa Odori Kaikan is also where you'll find the lower station of the Bizan Ropeway. After seeing and, perhaps, joining a dance performance, ride to the top of Mount Bizan for a nice panorama of the city below.

ENTERTAINMENT AND EVENTS

TOP EXPERIENCE

★ AWA ODORI
阿波おどり

www.awaodori.tokushima.jp; Aug. 12-15

"The dancing fool and the watching fool are both fools, so why not dance?" There could be no better tagline for Tokushima's—and Japan's—summer dance festival par excellence.

The Awa Odori Matsuri takes place during Ōbon, Japan's festival of the dead, when everyone traditionally returns to their hometown to honor their ancestors; it's as much a fête as a remembrance of those who have passed. The formula is simple: don geta (wooden sandals) a vivid *yukata* and follow the lead of those around you, dancing in unison. Some of the pros wear a combination of *happi*, or shortened *yukata*, worn with shorts or pants, and a headband or taco-shaped straw hat. Dance troupes known as *ren* range from groups created just before the festival to seasoned pros who practice all year. Slowly step along to the rhythm of the *taiko* drums, accompanied by the three-stringed shamisen and bamboo flutes, and wave your hands as gracefully as you can.

Every August, 1 million revelers flock to the city to participate in the Awa Odori. All of downtown is blocked off to traffic from evening on the days of the event, and from 6pm to 10:30pm, troupes of dancers are seen at practically every turn. You'll notice that the dancers tend to stick to the old-school, down-tempo two-step format earlier in the evening. But as dusk falls, the vibe intensifies until the party finally quiets down around 11pm.

If you plan to attend, book accommodations at least three months in advance—the earlier the better. If you have an interest in joining an official dance troupe, contact the **Tokushima International Association** (www.tia81.com), which assembles a ragtag group to dance in one of the officially designated zones on one of the nights.

AWA JŪROBE YASHIKI
阿波十郎兵衛屋敷

184 Miyajima Motoura, Kawauchi-chō; tel. 088/665-2202; http://joruri.info/jurobe; 9:30am-5pm Sept.-June, 9:30am-6pm July-Aug.; ¥410 adults, ¥300 high school and university students, ¥200 junior high and elementary students

Farmers in the rural Tokushima area have a centuries-old tradition of putting on community puppet shows. Head to this historic building, once lived in by Bandō Jūrobe, a local samurai who handed himself over to be executed so that his master's name would remain untainted. The tale of Jūrobe's plight inspired the puppet play *Keisei Awa no Naruto*, first performed in 1768. Every day a group of puppeteers, clad in black from head to toe, kneel behind the large puppets and control them in plain view of the audience. All of this takes place to a soundtrack of vocals and the three-stringed shamisen.

SPORTS AND RECREATION

HYŌTANJIMA BOAT TOUR

tel. 090/3783-2084; www.city.tokushima.tokushima.jp/kankou/taiken/hyoutanjima.html; 1pm-4pm Mon.-Fri. mid-Mar.-mid-Oct., 1pm-4pm and 5pm-8pm daily July 20-Aug. 31; adults ¥200, children ¥100; walk about 10 minutes' south of Tokushima Station

Tokushima is a town of rivers, with the Shinmachi and Suketo rivers chief among

dancers in Awa Odori

them. The island-like area between these two rivers is known as Hyōtanjima (Gourd-shaped Island). One of the city's lesser known attractions is an affordable boat tour that begins near the Ryōgoku Bridge in the Shinmachi Riverside Park and motors around Hyotanjima (about 30 minutes). It's a fun, budget-conscious way to see the heart of the city. Boats run about every 40 minutes.

CHŪŌ-KŌEN

1 Jōnai; www.city.tokushima.tokushima.jp/shisetsu/park/chuo.html; 24 hours; free

Tokushima's best green space, Chūō-kōen (Central Park) is a great place to unwind. You'll find the remnants of the city's former castle, a museum dedicated to it, and a lovely landscape garden dating from the 16th century. More specifically, the **Tokushima Castle Museum** (1-8 Jōnai; tel. 088/656-2525; www.city.tokushima.tokushima.jp/johaku; 9:30am-5pm Tues.-Sun; ¥300) has a model of the former castle and various artifacts from the lords who once ruled from the city. And the **Senshūkaku-teien** (additional ¥50 with castle museum ticket), located beside the museum, has ponds, stone bridges, and perfectly sculpted shrubs. This park isn't a must-see, but it is a nice place to unplug.

FOOD

MENŌ

1F Asahi Bldg., 3-4 Terashima Honchō Higashi; tel. 088/623-4116; http://7-men.com; 11am-midnight; from ¥500

A greasy spoon a short walk from JR Tokushima Station, this is the best-known shop in town for Tokushima's signature style of ramen, topped by stir-fried pork belly, green onions, bean sprouts, and sometimes raw egg, and served in a rich, brown broth made with pork bones and soy sauce. If you've got the appetite, order a bowl of white rice and pour the remaining soup over it after finishing the noodles. Many locals swear by this heavy finishing move. Select what you want based on the pictures on the ticket machine out front, insert the money required, and hold on to your tickets until you're seated. There's often a queue, but it tends to move fast.

YAKINIKU ORENCHI

1F Daisan Bldg. 2, 1-59 Sakaemachi; tel. 088/655-0691; http://0691.web.fc2.com; 6pm-3am; dishes from ¥300

This *yaki-niku* (grilled meat) restaurant in the heart of the Sakaemachi entertainment district is a good choice for a hearty meal either before a night out, or as a late-night meal after visiting the bars. Put cuts of locally sourced beef on the grill at your table, let them sizzle, and combine with trimmings—kimchi, salads, rice—of your choice. Look for the door with a window shaped like an electric guitar.

KARLITO'S BB MEX

1F Nishiyama Bldg., 2-38 Tomidamachi; tel. 088/635-6218; https://karlhammot7.wixsite.com/karlitosbbmex; 6pm-late daily; from ¥450

Who would have thought you could get tasty Mexican food in Tokushima? Karlito's whips up tacos, burritos, quesadillas, chimichangas, and more. There's a good selection of Mexican beers and tequilas, and a decent cocktail menu too. Funky decor and a lively crowd of locals and expats make it a fun place for a few drinks and nibbles too. The friendly staff speak some English and are happy to make various recommendations around town too.

BARS AND NIGHTLIFE

INGRID'S INTERNATIONAL MUSIC BAR

2-7-1 Sakaemachi; tel. 088/626-0067; www.facebook.com/ingridsinternationalmusicbar; 9pm-late daily

Going strong for two decades, this jovial bar is run by the warm, charming Filipina proprietor Ingrid. A steady flow of locals and expats makes this one of the city's more hopping spots at night, especially on the weekend. You'll find cozy couches, a wide selection of booze, and free karaoke; in fact, the whole bar can, in theory, join in thanks to a slew of wireless mics and four television screens on the walls to display the scrolling lyrics.

ACCOMMODATIONS

HOTEL SUNROUTE TOKUSHIMA

1-5-1 Motomachi; tel. 088/653-8111; https://en.sunroute.jp; from ¥8,000 d

Just a stone's throw from the main station, this hotel offers reasonably priced rooms that are simple but stylish. Bathrooms are well-appointed, and free Wi-Fi is available throughout. There are three restaurants on-site.

DAIWA ROYNET HOTEL TOKUSHIMA EKI-MAE

3-8 Terashima Honchō Higashi; tel. 088/611-8455; www.daiwaroynet.jp/tokushimaekimae; ¥10,300 d with breakfast

This hotel, in close proximity to the station, has clean, comfortable rooms that are more spacious than most Japanese business hotels: a good balance of convenience and comfort with a reasonable price tag. There's a breakfast buffet serving a range of Western and Japanese dishes.

AGNES HOTEL

1-28 Terashima Honchō Nishi; tel. 088/626-2222; www.agneshotel.jp; ¥12,000 d with breakfast

Located just across the street from JR Takamatsu Station, the Agnes Hotel has cozy, though minimal, rooms. Staff at the reception desk are notably friendly and helpful. There's an eatery that functions as a café by day, a chic restaurant by night, and a bakery that serves delightful pastries made in-house. Note that there are no rooms with double beds—only singles and twins.

INFORMATION AND SERVICES

To speak with friendly bilingual staff, head to **Tokushima International Strategies Center** (Clement Plaza 6F, 1-61 Terashimahon-chō Nishi; tel. 088/656-3303; www.topia.ne.jp; 10am-6pm daily). There are lots of English-language books and periodicals, as well as free Wi-Fi and computers that can be used to access the Internet. This cheery office is located in Clement Plaza, a shopping mall next to JR Tokushima Station.

Online, Tokushima Prefecture runs the excellent **Discover Tokushima** tourism portal (https://discovertokushima.net). Visit the website to find out about all kinds of attractions, adventurous activities, cultural experiences, accommodations, and more not only in Tokushima City, but also throughout the prefecture, from Naruto to the north and surf spots in southern Kaifu to the secluded Iya Valley to the west.

TRANSPORTATION

Getting There

TRAIN

Coming from **Tokyo** (5 hours 30 minutes; about ¥20,000 one way) or **Osaka** (3 hours 30 minutes; about ¥10,500 one way), you can simply take the *shinkansen* to Okayama, then transfer to a rapid train to Takamatsu and take a local or limited express train to Tokushima from there. Or, you can simply take a limited express train directly from **Okayama** to Tokushima. Also within Shikoku, you can directly reach Tokushima by train from **Awa-Ikeda** in the Iya Valley region (1 hour 40 minutes). You can also come from **Matsuyama** (3 hours 10 minutes), transferring at Utazu, and from **Kōchi** (2 hours 40 minutes), transferring at Awa-Ikeda.

BUS

If you prefer to take a bus, you can make the long journey from **Tokyo** (10 hours; about ¥10,000 one way) or **Osaka** (2 hours 30 minutes; about ¥4,000). It's also possible to travel by highway bus from most of **Shikoku's** major towns and cities. To learn more about bus options, check out **Tokushima Bus** (tel. 088/622-1826; www.tokubus.co.jp), **Shikoku Kotsu Bus** (tel. 088/372-1231; www.yonkoh.co.jp) and **JR Bus** (tel. 088/602-1090; www.jr-shikoku.co.jp/bus).

BOAT

Ferries run by **Nakai Ferry** (tel. 088/636-0750; http://nankai-ferry.co.jp) make the journey daily between Tokushima and **Wakayama** (2 hours by standard ferry, 1 hour by hydrofoil; adults ¥2,000, elementary school students and younger ¥1,000). A longer journey from **Kita-Kyushu** (17 hours; from ¥9,570 one way) or Tokyo (17 hours 30 minutes; ¥12,660 one way) is also possible via **Ocean Tokyū Ferry** (tel. 088/622-0489; www.otf.jp).

AIR

While not the cheapest route, you can also access the city by plane. **Tokushima Awaōdori Airport** (16-2 Asahino, Matsushige; tel. 088/699-2831; www.tokushima-airport.co.jp) services daily flights from Fukuoka, Tokyo, Nagoya, and Sapporo. Note that flight prices are sky-high during the summertime Awa-Odori Matsuri. You can reach **JR Tokushima Station** from the airport by **bus** (30 minutes; ¥440 one way).

Getting Around

Once you've made it to JR Tokushima Station, you're more or less in the center of downtown. Many food and entertainment options are also arrayed throughout the Sakaemachi district, and along the banks of the Shinmachi-gawa. You can access most of this **on foot.**

That said, having a car is recommended for exploring the surrounding area. If you want to rent a car, there's **JR Rent-a-Car** (1-4-2 Terashimahon-chō Nishi; tel. 088/622-1014; www.ekiren.co.jp; 9am-7pm daily) right in front of JR Tokushima Station. If you're flying into town, try **Toyota Rent-a-Car** (15-10 Asahino, Toyohisa Matsuhige-chō; tel. 088/699-6606; https://rent.toyota.co.jp; 8am-8pm daily), located at the airport.

Cars can be booked out surprisingly far ahead, especially during peak season. Reserve your car online as far in advance as possible.

★ Iya Valley 祖谷渓

Entering the misty Iya Valley ("Ancestor Valley") and the neighboring Ōboke Gorge in Tokushima's deep, rugged west, feels akin to entering some sort of lost world. Dangling vine bridges cross rushing rivers, with lush mountains shooting skyward on each side. Smoke rises from fairy-tale houses that are clustered in small settlements scattered across the rugged valley walls.

The Iya Valley is often divided into Nishi Iya (West Iya) and Oku Iya (Inner Iya), or Higashi Iya (East Iya). Nearby the valley are the Ōboke and Kōbōke gorges, through which the frothy Yoshino River flows. Given the remoteness of the terrain, it's no surprise that in 1185 the vanquished soldiers from the defeated Heike (aka Taira) clan found refuge in this remote swath of wilderness after losing on the battlefield at Yashima, near Takamatsu, to the Minamoto clan. Some of these conquered fighters stayed on and made the valley home, propagating hamlets that are now only glimpsed in fleeting remnants. Apart from precarious mountain roads and a one-man train car transporting the odd passenger, little has changed in the valley since then.

An innovative tourism initiative called the Chiiori Project, hatched by renowned American author and Japanologist Alex Kerr, has restored one of the valley's wonderful traditional homes, bringing it into the modern age while preserving its soul. It's possible to volunteer at the house, called Chiiori (House of the Flute), as well as stay overnight, tend to its organic garden, cook, attend workshops, and enjoy the rural splendor surrounding it.

It's more than bucolic bliss. The section of the nearby Yoshino-gawa near the Awa-Ikeda train station is home to Japan's best stretch of white-water rapids. This is a great out-of-the-way place to get wet. Iya Onsen, deeper into the valley itself, is a good place to soak in

Naruto Whirlpools

About 13 km (8 mi) north of Tokushima city, Naruto is a scenic town clinging to a craggy peninsula that overlooks a peculiar natural phenomenon: cavernous whirlpools that form underneath the nearby Ō-Naruto Bridge. The whirlpools can make for a worthwhile day trip from Tokushima if you time it right. On a good, frothy day, the whirlpools violently spinning in the Naruto Straits just below the Ō-Naruto Bridge are a sight to behold. These forces of nature are created when an enormous volume of water is pushed through the slender strait between Naruto and neighboring island of Awaji-shima during high and low tide.

You can witness this phenomenon either from the glass-bottom **Uzu-no-Michi Promenade** (772-0053 Naruto Park; tel. 088/683-6262; www.uzunomichi.jp; 9am-6pm Mar.-Sept., 9am-5pm Oct.-Feb., ¥510) below the O-Naruto Bridge, or from the deck of a tour boat operated by **Naruto Kankō Kisen** (264-1 Oge, Tosadomariura; tel. 088/687-0101; www.uzusio.com; 9am-4:20pm daily; rides ¥1,800-2,400). See the website for details, including the best times of day to see the whirlpools.

In truth, the whirlpools are hard to predict. There's a chance you could make the trip and not see much of a swirl. But if the timing is right—new moon and full moon days are prime—the pools swell to 20 meters (65 feet) across.

GETTING THERE

The easiest way to reach Naruto if you're coming from Tokushima is with your own wheels. If you have your own **car,** it's about 30 minutes' drive via the Yoshinogawa Bypass and Route 11. Otherwise, you can take a **bus** from Tokushima Station to the Uzu-no-michi bus stop (1 hour 15 minutes; ¥710 one way). From there, the boat dock from which to access the whirlpools is about 8 minutes **on foot.** Alternatively, you can take a **train** on the JR Naruto line from Tokushima to JR Naruto Station (35 minutes; ¥360). From Naruto Station, take either a **bus** or **taxi** to Uzu-no-michi bus stop and walk to the seaside from there. From JR Naruto Station, take a bus to Naruto Park (20 minutes; ¥310).

calmer—and warmer—waters. Tsurugi-san, east of the valley proper, makes for a great hike.

SIGHTS

Nishi Iya (West Iya)

KAZURA-BASHI

かずら橋

162-2 Nishi Iya Yamamura Zentoku, Miyoshi-shi; 0120/40-4344; 8am-5pm daily; ¥550; take a bus from Ōboke Station (20 minutes, 4-8 buses per day, ¥660)

This vine bridge is perhaps Iya's most recognizable spot. Although the bridge can get crowded at times, it's still an incredible construction.

This type of bridge, made of thick vines growing wild in the surrounding mountains, was once a necessity for valley dwellers to transport goods from one side of the valley to the other. Legend holds that Kōbō Daishi had the first such bridge built. According to another version of the story, survivors from the vanquished Heike clan built the bridges after fleeing into the depths of the valley with the intention of being able to destroy them in a hurry if their enemies approached. At one time, there were 13 of these bridges spanning the valley. Today, only three remain, and this is the most popular.

Crossing the 45-meter-long (148-foot) bridge is surprisingly unnerving. Thankfully, the only danger here is succumbing to a mild fear of heights. The river can be seen through the uneven slats, 14 meters (46 feet) below, but the bridge is secure. It's been shored up with steel cables, concealed by the vines, and is rebuilt every three years.

Across the bridge, back on terra firma, turn left and walk down the road that runs

1

2

alongside the river to your left. You'll soon come to a lovely waterfall pouring over the mountainside on the right, and a series of covered rest areas and staircases that lead down to the river on the left. Continuing down this same road will eventually bring you to a lovely riverside campsite.

On your way to Kazura-bashi on Route 32 (9 km/5.5 mi north), keep your eye out for one of the most accessible view points from which to admire the region. The view point is shared with a statue known as the **Manikin Peeing Boy,** who is appropriately peeing from the edge of a precipitous 200-meter-high (656-foot) cliff.

Oku Iya (Inner Iya)

NAGORO SCARECROW VILLAGE
名頃かかしの里

Passing the village of Ochiai as you drive along Route 439, deep into Oku Iya, you'll eventually begin noticing figures standing along the roadside and sitting under bus stop shelters. These figures are not human, but are hauntingly lifelike scarecrows (*kakashi*). Welcome to Nagoro, a hamlet that's come to be known as Scarecrow Village or the Village of the Dolls. All told, around 350 of these dolls sit on porches and behind windows, stand beside bicycles, sit as "students" in the now-closed local school, work in the fields, perform roadwork, and fish in the river.

These hauntingly life-like dolls are the brainchild of artist Ayano Tsukimi, who grew up in Nagoro and returned more than a decade ago. Tsukimi was shocked by how empty Nagoro had become in her absence and was struck with the idea of addressing the loneliness by crafting dolls and placing them in various poses around town. Adding to the poignant nature of this deeply personal effort, the first doll she ever made was meant to resemble her father. Many of the other dolls are designed to look like past residents.

Her project has not been commercialized in any way. The dolls simply fill the town, turning the village into an unlikely stop for travelers. To reach the hamlet, which is easy to miss, it's best to take a taxi or drive yourself, using a GPS for good measure.

OKU IYA NIJŪ KAZURA-BASHI
奥祖谷二重かずら橋

620 Higashi Iya Sugeoi, Miyoshi; tel. 0120/40-4344; 7am-5pm daily; ¥550

Deeper into the inner side of Iya, 3.5 km (2 mi) past Nagoro on Route 439, two more vine bridges come into view on the right side of the road. Compared to Kazura-bashi in Nishi Iya, these two vine bridges feel like they're in the middle of nowhere. Fewer people make it this far into the valley.

The higher, slightly more daunting of the two is known as the Otto no Hashi (husband bridge), while the slightly shorter one is the Tsuma no Hashi (wife bridge). Nearby, there's also a wooden vehicle that glides along a system of ropes known as the *yaen* (wild monkey), from which you pull yourself across the river using your own strength.

There's a campsite on the far side of the river, a gift shop serving a peculiar array of ice-cream flavors (soba anyone?) and a few places to access the riverside. If you've got your own wheels or the patience to use the limited public transport needed to get to this faraway corner of Japan, it's a great escape far beyond where most travelers go.

SPORTS AND RECREATION

Hiking

TSURUGI-SAN

Distance: 5 km (3 mi)

Time: 3 hours round-trip

Information and maps: http://best-hike-japan.com/hiking/mt-tsurugi-tsurugi-san; https://japanhike.wordpress.com/2008/04/26/tsurugisan

Trailhead: Near Mi-no-Koshi bus stop

Tsurugi-san, located at the eastern edge of the Iya region, is the island's second-tallest mountain (1,955 meters; 6,414 feet). The smooth-edged outline of the mountain is often

1: Ōboke Gorge and Yoshino River **2:** Kazura-bashi vine bridge in Nishi Iya (West Iya)

contrasted with jagged Ishizuchi-san, the loftier peak in Ehime Prefecture. Adding an element of mystique to the summit, the sword of the vanquished Heike emperor was purportedly laid to rest in the earth of the expansive plain atop the peak, known as Heike-no-baba, inspiring the nickname "Sword Peak."

To reach the top, you can ride a chairlift that whisks passengers to a stop 30 minutes' walk from the top. It's also possible to hike from a trailhead located near the Mi-no-Koshi bus stop (2 hours one way). Note that buses only run to Mi-no-Koshi late July to late August. It's best only to plan on hiking this mountain if you've got your own wheels. The mountain is a magnet for pilgrims, and at the top, you'll find a shrine, huts, and a series of wooden walkways that lead to superb vistas of the entire region.

Unfortunately, the top of Tsurugi-san has a disconcerting amount of concrete, a weather tower and other signs of development. To enjoy better views without so many dreary reminders of modern life, hike in the direction of the Jirōgyū Pass, then make the ascent to the nearby peak of **Jirōgyū** (1,929 meters/6,328 feet). From Jirōgyū, trace your steps back to the Mi-no-Koshi bus stop.

White-Water Rafting

The bluish-green stretch of the Yoshino River that flows through the Ōboke and Kōbōke gorges is known to be just the right level of frothy. Combined with the stunning scenery of the gorges themselves, the rapids are widely considered the best for white-water rafting in Japan.

HAPPY RAFT

221-1 Ikadagi; tel. 0887/75-0500; www.happyraft.com; mid-Mar.-mid-Oct. tours; half-day from ¥5,500, full day from ¥10,000

Of the slew of rafting outfits operating in the Yoshino River area, Happy Raft, based near Tosa Iwahara Station, is at the top of the game. Their bilingual river guides have vast experience working and rafting on the best rivers around the world, from New Zealand and the American West to Nepal. The river hits a certain sweet spot due to the fact that it's just difficult enough to be exciting without being notably dangerous, with many rapids in the Class III and IV range.

Happy Raft's guides know the quirks of the terrain, such as the best outcrops from which to jump into deep pools and the safest spots just to horse around. If you'd rather get wet while scuttling along the gorge walls, they conduct canyoning tours and have plans to offer trekking too. Check the website for up-to-date offerings, and if you'd like to stay overnight, they run a handful of cozy, bare-bones guesthouses overlooking the Yoshino River valley.

Onsen

IYA ONSEN

367-2 Matsuo Matsumoto; tel. 0883/75-2311; www.iyaonsen.co.jp; 7am-6pm non-staying guests; ¥1,700 bathing and cable car

If you go to the effort of reaching this remote pocket of misty mountains, be sure to stop at Iya Onsen. This excellent hot spring—the valley's one and only—is reached via a cable car that zips from Hotel Iya Onsen down to indoor and outdoor pools beside the Iya River below. The Heike clan is said to have plunged into these steamy pools after retreating in defeat at the hands of the Minamoto clan in the 12th century. This is a fantastic spot to soak year-round, but the views really pop in spring and autumn. If you've got time, stick around for an excellent meal at the hotel's restaurant, or better yet, stay for a night. Hotel Iya Onsen is located on Route 32, near the Peeing Boy statue.

FOOD AND ACCOMMODATIONS

Iya doesn't offer much in the way of restaurants, but most of the hotels in the region prepare meals for guests. Rice wasn't historically as plentiful here as in the rest of Japan due to the difficulty of cultivating it on the region's steep hillsides. Traditionally, a meal in Iya is likely to consist of grains, tubers, venison, and boar. As for staying, there are appealing options from swanky *onsen* resorts and guesthouses to restored thatched-roof farmhouses and places to camp. The Chiiori Project, launched in the 1970s by American author, art collector, and Japanologist Alex Kerr, aims to restore traditional houses dotting the lush Iya Valley and promotes sustainable tourism deeply rooted in the valley community.

★ CHIIORI

209 Higashi Iya, Miyoshi; tel. 0883/88-5290; www.chiiori.org; ¥20,520 pp for double without meals, cheaper with larger groups, meals ¥3,200 pp

Documented in the beautifully written memoir *Lost Japan*, Kerr bought Chiiori (House of the Flute) in a ramshackle state in 1971 and proceeded to renovate the home slowly, with locals' help, to its current gorgeous state. It has an immaculate kitchen and bathroom with cypress bathtub, beautiful antiques carefully arranged, a floor hearth, calligraphy scrolls, *shoji* (paper screens), and of course, stunning valley views. Catered dinners with ingredients from around the valley can be had if you request in advance.

TOUGENKYO-IYA

142 Higashi Iya, Ochiai, Miyoshi; tel. 0883/88-2540; www.tougenkyo-iya.jp; from ¥17,820 pp for two without meals, cheaper with larger groups, catered meals ¥3,200 pp, home-cooked dinner made by a local aunty ¥15,000 per group

A cluster of similarly stunning houses, overseen by the Chiiori Alliance & Trust (est. 2005), can be found deeper within the Iya Valley at the "Shangri-la" mountain hamlet of Tougenkyo-Iya. Here you'll find eight charming renovated farmhouses with painstakingly maintained thatched roofs, tucked away deep in the eastern reaches of this remote gully. Meals are available upon request.

HOTEL IYA ONSEN

367-28 Matsuo Matsumoto, Ikeda-chō; tel. 0883/75-2311; www.iyaonsen.co.jp; from ¥20,000 pp with meals

It's not cheap, but this hotel is worth every yen. this *onsen* ryokan is located in Nishi Iya and backs directly onto the valley. Meals are fantastic, rooms are spacious, and *onsen* options include both indoor and outdoor baths, with the latter sitting almost next to the river at the base of the valley. The hotel is adept at accommodating foreign guests, and most staff speak English. If you're going to splurge on lodgings on any leg of a Shikoku journey, you won't be disappointed by doing so here.

YOKI GUESTHOUSE AND CAFÉ

375-3 Nishiiyayamamura Ichiu, Miyoshi; yokicafeguesthouse@gmail.com; www.yokicafeguesthouse.com; rooms from ¥8,700

A solid, affordable option, this guesthouse has three private tatami rooms and a snug shared lounge with a fireplace—a nice touch in winter. Bathroom facilities and a kitchen space are shared. The property sits right beside Route 45 near the junction with Route 32, making it a convenient base for exploring the valley.

KAZURA-BASHI CAMPING VILLAGE

233 Nishiiyayamamura Kanjo, Miyoshi; tel. 090/1571-5258; check-in 9am-5pm Wed.-Mon., Apr.-Nov.; free showers, cooking equipment available; tent sites from ¥510, tents from ¥1,030, bungalows from ¥3,190 per night

After crossing Kazura-bashi, turn left and walk 0.5 km (0.3 mi) upstream, and you'll come to Kazura-bashi Camping Village. This spot is bare-bones, but it's a wonderful place to camp, or sleep in a bungalow, for a night. There's a good barbecue area, and cooking equipment can be rented as well as tents and bedding. Have someone who can speak Japanese call ahead on your behalf to make a reservation, including specifying anything you may want to rent.

INFORMATION AND SERVICES

For information on the region, stop at the **Miyoshi Tourist Information Center** (tel. 0883/76-0877; 9am-6pm daily) beside Awa Ikeda Station, or **Lapis Ōboke** (1553-1

Kamimyo, Yamashiro-chō; tel. 0883/84-1489; www.yamashiro-info.jp/lapis; 9am-6pm daily Apr.-Nov., 9am-5pm daily Dec.-Mar.), located about 25 minutes' walk north of Ōboke Station beside Route 32. This quirky facility serves as both a museum of the city's colorful geology and supernatural *yōkai* (ghost) folklore, as well as a tourism information center.

A great online resource for the region is **Iya Time** (www.iyatime.com), covering everything from things to see and do to small cafés and farmhouse lodgings in the Iya Valley, Ikeda, and Ōboke and Koboke gorge areas.

TRANSPORTATION

Getting There

TRAIN

Awa-Ikeda Station and **Ōboke Station** are the main entry points to the region by train. Both of these stations, on the **JR Dosan** line, lie between **Okayama** (1 hour 30 minutes; ¥4,000 one way) on Honshu, to the north, and **Kōchi** (1 hour; ¥2,930 one way) to the south. It's also possible to reach Awa-Ikeda from either **Takamatsu,** with a transfer at Tadotsu (1 hour, ¥3,000 one way), or directly from **Tokushima** (1 hour 15 minutes, ¥3,540 one way).

BUS

If you're coming from Osaka, you also have the option of taking a highway bus operated by bus operator **Shikoku Kotsu Bus** (tel. 0883/72-1231; www.yonkoh.co.jp) from Hankyū Umeda Station to the **Awa-Ikeda bus terminal** (4 hours; ¥4,650 one way, ¥8,370 round-trip).

Getting Around

BUS

Once you're in the valley region, there are sporadic public buses that run from **Ōboke Station** into Nishi Iya's core sights, such as Kazura-bashi. Outside of winter, limited buses run as far east as Tsurugi-san.

CAR

Your best bet is having your own wheels. About 30 minutes' walk north of Ōboke Station, a brief walk from the information center at Lapis Ōboke, you'll come to a small car rental outfit, run by a restaurant called **Mannaka** (1520 Yamashiro-chō Nishi; tel. 0883/84-1211; www.mannaka.co.jp; 9am-5pm). At only ¥5,000 for three hours and ¥9,000 for 24 hours, it's a good deal.

While it's not an altogether predictable means of transport, a final option is simply holding out your thumb. **Hitchhiking** in the area is known to be fairly common enterprise thanks to the friendly locals. If you're feeling adventurous, this is a good last resort. Of course, use your own intuition and common sense before hopping into someone's car.

TAXI

If you're not averse to spending a fair chunk of change—about ¥4,000 to Kazura-bashi, for example—Ōboke Station is a good place to catch a taxi. Have a station attendant call the taxi company (tel. 0883/87-2017) if none rolls up after you've been waiting in front of the station for a bit.

Matsuyama 松山市

Shikoku's largest metropolis, with a population of 450,000 and capital city of Ehime Prefecture, Matsuyama is loaded with history. You wouldn't necessarily sense this upon exiting its main train station, however, as drab buildings line the streets fanning out in all directions, largely the result of bombing during World War II. But forge ahead, past the immediate station area, and the city's gems soon come into view.

Chief among them is Matsuyama-jō, an impressive original castle perched atop a hill overlooking the city. Just southeast of the castle, the city's welcoming locals come to the lively area surrounding the Ōkaidō shopping arcade to eat, drink, and shop. The other major point of interest is legendary Dōgo Onsen, northeast of downtown, where Japan's first *onsen ryokan,* inspiration for the bathhouse in Miyazaki's movie *Spirited Away*, proudly occupies a prominent corner. Beyond the famed bathhouse, there's a vast, fading red-light district that makes for an interesting after-hours stroll for a particular sort of armchair anthropologist.

Matsuyama also likes to brandish its literary credentials. Natume Sōseki (1867-1916)—author of classics including *I Am a Cat*, *Botchan*, and *Kokoro*, and widely regarded as the godfather of modern Japanese literature—taught English in the city before devoting himself to writing full-time. Although the often-melancholic scribe's *Botchan* lightly skewers many aspects of life in Matsuyama during the tumultuous Meiji Restoration (1868), it didn't stop the city from erecting the **Botchan Wind-up Clock** in his honor at the entrance to the long arcade that runs through the Dōgo Onsen neighborhood, with figures of characters from the novel appearing at each new hour. Sōseki's one-time roommate in the city, the tragically short-lived haiku poet Masaoka Shiki (1867-1902), is another figure who boosts the city's literary cred.

Matsuyama moves at a leisurely pace. A tram glides from place to place, lending an old-world charm. While it's certainly possible to see the city's major attractions in a day, an overnight stay will give you the luxury of exploring without feeling rushed. It's also possible to use Matsuyama as a base for a few days longer if you plan to venture farther into Ehime's south, perhaps to Uchiko and Ōzu or Uwajima, or to the island's highest point, Ishizuchi-san, an hour and a half drive east.

SIGHTS

Matsuyama-jō
松山城

1 Marunouchi; tel. 089/921-4873; www.matsuyamajo.jp; 9am-5pm Feb.-July. and Sept.-Nov., 9am-5:30pm Aug., 9am-4:30pm Dec.-Jan.; ¥510; take tram line 5 from JR Matsuyama Station to Okaido tram stop (10 minutes; ¥160). From Okaido, walk north 5 minutes along Katsuyama's eastern side to ropeway/chairlift station (8:30am-5pm daily, seasonal variations; ¥270 one-way, ¥510 round-trip). Or walk 15 minutes to summit via path from lower ropeway station.

Looming above Matsuyama, atop the steep hill of Katsuyama, this white fortress has been added to, renovated, and in the case of the main keep, rebuilt after a lightning strike in 1784. The overall impact of entering the grounds is of stepping into one of Japan's best-preserved castles with some of the most dramatic vistas to boot.

The construction of the complex we see the remnants of in Matsuyama today began in 1602, when feudal lord Katō Yoshiakira envisioned a stronghold on the hill overlooking the city. Only 26 years later, Katō moved north to Aizu, and in 1635, the Matsudaira clan, relatives of the ruling Tokugawa regime in Edo, moved in. The Matsudaira lords stayed on as rulers of the region until 1868 when the Meiji Restoration brought Japan's feudal age to an end.

The classic fortress is replete with dark

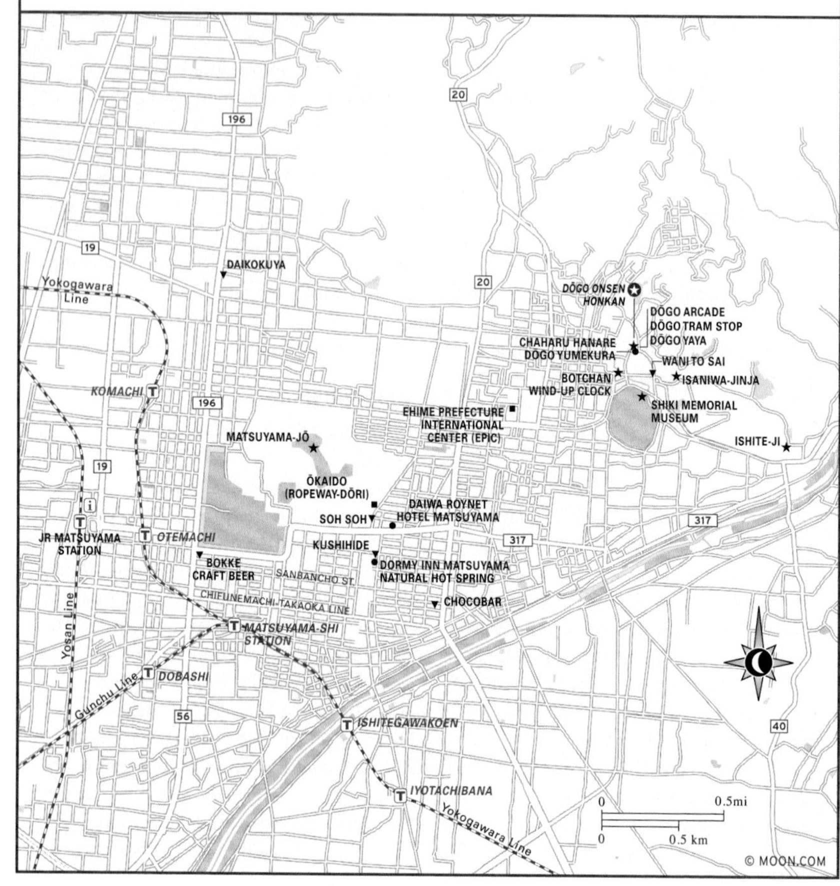

corridors, steep rickety stairs, and openings once intended to serve as the holes from which arrows and large rocks were shot and hurled at would-be invaders. From the highest floor are sweeping views of Matsuyama rolling toward the Inland Sea.

★ Dōgo Onsen Honkan
道後温泉本館

5-6 Dōgo-yunomachi; tel. 089/921-5141; https://dogo.jp; 6am-10pm, kami-no-yu 6am-11pm

When most people hear "Dōgo Onsen" they're thinking of this iconic complex, widely considered Japan's first *onsen* bathhouse. The bathhouse is famed among fans of legendary anime director Hayao Miyazaki due to its links with his animated masterpiece *Spirited Away*. Miyazaki famously drew inspiration from this venerable complex when envisioning the film's fantastical spirit-run bathhouse. Occupying a large block and dominating a corner about four minutes' walk northeast of the Dōgo tram stop, this archetypal *onsen* complex has two indoor baths, namely, the bigger,

1: Dōgo Onsen soaking bath **2:** Dōgo Onsen Honkan at night

1

2

more crowded Kami no Yu (Water of the Gods) and the smaller, mellower Tama no Yu (Water of the Spirits). Both baths are separated by gender.

Constructed in 1894, this sprawling bathhouse works its magic through its very layout: a labyrinth of corridors, chambers, and staircases, all made of wood. The baths in both the main, first-floor Kami no Yu and the more exclusive, second-floor Tama no Yu are made of granite. Beyond the tubs, there are shared lounges on the second floor and private spaces on the third floor to relax with a tea and snack after you've had a soak.

How deeply you can explore this vast bathhouse depends on which price plan you choose upon entering. At the higher end of the scale, you'll be able to lounge around in a *yukata* and take a peek into the Yushiden, where baths were built for visiting emperors in 1899. Although no emperor has soaked at Dōgo since 1952, the extravagant room speaks for itself. Among the memorabilia and pieces of history on display are painted mosaics of white herons. According to legend, the curative waters of Dōgo were discovered when a heron was seen mending its leg in the spring.

Isaniwa-jinja
伊佐爾波神社

173 Sakuradani-chō; tel. 089/947-7447; https://isaniwa.official.jp; 9am-5pm daily; free

About four minutes' walk southeast of Dōgo Onsen Honkan, this unique shrine is worth climbing the steep flight of steps at its entrance. According to legend, the atmospheric shrine stands on the site where Emperor Chuai (149-200) and Empress Jingū (169-269) often bathed in the primordial past.

For architecture geeks: This structure, built in 1667, is a National Treasure and was built in the atypical *hachiman-zukuri* pattern. In this architectural style, two structures with gabled roofs standing side-by-side are linked on the side without gables. This layout creates the appearance of two separate buildings, although there is in fact only one.

Shiki Memorial Museum
立子規記念博物館

1-30 Dōgo-kōen; tel. 089/931-5566; http://sikihaku.lesp.co.jp; 9am-6pm May-Oct., 9am-5pm Nov.-Apr.; ¥400

About five minutes' walk south of Dōgo Onsen Honkan, or four minutes southwest of Isaniwa-jinja, you'll come to a museum dedicated to the life of Masaoka Shiki (1867-1902), Matsuyama's favorite literary son. Masaoka's life was cut short by tuberculosis; his nom de plume, "Shiki," was derived from a legendary bird said to cough blood when it sings. During his short life, he shunned orthodoxy in Japan's two most beloved poetic forms, the haiku and tanka, inspiring the nation's poets for decades to come. The main thrust of Masaoka's message was to bring the art of poetry into daily life by letting go of the traditional haiku structure (three lines of five, seven, and five syllables, respectively). He would take the content beyond a timeworn focus on the seasons, and instead, write about whatever inspired him from daily life.

This museum explores Masaoka's brief, poignant life, as well as the history of Matsuyama. There's decent English-language signage, as well as English-speaking guides if you contact the museum ahead of your visit.

Ishite-ji
石手寺

2-9-21 Ishite; tel. 089/977-0870; www.88shikokuhenro.jp/ehime/51ishiteji; 24 hours daily; free

If you're up for a slightly longer stroll, about 15 minutes' walk east of the Shiki Memorial Museum you'll come to Ishite-ji (Stone Hand Temple), the city's most important (and quirky) temple; it's number 51 on the island's 88-temple circuit. Its peculiar name is linked to a legend in which a fading local lord, unable to reach Kōbō Daishi, perished with a stone in his hand. As the story goes, he was later reborn still clutching it.

Ishite-ji has a funhouse quality to it. Trundling down a stone pathway lined by wooden stalls hawking amulets, fortunes on strips of paper, and other suitably spiritual trappings, you soon reach the Niomon Gate, a National Treasure. Passing through the opulent entry and emerging into the temple's expansive grounds, you'll find a three-tiered pagoda, numerous statues, halls, buildings filled with paintings of various deities, a giant bronze bell, praying pilgrims kitted out in white outfits and conical hats, and an army of prowling cats.

Perhaps most intriguing is the golden inner temple, accessed via a cavernous passageway filled with statuary and murals that burrows some 200 meters (656 feet) through the earth behind the main hall. Exiting the other side, you'll come to a statue of the emaciated historical Buddha, pre-enlightenment, and a towering effigy of Kōbō Daishi on a hill behind this hidden, inner sanctum. If you've got time, Ishite-ji is a worthwhile detour from Dōgo. If you stop by, be sure to sample the grilled *mochi* (rice cake) sold on the grounds.

SPORTS AND RECREATION

Hiking

ISHIZUCHI-SAN

Distance: 7.2 km (4.5 mi) round-trip from upper station of Shimotani cable car; 9.2 km (5.7 mi) from Tsuchi-goya Hut

Time: 6-7 hours round-trip (from upper station of Shimotani cable car); 5-6 hours round-trip (from Tsuchi-goya Hut)

Information and maps: http://www.ishizuchi.com; English language map available online: http://www.ishizuchi.com/web/wp-content/uploads/2014/10/102a1bab9c7e6d293bd4432da75530ff.pdf; https://japanhike.wordpress.com/2008/06/12/mt-ishizuchi

Trailhead: upper station of Shimotani cable car (north side of mountain); Tsuchi Goya Hut (south side of mountain)

The highest mountain in western Japan at 1,982 meters (6,502 feet), Ishizuchi-san is a pointed, hammer-shaped peak and one of Japan's 100 Famous Mountains. Like Tsurugi-san, it's also a pilgrimage destination and makes for a challenging hike. Traditionally, women are forbidden from climbing the peak on July 1 when a mountain opening ceremony is held. There are numerous shrines dedicated to mountain deities as you make your way up.

You can hike from the top of a cable car line that begins from **Shimotani** cable car station, located near **Nishi-no-kawa** bus stop on the north side of the mountain (tel. 0897/59-0331; www.ishizuchi.com; 8am-6pm Jul.-Aug., irregular hours at other times of year; ¥1,030 one way, ¥1,950 round-trip). The cable car whisks passengers from an elevation of 455 meters to 1,300 meters (1,493 feet to 4,265 feet). From the upper station, it's a 6- to 7-hour hike round-trip. A less grueling trail begins at **Tsuchi-goya Hut** (1,500 meters, 4,921 feet) on the south side of the mountain. The round-trip hike on this trail takes five to six hours.

Whichever path you choose, the trails merge eventually and the path becomes increasingly steep as you approach the summit. At **Misen** (1,974 meters, 6,476 feet), you'll discover **Ishizuchi-jinja**, likely to be thronged with pilgrims, and you'll be rewarded with dramatic views stretching from the nearby mountains all the way to the Inland Sea. The **Ishizuchi-san Summit Hut** (tel. 080/1998-4591; http://ishizuchisan.jp/sansou/sub02-0.htm; ¥8,700 pp with two meals) is open from May through October. This lodge accommodates up to 50 in a large, simple shared space. If you don't mind roughing it for the night and enjoy a bit of camaraderie, this is a good option. Reservations must be made by phone or email at least 10 days in advance.

From here, you can clamber up the final jagged section of the mountain known as **Tengudake** (1,982 meters; 6,502 feet). Note that some sections of this final leg of the ascent require the use of chains drilled into rock faces. Thankfully, stairs are also available for those with less of a taste for adventure.

The trailhead for both the Joju and Tsuchi-goya routes can be reached directly by car. If you're limited to public transport, making it to Tsuchi-goya is complicated and limited due to the fact that buses only run on holidays and weekends. This means it's simpler to go via cable car if your only option is public transport. **Setouchi Bus** (tel. 0898/23-3450; www.setouchibus.co.jp; ¥1,000 one way) runs between JR Iyo-Saijo Station and the Shimotani cable car station. That said, given the challenge with reaching the top, it's best to pass on Ishizuchi-san if you don't have a car or have limited time.

SHOPPING

ŌKAIDO (ROPEWAY-DŌRI)

Ōkaido is a covered shopping arcade on a north-south axis in the center of town. A wide range of stores, from small mom-and-pop shops to large emporiums, line this thoroughfare. Many cafés, restaurants, and bars are also located along this street.

If you continue north from Ōkaido, the rooftop ends and the street becomes Ropeway Dōri, a prime souvenir hunting ground. This road has a slightly more upscale feel, with a range of established boutiques and small antique dealers. The restaurants and cafés here also have a more stylish edge.

DŌGO ARCADE

This covered walkway is another good souvenir shopping spot. Starting near Dōgo Onsen Honkan and running toward the Dōgo tram stop, restaurants and cafés share space with shops selling souvenirs One of the shops is devoted to Studio Ghibli merchandise, including items inspired by *Spirited Away.*

FOOD

Matsuyama is blessed with a lovely seaside location. Its mild climate results in a bounty of produce and the assurance of a regular fresh catch. Among its well-known local dishes is *taimeshi*, or rice mixed with sea bream.

★ NIKITATSU-AN

3-18 Dogokitamachi; tel. 089/924-6617; www.dogobeer.jp/nikitatsu-restaurant; 11am-9:30pm Tues.-Sun.; meals from ¥1,000

Nikitatsu is actually a sake brewer. Beside the shop that sells the highly regarded drink, you'll find a restaurant set in a garden villa. From the dark-wood interior, diners enjoy tranquil views onto the greenery just outside, as servers shuffle between tables in traditional garb. The menu includes a simple selection of set courses—fish, meat, and vegetables with rice, seasoned by soy sauce and fish broth—that goes down well with sake from next door.

KUSHIHIDE

3-2-8 Nibanchō; tel. 089/921-1587; 5pm-11pm Mon.-Sat.; ¥1,000 average meal

It's all about free-range, organic chicken here, prepared in a variety of styles, from *kara-age* (deep-fried) to yakitori (grilled on a stick). The offerings include a nice range of individual dishes, as well as set meals. An English menu is available. You'll know you found it when you spot a refined Meiji-era building with a white plaster exterior and a wooden sign and lamp hanging above the door. The service is friendly and the value is great.

SOH SOH

3-2-10 Ōkaido; tel. 089/998-7373; http://greenlabel-group.com; 11am-11pm daily; ¥1,000 average meal

Soh Soh is a nationwide chain with a legion of fans attracted to its balanced meals, which include a healthy dose of vegetables, and notably modest portions of meat and fish—in essence, nouvelle Japanese fare. The chic ambience is pleasant, too.

★ DAIKOKUYA

6-9-5 Honmachi; tel. 089/924-0557; www.daikokuya-udon.co.jp; 11am-10pm daily; ¥800-1,240 udon and rice dishes, multicourse meals ¥2,170-4,250

While *taimeshi* is sometimes served as sea bream sashimi atop rice, Daikokuya mixes the two elements together in an iron pot called a *kama* and whips up a dish known as *tai no kama meishi* (sea bream kettle rice). This is the dish to go for. Beyond this, the menu makes heavy use of seasonal ingredients. The noodles are great too—not too soft, not too firm.

YUMENOYA HANARE

Yoshida Bldg. 1F, 3-1-14 Sanbanchō; tel. 089/932-3939;6pm-midnight daily; dinner ¥3,000

If you're looking for an *izakaya* to provide a healthy flow of booze to go with the food, and feel torn by the city's bewildering number of choices, you won't go wrong here. The dishes are a fusion twist, drawing from Japan and the West, with ingredients sourced locally. Servers are friendly and speak enough English to help you navigate the menu.

BARS AND NIGHTLIFE

The bulk of Matsuyama's nightlife is concentrated along three parallel streets that run east to west: Ichibanchō, Nibanchō, and Sanbanchō. The airy, covered arcade known as Ōkaido cuts through the middle of these three strips, running north to south. The Dōgo area also has its share of nightlife, some of it on the seedier side.

BOKKE CRAFT BEER

5-6 Minami-horibata; tel. 088/906-8349; 5pm-midnight daily

If you're a craft beer fan, this is your place in Matsuyama. There's a broad spectrum of Japanese microbrews on tap in this smartly designed space with seating both in and out of doors. The menu also includes a good range of savory nibbles. It's a good place to socialize on weekends.

WANI TO SAI

1-39 Dōgo-yunomachi; tel. 080/3319-2765; www.facebook.com/wanitosai; 6pm-late daily

It would be safe to call this hideaway in Dōgo the city's most bohemian haunt. Wani to Sai (Alligator and Rhinoceros) has a peculiar circus theme—philistine art, sundry oddities, and marionettes—which is the direct product of the proprietor's life experience. He went to Italy to study fresco painting, only to redirect his efforts into studying marionettes, which he made and brought to life on the streets of Europe as a busker for eight years. His project today is running this fun dive bar, serving cocktails, European beers, Japanese comfort foods like ramen and *yaki-niku donburi* (rice topped with grilled meat) and more. It's located near the base of the stairs that lead to Isaniwa-jinja.

CHOCOBAR

1F First Kisuke Bldg., 2-6-2 Sambanchō; tel. 089/933-2039; 7pm-late daily

This lively shot bar is popular with locals and expats looking to tie one on to a hip-hop soundtrack. Sitting on a busy street corner, the place can get packed on weekends, with crowds spilling onto the sidewalk outside. There are hookahs too, if that's your kind of thing.

ACCOMMODATIONS

DAIWA ROYNET HOTEL MATSUYAMA

2-6-5 Ichibanchō; tel. 089/913-1355; www.daiwaroynet.jp/matsuyama; ¥10,000 d with breakfast

This neat, modern hotel is smack in the middle of the city. The rooms here are reasonably spacious and come with large bathrooms. English-speaking staff are happy to answer questions. There's a breakfast buffet, as well as a restaurant serving Asian cuisine throughout the day. It's a great pick for convenience and value.

DŌGO YAYA

6-1 Dōgo-takōchō; tel. 089/907-1181; www.yayahotel.jp; ¥11,000 d

A great midrange option near Dōgo Onsen, this hotel has a distinctly Japanese aesthetic, with *shoji* (paper screen) doors and windows veiled behind wooden slats—a sleek, modern touch. The rooms are compact but well-appointed with good bathrooms, and the friendly staff are welcoming. Guests are eligible for a discount at Dōgo Onsen. Breakfast buffet available.

★ CHAHARU HANARE DŌGO YUMEKURA

4-5 Yuzukichō, Dōgo; tel. 089/931-1180; www.yume-kura.jp; ¥56,160 for two in a twin room with breakfast and dinner

Flawless service is provided by friendly staff at

this luxe, modern *ryokan,* located across the road from Dōgo Onsen Honkan. The spacious rooms have private baths filled with local *onsen* water. There's no public bath in the hotel itself, but guests receive coupons to soak in Dōgo Onsen Honkan, right across the street. Excellent dinner and breakfast spreads are served in private dining rooms. Amenities down to the toiletries, robes, and towels are top-notch. If you can afford to splurge, this boutique *ryokan,* with only seven rooms, is an excellent choice.

INFORMATION AND SERVICES

Tourist information centers are located in **JR Matsuyama Station** (tel. 089/931-3914; 8:30am-8:30pm daily) and another next to the Botchan Wind-up Clock outside the **Dōgo Onsen tram stop** (tel. 089/921-3708; 8am-5pm daily).

There's also the more comprehensive **Ehime Prefecture International Center** (EPIC) (1-1 Dōgo Ichiman; tel. 089/917-5678; www.epic.or.jp; 8:30am-5pm Mon.-Sat.). Besides providing a good range of English-language materials on the city and free Wi-Fi, EPIC also holds classes on traditional arts and crafts and can set you up with a volunteer guide to introduce you to Matsuyama. EPIC is located about three minutes' walk from the Minami-machi tram stop on tram lines 3 and 5.

Another service offering free English-language tours of some of the city's main sights is **Team Camellia** (https://matsuyamavolunteerguide.jimdo.com).

TRANSPORTATION

Getting There

TRAIN

You can reach Matsuyama by limited express train on the **JR Yosan** line from **Takamatsu,** with a transfer at Tadotsu Station (2 hours 30 minutes; ¥6,390), or by a limited express train directly from **Okayama** on Honshu (2 hours 40 minutes, ¥7,030).

BUS

You can take a highway bus between Matsuyama's main **bus stop,** located directly in front of JR Matsuyama Station, and most major cities around Shikoku. Buses also run longer routes between Matsuyama and **Osaka** (5 hours 30 minutes) and **Tokyo** (12 hours). For timetables, routes, and fares, see the **JR Shikoku Bus** website (www.jr-shikoku.co.jp/bus/).

BOAT

It's possible to make the trip to Matsuyama over the Inland Sea from **Hiroshima** (1 hour 15 minutes, ¥7,100 by hydrofoil; 2 hours 30 minutes, ¥3,600 by standard ferry). For details, check the website of ferry and hydrofoil operator **Setonaikai Kisen** (tel. 082/253-1212; www.setonaikaikisen.co.jp; 7am-9pm daily).

AIR

It's possible to fly from any of Japan's main cities, and from Seoul and Shanghai, to and from **Matsuyama Airport** (2731 Minami Yoshidamachi; tel. 089/972-5600; www.matsuyama-airport.co.jp), located just west of town and easily reachable by a **bus** that runs twice hourly to and from the main bus station in front of JR Matsuyama Station (15 minutes; ¥310).

Getting Around

Matsuyama's two main train stations are **JR Matsuyama Station,** located west of the city's heart at Matsuyama-jō, and south of the castle, **Matsuyama-shi Station,** the main hub of the local Iyotetsu line. Most points of interest are found somewhere between the castle mount of Katsuyama and Dōgo Onsen, northeast of the city. The best way to shuttle between them is either **on foot,** by **bicycle,** or aboard the city's smoothly operating **tram** network.

TRAM

Matsuyama's main transport feature is its classic trams. In total, there are four tram lines.

Loop **lines 1** (clockwise) and **2** (counterclockwise) run around the large hill, Katsuyama, atop which Matsuyama-jō stands. **Line 3** links Matsuyama-shi Station, on the local Iyotetsu train line, to Dōgo Onsen. **Line 5** (number 4 is skipped over) goes from JR Matsuyama Station to Dōgo Onsen. Line 6 runs between Matsuyama-shi Station and the Honmachi 6 tram stop north of Matsuyama-jō.

To ride the tram, simply hop on via the back door and pay a flat ¥160 when you exit via the front door wherever you get off. You can also buy a **one-day pass** (adults ¥600, children ¥300) for unlimited tram rides at the **Iyotetsu Ticket Center,** located at Matsuyama City Station, or at any station on the Iyotetsu line. See the official **Iyotetsu** website (http://www.iyotetsu.co.jp) for more details.

BICYCLE

There's a city-run bicycle **rental service** located just outside JR Matsuyama Station. As you exit the station, turn right and you'll see a covered bicycle lot with a small adjacent office on the right side of the road (8-364-6 Sanbanchō; tel. 089/943-9511; 9am-6pm Mon.-Sat.; ¥300 per day).

Alongside serving as a tourist information center, the **Ehime Prefecture International Center** (EPIC) also provides bike rentals for as long as two weeks (1-1 Dōgo Ichiman; tel. 089/917-5678; www.epic.or.jp; 8:30am-5pm Mon.-Sat.). The **tourist information center** across from the Dōgo tram stop also offers bicycle rentals (tel. 089/921-3708; 8am-9pm daily Apr.-Sept., 8am-8pm daily Oct.-Mar.; ¥300 per day).

Around Matsuyama

UCHIKO
内子町

The historic town of Uchiko makes for a good combined day trip from Matsuyama. About 40 km (25 mi) southwest of Matsuyama, Uchiko became rich during the early 20th century thanks to a thriving wax industry. The remnants of that period of its past make Uchiko a great place to step back in time to the Taishō-era (1912-1926) and imagine daily life then from the perspective of the elite.

Centered in the historic Yōkaichi district, the townscape is a mix of grand old homes once occupied by well-heeled denizens, from wax moguls to the founder of the still-thriving beer giant Asahi. Many of the abodes in the **Yōkaichi Historic District** feature immaculate gardens and sprawling courtyards. All told, some 90 homes, once built by the town's well-heeled merchant class, line this 1.5 km-long (1 mi) street.

Sights

UCHIKO-ZA
内子座

1515 Uchiko; tel. 0893/44-2840; 9am-4:30pm daily; ¥400; walk 7 minutes northeast of Uchiko Station

This old-school kabuki theater is a beautiful structure dating to 1916 that was spruced up in the mid-1980s. It's still in use and hosts the occasional performance of kabuki or bunraku puppet theater. It's possible to go behind the scenes and under the stage to see how the magic is created through trapdoors, hidden passages, and a revolving stage. Have a Japanese speaker call ahead to inquire about upcoming performances.

ŌMORI WA-RŌSOKU
大森和ろうそく

2214 Uchiko; tel. 0893/43-0385; http://o-warousoku.com; 9am-5pm Wed.-Thurs. and Sat.-Mon.; free

After exploring the atmospheric kabuki theater, backtrack to the main street that you walked along from the station to get there. Turn right and continue walking northeast,

Cormorant Fishing in Ōzu

Some 1,300 years ago, fishermen developed the technique of *ukai*, a peculiar fishing method with cormorants, large black birds that dive into rivers to hunt for *ayu* (sweet freshwater fish). Traditionally dressed fishermen board long, narrow wooden boats with lanterns hanging from the front to attract *ayu*. Birds, with ropes tied around their long necks like leashes to prevent larger fish from being swallowed, swoop into the water to catch up to a half-dozen fish at a time. Unconsumed fish are collected by the fishermen.

Ōzu no Ukai (649-1 Ōzu; tel. 0893/57-6655; twice daily at noon and 6pm Jun.-Sept.; ¥4,000 per person for tour at noon, ¥6,000 per person at 6pm) gives demonstrations, which last about half an hour; *ukai* season stretches roughly from May through September.

away from the station. When you reach a four-way intersection with a bank in front of you, turn left and walk straight for two minutes. You'll come to this small shop selling candles on the left side of this road. Pull aside the *noren* (curtains) with candle motifs on them and step inside. This is Uchiko's last candle workshop where all work is still done the old-fashioned way: by hand. Watch the artisans at work and, if you feel inspired, pick up a few of the wax torches for which the town is known.

KAMIHAGA RESIDENCE
上芳我邸

Kamihaga Residence: 2696 Uchiko; tel. 0893/44-2771; www.we-love-uchiko.jp/spot_center/spot_c3; 9am-4:30pm daily; ¥500; 20 minutes' walk northeast of Uchiko Station

Of the various old homes that can be entered in the Yōkaichi Historic District, visit the **Kamihaga Residence,** a museum set in the grand old home and former workshop of the Kamihaga family, who were among the town's most influential wax producers. Inside the home is a museum that explores the town's once-booming wax industry. The home is also a fantastic example of an affluent Meiji-period residence; painted screens and exquisite pottery grace elegant rooms with tatami floors, alongside Western design accents, which were just coming into vogue when the home was built.

Food and Accommodations

ZUM SCHWARZEN KEILER

2885 Uchiko; tel. 0893/44-2900; https://ameblo.jp/zum-schwarzen-keiler; 5pm-9:30pm (last order 8:30pm) Thurs.-Tues.; 11:30-2:30pm (last order 2pm) and 5pm-9:30pm (last order 8:30pm) Sat.-Sun.; lunch sets from ¥1,250; dinner courses from ¥1,650; dishes from ¥250

If you're feeling like mixing it up and taking a break from Japanese fare, you're in luck. This restaurant, run by a German expat and his Japanese wife, serves a hearty range of sausages, schnitzels, pretzels, and other things you'd expect from Deutschland. There's a nice range of German beer and wine too.

NAKAHAGA RESIDENCE GUESTHOUSE

2655 Uchiko; tel. 0893/50-6270; http://kamihaga-club.com/?tid=8&mode=f4; twin rooms from ¥6,000 pp with breakfast

Set in an Edo-period storehouse, this guesthouse has been spruced up by local artisans but retains its old-world charm. It has a serene private garden out back that induces contemplation. Among the handful of small bed-and-breakfasts in the Yōkaichi district, this one is the most appealing. Better yet, you'll have the place all to yourself, because they only accommodate one booking per night for one to four guests. No meals are provided.

HOTEL COCORO.KURA

1949 Uchiko; tel. 0893/44-5735; www.uchi-cocoro.com; ¥9,800 d with breakfast

Another great option set in an old storehouse in the Yōkaichi area. This inn accommodates up to two groups per night. There's a private garden behind the building here too. The rooms have a stylish spin with clean minimal lines and a slightly more modern Japanese aesthetic. As an added bonus, each room has a pristine wooden tub for a soak.

Information and Services

Pick up English-language materials on the town and ask questions at the small **tourist information center** next to Uchiko Station (324 Uchiko; tel. 089/343-1450). For more in-depth guidance and the chance to ask questions, speak with the bilingual staff at the **Uchikochō Visitor Center** (2020 Uchiko; tel. 0893/44-3790; www.we-love-uchiko.jp; 9am-5:30pm Fri.-Wed. Apr.-Sept., 9am-4:30pm Fri.-Wed. Oct.-Mar.), located about 10 minutes' walk northeast of Uchiko Station.

In Ōzu, head to the tourist information center inside Iyo-Ōzu Station (tel. 0893/57-9161; 9am-6:30pm daily) for English-language information on the town.

Transportation

The easiest way to reach Uchiko and Ōzu is by **train** from **Matsuyama.** Uchiko is about 25 minutes south of Matsuyama on a limited express train (¥2,230). Coming by limited express from Uwajima in the south, you can reach Uchiko in about an hour (¥2,990).

Uchiko is very **walkable.** You can rent a **bicycle** beside Uchiko Station (9:30am-5pm daily; ¥350 for two hours).

ŌZU
大洲市

About 10 minutes by train west of Uchiko, the small town of Ōzu arose as a castle town during the Edo period (1603-1868). By the Meiji period (1868-1912), moneyed merchants' houses infused a nice blend of historical strata into the city's architecture. One Meiji-period residence worth a trip is just east of town: Garyū Sansō. This thatched-roof villa is graced by an exquisite garden and a pavilion overlooking the Hiji-kawa river. The town's most unique characteristic point is its *ukai* (cormorant fishing) demonstrations that take place in this river from June 1 to September 20 each year. This is one of the best places to see this singular fishing technique in action.

Sights

ŌZU-JŌ

903 Ōzu; tel. 0893/24-1146; www.ozucastle.jp; 9am-5pm daily; ¥500, ¥800 for joint ticket with Garyū-sansō

With a history stretching back to the 14th century, this diminutive castle has been refurbished numerous times, most recently in 2004. Traditional building methods and materials were used, imbuing it with authenticity. Climb to the top and look out over the lovely countryside scene and the Hijikawa River.

The castle is about 25 minutes' walk south of JR Iyo-Ōzu Station. You'll pass over the Hijikawa on the way. Alternatively, you can take a taxi (5 minutes; ¥900).

GARYŪ-SANSŌ

411-2 Ōzu; tel. 0893/24-3759; www.garyusanso.jp; 9am-5pm daily, last entry 4:30pm; adults ¥550, children ¥220

Fifteen minutes' walk east of the castle, this thatched-roof teahouse and garden is in a tranquil spot with views of the Hijikawa below. You'll pass through Ōzu's quaint old town on the way to reach this aesthetically refined villa, which required four years and a whopping 9,000 craftsmen to complete it in 1907. The grounds are equally alluring. If you make the trip to Ōzu, a visit to Garyū-sansō is a more moving experience than the town's castle.

Transportation

Ōzu is about 15 minutes farther south of **Uchiko** (¥260) by local train and 10 minutes by express train (¥1,510).

Kōchi 高知市

There's a subtropical vibe in sun-kissed Kōchi's air. As you exit the main station, palm trees line the main boulevards, gregarious locals banter in a carefree tone, and just south of downtown, Katsurahama Beach stands at the foot of cliffs renowned for being a prime spot to moon-gaze. These bluffs were once frequented by the city's favorite son, legendary samurai and political revolutionary Sakamoto Ryōma, a pivotal figure in advancing the Meiji Restoration of 1868. Sakamoto is hard to miss with his scowling visage glaring from so many billboards and shop signs around town.

Downtown, a townscape punctuated by rivers, is centered around a well-preserved, original castle. There's a vibrant dining scene, heavily featuring *katsuo no tataki* (flame-broiled bonito), as well as a smattering of lively nightlife. These draws make the city of Kōchi a good base for exploring elsewhere in the prefecture, or, if you're not in a rush, for a day or two of exploration, eating, and drinking in the city for its own sake.

Kōchi's colors are most visible during the spirited Yosakoi Matsuri in August, hands-down the best time to visit. The festival features a range of modern dance troupes frolicking in the streets and on stages to music ranging from hip-hop to traditional scores and high-speed anime soundtracks. This decidedly colorful, modern take on the summer dance *matsuri* is in many ways an ideal complement to neighboring Tokushima's more historically grounded, though also lively, Awa Odori festival. Both bashes attract huge crowds, so book accommodation well in advance.

SIGHTS

Kōchi-jō
高知城

1-2-1 Marunouchi; tel. 088/824-5701; http://kochipark.jp/kochijyo; 9am-5pm; ¥420; take tram from JR Kōchi Station to Kōchijō-mae tram stop and transfer at Harimayabashi (15 minutes, ¥200), or walk from JR Kōchi Station (20 minutes)

This stout castle in the center of town is one of Japan's 12 citadels still standing in original form since the end of the feudal era in 1868 when the Meiji Restoration swept the country. First completed in 1611, the current incarnation largely dates from 1748, after a rebuilding effort that followed a fire.

After passing the moat, make your way up through the grounds and enter the castle proper. You'll sense its age when you see its lived-in chambers, deep stairwells, and commanding watchtower. Uniquely, the main keep doubled as a residence for the lords of the Yamauchi clan who reigned over what was then Tōsa (Kōchi today) during the feudal era. From the top floor of the main tower, you'll be rewarded with excellent views of the city fanning out in all directions below.

Godai-san
五台山

A rewarding side-trip from downtown Kōchi, the peak of Godai-san, named after a mountain in China by visiting monks, boasts temple number 31 on the circuit of 88, **Chikurin-ji**, as well as the lovely **Makino Botanical Garden**, an expansive green space with walking paths, a greenhouse, and more. The mountain is also a great place to take in views of the city and Katsurahama Beach, a picturesque stretch of sand located south of town, though swimming is prohibited. To reach Godai-san, take the My Yu Bus from JR Kōchi Station (25 minutes, ¥600 for day pass). Alternatively, take a taxi from JR Kōchi Station to Godai-san (20 minutes, about ¥1,500).

CHIKURIN-JI
竹林寺

3577 Godai-san; tel. 088/882-3085; www.chikurinji.com; 8am-5pm daily for main hall, 8:30am-5pm daily

Kōchi

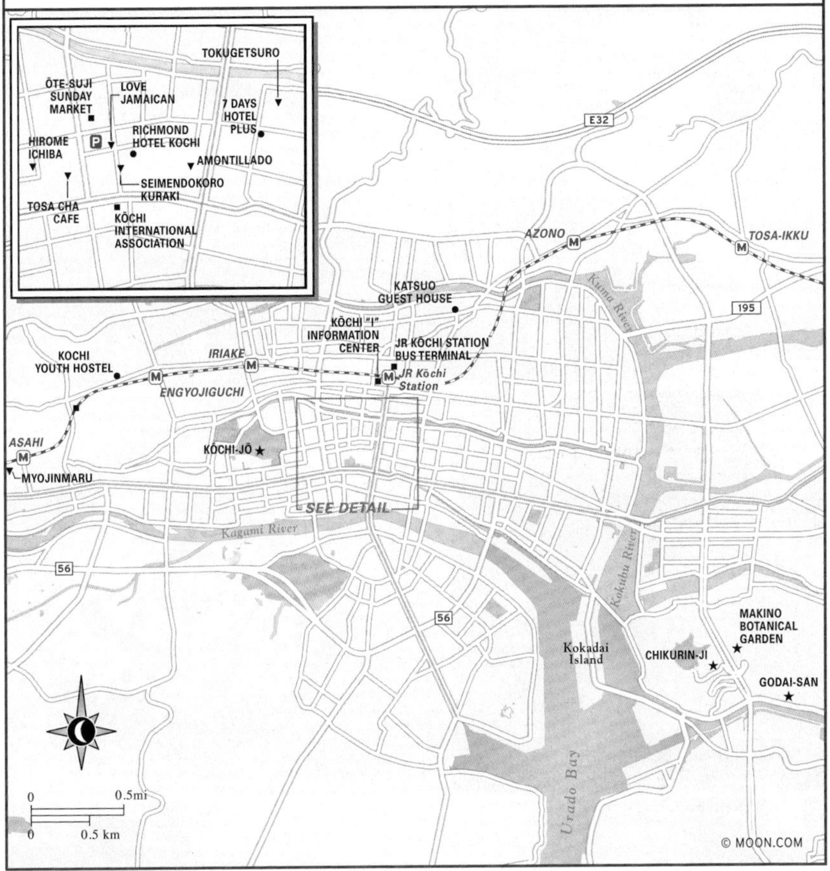

for treasure hall; free

Founded in 724 by a monk visiting from China, this temple (number 31 on the circuit of 88) has scholarly associations, venerating Manjusri, a bodhisattva of wisdom. As such, it attracts not only pilgrims but also a steady flow of students hoping for high marks on exams. A five-tiered pagoda, a tranquil garden, and a host of buildings dot the grounds. Inside its treasure hall are scrolls and various statuary with a decidedly Indian touch. The temple's spacious grounds are especially lovely in spring and autumn.

MAKINO BOTANICAL GARDEN
牧野植物園

4200-6 Godaisan; tel. 088/882-2601; www.makino.or.jp; 9am-5pm daily; ¥720 adults, free for high school students and younger

Located a pleasant 20-minute walk east of Chikurin-ji, this lush zone bears the family name of a prominent Kōchi-born botanist, Dr. Makino Tomitaro (1862-1957). Walk among 3,000 species of plant-life in 6 hectares (14.8 acres) of outdoor gardens and in a large greenhouse, and learn about Dr. Makino's contributions to his science at the on-site museum.

1
2
3
T-14
合流
4

FESTIVALS AND EVENTS

YOSAKOI ŌDORI MATSURI
よさこい祭

Aug. 9-12

Kōchi's flamboyant, kinetic Yosakoi Matsuri is one of the 10 largest festivals in Japan, and the energy level doesn't disappoint. Consecutive waves of dance troupes dressed in colorful costumes—many of them being playful twists on traditional forms—jump, shout, and groove through the city's downtown streets, fill covered shopping arcades, and perform in parks, on stages next to the castle, and various other locations. The atmosphere is fun and loud. Revelers spill into local restaurants and bars after the dancing stops, and street food stalls hum with energy into the night.

The best days are Aug. 10-11. This festival has a more modern flavor than Tokushima's **Awa Odori,** which is held immediately following Kōchi's big bash on August 12-15. The two festivals complement one another perfectly. If you can swing it, consider attending both. Just be sure to book accommodations as far in advance as possible to account for the inevitable crowds.

SHOPPING

ŌTE-SUJI SUNDAY MARKET

1.3-km (0.8-mi) stretch of Ōte-suji; 5am-6pm Sun. Apr.-Sept., 5:30am-5pm Oct.-Mar.

For more than three centuries, a street bazaar has buzzed on Sundays along Ōte-suji, the street leading to the Ōte-mon gate of Kōchi-jō. Nearly 500 stalls hawk everything from local fruits and vegetables to flowers, wooden crafts, and daily sundries. The atmosphere is friendly and boisterous. It makes a great introduction to the lively spirit of Kōchi.

1: roofline of Kōchi-jō **2:** detail of Kōchi-jō **3:** engraved manhole cover **4:** Yosakoi Ōdori Matsuri dancers

FOOD

★ HIROME ICHIBA

2-3-1 Obiyamachi; tel. 088/822-5287; http://hirome.co.jp; 8am-11pm Mon.-Sat., 7am-11pm Sun., open times of individual restaurants vary

Boisterous, sprawling, and brimming with variety, this indoor food court shares space with a market that serves a bit of everything Japanese. Near the castle downtown, at the end of the Obiyamachi covered arcade, this is a good place for a cheap, casual meal. After buying your dish and beverage of choice, find an empty seat at any of the large wooden tables. This is a good place to strike up a conversation over a few drinks too, particularly on the weekends.

TOSA CHA CAFÉ

2-1-31 Obiyamachi; tel. 088/855-7753; http://tosacha.net; 11am-7pm Thurs.-Tues.; set meals from ¥780, tea/coffee from ¥350

Kōchi has a tea-growing region in its warm southwest. This café serves black, green, oolong, chamomile, ginger, and mint tea made from leaves harvested in the Shimanto region. Healthy lunch sets and great desserts are also on the menu. The atmosphere is relaxing too, with outdoor seating and a nice wooden interior. This is a good choice if you're in the Obiyamachi area downtown.

★ MYOJINMARU

1-1-2 Motomachi, 1F Yachiyo Bldg.; tel. 088/820-6505; http://myojinmaru.jp; 5pm-11:30pm daily; courses from ¥5,000

This is an excellent place to sample Kōchi's local specialty, *katsuo tataki* (lightly seared bonito), in a relaxed setting. This dish is often served with garlic, ginger onions, and various herbs. Cozy and elegant with soft lighting, this branch of the restaurant is a laid-back alternative to the one next to Hirome Ichiba, which is often thronged with tourists.

Whale Watching and Surfing Cape Ashizuri

The farthest southern extremity of the whole island, Cape Ashizuri (**足摺岬**, Cape "Foot Stamping") is a surf-pounded landscape of jagged rocks and palm trees touching the Pacific. This rugged shoreline, and the wild stretch of coast leading toward it from the northeast and northwest, offers ample chances to hike, whale-watch, surf, star-gaze, and ultimately, get away from it all.

SURFING

Approaching Cape Ashizuri, **Ōkinohama** is a lovely stretch of sand nestled in a crescent-shaped bay with dependably good waves. There are basic amenities on-site—public parking, restrooms, showers—but not much else. Be sure to come stocked with food and other provisions from the supermarket in Tosa-Shimizu, about 20 minutes' drive south on Route 321.

WHALE-WATCHING

Former whaling companies lead whale-watching tours from various ports around Cape Ashizuri. Contact the **Tosa-Shimizu City Tourism Association** (303 Yorō, Tosashimizu-shi; tel. 0880/82-3155; www.shimizu-kankou.com; 8:30am-5pm daily) for more details on the tours available.

KONGŌFUKU-JI

Kongōfuku-ji (214-1 Ashizuri-misaki; 0880/88-0038; www.city.tosashimizu.kochi.jp/kanko/g01_kongofukuji.html; free), temple number 38 on the circuit of 88, is located beside Route 27 in the heart of Ashizuri. It was purportedly founded by the trailblazing monk Kūkai himself in 822 and is one of the toughest temples to reach on the island. Combined with its dramatic clifftop setting, it's one of the more exotic stops on the island's long pilgrimage circuit.

HIKING

After exploring the grounds of Kongōfuku-ji, cross the street in front of the temple. Here, a trail around 2 km (1.2 mi) long threads along the coast, stopping at a lighthouse, the **Ashizuri Observatory** and the **Tengu-Nose Observatory,** each with dramatic views. Stroll along this path to fully appreciate this beautiful stretch of coast.

TOKUGETSURO

1-17-3 Minami Harimaya-chō; tel. 088/882-0101; www.tokugetsu.co.jp; lunch courses from ¥6,480, dinner courses from ¥8,640

This elegant *kaiseki* restaurant has the trappings of a classic Japanese establishment, from the servers in kimono to calligraphy scrolls, tatami floors, and a landscape garden. Multicourse spreads are artfully presented and packed with refined flavors. The menu draws heavily on the bounty from the nearby sea, with options for meat too. Make a reservation at least a few days in advance.

SEIMENDOKORO KURAKI

1-10-12 Obiyamachi; tel. 088/871-4059; 11:30am-4pm and 5:30pm-midnight daily; ¥1,000

This popular ramen joint near the Obiyamachi shopping arcade serves its noodles in either pork or chicken-based soup, with an infusion of soy sauce (miso) or salt (*shio*), as well as a dose of fish powder. The noodles are then topped with vegetables and pieces of either chicken or pork. This is a popular choice among the late-night crowd, so don't be surprised if there's a queue if you show up after hours.

BARS AND NIGHTLIFE

AMONTILLADO

1-1-17 Obiyamachi; tel. 088/875-0599; www.facebook.com/irishpubamo; 5pm-2am daily

Even in Japan, sometimes you just need a pint. Come in here for a glass of Kilkenny or Guinness, and a chance to chat with friendly

the rugged Cape Ashizuri coast

ACCOMMODATIONS

If you want to stay in this remote part of Shikoku, ★ **Kaiyu Inn** (2777-12 Ōki; tel. 0880/82-8500; www.kaiyu-inn.jp; singles ¥7,000-23,000, ¥2,500 for each additional person) is a chilled-out beach house run by a friendly couple, a stone's throw from Ōkinohama.

GETTING THERE

Pressing on to Cape Ashizuri only makes sense if you're **driving** yourself. If you have a car, you can drive straight down the center of the peninsula on routes 321 and 27. If you're traveling by public transport from Kōchi Station, take the **Ashizuri limited express** to **Nakamura Station** (1 hour 40 minutes; ¥4,670). From there, about seven daily buses run south to Cape Ashizuri.

locals. There's live music on some nights, too. Happy hour is 5pm-8pm daily.

LOVE JAMAICAN

9-1 Ōte-suji; tel. 090/8973-4736; 10pm-late daily

This lively club is a good place to mingle with young locals on a dance floor. As the name suggests, the music leans reggae, with hip-hop sometimes added to the mix.

ACCOMMODATIONS

KATSUO GUEST HOUSE

4-7-28 Hijima-chō; tel. 070/5352-1167; http://katuo-gh.com; private rooms ¥3,800 pp

For a hostel a bit closer to downtown, this cheerful family-run guesthouse has a number of playfully themed dorm rooms with a mix of futons and bunk beds. There's also a shared kitchen, bathroom, and showers. Wi-Fi is available throughout. Located about 15 minutes' walk northeast of Kōchi Station.

RICHMOND HOTEL KŌCHI

9-4 Obiyamachi; tel. 088/820-1122; http://kochi.richmondhotel.jp; ¥7,500 d; walk 5 minutes from the Hasuikemachi-dōri tram stop, or walk 13 minutes southwest of Kōchi Station

Well located in the heart of downtown, this business hotel has well-appointed, clean rooms sized slightly above average. Prices are reasonable, with a decent breakfast provided. The hotel is attached to the Obiyamachi shopping arcade, which means plenty of restaurants, cafés, and nightlife are all around.

7 DAYS HOTEL PLUS

2-13-6 Harimayachō; tel. 088/884-7111; www.7dayshotel.com; ¥8,000 d; walk 10 minutes southeast of Kōchi Station

This hotel, in a convenient location, has petite, well-appointed rooms. The entrance and ground floor are bright and airy with a boutique feel. A simple continental-style breakfast is included. The hotel is located a short walk from a wide variety of restaurants and nightlife.

INFORMATION AND SERVICES

Stop at the **Kōchi "i" Information Center** (2-10-17 Kitahonmachi; tel. 088/826-3337; http://visitkochijapan.com; 9am-5pm daily), housed in a stylish complex called the Tosa Terrace, in front of the south exit at JR Kōchi Station. Here you'll find great English-language materials, from pamphlets to maps, and English-speaking staff who are ready to help with everything from recommending food options to activities. There's a separate **window** just for helping visitors with accommodations that stays open until 7:30pm daily. The office's website is also useful.

Another good resource in town is the **Kōchi International Association** (2F Marunouchi Bldg., 4-1-37 Honmachi,; tel. 088/875-0022; www.kochi-kia.or.jp; 8:30am-5:15pm Mon.-Sat., closed Sat. in Aug.). This center is located across the street from the southeast corner of the castle grounds. Come here for English-language books, magazines, and free Internet.

TRANSPORTATION

Getting There

TRAIN

JR Kōchi Station is on the **Dosan** line. This links it to **Kubokawa** in the prefecture's west; from there you can transfer to other trains and travel farther south into the Shimanto-gawa region by traveling to Nakamura Station (limited express 1 hour 45 minutes; ¥4,870), or travel north to Uwajima (3 hours; ¥4,860). To travel between Kōchi and **Matsuyama,** it's best to go via **Tadotsu Station** (4r hours 15 minutes, ¥10,670).

To travel from Kōchi to **Tokushima,** take the Dosan line north to Awa-Ikeda and transfer to the JR Tokushima line (three hours; ¥5,080). To reach Takamatsu Station, take the Dosan line north, transferring at Utazu Station (2 hours 20 minutes; ¥5,300). It's possible to travel directly between Kōchi and **Okayama** on Honshu via limited express train, too (2 hours 30 minutes; ¥6,160).

BUS

You can take a highway bus to or from Kōchi and most of Shikoku's major towns and beyond. Buses arrive and depart from **JR Kōchi Station Bus Terminal,** just north of JR Kōchi Station. See the **JR Shikoku Bus** website (www.jr-shikoku.co.jp/bus) for details, routes, and fares.

AIR

Domestic flights from Tokyo, Nagoya, Osaka, and Fukuoka land daily at **Kōchi Ryōma Airport** (www.kochiap.co.jp). It's located about a 40-minute **bus** ride east of JR Kōchi Station (¥720).

Getting Around

Entering via JR Kōchi Station, as most people do, you'll find yourself in the north part of the city. If you plan only to visit the castle and core downtown area, you'll be able to manage **on foot.** But if you plan to travel to Godai-san Beach, you'll definitely want to make use of the city's **tram** and **bus** networks.

TRAM

There are two tram lines in Kōchi. The **Sanbashi line** runs north to south from just outside the south exit of JR Kōchi Station to the port in the south, while the **Ino line** runs east to west. They intersect at Harimaya-bashi in the center of town. All rides cost flat fee of ¥200. To ride the tram, simply enter via the back side and take one ticket from the machine. When you reach your destination, drop your fare into the box beside the driver's seat as you exit from the front. If you need to switch to the other tram line, request a *norikae-ken* (transfer ticket) from the driver as you exit.

BUS

To reach Godai-san, you'll need to take the **My-Yu Bus.** The buses run on a loop that starts and ends at the **bus terminal** just outside the north exit of JR Kōchi Station. A one-day pass for the return trip is ¥600. A one-day unlimited pass is ¥1,000 and a two-day pass is ¥1,600. Pick up a pass and get information on the bus schedule from the **Kōchi "i" Information Center** at Tosa Terrace just in front of the south exit of JR Kōchi Station. If you're a foreign tourist, you can get a 50 percent discount if you show your ID when buying the pass.

BICYCLE

You can also rent a bicycle at **OK Parking** (1-chōme Otesuji; tel. 088/871-4689; www.ok-parking.jp/rental_bicycle/index.html; 8am-9pm, ¥500 per day). You'll find this facility about 12 minutes' walk southwest of JR Kōchi Station next to Otesuji-dōri, where the weekly Sunday market is held.

CAR

If you want to explore the surrounding region, it becomes increasingly hard to get around by public transportation the more remote you get. If it's an option, a car is undoubtedly the smoothest means of transport. **Toyota Rent-a-Car** (4-15 Ekimae-chō; tel. 088/823-0100; www.r-ehm.co.jp; 8am-8pm daily), located about 3 minutes' walk south of JR Kōchi Station, is a safe bet.

Kyūshū 九州

Japan's third largest island, Kyūshū is an appealing alternative to the usual Kantō and Kansai circuits on most travelers' itineraries. The subtropical, southernmost of Japan's four main islands, Kyūshū presents immense variety, from the ramen stalls and rowdy nightlife of cosmopolitan Fukuoka to the pottery kilns of Saga. Phoenix-like Nagasaki, rebuilt from the ashes of its tragic past, hums with *joie de vivre* today, volcanic peaks and fertile valleys swathed in cedar beckon hikers to the heart of the island. In Miyazaki, sea turtles and clued-in surfers flock to beaches pounded by the country's best waves. And in the far south, Sakurajima (Japan's Vesuvius), smolders imposingly across the bay from the laid-back city of Kagoshima.

Indeed, throughout the island—Japan's most intensely volcanic and

Highlights

Look for ★ to find recommended sights, activities, dining, and lodging.

★ **Fukuoka's Street Food Stalls:** Squeeze in beside locals at one of Fukuoka's hundred-plus food stalls to gorge on *tonkotsu* ramen or grilled meat on sticks, washed down with beer (page 617).

★ **Saga's Pottery Towns:** Pore over stunning pieces of porcelain and finely sculpted clay in the ceramics centers of Karatsu, Imari, and Arita (page 622).

★ **Aso-san:** Marvel at the vast expanse that is one of the world's largest calderas, epitomizing Kyūshū's volcanic terrain (page 646).

★ ***Onsen:*** From the touristy pools of Beppu to the serenity of Kurokawa Onsen, submerge yourself to the shoulders in some of Japan's best hot springs (page 651 and 654).

★ **Takachiho:** Delve deep into Shinto's roots at this remote sacred power spot, centered on a mossy gorge and a smattering of ancient shrines (page 656).

★ **The Nichinan Coast:** Take a drive down this dramatic, subtropical coastline, stopping at cliffside shrines, islands ruled by monkeys, and some of the best surf spots in Japan (page 662).

★ **Ibusuki's Hot-Sand Baths:** For a different take on warmth-induced R&R, bury yourself up to the neck in geothermally heated sand on Ibusuki's coast (page 672).

Kyūshū

Sea of Japan
HONSHU
Midobara
Kogushi
Yamaguchi
Yamaguchi Prefecture
Kano
Ogori
Shimonoseki
Tokuyama
Kudamatsu
Ube
YAMAGUCHI UBE
Kitakyushu
KITAKYUSHU
FUKUOKA'S STREET FOOD STALLS
Oshima
SEE "FUKUOKA OVERVIEW" MAP
Iki Island
Munakata
Shingu
Nogata
Yukuhashi
SHIKANOSHIMA
NOKONOSHIMA ISLAND PARK
NOKONOSHIMA
Madara
Fukuoka
FUKUOKA AIRPORT
Iizuka
Oshima
Maebaru
Kasuga
Fukuoka Prefecture
Nakatsu
Imi
Karatsu
JR CHIKUHI LINE
Chikushino
Takada
213
Ikitsuki
JR KARATSU LINE
Saga Prefecture
Ogori
Tosu
Furuichi
OITA
10
SAGA'S POTTERY TOWNS
202
Imari
Oita Prefecture
Fuko Island
OKAWACHIYAMA VILLAGE
210
Saga
Kurume
Hita
Kuro
Sasebo
Arita
Beppu
Oita
Saganoseki
Oshima
Ariakeno Bay
ONSEN
Yufuin
DAIKANBO LOOKOUT
Nagasaki Prefecture
Omura Bay
3
Omuta
KUROKAWA ONSEN
Taisen-Zan
Usuki
Matsushima
Omura
NAGASAKI AIRPORT
Arao
Ariake Sea
MICHI-NO-EKI ASO
ASO BASE BACKPACKERS
57
10
Isahaya
KUSASENRI PLATEAU
ASO-SAN
Saiki
ATOMIC BOMB HYPOCENTER PARK / NAGASAKI ATOMIC BOMB MUSEUM
Shimabara Peninsula
Kumamoto
ASO VOLCANO MUSEUM
Tsurumi-zaki
Nagasaki
KUMAMOTO PORT
KUMAMOTO AIRPORT
TAKAMORI DENGAKU
TAKACHIHO SHRINE
AMANO IWATO JINJA
GUNKANJIMA
Arie
Maruichibi
SEE "NAGASAKI" MAP
218
Tomochi
TAKACHIHO
Hondo
Yatsushiro
Kumamoto Prefecture
218
Nobeoka
KYUSHU
Shimoshima Island
Miyazaki Prefecture
445
Hyuga
Yatusushiro Bay
Hitoyoshi
Murasho
10
267
3
EBINO-KŌGEN ECO MUSEUM CENTER
KARAKUNI-DAKE
Kami-Koshiki
KIRISHIMA HOTEL
GIANT STORE
Sendai
KIRISHIMA-JINGŪ
10
Miyazaki
Shimo-Koshiki
KAGOSHIMA AIRPORT
KIRISHIMA-JINGŪ STATION
Kokubu
Oryuzako
YUNOHIRA LOOKOUT
Miyakonojo
SEE "KAGOSHIMA" MAP
KUROKAMI OBSERVATION POINT
Kagoshima
KUROKAMI BURIED TORII
UDO-JINGŪ
Izaku
ARIMURA LAVA OBSERVATORY
Aburatsu
Tarumizu
Kagoshima Prefecture
THE NICHINAN COAST
Oura
ROUTE 220
220
226
Kagoshima Bay
Kanoya
Ariake Bay
KŌJIMA
Makurazuki
Cape Toi
IBUSUKI'S HOT-SAND BATH
SARAKU SAND-BATH HALL
HEALTHY LAND TAMATEBAKO ONSEN
0
20 mi
0
20 km

home to one of the world's largest calderas (Aso-san)—smoking summits belch gases, clog the sky with ash and occasionally cause great destruction. No shortage of hot-spring waters bubble to the surface across this fiery landscape. *Onsen* meccas range from kitschy but fun Beppu to Kurokawa Onsen, one of Japan's most picturesque hot-spring villages, nestled in a green valley largely untouched by concrete-happy developers. If you'd like to try a novel take on geothermally induced relaxation, you can also bury yourself up to the neck in hot sand in far southern Ibusuki.

Volcanic forces beneath the earth are only one form of power associated with Kyūshū. The island is also a spiritual power-spot, with deep Shinto roots. In many ways, Kyūshū is the spiritual birthplace of Japan. According to legend, the small town of Takachiho in northern Miyazaki Prefecture is home to the cave where Amaterasu, the Sun Goddess, fled to escape her taunting brother. Today, Takachiho-jinja hosts dances inspired by these divine tales. The nearby scenic gorge, with a waterfall cascading directly over the rim into its waters, is one of the island's most picturesque spots.

ORIENTATION

Kyūshū is located southwest of both Honshu and Shikoku. South Korea is only 200 km (125 mi) from Kyūshū's northern shore. Although the island was home to nine states in ancient times—Kyūshū means "nine provinces"—today there are seven: **Fukuoka, Saga, Nagasaki, Kumamoto, Oita, Miyazaki,** and **Kagoshima.** It's easiest to divide these prefectures into three distinct regions: **northern Kyūshū, central Kyūshū,** and **southern Kyūshū.**

Trains are the best way to get around Kyūshū's distinct regions, which are well-connected by rail for the most part. Buses are good for reaching some more remote parts, while islands just offshore can be reached by ferry. It's possible to come to the island by ferry from western Shikoku too. Having a car is a godsend in the vast central region around **Aso-san,** some of the remote *onsen* villages like **Kurokawa,** and the spiritual hot spot of **Takachiho.** It's particularly crucial to have your own wheels if you plan to venture into the remote **Kunisaki Peninsula** in Oita Prefecture's northeast or down along the surfer's paradise that is the **Nichinan Coast** in the southeast of Miyazaki Prefecture.

Northern Kyūshū

The entry point for most visitors to the island, Northern Kyūshū is composed of **Fukuoka Prefecture** in the north-central part of the island, bordered by **Saga Prefecture** to the west, with **Nagasaki Prefecture** accounting for the island's northwest corner.

Fukuoka is the island's biggest city and Japan's eighth most populous. It's also a major transport hub with *shinkansen* (bullet train) links and an international airport. In neighboring Saga Prefecture, you'll find a number of pottery villages and historic towns. The city of **Nagasaki,** capital of the prefecture of the same name, is the island's second largest metropolis.

Central Kyūshū

Alternating between volcanic cones and verdant valleys, Central Kyūshū offers stunning vistas, historic towns, and hot springs, spread around the prefectures of **Kumamoto** and **Oita.** The region is among the most geothermally active on earth. East of Nagasaki, across the Ariake Sea, the city of **Kumamoto** is the capital of the prefecture of the same name, which accounts for a large section of the island's heartland. An old castle town, Kumamoto lies in the west of the prefecture, with **Aso-san** and the surrounding plateaus, and charming **Kurokawa Onsen** to the east. Northeast of Kumamoto lies **Oita Prefecture.** This is where you'll find the fashionable hot-spring town of **Yufuin** and

Previous: Takachiho Gorge; hot-sand baths in Ibusuki; Mount Aso.

Best Restaurants

★ **Chikae:** Watch chefs prepare fish selected from a central tank at this bustling seafood hot spot doing business in Fukuoka since 1961 (page 617).

★ **Tsukasa:** Start your exploration of Fukuoka's *yatai* (street-food stall) scene at this friendly riverside spot known for its yakitori and cod-roe tempura, but don't stop there (page 618).

★ **Kagetsu:** This restaurant set in an old geisha house is a classy place to dine on *shippoku,* Nagasaki's eclectic contribution to haute Japanese cuisine (page 637).

★ **Yokobachi:** With indoor and outdoor seating and a sprawling booze menu, this lively *izakaya* is the best place to sample Kumamoto's specialties, including its famed *basashi* (horse sashimi) (page 644).

★ **Takamori Dengaku-no-Sato:** Dine on skewered vegetables, meat, and fish cooked in an *irori* (sunken hearth) at this atmospheric, wood-beamed farmhouse set in a forest near Aso-san (page 649).

REGIONAL SPECIALTIES

Fukuoka is a foodie haven. The city's specialties include ***tonkotsu* ramen,** served in a flavorsome soup made by simmering pork bones and fatback for upward of half a day. Fukuoka is also known for its surprisingly tasty ***motsu-nabe*** (offal hotpot).

Nagasaki has a highly eclectic cuisine, mirroring its cosmopolitan past. The city's most famous dish is ***chanpon,*** essentially ramen noodles served in salty soup with slices of pork and squid. Nagasaki is also known for ***shippoku,*** a unique spin on haute *kaiseki* fare that's been influenced by Chinese and Portuguese cooking. A downright fanciful Nagasaki dish is **"Turkish rice,"** a hodgepodge of spaghetti, rice, and *tonkatsu* (breaded and deep-fried pork cutlet). It has no ties to Turkey—the chefs who first whipped it up named it as such as it all felt rather exotic to them, like the country of its namesake.

In Kyūshū's far south, the city of Kagoshima is known for its ***shōchū,*** a distilled spirit that is made with sweet potato, barley, soba, rice, and occasionally corn. The city is also known for its dishes made with ***kurobuta*** (black Berkshire pork) and its ***satsuma-age,*** or deep-fried fish paste.

the amusement park-like geothermal mecca of **Beppu.**

Southern Kyūshū

Kyūshū's south includes **Miyazaki Prefecture** in the east and **Kagoshima Prefecture** in the west. This is the southernmost point of Japan's four main islands. As such, the vibe is laid-back and far removed from the economic and political juggernaut of Tokyo or the nation's historic heartland of Kansai. It's a good place to slow down and enjoy a low-key corner of Japan, minus the crowds.

PLANNING YOUR TIME

By Japanese standards, Kyūshū is vast. You could spend weeks slowly discovering its beauty, much of it hidden deep within its volcanic landscape and along its rugged coastline. To make it worth your while, aim to spend a minimum of **five days** on the island, or better yet, a **week.** Even still, that will only allow you to scratch the surface. Kyūshū is best approached as a stand-alone destination, or in combination with neighboring Shikoku or Western Honshu. If you have the luxury of time, it's also possible to combine it with a trip into either Tokyo or Kyoto and Kansai.

The best time to visit Kyūshū is either

Best Accommodations

★ **Sakamoto-ya:** You can expect top-notch service and plenty of historic ambience at Nagasaki's oldest *ryokan* (page 640).

★ **Yamada Bessō:** This family-run inn in the heart of Beppu is an authentic *ryokan* with an atmosphere that is rich in antique charm (page 652).

★ **Sansou Murata:** This rambling *onsen* resort artistically made of wood and stone is one of the top places to stay in the stylish hot-spring town of Yufuin (page 655).

★ **Ibusuki Syusui-en:** If you've got the funds, this upscale *ryokan* is an ideal place to crash after reaching a state of peak relaxation at Ibusuki's nearby hot-sand baths (page 675).

spring (mid-March through early May) or **autumn** (mid-October through November). As elsewhere in Japan, these two seasons are times of great beauty, as cherry blossoms pop and the leaves blaze red and orange. That said, there's really no time of year when the island cannot be visited, so long as you're prepared to deal with **rainy season** (*tsuyu*) from late May through June, hot and sticky days throughout July and August, and the potential for **typhoons** in September and October. Though temperatures are cold from December through February, **winter** is a touch milder on most of the island than in the regions to the north and snow is rare.

To make the most of your time, **Fukuoka** is the best base for traveling throughout the north of the island. From there, you can make day trips around **Fukuoka Prefecture,** as well as **Saga Prefecture** and even **Nagasaki,** which itself is worth spending a few days exploring. East of Nagasaki, the city of **Kumamoto** is a good jumping-off point for venturing into the island's rugged, volcanic heartland. The city of **Kagoshima** is a great base for maneuvering in the island's south, from **Ibusuki** to **Kirishima-Yaku National Park.**

Itinerary Ideas

ONE DAY IN FUKUOKA

1 Start your day walking from Hakata Station to **Tōchō-ji,** which houses a massive wooden Buddha statue.

2 Next move to **Kushida-jinja,** the city's most significant shrine.

3 Swing by the **Fukuoka Asian Art Museum.**

4 After that, go for lunch at **Toriden Hakata Honten,** a chicken hot-pot restaurant near the museum.

5 After lunch, hop on the Kūkō line at Nakasukawabata Station and head west to Akasaka Station. Go for a tea tasting at **Yorozu**, a chic space in which to get a sense of the depth of Japan's tea tradition, which has deep roots in Kyūshū.

One Day in Fukuoka

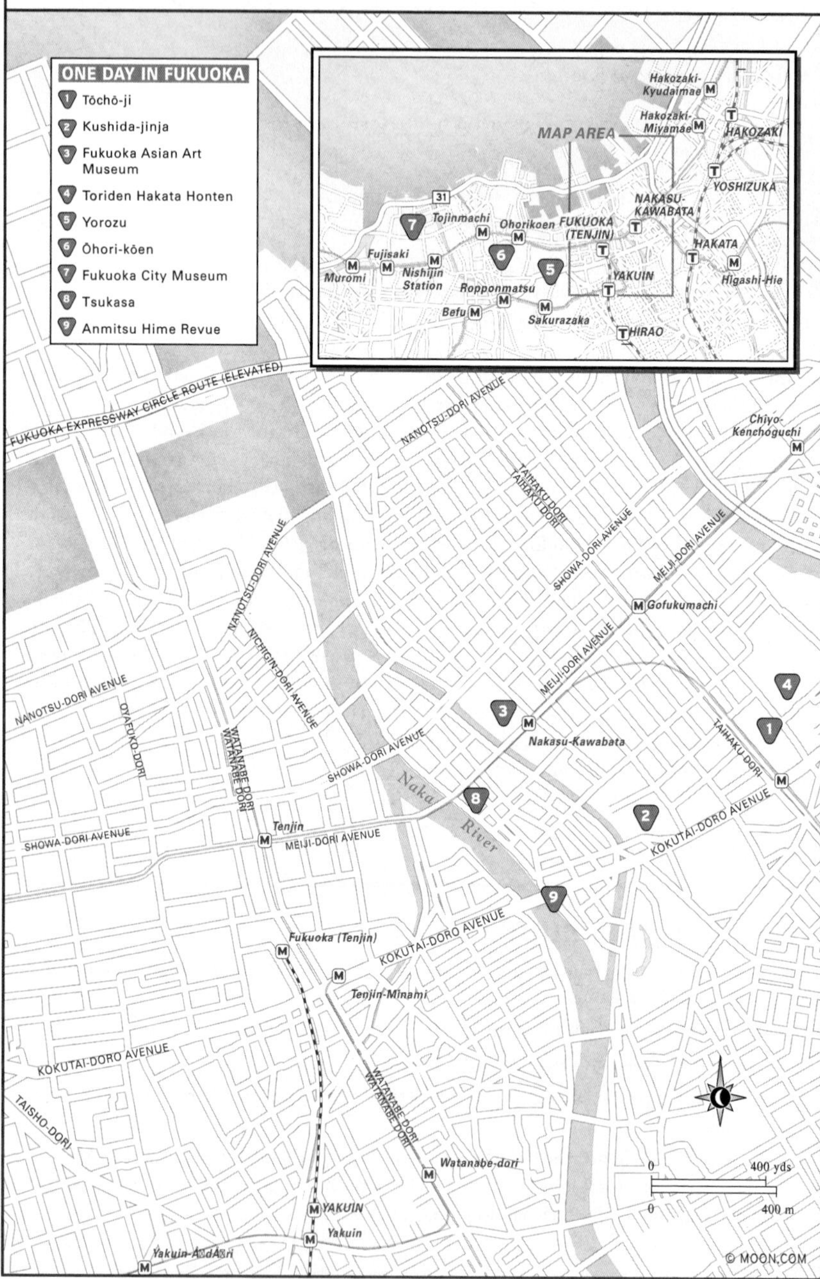

One Day in Nagasaki

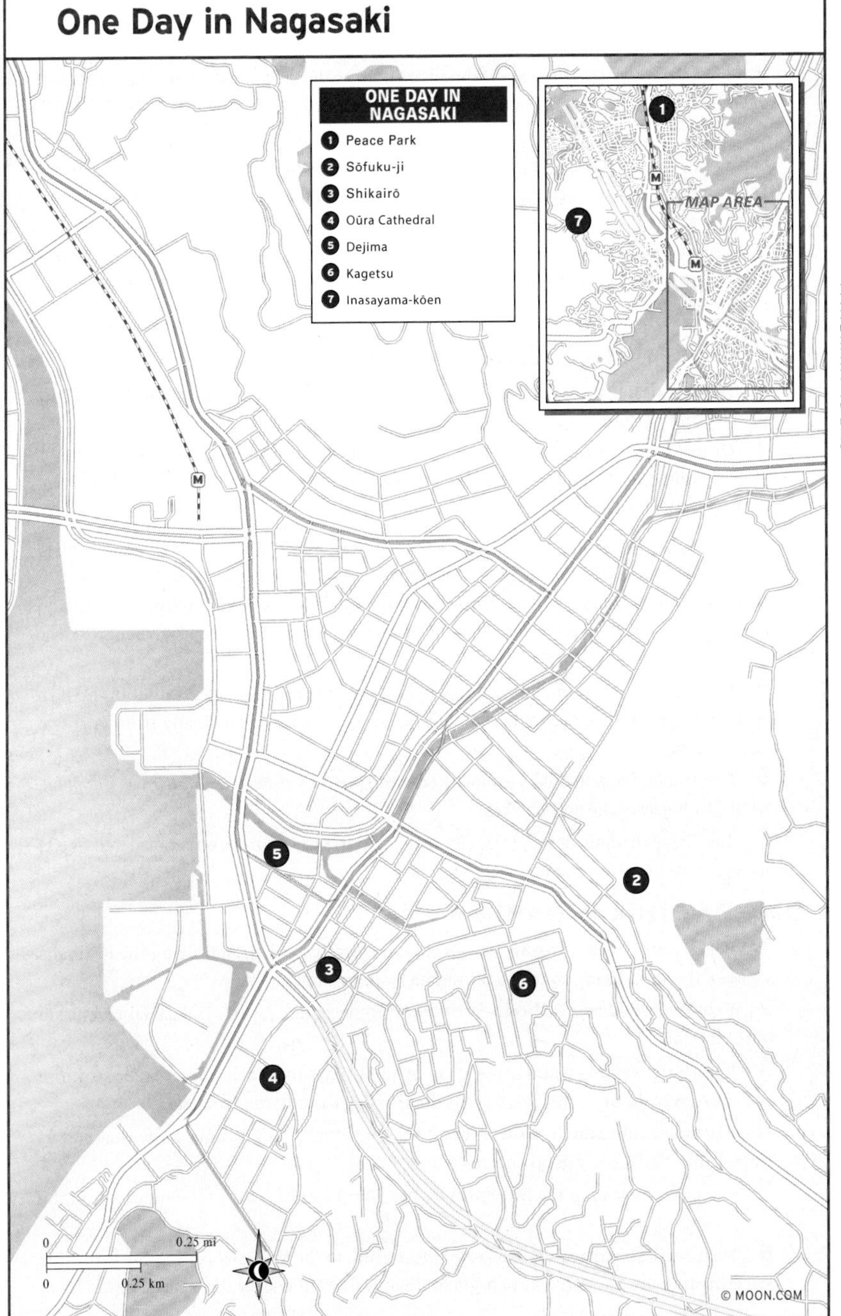

6 Next walk north to the sprawling park of **Ōhori-kōen.** Explore the Japanese garden and Fukuoka Castle ruins.

7 Head to the excellent **Fukuoka City Museum,** sure to scratch your history itch. After that, make your way to the neighborhood of **Daimyō**, located about 15 minutes' walk east of Ōhori-kōen, where youth-oriented shops predominate.

8 As dinnertime approaches, make your way to **Nakasu Island**'s collection of *yatai*, facing the waterfront of the Nakagawa river. Sample some street food here first—**Tsukasa** is famous—then make your way west to Tenjin's *yatai* zone, which has a more local vibe.

9 After you've filled up, explore Tenjin's lively nightlife scene, starting with a bawdy show at **Anmitsu Hime Revue.** Note that the bars often don't start hopping until around midnight.

ONE DAY IN NAGASAKI

1 Begin your day by paying your respects at **Peace Park** on the northeast side of town. Aim to arrive around 9am.

2 Cross Meganebashi, also known as Spectacles Bridge, to Teramachi ("Temple Town"). Stop by **Sōfuku-ji,** a temple whose design is heavily influenced by Chinese aesthetics, reflecting the city's deep historical ties to China.

3 Make your way to nearby Chinatown (Shinchi), Japan's oldest, for lunch. Try **Shikairō,** where Nagasaki's famed *chanpon* dish originated.

4 After lunch, head up Dutch Slope, stopping by **Ōura Cathedral.** This district and these specific sights serve as reminders of Nagasaki's long history of engagement with the West.

5 Walk downhill and make your way to **Dejima,** the artificial island built in the 17th century to contain increasingly interruptive foreign traders, principally from Portugal and Holland.

6 For dinner, try Nagasaki's uniquely eclectic spin on *kaiseki ryōri* known as *shippoku*. **Kagetsu** is one of the best choices.

7 Take in nighttime views of the city from atop **Inasayama-kōen,** considered one of Japan's most beautiful nighttime panoramas.

ONE DAY IN KAGOSHIMA

1 Begin your day at **Sengan-en.** Explore the lovely gardens, admiring the dramatic views of the smoldering cone of Sakurajima looming across the bay.

2 Visit the neighboring **Shoko Shuseikan** to see where Japan's industrial revolution officially started.

3 Return to downtown and make a trip up to **Shiroyama Park**'s observatory. Admire the views over the city with Sakurajima dominating the horizon from afar.

4 Eat lunch downtown. **Kumasotei,** an eatery near Shiroyama Park that serves Kagoshima classics, is a good choice.

5 After lunch, head to the **Museum of the Meiji Restoration** for a quick fix on the city's history.

6 Next, walk six minutes northeast of the musum to the Kajiya-chō streetcar stop. Ride streetcar line no. 2 to Suizokukan-guchi, then walk to the ferry terminal. Board one of

One Day in Kagoshima

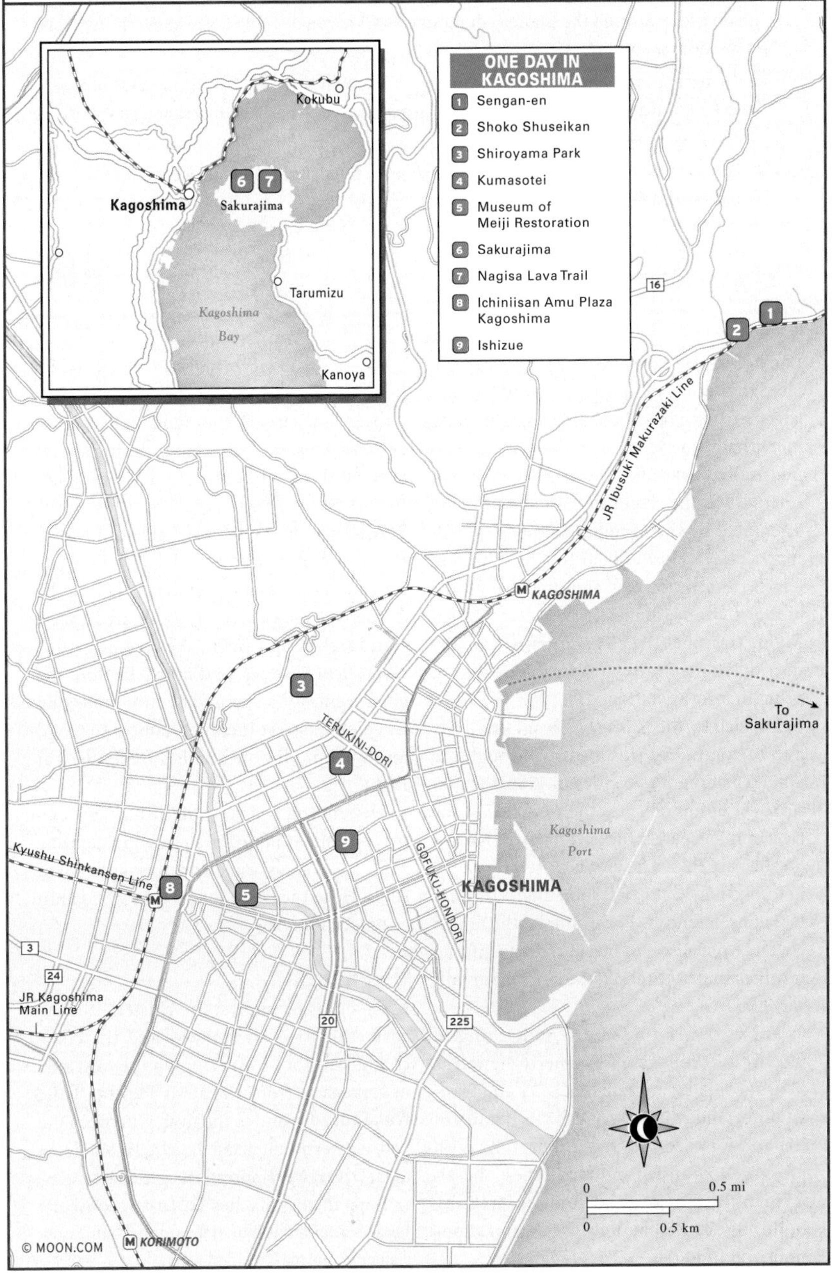

ONE DAY IN KAGOSHIMA

1. Sengan-en
2. Shoko Shuseikan
3. Shiroyama Park
4. Kumasotei
5. Museum of Meiji Restoration
6. Sakurajima
7. Nagisa Lava Trail
8. Ichiniisan Amu Plaza Kagoshima
9. Ishizue

Kokubu
Kagoshima
Sakurajima
Tarumizu
Kagoshima Bay
Kanoya
16
JR Ibusuki Makurazaki Line
KAGOSHIMA
To Sakurajima
TERUKINI-DORI
Kagoshima Port
GOFUKU-HONDORI
KAGOSHIMA
Kyushu Shinkansen Line
3
24
JR Kagoshima Main Line
20
225
0 0.5 mi
0 0.5 km
KORIMOTO

the ferries that depart regularly for the 15-minute journey across the bay to the foot of **Sakurajima,** Japan's answer to Mount Vesuvius.

7 Walk along the **Nagisa Lava Trail** and try out the free footbath. If you rent a car, you can do a loop around the island (1-hour drive). Cars can be rented near the ferry terminal for as short as two hours.

8 After exploring Sakurajima, return to downtown by ferry. Eat dinner at **Ichiniisan Amu Plaza Kagoshima,** famed for its *kurobuta* (black pork) shabu-shabu (hot pot). Be sure to reserve a day or two in advance.

9 End your day by getting schooled on *shōchū,* Kagoshima's booze of choice, at the stellar bar **Ishizue.**

Fukuoka

Located closer to Seoul than Tokyo, with Shanghai not much farther, Fukuoka's engagement with the rest of Asia stretches back more than two millennia. Its harbor—as economically vital today as it has been for centuries—was the site of the ill-fated invasion attempted by the Mongols in the 13th century. Today, international freight ships and ferries running to Seoul and Shanghai ply the harbor's waters, domestic and international flights transit at the city's international airport, and bullet trains arrive from Honshu at its main railway station.

Divided by the Nakagawa river, this lively hub of commerce was formed through the amalgamation of two cities in 1889: the castle town of Fukuoka on the west side of the river and the mercantile port town of **Hakata** on the east side. The city is generally called Fukuoka now, but you'll sometimes still hear Hakata referenced. For example: the famed Hakata ramen, served in a pork-bone infused broth, or Hakata Station, the city's main railway hub.

Fukuoka has undergone something of facelift in recent years. Formerly viewed as little more than an industrial city and transit point, today it is lauded for its quality of life and forward-looking mindset. As with most well-rounded modern cities, there's a sprinkling of art and some interesting buildings, as well as a good range of shopping and food.

Beyond the city's handful of sights, its main draw is its atmosphere at night and its street food, served from food stalls known as *yatai,* clustered in outdoor dining spaces arrayed throughout the city. The best place to experience this in action is either in the **Tenjin** district on the west side of town or the island of **Nakasu,** which sits about 15 minutes' walk east of Tenjin in the middle of the Nakagawa river. In both areas, food stands whip up ramen, skewers of grilled meat, hearty stews, and more. Explore the city's sights for a day, and be sure to soak up its colorful street life, then sample the food and wash it all down with a frosty beer at night.

Depending on your stamina, you can party all night in Tenjin's rambling nightlife zone, 15 minutes' walk west of Nakasu's food stalls. Here, the party doesn't get started until around midnight.

Orientation

Most sights of interest are clustered in the eastern district of **Hakata** and the city's coastal area of **Momochi.** On the west side of Nakagawa from Hakata is **Tenjin,** while **Nakasu,** an island in the river, is between the two. Between Tenjin and the eastern Momochi area, **Ōhori Park** spreads its greenery.

Beyond the city lies **Dazaifu,** southern Japan's ancient hub of officialdom that is now a sleepy, temple-studded town.

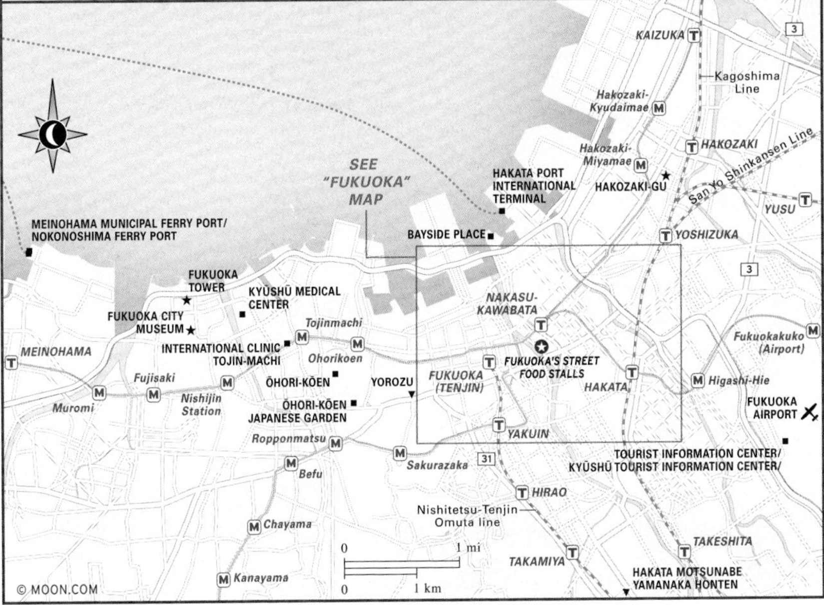

SIGHTS

Hakata

SHOFUKU-JI
聖福寺

6 Gokushomachi, Hakata-ku; tel. 092/291-0775; http://shofukuji.or.jp; 24/7; free

Founded in 1195 by Eisai, the monk who introduced tea and the Rinzai sect of Buddhism from China, this was the first Zen temple in Japan. The buildings, razed and rebuilt numerous times throughout the ages, cannot be entered. Visitors can, however, freely roam through the leafy grounds, believed to be the place where tea plants were first cultivated in Japan.

TŌCHŌ-JI
東長寺

2-4 Gokushomachi, Hakata-ku; tel. 092/291-4459; 24/7; free

It doesn't quite claim the heft of Nara's Daibutsu (Great Buddha) statue, but Fukuoka's very own wooden *daibutsu* is housed here. It's no lightweight either, clocking in at 10.8 meters (35 feet) high and weighing 27 tonnes (30 tons), making it the largest wooden figure of the enlightened one in Japan.

The temple's founding stretches far back into antiquity in 806, when Shingon sect founder Kūkai (aka Kōbō Daishi) purportedly did the honors just after his return from studying in China, making it the first Shingon temple in Japan. The mammoth wooden effigy was carved very recently, however, in 1992.

Be sure to pass through the Pilgrimage of Heaven and Hell, a pitch-black path accessed from the beneath the left side of the wooden figure. As you enter the corridor, note the macabre paintings of suffering experienced in various Buddhist hells. Don't let them phase you; pass through the inky darkness while gripping a handrail and continue until you emerge into the light on the other side. As you come to this other side, keep your

Fukuoka

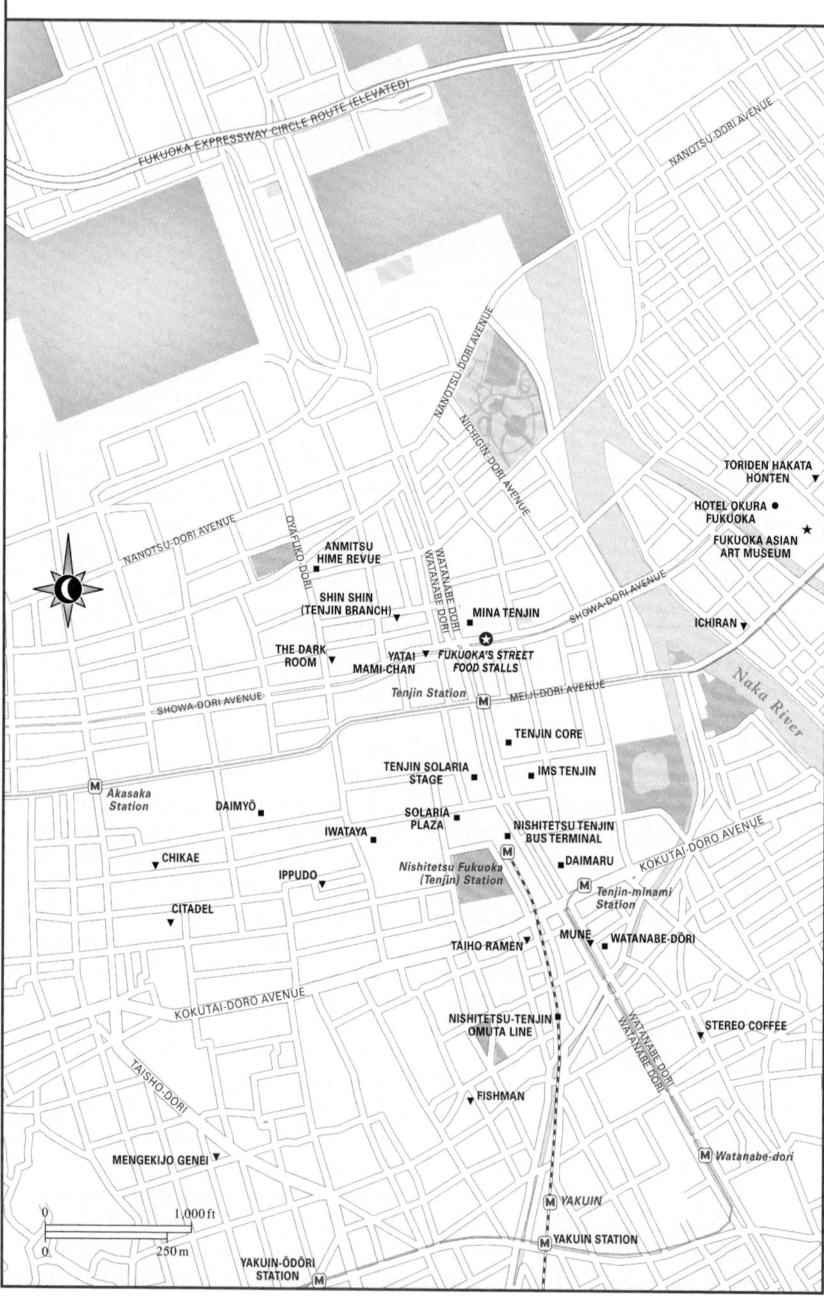

FUKUOKA EXPRESSWAY CIRCLE ROUTE (ELEVATED)
NANOTSU-DORI AVENUE
NANOTSU-DORI AVENUE
NICHIGIN-DORI AVENUE
TORIDEN HAKATA HONTEN
HOTEL OKURA FUKUOKA
FUKUOKA ASIAN ART MUSEUM
NANOTSU-DORI AVENUE
OYAFUKO-DORI
ANMITSU HIME REVUE
WATANABE DORI
WATANABE DORI
SHIN SHIN (TENJIN BRANCH)
MINA TENJIN
SHOWA-DORI AVENUE
ICHIRAN
THE DARK ROOM
YATAI MAMI-CHAN
FUKUOKA'S STREET FOOD STALLS
Tenjin Station
MEIJI-DORI AVENUE
SHOWA-DORI AVENUE
Naka River
TENJIN CORE
TENJIN SOLARIA STAGE
IMS TENJIN
Akasaka Station
DAIMYŌ
SOLARIA PLAZA
IWATAYA
NISHITETSU TENJIN BUS TERMINAL
KOKUTAI-DORO AVENUE
CHIKAE
Nishitetsu Fukuoka (Tenjin) Station
DAIMARU
IPPUDO
Tenjin-minami Station
CITADEL
MUNE
WATANABE-DŌRI
TAIHO RAMEN
KOKUTAI-DORO AVENUE
NISHITETSU-TENJIN OMUTA LINE
STEREO COFFEE
WATANABE-DORI
WATANABE-DORI
TAISHO-DORI
FISHMAN
MENGEKIJO GENEI
Watanabe-dori
0
1,000 ft
0
250 m
YAKUIN
YAKUIN STATION
YAKUIN-ŌDŌRI STATION

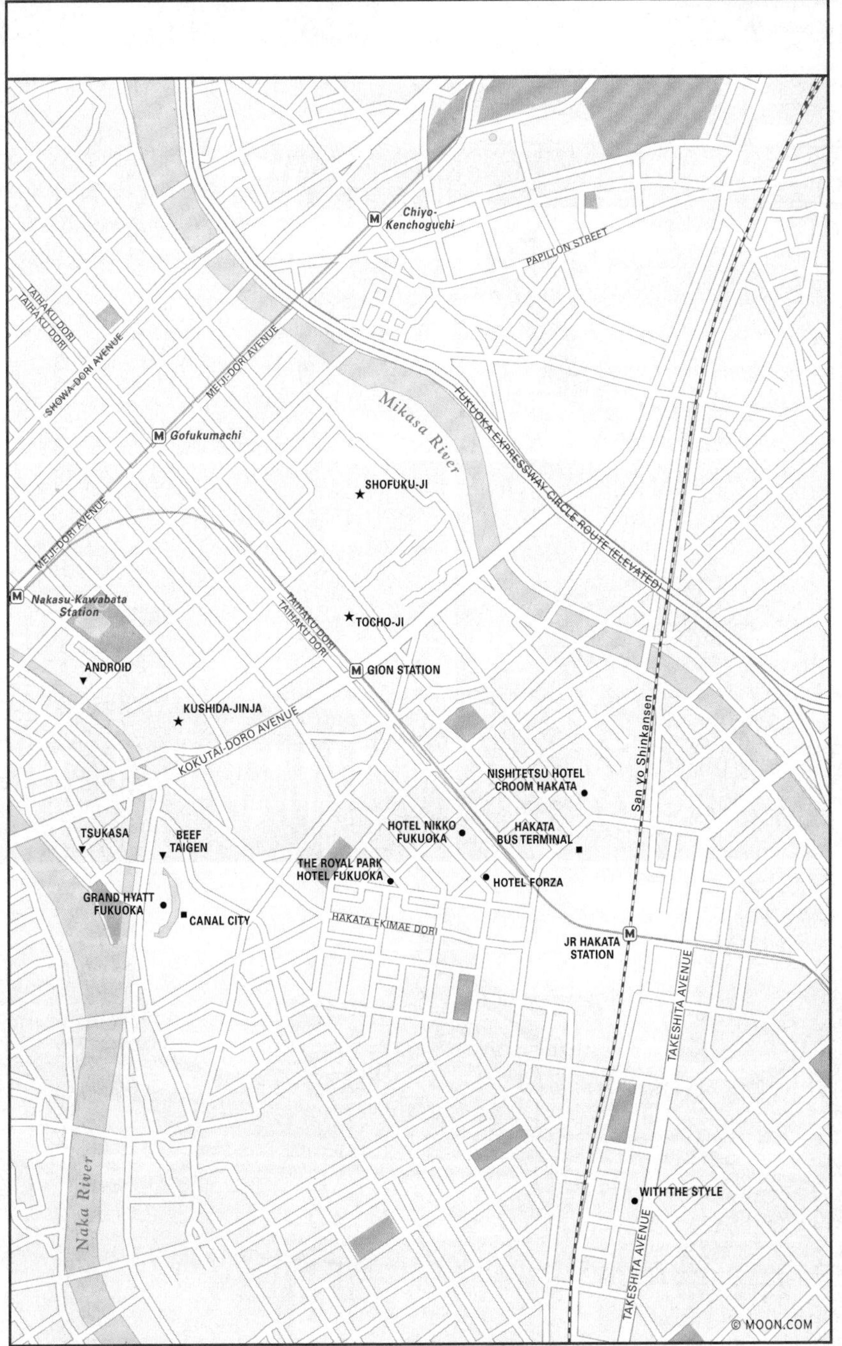

Chiyo-Kenchoguchi
PAPILLON STREET
TAIHAKU DORI
TAIHAKU DORI
SHOWA-DORI AVENUE
MEIJI-DORI AVENUE
Mikasa River
FUKUOKA EXPRESSWAY CIRCLE ROUTE (ELEVATED)
Gofukumachi
SHOFUKU-JI
MEIJI-DORI AVENUE
Nakasu-Kawabata Station
TAIHAKU DORI
TAIHAKU DORI
TOCHO-JI
ANDROID
GION STATION
KUSHIDA-JINJA
KOKUTAI-DORO AVENUE
San yo Shinkansen
NISHITETSU HOTEL CROOM HAKATA
HOTEL NIKKO FUKUOKA
HAKATA BUS TERMINAL
TSUKASA
BEEF TAIGEN
THE ROYAL PARK HOTEL FUKUOKA
HOTEL FORZA
GRAND HYATT FUKUOKA
CANAL CITY
HAKATA EKIMAE DORI
JR HAKATA STATION
TAKESHITA AVENUE
Naka River
WITH THE STYLE
TAKESHITA AVENUE
© MOON.COM

1
2
3
4

eyes peeled for a visual depiction of heaven, bathed in soft light. This imaginary journey into the Buddhist underworld is unexpectedly stirring.

KUSHIDA-JINJA
櫛田神社

1-41 Kamikawabatamachi, Hakata-ku; tel. 092/291-2951; www.jinja.in/single/63655.html; 8am-6pm daily; free; take the subway to Gion or Nakasu station

This compact shrine, also known as Okushida-san, is viewed by locals as the spiritual heart and guardian of the city. Thought to have been founded in 757, the shrine is devoted to the god Ohata Nushima-Mikoto, believed to be an ancestor of the Watarai line of priests who preside over Shinto's holiest of holies, Mie Prefecture's Ise Jingu. The shrine comes to the fore during the famed Hakata Gion Yamakasa Matsuri, held during the first half of July every year.

Most believers come to pray for prosperity and a long life. Appropriately, there's a millennium-old gingko tree in the shrine's courtyard and a number of stones said to have been anchors used on the ships of the would-be Mongol invaders, although they were more than likely used aboard Chinese trading fleets. Also take a peek at the *tengu* masks displayed in the main shrine building, with noses so long they put Pinocchio to shame.

FUKUOKA ASIAN ART MUSEUM
福岡アジア美術館

7-8F Riverain Center Bldg. 7, 3-1 Shimokawabatamachi, Hakata-ku; tel. 092/263-1100; http://faam.city.fukuoka.lg.jp; 10am-7:30pm Thurs.-Tues.; ¥200 adults, ¥150 students

This renowned collection of Asian art offers a glimpse of sculptures and paintings created by artists across more than 20 Asian countries, from India and Pakistan to Myanmar and Japan. There are nearly 3,000 works from the late 19th century, comprising the permanent collection, with regularly changing special exhibitions.

Past exhibitions have ranged from woodcut prints emblazoned with anticolonial imagery to paintings made from ivory and painted glass. These special exhibitions charge a separate admission fee. There's good English signage throughout. The museum is located on the seventh and eighth floors of the Hakata Riverain shopping mall.

Momochi

FUKUOKA CITY MUSEUM
福岡市博物館

3-1-1 Momochihama, Sawara-ku; tel. 092/845-5011; http://museum.city.fukuoka.jp; 9:30am-5:30pm Tues.-Sun.; ¥200; take the Kuku subway line to Nishijin Station

Fukuoka has a long history of trade and exchange with the rest of Asia, particularly via Korea and China. This museum elucidates this past and provides ample English signage in 11 galleries. A relic of note is the gold seal gifted to a diplomat in AD 57 by Emperor Gwang Wu of Han Dynasty China. Discovered in Hakata Bay in 1784, it indicates just how far back Japan's ties go with its ancient neighbor to the west.

FUKUOKA TOWER
福岡タワ

2-3-26 Momochihama, Sawara-ku; tel. 092/823-0234; www.fukuokatower.co.jp/en; 9:30am-10pm daily; ¥800 adults, ¥500 ages 6-15, ¥200 ages 4-5; take Kūkō subway line to Nishijin Station, then walk 18 minutes north of exit 1

At 243 meters (797 feet) tall, this largely vacant broadcast tower beside Hakata Bay in the Momochi district was built in 1989 to celebrate Fukuoka City's 100th anniversary. It's the city's loftiest structure and Japan's highest coastal tower. Its three-story observation deck hovers 123 meters (403 feet) above the ground, affording good views of the city and bay.

1: Shofuku-ji **2:** Tōchō-ji **3:** Fukuoka Tower at night **4:** Kushida-jinja

SPORTS AND RECREATION

Fukuoka is touted as one of the most livable cities, not only in Japan but in the world. **Fukuoka Walks** (https://fukuokawalks.com) helps visitors to get a sense of the city, through city walking tours, food tours, and everything in between, offered by friendly English-speaking guides. Fukuoka's livability also seems justified by the many parks and rural island escapes nearby. Among the plethora of options, the following are the most accessible and worthwhile.

Ōhori-kōen

1-2 Ohorikōen, Chūō-ku; tel. 092/741-2004; www.ohorikouen.jp; take Kūkō subway line to Ōhori-kōen Station, then walk 5 minutes southwest; 24/7; free

Essentially Fukuoka's Central Park, this expansive green zone, built from 1926 to 1929, in the heart of downtown wraps around a large central pond that once served as the moat to Fukuoka Castle. The park took its design cues from Hangzhou, China's West Lake. Three islands in the pond are linked to the rest of the park by tastefully hewn stone bridges.

Located within the park is the expansive **Ōhori-kōen Japanese Garden,** (1-7 Ōhorikōen; tel. 092/741-8377; 9am-6pm Tues.-Sun. Jun.-Aug., 9am-5pm Sept.-May; ¥240 adults, ¥120 children), which sits within a walled-in space of 12,000 square meters (129,166 square feet). Behind the white-plaster walls, streams, a waterfall, a sizable pond, teahouses, a dry garden, and more set the scene, which was created by Nakane Kinsaku, the famed garden architect who also conjured the beautiful gardens of Shimane Prefecture's Adachi Museum and Kyoto's Nijo-jō. Across the street, roughly 150 meters (492 feet) southeast of the garden sits Gokoku-jinja, a golden shrine approached via a path that leads you through mammoth tori gate.

Bay Islands

NOKONOSHIMA

http://nokonoshima.com; take Kūkō subway line to Meinohama Station, then ride Nishitetsu bus from Meinohama-eki Kitaguchi (in front of station's north exit) to Meinohama ferry terminal (10 minutes; ¥230); or take bus 300 or 301 from Nishitetsu Tenjin bus terminal to Meinohama ferry terminal (15 minutes; ¥360); from Meihnohama, take ferry to island (10 minutes; ¥230)

For a breather from the city, this lovely island is about 10 minutes away by ferry. With a circumference of 12 km (7.5 mi), the island is lined with walking paths that offer lovely views of the sea and Fukuoka's skyline across the bay.

On the north side, **Nokonoshima Island Park** (1624 Noko, Nishi, Nishi-ku; http://nokonoshima.com/en; 9am-5:30pm Mon.-Sat., 9am-6:30pm Sun., and holidays Mar.-Nov.; ¥1,200 adults, ¥600 elementary and junior high school students, ¥400 3 years and older) is swathed in flowers that change with the seasons. Yellow rape blossoms and pink cherry blossoms explode with color in spring. Cosmos bloom in the first half of October, camellias pop from December to early February, Japanese narcissus petals open in January and early February, and scarlet sage blooms from August to early December.

Next to the ferry terminal on Nokonoshima, **Noko Market** rents bicycles (¥300 per hour, ¥1,000 per day). You can also pick up an English map here. To reach the island, take bus 300 or 301 from Nishitetsu Tenjin bus terminal to Meinohama Municipal Ferry Port (20 minutes; ¥360).

SHIKANOSHIMA

take bus 46 or 90 from Hakata bus terminal to Hakata Wharf at Bayside Place, then take ferry (15 minutes; ¥670)

Another nearby island, Shikanoshima is a great place to go for cycling and seafood. While it fills up in summer, it's less touristy than Nokoshima, where the flowers of Island Park often bring the masses. Rent a bicycle at **Shikashima Cycle** (417-1 Shikashima, Higashi-ku; tel. 050/3459-2956; http://shikashima-cycle.com; 9am-6pm Wed-Mon; ¥2,000 three hours), located near the ferry terminal. There's a café attached to the shop that serves good drinks and light meals. To reach this island, hop on the ferry from Bayside Place (30 minutes; ¥670 one way).

A caveat: You will not be permitted to visit the island's rustic **Shikaumi Shrine** (877 Shikanoshima, Higashi-ku; tel. 092/603-6501; 6am-5:30pm daily) if you're pregnant, traveling with a baby less than 100 days old, menstruating, or in mourning. These somewhat off-putting restrictions are based on a very ancient Shinto tradition, dating from times when Japan was more of a man's world. However, if none of these restrictions applies to you, you will enjoy this sight, set in a forest with views of the bay and dedicated to the three sea gods.

FESTIVALS AND EVENTS

HAKATA YAMAKASA GION MATSURI
博多祇園山笠

www.hakatayamakasa.com; July 1-15; free

Fukuoka's biggest festival centers around Kushida-jinja (1-41 Kamikawabatamachi, Hakata-ku; tel. 092/291-2951; www.jinja.in/single/63655.html; 8am-6pm daily; free), a compact shrine, also known as Okushida-san, viewed by locals as the spiritual heart and guardian of the city. A festive atmosphere builds July 10-14, with parades and practice runs taking place, until 4:59am on July 15, when seven teams of men—one for each of Hakata's seven districts—clad in loincloth-like *fundoshi* transport multilevel floats known as *yamakasa*, which depict figures and scenes from the city's past, on their shoulders in a procession starting from Kushida-jinja. The smaller sized floats stand 5 meters (16 feet) tall and weigh a ton; the larger ones stand twice as high and weigh a whopping two tons.

Up to around 30 team members hoist these massive floats at any given time, while three or four team members ride up top, directing the changing of team members when they spot specific members starting to flag. The festival is said to have been inspired by the story of Shoichi Kokushi, a 13th-century Buddhist priest, who was said to have been carried through town on a platform so that he could pray and toss holy water onto the populace, which was suffering from a plague. Today, the raucous proceedings involve a lot of noise and a lot of water being doused onto the profusely sweating teams as they move through the streets.

The viewing areas near Kushida-jinja fill up many hours early, but it's possible to see the event elsewhere along the route, including the intersection of Meiji-dōri and Higashimachi-suji, which affords views of the oncoming teams at a distance, and Showa-dōri and Taihaku-dōri, where it's possible to glimpse each float pass by twice, running along parallel lanes.

HOJŌYA
放生会

1-22-1 Hakozaki, Higashi-ku; tel. 092/641-7431; www.hakozakigu.or.jp/omatsuri/houjoya; 10am-10pm Sept. 12-18; free

Another of Fukuoka's great festivals, Hojoya takes place from September 12-18 every year. More than a million people flock to the grounds of **Hakozaki-gu** to thank the gods for nature's blessings, and to pray for success in business and safety for family members. Some 500 food, drink, and game stalls line the path leading up to the shrine, and a lively atmosphere pervades for the duration of the event. To experience the festival in full swing, aim to arrive in the evening, especially on the weekend days.

KYŪSHŪ BASHŌ SUMO TOURNAMENT

www.sumo.or.jp; mid-Nov.; seats ¥3,500-15,000

Every year in mid-November, a sumo bash takes place at the **Fukuoka Kokusai Center** (2-2 Chikko Honmachi, Hakata-ku; tel. 092/272-1111; www.marinemesse.or.jp/kokusai). Tickets are same-day only, and fans start lining up at the complex around daybreak to snag them.

SHOPPING

Tenjin

WATANABE-DŌRI

All the big-name *depaato* (department stores) line a three-block stretch of this busy thoroughfare in Tenjin. Peruse the shops at these stores if you're interested in glitz and big-name brands. True to the Japanese *depaato* tradition, the basement food courts are also a revelation.

Starting from the intersection of Shōwa-dōri and Watanabe-dōri, there's **mina tenjin** (4-3-8 Tenjin, Chūō-ku; tel. 092/713-3711 www.mina-tenjin.com; 10am-8pm daily). Next, you'll come to **Tenjin Core** (1-11-11 Tenjin, Chūō-ku; tel. 092/721-8436; www.tenjincore.com; 10am-8pm daily) and **IMS Tenjin** (1-7-11 Tenjin, Chūō-ku; tel. 092/733-2001; http://ims-tenjin.jp; 10am-8pm daily), both on the left side of the street as you move south.

Veer to the west here and you'll come to the **Solaria Plaza** (2-2-43 Tenjin, Chūō-ku; tel. 092/733-7777; www.solariaplaza.com; 10am-10:30pm daily) and the 260-year-old **Iwataya** (2-5-35 Tenjin, Chūō-ku; tel. 092/721-1111; www.i.iwataya-mitsukoshi.co.jp; 10am-8pm daily) on the left. Backtrack to Watanabe-dōri and turn right. A few minutes' walk brings you to **Daimaru** (1-4-1 Tenjin, Chūō-ku; tel. 092/712-8181; www.daimaru.co.jp/fukuoka; 10am-8pm daily), another *depaato* stalwart.

DAIMYŌ

For a more boutique, youth-oriented vibe, walk about 10 minutes west of Tenjin to Daimyō, an enclave of cool. This is Fukuoka's more mature—think 20s through mid-30s—answer to Harajuku, minus the ultra-*kawaii* schoolgirl chic. The neighborhood is brimming with inventive little cafés, purveyors of fashion, restaurants, and bars.

Hakata

CANAL CITY

1-2 Sumiyoshi, Hakata-ku; tel. 092/282-2525; https://canalcity.co.jp; 10am-9pm daily

This sprawling mecca of commerce—the city's largest mall—was created by Jon Jerde, who also designed Tokyo's mammoth urban renewal project, Roppongi Hills. Like its Tokyo counterpart, Canal City has everything you could imagine under one roof: a multiplex cinema with capacity for more than 2,500, hotels, eateries, bars, some 250 name-brand shops and, as the name suggests, a manmade canal in its inner courtyard. Here, fountains of water spray skyward every 30 minutes and there's a light show every evening.

FOOD

No other city in Japan is more closely associated with street food than Fukuoka. *Yatai* spill into byways across town from evening into the booze-fueled wee hours, with many only closing on Sunday. As evening falls, locals pile in, elbow to elbow, dipping chopsticks into bowls of *tonkotsu* ramen (served in a rich pork-bone broth), sipping offal stew and plucking grilled chunks of meat and vegetables from skewers.

Tenjin

YATAI MAMI-CHAN

2-2 Tenjin, Chūō-ku; tel. 090/1921-0389; http://yataimamichan.daa.jp; 6pm-1:30am Mon.-Sat.

Situated right on Shōwa-dōri on the backside of Fukuoka Honten Bank, this welcoming street food stall is run by the amiable Mami-chan herself. She loves to welcome foreign travelers and even has a website and an English menu. Good picks include roast pork and the spicy Chinese favorite, *mabo tofu*.

MUNE

4-10-10 Watanabe-dōri, Chūō-ku; tel. 090/8665-1692; 7pm-2am Mon.-Sat.

Another good food stall choice in the Tenjin area is Mune, about 8 minutes' walk south of Yatai Mami-chan. It's located on the *yatai* stronghold of Watanabe-dōri. Try the mentai *tamagoyaki* (rolled omelet stuffed with Pollock roe), followed by a piping bowl of rich Hakata ramen topped with pickled ginger, sesame seeds, and pork.

1: street stalls in Fukuoka **2:** Chikae **3:** ramen chain Ippudo

1

2

3

The Capital of *Tonkotsu* Ramen

The northern hub of Sapporo is renowned for its ramen, served in a hearty miso-infused broth and topped with butter and corn. Meanwhile, almighty Tokyo is the undisputed king of variety and quality of all things culinary, including the beloved noodle dish. But few would dispute the notion that the southern metropolis of Fukuoka—more specifically, Hakata—is the *tonkotsu* ramen capital of Japan.

Fukuoka's flag was firmly planted on the noodle map thanks to Hakata's widely loved spin on ramen, which was originally created on the city's east side in the mid-20th century. Although the downhome dish was first meant to serve as fuel for those working tough shifts in the city's seafood markets, today, feasting on a bowl of *tonkotsu* is a de rigueur experience for any visit to Fukuoka.

Tonkotsu's cloudy, flavor-laden broth is made by cooking pork bones, cuts of fatback, and other ingredients for upwards of 12 hours. Once served, it can be positively frothy, afloat with drops of fat. It proves too much for some; for others, it's heavenly. Ramen hunters in the know often order their noodles *katame* (firm), akin to al dente, as the thin strands quickly soften in the piping-hot soup. If you want a heaping portion, you can call for *kaedama,* or noodle refill that many shops offer for free or cheap.

Besides noodles, a proper bowl of *tonkotsu* is loaded with *cha-shu* (pork strips), hard-boiled egg marinated in soy sauce, and a generous sprinkling of piquant spring onion. Other condiments often arrayed around the counter of a *tonkotsu* joint include but are not limited to grinders full of roasted sesame seeds, pickled mustard greens, *beni-shōga* (ginger with a reddish hue), roasted sheets of seaweed, chili paste, and raw garlic cloves that you can press straight into your bowl.

WHERE TO TRY IT

Appropriately, Fukuoka is home to the main shops of nationwide chains **Ichiran** (5-3-2 Nakasu; tel. 092/262-0433; www.ichiran.co.jp; 24/7; from ¥790), operating since 1960 and widely considered the first *tonkotsu* ramen-dedicated shop in Japan, and **Ippudo** (1-13-14 Daimyō, Chūō-ku; tel. 092/771-0880; from ¥720), a wildly popular chain in business since 1985 that has begun to pop up overseas in recent years.

This barely scratches the surface. The city is home to a few thousand ramen shops, according to some estimates. To get acquainted, take your pick from among the surfeit of ***yatai*** (street-food stalls) and mom-and-pop shops where cauldrons of pungent, fatty broth simmer around the clock.

SHIN SHIN (TENJIN BRANCH)

3-2-19 Tenjin, Chūō-ku; tel. 092/732-4006; www.hakata-shinshin.com; 11am-3am Mon.-Sat.; ¥650-950; take the Kūkō subway line to Tenjin Station, then walk 3 minutes, or take the Nishitetsu-Tenjin Omuta line to Nishitetsu Fukuoka (Tenjin) Station and walk 5 minutes

This is one of Fukuoka locals' favorite Hakata (*tonkotsu*) ramen joints, as indicated by the occasionally long lines and flurry of celebrity autographs adorning the walls. The soup, somewhat tame by Fukuoka standards, is complemented nicely by well-seasoned slabs of soft pork. There's an English menu, which also includes other delicious dishes like the miso *chanpon,* in which noodles are boiled directly in the miso-based soup.

TAIHO RAMEN

1-23-8 Imaizumi, Chūō-ku; tel. 092/738-3277; www.taiho.net; 11am-midnight daily; ¥600-930; take the Nanakuma subway line to Tenjin-minami, then walk 4 minutes

For an even stronger broth, head to this Taiho Ramen outpost in Tenjin-imaizumi. The original shop is located south of the city in the suburb of Kurume, but the noodles and creamy soup are legit here, too. The soup is milky, even frothy. This is another great bowl and a good option about 10 minutes' walk south of Shin Shin in case the latter has a long queue.

☆ Fukuoka's Street Food Stalls

The lively street food scene in Fukuoka adds to the city's inviting atmosphere. Some 150 of these makeshift dining rooms, called *yatai*, dot the city, each one generally seating anywhere from six to nine patrons at a time. Each is fronted by a red lantern indicating its specialty, whether it's ramen, yakitori, or any other food creation that lends itself well to a quick bite and an accompanying beer. For most of the year they are open to the elements. Thin plastic sheets in place of walls soften the bite of the cold during winter. Most are concentrated around the crossing of **Tenjin Shishi-dōri** and **Shōwa-dōri,** west of the Nakagawa, as well as the southwestern bank of **Nakasu Island.**

Picking a *yatai* is usually about where you are, what you feel like, or what smells good; here are a few excellent stalls to get you started:

- **Yatai Mami-chan** (Tenjin, page 614)
- **Mune** (Tenjin, page 614)
- **Tsukasa** (Nakasu, page 618)

MENGEKIJO GENEI

2-16-3 Yakuin, Chūō-ku; tel. 092/732-6100; 11:30am-2:30pm and 6pm-10:30pm Mon.-Sat., 11:30am-5pm and 6pm-10pm Sun.; ¥1,000; take the Nanakuma subway line to Yakuin-ōdōri station, then walk 5 minutes northwest

For a quality bowl of *tonkotsu* ramen in a quirky setting, come to this "noodle theater," as the restaurant's name literally translates. The seating area in this amphitheater-like space is oriented so that diners face the kitchen, akin to a stage where the chef's cooking is the performance. The broth here really packs a flavorsome punch that can be kicked up a notch with the signature sauce.

★ CHIKAE

2-2-17 Daimyō; tel. 092/721-4624; https://chikae.co.jp; 5pm-10pm Mon.-Fri., 11:30am-10pm Sat.-Sun. and public holidays; a la carte from ¥800, lunch sets ¥3,000, dinner courses ¥5,000-20,000; take the Kūkō subway line to Akasaka Station, then walk 5 minutes

This local institution has been doing brisk business since 1961. The first floor is a buzzing hive of fish consumption, with seats for 200 surrounding a central counter made of gingko wood. Fish are plucked straight from rows of tanks in the center of the main counter, as kimono-clad servers attend to customers and an army of cooks assemble slap-up seafood feasts in the kitchen beyond. Order various items a la carte, from sashimi to hot pot, or try one of the good-value lunch sets. Expect to wait in line, especially at lunch time. Private rooms available by reservation.

FISHMAN

1-4-23 Imaizumi, Chūō-ku; 092/717-3571; www.m-and-co.net/fishman; 11:30am-2:30pm and 5:30pm-midnight daily; ¥680-2,300; take the Nanakuma line or Nishitetsu-Tenjin Omuta line to Yakuin Station, then walk 6 minutes

Another great seafood option, this shop is stylish and inviting, with its interior of warm wood and minimal industrial lighting. The chefs in the open kitchen whip up dishes with an innovative spin, and creatively present them too, as seen in the spiral wooden staircase-like platters of sashimi. Staff speak some English and can help with the menu.

STEREO COFFEE

3-8-3 Watanabe-dōri, Chūō-ku; tel. 092/231-8854; http://stereo.jpn.com; 8am-10pm daily, closed every second Wed; drinks ¥350-680, dishes ¥550-680

This indie standing-only coffee shop is a great spot for a caffeine hit. The coffee menu includes an impressive range of beans, which are all freshly ground. There's also a great sound system, and DJ and part-owner Yusuke Watanabe provides a steady stream of smooth tunes. The second floor serves as an art gallery, exhibiting work by budding artists. They also serve hot sandwiches.

Nakasu Island

★ TSUKASA

1-8 Nakasu, Hakata-ku; tel. 092/413-9248; www.yatai-tsukasa.com; 5:30pm-1am daily

In the Nakasu Island area, Tsukasa is a wonderful food stall that sits beside the waterfront along the southwestern bank. Admittedly, it's known to occasionally attract a queue of tourists, but the pull of its setting on the waterfront and its classic *yatai* ambience cannot be denied. The menu has everything from grilled asparagus and pork to fantastic cod-roe tempura. For ambience alone, this stretch of riverfront is the best place to go for full *yatai* immersion. Pick any stall that draws your attention, order some food with your booze of choice, and enjoy the friendly chatter with curious locals. You won't go wrong.

Hakata

TORIDEN HAKATA HONTEN

10-5 Shimokawabata-machi, Hakata-ku; tel. 092/272-0920; https://toriden.com; 11:30am-11pm daily; lunches ¥2,800, dinner courses ¥3,800-4,800; take the Hakozaki or Kūkō subway line to Nakasu-Kawabata Station, then walk 3 minutes

It takes six hours to make the creamy soup used in the excellent *mizutaki* (chicken hot pot) at this Kyūshū-centric restaurant, which sources all ingredients from the island. First, eat vegetables and chicken cooked in the delicious broth at your table. Finish with either *zosui* (rice porridge) or ramen noodles. The portions are generous, too. Recommended.

BEEF TAIGEN

1-2-1 Sumiyoshi, Hakata-ku; tel. 092/283-4389; www.taigen.jp; 11:30am-10pm daily; dishes ¥1,000-2,500; courses ¥11,000; take the Kūkō subway line to Gion Station, then walk 10 minutes

This stylish *yakiniku* (barbecue) joint serves only high-grade beef from Kagoshima Prefecture, along with side salads, miso soup, rice, and various vegetable dishes. It gets crowded at lunchtime, when its much-loved sets—including beef sausage, breaded and deep-fried beef cutlets, and more—are sold for ¥1,200 each, but it's a bit less crowded at dinnertime.

Ōhori-kōen

YOROZU

2-3-32 Akasaka, Chūō-ku; tel. 092/724-7880; www.yorozu-tea.jp; 3pm-midnight Mon.-Sat.; tea and sweets sets ¥1,500-3,000

Yorozu does tea-tasting courses with traditional Japanese sweets, in a similar vein to Sakurai Tea Experience in Tokyo, where preparing tea is elevated to an art. This is a chic space that has a nice *wabi-sabi* (Japan's traditional answer to shabby-chic) vibe to it.

BARS AND NIGHTLIFE

A thick concentration of bars, clubs, and unsavory establishments aimed at tipsy businessmen with stratospheric expense accounts clog the island of Nakasu, along with cheap, friendly food stalls. It's certainly an interesting place to wander at night in urban-anthropologist fashion, but many of the bars on the island are exorbitantly priced and discriminate against foreign travelers without batting an eyelid. Friendlier, more reasonably priced bars and clubs line the streets of Tenjin, about 15 minutes' walk west of Nakasu. The thoroughfare of **Oyafukō-dōri** and the streets to its east are the heart of the action. That said, fun awaits in all corners of the city if you know where to look.

BPC Fukuoka (www.facebook.com/bpcfukuoka) is a fun way to explore Fukuoka's pub scene (BPC stands for "British Pub Crawl"). Run by a friendly Brit living in the city.

Tenjin

CITADEL

1-8-40 Daimyō, 2F, Chūō-ku; tel. 092/688-4190; www.facebook.com/citadeldaimyo; 5pm-3am Tues.-Sun.

This watering hole in the trendy, youth-centric

neighborhood of Daimyō is renowned for its coffee-based cocktails. Barman and master mixologist Yoshi incorporates everything from citrus accents to melon rum with coffee, and manages to balance all the elements perfectly.

THE DARK ROOM

3-4-15 Tenjin, Chūō-ku; tel. 092/725-2989; 8pm-3am daily

This industrial-chic bar is a good spot for fans of alternative and indie rock, with an impressive music library of about 50,000 songs. It's owned by an American who brings his kitchen chops to the fore from Thursday to Saturday, whipping up a menu from scratch. It gets hopping on Friday and Saturday nights.

ANMITSU HIME REVUE

2F MT 20 Bldg., 3-7-13 Tenjin, Chūō-ku; tel. 092/725-2550; www.okama.com; ¥4,500

Audience participation is a big part of the show at this revue. High-energy performers in glittery, frilly, flamboyant costumes dance, croon, and act out slapstick routines amid a cacophony of playfully exaggerated Japanese motifs. Although it's often billed as a drag queen show, both men and women perform, and while some of the humor is a touch bawdy, nothing is overtly inappropriate for kids. You won't understand anything spoken, but it won't matter. The show itself will mesmerize you, and the genuine vibe exuded by all performers will charm you and leave you beaming. It's tucked away on the second floor of a building on Oyafukō Street in the heart of Tenjin. Recommended.

Hakata

ANDROID

B1F Shin-Kawabata Bldg., 11-1 Kamikawabata-machi, Hakata-ku; tel. 092/291-2760; 6pm-1:30am Mon.-Fri., 7pm-1:30am Sat., 7pm-11:30pm Sun.

Sip cocktails or throw back a few shots to a thoughtfully curated electronic soundtrack at this subterranean hideout on the east side of the Naka-gawa. Soft lighting illuminates the space, which has a subtly sci-fi aesthetic. Comfy seating includes sofas and soft chairs.

ACCOMMODATIONS

Hakata

HOTEL FORZA

2-1-15 Hakata Ekimae, Hakata-ku; tel. 092/473-7113; www.hotelforza.jp/hakataguchi; ¥12,000 d; 5 minutes' walk from JR Hakata Station

This modern hotel just west of Hakata Station has clean, well-appointed rooms. Sitting on a quiet street, yet close to the action, this hotel is extremely convenient for exploring the city. The rooms are spacious and all are non-smoking. There's a good breakfast on offer, which includes both Japanese and Western fare.

NISHITETSU HOTEL CROOM HAKATA

1-17-6 Hakata Ekimae, Hakata-ku; tel. 092/413-5454; https://nnr-h.com/croom/hakata; ¥17,000 d; 5 minutes' walk north of JR Hakata Station

The bright, stylish rooms in this conveniently located modern hotel are on the petite side, but the hotel's other facilities shine, including a shared hot-spring to complement the well-stocked, though small, en-suite bathrooms. There are four restaurants on-site. Female-only floors available.

HOTEL OKURA FUKUOKA

3-2 Shimokawabata-machi, Hakata-ku; tel. 092/262-1111; www.fuk.hotelokura.co.jp; ¥17,500 d; take the Kūkō subway line to Nakasu-Kawabata Station, then walk 5 minutes

This elegant hotel sits just east of the Naka-gawa, near Canal City. Genial staff, including a very helpful concierge, are ready to help. Rooms are petite but well-appointed. On-site restaurants include Japanese and Chinese fare, a patisserie, and craft beer, and there's a health club with a pool (¥2,000 for a swim).

GRAND HYATT FUKUOKA

2-81-1 Sumiyoshi, Hakata-ku; tel. 092/282-1234; https://fukuoka.grand.hyatt.com/en/hotel/home.html; from ¥27,000 d; take the Hakozaki or Kūkō subway line to Nakasu-Kawabata Station, then walk 10 minutes south

Connected to Canal City, with chic, modern Japanese decor, this luxury hotel is a cut above most properties in the city. Its stylish, open rooms are relaxing and packed with amenities, including a range of dining options and a fitness center with indoor pool. To avoid paying out of pocket for breakfast and access to the fitness center (¥2,000 per person for each amenity), book a club room for around an extra ¥10,000. With a club room, you'll also get afternoon tea and cocktails in the rooftop lounge in the evening.

WITH THE STYLE

1-9-18 Hakataeki-minami, Hakata-ku; tel. 092/433-3900; www.withthestyle.com; ¥40,000 d; 8 minutes' walk southeast of JR Hakata Station

This is hands-down the city's most modish hotel. Step into the soothing lobby and feel the city fade away. Bathrooms are stocked with carefully chosen products. Each of the 16 suites has stylish, mid-20th-century American furniture, quirky artwork, and a complimentary minibar. All rooms have a space to chill, as well as a leafy balcony or terrace. The Penthouse serves complimentary breakfast and brunch (7am-1pm daily) and complimentary welcome drinks (4pm-midnight daily). There's also a guests-only rooftop spa-jacuzzi, available 24/7 by reservation only.

INFORMATION AND SERVICES

There are tourist information offices on the main concourse of **Hakata Station** (tel. 092/431-3003; 8am-9pm daily), on the ground floor of **Lion Plaza** in Tenjin (tel. 092/751-6904; 9:30am-7pm daily).

Fukuoka Now (www.fukuoka-now.com) is a great city-focused website and a free monthly print zine that can be picked up in a range of expat-friendly restaurants, shops, hotels, and tourist information centers. The media outfit has also created a good English-language map of the city, which is usually stocked alongside the magazine.

JR KYŪSHŪ TRAVEL AGENCY

1-1 Chūō-gai; tel. 092/431-6215; 10am-8pm Mon.-Sat., 10am-6pm Sun.

For assistance in English with making reservations and arranging various travel logistics within Kyūshū and elsewhere in Japan, stop by the JR Kyūshū Travel Agency, situated in JR Hakata Station.

INTERNATIONAL CLINIC TOJIN-MACHI

1-4-6 Jigyo, Chūō-ku; 9am-1pm and 2:30pm-5:30pm Mon.-Tues. and Thurs.-Fri., 9am-1pm Sat.; tel. 092/717-1000; www.internationalclinic.org

If the need for medical attention arises, a good option is the International Clinic Tojin-machi, a private clinic run by a general practitioner from the Netherlands, located a short walk east of Tojin-machi subway station on Meiji-dōri. The staff all speak English.

KYŪSHŪ MEDICAL CENTER

1-8-1 Jigyohama; tel. 092/852-0700; www.kyumed.jp

If you don't mind waiting with potentially large crowds of other patients for care, the Kyūshū Medical Center has English-speaking doctors on staff.

TRANSPORTATION

Getting There

TRAIN

A slightly confounding fact: Fukuoka has no main station called Fukuoka. Instead, the main terminal is found slightly east of the heart of town at **JR Hakata Station,** named after the former city of Hakata on the eastern banks of the Naka-gawa. JR Hakata Station is served by the *shinkansen,* meaning that it's possible to travel all the way to the city by bullet train from the hubs of Kansai—**Kyoto** (2 hours 45 minutes; ¥16,060), **Osaka** (2 hours 30 minutes; ¥15,310) and beyond—**Tokyo** (5 hours; ¥22,950), or even farther north.

JR Hakata Station is also where the Kyūshū *shinkansen* line starts, linking the city to hubs deeper into the island, from **Saga** (40 minutes; ¥2,450), **Kumamoto** (40 minutes; ¥5,130) and **Kagoshima's** main hub, Kagoshima Chūō Station (1 hour 40 minutes; ¥5,510). To reach **Nagasaki,** take the Kamome Limited Express train from Hakata (2 hours; ¥4,710).

From Fukuoka's **Nishitetsu-Fukuoka Station** in Tenjin, on the west side of the Naka-gawa, you can access many smaller towns on the island, including **Dazaifu** (30 minutes; ¥400), via Nishitetsu-Futsukaichi Station.

AIR

Given its position in the south of Japan, flying into Fukuoka may be a good option, depending on where you're coming from. **Fukuoka Airport** (www.fuk-ab.co.jp)—split into a domestic wing (tel. 092/621-6059) and an international wing (tel. 092/483-7007)—is surprisingly close to downtown, too. The domestic terminal is served by flights from all over the country, while the international terminal is covered by airlines around East and Southeast Asia.

You can access downtown from the domestic terminal by simply hopping on the **subway,** which is a mere 5 minutes' ride from Hakata Station (¥260) and just over 10 minutes to Tenjin (¥260). Free **shuttle buses** link the international terminal to the domestic one (15 minutes). Alternatively, you can take a **bus** from the international terminal to JR Hakata Station (15 minutes; ¥260) or Nishitetsu-Fukuoka Station (30 minutes; ¥310).

BUS

Highway buses service the **Nishitetsu Tenjin Bus Terminal** (2-1-1 Tenjin, Chuo-ku; tel. 0570/001-010), near Nishitetsu-Fukuoka Station, and the **Hakata Bus Terminal** (aka Hakata Kōtsū Center; 2 Hakataekichūōgai, Hakata-ku; tel. 0120/489-939), adjacent to JR Hakata Station. Given the length of the journey and relatively modest monetary savings, taking the train or even flying is a more appealing option if you're coming from other regions of Japan. That said, traveling to or from Fukuoka by highway bus may be an option worth considering for trips within Kyūshū. For detailed timetables and routes, visit www.nishitetsu.jp/en/highway_bus.

FERRY

Underscoring just how near South Korea is to Fukuoka, the city is linked to Busan, South Korea, by a convenient daily ferry departing from **Hakata Port International Terminal** (14-1 Okihama-machi; tel. 092/282-4871; www.hakataport.com), which can be reached by **bus no. 88,** which leaves from bus stop F in front of JR Hakata Station, or **bus no. 80** at bust stop 2A in front of Tenjin Solaria Stage (2-11-3 Tenjin, Chūō-ku; tel. 092/733-7111).

Ferry operator **Beetle** operates hydrofoils three times a day from Hakata to Busan (www.jrbeetle.co.jp; 3 hours; ¥13,000 one way, ¥26,000 return), and the **Camelia Line** (www.camellia-line.co.jp; 5 hours 30 minutes; from ¥9,000 one way, ¥17,100 return) trundles along the same route at a more moderate speed, departing once daily at 12:30pm.

Getting Around

Fukuoka is easily navigable by subway and **on foot.** The easy-to-use **subway** has three lines, the most convenient being the **Kūkō line,** running from the airport's domestic terminal through the heart of the city with stops at Hakata and Tenjin (http://subway.city.fukuoka.lg.jp; single rides from ¥200, one-day pass ¥620 adults, ¥310 children).

There's also a **bus network** (www.nishitetsu.jp/en/bus) running through town (¥100 flat rate for single rides within city center, including Hakata and Tenjin; one-day pass ¥900). Convenient stops include the **Hakata Bus Terminal** (aka Hakata Kōtsū Center; 2 Hakataekichūōgai, Hakata-ku; tel. 0120/489-939), next to JR Hakata Station, and **Nishitetsu Tenjin Bus Terminal** (2-1-1 Tenjin, Chuo-ku; tel. 0570-001-010), near Nishitetsu-Fukuoka Station.

☆ Saga's Pottery Towns

A rural patchwork of charming villages and terraced rice fields leading down to the sea, the Saga Prefecture's good clay makes renowned pottery, from exquisite porcelain tea cups to earth-tone jars. The prefecture's famous ceramics come predominantly from historic kilns in the towns of Karatsu, Imari, and perhaps most famous of all, Arita, where the first porcelain was produced in Japan.

KARATSU

Collectively, Karatsu's ceramics are known as Karatsu-yaki (Karatsu ware). From humble earthen vases to showpieces by renowned potters that cost as much as a car, the exquisite wares produced in Karatsu are fired at 1,000°C (1,832°F), then coated in heavy glaze with earthy brown or black coloration. Other pieces are covered with white glaze with a cracked finish and adorned with floral patterns.

Stop by **Nakazato Tarōemon Shop and Kiln** (3-6-29 Chōda; tel. 0955/72-8171; www.nakazato-tarouemon.com; 9am-5:30pm Thurs.-Tues.). Although master potter Nakazato Tarōemon (1923-2009) has passed, the Nakazato family's shop, which doubles as a gallery and museum, is the most accessible of the 30 or so studios and kilns dotting Karatsu. There are plenty of antique pieces dating to the early days of Karatsu's exquisite pottery tradition. After taking in the visual feast of the shop, cross the street and check out the kiln.

To reach Karatsu from Fukuoka, hop on the Kūkō (Airport) subway line at either Tenjin or Hakata station and ride for about 15 minutes to Meinohama. Here, you'll either transfer to the JR Chikuhi line or simply stay put on the train you started on— it varies by train—and ride the rest of the way to JR Karatsu Station (total trip: 1 hour 20 minutes; ¥1,140).

IMARI

Tiles form blue and white motifs of dragons, flowers, and geometric patterns on Inari's signs, walls, and bridges. The town is known for its more delicate approach to porcelain: situated next to the sea, Imari was the port from which finished pieces crafted in Saga Prefecture were sent for distribution throughout Japan and the world beyond. Among collectors, porcelain that reached the outside world via Imari that dates to the Edo period (1603-1868) is now referred to as Koimari (Old Imari).

The first floor of the **Ceramic Merchant's Residence Museum** (555-1 Imari-chō Ko; 10am-5pm Tues.-Sun.; free) exhibits a precious collection of antique Koimari dating to the 18th and 19th centuries. For a fuller appreciation of Imariware's refined beauty, leave downtown and head to **Ōkawachiyama Village** (www.imari-ookawachiyama.com), one of the region's two

DAZAIFU
太宰府

For a dose of history close to the city of Fukuoka, head to Dazaifu, an ancient town set against a backdrop of sylvan slopes. Dazaifu was once the locus of administrative affairs for Kyūshū, and today its legacy is seen in the handful of important religious complexes strewn throughout the town. Founded in the late 7th century, the town was the island's administrative hub for more than five centuries, with the port of Hakata to the north serving as an important point of contact with the rest of Asia.

Chief among the town's various sacred sites is Dazaifu Tenmangu, a shrine famed for its plum blossoms in early spring that honors the exalted scholar and poet Sugawara Michizane. The other main attraction in the town is the excellent Kyūshū National Museum, which offers an insightful glimpse into the island's history and heritage. The town makes for a pleasant day trip from Fukuoka or a stop en route to Nagasaki.

major production sites, and stroll streets lined with some 30 galleries and workshops, as well as cafés and eateries.

Buses run from Imari Station to Ōkawachiyama roughly once ever two hours (15 minutes; ¥170). If there's a long wait until the next bus, taking a taxi will set you back about ¥1,800. Or, if you feel like exploring the area on your own two feet, it's roughly a 1-hour walk southeast of Imari Station. Imari is easily reached from Karatsu via the JR Chikuhi line (50 minutes; ¥650). If you're coming from Arita, take the Matsūra-tetsudō line (25 minutes; ¥460). Note that this private line isn't covered by the JR pass. Once you've arrived at Imari, either take a bus (¥170), which shuttles to and from the station about five times daily, or a taxi (one-way about ¥2,000) to the Ōkawachiyama pottery district.

Arita porcelain

ARITA

The region's relationship with the clay arts began here in 1615, when a Korean potter named Ri Sampei uncovered kaolin clay, a necessary mineral for making porcelain, in the mountains just outside town. Lee's discovery was followed by an influx of Koreans who also set up shop. Early porcelain produced in the town was mostly blue and white, often with floral motifs. The style evolved into the more vividly colorful Kakiemon style, which caught the eye of European traders by the mid-17th century.

The **Kyūshū Ceramic Museum** (3100-1 Toshaku, Nishimatsuura-gun; tel. 0955/43-3681; http://saga-museum.jp/ceramic; 9am-5pm Tues.-Sun.; free) is the best overall introduction to Kyūshū's illustrious history with the clay arts. **Kakiemon Kiln** (Tei-352 Nanzan, Nishimatsuura-gun; tel. 0955/43-2267; http://kakiemon.co.jp; 9am-5pm daily; free), **Kouraku Kiln** (Hei-2512 Maruno; tel. 0955/42-4121; http://kouraku-kiln.com; 8am-5pm Mon.-Sat.; free) and **Imaemon Gallery** (2-1-15 Akaemachi, Nishimatsuura-gun; tel. 0955/42-3101; www.imaemon.co.jp; 8am-5pm daily, closed first Sun. of month; free) are all excellent places to see porcelain as a living art.

Coming from Imari, take the Matsūra-tetsudō line to Arita Station (25 minutes; ¥460). Starting in Fukuoka, hop on the limited express train, bound for Sasebo, at Hakata Station (about 1 hour 15 minutes; ¥3,270).

Sights

DAZAIFU TENMAN-GŪ
太宰府天満宮

4-7-1 Saifu; tel. 092/922-8225; www.dazaifutenmangu.or.jp; 6:30am-7pm daily; free; take the Nishitetsu line to Dazaifu Station, then walk 5 minutes east

If you're studying for an exam, you'd be wise to visit this shrine, dedicated to Tenman-Tenjin, the god of scholarship. Tenjin is actually the deified form of poet, politician, and scholar Sugawara no Michizane (845-903), the first person in Japan's history to be elevated to divinity after dying in exile in Dazaifu, where he was banished after his great gifts began to create tensions with the ruling Fujiwara clan in Kyoto. Soon after the great scholar's death, Japan suffered a series of natural calamities, which people began to suspect were being inflicted by Michinaze's angry spirit. People began to make offerings to his spirit in an effort to appease him. Thus, the practice of worshipping at Tenmangū shrines was born.

This sprawling shrine complex, built at the location of Michinaze's grave, is the most important Tenmangū shrine, along with Kyoto's

Kitano Tenmangū. A long walkway lined with shops hawking *mochi* (rice cake) dumplings, soft-serve ice cream, and gimmicky souvenirs leads to the shrine's *torii* gate entrance. You'll see three bridges that reach across a small carp-filled lake that is shaped like the character for "heart" and edged by plum trees, which erupt with pink blossoms from late-February to mid-March. One famous tree named Tobiume, to the right of the main hall, is more than 1,000 years old. Plum trees are common at Tenmangū shrines nationwide.

The main hall, built in 1591, is continuously packed with visitors, especially university applicants who have come to buy amulets designed to boost their chances of scholastic success. On the grounds, the **Kankō Historical Museum** illustrates the life story of Tenjin, while the **Daizaifu Tenman-gū Museum** presents relics from his bookish human life.

KYŪSHŪ NATIONAL MUSEUM
九州国立博物館

4-7-2 Ishizaka; tel. 092/918-2807; www.kyuhaku.jp; 9:30am-5pm Tues.-Sun.; ¥430 adults, ¥130 students

Looming in the hills east of Daizafu Station, this enormous complex resembles an international airport or basketball stadium more than a history museum. It opened to major fanfare in sleepy Dazaifu in 2005. It's only one of four national museums in Japan, the others being in Tokyo, Kyoto, and Nara. Each of these four museums has its own spin on Japanese history; Dazaifu's explores Japanese history through its interactions with the rest of Asia, many of which were made in Kyūshū.

A series of elevators shooting through futuristic tunnels bring you to the fourth floor of the sprawling complex, where a large collection of relics from across Asia is displayed with Japanese and English signage. If you're making the trip to Dazaifu, be sure to visit this unlikely museum, notable both for its form and content.

KOMYOZEN-JI
光明禅寺

2-16-1 Saifu; tel. 092/922-4053; www.dazaifu.org/map/tanbo/tourismmap/2.html; 8am-4:30pm daily; ¥200

Two phenomenal rock gardens, one of them also incorporating moss and maple trees, lie hidden within the grounds of this low-profile Zen temple. Located a short walk south of Tenmangū and about 5 minutes' walk east of Dazaifu Station on the way to Kyūshū National Museum, this tranquil temple and its

Dazaifu Tenman-gū

stunning grounds offers a bit of respite. The temple's open hours are unpredictable, so it's wise to call before making the trip.

Food

KASANOYA

2-7-24 Saifu; tel. 092/922-1010; www.kasanoya.com; set meals ¥750-1,080; 4 minutes' walk east of JR Dazaifu Station on the way to Tenman-gū

This is the place to try Dazaifu's local sweet of renown, *umegaemochi,* a *mochi* (rice cake) dumpling filled with sweet red bean paste. You can buy it outside and nibble it on the go—just look for the queue in front of the shop—or sit inside and have it with a cup of tea. Lunch sets including things like udon and soba noodles are also on offer.

UME-NO-HANA

4-4-41 Saifu; tel. 092/928-7787; www.umenohana.co.jp; 11am-10pm daily; lunch ¥1,620, dinner ¥3,920-5,200; 3-minute walk from the side streets east of Kōmyōzen-ji

Come here for a delicious tofu lunch in picturesque surroundings. Seating is in elegant tatami rooms overlooking a garden. Prices aren't exactly cheap, although the quality speaks for itself and lunch sets are a good value. The variety of items is a revelation: smoked tofu cheese, steamed buns stuffed with tofu and tofu skin to name a few. Reserve a day ahead for dinner. For lunch, aim to arrive by noon. Otherwise, be prepared to potentially wait for a bit.

Information and Services

You can speak to friendly staff and pick up a smattering of printed materials in English at the **tourist information center** located inside Nishitetsu Dazaifu Station (tel. 092/925-1880; 9am-5pm daily).

Getting There and Around

Dazaifu is easily reached from Fukuoka. From **Nishitetsu Fukuoka Station,** situated in Tenjin, take the **Nishitetsu line** to **Nishitetsu Futsukaichi Station,** and switch to the train bound for **Nishitetsu Dazaifu Station** (30 minutes; ¥400).

If you're making your way directly to Daizaifu from **Fukuoka Airport,** you can also hop on a **bus** directly from the latter (30 minutes; ¥500).

Inquire at Nishitetsu Dazaifu Station about **bicycle rentals** (¥500 per day).

Nagasaki

Situated at the northwestern corner of Kyūshū is Nagasaki Prefecture. This area's history is steeped in interactions with the outside world, and the prefecture's capital city of Nagasaki is sadly known more for its tragic past than its dynamic present. On your first visit to Nagasaki, you might experience cognitive dissonance. Exploring the remnants of the city that were ravaged by the A-bomb is understandably at the top of most visitors' itineraries to the city.

Venture beyond the monuments and museums dedicated to this single destructive act, however, and you'll find yourself in a cosmopolitan city that is zestfully alive in the present. Loose comparisons to San Francisco are often made to modern-day Nagasaki, a cheerful and cosmopolitan city. Trams glide through downtown, an attractive harbor lies to one side, and streets climb the hills behind the city, which looks spectacular from atop the peak of Inasayama.

There are many reminders of the city's long engagement with Christianity, including Ōura Cathedral, one of Japan's oldest. Reminders of the foreign traders who once thrived in the city are concentrated around a hilly neighborhood replete with European architecture known as the Dutch Slope. The city's burgeoning Chinese community has also made

Nagasaki

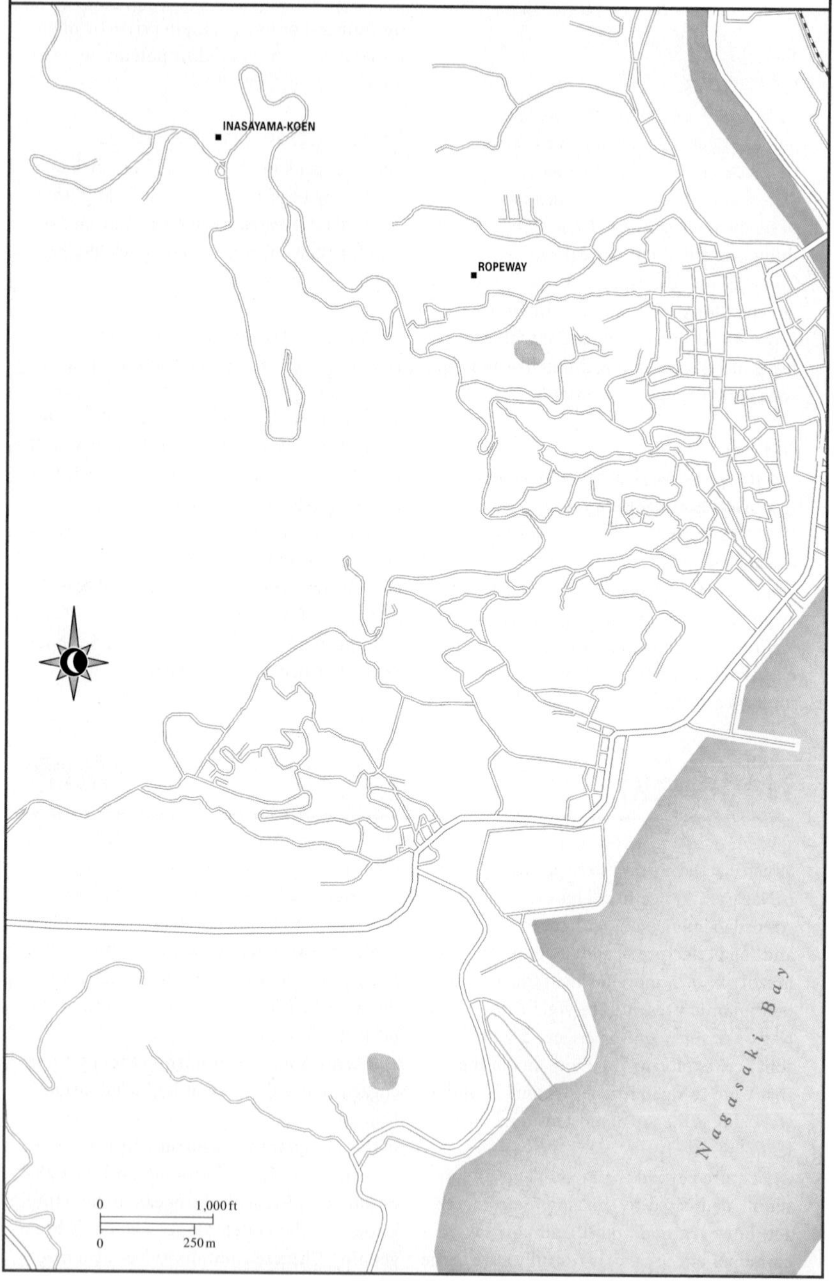

INASAYAMA-KOEN
ROPEWAY
Nagasaki Bay
0 1,000 ft
0 250 m

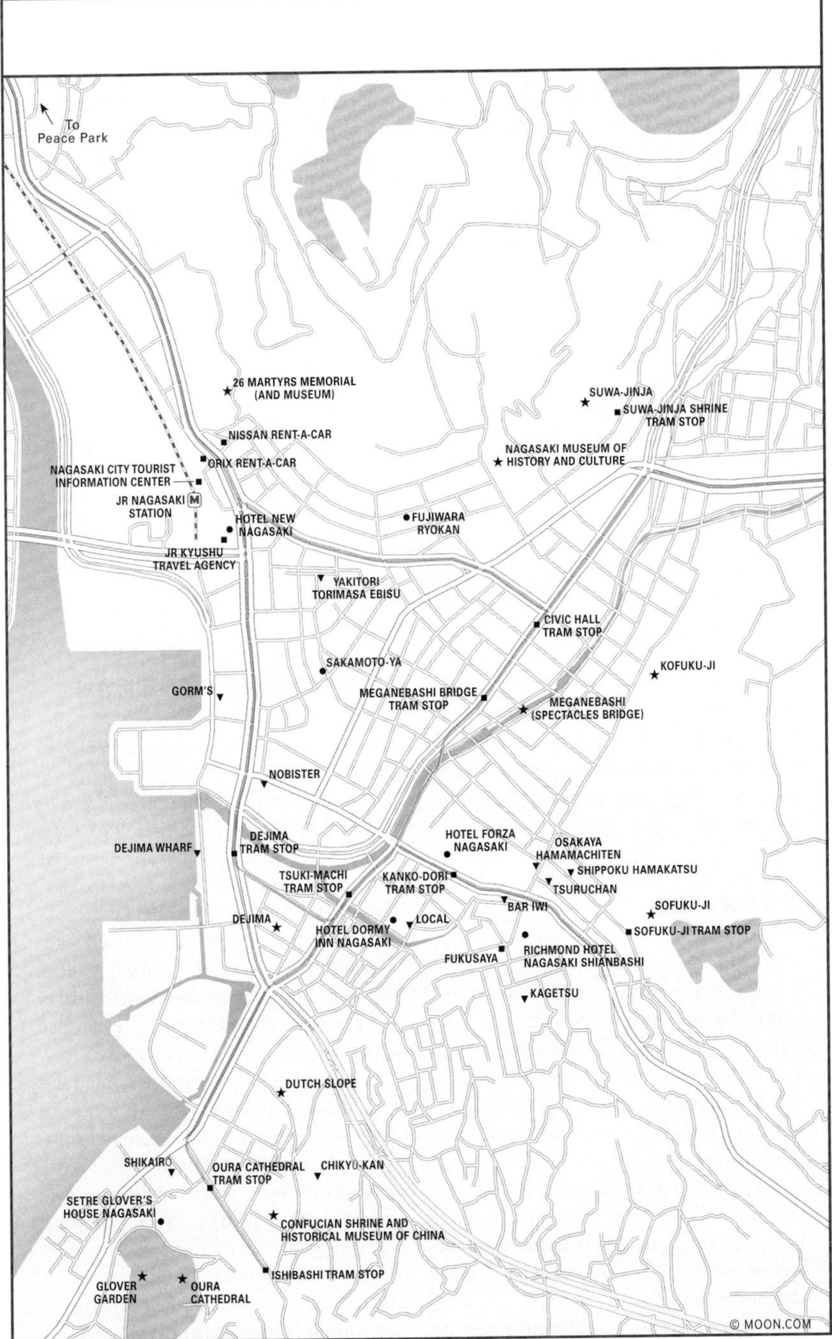
To
Peace Park
26 MARTYRS MEMORIAL
(AND MUSEUM)
NISSAN RENT-A-CAR
ORIX RENT-A-CAR
NAGASAKI CITY TOURIST
INFORMATION CENTER
JR NAGASAKI
STATION
HOTEL NEW
NAGASAKI
JR KYUSHU
TRAVEL AGENCY
SUWA-JINJA
SUWA-JINJA SHRINE
TRAM STOP
NAGASAKI MUSEUM OF
HISTORY AND CULTURE
FUJIWARA
RYOKAN
YAKITORI
TORIMASA EBISU
CIVIC HALL
TRAM STOP
SAKAMOTO-YA
KOFUKU-JI
GORM'S
MEGANEBASHI BRIDGE
TRAM STOP
MEGANEBASHI
(SPECTACLES BRIDGE)
NOBISTER
DEJIMA WHARF
DEJIMA
TRAM STOP
HOTEL FORZA
NAGASAKI
OSAKAYA
HAMAMACHITEN
SHIPPOKU HAMAKATSU
TSURUCHAN
TSUKI-MACHI
TRAM STOP
KANKO-DORI
TRAM STOP
BAR IWI
SOFUKU-JI
SOFUKU-JI TRAM STOP
DEJIMA
LOCAL
HOTEL DORMY
INN NAGASAKI
FUKUSAYA
RICHMOND HOTEL
NAGASAKI SHIANBASHI
KAGETSU
DUTCH SLOPE
SHIKAIRO
OURA CATHEDRAL
TRAM STOP
CHIKYU-KAN
SETRE GLOVER'S
HOUSE NAGASAKI
CONFUCIAN SHRINE AND
HISTORICAL MUSEUM OF CHINA
ISHIBASHI TRAM STOP
GLOVER
GARDEN
OURA
CATHEDRAL
© MOON.COM

its mark in Chinatown, which includes one of the only Chinese-built Confucian shrines outside the motherland. Given this mélange of cultures, it's no surprise that culinary offerings in the city are eclectic. Nightlife, some of it salacious, is close at hand in the neighborhood of Shianbashi too.

About 20 km (12 mi) off the coast lies the city's most enigmatic attraction, Gunkanjima (Battleship Island). This island is the eerie site of phenomenal modern ruins—decrepit schools, derelict hospitals, crumbling apartment blocks—all abandoned, in what was once the most densely populated place on earth. To take all of this in properly, plan to spend a few days in Nagasaki, a city that is likely to surprise you.

SIGHTS

Peace Park and Around

The heart of the mellow suburb of **Urakami,** north of downtown, is where you'll find the hypocenter, where the atomic bomb landed and changed the city forever. The tragic event is commemorated at a number of sights in the area, which can easily be explored on foot. From Nagasaki Station, hop on tram line 1 or 3 and ride 10 minutes to the Matsuyamamachi tram stop. From here, everything is a short walk away.

NAGASAKI ATOMIC BOMB MUSEUM
長崎原爆資料館

7-8 Hirano-machi; tel. 095/844-1231; https://nagasakipeace.jp/english/abm.html; 8:30am-6:30pm May-Aug., 8:30am-5:30pm Sept.-Apr.; ¥200 adults, ¥100 students and schoolchildren

This harrowing museum documents the city's past leading up to August 9, 1945, its unthinkable annihilation by the bomb, and its reconstruction. It also tells the sobering history of the development of nuclear weapons.

Upon entering the museum, the first section gives a glimpse of what Nagasaki was like before the bombing. This leads to the second section, which gives some sense of the catastrophic event.

Items and photographs documenting the carnage left by the blast are displayed in heart-wrenching exhibits: a water tank with twisted legs from a middle school that stood near the hypocenter, rosaries left by churchgoers at Urakami Cathedral when the bomb went off, singed clothing, contorted rocks and trees, warped glass, melted coins, and a clock with the hands frozen at 11:02, the time of the blast. The aftermath, including radiation damage and accounts from survivors, is also explored in detail. Note that some of the photographs and items displayed can be very disturbing, particularly for children.

The museum invites visitors to consider deeper questions related to the existence of nuclear weapons in the present. It explores the surge in antinuclear activism across the globe, and closes with an unsettling matter-of-fact list of the nations that currently have nuclear arsenals.

NAGASAKI NATIONAL PEACE MEMORIAL HALL FOR THE ATOMIC BOMB VICTIMS
国立長崎原爆死没者追悼平和祈念館

7-8 Hirano-machi; tel. 095/814-0055; www.peace-nagasaki.go.jp/en; 8:30am-6:30pm May-Aug., 8:30am-5:30pm Sept.-Apr.; free

This deeply stirring memorial, designed by architect Kuryū Akira, opened in 2003. Enter the outdoor space that houses the memorial, encircled by trees, and take in the expansive pool of water. This basin signifies the harrowing ordeal experienced by survivors left without water in the wake of the blast. As dusk falls, lights beneath the water's surface flicker briefly in honor of the 70,000 people who died in the blast.

After reading the inscriptions around this basin, descend into the first basement level. Here, you'll discover memoirs penned by survivors. Also on the first basement floor are 12 columns with books bearing the names of all victims. On the second basement floor, you'll encounter pictures of victims, audio and video related to the bombing, and harrowing accounts from victims about their experiences receiving medical care after the blast.

While the atmosphere at this memorial is undeniably somber, the combination of light, water, and serenity inspire a glimmer of hope for a future that is free of nuclear weapons.

ATOMIC BOMB HYPOCENTER PARK
原爆落下中心地公園

6 Matsuyamamachi; https://nagasakipeace.jp/english/map/zone_inori/genbaku_rakka_hi.html; free

Leaving the memorial, walk about four minutes north to this park. Steps arranged in concentric circles lead down to a central black column made of polished stone, which marks the spot just below where the bomb detonated. Near this pillar, a remnant of a wall that once belonged to the original Urakami Cathedral still stands.

PEACE PARK
平和公園

9 Matsuyamamachi; free

After visiting the hypocenter, walk north about five minutes to Peace Park. Every August 9, there's a memorial ceremony held here to honor the victims of the tragic blast, as well as a vocal antinuclear protest. There's a fountain shaped like a dove and a sculpture garden graced by peace-themed works made by artists from around the world.

The centerpiece of the park is the Nagasaki Peace Statue. Standing 9.7 meters (32 feet) high and weighing 9 tonnes (10 tons), the bronze statue was created by Kitamura Seibō in 1955. The muscular effigy is loaded with symbolism: His right hand points skyward as a reminder of the dangers of atomic weaponry. The left hand, extended outward, is a call for eternal peace. The figure's serene face and closed eyes also indicate prayer for the souls of those who died in the blast. The black vault beneath the statue contains all names of those who died in the explosion, as well as those who passed years later.

Central Nagasaki

Central Nagasaki extends roughly from the area around Nagasaki Station at the northwest corner, to **Suwa-jinja shrine** in the northeast and **Sōfuku-ji temple** in the south. You can hop on the city's convenient **tram,** but if the weather is nice, Nagasaki lends itself to exploration on foot. As you make your way through the central part of town, be sure to stroll along the stretch of riverside graced by **Meganebashi bridge,** named for the appearance of spectacles it creates when its two arches are reflected

Nagasaki Peace Memorial

Fat Man

SECOND ATOMIC BOMBING

Three days after Hiroshima was decimated, on August 9, 1945, Nagasaki became the second city to be eviscerated by an atomic bomb. Departing from North Field airbase in the Mariana Islands near Guam, the B-29 bomber known as *Bockscar (Bock's Car)* made the long journey northwest to the skies over Kyūshū. The originally intended target was the city of Kokura on the northeastern coast of the island, which was spared by cloud cover. Diverting southwest, the aircrew turned southwest to Nagasaki instead.

Fat Man bomb

A few minutes before 11am, the plane was over Nagasaki. When there was a break in the clouds, the crew dropped the 4.9-tonne (5.4-ton) bomb, nicknamed "Fat Man," which had an explosive force equivalent to 19,000 tonnes (21,000 tons) of TNT. ("Little Boy" detonated three days before, equated to 14,500 tonnes (16,000 tons) of TNT.) The bomb missed its target, the Mitsubishi Arms Factory, detonating instead at 11:02am, about 500 meters (1,640 feet) above what was then Asia's largest Catholic church, Urakami Cathedral.

DEVASTATION

As in Hiroshima, the destruction was immediate and mindboggling. At the time of the blast, a mushroom cloud climbed 13,716 meters (45,000 feet) over the city. Temperatures at the hypocenter are estimated to have reached up to an unfathomable 4,000°C (7,232°F), while devastating winds stronger than a hurricane—70 km (105 mi) per hour—furiously lashed through downtown. Everything within a kilometer (0.6-mi) radius of the hypocenter was eviscerated, and 74,000 died in an instant. Another 75,000 were critically injured in the blast, with roughly the same number dying in the aftermath. By the time fires began to spread outward from the hypocenter, about one-third of the city was subsumed in the blaze.

The carnage could have been even worse, were it not for Nagasaki's topography. The ring of hills around the city prevented the blast and ensuing fires from spreading too far into the outskirts. Six days after the dreadful blast, Japan formally surrendered, bringing World War II to a close.

in the Nakashima River. Another section of Central Nagasaki worth meandering through is **Teramachi** ("Temple Town"), which lies about 8 minutes' walk east of the famed bridge. As the name suggests, temples abound here, with the most famous being **Kōfuku-ji.** Along with Sofuku-ji, this temple displays heavy architectural influence from China's Ming Dynasty.

26 MARTYRS MEMORIAL (AND MUSEUM)
日本二十六聖人記念館

7-8 Nishizaka-chō; tel. 095/822-6000; www.26martyrs.com; 9am-5pm daily; Memorial free, museum ¥500adults, ¥300 high school students, ¥150 elementary school students; walk 7 minutes northeast of JR Nagasaki Station

From this wall protrude 26 reliefs that commemorate a haunting incident in Nagasaki's history. It was at this post that 20 Japanese

Christians, including a few boys aged 12 and 13, and six Spanish friars were crucified in 1597. It is said that one of the martyrs, Paulo Miki, delivered a final sermon as he hung on the cross and even forgave those who executed him. Beyond the wall, a museum explores the history of Christianity in Nagasaki and the brutal crackdown on the religion that was in full swing from the late 16th century.

NAGASAKI MUSEUM OF HISTORY AND CULTURE
長崎歴史文化博物館

1-1-1 Tateyama; tel. 095/818-8366; www.nmhc.jp; 8:30am-7pm daily, closed third Tues. every month; ¥600; take tram line 3 to Sakuramachi, then walk 6 minutes northeast

This smart museum illuminates Nagasaki's storied, cosmopolitan past. A permanent exhibition spread across two floors explores the city's long history of engagement with the outside world, even at a time when the rest of Japan was sealed shut during the Edo period. Relics, art, documents, and various tools and visual illustrations are used to convey the city's storied exchange with powers from abroad.

There's also a section showing off Nagasaki's influence on refined crafts like porcelain and lacquerware, and another offering a glimpse into daily life in the city's heyday. Perhaps the most impressive section of the museum is its reproduction of the Nagasaki Magistrate's Office, where dignitaries were entertained in an elegant, expansive tatami room and smugglers were dealt with in a (reproduced) interrogation room. If you want to visit one museum during your time in the city, make it this one.

SUWA-JINJA
諏訪神社

18-15 Kaminishiyamamachi; tel. 095/824-0445; www.osuwasan.jp; 24/7; free; take tram line 3 to Suwa-jinja Shrine tram stop, then walk a 10 minutes northwest

Beloved by locals, who sometimes refer to it as "O-suwa san," this Shinto shrine was founded in 1625. The deities enshrined here are the god of divine favor (Suwa no Okami), the god of matchmaking (Morisaki Okami), and the god of safe sea travel (Sumiyoshi no Okami). To reach the sprawling shrine, you'll need to plod up a series of stairways (almost 200 steps) to the top of a leafy hillock where the grounds are situated.

A variety of stone guardian dogs stand guard around the grounds. The faithful sprinkle water into impressions on their heads. The

26 Martyrs Memorial

particularly stout "turntable guardian dog" statue was once the object of choice for prostitutes who would pray to it to conjure storms that would delay sailors from coming to shore just a bit longer. The shrine is at its most lively every October 7-9, when its hosts the city's massive Kunchi festival.

SŌFUKU-JI
崇福寺

7-5 Kajiyamachi; tel. 095/823-2645; 8am-5pm daily; ¥300; take tram line 1 to Sōfukuji Temple tram stop, then walk 3 minutes north

This blazing-red temple, built in 1629, stands on the side of a hill. This temple belongs to the Zen sect known as Ōbaku, and like many of the temples in Nagasaki, a Chinese monk oversaw its building. Entering the temple grounds, you may be struck by the palpably different atmosphere here from what you have experienced in the vast majority of temples in Japan.

The imposing Ryugumon (Gate of the Dragon Palace) entrance gate is a prime example of such Ming dynasty flourishes. This bright red entryway stands two stories high and is flanked by two stone guardians. Although the gate was first built in 1673, it succumbed to the elements numerous times and the current iteration dates to 1849. After passing through the gate and walking up the hill to the temple main grounds, you'll see a number of halls housing a host of statues, including the Chinese goddess of the sea, Mazu ("Maso" in Chinese).

Elsewhere in the temple's inner sanctum, you'll find a temple bell made in 1647 and a massive cauldron in which food was made by resident priest Qianhai to feed starving residents during a famine in 1681. The Buddha Hall was designed in China and constructed with Chinese wood, transported to Nagasaki and assembled in 1646, making it one of the city's oldest buildings.

Ample English signage elucidates all of this and more throughout the complex. Overall, this temple is the best example of a Chinese-constructed place of worship in the city.

Southern Nagasaki

Think of southern Nagasaki as starting near the mouth of the Nakashima River with **Dejima,** a manmade island, and **Chinatown** at the northern edge. While the tram network can save you a bit a time and energy, it only takes about half an hour to walk between the following sights, and walking is recommended if the weather cooperates.

Much of this area has been shaped by the city's historic Dutch presence. The cobblestone streets of the Dutch Slope, 10 minutes south of Dejima, or Oranda-zaka (Oranda being the Japanized pronunciation for Holland) evoke the bygone era when Holland was all the rage in Nagasaki. It's a picturesque streetscape to ramble along as you make your way through the south side of the city.

DEJIMA
出島

tel. 095/829-1194; http://nagasakidejima.jp; 8am-6pm daily; ¥510 adults, ¥200 high school students, ¥100 elementary and junior high school students; take tram line 1 to Dejima tram stop, then walk 5 minutes south

Dejima was originally a manmade island built in 1636 to house the Portuguese and contain their evangelical activity. Soon after the construction of the district, the Portuguese were booted out of Japan for their persistent missionary efforts. From that point on, a small contingent of resolutely secular Dutch traders was then allowed to move its base of operations to Dejima. Although it's no longer an island, the whiff of its historic Dutch presence remains: Reconstructed warehouses, merchants' homes, walls and gates line the streets, which would have been the only window onto the outside Western world for nearly two centuries.

The buildings feature seamless integration of Japanese and Western styles, such as rooms with tatami-mat floors and walls exotically covered in wallpaper. Displays tell the story of

1: Confucian Shrine **2:** Glover Garden
3: Dejima Wharf

孔子廟
1
2
3

the growth of trade in Nagasaki, cultural exchange, and the city's long history of studying overseas advancements in science and technology, from medicine to botany, in what was once coined *Rangaku* ("Dutch studies").

Plan to spend a few hours ambling through the area, which is well marked and easily navigable thanks to abundant English signage and free maps.

CONFUCIAN SHRINE AND HISTORICAL MUSEUM OF CHINA
長崎孔子廟中国歴代博物館

10-36 Ōuramachi; tel. 095/824-4022; http://nagasaki-koushibyou.com; 8:30am-5:30pm daily; ¥600 for both shrine and museum; take tram line 1 to the Ishibashi tram stop, then walk 2 minutes

Given China's deep ties to Nagasaki, it's fitting that one of only a handful of shrines in Japan dedicated to the great Chinese sage Confucius is found in the city. It's said to be the only one built with Chinese labor outside the motherland. Originally built in 1893, the Confucian Shrine (Kōshi-byō) was ravaged by fire that rippled across the city following the dropping of the A-bomb. Although it's a reconstruction, the shrine still packs a strong atmospheric punch.

As you enter, pass through a garden, crossing a bridge over a pond as the opulent buildings topped by yellow sweeping roofs come into view. The quad that fronts the complex is lined by 72 statues of the disciples of Confucius. The centerpiece of the main hall is a statue of the great sage himself, seated in repose. Beyond the shrine there's a small museum displaying a number of Chinese relics—archaeological discoveries, statues, porcelain and more—as well as exhibits about the shrine.

ŌURA CATHEDRAL
大浦天主堂

5-3 Minamiyamate-machi; tel. 095/823-2628; 8am-6pm daily; ¥1,000; take tram line 1 to Ōura Cathedral Station tram stop, then walk 6 minutes

About 10 minutes' walk southwest of the Confucian shrine is Ōura Church. Serving as yet another reminder of just how diverse Nagasaki was by Edo-period standards, this Catholic cathedral was completed in 1864, just before the Meiji Restoration led to the opening of Japan to the outside world.

Its construction was overseen by two French priests, who catered to the growing community of foreign traders living in the city. The Catholic cathedral honors the 26 martyrs who were crucified in the city in 1597. Within the church's old seminary and bishop's living quarters, there's a small museum on Christianity's history in Japan, including the period in which "hidden Christians" were forced to live in self-exile to preserve their lives. This museum accounts for the hefty admission fee. If you don't have a strong interest in the religion's history in Japan, you can simply appreciate the structure from outside.

The first Western-style structure to be deemed a national treasure, the church is still actively used today. In 2018, the cathedral and a smattering of other sites related to the history of Christianity in Nagasaki were also added to UNESCO's World Heritage list.

GLOVER GARDEN
グラバー園

8-1 Minamiyamate-machi; tel. 095/822-8223; www.glover-garden.jp; 8am-9:30pm May-mid-Jul., 8am-6pm mid-Jul.-Apr.; adults ¥610, high school students ¥300, junior high and elementary students ¥180; take tram line 1 to the Ōura Cathedral Station tram stop, then walk 6 minutes

Located next to Ōura Cathedral, this open-air museum is a great place to imagine how the well-heeled foreign business community lived in the 19th century. Several mansions and other buildings with arches and porticoes done in Greco-Roman style, and spacious wooden verandas, dot this lovely garden. Notice that some of the buildings have Japanese-style roofs. As the gardens sprawl across a hilltop, accessible by escalators, it also provides great views of the city and harbor.

The main residence once belonged to Thomas Glover (1838-1911), an influential Scottish trader who helped bring what were

Gunkanjima: Battleship Island

Formally called Hashima, this island with a peculiar history lies about 20 km (12.4 mi) south of Nagasaki Harbor, and was home to a once-bustling **coal mine** that shut down in 1974. The nickname Gunkanjima ("Battleship Island," **軍艦島**) comes from its resemblance to a warship floating on water. You might recognize it from its appearance in the James Bond flick ***Skyfall,*** in which James is taken hostage and dropped off on an abandoned island—supposedly near Macau—where baddie Raoul Silva awaits.

The lord of Saga found the island's coal deposits in 1810, spurring the creation of a full-scale mining operation by the late-19th century, after which the **Mitsubishi Corporation** snapped up the property. Some of the island's history is a bit dark, particularly that of the Korean and Japanese **slave laborers** who worked there in the 1930s and '40s.

As the island's population swelled, buildings were squeezed into the already cramped quarters. The entire island is surprisingly small, at 150 meters (492 feet) wide by 480 meters (1,575 feet) long. At its peak in the 1950s, the community grew to around 6,000 people, making it one of the most **densely populated** places in human history. Gunkanjima's coal mines abruptly shut down in April 1974 and its denizens disbanded. Today, all that's left is the husk remains of dilapidated housing blocks, crumbling schools, restaurants, a hospital, a public bath, and of course, the once massive mining operations—essentially, what is known in Japanese as ***haikyo*** (modern ruins).

HOW TO VISIT

Access to the island was blocked and its concrete ruins were left to weather the elements until 2009, when a newly built boat dock opened for tours. **Guided tours** now usher visitors to three observation decks to gaze across the concrete wasteland. Access to the structures is forbidden due to danger of collapse. Many tour boat operators now make the journey to the island multiple times each day. Tours typically cost about ¥3,500-4,500 per person and last about three hours, including the time it takes to travel to and from the island (1 hour, one-way). Check out **Gunkanjima Concierge** (www.gunkanjima-concierge.com) and **Gunkanjima Cruise** (www.gunkanjima-cruise.jp).

It's a surprisingly common occurrence for the tour boats to be unable to moor at the island's dock, even on sunny days. Further, the tours themselves feature a lot of Japanese language over loudspeakers and the boats can be crowded. If you're keen to make the trip anyway, reserve a seat ahead of time, and be sure to take sunscreen and use the bathroom before stepping off the ship, as no facilities are present on the island.

then cutting-edge technologies to Japan, such as industrialized coal mining, modern shipbuilding techniques, and even the steam locomotive. He also helped usher in the Meiji Restoration, which finally brought Japan's Edo period to an end.

INASAYAMA-KŌEN
稲佐山

www.nagasaki-ropeway.jp; 9am-10pm daily; ¥1,230 round-trip

If you're not going to Glover Garden, which offers excellent views of the city from the south side, head to this park, perched on a 333-meter-high (1,092-foot) hill overlooking downtown from the west. To reach the park, take tram line 3 to the Takaramachi tram station, then walk five minutes to the lower station of the **ropeway** (9am-10pm daily, closed first 10 days of Dec.; ¥720 one-way, ¥1,230 round-trip) that goes to the top of the hill. Alternatively, take city bus no. 3 or 4 from in front of JR Nagasaki Station to the Ropeway-mae bus stop, then ascend the steps in the grounds of the nearby shrine. You'll find the lower ropeway station nearby.

FESTIVALS AND EVENTS

CHINESE NEW YEAR

Late-Jan. to mid-Feb.; free

Dragon dances and acrobatic performers fill the streets and lanterns are festooned throughout Chinatown every lunar new year. Visit the neighborhood if you're here at the right time to feel the deep cultural influence of the city's Chinese community.

PEIRON (DRAGON-BOAT RACES)
ペイロン (竜船競漕)

www.minatomatsuri.com; late-Jul.; free

Boats measuring 14 meters (46 feet) long are rowed with great speed by 26-man teams for two days in late July (starting 9am). This tradition was introduced in the mid-17th century by the city's Chinese community, who took to the harbor to race in efforts to placate the wrath of the sea god. Both nights also feature massive displays of fireworks, lasers, and music, with the first night being slightly more epic than the second.

SHŌRŌ-NAGASHI (SPIRIT-BOAT PROCESSION)
精霊流し

Aug. 15; free

On the last night of the Ōbon festival, locals parade floats, impressively made from wood, bamboo, and other natural materials, through the city, before releasing them into the harbor. These glowing barges are said to carry the spirits of the ancestors, symbolized by the lanterns they are topped with. As they drift farther offshore, they are naturally subsumed by the waves.

NAGASAKI KUNCHI
長崎くんち (長崎伝統芸能振興会)

http://nagasaki-kunchi.com; Oct. 7-9; free

With roots that stretch back more than four centuries, this syncretic festival draws on the city's Dutch and Chinese ties with colorful aplomb. Dance groups kitted out in ostentatious attire represent the city's neighborhoods, as serpentine dragon puppets and floats in the shapes of lions, dragons and ships from both China and Holland are dragged through the streets, to the beating of drums and clanging of cymbals.

The bulk of the action takes place around Suwa-jinja, but spills into Chūō Park, located a few minutes' walk west of Meganebashi in the center of town, and the plaza at JR Nagasaki Station. For a good viewing spot, aim to arrive as early as possible. Sometime around 7am or even earlier is a good bet. Don't fret if you don't snag a perfect seat though. The revelry spills into the streets around town as the days drag on and a buzz fills the air throughout. English-language festival information is readily available at the tourist information center.

FOOD AND BARS

Nagasaki's menu of hybrid dishes attests to its cosmopolitan past, in which Portuguese missionaries and merchants and traders from China had a significant presence. In 1899, Chinese students yearning for a taste of home inspired the creation of *chanpon*, or ramen noodles, squid and pork served in a salty, opaque soup. *Sara-udon* puts a southern Chinese spin on this dish, instead covering crispy, fried noodles with a thick sauce containing the same elements.

At the higher end, *shippoku* is a local take on Japan's vaunted *kaiseki* tradition, given both Chinese and Portuguese spin. This multicourse feast includes dishes from all three cultures. Like *kaiseki*, it's not cheap, but makes for an experience as much as a meal.

Then there's the altogether fanciful "Turkish rice". Despite its name, the dish has no link whatsoever to Turkey. The gastronomic pastiche combines spaghetti, rice and *tonkatsu* (breaded pork cutlet), all slathered in curry sauce. Curry must have struck the inventors of the concoction as being vaguely exotic in the same way that Turkey once was seen. As unlikely as it may sound, this dish is now a staple on cafe menus across the city.

Shippoku

★ KAGETSU

2-1 Maruyama-machi; tel. 095/822-0191; www.ryoutei-kagetsu.co.jp; noon-3pm and 6pm-10pm Wed.-Mon.; lunch boxes ¥5,400 (Mon.-Fri.), lunch courses from ¥10,240, dinner courses from ¥15,000; take tram no. 1 or 4 from Sōfuku-ji tram stop, then walk 5 minutes

Occupying a 17th-century wooden structure that once served as a geisha house, this *shippoku* restaurant looks like the archetypal set for a restaurant scene in a samurai flick. You'll find tatami floors with low tables, windows looking out onto a dreamy garden, and servers shuffling about in kimono as they deftly balance trays loaded with lacquer bowls filled with delicacies. There are even gashes in a few wooden beams left by katana blades. If you want to go all out and experience Nagasaki's unique *shippoku* tradition, this is the preeminent spot. That said, you'll appreciate it much more if you're with someone who speaks Japanese to help make sense of the meal. At least two people are required to order a full *shippoku* course. If you can stomach the prices, a meal here will be an experience you'll not soon forget. Reservations, made as far in advance as possible, are essential.

SHIPPOKU HAMAKATSU

6-50 Kajiya-machi; tel. 095/826-8321; www.sippoku.jp; 11:30am-10pm daily; lunch (11:30-3pm, last order 1:30pm) from ¥1,480, afternoon tea sets (1:30pm-5pm, last order 4pm) from ¥2,800, dinner from ¥3,800; take tram no. 1 or 4 from the Shianbashi tram stop, then walk 3 minutes

Although lacking the timeworn ambience of Kagetsu, this sleek, modern restaurant is a less exorbitant place to sample *shippoku* (though it's still not cheap). Lunch and dinner courses are prepared in several tiers. At the higher end, courses can cost upwards of ¥13,800. Book a table at least a few days in advance to be safe. At least two people are required to order a full course.

Barbecue

OSAKAYA HAMAMACHITEN

11-11 Hamamachi; tel. 095/820-9198; 5pm-1am Sun.-Thurs., 5pm-3am Fri.-Sat.; dishes ¥780-3,800, average meal ¥8,000; take tram no. 1 or 4 from the Shianbashi tram stop, then walk 2 minutes

Come here if you're in the mood for a carnivorous feast. Excellent beef and pork platters, vegetable medleys, and a robust assortment of sake fill the menu. You'll barbecue the meat and added trimmings at your table. Making matters easier, there's an English menu and some staff speak English. Reserve a day or more in advance to ensure a seat. Recommended.

Yakitori

YAKITORI TORIMASA EBISU

6-2 Ebisumachi; tel. 095/895-7227; www.torimasa.net; 5:30pm-midnight, last order 11:30pm daily; skewers ¥120-500; walk 7 minutes southeast of JR Nagasaki Station, or take tram line 3 to the Sakuramachi tram stop, then walk 3 minutes

For char-broiled goodness, come to this excellent yakitori shop east of JR Nagasaki Station. Along with chicken, the menu extends to beef, pork, seafood, and lamb, with a range of vegetables too. Staff and diners alike are friendly and open, and there's an English menu. This is a great place for a fun, hearty meal washed down with cold beer or hot *sake*.

Cafés and Light Bites

NOBISTER

1-3 Edomachi; tel. 095/829-0831; http://nobister.com; 11:30am-2:30pm Mon.-Sat.; plates from ¥750, lunch course from ¥1,500; take tram line 1 or 2 to the Ōhato tram stop, then walk 1 minute

This friendly café serves vegetable-packed curries, sandwiches with lean cuts of meat, freshly baked bread, healthy lunch sets, delicious smoothies, and a range of vegan fare. There's an English menu. Take-out is also available.

TSURUCHAN

2-47 Aburaya-machi; tel. 095/824-2679; 9am-9pm daily; Turkish rice ¥1180

This café claims to have whipped up the first plate of Turkish rice in 1925. While the traditional variety includes a *tonkatsu* cutlet (breaded, fried pork), the menu here extends to beef and chicken, and offers a cream sauce in place of the customary curry-based gravy. If you're the type who likes to try something once just to say you did it, you may as well go to the source, and that source would be Tsuruchan for Nagasaki's most peculiar dish.

FUKUSAYA

3-1 Funadaiku-machi; tel. 095/821-2938; www.fukusaya.co.jp; 8:30am-8pm; take tram no. 1 or 4 from the Shianbashi tram stop, then walk 3 minutes

Overseas culinary influence can be tasted in Nagasaki's signature dessert and favored souvenir, the Castella sponge cake. Made with flour, eggs, sugar, and syrup, this dessert first arrived with Portuguese traders in the 16th century. This shop has been making the block-shaped sweet since 1624.

International

SHIKAIRŌ

4-5 Matsugaemachi; tel. 095/822-1296; http://shikairou.com; 11:30am-3pm and 5pm-8pm daily; ¥970 (signature dish, chanpon); take tram line 5 to the Ōura Cathedral tram stop, then walk 2 minutes

This cavernous Chinese joint with sweeping views of the harbor admittedly has a tourist-track feel, but it stakes a legitimate claim as the originator of Nagasaki's beloved *chanpon* dish. Although it's set in a modern building now, it's said to have whipped up its first batch of the dish in 1899. The menu extends to *gyoza* (fried pork dumplings), fried spring rolls, and other Sino fare. Keep an eye out for the complex with massive red pillars and an entrance topped with a Chinese-style roof. It's a short walk from Glover Garden (5 minutes) or Ōura Cathedral (8 minutes).

DEJIMA WHARF

1-1-109 Dejimamachi; tel. 095/828-3939; http://dejimawharf.com; hours vary by stand; prices vary; take tram line 1 to the Dejima tram stop, then walk 3 minutes

This is a good place to go if you're feeling hungry and spontaneous. Seafood, steak, Italian, Chinese dishes, and more are served at this assortment of harbor-facing restaurants, housed in a two-story wooden building. It's an especially appealing spot to dine at lunchtime during the warmer months, given the great al fresco seating areas.

CHIKYŪ-KAN

6-25 Higashiyamate-machi; tel. 095/822-7966; http://higashiyamate-chikyukan.com/j_frame.htm; 10am-5pm Thurs.-Mon., restaurant noon-3pm Sat.-Sun.; price varies with menu; take tram line 5 to the Ishibashi tram stop, then walk 3 minutes

In the name of cultural exchange, this charming space invites someone from overseas every weekend to cook a reasonably priced meal from their home country. Representatives from more than 70 nationalities, many of them university exchange students, have donned the chef cap so far. It's housed in a 19th-century period piece of a building on the Dutch Slopes, where a much earlier form of intercultural exchange flourished. On weekdays, it's a laid-back, amiable café that hosts language exchange meetups. Look for the old house with countries' flags—changed weekly—flying from the second-floor veranda.

GORM'S

9-10 Motofuna-machi; tel. 095/893-8795; https://gorms.owst.jp; 11:30am-2pm and 6pm-9:30pm Wed.-Mon.; lunch from ¥1,000, dinner from ¥4,000

The Nagasaki outpost of this Danish chain sells great pizza, as well as pasta, salads, and desserts. The cozy interior is all clean lines, elegant lighting, wood, and chic Scandinavian furniture. It's a little pricy, but makes for a good break from Japanese fare. Be forewarned that a salad is served to every diner as part of a ¥550 "service charge."

Bars

BAR IWI

1-7 Motoshikkuimachi; tel. 080/8887-9514; 8pm-late Mon.-Sat.

With its all-black interior—drawing in those rugby fans—and an abundance of Ultraman figurines, this bar is a friendly spot to mingle with locals and expats over reasonably priced drinks.

LOCAL

7-8 Dōza-machi; tel. 095/823-0022; 5pm-2am daily

This cheery bar has a good range of imported beers on tap and a smattering of craft brews in the bottle. The first floor is standing only, while the second floor has limited seating.

ACCOMMODATIONS

Under ¥10,000

FUJIWARA RYOKAN

6-12 Uwamachi; tel. 095/822-2378; www.fujiwara-ryokan.jp; ¥9,000 d; walk 10 minutes east of JR Nagasaki Station, or take tram line no. 3 to Sakura-machi Station, then walk 2 minutes

Simple, clean tatami rooms with futons come stocked with plenty of useful English-language information on the city at this welcoming *ryokan*. Two rooms have private bathrooms, while another two share one. The amiable owner, Mr. Fujiwara, speaks basic English and is eager to help. Coin-operated laundry is available.

¥10,000-20,000

HOTEL DORMY INN NAGASAKI

7-24 Dozamachi; tel. 095/820-5489; www.hotespa.net/hotels/nagasaki; ¥12,000 d; take tram line 1 or 4 to the Kanko-dōri tram stop, then walk 4 minutes

This modern business hotel has compact, tidy rooms and is conveniently situated near Chinatown. Each room has a petite en-suite bathroom, complemented by shared bath and sauna facilities divided by gender. There's a decent breakfast buffet option, comprising a mix of cuisine types: Japanese, Western, Chinese.

RICHMOND HOTEL NAGASAKI SHIANBASHI

6-38 Motoshikkuimachi; tel. 095/832-2525; https://richmondhotel.jp/nagasaki; ¥13,000 d; take tram line 1 or 4 to the Shianbashi tram stop, then walk 1 minute

Conveniently located near a lively entertainment area with lots of restaurants and shops. Rooms are slightly above average in size and are well-appointed, with each one including a smart phone that can be used around town during your stay (calls and data). The breakfast buffet includes local dishes and Western staples, and is good for the price. This is a very good midrange choice in the heart of the action.

HOTEL FORZA NAGASAKI

4-11 Hamamachi; tel. 095/816-2111; www.hotelforza.jp/nagasaki; ¥14,000 d; take tram line 1 or 4 to the Kanko-dōri tram stop, then walk 1 minute

This well-located modern hotel sits at the end of a shopping arcade. Modern rooms with a stylish touch, helpful staff at the front desk and a location in the heart of town make it a great choice. A restaurant serves Japanese and Western-style breakfast, and there's a shared lounge with free coffee. There's a small sofa and table squeezed into most rooms for a little chill-out space. All rooms are non-smoking.

¥20,000-30,000

SETRE GLOVER'S HOUSE NAGASAKI

2-28 Minami Yamatemachi; tel. 095/827-7777; www.hotelsetre-nagasaki.com; from ¥29,000 d; take tram line 5 to the Ōura Cathedral tram stop, then walk 5 minutes

Housed in a handsome Western-style building with antique furniture and romantic vibes, this classy hotel oozes a vaguely European charm. It's a short walk from Glover House and Ōura Cathedral. Rooms are spacious and well-appointed. A swanky on-site restaurant serves Nagasaki's three core cuisines—Japanese, Chinese and Western—and all guests have access to a plush lounge with complimentary drinks, comfy seating, and soft lighting. Staff are friendly and eager to help. This property is not quite high-end luxury, but it's very comfortable and well-appointed—easily one of the city's best accommodations.

★ SAKAMOTO-YA

2-13 Kanayamachi; tel. 0120/268-8210; www.sakamotoya.co.jp; from ¥30,000 d; take tram line 1 or 2 to Gotomachi Station, then walk 5 minutes

In business since 1894, this is the city's oldest hotel. Its heritage shows in the wooden structure, tatami floors, sliding *fusuma* doors, and alcoves containing calligraphy and flower arrangements in ceramics fired in the island's kilns. There are only 11 rooms, each with a private bathroom with a cypress tub, and private gardens for those on the first floor. Service is highly personalized. Japanese meals are served, with the city's signature *shippoku* spreads available upon request. This is a great choice for the classic *ryokan* experience.

INFORMATION AND SERVICES

On the first floor of Nagasaki Station near the main ticket gate you'll find the **Nagasaki City Tourist Information Center** (tel. 095/823-3631; https://travel.at-nagasaki.jp; 8am-8pm daily). Staff here speak a smattering of English, and maps and pamphlets in English are available.

If you ask for more than directions or a simple recommendation—or perhaps for help with making a quick reservation—you may be referred to the city's **call center** (tel. 095/825-5175) geared toward answering the questions of foreign tourists. It's a slightly annoying state of affairs, but this is currently Nagasaki's model for fielding the queries of foreign visitors.

If you want more attentive in-person assistance with domestic bookings, head to the **JR Kyūshū Travel Agency** (tel. 095/822-4813; 10:30am-7pm Mon.-Fri., 10am-6pm Sat.-Sun.), situated in JR Nagasaki Station.

For information on the city and surrounding prefecture, you may have better luck online. Try **Nagasaki Prefecture's website** (www.visit-nagasaki.com), which provides extensive information on things to see and do not only in the city, but around the prefecture.

If you'd like to join a free guided walk in English, led by a local volunteer, check out the website of the organization **Nagasaki Walks** (www.keirinkai.or.jp/nagasaki-walks).

GETTING THERE

Train

JR Nagasaki Station sits at the northwestern edge of the heart of downtown. It's serviced by local train lines that run to various parts of the island. The **Kamome limited express** runs to **Fukuoka** (2 hours; ¥4,710) and to Shin-tosu, from which you can continue to **Kumamoto** by *shinkansen* (2 hours 15 minutes; ¥7,990).

Air

Nagasaki Airport (tel. 095/752-5555; www.nagasaki-airport.jp) is a fair distance from the city center, about 40 km (25 mi) north of town on an artificial island in Ōmura Bay. Along with servicing flights to and from a variety of domestic hubs—Tokyo, Osaka (Itami and Kansai International), Kobe, Okinawa, Nagoya—a smattering of international flights link the city to Seoul and Shanghai. Buses run between the airport and the **Kenei bus terminal,** located adjacent to JR Nagasaki Station (40 minutes to 1 hour; ¥900).

Bus

Highway buses serving routes throughout Kyūshū come and go from the **Kenei bus station** (3-1 Daikoku-machi; tel. 095/826-6221), located across the street from JR Nagasaki Station. Destinations include Fukuoka, Kumamoto, Miyazaki, Kagoshima and beyond. See the website of the **Nagasaki Prefecture Transportation Authority** (www.keneibus.jp) for timetables and fares.

GETTING AROUND

Tram

Although Nagasaki is pretty spread out, it's blessed with a brilliant tram network that drastically simplifies getting around town (until around 11:30pm; single ride ¥120, one-day pass ¥500). There are **five color-coded lines,** of which no. 2 is only used for occasional events. Aside from being a handy means of transport, many of the tram cars are period pieces straight out of the early 20th century.

If you want to transfer to another line, which requires a *noritsugi* (transfer pass), **Tsuki-machi** is the only stop where you can do it for free. If you're taking a single ride on the tram network, simply drop your fare into the box beside the driver's seat as you exit the tram. Pick up a day pass at the tourist information center in **JR Nagasaki Station** or from a number of hotels.

Car

If you're looking to venture from Nagasaki to other regions of the island, having your own wheels is a good idea. There are a number of car-rental options around JR Nagasaki Station, including reliable chains like **Nissan Rent-A-car** (2-9 Daikoku-machi; tel. 095/825-1988; https://nissan-rentacar.com) and **Orix Rent-a-car** (1-22 Daikoku-machi; tel. 095/827-8694; https://car.orix.co.jp).

Central Kyūshū

The central region of the island is dominated by the large prefectures of Kumamoto on the western side and Oita in the east. Fukuoka Prefecture borders both Kumamoto and Oita to the north, while Kagoshima Prefecture lies to the southwest of Kumamoto and Miyazaki Prefecture is southeast of Kumamoto and south of Oita.

Kumamoto's capital city of the same name lies about 10 km (6.2 mi) inland from Ariake Bay. The Shimabara Peninsula and Nagasaki Prefecture are on the other side of the water to the west. The massive caldera of Aso-san lies about 50 km (31 mi) east of the city of Kumamoto, while the remote hot-spring village of Kurokawa Onsen is roughly 30 km (18.6 mi) north of there.

From Kurokawa Onsen, crossing the border into Oita Prefecture, the quaint *onsen* town of Yufuin is about 50 km (31 mi) to the northeast. The kitschy *onsen* mecca of Beppu, with its theme-park ambience, is another 25 km (15.5 mi) east of there on Oita's coast.

KUMAMOTO
熊本

The largest city in Central Kyūshū, Kumamoto is the island's most centrally located hub. Most of Kumamoto's action takes place in the northeast of town. Its main attraction is its castle, a scaled-down replica of the original 17th-century fortress. It serves well as a base for exploring the island's craggy interior, including the smoking cone of Aso-san.

Note that a series of earthquakes, topping out at 7.0 magnitude, struck Kumamoto in April 2016, dealing significant damage to the city and surrounding region. Train lines were ravaged, schools, office blocks, and homes collapsed, and more than 200 fatalities occurred. Historic and spiritual sights as far away as Aso-jinja were badly damaged, with some even toppling over. The rebuilding is ongoing and is expected to continue for decades to come.

Sights

KUMAMOTO-JŌ
熊本城

1-1 Honmaru, Chūō-ku; tel. 096/352-5900; www.manyou-kumamoto.jp; 8:30am-6pm Mar.-Nov., 8:30am-5pm Dec.-Feb.; ¥500; from JR Kumamoto Station, take tram line A or B to the Kumamotojō-mae tram stop

Considered one of Japan's top three citadels, Kumamoto-jō cuts a striking profile. Its looming black keep is topped by a gently curving roofline accented by white-fronted eaves. Its imposing stone wall wraps 5.3 km

Shimabara Peninsula

Lying east of the city of Nagasaki, the Shimabara Peninsula's main draws are the undulating volcanic landscape in **Unzen Amakusa National Park** (www.unzen-geopark.jp) and the historic seaside town of **Shimabara.**

UNZEN-DAKE

The main volcanic peak in Unzen Amakusa National Park is Unzen-dake (1,483 meters/4,865 feet). As recently as 1991, the tempermental cone erupted, killing dozens of scientists and journalists who lingered too long near the peak attempting to document the blast, and forcing thousands to flee from surrounding towns. A visit to this peak makes for a good day trip from Nagasaki if you want to engage in some hiking and *onsen* R&R.

Once in the village of **Unzen Onsen,** stop by the **Mount Unzen Visitor Center** (320 Unzen; tel. 0957/73-3636; http://unzenvc.com; 9am-5pm Fri.-Wed., closed on Fri. if Thurs. is a holiday), which stocks a variety of English-language information and can store your luggage (10am-4:30pm; ¥300 pp). You can also get information at the **Unzen Tourist Association** (320 Unzen; tel. 0957/73-3434; www.unzen.org; 9am-5pm daily).

About 5 minutes' walk northeast of the Mount Unzen Visitor Center, you'll discover a series of ***jigoku,*** or sulfurous boiling "hell" pools and seething steam vents, akin to the ones found in Beppu, minus the tourist throngs. It's possible to walk among these gurgling pools, which conjur an otherworldly scene (24/7; free). You can also take a dip in one of the village's *onsen* pools; try **Kojigoku Onsen** (500-1 Unzen; tel. 0957/73-2351; https://hpdsp.jp/seiunso/hot_spring/#422995; 9am-9pm daily; ¥420 adults, ¥210 children).

Head to the **Unzen Ropeway** (551 Unzen; tel. 0957/73-3572; http://unzen-ropeway.com; 8:30am-5:20pm daily; ¥630 one way), from where a number of hiking trails begin. One popular trail threads along a ridge to the nearby peak of **Fugen-dake** (1,359 meters/4,458 feet; hike 2.1 km/1.3 mi one way, 2 hours round trip).

SHIMABARA

A little over 20 km (12 mi) east of the Unzen area lies the town of Shimabara. Here, you'll find the

(3.3 mi) around it, and gaping moats bisect the grounds. It was, in many ways, the perfect citadel, which was exactly its intended purpose.

Originally built by local lord Katō Kiyomasa (1562-1611) over a seven-year period that culminated in 1607, the Kato clan's time in the fortress was short-lived. The castle was transferred to the Hosokawa clan 50 years after the complex was built. The Hosokawa clan ruled the region from the great black castle for the next two centuries.

Today, all but a few structures such as the **Uto Turret,** are reproductions. The originals were wiped out in the battle that saw Saigō Takamori, the legendary "last samurai," lead his rebel forces against the newly ensconced Meiji imperial army, which fought from within the castle. Although the imperial troops prevailed and Saigō's men were forced to retreat after a two-month onslaught, the fighting dealt a heavy blow to the castle. Further, regardless of the imperial victory, the keep had burned down prior to the siege.

A museum within the reconstructed keep tells the illustrious history of the castle and the brutally elegant trappings of the samurai way. Along with the keep, there are a variety of structures that are likewise reproductions, including dozens of turrets and gates. Other impressive structures on the grounds include the atmospheric **Former Hosokawa Residence**—closed due to earthquake damage at the time of writing—located in the northwest part of the grounds, and the stunning reproduction of the **Honmaru Goten Palace.**

Sadly, the castle took another serious blow

reconstructed white-walled **Shimabara Castle** (1-1183-1 Jonai; tel. 0957/62-4766; https://shimabarajou.com; 9am-5:30pm daily; adults ¥540, high school, junior high and elementary school students ¥270), located 10 minutes' walk west of Shimabara Station. There's also a **samurai district** (Teppō-machi area) set on a street lined with mostly inhabited samurai homes—some can be entered for free (9am-5pm daily). A neighborhood known as the **City of Swimming Carp** is famous for its canals filled with crystal-clear spring water teeming with multihued koi (carp). And stop by the **Shimeisō tea house** (2-125 Shinmachi; tel. 095/763-1121; 9am-6pm daily; ¥300), which stands above a lovely pond of spring water.

South of town, the **Mount Unzen Disaster Museum** (1-1 Heiseimachi; tel. 0957/65-5555; www.udmh.or.jp; 9am-6pm daily; adults ¥1,000, high school and junior high school students ¥700, elementary school students ¥500) commemorates and illuminates the 1991 eruption of Unzen-dake that caused vast destruction in the region.

GETTING THERE AND AROUND

To reach **Shimabara Station** from Nagasaki Station, you must first travel to Isahaya Station. To do this you can either take the **JR local train** (about 30 minutes; ¥460) or the **limited express train** (20 minutes; ¥1,280). From Isahaya Station, transfer to the local Shimabara Railway to Shimabara Station (1 hour 10 minutes; ¥1,430). From Nagasaki Station, **buses** run three times daily to **Unzen Onsen** (1 hour 40 minutes; ¥1,800). Hourly buses run from Shimabara Station to Unzen Onsen (55 minutes; ¥830).

The best way to get around the peninsula, however, is with your own wheels. There are plenty of rental outlets near Nagasaki Station, Isahaya Station, and Shimabara-gaikō Station. From Shimabara Port, accessible by bus from Shimabara Station (¥170), you can also catch a ferry across the Ariake Bay to Kumamoto. Ferry operators servicing this route include **Kyūshō Ferry** (tel. 096/329-6111; www.kyusho-ferry.co.jp; 1 hour; ¥780, ¥2,310 with economy-size car) and hydrofoil company **Kumamoto Ferry** (tel. 096/311-4100; www.kumamotoferry.co.jp; 30 minutes; ¥1,000). Once in Kumamoto, buses run from Kumamoto port to Kumamoto Kōtsū Center (35 minutes; ¥550).

in 2016 when a 7.0-magnitude earthquake struck Kumamoto. The main keep's interior is expected to reopen to the public in 2021, while the sobering fact is that it could take another 20 years to completely repair all the damage done.

The good news is that you can still admire the sprawling fortress from a distance. A good walking route begins at **Sakuranobaba-Josaien,** where you'll also find the castle's tourist information center, and walk uphill to the **Ninomaru turret.** This is the only structure on the grounds that remains open to visitors. Walking a loop around the castle takes around an hour, two if you're walking at a leisurely pace. In late March and early April, some 800 cherry trees fill the grounds with an ocean of pink blossoms—understandably a popular time to visit.

Food

Kumamoto is best known for its *basashi* (horsemeat sashimi). While this may sound off-putting, if you're willing to entertain the thought, it's surprisingly tasty, especially when liberally seasoned with garlic, ginger, and a dipping sauce. Another local favorite is *karashi-renkon* (slices of deep-fried lotus root, stuffed with miso paste and hot mustard).

KOME NO KURA

2F, 1-6-27 Shimotōri; tel. 096/212-5551; 5pm-midnight daily; dishes ¥250-950; take tram line A or B to the Hanabata-chō tram stop, then walk 5 minutes

This sleekly understated *izakaya,* tucked away on the second floor of a building in the Shimotōri shopping arcade, has a menu devoted to local favorites, alongside other Japanese fare. Served on low tables in snug private booths behind dark-wood sliding doors, the menu has enough English and photos for you to know what you're ordering. You'll know you've found it when you spot the black, white, and red square-shaped sign with the words "Dynamic Kitchen" in the upper left corner.

★ YOKOBACHI

11-40 Kamitoricho, Chūō-ku; tel. 096/351-4581; www.yokobachi.com; 5pm-midnight daily; dishes ¥350-2,400, courses from ¥2,500

With its verdant inner courtyard, tatami rooms, al fresco seating in warmer months, and creative menu, this *izakaya* is among the best places to dine in the city. Try the *karashi-renkon*, skewers of Higo beef, as the local form of wagyu (high-grade Japanese beef) is known; a *basashi* platter; or a Caesar salad topped with lotus-root chips, sweet potato, parmesan, and pancetta. There's an extensive alcohol menu, with a nice range of *shōchū* and a *nomihōdai* (all-you-can-drink) plan (90 minutes; ¥1,500). Reserve a table a few days early to be safe. Recommended.

AND COFFEE ROASTERS

11-22 Kamitori-chō; tel. 096/273-6178; www.andcoffeeroasters.com; 9am-8pm daily; ¥300-420; take the local Dentetsu Fujisaki line to Fujisakigu-mae Station, then walk 5 minutes

This hip, local café makes artisan coffee in a minimal, laid-back space. The friendly staff take their craft seriously. Upstairs, there's a small seating area. It's a great place for a caffeine hit.

Nightlife and Entertainment

It may lack the buzz of bigger cities, but Kumamoto does see its fair share of after-hours action. For starters, meander through some of the side streets branching off from the Shimotōri shōten-gai (covered arcade), south of Kumamoto-jō. You're bound to discover a few unlikely gems.

GOOD TIME CHARLIE

5F, 1-7-24 Shimotori, Chūō-ku; tel. 096/324-1619; 8pm-2am Thurs.-Tues.; take tram line A or B to Hanabatachō Station, then walk 3 minutes

One of Kumamoto's favorite sons, Charlie Nakatani is a goateed Japanese gentleman known for his trademark black cowboy hat, aviator sunglasses, and jeans, and for strumming a guitar and singing with a distinctly

Kumamoto-jō

country twang. Charlie singlehandedly brought country music to his homeland, and this bar in Kumamoto is his home base. Plastered to the hilt with photos of country greats and trimmings of Americana, it's clear where Charlie derives his inspiration. Whether you're into country music or not, visiting this bar, which hosts regular gigs, is an enjoyable, slightly surreal experience.

GLOCAL BAR VIBES

1-5-6 Shimotori, Chūō-ku; tel. 080/8350-9624; https://vibes222.wixsite.com/glocalvibes; 8pm-11:30pm Mon.-Sat.

With barman Nori-san as your guide, this is an excellent spot to dive into the wonders of *shōchū* Kumamoto has a reputation for producing a slightly sweet, rice-based variant of the distilled spirit so closely associated with Kyūshū. The huge range of *shōchū* is reason enough to visit the bar, but enthusiastic, English-speaking Nori-san elevates it to an unforgettable experience. Highly recommended.

Accommodations

DORMY INN KUMAMOTO

3-1 Karashimacho, Chūō-ku; tel. 096/311-5489; www.hotespa.net/hotels/kumamoto; ¥12,000 d; take tram line B to Nishi-Karashima-chō Station, then walk 3 minutes

Clean, modern, and well-located, this business hotel is a good basic choice for a night in the city. English-speaking staff at the front desk are helpful, and the rooftop hot-spring bath is a nice addition to each room's en-suite bathroom. The rooms are on the petite side, but not overly so by Japanese standards.

KUMAMOTO HOTEL CASTLE

4-2 Jōtō-machi; tel. 096/326-3311; www.hotel-castle.co.jp; ¥16,000 d; take tram line A or B to the Kumamoto Castle/City Hall tram stop, then walk 5 minutes

This upscale hotel is well-located, only a short walk from the city's prime attraction, after which it is named. Amiable staff provide great service, and the rooms are tastefully decorated, with many boasting castle views. Head to the elegant restaurant and bar on the 11th floor for arresting views of the fortress at night. Given its prime location and high standard of service, the rooms are a bargain.

Information and Services

There's a **tourist information center** in JR Kumamoto Station (tel. 096/327-9500; 8am-7pm daily). Just southwest of Kumamoto-jō, there's also a well-run tourist information center in the **Jōsaien complex** (1-1-3 Ninomaru, Chūō-ku; tel. 096/322-5060; 9am-5:30pm daily). Online, visit www.manyou-kumamoto.jp for information on the city of Kumamoto, and www.kumanago.jp to glean more about the prefecture.

Getting There

TRAIN

JR Kumamoto Station sits a few kilometers (just under 2 mi) south of the heart of town. It's serviced by the *shinkansen* and local lines. Take the *shinkansen* if you're coming from JR Hakata Station in **Fukuoka** (40 minutes; ¥5,130) or Kagoshima-Chūō Station (45 minutes; ¥6,940) in the southern hub of **Kagoshima.** Coming from **Nagasaki,** take the Kamome Limited Express train to Shin-Tosu, then transfer to the *shinkansen* (2 hours 30 minutes; ¥7,990).

AIR

Kumamoto Airport (tel. 096/232-2810; www.kmj-ab.co.jp), situated east of downtown, services domestic flights from Tokyo, Osaka, Nagoya and Naha. Buses make the roughly 20-km (12-mi) trip to JR Kumamoto Station (1 hour; ¥800), making stops at the main bus station of **Kumamoto Kōtsū Center** (7-20 Sakura-machi, Chūō-ku; tel. 096/325-0100; 7am-9:30pm daily) on the way.

BUS

The **Kumamoto Kōtsū Center** (7-20 Sakura-machi, Chūō-ku; tel. 096/325-0100; 7am-9:30pm daily) is a provisional bus terminal, servicing long-distance routes around Kyūshū and beyond (**Kyoto,** 12 hours, ¥6,000-11,500 depending on day; **Nagoya,** 12 hours, ¥8,000-12,500 depending on day). For detailed routes and fares to and from Kumamoto, and elsewhere in Kyūshū, visit the website of **Kyūshū Booking** (https://kyushubusbooking.com).

BOAT

It's possible to travel by regular ferry, operated by **Kyūshō Ferry** (tel. 096/329-6111; www.kyusho-ferry.co.jp; 1 hour; ¥780), or a snappy hydrofoil, run by **Kumamoto Ferry** (tel. 096/311-4100; www.kumamotoferry.co.jp; 30 minutes; ¥1,000) to and from the **Shimabara Peninsula,** which lies west of Kumamoto across the Ariake Bay, en route to **Nagasaki.** Buses run between Kumamoto Kōtsū Center and Kumamoto port (35 minutes; ¥550).

CAR

If you plan to venture into the heart of the island, to Aso-san and beyond, a car will prove indispensable. There are a number of rental agencies scattered around both the east and west sides of JR Kumamoto Station. On the road running just in front of the station's east side, **Nissan Rent-a-car** (1-14-1 Kasuga, Nishi-ku; tel. 096/356-4123; https://nissan-rentacar.com; 8am-8pm daily) and **Toyota Rent-A-car** (1-14-28 Kasuga, Nishi-ku; tel. 096/311-0100; https://rent.toyota.co.jp; 8am-8pm daily) are both trusty options.

Getting Around

TRAM

While Kumamoto's main train station is admittedly a little out of the way, thankfully its tram system (6:30am-11pm daily; single ride ¥170; one-day pass ¥500) makes it easy to get into and around downtown. The network is simple, with two lines that begin east of the city and move toward downtown. These lines branch out when they reach the Karashima-chō tram stop, with **line A** moving southward toward JR Kumamoto Station and **line B** running north and doing a circuit around Kumamoto-jō. Pay for either single rides or day passes on the tram. If you plan to transfer between the lines, you must do so at the Karashima-chō tram stop. Request a *norikae-kippu* (transfer ticket) to change trams for free.

LOOP BUS

Roughly every 30 minutes, a loop bus departs from the **Kumamoto Kōtsū Center** and makes a loop around the castle (9am-5pm daily; single ride ¥150, one-day pass ¥400). This is a convenient way to access the city's major sights.

TOP EXPERIENCE

★ ASO-SAN
阿蘇山

Traveling east from Kumamoto, the road dips, curves, and ultimately rises up the side of the formidable Aso Caldera, a very ancient and still active volcano that is, to put it mildly, massive. From east to west, its caldera spans 18 km (11 mi); from north to south, 24 km (15 mi). Its circumference is more than 120 km (75 mi) around. The spread is so vast, entire villages and swaths of farmland exist within its basin. The main crater formed some 90,000 years ago after a mega-volcano imploded. A lake's worth of water then accumulated, and a number of diminutive additional cones rose as the moody volcano continued to gush. This cluster of five cones is known as Aso-san, one of the world's largest calderas.

The most heavily trafficked road into Aso-san's vast interior is the **Aso Kankō Toll Road.** Starting from **JR Aso Station,** take the road southward and the perfectly symmetrical cone of **Komezuka,** which literally means "Hill of Rice," comes into view. Legend holds that the peak was once a large mound of rice owned by the local god Takeiwatatsu-no-mikoto. When the townspeople in the area were struck with hunger, they pleaded with the god for food. He generously agreed to give a portion of his mountain-sized stockpile to the starving villagers. The divine scoop of sustenance resulted in the crater seen atop the mountain today.

As the road bends eastward, the **Kusasenri Plateau** unfolds as a calm scene of marshes and fields of grazing cows and horses, with **Naka-dake** (1,506 meters/4,940 feet) looming beyond. This peak, accessed by ropeway, is Aso-san's only active cone. Note that gas levels near Naka-dake can become dangerously high, a particular problem if you have any kind of respiratory condition.

While it's generally safe to visit if you take proper precautions, Aso-san erupted as recently as October 2016, causing significant damage to the area around the peak. Also note that the earthquake that struck Kumamoto in April of the same year dealt a major blow to some of the area's sights. Among them, the ancient shrine **Aso-jinja** was sadly all but flattened.

Sights

DAIKANBŌ LOOKOUT
大観峰展望所

24/7; free

Located on the caldera's northern rim, this scenic viewpoint sits on one of seven promontories (aka "noses") that extend into the basin from its edge. While this used to be a strategic place for the Aso clan to gaze long distances in ancient times, today it serves as a lookout for buses full of tourists. The 360-degree views of the entire caldera are splendid. The five main peaks of Aso-san—all visible here—are said to resemble the outline of Buddha sleeping ("Nehanzo") on the basin floor. When clouds occasionally roll into the valley at just the right elevation, the enlightened one appears to be floating supine on them.

This is the best place to see Aso-san in all its majesty from a distance. It's a particularly good option if you're driving your own car and want to see the mountain in passing without spending too much time. To reach the viewpoint, from JR Aso Station on the JR Houhi Main Line, take the Kyūshū Sanko bus heading northward toward Tsuetate. Get off at the Daikanbo Iriguchi bus stop. From there, follow the walking path to the left of the toilets in the parking area. You can either return the same way you came (10 minutes each way), or walk a longer loop that takes about 40 minutes total. It's wise to bring a jacket any time of year as it can get quite windy. Also, check the weather before making the trip. Sometimes fog rolls in and totally obscures the view.

Aso-san

KUSASENRI PLATEAU
草千里高原

Distance: 5.5 km (3.4 mi)

Time: 1.5 hours round trip (Kijima-dake), 3 hours round trip (Naka-dake)

Information and maps: Aso Volcano Museum information desk; www.explore-kumamoto.com/kusasenri-plateau

Trailhead: Aso Volcano Museum

Taking the Kyūshū Sanko bus (¥650 one-way) or driving your own car (¥800 for toll road) southward from JR Aso Station for about 40 minutes, you'll arrive at this grassy plain. Horses and cattle graze and drink from shallow crater lakes, while Mount Naka-dake looms just beyond. This is a great place to get up close and personal with this otherworldly landscape.

The **Aso Volcano Museum** (tel. 0967/34-2111; www.asomuse.jp; 9am-5pm daily) is across the street from the parking lot for the Kusasenri area. Although you wouldn't be missing much to skip it, there is a live feed of the happenings of the volcano's interior supplied by two heat-resistant cameras installed in the most active spot inside the volcano.

More significantly, this is a good starting point for exploring the unearthly terrain on foot. A 5.5-km (3.4-m) path that takes you to the top of **Kijima-dake** starts from behind the museum (30 minutes one-way).

Once you've reached the top and have gazed into the crater of this now extinct volcano, you can either return the way you came or descend into the belly of Kijima-dake, before trundling down a ski slope that merges with a path running beside the road to nearby **Naka-dake.** The one-way hike, from the Kusasenri parking lot to Kijima-dake and on to Naka-dake, totals about one and a half hours. This is a good option if you want to explore the area on foot.

If you plan to also take the ropeway, or shuttle bus, to the top of Naka-dake to peer into its steamy vent, you can do so from this point. You can return via the ropeway (or bus), then make the return hike along the same trail. Alternatively, if you're relying on public transport, you can take a bus to Asosan-nishieki bus stop, in front of the ropeway's lower station, ride the ropeway (or bus) to the summit, then return via the ropeway (or bus) and starting from Asosan-nishieki bus stop, even walk down the trail to Kusaneri and catch a bus from the Aso Volcano Museum.

MOUNT NAKADAKE
中岳

www.aso.ne.jp/~volcano/info; to reach the bottom cable car station, take the Kyūshū Sanko bus (¥650 one-way) to Asosan-nishieki bus stop or drive (¥800 toll road) south from JR Aso Station for about 40 minutes

If conditions are right, Naka-dake is the most awe-inspiring sight at Aso-san. However, conditions could include dangerous levels of poisonous gases or the potential for an eruption. If the volcano is cooperating on the day of your visit, quite a scene awaits. Inside the crater, a lake infused with a heavy layer of gray ash gurgles as sulfurous steam wafts in the air.

You can reach the top of the crater and gaze upon this unearthly landscape, by walking 30 minutes uphill from the Asosan-nishieki bus stop at the bottom station of the **Mount Aso Ropeway** line (808-5 Kurokawa; tel. 0967/34-0411; www.kyusanko.co.jp/aso/lang_en). At the time of writing, the ropeway itself was closed. It's uncertain when or if it will be operational again. It is, however, possible to board a shuttle bus in lieu of the ropeway and travel by road to the top of the crater (www.kyusanko.co.jp/aso/pdf/alsinfo_en.pdf; 9am-5pm daily; adults ¥750 one way, ¥1,200 return; children ¥370 one way, ¥600 return). You can also make this same journey yourself via a toll road (¥800) if you've got your own wheels. Once on top, you can walk along a stretch of the crater's edge, but access to its north side is forbidden due to the deaths of two tourists in 1997 who were struck by a sudden blast of lethal fumes.

While the odds of a full-scale eruption while you stand atop the peak are slim, eruptions did lead to loss of life in 1958 and 1979. Other sizable discharges happened in 1989, 1990, 1993, and 2016. If the earth starts to wobble or ominous clouds of ash begin to spew, keep your eyes peeled for the emergency bunkers arrayed around the mountain and take cover in one of them.

Be sure to check on daily conditions before making the trip to Naka-dake. It's not uncommon for the peak to be closed. And if you happen to have a respiratory ailment of any kind, don't go regardless of how the volcano is behaving that day.

Food and Accommodations

★ TAKAMORI DENGAKU-NO-SATO

2685-2 Ōaza-Takamori; tel. 0967/62-1899; www.dengakunosato.com/index.html; 10am-7:30pm daily late-Mar.-Nov., 10am-5pm Mon.-Fri. and 10am-6:30pm Sat.-Sun. Dec.-late-Mar.; sets ¥1,790-2,850; take the Minamiaso Tetsudo local railway line to Takamori Station, then take a taxi (10 minutes; less than ¥1,000 one way)

Set within an atmospheric grove, this repurposed thatched-roof farmhouse is fitted with *irori* (floor hearths), around which diners sit on floor-cushions. Fish, meat, vegetables, and tofu are deliciously glazed in miso paste and speared on skewers, then slowly grilled in the pit. This is an ancient form of rural cooking. A local spin includes the use of the taro root, which proliferates in the region. It's an experience as much as it is a meal.

ASO BASE BACKPACKERS

1498 Kurokawa, Aso-shi; tel. 0967/34-0408; www.aso-backpackers.com; dorms ¥2,800, twins ¥6,000, ¥6,600 d; walk 3 minutes south of JR Station

This spotless, cedar-scented hostel is a great base for exploring the region, and to meet fellow travelers. There are dorms (mixed and female-only) and private rooms, all of which share a bathroom. There's a shared lounge, kitchen and balcony. The atmosphere is more akin to a cabin—including a wood-burning stove and mountain views—than a backpacker hub. The friendly staff speak English and are happy to help. It shuts down during the coldest part of the winter (check the website for dates). Recommended.

Information and Services

If you want to learn more about longer hikes in the area, stop by the **Michi-no-Eki Aso** tourist information center (1440-1 Kurokawa; tel. 096/735-5077; www.aso-denku.jp/denku; 9am-6pm daily) a one-minute walk east of JR Aso Station. Here you can pick up an English-language hiking map of the caldera and speak to friendly English-speaking staff who can help with transportation logistics, reservations, and local recommendations. It's a good spot to pick up food before a hike too.

Online, to learn more about the wide range of activities on offer around Aso-san, from riding horses to paragliding, check out the region's tourism portal at www.asocity-kanko.jp.

Getting There and Around

Unfortunately, the train line that once linked Kumamoto city and Aso was put out of commission by the large quake that struck the region in 2016. The best way to reach Aso-san from Kumamoto city is by **car.** There are numerous car rental outlets around JR Kumamoto Station. If you're coming to Aso-san from Beppu, to the east, take the Aso Boy limited express train straight to **JR Aso Station** (2 hours 15 minutes; ¥3,880).

It's also possible to arrive in front of JR Aso Station by **bus.** Destinations served by bus to and from Aso include Beppu, Kurokawa Onsen, Yufuin, and Kumamoto Airport.

Once you've arrived, buses shuttle from JR Aso Station to as far as the Kusasenri Plateau (¥570), but renting a car is a better option. **Toyota Rent-a-Car** (1478-1 Kurokawa; tel. 0967/35-5511; https://rent.toyota.co.jp; 8am-8pm Apr.-Oct., 8am-6pm Nov.-Mar.) has an outlet just east of JR Aso Station. Given the popularity of exploring the region by car, try to reserve your car online at least a week or two before you plan to arrive.

BEPPU
別府

Beppu is brash, kitschy, and fun. Think of it as geothermal Disneyland. Beyond the aging hotel facades, the earth tells its own story through the cloud of steam, wafting from 2,500 springheads and hanging above the hilly town at all times.

The variety of baths in Beppu is daunting. This sprawling *onsen* resort is blessed with more fiery water than any other in Japan. A whopping 100 million liters of hot water gurgles to the surface of this geothermal nexus every day, second only to Yellowstone National Park in volume of hot-spring water. It's possible to immerse yourself in hot muddy pools, bury yourself up to the neck in steaming sand, and sweat it out sauna-style. And, of course, practically every *ryokan* in town has its own private baths, from en-suite tubs to shared outdoor pools. While Beppu is known to draw a crowd, you'll find a few secret baths outside downtown with more elbow room.

Beyond bathing, the town is also famous for its array of "hells," akin to some of the boiling pools seen, for example, at Yellowstone National Park. These seething cauldrons are purely for observation. The town's excess steam is even put to use in food preparation: it's possible to steam-cook a meal with heat rising directly from the earth.

Sights

BEPPU CITY TRADITIONAL BAMBOO CRAFTS CENTER
別府市竹細工伝統産業会館

8-3 Higashi-sōen; tel. 0977/23-1072; www.city.beppu.oita.jp/06sisetu/takezaiku/takezaiku.html; 8:30am-5pm Tues.-Sun.; ¥300 adults, ¥100 junior high and elementary school students; from JR Beppu Station, take bus 22 or 25 to the Takezaiku-densankan-mae bus stop

One of the simple pleasures of any trip to Japan is deeply immersing yourself in a bamboo grove. The area around Beppu is awash in bamboo. This sturdy plant, the fastest grower of all perennials, symbolizes prosperity and purity of mind in Japan. Moreover, the Japanese have learned to use the shoots in a multitude of ways, from eating it to employing it as a raw material for making crafts (toys, baskets) to construction (fences, ladders). To get a sense of how deep Japan's mastery of this versatile plant goes, pay a visit to this museum.

From woven baskets to delicate works of art, the displays here will leave you with a new appreciation for this amazing plant and just how creatively Japan has learned to use it. You can also try your hand and making something from bamboo in one of the workshops held on the second floor. Reserve more than a week ahead, because the classes are popular.

HELL CIRCUIT (JIGOKU MEGURI)
地獄めぐり

www.beppu-jigoku.com; tel. 0977/66-1577; 8am-5pm daily; ¥400 for single "hell" entry, ¥2,000 for combination ticket; both single and combination tickets can be purchased at any given "hell"

This is where Beppu brandishes its kitsch credentials. If you aren't put off by tacky motifs and assorted schlock, these infernal pools can be a bit of fun to see. There's a combination ticket that allows you to move freely between seven boiling pools, each with its own quirks. Of the seven hells covered by the combination ticket, five dot the Kannawa area, about 4 km (2.5 miles) northwest of JR Beppu Station, while the other two are located in the more secluded district of Shibaseki, around 2.5 km (1.6 mi) north of Kannawa. If you're keen to roll around in the kitsch, by all means, dutifully visit each hell. But if you'd rather just get a taste and avoid the cheesier displays, Umi Jigoku and Oniishibozu Jigoku in Kannawa should suffice.

To reach the Kannawa and Shibaseki districts, note that the closest train stations are Beppudaigaku (from Beppu Station, 4 minutes; ¥210) and Kamegawa (from Beppu Station, 7 minutes, ¥210) on the Nippo line. Buses run to the respective neighborhoods from both stations. Once in the Kannawa or Shibaseki area, it's possible to walk between each district's respective pools.

★ *Onsen*

TAKEGAWARA ONSEN

16-23 Motomachi; tel. 0977/23-1585; www.gokuraku-jigoku-beppu.com/entries/takegawara-onsen; 6:30am-10:30pm daily; ¥100 onsen, ¥1,030 sand bath; walk 10 minutes east of JR Beppu Station

This nostalgic wooden bath house is Beppu's most famous. Built in 1879, the complex stands in the heart of a red-light district. Immerse yourself in the piping hot water filling its timeworn pools. Or, rent a *yukata* and get buried in steamy black sand, followed by a soak in the pool. Whether you opt for water or sand, you'll be sure to get a strong dose of retro charm.

BEPPU BEACH SAND BATH (AKA KAIHIN SAND BATH)

tel. 0977/66-5737; www.gokuraku-jigoku-beppu.com/entries/kamegawa-hamada-onsen; 8:30am-6pm Apr.-Oct., 9am-5pm Nov.-Mar.; ¥1,030; from JR Beppu Station, take the Nippo line to Beppudaigaku Station (4 minutes, ¥210) and walk 7 minutes east

In northern Beppu, this beachside sand bath is another local icon. The spot along the Shōnin-ga-hama beachfront can get very crowded, so plan on going earlier in the day. The system is simple: suit up in a *yukata* and lay on your appointed beach plot, beneath a multicolor parasol. A staff member will then cover you with hot black sand up to your neck. Sit there for 15-20 minutes, then emerge refreshed.

ONSEN HOYŌLAND

tel. 0977/66-2221; http://hoyoland.webcrow.jp; 5-1 Myōban; 9am-8pm; ¥1,100; about 15 minutes by taxi from Beppudaigaku Station, or 15 minutes' walk west of Umi Jigoku in the "hell circuit"

About 5 km (3 mi) west of the sand baths of Shōnin-ga-hama, this tumbledown complex is showing signs of age. Knowing its deeper history, this shabbiness only adds to the appeal of this bucolic, open-air scene. Bathing in these large vats of steamy mud is thought to stretch back as far as the 8th century. There are gender-separated changing rooms, but the mud baths themselves are mixed. While the mud obscures anything from view in the pools, a modesty towel is advised for covering up in the other areas. Nearby, there are also traditional, gender-separated baths of hot water, as well as steam baths.

Local buses run to this *onsen*, which is which is a good one to visit either before or after observing the Kannawa district's group of five "hells."

Umi Jigoku hell

SHIBASEKI ONSEN

4-1 Noda; tel. 0977/67-4100; www.gokuraku-jigoku-beppu.com/entries/shibaseki-onsen; 7am-8pm, closed second Wed. of month; ¥210; 35 minutes' walk, or a 10-minute taxi ride, from Kamegawa Station

Set beside a stream and surrounded by nature, this tranquil *onsen* in the hills outside of town feels a world apart from the crowded pools elsewhere in Beppu. In use since the Kamakura Preriod (1192-1333), there's a steam bath and two pools. One of the pools is deemed lukewarm (*nuruyu*), despite being pretty toasty. The second is labeled as hot (*atsuyu*), although it may feel borderline scalding for some. To be safe, enter *slowly*. It's possible to rent a private pool, intended for families (*kazoku-buro*), for up to four people (¥1,620 per hour). As an aside, this *onsen* is notable for its lax policy toward bathers with tattoos.

Local buses run to this *onsen*, and it is within easy reach of the two hells of the residential Shibaseki district, Chinoike Jigoku and Tatsumaki Jigoku, which are both about 12 minutes' walk to the east.

Food

HAJIME ZUSHI

1-4-13 Kitahama; tel. 0977/25-8421; 6pm-11pm Mon.-Sat.; courses ¥1,500-3,000; walk 6 minutes east of JR Beppu Station

This welcoming sushi spot is routinely packed thanks to its reputation for sourcing only top-notch fish. The gregarious staff exert a pull of their own as well. Be sure to try the rewowned *anago* (conger eel). The price-to-quality ratio is fantastic. Reserve a day or more in advance to snag a seat.

GYŌZA KOGETSU

1-9-4 Kitahama; tel. 0977/21-0226; 2pm-9pm Wed.-Mon.; ¥600 per plate

Gyoza (fried dumplings) and beer—that's the entire menu. The former is cooked to crisp-perfection; the latter is sold by the ice-cold bottle. The shop is tucked down a side-street behind a shopping arcade. A menagerie of *maneki-neko* (lucky cat) figurines stands poised in the window. This place has an ardent fan base, so be prepared to wait in line.

TOYOTSUNE HONTEN

2-12-24 Kitahama; tel. 0977/22-3274; www.toyotsune.com; 11am-2pm and 5pm-10pm daily; lunch ¥860-1,650, dinner courses ¥3,240-4,320; walk 10 minute east of JR Beppu Station

This down-to-earth restaurant serves Beppu's culinary fortes: *fugu* (blowfish), *toriten* (chicken tempura), Bungō beef (the local wagyu variant), and the fresh catch of the day. Check out the *shōchū* list too if you feel like sampling some of the local firewater.

JIGOKU MUSHI KŌBŌ

5-Kumi Furomoto; walk 15 minutes east of Umi Jigoku

Come here to cook your own food in vats, using steam rising from *onsen* waters below. Tickets for chicken, pork, seafood, and vegetable sets can be purchased from a vending machine there. Alternatively, bring your own ingredients and pay to use the vats. While Kannawa's hells are admittedly tacky, this DIY culinary experience in the same area is fun. Plan on working it into your tour of the area's hells.

Accommodations

★ YAMADA BESSŌ

3-2-18 Kitahama; tel. 0977/24-2121; http://yamadabessou.jp; ¥19,000 d without meals; walk 7 minutes from JR Beppu Station

This family-owned gem is showing signs of wear, but it only adds to the charm. In business more than eight decades, the *ryokan* is set in a garden and housed in a quaint wooden building with inviting tatami rooms. Its rich tapestry of antique items conjures an early Shōwa-Period dream. Most of the rooms don't have their own bath, but the inn does have atmospheric shared pools (gender-separated).

SHINKI-YA

2-kumi; tel. 0977/66-0962; www.shinkiya.com; ¥18,800 d with two meals

There are seven cozy tatami rooms at this charming, family-owned ryokan hidden away in a quiet corner of Kannawa, north of Beppu's tourist fray. Most of the rooms have a toilet and sink, but hot-spring bathing is communal (gender-separated). Meals akin to feasts, including food cooked with *onsen* steam, are optional at an elevated rate. Recommended.

HOTEL UMINE

3-8-3 Kitahama; tel. 0977/26-0002; www.hotelumine.com; ¥34,560 d with breakfast; walk 12 minutes east of JR Beppu Station

This is one of Beppu's top luxury properties, right on the beach, and the rates reflect that. Each room is bright and airy with elegant furniture made of wood and leather, a living-room area, and its own wooden *onsen* tub. There are views of the ocean, just beyond the property, too. Meals are terrific, and service is just as personalized as you'd expect in a high-end resort.

KANNAWA-EN

6-kumi Miyuki; tel. 0977/66-2111; www.kannawaen.jp; ¥34,000 d with meals

This property offers a similarly high-end experience to Hotel Umine, offering plush rooms with private *onsen* tubs, exquisite *kaiseki* and teppanyaki meals, impeccable service, and alluring shared pools. It has a fantastic garden with an artificial waterfall feeding into a central pond, teahouses, a swimming pool, and even an on-site *Noh* theater. In short, stay here if you can afford to splurge. It's an oasis of calm set in the middle of Kannawa's hells.

Information and Services

TOURIST INFORMATION

The easiest place to go for English information and bilingual help is **Beppu International Plaza** (12-13 Ekimae-machi; tel. 0977/21-6220; 8:30am-5pm daily), located in JR Beppu Station near the central east exit. There's also a branch in **Kannawa** (4-kumi, Miyuki; tel. 0977/66-3855; 9am-5pm daily), a short walk east of the area's various "hells" in the north side of town. Besides providing useful information on Beppu, these offices provide services like baggage storage and delivery. Beppu International Plaza also maintains a good English-language website (https://biplaza.jp).

MEDICAL SERVICES

If you need medical help, the **Beppu Medical Center** (1473 Uchikamado; tel. 0977/67-1111; https://beppu.hosp.go.jp) is about 20 minutes' walk west of Kamegawa Station, two stations north from Beppu Station on the JR Nippō line.

Getting There

TRAIN

JR Beppu Station, located in the heart of town, is well-connected to Kyūshū's key hubs. Coming from **Hakata,** the easiest route is to take the *shinkansen* train to Kokura, where you'll transfer to the Sonic limited express train on the JR Nippō line, which runs to JR Beppu Station (1 hour 40 minutes; ¥7,740). You can also take the Sonic limited express train directly to and from Hakata from Beppu (2 hours; ¥5,570).

Coming from JR Miyazaki Station in the south, take the Nichirin limited express to **Ōita Station,** then transfer to the Sonic limited express until Beppu (3 hours 20 minutes; ¥6,000). Farther south in Kagoshima, hop on the *shinkansen* to Hakata on the other end of the island (1 hour 30 minutes; ¥10,650), then follow the same route from Hakata described above to reach Beppu from there.

Coming from Aso in the west, take the **Aso Boy** limited express (2 hours 15 minutes; ¥3,880) straight to Beppu. Note that only three of these trains run each day. If you're coming from Nagasaki, first take the Kamome limited express to Hakata, then transfer to the Sonic limited express and ride until Beppu (4 hours; ¥10,170). From Kumamoto, the previously more direct route has been suspended since 2016 due to the large quake that struck the region. For the time being, you'll need to take the *shinkansen* north to Kokura, then hop on the Sonic limited express that runs directly to Beppu (2 hours 15 minutes; ¥11,640).

AIR

Ōita Airport (tel. 0978/67-1174; www.oita-airport.jp) services flights from Tokyo, Osaka, Nagoya, and Seoul. **Buses** shuttle between the

☆ Beppu *Onsen* Alternatives

There's no denying Beppu's kitschy geothermal amusement park is tons of fun, but it may leave something to be desired in terms of relaxation. Luckily, there are a few alternatives.

TOP EXPERIENCE

KUROKAWA ONSEN
黒川温泉

Kurokawa Onsen is an understated mountaintop gem, easily ranking among Japan's most atmospheric hot-spring towns. All told, 24 *rotemburo* (open-air public baths) dot the town, which has a number of rustic public bath houses as well (8:30am-9pm daily for day visitors). Some highlights, all of which double as exquisitely traditional *ryokan* serving *kaiseki* meals, include **Kurokawa-sō** (6755-1 Manganji, Kurokawa; tel. 0967/44-0211; www.kurokawaso.com; ¥17,600 pp with 2 meals); the iconic **Shinmei-kan** (6608 Manganji; tel. 0967/44-0916; www.sinmeikan.jp; ¥34,500 d with 2 meals); the lovely riverside **Fujiya** (6541 Manganji; tel. 0967/48-8117; www.ryokan-fujiya.jp; ¥40,000 d with 2 meals); and highly atmospheric and centrally located **Okyaku-ya** (6546 Manganji; tel. 0967/44-0454; www.okyakuya.jp; ¥23,250 d with 2 meals).

Food

For something hearty and filling head to **Ufufu** (6606 Manganji; tel. 0967/44-0651; http://oyadokurokawa.com/restaurant; noon-2pm Fri.-Wed., 6:30pm-8pm Fri.-Wed., open Thurs. if public holiday; lunch ¥900-2,000, dinner courses ¥4,000-8,000). This restaurant, attached to the Oyado Kurokawa *ryokan,* offers excellent *yakiniku* and yakitori meals.

Information and Services

A **nyūto tegata** (wooden *onsen* pass), gives you access to the *rotenboro* (open-air baths) of any three of the 24 participating *onsen ryokan* around town. You can pick up one of these passes for ¥1,300 (children ¥700) at the **Kurokawa Onsen Ryokan Association Information Center** (Kurokawa Sakura-dōri; tel. 0967/44-0076; 9am-6pm daily) or at the reception desk of any of participating *ryokan.* Without this pass, the cost is ¥600 per bath. Before you set off, be sure to ask which *onsen* are open that day, as some will sporadically be closed. Check out www.kurokawaonsen.or.jp/eng_new for more information.

Getting There

Buses link Kurokawa Onsen to many spots around the island, with the closest being **Aso** (1 hour; ¥990) and **Beppu** (2 hours 30 minutes; ¥2,980), passing **Yufuin** on the way (¥2,370). If you have

airport and the beachside area of Kitahama (40 minutes; ¥1,500), terminating at JR Beppu Station (50 minutes; ¥1,500).

BUS

Long-distance buses run mainly to the **bus terminal** beside JR Beppu Station and to the Kamenoni bus terminal (102-2-10 Kitahama; tel. 0977/23-5170; www.kamenoibus.com), located near the Kitahama beach area. Taking a highway bus is particularly a good option if you're traveling from JR Kumamoto Station (5 hours; ¥3,960), which is currently only reachable by train via a circuitous route due to the blow dealt to the region's railway network in the large 2016 earthquake.

BOAT

Ferries operated by **Ferry Sunflower** (tel. 0977/22-2181; www.ferry-sunflower.co.jp) travel between Beppu and Osaka. Coming from Shikoku, **Uwajima Unyu Ferry** (tel. 0977/21-2364; www.uwajimaunyu.co.jp) runs ferries to Beppu from Yawatahama, which is reachable from Uwajima on the Uwakai limited express (40 minutes; ¥2,130). Check the websites of both ferry operators for more details on routes, timetables, and fares.

a **car,** however, you'll be able to reach the remote town and explore the surrounding region more easily.

Kurokawa Onsen

YUFUIN
湯布院

Yufuin is a slightly hipper onsen resort with chic cafés, restaurants, and fashionable shops selling artfully made Japanese crafts. Though the town's other public baths are reserved for local residents, three excellent *ryokan* with *onsen* open to day-trippers are scattered throughout the area: **Baien** (2106-2 Yufuin-chō Kawakami; tel. 0977/28-8288; www.yufuin-baien.com; 11am-4pm daily, last entry 3pm; ¥700), **Tsuka no Ma** (444-3 Yufuin-chō Kawakami; tel. 0977/85-3105; https://tsukanoma.club; 9:30am-6:30pm daily, last entry 6pm; ¥800), and **Shitan-yu** (1585 Yufuinchō Kawakami; tel. 0977/84-3111; 9am-11pm daily; ¥200).

Food

For a snack with a view, try **Café la Ruche** (1592-1 Kawakami; tel. 0977/28-8500; www.chagall-museum.com/cafe/index.html; 9am-5pm Mon.-Sat., 7:30am-5pm Sun.; ¥864-1,836). And if you decide to stay the night in Yufuin, you have two very different options: **Country Road Youth Hostel** (441-29 Yufuinchō Kawakami; tel. 0977/84-3734; http://countryroadyh.com; dorms ¥3,800, private single ¥4,500, ¥8,600 d); and ★ **Sansou Murata** (1264-2 Yufuin-chō Kawakami; tel. 0977/84-5000; www.sansou-murata.com; ¥80,000 d), a truly luxurious *onsen* retreat.

Information and Services

For a fuller picture of what's on offer in Yufuin, stop at the **tourist information center** inside JR Yufuin Station (tel. 0977/84-2446; http://yufuin.or.jp/global/; 9am-5:30pm daily). Pick up a copy of the English-language map showing the town's prime galleries and *onsen* pools.

Getting There

Coming from **Beppu,** take the Sonic limited express train to Ōita, then transfer to the local JR Kyudai line to **Yufuin Station** (1 hour 20 minutes; ¥1,930).

Getting Around

BUS

Downtown Beppu is navigable **on foot,** but you may want to make use of the town's efficient bus network if you plan to visit the various hells dotting Kannawa on the north side of town. There are a number of bus routes, most of which depart from outside **JR Beppu Station.** To be sure you're catching the correct bus, and that you're clear on the correct stop to wait for the bus, check with the staff of the **Beppu International Plaza** housed in the station.

There are a few bus passes worth knowing about. The **"mini" pass** (¥900) allows unlimited travel within Beppu's city limits for a day. The **"wide" pass** (¥1,600) covers all buses within Beppu, as well as the bus to the nearby *onsen* hub of Yufuin. You can purchase one of these passes at the Beppu International Plaza or ferry terminal.

CAR

If you plan to venture farther afield, renting a car is a good option. Situated inside JR Beppu Station, **Eki Rent-a-car** (tel. 097/724-4428; www.ekiren.co.jp) is a good bet.

Miyazaki Prefecture 宮崎県

Bordering Oita to the north and Kumamoto to the west, sun-drenched Miyazaki comprises the beautiful southeastern corner of Kyūshū. Thanks to its latitude, Miyazaki is blessed with a mild climate. This makes it a nice destination year-round and a place where tropical fruit can grow—mangos anyone?

Misty mountains in the north buzz with mystic significance due to their ties to Japan's creation myths. The fetching coast invites unplugging. Catch rays, or waves, and if you have a car, trundle down the gorgeous Nichinan Coast, renowned as a magnet for surfers. This laid-back enclave serves as an escape for stressed urbanites—a rare corner of Japan that seems designed for sun worship, beach bumming, and unleashing one's inner flower child.

★ TAKACHIHO
高千穂

Tucked away in Miyazaki's northern mountains, the Takachiho region is the backdrop to some of Japan's core mythology. It is said that the gods beamed down to Takachiho-yama and created the whole archipelago from there.

Takachiho is also one of two contested spots, along with Kirishima National Park's Mount Takachiho-no-mine, where the sun goddess Amaterasu's grandson Ninigi no Mikoto is said to have descended to earth to establish Japan's imperial line.

To fully appreciate the magical atmosphere of Takachiho, plan to spend a night in the area. This makes the effort to reach the remote region more worthwhile. It also gives you a chance to slow down and savor the atmosphere of the place where Japan's most core myths were born.

Sights

TAKACHIHO SHRINE
高千穂神社

Set in a dense grove of cedars, some several hundred years old, this tranquil shrine is unassuming. As dusk falls each day, the sacred space comes alive as professional dancers don masks to do a condensed reenactment of what is perhaps the most famous episode in all Shinto myth. Takachiho is also said to be the site of the cave where the sun goddess

Takachiho Gorge

Divine Dirty Dancing

Not far from Aso-San, but actually in the northern mountains of Miyazaki prefecture, is Takachiho, whose deep Shinto roots are vibrantly alive today, as seen in the area's sacred dances known as *kagura*. The dances are performed across the villages and valleys of Takachiho, and the locals who keep them alive enact Shinto myths involving Amaterasu Omikami (the Sun Goddess), her brother Susano'o (the Storm God), and a host of other deities.

Tired of her brother's shenanigans—trashing her palace and ravaging her rice fields—Amaterasu fled to a cave. She blocked the entrance with a large stone, thus depriving the world of her light. **Amano Iwato Jinja,** set in a grotto, marks the spot where Amaterasu is said to have gone into hiding. Dismayed, a throng of deities convened to formulate an ingenious (and rather cheeky) plan to coax her out. In short, the goddess Ame-no-Uzume (appropriately, the Goddess of Mirth and Revelry) cavorted in a manner so provocative it sent the other gods into a resounding fit of laughter. Hearing the commotion, the Sun Goddess couldn't help but take a peek outside the cave. Tajikarao (the God of Power) stood nearby and hauled away the boulder. And thus, her light returned to the world.

This tale is reenacted—sometimes in snippets, other times in full—throughout the year. For a glimpse, a drastically condensed one-hour performance depicts a few scenes of the story at **Takachiho Shrine** every evening. Aim to arrive at least 30 minutes, or even an hour, early for seats offering good views of these *yokagura* (night *kagura)* dances.

If you're keen and timing is right, the full divine saga is acted out by more than 20 troupes of local dancers, from kids to grannies, in 33 parts during winter weekends (Sat. nights, mid-Nov. to mid-Feb.). These epic performances test the endurance of the audience as well as the dancers, taking place through the night and into the next morning. These *satokagura* (village *kagura*) performances are held at shrines, public halls and in private farmhouses to the accompaniment of flutes and drums. The atmosphere is light and laid-back, and a sense of humor pervades. Contact the **Takachiho Tourism Association** a few months in advance if possible to learn more or reserve a place.

Amaterasu hid her light from the world for a time when she grew weary of her brother's pranks. Nearby, Takachiho Gorge presents a pleasing natural scene, with waterfalls spilling over precipitous rock walls into the Gokase River below.

To reach the shrine, walk south along Route 50 for 10-15 minutes from the Takachiho Bus Center. It's recommended to combine a trip to the shrine with a visit to Takachiho Gorge, located just a bit farther south along Route 50.

AMANO IWATO JINJA
天岩戸神社

Iwato, Takachiho; tel. 0982/74-8239; http://amanoiwato-jinja.jp; 24/7; free; buses run once every 1 or 2 hours from Takachiho Bus Center (15 minutes, ¥300 one-way), or you can take a taxi (10 minutes; ¥2,500 one-way)

This shrine, located next to the Iwato-gawa river about 10 km (6.2 mi) northeast of Takachiho's town center in the village of Iwato, is situated near the cave where Amaterasu went into hiding. Set among towering cedar trees, the shrine complex sits across the Iwato-gawa from the cave, which cannot be entered. If you ask the priest at the entrance to the shrine, it's possible to get a brief tour in Japanese of the precincts, including a stop at a viewing platform behind the shrine that looks across the Iwato-gawa toward the cave.

For the full impact of this holy site, don't stop here. Walk briefly north along the road that brought you to Amano Iwato Jinja, and descend along the walkway that leads to the river below. You'll know you're on the right path when you begin to see small piles of rocks on either side of the trail. With bigger stones at the bottom and increasingly smaller ones toward the top, these delicately made stacks are left by pilgrims to commemorate their sojourn to this spiritually charged spot. The deeper you push into this forest, the more of these markers appear.

This footpath ends at **Amano Yasukawara,** a shrine dramatically set inside the grotto said to be the place where the gods plotted their scheme to draw out the sun goddess. The air in the cave and the path leading to it is charged with a sense of the sacred, making it well worth the slight detour.

Food

NAGOMI

1099-1 Mitai; tel. 0982/73-1109; http://takachiho.ja-miyazaki.jp/nagomi.php; 11am-2:30pm and 7pm-9pm daily, closes second Wed. every month; lunch ¥1,700-3,500, dinner ¥2,000-4,300; walk 6 minutes from Takachiho Shrine

Set in the **Gamadase Ichiba** complex, which houses a number of markets hawking local produce, this restaurant serves beef hot-plate set meals prepared by chefs in the kitchen, and *yakiniku* (Korean barbecue), which you grill yourself at the table. Beef comes straight from the butcher next door and is reasonably priced according to grade.

CAFÉ MERCHEN

1101-12 Mitai; tel. 0982/72-2439; http://takachiho-kanko.info/gourmet/detail.php?log=1428993708; 11am-4pm and 7pm-11pm Mon.-Sat.; ¥700-1,100; walk 3 minutes from Takachiho Shrine

Pizza, pasta, salad, curry rice: these simple *kissaten* (old-school café) classics are served here. It's a tiny space with one woman running the shop, so be prepared to wait a bit for your food to arrive if you're in a large group or when the restaurant is busy. Good food at very reasonable prices, in the heart of town.

Accommodations

B&B UKIGUMO

983-7 Mitai; tel. 0982/82-2703; www.takachiho-ukigumo.com; ¥4,800 d pp; walk 5 minutes from Takachiho Shrine

This cozy inn has clean, simple tatami rooms with en-suite bathrooms. The owner speaks English and is eager to help. A simple, hearty Western-style breakfast is included for all guests. As a bonus, its location offers great views of the gorge. Recommended as a budget option.

SOLEST TAKACHIHO HOTEL

1261-1 Mitai; tel. 0982/83-0001; www.solest-takachiho.jp; from ¥16,000 d

Opened in spring 2018, this brand-new chic hotel has sleek, spacious rooms with contemporary decor. There's a well-rounded breakfast spread, including both Western and Japanese-style dishes. Staff don't speak much English, but they're amiable and keen to help where they can. It's located right in the middle of town, making it a good base for exploring the area.

Information and Services

Located in the heart of town, across the street from the Takachiho Bus Center, the **Takachiho Tourism Association** (809-1 Mitai, Takachiho; tel. 0982/72-3031; 8:30am-5pm daily) provides basic English-language information on the area. Online, the town's English-language tourism portal (http://takachiho-kanko.info/en) is also a helpful resource.

Note that there's a notable dearth of ATMs in Takachiho. It's wise to withdraw cash before arriving if you can. If you need to pull out money in town, there's an ATM at the **post office** (27-2 Mitai, Takachiho; tel. 0982/72-2615; ATM hours 8:45am-7pm Mon.-Fri., 9am-5pm Sat.-Sun. and holidays).

Getting There

Takachiho isn't the easiest place to reach. This is largely due to the extensive damage done to infrastructure in the surrounding area by the quake that hit Kumamoto in 2016. **Driving** or taking a **bus** is necessary at the time of writing.

If you're traveling from **Kumamoto,** the easiest way to reach the outpost is by driving. Otherwise, two daily buses depart from the bus terminal in front of Kumamoto Station and travel to **Takachiho Bus Center** (3 hours 30 minutes; ¥2,370), stopping at Kumamoto Airport (2 hours; ¥2,160) on the way. Coming from **Aso,** you'll need to take a bus to **Kumamoto Airport** (7 daily; about 1 hour), then change to one of the two buses that travel from the airport to Takachiho each day.

Coming from the east, the best starting point is **Nobeoka,** which is a straight-shot on the **Nichirin limited express** from **Beppu** (2 hours 15 minutes; ¥4,230) and Miyazaki (1 hour; ¥3,100). At Nobeoka, transfer to one of the hourly buses that run to Takachiho Bus Center (1 hour 30 minutes; ¥1,790).

It's also possible to travel directly to Takachiho from **Fukuoka.** Buses travel from the bus terminal near Hakata Station to Takachiho Bus Center four times each day (3 hours 30 minutes; ¥4,020). You can either buy your ticket on the spot or make a reservation online via https://global.atbus-de.com/route_lists/?locale=en.

Getting Around

Once you've arrived in Takachiho, if you're only planning to visit the sights situated near the heart of town and the gorge, you can do it **on foot** if you're willing to walk a bit (the gorge is about 40 minutes' walk one-way from the heart of town). Amano Iwato Jinja is far enough to warrant hailing a **taxi** or hopping on one of the sporadic public **buses** that depart from **Takachiho Bus Center.**

If you'd prefer to get around on two wheels, you can rent a **bicycle** at the Takachiho Tourism Association (¥300 per hour, ¥1,500 per day).

Having a **rental car** is another great way to get around. Note that you'll need to rent a car elsewhere, such as Kumamoto, Aso, or Miyazaki, before making your way to remote Takachiho.

AOSHIMA
青島

Miyazaki's coast evokes the Mediterranean or Baja California more so than it does the bulk of Japan: palm trees, surf towns, pounding waves, and a pervading hippy ethos. As you make your way down the prefecture's lovely coast—a car is all but essential—the small island of Aoshima is worth a stop.

Located just south of Miyazaki City, this small spit of land is connected to the shore by a footbridge. It's a tranquil place, fringed by sandy beaches with a dense crop of jungle at its center. The main draw is Aoshima-jinja, a shrine said to bestow good fortune on married couples. The walk to the shrine, alone on silent sandy beaches, is entrancing. With more than 5,000 trees and a few hundred subtropical plants, the island has a distinct "not-in-Japan" atmosphere.

As you walk around the island's 1.5-km (0.9-mi) circumference, look out to the ocean just off the beach and take note of the peculiar basalt rock formations known as *oni-no-sentaku-ita* ("devil's washboard"), which emerge at low tide. This peculiar phenomenon, sculpted by waves, looks as if an intelligence shaped them.

Sights

AOSHIMA SHRINE
青島神社

2-13-1 Aoshima; tel. 0985/65-1262; https://aoshima-jinja.jp; 8am-5pm daily for shrine, 8am-5pm daily Sept.-Jun. and 8am-6pm Jul.-Aug. for museum; shrine free, museum ¥600

Walk through the gauntlet of souvenir vendors on the approach to this lovely island, pass under the *torii* gate, and make your way to this shrine. In many ways the nerve center of this island, which is considered a spiritual "power spot," this shrine draws a steady stream of couples and those in search of love. Even Emperor Akihito visited with Empress Michiko when they were still Crown Prince and Princess, spurring couples nationwide to flock to the sacred site for luck in matters of the heart.

At the main shrine, amulets are sold at the shrine both for those already partnered, as well as singles seeking love. Follow a side path that leads to the right of the main shrine, and you'll discover an inner shrine beyond. Here, you can purchase small clay disks. Lob them at the target nearby in the hopes of attracting good luck.

Also on the shrine grounds is a small museum called the **Legend of Hyūga Hall.** Offering a different spin on Shinto myth from the dances of Takachiho, this museum uses wax effigies to illustrate stories surrounding some of Shinto's most important characters, from the sun goddess to Japan's first legendary leader, Emperor Jimmu. English signage included.

Surfing

Beginners will appreciate the relatively calmer swells at **Aoshima Beach** (2-2-233 Aoshima; tel. 0985/65-1055; www.aoshimabeachpark.com; 9am-6pm daily late Apr.-late Oct.) just west of Aoshima.

Farther down the coast from Aoshima, **Uchiumi** (aka Curren's Point, named after American surfer Tom Curren, who first scouted the spot), is located between Uchiumi Station and Kouchiumi Station, about eight minutes' drive south of Aoshima.

Closer to the heart of Miyazaki city, the beachfront of **Kisaki-hama** is another good surf spot. This beach is located on the far side of a large sports park near Undōkōen Station, three stops north of Aoshima Station on the Nichinan line.

SURF CITY

2-1-11 Aoshima; tel. 050/3571-3238; http://surfcity-miyazaki.jp; 9am-10pm Tues.-Fri., 7am-6pm Sun. and holidays; walk 8 minutes north of Aoshima Station

If you'd like to try to catch some waves at Aoshima Beach, Surf City, where some staff speak English, is one of the surf shops in the area.

SURFSHOP NEWWAVE

1315-1 Kumano; tel. 0985/58-2155; http://newwavesurf.net; 10am-8pm Wed.-Mon.; walk 15 minutes north of Undōkōen Station on your way to the beach

Stop here for rentals around Kisaki-hama.

Food

FUJIYAMA PUDDING

2-11-1 Aoshima; tel. 070/5502-5670; walk 3 minutes east from JR Aoshima Station

This cafe, housed in an all-white building, makes a mean taco rice. Coffee is also great, as are the homemade puddings, with flavors including Uji green tea and Okinawa black sugar. The relaxing interior is all warm wood, down to the coasters. This is a good spot for lunch or a light dinner.

AOSHIMA BEACH PARK

2-2-233 Aoshima; tel. 0985/65-1055; www.aoshimabeachpark.com; 9am-6pm daily late Apr.-late Oct.

From spring through autumn, a collection of transient beachside bistros pop up in the form of shipping containers a stone's throw from the entrance to Aoshima. They may not be permanent, but the shopfronts are thoughtfully designed. The restaurants serve a range of foods, from burgers and tacos to Thai cuisine. It's a great laid-back option when the weather is conducive.

COAST LIFE

4710-13 Kaeda; tel. 0985/75-0673; www.coastlife.jp; 11am-3pm and 6pm-10pm Fri.-Wed.; Wed. lunch only; ¥1,500; take the JR Nichinan line from Aoshima Station to Sosanji Station, then walk 10 minutes toward the coast

"Coffee Wine Oyster and Beef" is the restaurant's stated credo, and this pretty much sums it up. It does all four, along with a good range of other items, very well, including sandwiches, risotto, and steak. Then there's the sterling beachside setting and calm-inducing vibes of the leafy, wood-paneled interior. It's a 25-minute walk north of Aoshima.

Accommodations

B&B PIER

7450-4 Kaeda; tel. 0985/652-061; from ¥6,000 d; walk 1 minute from Kodomonokuni Station, 1 stop from Aoshima Station on the JR Nichinan line

This crisp-white bed-and-breakfast houses clean, bright rooms, and a shared lounge and kitchen. All rooms share a bathroom. Breakfast is provided for all guests, as are free loaner bicycles. The affable owner is happy to advise on local attractions, and when available, to help you get around.

CINEMA HEAVEN

3983 Uchiumi; info@cinema-heaven.com; www.cinema-heaven.com; tent rentals ¥2,000, yurt rentals from ¥10,000, airstream rentals from ¥22,000; 7 minutes' drive south of Aoshima, off Route 220

This bohemian restaurant-café has a campsite (complete with yurts) and an art gallery. It also hosts occasional music events, runs a surf shop, and provides car rentals geared toward those who want to explore the coast. It's a unique mix of what makes the Nichinan Coast feel so distinct from workaday Japan: unrushed and inviting, with more than a dash of hippy ethos. Located just above Curren's Point, this is a recommended stop on your way down this sun-drenched coast.

GIN KHAAO

4028-4 Futo 1, 1F-1 Ushio no Mori, Nichinan-shi; tel. 090/8639-5614; www.ushio.co; 11am-3pm and 6pm-9:30pm Wed.-Mon.; dishes from ¥750; drive 15 minutes south of Aoshima beside Route 220

Picnic tables, benches, and metal chairs ensure this Thai eatery is anything but fussy. Festive Thai-style lights hang from the ceiling, Singha Beer posters adorn the walls, and the menu features deliciously sweet, sour, and spicy dishes (curries, spicy salads, Thai-style fried chicken) scrawled in chalk on a blackboard. This blackboard hints at the fact that the building was originally a school, which closed in 2011 after 120 years of operation. The building reopened in 2014 as the **Ushio no Mori** (Tide Forest) complex, the brainchild of Miyazaki native Shoji Ogura, who's lived in Hawaii and Australia. Alongside Thai food, you'll also find a shop selling aroma therapy oils, a hula classroom, and more. This is a good offbeat dining option as you make your way down the coast.

Getting There and Around

You can travel by train from Miyazaki Station, on the JR Nichinan line to **Aoshima Station** (25 minutes; ¥370). The island itself is a bit over 10 minutes' walk east of the station. There's also an hourly **bus** that departs from near the west exit of Miyazaki Station and travels to the west side of a botanical garden that sits a few minutes' walk from the bridge that leads to the island.

If you'd like to **cycle** from Miyazaki and explore some of the northern stretches of the Nichinan Coast extending southward, or even make a multiday journey on two wheels, there's a **Giant Store** (4-1-32 Tachibana-dōri-nishi, Miyazaki; tel. 0985/72-4307; https://giant-store.jp/miyazaki; 9am-7pm Thurs.-Tues.) about 15 minutes' walk west of Miyazaki Station. Note that this option only makes sense if you plan on doing a substantial journey, as the bicycles aren't cheap, starting with city bikes from ¥3,000 for five hours or ¥4,000 for one day, and going up from there.

Kagoshima Prefecture 鹿児島県

Entering Kagoshima Prefecture feels like arriving in the Mediterranean, or somewhere in Southeast Asia, perhaps. There's a subtropical vibe to this sun-drenched place, where more palms grow than pines. In the north, you can traipse among lush volcanic peaks in Kirishima-Yaku National Park, a dramatic landscape that spills across the border with neighboring Miyazaki. In the south, bury yourself to the neck in hot sand on the beach in Ibusuki. And in the balmy capital city of Kagoshima, southern Kyūshū's largest metropolis, you can sip *shōchū* in the shadow of "Japan's Vesuvius" (Sakurajima).

☆ Nichinan Coast Scenic Drive

the Nichinan Coast

This lush stretch of shoreline extends roughly 100 km (62 mi) from Aoshima in the north to Cape Toi in the south. Studded with palm trees, this coastline evokes the Hawaiian Islands more than mainland Japan. Above all, it's a gorgeous place to take a scenic drive. Heading south along Route 220 from Aoshima, you'll see the coastline become increasingly dramatic. Wild monkeys frolic in the surrounding mountains, and horses gallop along the plains above Cape Toi.

- About 4 km (2.5 mi) south of Aoshima you'll reach **Horikiri Pass.** The same "devil's washboard" striated rock formations seen at low tide around Aoshima can be seen covering large sections of the coast at the base of cliffs that drop beside the road.
- 30 minutes south of Horikiri Pass is **Udo-jingū** (3232 Ōaza Miyaura; tel. 0987/29-1001; www.udojingu.com ; 6am-7pm Apr.-Sept., 7am-6pm Oct.-Mar.), a unique shrine ensconced in a grotto carved into cliff above the crash of ocean waves. After descending down a stone staircase set into the side of the cliff, you'll come to the main shrine, set in a cave.
- Continuing south from Udo-jingū, drive another 50 minutes along the coast until you reach **Kōjima.** This small island about 400 meters (984 feet) offshore is home to a troupe of monkeys made famous by Kyoto University scientists who observed them washing sweet potatoes in the ocean before taking a bite. No guarantee you'll spot the critters performing the cleaning ritual, but boats run from Ishinami Beach to the island. Fares typically run about ¥1,000 per person or ¥3,000 per boat.
- **Koigaura Beach** is a highly regarded spot among surfers across Japan, about 10 minutes' drive south of Kōjima.
- Forty minutes south of Kōjima, you'll reach the end of the Nichinan Coast at **Cape Toi.** The sea cliffs here are the dramatic southern tip of Miyazaki Prefecture. The soaring **Cape Toi Lighthouse** sits atop a vast plateau that looms 255 meters (836 feet) above the ocean below.

If you need a meal or even to bed down for the night after the drive, **Tagiri Hotel Dining and Spa** (152 Ichiki; 0987/77-0238; www.tagirihotel.com; from ¥14,000 for two people), housed in a former roadside spa-inn, is unique and recommended, and there is an on-site restaurant (10am-4pm, lunchtime 11:30am-2pm Fri.-Mon.; mains ¥800). Find the path that leads through a thicket of trees behind the property to a secluded stretch of beach.

KIRISHIMA-YAKU NATIONAL PARK
霧島錦江湾国立公園

This region's otherworldly terrain, which has more than a hint of lunar quality, was the first to be designated a national park in Japan. The volcanically active Kirishima range straddles the prefectural border of Miyazaki and Kagoshima. A second far-removed section of the park—accounting for the "Yaku" portion of its name—is located to the south on the island of Yakushima, an emerald, sylvan wonderland reached by ferry from Kagoshima.

Given their otherworldly appearance, it's no surprise that the peaks of the Kirishima region serve as the backdrop to many Japanese myths. While it's disputed with the Takachiho region, the Kirishima range is also said to be the place where Ninigi no Mikoto, the sun goddess Amaterasu's grandson, descended to earth and founded the Japanese imperial line.

In this mystical landscape, trails weave through grassy plateaus, around calderas and electric-blue lakes set in craters, and down hillsides laden with a substantial layer of red dust. After rambling through the otherworldly landscape, recuperate with a soak in one of the region's *onsen* pools. One of the cones in the park, Shinmoe-dake, spewed ash and smoke thousands of feet skyward as recently as March 2018. Increased volcanic activity, including but not limited to Shinmoe-dake's recent belch, has caused some of the park's hiking trails to close indefinitely.

Be sure to check conditions before setting off for any forays into the park. Besides noxious gases and ash, the region also receives its fair share of storms, especially during the rainy season from mid-May through June. Temperatures also plummet in the dead of winter. While it's certainly possible to take a day hike here, to fully enjoy the park, it would be better to stay at least one night, or even longer—a particularly appealing prospect if you book a room at one of Kirishima Onsen's attractive *ryokan*.

Sights

KIRISHIMA-JINGŪ
霧島神社

2608-5 Kirishimataguchi; tel. 0995/57-0001; www.kirishimajingu.or.jp; 24/7; free

Dedicated to Ninigi-no-mikoto, the god who touched down on nearby Takachiho-no-mine, this shrine stretches back into deep antiquity. The current complex was constructed with the backing of the Shimazu clan in 1715, although the original was built in the 6th century. The backdrop of surrounding peaks, with a view all the way to Sakurajima on clear days, is a phenomenal sight. From JR Kirishima-Jingū Station, take the Iwasaki bus bound for Kirishima-Iwasaki Hotel, and get off at Kirishima-Jingū Mae bus stop to reach the shrine (15 minutes; ¥250; one bus every 1-2 hours).

Hiking

Due to recent Shinmoe-dake volcanic activity, many of Kirishima-Yaku's scenic trails remain closed to the public. Standout hikes include the **Ebino-Kōgen Circuit** (5.2 km/3.2 mi; 2 hours), a leisurely walk through crater lakes; **Karakuni-Dake** and **Onami-Ike Crater Lake** (9.7 km/6 mi; 6.5 hours), which traces the rim of a caldera and circles around a crater lake; and **Takachiho-no-mine** (6.8 km/4.2mi; 3 hours), a mountain ascent, but almost all of these hikes have recently been closed due to unsafe conditions.

The best strategy is to start out at one of Kirishima-Yaku's excellent visitor centers—the **Ebino-kōgen Eco Museum Center** or the **Kirishima City Tourism Information Center**—to see what hikes are available. Friendly staff will be able to provide maps and advise you on the best routes.

Food and Accommodations

Lodging and food options are clustered around the park's peaks in **Ebino-kōgen,** and in the area leading up to **Kirishima-jingū.** Perhaps the most important thing to keep in mind in these areas is that restaurants close early. If you're not staying in a *ryokan* that provides meals, aim to buy all the food you'll need for the evening before setting off for a day of hiking. If you're staying at one of the area's many *ryokan*, meals are provided.

EBINO-KŌGEN CAMPGROUND

1470 Ōaza Suenaga; tel. 0984/33-0800; www.city.ebino.lg.jp/display.php?cont=140328154326; campsite ¥830, tent rental ¥1,440, cabin ¥1,650 pp

This is a wonderful base for exploring the park. You'll have the option of pitching your own tent, renting a tent, or staying in a cabin. It's situated about 10 minutes' walk south of the Ebino-kōgen Eco Museum Center, amid pines and bisected by a murmuring stream. There's an *onsen* on-site (5pm-8pm daily). Restrooms are clean by campground standards. The price spikes a bit in mid-summer and the campground closes for a time in winter. Cooking utensils, blankets, and more are available for rent.

KIRISHIMA HOTEL

3948 Makizono-chō, Takachiho; tel. 0995/78-2121; www.kirishima-hotel.jp; ¥32,400 d with meals

Situated on the Kirishima-jingū side of the park, this *onsen* hotel has clean, though somewhat dated, rooms with en-suite baths. The staff are helpful, and the restaurant serves decent Japanese fare. But most enticing are the singular *onsen* baths. The pools here are neither the standard open-air type nor indoor the variety. Instead, a large central pool sits within a cavernous hall, with a number of smaller baths dotting the periphery. A large section of the baths are mixed-gender, but there's a corner reserved for women only. Further, only women are allowed to enter from 7:30pm until 10pm every day. Although the rates are a bit on the high side, finding good deals online is not uncommon.

Information and Services

To get a feel for the park—from its flora and fauna to updated on recent volcanic activity and a 3-D display of the landscape—stop by the **Ebino-kōgen Eco Museum Center** (1495-5 Suenaga, Ebino; tel. 0984/33-3002; www.ebino-ecomuseum.go.jp; 9am-5pm daily). This tourist information center is located near the trailhead of the Ebino-kōgen Circuit, described above. You can pick up good English-language maps of the trails that weave through the park, and ask the friendly staff any burning questions you may have.

hiking Kirishima

Beside the imposing *torii* shrine gate on the south side of Kirishima-jingū is the **Kirishima City Tourism Information Center** (2459-6 Taguchi, Kirishima; tel. 0995/57-1588; 9am-6pm daily Apr.-Sept., 9am-5pm daily Oct.-Mar.). The Kirishima City Tourism Association also maintains a website (http://kirishimakankou.com) and operates an English-language help hotline (tel. 0995/78-2115).

For a good rundown of some of the park's more popular hikes online, visit www.env.go.jp/en/nature/nps/park/guide/kirishima/recommend/index.html.

Getting There

Given the remoteness of the region, the best way to reach Kirishima is with your own wheels. That said, it's possible to arrive via **rail.** If you're approaching the park from the east, from JR Miyazaki Station, take the JR Nippō line to Miyakonojo, then transfer to the JR Kitto line bound for Hayato and ride until **Kobayashi Station** (2 hours; ¥1,650). This will put you on the northeast side of the park.

Coming from the south, take the Kirishima limited express train from Kagoshima-Chūō Station directly to **Kirishima-jingū Station,** situated on the south side of the park. The station is located about 7 km (4 mi) south of the village that sits near the southern edge of the sprawling shrine complex after which the station is named. Regular buses shuttle to and from Kirishima-jingū Station and the small village near the shrine's grand southern gate (15 minutes; ¥480).

Getting Around

Having a **car** to get around Kirishima is all but essential. That said, a few daily buses run between **JR Kirishima Station** in the south to **Maruo,** before trundling on to **Ebino-kōgen** in the park's northwest (¥990). The likelihood of missing a connection or waiting ages for the next bus to arrive makes driving a significantly more appealing option.

KAGOSHIMA
鹿児島

The parallels between Kagoshima and Naples are notable. Both are sunny cities in warm climes and both sit beside looming volcanos. Sakurajima, Kagoshima's Vesuvius, hasn't wiped out a city Pompeii-style, but that doesn't stop the very active cone from occasionally clogging the skies with black ash, obscuring the sun, and coating everything in its path—umbrella recommended.

Occasional haze aside, the city is renowned for its gregarious disposition. Its denizens are widely considered to be some of the friendliest in Japan. As for sights, there are a few good museums focused on local history, and Sengan-en, a lovely garden with the dramatically borrowed scenery of Sakurajima in the background. Last but not least, the city presents an array of dining options, complemented by a seriously good *shōchū* scene. This is the best place in Japan to imbibe the spirit.

Sights

SENGAN-EN
仙巌園

9700-1 Yoshinochō; tel. 099/247-1551; www.senganen.jp; 8:30am-5:30pm daily; ¥1,000 garden and house, ¥1,300 garden, house, and museum; from Kagoshima-Chūō Station, take the Machimeguri Bus (35 minutes) or the City View Bus (50 minutes)

Japanese garden planners have elevated the ancient Chinese concept of borrowed scenery to a high art. This principle entails visually incorporating neighboring landmarks or natural scenery, from man-made structures to mountains, into the views seen from a garden. Perhaps nowhere else is this principle more dramatically actualized than the landscape garden of **Sengan-en.** Across the bay from the garden's undulating terrain, dotted by thickets of tropical vegetation and laced with footpaths, looms the smoldering cone of Sakurajima.

The garden, located north of downtown Kagoshima next to the bay, was designed by the 19th lord of the Shimazu clan in 1658. The Shimazu lineage ruled the Satsuma domain

Kagoshima

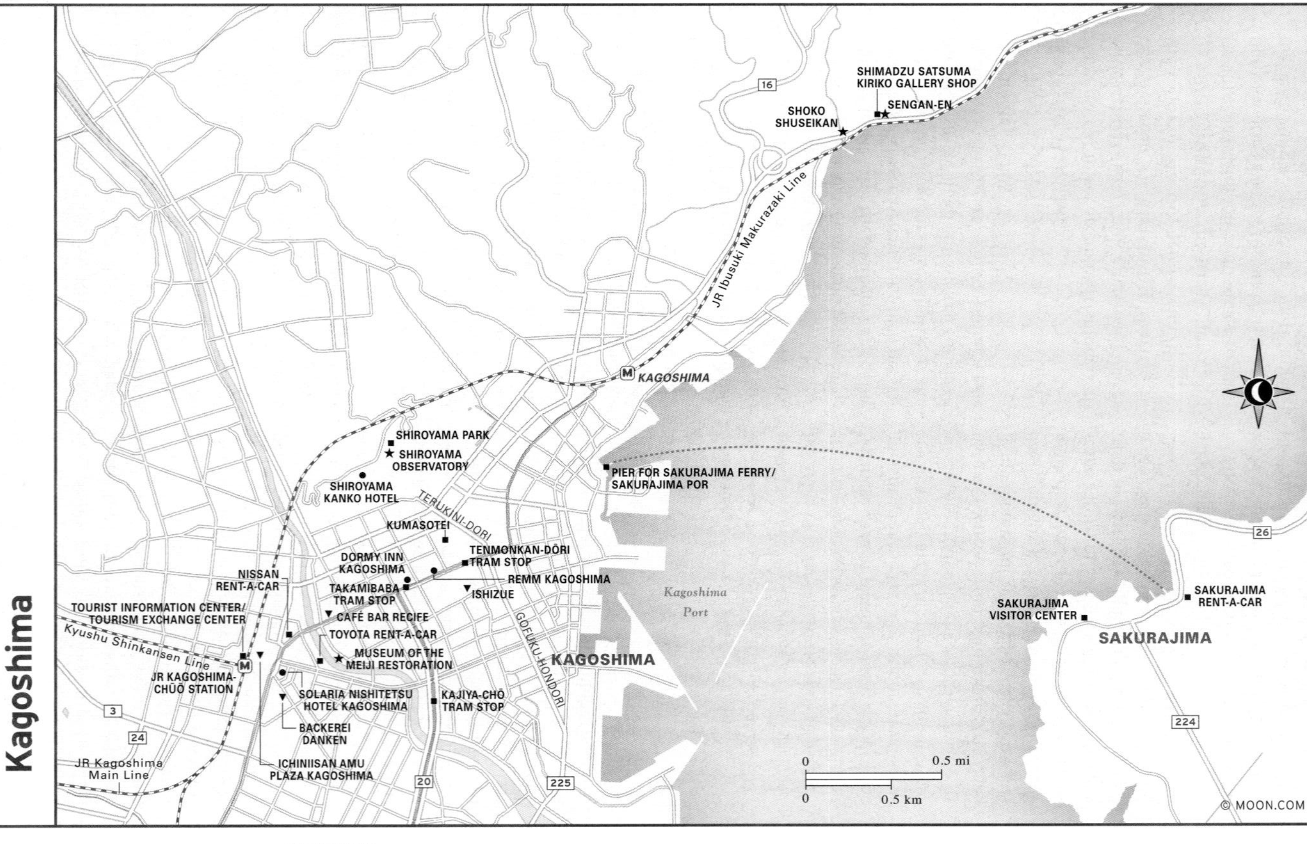
SHIMADZU SATSUMA KIRIKO GALLERY SHOP
SENGAN-EN
SHOKO SHUSEIKAN
16
JR Ibusuki Makurazaki Line
KAGOSHIMA
SHIROYAMA PARK
SHIROYAMA OBSERVATORY
SHIROYAMA KANKO HOTEL
PIER FOR SAKURAJIMA FERRY/ SAKURAJIMA POR
TERUKINI-DORI
KUMASOTEI
TENMONKAN-DŌRI TRAM STOP
DORMY INN KAGOSHIMA
REMM KAGOSHIMA
NISSAN RENT-A-CAR
TAKAMIBABA TRAM STOP
ISHIZUE
TOURIST INFORMATION CENTER/ TOURISM EXCHANGE CENTER
CAFÉ BAR RECIFE
TOYOTA RENT-A-CAR
Kyushu Shinkansen Line
MUSEUM OF THE MEIJI RESTORATION
JR KAGOSHIMA-CHŪŌ STATION
SOLARIA NISHITETSU HOTEL KAGOSHIMA
KAJIYA-CHŌ TRAM STOP
BACKEREI DANKEN
GOFUKU-HONDORI
KAGOSHIMA
Kagoshima Port
ICHINIISAN AMU PLAZA KAGOSHIMA
JR Kagoshima Main Line
3
24
20
225
26
SAKURAJIMA RENT-A-CAR
SAKURAJIMA VISITOR CENTER
SAKURAJIMA
224
0 0.5 mi
0 0.5 km
© MOON.COM

The Last Samurai

Of all the fabled warriors populating Japanese history, perhaps the most romanticized, to the point of directly inspiring a Hollywood flick, was "last samurai" **Saigō Takamori.** Born in the Satsuma Domain (modern-day Kagoshima) in 1828, Saigō went on to symbolize the profound crossroads where Japan found itself following the Meiji Restoration of 1868. At different stages of his life, he was a standard-bearer of feudalistic samurai tradition and a forward-looking modernizer.

At six feet tall, Saigō was massive by Japanese standards in the 19th century. Besides being loyal to the samurai ethos on the battlefield, Saigō also began doing calligraphy and penning poetry while he was exiled following his feudal lord's death, using the nom de plume Saigō Nanshu.

Saigō's worldview was shaped by the heady forces of the time, in which the Meiji Emperor briskly set out to modernize Japan after two centuries of self-imposed isolation from the world beyond. That was spectacularly brought to an end with the arrival of Commodore Perry's black ships in 1852. As the new imperial government took the reins and old feudal ways died, many samurai were left adrift.

In 1868, Saigō led the warriors who successfully overthrew the Tokugawa shogunate in 1868, ushering in the **Meiji Restoration.** In the ensuing years, Saigō swung between Satsuma and Tokyo, where he served for a time as head of the Imperial Guard. He became increasingly disillusioned by the new state of affairs, however, scoffing at Tokyo's increasing bureaucracy and what he felt was an overly forced push to Westernize. In 1871, all samurai were forced to lop off their topknot and adopt a Western hairstyle. Publicly brandishing a *katana* was outlawed in 1876. In response to these trends, Saigō poured his energy into a military academy in Satsuma.

Tensions boiled over in January 1877, when Saigō commandeered an army 40,000-strong in what has become known as the **Satsuma Rebellion.** He and his comrades executed a two-month siege against 60,000 imperial troops holed up in Kumamoto Castle, but were ultimately forced to flee south to Shiroyama, a peak beside Kagoshima city. Here, Saigō was critically wounded and asked one of his troops to kill him in a manner befitting a samurai.

Today, Saigō's legacy is felt far beyond Kagoshima. Japan's reverence for this rebel runs so deep that Saigō was officially pardoned by the emperor in 1891. If you don't make it to his hometown, even in Tokyo's famed **Ueno Park** he is commemorated in a bronze statue, wearing a *yukata*, with a *katana* on one side and his dog on the other.

for almost seven centuries, until the Meiji Restoration in 1868. And based on this garden, the Satsuma lords knew how to live: palms, pines, ponds, shrines, butterflies flitting among exotic flowers, stone lanterns, a bamboo grove, colorful koi (carp), and meandering paths are all lovely to explore.

Also on the grounds is the rambling 25-room villa (**Goten,** "the house") where the Shimazu clan once lived. Even with 25 rooms, the property is only one-third the size of the original. A few remnants of the **Shuseikan Industrial Complex,** which once stood on the grounds, also remain, from a factory set up in the garden for iron production during the industrial revolution.

SHOKO SHUSEIKAN
尚古集成館

Admission to the museum is included in the garden ticket (¥1,300)

Located next to the garden, just outside its main gate, this museum is housed in a long stone building that was once Japan's first factory and is now a UNESCO World Heritage site. The museum illustrates the history of Japan's industrialization and delves into the Shimazu family's important role in it. Items on display include steam engines, cannons, scrolls, military relics, locally made pottery, and examples of the city's famed cut glass. There's good English signage throughout. Plan to stop by after visiting the neighboring gardens if you're keen to dig deeper into the Shimazu clan's part in Japan's journey toward becoming an industrial juggernaut.

MUSEUM OF THE MEIJI RESTORATION
維新ふるさと館

23-1 Kajiyachō; tel. 099/239-7700; http://ishinfurusatokan.info; 9am-5pm daily; ¥300

Despite its location in Japan's southern periphery, Kagoshima has had an outsized influence on Japan's history. This is particularly true of the Meiji Restoration of 1868, when the feudal age ended and power returned to the emperor. This museum explores Kagoshima's pivotal role in that tumultuous period of Japan's history and the vital role played by Kagoshima in modernizing Japan. The displays reveal episodes from this exciting period of the nation's history, such as the ill-fated Satsuma Rebellion, led by Saigō, and the decision to send Satsuma's best and brightest young minds to study in the West.

Some of the exhibits have English signage, while others do not. For deeper understanding, download the museum's English audio guide or take the English headsets available at the reception desk. If you're interested in Japanese history, this museum is worth an hour of your time.

SHIROYAMA PARK
城山公園

22 Shiroyamachō; tel. 0942/72-2111; 24/7; free; take the City View Bus (25 minutes) or walk (35 minutes) from Kagochima-Chūō Station

Atop Mount Shiroyama (107 meters, 351 feet) near the heart of downtown, this park is located on the site where the Satsuma Rebellion came to an end with the Battle of Shiroyama. It's crisscrossed with trails and is home to the **Shiroyama Observatory** (22-13 Shiroyamachō; tel. 099/298-5111; www.kagoshima-kankou.com/guide/10525; 24/7; free). This lookout is a great place to snap a photo of the city from above, with the bay and Sakurajima hovering in the distance.

Shopping

SHIMADZU SATSUMA KIRIKO GALLERY SHOP

9700-1 Yoshinochō; tel. 099/247-1551; www.senganen.jp/en/food-shopping/shimadzu-satsuma-kiriko-gallery-shop; 8:30am-5:30pm daily

The Shimadzu Satsuma Kiriko Gallery, situated in the Sengan-en grounds adjacent to the Shoko Shuseikan museum, is a great place to buy pieces of *kiriko* (cut glass), an art form with a long history in Kagoshima. The exquisite pieces are crafted at Satsuma Kiriko Glassworks, which sits behind the Shoko Shuseikan.

Food and Bars

KAGOSHIMA FISH MARKET TOUR

tel. 099/226-8188; www.gyokago.com; 6:45am-8am Sat. Mar.-Nov.; adults ¥1,500, children ¥800

Tokyo's grand seafood bazaar at Toyosu (formerly Tsukiji) can feel overwhelming. Kagoshima's much smaller-scale market is a great alternative. These tours, held on Saturday mornings from March to November, are collectively organized by a group of hotels and *ryokan* around town, many of which provide pickup on the morning of the tour. After exploring the market, the guides will be happy to direct you to some of the best shops for a breakfast sushi spread. Sushi may not seem like a logical breakfast choice, but when in Rome...

Reserve your spot as early as possible to give the tour company time to arrange an English interpreter. Very young children are not permitted, but kids from elementary school age and up are welcome.

ICHINIISAN AMU PLAZA KAGOSHIMA

1-1 Chūōchō; tel. 099/252-2123; http://ichiniisan.jp/access/kagoshima/amu.html; 11am-11pm daily; dishes ¥300-1,080, lunch sets ¥850-1,000, dinner courses ¥3,800-6,500; walk 4 minutes east of JR Kagoshima Chūō Station

It's all about the pork at this local favorite—in particular, Kagoshima's renowned kurobuta ("black pork"), which refers to the color of the pig's skin. The juicy, tender meat is is

Shōchū: Kagoshima's Drink of Choice

When it comes to booze made in Japan, most think of rice wine, or *nihonshu*—often referred to incorrectly as *sake* (alcohol) overseas. Kagoshima breaks that stereotype with its own variety of firewater known as *shōchū*. The denizens of the balmy city not only consume the spirit more than those of any other locale in Japan, but the city also produces more of the stuff, with around 800 types, than anywhere else.

This distilled spirit is made with **sweet potato** (Kagoshima's preferred base), **barley, soba, rice,** and rarely, **corn.** It packs a punch with an alcohol content of 15-25 percent alcohol by volume, with some heavyweight varieties creeping toward 40 percent. Unlike *nihonshu*, which has inspired a subculture of aficionados and sommeliers akin to that of wine, Kagoshima's favorite tipple was long plagued by a somewhat tawdry image. This has changed, however, and today *shōchū* has slowly garnered its own rightful following. It's often compared to vodka, but *shōchū* tastes less stringent, going down smoothly neat, on the rocks, with warm water *(oyuwari)*, mixed with soda water *(chūhai)*, or infused with fruit (lemon, apple, grapefruit, lime, lychee, grape, the list goes on...) in the form of a *sawā* (sour).

A few things to note: rice-based *shōchū* is a bit milder than the full-bodied sweet potato variety, while the rare corn-based variety can reach 35 percent or more. One of the city's best-loved lines is **Shiranami.** Good, reasonably priced, and widely available varieties include **Kaidō, Kuro,** and **Kojika.** For something higher-end, try **Maō** and **Mori Izō.** If you're feeling unsure, just ask the bartender or server, *"O-susume wa nan desu ka?"* ("What's your recommendation?").

Kyūshū brims with purveyors of the beverage, but Kagoshima is the best place for a deep dive. Hands down, **Ishizue** is the place to go for this. If you're keen to hunt down a distillery, the owner can point the way. The added bonus of going to a shop that takes its quality seriously is that the pricier varieties are less likely to leave you in agony the next morning.

fantastic when eaten as shabu-shabu (hot pot made at the table with thin slices of pork, vegetables, and sometimes noodles). There are some great-value lunch sets as well, with thinly sliced boiled pork, rice, greens, and soup. Reserve ahead a day in advance for dinner if you can.

BACKEREI DANKEN

16-3 Chūōchō; tel. 099/214-9550; http://danken.jp; 7am-7pm Tues.-Sun.; baked goods from ¥180; walk 6 minutes southeast of JR Kagoshima Chūō Station, on Konan-dōri

This bakery serves excellent pastries packed with raisins, cinnamon, and chocolate, as well as savory items like sandwiches and calzones. It's a great spot to grab something on the go if you want to eat by the bay or in a park. They serve good coffee, too.

KUMASOTEI

6-10 Higashisengoku-chō; tel. 099/222-6356; www.kumasotei.com; 11am-2pm, 5-10pm daily; lunch courses ¥1,620-4,320, dinner courses ¥3,240-10,800; walk 4 minutes north of Tenmokan-dōri tram stop

With its dark wood interior and plenty of *shōchū* bottles on display, this restaurant sets the scene for a Satsuma-themed feast. Regional dishes from *kurobuta shabu-shabu* (hotpot with black pork), *kurobuta tonkotsu* (Satsuma black pork stewed in raw sugar, miso and *schōchū*), *satsuma-age* (deep-fried fish paste), *kibinago sashimi* (sashimi served with vinegared miso dipping sauce), and of course, lots of *shōchū*. The spreads are quite diverse and filling, with numerous small dishes. English menu available.

CAFÉ BAR RECIFE

1-3 Kajiyachō; tel. 099/213-9787; www.recifetereza.com; noon-11pm Sun. and Wed.-Thurs., noon-midnight Fri.-Sat.; lunch ¥1,000, dinner from ¥2,000; take tram line 2 to the Kajiya-chō tram stop, then walk 2 minutes

This bar and restaurant has a laid-back

Brazilian vibe, oozing effortless charm. It serves good food—Latin American fare, salads, chicken dishes, taco rice—and has a solid but not pretentious wine list. There are occasional DJ events, with the space functioning more as a bar at night. When it's warm, the rooftop terrace is an inviting place to while away an evening.

ISHIZUE

6-1 Sennichichō; tel. 099/227-0125; www.honkakushochu-bar-ishizue.com; 8pm-3am daily; take tram line 1 or 2 to the Temmonkan-dōri tram stop, then walk 2 minutes

This intimate, wood-paneled bar is the best place to drink *shōchū* on home turf. Having once worked in a distillery himself, the bar's owner is a master of the spirit, which exhibits an impressive range of qualities across the 1,500 bottled varieties behind the counter. Look for a sign at street level that reads "Bar 4F." Highly recommended.

Accommodation

DORMY INN KAGOSHIMA

17-30 Nishisengokuchō; tel. 099/216-5489; www.hotespa.net/hotels/kagoshima; from ¥9,000 d; walk 2 minutes from Takamibaba Station (accessible on tram lines 1 and 2), or walk 5 miutes from Tenmonkan Airport Shuttle Bus Stop

Clean, modern (if petite) rooms with the essentials are offered at a reasonable price at this centrally located hotel. There are shared hot-spring baths both inside and out, as well as en-suite facilities. It's good value for money, if you just want a clean, convenient place to sleep. Breakfast buffet is optional. Front desk staff speak English and are happy to help. Complimentary shuttle pickup from JR Kagoshima Chūō Station available with reservation.

REMM KAGOSHIMA

1-32 Higashisengokuchō; tel. 099/224-0606; www.hankyu-hotel.com/hotel/remm/kagoshima; ¥10,000 s, ¥15,000 d; walk 2 minutes from Takamibaba Station (accessible on tram lines 1 and 2), or walk 2 minutes from Tenmonkan Airport Shuttle Bus Stop

Another good, modern hotel in the heart of town, Remm has slightly more spacious rooms and a stylish on-site restaurant serving breakfast. Helpful staff speak English at the 24-hour front desk. There are shops, cafés, and restaurants aplenty in the area.

SOLARIA NISHITETSU HOTEL KAGOSHIMA

11 Chūōchō; tel. 099/210-5555; www.solaria-hotels.jp/kagoshima; ¥13,800 d; in front of JR Kagoshima Chūō Station

Some of the rooms at this modern hotel offer sweeping views of the city and Sakurajima looming beyond. Smartly decorated rooms are compact, with en-suite bathtubs. There's a French restaurant on-site that serves a breakfast buffet of Japanese and Western food, as well as French fare during lunch and dinner hours. Coin laundry facilities are on-site. Request a room facing the bay.

SHIROYAMA KANKO HOTEL

41-1 Shinshoinchō; tel. 099/224-2211; www.shiroyama-g.co.jp; ¥27,000 d; use complimentary shuttle service

One of the city's best places to stay, this hotel on the slopes of Mount Shiroyama boasts arguably better views than those had from Shiroyama Park. There are vistas of the smoldering cone of Sakurajima throughout the property, including from an open-air *onsen* on-site. There's also a spa with a mist sauna, flower bath, and masseuses on staff. A good breakfast buffet with Western and Japanese dishes is served in one of seven restaurants on-site, and the Sky Lounge offers gorgeous views of the volcano across the bay. A helpful English-speaking concierge service is happy to assist with reservations. Complimentary shuttles run between the inn and the airport as well as other places around town. Recommended.

Information and Services

There's a well-run **tourist information center** on the second floor of JR Kagoshima-Chūō Station's Sakurajima exit (tel. 099/253-2500; 8am-7pm daily). You can pick up

English-language maps and a handy city guide booklet there.

About 6 minutes' walk east of JR Kagoshima-Chūō Station, the **Tourism Exchange Center** (Kankōkoryū Center, 1-1 Uenosono-chō; tel. 099/298-5911; www.kagoshima-kankou.com/for/attractions/52888; 9am-7pm daily) also stocks various English-language material on the city, and the helpful staff can assist with bookings.

Online, visit the website run by the **Kagoshima Internationalization Council** (http://kic-update.com) for a rundown on things to see and do, as well as dining and events listings around town and beyond. The prefectural website gives a broad view of activities and experiences on offer in the prefecture (www.kagoshima-kankou.com).

Getting There

TRAIN

If you're arriving in Kagoshima by *shinkansen,* your terminus will be **Kagoshima-Chūō Station,** located on the west side of town. It's possible to arrive by *shinkansen* from Kumamoto (45 minutes; ¥6,940) and Hakata (1 hour 15 minutes; ¥10,450), or farther afield, from Hiroshima (2 hours 30 minutes; ¥17,670) and Shin-Osaka (3 hours 45 minutes; ¥22,210).

As for local trains, the JR Nippō line's southern terminus is **JR Kagoshima Station,** situated on the north side of town. This line terminates in Kagoshima after traveling south all the way from Kokura in northeastern Kyūshū, hugging the east coast of the island, with stops at other key hubs such as Beppu and Miyazaki. If you're coming from Beppu, you can travel using limited express or local trains all the way down the eastern coast if you're happy to move at a snail's pace. For example, you can take the Nichirin Limited Express from Beppu, transferring to the Kirishima Limited Express at Miyazaki, then ride the rest of the way to Kagoshima for a total trip-time of more than 6 hours (¥10,130). Sticking only to local trains can extend that journey to upwards of 8 hours.

If you have a JR pass or don't mind absorbing the shock of a higher fare, a faster option for traveling to Kagoshima from Beppu is to first head north to Kokura on the Sonic Limited Express, then transfer to the *shinkansen* and travel directly to Kagoshima-Chūō Station from there (3 hours 30 minutes; ¥15,650). Coming from Miyazaki is thankfully a much simpler (and quicker) affair. Just hop on the Kirishima Limited Express and ride directly to JR Kagoshima Station (2 hours; ¥4,230).

AIR

Kagoshima Airport (www.koj-ab.co.jp) has links to Asian hubs Seoul, Shanghai, Taipei, and Hong Kong, as well as domestic connections to Tokyo, Nagoya, Osaka, and Okinawa. Until around 9pm, buses shuttle from the airport to downtown, about 30 km (19 mi) to the south, stopping at Kagoshima-Chūō Station (45 minutes; ¥1,250) and the central Tenmonkan shopping district (1 hour; ¥1,250). Select buses continue on to Kagoshima's ferry ports.

BUS

Highway buses serve the bus terminal near the east exit of Kagoshima-Chūō Station and from the bus stops (1 Sennichi-chō) in front of Tenmonkan's **Takashima Plaza** and next to the Tenmonkan-dōri tram stop. Destinations include the island's main hubs, such as Miyazaki, Nagasaki, and Fukuoka. Although timetables and fares are detailed on the JR Kyūshū Bus website (www.jrkbus.co.jp), the lack of even basic English functionality makes booking a challenge. Inquire at the Tourism Exchange Center for assistance.

BOAT

Kagoshima is a prime jumping-off point for traveling to Japan's southwest islands, starting with Yakushima, and Okinawa beyond. If you're bound for lush Yakushima, head to **South Pier** (Minami-futō), located next to the Dolphin Port shopping complex (5-4 Honkōshin-machi; tel. 099/221-5777; www.

dolphinport.jp). From there, both daily regular ferries (one daily, 4 hours; ¥4,900) and jetfoils (six or seven daily, 1 hour 45 minutes to 2 hours 45 minutes; ¥8,800) travel to and from Yakushima. To reach the South Pier, either take the **City View Bus** (every 30 minutes; 9am-6:20pm; ¥190) to Dolphin Port or hop on a bus bound for the jetfoil terminal from either JR Kagoshima-Chūō Station or Tenmonkan.

Getting Around

TRAM

Kagoshima is served by a convenient tram network (6:30am-10:30pm; single journey ¥170, one-day pass ¥600). Two lines start from **JR Kagoshima Station** and trundle toward the central **Tenmonkan** shopping district. At Takamibaba, **line 1** forges southward into the burbs, while the better situated **line 2** stops at **JR Kagoshima-Chūō Station** and other places in the heart of town. Pay for a single trip as you exit the tram. Buy a one-day pass at the tourist information center. Note that the one-day pass can also be used on the City View Bus (see below).

BUS

Don't bother with Kagoshima's arcane city bus system, but the clearly marked **City View Bus** (every 30 minutes; 9am-6:20pm; single journey ¥190, 1-day pass ¥600) is a convenient way to take in the city's main sights. Beginning from the **E-4 bus terminal** outside JR Kagoshima-Chūō Station's east exit, these buses follow three routes around the city. To learn more about the routes, visit www.kotsu-city-kagoshima.jp/en/e-tourism/e-sakurajima-tabi. Note that the one-day pass, which can be purchased at the tourist information center, is also valid on the tram network.

CAR

Car rental outlets abound near JR Kagoshima-Chūō Station. Good options include **Toyota Rent-A-Car** (5-46 Chūō-chō; tel. 099/250-0100; https://rent.toyota.co.jp; 7am-9pm daily), about 8 minutes' walk east of the station, and **Nissan Rent-a-Car** (4-43 Chūō-chō; tel. 099/250-2123; https://nissan-rentacar.com; 8am-9pm daily), 5 minutes' walk northeast of the station.

IBUSUKI
指宿

Ibusuki is an *onsen* town in the far south of the Satsuma Peninsula where you can do something you probably never knew was possible: bury yourself up to the neck in beach sand that's heated by *onsen* water running just below the ground. It's said to relax, detox, and soften the skin. The singular experience alone justifies a day trip from Kagoshima; from there it's about an hour on the train.

★ Hot-Sand Baths

SARAKU SAND-BATH HALL

5-25-18 Yunohama, Ibusuki; tel. 0993/23-3900; http://sa-raku.sakura.ne.jp; 8:30am-noon and 1pm-9pm Mon.-Fri.; sand bath and onsen ¥1,080; walk 20 minutes from Ibusuki Station or take a taxi (5 minutes)

Here's how it works: First, buy a ticket at the Saraku Sand-Bath Hall, located about 1 km (0.6 mile) from Ibusuki Station. Head to the locker room to suit up in a rental *yukata* and pick up a towel to bundle your head, to keep your hair clean as you lay directly on the beach.

Next, go outside to find a comfy-looking plot along Surigahama Beach. Finally, wrap your head and lay down for one of the staff to cover you in the beach's hot gray sand, which puts off a slightly sulfurous odor. While this may sound unpleasant, the soft embrace of the sand and feeling of heat emanating from underneath is more akin to curling up in a cocoon.

After a few minutes, the staff offer to shovel more warm sand over you, sucking you further into the womb-like state. The choice is yours. Most sand-bathers stay put for up to 15 or 20 minutes. After that, arise like Lazarus, shake off the sand, and go hop in the shower. You'll have to return the *yukata*, but you can keep the towel as a souvenir.

Onsen

HEALTHY LAND TAMATEBAKO ONSEN

3293 Yamagawafukumoto, Ibusuki; tel. 0993/35-3577; www.seika-spc.co.jp/healthy; 9:30am-7:30pm Fri.-Wed., closed Fri. if Thurs. is national holiday; ¥510 for rotenboro; drive 15 minutes along Route 226 (9 km/ 5.6 mi) south of Saraku Sand-Bath Hall, or walk 40 minutes, or take a taxi (12 minutes) from Oyama Station on the Ibusuki Makurazaki line

Post-sand bath, if you want to relax even more, the town's traditional hot-water *onsen* await. This public bath is a good bet. Although it has both indoor and sand baths of its own, its gender-separated *rotenboro* (outdoor baths) that sit near the beach are the best offerings.

Food and Accommodations

MENYA JIRO

1934-4 Nishikata; tel. 0993/26-4358; www.menyajiro.com; 11:30am-3pm and 6pm-9:30am Thurs.-Tues.; ¥700-900; walk 3 minutes from JR Ibusuki Station

This ramen joint serves Kagoshima-style ramen: homemade noodles in a gentle broth made from pork and chicken, combined with a dash of sweet Kagoshima-made soy sauce and some burnt garlic. Locals add rice to the soup after polishing off the noodles. This is a good place for a quick meal.

AOBA

1-2-11 Minato; tel. 0993/22-3356; https://aoba-ibusuki.com; 11am-2:30pm and 5:30pm-9:30pm Thurs.-Tues.; dishes from ¥480; walk 1 minute north of JR Ibusuki Station

Cheap local dishes are served here, from *kurobuta* set meals and locally caught eel to what is for many Westerner's the paranoid-inducing *kurosatsuma-dori sashimi* (thinly cut raw chicken). There's a good range of *shōchū* on the shelves, too. Look for the yellow *noren* (curtain) hanging in front of the entrance.

KAWAKYU

4-10-12 Omure; tel. 0993/23-4020; https://hydeo41012.wixsite.com/kawakyu-official/home-1; from ¥10,800 d; walk 20 minutes northeast of JR Ibusuki Station, or contact ahead for pickup from the station

This low-key *ryokan* beside a river in a residential area has clean, compact tatami rooms and a shared bathroom. Run by a wonderful family, the property has *onsen* facilities on-site. It's located a little bit outside downtown, but the owner is happy to shuttle guests to and from the station and to the town's famed

hot-sand baths

Sakurajima: Japan's Vesuvius

Across Kinko Bay from Kagoshima the impressive contours of Sakurajima (桜島) dominate the view. This hyperactive volcano hovers imposingly on the horizon east of town, rising 1,117 meters (3,665 feet) skyward at its highest point, with two lower craters, and commanding a circumference of about 50 km (31 mi).

Since Sakurajima's first recorded eruption in 708, the peak has been continuously temperamental. The volcano was an island until a major blast in 1914 created a land bridge stretching eastward to the Osumi Peninsula. The last major eruption was in 1955, with several smaller, though substantial, eruptions taking place in 1994, 1995, and 2013. On average, the back of the crater spews ash between 100 and 200 times a year, amounting to 100 millimeters (4 inches) annually. This dust-fall often turns the sky red at night and blocks out the sun.

While this may all sound quite ominous, this volcano is, in fact, a popular sight for travelers to visit. Here are some ways to get close:

- **Nagisa Lava Trail and Foot Bath** (1722-3 Yokoyama-chō; www.sakurajima.gr.jp/tourism/000677.html; 9am-sunset daily; free): This 3-km (1.7-mi) trail runs along the waterfront, extending to the west of the ferry terminal, crossing over a lava field created by an eruption in 1914 that has since been slowly reclaimed by vegetation. The free **Nagisa Park Foot Bath,** about 10 minutes' walk west of the ferry terminal, is a great place to rest your feet and enjoy the view after the walk.

- **Arimura Lava Observatory** (952 Arimura; 24/7; free): Although no actual observatory awaits, this sheltered area has several vantage points from which to view fields where lava flowed relatively recently. This area is located about 15 minutes' drive southeast of the ferry terminal along Route 224.

- **Kurokami Buried Torii** (647 Kurokami-chō; www.sakurajima.gr.jp/tourism/000352.html; 24/7; free): This gate once stood 3 meters (9.8 feet) tall in front of Kurokami Shrine. Today, only its top portion protrudes from the ground, with the remainder having been buried by volcanic ash in the major eruption that rocked the island in 1914. While you're in the area, walk south from the buried shrine gate for about 10 minutes (1-minute drive) along Route 26 to the **Kurokami Observation Point.** Here you'll have good views of the volcano's active Showa Crater. To reach the gate, drive about 10 minutes northeast from the Arimura Lava Observatory, changing from Route 224 to Route 26.

- **Yunohira Lookout** (1025 Koike-chō; www.sakurajima.gr.jp/tourism/000350.html; 9am-5pm daily; free): Drive 10 minutes east of the ferry terminal to this high perch, which offers stellar views of the volcano and the city on the far side of the bay.

To glean more insight into Sakurajima, stop by the **Sakurajima Visitor Center** (1722-29 Yokoyama-chō, Sakurajima; tel. 099/293-2443; www.sakurajima.gr.jp/svc/english; 9am-5pm daily).

GETTING THERE

Ferries run between a pier in Kagoshima (4-1 Honkōshinmachi; tel. 099/223-7271; www.city.kagoshima.lg.jp/sakurajima-ferry) and **Sakurajima Port** (61–4 Yokoyama-chō; tel. 099/293–2525) on the west side of the island. The journey across is quick and cheap (15 minutes; ¥160), and ferries are plentiful, running 24/7 a day. Pay the fare on the Sakurajima side.

By far, the best way to explore Sakurajima is by car. This allows you to travel more quickly to the more picturesque north shore of the island and to do a full loop, which generally takes about 1 hour, if you're keen. You can rent one at **Sakurajima Rent-A-Car** (60 Yokoyama-chō, Sakurajima; tel. 099/293-2162; 8am-6pm; ¥4,800 2 hours, ¥11,000 1 day), located about 10 minutes' walk east of the island's ferry terminal.

sand baths. Great breakfasts and dinners (both Japanese-style) are available—a recommended choice given that the hotel is a bit outside downtown.

★ IBUSUKI SYUSUI-EN

5-27-27 Yunohama; tel. 0993/23-4141; www.syusuien.co.jp; from ¥27,000 pp with meals

This luxury property has all the makings of a premium *ryokan* experience: expansive tatami rooms with en-suite bathrooms, antique furniture, scroll-paintings hanging in alcoves, incredible service by staff clad in kimono, and fantastic *kaiseki* meals. There's also a public *onsen* on-site. Admittedly, it's pricey. But it's an ideal place to idle in a kimono, dine on lavish seafood spreads and sip *matcha* (powdered green tea) while gazing onto a landscape garden. It's only a few minutes' walk south of the town's famed sand baths, or about 20 minutes' walk southeast of JR Ibusuki Station. Recommended.

Information and Services

There's a **tourist information desk** in JR Ibusuki Station (tel. 0993/22-4114; 9am-5pm daily). Alongside English-language maps, the staff here can help with making reservations.

For more robust services and a more generous supply of printed materials in English, head to the **Ibusuki Sightseeing Information Center** (2-5-33 Minato; tel. 0993/22-3252; www.ibusuki.or.jp; 9am-5pm daily). Staff here are also happy to help with directions and recommendations. It's located about 6 minutes' walk east of JR Ibusuki Station.

Getting There

From JR Kagoshima-Chūō Station, both local and limited express trains run directly to Ibusuki Station. You can either take the local **JR Ibusuki Makurazaki** line (1 hour 20 minutes; ¥1,000) or the **Ibusuki-no-Tamatebako** limited express train (50 minutes; ¥2,140). Note that seats must be reserved for this particularly stylish limited express, which runs three times daily. Its interior is fitted with pine paneling and is furnished with special seats that face the ocean.

Buses also run between Kagoshima and Ibusuki (1 hour 15 minutes; ¥950).

Getting Around

Once you're in Ibusuki, the "My Plan" bus deal allows you unlimited rides around town for one day (¥1,100 adults, ¥550 children).

Another alternative is renting an **electric bicycle** from the tourist information desk in Ibusuki Station (¥500 for 2 hours).

Okinawa and the Southwest Islands

At Japan's southwestern edge, a cluster of island chains stretches some 700 km (435 mi) into the East China Sea. Laid-back, with a climate that alternates between subtropical and tropical, these islands—about 160 in all—show a side of Japan that many outsiders don't know exists, with tangled jungles, azure waters, coral reefs, white-sand beaches, and mangrove swamps. Most of these islands are located at roughly the same latitude as Miami, so the islands enjoy an average annual temperature of 24°C (75°F).

They begin in the north with lush, mountainous Yakushima, a UNESCO World Heritage Site, and extend to the far-flung Yaeyama Islands off the eastern coast of Taiwan. In between, the prefecture's main and largest island of Okinawa-Hontō buzzes with life, the nearby

Highlights

Look for ★ to find recommended sights, activities, dining, and lodging.

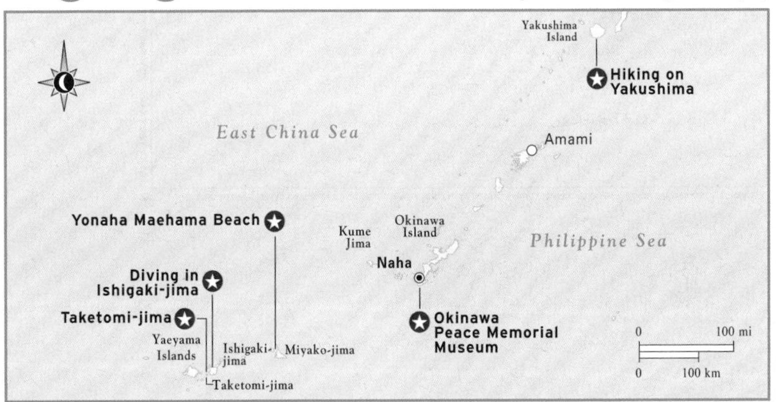

★ **Okinawa Peace Memorial Museum:** This museum offers a sobering reminder of the horrors of war on an island where one of World War II's bloodiest battles took place (page 695).

★ **Hiking on Yakushima:** Covered in dense cedar forest, this mossy, subtropical island makes for lovely hikes (page 700).

★ **Yonaha Maehama Beach:** Maehama's white sands continue for miles and gently descend into warm, crystal-clear waters that are great for swimming and water sports (page 708).

★ **Diving in Ishigaki-jima:** This island refuge is considered by many to be the best place to scuba dive in the country (page 712).

★ **Taketomi-jima:** Cycling or walking through the villages of this island offers a chance to experience Okinawa's living traditional culture (page 715).

Okinawa and the Southwest Islands

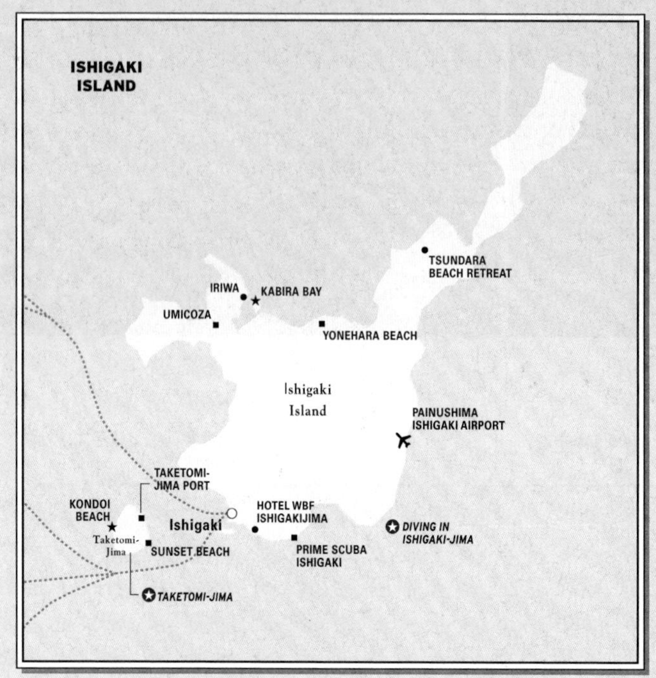

East China Sea

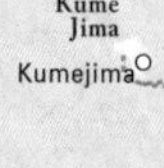

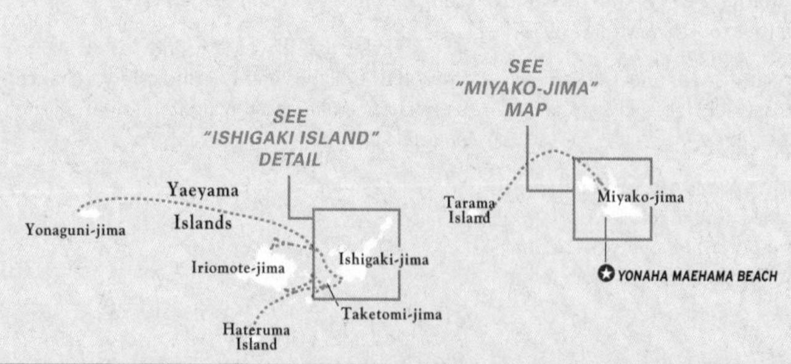

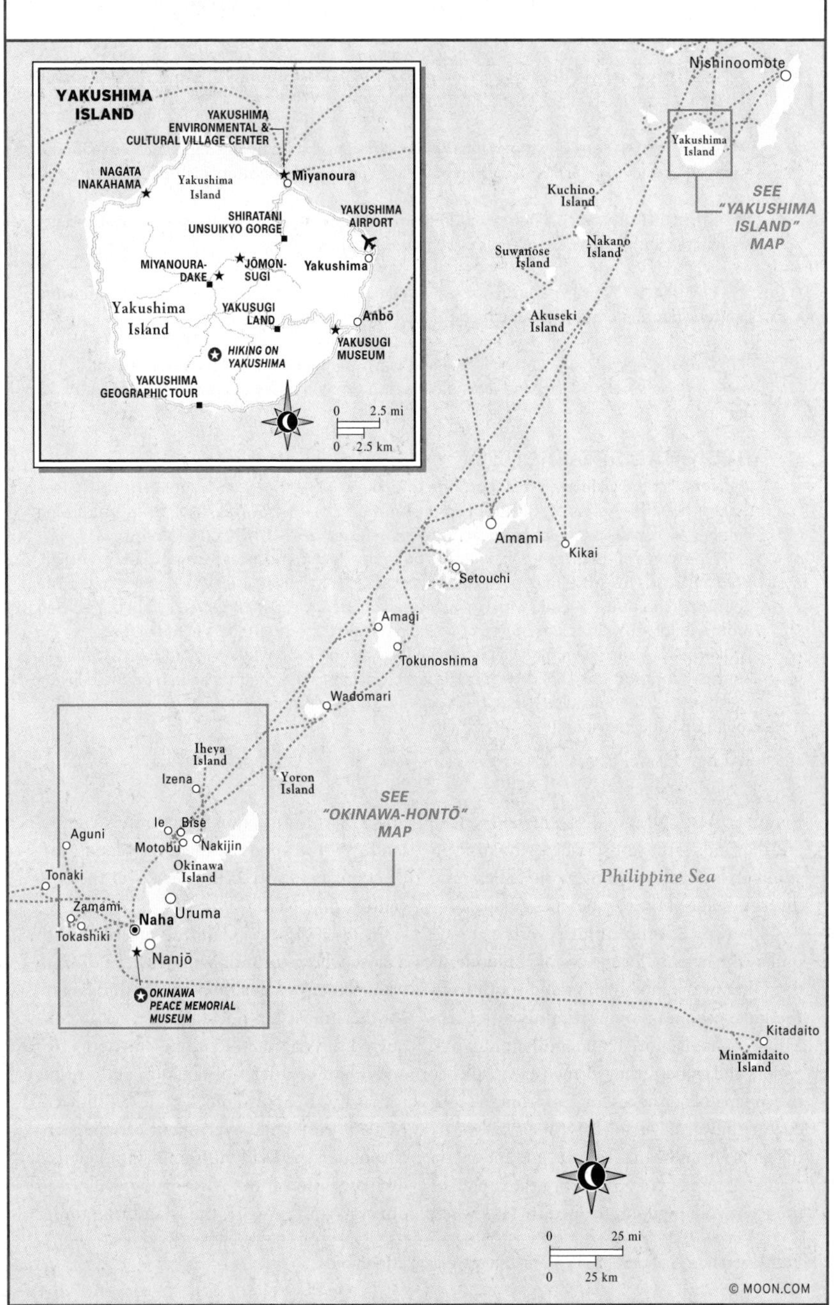

YAKUSHIMA ISLAND
YAKUSHIMA ENVIRONMENTAL & CULTURAL VILLAGE CENTER
Miyanoura
NAGATA INAKAHAMA
Yakushima Island
SHIRATANI UNSUIKYO GORGE
YAKUSHIMA AIRPORT
Yakushima
MIYANOURA-DAKE
JŌMON-SUGI
Yakushima Island
YAKUSUGI LAND
Anbō
YAKUSUGI MUSEUM
HIKING ON YAKUSHIMA
YAKUSHIMA GEOGRAPHIC TOUR
0 2.5 mi
0 2.5 km
Nishinoomote
Yakushima Island
SEE "YAKUSHIMA ISLAND" MAP
Kuchino Island
Nakano Island
Suwanose Island
Akuseki Island
Amami
Kikai
Setouchi
Amagi
Tokunoshima
Wadomari
Iheya Island
Izena
Yoron Island
SEE "OKINAWA-HONTŌ" MAP
Ie
Bise
Aguni
Motobu
Nakijin
Okinawa Island
Tonaki
Zamami
Naha
Uruma
Tokashiki
Nanjō
OKINAWA PEACE MEMORIAL MUSEUM
Philippine Sea
Kitadaito
Minamidaito Island
0 25 mi
0 25 km

Best Restaurants

★ **Ashibiuna:** Overlooking a gravel garden fringed by subtropical plants, this Okinawan restaurant is set in an atmospheric old home (page 690).

★ **Nuchigafu:** For a pit stop or meal with a difference, drop by this sophisticated teahouse and restaurant known for its Okinawan bubble set amid Naha's pottery district (page 690).

★ **Shimaumui:** Catch a masterful live performance on the three-stringed *sanshin* and get acquainted with Okinawan folk music at this *izakaya* (page 691).

★ **Panorama:** This hyperlocal hotspot in Yaksuhima's north is a friendly *izakaya* to unwind in after a day exploring the island (page 702).

★ **Usagi-ya Honten:** Eat local fare and wash it down with a glass of local spirit at this lively *izakaya* where a folk band jams nightly and the whole restaurant often ends up on its feet (page 714).

REGIONAL SPECIALTIES

Key items on the Okinawan menu include tofu-like ***fu,*** bitter ***goya*** (melon), ***umibudo*** (sea grapes), ***mozuku*** seaweed, and the deep-purple sweet potato known as ***beni-imo.*** A surprising number of Okinawan classics are in fact stir-fries, referred to as ***champuru*** locally.

The presence of US military personnel has brought eclectic influences to the Okinawan kitchen, from **SPAM** to Tex-Mex-influenced **taco rice.** Another local classic is **Okinawan soba.** The noodles in this dish are made with wheat instead of buckwheat, then served a light pork-based broth with green onions and chunks of boiled pork and tossed with slices of red ginger.

Okinawa is also known for its own its own local alcoholic brew, ***awamori,*** which can be as high as 120-proof. This fiery drink is made with Thai Indica rice that has been fermented in kōji yeast extract, then distilled. Don't be shocked if you encounter a jar of *awamori* containing a coiled-up habu (pit viper).

Keramas draw divers to deep emerald waters, and the sands of the sun-splashed Miyako chain summon loungers, swimmers, snorkelers, and divers to some of the best beaches in Japan.

Okinawa's eclectic culture exerts as much pull as the terrain. The ancestors of modern-day Okinawans mostly migrated south from the Japanese mainland, bringing with them a dialect that is more than a millennium old. Sailors and traders, they formed a key link between Japan and the rest of Asia from the 14th century onward. During this time, boats bearing goods from China, Taiwan, and Indonesia ferried in and out of Naha, once the capital of the Ryūkyū Kingdom, formed in 1429 when Sho Hashi united these disparate slivers of land. With weapons banned, the islands' distinct culture evolved in peace over the next century and a half.

In 1609, this period of tranquility came to a close when the Shimazu clan set sail from what is today Kagoshima on Kyūshū, Japan's southernmost main island, and easily conquered the unarmed Ryūkyū Kingdom. Two and a half centuries of taxation and exploitation by the mainland Japanese followed. In 1879 the Meiji government officially incorpotated the Ryūkyū Islands into Japan as Okinawa Prefecture. After being decimated during World War II, the islands fell under

Previous: Shisa guardian; hiking on Yakushima; diving in Iriomote.

Best Accommodations

★ **The Naha Terrace:** Put yourself in the center of Naha's action at this smart hotel with a bar featuring live jazz shows every night and upper-floor rooms with sweeping views (page 693).

★ **Sankara Hotel & Spa:** Lounge amid Balinese vibes at this luxury resort and spa on the southeastern coast of the lush isle of Yakushima (page 703).

★ **Private Resort Hotel Renn:** Stay a stone's throw from one of Japan's best beaches on Miyako-jima at this chic B&B with a rooftop balcony affording lovely ocean views (page 710).

★ **Iriwa:** This guesthouse near Ishigaki-jima's Kabira Bay has all the markings of a beach house—surfboards, tropical plants—and hosts who relish introducing their island to guests (page 714).

★ **Tsundara Beach Retreat:** If your aim is to have a stretch of beachfront all to yourself, you won't go wrong with this private beach house in Ishigaki-jima's remote north (page 715).

US control until 1972, only being returned to Japan upon agreement that US bases were allowed to remain—a source of heated controversy to this day.

The Ryūkyū legacy lingers today in the prefectural capital of Naha. Elsewhere, the islands' subtropical roots are seen in market stalls overflowing with mangoes, bananas, star fruit, papayas, and durian—famed across tropical Asia for its stench—alongside scarlet octopuses and turquoise parrot fish. Twangy notes plucked from the snakeskin-covered *sanshin*, akin to the banjo, float in the air on balmy nights. Meanwhile, locals and refugees from the mainland run dive shops, play in bands, and gush about the slow pace and warmer climes of their home, a world away from urban Japan.

PLANNING YOUR TIME

Although snowcaps sometimes form on the peaks of Yakushima from December through February, winter doesn't really come to Japan's southwest islands. In **winter,** the islands see temperatures similar to those felt in Tokyo during spring. This means cherry blossoms bloom as early as December or January, while the prefecture's official red *deigo* flower, bougainvillea, yellow tabebuias, and white Easter lilies color the islands year-round.

Typhoons occasionally sweep through from June through October, with regular cloudbursts occurring during the **rainy season** from late May through June. Aside from these times (when transport networks can temporarily be interrupted), the islands are pleasant to visit year-round.

Domestic tourists swarm the islands' beaches during the **Golden Week holidays** in late April and early May, as well as during the peak **summer** months of June through August. The best time to visit—both for weather and crowds—is from March through the first three weeks of April, and the latter three weeks of May, before the rainy season begins.

The northern half of the Ryūkyū archipelago comprises the **Satsunan-shotō**—further broken into the smaller chains of the Ōsumi, Tokara, and Amami Islands—while the southern half of the archipelago contains the **Ryūkyū-shotō,** which includes the Okinawa, Miyako, and Yaeyama chains, as well as the farther flung Daitō and Senkaku Islands. Jumping between these various chains is relatively straightforward thanks to extensive flight and ferry networks.

The islands are all relatively small and don't require a huge amount of time to see, so plan

Itinerary Ideas

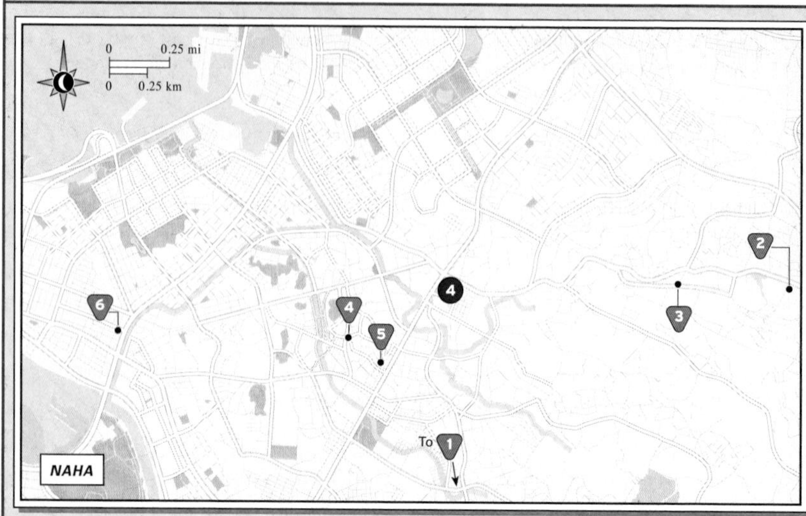

NAHA AND THE OKINAWA PEACE MEMORIAL

1. Okinawa Peace Memorial Museum
2. Ashibiuna
3. Shuri Ryusen
4. Tsuboya Pottery Street
5. Nuchigafu
6. Shimaumui

THE BEACHES OF THE KERAMA ISLANDS

1. Zamami-jima
2. Furuzamami Beach
3. Aka-jima
4. Sakaemachi Arcade

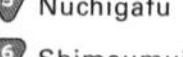

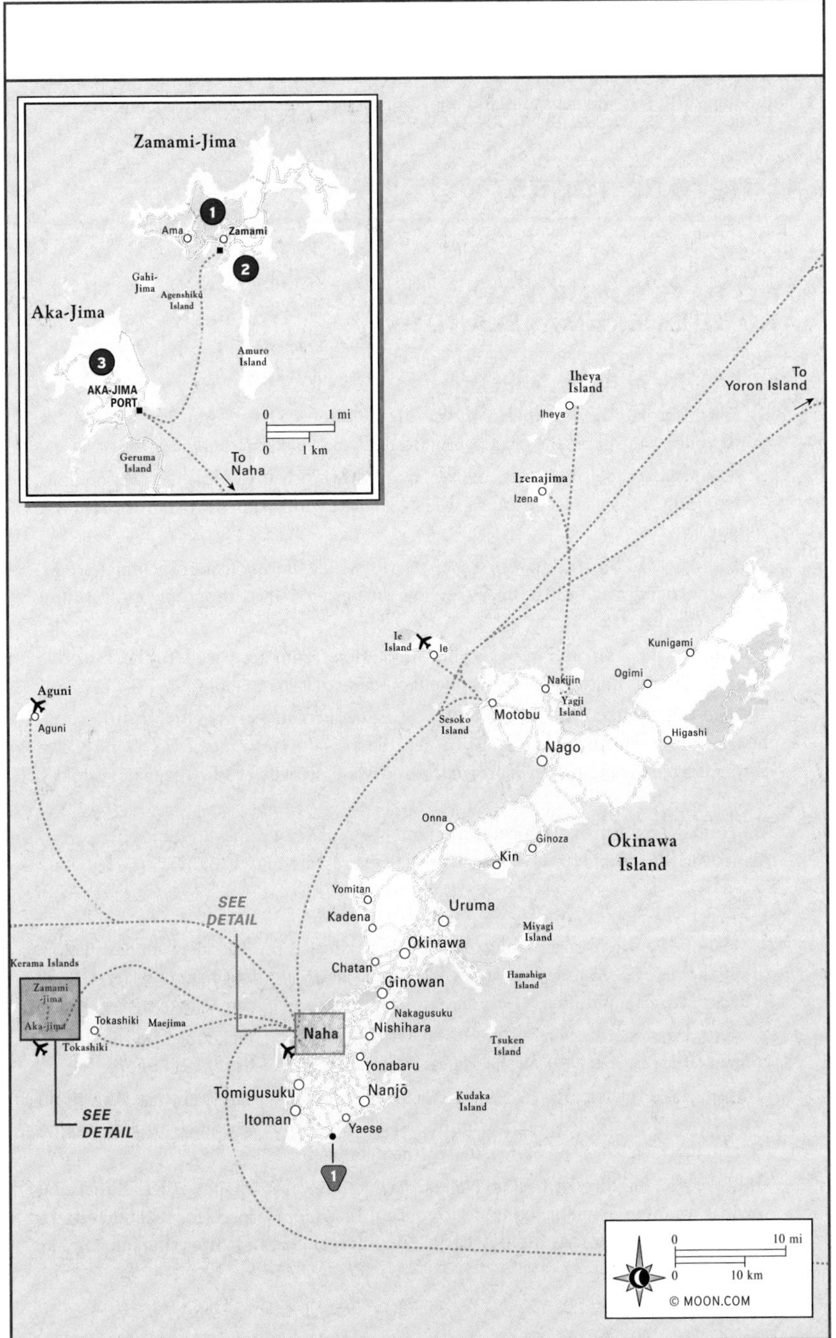

Zamami-Jima
Ama
Zamami
Gahi-Jima
Agenshiku Island
Aka-Jima
Amuro Island
AKA-JIMA PORT
Geruma Island
To Naha
0 1 mi
0 1 km
Iheya Island
Iheya
To Yoron Island
Izenajima
Izena
Ie Island
Ie
Aguni
Aguni
Kunigami
Ogimi
Nakijin
Yagji Island
Motobu
Sesoko Island
Higashi
Nago
Onna
Ginoza
Kin
Okinawa Island
Yomitan
Kadena
Uruma
SEE DETAIL
Miyagi Island
Okinawa
Chatan
Ginowan
Hamahiga Island
Kerama Islands
Zamami-jima
Aka-jima
Tokashiki
Maejima
Tokashiki
Nakagusuku
Naha
Nishihara
Tsuken Island
Yonabaru
Tomigusuku
Nanjō
Kudaka Island
Itoman
Yaese
SEE DETAIL
0 10 mi
0 10 km
© MOON.COM

to spend somewhere between **three days** and **a week** in the southwestern islands. If your only aim is to soak up rays on a beach, a weekend should suffice. If you plan to island hop, hike, or dive, consider spending five days or longer. Note that reaching many of the smaller islands requires first traveling into a bigger hub before hopping aboard a ferry.

Itinerary Ideas

TWO DAYS ON OKINAWA-HONTŌ AND THE KERAMA ISLANDS

Day 1: Naha and the Okinawa Peace Memorial

1 Start your morning southwest of Naha at the **Okinawa Peace Memorial Museum,** doing your best to grasp the pivotal, brutal battles that took place on the island.

2 Change the mood a bit with an Okinawan-style lunch at **Ashibiuna,** overlooking a subtropically influenced landscape garden, complete with geometric patterns raked into its gravel.

3 Head over to **Shuri Ryusen,** a shop nearby selling *bingata* (colorful Okinawan textiles). The friendly staff will be happy to show you upstairs, where the pros work at crafting exquisite patterns.

4 Hop on the train and head to Makishi Station. From here, walk to the **Tsuboya Pottery Street.** Enjoy popping in and out of the street's many shops.

5 End your stroll down Tsuboya Pottery Street with a cup of tea at **Nuchigafu,** set in a historic house specializing on a quiet corner. The specialty is *bukubuku cha*, a kind of cold tea made from a combination of brown rice and white rice with crushed peanuts sprinkled on top.

6 Head out for dinner at **Shimaumui** for more Okinawan dishes and enjoy live performances on the *sanshin* (three-stringed instrument resembling a banjo).

Day 2: The Beaches of the Kerama Islands

1 Around 9am, hop on a jet foil bound for the nearby Kerama Islands. Your destination: the idyllic isle of **Zamami-jima,** accessible from Naha in less than an hour by ferry. Book your ticket to Zamami-jima at least one day in advance, and be sure to note all ferry times.

2 Spend your morning on **Furuzamami Beach,** swimming and lounging to your heart's content. There's a snack bar on the southside of the promenade if you get hungry.

3 Next, take a boat for the 15-minute ride to the nearby spit of land known as **Aka-jima.** While away the early afternoon swimming, snorkeling, scuba diving, or strolling around the island, which is lush and populated by the Kerama deer.

4 Take a jet foil directly back to Naha from Aka-jima around 4pm. After all that sun, you may want some time at your hotel to cool off. Then join the locals for street food and a rowdy night out at **Sakaemachi Arcade,** sampling yakitori and wandering into any bar that appeals to you.

Okinawa-Hontō 沖縄本島

The biggest and most populated (1.3 million) island in the extensive Ryūkyū chain, Okinawa-Hontō was once the beating political heart of the Ryūkyū Kingdom. The island's elongated shape—12 km (70 mi) from north to south with 476 km (295 mi) of jagged coastline—inspired the name Okinawa, which literally translates as "offshore rope." The original inhbaitants pictured it as a rope floating on the sea. Today the island is the main entry point for those traveling to the Ryūkyū Islands, with the capital city of Naha being the main urban center.

South of Naha, memorials commemorate the horrific Battle of Okinawa and the island's pivotal role in the war. In the central section of the island you'll find good beaches, particularly around the Motobu peninsula. And in the Yambaru region in the north, rustic fishing hamlets on the coast and farming villages in the verdant hills are home to some of the world's longest living people, with more than 30 centenarians per 100,000.

Controversially, the island has a huge US military presence. On one hand, this means ample access to overseas goods and a bit more widespread use of English than elsewhere in Japan. On the other hand, these bases are a constant reminder of ghosts of the island's past. Aside from a handful of sites of cultural and historical significance, Okinawa-Hontō is best used as a base for traveling by boat or plane to other less intensely developed islands where old ways and pristine stretches of sand are in abundance.

NAHA
那覇

Modern-day Naha, Okinawa's prefectural capital and its largest metropolis with a population of more than 300,000, is a thoroughly modern city, laid out on a grid thanks to the city's utter destruction during World War II. The city's main thoroughfare is Kokusai-dōri, a lively if garish strip lined with restaurants, bars, clubs, and kitsch souvenir shops. But veer off the main drag and you'll discover pockets of local color where Okinawan culture survives.

South of Kokusai-dōri are the bustling bazaars of Ichiba-dōri and Heiwa-dōri, as well as the raucous Makishi Public Market, overflowing with tropical seafood, fruits and vegetables. To experience a more home-grown side of the city, wander through these rambling arcades and visit the Tsuboya pottery district. At night, head to the charming if slightly run-down Sakaemachi Ichiba shopping arcade and the surrounding streets lined with tumble-down bars and restaurants full of friendly locals.

Sights

SHURI CASTLE
首里城

1-2 Kinjō-chō; tel. 098/886-2020; http://oki-park.jp/shurijo; 8:30am-7pm daily Apr.-Jun. and Oct.-Nov., 8:30am-6pm daily Dec.-Mar., 8:30am-8pm daily Jul.-Sept.; ¥820; take Okinawa Monorail to Shuri station (end of the line)

Shuri Castle was wrecked in World War II, when it served as the Japanese military's headquarters, and then was rebuilt in 1992 and designated a UNESCO World Heritage Site. Unfortunately, Shuri Castle was very badly damaged by a devastating fire in October 2019. At the time of writing, the cause of the fire, along with plans for rebuilding this precious cultural landmark, were unknown.

Until the fire, it was one of the few visual reminders of the Ryūkyū Kingdom left in Okinawa. Overlooking Naha's urban sprawl from a hilltop, the original structure was constructed in the late 14th century during the rise of the Ryūkyū kings, who maintained it as their base of power until Okinawa was formally annexed by Japan in the 19th century.

To reach Shuri Castle, take the Okinawa Monorail to Shuri station at the end of the

Okinawa-Hontō

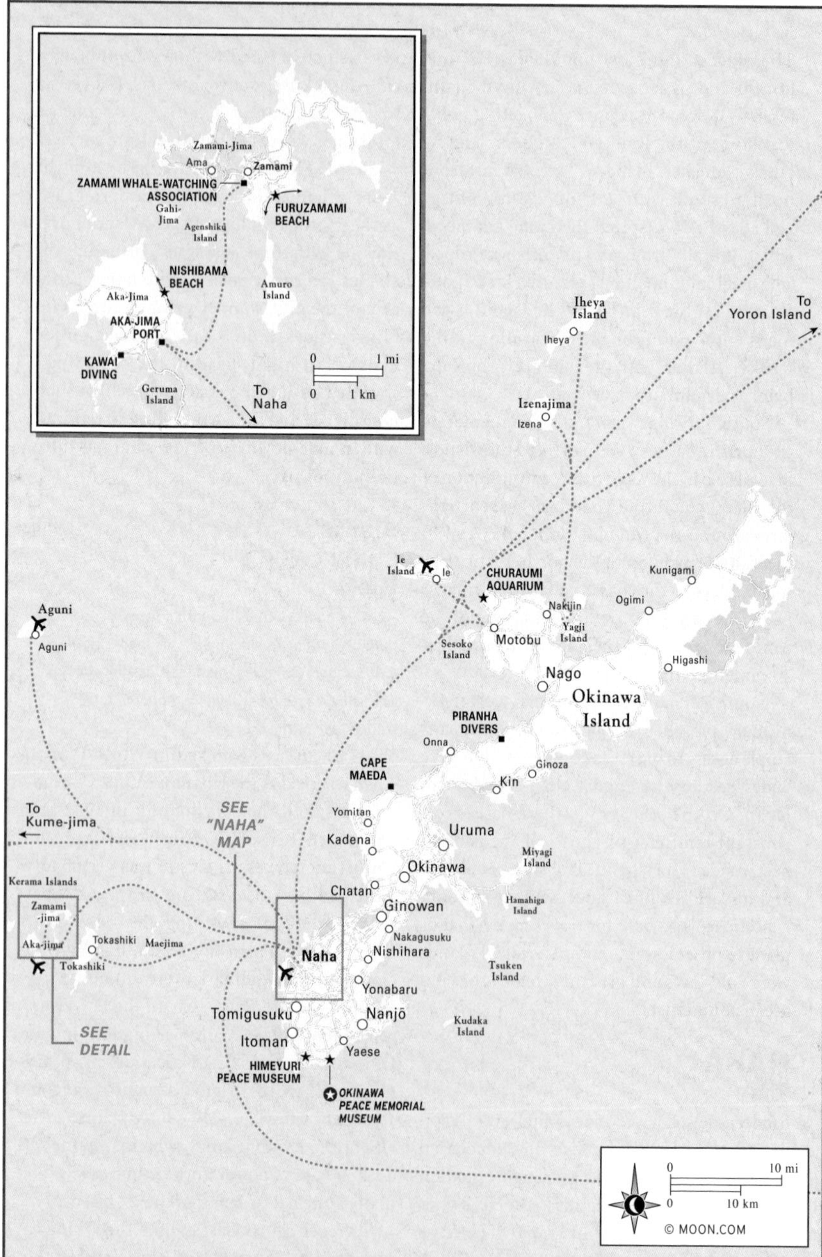

Naha

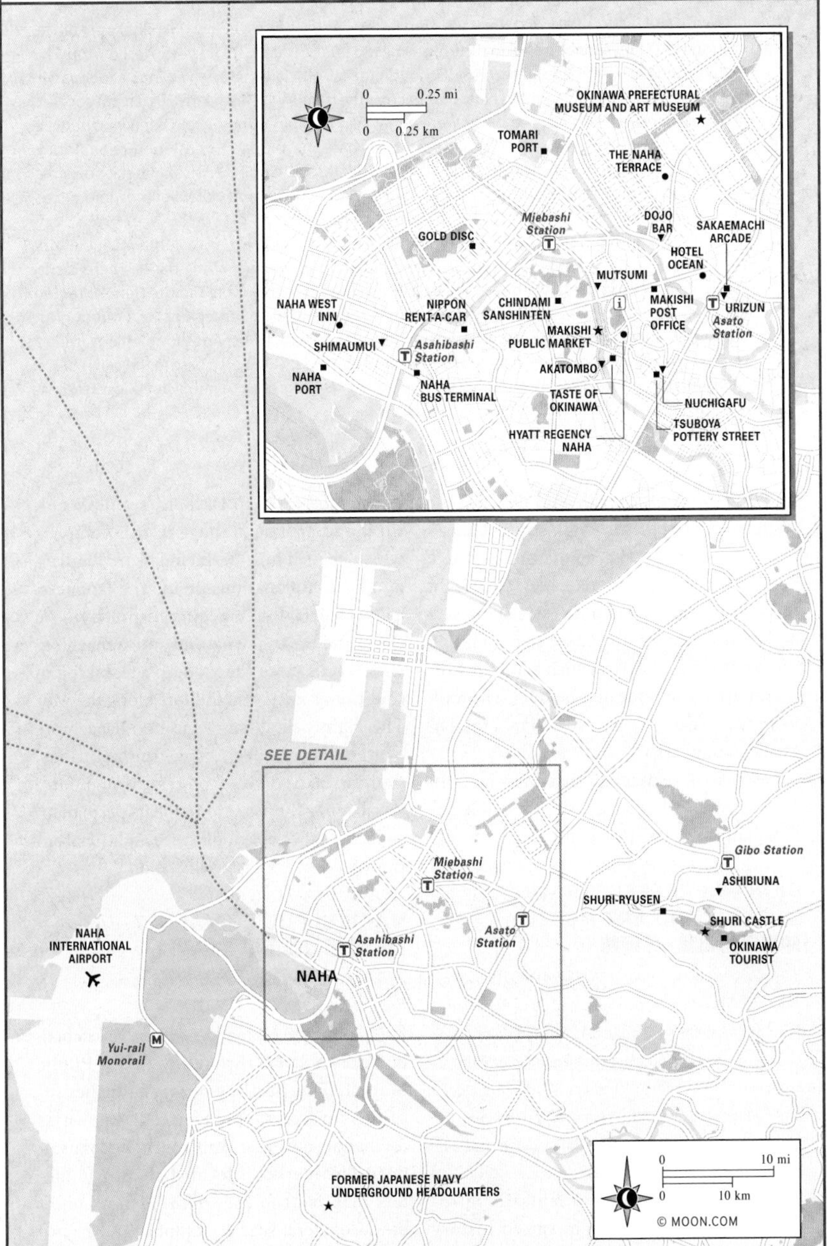

0 0.25 mi
0 0.25 km
OKINAWA PREFECTURAL MUSEUM AND ART MUSEUM
TOMARI PORT
THE NAHA TERRACE
DOJO BAR
SAKAEMACHI ARCADE
Miebashi Station
GOLD DISC
HOTEL OCEAN
MUTSUMI
NAHA WEST INN
NIPPON RENT-A-CAR
CHINDAMI SANSHINTEN
MAKISHI POST OFFICE
URIZUN
Asato Station
MAKISHI PUBLIC MARKET
SHIMAUMUI
Asahibashi Station
NAHA PORT
AKATOMBO
NAHA BUS TERMINAL
TASTE OF OKINAWA
NUCHIGAFU
TSUBOYA POTTERY STREET
HYATT REGENCY NAHA
SEE DETAIL
Gibo Station
ASHIBIUNA
SHURI-RYUSEN
SHURI CASTLE
OKINAWA TOURIST
Miebashi Station
Asato Station
Asahibashi Station
NAHA
NAHA INTERNATIONAL AIRPORT
Yui-rail Monorail
FORMER JAPANESE NAVY UNDERGROUND HEADQUARTERS
0 10 mi
0 10 km
© MOON.COM

US Military Bases

Since the end of World War II, Okinawa-Hontō has been subject to a heavy US military presence, with some 27,000 service personnel currently based on the island. Tokyo pays Washington $1.8 billion annually for this added security. Although the US officially returned Okinawa to Japan in 1972, they negotiated the right to have bases across the island, which is nearly 20 percent covered by US military installations. The bases were initially an economic engine for Okinawa, but were left in shambles after the war. In recent decades the bases have created constant friction. Today, American fighter jets and helicopters routinely whoosh through the otherwise calm skies over the island, while an air crash in 2016 and a series of high-profile sexual and violent crimes committed by service personnel have exacerbated the already tense situation.

Waves of anti-base protests have built in intensity over the years, with some 90,000 angry citizens taking to the streets in April 2010 demanding total removal of the bases. There is currently a plan to relocate the large Marine base from Futenma to the more remote Henoko region in the north, and to move about half of the marines on the island to other locations throughout the Pacific, including Hawaii and Guam sometime in the mid-2020s. Another plan is slated to return about 1,000 hectares of land to Japan around the Kadena Air Force base in the early-2020s. Although these stop-gap measures suggest incremental progress, the public remains steadfast in its push to have the bases removed entirely.

line. Exit on the west side and descend the staircase to street level. Walk straight ahead from here, crossing first a busy thoroughfare and then crossing a second street. Turn right on here and walk along the left side of this second smaller street until you see signs pointing the way to Shuri Castle, which is on the hillside above the left side of this street. The walk from the station to the castle takes a total of about 20 minutes.

Because of damaged caused by the 2019 fire, research whether a visit is possible before planning a trip to the site.

OKINAWA PREFECTURAL MUSEUM AND ART MUSEUM
沖縄県博物館・美術館

3-1-1 Omoromachi, Naha; tel. 098/941-8200; http://okimu.jp; 9am-6pm Tues.-Thurs. and Sun., 9am-8pm Fri.-Sat.; museum ¥410 adults, ¥260 high school and college students, ¥150 elementary and junior high students; art museum ¥310 adults, ¥210 high school and college students, ¥100 elementary and junior high students; ride monorail to Omoromachi station, then walk 10 minutes northwest

These museums provide a fantastic introduction to Okinawa's rich, varied history and culture. There's a history section and a wing dedicated to Okinawa's unique cultural and artistic heritage in this complex, which opened in 2007. Included are English-language explanations beside the Japanese. The historical side begins in pre-Ryūkyū times and traces the natural and archaeological records up to the modern age, taking in traditional crafts and folklore along the way. The slightly smaller art museum has a more contemporary edge, displaying paintings, sculptures, and video pieces throughout a number of galleries. Alongside its permanent collection, special exhibits with additional entrance fees are occasionally held.

MAKISHI PUBLIC MARKET
第一牧志公設市場

2-10-1 Matsuo; https://kosetsu-ichiba.com; 10am-8pm daily

For a look into Okinawa's collective kitchen, be sure to stroll through Makishi Public Market. This bustling bazaar branches off of the covered shopping arcade known as Ichibahon-dōri that runs south of Kokusai-dōri. The market is located about 200 meters (656 feet) to the south. Fish mongers hawk lobsters, scarlet octopus, and parrot fish, while produce merchants offload local vegetables, mangoes, papaya, and pineapples. Upstairs, hole-in-the-wall eateries will prepare fish you've just bought downstairs. All told, some 400 shops fill the rowdy marketplace, which has an atmosphere more akin to Bangkok than anywhere in mainland Japan.

Shopping

TSUBOYA POTTERY STREET

1-21-14 Tsuboya

Tsuboya Pottery Street is an atmospheric thoroughfare has been at the center of Naha's thriving ceramics trade since 1682. Today, the shops along this historic street hawk decorative objects, thimble-sized *awamori* cups and pairs of leonine shisa guardian figurines: The one with its mouth agape welcomes good fortune, while the one with mouth closed keeps it from escaping. Kiyomasa Toki (1-16-7 Tsuboya; tel. 098/862-3654; 10am-7pm daily), a shop with 320 years of history, stands out. Whether you're shopping or not, it's worth strolling down this street to soak up the atmosphere.

CHINDAMI SANSHINTEN

1-2-18 Makishi; tel. 098/869-2055; http://chindami.com; 11am-8pm daily

After a few days in Okinawa, if the haunting sound of the three-stringed *sanshin* has seeped sufficiently into your brain that you are intrigued by the possibility of learning to play the instrument yourself, you're not alone. Chinadami Sanshinten, situated down a side-street about 10 minutes' walk south of Miebashi monorail station, is the best place in Naha to peruse models of this lacquer-necked banjo-like instrument covered in python skin. Owner Higa-san is a *sanshin*-maker renowned for his craft. He doesn't speak English, but happily offers a basic lesson to anyone with a hankering to learn.

SHURI-RYUSEN

1-54 Shuri Yamagawa-chō; tel. 098/886-1131; www.shuri-ryusen.com; 9am-6pm daily; walk 15 minutes south of Gibo station

Shuri Ryusen is a wonderful, family-owned shop that sells Okinawa's hand-painted, batik-like variety of textile known as *bingata*. The first floor of this handsome building is overflowing with vivid hand bags, pillows, handkerchiefs, scrolls, and much more. DIY workshops are held on the second floor, while the masters can be seen at work on the third floor. Shuri Castle is a 10-minute walk east of the shop.

Shisa guardian

Okinawan Cuisine

Okinawan cuisine differs markedly from food on the mainland. Simple, home-grown, and exceptionally healthy, the diet is rich in soy, bitter **gōyā** (melon, renowned for its cancer-fighting properties and for being nearly unpalatable), **umibudo** (sea grapes), **mozuku** seaweed, ginger, turmeric, and the ubiquitous **beni-imo,** a vibrantly purple sweet potato packed with vitamins A and C, fiber, folic acid, and beta-carotene. For protein, **pork** is the meat of choice. Thanks to this nutritious intake, the people of the Ryūkyū Islands are among the longest-living in the world.

Before sampling the island's nutritious edibles, dispense with ideas of elaborate creations on lacquer trays. Instead, think soul food that is healthy despite the fact that much of it is whipped up in a frying pan. Classic dishes include various **champuru** (stir fry), which usually includes a mix of tofu-like **fu,** eggs, pork—or Spam—and bitter *goya.* **Okinawan soba** is a popular noodle dish. Instead of buckwheat, traditionally used in soba noodles, these noodles are made from wheat and served in a warm, light pork-based broth topped with green onions and hunks of boiled pork, and tossed with red ginger.

A few culinary hybrids have been hatched on the island as well, largely due to the US military presence. A famed fusion dish, **taco rice,** is a reasonably priced Tex-Mex spin-off: a bed of rice topped with the main ingredients of a taco. This dish was created on the island but is now widespread throughout Japan. For truly intrepid gourmands, dig deep and you may discover one of the island's more peculiar culinary offerings: **raw goat** (***yagi sashimi***).

If Okinawan cuisine has piqued your curiosity and you'd like to learn how to whip up a few classics at home, they're relatively simple: **Taste of Okinawa** (1-6-21 Tsuboya; tel. 098/943-6313; https://tasteof.okinawa) is a craft beer bar and restaurant that offers one-off cooking classes (3:30pm-6:30pm Tues.-Sun.; ¥6,500 adults, ¥3,500 children).

Food

★ ASHIBIUNA

2-13 Shuri, Tonokura-chō; tel. 098/884-0035; www.ryoji-family.co.jp/ryukyusabo.html; 11:30am-3pm, 5:30pm-midnight daily; ¥1,000 lunch, ¥2,000 dinner; coming from Shuri monorail station, you'll see the restaurant on the left side of the road that leads uphill to Shuri Castle

This cozy restaurant is inside an old home with indoor and outdoor seating and a menu that is strictly Okinawan: *soki soba* (white noodles served with pork spare rib and leak in pork-bone and chicken broth), *goya-chanpuru* (stir-fried bitter melon), sashimi, tofu, and more. Lunch sets come with *mozoku* seaweed and vinegar, pickled vegetables, and either white or Jyushi-Okinawan mixed rice. To add some kick to your meal, add a few drops of the *koreguzu* hot sauce made with pickled chilis in *awamori* (a rice-based alcoholic drink).

MUTSUMI

2-1-16 Makishi; tel. 098/867-0862; ¥1,000

If you want to indulge in Okinawa's penchant for greasy-spoon delights, Mutsumi doesn't disappoint. Located just north of Kokusai-dōri, this no-nonsense shop, with swivel office chairs at wooden plastic-topped tables and a TV broadcasting local variety shows, has been serving the good stuff since 1958: pottage, *tonkatsu* (fried, breaded pork cutlet), cheese-stuffed omelette wedges, and plenty of SPAM, brought to the islands by US troops after World War II. Pictures of the hearty, simple, satisfying offerings are plastered on the walls.

★ NUCHIGAFU

1-28-3 Tsuboya; tel. 098/861-2952; 11:30am-5pm, 5:30pm-10pm Wed.-Mon.; ¥1,200 tea set, ¥3,000 dinner

For something refined, head to Nuchigafu, a restaurant and teahouse located down an alley at the southeastern edge of the atmospheric Tsuboya Pottery Street. Set in a beautiful historic building, the restaurant is primarily known for its *buku buku cha.* This local specialty drink is a tea made of polished white rice (occasionally substituted with brown rice) with an unlikely top-layer of mashed peanuts. The cold beverage is served in a lacquer bowl and stirred with a bamboo whisk that produces a layer of foam on top; it's refreshing and unique. Combine a stop here with your visit to the nearby pottery street.

AKATOMBO

2-21-16 Matsuo; tel. 098/866-9535; 10am-9pm daily; ¥1,000; walk 10 minutes southwest of Makishi monorail station or 6 minutes west of Tsuboya Pottery Street

One of Okinawa's most iconic dishes is taco rice, a dish that celebrity chef Anthony Bourdain referred to as a "booze-mop." To taste this delicious concoction of rice topped with ground beef, shredded cheese, tomatoes, lettuce, and salsa, go to the old-school al fresco Akatombo (Red Dragonfly). This place serves what is arguably the best rendition of this beloved dish in town. Note that there's only one table, however, so plan to get takeaway.

URIZUN

388-5 Asato; tel. 098/885-2178; http://urizun.okinawa/index.html; 5:30pm-midnight daily; ¥3,000; walk 3 minutes northeast of Asato monorail station

Urizun is a great down-home *izakaya* (pub) serving up Okinawan classics in the heart of Naha. Dark wood tables and walls, jars of *awamori* lined up on shelves, and tatami floors create a cozy vibe. Anything on the menu will be good. Try the *rafute,* (soft pork belly left to stew in brown sugar and soy sauce) or any one of the *chanpuru* dishes.

Nightlife

★ SHIMAUMUI

B1 Ichibankan Bldg., 4-4-6 Higashimachi; tel. 080/8376-4348; www.shimaumui.net; 7pm-2am Thurs.-Mon.; ¥3,000; walk 4 minutes north of Asahibashi monorail station

A highlight of any trip to Okinawa should include a night out at a bar or restaurant with a live band playing *Ryūkyū minyo*, as the island's folk music is called. Shimaumui is an excellent spot to get acquainted with the island's beautiful, yet melancholy musical tradition. Famed singer Misako Oshiro owns this restaurant, where she routinely croons, accompanied by the twangs of a *sanshin* and an occasional *taiko* drum beat. The performance starts at 8pm and comes with a ¥1,000 cover charge, added to whatever food and drinks you order. The menu is mostly Okinawan fare.

DOJO BAR

101 Asato; tel. 098/911-3601; www.dojobarnaha.com; 6pm-1am Mon.-Thurs., 6pm-2am Fri.-Sun.; walk 6 minutes north from Makishi monorail station

Dojo Bar is a friendly watering hole run by a Brit named James with an appropriately Okinawan theme: karate. You don't have to be a black belt to drink here, but the bar is known to attract martial arts aficionados from around the globe. The drink menu includes original cocktails with names like the *tobigeri* (flying kick) and tasty nibbles from pizza to local favorites like marinated salt pork.

GOLD DISC

B1 Matsu-machi Peatsuti Bldg., 1-14-19 Matsuyama; tel. 098/868-1268; 6pm-1am Mon.-Thurs., 6pm-2am Fri.-Sat., 6pm-midnight Sun.; ¥1,500 cover

Gold Disc is an institution. Situated in a somewhat sordid area, this bouncing music club hosts nightly bands that rock out hits from the 1950s and 1960s, from Elvis to Ray Charles and the Supremes. Think guitarists with ducktails and dancers in polka-dotted circle skirts.

SAKAEMACHI ARCADE

381 Asato; tel. 098/886-3979; walk 2 minutes northeast of Asato monorail station

If you feel like having a little urban adventure, head to the Sakaemachi Arcade. The area is a marketplace by day, but from 6pm on, *izakaya,* ramshackle bars, and hazy yakitori joints fill with a diverse crowd. Mom-and-pop shops, tucked down covered lanes snaking around the market area, give glimpses of

琉球茶房
1
2
3

Awamori, Okinawan Firewater

If you ever enter a bar in the southwest islands and spot a jar of ominous looking fluid in a jar, complete with coiled pit viper, beware. This is *habushu,* named after the *habu* pit viper and a dramatic variety of *awamori,* the fire water of choice among Okinawans. A distant cousin of vodka, whisky, and rum that packs a serious punch, *awamori* is typically in the range of 60-80 proof. Some of the fiercest labels sport a proof as high as 120. There are many takes on the liquor, which is infused with ingredients from spices to honey.

The fiery drink is based on Thai Indica rice, highlighting Okinawa's proximity to Southeast Asia. The rice is fermented in a yeast extract called *koji* before being single-distilled. A high-end bottle of *awamori* is aged in a clay jar in the dark, cool recesses of a cave for upwards of three years. One of these prized bottles can set you back tens of thousands of yen (hundreds of dollars). Whatever variety of *awamori* you order, drink it on the rocks, neat or *mizu-wari* (its bite quelled with water). And if you take the *habushu* plunge, know that you'll be rewarded for your courage. This serpentine spirit is believed to bestow physical healing or—ahem—stamina.

another side of Naha. Rather than go to a specific bar, just wander the lanes and enter any place that draws you.

Accommodations

OKINAWANOYADO AJIMAA MAKISHI

2-1-18 Makishi; tel. 098/975-9851; www.ajimaa.com; ¥5,000

This is a good, no-frills budget option located 7 minutes' walk west of Makishi monorail station. The small pension has 11 Japanese-style rooms with tatami floors and futons. Bathrooms and a small common area are shared. No meals are served, but a plethora of food options are right outside the inn's door.

NAHA WEST INN

1-16-7 Nishi; tel. 098/862-0048; http://78west-inn.jp/en/index.html; ¥12,000 d

Located 9 minutes' walk west of Asahibashi monorail station, 12 minutes' walk from the beach, and 15 minutes' walk from Kokusai-dōri, Naha West Inn is close to the heart of the action, but just far enough outside it to be relaxed. The rooms are spacious and clean, ranging from twins to doubles that look more like designer lofts than hotel rooms. Good value in a good location. Rooms have private bathrooms.

★ THE NAHA TERRACE

2-14-1 Omoromachi; tel. 098/864-1111; www.terrace.co.jp/en/naha; ¥18,000 twin

The Naha Terrace is a great hotel that's within walking distance of basically everywhere you'll want to go within the city, yet it is just far enough from the bustle to feel private, even quiet. It offers western and Japanese-style breakfasts, a bar with live jazz every night, and staff who are chipper and eager to help. There are small decorative touches throughout like tropical flowers in the lobby and large windows overlooking the city in the upper-level rooms, many of which have large soaking tubs.

HOTEL OCEAN

2-4-8 Asato; tel. 098/863-2288; www.hotelocean.okinawa; ¥15,000

Hotel Ocean is a sound choice for a midrange place to bunk down in the center of Naha. Only 2 minutes' walk from Makishi monorail station, the hotel has both Japanese (tatami) and Western-style rooms. The Makishi Public Market is only 7 minutes away on foot. Staff are friendly and the environment is family-friendly, with a children's play space on the first floor. Okinawan-style breakfast is served.

1: entrance to Ashibiuna **2:** "sea grapes" seaweed **3:** Okinawa soba at Ashibiuna

HYATT REGENCY NAHA

3-6-20 Makishi; tel. 098/866-8888; https://naha.regency.hyatt.com; ¥25,000 twin

Hyatt Regency Naha offers luxury at a relatively low price. Only open since 2015, this new hotel is in a good location between Makishi monorail station (8 minutes' walk) and Tsuboya Pottery Street (3 minutes' walk), and is less than 5 minutes' stroll from Kokusai-dōri too. The hotel is not quite as luxe as some locations in the Hyatt chain, but the price tag isn't as high either.

Information and Services

Upon arriving in Naha, stop by the tourist information counter (tel. 098/857-6884; 9am-9pm daily) in the first-floor arrivals terminal of Naha International Airport. Here, you'll find English-language literature on Naha and friendly bilingual staff.

There are also a few good places in town to go for help with arranging travel logistics, to pick up English-language pamphlets, and more. One of them is **Okinawa Tourist** (1-2-3 Matsuo; tel. 098/862-1111; 9:30am-7:30pm Mon.-Fri.; 9:30am-4:30pm Sat.), conveniently located on the main drag of Kokusai-dōri, three minutes' walk from Prefectural Office monorail station. Another option is the **Tourist Information Office** in Makishi (3-2-10 Makishi; tel. 098/868-4887; 9am-8pm daily). Here you'll find helpful English-speaking staff and loads of English-language material. The Naha Traditional Arts and Crafts Center, featuring Okinawan arts and crafts, is housed in the same building.

For postal service, a convenient option is **Makishi Post Office** (3-13-19 Makishi; tel. 098/863-3880; 9am-5pm Mon.-Fri.) just outside Makishi monorail station on Kokusai-dōri.

Transportation

GETTING THERE

Naha is easily accessed by plane, with daily flights coming into its **Naha International Airport** from Tokyo, Osaka, Nagoya, Fukuoka, Kagoshima, and more. Domestic flights can be quite cheap if booked more than a month in advance (e.g., as little as ¥10,000 or less one way on discount airlines such as Vanilla Air, Jetstar Japan, and Skymark). Coming from abroad, direct flights also make the journey from Taipei, Hong Kong, Shanghai, and Seoul.

It's far less convenient, but you can travel to Naha by **ferry,** arriving in Naha Port (10 minutes' walk south of Asahibashi monorail station) from Kagoshima. Operated by **A Line Ferry** (tel. 099/226-4141; www.aline-ferry.com) and **Marix Line** (tel. 099/225-1551; www.marix-line.co.jp), these ferries depart from Kagoshima New Port every other day and make the 25-hour journey to Naha. Fares range from about ¥15,000 for second class and from about ¥29,000 for first class.

GETTING AROUND

Naha's Yui-rail **monorail** is the only form of public transport beyond buses in Okinawa-Hontō. Most of the city's attractions are easily accessed by the monorail, which is cheap and runs right through the center of downtown. The monorail line begins at Naha International Airport in the city's south and ends at Shuri, near Shuri Castle, in the north. Single journeys range in cost from ¥150 to ¥330, and an unlimited pass can be purchased for one day (¥800 adults, ¥400 children) or two days (¥1,400 adults, ¥700 children). Ask for details at any monorail station.

Besides the monorail, Naha also has a city **bus** network, but navigating it can be confusing; stick to the monorail when possible. Of course, **taxis** are available too, though they are not cheap.

SOUTH OF NAHA

The area south of Naha, colloquially known as Nanbu, was the setting where the bloody Battle of Okinawa, which lasted from April to June 1945, saw its last days play out. Japanese troops held out as long as they could, as US forces invaded and overtook the island.

The death toll was stratospheric, with some 200,000 people, including more than 100,000 civilians and 12,500 US troops, dying in the battle.

Museums and monuments dot the area south of Naha, providing a somber reminder of the horrific battle and paying tribute to those who died in the fighting, from soldiers committing mass suicide to civilians trapped in the crossfire. For a sense of the profound scar left on Okinawa's psyche by the war, make time for a half-day or day trip to the island's deep south, where some of the bloodiest combat of the whole battle took place.

★ OKINAWA PREFECTURAL PEACE MEMORIAL MUSEUM
沖縄県平和祈念資料館

614-1 Aza Mabuni; tel. 098/997-3844; www.peace-museum.pref.okinawa.jp; 9am-5pm daily; ¥300 adults, ¥150 children

War memorials are spread across the town of Itoman, occupying the southern tip of the island, centered on **Peace Memorial Park.** Once you've reached the park, head to the Okinawa Prefectural Peace Memorial Museum.

This complex gives you a moving look at the days leading up to the bloody Battle of Okinawa, the horrors experienced by those who were caught in the battle itself, from civilians to troops on both sides, and the long slog to rebuild Okinawa from rubble after the war. The museum's displays may feel one-sided on some points, but the overarching message of its exhibits is one that all can agree on: War is terrible and should be avoided at all costs. Clear English-language signage is available throughout the museum.

Also within Peace Memorial Park is the **Cornerstone of Peace.** Rows upon rows of granite slabs bear the names of all who died in the horrific battle, from Japanese civilians and soldiers to American, British, Taiwanese, and Korean civilians and service personnel. To reach the museum, take bus no. 89 from Naha Bus Terminal outside Asahibashi monorail station to Itoman Bus Terminal (1 hour, departs several times hourly; ¥580). At Itoman, take bus no. 82 until Heiwakinendo Iriguchi bus stop (20 minutes, departs once or twice hourly; ¥470).

HIMEYURI PEACE MUSEUM
ひめゆり平和祈念資料館

671-1 Ihara; tel. 098/997-2100; www.himeyuri.or.jp; 9am-5:30pm daily; ¥310 adults, ¥210 high school students, ¥110 elementary and junior high school students; take bus no. 89 from Naha Bus Terminal to Itoman Bus Terminal (1 hour, ¥580). At Itowan Bus Terminal, transfer to bus number 82, 107, or 108 and ride to Himeyuri-no-to bus stop (20 minutes, once or twice hourly, ¥320)

The Himeyuri Peace Museum commemorates the tragic experience of 240 high school-aged girls who were forced to serve as nurses in the last months of the war, nursing maimed Japanese troops in hidden caves dotting the area around Itoman. The museum brings contracts artifacts like some of the girls' pre-war diaries, with journal entries written by some of them during their time working under horrendous conditions as the battle raged on. A photographic portrait of each girl is also on display in the museum. The vast majority of the girls did not make it through the battle alive.

FORMER JAPANESE NAVY UNDERGROUND HEADQUARTERS
旧海軍司令部壕

236 Aza Tomishiro, Tomigusuku; tel. 098/850-4055; http://kaigungou.ocvb.or.jp; 8:30am-5pm daily Oct.-Jun., 8:30am-5:30pm Jul.-Sept.; ¥440 adults, ¥220 children; take bus no. 55 or 98 to Tomigusuku Minami bus stop (20 minutes, ¥260, then walk 5 minutes

These underground tunnels south of Naha give a dismal glimpse into the dank space—dug entirely with hand tools—where the Japanese navy ran their operations in the final days of the war. Displays of naval documents, weapons (including a crudely handmade spear), uniforms, and soldiers' letters to their families, tell the story of Admiral Ota and his 174 men, all of whom met their demise in this cold, bleak labyrinth of tunnels in June 1945, as the war's end drew close. Ota and his commanding officers committed suicide, while some 400 sailors were either killed by grenade blasts or took their own lives toward the final days of the war. It's a sobering testament to the horrors of war. Outside the museum, a monument at the top of a hill overlooking Naha and the ocean beyond commemorates the men whose lives were lost at this site.

Transportation

GETTING THERE

If you plan to venture beyond Naha, there are regional **buses** running throughout the island. The main hub from which to leave the capital by bus is **Naha Bus Terminal,** just south of Asahibashi monorail station.

That said, the easiest way to get around the island by far is simply to rent a car. Pick one up in the arrivals hall at Naha Airport. If you're already in Naha and haven't rented one yet, head to **Nippon Rent-A-Car** (1-1-1 Kumoji; tel. 098/867-4554; www.nrgroup-global.com; 8am-8pm daily) just outside the Prefectural Office monorail station. Another option is a branch of **Toyota Rent a Car** (4-1 Omoromachi; tel. 098/860-1530; https://rent.toyota.co.jp; 9am-8pm daily) just outside Omoromachi monorail station.

MOTOBU PENINSULA
本部半島

A few hours' drive to the north of Naha, the Motobu Peninsula offers a very different set of attractions. In the heart of the peninsula is Ocean Expo Park, where you'll find the fantastic, if crowded, **Churaumi Aquarium.** And off the coast of the small neighboring island of Kōri-jima, divers can explore underwater wreckage from World War II.

If you make the trip to the aquarium, be sure you take time to walk about 15 minutes north to the small hamlet of **Bise.** This little slice of traditional Okinawa has a famous path around 1 km (0.6 mi) long that is lined with fukugi trees. More than 200 red-tile roofed homes dot the grid-like area, forming a tunnel of shade. To reach this little pocket of residential bliss, walk north on Route 114 for about 10 minutes, veering left at the fork in the road in front of Hotel Orion Motobu Resort and Spa Galaxy. Passing by the hotel on your left, continue along this road for another five minutes or so until you reach the tunnel of shrubbery. Here, wander and soak up the ambience. This is what Okinawa was before concrete crept in.

Sights

CHURAUMI AQUARIUM
美ら海水族館

424 Ishikawa, Motobu-chō; tel. 098/048-3748; http://oki-churaumi.jp; 8:30am-8pm Mar.-Sept., until 6:30pm Oct.-Feb.; ¥1,850 adults, ¥1,230 high school students, ¥610 elementary and junior high school students; after 4pm ¥1,290 adults, ¥860 high school students, ¥430 elementary and junior high school students

This truly massive aquarium on the Motobu Peninsula is an awe-inspiring collection of marine life. Part of Ocean Expo Park, the aquarium is the undisputed champion of Japanese aquariums. Its Kuroshio Tank is among the world's biggest, as evidenced by the gigantic whale sharks swimming inside it alongside majestic manta rays and small schools of multihued tropical fish.

To access the aquarium by car—about 2 hours' drive one way—take the Okinawa Expressway (¥1,020 one way) to Nago at its northern end. From there, take local roads running through the Motobu Peninsula to Ocean Expo Park. If you don't have your own wheels, take the Yanbaru Express Bus (http://yanbaru-expressbus.com; ¥2,000 one way), which goes directly to the aquarium from Furujima monorail station six times daily. Alternatively, take Expressway bus no. 111 from Naha Bus Terminal just outside Asahibashi monorail station (1.5 hours; ¥2,100 one way) to Nago Bus Terminal. From Nago, transfer to infrequent local bus no. 70

1: Okinawa Peace Memorial Park
2: Churaumi Aquarium

1

2

for the last leg of the trip (50 minutes; ¥880 one way), which ends at Kinen Kōen Mae bus stop in front of Ocean Expo Park.

Transportation

To venture beyond Naha, you can hop on one of the regional **buses** running throughout the island. The main hub is the **Naha Bus Terminal.**

The easiest way to get around the island is renting a car. Pick one up in the arrivals hall at Naha Airport, or if you're already in Naha, head to **Nippon Rent-A-Car** (1-1-1 Kumoji; tel. 098/867-4554; www.nrgroup-global.com; 8am-8pm daily) or **Toyota Rent a Car** (4-1 Omoromachi; tel. 098/860-1530; https://rent.toyota.co.jp; 9am-8pm daily).

NORTH OF NAHA

Diving

North of Naha, there are some excellent diving opportunities along the western coast of Okinawa-Hontō. About 50 minutes' drive north of Naha, Cape Maeda is one of the island's most popular diving spots, known for its underwater Blue Cave and colorful schools of fish. Note that this popular spot is beginner-friendly.

Farther up the island's west coast, a fantastic dive of intermediate difficulty is the Manza Dream Hole. Descend about 6 meters (20 feet) and enter an expansive chamber teeming with thousands of fish. Exit through a wall of fish, past fan corals and garden eels poking their heads out of the sand below. For something even more challenging, advanced divers can consider going farther north to the final resting place of the sunken American warship the USS Emmons, off the coast of Kōri-jima, a speck of land near the northeastern coast of the Motobu Peninsula. The ship is 100 meters (328 feet) long and remains largely intact.

English-speaking dive outfits operating in the region include **Piranha Divers** (tel. 098/967-8487; www.piranha-divers.jp), **Reef Encounters** (tel. 098/995-9414; www.reefencounters.org), and **Natural Blue Diving Company** (tel. 090/9497-7374; www.naturalblue.net/jp). Inquire with them about potential underwater adventures.

Transportation

Regional **buses** leave from **Naha Bus Terminal.** Pick up a rental car at Naha Airport, **Nippon Rent-A-Car** (1-1-1 Kumoji; tel. 098/867-4554; www.nrgroup-global.com; 8am-8pm daily) or **Toyota Rent a Car** (4-1 Omoromachi; tel. 098/860-1530; https://rent.toyota.co.jp; 9am-8pm daily).

Yakushima 屋久島

Lying off the southern coast of Kyushu, the subtropical island of Yakushima is famed for its dense cedar forests draped in vivid green moss. Traipsing among these mystical trees, it's not hard to see how the island inspired anime master Hayao Miyazaki's vision of the world in his classic film *Princess Mononoke,* with its environmentalist message.

Like the mining company in Miyazaki's realm, which fights with the gods of a fictionalized forest, Yakushima once faced struggles of its own. The island suffered as a result of large-scale logging operations during the Edo period (1603-1868), when cedar shingles were a preferred material for rooftops. Thankfully, the forests recovered and today the island is a national park, sections of which were declared a Natural World Heritage Site by UNESCO in 1993.

Today, the forests of Yakushima are just the sort of woodlands that remind us of the magic of trees. Some of the cedars on the island are more than 7,000 years old. These ancient wonders are lovingly called *yakusugi* (*yaku* taken from the island's name and *sugi* meaning cedar). Moreover, the island's flora is

The Ryūkyū Kingdom

Okinawan history reminds us that Japan is home to a forgotten royal family. The **Sho dynasty,** founded by Sho Hashi, ruled over the Ryūkyū Kingdom for more than four centuries (1429-1879) from Shuri Castle in Naha. The kingdom stretched from the Amami Islands in the north, in modern-day Kagoshima Prefecture, to the Sakishima Islands in the south, which include the Miyako Islands and Yaeyama Islands, east of Taiwan. Today, the descendants of the Sho dynasty may speak their arcane court dialect at family gatherings, but they otherwise live as members of mainstream Japanese society.

Rewind the clock to the Ryūkyū Kingdom's heyday, however, and life for the Sho kings was a very different story. From the 15th century through the 19th century, the Ryūkyū Kingdom was an important star in East Asia's constellation of power, alongside Japan and Korea, with China being the main planet they all orbited around. Rather than rule by force, the Ryūkyū kings maintained a weapons-free realm and were known as being straight shooters and savvy diplomats, earning the kingdom the nickname the **"country of courtesy."** Although geographically tiny, the Ryūkyū Kingdom wielded vast influence through its strategically located shipping ports, which saw ships sail from Siberia in the far north to Thailand (then Siam) and Sumatra in the south. The wide range of goods traded along this vast stretch of ocean included Japanese swords, folding fans, lacquerware, herbs used in Chinese medicine, ivory from India, and frankincense from the Middle East.

With a long history as a vassal state to China, the Ryūkyū Kingdom was put between a rock and a hard place by Japan in 1590 when warlord Toyotomi Hideyoshi asked the kingdom to supply men as troops in his quest first to take over Korea, then China. The Ryūkyū kings refused to comply with Toyotomi's request, prompting an invasion by the **Satsuma clan** who set sail to invade the peaceful Ryūkyū chain in 1609. The kingdom was subdued and forced to pledge loyalty to the Satsuma clan, who took over the island's lucrative trade routes.

This uneasy arrangement came to a head in 1875 when Japan officially demanded that Naha end its tributary relationship with China. Okinawa was officially made an overseas territory of Japan at the end of the **Sino-Japanese War** (1895-1896). In 1972, Okinawa officially became the country's 47th prefecture when it was returned to Japan by the US occupying forces. Today, Okinawa sees the least investment of all Japanese prefectures. Further, sentiment is widespread that the prefecture is routinely neglected by Tokyo. Given this state of affairs, a growing number of Okinawans feel that their unique language, culture, and heritage make their homeland a prime candidate for **independence.**

profuse, ranging from subtropical in the lower elevations to subarctic toward the top of the island's mountainous core.

Yakushima is also highly mountainous, with some of the peaks at its center reaching almost 2,000 meters (6,561 feet) high. Particularly in its mountainous interior, precipitation is near constant, a fact humorously acknowledged by the local saying that it rains 35 days a month on the island. With annual precipitation of 5-10 meters (16-32 feet), on the coast and inland, respectively, Yakushima is one of the rainiest places in Japan, and in the world. Despite its southern altitude, it often gets an ample dump of snow in the higher elevations during winter, too. Away from its misty interior, the northwestern coast is lined by appealing sandy beaches where sea turtles lay their eggs from May to July. On the western side of the island you'll also find the tallest and most impressive of the island's four major waterfalls, **Ōkonotaki,** a cascade that spills 88 meters (288 feet) over a granite wall, hammering into a pool below. It's possible to get close to the falls, which send a cool swath of mist throughout the surroundings. The falls are a short walk from the Ōkonotaki bus stop.

In terms of basic orientation, the island's two main towns are **Miyanoura,** which sits on the north shore, and the two-horse town of **Anbō** on the east coast. The excellent hike of Shiratani Unsuikyō is best reached from

Miyanoura, while the **Yakusugi Land** nature park lies west of Anbō.

To make a trip to Yakushima worthwhile, plan on staying for a night or two. Furthermore, rent a car if you can. Having your own wheels will allow you to bypass the island's patchy bus schedule.

SIGHTS

YAKUSUGI MUSEUM
屋久杉自然館

2739-343 Anbō, Kumage-gun; tel. 0997/46-3113; www.yakusugi-museum.com; 9am-5pm daily, closed first Tues. every month; ¥600 adults, ¥400 high school and college students, ¥300 children

Before venturing into the island's misty interior to see the its ancient wonders in the wild, visit the Yakusugi Museum. This compact, artfully presented museum offers a glimpse into the long history of the island's stunning cedar trees.

Exhibits give deep context on the island's long journey toward preservation, explaining how it came to be claimed as a World Heritage site by UNESCO and how it serves as a testament to the ability of humans to live in harmony with nature. Be sure to pick up an English-language audio guide. The museum is locaated on the eastern side of the island about 3 km (1.9 mi) inland from the coast on Route 592, the road that leads to Yakusuki Land. It can be reached by bus from Anbō.

NAGATA INAKAHAMA
永田いなか浜

The island's famous flora isn't its only draw. The coasts of Japan are the part of the northern Pacific where loggerhead sea turtles come to lay their eggs. Nearly half of the loggerhead turtles who give birth in Japan do so on Yakushima. Along the lovely stretch of beach known as Nagata Inakahama, in the island's northwest, the bulk of these sea turtles lay their eggs starting from May and nest through July, until the beach fills with hatchlings in August.

To see the turtles in action, make a visit to the **Nagata Sea Turtles Association** (tel. 0997/45-2280; http://nagata-umigame.com; 1pm-5pm daily Apr. 1-Aug.31; ¥1,500 adults, children free for nighttime tour) a nonprofit group that leads tours to the beach at night from May through August. Note that the main purpose of these tours is to protect the turtles and their babies. Resist the urge to walk through the sand without a tour group during turtle season, lest you disturb the creatures' delicate habitat. The beach is located near the Inakahama bus stop, reached via the bus that runs from Miyanoura to Nagata.

★ HIKING

Yakushima's prime attraction is its dense primeval forests, ideally explored on foot. The forest zones here merely scratch the surface of the island's vast hiking options. If you're keen to go deeper into the island's interior, **Yakumonkey** (www.yakumonkey.com), an excellent resource about the island, sells a popular guidebook chock-full of information on sights, hiking trails, and sundry practicalities. This guide should more than suffice for ambitious wanderers.

If you'd like to explore alongside a locally knowledgable guide, **Yakushima Life** (www.yakushimalife.com), **Yakushima Experience** (www.yakushimaexperience.com), **Yes! Yakushima** (www.yesyakushima.com) and **Yakushima Geographic Tour** (http://yaku-geo.com) are all English-speaking tour providers that lead treks on the island, from custom hikes to overnight journeys. Check their websites for more details. Further, if you're in need of apparel to protect you from Yakushima's oftentimes relentless rain, stop by **Nakagawa Sports** (421-6 Miyanoura; tel. 0997/42-0341; http://yakushima-sp.com; 9am-7pm daily, closed every second Wed.). This shop in Miyanoura rents and sells everything from waterproof footwear to camping supplies at reasonable prices.

If you plan to summit any of the island's drizzly peaks, such as its highest point **Miyanoura-dake** (1,935 meters/ 6,348 feet), bear in mind that the temperature difference between sea level and the highest points inland is about 11°C (19.8°F). Wear waterproof footwear and fast-drying clothing, and carry a change of clothing. Be sure to tell the reception desk at your hotel, register at the nearest Tourist Information Center, or jot the details of your intended hike at the trailhead on a form called a *tōzan todokede* before striking out on any long-distance hike.

During prime hiking season, from March to November, private cars are not permitted to make the 30-minute journey from Anbō to the Aarakawa Trailhead. This is meant to prevent traffic jams caused by the rush of hikers. You must instead take a shuttle bus that departs from the Yakusugi Museum (35 minutes; ¥1,380 round-trip, ¥1,000 for conservation efforts). Purchase a bus ticket at least a day before you plan to go on the hike. Tickets are available at the airport or the tourist center in either Miyanoura or Anbō (page 703). Buses depart the Yakusugi Museum parking lot in the early morning (5am-6am) and return between 3pm and 6pm. Many hotels provide their guests with transport to the Yakusugi Museum for this purpose.

YAKUSUGI LAND

tel. 0997/42-3508; http://y-rekumori.com; 9am-5pm daily; ¥300

A wonderful introduction to the island's forest magic, Yakusugi Land's network of trails leads to some of the island's most accessible ancient trees. This is a good choice if your time limited and ease of access is your main priority, with well-maintained trails (1-4.5 km/.6-3 mi) suitable for beginners and children. Four hiking courses, ranging in length from 30 minutes to 2.5 hours, allow you to tailor the length of your walk. They all follow the same basic route, with each looping back to the trailhead. The easiest section of the trail is made of a wooden boardwalk. As you progress farther into the woods, the trail and the terrain slowly change. The longest hike ends atop Tachudake (1,457 meters/4,780 feet).

As you venture into these woods, you'll cross a suspension bridge that takes you over a river set in a mossy gorge. Deeper in the woodlands, you'll find the area is populated with trees more than 1,000 years old. English signage is found throughout, and English pamphlets can be picked up at the trailhead. There are two daily round-trip bus services between Anbō and Yakusugi Land

coastline hike on Yakushima

(40 minutes; ¥740 one way). A taxi ride from Anbō will take about 30 minutes and cost about ¥4,000.

SHIRATANI UNSUIKYŌ GORGE

Miyanoura; tel. 0997/42-3508; http://y-rekumori.com; 24/7; ¥300

Another pristine area of the island to marvel at its wondrous trees is Shiratani Unsuikyō Gorge. This park is lined with trails—Edo-period footpaths, wooden walkways, trails of stone—ranging from one to five hours in length. The full loop is 10 km (6.2 mi) and takes roughly 4 hours to complete. It's a popular spot to see yakusugi without being forced to walk any overly strenuous trails. The sylvan scenes found along the paths that run along the gorge are so archetypal they almost look unreal. From a lookout rock called Taiko-iwa, the woodlands of the island stretch out like an endless green carpet. To access the trailhead, take a bus from Miyanoura to Shiratani Unsuikyō Gorge bus stop (30 minutes; ¥550). There are upward of five round-trip journeys per day.

JŌMON-SUGI

Miyanoura; 24/7; free

Jōmon-sugi is the granddaddy of all the island's yakusugi trees. The giant Cryptomeria is something like the island's mascot. It was luckily spared the saw during the Edo period logging days due to its asymmetrical shape. It's not particularly tall at about 25 meters (82 feet), but it makes up for it with its exceptionally rotund trunk measuring 5 meters (16 feet) around, with gnarled vertical ridges and limbs sprouting from its top in random directions. Its fabled look is in keeping with the fantastical surroundings, swathed in moss and veiled in mist. Aged somewhere between 2,000 and 7,200 years, this tree dates to the Jōmon period (14,000-300 BCE), after which it is named.

The only way to reach this near-mythical tree is on foot along a trail that begins from a trailhead at **Arakawa-tozanguchi** (19.5 km/12.1 mi; about 10 hours round trip). You'll follow an old railroad track before switching to a mix of dirt, wooden boardwalks, and steps. If you're in good physical condition and feel confident about your ability to keep a solid pace, it's possible to make the journey in a long day trip. To pull this off, leave before dawn to ensure you finish by sunset.

If you'd rather not push too hard, the unstaffed **Takatsuka Hut** is about 200 meters (656 feet) beyond the tree. Pack your own food, toiletries, and water if you plan to stay at this bare-bones lodging. Mercifully, the trail is well marked in English.

To reach the trailhead, you must first take a **shuttle bus** (35 minutes; ¥1,380, plus ¥2,000 for conservation efforts) from the Yakusugi Museum in the town of Anbō, roughly 15 km (9.3 mi) to the southeast. Note that these buses depart very early in the morning, between 5am and 6am, then return from Arakawa-tozanguchi between 3pm and 6pm. It's possible to also drive yourself to the trailhead from December through February, but private cars are prohibited on the road leading up to the trailhead at Arakawa-tozanguchi from March through November to prevent congestion. Buy your ticket for the shuttle bus at least one day ahead of your planned hike either at the tourist information center in either Miyanoura or Anbō. Some of the island's hotels also sell tickets, as does the airport.

FOOD

★ PANORAMA

60-1 Miyanoura; tel. 0997/42-0400; http://panoramayakushima.com; 6pm-11pm Thurs.-Tues.; plates ¥300-900; walk 5 minutes south of Miyanoura Port

Set in a nicely madeover former hardware store with long picnic-style tables and seats along a bar in front of an open kitchen, this stylish neighborhood *izakaya* in Miyanoura serves a menu of dishes made with locally sourced produce and seafood caught just offshore. Dishes are diverse, from pizza and chicken liver pâté with baguette to braised pork belly over rice, fried flying fish, poke (Hawaiian-style marinated sashimi), and more. The atmosphere is casual and friendly, and the drinks menu includes craft beer and *shōchū* brewed on the island and fruit-infused sodas made in-house. English menu available.

RENGAYA

410-74 Anbō; tel. 0997/46-3439; lunch 11am-2pm daily, dinner 6pm-10pm daily; lunch from ¥1,000, dinner sets ¥1,600-2,500; walk 5 minutes north from Anbō Port

This boisterous barbecue joint in Anbō serves venison, beef, vegetables, and more to be grilled at your table, preferably washed down with an ice-cold beer. It's a cozy spot to fueld up before a hike or to unwind after traipsing through the island's verdant interior.

ACCOMMODATIONS

SŌYŌTEI

521-4 Nagata; tel. 0997/45-2819; http://soyotei.net; ¥15,000 pp with 2 meals; walk 3 minutes west of Nagata Inakahama bus stop

This family-owned *ryokan* is about 40 minutes' drive west of Miyanoura Port near the lovely beach of Nagata Inakahama. There are 11 semidetached Japanese-style rooms, each with a verandah facing the ocean. Each room has its own toilet but shares a number of baths, both indoor and open-air, supplied with *onsen* water. There's a communal dining hall looking out to the ocean where seafood-heavy meals are served twice daily.

★ SANKARA HOTEL & SPA

553 Haginoue, Mugio; tel. 0997/47-3488; https://sankarahotel-spa.com; from ¥47,300 pp with 2 meals; drive 20 minutes (10 km/6.2 mi) southwest of Anbō Port

On the island's southeast coast, overlooking the ocean, this world-class accommodation offers plush villas decked out in Balinese-style decor with plenty of teak, with all the bells and whistles you'd expect at a luxury property. There are two one-site restaurants—the casual Ayana and more formal Okas—where the chefs adroitly concoct exquisite French fare using locally sourced ingredients, as well as a pool, spa, and library. The staff are incredibly attentive, freely sharing knowledge about the island's hidden gems, and exhibit the same level of omotenashi (hospitality) you'd expect at one of Kyoto's most exclusive *ryōkan*. It's possible for guests to rent a car from the hotel with an advanced reservation (¥1,500 per hour). Highly recommended.

INFORMATION AND SERVICES

Before heading into the island's wilderness, bulk up on information at the **Tourist Information Center** (tel. 0997/42-1019; 9am-5pm daily), connected to the ferry terminal in the port town of Miyanoura on the island's north coast. Also in Miyanoura, **Yakushima Environmental & Cultural Village Center** (823-1 Miyanoura; tel. 0997/42-2911; 9am-5pm daily Tues.-Sun., closed Tues. if Mon. is national holiday; ¥520 adults, ¥360 high school students, ¥260 elementary and junior high students) screens the 25-minute film *Yakushima, Symphony of Forest and Water* at 20 minutes past each hour—basic English subtitles included—and is a good place to get acquainted with the hiking trails of the island.

Another **Tourist Information Center** (187-1 Anbō; tel. 0997/46-2333; 8:30am-6pm daily) can be found about 4 minutes' walk north of MOS Burger, near Anbō Bridge in the town of Anbō in the island's southeast.

Online, a wealth of free English-language information, from hotel and restaurant listings to maps and bus timetables, can be downloaded: http://yakukan.jp/doc/index.html.

Note that **ATMs** are hard to come by on the island. Plan to handle any banking matters before arriving in Yakushima—or make any withdrawals at one of the eight post office ATMs around the island. The most convenient to reach is the post office in Miyanoura. Post office ATMs are open on weekdays from 8:45am to 6pm, and on weekends and national holidays from 9am to 5pm.

TRANSPORTATION

Getting There

Daily flights are available between Kagoshima (35 minutes; discount fares from ¥10,000 one way), Osaka (one hour 40 minutes; discount fares from ¥26,000) and Fukuoka (one hour; discount fares from ¥18,000) to **Yakushima Airport** (501 Koseda; tel. 0997/42-1200), located between Anbō and Miyanoura on the island's northern coast.

If you prefer to go by boat, jetfoils run to Miyanoura port (1 hour 50 minutes) five times daily (less during winter), from Kagoshima's high-speed ferry terminal south of Minamifutō pier. High-speed ferries also travel twice daily to the town of Anbō (2 hours). The hydrofoil operator is **Tane Yaku Jetfoil** (tel. 099/226-0128 in Kagoshima, 0997/42-2003 in Miyanoura; www.tykousoku.jp; ¥8,300 one way, ¥15,000 round-trip). Book tickets in advance by asking for assistance from your accommodation or filling in a ticket request form on the website of English-speaking agent Yakushima Travel (www.yakushimatravel.com/ticket-english.html). Or, do it the old fashioned way: Go to the jetfoil terminal window and purchase a ticket in person.

Slower car ferries operated by **Ferry Yakushima 2** (http://ferryyakusima2.com) bound for Miyanoura also depart from Kagoshima New Port once every morning and return in the afternoon (4 hours; ¥4,900 one way, ¥8,900 round-trip).

Getting Around

The easiest way to travel around Yakushima is by **rental car.** There are rental shops at Miyanoura port and at Yakushima Airport.

If you're not planning to have your own car, buses also move about once per hour around Yakushima's main road that runs along its coast. There are two bus operators: **Tanegashima-Yakushima Kotsu** and **Matsubanda Kotsu** (www.yakushima.co.jp/index-5.php). The one stretch of the island where buses don't run as often is between Nagata and Okonotaki, which is only reachable by bus twice per day. Limited buses also run into the island's interior from Miyanoura and Anbō. Check the timetable at either bus terminal before making any journeys inland, as getting back can be a challenge due to long time lags.

You can also buy a pass for one day (¥2,000), two or three days (¥3,000), or four days (¥4,000) for buses operated by Tanegashima-Yakushima Kotsu. Inquire at either Miyanoura or Anbō bus terminal for details.

Kerama Islands 慶良間諸島

TOP EXPERIENCE

Only 35 km (22 miles) west of Okinawa-Hontō, the Kerama Islands are the first port of call for those venturing to Okinawa's *sakishima* (outer islands). These islands—some 20 in all—are renowned for their crystal-clear waters teeming with manta rays, sea turtles, and tropical fish that beckon divers and snorkelers. Start your exploration of the Keramas on Zamami-jima. While the island is already relatively unspoiled, go just a bit farther to the small spit of land known as Aka-jima, or farther out to Kume-jima, to discover some of the most pristine, uncrowded beaches and best waters for diving in all of Japan.

ZAMAMI-JIMA 座間味島

Zamami-jima, the most developed of the lovely Kerama Islands, is less than an hour from Naha by jetfoil. Its beaches are excellent places to swim or relax under a parasol in the sand.

Sports and Recreation

The turquoise waters of Zamami-jima and the small, neighboring islets of Gahi-jima and Agenashiku are great for snorkeling and diving. The islands are a hot spot for whale watching during winter, too. From late-December through early-April, it's possible to board a tiny boat to get up close to the whale pods that congregate here.

FURUZAMAMI BEACH

About 20 minutes' walk southeast of the port and main village on the island

The island's main prime sweep of oceanfront is Furuzamami Beach. This pristine expanse of white sand goes on for about 700 meters (2,296 feet). Showers, toilets, food vendors, and snorkel rentals (¥1,000) make it a convenient choice for a day at the beach for those coming from Naha.

While Furuzamami Beach is by no means thronged with crowds throughout most of the year, it can become slightly crowded in summer. If you yearn for a bit more isolation, board a boat at Zamami-jima's port and ride about five minutes (¥1,500 round-trip) south to the two tiny neighboring islands of **Gahi-jima** and **Agenashiku-jima.** The beaches on these smaller islands lack the amenities of Furuzamami Beach, but crowds are thinner and the crystal-clear water is home to abundant coral.

DIVE CENTER NO-Y

878 Zamami; tel. 098/987-3262; http://kerama-zamami.com; single boat dives from ¥5,400 plus equipment rental, 2-hour whale-watching tour ¥5,400

Dive Center No-Y, 5 minutes' walk north of Zamami Port, is a guesthouse that offers tours of up to three dives in a day. Dive Center No-Y also provides whale-watching tours that depart from Naha, run to Zamami-jima, then return to Naha. See the website for details.

DIVE-INN-HAMA

97 Zamami; tel. 098/987-2013; http://diveinnhama.jp; boat dives from ¥6,000 plus equipment rental

Another option for dive excursions and rentals, Dive-Inn-Hama is a dive shop that also doubles as lodging. The shop is only two minutes' walk from Zamami Port. Its website is Japanese-only, but the staff speak limited English.

ZAMAMI TOUR OPERATION

19-2 Zamami-son; tel. 080/1766-6745; www.zamami.ne.jp; 8:30am-5pm; single boat rides ¥1,500-2,500, snorkeling and beach equipment rentals ¥500-1,500

This company fronts the beaches of Gahi-jima and Agenashiku-jima; the water here is an excellent place to snorkel. Get in touch with Zamami Tour Operation to arrange boat transport between these islands and to get set up with a snorkeling session.

Furuzamami Beach

ZAMAMI WHALE-WATCHING ASSOCIATION

tel. 098/896-4141; www.vill.zamami.okinawa.jp/whale; 2-hour whale-watching tour ¥6,000 adults, ¥3,000 children 6-11, free children under 5

Another whale-watching outfit that leads tours around the island is Zamami Whale-Watching Association.

Food

ZAMAMI BURGER

126 Zamami; tel. 098/987-3626; noon-8pm daily; average ¥1,000; walk 4 minutes' north from Zamami Port

This foreign-owned burger joint is located in the Zamamia International Guesthouse. The eatery serves straightforward, delicious burgers, fries, and more through both lunch and dinner hours. A good spot for a casual, filling meal.

MARUMIYA

432-2 Zamami; tel. 098/987-3166; www.vill.zamami.okinawa.jp/guidemap/detail/138; lunch 11am-2:30pm Thurs.-Tues., dinner 6-10:30pm Thurs.-Tues.; lunch specials from ¥800; walk 6 miles north of Zamami Port

This mom-and-pop shop serves up greasy spoon Okinawan classics like *gōya champurū* (bitter gourd stir-fry) and Okinawan-style soba, as well as otherwise standard Japanese fare (sashimi, tonkatsu, and more). Think home-cooking. The staff are very welcoming, too. It fills up fast with locals during lunch hours. English menu available.

Accommodations

AMA BEACH CAMPGROUND

Next to Ama Beach; tel. 098/987-3259; www.vill.zamami.okinawa.jp/enjoy/New%20campground%20fee%20and%20guide%20from%202019.4.1.pdf; tent rentals from ¥1,000 pp; walk 25 minutes west of Zamami Port

Right beside the quiet stretch of sand that is Ama Beach, this well-equipped campground has a cooking area, showers (¥300 pp for each shower, to be paid at reception), a reception area that holds luggage (¥200 per day for each piece), and more. Other camping supplies can also be rented, from sleeping bags (¥500 per night) to mats (¥300 per night). Reserve at least a day ahead to ensure you get everything you need.

ZAMAMIA INTERNATIONAL GUESTHOUSE

126 Zamami; tel. 098/987-3626; http://zamamia-guesthouse.com; private twins ¥3,500 pp, mixed dorms ¥3,000 pp, female-only dorms ¥3,000 pp

This bare-bones, budget guesthouse is clean, cheerful, and run by helpful foreign staff. The rooms are a mix of female-only and mixed dorms, as well as private twin rooms. All bathrooms and toilets are shared. Zamami Burger is also housed on-site. There's also a large communal lounge.

Information and Services

Virtually everything you'd need to find for your exploration of the island and its surroundings can be found at the **Tourism Information Center** (1-1 Zamami; tel. 098/987-2277; 9am-5pm daily) next to Zamami Port. An English-speaking staff member is usually present and there are plenty of English-language materials about the island and its surroundings. Online, the **Zamami English Guide** (www.zamamienglishguide.com/zamami) gives the low-down on logistics, outdoor activities and more on the island.

Transportation

From Naha's Tomari Port, the **Queen Zamami 3** operates two high-speed ferries most of the year and three during peak season in Apr.-Sept. (50 minutes; adults ¥3,140, children ¥1,570). There's also one normal ferry run by **Ferry Zamami** (2 1.5 hours; adults ¥2,120, children ¥1,060) that runs to Zamami Port every day, making a stop by the neighboring island of Aka-jima on the way. To book either one of these ferries, contact the Zamami Village Ticket Office at Tomari Port (tel. 098/868-4567, service center 10am-5pm daily). Learn more about reserving a seat at www.zamamienglishguide.com/ferries, where you'll find ferry timetables, and https://zamamitouristinfo.wordpress.com/getting-here, which provides a link to a reservation page.

Getting around the island on foot is entirely possible, although bicycles and motor scooters can be rented at the port. There's also a bus that runs from the port to Furuzamami Beach (5 minutes; ¥300).

AKA-JIMA

阿嘉島

This tiny island, 15 minutes by boat from Zamami-jima, embodies a laid-back island vibe. Time flows slowly here, even compared to sleepy Zamami-jima.

Graceful Kerama deer—petite, skillfully swimming descendents of the deer imported by conquerors from the Japanese mainland during the early 17th century—poke around this little slice of paradise, where the pristine beaches seem designed for whiling away long, lazy days in the sun.

If your aim is to chill out and gaze at the azure seas surrounding the island on all sides, head for the main stretch of sand, **Nishibama Beach.** If you feel like exploring, just strike off and wander; the island is easy to negotiate on foot and is bordered by soft sand at almost every turn.

If you feel like exploring the island's underwater seascape, teeming with small tropical fish, **Marine House Seasir** (tel. 098/987-2973; www.seasir.com; single beginner dives from ¥12,000, double dives from ¥19,100 for certified divers, plus equipment rental) and **Kawai Diving** (153 Aka; tel. 098/987-2219; http://oki-zamami.jp/~kawai; single dives from ¥7,000, plus equipment rental) are dive operators that also run guesthouses within a few minutes' walk of each other in Aka Village, near the island's south coast.

Transportation

GETTING THERE

Queen Zamami 3 (tel. 098/868-4567; www.zamamienglishguide.com/ferries) runs jetfoils directly from Naha to Aka-jima twice a day (1 hour 10 minutes; ¥3,140 adults, ¥1,570 children), and one daily standard ferry (1.5 hours; ¥2,120 adults, ¥1,060 children). Boats also run four times daily between Zamami Port and Aka-jima (15 minutes; ¥300 one way).

Miyako-jima 宮古列島

The main island of the Miyako chain, Miyako-jima, is home to some of Japan's best beaches, centered on Yonaha Maehama Beach in the island's southwest. If you're an advanced diver, take note of the tiny islands of Irabu-jima and Shimoji-jima, which are slightly farther out to sea but accessible by bridge from Miyako-jima. Each of these islands is a cave-diving mecca.

The island's main hub is Hirara (pop. 33,000), a laid-back town in the west full of weather-beaten concrete blocks slowly being claimed by nature via lush climbing plants; his adds to the island's far-flung tropical appeal and reminds you that you're not on the mainland anymore.

BEACHES

SUNAYAMA BEACH

砂山ビーチ

Sunayama Beach (Sand Mountain) is about 4 km (2.5 mi) north of Hirara (pop. 33,000). The beach is known for its picturesque rock formations, including an iconic arch carved out by waves crashing against a giant block of coral. Amenities include a shop that rents water sports equipment, as well as toilets and showers. The beach is easily accessible from Hirara, making it a good choice if you don't have your own wheels to get around the island. Take a bus or drive to the large sand dune looming behind the beach. Descend to waterfront from there.

Miyako-jima

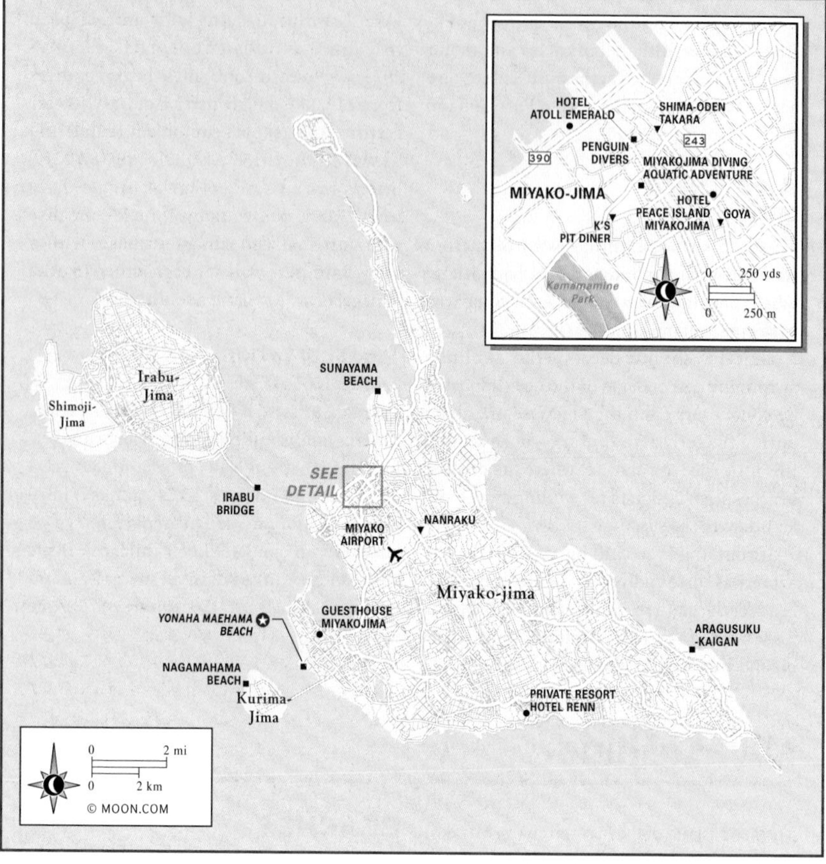

★ YONAHA MAEHAMA BEACH
与那覇前浜ビーチ

This 7-kilometer (4.3-mile) long tract of silky, white sand at the southwest corner of the island is easily one of Japan's best beaches. The water is warm and clear, making it ideal for water sports. It's also an idyllic vantage point to watch the sun dip below the horizon. There are ample facilities on the beach: showers, toilets, rental shops offering beach chairs, parasols, banana boats, and jet skis (which *can* get a little noisy during peak season). Access the beach either by local bus or rental car. It's located about 20 minutes' drive south of Hiara, just north of the bridge that links Miayko-jima to the neighboring island Kurima-jima.

NAGAMAHAMA BEACH
長間浜

Particularly during peak season, the sands of Yonaha Maehama are thronged with holidaymakers. Thankfully, there's an alternative not far away with a fraction of the crowds. Across the bridge just north of Yonaha Maehama, the small island of **Kurima-jima** is home to the excellent Nagamahama Beach on its northwest shore. If you choose to go to this hidden gem of a beach, be sure to bring everything with you that you'll need, including a snorkel and goggles as coral is abundant just offshore. There are no rental shops, jet skis or banana boats here.

ARAGUSUKU-KAIGAN
新城海岸

A good snorkeling spot on Miyako-jima is the Aragusuku-kaigan, a fine stretch of beach found along the southern portion of the island's eastern shore. The shallow water here teems with tropical fish. There are toilets and showers on the beach, and during the summer months a rental shop offers beach supplies. The beach is about 30 minutes' drive from Hirara.

DIVING

Just off the western coast of Miyako-jima, the tiny islets of **Irabu-jima** and **Shimoji-jima,** connected to each other by a bridge, are a beloved haunt of cave divers. **W-Arch,** off the coast of small neighboring islet Irabu-jima, is a great choice for beginners. The menacingly named Satan's Palace, off the tiny nearby island of Shimoji-jima, is for advanced divers only. Also off the coast of Shimoji-jima is the "Antonio Gaudi" cave system, replete with submarine archways reminiscent of the Spanish architect's surreal signature style.

A slew of other colorfully named formations lie submersed around these two islands. To learn more about the fantastic diving opportunities in the waters of Irabu-jima and Shimoji-jima, check out the offerings of **Miyakojima Diving Aquatic Adventure** (543-1 Shimozato, Hirara; tel. 0980/79-5009; www.miyako-aquaticadventure.com; one boat dive ¥7,500 plus equipment rental) and **Penguin Divers** (40 Shimozato, Hirara; tel. 0980/79-5433; www.diving-penguin.com; two cave dives ¥13,000 plus equipment rental). Both dive shops have English-speaking staff. Note that their offices are actually located in Hirara on Miyako-jima.

Transportation

Thanks to the completion of the Irabu Bridge in 2015, a boat is no longer needed to cross from Miyako-jima to Irabu-jima and closely neighboring Shimoji-jima (accessible from Irabu-jima by bridge). The 3,540-meter (2.2-mile) bridge is the longest toll-free bridge in Japan. Make your way across by local **bus** or **rental car.**

Yonaha Maehama Beach

Food

The best place to get a drink or a meal on Miyako-jima is in its main town of Hirara.

NANRAKU

568 Nishizato; tel. 0980/73-1855; 6pm-midnight; ¥2,500

This restaurant is an institution, as attested to by the celebrities' signatures adorning the walls. The key word here is local: Ingredients—from vegetables to beef to fish—all come from Miyako. The chef hails from Miyako. Be sure to try some *umibudō* (literally "sea grapes," a kind of edible seaweed), pulled from the waters just offshore, or beef sashimi sourced from Miyako farms too.

GOYA

570-2 Nishizato; tel. 0980/74-2358; https://zumi-goya.com; 5:30pm-midnight Fri.-Wed.; ¥3,000

At Goya you'll find solid *izakaya* fare: sashimi, *benimo* (purple sweet potato) croquettes, various grilled meats, and more. The main draw is its spirited musical performances. Diners share long tables, and a live band jams every night (¥320 cover charge). Dancing is encouraged, and facilitated by the Orion beer on tap and the wide range of *awamori* on offer.

SHIMA-ODEN TAKARA

172 Nishizato; tel. 0980/72-0671; ¥2,500

An *izakaya* with a menu focused on *oden*, a style of cooking that involves stewing a variety of things—from boiled eggs and deep-fried tofu to radish and pig's feet—in a soy-based broth, often eaten with a dab of hot mustard. The restaurant has a classic island feel, with counter seats and tatami-mat floor-seating in private booths separated by bamboo curtains. Reserve a day in advance or plan to come after 9pm to ensure a seat.

K'S PIT DINER

517 Shimozato; tel. 090/1821-1098; 11:30am-3pm and 6pm-11pm Tues.-Sun.; ¥1,200

Sometimes you just want a burger and fries. When you do, head to this old-school American-themed diner—down to the red, white and blue checkered plates—in the middle of Hirara.

Accommodations

GUESTHOUSE MIYAKOJIMA

233 Shimojiyonaha; tel. 03/4510-8459; https://blogs.yahoo.co.jp/yonaha233mair/52847131.html; ¥7,000 d with private bath

Aside from its stellar location near Yoneha Maehama Beach, the hotel has a variety of room types to suit a range of budgets, from dorm beds to doubles with private baths.

HOTEL PEACE ISLAND MIYAKOJIMA

310 Nishizato; tel. 0980/74-1717; http://peace-k.jp/miyako; ¥13,000 with breakfast

Hotel Peace Island Miyakojima is clean and friendly. While the aesthetics are not a selling point, each room has a washing machine with built-in dryer. Staff are helpful and its location is central.

HOTEL ATOLL EMERALD

108-7 Shimozato; tel. 0980/73-9800; www.atollemerald.jp; ¥25,000

Hotel Atoll Emerald is a good hotel in the middle of town, which means easy access to food and shops, but a bit more travel to reach the prime beaches. It has clean, modern Western and Japanese-style rooms, views of the ocean, and amiable staff.

★ PRIVATE RESORT HOTEL RENN

422-2 Gurikubetomori; tel. 0980/77-7859; www.resort-renn.jp; ¥42,000

This property offers charm, privacy, peace and quiet, and a helpful host, Mr. Renn. This intimate, elegant bed-and-breakfast is smack in the middle of the southern coast of the island, with easy access to both Yoneha Maehama Beach to the west and Nishi Henna-zaki to the east. The three rooms are big and clean with balconies. There's also a shared rooftop lounge with stellar ocean views. Continental breakfast is provided, courtesy of Mr. Renn's mother. If you will have a rental car and want to splash out on digs a cut above the rest in town, this is a very good pick.

Information and Services

The best place to pick up information in Miyako is actually at the airport. So don't forget to swing by the tourist information desk run by the **Miyako Tourism Association** (tel. 0980/72-0899; 10am-5:30pm daily). There's also a branch in the center of Hirara, about 20 minutes' walk southeast of the port on the second floor of a building across the street from a twon hall(187 Nishizato; tel. 0980/73-1881; 9am-6pm daily). Check out the association's website too (https://miyako-guide.net).

The **Hirara-Nishizato Post Office** (142 Nishi-zato, Hirara; 9am-5pm Mon.-Fri.) has a Japan Post Bank ATM (8am-7pm Mon.-Fri., 9am-6pm Sat., 9am-5pm Sun. and holidays), and the **Bank of the Ryukyus** (240-2 Nishizato, Hirara; tel. 098/72-2251; 7am-10pm Mon.-Fri., 8am-9pm Sat.-Sun. and holiday-s9am) also services foreign cards.

Transportation

GETTING THERE

Miyako-jima is one of the easier islands to reach. Direct flights to and from **Miyako Airport** run from Tokyo's Haneda Airport (3 hours), Osaka's Kansai Airport (2 hours), Naha Airport (45 minutes), and Ishigaki Airport (35 minutes).

GETTING AROUND

Miyako-jima is about 15 km (9.3 mi) across from east to west and 25 km (15.5 mi) north to south. Renting a **car** will give you the most freedom to explore the beaches that are scattered around the island, and visit neighboring islands that are accessible by bridge. Renting a car is easy at Miyako Airport or in Hirara.

The next best way to get around is actually by **bicycle.** Simply ask your accommodation's front desk, as most inns around Hirara offer bicycle rentals. The island is remarkably flat, which makes cycling a pleasureable way to explore.

There is a local **bus** network, but connections are very infrequent. That said, if you have no other option, buses do shuttle between the airport and Hirara (10 minutes; ¥210), and from Hirara to Yoneha-Maehama Beach and the neighboring island of Kurima-jima (30 minutes; ¥390).

Yaeyama Islands 八重山諸島

Of all the southwest isles, the Yaeyama Islands offer the broadest and deepest experience of Okinawa. In Japan's far southern frontier, these remote islands feel like they belong in Southeast Asia. Life here moves at a laid-back pace, completely out of sync with the mainland. Even the rhythms of relatively chilled-out Naha seem frantic by comparison.

The main island and gateway to the chain is Ishigaki-jima, where relaxed, friendly locals, excellent diving, and beaches abound. From Ishigaki, ferries shuttle back and forth daily to tiny Taketomi-jima, which offers the best possible glimpse of living Okinawan culture. Saunter or cycle through its rustic car-free villages on streets made of crushed coral and admire the cultural hybrid of architectural styles in its old homes, adorned with red-tiled roofs and dog-lion *shisa* guardians. Beyond Taketomi-jima, the landscape of Iriomote-jima, also reached by ferry, befits an *Indiana Jones* film set, with its dense mangrove swamps and jungles that almost call for a machete.

And at Japan's farthest southwestern corner, the far-flung Yonagumi-jima is home to the Atlas moth, the world's largest. This island is a magnet for divers, who come to witness the multitude of hammerheads that swarm through its waters during winter, and, more famously, to glimpse enigmatic underwater formations off the island's coast that appear man-made, although the jury is out.

ISHIGAKI-JIMA
石垣島

Ishigaki-jima is the gateway to the naturally diverse and culturally distinct Yaeyama Islands, which include Japan's southernmost and westernmost bodies of land. Ishigaki boasts great beaches and gorgeous underwater terrain, making it a diving mecca in its own right. Yet, it's also a key transport hub for the Yaeyama chain as a whole. Both the region's major airport and ferry terminal are located on the island. The city of Ishigaki, its main hub, also has a lively dining and social scene.

Sights

KABIRA BAY
川平湾

The waters of Kabira Bay are reserved for very rare black pearl cultivation, so it's forbidden to swim. It's a lovely view, though, with some small rocks dotting the seascape. The beach fronting this picturesque scene is white sand. If you are hankering to get out on the water, it's possible to take a ride through the bay in a glass-bottomed boat which depart from near the premises of the tour operator, **Kabira Marine Service** (934 Kabira; tel. 0980/88-2335; www.kabiramarine.jp; 9am-5pm daily; 30 minutes; adults ¥1,030, children ¥520). Look down and you'll see a host of tropical fish at play.

Beaches

YONEHARA BEACH
米原海岸

Yonehara Beach is Ishigaki's prime stretch of sand. Located on the island's north coast, east of Kabira Bay, it has all the amenities of a major beach—showers, toilets, snorkel rentals—and allows camping. There are good sections of coral reef, but the current is strong, so don't go out too far if you're not a skilled swimmer.

SUNSET BEACH

Sunset Beach is a tranquil spot on the western side of the finger of land extending from the north of the island. It's a great place to snorkel and to watch the sun dip below the horizon. Showers and toilets are available, and parasols and beach chairs can be rented.

★ Diving

Ishigaki is one of the best places to dive in Okinawa, which makes it a strong contender for best dive spot in Japan. Coral reefs are found near Kabira Bay, Yonehara Beach, and beyond. But the island's most famous spot of all is known as the **Manta Scramble,** a natural occurrence that takes place each autumn near Kabira Bay: Manta rays congregate to be cleaned by a proliferation of plankton that builds up in the area. Divers come to the site en masse every autumn to dive below the rays and watch them circle and feed on the plankton, which also scrub them down. Among the island's many other stellar dive spots, **Osaki Hanagoi Reef** stands out. This reef is like a multihued coral jungle teeming with oceanlife.

There are so many dive spots around the island that it pays to consult local pros to find out what your options would be. The English-speaking members of **Prime Scuba Ishigaki** (345-9 Maezato; tel. 0980/87-5980; www.primescuba-isg.com; 8:30am-6pm daily) are the real deal. **Umicoza** (1287-97 Kabira; tel. 0980/88-2434; https://umicoza.com) is another reputable English-speaking outfit on the island.

Food

Just like elsewhere in Okinawa, Ishigaki-jima is home to loads of charming *izakaya* serving up Ryūkyū classics like *goya chanpuru* (bitter melon stir-fried with tofu, eggs, and pork),

1: Kabira Bay, Ishigaki-jima **2:** diving in the waters off Ishigaki-jima

1
2

mozoku seaweed tempura, locally caught fish served raw or grilled, and more.

SHIMANO TABEMONOYA PAIKAJI

219 Okawa; tel. 0980/82-6027; 5pm-midnight daily; ¥3,500

A homey, lively, and well-lit space with friendly staff. This is a great choice for dinner. Book a day in advance to ensure a seat. One caveat: the restaurant can get pretty smoky as the evening wears on.

★ USAGI-YA HONTEN

1-1 Nakamura Heights 102; tel. 0980/88-5014; http://usagiya-ishigaki.com; 5pm-11:45pm daily, last order 10:45pm; dishes ¥380-3,580

Usagi-ya is more than a meal; it's an experience. The friendly staff, dressed in Okinawan-style *yukata,* double as drummers and dancers for the nightly performances. An acoustic guitarist and a *sanshin* strummer jam 7pm-9pm nightly. The offerings are filling and delicious: green papaya salad, teppanyaki hot plate with locally sourced beef and vegetables (green and yellow bell peppers, potato wedges, bean sprouts, and a citrus-based dipping sauce). There are ample *awamori* options from distilleries around the Southwest Islands and of course cold Orion is on tap. By the end of the evening, don't be surprised if the entire restaurant is on its feet dancing.

CAFÉ IMAGINE

644-41 Fukai; tel. 0980/88-2377; http://cafeimagine.business.site; 11am-5pm daily; ¥1,200

This is an unsuspecting bistro with a surf-bar vibe located near Yonehara Beach. The menu offers simple, delicious, and reasonably priced dishes like taco rice, pasta, and pizza made with care. The owner also whips up mean smoothies using fruit sourced from around the island. An ideal place for lunch on a day out at the beach.

Accommodations

★ IRIWA

599 Kabira; tel. 0980/88-2563; ¥2,500 dorm, ¥7,600 d

A rooftop terrace with ocean views, a shared living room and kitchen, and welcoming English-speaking hosts who want to introduce guests to the underwater wonders of Ishigaki-jima (with snorkel) are just a few of this guesthouse's selling points. If you enjoy communal living, it doesn't get much better than Iriwa, an island-chic guesthouse—surfboards and potted plants in the lounge—that

beef hotplate at Usagi-ya Honten

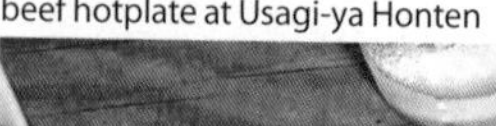

sits near Kabira Bay. All rooms but one share bathroom facilities. Book far (months) in advance, because Iriwa has developed a name for itself.

HOTEL PATINA ISHIGAKIJIMA

1-8-5 Yashima-chō; tel. 0980/87-7400; www.patina.in; ¥11,000 d

Hotel Patina Ishigakijima is a sleek, reasonably priced hotel about 10 minutes' walk from the pier. It's ideal for those planning to use Ishigaki as a base to explore other islands in the Yaeyama chian by ferry. There are free laundry facilities on-site. Bicycles and scooters are available for rent.

HOTEL WBF ISHIGAKIJIMA

86 Tonoshiro; tel. 0980/87-9010; www.hotelwbf.com/ishigakijima; ¥20,000 d

Hotel WBF Ishigakijima is a new, modern hotel with designer loft-style rooms. If minimalist architecture isn't your style, it might not be the choice for you. That said, it's 10 minutes' walk to the port, which makes it a great choice for those seeking to island hop in the Yaeyamas. There's a rooftop terrace and free bicycles are available for staying guests.

★ TSUNDARA BEACH RETREAT

895-2 Nosoko; tel. 090/7587-2029; www.tsundarabeach.com; 2 adults ¥40,000 per night for 2-night minimum (¥10,000 per additional adult, ¥4,000 per night for children under 12), plus ¥10,000 cleaning fee

Located on the peninsula in Ishigaki-jima's far north, this amply sized detached cottage (100 sq meters/1,076 sq feet) is fully private and only hosts single visitors or a group of up to four at any given time. It has direct access to the beach and sits on a lush plot of land awash in green. There's one bedroom, with extra hideaway beds in the living room, a full kitchen, and laundry facilities. Outside, there's a patio where you can barbecue or lounge in beach chairs. Walk down to the private beach to swim, go stand-up paddleboarding, snorkel, or sunbathe, as you please. It's owned by an American couple who also lives on the grounds in a separate house. They speak flawless Japanese and are happy to help guests maximize their stay on the island. A great place to go for a peaceful escape.

Information and Services

To pick up English-language information on the island, your best bet is to stop by the information desk (7:30am-9pm daily) at the airport upon arriving on the island. The ferry terminal also has a smattering of English-language material on hand. Head to the **Yaeyama Post Office** to withdraw cash (12 Ōkawa; 8am-9pm daily; ATM in operation).

Transportation

GETTING THERE

It's possible to fly direct to **Painushima Ishigaki Airport** (tel. 0980/87-0468, www.ishigaki-airport.co.jp; 7:30am-9pm) from both Narita Airport and Haneda Airport in Tokyo, Kansai International Airport in Osaka, as well as from Naha, Miyako, and Yonaguni-jima.

Ishigaki-jima can also be reached by direct ferry from other islands within the Yaeyama chain, including Iriomote-jima and Taketomi-jima. The ferry operators servicing these routes are **Anei Kankō** (tel. 0980/83-0055; www.aneikankou.co.jp), **Yaeyama Kankō Ferry** (tel. 0980/82-5010; www.yaeyama.co.jp), and **Ishigaki Dream Kankō** (tel. 0980/84-3178; www.ishigaki-dream.co.jp).

★ TAKETOMI-JIMA
竹富島

A 15-minute ferry ride from Ishigaki Port brings you to Taketomi-jima, the island with perhaps the best sense of cultural identity in all Okinawa. The sole settlement has a population hovering around 300. There are no supermarkets or convenience stores, nor are there any stop lights.

As you exit the island's sole dock, fluttering butterflies hover around you and flowers line the roads, which are made from ground-up coral stones. Cars do exist on the island, but they are rarely seen or heard. The traditional homes are fenced in by walls made from coral and lined by *fukugi* trees, meant to protect them from being battered by typhoons. They are also elevated by stones to ward off dampness and invading insects. The exaggerated eaves of the roofs are meant to increase shade and keep cool air flowing indoors. *Shisa* guardians—lion-dog hybrid talisman figures, cultural artifacts of the mingling of Chinese and Ryūkyū culture—stand atop gates, on roofs, and at entranceways to schools and banks; they are meant to ward off evil spirits.

Just meandering through these streets and enjoying the peace and quiet will likely be enjoyable enough. In the town, *sanshin*-strumming bards drive tourists in **water buffalo carts** and regale them with ballads written on these islands. It's possible to ride in one of these carts (30 minutes; ¥1,200), but the drivers typically don't speak any English. There are a few nooks and crannies of this picturesque little island in the antipodes of Japan—a bike is perfect if you really want to explore.

Kondoi Beach
コンドイ浜

Kondoi Beach is the best waterfront on the island. It's less a swimming or snorkeling spot and more a place just to chill out; there are ample tables for picnics, as well as an army of local cats. Basic facilities such as toilets and showers are on-site. The beach is relatively shallow, which makes it a good choice for families traveling with children. Another selling point: It rarely gets thronged like some of the more popular beaches across the region. The beach is located about 1.5 km (1 mi) from the village at the island's core.

Cycling

The magic of Taketomi-jima is best experienced from the seat of a bicycle. Trails weave through the fields of flowers, leading to beaches without another soul on them. Butterflies flit across the paths as you ride along. Elsewhere, graveyards and rustic shrines with none of the pomp seen on the mainland lie enshrouded by groves of trees.

Simply rent a bicycle (¥300 per hour; ¥1,500 for a day) at one of the many clearly marked **bicycle rental shops** in the town center and explore. Look for staff members from these rental shops who come to greet arriving travelers on ferries arriving at the port.

Transportation
GETTING THERE

Reaching Taketomi-jima from Ishigaki-jima is a cinch. Three **ferry** operators run boats dozens of times daily from Ishigaki Port, departing every 30 minutes between 7:30am and 5:30pm (¥600 one way, ¥1,330 round-trip). Go to the ticket counter inside Ishigaki Port and purchase a ticket there. The process is straightforward. Just be sure to catch the last ferry for the day if you're planning on returning to Ishigaki-jima.

IRIOMOTE-JIMA
西表島

The second largest island in all of Okinawa, Iriomote-jima has a mere couple of thousand residents. Its landscape is wild, untamed, and fundamentally different from the rest of Japan. Nearly 90 percent of this subtropical island is covered in mangrove forests, with rivers coursing through it. Waterfalls crash over its precipitous interior, which is home to a rare breed of wildcat, the Iriomote lynx, a housecat-sized subspecies of leopard, only 100 of which are thought to exist. In many ways, it is the southern subtropical complement to Shiretoko National Park in the far northern frontier of Hokkaido.

Beaches
IDA-NO-HAMA
イダの浜

Ida-no-hama is a spectacular beach on the west coast of Iriomote. The beach sits in a quiet, isolated bay that can be reached by

1: Kondoi Beach **2:** traditional Okinawan homes **3:** Taketomi-jima's sandy streets

1
2 
3

Okinawa's Best Diving Spots

Far-flung **Yonaguni-jima** is the westernmost inhabited island in Japan. At the edges of this 28.5-square-km (11-square-mi) chunk of land, foamy seas crash into soaring cliffs. The main draw for most visitors to the island is the chance to dive off its coast.

There are two main points of interest to divers who make the journey to Yonaguni. One is **Irizaki Point,** where hammerheads are known to congregate. Perhaps the more famous diving site associated with the island, however, is **Kaitei Iseiki,** a peculiar underwater structure that looks like it could indeed be the remnants of some lost civilization subsumed by the deep, Atlantean-style.

Beneath the waters off the coast of Yonaguni-jima lies a massive stone enigma known as **Kaitei Iseki.** Although controversial, what appear to be underwater megalithic ruins off the coast of the island attract many divers. The stone step-like structures appear to be the remnants of a man-made settlement dating back to as early as 10,000 BC.

Although divers are the only ones who can see it up close, it's possible it's also possible for those without a scuba license to survey this submarine enigma. **Mosura no Tamago** (4022-380 Yonaguni; tel. 0980/87-2112; ¥3,700) leads glass-bottom boat tours over Kaitei Iseki.

English-speaking dive operators on the island include **Sou-Wes Diving** (59-6 Yonaguni; tel. 0980/87-2311, http://www.yonaguni.jp/en/index.html; ¥12,000 two boat dives, plus equipment rental) and **Yonaguni Diving Service** (3984-3 Yonaguni; tel. 0980/87-2658; ¥12,500 two boat dives, plus equipment rental). If you do make the journey, note that the proprietors of Yonaguni Diving Service also run an inn called **Minshuku Yoshimaru-sō** (3984-3 Yonaguni; tel. 0980/87-2658; www.yonaguniyds.com/yoshimaru; dorm with 2 meals ¥6,000, private room with 2 meals ¥7,050).

Three daily flights go between Ishigaki and Yonaguni (30 minutes; ¥7,500-13,000 one way), while

taking a boat from Shirahama to the isolated village of Funauki, and walking from there. Only 4-5 ferries make this trip daily, but the journey is worth it. Behind the beach, the wild jungle of the island looms, while turquoise water laps against the sand. The spot is stunning. And under the water, coral and tropical fish are in abundance.

HOSHISUNA-NO-HAMA
星砂の浜

Hoshisuna-no-hama (Star Sand Beach) is at the northern edge of Iriomote and is composed of star-shaped grains of sand that are, in fact, skeletons of miniscule one-celled organisms that dwell in sea grass. Moving past these protozoa, proceed to the waters with a snorkel and goggles to explore what's happening beneath the water. An impressive array of colorful fish can be seen darting in and out of the coral seascape off this beach. Note that there are no public toilets or showers.

Sports and Recreation

Iriomote has a dramatic landscape that is 90 percent covered by jungle and lined by rivers and waterfalls. It's also blessed with white-sand beaches, making it a playground for nature junkies. Taking a cruise down the **Urauchi-gawa**, a river that flows amid dense mangrove swamps, is one of the most popular ways the get a taste of the island's wild natural beauty.

URAUCHI-GAWA KANKŌ

tel. 0980/85-6154; www.urauchigawa.com

The most well-known provider of boat tours through this unique ecosystem is Urauchi-gawa Kankō. The tour starts at the river's mouth, and journeys 8 km (5 mi) inland (1 hour; ¥1,800 round-trip) to a point where it's possible to walk an additional 2 km (1.2 mi) to the waterfall **Mariyudō-no-taki**, which leads to a second waterfall, **Kanpire-no-taki**.

one daily flight operates between Naha and Yonaguni (95 minutes, ¥17,000-33,000 one way). On the island, public bus transport is so infrequent, it's best to rent a car at the airport upon arrival.

If you can't make it to remote Yonagi-jima, there are many other excellent places to dive in Okinawa:

- **Zamami-jima:** About 50 minutes' ferry ride west of Naha, the beginner-friendly island of Zamami-jima in the Kerama Island chain is a secluded diving mecca. Its phenomenally clear water teems with more than 200 kinds of coral. Nearby, the slightly smaller and less crowded **Aka-jima**, a 15-minute ferry ride away, is an equally great place to dive. Compared to Okinawa-Hontō, diving anywhere in the Keramas is more affordable to boot.
- **Miyako-jima:** Accessible by direct flight not only from Naha and nearby Ishigaki-jima, but also from Tokyo and Osaka, Miyako-jima is famed for cave diving, with some stellar spots next to a few small spits of land just off its shores. The best spots for underwater exploration in the Miyako chain are Irabu-jima and Shimoji-jima, where a series of arches, caves, and surreal passageways offer an exciting realm for advanced divers to explore.
- **Ishigaki-jima:** Dive with schools of manta rays at the Manta Scramble in Kabira Bay or in the habitat of cuttlefish and anthias in the multihued Osaki Hanagoi Reef off the west coast of the island. Ishigaki-jima, the gateway to the Yaeyama Islands, is synonymous with diving, which means ample infrastructure. Many of the best spots are accessible for beginners, too.

Note that the best time to dive in Okinawa is from April through June. After that, typhoons sporadically whip through the archipelago, especially from July through September. The water temperature dips to as low as 15°C (59°F) during the winter months.

IRIOMOTE OSANPO KIBUN

tel. 0980/84-8178; www.iriomote-osanpo.com; ¥6,000 half day, ¥10,000 full day

Kayaking makes it possible to see the Urauchi-gawa from closer to the water. A great outdoor tour provider on the island that offers kayaking trips is Iriomote Osanpo Kibun. Moving out to the coast, Iriomote Osanpo Kibun also offers snorkeling tours on the reefs that ring the island.

SIMAMARIASIBI TREKKING ACTIVITIES

972 Taketomi-chō; tel. 0980/84-8408; www.simamariasibi.com; excursions range from 5-10 hours; ¥10,000-34,000 depending on length of time and number of participants

Iriomote is also a fantastic place to trek. It's essentially a large expanse of jungle punctuated by rivers and waterfalls. That said, it's tricky terrain that can be notoriously disorienting. It's unwise to venture into the interior without a paid guide. If you're keen to hike on this wild island, get in touch with Simamariasibi Trekking Activities. This Iriomote-based outfit leads people on excursions from canyoning and caving to summiting mountains in the rugged interior. Iriomote Osanpo Kibun also provides trekking tours to gorgeous spots like the waterfall **Pinaisāra-no-taki.**

Food

LAUGH LA GARDEN

550-1 Uehara, Taketomi; tel. 0980/85-7088; lunch 11:30am-2pm, dinner 6pm-9pm Fri.-Wed.; walk 3 minutes west of Uehara Port; ¥600-900

Across the road from the pier with a verandah that looks out to sea, this casual eatery serves reasonably priced lunch and dinner sets. Choices range from hamburgers and hot dogs to Okinawan classics like pork cutlets sourced from neighboring islands and *gōya champurū* (bitter gourd stir-fry). There's a robust alcohol menu, too.

KITCHEN INABA

742-6 Uehara; tel. 0980/84-8164; http://kitcheninaba.com; lunch 11:30am-2:30pm Tues.-Sun., dinner 6pm-8:30pm Tues.-Sun.; ¥350-1,800; drive 7 minutes west from Uehara Port, or drive 4 minutes south of Hoshizuna-no-hama

For island food with a slightly more refined touch, this restaurant on the west side of Uehara does the trick. Serving local dishes like *inushishi-sashimi* (wild boar sashimi) and crab soup, as well as items with a subtropical twist like papaya salad. Reserve ahead if you plan to go for dinner. A good choice if you're on the west side of the island.

Accommodations

IRUMOTE-SŌ

870-95 Uehara; tel. 0980/85-6255; www.ishigaki.com/irumote; dorm with dinner from ¥5,300, private room for 1 with shared toilet/bath and dinner from ¥6,000, private twin room with in-suite bath/shower and dinner from ¥14,500; walk 20 minutes southeast of Uehara Port, or arrange free pick-up at port

Friendly staff who are eager to help with arranging logistics for activities around the island, clean rooms, lush palm-studded grounds, and seaside views make this a great budget option in Uehara. The rooms are Japanese-style with tatami floors and futons, some with private bath/shower and some shared. Arrange ahead for pick-up at Uehara Port to avoid the slightly long uphill walk to the inn. Given the meager increase in price from dorm to private room, it pays to go with the latter. The amiable hostess serves tasty, optional home-cooked dinners. Opting out of them will cut the rate by ¥1,200.

Transportation

GETTING THERE

High-speed ferries run to and from Ishigaki and two ports on Iriomote, namely, **Ōhara Port** (40 minutes, up to 27 daily; ¥1,570) in the island's east and **Uehara Port** (1 hour, up to 20 daily; ¥2,060) in the west. Tickets can be purchased directly from Ishigaki Port on the day of travel.

GETTING AROUND

Up to nine daily **buses** run between Ōhara Port and the town of Shirahama in the island's northwest, passing Uehara Port on the way (1.5 hours; ¥1,240). You can catch the bus anywhere along this road, which wraps halfway around the island, by simply flagging down a bus with your hand.

Background

The Landscape

GEOGRAPHY

Despite the insistence of many Japanese people, their country is not a small place. At 377,915 square km (145,914 square mi), it's a bit larger than Germany and slightly smaller than California. From the northeastern tip of Hokkaido to far southwestern Okinawa, the bow of islands extends 3,008 km (1,869 mi), or roughly the same length, north to south, as the continental US. This gives the country a wide range of climates and landscapes, and a vast coastline.

With so much natural splendor, it's no surprise that Japan is home

to 33 **national parks.** The first was created in 1934, following the birth of mountaineering among Japanese in the early 20th century and subsequent growth in eco-consciousness.

Oceans and Coastline

Perhaps the most constant feature is the ocean. The Sea of Japan (which is controversially known as East Sea in South Korea) lies to the west, with the Korean peninsula and China on the other side. The Pacific stretches eastward, with the US mainland lying more than 8,000 km (about 5,000 mi) to the east. The lack of land borders has allowed Japan to develop its unique cultural universe.

Thousands of islands comprise Japan, but four make up the bulk of the nation's landmass: the main island of Honshu, earth's seventh-largest; Hokkaido in the north, which is roughly the size of Ireland; and bordering the Inland Sea with western Honshu in the nation's southwest: rustic Shikoku and volcanic Kyūshū. All told, some 27,000 km (16,777 mi) of coastline encircle these islands, from the white-sand beaches of Okinawa and sand dunes of Tottori to the pebbled promontories of Tohoku and cliffs of outlying Sado-ga-shima.

Mountains

Inland, the landscape is roughly 70-80 percent mountainous, pushing people and agriculture to the coastal fringes, comprising 20-30 percent of the land. Jagged peaks and foothills swathed in dense forest dot the sparsely populated natural wonderland of Hokkaido in the north, drawing legions of trekkers in the warmer months and powder hounds in winter. Honshu's geographic heart is in the Japan Alps (North, Central, and Southern), where you'll find most of the nation's tallest peaks, some of which top 3,000 meters (9,842 feet). Elsewhere on Honshu are the Hida and Kiso ranges, as well as Japan's tallest and one of the world's most recognizable peaks, the sublime Mt. Fuji (3,776 meters/12,388 feet). As you move southwest or northeast of Honshu, the mountains dip to rolling foothills. Down south, Shikoku is shot through with more modest peaks, while craggy Kyūshū is awash in volcanic activity.

Geothermal Activity and Volcanoes

Geothermal activity is rife in the country. Part of the Ring of Fire, Japan is located directly on the Pacific Plate ridgeline. The country's share of volcanic eruptions and earthquakes attest to that fact. Even Fuji itself is a volcano, which last erupted in 1707. All told, about 70 volcanoes dot Japan, including the famed cones of Aso-san and Sakurajima on Kyūshū.

Though occasional eruptions send shivers down the public's collective spine, cataclysmic events are rare. Nonetheless, even minor flare-ups have caused deaths, such as the unexpected eruption of Mount Ontake on September 27, 2014. Eruptions are but a side note for most Japanese, however, who take advantage of the country's intense geothermal activity by periodically plunging into the waters of a hot *onsen* bath.

Rivers and Lakes

They may lack the gravitas of great rivers like the Mississippi or Mekong, but plenty of rivers course through Japan. The longest is the Shinano River (Shinanogawa) of Niigata (370 km; 230 mi). Other notable rivers include the Tehiogawa (Hokkaido), the Tonegawa, which runs from Niigata to Chiba east of Tokyo and serves as a major source of freshwater for the capital region; Tokyo's Sumidagawa, running through the old part of downtown (Shitamachi); Osaka's concrete-embanked Yodogawa, a key historic lane of commerce; and Kyoto's pleasant Kamogawa, lined with paths well suited for a summer evening stroll. Especially in the mountains, many rivers are short and fierce, whipping through narrow

Previous: paper lanterns in Kyoto

canyons on their way from mountains to the sea, with many dropping as much as 1,000 meters (3,280 feet) in elevation in the course of traveling less than 50 km (31 mi). Some of these waterways are ideal for canoeing, while those producing rapids are unsung meccas for white-water rafting, particular in Shikoku and in the mountains of central Honshu. To the chagrin of many environmental activists, a major proportion of the country's waterways have been dammed for electricity, water storage, irrigation, or other traditional industries.

Lakes are strewn across the archipelago, many of which either are fed by natural springs found upriver or placidly occupy extinct volcanic craters. The largest is Lake Biwa (Biwa-ko), which lies northeast of Kyoto. Other prominent lakes include the Fuji Five Lakes (Lake Kawaguchi and Lake Yamanaka being most famous), which frame the iconic peak; Hokkaido's Lake Akan; and the Tohoku region's Tazawa-ko, Japan's deepest, and Towada-ko, Honshu's largest crater lake.

CLIMATE

The vast majority of Japan has four neatly delineated seasons, but there are variations. The northern extremities of the country, particularly Hokkaido, fall into the Northern Temperate Zone, producing conditions similar to those of New England. Meanwhile, Okinawa and much of the far southwest enjoy subtropical warmth most of the year.

Several distinct climatic zones are delineated by mountain ranges and ocean straits. From northern Kyūshū to Shikoku and up the eastern half of Honshu, the climate is defined by mild springs; hot, sticky summers; cool autumns; and chilly, crisp winters with the occasional dusting of snow or (even more rare) heavy snowfall.

Northern Honshu

Along the western side of the country, the differences between the four seasons are dramatic. Although the western side of the country may see less rain, this is compensated for with a heavy dump of snow in winter. In some places, up to 3 meters (9.8 feet) of powder accumulate during the colder months. Some parts of northwestern Tohoku—Yamagata, Akita, Aomori prefectures—see some of the heaviest snowfalls on earth. Winds from Siberia and Mongolia howl over the Sea of Japan and make landfall on these snowy realms.

Central Honshu

In the mountainous interior of Central Honshu, a highland climate prevails. Snow piles up in the Japan Alps and surrounding ranges during winter, producing excellent winter sports conditions. Summers are warm, but less intensely humid than the coastal population centers. As a general rule of thumb, the temperature dips about 5°C (9°F) for every 1,000-meter increase in altitude.

Hokkaido

The far northern island of Hokkaido experiences long, bitter winters with heavy snowfall and pleasant summers that lack the oppressively sweltering humidity felt throughout much of the country. The northern island also sees less rain. The warmer seasons are shorter than in the rest of Japan, with spring coming late (around early May) and autumn coming early (around late September or early October).

Inland Sea

Moving south, the Inland Sea region, which includes northern Shikoku and the southern Sany'yō coast of Western Honshu, has a distinct climate of its own. This idyllic section of the country is largely sunny, but droughts can occur in the region. Moreover, the overwhelming floods that ravaged this mostly sun-drenched region in 2018 are a reminder that it's not immune to inclement weather.

Southern Islands

Farther south, from southern Kyūshū to Okinawa, winters, spring, and autumn are significantly milder than elsewhere in the country, while summers are hot. The saving grace is that many of the islands are slightly cooled by a year-round sea breeze.

Tsuyu

From late-May or early-June, *tsuyu* (rainy season) descends on much of the country. Showers vary from heavy to nonexistent during this period. Then, from July through September, typhoons that begin farther south in the tropical Pacific begin to work their way across Japan, starting in Okinawa and moving north. These storms often batter the southern half of the country, before gradually tapering off as they reach Tohoku. Hokkaido, separated from Honshu by the Straits of Tsugaru, is generally spared. These mid-summer squalls can be unpleasant and can occasionally turn dangerous. Take any forecasted typhoon into consideration when planning a trip, but not to the extent of avoiding the country altogether.

Extreme Weather Events

In recent years, in line with broader climate change sweeping the globe, Japan has had record-high temperatures in summer and winters that are either short and mild, or in some cases bitterly cold. Extreme rainfall, including floods and landslides, have also spiked in recent years. Most notably, in the summer of 2018 floods devastated large swaths of western Japan. The cataclysmic floods killed nearly 200 people, left thousands without water and electricity, and forced millions to evacuate.

ENVIRONMENTAL ISSUES

At a glance, Japan is stunning, with craggy spines blanketed in forest, pristine rivers coursing through steep ravines, and sweeping seaside cliffs plummeting into unspoiled bays. Look closer, however, and blemishes reveal a harsh truth: the postwar development rush has not been kind to the environment. The country's environmental issues are many, afflicting both land and sea.

Construction and consumer waste have blighted the landscape, and sustainable forestry has been supplanted by boundless *sugi* (cedar) plantations. Offshore, the oceans have been severely depleted by overfishing, Japanese ships sustain a highly contentious whaling industry, and smaller boats execute a deplorable dolphin hunt. Meanwhile, the nuclear catastrophe flowing out from Fukushima has seeped into the surrounding earth and spread to all corners of the planet, carried by ocean currents.

Construction

Japan has a bad track record with overuse of timber from developing countries in the tropics. Despite environmentalists' best efforts from the 1990s on, Japan's ravenous construction industry continues to use imported tropical timber at unsustainable rates.

Another issue fueled by the construction industry that plagues both city and countryside is a glut of concrete, eagerly laid by fat cats over beaches, hillsides, rivers, and streams from Hokkaido to Okinawa. While this more of an aesthetic issue than a health hazard, the "visual pollution" created by the onslaught of concrete in the postwar construction frenzy can be jarring. Pick up a copy of Alex Kerr's meticulously researched tom *Dogs and Demons* to learn more about this issue. Brace yourself before reading.

Overfishing

Japan's dietary dependence on seafood is taxing on the world's fish stocks. To lessen your own footprint, keep an eye on your consumption of the hardest hit species, such as *uni* (sea urchin) and *hon-maguro* (bluefin tuna). Japan agreed to halve its quota for southern bluefin tuna to 3,000 tonnes (3.3 tons) per year from 2005 to 2012, after overshooting the former quota of 6,000 tonnes (6.6 tons) by a whopping 1,800 tonnes (1.1 tons) in 2005.

Waste and Pollution

The proliferation of plastic and staggering levels of consumption of every kind make waste management a perennial challenge. All told, 45.4 tons of municipal solid waste are generated annually in Japan, the eighth highest worldwide, with 20.8 percent of that being recycled. It's worth noting that many of Japan's artificial islands have been built on reclaimed land packed deeply with all manner of garbage. This has resulted in contaminated ground in many cases. A dramatic example is Tokyo's Toyosu fish market, which replaced the legendary market at Tsukiji in 2018.

Disposable wooden chopsticks (*waribashi*), which are dispensed freely by restaurants and convenience stores, further contribute to the excess of waste. About 130 million pairs of chopsticks are discarded daily; to avoid wasting wood and adding to the landfill, consider picking up a pair of "my hashi" (my chopsticks), which are stored in a case and reused. These chopsticks kits are sold in lifestyle shops like Tokyu Hands and Loft, and in some convenience stores. For perspective, some estimates place the toll for the production of these throw-away chopsticks at 400,000 cubic meters of forest annually.

Fukushima and Nuclear Power

The ongoing nuclear crisis in Fukushima is the most pressing environmental issue facing Japan today. When the mega-quake struck off the coast of Tohoku on March 11, 2011, six reactors melted down. Since then, radioactive fuel has been leaking from the complex, into which up to 150 tons of groundwater leaks daily. And this is an improvement. The figure once stood at 400 tons before TEPCO installed pumps and its $300 million ice wall.

Aside from the region immediately surrounding Fukushima's reactors, the country is officially deemed safe for visitors and citizens. Nonetheless, groups of concerned citizens, scientists, and activists have taken radiation monitoring into their own hands. To find current radiation levels (from non-government sources), visit Safecast (https://blog.safecast.org) or the Citizens' Nuclear Information Center (www.cnic.jp) online.

Meanwhile, there are signs of hope that a deeper environmental consciousness is slowly taking hold. Civil consciousness surrounding nuclear energy has taken off significantly in the years following Fukushima. Protestors routinely gather in Tokyo's public squares and in front of government offices to voice their opposition to the use of nuclear power. But it remains to be seen whether their voices will be heard. Under PM Shinzo Abe, the government has pushed to keep nuclear power.

Plants and Animals

When it comes to flora and fauna, it helps to think of Japan as being divided into three broad regions: temperate in the center (Honshu, Shikoku, and Kyushu), subarctic in the north (Hokkaido), and subtropical in the far southwest (Okinawa and the other southwestern island chains).

Within these three zones, remarkable variations exist in the plant life, from the old-growth beech forests of Tohoku to the mangrove swamps of Iriomote-jima. Wildlife species range from large brown bears in Hokkaido to mountain-dwelling snow monkeys, and giant salamanders in riverbeds on Honshu.

To delve deep into the archipelago's natural world, Japan Nature Guides (www.japannatureguides.com) offers a range of services to help with birdwatching tours and other excursions, as well as in-depth guidebooks about wildlife of the islands.

TREES

Roughly two-thirds of Japan is forested, even after the post-World War II construction boom. While forests envelope much of Japan today, around half of this cover is comprised of *matsu* (pine) and *sugi* (cedar) plantations.

These cookie-cutter forests once served the lumber industry, falling into disuse in the

1970s when the nation began to import timber from its tropical neighbors at an eyebrow-raising rate. Historically, the Kiso Valley of Nagano Prefecture has been famous for its prized timber. The imperial seal of approval has meant that the wood from this region has long been used in the construction of key structures, with Tokyo's most venerable shrine, Meiji Jingū, among them.

Beyond the ubiquitous pines and cedars, other common species include hinoki (Japanese cypress), a smattering of bamboo varieties, and a host of deciduous trees, from oaks to maples that blaze with earthy colors every autumn, and, of course, the beloved cherry tree, famed for vivid pink petals that dazzle every corner of the nation every spring. The last surviving virgin beech forest in Japan envelopes the Shirakami Sanchi mountain range straddling Akita and Aomori prefectures. This precious pocket of primeval forest, encompassing 169.7 square km (65.5 square mi), was saved from logging by citizen protests in the 1980s. The forest was declared a UNESCO World Heritage Site in in 1993.

As you travel south, you'll also notice an increase in palm trees. Miyazaki Prefecture's Nichinan Coast, for example, resembles southern California more than it does most of Honshu's coast. In the far south, some of Okinawa's islands are swathed in forest that resembles jungle. Iriomote-jima's dense mangrove swamps are a prime example.

FLOWERS

Japan has a reverence for flowers. Plum blossoms, which bring winter to a close, are soon followed by waves of pink *sakura* (cherry blossoms): nature's way of announcing the arrival of spring. These beloved blossoms erupt northward, first popping in Okinawa in February, and finishing their journey in Hokkaido in May. The unofficial national flower of Japan, *sakura* has an outsized presence in the nation's psyche.

Meanwhile, violet wisterias bloom around the end of April; hydrangeas and irises flourish in June; and lotus blossoms, sunflowers, and lavender cover fields like patches of a quilt in July and August. These waves of summer blooms draw enthusiasts to wildflower hot spots, while hikers marvel at similar displays in mountain meadows nationwide.

Heading into autumn, spider lilies unfold their spindly arms in September and October, while the chrysanthemum, Japan's official national flower, blooms from September to November. Though it's not a flower, the transformation of leaves into blazing reds, yellows, oranges, and earthy browns in October through early December is relished with a similar ardor.

MAMMALS

A vast range of mammals inhabit Japan. Kyushu, Shikoku, Honshu, and Hokkaido fall into the Palaearctic region, home to temperate and subarctic mammals, many of which have links to East Asia. Kyūshū and the Okinawa Prefecture fall into the Oriental region, a balmier zone inhabited by subtropical and tropical animals linked to Southeast Asia.

Starting with Hokkaido in the far north, we find a subarctic menagerie: Ussuri brown bears (black grizzly) live here, along with arctic hares, Eurasian red squirrels, Siberian flying squirrels, and the cute northern pika, to name but a few. Sadly, the Hokkaido (Ezo) wolf, which once stalked the island, is now extinct.

Moving south, the iconic Japanese macaque (also referred to as a "snow monkey"), which is endemic to Japan, is perhaps the most recognizable mammal of all. These ornery primates live in an area that stretches from the northern periphery of Honshu to the emerald island of Yakushima, off the southern coast of Kyūshū. Atop Hondo's food chain is the Asiatic black bear, smaller than its cousins in Hokkaido. Some 15,000 of these bears are believed to roam the forests and mountains of Honshu. The species was totally wiped out on Kyūshū by the 1950s and is considered all but extinct on Shikoku.

Other land-dwelling mammals include

the endemic Japanese serow, which looks like cross between a goat and an antelope, and lives in mountains and forests from northern Honshu to Shikoku and northern Kyūshū; the wild boar (*inushishi*); Japanese sika deer; the tanuki, or raccoon dog; and red foxes, which feature heavily in Shinto myth. Note that the "fox villages" found in some parts of Honshu are sad affairs with cooped-up foxes and are not worth visiting. Hondo's coastal mammals include sea lions and fur seals, while endangered otters flit through some of Shikoku's remote rivers. Like the Ezo Wolf, the Japanese wolf that once prowled the woodlands of Hondo is extinct.

In the subtropical southwest, a few interesting mammalian species include the large Ryūkyū flying fox (Ryūkyū fruit bat), the severely endangered Iriomote lynx, and on the Amami Islands just north of Okinawa, the endangered, dark-furred Amami rabbit and the mysterious, endangered Amami spiny mouse, a sexually flexible rodent which lacks Y chromosomes.

It's also worth noting that Japan has a few native dog breeds, namely the medium-sized shiba and the larger akita, which are both Spitz types (pointed ears, thick fur). The Tosa inu, considered dangerous and banned in certain countries, is a rare breed that originated in the old province of Tosa (modern-day Kōchi Prefecture on Shikoku). Cats are ubiquitous and beloved across Japan as well. In a few cases, they have proliferated to such a degree that they have come to occupy their own islands, such as Aoshima, off the coast of Shikoku in the Inland Sea, where felines outnumber humans.

SEALIFE

All told, some 3,000 species of aquatic life inhabit Japan. This remarkable diversity of marine life is partly due to a few distinct ocean currents. Warm water flows from Taiwan to Okinawa and the southwest islands, branching off into two separate currents when it hits Kyushu. Meanwhile, coming from the north, the cold waters move towards northeastern Hokkaido, veering south towards northeastern Honshu.

Japan's most colorful sea life is found in the subtropical waters of Okinawa and the Southwest Islands, where anemone, butterfly fish, parrot fish, sea turtles, and many species of shark dart among vibrant coral reefs in the deep-blue waters. From January through March, humpback whales flock to the waters of Okinawa, escaping the frigid waters of Alaska's Aleutian Islands, 5,100 km (3,169 mi) to the north.

In the Pacific south of Shikoku and Honshu swim Loggerhead turtles, dugongs, and dolphins. The frigid waters off Hokkaido teem with humpback whales, gray whales, blue whales, orcas, and giant crabs. And elsewhere, a range of marine life teems in the oceans surrounding Japan, from dolphins and flying squid to sea bream, surgeonfish, tuna, seabass, sting rays, sharks, and snappers, to name but a few.

Freshwater fish living in the nation's rivers, lakes, and streams include carp, *ayu* (sweet fish), eel, and more.

BIRDS

Perhaps the most recognizable of Japan's numerous avian species is the red-crowned crane of Hokkaido, a lithe creature with a red crop of feathers atop its head. Throughout the country, there are many types of ducks, geese, swans, herons, kingfishers, pheasants, black kites, hazel grouses (Hokkaido), and cormorants. The Blakiston's fish owl, which lives only on Hokkaido, is one of the world's largest owls. The crested serpent eagle lives and hunts on some of the subtropical southwest islands, while the Steller's sea eagle, an imposing bird of prey, soars over northern Hokkaido.

REPTILES

Turtles and small lizards such as geckos are found throughout much of Japan, but make their strongest showing in the subtropical islands of Okinawa.

All told, some 50 species of snake live in Japan. As one of the Chinese zodiac's 12 animals, snakes have a potent symbolic significance in Japan, and elsewhere in East Asia, where they are traditionally thought to serve as divine messengers. While most of them are harmless, there are a few poisonous species in the islands extending southward from Kyūshū. Of particular note, the thick habu (pit viper), which can grow to 2 meters (6.6 feet) in length or more, as well as coral snakes, slither through Okinawa's balmy forests.

INSECTS AND ARACHNIDS

To the chagrin of many residents in Japan's urban centers, *gokiburi* (cockroaches) are common any time of year in humid parts of the country, and most common during summer in drier climes. Another insect that sometimes finds its way into homes is the *gejigeji* (house centipede), which looks positively terrifying, though it's harmless and is only interested in eating other insects.

Outdoors, the hum of cicadas peaks at around 120 decibels during summer, making a walk through a forest or park as loud as a rock concert. Mosquitoes can be a nuisance in the warmer months and near any fresh water source.

Generally speaking, Japan's insects are relatively harmless and few are poisonous, but there are some insects to avoid. The vividly colored, spiked caterpillar known as the *denkimushi* (electric bug) secretes poisonous chemicals from small prickly stingers when touched, giving what feels like an electric shock. Leeches are common in the mountains, both on land and in water. Measuring up to 38 centimeters (15 inches), the *mukade* (giant centipede) has a highly poisonous bite. Just seeing one is likely sufficient to dissuade you from getting too close, though; they're considered malevolent in Japanese folklore. The most dangerous of all is the Japanese Giant Hornet, a subspecies of the Asian giant hornet, the world's largest. They can be aggressive if provoked, and their sting is extremely painful and may require a trip to the hospital.

Most of Japan's spiders are harmless. Although massive, the Huntsman spider, with a span as wide as a dinner plate, is harmless to humans. The Jorō spider, on the other hand—a species with black and yellow legs and a very vividly colored body—is poisonous; its bite isn't deadly, but is serious. The most dangerous spider found in Japan is the redback spider, believed to have been introduced from Australia by cargo ships carrying wood chips. A bite from a redback can occasionally be deadly. Unfortunately, these spiders have been seen in more than 20 of Japan's prefectures, largely toward the west of the country.

AMPHIBIANS

Around 40 frog species live in Japan, including the Japanese rain frog, Japanese tree frog, and American bullfrog, which is common in ponds. A number of toad species are also found across the country. An amphibian of particular note is the Japanese giant salamander, the second-largest salamander in the world. Endemic to the rocky bottoms of swiftly flowing streams in southwestern Japan, the giant salamander reaches up to 1.5 meters (5 feet). In folklore, they are referred to as *hanzaki*, a name that suggests they remain alive even if they've been chopped in half (*han*). They are also popularly known as *ōsanshōuo* (giant pepper fish), a name that stems from the white, sticky mucus that smells like peppers, which they secrete when provoked by a predator.

History

ANCIENT CIVILIZATION

For a period of time around 18,000 BC, there was a land bridge linking Japan to the Asian continent. Japan's first inhabitants traveled over this bridge from the mainland. This overland link to the rest of Asia vanished when sea levels rose around 10,000 BC. Architectural touches and some facial features of the Japanese population today suggest that Polynesian seafarers may also have made the long journey north to the islands in the ancient past. In truth, the origins of Japanese people are highly complex and debated, with genetic input believed to originate in groups all around Asia, from Tibetans and Koreans to Han Chinese.

Jōmon Period

The earliest civilization emerged in Japan during the Jōmon period (14,000-300 BC), a hunter-gatherer culture known for its "cord-marked" pottery made by pressing cords onto wet clay. This pottery tradition is thought to be among not only the oldest in East Asia, but the whole world.

Yayoi Period

During the following Yayoi period (300 BC-AD 300), rice cultivation techniques and metalworking arrived from mainland Asia. The period's name is derived from the place in present-day Tokyo where bronze artifacts dating to the period were first unearthed.

An intriguing semi-mythical figure from this period was Queen Himiko (AD 183-248), who reigned over the realm of Yamatai. The name Himiko (Sun Child) hints at her divine descent from the sun goddess Amaterasu. She was an unmarried priestess purporting to wield significant shamanic power. Although Himiko does not appear in any of Japan's ancient records, she was mentioned in those of China, where she established diplomatic ties.

Scholars debate who Himiko really was and where Yamatai was located, although the region around Nara has been proposed. Around 100 kingdoms were arrayed throughout the islands during Himiko's reign, of which she may have overseen a loose grouping of about 30. Her ruling over this small federation led the Chinese to view her as the leader of all Japan.

EARLY HISTORY

Yamato Period (250-710)

KOFUN PERIOD (250-538)

The first section of the Yamamoto period, the Kofun period was named after a type of burial mound used for the period's elite. These megalithic tombs ranged from relatively modest square-shaped mounds to massive mounds shaped like keyholes hundreds of meters long, surrounded by moats and laden with sometimes thousands of artifacts. All told, more than 160,000 Kofun have been discovered around Japan, with a heavy concentration around modern-day Kansai and Western Honshu.

During this period, the Shinto religion began to take shape, its principles and practices growing from older beliefs from the Yayoi period. During the Kofun period, a plethora of small kingdoms existed in Japan. The Yamato Clan, which would eventually become the imperial family, rose to the top of that power structure. Contact with China and Korea also grew, with Japan taking on a more formal political identity of its own.

ASUKA PERIOD (538-710)

As the Kofun period drew to a close, the Yamato clan had fully established itself as the imperial family of Japan. The key features of the Asuka period were the introduction of Buddhism in the mid-sixth century and the adoption and adaptation of Chinese characters to form Japan's own written script. Coinage, in the form of the *Wado kaiho*, was also introduced. Japan began to borrow heavily from China, perceived as a highly civilized role model. The period is named after Asuka, the capital during the period that today is northern Nara Prefecture.

The first bona fide historical emperor rose to power during this period, Emperor Kimmei (509-571). Empress Suiko (554-628), and Prince Shōtoku (574-622) were by far the period's most prominent leaders. As Suiko's regent, Shōtoku initiated government reforms, stamped out corruption and entrenched nepotism, and established embassies with the Chinese Sui Dynasty around 607 CE.

Shōtoku is believed to have drawn up Japan's first constitution, the Jushichijo-kenpo (Seventeen Article Constitution) in 604 CE. This document centralized Japan's government and emphasized the Confucian principle of *wa* (harmony).

Shōtoku heavily promoted Buddhism, erecting 46 monasteries and temples, including Hōryū-ji in modern-day Nara, the only monastery still standing that was originally built in the Asuka period. This initial push to adopt Buddhism would significantly alter Japan's spiritual development over the longer term and signal to its more powerful neighbors that the country had "arrived." In addition to an increasingly sophisticated system of government and a deeper spiritual life, the Asuka period also saw a creative boom as music and literature flourished in and around the imperial court.

Within this milieu, the upstart Fujiwara clan rose to prominence through a coup in AD 645, wresting power from the Soga clan, which had controlled the government since 587. Inspired by China, Emperor Kōtoku reshaped the new government through the Taika Reform of 645, shortly after the death of Shōtoku. The sweeping changes of these reforms included introducing a codified system of law, nationalizing land, replacing forced labor with a tax system, reshuffling social classes, introducing an examination-based recruitment system for the civil service, and establishing the emperor's absolute authority. With the elevation of Emperor Tenjin (626-672), along with his senior minister Nakatomi no Kamatari (614-669), who was granted the surname Fujiwara, the Fujiwara clan ascended to a position of great power, where they would remain for centuries to come.

Nara Period (710-794)

During the brief Nara period, the capital relocated to Nara during 710-784. Until this time, the capital moved every time an emperor or empress died. Todai-ji, the world's largest wooden building which houses the towering Great Buddha, was built during this time. By the end of the Nara period, the capital's population swelled to around 200,000.

Two seminal texts were penned during the Nara period, placing the nation's mythical founding in the ancient past. According to the legends recorded in the 8th century, the Kojiki, Japan's oldest written chronicle, and the Nihon Shoki (aka Nihon-gi), the second oldest, say that the mythical first emperor, Jimmu Tenno, established the nation of Japan on February 11, 660 BC. This is why the National Foundation Day holiday is held on February 11 each year. Others put his actual existence, if he existed at all, closer to AD 100.

In many ways, the Nara period saw a continuation of trends that began in the Kofun and Asuka period. The city itself, then known as Heijokyō, was modeled after the Tang Dynasty's capital of Chang-an and was laid out on a Chinese grid pattern. Its architecture was similarly Chinese in appearance. A Confucian university was built and the government became increasingly bureaucratic, mimicking the mandarins of the Tang court.

Smallpox outbreaks (735-737) killed 25-35 percent of the population. Faced with widespread poverty, and occasionally struck with famine, the remaining citizens became resentful of the increased meddling of the Yamato court in Japan's outlying areas, and the largely agrarian provinces grew restless. The government in Nara responded by establishing military outposts in the provinces. Fujiwara no Hirotsugu raised an army in Dazaifu, Kyūshū, then led a rebellion in 740 that was quashed by a 17,000-strong army sent by Emperor Shomu (724-749 CE).

It's worth noting that three empresses ruled during the Nara period: Gemmei ruled AD 707-715; Gensho ruled 715-724; and Koken ruled 749-758 and again as Shōtoku 764-770. This would be the last empress for 800 years. Women were also able to own land during this time.

Heian Period (794-1185)

As the Nara period drew to a close, Emperor Kammu (AD 736-806) moved the capital in 794 to Heiankyō (modern-day Kyoto), where the imperial court remained for more than a millennium. This marked the start of a pivotal stage in Japan's history, the Heian period.

During this time, Japan began to wean itself off Chinese influence, taking on an isolationist stance that would greatly intensify in the ensuing centuries. Although the flow of cultural and commercial exchange did continue, Japan became less politically engaged with China. Scholars, monks, and creatives went on study missions to China to glean ideas on topics ranging from medicine to painting techniques. These exchanges gradually wound down, however, and Japanese civilization began to take on its own distinct characteristics.

During this time, Shinto and Buddhism began to fuse, becoming both the state religion as well as the faith of commoners. Buddhism flourished, with Shingon Buddhism being founded by Kūkai (774-835), or Kobo Daishi. The Tendai sect was also founded during this era by Saicho (767-822).

It was during this period that Japan began to hone its own artistic style, introducing a broader range of subjects to painting and other art forms. The life of the court was rife with romance, conjuring the classic image of courtiers in elaborate silk costumes, poets, trysts, and intrigue. This led to a remarkable leap forward in the literary arts, with the penning of classic works of literature in the early 11th century such at *The Tale of Genji* by Lady Murasaki Shikibu and *The Pillow Book* by Sei Shōnagon. Beyond literature, court artists actively developed the arts of screen paintings, scrolls, calligraphy, and music, and enjoyed teasing their intellects with the complex strategy board game known as *go*.

Politically, the period was marked by significant influence exerted by the Fujiwara clan, who eventually fell into a feud with lesser nobles, including the Taira (aka Heike) and Minamoto (aka Genji) families. Under the helm of Taira no Kiyomori (1118-1181), the Taira clan challenged the Fujiwara and Minamoto, and emerged victorious in 1160, ruling for 20 years. Taira rulers succumbed to corruption and vice and were supplanted by the victorious Minamoto clan, led by Yoritomo Minamoto (1147-1199), in the Genpei War (1180-1185), waged for control of the imperial throne.

Following the war's final conflict, the Battle of Dannoura, Tomomori, who led the Taira forces, and Antoku, the would-be young Taira emperor, committed suicide. Yoritomo then granted himself the title of Shōgun (Generalissimo) upon the death of Emperor Go-Shirakawa in 1192, an honor normally only granted to a general. With this bold move, the illustrious Heian period came to an end, ushering in the beginning of Japan's military-dominated feudal age.

FEUDAL JAPAN

Kamakura Period (1185-1333)

Japan's long, tumultuous feudal era would last seven centuries, beginning with the Kamakura period. Major political change came with this new era, including control of the government falling under the newly declared shogunate and military ruler, Yoritomo Minamoto.

Although Yoritomo officially operated under the distant emperor, in truth, he was the new de facto head of government. While the emperor remained in Heiankyo (Kyoto), Yoritomo set up his new *bakufu* (tent government) in Kamakura. A lord-vassal system emerged, and the age of the samurai was born.

Staunch loyalty was a hallmark of the new cultural ethos, which was markedly militaristic in tone.

When Yoritomo died under suspicious circumstances in 1199, his widow, Masako, began to lay the foundation for the Hōjō Shogunate, under her own family. By the late Kamakura period, the state was tried by invasion attempts by Kublai Khan, who led forces from Mongolia across the Sea of Japan in 1274. Khan's men were thwarted by Japanese forces in the first attempt. He tried again in 1281, bringing with him a 100,000-strong armada. This time Japan was spared by a kamikaze (divine wind) that sunk half of the mighty fleet, while spirited warriors in Kyūshū finished the job. This is the origin of the name that would later be given to World War II pilots who were said to be imbued with the spirit as they went on suicide missions.

Khan's expansionist adventures may have failed, but things began to unravel internally due to increased regional infighting. Emperor Go-Daigo and his court made efforts to bring full control of the government under the throne. These plans included hatching a plot to do away with the *bakufu*. When the conspiracy was discovered, Go-Daigo was exiled to far-flung Oki Island off the coast of modern-day Shimane Prefecture.

Meanwhile, local chieftains in the Kinai area, comprising Kyoto and Nara today, assembled an army and took the Kamakura *bakufu* by storm. Two vassals of the ruling Hōjō clan who had become disgruntled, Ashikaga Takauji and Nitta Yoshisada, helped clinch the victory for the imperial forces, wiping out the majority of Hōjō elites. This effectively brought the Kamakura period to a close.

Muromachi Period (1333-1568)

Following the overthrow of the Kamakura *bakufu*, exiled Emperor Go-Daigo returned from exile to Kyoto and swiftly instituted reforms aimed at restoring imperial rule. He appointed Morinaga as his military chief and sent family members to serve as administrators in the outlying provinces.

Many warriors felt that Go-Daigo unfairly rewarded his own family, while neglecting the men who fought on his behalf. In response, Ashikaga turned on Go-Daigo and forced the emperor to the Yoshino Mountains outside Nara in 1336. Go-Daigo then established the Southern Court near Nara, while Ashikaga appointed a puppet emperor in Kyoto. These two rival courts were engaged in an ongoing feud for the next six decades, until Takauji's grandson Yoshimitsu finally settled the score in 1392 CE, after which the imperial line descended through the Northern Court of Kyoto.

When Go-Daigo fled to Yoshino, Ashikaga Takauji established a *bakufu* of his own in Kyoto. From Kyoto, Takauji's grandson Yoshimitsu neutralized all rivals and was declared prime minister. He resuscitated trade and diplomatic relations with China, then in the Ming Dynasty.

Despite these advancements, the era was largely characterized by an ongoing state of civil war between regional lords (daimyo) and their loyal armies of *bushi* (samurai warriors). There was also widespread economic instability, famine, and disagreement over who would become the next shogun.

Combined, these developments created the perfect conditions for the breakout of the Onin War (1467-1477), which erupted around the midway point of the Muromachi period, marking the beginning of the Sengoku (Warring States) period (1467-1600). The eastern Hosokawa faction, backed by the shōgun and emperor, clashed with the western Yamana faction, supported by the powerful Ōuchi family. Fires raged in the capital, decimating temples and grand homes. Fighting gradually bled into the provinces, where local samurai led defensive uprisings against *shugo* (military governors) who oversaw large swaths of land. Amid the chaos, some of these samurai ended up established themselves as local lords.

The warrior class undoubtedly set the

cultural tone during this period. The ideals of Zen Buddhism, such as austerity, simplicity, and self-discipline, meshed well with the samurai class. This led to the rise of refined arts such as ikebana (flower arrangement), *Noh* theater, *renga* (linked verse) poetry, and the painstaking social ritual that is the tea ceremony. In short, Kyoto's creative pulse really came to life at this time. Fleeing the volatile capital, many priests and aristocrats dispersed to surrounding towns, facilitating the spread of Kyoto's rarefied culture into the outlying provinces.

In 1543, a Portuguese ship was blown ashore on the small island of Tanega-shima, off the southern coast of Kyūshū. The exotic foreigners, who were the first Europeans to arrive in Japan's history, came bearing guns and Christianity. This disruptive foreign faith took off. Many daimyo adopted the new faith in hopes of facilitating commerce with European merchants and accessing the revolutionary weapons the Europeans brought with them.

True to the violent times, the arcane art of musket construction became prized knowledge among daimyo, who clamored to get their hands on the new military technology. A warlord with a particular affinity for firearms was the ruthless Oda Nobunaga (1534-1582). Although he never became shogun, he did manage to topple Kyoto and seize control of it in 1568, deposing Ashikaga Yoshiaki in 1573 and effectively bringing the Ashikaga shogunate to a close. This made Nobunaga Japan's de facto supreme leader.

Azuchi-Momoyama Period (1568-1600)

During this short period, Nobunaga and his brilliant successor, Toyotomi Hideyoshi (1537-1598), brought order to the chaos of the day. Betrayed and wounded by one of his generals, Nobunaga committed suicide in 1582. Power was then given to Toyotomi Hideyoshi (1537-1598), one of Nobunaga's favorite, most brilliant generals. Hideyoshi swiftly consolidated power and started the practice of requiring daimyo's families to reside in Kyoto, effectively as hostages. Castles, built and refortified by regional daimyo, mushroomed around Honshu and Kyūshū during this turbulent period. This fortress-building spree makes perfect sense in light of events to come.

Hideyoshi's main rival was Tokugawa Ieyasu (1543-1616), a local lord originally from a domain near modern-day Nagoya. Ieyasu decided to pledge his fealty to Hideyoshi, who allowed Ieyasu to remain in charge of his own domain. Meanwhile, Ieyasu diligently built up and strengthened his domain. In 1586, he even moved his base farther east, away from Hideyoshi, where he laid in wait for his time to pounce.

Toward the end of his life, Hideyoshi became feverish with expansionist dreams. He launched two invasions of Korea, with the hopes of going on to topple China and control Asia. This had long been the dream of his predecessor Nobunaga. The attempted invasions failed miserably, however, and severely damaged ties between Japan and Korea. During the second invasion, Hideyoshi died in Kyoto.

Following Hideyoshi's death, his young son Hideyori was placed behind the protective walls of Osaka Castle until he was old enough to rule. This, however, was not to be. Ieyasu seized power in the Battle of Sekigahara (1600), widely considered one of the most epic battles in Japanese history.

Edo Period (1603-1868)

In 1603, Tokugawa Ieyasu became shogun, and established his base in Edo, which would one day become Tokyo. Under the Tokugawa Shogunate, Japan enjoyed relative peace for more than 250 years. A policy called *sankin kotai* forced daimyo and their families to alternate between the new capital Edo and their home state, controlling the daimyo and keeping any hidden ambitions in check.

During this time, Japan strictly enforced the *sakoku* (closed country) policy, largely spurred on by meddling by foreign missionaries. In 1614, Portuguese missionaries began to be expelled from what had become a vibrant base of Christian activity around Nagasaki and elsewhere on Kyūshū. Christianity was flat-out banned following the Shimabara Rebellion (1637-1638), forcing believers into hiding.

In 1638, all foreigners were kicked out of the country, save for a cadre of Dutch traders who swore allegiance to commerce above religion. Allowed only to trade, these crafty merchants were relegated to a small, artificial island off the coast of Nagasaki known as Dejima, which still exists in the city today. As a result, all Western medical and scientific knowledge came via the Dutch during this age of intense isolation.

By the early 18th century, Edo had a population of more than 1 million, making it the world's largest city at the time, as it is today. Osaka became a mighty mercantile center, while Kyoto became a hub of leisure and luxury. Four social classes emerged: the samurai, farmers, artisans, and merchants. These social classes were based on the ancient Chinese ideal of the "four occupations," derived from Confucian thought. Existing above these classes were the emperor, imperial court, shogun, and daimyos.

Though in European feudal society, the serfs (farmers) were at the bottom, in Japan, the group at the bottom of the hierarchy was the merchants—viewed as self-serving and less crucial than farmers and artisans. This didn't stop the mercantile class from carving out a vibrant place in society, though. With money in their pockets, the increasingly rich merchants developed a penchant for indulging in the arts, entertainment, and culinary pursuits. Woodblock prints known as *ukiyo-e* depict many of the favored pastimes from this *ukiyo* (floating world), including sumo tournaments, kabuki, and sprawling pleasure quarters such as Edo's Yoshiwara.

By the early 19th century, the shogunate's power had begun to wane, just as the merchant class saw its influence rise. Moreover, foreigners began trying to make contact with the government. Commodore Perry's Black Ships sailed into Edo Bay on July 8, 1853, gunboat-diplomacy style. After firing blank shots from 73 cannons—which Perry claimed was in celebration of American Independence Day—Perry sent a letter to the shogunate threatening to destroy them if they didn't comply, promising to return again a year later.

Only six months later, Perry returned with a crew of 1,600 men aboard 10 ships. They sailed into Kanagawa, negotiated the Convention of Kanagawa, signed on March 31, 1854. The treaty granted access to the ports of Shimoda, Shizuoka Prefecture, and Hakodate on Hokkaido. Soon after, Townsend Harris was appointed the first American diplomat to Japan. Other countries and ports followed.

From the time of Perry's arrival until the Meiji Restoration, sentiment against foreign powers and the shogunate became rife among the public, who increasingly yearned for the emperor to be put atop the government again. On the other hand, there was also a growing sense that adopting Western science and military technology was indeed the only hope for Japan in the new age. The tension between these two contradictory impulses set the stage for the next major sea change in Japan's history.

Meiji Period (1868-1912) and the Lead-Up to World War II

By 1867, the Tokugawa shogunate was crumbling under the weight of pressure from internal politics and anti-shogunate sentiment. Emperor Mutsuhito (1852-1912), posthumously renamed Emperor Meiji, was reinstalled as the head of state in the Meiji Restoration of 1868. With this monumental gesture, the feudal age came to a close and the radically transformative Meiji Period began.

In the early Meiji years, real power was wielded by oligarchs who pulled strings from the freshly renamed Edo. Tokyo, which literally means Eastern Capital, was officially made the new capital. There was a sense that Japan desperately needed to play technological, economic, and political catch-up with the West to resist colonization. Japanese scholars were sent West, and Western scholars were invited to Japan.

The ensuing changes were swift and dramatic. The first railway was built, linking Yokohama to Shinbashi in Tokyo. A new constitution was drafted, based on Prussian and English models, and nationalized industries were formed, then sold to chosen entrepreneurs. This led to the rise of conglomerates known as zaibatsu, many of which still exist today, such as Mitsubishi, Sumitomo, and Mitsui.

Amid these heady developments, State Shinto replaced the Shinto-Buddhist mix that had been in favor for centuries. This was a symbolic return to a more "pure" Japanese state, with the emperor at the top. The ban on Christianity was lifted and the rigid four-tier class system was suddenly disbanded. This led to massive upheaval for a few years, but ultimately all, save for the imperial class, were equal under the law, though women were neglected.

Japan also became militarily expansionist, annexing Korea after the Sino-Japanese War (1894-1895). Next came the Russo-Japanese War (1904-1905), which Japan also won. This victory elevated Japan's reputation as a force to be reckoned with, and won Taiwan and Liaoning peninsula as colonies.

By historical standards, the Meiji Period ended with the death of the emperor on July 30, 1912. The decades that followed, leading up to the outbreak of World War II (1939-1945), were defined by Japan's increasing military and economic confidence, solidifying Japan's newfound status as the preeminent power in modern East Asia.

When World War I (1914-1918) broke out, Japan sided with the allies. In 1914, Japan gave Germany an ultimatum: remove all ships from the waters of Japan and China and let go of the port city of Tsingtao in China's northeast. Germany agreed, and by early 1915, Japan controlled the entire Shantung Peninsula, on which Tsingtao sits. By extension Japan was able to gain control over China, laying the groundwork for Japan to exploit China's vast pool of labor and rich natural resources.

In 1923, the Great Kanto Earthquake led to immense loss of life in the region surrounding the capital, with around 100,000 killed. Highlighting deeply entrenched discrimination, Japan's ethnic Korean community were falsely blamed for widespread looting and additional loss of life following the disaster. Tragically, many ethnic Koreans were hunted down and lynched by angry mobs.

World War II (1939-1945)

In the years leading up to the outbreak of World War II, Japanese forces became embroiled in a growing number of skirmishes in Manchuria. By 1937, Japan was engaged in all-out war with China, with imperial troops sacking Shanghai and advancing on Nanjing. Over several months, a staggering number of people were raped and murdered in what would become known as the Rape of Nanking. The total number of victims in the atrocity perpetuated by Japanese troops in Nanking is still debated by scholars, with some estimates as high as 400,000.

As war officially broke out in Europe, and France was defeated in 1939, Japan swooped in and overtook French Indo-China. When Japan came to blows with the US over Washington's demands that Japan stop its advance through China, the US halted oil exports to Japan. This led to Japan's devastating attack on Pearl Harbor (December 7, 1941), which officially brought the US into the war.

In 1942, an emboldened Japan proceeded to occupy a number of other countries in the region, including the Philippines, Dutch East Indies, Burma, Malaya, Hong Kong, and Guam, among others. The turning point came in June 1942 at the Battle of Midway, in which the Allied forces managed to wipe out most of Japan's carrier fleet.

After Midway, US forces proceeded to "island hop" and route Japan's lines of support on the advance toward the Japanese archipelago itself. By 1944, US planes were doing bombing missions over Japanese cities, including devastating firebombing runs over Tokyo.

The war came to a dramatic, decisive end when the US dropped atomic bombs on Hiroshima (August 6, 1945), and then Nagasaki (August 9, 1945). Both bombs killed tens of thousands in an instant, and hundreds of thousands more through subsequent fires and radioactive fallout. Faced with utter ruin, Emperor Hirohito formally surrendered on August 15, 1945 via radio. This was the first time that the Japanese people had ever heard the voice of the emperor, who until then had been believed to be a god. Along with surrendering, the emperor renounced his divine status.

Emperor Hirohito was loathed across Asia until his passing in 1989. To this day, the barbaric incident in Nanking is a source of intense friction between the governments of Japan and China. In Korea, Japan's wartime use of Korean "comfort women," who were forced to serve as sex slaves, is still a source of ire.

Post-War Japan

After the war, the US military occupied Japan and the imperial military and navy were completely disbanded. Under General Douglas MacArthur, a new postwar constitution was written and came into effect in 1947. The constitution created a parliamentary system that gave adults age 20 and over (now 18) the right to vote. The document included a pacifism clause, under which Japan was forced to pledge not to have a military with the intent or capability of waging war. The emperor's status was brought down to serving as a ceremonial figurehead.

In 1951, Japan inked a peace treaty with the US and other former foes, although it's worth noting that Japan and Russia still haven't formally signed a peace treaty. This is reflected in the existence of disputed islands off the coast of Hokkaido. Japan was finally given independence and the US withdrew, although a handful of US military bases remain.

From the late 1940s to the early 1950s, Japan was heavily engaged in nation building and rebuilding. From the nuclear bombing of Hiroshima and Nagasaki to firebombing raids across the nation, much of urban Japan was in shambles. Many citizens were on the verge of starving.

American influence began to creep into everything from pop culture to the nation's diet—most notably, bread and wheat products—which led to an explosion of cheap, homegrown dishes like ramen, and the takeoff of Japan's own music and pop cultural sensibility. The 1950s were also the dawn of what would become known as an "economic miracle," with Japan's industry and economy astonishingly ascending to become the world's second-largest after the US by the 1960s. Economic growth roared through the 1970s and early 1980s. At the peak of Japan's growth, people were splashing around ¥10,000 bills in the way most would spend a ¥1,000 note today.

The 1950s also saw major realignment in international relations, with Japan joining the United Nations in 1956. It went on to hold the 1964 summer Olympics in a radically transformed Tokyo—having gone from rat-infested and polluted to a showcase to the world—and unveiled the first *shinkansen* (bullet train) that same year. In 1972 Okinawa, was finally handed back to Japan, although a heavy US military presence still controversially persists on the island today. That same year, the Japanese prime minister went to China, normalizing relations, and Japan closed its embassy in Taiwan. A decade later, in 1982, Honda opened its first factory in the US.

Emperor Hirohito was never tried for war crimes; he passed away on January 7, 1989, marking the end of the Shōwa Era, which was the longest of any in Japan's long history.

Late 20th and Early 21st Century

Rule passed on to Hirahito's son Akihito, giving birth to the Heisei (Peace Everywhere) Era. To the shock of diehard traditionalists, the emperor married a commoner. To top it off, there was no male heir for a long stretch, spurring talks of a female to ascending to the throne for the first time in millennia.

From around 1986 the economy reached "bubble" proportions, fueled by inflated real estate and stock prices, until it popped in 1992. Stagnation stretched from 1991 until 2010, a period that is often called the "lost decades."

Underscoring the downturn were a series of calamities, starting with the 6.9-magnitude Great Hanshin Earthquake that struck Kobe on January 17, 1995. This natural disaster was followed two months later by the heinous sarin nerve gas attack on the Tokyo subway, carried out by members of the Aum Shinrikyo doomsday cult on March 20. Another major disaster rocked the nation 16 years later on March 11, 2011, when the 9.0-magnitude Great Tohoku earthquake and tsunami not only killed an estimated 18,000, but also triggered the ongoing meltdown at Fukushima's nuclear plants.

Japan's relations with its neighbors, namely, Korea and China, began to improve in the early 2000s, beginning with Prime Minister Koizumi Junichiro's visits to Seoul in 2001 and Pyongyang in 2002. Then Chinese Prime Minister Wen Jiabao addressed Japan's parliament and touted the two nations' strengthening ties in April 2007, by which point Shinzo Abe had succeeded Koizumi as Prime Minister.

To the dismay of peaceniks, the government approved a reinterpretation of the pacifist Article 9 of the postwar constitution in July 2014. This reinterpretation calls for allowing Japan's self-defense forces to engage in "collective self-defense," which includes coming to the aid of allies if attacked. This controversial shift in tone has ignited furious debate: Some feel that the change is flat-out illegal, while others insist it's necessary to keep up with the changing times. Prime Minister Abe has declared that 2020 would be a deadline to finalize the revision of the article.

Emperor Akihito shocked the nation in August 2016 with a televised address in which he expressed his desire to abdicate: the first time this has been done in about two centuries. The Heisei era finally ended on April 30, 2019, with the dawn of the Reiwa Period on May 1, 2019. On that day, Crown Prince Naruhito officially ascended to the throne to become the 126th emperor of Japan.

Naruhito has broken with tradition in a number of ways, having studied overseas at Oxford, married a commoner, and been surprisingly candid about the struggles that he and his wife, Empress Masako (nee Owada), have had with their unfruitful attempts to have a male heir.

With the dawn of the Reiwa era, soul searching about the legacy of the turbulent Heisei era is ongoing. Only time will tell what the tone of the new era will be.

Government and Economy

ORGANIZATION

Japan is a constitutional monarchy with a parliamentary system. According to the postwar constitution, the emperor is head of state, but is expressly restricted from participating in politics. Pacifism is a key element of the constitution. Japan is banned from having atomic weaponry or maintaining a standing army, although it does maintain self defense forces, which in recent years have gone on missions abroad but never engaged in combat.

The government is led by a prime minister who is elected from a majority ruling party of the government, known as the National Diet (legislative), plus Cabinet members (executive branch). The Diet is split between two parts, the House of Representatives (lower house), which is more powerful in practice, and the House of Councillors. Together, both houses draft and ratify all bills. The judiciary is headed by the Supreme Court, with three levels of lesser courts under it. A majority vote is needed to elect an official or pass a bill.

POLITICAL PARTIES

In theory, a range of parties occupy Japan's political spectrum. In practice, the Liberal Democratic Party (LDP), which leans toward the conservative edge of the spectrum, has ruled the roost more or less from the time it formed in 1955, with only brief interludes. At the time of writing, the Prime Minister is Shinzo Abe. His current stint in power began in 2012, making him the second-longest sitting leader in postwar Japan. Another party that wields significant influence is the Komeito. This small fringe party is a stalwart coalition party of the LDP, as well as the political arm of the mainstream religious group Soka Gakkai, to which many ascribe cultish undertones.

The main opposition party was once the Democratic Party (DP), which was virtually wiped out in the 2017 general elections. The party then splintered into two factions: the Constitutional Democratic Party of Japan (CDP) and the Democratic Party for the People (DPP). Further toward the fringe are the Japanese Communist Party (JCP) and the Social Democratic Party of Japan (SDPJ).

Scandals have swirled around Prime Minister Abe; among them was his alleged donation to a nationalist elementary school, which was able to buy government land for a fraction of its price. Abe's image took another hit when his friend and former Administrative Vice Finance Minister Junichi Fukuda was accused of committing sexual harassment in 2018. Abe has also been revealed to be a member of Nippon Kaigi (Japan Conference), a right-wing group of lobbyists intent on restoring Japan to the supposed glory of its imperial days before World War II; that would mean trashing the postwar constitution as well as human rights, doing away with sexual equality and booting out foreigners.

ELECTIONS

Japan holds three types of elections: a general election for the House of Representatives, which is supposed to occur every four years, but snap elections are common; an election for the House of Councillors, held every three years; and local government elections held every four years.

Political campaigning, though heavily regulated, can be quite an intrusive affair. The preferred method is good old-fashioned posters and vans patrolling streets with megaphones blaring recorded campaign announcements. Despite this, recent voter turnout has been lackluster. In the 2017 election for the House of Representatives, election turnout was around 54 percent, just above the nearly 53 percent turnout of 2014, which was the lowest in postwar Japanese history. Since 2018, citizens aged 18 and over have a legal right to vote. (This age was initially set at 20, then lowered to 19 in 2016.) Despite the drops in voting age, young people remain largely unengaged, except for short-lived examples like the Students Emergency Action for Liberal Democracy (SEALDs), which led anti-LDP protests in 2015 and 2016.

AGRICULTURE

Japan conjures images of rice fields and rolling tea plantations. Yet, very little of Japan's land is actually suitable for cultivation, and it's shrinking—from 15.4 percent of the country in 1961 to 11.5 percent in 2015. Terrace farming allows for maximum use of limited space. Japan has one of the highest levels of crop yield per area of any country in the world.

Due to a decline in rice consumption, and wheat production facing a setback due to typhoon damage, the nation's food self-sufficiency dropped to 38 percent in 2016, the lowest in 23 years at that time. The government has set a rather ambitious target of raising that figure to 45 percent by 2025.

Japan's agriculture sector is highly subsidized, even coddled, and sheltered from outside influences. Japanese farmers always take precedence, even if it means consumers paying top yen. This is particularly true for rice, by far Japan's most protected crop, with tariffs of up to 778 percent. Quotas have at least expanded through recent trade deals under the Trans-Pacific Partnership (TPP) and with the European Union.

INDUSTRY

Toyota. Honda. Sony. Nintendo. Nikon. Canon. Fuji. Toshiba. Panasonic. Softbank. Nippon Steel. Shiseido. Uniqlo. Muji. The list goes on. Japan is known globally as a juggernaut of industry and commerce, producing vehicles, electronics, ships, (bio)chemicals, machine components, tools, and increasingly softer items like snacks, cosmetics, fashion, lifestyle goods, and so much more. By far, Japan's main exports are vehicles, followed by machinery. As of 2012, Toyota was the largest vehicle producer in the world.

From the Meiji period through WWII, a cluster of zaibatsu exerted an outsized influence on the Japanese economy. The four biggest zaibatsu were still-surviving Mitsubishi, Mitsui, Sumitomo, and the disbanded Yasuda group. Sumitomo is the oldest of the lot, having been founded during the Edo period in 1615.

Following World War II, the *keiretsu* ("system" or "grouping of enterprises"), a new form of business grouping that is arranged horizontally and vertically, emerged. The members of these newer business groupings all own shares in each other's stock and are served by the same bank at the center, the idea being to reduce the risk of stock market turbulence and any potential takeover attempts. Former zaibatsu Mitsubishi, Mitsui, and Sumitomo have lived on as members of the "Big Six" *keiretsu,* along with Fuyo, Sanwa, and the Mizuho Financial Group.

When Sony released its Walkman in 1979, the product represented a major turning point for personal gadgets, ultimately leading to the ubiquitous MP3 player. While Japan has been knocked off its pedestal somewhat by electronics brands in South Korea and China, it remains a giant in the field.

DISTRIBUTION OF WEALTH

Japan has a robust middle class, with GDP per capita at $34,428.10 in 2017, making it 23rd globally. On paper, it is among the most equal economies in the world, but poverty does exist. Just walk under an overpass near a major train station and you'll notice small homeless communities, who by and large opt to rummage through garbage rather than beg.

Under current laws, part-time workers do not have the same access to nationalized healthcare or to the pension system, leaving those not adequately plugged into the system in a precarious position. For those who do pay into the pension system, the returns are miniscule. For this reason, some elderly people can't afford to stop working, and many of them reside in rural areas, where resources are dwindling due to depopulation.

Generally speaking, moneyed Japanese tend to prefer subtle displays of wealth. There is also a widespread attitude among Japanese that it is virtually immoral for company executives to receive the kinds of exorbitant salaries that are commonplace in the West. This outlook can be traced back to the postwar years when buckling down and rebuilding the nation took precedence over personal gain.

TOURISM

Tourism has been a bright spot in Japan's otherwise sluggish economy in recent years. When the 2011 Tohoku earthquake and tsunami battered the country's economy and morale, inbound tourist numbers dipped to 6.2 million. Inspired by Tokyo winning the bid to host the 2020 Summer Olympics, the government set about to change that trend, aiming to attract 20 million annual visitors by 2020. By 2015, the number of overseas visitors positively exploded, shooting up to 19.7 million. The figure just kept climbing, hitting 31.2 million in 2018. With the initial target already long surpassed, the government hopes to see 40 million inbound visitors by 2020.

There's been a corresponding flood of positive press about Japan as a travel destination, from glossy travel magazine features to travel documentaries. Anthony Bourdain, the late chef, writer, and host of television shows *No Reservations* and later *Parts Unknown,* liberally praised Japan in a handful of episodes he filmed there. It's appropriate that Mt. Fuji itself, primordial symbol of the nation, and *washoku* (Japanese cuisine) as a whole were both bestowed heritage status by UNESCO in 2013.

The downside to this massive boost in soft power is that some places are now routinely clogged with camera-toters. Kyoto, which is visited by 25.9 percent of international visitors to Japan, is a prime example. From 2013 to 2017, Kyoto saw international tourist numbers surge by 279 percent. Tokyo (visited by 46.2 percent of inbound travelers) and Osaka (38.7 percent) have also been positively flooded by international tourists. Most of these visitors are coming from a number of Asian countries benefitting from recently relaxed visa laws—such as Thailand, China, and the Philippines—and a glut of cheap intra-Asia flights.

With this surge comes a shortage of accommodation, especially during high season, and a high likelihood that you'll be gazing upon the more famous sights with a multitude of others. Prominent restaurants and shops are often overrun, too.

People and Culture

DEMOGRAPHY AND DIVERSITY

Japanese society is exceptionally homogenous, with less than 2 percent being foreign-born. The refrain of *ware ware Nihonjin* (we Japanese) is commonly heard, though the tone might be humble or proud. At the far-right end of the spectrum, it's downright xenophobic, underlying a pervasive belief that being 100 percent ethnically Japanese is a thing to be desired.

Zainichi

Chinese and Koreans have a long history of living on the fringes of Japanese society. The Zainichi Koreans community took shape after World War II, when Koreans living on Japanese soil were stripped of their nationality, becoming essentially stateless. Many of these unfortunates caught up in geopolitical chaos were thrown out with the bathwater when Korea was divided into North and South, forcing people to choose sides. Even today, members of the Zainichi community are often treated as outcasts and second-class citizens. Until the 1980s, they were forced to relinquish their Korean names and adopt Japanese names to become Japanese. Although the majority have naturalized, discrimination remains entrenched.

Burakumin

The community that's faced, perhaps, the most discrimination in Japan, however, is the *burakumin* (hamlet people). Akin to India's "untouchables," this class comprises people employed in professions deemed "unclean," from sanitation staff, to slaughterhouse workers, undertakers, and even executioners (the death penalty is still enforced in Japan). Today, those of *burakumin* descent still face discrimination in everything from marriage to employment prospects, often being pushed into unskilled labor and low-income jobs. The government passed a law in 2016 that was meant to discourage discrimination against burakumin. Many have criticized the bill, however, saying it lacks teeth, because violators cannot be fined or imprisoned.

Immigration

Demographics and economics are forcing things to change. Japan's complex relationship with foreigners or *gaikokujin* ("foreigners";

sometimes called by the more colloquial, slightly derogatory *gaijin*) is gradually evolving. A recent influx of Asian immigrants, hesitantly encouraged by the government due to labor shortages, is coming from Nepal, Vietnam, the Philippines, and beyond. This new wave of immigrants, which is often forced to speak Japanese at a higher level than many Westerners who come to work in Japan, is visible in the service industry, and many attend Japanese universities.

One trend indicating a change in Japan's makeup is the rise of mixed-race and mixed nationality marriages. The social impacts of this shift are not yet obvious, but the growing number of *haafu* ("half" or mixed) people has become a hot topic in the media. At best, mixed Japanese are put on a pedestal for their "exotic" looks. At worst, mixed-birth Japanese are treated like foreigners in their own country. To combat negative attitudes, many have copped onto the idea that *haafu* aren't "half," they're "double," with roots in more than one culture. To put a human face on this social problem, check out the documentary *Hafu—The Mixed-Race Experience of Japan,* directed by Megumi Nishikura, a filmmaker born to a Japanese mother and American father.

Population Decline

Recent immigration trends may be the tip of a much larger iceberg. For the first time in recorded history, Japan's population began to decline in 2016, when the census counted 127.1 million, down 0.7 percent from 2010. Estimates vary, but some numbers peg Japan's projected population in 2060 at around 87 million. At that point, 40 percent of the population will be 65 and up. This has myriad implications, from a smaller workforce to increased need for imported goods to satiate the consumer habits of pensioners, which will in turn limit the growth of GDP.

The rise in retirees will also strain the government's pension system. Japan has the second-largest debt load—and growing—of any nation. One government response has been to raise the retirement age from 60 to 65 for employees in the private sector. While there's still time to find solutions, these trends paint an unsettling picture.

INDIGENOUS CULTURES

Ainu

A group known as the Ainu is the indigenous population of Hokkaido, or Ezo as it was once known. Ainu settlements could also be found in Tohoku, or northeastern Honshu, as well as some of the Russian Far East, such as the vast Kamchatka Peninsula and Sakhalin Island.

The Ainu are of mysterious origin, with possible links to the Jomon people of ancient Japan. They also have strong genes from the Okhotsk region of the Russian Far East. Under the Hokkaido Former Aborigines Protection Act of 1899, the Japanese government tried to assimilate the Ainu into mainstream society, banning the teaching of their own language and customs in schools until the act was finally repealed in 1997. There are only a handful of native Ainu speakers left, but some youngsters are trying to learn and revive the ancient tongue with no ties to Japanese.

As an indicator of their status in modern Japan, consider the fact that the Ainu were only officially recognized as the nation's indigenous culture in early 2019. Today, there are a mere 20,000 people who self-identify as Ainu, although the actual number of those who are unaware of their Ainu heritage is likely higher.

Ryūkyūan People

On the opposite side of the country, in the far south, the Ryūkyūan people are the indigenous inhabitants of Okinawa. From the 15th to the 19th centuries, the Ryūkyū Kingdom served as a tributary state to China. The kingdom was a key player in maritime trade and diplomacy, with a peace-loving reputation.

Genetically, they have strong ties to the ancient Jomon and Yamato people, as well as Chinese and Korean blood. The Ryūkyū Islands were first occupied by Japan via the Satsuma domain in southern Kyūshū in the early 17th century. The Ryūkyū Kingdom remained semi-autonomous for a time, but was gradually forced to serve as a tributary state to both China and the Satsuma domain.

Mirroring the experience of the Ainu in Hokkaido, the government banned the Ryūkyū language, customs, and more, stirring widespread resentment. Despite this treatment, many Ryūkyūans fought as imperial troops in World War II, which brought devastating battles to Okinawan shores.

Today, some 1.3 million Ryūkyūans live in Okinawa Prefecture, with about 600,000 abroad, mostly in Hawaii. Akin to Scotland, there is an independence movement in Okinawa, largely fueled by the heavy presence of US military bases on the islands.

RELIGION

There's a saying that most Japanese are born Shinto, are (sometimes) married Christian (aesthetically, anyway), and die Buddhist. In many ways, this truism is a good summary of the nation's spiritual life, which is highly pragmatic and involves a lot of mixing. From a Judeo-Christian or Western perspective, religion is a slippery concept in Japan.

Today, ask someone in Japan if they're religious and chances are they'll say they're not. Many will go as far as saying that Japan as a whole is not a very religious country. Yet, you won't have to look far to see throngs at Buddhist temples where they wave holy incense smoke around their heads and bodies, or at Shinto shrines where they toss coins into wooden boxes, ring bells to summon the resident kami (god), bow, clap their hands, and pray.

In the distant past, Shinto and Buddhism, Japan's two key faiths, mingled freely. Shrines and temples were often combined into single complexes until the late 19th century when they were crudely ripped apart. This government action set the stage for what would eventually become the creation of State Shinto. During the years leading up to World War II, the state labeled Buddhism and Christianity, among others, as religions, but conspicuously left Shinto off the list, classifying the Japanese system of nature worship as more of a proto-philosophy than a religion. This status was nullified after the end of the second world war, when the emperor publicly broadcasted that he relinquished claims to divinity. From that point on, Shinto was classified as a religion like any other. Nonetheless, the notion that Shinto is the spiritual fabric of the Japanese nation, beyond any kind of religious faith, persists.

Shinto

Of the two primary religions that color life for the vast majority of Japanese—Buddhism and Shinto—Shinto can claim to be the indigenous faith. Literally translated as "way of the kami," Shinto is predicated on the belief that kami (deity, gods, or divine beings) live in all things. Kami are believed to inhabit natural objects, from rocks to mountains to trees, encircled by thick ropes festooned with intricately cut white paper on many shrine grounds.

Today, shrines remain busy as ever, due to the widely held belief that kami can be called upon for help through prayer, or through specific rituals that often involve music and dance. Before beseeching a kami, purification is key. You'll notice water basins with bamboo scoops on long handles near the entrance to any shrine. All visitors to shrines are expected to carry out a simple purification ritual at these *temizuya* (water ablution pavilions).

Cleansed, one is prepared to enter the shrine grounds. Known as *jinja, jingū,* or sometimes simply bearing the suffix *-gū,* shrines are usually open-air, save for an inner sanctum or main hall, which can only be entered directly by priests. Shrines at the more elaborate end are often patronized by the Imperial family and approached via expansive paths lined by imposing *torii* gates. Meanwhile, small roadside structures that resemble the humble "spirit houses" seen in parts of Southeast Asia are often fronted by a single, humble torii gate.

Famous shrines include Ise Jingū, Shinto's

holiest spot; Izumo Taisha, the grand shrine in Shimane Prefecture; Miyajima's Itsukushima-jinja, famed for its "floating" *torii* gate; Tokyo's Meiji Jingū and Nikkō's opulent Tōshō-gū. Most ordinary Japanese visit shrines for births, to celebrate various rites of passage, sometimes for traditional weddings, for purification rites, or to receive blessings for things ranging from new homes to business ventures and new cars.

Buddhism

By far the foreign faith with the most lasting impact on Japan has been Buddhism, specifically the Mahayana ("Great Vehicle") strain. First brought to the country from Korea in the 6th century, it's been both demonized and patronized by different governments. Buddhism saw major leaps in sophistication from the 7th through 9th centuries, largely benefitting from its deepening in China. It was essentially combined with Shinto for centuries, until the two were split in the late 19th century. Even today, many Japanese may scratch their heads if you ask them to explain the difference between a temple and a shrine.

Contrasting with Shinto's here-and-now focus on life—births, blessings, rites of passage, *matsuri* (festivals)—Buddhist temples are associated with the hereafter. Most Japanese ultimately have Buddhist funeral rites. Graveyards are often situated next to temples. It's also common, especially in rural Japan, to see a small Buddhist altar, usually kept in an elaborate wooden cabinet, known as a *butsudan,* prominently displayed in a family's living space. These miniature altars, which often contain statues of the Buddha or various deities and scrolls inscribed with sacred text, are meant to honor deceased loved ones.

Known as (ō)tera or simply having the suffix *-ji,* like shrines, temples also range from towering wooden edifices housing giant bronze bells to small structures akin to local chapels in the West. Famous temples include Nara's massive Todai-ji, the world's largest wooden structure which houses the world's largest bronze statue of Buddha; Kinkaku-ji, Kyoto's postcard-perfect gilt icon, as well as Kyoto's hillside complex Kiyomizu-dera; the mesmerizing cluster of temples and adjacent cemetery atop the mountain sanctuary of Kōya-san; and Hase-dera, known for its towering wooden statue of Kannon (goddess or bodhisattva of mercy) in Kamakura, a town littered with majestic temples.

The main Buddhist sects include Tendai, the nation's oldest, founded at Hiei-zan in Kyoto; the more esoteric Shingon, founded at Kōya-san; Jodo, or Pure Land, which emphasizes faith in the Buddha over ritual; Nichiren, named for its founder, the monk Nichiren, centered on habitually reciting sections of the Lotus Sutra; and the austere school of Zen, heavily weighted toward strict meditation and asceticism, and once prized by the samurai class.

New Religious Movements

Alongside the mainstays of Shinto and Buddhism, a number of *shinshukyō* (new religions) have mushroomed in Japan since the mid-19th century. These new faiths are often centered around a charismatic leader, and range from bona fide religions to downright cults. Given this reputation, *shinshukyō* have an unsavory reputation among much of the public.

The most famous new religion is Soka Gakkai, a strain of Nichiren Buddhism with a major presence overseas. The influential group has claimed celebrity members such as rock star Courtney Love, actor Orlando Bloom and jazz legend Herbie Hancock. Many who have left the group have brought attention to its cultish tendencies, as well as the right-leaning agenda being pushed by its political arm, the Komeito party.

Another *shinshukyō* of note is Ōmoto (aka Sekai Kyuseiko), based on the teachings of Deguchi Nao (1837-1918), a peasant healer and oracle who channeled apocalyptic, messianic and "new world" prophecies in the late 19th century. Her teachings were later systematized by her son-in-law Deguchi Onisaburō

(1871-1948), who claimed he would become the leader to establish the "new world" prophesied by Nao. Although this didn't come to pass, the movement did garner around 2 million followers at its peak between the first and second world wars.

The most infamous of all of the numerous new religious movements to pop up in Japan is Aum Shinrikyō (supreme truth, often shortened as "Aum"). The cult was formed in 1984 by Shoko Asahara (birth name: Chizuo Matsumoto), who was born into a poor family of tatami mat makers. Asahara, who was blind since childhood, claimed divinity. The doomsday cult he founded combines teachings from Buddhism, Hinduism and apocalyptic Christian prophecies. Aum made global headlines on March 20, 1995, when a group of its members carried out the worst terrorist attack in Japanese history, using sarin nerve gas during morning rush hour on the Tokyo subway. The chemical attack killed 12 commuters and forced some 6,000 others to seek medical help.

Asahara and six followers were executed by hanging in July 2018. Six other members remain on death row at the time of writing. At its peak, Aum had tens of thousands of members around the globe. Today, under the new name of Aleph, it still operates at the fringes, underground, with some estimates claiming its membership numbers 1,500 and growing. Documenting the dark chapter of Japan's history, novelist Haruki Murakami interviewed 60 victims of the attack. The result is his chilling non-fiction book *Underground: The Tokyo Gas Attack and the Japanese Psyche.*

Christianity

Unlike Buddhism, Christianity received a tepid greeting upon reaching Japanese shores. Arriving with Portuguese merchants and missionaries in Kyūshū in 1542, it was initially tolerated and swiftly grew. By 1587, the tides had turned. Faced with the growth of European colonization in the East, Toyotomi Hideyoshi banned missionary activity in Japan. More infamously, Hideyoshi had 26 people executed in Nagasaki. The faith was outright banned by Tokugawa Ieyasu following the Shimabara Rebellion (1637-1638), after which thousands of Christians went into hiding. These *kakure kirisutian* (hidden Christians) remained in hiding for more than two centuries. This suppressed community remained in hiding until the arrival of Commodore Perry's fleets in 1853-1854. With the Meiji Restoration of 1868, freedom of religion was declared.

Today, Christianity has only a minor presence in Japan, representing about one percent of the population. Sometimes Christians are seen smiling and greeting passersby in the streets, ready with leaflets or to extend an invitation to mass. Faith aside, Christian wedding ceremonies are big business even among unbelieving Japanese. Held at mock wedding chapels, these ceremonies are often officiated by token foreigners playing the role of priest or pastor. Moreover, Christian holidays like Christmas and Valentine's Day have gained a purely secular, commercial foothold. Decorations are often festooned and holiday-appropriate chocolates and other goods are hawked at shops during these times.

LANGUAGE

As far as linguists can tell, Japanese is related to the Altaic language family, but is not officially included in it. Together with the Ryūkyū languages, Japanese falls under the stand-alone Japonic language family. It is grammatically similar to Korean, but has no other clear links. The Japanese language has a reputation as being difficult to learn. In truth, it's not too hard to get the hang of the highly systematic Japanese pronunciation system.

Although the Tokyo dialect is the official version of Japanese, dialects known as *ben* maintain a strong hold on many parts of the country. Moving to the margins—rural Tohoku or southern Kyūshū, for example—the chance that something may be lost in translation, even among two Japanese, is very real. A particularly colorful dialect, often spoken in a gangster-like staccato with thick intonation, is Kansai-ben, spoken particularly in Osaka and around. Kansai-ben has been popularized by an ever-expanding stable of zany comedians who emerge from the city, known for its flamboyant street life and razor wit. For fun, try saying "*okini*" (thank you) instead of the standard "*arigato gozaimasu*" when leaving a shop or restaurant in Osaka or elsewhere in Kansai.

On the other hand, the written language is a convoluted affair, requiring much more effort to master. In any selection of Japanese text, you'll likely see a combination of three scripts: kanji, hiragana, and katakana. The most complicated aspect of learning to read and write Japanese is coming to grips with thousands of kanji, derived from Chinese characters that were adapted to fit the Japanese pronunciation system. Although there are around 50,000 kanji in use, Japanese are supposed to learn about 2,100 by the time they graduate from secondary school.

Making matters more complex, there is also hiragana, originally called *onnade* (women's script), a cursive script derived from Chinese characters originally created so that women could have the ability to write. By the 10th century, it was ubiquitous throughout Japanese society. The other syllabary, katakana, is also derived from Chinese characters. These boxy, angular characters, are now primarily used to write foreign loanwords, onomatopoeia, and scientific terms, or to emphasize a given word or phrase.

LITERATURE

Traditional

With roots stretching back more than a millennium, Japan can rightly be proud of its literary tradition. In the eighth century, a collection of orally transmitted ancient myths known as the *Kojiki* was written down. Around the same time, a chronological account of Japan's origins was recorded in the *Nihonshiki*.

Some of Japan's earliest literature was written in verse. In the Asuka Period (538-710), much of the poetry was being penned that would later be compiled in the *Manyoshu (Collection of 10,000 Leaves).* This poetry anthology, which actually contains about 4,500 (not 10,000) poems, was put together around 760 CE, making it the first anthology in Japanese literature.

By the Heian period, women of the imperial court were writing groundbreaking works that would form the foundation of the novel. Specifically, *Genji Monogatari* (*The Tale of Genji*), considered the world's first novel, was penned by Lady Murasaki Shikibu, the pen name of an unidentified courtesan who lived in the late 10th and early 11th centuries. This tome, which describes the court dalliances of Prince Genji, was written in the first decade or so of the 11th century. Another notable example, *The Pillow Book* was written by courtesan Sei Shōnagon (966-1017 or 1025). Essentially a diary, the book offers an intimate glimpse of the intricacies and indulgences of Heian court life.

In the 13th century, the dramatic recounting of the battles between the Heike and Genji clans was put down in written form in Heike Monogatari (The Tale of the Heike). The saga tells the story of the Heike losing to the Genji clan in 1185. This classic story forms the basis of many theatrical performances.

By the Edo period, starting from 1682, writer Iharu Saikaku began scrawling the comedic tome *The Life of an Amorous Man,* based loosely on *The Tale of Genji*. The humorous novel was laced with ribald tales of the lavish exploits of Osaka's hedonistic merchant class. Equally renowned for his poetic prowess, Saikaku worked in what was known as *haikai renga* (or *hokku*), or linked-verse, which laid the groundwork for haiku.

Although the name "haiku" didn't stick until the 19th century, the form emerged in the 17th century as a response to Japan's older, more rarified forms. Composed of three lines, a haiku contains a total of 17 syllables. The lines, split into five, seven, and five syllables, respectively, are unrhymed. More than anyone else, the wandering poet Matsuo Bashō immortalized Japan through his masterful haiku in the later 17th century. Bashō's poems are still the gold standard for haiku, exploring themes related to nature and the transient beauty of life. Later haiku masters include Buson (1716-1784), Kobayashi Issa (1763-1828), Masaoka Shiki (1867-1902), Kawahigashi Hekigotō (1873-1937), and Takahama Kyoshi (1874-1959).

Modern

Moving into the modern era (late-19th and early-20th centuries), a new coterie of forward-thinking scribes began to write short stories with a naturalistic flavor, which bore noticeable Western influence. Among the first authors of "I-novels," as first-person accounts were called in Japan, was Natsume Sōseki (1867-1916). His most famous works include *Wagahai wa Neko de Aru (I Am a Cat), Botchan*, and *Kokoro*.

Other giants from the early modern period include Jun'ichirō Tanizaki (*Sasame Yuki*) and Ryunosuke Akutagawa (*In a Grove*). Yasunari Kawabata (*Izu no Odoriko, Asakusa Kurenaidan, Yukiguni*) became the first Japanese writer to win the Nobel Prize in Literature in 1968.

Writers who were working in the mid- to late-20th century include the controversial Yukio Mishima (*Confessions of a Mask, The Sound of Waves, The Sailor Who Fell from Grace)* a raging nationalist who visited the Tokyo headquarters of the Japan Self-Defense Forces calling for them to restore the emperor to power and overturn the pacifist constitution. He summarily committed *seppuku*—ritual suicide samurai-style—on a balcony as shocked troops watched from below.

A singular writer who came to prominence in the 1960s was Abe Kobo (*Woman in the Dunes*), a surrealist master who often draws comparisons to Franz Kafka. Oe Kenzaburo, whose work is interwoven with a deep strain of humanism, won the Nobel Prize in Literature in 1994.

Contemporary

Contemporary literature in Japan is dominated by the post-modern juggernaut Haruki Murakami (*The Wind-Up Bird Chronicle, Norwegian Wood*, the *1Q84* trilogy and *Kafka on the Shore*). His whimsical world of talking frogs, psychic prostitutes, dancing gnomes, and scenarios wherein the supernatural and strange intrude onto the workaday world in bizarre, often comical and even erotic ways has amassed a giant cult following worldwide. A contemporary giant with a much darker gaze is Ryū Murakami (*Almost Transparent Blue* and *Coin Locker Babies*).

There are also a number of influential female writers making their mark in Japanese literature today. Some of the biggest include Yoko Ogawa (*The Diving Pool*); Banana Yoshimoto (*Kitchen*); Risa Wataya, who became the youngest author ever to win the Akutagawa Prize in 2003 for her novel *Keritai senaka;* Hitomi Kanehara (*Snakes and Earrings*), who shared the Akutagawa Prize in 2003 with Wataya; Sayaka Murata (Convenience Store Woman) and the novelist Mieko Kawakami (*Breasts and Eggs, Ms. Ice Sanwich*), a writer's writer whom Haruki Murakami has praised for her work, which spans many genres and is often written in her native Osaka dialect.

Generally speaking, to dig deeper into contemporary literature, seeking out recent winners of the semi-annual Akutagawa Prize for up-and-coming writers is a good starting point. An excellent anthology of short stories published annually is *Monkey Business*.

Manga

Japanese literature can't be discussed without mentioning manga ("whimsical pictures"), as graphic novels or comics are known. Japan has a voracious appetite for manga, which accounts for nearly a quarter of all book sales in the country. Readers span every age group, gender, and socioeconomic status. The popularity of this form of storytelling can loosely be traced back to the country's long history of caricature, seen in the woodblock prints known as *kiboyoshi*. The transition to manga came with the introduction of American comic books during the postwar occupation. In the ensuing decades, the form took on a life of its own, with a variety of quirks, genres, and styles. Topics range from high school antics and tales involving Jesus and Buddha teaming up and making mischief (*Saint Young Men*) to the psychedelically grotesque creations of visionary artists like Shintaro Kago and infamously graphic porn involving gigantic octopi.

Popular manga series, some running for many years, can be collected in massive volumes known as *tankobon*. The sprawling, violent, cyberpunk masterpiece *Akira,* which explores dystopian themes in a post-apocalyptic future, was serialized from 1982 to 1990. Like many hit manga series, *Akira* was made into an animated film in 1998. *Ghost in the Shell,* a brilliant post-cyberpunk sci-fi franchise that explored the nature of consciousness through a counter-cyberterrorist organization active in the mid-21st century, ran from 1989 to 1990. It too spawned a classic animated film in 1995.

VISUAL ARTS

Japan has a vibrant arts tradition, ranging from ancient Buddhist sculptures and landscape paintings of austere beauty to cheeky post-modern sculpture. Among Japan's most notable arts are painting, calligraphy, woodblock prints (*ukiyo-e*), ceramics, lacquerware, *ikebana* (flower arrangement) and a bleeding-edge contemporary scene.

Concepts

WABI-SABI

Of the many concepts to be aware of when viewing traditional Japanese art, a recurring aesthetic ideal is *wabi-sabi*. Many non-Japanese are vaguely aware of this term and may have an inkling about its meaning, but it's a remarkably deep principle. In essence, it is the appreciation of things that are blemished, rustic, earthy, asymmetrical, incomplete, transient, authentic, and, in a word, imperfect. This sensibility is deeply Buddhist, in its positing that there is no inherent eternal essence to things, and further, that life is impermanent. *Wabi-sabi* took root in Japan in the 15th century, when tea ceremony founder Sen no Rikyū and others sought to rebel against the extravagant tastes of the time.

MA

Another key element that runs through much Japanese art is the spatial concept of *ma* (negative space). This idea highlights the importance of the empty space or gap between objects in a scene. You'll notice a preponderance of blank space in many landscape paintings, calligraphy scrolls, which evokes the focus of the scene at hand all the more dramatically by the lack of "busyness" around it. This sensibility also accounts for the visual power that a simple flower arrangement or scroll will exude when placed within an otherwise spare tatami-mat room.

KAWAII

Then, there's kawaii, a cloyingly saccharine sense of cuteness. Almost a household word now in the West, *kawaii* is the very life force of phenomena such as Hello Kitty.

Traditional Art Forms

PAINTING

Painting in Japan began with ink or black paint landscapes on *washi* paper, with deep influence from China. From the Heian period on, paintings that would later be known as *yamato-e* tended to depict court life, often from an aerial point of view. Starting in the Muromachi period, the ruling class began to patronize the arts. During this time, the Tosa and Kano schools took shape.

The Tosa school shared characteristics with the older *yamato-e* tradition, with lots of fine brushwork depicting elegant historic scenes. The Kano school, meanwhile, set the scene for the marvelous sliding doors, folding screens, temple ceilings, and more, splashed with paintings of nature, and mythological creatures such as dragons and phoenixes.

Following the Edo period, contact with the West shook up Japanese painting, which split into the schools of *yōga* (Western-style painting) and *nihonga* (Japanese-style painting). Nihonga is distinct from older styles of painting in that it's influenced by Western techniques such as shading.

CALLIGRAPHY

Originally imported from China, *shodo* (calligraphy) is deeply entrenched in the Japanese psyche. Throughout Japan's history it's been prized by the upper classes and is essentially the first art form taught to elementary school students today, along with learning kanji and kana characters. There are a variety of styles, from the blocky, clear-cut *kaisho* to *gyosho* (running hand, informal, semi-cursive) to *sosho* (fully cursive, formal, illegible to all but the initiated).

UKIYO-E (WOODBLOCK PRINTS)

Ukiyo-e (pictures of the floating world) evoke the fleeting pleasures and realm of the senses. These paintings became synonymous with the pleasure quarters of the Edo period. As such, they depict almost crude scenes in vivid colors. Kabuki, sumo, geisha, as well as landscape scenes are figure prominently in *ukiyo-e*. This style inspired the Japonisme movement in the West, which attracted such luminaries as Van Gogh and Manet.

CERAMICS

Jomon-era pottery represents some of the oldest fired clay in human history. What began as functional over time took on added layers of complexity and beauty starting with the advent of the tea ceremony in the 16th century. Potters often worked deep in the mountains, where ideal clay was readily available, and Koreans with superior techniques were often employed in the early days.

A smattering of towns became famous around Japan for their distinct ceramics styles. To name but a few: Arita in Saga Prefecture, Bizen in Okayama Prefecture, Mashiko in Tochigi Prefecture, and Hagi in Yamaguchi Prefecture. In the far south, Okinawan pottery, known by the name of *yachimun*, has a distinct aesthetic of its own.

LACQUERWARE

Shikki (lacquerware), also referred to sometimes as *nurimono*, is a delicate art form done by applying layer upon layer of sap from the lacquer tree to an object, from Buddhist statues and painted panels to tea pots and bento lunch boxes. Once an object is lacquered, pigments are added for color—black and red are common—and then the object is sometimes spruced up with inlays of silver, gold, or pearls. Aside from being beautiful, lacquerware items are durable, with lacquered wood known to endure millennia.

IKEBANA

Likely introduced along with Buddhism, the art of *ikebana* (flower arrangement) involves the careful placement of flowers, usually in a vase, in a way that uses both the florets themselves as well as the empty space around them to elicit a certain aesthetic response. An arrangement can also carry symbolic meaning. Several distinct schools have evolved, each with its own philosophy.

Contemporary Artists

Much of contemporary Japanese art has a pop touch. Perhaps the biggest name overseas from Japan's contemporary scene is Yayoi Kusama. Active since the 1950s, Kusama has created a singular body of colorful, polka-dotted tentacle-like sculptures, geometric, dot-infused abstract paintings, and immersive installations. Takashi Murakami, whose work is heavily influenced by manga and anime, is another heavyweight. He launched a post-modern artistic movement known as Superflat, which seeks to "flatten" a range of artistic forms, from graphic art and animation to pop culture and the fine arts. Murakami also founded the Kaikai Kiki artist collective, which has launched the careers of a number of new young talents, including Chiho Aoshima and Yoshitomo Nara.

Other notable artists mining a similar

vein of inspiration include Ai Yamaguchi, who paints young Edo-era female prostitutes; Mr., a former apprentice of Murakami who draws heavily on otaku culture; and Madsaki, a sometimes accomplice of Murakami whose work has a vandalistic street-art quality. Meanwhile, Hush is a street artist whose complex work combines pop and traditional motifs; and Tomoo Gokita is worth noting for his surrealist black-and-white noir paintings. For something uplifting, check out the color-drenched photographs of Ninagawa Mika.

Also worth noting is provocateur Aida Makoto, who works in a variety of mediums and tackles the bugbears of Japanese history, dark facets of the nation's psyche, and more. Among his works are a manga-style painting of a phallic mushroom cloud, a cardboard castle built to look like the cardboard homes lived in by many of Japan's homeless, and post-apocalyptic scenes depicted as a traditional landscape painting.

Plenty of biennales and triennales (art festivals held every other year, or every third year, respectively) highlight Japan's buzzing contemporary art scene. Some of the most prominent ones are the Echigo-Tsumari Art Triennale (www.echigo-tsumari.jp), the Setouchi Triennale (https://setouchi-artfest.jp) and the Yokohama Triennale (www.yokohamatriennale.jp), to name a few.

MUSIC

Traditional

Japan's musical heritage can be traced back to a troupe of Korean musicians who made the journey to Japan in the mid-5th century, and the arrival of Buddhism a century later. With the religion came a range of instruments, including the three-stringed shamisen, akin to a banjo; the biwa, a four-stringed lute shaped like a pear with a short neck often played by wandering monks; the koto, a 13-stringed zither; a variety of wind instruments, from the shakuhachi (five-holed bamboo flute) to panpipes to the oboe; and a range of percussion instruments from gongs to taiko drums of various sizes. (If you enjoy a good percussion show, check out the infectious beats of Kodō, a Sado Island-based taiko troupe of world renown.)

Of these instruments, the shamisen is particularly versatile, being the main instrument used in *minyo* (folk music). There are a variety of folk music styles across Japan, with strong variants coming from Aomori in Honshu's far north and Okinawa in the country's southwest, where musicians play a snakeskin-wrapped local variant of the shamisen known as the *sanshin*. Shamisen musicians from up north who are making a splash in Japan's music scene include Agatsuma Hiromitsu and the Yoshida Brothers. To hear the Okinawan *sanshin*, seek out Nagama Takao and Hirayasu Takashi.

Contemporary

Japan is a country of audiophiles and deeply informed connoisseurs. Today, Tokyo is one of the best cities in the world to listen to music, with its deep network of dedicated DJ bars, jazz joints, classical music cafés, and thumping techno clubs. Likewise, record stores overflowing with rare vinyl of all genres dot the city. This isn't limited to the capital, however, with thriving music scenes found in Osaka, Kyoto, Kobe (known for jazz), and Sapporo.

ENKA

More than a century ago, trailblazing Japanese singers began to blend Western and Japanese music into a new genre that would become *enka* (roughly meaning "speech song" or "performance song"). Still immensely popular even today, *enka*, particularly from the postwar years, is the go-to genre for drunk, tone-deaf salarymen at hostess bars where mama-sans know and can skillfully croon all the classics. The nostalgic themes of *enka* songs cover the usual range of topics that were routinely touched upon in Western music in the early to mid-20th century, such as heartbreak, homesickness, and loneliness.

Some of *enka*'s leading lights include early pioneer Koga Masao, who composed a staggering 5,000 songs in his lifetime, and Misora Hibari, a legendary songstress who began performing from age nine. The younger cadre of *enka* stars includes "prince" Hikawa Kiyoshi and Jerome Charles White, Jr. (aka Jero), a young singer from Pittsburgh of Japanese and African American ancestry, known for performing in a hip-hop getup.

J-POP

Meanwhile, youth culture began to hatch its own style: J-Pop (Japanese pop). This bubblegum juggernaut of a genre was popularized by Hamasaki Ayumi, the queen, and boy-band SMAP, helmed by all-purpose celebrity Kimura Takuya. When SMAP disbanded in 2016 it was a national event. Kyary Pamyu Pamyu is a recent J-Pop singer whose saccharine hit songs and colorful fashion sense helped popularize Harajuku's kawaii aesthetic.

Another spin on the J-Pop shtick is the idol group genre, with acts like AKB48, comprising nearly 140 young female members; and Arashi (Storm), a five-member boy band, atop the heap. Meanwhile, the irresistibly catchy kawaii metal group Babymetal is composed of three young female members clad in goth-Lolita style outfits, singing bubbly tunes to a metal soundtrack, energetically dancing and beaming lots of smiles. And then there's Ladybaby, a J-Pop group with a metal edge composed of two teens donning schoolgirl uniforms and a burly wrestler from Australia suited up in knee-high socks and a pink dress.

DJS

Digging a bit deeper, DJ Krush is a renowned spinner of jazz, soul, and hip-hop instrumentals; while DJs like Ken Ishii and Satoshi Tomiie, and deeper still, Nobu, Wata Igarashi, So, Hiyoshi, Haruka, Takaaki Itoh, and so many more, provide the soundtrack of Japan's burgeoning techno, house, and underground music scenes.

THEATER

Noh

With elaborate wooden masks and enigmatic music, *Noh* is a highly refined and regimented form of theater that is downright baffling to the uninitiated. Truth be told, the arcane language (even for Japanese), long periods of inaction, and rarefied atmosphere of *Noh* are not everyone's cup of tea. But with patience, the world of *Noh* proves fascinating.

Noh plays take place on a beautiful, yet austere stage, traditionally made of *hinoki* (cypress) and backed by the painted image of a single pine tree. Much of the story in a *Noh* play is told through an arcane system of gestures, movements, and subtle expressions.

There are two main characters in a play: a *shite* (pronounced "she-te"), which is often a restless ghost; and a *waki,* which steers the shite to the climax of the play. The roots of *Noh*, Japan's oldest form of theater, are found in ancient Shinto dances. It is traditionally a male-dominated art, although women are gradually making headway in the modern age. Traditionally, female and otherworldly roles are depicted with the masks that Noh is known for, while male roles are done without masks. There are prominent families of Noh actors in Japan, well ensconced in society's upper rung.

There's an accompanying form of theater known as *kyōgen,* performed during the intermission of a *Noh* play. *Kyōgen* actors perform short humorous skits meant to both add context or comment on the happenings of the ongoing Noh play, but also to serve up a bit of comedic relief.

Kabuki

What began with former shrine maidens dancing would eventually become the theatrical art form known as kabuki (song-dance-skill). The pivotal moment came in 1603 when former shrine maiden Izu no Okuni and a number of other female dancers arrived in Kyoto and invoked the ire of the authorities with their suggestive performances.

After several crackdowns, the government decreed that only adult men could play roles in kabuki. Hence the creation of the *onnagata* (men who play women's roles), a mainstay in the kabuki world to the present day. Typical kabuki stories revolve around betrayal, samurai clashes, and dramatic suicides. Kabuki reached its apex in popularity during the Edo period, when it was voraciously patronized by the moneyed merchant class in cities like Osaka, which developed sprawling pleasure quarters.

Today, the style of theater is by far Japan's most recognizable overseas, thanks to its elaborate attire; heavily made-up actors; intense music known as *nagauta* (long song), played on shamisen, *taiko* drums, and flutes; and dramatic style of acting.

Bunraku

Bunraku is a style of theater that emerged in Osaka in the early part of the 17th century, employing puppets that are up to half the size of a grown adult. Rather than being manipulated by strings, a single bunraku puppet is controlled by three puppeteers: a leader and two others dressed in black from head to toe.

Bunraku grew out of the older tradition known as *jōruri,* in which minstrels told legends accompanied by a shamisen or biwa. The story being told, typically involving heroic feats and legends, is chanted by a narrator with exceptional vocal range who is separate from the puppeteers. Many of these tales were penned by Chikamatsu Monzaemon (1653-1724), regarded as Japan's very own Shakespeare.

The puppeteers, meanwhile move the puppets to reflect the story as it unfolds with a shamisen being strummed in the background. The result is a surprisingly lifelike performance with theatrical precision and flair that most would never imagine possible with puppets.

Contemporary Theater

Starting in the 1960s, coinciding the countercultural explosion taking place globally, new currents reached the theater scene, spawning the *angura* (underground) scene and, soon after, the "fringe theater" movement. Playwrights and thespians with an eye on creative revolution staged performances in public places, basements—anywhere they could.

Alongside those who favored overturning convention, there were some artists who connected with Japan's well of tradition. Director and playwright Kara Jūrō, for one, noted how kabuki was initially performed in the open-air. *Noh* was also. Other playwrights who were central to the *angura* period included Shūji Terayama; Abe Kōbō, the novelist of *Woman in the Dunes* fame; Shimizu Kunio; and Minoru Betsuyaku, famous for advancing "theater of the absurd" in Japan.

CINEMA

Japan's film history is peppered with illustrious names. As early as the 1930s, Japan was pumping out around 500 feature films annually.

Notable Directors

One of the earliest masters to emerge was Mizoguchi Kenji, who had been active since the 1930s but is best known for his 1954 samurai drama *Ugetsu Monogatari.*

The golden age of Japanese cinema was the 1950s. Akira Kurosawa (*Rashōmon, The Seven Samurai, Yōjimbō, Ran*) would cement his universally revered reputation during this time, along with Ozu Yasujirō (*Tokyo Story, An Autumn Afternoon*). The 1950s also saw the release of the original *Gojira* (*Godzilla*).

The 1960s saw the birth of a new genre of *yakuza* (mafia) flicks, many of which were directed by Suzuki Seijun, whose unflappable depiction of slick violence would later inform directors from Quentin Tarantino to compatriot Kitano Takeshi. The classic Tora-san series of films, among Japan's highest grossing of all time, debuted in 1969 with *Otoko wa Tsurai yo* (*It's Tough Being a Man*). The series ran until 1996, when the actor who played Kuruma Torajirō (Tora-san) passed away.

Kitano Takeshi (aka Beat Takeshi), a man

of many talents from standup comedy to acting, made his first big directorial splash with Hana-bi (*Fireworks)* in 1997. Also gaining stature around this time were Japanese horror directors like Nakata Hideo (*Ring)* and Takashi Shimizu, who directed the Ju-on (*The Grudge)* series.

Takashi Miike, a director with a cult following whose splatter quotient would put Quentin Tarantino's most violent work to shame, also came to prominence in the mid-1990s and early 2000s, with films like the horror romance *Audition*, adapted from Ryū Murakami's novel of the same name; *yakuza* tale *Dead or Alive;* and hyper-violent *Ichi the Killer,* for which vomit bags were distributed ahead of its screening at film festivals in Toronto and Stockholm. Miike's more recent output has been less gratuitously violent, with films like *Hara-Kiri: Death of Samurai* telling a straightforward samurai story, and *Shield of Straw,* a political thriller, being nominated for the Palme d'Or in Cannes in 2013.

New voices have since emerged such as Kiyoshi Kurosawa, whose film *Tokyo Sonata* garnered praise at the Cannes Film Festival in 2008. Takita Yōjirō's *Departures* won the Oscar for best foreign-language film in 2009. And in 2013, Hirokazu Kore-eda snagged the 2013 Jury Prize in Cannes for his excellent *Like Father Like Son.*

Anime

Like manga, anime is geared toward all age groups and social classes in Japan. It covers everything from history to love stories, to surreal fantasy, sci-fi, and entertainment for kids. In many ways, anime achieved liftoff in the 1960s with the legendary Tezuka Osamu's *Astro Boy* television series. Sharing the airwaves with *Astro Boy* were a host of other hit shows with names like *Space Battleship Yamato* and *Battle of the Planets* were beginning to cast a spell over Japan's youth.

Other developments in the early days of anime included some of Toei's big releases, beginning with *Hakujaden* (*Tale of the White Panda)* in 1958. The Toei animated flick *Little Norse Prince* was directed by the late Takahata Isao (1935-2018), who would form Studio Ghibli with the genius director Hayao Miyazaki in 1985.

Mentioned above as a manga series, the anime film adaptations of *Akira,* directed by Ōtomo Katsuhiro, and *Ghost in the Shell,* directed by Oshii Mamoru, are both mind-expanding explorations of metaphysical and post-apocalyptic themes, interlaced with plenty of bizarre characters, psychedelic imagery, and philosophical speculation. The late anime master Kon Satoshi (1963-2010) also produced a challenging and unique body of work in his short life. For something offbeat and unique, check out the 2006 film *Tekkonkinkreet.* The film is notable for being the first major anime feature made by a non-Japanese director, the American-born Michael Arias.

Looming above all these names, however, is anime maestro Hayao Miyazaki, the oft-grinning, bespectacled genius and co-founder of Studio Ghibli. Although he'd been churning out brilliant films since the 1980s, Miyazaki finally broke onto the international stage by winning the Oscar for best animated feature in 2001 for his masterpiece *Spirited Away.* From his deep oeuvre, some of the other standouts include *Princess Mononoke, My Neighbor Totoro,* and more recently, *The Wind Rises,* which has stoked controversy over the implications of its antiwar tone.

DANCE

Traditional

Buyō is the umbrella term for all forms of traditional Japanese dance. It extends from the dances performed by geisha to the theatrical movements of kabuki and *Noh.* All forms of *buyō* ultimately stem from ancient folk and Shinto dances. The movements of traditional Japanese dance tend to be slow, graceful, and contained. This is largely due to the fact that they were traditionally performed while wearing a kimono, which restricts movement. All told, there are a few hundred different varieties of *buyō* today.

Contemporary

Japan's contemporary dance scene exists on a spectrum between the gleeful, all-female musical extravaganza known as the Takarazuka Revue and the evocative, grotesque form of dance known as *butō,* which emerged from the urge to discard the stringent rules found in most forms of traditional Japanese dance, while tapping into something more ancient and primal. Visionary dancer Hijikata Tatsumi performed the first *butō* dance in 1959. A *butō* dancer is in an intensely vulnerable state, usually naked or close to it. Unsurprisingly, *butō* has been considered scandalous by many. This has only inspired many dancers to push even harder against boundaries and discover more cracks in the edifice of society.

Essentials

Transportation

GETTING THERE

From North America

Tokyo's Narita International Airport (NRT) and Haneda Airport (HND) are linked by direct flights to a number of North American cities. Some carriers also fly direct to Osaka's Kansai International Airport (KIX). Delta also offers limited direct flights to Nagoya's Chubu Centrair International Airport (NGO).

Generally speaking, prices vary widely, with flights from the West Coast of North America being slightly cheaper than those from the

Getting to Japan From North America

Departure Airport	Arrival Airport	Carriers
New York City (JFK) Detroit (DTW) Chicago (ORD) Los Angeles (LAX) San Francisco (SFO) Honolulu (HNL) Vancouver (YVR) Toronto (YYZ)	Tokyo (NRT) Tokyo (HND)	Delta Air Lines United Airlines American Airlines Air Canada All Nippon Airways Japan Airlines
Detroit (DTW) Honolulu (HNL)	Nagoya (NGO)	Delta Air Lines Japan Airlines

East. Although less convenient in terms of access to Tokyo proper, Narita is usually cheaper than Haneda. Deals can be found if you're willing to endure layovers. Moreover, avoiding peak season and buying as far in advance as possible (aim for three months or more) will naturally drive fares down. To fly economy from anywhere in North America, have a rough budget in mind of about $1,000 US, give or take. A stopover can bring prices down to as low as $500 US during off-season from some airports.

From Europe

Direct flights to and from the United Kingdom are getting cheaper. Carriers offering direct flights from London Heathrow (LHR) include British Airways (to NRT and HND), All Nippon Airways (to HND), and Japan Airlines (to HND). British Airways now flies direct to Osaka's KIX, too. It's generally cheaper to transfer in another European or Asian city en route.

Various carriers provide direct flights to Japan (mostly NRT and HND, but also sometimes KIX and NGO) from many European cities, including: Amsterdam (AMS), Brussels (BRU), Paris (CDG), Munich (MUC), Frankfurt (FRA), Zurich (ZRH), Vienna (VIE), Copenhagen (CPH), Helsinki (HEL), Madrid (MAD), Rome (FCO), Milan (MXP), Warsaw (WAW), and Moscow (SVO and DME).

Broadly speaking, if you're flying from Europe the budget is in the same ballpark as what it is from North America. Plan on spending roughly €850 (£750) for an economy class seat. A stopover will bring that figure down, and if you book several months in advance—three months or more is a good benchmark—you may land a bargain.

From Australia and New Zealand

It's possible to fly direct to Tokyo from Sydney, Melbourne, Perth, Brisbane, and Cairns in Australia, while most (but not all) flights from New Zealand first route through Australia, usually Sydney. Most of these flights land in NRT, although some do service HND. Carriers servicing these routes include Japan Airlines, All Nippon Airways, Qantas, and budget Japanese airline Jetstar, in addition to Air New Zealand from Auckland. There are limited direct flights to Osaka's KIX from Sydney, Cairns, and Auckland.

A stopover in another Asian city will likely make a flight significantly cheaper, but will

Previous: Randen Keifuku Electric Railroad in Kyoto

tack on quite a bit of travel time. Rock-bottom prices can occasionally be snagged through budget carriers like Jetstar or AirAsia, but don't expect a plush ride. Again, try to book tickets three or more months in advance to avoid paying top dollar.

Given that Japan is about the same distance from Australia and New Zealand as it is from North America or Europe, the budget is similar. Plan on paying about A$1,400 (NZ$1,500) for an economy class seat.

South Africa

There are no direct flights between South Africa and Japan, making for a very long journey. Major Middle Eastern carriers do fly to Tokyo from South Africa's major airports, Johannesburg (JNB) and, to a lesser extent, Cape Town (CPT). These carriers include Emirates, requiring an interchange in Dubai; Etihad, with a layover in Abu Dhabi; and Qatar Airways, with a transfer at Doha. It's also possible to fly from South Africa to Tokyo on Singapore Airlines via Singapore, Cathay Pacific via Hong Kong, or British Airways via London.

As with booking flights from other regions, try to buy tickets three or more months in advance to avoid price gouging. Expect to pay similar to the other regions described above: R150,000 for an economy seat. Tickets from Cape Town tend to be slightly more expensive than from Johannesburg.

GETTING AROUND

Train

Japan's rail network is world-famous for its cleanliness, safety, and punctuality. It's extensive, linking northernmost Hokkaido to far-flung southern Kyūshū. It can be daunting to get the hang of all the transfers and ticket deals, but thankfully, it's possible to catch on fast.

The main train operator nationwide is **Japan Railways** (JR), which has numerous regional branches. There is also a slew of private operators—**Odakyu, Tokyū, Hankyū, Kintetsu,** and more—each with their own fare and ticketing system. Regardless of the train network you're on, larger stations will have their own ticket office. Buying tickets at these offices is often the way to go if the machines feel too daunting (though most ticketing machines can be switched to English). The staff at ticket counters are generally experienced with helping overseas travelers. However you buy it, once you've got your ticket in hand, simply put it in the slot at the ticket gate, and then pick it back up after passing through. Hold on to your ticket for the duration of the trip, as you'll need to insert it again at the ticket gate of your destination. If you happen to lose a ticket, there's a chance you may have to pay for your journey again on arrival.

Another factor of train travel in Japan is speed: some routes are local, and others are express or limited express train (slightly faster), while the *shinkansen* (bullet trains that reach up to 30kmph/199 mph) is the way to go for long-haul trips. To save on fare, the **Japan Rail Pass** is a good idea if you plan to travel extensively over long distances. A number of regional passes are also sold.

If all this sounds intimidating, don't fret. Staff at train stations are happy to help and comfortable with overseas travelers. Just be ready to bridge the communication gap with a smile and a sense of humor.

SHINKASEN

Shinkansen run on an altogether different rail network than regular trains. There are two classes: **ordinary** (already a pleasant experience) and the pricier **Green Car,** akin to first class. Most of the cars of a *shinkansen* have reserved seats, which can be secured either at a ticket office or a ticket vending machine. Even if you have a Japan Rail Pass, you'll still need to stop by the ticket office if you want to sit in a reserved seat. For an unreserved car, you can simply queue and board with the JR pass in hand. Reserved seats are recommended as unreserved cars often fill up completely.

Note that *shinkansen* often depart and arrive from entirely different areas within a station and sometimes from altogether separate stations. If *shinkansen* trains run through the same station also serviced by local trains, you'll likely have to go through another set of gates to enter the *shinkansen* area. Allow at least 10 minutes to get to get to the correct platform and find the correct car.

One more point to be aware of is that the ticketing system for *shinkansen*, as well as for limited express (see below), means that you will have two tickets instead of one. There's a *joshaken* (base fare ticket), which covers the journey itself, and the *tokkyūken* (special fare ticket), which allows you to travel aboard one of the more expensive, high-speed trains. Counterintuitively, you'll need to simultaneously put both tickets into the ticket machine as you enter the gate.

LOCAL, RAPID, EXPRESS, AND LIMITED EXPRESS TRAINS

There are several different categories of local trains. Local (**普通**, *futsū / kaku-eki-teisha*), trains are the most common. Local trains are the slowest and make the most stops. Rapid (**快速,** *kaisoku*) or, trains skip some stations, while express (**急行**, *kyūkō*), or, trains generally skip even more, thus speeding up the journey. There's no extra expense to hop on either a rapid or express train.

To ride a limited express (**特急**, *tokkyū*) train, fares do jump. Moreover, these trains often have both unreserved and reserved seating, akin to the *shinkansen*, and carry a surcharge that can be bought on board or at the ticket office in advance. Like the *shinkansen*, limited express trains also require an additional ticket—one to cover the journey, the other to cover the added expense of riding in an extra-speedy train. Insert both into the machine at the ticket gate as you enter, and hold on to both tickets for the duration of your journey.

JAPAN RAIL PASS

The Japan Rail Pass (JR Pass, www.japanrailpass.net) can be purchased for either one, two, or three weeks, during which pass holders are able to travel freely on all JR lines, including *shinkansen*, as well as local buses in the JR network nationwide and the JR-West ferry that runs to Miyajima. Simply flash the pass to the staff each time you pass through the ticket gates at any JR station, bus station, or ferry terminal in the case of Miyajima, and hop aboard.

There are two grades available for the pass: regular and Green Car (first class). For the ordinary seat level, one week costs ¥29,650 per pass, two weeks costs ¥47,250, and three weeks will set you back ¥60,450. Upgrading to the Green Car will cost ¥39,600 for one week, ¥64,120 for two weeks and ¥83,390 for three weeks. For children ages 6-11, rates are lower, while children under six can ride for free as long as they are accompanied by an adult with a JR Pass and no other passenger needs their seat.

Note that the fastest categories of *shinkansen*, known as Nozomi and Mizuho, are not covered by the pass. Another thing to be aware of is that even with the JR Pass, you'll still need to go to the ticket office to get a ticket for the reserved seat.

For many travelers, the pass is a no-brainer. Even a Tokyo-Kyoto round-trip on the *shinkansen* will justify the seven-day pass for most travelers after taking into account the additional travel done on JR lines within either city. That said, the JR Pass isn't for everyone. Consider whether you will be doing enough travel to justify the cost of the pass. If you're traveling on a sumptuous budget, it's doubtful that the savings made with a JR Pass will feel worthwhile in exchange for the hassle of having to take on the limitations of the pass. If money is no object, you'll likely be happier booking transportation when and in what form you desire it.

If you'd like to book a JR Pass, you must be a **foreign traveler** entering Japan on a "temporary visitor" tourist visa. After you've bought a pass online and chosen a starting date for the pass, you'll receive a voucher at your home address, which can be exchanged for a proper pass at selected train station offices once you've arrived in Japan.

The Almighty IC Card

Your first order of business on entering a Japanese train station for the first time should be to get a rechargeable smart card, known as an IC card in Japanese. These touch-cards are available from select vending machines at a station's ticketing counter. If you have an IC card, you can recharge it any time you are running low on funds at one of the IC card vending machines at any station.

Each region has its own, with **Suica** and **PASMO** being the variety sold in the JR East network, which includes Tokyo. The JR West network, including the Kansai region, issues the **ICOCA** card, but the cards are largely swappable, no matter where in Japan they are purchased. The **Suica** card, available at stations in the JR East network, is perhaps the most flexible.

IC cards will allow you to travel on local, rapid, and express trains, as well as subway networks in most cities. For *shinkansen* (bullet train) or limited express train journeys, you'll need to buy a ticket in advance or have the **JR Rail Pass.** The added bonus of having an IC card is that you can use it at vending machines inside stations and to make purchases at many convenience stores, whether inside a station or deep in a residential area.

The JR Pass can only be purchased **outside Japan**—you cannot purchase it once you are in country. Also, you have to exchange the purchase voucher for the actual pass within three months of purchasing the voucher, so don't buy it too early.

INTERNET RESOURCES

There are some very useful sites to be aware of when it comes to train travel in Japan. **HyperDia** (www.hyperdia.com) provides step-by-step route information. All you do need to do is input the station you're leaving from and where you're going. You can also adjust the date and time, selected for either departure or arrival. **Jorudan** (https://world.jorudan.co.jp/mln/en) does the same thing. When all else fails, **Google Maps** (www.google.com/maps) is not only a trusty way to navigate a city street by street, but also allows you to compare how long it would take to make a journey by train, taxi, or on foot.

Bus

Traveling by bus is less comfortable and slower than train or plane, but it scores points for value, and sometimes it's the only option for reaching remote areas. Most towns and cities have their own local bus networks, which can come in handy in some places, but in others, it's quicker to simply walk or pay a bit more and take a taxi.

For longer journeys, highway buses operate during both daytime and nighttime, often arriving and departing near major train stations. Main bus terminals are sometimes set apart in slightly inconvenient spots, so be sure you know where your bus terminal is before a major journey.

There are eight regional variants of **JR Bus.** Some JR Bus routes can be booked at the website of **Japan Expressway Bus Net** (www.kousokubus.net/JpnBus/en). **Willer Express** (http://willerexpress.com/en) is another major highway bus operator, which offers some good deals. It's one of the few highway bus operators in Japan that allows for relatively easy online reservations in English. Willer also offers the **Japan Bus Pass** (http://willerexpress.com/st/3/en/pc/buspass), which covers all long-distance journeys for either three days (¥10,200 Mon.-Thurs., ¥12,800 all days), five days (¥12,800 Mon.-Thurs., ¥15,300 all days), or seven days (¥15,300 Mon.-Thurs.).

A number of other regional discount bus passes are available, including: the **Hokkaido Budget Bus Pass** (www.budget-buspass.com/purchase), the **Tohoku Highway Bus Ticket** (www.tohokukanko.jp/en/transport/detail_1001089.html), the **Shoryudo Highway Bus Ticket** (www.meitetsu.co.jp/eng/ticket-info/shoryudo.html), covering much of Central Honshu, and the Kyūshū-centric **SunQ Pass** (www.sunqpass.jp).

It's recommended to reserve seats ahead for any long journey, particularly if it's on a popular route. Unfortunately, many bus reservation websites are only usable in Japanese. A few exceptions to this rule include the website of Willer (see above), and the websites of **Japan Bus Lines** (http://japanbuslines.com/en).

For more information on the various types of buses and how to make them work for you, visit the website of the **Nihon Bus Association** (www.bus.or.jp/en).

Car

Given Japan's fantastic rail network, renting a car may not be the most intuitive choice, but in some regions—rural or mountainous areas, Hokkaido, the Noto Peninsula, and Okinawa—it's often the best way to go. On the flipside, cars can be downright inconvenient in urban areas, where you'll be contending with traffic, lots of narrow one-way streets, and extortionate rates for parking, which is often hard to find.

If you're traveling in a part of the country where having your own wheels makes sense, roads are well-paved and maintained, and most drivers are conscientious and follow traffic laws, speed limits aside. Driving is on the **left** side of the road like it is in the UK, which may be challenging for drivers from the United States. Traffic laws are essentially the same as what you'd expect anywhere else. If you're on a motorcycle, you'll need a helmet.

Drivers from most countries need an **International Driving Permit** (IDP). Apply for it in advance in your home country or the country of your driver's license.

SPEED LIMITS

The average speed limit hovers around 30 kilometers (19 miles) per hour on smaller streets, 40 kilometers (25 miles) per hour on medium-sized streets in cities, 80-100 kilometers (50-62 miles) per hour on expressways, and 50-60 kilometers (31-37 miles) per hour elsewhere. Signage is usually in Japanese and *romaji* (Roman alphabet). This comes in handy when navigating the country's extensive expressway network. Tolls are often hefty.

GAS

Gas stations, known as *gasorin sutando* ("gasoline stands"), are plentiful in most towns and at service areas (rest stops), dotting all expressways. They are often full-service, although self-service is increasingly common, and they may close at night. Gas prices have ebbed and flowed in recent years, but tend to hover around ¥140 per liter (0.26 gallon). Credit cards (*kurejitto kaado*) and cash (*genkin*) are both accepted. To keep matters simple, just request *mantan* ("full tank") when pulling into a full-service station. Note that rental car companies require all cars to be brought back with the tank full.

CAR RENTALS

Typically, car rentals start from ¥5,000 per day, plus daily insurance fees. Some car rental agencies give discounts for multiday rentals. Many rental cars from major agencies have navigation systems with English-language functionality. Having this set up before you hit the road will drastically simplify the task of navigating. Politely ask the car rental staff to switch the GPS system to English before you leave the agency—you'll be grateful you did later. If there's no English option for a given car's GPS, don't panic. The easiest solution is to punch in the phone number of your destination.

Japan's biggest car rental outlets include **Toyota Rent-A-Car** (https://rent.toyota.co.jp), **Nippon Rentacar** (www.nipponrentacar.co.jp), **Nissan Rent-A-Car** (https://nissan-rentacar.com), **Orix Rent-A-Car** (https://car.orix.co.jp), **Ekiren** (www.ekiren.co.jp), and **Times Car Rental** (https://rental.timescar.jp).

Although most of these agencies have some kind of English-language reservation system, **Japan Experience** (www.japan-experience.com/car-rental-japan) assists foreign travelers with making car rental reservations. **Rental Cars** (www.rentalcars.com) and **ToCoo!**

Travel (www2.tocoo.jp/en) also offer English support with car rentals.

Plane

Japan's far-reaching flight network is best used if you're traveling a long distance domestically (e.g. from Sapporo to Osaka, Tokyo to Fukuoka, Hokkaido, or Okinawa).

Carriers flying domestically include Japan's big major airlines, including **Japan Airlines** (www.jal.co.jp), or JAL, and **All Nippon Airways** (www.ana.co.jp), or ANA, as well as a host of low-cost carriers such as **Jetstar** (www.jetstar.com), **Peach** (www.flypeach.com), **Vanilla Air** (www.vanilla-air.com), and **Skymark Airlines** (www.skymark.co.jp). While some of these domestic carriers offer one-way deals as low as ¥2,000, excluding taxes, there's always a catch. Often, baggage weight limits are unrealistically strict, seating is spartan and add-on fees accumulate for a number of minor reasons.

JAL and ANA often cut fares significantly for flights purchased at least a month early, so book as far ahead as you can. Both carriers also offer air passes with flat fees for tourists on domestic flights. Check out ANA's **Experience Japan Fare** (www.ana.co.jp/en/ph/promotions/share/experience_jp; ¥10,800 per leg). If you're planning to specifically visit Okinawa, JAL subsidiary Japan Transocean Air (JTA) offers the **Okinawa Island Pass** (www.churashima.net/jta/company/islandpass_en.html). This pass, which must be purchased overseas, gives travelers the ability to hop between Okinawa Hontō, Miyako-jima, and Ishigaki-jima (up to five flights total) at discounted rates.

Here are a few destinations with airports that make sense to fly into to cut time on your journey.

- Travel to remote, northern **Hokkaido** is made easier with Sapporo's **New Chitose Airport** (www.new-chitose-airport.jp), **Hakodate Airport** (www.airport.ne.jp), and **Asahikawa Airport** (www.aapb.co.jp) for travelers interested in visiting Daisetsuzan National Park.
- If you're beginning a trip in **Kyoto** or **Kansai,** it may make sense to fly into Osaka's **Kansai International Airport** (Osaka, KIX; www.kansai-airport.or.jp) or **Osaka International Airport.**
- **Shikoku's** airports are also worth considering if you're starting from Greater Tokyo or anywhere north of there; key flight hubs include **Takamatsu Airport** (www.takamatsu-airport.com), **Tokushima Airport** (www.tokushima-airport.co.jp), **Kōchi Ryōma Airport** (www.kochiap.co.jp), and **Matsuyama Airport** (www.matsuyama-airport.co.jp).
- It can also make sense in some cases to reach **Kyūshū** by air; though there are other airports on the island, **Fukuoka International Airport** (www.fuk-ab.co.jp) is your best bet.
- **Okinawa** can only be reached by ferry or plane, plane being more efficient. **Naha Airport** (www.naha-airport.com), on the main island of Okinawa-Hontō, is by far the region's major flight hub. Flights, or ferries, to other more far-flung islands can be caught from there.

Ferry

Although Japan's main islands are linked by bridges and undersea tunnels, ferry is the only option for reaching some of the more remote corners of the archipelago, including many islands in the Inland Sea, Yakushima off the coast of Kagoshima, and Okinawa's constellation of small islands.

You can usually buy tickets through individual ferry companies or through major travel agencies. Note that the water on some ferry routes can be notoriously choppy, so it pays to ask about this if you're prone to sea sickness.

While it's a plodding way to get around, if you'd like to get your sea legs and travel Japan (mostly) by boat, the **Japan Ferry Pass 21** (http://jlc-ferry.jp/jfp21) allows holders, who must be non-residents of Japan, to take up to six trips in a 21-day period for only ¥21,000. The pass only covers second-class travel, but holders can upgrade if they pay a bit more. The pass can't be used during Golden Week (late April through early May, dates vary by year), Ōbon (mid-August) or at New Year. All ferries taken with the pass must be reserved at least five days ahead.

The best places to buy a ferry ticket are either at a travel agent or the ferry terminal itself. A ferry ticketing website that covers a good range (but not all) routes, which has an English reservation system, is **Direct Ferries** (www.directferries.com).

Visas and Officialdom

PASSPORTS AND VISAS

Travelers from 68 countries, including the US, Canada, UK, Australia, and New Zealand, as well as most European nations, receive short-term visas on arrival in Japan. The majority of these visas are for 90 days, with extensions of up to 90 days possible for a handful of countries, including the UK, Germany, and Switzerland, with a trip to the immigration office required. For a full list of visa-exempt nations, visit www.mofa.go.jp/j_info/visit/visa/short/novisa.html. Note that South African nationals must apply for a tourist visa at their nearest embassy or consulate.

Before traveling to Japan, check your passport's expiration date. It must be valid for at least six months from the date of your flight and entry into the country. Further, an onward ticket is required to enter the country.

Customs

Upon arriving in Japan, you'll be asked to fill out a customs declaration form. For this, have the address and phone number of where you plan to stay ready at hand. Simply writing the name of a city where you'll be staying won't be accepted.

A few official limitations to be aware of at customs: up to three 760-mililiter bottles of alcoholic beverages; 400 cigarettes, regardless of origin; all goods meant for personal use besides these two items may not exceed ¥200,000 in total value; a maximum amount of cash or travelers checks on hand no higher than ¥1 million; no more than 1 kilogram (2.2 pounds) of gold.

VACCINATIONS

Japan has an advanced medical system and is extremely safe from the perspective of communicable illnesses. No immunizations are required.

Festivals and Events

Throughout the year, matsuri (festivals) are held in every corner of Japan, commemorating historical events, nodding to the seasons, celebrating historic personalities, revering kami (gods), and carrying out Buddhist rites. If you can work a festival into your itinerary, you'll be rewarded with a glimpse of Japan that escapes most visitors. Japanese people are at their most casual and relaxed during festival time, making this a great time to mingle with locals.

TWICE-YEARLY

TAKAYAMA MATSURI

Takayama's old town, Apr. 14-15, Oct. 9-10

Considered one of Japan's three most visually stunning festivals, the Takayama Matsuri held twice yearly, in spring and autumn, throngs gather in the heart of the old town to witness a dozen towering floats strutted through the streets. The spring half of the event is known as the Sannō Matsuri and the autumn edition is known as the Hachiman Matsuri. The biggest thrill comes in the evenings when the colorfully decked-out floats roll through town ridden by mechanical dolls.

FUJIWARA FESTIVAL

Hiraizumi; May 1-5, Nov. 1-3; free

Once in spring and again in fall, various games, dances and a memorial service to honor the Fujiwara clan also take place during the festival. In autumn, the Fujiwara lords are again honored. There's also a parade of children in kimono, a Noh play on the stage at Chūson-ji, and various traditional dances.

SPRING

KANDA MATSURI

Tokyo, weekend closest to May 15

One of Tokyo's three biggest festivals. with hundreds of floats and *omikoshi* (portable shrines) carried by sweaty participants to the great shrine of Kanda Myōjin. It's a spectacle to behold.

SANJA MATSURI

Tokyo, third weekend of May

The largest festival in Tokyo celebrates the three founders of Tokyo's most famous Buddhist temple, Sensō-ji in Asakusa. The most visually stunning aspect is about 100 elaborate mikoshi (portable shrines), which symbolically house deities. The neighborhood around Sensō-ji overflows with *yatai* (foot stalls), games, and plenty of locals beating drums, playing bamboo flutes, and milling around in yukata (lightweight kimono).

SUMMER

HYAKUMANGOKU MATSURI

Kanazawa, early June

The city's biggest festival, spanning three days in early June each year, commemorates Kanazawa's founding by Lord Maeda Toshiie on June 14, 1583. A procession of locals in 16th-century attire marches through the streets, a special tea ceremony is held in a variety of styles, Noh is performed in the ethereal glow of torch light, 1,500 floating lanterns drift down the lazy Asano-gawa, and thousands of youngsters advance through the streets bearing red lanterns and beating taiko drums.

GION MATSURI

Kyoto, throughout July

One of Japan's most iconic festivals, Kyoto's Gion Matsuri takes place during the sweltering month of July each year. It is rounded off with a parade of truly astounding floats pushed through the streets of Gion by revelers in traditional garb. The festival culminates July 14-17, when Kyoto's city center is blocked off to traffic and residents mill about in yukata, drinking beer and nibbling on grub from food stalls.

HAKATA YAMAKASA GION MATSURI

Fukuoka, July 1-15

Fukuoka's biggest festival, a festive

atmosphere builds July 10-14, with parades and practice runs taking place, until 4:59am on July 15, when seven teams of men—one for each of Hakata's seven districts—clad in loinclothlike fundoshi transport multilevel floats known as *yamakasa,* which depict figures and scenes from the city's past, on their shoulders.

TENJIN MATSURI

Osaka, July 24-25

Regarded as one of Japan's three blowout festivals, practically all of the city participates in this massive festival. Following a ritual and prayers on the first day, the festival reaches a crescendo on the second day when (starting from around 3:30pm) locals wearing traditional garb pull opulent portable shrines the size of cars, known as mikoshi, from Tenmangū through the surrounding streets, then proceed to glide through the Ō River in swarms of boats. The evening ends with a huge fireworks show along the Ō River.

MATSUMOTO-JŌ TAIKO MATSURI

Matsumoto, last weekend of July

During the last weekend of July every year, some of Japan's best taiko, or traditional drum, troupes converge on Matsumoto to beat hearty rhythms with hefty batons. Their high-energy performances against the stunning backdrop of one of Japan's most pristine original castles make for an impressive introduction to Japan's rich tradition of percussion.

AOMORI NEBUTA MATSURI

Aomori, Aug. 2-7

Every August in Aomori city, reaching a crescendo the night of August 5, locals parade large, luminous papier-mache lanterns through heaving streets. The ornate floats depict samurai warriors, mythical figures, animals, and more. Revelers fill the streets wearing colorful, lightweight summer kimonos (yukata), nibbling on summer fare—yakitori, grilled corn—and downing beers.

KANTŌ MATSURI

Akita City, Aug. 3-6

The Kantō ("pole lantern") festival is among Japan's most visually impressive summertime spectacles. Daytime events are held around town, but the real buzz surrounds the nighttime performances that take place as dusk falls. Some 230 bamboo poles are hoisted aloft by Akita citizens, young and old, to the sound of flutes, shouts, and taiko drums. Topped with up to 46 lanterns warmly lit by candles within and sacred offerings of intricately cut white paper known as *gohei* that flap in the breeze.

TANABATA MATSURI

Sendai, Aug. 6-8

It's all about love at the Tanabata Matsuri (Star Festival), one of Tohoku's biggest summer festivals. Kicking off the festivities on the evening of August 5 (from 7pm), upward of 15,000 fireworks are launched in Nishi-kōen, next to the bank of the Hirose River on the west side of town. The streets fill with sentimental revelers who are encouraged to (literally) wish upon a star by writing out their desires on paper strips known as *tanzaku,* which are then affixed to bamboo strewn throughout the city, and to freely reveal their bottled-up feelings.

YOSAKOI ŌDORI MATSURI

Kōchi, Aug. 9-12

Kōchi's flamboyant, kinetic Yosakoi Matsuri is one of the 10 largest festivals in Japan, and the energy level doesn't disappoint. Consecutive waves of dance troupes dressed in colorful costumes jump, shout, and groove through the city's downtown streets, fill covered shopping arcades, and perform in parks, on stages next to the castle, and various other locations.

AWA ODORI MATSURI

Tokushima, Aug. 12-15

The Awa Odori Matsuri takes place during Ōbon, Japan's festival of the dead, when everyone traditionally returns to their hometown to honor their ancestors; it's as much a

remembrance of those who have passed. The formula is simple: don *geta* (wooden sandals), a vivid *yukata* and follow the lead of those around you, dancing in unison.

SHŌRŌ-NAGASHI (SPIRIT-BOAT PROCESSION)

Nagasaki, Aug. 15

On the last night of the Ōbon festival, locals parade floats, impressively made from wood, bamboo, and other natural materials, through the city, before releasing them into the harbor. These glowing barges are said to carry the spirits of the ancestors, symbolized by the lanterns they are topped with. As they drift farther offshore, they are naturally subsumed by the waves.

DAIMON-JI GOZAN OKURIBI

Kyoto, Aug. 16

Another iconic Kyoto summer festival, this is an occasion to bid farewell to deceased spirits believed to visit the living during the holiday of Ōbon, celebrated in mid-August in Kyoto. Blazing fires in the shape of Chinese characters are lit and left to burn for about 40 minutes on the slopes of five mountains surrounding the city.

KŌENJI AWA ODORI

Tokyo, last weekend of Aug.

Kōenji Awa Odori is a pulsating, fun, and rowdy festival, by far Tokyo's best awa-odori dance festiva. Although not quite as large as the one in Tokushima, more than 1 million people flock to the suburb of Kōenji to watch as troupes of drummers, flutists, shamisen players, and dancers weave through the neighborhood's streets. This is one of my personal favorites.

FALL

TOKYO JAZZ FESTIVAL

Tokyo, Sept.

Tokyo Jazz Festival brings together a world-class lineup of jazz stars from Japan and abroad for Japan's biggest jazz event. It's definitely recommended for serious devotees of the art.

JOZENJI STREETJAZZ FESTIVAL

Sendai, second weekend of Sept.

Buskers from across Japan jam in Sendai's downtown, drawing hundreds of thousands to the city center for this impressively free festival. Performances take place in the downtown area in parks, shopping arcades, and beyond, rain or shine. If jazz isn't your thing, there are also performances of other musical genres, from Latin and pop to rock and gospel.

WINTER

DŌSOJIN MATSURI (NOZAWA FIRE FESTIVAL)

Nozawa Onsen, Jan. 15

Considered one of Japan's top three fire festivals, 25- and 42-year-old men of the town fight with the rest of the village men in a literal flame battle. First, some 100 villagers build a towering wooden shrine, which, after being blessed by a Shinto priest, is defended at its base by the 25-year-olds, while the 42-year-olds guard the top. Encroaching hordes wielding torches descend on the structure with the goal of burning it to the ground. Throughout the event, participants and spectators alike are primed with a continuous flow of sake by—no joke—the local fire department.

SAPPORO SNOW FESTIVAL

Sapporo, early Feb

During the Sapporo Snow Festival, intricate, sometimes towering sculptures are made from snow and ice by teams from around the globe. Vendors sell roast corn, potatoes drenched in butter, sausages, beer, and hot cocoa, as well as a sampling of regional specialties from around Japan. Crowds gleefully mill about the city or sit under large outdoor heaters, contentedly nursing hot wine in routinely below-freezing temperatures.

Food and Drink

EATING IN

Eating a meal at someone's home in Japan is a great pleasure and a revelatory cultural experience. Most Japanese don't expect foreigners to have expert command of the multitude of nuanced table manners, but mastering a handful of small things will make a first-rate impression on your hosts. Note that most of the following also holds true for eating at restaurants.

First things first, sit tight until everyone is seated. If alcohol is being served, the meal will normally begin with a toast. In a Japanese home, more often than not, meals consist of many shared dishes, clustered in the center of the table. In this situation, turn your chopsticks around and use the opposite ends to take food from the individual shared dishes. Alternatively, some dishes may have chopsticks, or other utensils, solely used for serving. Use these instead of your own chopsticks if they are available.

A few pointers on chopsticks. Try to practice using them before making your trip. You'll feel more confident and will enjoy dining situations more. Western utensils will often simply not be available. Don't use your chopsticks to point or gesticulate. It's also considered rude to spear any form of food with chopsticks.

While you'll want to use your chopsticks to lift the food to your mouth from each small dish, when eating from a small bowl of rice in particular, it's customary to lift the bowl close to your mouth and take the rice from there with your chopsticks. In the case of miso soup, sip it directly from the small bowl. But don't lift other bowls in this manner, especially larger ones. Another point: Put soy sauce or any other kind of dipping sauce into a small dish that will be provided with the rest of the dishes, rather than pouring sauce directly onto your food, especially white rice.

When drinking, it's considered good manners—and good for social bonding—to refill the glass of anyone sitting next to you. They will likely offer to do the same. Just hold your glass in their direction. Try not to leave food uneaten—as much as you can manage. A counterintuitive "do," however, is slurping noodles, especially when served in soup. Finally, at the end of a meal try to put all your dishes back in their original places. Then, give your complements to the host by saying a hearty *gochisōsama deshita* ("It was a feast!").

A final word on coming prepared for a meal at someone's home: Bring a bottle of booze (wine, *nihonshū*, etc.), some nicely packaged tea, or a dessert that everyone can share. If you'd like to experience a meal at someone's home during your trip but don't know anyone, **Nagomi Visit** (www.nagomivisit.com) matches travelers and English-speaking locals living across Japan for a home-cooked meal.

EATING OUT

The sheer range of restaurant offerings in Japan can be daunting. Many restaurants in Japan specialize in only one type of dish. Many meals that leave a lasting impression will likely be from a chef who embodies the traits of a *shokunin*, someone who brings a sense of pride to their work. Another thing to note is an emphasis on seasonality.

Some general restaurant types include:

- **"Family restaurants"** (think: Denny's and similar), where a range of set meals and items can be ordered a la carte.
- ***Shokudo* canteens,** which are essentially cafeterias that serve simple set meals of home-cooked Japanese fare.
- **Cafés,** in the modern sense, and their antecedents, ***kissaten,*** which are nostalgic coffeehouses preserved with their old brewing methods and atmosphere intact since the postwar years.

- ***Izakaya,*** or pub-cum-restaurants with sometimes quite extensive food offerings, featuring lots of small dishes that are typically shared by the whole table (think grilled meat on sticks and various dishes that pair well with booze).
- The humble ***yatai,*** or street stall commonly seen at traditional festivals, and famously arrayed throughout the city of Fukuoka.
- The ***yokochō,*** or culinary alleyway, is another phenomenon abundant throughout Japan.

If you follow basic etiquette, your experience dining out in Japan will be smooth. First things first, when entering a restaurant, you'll be greeted with *Irasshaimase* ("Welcome, come in"). A server will likely come to you and ask *Nan mei sama desu ka*? ("How many are in your party?"). While answering in Japanese may feel like an achievement, it's perfectly fine to just hold up the number of fingers to indicate how many you'll be dining with. Now is the time to either request a smoking seat (*kitsuen seki*) or non-smoking (*kin-en seki*). Note that many restaurants permit smoking anywhere, so you may have to endure a bit of secondhand smoke.

A vast range of seating styles are found at restaurants in Japan. Besides tables (or counters) and chairs, some restaurants have tables that sit close to the ground with seating that ranges from thin cushions on a tatami floor, known as *zashiki* style, to sunken spaces in the floor beneath the table where diners put their legs. As with tatami floors in any environment, always remove your shoes before stepping on the tatami mats.

A common feature of a restaurant meal is being presented with a wet towel known as an *oshibori*, which is often either chilled or heated (depending on season). Use this to clean your hands before eating; resist the urge to wipe your face or neck with it.

If dining with a group, once everyone has placed their order, it's considered good manners to wait until everyone's food has arrived to begin eating. When it comes time to call for the check, call over a server again with a polite *sumimasen* ("excuse me"), then say *o-kaikei onegaishimasu* ("check please"). Japan is still very much a cash-based society. Unless you're at a high-end restaurant, plan on paying with cash. **Tips** are simply not accepted in Japan. If you do try to give a tip, you'll likely be chased down by the staff to return your "forgotten change." Be aware, however, that some upscale restaurants may add a 10 percent service charge or a seating charge ranging from ¥200 to upward of ¥1,000 at swankier establishments.

Unless you're going to a 24-hour chain restaurant or convenience store, you're unlikely to find good food outside typical opening times. Breakfast is usually eaten at home, but cafés will often serve "morning sets" from around 8am until 10am or 11am. Lunch is typically served from 11:30am to 2pm or 3pm, while dinner hours are usually from 5pm or 6pm until 10pm or11pm.

To make a reservation, language barrier can be a real challenge. Your best bet is to ask the staff at your accommodations to call on your behalf.

REGIONAL SPECIALTIES

On the casual end of the spectrum, popular options when dining out include ***donburi*** (rice bowls topped with various types of meat or fish) and a glut of noodles, from **ramen** (typically thin noodles), to ***udon*** (thick noodles made of wheat flour), to ***soba*** (thin noodles made from buckwheat). It's worth noting that ramen alone is said to have 26 varieties, served in a range of soups (*tonkotsu*, or pork bone-based, miso-based, soy sauce-based, etc.). *Udon* and *soba* can also be served in broth, or separately and dipped in a side bowl of broth or sauce. Another heartier casual option is ***tonkatsu,*** or breaded and deep-fried pork cutlet often served with rice, shredded cabbage and various condiments and sauces. Another great casual mainstay is the **yakitori** shop. Here you'll find most parts of a chicken (and many vegetables) slow-grilled on skewers over charcoal.

While most of the above will be prepared by a chef and served to you at a table or counter, you'll also prepare some types of meals at your table. Common examples include **okonomiyaki,** a savory pancake stuffed with vegetables, seafood, meat, cheese, and more, cooked on a griddle built into your tabletop, then dabbed in a sweet, savory sauce; **sukiyaki,** a hotpot dish containing choice thin cuts of beef and vegetables, thoroughly boiled in a pot then dipped in a dish of raw egg (it's safe!); **shabu-shabu,** which is similar to *sukiyaki*, but the meat (and sometimes fish) is merely parboiled then dipped in sauce infused with sesame or citrusy *ponzu*. Another DIY classic is **yakiniku** (Korean BBQ), which consists of meat, vegetables, and more, brought to your table where you'll cook them at a grill that is either built into the table or on a brazier that will be brought to you by the staff.

At the haute end of the spectrum, **kaiseki ryōri,** which grew out of the traditional tea ceremony, is essentially a multicourse banquet, often served at a plush *ryokan* or exclusive restaurant. *Kaiseki* dishes are highly seasonal and include a range of often inventive concoctions made with all manner of ingredients that are only limited by the imagination of the chef. Tempura, a style of cooking in which vegetables, seafood, and more are battered and deep-fried, can also get pricey at the higher end of the spectrum. And of course, the price of an upmarket sushi or sashimi spread can be exorbitant.

DRINKS AND ALCOHOLIC BEVERAGES

The legal drinking age in Japan is 20. It's worth saying a few words about Japan's most famous alcoholic beverage, **nihonshū** (rice wine; literally, "drink of Japan"). Although *nihonshū* is widely referred to overseas as *sake*, this word literally just means "alcohol." Breweries across the islands make *nihonshū* every winter using a mix of water, a special type of polished rice, and a yeast extract known as *koji*.

While a sommelier approaches *nihonshū* with the same level of nuance you'd expect of wine in the West, at a the most basic level, *nihonshū* is usually described as being either *kara-kuchi* (dry) or *ama-kuchi* (sweet). Typical ways of drinking it include *jō-on* (room temperature), *reishu* (chilled), or *nurukan* (heated). It's often poured from a small ceramic flask known as a *tokkuri* into drinking cups known as *o-choko*. When it comes to choosing *nihonshū*, as well as how to drink it, your best bet will be to simply ask for a recommendation from the staff at a bar or restaurant. It's easy to get carried away when drinking *nihonshū*, which can be deceptively smooth, but be careful: It ranges in strength from 15 to 22 percent.

O-cha is the general term for tea, and the default is green tea. While **matcha** is the type of tea around which tea ceremony is based, there are a number of other teas to sample in Japan. Roasted *matcha* is known as *hōjicha*, which is a darker brown color and less caffeinated. Warm *hōjicha* is often served for free at restaurants. A refreshing tea that tastes great chilled is *mugicha*, made with roasted barley. Sometimes you'll come across *kōcha* (black tea) too, although the aforementioned types of the beverage are more common.

DIETARY RESTRICTIONS

Eating out in Japan can admittedly be tricky if you've got dietary restrictions, from being vegetarians or vegan, to dealing with gluten intolerance or other allergies, to having religious commitments that forbid certain products (halal, kosher). To smooth things, consider carrying cards that explain in Japanese exactly what you can't eat. **Just Hungry** provides free, printable cards that do just that (www.justhungry.com/japan-dining-out-cards). In a pinch, simply saying you have an allergy to a specific ingredient will ensure that the restaurant staff does due diligence to confirm whether it's present in a specific dish or not.

A good option for vegetarians is *shōjin-ryōri*, served at Buddhist temples. *Kaiten-zushi* (conveyor belt sushi) provides a surprising number of veggie sushi (cucumber roll, pickled vegetable sushi, etc.), as well as some side dishes and desserts. Convenience stores are another unlikely option, selling a range of salads, pickled vegetables, tofu dishes, egg sandwiches, and more.

A few other good resources for finding food options with dietary limitations include the website **Happy Cow** (www.happycow.net), a global database of vegan restaurants, and the online, Japan-specific restaurant guide **Bento** (https://bento.com), which allows you to apply vegan or vegetarian filters to search results. **Halal Gourmet** (www.halalgourmet.jp) is a good source for Muslim-friendly dining options. If you must avoid gluten, be aware that some types of soy sauce may contain wheat. The **Legal Nomads** website has compiled a good guide to eating gluten-free in Japan (www.legalnomads.com/gluten-free/japan).

Accommodations

Japan has an eclectic range of accommodations, ranging from hyper-modern to traditional, with all types available for every budget. Even modest accommodations are usually well-maintained. Moreover, travelers are routinely wowed by Japan's justifiably famous hospitality (*omotenashi*).

That said, room rates in Japan can run quite high, and the rooms quite small. To avoid being charged sky-high rates, plan and book as far in advance as possible, especially during peak season (*hanami*, or cherry blossom season, in late March or early April; Golden Week holidays in late April and early May; or the Ōbon holidays in August).

The following websites tend to be particularly helpful for reserving accommodations in Japan, particularly *ryokan* and *minshuku*:

- **Travel Rakuten** (https://travel.rakuten.com)
- **Japanese Guest Houses** (www.japaneseguesthouses.com)
- **Ryokan Collection** (www.ryokancollection.com)
- **Japanese Inn Group** (www.japaneseinngroup.com)
- **Jalan** (www.jalan.net)
- **Japan Hotel Association** (www.j-hotel.or.jp)
- **JAPANiCAN**, run by travel agency giant JTB Group (www.japanican.com/en)
- **Japan Hotel & Ryokan Search**, run by Japan National Tourism Organization (www.jnto.go.jp/ja-search/eng/index.php)

HOTELS

There is a plethora of different types of Western-style hotels. At the cheaper end of the spectrum, **business hotels** are compact, no-frills options that are normally located near transport hubs. What they lack in soul, they make up for in reasonable rates. Singles tend to go from around ¥8,000, while doubles usually go for about ¥12,000 per night. There's often an optional breakfast buffet on offer.

Midrange options are readily available in Tokyo and Kyoto, where hotels with a truly boutique touch are only recently gaining more traction. At the higher end, the sky is the limit to how much you could spend on a luxury room.

RYOKAN

A *ryokan* is the most quintessentially Japanese accommodation: tatami-mat floors, futons instead of beds, and meals served to your room, all within the walls of a creaky, old wooden building. A deep sense of hospitality is something that respected *ryokan* are known for. A *ryokan* is much more than just a place to sleep. Most offer the option of an elaborate dinner and breakfast, often served to your room where you eat while lounging in a *yukata* (lightweight kimono).

Ryokan are often located in *onsen* towns.

As such, many have a private, in-house *onsen* (hot spring), which can typically be rented hourly for ¥2,000-4,000, or a shared, gender-separated *onsen* that can be used by guests and sometimes visitors during specific hours only.

Both cheap and expensive *ryokan* exist. For the full experience, expect to spend in the range of ¥15,000-25,000 per person.

BED-AND-BREAKFASTS

A traditional Japanese bed and breakfast, or *minshuku*, is typically family-owned and often set in a private home that's been converted into a lodging. They're similar to *ryokan* but tend to charge more affordable rates, and are often clustered around ski resorts, mountain towns, and hot-spring areas. More often than not, guests share toilet and bathroom facilities. Expect to pay in the range of ¥5,000-12,000 per person.

HOSTELS

If you don't mind sharing bathroom facilities and potentially even the room itself, there are a growing number of hostels in Japan, particular in larger cities. Most hostels are either part of the **Japan Youth Hostel** (JYH) network (www.jyh.or.jp/e) or operate independently or as part of a small chain. Bedding will be included in the price. Room types include both dormitory and private, with a private room in an independent hostel costing around the same or more than a private room in a business hotel. This is worth considering if you're keen to have privacy, as a business hotel room has the added benefit of a private bathroom.

JYH membership gives you a discount on prices of member hostels (usually starting around ¥3,300 for members, from ¥4,000 for non-members). JYH-member hostels often offer food (breakfast and dinner) for a small fee, but the kitchen can't be used freely by guests. They may also have a curfew. Check the JYH website to see what properties are available. Make sure you've read the fine print so that you're not surprised by strict conditions around points like the timing for check-in and check-out or whether there's a curfew.

At independently run hostels, dorm beds tend to start from around ¥2,000 at the low end, although a more realistic starting figure is ¥3,000. Normally, private hostels will have a shared kitchen and lounge. Curfews will be less common, too. Chains include **J-Hoppers** (https://j-hoppers.com), **K's House** (https://kshouse.jp/index_e.html), and **Khaosan** (http://khaosan-tokyo.com/en).

CAPSULE HOTELS

A night spent in a capsule hotel could be either a matter of urban survival for a drunk salaryman or a one-off novelty for the experience-seeking traveler. A capsule hotel is literally what its name suggests: a capsule or pod in which you can bed down for a night, with lockers outside for your luggage. You'll likely have just enough room to crawl in and lay down.

Naturally, you'll be using a shared toilet and bath. Most capsules have air conditioning, a power outlet, and a small television. Don't expect much in the way of privacy, and note that not all chains accept female guests. If a chain does accept female guests, the floors are usually segregated by gender.

Given their nature, a capsule hotel isn't a practical choice for more than an overnight stay. If you plan to stay in one of these cubes for more than a night, you'll have to actually check out each morning and then check back in. Prices hover around ¥3,500-6,000 or a bit higher for more stylish options.

TEMPLE STAY (*SHUKUBO*)

The *shukubo* (temple stay) phenomenon allows travelers to sleep in a temple. This highly recommended experience is a great way to see inside a Buddhist temple and offers guests a chance to potentially join in morning meditation or some form of ritual, such as prayers or fire ceremonies.

Two meals will be served of the Buddhist vegetarian variety known as *shōjin-ryōri*,

Love Hotels

Another "only-in-Japan" accommodation is the ubiquitous love hotel. As the euphemistic name suggests, these establishments are geared toward those engaged in the pursuit of "love." Let's face it—space and privacy are hard to come by in many Japanese homes, hence the explosion of this novel form of accommodation. Appropriately, they tend to be clustered around entertainment districts or near highway exits.

These hotels have increasingly snuck onto mainstream booking websites. The easiest way to tell if you've stumbled upon a love hotel listing will be if it happens to say "adults only" or something to that effect in the description. These rooms will usually contain an array of condoms and sex toys (handcuffs, blindfolds, whips), and are often decked out in lavish (if dated) bathing facilities. Don't worry—the cleaning crews are said to do a legendarily thorough job.

On the street, the easiest way to spot a love hotel is by its placard out front containing by-the-hour rates. More often than not, rather than dealing with a receptionist (the shame!) you'll be selecting your room from an electronic board that shows vacancies. Note that same-sex couples aren't always admitted, and multi-night stays usually aren't allowed. Prices can differ wildly depending on the area and rise dramatically on the weekends or for overnight stays. Generally speaking, renting a room to "rest in" for a few hours usually costs from around ¥3,000, while overnight stays start from about ¥6,000.

Despite the overtly risqué nature of love hotels, they can actually make for a fun experience. Rooms are often decked out in whacky themes and offer a firsthand glimpse into Japan's collective private life.

and rooms tend to be traditional (tatami mat, futon, with *yukata* for guests to wear). Depending on the temple, both shared and private rooms can be chosen, of which some have private bath and toilet facilities, while others are shared. While there are temples around the country that offer *shukubo* lodgings, the best place to experience a temple stay is in one of the dozens of temples that offer lodgings in the sacred hermitage of Kōya-san.

AIRBNB

Despite making massive inroads to so many tourism hot spots around the globe, Airbnb's footprint in Japan is notably small. This is largely due to new accommodation laws that came into effect in 2018, which imposed more stringent laws for shared accommodations, from making it mandatory for all rented rooms to have clearly marked emergency exits to requiring those running Airbnb rooms to have a license number. This doesn't mean that Airbnb isn't an option. Have a look on the website and peruse rooms if you're a fan of the service. Just be aware that the company's reach isn't as deep in Japan as it is in most places around the world.

Conduct and Customs

Japanese people have a reputation for being a bit buttoned-up. There is some truth to this, as seen in the complex etiquette that governs social interactions. While foreigners are granted quite a bit of leeway, if you observe basic customs it will be reciprocated with friendliness and appreciation. Keeping things as simple as possible, here are some fundamentals.

GENERAL TRAVEL ETIQUETTE

One important area of etiquette in Japan revolves around footwear. **Remove your shoes** in the *genkan* (entryway) of anyone's home you visit, without fail. Some restaurants will also require patrons to remove their footwear at the entrance, and castles or old-school *ryokan* also require you to slip out of your shoes at the door.

On the subject of floors, be sure to carefully handle **luggage** indoors. Try not to roll, let alone drag, any luggage across wooden or tatami floors. In fact, try to avoid putting luggage on tatami floors altogether, whether at someone's home or in an old *ryokan*.

In public, use common sense when it comes to **noise** levels. Keep your voice down on public transit, especially if you get onto a train or bus and no one around you is talking.

HOUSES OF WORSHIP

When visiting shrines (Shinto) and temples (Buddhist), the etiquette is quite similar. At a **shrine,** bow before walking through the *torii* gate that marks the entrance. After passing through the *torii*, walk along either side, but not the center, of the path that leads to the shrine. It's believed that the *kami* (gods) proceed down the center of the path. After walking farther into a shrine's ground, you'll come to a water basin, where it's customary to fill the ladle resting on the basin, pour a small amount of water on your left hand, followed by your right, and rinse your mouth with it. Finally, tilt the ladle upright so the small remaining bit of water runs down the handle, thus cleansing the ladle itself. If you want to say a prayer, toss in a coin (¥5 is standard), then ring the bell hanging over the offering box, deeply bow twice, clap your hands two times, pray silently, then bow once more and walk away.

When visiting a **temple,** you can essentially follow these same guidelines, minus clapping your hands. Note that not all temples have purification basins. Some have large incense burners where you can purchase incense as an offering for a small fee (usually around ¥100). If you choose to do so, light the incense from the other incense already protruding upright from within the ash that fills the burner, wave it around your head and body, then stick the bundle of incense sticks into the burner along with the others.

Photography can be limited at shrines and temples. Watch out for signs and heed them.

PUBLIC BATHING

Public bathing is another area where etiquette matters. When visiting an ***onsen,*** the most important rule is that you must thoroughly wash *before* you enter. Also, if you're using a small privacy towel, often supplied at *onsen*, don't let it get into the pool. Instead, either fold it up and lay it next to the edge of the pool where you're soaking or put it on top of your head.

Japan's conservative attitudes on **tattoos** is most apparent when it comes to *onsen*, the majority of which do not permit people with tattoos to use their baths. This is slowly changing. More young people are getting tatted up, but tattoos unfortunately still have a strong association with members of the *yakuza* (mafia) who have a long history of getting inked. You can avoid issues by covering any visible ink with clothing when in professional or formal situations.

ATTIRE

On the subject of attire, aim to dress slightly more formally than you may be used to. On average, Japanese people are quite dapper and, cutting edge trendsters aside, modest. You'll notice that many men wear suits, especially while working, while women tend to dress in classic cuts.

SMOKING

Be aware the smoking is still considered very normal in Japan. That said, smoking on the street isn't permitted, except in designated areas. Frustratingly for many, smoking is often permitted indoors, including in restaurants and bars. Some restaurants will have a smoking (*kitsuen*) and non-smoking (*kinen*) sections.

PHOTOGRAPHY

Ask before taking photos of people. Not only out of courtesy, but also the law. Taking photos in which people in public spaces are visibly recognizable and publishing them without their permission is illegal.

Also, watch out for places, especially at religious structures and museums, where photography is forbidden.

Health and Safety

Japan sets a high benchmark for cleanliness and safety. Your chances of encountering any serious physical danger in the country are very low. Nonetheless, arm yourself with basic knowledge on a few things to be aware of during your trip.

EMERGENCIES

If you need emergency medical assistance, dial 119. Most operators only speak Japanese, but they will transfer your call to someone who speaks English. Japanese hospitals and clinics only accept Japanese medical insurance. Foreigners will generally be asked to pay upfront and claim it back after returning home. Just be sure to get medical/travel insurance before your trip. If you do find yourself in need of medical assistance, the standard of care is high, but little English is spoken. Large university-affiliated hospitals, typically in major cities, tend to have more English-speaking doctors on staff, as do pricey international clinics, which are also usually in urban centers.

CRIME

Alongside being a very clean, safe place in terms of health, Japan is also blessed with some of the lowest crime rates in the world. Still, resist the temptation to lull yourself into a false sense of security. To call the police about a crime or accident, dial 110. For English-language help with emergency services assistance, available 24/7, dial 0120/461-997 (www.jhelp.com/en/jhlp.html). Alternatively, contact your embassy if you're not in immediate danger. On the flipside, if stopped by police, be polite and cooperative. If they ask to see your ID, you are legally obligated to show them. Sometimes foreigners are stopped in this manner. The more cooperative you are, the quicker you'll likely be on your way.

Petty theft is thankfully a rarity. If you've lost something, or suspect if may have been stolen, go to the closest *kōban* (police box). Chances are someone has handed it in. Likewise, if you lose something on a train, go report the matter to the station staff when you get off the train. Tales of kindly train attendants recovering wallets and high-end cameras are commonplace.

One common crime is drink spiking, which occurs routinely in small, dodgy corners of select nightlife zones such as parts of Tokyo's Roppongi and Kabukicho districts. If you happen to go out in one of these two areas, keep an eye on your drink to be safe. Also, never follow a tout into any establishment in either neighborhood

ILLICIT DRUGS

When it comes to drugs, beware that Japan has a zero-tolerance policy, with even first-time offenders usually charged (and jailed) or deported. In the event of arrest, try to contact your local embassy. They won't provide legal aid but may be able to recommend a lawyer or translator. You may not be given this option, however, with Japanese detention laws being rather severe, with police having the right to detain anyone without charges for up to 23 days. Japan's controversial detention practices were dramatically revealed in the high-profile detention saga of Brazilian-born French ex-chairman and CEO of Nissan, Carlos Ghosn, in 2018.

NATURAL DISASTERS

Being caught up in a natural disaster is more likely than falling victim to a crime in Japan. Foremost, there are regular earthquakes, which are usually small, but the "big one" always looms. If you happen to be unlucky enough to be in the country when the next big one strikes, drop close to the ground, cover your head and neck—either under a table or under your backpack; whatever is at hand—and hold onto something to keep your footing steady.

While rare, devastating tsunamis do sometimes strike after significant tremors. Typhoons, which sweep through the country from July through early October, as well as occasional landslides, volcanic eruptions, extreme heat waves at the peak of summer, and occasional snowstorms in the depths of Tohoku and Hokkaido during winter are other potential natural dangers.

Information on weather, earthquakes, and more is available in English on the website of the Japan Meteorological Agency (www.jma.go.jp/jma/indexe.html). The same information is also disseminated by the national broadcaster, NHK, in up to 18 different languages on their NHK World website (www3.nhk.or.jp/nhkworld).

Practical Details

WHAT TO PACK

First things first, note that storage on public transport is often limited, so you should opt for a small bag if possible. Also, before packing anything else, be sure to take a small **gift**—something linked to where you're from is best—for anyone whose home you may be visiting. This little gesture goes a long way in Japan.

When it comes to attire, everyday dress tends to be a bit more **formal** than you may be used to. For perspective, many salarymen go to work in a suit every day. For dinner in an upscale restaurant, men should pack a dress shirt; for women, a smart-casual dress or blouse should do the trick. And, of course, be sure to pack for the season. Depending on where you're going and when, you may need proper winter attire or only loose, breathable clothing. Layers that you can add or remove are almost always a good bet.

Bring a **plug adapter** from home if you're traveling from a country with a different system. (Outlets in Japan are two-prong, like in the United States.) You can check if you'll need an adapter at https://world-power-plugs.com/japan. Most electronic stores will sell them, but may only have the Japan to international version if not in a tourist hot spot/large city.

To be on the safe side, bring all **medicines** with you that you may need during your trip, preferably in the original packaging. Pharmacies (*yakyoku*) are plentiful—simply look for the internationally recognizable red cross symbol out front—but there are fewer over-the-counter medicines in Japan than overseas. In a pinch, most pharmacists can usually speak limited English and will likely be able to read and write some, too. On that subject, certain antidepressants and painkillers, which are mostly legal overseas, are illegal in Japan unless they're under a certain strength. To learn more, read the information on classes of drugs and how to bring those that are legal into the country, as explained by the **Ministry of Health, Labour and Welfare** (www.mhlw.go.jp/english/policy/health-medical/pharmaceuticals/01.html), which has also provided a helpful Q&A page on the matter (www.mhlw.go.jp/english/policy/health-medical/pharmaceuticals/dl/qa1.pdf).

BUDGETING

Japan isn't the cheapest country, but it's less prohibitively expensive than what its reputation suggests. Your main costs will come from transportation and accommodation. **Book in advance** to increase your chances of landing a deal. Further, if you'll be traveling long distances in a short period of time, it will likely pay to get a **rail pass.** Otherwise, budget quite a bit more (at least ¥10,000 per leg) for transportation—*shinkansen* in particular are pricey, and it doesn't take long for a taxi meter to top ¥2,000. Food, drink, and entertainment costs can be as high or low or as you like, as the proliferation of Michelin stars going to affordable ramen restaurants attests.

A good baseline daily budget would be around ¥8,000. This will typically get you a hostel bed (¥3,000), three cheap meals a day (¥500-1,000 each), basic transportation, and perhaps one splurge such as a café pit stop or a moderate entry fee. A good midrange daily budget would be around ¥10,000-25,000 (business hotel or private room in guesthouse from ¥8,000, dinner ¥3,000 per person at an *izakaya* or restaurant, and extra funds of roughly ¥6,000-9,000 for miscellaneous things like admission fees or local tours). For a bit more luxury, the prices jump quite a bit. A night in a good hotel will likely start from around ¥25,000, while an upmarket dinner will likely cost at least ¥10,000 per person.

To trim food costs, try to eat a big lunch. Many good restaurants offer ¥1,000-2,000 lunch sets that can be surprisingly satisfying. Alternatively, see what surprisingly substantial food items convenience stores sell, or go to a supermarket or department store food hall around 30 minutes to an hour before closing time to hunt for discounted *bento* (boxed meals).

- **Sandwich:** ¥300-500
- **Cup of coffee:** ¥300-500
- **Beer:** ¥500 for draft beer at local *izakaya*
- **Lunch:** ¥1,000 for a rice bowl topped with meat or fish
- **Dinner:** ¥1,500 for midrange meal without drinks; ¥3,000 for a meal at an *izakaya* with drinks
- **Train ticket (local):** from around ¥180 if traveling only a few stops
- **Train ticket (regional):** ¥3,000-8,000 for journeys on limited express trains; ¥8,000-25,000 for longer *shinkansen* trips
- **Hostel bed:** ¥3,000
- **Business hotel or private guesthouse:** ¥8,000
- **Small *ryokan* (often with 2 meals):** ¥12,000

MONEY

Japan's currency is known as the yen (pronounced "*en*"). Its symbol is ¥, and its abbreviation is JPY. Banknotes come in denominations of ¥1,000, ¥5,000, and ¥10,000. Coins include the small, lightweight silver ¥1, the copper ¥5 (with a hole in the center), the copper ¥10, the nickel ¥50 (with a hole in the center), the nickel ¥100, and the hefty copper-nickel blend worth ¥500. Vending and ticketing machines will often take ¥10, ¥50, ¥100, and ¥500 coins, but not ¥1 or ¥5. Generally, shops do not let you break bills without purchasing something. But, when paying, most shops will have change for a ¥10,000 note, unless you're at a flea market or street stall.

At the time of writing, the exchange rate was as follows for a range of currencies: US$1 = ¥107, £1 = ¥132, €1 = ¥117, AU$1 = ¥72. Check for latest rates at www.xe.com or www.oanda.com. Note that ATM exchange rates are often better than those offered by money changers, especially those at the airport. Reputable, but smaller exchange offices in big cities, close to train stations, will often have better rates. For US travelers, thinking of ¥100 as US$1 makes the conversion easier—just think of the last two digits of any price as cents, and you have a US dollar estimate: ¥1,750 is roughly $17.50.

ATMs are on nearly every corner in the downtown of most big cities. Give a pre-trip travel notice to your card provider, and you'll likely not have an issue using your card at select ATMs. Be aware that making a withdrawal may incur a small fee (¥216). A good rule of thumb is to look out for 7-Eleven ATMs (Seven Bank), which tend to be the most accessible for those with overseas cards. Beyond the cities, ATMs are a bit harder to find. If you're heading into the countryside, withdraw enough cash to cover you until you plan to be back in a larger town.

Japan is quite slow to the credit card game. A surprising number of businesses still only accept cash. To be safe, plan on paying for the bulk of your trip with cash.

COMMUNICATIONS

Cell Phones

To dial a number in Japan from overseas, first dial your country's exit code (00, 011, 0011, depending on country), then Japan's country code (81), followed by the number. If the number you're trying to dial begins with a 0, drop that digit, then dial it from the second digit on. To dial direct to an overseas line from Japan, follow the same procedures you would if calling Japan from overseas. First, dial the international dialing access code (010), followed by the country code where you're calling (e.g., 1 for dialing to the US), then the number. To dial a domestic number from within Japan, just dial it as is.

Japan's largest players in the mobile market are **NTT Docomo** (www.nttdocomo.co.jp/english), **Softbank** (formerly Vodafone; www.softbank.jp/en/mobile), and **au** (owned by KDDI; www.au.com/english).

Assuming you have a cell phone that is both unlocked and works on a Japanese network, you can also buy a **prepaid Japan SIM card** for it. Note that SIM cards on offer for foreign travelers often only allow for data usage. This means you'd only be able to make voice calls on internet-based apps like Skype and WhatsApp. If your phone has Wi-Fi connectivity, of course you'll be able to access the internet anytime you have Wi-Fi access.

The best prepaid card on offer right now is available through **Mobal** (www.mobal.com). You'll get unlimited cellular data, English-language support, and the ability to make and receive voice calls—a rarity among the main prepaid SIM card options—for any plan above the 30-day option (¥7,500). They send their SIM cards worldwide, so you can place your order and receive it before ever setting foot on a plane. Alternatively, you can reserve in advance, then fetch it on arrival at the airport.

For something a bit less expensive, but without voice calls and with limits on data usage, vending machines stocked with **U-Mobile SIM cards** (for one or two weeks) are found scattered around Narita Airport. You can also just walk into a major electronics shop (Bic Camera, Yodobashi Camera, Labi) and pick up a store-branded prepaid SIM card with limited data and no voice calls. These cards tend to run around ¥4,000 for a week or so of use.

Internet Access

Despite its high-tech reputation, finding Wi-Fi in Japan can be surprisingly challenging. It's often available in cafés, at some restaurants, and even in some public spaces (at train stations, etc.), but it tends to be slow or require an inconvenient amount of hoop-jumping to get what is often only 30 minutes to 1 hour of very patchy access. As a saving grace, most accommodations do offer some form of internet, whether Wi-Fi in the rooms or (bare minimum) a shared computer for emails and basic web surfing in a shared lounge.

The best way around this is to rent a pocket Wi-Fi router for internet access when you're on the go. The best pocket Wi-Fi provider is **Ninja WiFi** (https://ninjawifi.com), which offers up to 10GB of daily data use from ¥900 per day. Conveniently, it's possible to rent a Ninja WiFi pocket router along with a JR Pass, allowing you to pick up both of them at once at the airport or have them delivered to your accommodation. You can read more about this option at www.jrpass.com/pocket-wifi.

Shipping and Postal Service

Post offices are widespread throughout Japan, as are red post boxes often seen sitting beside the road. Post offices and post boxes alike are marked with a 〒 symbol. **Japan Post** (www.post.japanpost.jp/index_en.html) runs a useful English-language website where you can search for the nearest post office. It's easy to send letters, postcards, and packages anywhere on the globe for reasonable rates from any Japan Post branch. You'll have the option of attaching a tracking number to your shipment and more.

When you're on the ground, Japan's well-oiled luggage forwarding service, known as *takkyūbin*, is a major boon. This service eliminates the need for you to lug your baggage up steep staircases or through crowded train stations. Most service desks providing this service can be found at airports and train stations. Be aware that you'll need to fill a day-pack with your necessities if using one of these services, as you'll likely be waiting for your bag the day after you've sent it. To learn more about this handy service, check out the helpful **Luggage-Free Travel** website (www.luggage-free-travel.com). Rates tend to be around ¥2,000, give or take, per item.

OPENING HOURS

All offices are closed on **public holidays,** but many businesses (shops, museums, restaurants, cafés) will often be open but closed on the day after the public holiday. Department stores and many shops often operate from around 10am-8pm daily. Museums and galleries likely stay open 9am-5pm, with last entry around 4:30pm or even 4pm. They are often closed on Monday, unless Monday is a public holiday, in which case they close on Tuesday.

Bars tend to open from 5pm at the earliest, but more often start serving from around 6pm or later, then stay open until midnight or in some cases, much later. **Restaurants** normally open for lunch from 11:30am-2pm or 3pm, then again open for dinner from 6pm-10pm or 11pm (last orders tend to be taken 30 minutes or even 1 hour before closing time). Later opening hours tend to be more common in cities or for chains.

Banks tend to be open from 9am-3pm (counter can be until 5pm as well) Monday-Friday and are closed on public holidays. Some banks may be closed on Sunday and only open until 5pm or earlier on other days. Meanwhile, **post offices** are usually open 9am-5pm Monday-Friday, with some large branches maintaining longer hours and offering services on Saturdays and sometimes even Sundays (limited hours). Truly large ones will have pickup points for mail that are open 24/7.

Public Holidays

Restaurants, shops, and most tourist attractions are still open on national holidays, with the exception of New Year, when almost everything closes down. Another point to be aware of: holidays are moved to the following Monday if they happen to fall on a Sunday. Further, if there are two national holidays within two days apart, the day between them also becomes a holiday. This sometimes happens during **Golden Week** in late April to early May, when a handful of holidays are clustered close to each other.

- Jan. 1: **New Year**
- Jan. (second Mon): **Coming of Age Day**
- Feb. 11: **National Foundation Day**
- Feb. 23: **The Emperor's Birthday**
- Mar. 20 or 21: **Spring Equinox Day**
- Apr. 29: **Shōwa Day**
- May 3: **Constitution Day**
- May 4: **Greenery Day**
- May 5: **Children's Day**
- Jul. (third Mon): **Ocean Day**
- Aug. 11: **Mountain Day** (moved to Aug. 10 for 2020 only to make a long holiday coinciding with the 2020 Tokyo Olympics closing ceremony)
- Sept. (third Mon): **Respect for the Aged Day**
- Sept. 22 or 23: **Autumnal Equinox Day**
- Oct. (second Mon): **Health and Sports Day**
- Nov. 3: **Culture Day**
- Nov. 23: **Labor Thanksgiving Day**

ŌBON

Ancestors who have passed on are believed to return to the land of the living during this important Buddhist holiday. Lanterns are festooned in front of homes and around towns intended to guide the spirits to their destination, dances are performed at local festivals by everyone from children to the elderly, and people tend to the graves of their ancestors and leave offerings of food at temples and home altars. The festival is brought to a close by releasing floating lanterns into rivers, lakes, and the ocean to light the way back to the spirit world for the ancestors who have visited.

This day was traditionally celebrated form the 13-15 on the seventh month of the year on the lunar calendar (August). Today, however, many regions follow the solar calendar, which makes it fall in July (July 13-15). Semi-officially, August is the month that is treated like a holiday, with August 10-17 being one of the busiest tourist seasons in Japan, as companies nationwide let their staff take off. It's best to either avoid traveling during this peak time, or to book accommodations, flights, and more *well* in advance.

WEIGHTS AND MEASURES

Japan is on the **metric system.** All weights, measures, and distances on road signs will be in metric units.

When it comes to voltage, **100V** is the norm, unlike the 110-120V standard for the US or Europe's 220-230V. That said, the plugs are the same type as those used in the US, with two flat prongs.

TOURIST INFORMATION

More often than not, you'll find a little tourist information center inside or near main train stations or close to popular tourist spots. Staff tend to be more proficient in English on average in bigger cities, but English-language help becomes hit or miss in the countryside. Thankfully, there are usually a healthy number of English-language leaflets.

While you can't expect every tourist office to handle all of your logistical needs, many helpful members of staff will be willing to assist with things like booking onward travel, booking tickets, reserving accommodations, and more.

Traveler Advice

ACCESS FOR TRAVELERS WITH DISABILITIES

The keyword for accessibility when traveling with a disability is *baria-furii* ("barrier free"). Accessibility in Japan is improving in cities, mostly due to an aging population and the Olympics, but the issues remain in rural areas.

On the street, traffic lights are synced up with different songs that indicate when it's safe to cross. And train platforms have raised dots and lines worked into the pavement as tangible guidance. A good rule of thumb for wheelchair users would be to contact any tourist sites or restaurants ahead of time to ask about access such as a separate entrance with a ramp. Many sites marked as "accessible" will unfortunately still have gravel pathways or sharply inclined slopes.

Most train lines will have a car or several cars for wheelchair users, while the priority seats at each end of the carriage, near the doors, are reserved for elderly, pregnant, and disabled people. Also note that most trains have a gap between train and platform. To board, the best thing to do is often inform a staff member. They will then bring a portable ramp to lay down and help you on. They will also call ahead to the station you're getting off at, where another member of staff will be there at your car with a ramp to help you get off. Buses usually have priority seats too, which are sometimes stowaway seats that are often marked with a different color of upholstering.

The multilingual **Japan Accessible Tourism Center** website (www.japan-accessible.com) has extensive information about wheelchair accessibility. It also includes good information about hotels and more for a number of cities. For accommodations that do have barrier-free rooms, book as far in advance as you can to secure them.

WOMEN TRAVELERS

Japan is a very safe country, including for women travelers. There are incidences of groping or unwanted contact on crowded trains, but they are not common. In cities, trains and metros often have dedicated women-only cars to decrease the possibility of inappropriate behavior from men. Open harassment, such as catcalls and gestures, is practically nonexistent.

Although sexism is in many ways still rooted in Japanese society, it primarily affects women living in Japan. Some capsule hotels don't allow women guests, but otherwise, there are few ways in which women travelers are limited in their experience of the country.

TRAVELING WITH CHILDREN

There's plenty of kid-friendly stuff to do in Japan, from beaches and attraction parks to arcades, pop culture sites, outdoor activities, and more.

Be aware that you'll likely end up walking significant distances in big cities. Further, there are often elevators in train stations, but few ramps exist near many tourist sites. Children ages 6-11 receive half-price train fare (including for the *shinkansen*), while those under 6 are free. There is priority seating and trains and city buses for pregnant women and those with small children.

When dining out, note that picky eaters can be placated with Western-style foods like sandwiches at convenience stores, cafés, and more. There are plenty of bakeries and family restaurants with kids menus in Japanese towns, too. Note that highchairs aren't ubiquitous in Japan.

When choosing accommodation, be aware that hotels can usually provide cots, assuming there's space. Even double rooms can be quite small in Japanese hotels. Quad rooms or two double beds are rare, although triple rooms are occasionally available. For these reasons, staying in a traditional accommodation such as a *ryokan* or *minshuku* might be easier if you want everyone to be in one room. A room in one of these traditional digs will probably be one large tatami room with several futons.

If you're traveling with an infant or a toddler, when it comes time to change a diaper, changing stations are usually found in the women's bathrooms in (large) train stations, department stores, larger shops, and malls. You can pick up diapers and other basics at larger pharmacies and at some larger supermarkets. Breastfeeding in public isn't common and is somewhat frowned upon. It will likely go unnoticed if you find a corner and cover up.

SENIOR TRAVELERS

With its aging population, Japan has relatively good infrastructure for senior travelers. Be aware, though, that there are still lots of steps and little ledges (often unmarked) that you'll have to navigate. There are priority seats for seniors on trains and buses. Some tourist attractions offer discounts (even some domestic travel tickets), but are often either unmarked or only explained in Japanese.

LGBTQ TRAVELERS

LGBTQ travelers are unlikely to encounter any discrimination, especially in urban areas like Tokyo and Osaka. If anything, Japan is relatively accepting, although prejudice does still exist. Homosexuality is legal, but gay marriage isn't. Foreign marriages aren't recognized in Japan, but partnership certificates are available in several cities or districts.

Same-sex couples should not have a problem getting reservations or staying in a hotel. Regardless of sexual orientation, overt displays of affection are not very welcome in public. For trans people, the main issue may be *onsen* and bathrooms, as you'll be expected to go to one that matches your physical sex. The best solution is to rent a private *onsen*.

By far, Tokyo is Japan's main LGBTQ hub. The city's LGBTQ community throws the large **Tokyo Rainbow Pride** (https://tokyorainbowpride.com) parade in May each year as part of a multiday celebration.

For up-to-date information on what's happening in Japan's LGBTQ community, particularly in Tokyo, check out the website of **Utopia Asia** (www.utopia-asia.com). LGBTQ groups on Meetup.com are active in Tokyo, too.

TRAVELERS OF COLOR

Only about 2 percent of Japan's population is foreign-born. There's not a whole lot in the way of diversity, especially of those who look significantly different. People are mostly polite to foreigners, although the occasional microaggression and even overtly racist behavior do occasionally occur. Those with East Asian features will be assumed to speak Japanese. Expect some confusion if you don't. In general, this can make visiting Japan more of an "invisible tourist" experience for those of East Asian descent. Sadly, those perceived to have Korean features report having been the victims of derogatory comments from older Japanese.

Some travelers report that if you're black or brown, some people may appear to avoid sitting next to you on trains—this may happen to foreigners of other ethnicities too, and in some cases, small children may stare. Don't expect too much of this kind of behavior, though.

Unfortunately, blackface makes an occasional appearance on primetime television. The situation is changing, though, and social discourse around diversity is on the rise. A good reference for black travelers is the ***Black Eye*** column in *The Japan Times*, written by American expat Baye McNeil; **The Black Experience Japan** (www.blackexjp.com), where you'll find videos, interviews and more, as well as Facebook groups and pages such as **Black in Japan** (www.facebook.com/groups/BlackinJapan).

TOUR GUIDES AND OPERATORS

For a service that can connect you with various professional tour guides who can also serve as interpreters on the go, there is the **Japan Guide Association** (tel. 03/3863-2895, www.jga21c.or.jp; fee varies by tour). Its website allows you to search for licensed guides nationwide. The Japan National Tourism Organization (JNTO) also offers a system of goodwill guides who work on a volunteer basis around the country. If you employ their services, just be aware that you will need to cover their transportation, admission to any sites or events, and meals eaten during the tour. For a nationwide list of goodwill guide groups, visit www.japan.travel/en/plan/list-of-volunteer-guides.

For a more tailored experience, there are a number of stellar tour bespoke trip outfits:

Boutique Japan (https://boutiquejapan.com) excels in this area. This small Japan-focused tour operator specializes in immersive private itineraries throughout the country. They offer high-end trips, especially for travelers deeply interested in off-the-beaten-path cultural and culinary experiences. Each trip is completely unique.

Be Here (http://behere.asia) operates with a similar philosophy, albeit with less of a focus on high-end accommodation and food (although these things can be part of a tour, too!). These tours tend to put travelers in touch (literally) with local arts and crafts, and put a premium on learning in a hands-on way by taking a cultural deep dive into out-of-the way corners of the country.

Shikoku Tours (https://shikokutours.com) provide a wide range of reasonably priced tours around all corners of Shikoku. They offer single-day and multiday tours to the remotest parts of the island, from white-water rafting and exploring rustic *onsen* to doing legs of the 88-temple pilgrimage route by taxi. The staff are friendly, good-humored, and really know their stuff.

Hokkaido Wilds (https://hokkaidowilds.org) is not a tour provider per se, but is the work of an adventure sports-loving collective based on the northern island that has created an excellent online resource. On their website, you'll find loads of free, self-guided bicycle, skiing, hiking, and canoeing tours, and various other practical information on the island's deep wilderness.

As its name suggests, **Walk Japan** (https://walkjapan.com) offers a variety of trips through the country, undertaken on your own two feet. Self-guided and custom tours are possible.

If you'd prefer to get around by bicycle, there are a number of tour providers that both lead tours and create self-guided tour plans, as well as rent touring bicycles. **Cycle Japan** (https://cyclingtoursjapan.com) and **Bike Tour Japan** (https://biketourjapan.com) both offer enticing rural journeys, including both led and self-guided. If you prefer to design your own tour, check out **Japan Cycling** (www.japancycling.org).

Resources

Glossary

annaijo (案内所): information desk
bijutsukan (美術館): art museum
cha (茶): tea; often *o-cha*
chūi (注意): caution
dōzo: please, go ahead
eki (駅): train station (eki)
futsū (普通): regular; for trains, *futsū* means local, making all stops
-gai (街): district
gaijin: shortening of *gaikokujin;* although often casually used, it is an impolite term for foreigner
gaikokujin: foreigner
genkin: cash
geta: traditional Japanese wooden sandals; shoe storage closets are called *getabako* (*geta* box)
gohan: rice
goran kudasai: please look around; often heard in shopping areas
goyukkuri: please take your time (often used with dozo)
hakubutsukan (博物館): museum
hashi (橋): bridge, sometimes changes to *-bashi* when part of a name
hashi (箸): chopsticks, often *o-hashi*
hiragana: Japanese phonetic alphabet used for Japanese words
irrashaimase: Welcome! Often heard when entering an establishment
izakaya: Japanese pub with bar bites but not full meals
jiyūseki (自由席): open seating, as opposed to reserved (e.g., on trains)
kaikei: bill, check (at restaurant)
kaiseki ryōri: traditional Japanese multi-course meal
kaisoku (快速): rapid (for trains)
kaku-eki-teisha: local train; literally, stopping at all stations
kami: god
kanji: Chinese character-based Japanese writing system
katakana: Japanese phonetic alphabet used to write foreign words
kawa: river (川), sometimes changes to *-gawa* when part of a name
kawaii: cute
kin-en (禁煙): no smoking
kissaten: café
kitsu-en (喫煙): smoking
kōban (交番): neighborhood police booth
kōen (公園): park
koto: Japanese zither
kushikatsu: deep-fried pork skewers
kyūkō (急行): express (for trains)
madoguchi (窓口): ticket window
maiko: geisha in training
maki: form of sushi with items rolled into the center of a tube of rice and seaweed
manga: comic book
matsuri: festival
-meisama: party of [number], e.g., *nimeisama* is party of two; this is only used by restaurant employees when confirming the number of customers in a party, not the other way around—use *futariseki* to ask for a table of two
minasan: everyone (often heard when addressing, or trying to get attention from, a group)

misoshiru: miso soup

mochi: sweet rice cake, often *o-mochi*

nigiri: form of sushi with an oblong ball of rice topped with a piece of fish

okonomiyaki: Japanese savory pancake

okyakusan/okyakusama: customer

otsumami: snacks

otsuri: change (when making a purchase)

rotenburo: open-air *onsen*

ryokan: traditional Japanese inn

ryokō/ryokōsha: travel/traveler

sakura: cherry blossom

shakuhachi: traditional Japanese flute-like instrument

shamisen: traditional Japanese guitar-like instrument

shima (島): island; *shima* sometimes changes to *-jima* when paired with the name of the island

shiteiseki (指定席): reserved seating (e.g., on trains)

shosho omachikudasai: please wait a momment

shōjin-ryōri: Buddhist vegetarian food

shokuji: meal

shukubo: temple lodging

takoyaki: octopus dumpling

tera: temple; often *o-tera; tera* sometimes changes to *-dera* when paired with the name of the temple

tokkyū (特急): limited express (for trains)

tomare (止まれ): stop

tonkatsu: pork cutlet

torii: gate at Shinto shrines

uketsuke (受付): reception desk

washiki: Japanese-style toilet

yakiniku: grilled meat

yakitori: grilled chicken on skewers

yama (山): mountain; **山** is also read *san* and sometimes *zan* when paired with the name of the mountain

yakuza: Japanese mafia

yokochō: culinary alleys; side streets lined with food stands

yōshiki: Western-style toilet

yukata: lightweight kimono worn in the summer or as loungewear at *ryokan*

Japanese Phrasebook

ALPHABETS AND WRITING

The phonetic alphabets used in Japanese (hiragana and katakana) are made up of five vowels, same as English (*a, i, u, e, o*), 39 consonant-noun pairs (*ka, ki, ku, ke, ko, sa, shi su, se, so*, etc.), plus one single consonant (*n*) and one single particle (*o*). The consonants *k, s, t, n, h, m, and r* are paired with each of the five vowels, with a few exceptions: there's *shi* instead of si; *chi* instead of ti; *tsu* instead of tu; *fu* instead of hu. *Y* is only paired with a, u, and o (*ya, yu, yo*); and *w* is only paired with a (*wa*).

This base 46-letter alphabet is extended with symbols that look like straight quotes (") on the k set to make the g sound (so, *ka* becomes *ga, ki* becomes *gi*, etc.); the *s* set to make the *z* sound (except for *shi*, which becomes *ji*), the *t* set to make the *d* sound (except for *chi*, which becomes *ji*, and *tsu*, which becomes *zu*), and the *h* set to make the *b* sound. A symbol that looks like the degree symbol (°) also can appear with the *h* set to make the *p* sound.

Kanji is the writing system that uses Chinese characters and is not phonetic. Kanji is what makes reading even the most basic signs and notices, let alone newspapers, a bit intimidating. (For reference, 2,136 characters are listed as *jōyō kanji*, or commonly used kanji.) Latin characters are called *romaji* in Japanese, and many signs are also written in *romaji*, especially in cities.

PRONUNCIATION

Despite the difficult-looking characters, Japanese words are pronounced phonetically, so try saying them the way they look, and you won't

Hiragana and Katakana

English	wa	ra	ya	ma	ha	na	ta	sa	ka	a
hiragana	わ	ら	や	ま	は	な	た	さ	か	あ
katakana	ワ	ラ	ヤ	マ	ハ	ナ	タ	サ	カ	ア
English		ri		mi	hi	ni	chi	shi	ki	i
hiragana		り		み	ひ	に	ち	し	き	い
katakana		リ		ミ	ヒ	ニ	チ	シ	キ	イ
English		ru	yu	mu	fu	nu	tsu	su	ku	u
hiragana		る	ゆ	む	ふ	ぬ	つ	す	く	う
katakana		ル	ユ	ム	フ	ヌ	ツ	ス	ク	ウ
English	-n	re		me	he	ne	te	se	ke	e
hiragana	ん	れ		め	へ	ね	て	せ	け	え
katakana	ン	レ		メ	ヘ	ネ	テ	セ	ケ	エ
English	o	ro	yo	mo	ho	no	to	so	ko	o
hiragana	を	ろ	よ	も	ほ	の	と	そ	こ	お
katakana	ヲ	ロ	ヨ	モ	ホ	ノ	ト	ソ	コ	オ
English					ba/pa		da	za	ga	
hiragana					は″/は°		た″	さ″	か″	
katakana					ハ″/ハ°		タ″	サ″	カ″	
English					bi/pi		ji	ji	gi	
hiragana					ひ″/ひ°		ち″	し″	き″	
katakana					ヒ″/ヒ°		チ″	シ″	キ″	
English					bu/pu		dzu	zu	gu	
hiragana					ふ″/ふ°		つ″	す″	く″	
katakana					フ″/フ°		ツ″	ス″	ク″	
English					be/pe		de	ze	ge	
hiragana					へ″/へ°		て″	せ″	け″	
katakana					ヘ″/ヘ°		テ″	セ″	ケ″	
English					bo/po		do	zo	go	
hiragana					ほ″/ほ°		と″	そ″	こ″	
katakana					ホ″/ホ°		ト″	ソ″	コ″	

be as far off as you might think. Following the pronunciation tips below, especially for the vowels, will increase your success.

Vowels

Speakers of Spanish will have no problem pronouncing the vowels in Japanese, as they are pronounced the same way. Japanese puts vowels in a different order than in English, and we've used the Japanese order.

SHORT VOWELS

a pronounced *ah*, like ta-da

i pronounced *ee*, like saying the vowel "e" in English

u pronounced *oo*, like food; sometimes reduced or silent when at the end of a word (e.g., *desu* often sounds like *des*)

e pronounced *eh*, like educate

o pronounced somewhat like *oh* but with a lighter touch; words like "go" and "no" in English end with a slight "u" sound—the same words/syllables with a short "o" in Japanese are pronounced without that "u" at the end

LONG VOWELS

Long vowels in Japanese are indicated by a macron over the vowel (ō) or by a repeated letter (aa, ii, uu, ee). When a macron hasn't been used, the long o is spelled either *oo* or *ou*, depending on its hiragana spelling. Long vowels are pronounced by simply holding the sound of the short vowel for longer. (There is a slight pronunciation difference between *oo* and *ou*, but not one beginners should worry about.)

VOWEL COMBINATIONS

Vowel combinations are essentially pronounced as each vowel would be individually, although a few are more distinct.

ai pronounced like a long *i* in English, e.g., *tai* is pronounced tie

ao pronounced somewhat like *ow*, like in renown

ei pronounced like a long *a* in English, like in ace

Consonants and Consonant-Vowel Combinations

Consonants in Japanese are generally pronounced as they are in English, keeping the following notes in mind. Note that the Japanese alphabet does not use the consonants c by itself (although ch is used), l, q, v, or x. Nor is the sound "th" used.

g at the beginning of a word, always hard, as in *game*, no matter what vowel follows it; in the middle of a word, often pronounced like the g in *song*, but pronouncing it as a hard g in all cases is fine

r somewhere between the English r and l, but just pronouncing it as an English r is fine

tsu this combination is rare in English, but there is a Japanese word commonly used in English that includes it: tsunami

When two consonants are together, there is usually a slight pause between them.

In some cases, when preceded by a certain sound, words that would normally be said/written with a *k* are pronounced/written with a *g*, an *s* with a *z*, a *t* with a *d*, and an *h* with a *b* or a *p*. An example of this is *hyaku* (100) changing to *-byaku* in some cases (as in *sanbyaku* or 300) or *-pyaku* in others (as in *roppyaku* or 600).

Intonation

Japanese is not a tonal language, and stresses on syllables are subtle. Beginners should try to speak without putting too much emphasis on any particular syllable.

PHRASES

Although macrons are used in the rest of the book, long vowels in this phrasebook are depicted with repeated letters (or ou when relevant) to help with pronunciation. The particle *o* (**を** in hiragana) is spelled "wo" in romaji, but in this phrasebook "o" is used since that is how it is pronounced. Similarly, the particle **は** is spelled with the *ha* hiragana, but in this phrasebook, it's spelled "wa" to reflect the pronunciation.

Many Japanese nouns below start with "o," although if you were to look them up in an English-Japanese dictionary, the word without the "o" would appear. The "o" prefix makes the word more polite.

General

Excuse me Sumimasen

Do you speak English? Eigo o hanasemasu ka?

Hello (during the day) Konnichiwa

Hello (after dark) Konbanwa

Good morning Ohayougozaimasu (only said first thing in the morning)

Good night Oyasuminasai (literally, get rest; only said when turning in for the night)

Good-bye Sayounara

Thank you Arigatou (casual)/arigato gozaimasu (polite)

please onegaishimasu (literally, "I wish for this")

I'm sorry Gomennasai

yes hai

no iie

I don't understand Wakarimasen

I don't speak Japanese. Nihongo o hanasemasen.

Could you write that down? Sore o kaitekuremasen ka?

Where is/where are…? …wa doko desu ka?

Where are the restrooms? Otearai wa doko desu ka?

Do you have this in Latin characters/ English? Romaji/Eigo de kaitearu no arimasu ka?

I would like…/may I have… …kudasai (literally, "please give me") or ….onegaishimasu (e.g., *miso ramen kudasai* is "I would like/may I have the miso ramen")

I'm looking for… …o sagashite imasu (e.g., deguchi o sagashite imasu—I'm looking for the exit.)

How much is this? Ikura desu ka?

Can you take our picture? Shashin o totte kuremasenka?

Note: "How are you" is a useful phrase in English, but it is not as ubiquitous in Japanese conversation and does not have an easy Japanese equivalent. The closest is *genki desu ka?,* which translates to "are you healthy?" and would be odd to say to someone upon entering a shop, for example.

Terms of Address

In Japanese, the terms "I," "me," and "you" are generally omitted from sentences. "You," in particular, should be avoided. When you are being addressed by a sales person or someone in the service industry, most likely you will be called *okyakusama* (customer) or, if your name is known, by your last name with *-san* or *-sama.*

Mr./Mrs./Ms. … …-san (regular), -sama (very polite, used for people in a higher station than the speaker); for example, Ms. Suzuki is Suzuki-san or Suzuki-sama

I/me watashi

My name is … …to moushimasu (Note: Japanese people go by their last names, and first names are generally only used with friends and family. Foreigners can use either to introduce themselves—use whichever name they would like to be called by.)

adult otona

child kodomo

Directions and Transportation

(travel) information desk (ryokou) annaijo (旅行)案内所

map chizu 地図

here koko

there soko

over there asoko

left hidari 左

right migi 右

up ue 上

down shita 下

straight massugu

north kita 北

south minami 南

east higashi 東

west nishi 西

entrance iriguchi 入口

exit deguchi 出口

in front of mae

behind ushiro, ura

next to tonari

road douro/-douri (as part of a name) 道路/通り

street michi 道

signal shingou

bridge hashi/-bashi 橋

address juusho 住所

bicycle jitensha 自転車

car kuruma 車

taxi takushii タクシー

subway chikatetsu 地下鉄

train ddensha 電車

train station eki 駅

train platform hoomu ホーム

[Number] track number [number]-ban sen [number character]番線

[Number] train car [number]-gousha [number character]号車

What track number/train car? Nan ban sen/nan gousha desu ka?

plane hikouki 飛行機

airport kuukou 空港

bus basu バス

bus stop/station basu tei

ticket window madoguchi 窓口

How do I get to…? Douyatte…ni ikimasuka?

How far is it to… …wa dono gurai desu ka?

Is it close/far? Chikai/toi desu ka?
I want to go to… …ni ikitai desu.
kilometer kiro (also used for kilogram) キロ
I would like [one, two, etc.] (tickets) (Kippu) [ichi, ni, etc.]-mai kudasai. Note that including *kippu* is optional since what you are requesting would be clear from the context.
one-way katamichi 片道
roundtrip oufuku 往復
luggage nimotsu 荷物

Accommodations

hotel hoteru ホテル
traditional inn ryokan 旅館
key kagi 鍵
room heya 部屋
single room hitoribeya
double room futaribeya
western-style rooms (i.e., beds not futons)/Japanese-style rooms youshitsu/washitsu
I want to check in Cheku in onegaishimasu.
I want to check out Cheku aoto shimasu.
Can I get another key? Kagi mou hitotsu onegaishimasu. (If asking for more than one, change "hitotsu" to the counter number you want.)
Can I get another towel/ blanket? Taoru/Moufu mou ichimai onegaishimasu. (If asking for more than one, change "ichi" to the number you want.)
I can't get into my room. Heya ni hairemasen.
Is breakfast/are meals included? Asagohan/shokuji tsuki desu ka?
What time does breakfast start/ end? Asagohan wa nanji kara/made desu ka?

Food and Drink

breakfast asagohan 朝ご飯
lunch hirugohan 昼ご飯
dinner bangohan 晩ご飯
restaurant resutoran レストラン
A table for one/two, please Hitori/futari seki onegaishimasu (if asking for more than two people, change *hitori-/futari* seki to *[number]-nin* seki)
chopsticks ohashi
fork fooku
spoon supuun
knife naifu
napkin napukin
menu mennyu
water omizu お水
coffee koohii コーヒー
tea ocha お茶
cream kuriimu
beer biiru ビール
sake osake 酒
wine wain
milk gyuunyuu/miruku
bread pan
egg tamago 卵
fish sakana 魚
shrimp ebi 海老
Meat niku 肉
pork buta 豚肉
beef gyuuniku/biifu 牛肉
chicken toriniku/chikin 鶏肉
ramen ramen ラーメン
sushi sushi 寿司
sugar sato
I would like to order Chuumon onegaishimasu
I would like the check Okaikei onegaishimasu
to eat taberu 食べる
to drink nomu 飲む
I cannot eat… …o taberaremasen.
I cannot drink… o nomemasen.
vegetarian/vegan bejitarian/biigan

Money and Shopping

money okane お金
bank ginkou 銀行
post office yuubinkyoku 郵便局 (Note: Post offices in Japan perform banking functions and are a reliable place to find an ATM.)
shop mise 店
How much is this? Ikura desu ka?

Can I pay by credit card? Kaado de harattemo ii desu ka?

Can I try this on? Shichaku shitemo ii desu ka?

postcard hagaki

souvenir omiyage

Problems and Health

Help me! (emergency) Tasuketekudasai!

I lost... ...o nakushimashita

My...was stolen. ...ga nusumaremashita.

wallet saifu

phone/cell phone denwa/keitai denwa

passport pasupouto

I don't feel well Guai warui desu.

I feel sick to my stomach Onaka ga itai desu.

(I need to go to the) hospital/ doctor Byouin/isha (ni ikanakereba narimasen). **病院/医者**

It/that hurts Itai desu

fever Netsu **熱**

drugstore yakkyoku **薬局**

medicine kusuri **薬**

earthquake jishin **地震**

typhoon taifuu **台風**

embassy taishikan **大使館**

police keisatsu **警察**

Numbers

1 ichi **一**

2 ni **二**

3 san **三**

4 yon/shi **四**

5 go **五**

6 roku **六**

7 nana/shichi **七**

8 hachi **八**

9 kyuu/ku **九**

10 juu/too **十**

14 juuyon (not juushi) **十四**

17 juushichi/juunana (both okay) **十七**

20 nijuu **二十**

30 sanjuu **三十**

40 yonjuu **四十**

50 gojuu **五十**

60 rokujuu **六十**

70 nanajuu **七十**

80 hachijuu **八十**

90 kyuujuu **九十**

100 hyaku **百**

300 sanbyaku **三百**

400 yonhyaku (not shihyaku) **四百**

600 roppyaku **六百**

700 nanahyaku (not shichihyaku) **七百**

800 happyaku **八百**

1,000 sen **千**

10,000 man **万**

For numbers greater than 10, just combine the words for each digit. For example, 14 is *juuyon*: *juu* for the 10s digit and *yon* for the 1s digit. Similarly, for three-digit numbers, combine the various units: 256 is *nihyaku gojuu roku.*

Counting

Counting is complicated in Japanese because how you count depends on what you are counting. For example, the counter for small items (e.g., small fruits) is *-ko* (ikko, niko, sanko, etc.), the counter for flat items is *-mai* (e.g., tickets, postcards, shirts, etc.), for long narrow items (e.g., bottles of beer) is *-hon* (which changes to *-pon* for three and six), and the list goes on. A good default is *-tsu,* which is also meant for small items but only goes up to nine items. Beyond nine items, just try using the number with no counter.

1 hitotsu

2 futatsu

3 mittsu

4 yottsu

5 itsutsu

6 mutsu

7 nanatsu

8 yattsu

9 kokonotsu

Time

day nichi **日**

today kyou **今日**

yesterday kinou **昨日**

tomorrow ashita **明日**

morning asa **朝**

before noon/am gozen **午前**

noon hiru **昼**

afternoon/pm gogo 午後
evening ban 晩
night yoru 夜
[number] o'clock [number] ji (e.g., goji) [number] 時
What time is it? Nanji desu ka?
What time are we leaving? Nanji ni shuppatsu shimasuka?

Days of the Week

Monday getsuyoubi 月曜日
Tuesday kayoubi 火曜日
Wednesday suiyoubi 水曜日
Thursday mokuyoubi 木曜日
Friday kinyoubi 金曜日
Saturday doyoubi 土曜日
Sunday nichiyoubi 日曜日

Months

January ichigatsu 一月
February nigatsu 二月
March sangatsu 三月
April shigatsu (not yongatsu) 四月
May gogatsu 五月
June rokugatsu 六月
July shichigatsu (not nanagatsu) 七月
August hachigatsu 八月
September kugatsu 九月
October juugatsu 十月
November juuichigatsu 十一月
December juunigatsu 十二月

Dates

To express dates, the first part of the month doesn't follow the same pattern as the rest of the month. After the 10th, the dates follow the pattern *number + nichi*. There are a few exceptions, which are listed below. Also, except for *tsuitachi,* the dates also double as the counter for the number of days.

1st tsuitachi 一日
2nd futsuka 二日
3rd mikka 三日
4th yokka 四日
5th itsuka 五日
6th muika 六日
7th nanoka 七日
8th youka 八日
9th kokonoka 九日
10th tooka 十日
14th juu-yokka 十四日
17th juu-shichinichi 十七日
20th hatsuka 二十日
21th nijuu-ichinichi 二十一日
24th nijuu-yokka 二十四日
27th nijuu-shichinichi 二十七日

Suggested Reading

HISTORY

Embracing Defeat: Japan in the Aftermath of World War II (John W. Dower, 1999). This engaging tome explores Japan's rough road to recovery through the prism of the years after World War II. The book draws on numerous first-person accounts, documentary photographs from the period, and piercing historical analysis. This book, which won both the Pulitzer and the National Book Award for Nonfiction, is a powerfully focused lens onto the ways that World War II altered Japan's psyche and destiny forever.

Lafcadio Hearn's Japan: An Anthology of his Writings on the Country and Its People (1997). Lafcadio Hearn was the West's first great interpreter of things Japanese. During his time working as an English teacher in Matsue and Kyūshū, and later as a journalist in Kobe and a professor of literature in Tokyo, he penned a number of influential early works on the country.

CULTURE

A Geek in Japan: Discovering the Land of Manga, Anime, Zen, and the Tea Ceremony (Hector Garcia, 2019). Just released in revised and expanded form, this hit explores

Japanese pop culture from A to Z. It also unravels many arcane social constructs and rituals, and elucidates topics ranging from architecture to video games. It's beautifully illustrated with hundreds of photos, too, making it a great visual primer on contemporary Japan as a whole.

Yokai Attack! (Hiroko Yoda and Matt Alt, 2012). This fun, light series consists of three books: *Yokai Attack: The Japanese Monster Survival Guide, Ninja Attack: True Tales of Assassins, Samurai, and Outlaws,* and *Yurei Attack: The Japanese Ghost Survival Guide.* Each volume explores a different aspect of Japan's rich lore, ranging from the supernatural (*Yokai Attack* and *Yurei Attack*) to historical figures (*Ninja Attack*) with serious battlefield cred. Playful illustrations breathe life into the outlandish tales contained in the books.

SOCIETY

Tokyo Vice: An American Reporter on the Police Beat in Japan (Jake Adelstein, 2010). In this colorful memoir, American investigative journalist Adelstein tells all about his 12 years of reporting on Tokyo's underworld, from murder and corruption to human trafficking and plenty of *yakuza* (mafia).

You Gotta Have Wa (Robert Whiting, 2009). Baseball is a bigger deal than sumo in Japan. This brilliant blend of baseball and social commentary gives a humorous, behind-the-scenes glimpse at what happened when American sluggers began to move to Japan, where the decidedly American game has taken on a life of its own, including a very Japanese preoccupation with harmony (*wa*) above winning.

FOOD AND DRINK

Rice, Noodle, Fish: Deep Travels Through Japan's Food Culture (Matt Goulding, 2015). This lauded book is written in a literary voice and comes with a visual feast of images from across Japan's exceptional culinary world. Goulding explores the food culture of Japan's great cities—Tokyo, Osaka and Kyoto—but also ventures farther afield to Hiroshima, Fukuoka, Hokkaido, and the remote Noto Peninsula.

Food, Sake, Tokyo (Yukari Sakamoto, 2010). This book follows chef, sommelier, and writer Yukari Sakamoto through Japan's vast capital, exploring its department store food halls, sake bars, *izakaya*, markets, and more. The book brilliantly decodes arcane dishes, explains a range of exotic ingredients, gives the lowdown on which fish are in season at various times of year, gives a sake primer, and introduces Tokyo's brilliant food culture.

TRAVEL WRITING

The Inland Sea (Donald Richie, 1971). This timeless book, written by Japan's foremost interpreter of the 20th century, is an elegiac hymn to the joys of traveling in "old Japan"—specifically, the dazzling Inland Sea. Part memoir, part travel narrative, Richie muses on what was then—and only more so now—a vanishing way of life. He describes the seascape, the tiny island towns, and his encounters with a host of characters with great humanity, humor, and warmth. The result is a dreamlike travelogue on Japan that remains unsurpassed.

The Roads to Sata: A 2,000-Mile Walk Through Japan (Alan Booth, 1997). This insightful, often hilarious travelogue recounts the author's walk from the northern tip of Hokkaido to Kyūshū's far south, along back country lanes. His poignant descriptions of rural Japan, and the people he met along the way—from fishermen to bar owners—reveal a salty side of Japan that remains hidden to the vast majority of foreign visitors.

MEMOIR

Lost Japan: Last Glimpse of Beautiful Japan (Alex Kerr, 1993). This beautifully written and award-winning book—impressively first written in Japanese, then translated into English—weaves together three decades of the author's rich life experience in Japan. Kerr takes readers deep into the kabuki theater scene, Tokyo's boardrooms during the heady 1980s (before the bubble had popped), Kyoto's rarefied traditional arts, and the remote Iya Valley of Shikoku where he would ultimately make a home. Juxtaposing all this beauty is a sense that Japan's ancient traditions and natural splendor have been blemished by the country's race to modernize.

The Lady and the Monk: Four Seasons in Kyoto (Pico Iyer, 1992). This book recounts the year that celebrated travel writer Pico Iyer first came to Japan to study Zen Buddhism at a monastery—a goal that didn't last long—and ultimately fell in love with a woman who would eventually become his wife. The book is very much a love letter penned by a besotted young Iyer. He followed up this work recently with *Autumn Light* (2019), a deeply mature, meditative book on the passage of time, ageing, and how decades living in Japan have informed his outlook on life.

Internet Resources and Apps

TRAVEL

www.japan.travel/en

The Japan National Tourism Organization (JNTO) promotes travel to Japan and provides a good deal of English-language information on its website. It's a good place to go for trip ideas and suggested itineraries, and to download maps (www.japan.travel/en/things-to-do).

www.outdoorjapan.com

Outdoor Japan's website and full-color, seasonal print magazine cover Japan's wild side. It's a great resource for discovering outdoor adventure opportunities in off-the-radar areas.

NEWS AND MEDIA

www.japantimes.co.jp

The Japan Times is Japan's largest English-language newspaper. It's a good resource for keeping up on news, learning about local happenings, and checking out event listings.

https://gaijinpot.com

GaijinPot is a portal for the foreign community in Japan that runs great content on everything from culture and travel to what it takes to set up a life in Japan. Its Japan 101 section is packed with practical information on topics ranging from banking to doctors.

www.kansaiscene.com

In addition to the website, Kansai Scene free print zines are found at more than 300 pickup points in Kyoto, Osaka, Nara, Hyogo, Shiga, and Wakayama prefectures. It's a great portal into the Kansai region, including features about culture and happenings in the region, food and nightlife options, and event listings.

FOOD

https://tabelog.com/en

Tabelog's national restaurant database is comprehensive, including information like business hours, average prices, etc. You can search restaurants by location and cuisine type, as well as make informed decisions on where to eat based on user rankings. Anything with a rating above 3.5 stars tends to be dependably good.

https://gurunavi.com

Gurunavi is a good supplement to Tabelog, which scores points for its user rating system (allowing for discernment), but is more limited in its English-language coverage.

Gurunavi, however, lacks Tabelog's useful user rating system. If you use both websites creatively, you'll usually be able to find a good choice for a meal anywhere you go.

TICKET RESERVATION SERVICES

www.ticketsgalorejapan.com

Tickets Galore Japan, a ticket proxy service, is a godsend. Basically, you contact the service about ticket(s) for an event you'd like to attend. The service then buys the ticket(s) on your behalf, charging a reasonable service fee. This saves massive hassle and potentially losing out on great events, as buying tickets for events in Japan—let alone from overseas—can be quite convoluted at the best of times.

TRANSPORTATION

www.hyperdia.com/en

While in Japan, Hyperdia, a user-friendly train trip-planning website, will quickly become your new friend. The website allows you to input your starting point and destination, then gives you a full itinerary for a train journey, accurate to the minute. There are many other search options, such as boxes where you can select what categories of train (local, express, etc.) you'd like to include in the search results. Note that it is available as a smartphone app for both Android and iOS.

ONLINE LANGUAGE SERVICES

https://jisho.org

Denshi Jisho, and easy-to-use online dictionary, has a mercifully simple user interface. It'll come in handy when you're searching for the name of a dish or asking for medicine at a pharmacy.

https://translate.google.com

It may seem too obvious to mention, but Google Translate also does a great job with translating on the fly.

MONEY

www.xe.com

XE is a user-friendly, up-to-date currency conversion website that also has an app for both Android and iOS. Download it so you can convert prices in yen on the fly.

HEALTH

Japan Hospital Guide

In case you need to find a hospital on the road, this app draws on data from Google Maps to provide information on hospitals and clinics. All pertinent details—opening hours, phone numbers, and more—are given. Be aware that you'll have to allow your smartphone to know your location for the app to work.

CHAT APPS

https://line.me/en

If you plan to make any new friends in Japan, forget WhatsApp. The chat app of choice here, hands down, is Line. It's available on both iOS and Android, and has an English option, so downloading it and setting it up is pretty self-explanatory.

Index

A

B

C

D

E

F

G

H

I

J

K

L

M

N

S

T

INDEX

U V

W

Y

Z

Acknowledgments

Putting together a guidebook on a country as dense and complex as Japan wouldn't have been possible without the help of many bright, generous people along the way. Foremost, I want to thank Tom Vater for introducing me to the brilliant staff at Avalon Travel after I discovered an ad posted on Craigslist. And huge thanks to everyone at Avalon who has helped make this book a reality: Nikki, Kristi, Grace, Megan, Hannah, Ravina, Albert, and many more who have had a hand in the project. Thank you all for your sage guidance, hard work, flexibility and patience with bringing this lengthy book to completion!

Japan-side, I want to first express gratitude to Jeff W. Richards, a fantastic editor, writer and friend. Jeff, your assistance with making introductions at key times and generally bouncing around ideas has been invaluable. Huge thanks also to Kirsty Bouwers who helped greatly with a number of nitty-gritty tasks: research, contacting tourism boards, hunting down and cataloging images, and much more. And Nana Egawa, thank you so much for your help with many things, from simplifying transport logistics and making phone calls to road-testing itinerary ideas and driving me around some remote corners of Honshu. It's been a pleasure!

I want to thank Michinori Yamasaki at the JNTO for introducing me to a number of tourism offices across the country. I also want to give a special thanks to Kyoto City Tourism Association whose friendly staff provided a cache of lovely images of their city.

In Tokyo, Yukari Sakamoto generously shared her deep knowledge of things culinary. Chris Betros offered helpful advice on accommodations, while Emi Schemmer and Kelly Wetherille shared their informed takes on shopping. Dan Grunebaum and Santa Nakamura shared insight on the nightlife scene, while Dr. John Skutlin shed light on some of the city's edgier subcultures. Thank you all!

Outside Tokyo, Chris Cooling, an old Japan hand in the truest sense, significantly deepened my appreciation of Yokohama and beyond. Tomomi Watanabe, who drove me around Sado-ga-shima, and Silvana Imperatori and the rest of the staff behind Sado's stellar Earth Celebration, made my trip to that magical island a special one. A chance meeting with Yuki Sasamori and Yusuke Ogasawara led to new friendships and greatly enriched my appreciation of Sendai and Tohoku as a whole. Audrey Foo generously imparted lessons gleaned from her travels and shared some great photos. Sanjana Pegu and Pratik Shinde did the same. And Lance Kita enlightened me on the subtler nuances of Tokushima's Awa Odori dance festival. I appreciate all of your help.

Closer to home, Andrew Faulk, stellar photographer and friend, thank you for the portrait session. Likewise, thanks to my dear friends David Freeman and Brendon Gooden for accompanying me on a number of mountain excursions and sharing insights gleaned from your own travels. Thanks to Evan, my brother, who visited and gave me a chance to show him around. Mom and Dad, thank you for your tremendous support, your thoughts on Japan, and for instilling a love of travel in me at a young age. Arin Vahanian, my old Tokyo roommate, thank you for your unwavering friendship through the years and feedback as I wrote this book. And Ushna Iyer, I'll always treasure our many adventures. Kyoto and Kōya-san will never be the same. Thank you for the chance to introduce Japan to you, and for listening and giving feedback on so many ideas as I wrote this book.

Finally, thanks to all the wonderful Japanese people who have opened their amazing country up to me over the years, including the Saga family, in whose home my Japan journey began, Risa Mano-Cîrneală and her family and friends, the Nakamura family, and so many others. *Arigatō gozaimasu!*

List of Maps

MAP SYMBOLS

Expressway	City/Town	Airport	Golf Course
Primary Road	State Capital	Airfield	Parking Area
Secondary Road	National Capital	Mountain	Archaeological Site
Unpaved Road	Point of Interest	Unique Natural Feature	Church
Feature Trail	Accommodation	Waterfall	Gas Station
Other Trail	Restaurant/Bar	Park	Glacier
Ferry	Other Location	Trailhead	Mangrove
Pedestrian Walkway	Campground	Skiing Area	Reef
Stairs			Swamp

CONVERSION TABLES

°C = (°F - 32) / 1.8
°F = (°C x 1.8) + 32
1 inch = 2.54 centimeters (cm)
1 foot = 0.304 meters (m)
1 yard = 0.914 meters
1 mile = 1.6093 kilometers (km)
1 km = 0.6214 miles
1 fathom = 1.8288 m
1 chain = 20.1168 m
1 furlong = 201.168 m
1 acre = 0.4047 hectares
1 sq km = 100 hectares
1 sq mile = 2.59 square km
1 ounce = 28.35 grams
1 pound = 0.4536 kilograms
1 short ton = 0.90718 metric ton
1 short ton = 2,000 pounds
1 long ton = 1.016 metric tons
1 long ton = 2,240 pounds
1 metric ton = 1,000 kilograms
1 quart = 0.94635 liters
1 US gallon = 3.7854 liters
1 Imperial gallon = 4.5459 liters
1 nautical mile = 1.852 km

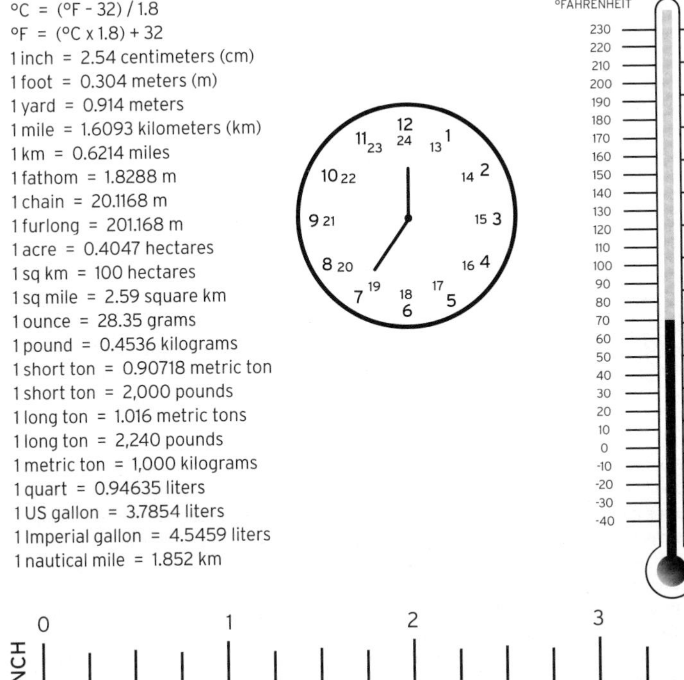

°FAHRENHEIT °CELSIUS

WATER BOILS

WATER FREEZES

INCH

CM

Photo Credits

Title page photo: JNTO; page 2 © JNTO; page 3 © Jonathan DeHart; page 6 © (top left) © Kyoto Convention & Visitors Bureau; (top right) Jonathan DeHart; (bottom) Anucha Pongpatimeth | Dreamstime.com; page 7 © (top) Jonathan DeHart; (bottom left) Kirsty Bouwers; (bottom right) JNTO; page 8 © (top) Kyoto Convention & Visitors Bureau; page 9 © (top) JNTO; (bottom left) JNTO; (bottom right) Shimane Prefectural Goverment/JNTO; page 10 © Nataliya Hora | Dreamstime.com; page 12 © JNTO; page 13 © (top) Yasufumi Nishi/JNTO; (bottom) Eudaemon | Dreamstime.com; page 15 © (top) Jonathan DeHart; (bottom) JNTO; page 16 © (top) Jonathan DeHart; (bottom) Audrey Foo; page 17 © Kyoto Convention & Visitors Bureau; page 18 © Jens Tobiska | Dreamstime.com; page 19 © Eyeblink | Dreamstime.com; page 20 © Steve Vidler / Alamy; page 21 © (top) Jonathan DeHart; (bottom) Crisfotolux | Dreamstime.com; page 22 © (bottom) Shinokamoto | Dreamstime.com; page 25 © Tohoku Tourism; Jonathan DeHart; page 27 © Kyoto Convention & Visitors Bureau; Jonathan DeHart; page 29 © (bottom) JNTO; page 30 © (top) F11photo | Dreamstime.com; page 31 © (bottom) JNTO; page 32 © Kyoto Convention & Visitors Bureau; Jonathan DeHart; page 33 © (bottom) JNTO; page 34 © Kyoto Convention & Visitors Bureau; JNTO; page 37 © Blanscape | Dreamstime.com; Jonathan DeHart; page 38 © Jonathan DeHart; Jonathan DeHart; page 39 © Jonathan DeHart; page 41 © (bottom) Thitichot Katawutpoonpun | Dreamstime.com; page 42 © (top) Photos7384 | Dreamstime.com; page 43 © Sean Pavone | Dreamstime.com; page 44 © (top left) Daboost | Dreamstime.com; (top right) Mosaymay - Dreamstime.com; page 58 © Blanscape | Dreamstime.com; page 62 © (top) Sanga Park | Dreamstime.com; (bottom) JNTO; page 65 © (top right) Cowardlion | Dreamstime.com; (bottom) Niphon Subsri | Dreamstime.com; page 72 © (top left) Jonathan DeHart; (top right) Torsakarin | Dreamstime.com; (bottom) Cowardlion | Dreamstime.com; page 79 © Roninz22 | Dreamstime.com; page 81 © JNTO; page 85 © (top) Cowardlion | Dreamstime.com; (bottom) Cowardlion | Dreamstime.com; page 91 © (top left) Erik Lattwein | Dreamstime.com; (top right) Jonathan DeHart; (bottom left) Jonathan DeHart; (bottom right) Jonathan DeHart; page 97 © (top) Erik Lattwein | Dreamstime.com; (left middle) Aleksandra Watanuki | Dreamstime.com; (right middle)Nui7711 | Dreamstime.com; (bottom) JNTO; page 101 © Kirsty Bouwers; page 106 © (top left) Jonathan DeHart; (top right) Jonathan DeHart; (bottom) JNTO; page 112 © Jonathan DeHart; page 119 © Watcharapong Thawornwichian | Dreamstime.com; page 121 © Hamamatsu Visitors and Convention Bureau/JNTO; page 123 © (top left) Jonathan DeHart; (top right) Jonathan DeHart; (bottom left) Sakurai Japanese Tea Experience; (bottom right) Jonathan DeHart; page 131 © Tupungato | Dreamstime.com; page 135 © Yasufumi Nishi/JNTO; page 146 © (top) Park Hyatt Tokyo; (left middle) Park Hyatt Tokyo; (right middle) Park Hyatt Tokyo; (bottom) Pablo Hidalgo | Dreamstime.com; page 158 © Kanagawa Prefecture; page 159 © (top left) JNTO; (top right) Dumrongsin Phitchphan | Dreamstime.com; page 170 © (top) Ixuskmitl | Dreamstime.com; (bottom) Cowardlion | Dreamstime.com; page 180 © (top left) Sergio Torres Baus | Dreamstime.com; (top right) Tupungato | Dreamstime.com; (bottom) Bennymarty | Dreamstime.com; page 182 © (top) Mrnovel | Dreamstime.com; (bottom) Kamakura City Tourist Association; page 189 © (top left) Maria Vazquez | Dreamstime.com; (top right) JNTO; (bottom) Pablo Hidalgo | Dreamstime.com; page 196 © (top) JTA/JNTO; (bottom) Navapon Plodprong | Dreamstime.com; page 201 © (top left) Milezaway | Dreamstime.com; (top right) Retina2020 | Dreamstime.com; (bottom) Kanagawa Prefecture; page 205 © Esmehelit | Dreamstime.com; page 206 © (top) Kanagawa Prefecture; (left middle) Kanagawa Prefecture; (right middle) Kanagawa Prefecture; (bottom) Kanagawa Prefecture; page 214 © (top) Luciano Mortula | Dreamstime.com; (bottom) Nattama Dechangamjamras | Dreamstime.com; page 217 © (top) Worldwidestock | Dreamstime.com; (bottom) Phurinee Chinakathum | Dreamstime.com; page 221 © Sean Pavone | Dreamstime.com; page 225 © Umarin Nakamura | Dreamstime.com; page 226 © (top left) JNTO; (top right) Jonathan DeHart; page 234 © (top left) Khuntapol | Dreamstime.com; (top right) Vodickap | Dreamstime.com; (bottom) Cowardlion | Dreamstime.com; page 243 © (top) Jonathan DeHart; (left middle) Jonathan DeHart; (right middle) Psstockfoto | Dreamstime.com; (bottom) Jonathan DeHart; page 246 © (top) Pipa100 | Dreamstime.com; (bottom) Imron Muhammad | Dreamstime.com; page 248 © Juite Wen | Dreamstime.com; page 256 © (top left) Nuvisage | Dreamstime.com; (top right) Katinka2014 | Dreamstime.com; (bottom) Katinka2014 | Dreamstime.com; page 262 © (top left) Guyn | Dreamstime.com; (top right) Jonathan DeHart; (bottom) Toyama Prefectural Tourism Association/JNTO; page 264 © Anujak Jaimook | Dreamstime.com; page 270 © (top) Matsumoto city/JNTO; (bottom) Tobyhoward | Dreamstime.com; page 273 © JTA/JNTO; page 277 © Umarin Nakamura | Dreamstime.com; page 283 © Navapon Plodprong | Dreamstime.com; page 284 © Nuvisage | Dreamstime.com; page 287 © Noppakun | Dreamstime.com; page 288 © (top left) Jonathan DeHart; (top right) Kuruneko | Dreamstime.com; page 300 © (top) David Evison | Dreamstime.com; page 302 © (top left) Joymsk | Dreamstime.com; (top right) Kyoto Convention & Visitors Bureau; (bottom) Raul Garcia Herrera | Dreamstime.com; page 306 © Elisa Bonomini | Dreamstime.com; page 311 © Kyoto Convention & Visitors Bureau; page 312 © (top) Kyoto Convention & Visitors Bureau; (left middle) Cebas1 | Dreamstime.com; (right middle) Jonathan DeHart; (bottom) Sean Pavone | Dreamstime.com; page 314 © Sergio Torres Baus | Dreamstime.com; page 317 © Umarin Nakamura | Dreamstime.com; page 321

© Nicholashan | Dreamstime.com; page 322 © Liyi Lee | Dreamstime.com; page 324 © Finallast | Dreamstime.com; page 325 © Kyoto Convention & Visitors Bureau; page 329 © Kyoto Convention & Visitors Bureau; page 332 © Kyoto Convention & Visitors Bureau; page 336 © Jonathan DeHart; page 339 © Kyoto Convention & Visitors Bureau; page 347 © Kyoto Convention & Visitors Bureau; page 354 © JNTO; page 355 © (top left) JTA/JNTO; (top right) Himeji Convention & Visitors Bureau/JNTO; page 367 © Tapiocatong | Dreamstime.com; page 369 (top) Cowardlion | Dreamstime.com; (bottom) © Edmond Leung | Dreamstime.com; page 374 © JNTO; page 378 © (top left) Jonathan DeHart; (top right) Jonathan DeHart; (bottom left) JNTO; (bottom right) Jonathan DeHart; page 379 © Eudaemon | Dreamstime.com; page 386 © (top) Dreamstime Agency | Dreamstime.com; (bottom) Sean Pavone | Dreamstime.com; page 392 © F11photo | Dreamstime.com; page 396 © JNTO; page 398 © (top) JNTO; (bottom) Toyooka City/JNTO; page 400 © (top) JNTO; (bottom) JNTO; page 402 © (top) JNTO; (bottom) Jonathan DeHart; page 407 © (top) JNTO; (bottom) Cowardlion | Dreamstime.com; page 410 © Sean Pavone | Dreamstime.com; page 411 © (top left) JTA/JNTO; (top right) DiegoFiore | Dreamstime.com; page 419 © (top left) JNTO; (top right) Cowardlion | Dreamstime.com; (bottom left) Jlobo211 - Dreamstime.com; (bottom right) Pipa100 | Dreamstime.com; page 421 © Jonathan DeHart; page 427 © (top left) Kuan Leong Yong | Dreamstime.com; (top right) Vichaya Kiatyingangsulee | Dreamstime.com; (bottom) Phuongphoto | Dreamstime.com; page 433 © Audrey Foo; page 436 © (top) Jonathan DeHart; (bottom) Cowardlion | Dreamstime.com; page 438 © Cowardlion | Dreamstime.com; page 440 © JNTO; page 443 © Shimane Prefectural Goverment/JNTO; page 447 © Leung Cho Pan | Dreamstime.com; page 448 © (top left) Tohoku Tourism; (top right) Tohoku Tourism; page 454 © Phillip Maguire | Dreamstime.com; page 459 © Leung Cho Pan | Dreamstime.com; page 461 © (top left) Jonathan DeHart; (top right) Jonathan DeHart; (bottom) Sean Pavone | Dreamstime.com; page 464 © (top) Shirototoro | Dreamstime.com; (bottom) Jonathan DeHart; page 469 © Tohoku Tourism; page 473 © (top left) Akita Prefecture/JNTO; (top right) Jonathan DeHart; (bottom) Tohoku Tourism; page 475 © Tohoku Tourism; page 478 © (top) Hiro1775 | Dreamstime.com; (bottom) Piti Sirisriro | Dreamstime.com; page 481 © Jonathan DeHart; page 483 © Motive56 | Dreamstime.com; page 485 © Feathercollector | Dreamstime.com; page 486 © (top left) Rangsiroj Akrachaka | Dreamstime.com; (top right) Videowokart | Dreamstime.com; page 497 © (top left) Artitwpd | Dreamstime.com; (top right) Keechuan | Dreamstime.com; (bottom) Simone Matteo Giuseppe Manzoni | Dreamstime.com; page 499 © Shawn Wee | Dreamstime.com; page 501 © (top) Jonathan DeHart; (left middle) Jonathan DeHart; (right middle) Jonathan DeHart; (bottom) Sean Pavone | Dreamstime.com; page 504 © Cross Hotel Sapporo; page 508 © (top left) Samantha Tan | Dreamstime.com; (top right) Wing Travelling | Dreamstime.com; (bottom) Jonathan DeHart; page 511 © Chung Jin Mac | Dreamstime.com; page 515 © (top left) Hokkaido Wilds; (top right) Aiaikawa | Dreamstime.com; (bottom) Sean Pavone | Dreamstime.com; page 521 © (top left) Sean Pavone | Dreamstime.com; (top right) Niradj | Dreamstime.com; (bottom) Blanscape | Dreamstime.com; page 525 © Jens Tobiska | Dreamstime.com; page 529 © Wangyining - Dreamstime.com; page 530 © Yung Chao Chen | Dreamstime.com; page 531 © Andreas Zeitler | Dreamstime.com; page 534 © Nuvisage | Dreamstime.com; page 536 © Niels Vos | Dreamstime.com; page 542 © JNTO; page 543 © (top left) JNTO; (top right) JNTO; page 549 © JNTO; page 552 © Yasufumi Nishi/JNTO; page 555 © (top) Jonathan DeHart; (bottom) Jonathan DeHart; page 559 © (top) Chun-Chang Wu | Dreamstime.com; (bottom) Jonathan DeHart; page 564 © Shutterstock.com 639430897; page 567 © Jonathan DeHart; page 572 © (top) Contrail1 | Dreamstime.com; (bottom) Aagje De Jong | Dreamstime.com; page 579 © (top) JNTO; (bottom) ©JTA/ JNTO; page 590 © (top) Mrnovel | Dreamstime.com; (left middle) Jonathan DeHart; (right middle) Mrnovel | Dreamstime.com; (bottom) Jonathan DeHart; page 593 © Tomoki1970 | Dreamstime.com; page 596 © JNTO; page 597 © (top left) JNTO; (top right) JNTO; page 610 © (top) Ixuskmitl | Dreamstime.com; (left middle) Raúl Rodríguez Arias | Dreamstime.com; (right middle) Julia Burlachenko | Dreamstime.com; (bottom) Ixuskmitl | Dreamstime.com; page 615 © (top left) Kirsty Bouwers; (top right) Audrey Foo; (bottom) JNTO; page 623 © Pipa100 | Dreamstime.com; page 624 © Cowardlion | Dreamstime.com; page 629 © Diego Grandi | Dreamstime.com; page 630 © JNTO; page 631 © JNTO; page 633 © (top left) Motive56 | Dreamstime.com; (top right) Galinasavina | Dreamstime.com; (bottom) Sanga Park | Dreamstime.com; page 644 © Sean Pavone | Dreamstime.com; page 647 © Daisuke Yatsui/JNTO; page 651 © Pipa100 | Dreamstime.com; page 655 © JNTO; page 656 © JNTO; page 662 © JNTO; page 664 © Kagoshima Prefectural Tourist Federation/JNTO; page 673 © JNTO; page 676 © Y.Shimizu/JNTO; page 677 © (top left) Yasufumi Nishi/JNTO; (top right) JNTO; page 689 © Phillip Maguire | Dreamstime.com; page 692 © (top left) Jonathan DeHart; (top right) Jonathan DeHart; (bottom) Jonathan DeHart; page 697 © (top) JNTO; (bottom) Krisada Wakayabun | Dreamstime.com; page 701 © Yasufumi Nishi/JNTO; page 705 © Photos7384 | Dreamstime.com; page 709 © Eyeblink | Dreamstime.com; page 713 © (top) JNTO; (bottom) JNTO; page 714 © Jonathan DeHart; page 717 © (top left) Jonathan DeHart; (top right) Jonathan DeHart; (bottom) Y.Shimizu/JNTO; page 721 © Xvaldes | Dreamstime.com; page 754 © Kyoto Convention & Visitors Bureau

Beachy Getaways

MOON.COM
@MOONGUIDES

MOON JAPAN
Avalon Travel
Hachette Book Group
1700 Fourth Street
Berkeley, CA 94710, USA
www.moon.com

Editor: Megan Anderluh
Managing Editor: Hannah Brezack
Copy Editor: Barbara Schultz
Graphics Coordinator: Ravina Schneider
Production Coordinator: Ravina Schneider
Cover Design: Faceout Studio, Charles Brock
Interior Design: Domini Dragoone
Moon Logo: Tim McGrath
Map Editor: Albert Angulo
Cartographers: Moon Street Cartography (Durango, CO), Karin Dahl, Albert Angulo
Indexer: Gina Guilinger

ISBN-13: 978-1-63121-711-1

Printing History
1st Edition — February 2020
5 4 3 2 1

Front cover photo: Honshu Island © Hemis / Alamy
Back cover photo: © Luis Henrique De Moraes Boucault | Dreamstime.com

Printed in Canada by Friesens